Canon Professor Anthony C. Thiselton

PATERNOSTER THEOLOGICAL MONOGRAPH SERIES

# Anthony C. Thiselton
### and
# The Grammar of Hermeneutics
### The Search for a Unified Theory

PATERNOSTER THEOLOGICAL MONOGRAPH SERIES

Trevor A. Hart, Head of School and Principal of St Mary's College, School of Divinity, University of St Andrews, Scotland, UK

Anthony N.S. Lane, Professor of Historical Theology and Director of Research, London School of Theology, UK

Anthony C. Thiselton, Emeritus Professor of Christian Theology, University of Nottingham; Research Professor in Christian Theology, University College Chester; and, Canon Theologian of Leicester Cathedral and Southwell Minster, UK

Kevin J. Vanhoozer, Research Professor of Systematic Theology, Trinity Evangelical Divinity School, Deerfield, Illinois, USA

A full listing of titles in this series appears at the end of this book

PATERNOSTER THEOLOGICAL MONOGRAPH SERIES

# Anthony C. Thiselton

## and

# The Grammar of Hermeneutics

### The Search for a Unified Theory

*A Study Presented to Anthony C. Thiselton in Recognition of Fifty Years of Outstanding Contribution to the Discipline of Hermeneutics*

Robert Knowles

Foreword by Anthony C. Thiselton

Copyright © Robert Knowles 2012

First published by Paternoster, 2012

Paternoster is an imprint of Authentic Media
52 Presley Way, Crownhill, Milton Keynes, Bucks, MK8 0ES

www.authenticmedia.co.uk
Authentic Media is a division of Koorong UK, a company limited by guarantee

09 08 07 06 05 04 03   8 7 6 5 4 3 2 1

The right of Robert Knowles to be identified as the Author of this Work
has been asserted by him in accordance with the Copyright, Designs
and Patents Act 1988.

*All rights reserved. No part of this publication may be reproduced, stored in a retrieval system, or transmitted, in any form or by any means, electronic, mechanical, photocopying, recording or otherwise, without the prior permission of the publisher or a license permitting restricted copying. In the UK such licenses are issued by the Copyright Licensing Agency, 90 Tottenham Court Road, London W1P 9HE.*

**British Library Cataloguing in Publication Data**
A catalogue record for this book is available from the British Library

ISBN 978-1-84227-637-2

Typeset by Robert Knowles
Printed and bound in Great Britain
by Lightning Source, Milton Keynes, UK

# Series Preface

In the West the churches may be declining, but theology—serious, academic (mostly doctoral level) and mainstream orthodox in evaluative commitment—shows no sign of withering on the vine. This series of Paternoster Theological Monographs extends the expertise of the Press especially to first-time authors whose work stands broadly within the parameters created by fidelity to Scripture and has satisfied the critical scrutiny of respected assessors in the academy.

Such theology may come in several distinct intellectual disciplines—historical, dogmatic, pastoral, apologetic, missional, aesthetic and no doubt others also. The series will be particularly hospitable to promising constructive theology within the evangelical frame, for it is of this that the church's need seems to be greatest.

Quality writing will be published across the confessions—Anabaptist, Episcopalian, Reformed, Arminian and Orthodox—across the ages—patristic, medieval, reformation, modern and counter-modern—and across the continents. The aim of the series is theology written in the twofold conviction that the church needs theology and theology needs the church—which in reality means theology done for the glory of God.

*Dedicated to Dorothy and Francis Knowles, my parents – and to Anthony C. Thiselton, Donald A. Carson, and Roy Kearsley, my teachers in the Christian Faith*

# Contents

Foreword and Commendation — xvii
Author's Preface and Acknowledgements — xxiii
Abbreviations — xxv

**Introduction The Need for a Fresh Study on Anthony C. Thiselton's Hermeneutical Theory** — 1
A. Anthony C. Thiselton — 1
B. The Discipline of Hermeneutics — 6
C. Scope, Approach, Presentation, and Comments on Language-Uses — 22

**Chapter 1 Widening Dialogue Towards Critical Synthesis: The Emergence of Thiselton's Hermeneutical Programme from 1959 to 1970** — 28
A. Preliminary Comments: Where to Begin — 28
B. Thiselton's "First Period" Hermeneutical Reflections: from 1959 to 1970 — 30
   1. *1959-1964: 1 Corinthians, Wittgenstein and Austin, and Continental Hermeneutics* — 30
   2. *1965: Mixed Response to Continental Hermeneutics* — 31
   3. *1966: Uniting the Pre-Cognitive and the Cognitive* — 31
   4. *1967: Tensions Between Continental and Anglo-American Traditions* — 32
   5. *1968: Pannenberg, Wittgenstein, and Dialogue Between Traditions* — 34
   6. *1969: Widening Dialogue: Philosophical and Theological Traditions* — 34
   7. *1970: Thiselton's Hermeneutical Programme: Widening Dialogue Towards Critical Synthesis* — 38
C. Conclusion: "Widening Dialogue Towards Critical Synthesis" as a Hermeneutical Axiom — 45

**Chapter 2 Widening Dialogue of Historical Response vs. Hermeneutical Foreclosure: The Immersion of Thiselton's Hermeneutical Programme in the Processes of Traditions, 1970 to 1978/80**     47

A. Preliminary Comments: How to Continue     47

B. The Background Context of Thiselton's "Second Period" Writings     49

   1. *Thiselton as an Author, as an Academic, and as an Anglican Churchman: Thiselton's Relationship to Evangelicalism and to Anglicanism*     49

      A) THISELTON'S HERMENEUTICAL CHALLENGE TO EVANGELICALS AT NEAC '77     50

      B) THISELTON'S SELF-CRITICAL, MODERATE, CONSERVATIVE EVANGELICALISM     54

      C) THISELTON'S SUBTLE RELATIONSHIP TO "ANGLICANISM" AND TO "LIBERALISM"     57

      D) WIDENING DIALOGUE WITH MULTIPLE TRADITIONS VS. HERMENEUTICAL FORECLOSURE     59

   2. *Historical Context: Thiselton's Immersion in Processes of Traditions*     59

      A) TRENDS AND ISSUES IN BIBLICAL INTERPRETATION     59

      B) TRENDS AND ISSUES IN SYSTEMATIC THEOLOGY     67

      C) TRENDS AND DEBATES IN PHILOSOPHY, HERMENEUTICS, AND PHILOSOPHICAL THEOLOGY     69

      D) TRENDS AND ISSUES IN THE CHURCH     77

      E) CONTEXTS AND ISSUES IN TERTIARY EDUCATION     78

      F) ISSUES IN THE BROADER SECULAR CULTURE OF BRITAIN AND THE WEST     79

C. Conclusion: "Ever-Widening Dialogue of Historical Response" as Implicit Hermeneutical Axiom vs. Hermeneutical Foreclosure     80

**Chapter 3 Hermeneutics, Unity, and Epistemology: Unifying Hermeneutics Christologically and Eschatologically, and, Towards a Unified Hermeneutical Critique of Epistemology**     82

A. Preliminary Comments: Approach to Chapters 3 to 7     82

B. Relating Theology and Philosophy during Hermeneutical Theory-Construction: Unifying Hermeneutics Christologically and Eschatologically     86

    1. *Dialogue Between Biblical Studies and Hermeneutics in Thiselton*    86
    2. *Dialogue Between Systematic Theology and Hermeneutics in*
       *Thiselton*    90
C. Dialogic Theory-Construction: Towards a Unified
   Hermeneutical Critique of Epistemology    100
    1. *Straightforward Fideism, or Warranted Inclusion of Theological*
       *Considerations?*    100
    2. *Philosophical Problem: Continental Epistemological Dualism and its*
       *Effect on the Character and Role of Conceptualization in Hermeneutics*    102
    3. *Towards a Warranted Theological Solution: Pannenberg's*
       *Eschatological Epistemology*    114
    4. *Philosophical Problem: The Spell of Kierkegaard's One-Sided Notion*
       *of Truth*    117
    5. *Towards a Warranted Theological Solution: A Biblical Multiform*
       *Notion of Truth*    120
    6. *Mutual Dialogic Warrant: Rationality, Perception, and Self-*
       *Deception in Philosophy and Theology*    131
        A) HISTORICAL-SCIENTIFIC RATIONALITY IN PANNENBERG
          AND T.F. TORRANCE    131
        B) PERCEPTION IN THE LATER WITTGENSTEIN, D.D. EVANS,
          I.T. RAMSEY, AND C.S. LEWIS    132
        C) SELF-DECEPTION AS AN EMPHASIS IN FREUD'S
          PSYCHOANALYSIS    136
    7. *Concluding Comments on Thiselton's Appeals to Mutual Dialogic*
       *Warrant*    136
D. Conclusion: Towards a Christological and Eschatological
   Unification of Hermeneutics and Towards a Unified
   Hermeneutical Critique of Epistemology, through Dialogue
   Between Philosophy and Theology    137

**Chapter 4 Hermeneutics, Language, Cultures, and Selves:
Towards Unified Hermeneutical Critiques of Language,
Western Culture, and Human Selves**    **140**
A. Preliminary Comments: Justifying Our Approach    140
B. Dialogic Theory-Construction: Towards a Unified
   Hermeneutical Critique of Language    141
    1. *The Philosophical Clarification of a Prior Biblical and Theological*

|   |   |
|---|---|
| Account of Language | 142 |
| 2. The Theological Shaping of Thiselton's Hermeneutical Critique of Language | 144 |
| 3. Thiselton's Appeal to the Later Wittgenstein and its Resonance with Theology, Eschatology, and Christology | 147 |
|     A) LINGUISTIC TRANS-CONTEXTUALITY, "ENFLESHED WORD", AND HISTORICAL ESCHATOLOGY | 148 |
|     B) LINGUISTIC TRANS-TEMPORALITY AND HISTORICAL TRADITION | 151 |
|     C) LANGUAGE-GAMES AND HISTORICAL SETTING | 157 |
|     D) SPEECH-ACTION AND PARTICULAR "ENFLESHED WORD" | 159 |
|     E) THE LEGITIMACY OF THISELTON'S APPEAL TO THE LATER WITTGENSTEIN | 163 |
| 4. Thiselton's Appeal to Linguistic Philosophy and its Resonance with Theology, Eschatology, and Christology | 163 |
| 5. Accommodation of the Saussurian Tradition to the Later Wittgensteinian Tradition | 167 |
|     A) THISELTON'S APPEAL TO SAUSSURE'S FOUR PRINCIPLES OF GENERAL LINGUSITICS | 168 |
|     B) THISELTON'S EXTENSION AND QUALIFICATION OF SAUSSURIAN INSIGHTS | 171 |
|     C) "LINGUISTIC SEMANTICS" AS A "SUPPLEMENT" TO "PHILOSOPHICAL SEMANTICS" | 175 |
| 6. Testing and Validating the Later-Wittgensteinian-Saussurian Alliance | 176 |
|     A) CRITICISM OF TRADITIONAL AND POSITIVIST ASSUMPTIONS AND APPROACHES | 176 |
|     B) CRITICISM OF "NATURAL" AND CONTINENTAL ASSUMPTIONS AND APPROACHES | 179 |
|     C) VALIDATING THE LATER-WITTGENSTEINIAN-SAUSSURIAN ALLIANCE THROUGH APPLICATION | 183 |
| 7. Implications of this Exposition of Thiselton's Unified Hermeneutical Critique of Language | 184 |
| C. Dialogic Theory-Construction: Towards a Unified Hermeneutical Critique of (Western) Culture | 187 |
| D. Dialogic Theory-Construction: Towards a Unified Hermeneutical Critique of Human Selves | 192 |

E. Conclusion: Towards Unified Hermeneutical Critiques of Language, Western Culture, and of Human Selves, through Dialogues Between Philosophy and Theology — 204

## Chapter 5 Hermeneutics and Responsible Interpretation: Towards a Unified Critique of Hermeneutical Understanding — **206**

A. Preliminary Comments: Responsible Interpretation — 206
B. The Need for a Transformed Hermeneutical Paradigm: Re-Addressing the Problem of Intelligibility Across Historical Distance — 208
   *1. The Inadequacy of Earlier Solutions to the Problem of Intelligibility Across Historical Distance* — 208
   *2. The (Ongoing) Urgent Need for a Transformed Paradigm for Hermeneutics* — 211
C. Dialogic Theory-Construction: Towards a Unified Critique of Hermeneutical Understanding as Responsible Interpretation — 216
   *1. Involved Subjectivities vs. Absolute Relativism, Subjectivism, Solipsism, and Individualism* — 216
   *2. Understanding as a Progressive Process: The Hermeneutical Circle (or Spiral)* — 222
      A) RE-HISTORICIZED HISTORICAL-EXPERIENTIAL UNDERSTANDING AND RE-HISTORICIZED SUBJECT-OBJECT CONCEPTUALIZATION — 222
      B) HERMENEUTICAL UNDERSTANDING AND SCIENTIFIC EXPLANATION, PARTICULAR AND GENERAL, AND PARTS AND WHOLES — 227
      C) DISTANCING AND FUSION THROUGH QUESTION AND ANSWER: TOWARDS RE-HISTORICIZED OBJECTIVITY AND RE-HISTORICIZED SELF-INVOLVEMENT — 230
         i) Distancing: Towards Re-Historicized or Historical Objectivity — 231
         ii) Fusion: Towards Re-Historicized or Historical Self-Involvement — 241
         iii) The Dialogic Relationship between Distancing and Fusion — 250
         iv) Question and Answer — 252
   *3. In Anticipation of Later Discussions: A Brief Note on Plural Interpretative Outcomes* — 252
   *4. Answering Critics in Relation to Thiselton's Critique of*

  *Hermeneutical Understanding*    259
D. Conclusion: Towards a Unified Critique of Hermeneutical
  Understanding as Responsible Interpretation, through Dialogue
  Between Philosophy and Theology    263

## Chapter 6 Hermeneutics and History: Widening Dialogue Towards a New Historical Unification of Hermeneutical Theory as a Precondition for Responsible Interpretation    272

A. Preliminary Comments: Justifying a Fresh Interpretation of
  The Two Horizons    272
B. The Direct Affect of Theory on Practice: A Pre-
  Understanding of Broadening Philosophical and Theological
  Dialogues as a Precondition for Responsible Interpretation    276
  *1. The Direct Affect of Theory on Practice: The Cruciality of*
    *Broadening Pre-Understanding*    276
  *2. Recovering Responsible Practice: Broadening Pre-Understandings*
    *Beyond Those of the New Hermeneutic (and Beyond Those of Later*
    *Approaches)*    292
C. Dialogic Theory-Construction: Towards the Unification of
  Stratum Two and Stratum Three Hermeneutical Theory in a
  Unified Hermeneutical Critique of History    299
  *1. Anticipations of History-as-a-Whole as the Universal Context(s)*
    *for Understanding*    301
  *2. The Unity of Historical Reality as the Ground for the Possibility*
    *and Unity of Language and of Understanding*    302
  *3. The Process of Historical Dialectic as Earthed in the Processes of*
    *Traditions*    321
D. Widened Dialogue Towards Critical Synthesis: Thiselton's
  Transformed Hermeneutical Paradigm and Its Tradition-
  Refinement of Gadamer's Hermeneutical Circle    339
  *1. The Importance of Gadamer's Thought for Thiselton's*
    *Hermeneutical Circle*    340
  *2. Thiselton's Tradition-Modification of Gadamer's Hermeneutical*
    *Circle*    343
  *3. Thiselton's Transformed Paradigm as the Awaited Paradigm-Shift*
    *for Hermeneutics*    368
E. Conclusion: Widening Dialogue Towards a New Historical

Unification of Hermeneutical Theory as a Precondition for
Responsible Interpretation — 384

**Chapter 7 Hermeneutical Unity, Objectivity, and Foreclosure: Towards a Christological Unification of Hermeneutics, a Unified Hermeneutical Critique of Historical Objectivity, and a Critique of Hermeneutical Foreclosure** — 396

A. Preliminary Comments: Hermeneutical Unity, Objectivity, and Foreclosure — 396

B. Towards a Provisional Christological Unification of Hermeneutics Embracing Metacritical Explanation and Metacritical Evaluation — 400

   *1. Thiselton's Critical Widening of Dialogue with Theological Traditions* — 400

   *2. Contrasting Evaluations of Whether or Not Thiselton is Straightforwardly Fideistic* — 401

   *3. Dialogic Warranting of the Inclusion of Theological Considerations in Hermeneutics* — 402

   *4. Christological Metacriteria and Broadened Philosophical Dialogue* — 403

   *5. Dialogic Warrant as a Context of Understanding for Thiselton on Biblical Authority* — 408

   *6. Problems with Broadly Positivist Approaches and with Broadly Existentialist Approaches* — 410

   *7. Responses to Critics of Thiselton's View of Revelation* — 411

C. Dialogic Theory-Construction: Towards a Unified Hermeneutical Critique of Historical Objectivity — 413

D. Plea for Responsible Interpretation Against Kinds of Hermeneutical Foreclosure: The Two Horizons and a Response to Thiselton's Critics — 430

   *1. Friendly Criticisms of Thiselton's Thinking: Straightforward Hermeneutical Foreclosure* — 430

   *2. Pseudo-"Post-Structuralist" and Broadly Socio-Pragmatic Criticisms of Thiselton's Thinking: Asserted, "Legitimized", and Canonized Hermeneutical Foreclosure* — 444

      A) RESPONSE TO A.K.M. ADAM IN RELATION TO S. FISH, J. DERRIDA, AND R. BARTHES — 445

      B) RESPONSES TO A FIRST GROUP OF "FISHIAN" CRITICISMS:

| | |
|---|---|
| W.G. JEANROND, M.G. BRETT, V.S. POYTHRESS, AND S. PERRY | 469 |
| C) RESPONSES TO A SECOND GROUP OF "FISHIAN" CRITICISMS: | |
| W.J. LYONS AND S. WOODMAN | 476 |
| i) W.J. Lyons' "Oxford Article" | 476 |
| ii) W.J. Lyons' *Canon and Exegesis* | 483 |
| iii) S. Woodman's Thesis Contribution | 530 |
| D) CONCLUDING COMMENTS | 548 |
| *3. Hostile Criticism: The Drama Triangle of Disowned Projected Hermeneutical Foreclosure* | 550 |
| *4. Interpretative Irresponsibility and Kinds of Hermeneutical Foreclosure* | 564 |
| E. Conclusion: Towards a Christological Unification of Hermeneutics, a Unified Hermeneutical Critique of Historical Objectivity, and a Critique of Hermeneutical Foreclosure | 566 |

**Chapter 8 Conclusions: The Value of Anthony C. Thiselton's Formative Thinking for the Discipline of Hermeneutics** — 572

**Appendixes** — 611

Appendix 1: Footnote Abbreviations Other Than Journals — 611

Appendix 2: Anthony C. Thiselton's Degrees, Honors, Main Academic Posts and Involvements in Societies and on Editorial Boards — 617

**Bibliography** — 619

**Author Index** — 659

**Subject Index** — 673

# Foreword

I am delighted to commend this volume by Dr. Robert Knowles very warmly. His research into my work and critical responses to it is breath-taking in its thoroughness, scope, and detail. Yet he is faithful to the themes of my thought. He has explored and assessed my hermeneutical theory and practice over more than forty years, and traced stages in its development. He rightly argues that my work constitutes a distinctive approach that resists assimilation into the thought of any other particular named thinker. He contributes distinctive and constructive arguments of his own on the nature of hermeneutics, and these deserve careful attention. A number of themes expounded in this volume deserve note in this Foreword.

(1) While he rightly recognizes that I draw on the insights of certain other thinkers selectively for particular purposes, Dr. Knowles convincingly shows that this is not a sufficient reason for some critics to identify my work as "Wittgensteinian", "Gadamerian", or as replicating Pannenberg or Moltmann. This is not to deny that I am indebted to Pannenberg and to Moltmann for certain ideas. He identifies my concern for contingency, particularity, and logical "grammar", behind which the later Wittgenstein stands as one influence among others. I share Wittgenstein's suspicions of over-easy generalizations, and I share with many analytical philosophers an urge for clarity in conceptual grammar. In the British tradition of philosophy, I owe much to J.L. Austin's early formulation of speech-act theory. But this has necessarily been modified and supplemented in the more recent writings of D.D. Evans, John Searle, Nicholas Wolterstorff, and other works, and I enter into conversation creatively and critically with these also.

Dr. Knowles carefully traces points of my indebtedness to Gadamer and to Ricoeur, without whom hermeneutics would not appear in the shape which it holds today. But in neither case, as he points out, do I replicate their thought as such. Gadamer assists us in seeking to prevent us from imposing our own prior concepts onto that which we seek to understand. He gives due place to the historical nature of understanding. Ricoeur explores the dual aspects of a hermeneutic of suspicion and a hermeneutic of retrieval in suggestive ways, and approaches biblical texts in ways that deserve serious attention. But the main agenda of Gadamer and Ricoeur, as Knowles demonstrates, is different from mine. For one thing mine includes more concerns that stem more explicitly from

Christian theology.

In Christian theology I draw more from Pannenberg and Moltmann perhaps to a greater extent than from many other writers. But this does not imply that my theology replicates theirs. Indeed this could not be the case, since these two thinkers display differences from each other. As Dr. Knowles rightly argues, it is profoundly *anti*-hermeneutical to try to categorize me as a version of this or that thinker, as if to place me in a static box. I share with Robert Knowles and with the later Wittgenstein a passionate dislike of over-ready generalization, and with Knowles and with Gadamer a dislike of confrontational "positions" rather than continuing explorations of meaning and truth. Polemical and static "positions" makes for misleading evaluations and for cheap and over-easy didactic methods in the classroom or lecture-room. Knowles has paid me the honour of granting to my thought the "respect for otherness" which Betti, Gadamer, and Ricoeur identify as the heart of hermeneutics.

(2) Dr. Knowles has shown enormous care, diligence and generosity, in formulating and suggesting counter-replies to criticisms of my work that are misplaced or based on misunderstanding. A heavy load of university teaching, doctoral supervision, and administration as Head of Department, in addition to considerable work for the Church of England, had left me too busy writing the next book in earlier years to read the huge range of the book reviews and critiques of my work which writers produced. Since I never replied to my critics, Dr. Knowles has produced welcome and original work in this respect.

Some sympathetic writers and critics, as Dr. Knowles indicates, were warm and appreciative. But only his amazingly meticulous research into earlier years has brought to my attention the astonishingly varied range of reasons why some found fault with my work. Some criticisms are flagrantly unjust because they have missed the point that I had tried to make, or because they arose from over-hurried or careless reading. I am more than grateful to Dr. Knowles for exposing these in their true light. He has performed a significant service by showing how many of these critical polemics were based on assumptions that were at variance with what I had aimed to achieve. His painstaking research exposes just how vital the hermeneutical process of *listening* is, before writers jump in with premature criticisms. His distinguishing at one point between "friendly" critics and "hostile" critics is also illuminating.

(3) Dr. Knowles has so saturated himself in my work over many years of reading and research that he accurately brings to the fore my most central concerns. He shows clearly how my concerns for history and for extra-linguistic situations constitute vital ingredients of my thought, and even more to the point he ascribes a proper role to Christology and to eschatology in my theology. He expounds the place that I wish to give to epistemology, as well as my emphasis on the need to go beyond rationalism, empiricism, and positivism. He faithfully identifies and defends my concern not to fall into the opposite error of showing excessive or uncritical hospitality to radical aspects of postmodernism.

Positivism is not value-neutral, but neither are meaning and truth exempt from public debate and public criteria of evaluation. Dr. Knowles defends me against the misleading accusation of fideism. He further shows that interpretation cannot give undue privilege to "the present horizon" if it is to avoid splitting a more unified approach to hermeneutics into fragments or into dichotomies. A radically pragmatic approach, he rightly argues, would dissolve genuinely "historical" understanding into social constructionism, or into narrative speech-acts which have no due basis in history and truth. Similarly he defends my claim that Derrida's semiotics are clearly not the only possible development or entailment of Saussure's general linguistics.

In more positive and practical terms, Dr. Knowles demonstrates my concern for appropriation, listening, actualization, application, agency, transformation, and Christian theology, and my passion to preserve the formative power and the "otherness" of the horizons of the biblical text.

(4) Much of the distinctive argument of this volume turns on the search for a unified approach to hermeneutics. Dr. Knowles well captures the mood of my extended critique of Bultmann to the effect that Bultmann fragments hermeneutics into a dichotomy between description and address, between history and faith, between law and grace, and so on. He traces my concern for a more unifying focus in various other case studies and issues. I have always valued Pannenberg's emphasis upon the wholeness of truth, and Ricoeur's use of multiform, multilevel, models without his falling into an uncontrolled radical pluralism.

Dr Knowles contributes original thinking of his own on the issue of a "unified" hermeneutical theory and practice. Yet the starting-point for this is true to my thinking. He avoids the endless polarizations of *either/or* categorizations that vitiate hermeneutics. I am at one with Dr. Knowles in seeking meaning, truth and relevance first of all in contingent and particular contexts, rather than setting one "positional" system against another. Such a strategy of confrontation invites abstraction, and encourages rushing in to speak before adequately listening.

(5) I was at first surprised by the high ratio of attention to my earliest works. I had forgotten much of what I wrote before 1980. Further, I often regret that much more attention is given publicly to *The Two Horizons* than to *New Horizons in Hermeneutics*. The latter was written to offer a more personal and more practical exposition of my hermeneutics than that which *The Two Horizons* presented. Nevertheless, as Dr. Knowles has shown, the years between 1964 and 1979 were formative years. He identifies the 1977 NEAC Conference as influential and formative for certain traditions of thought within the Church of England, and he notes the wide and ongoing impact of some publications from the 1970s on speech-act theory and semantics. Even in those early years I was concerned to explore the basis of speech acts in states of affairs and in conditions of truth for their presuppositions. Later I developed several implications of this for Christology.

(6) Dr. Knowles has not simply expounded and defended my work. He has brought to bear on the whole debate on hermeneutics a structure of his own that

not only clarifies my work, but also illuminates the shape of the subject in its own right. He distinguishes what he calls "seven conversations" that run through the subject and, equally, through my work. If we confuse these conversations, he argues, we miss much of the thrust of my work, and we lose sight of a more unified understanding of hermeneutics.

These seven conversations include issues under the headings of: dialogue, history, epistemology, and language, (Western) culture, selfhood, and the hermeneutical task. In turn, these conversations which arise from Dr. Knowles' explorations and structuring of my work, give rise to a series of six distinctive question-and-answer perspectives. The first of these responds to the need for a unified approach to hermeneutics. Knowles structures my work in terms of a scheme of "three strata" which involve respectively a level of dialogue and pre-understanding; a level of theoretical background; and a level of engaging in the hermeneutical task.

To trace all the details here would make this Foreword and Commendation too long. But in summary they include (in my own paraphrase, numbering, and sequence): (i) addressing the problems of complexity and abstraction; (ii) establishing widening dialogues with multi-disciplinary resources, as well as establishing greater openness; (iii) seeking a more unified philosophy of history; (iv) exposing unnecessary or artificial dichotomies and polarizations; (v) recognizing the priority of historical understanding over de-contextualized language; (vi) widening dialogue, formulating theory and proposing concrete practice, as ways of achieving responsible interpretation that avoids foreclosing further dialogue by imposing premature conclusions; and (vii) seeking to expose self-deception and aggressive power-play, not least because this undermines genuine hermeneutics and privileges entrenched "positions". This last level involves a positive *theological* recognition first of an eschatology in which Christians, like others, are still *en route*; and second, the definitive example of the patience and love of Christ, who refused short cuts to fulfilling the will of God, and rejected "violence", rather than the cross, as God's way of bringing in his kingdom.

I value the distinctive approach in terms of which Dr. Knowles has organized such a complexity of far-reaching issues. It coheres well with my thought and work, and illuminates it. This distinctive attempt to formulate these structural distinctions may also help us to avoid category mistakes when we engage in discussions of hermeneutics, and even to avoid some misunderstandings of my thought. A very small price to pay is that Dr. Knowles' recognition of the complexity of these multiform issues means that he rightly refuses to cut corners, and for a casual reader this volume will not always be the easiest reading. However, I have read it through, and cannot see where detailed argument could be omitted without undue simplification. Indeed much of Dr. Knowles' genius is to expose oversimplifications that have led to misunderstanding. Initially his attribution of "three strata" within my thought may seem daunting, but this no longer remains the case once we he explains that these denote the three respective operations of (i) widening our horizons and perspectives as much as possible; (ii) theoretical explorations of concepts, history, epistemology, language, culture, and the self; and (iii) responsible interpretation and hermeneutical understanding and application.

(7) From time to time Dr. Knowles gently suggests that I have left room for more explicitly theological developments in hermeneutics that I should have explored. I agree with this critique, and indeed it so happens that I anticipated it by producing a volume of more than eight hundred pages that addresses explicitly theological issues in relation to hermeneutics: *The Hermeneutics of Doctrine* (Eerdmans: 2007). *The Hermeneutics of Doctrine* attempts to avoid both abstraction and "premature closure" in approaching doctrine, but this does not mean that it includes no solid doctrinal content. It works with precisely the agenda that Dr. Knowles identifies, and I have described in section (6) above.

I commend the painstaking and thorough work of Dr. Knowles very warmly, in part as an accurate exposition of my work; in part as a corrective to some misunderstandings of it; but also in part as a distinctive hermeneutics that stands on its own feet. It faithfully expounds my thought, and provides a distinctive, original, and timely contribution to the subject. I am deeply grateful to Dr. Knowles for the years of meticulous research that he has spent on my writings, on critiques from other writers, and on his own approach to hermeneutical theory and practice.

Canon Professor Anthony C. Thiselton
*Formerly Head of Theology, University of Nottingham*
*October 2011*

# Preface and Acknowledgements

This study aims to ensure that Anthony C. Thiselton is heard aright. It is necessary to hear Thiselton aright for reasons that many will already appreciate. He is a world-ranking scholar of the very highest caliber; he has an unrivalled encyclopedic knowledge of the literature in his fields of study (hermeneutics and 1 Corinthians in particular); and he has contributed numerous outstanding writings to those same fields himself.

However, it is also necessary to hear Thiselton aright for a reason that many may not yet appreciate: the actual content of what Thiselton says and the relevance of that content for the discipline of hermeneutics today are often woefully neglected, badly misunderstood, or even unfairly attacked.

On the one hand, the discipline of hermeneutics is disorganized, exceedingly complex, seemingly abstracted from interpretative practice, and beset by multiple theoretical dichotomies and by other theoretical problems. Moreover, the discipline of hermeneutics is polarized into diverse disciplines, traditions, schools and thinkers who seem either to ignore one-another completely or to collide in spectacular fashion. Given this situation, it is not surprising that there seems to be little agreement over what constitutes "responsible interpretation" today.

And yet, on the other hand, we have Thiselton: an encyclopedic and world-ranking authority on hermeneutics, yes; but also a thinker whose work has not yet been adequately received. The discipline of hermeneutics is in disarray; – and yet its main champion (at least in theological circles) is not heard aright.

This situation does not make sense. Therefore, the present study attempts to address this situation by expounding the formative core of Thiselton's thinking so that his profound contribution to the discipline of hermeneutics might actually be allowed to transform that same discipline.

Thiselton already *has* a transformed hermeneutical paradigm. This study is offered in the hope that others might transform their hermeneutical paradigms as well. Then, there will surely be more "Transforming Biblical Reading" (to use Thiselton's language). And then, surely, the Word of God will strike home afresh.

Originally, this study was submitted as a PhD thesis to Cardiff University, UK, in 2005 (awarded 2006). I remain grateful to all those who facilitated this process, namely: Professor Paul Ballard and Professor Stephen Pattison - successive Heads of Departments at the School of Religious and Theological Studies at Cardiff

University; Rev. Dr. Hugh Matthews and Rev. Dr. John Weaver - successive Principals of South Wales Baptist College (my particular college within Cardiff University); Professor Francis Watson, Professor Josef Lössl, and Dr. John Watt, who examined the project; and my successive Tutors, Rev. Dr. Ian Tutton and Dr. Roy Kearsley. In particular, my thanks go to Professor Lössl, for his kind commendation of this work, and to Dr Kearsley, for his sagely input and kind encouragement throughout most of my PhD period (and occasionally afterwards), and for his kind remarks concerning the project as it is now.

I would especially like to thank Tim Smith, Chris Jensen, Rev Ted Fell, Rev Kieran and Catherine Webster, Matthew and Helen Crockett, Mark and Julie McKee, Dave and Anne Carlos, Rev David and Sue Morrell, Gerwyn and Ruth Miles, and Julie Robinson for their kind encouragement and assistance. Special thanks are also due to all those who continue to come together to finance my work as a whole. They are too numerous to list here, but their ongoing support made the present study possible. In particular, I'd like to thank Rev Dave Cave, Rev Geoffrey Fewkes and Rev Pete Orphan – successive Pastors of Pantygwydr Baptist Church, Swansea - for continuing to allow their church to handle my finances. In this respect, I would also like to thank Paul Carter and Eric Matthews, successive Treasurers at Pantygwydr, for all their hard work. I hope that this arrangement might continue as I have another volume on hermeneutics in mind!

Over the last few years, this study has grown to more than twice its "PhD" size, and has undergone a complete transformation. Professor Thiselton has remained in contact with me for this whole period. He has helped me much more than I could reasonably have expected him to – though *without* telling me what to say (except for very occasional corrections). He did not spare me the trouble of thinking! I would like to thank Professor Thiselton not only for all his help, but also for completely transforming my horizons, my faith, and my biblical reading.

Professor Donald A. Carson unknowingly started this whole project off when a friend, Rev John Smuts, gave me tapes of Professor Carson's talks on hermeneutics at Word Alive, Spring Harvest, UK, 1993. I would therefore like to thank Professor Carson (and Rev Smuts!) for lighting the blue touch-paper. I would also like to thank Professor Carson for his great contribution to my faith, to the global Church, and for his kind commendation on the cover of this book.

I would also like to thank Dr. Mike Parsons of Paternoster, and Paternoster itself, for agreeing to publish such a large project; Rev Dr. Derek Tidball for his proof-reading of parts of the work; and Jon Pott of Wm.B. Eerdmans Publishing Co. for giving me free reign with *The Two Horizons*.

Finally, I am especially thankful to my mother and father, Dorothy and Francis Knowles, who have always been a great support to me. Sadly, my Dad died in 2005 and so never saw this project. It is therefore submitted in his memory.

*Robert Knowles*
*Cardiff*
*November 2011*

# Abbreviations

| | |
|---|---|
| *AmJTh* | American Journal of Theology |
| *AmQ* | American Quarterly |
| *Anv* | Anvil |
| *ARC* | ARC |
| *AThRev* | Anglican Theological Review |
| *AUSStud* | Andrews University Seminary Studies |
| *Bib* | Biblica |
| *BibInterp* | Biblical Interpretation |
| *BibSac* | Bibliotheca Sacra |
| *BJRULibM* | Bulletin of the John Rylands University Library of Manchester |
| *CalThJ* | Calvin Theological Journal |
| *CBQ* | Catholic Biblical Quarterly |
| *CEN* | Church of England Newspaper |
| *CGrad* | The Christian Graduate |
| *ChLit* | Christianity and Literature |
| *Chman* | The Churchman |
| *Chn* | The Christian |
| *ChSRev* | Christian Scholar's Review |
| *ChTim* | Church Times |
| *CovQ* | Covenant Quarterly |
| *CRevBRel* | Critical Review of Books in Religion |
| *CrThRev* | Criswell Theological Review |
| *CTday* | Christianity Today |
| *CThM* | Currents in Theology and Mission |
| *Egel* | Evangel |
| *Enc* | Encounter |
| *EpRev* | Epworth Review |
| *Ety* | Eternity |
| *EuJTh* | European Journal of Theology |
| *EvanQ* | Evangelical Quarterly |
| *ExA* | Ex Auditu |
| *ExTim* | Expository Times |
| *FMn* | Faith and Mission |

| | |
|---|---|
| *FTht* | Faith and Thought |
| *FUty* | Faith and Unity |
| *Gly* | Glyph |
| *Greg* | Gregorianum |
| *GThJ* | Grace Theological Journal |
| *HeyJ* | Heythrop Journal |
| *IJPhRel* | International Journal for the Philosophy of Religion |
| *IJSTh* | International Journal of Systematic Theology |
| *Interp* | Interpretation |
| *JAARel* | Journal of the American Academy of Religion |
| *JACE* | Journal of the Association of Christian Economists |
| *JBLit* | Journal of Biblical Literature |
| *JDh* | Journal of Dharma |
| *JEThS* | Journal of the Evangelical Theological Society |
| *JLitTh* | Journal of Literature and Theology |
| *JPsychTh* | Journal of Psychology and Theology |
| *JRel* | Journal of Religion |
| *JRelHist* | Journal of Religious History |
| *JStudOT* | Journal for the Study of the Old Testament |
| *JThStud* | Journal of Theological Studies |
| *LitTh* | Literature and Theology |
| *ModTh* | Modern Theology |
| *MQRev* | Michigan Quarterly Review |
| *NB* | Nota Bene |
| *NDEJ* | Notre Dame English Journal |
| *NLitHist* | New Literary History |
| *NovTm* | Novum Testamentum |
| *NTStud* | New Testament Studies |
| *NZSThRelPh* | Neue Zeitschrift fur Systematische Theologie und Religionsphilosophie |
| *PEcc* | Pro-Ecclesia |
| *PRelStud* | Perspectives in Religious Studies |
| *Prem* | Premise |
| *PSChFJASA* | Perspectives on Science and Christian Faith: Journal of the American Scientific Affiliation |
| *PSemB* | Princeton Seminary Bulletin |
| *RefRev* | Reformed Review |
| *RefThRev* | Reformed Theological Review |
| *RelLit* | Religion and Literature |
| *RelStud* | Religious Studies |
| *RelStudRev* | Religious Studies Review |
| *ResPhen* | Research in Phenomenology |
| *RestQ* | Restoration Quarterly |
| *RevHstPhRel* | Revue D'Histoire et de Philosophie Religieuses |

| | |
|---|---|
| *RevMet* | Review of Metaphysics |
| *Scrip* | Scriptura |
| *Sem* | Semeia |
| *SJT* | Scottish Journal of Theology |
| *Sob* | Sobornost |
| *SWJTh* | Southwestern Journal of Theology |
| *TAB* | Transactional Analysis Bulletin |
| *Th* | Theology |
| *Them* | Themelios |
| *Thom* | The Thomist |
| *ThStud* | Theological Studies |
| *ThT* | Theology Today |
| *TRevCTLit* | Texte: Revue de Critique et de Theorie Litteraire |
| *TrinJ* | Trinity Journal |
| *TSF* | TSF Bulletin |
| *Tyn* | Tyndale Bulletin |
| *WThJ* | Westminster Theological Journal |
| *WW* | Word and World |

*N.B. An additional key to abbreviations of titles of writings cited in the footnotes may be found in Appendix 1.*

INTRODUCTION

# The Need for a Fresh Study on Anthony C. Thiselton's Hermeneutical Theory

Undoubtedly, a fresh study on the hermeneutical theory of Anthony C. Thiselton is long overdue. The justifications for this assertion emerge from two sources: a consideration of several observations related to Thiselton himself, and a consideration of several observations concerning the discipline of hermeneutics more broadly. Here, in our Introduction, we will examine each of these two sets of observations and justifications in turn, and will then conclude with a few comments on the scope, approach, presentation, and on a few of the language-uses of the present study.

### A. Anthony C. Thiselton

Thus, a fresh study of Thiselton's hermeneutical theory is shown to be necessary when three sets of observations about *Thiselton* are juxtaposed – as follows.

(1) Thiselton is widely regarded as a *world authority in biblical hermeneutics* - notably in relation to his most famous work, *The Two Horizons* (1980).[1] Thus, amongst friendly commentators, G.R. Osborne views Thiselton as 'the leading hermeneutical thinker of this generation'.[2] Conversely, one of Thiselton's most vehement critics, A.K.M. Adam, names Thiselton as 'the most sophisticated hermeneutician of his school'.[3] Indeed, *The Two Horizons* was reviewed by over thirty writers, and Thiselton's subsequent work, *New Horizons in Hermeneutics* (1992), received only marginally less attention.[4]

Certainly, whether reviewers were friendly or not, regard for Thiselton's stature

---

[1] Thiselton, A.C., *The Two Horizons: New Testament Hermeneutics and Philosophical Description with Special Reference to Heidegger, Bultmann, Gadamer, and Wittgenstein* (Exeter: Paternoster Press, 1980).
[2] Osborne, G.R., cited in: Goddard, J.M. ed., 'Review of A.C. Thiselton's *The First Epistle to the Corinthians*', NB 8.1 (Feb.-Apr. 2001), 4.
[3] Adam, A.K.M., 'Review of A.C. Thiselton's *Interpreting God and the Postmodern Self*, Interp 51.4 (Oct. 1997), 438.
[4] See, Thiselton, A.C., *New Horizons in Hermeneutics: The Theory and Practice of Transforming Biblical Reading* (London: HarperCollins; Grand Rapids: Zondervan, 1992), and our bibliography.

was almost unanimous following the publication of *The Two Horizons* in 1980. Thus, according to D.S. Dockery, *The Two Horizons* constituted 'the most comprehensive discussion of hermeneutical theory in print to date'.[5] P.R. Keifert, who was by no means uncritical of *The Two Horizons*, agreed, writing, 'the work is encyclopedic in its scope and deserves John Macquarrie's description of it as "the most comprehensive discussion of the hermeneutical question I have ever read"'.[6] Sandra M. Schneiders noted that *The Two Horizons* was nominated as a 'major contribution' to hermeneutics by 'numerous eminent reviewers',[7] and Robert Morgan urged that 'the importance' of the work could 'scarcely be overstated'.[8] Walter Wink called it 'the one book to read' in relation to 'the hermeneutical discussion', a 'monument to the conclusion of one stage in the hermeneutical debate'.[9]

More recently, writing of *New Horizons in Hermeneutics*, Walter Moberly speaks of Thiselton's 'astonishing breadth of reading… in theology… philosophy, social sciences, linguistics and literary theory'. Indeed, 'more than any other scholar in Britain', Thiselton 'has pioneered the rediscovery of the importance of hermeneutics in biblical and theological study'.[10] For Francis Watson, Thiselton's 'expertise' 'in hermeneutics' 'is probably unrivalled in… scope' whilst,[11] for Stephen D. Moore, Thiselton's 'versatility is remarkable, his erudition extraordinary. He ranges effortlessly from pre-modern theories of biblical interpretation to postmodernist theories of textuality and reading'.[12]

Nor is Thiselton's 'expertise' (to use Watson's term) merely theoretical. In 2001 D.A. Carson predicted 'that everyone will soon recognize that the best commentary on 1 Corinthians is that of Anthony C. Thiselton', a view

---

[5] Dockery, D.S., 'Review of A.C. Thiselton's *The Two Horizons*', *GThJ* 4.1 (Spr. 1983), 133; cf. Dockery, D.S., 'New Testament Interpretation: A Historical Survey', in *Interpreting the New Testament: Essays on Methods and Issues* (eds. D.A. Black and D.S. Dockery; Nashville, TN.: Broadman & Holman Publishers, 2001), 34.

[6] Keifert, P.R., 'Review of A.C. Thiselton's *The Two Horizons*', *WW* 1 (Fall 1981), 408; cf. Macquarrie, J., 'Review of A.C. Thiselton's *The Two Horizons*', *RelStud* 16.4 (Dec. 1980), 496-497.

[7] Schneiders, S.M., 'Review of A.C. Thiselton's *The Two Horizons*', *JRel* 62.3 (Jul. 1982), 308-309; cf. Schneiders, S.M., *The Revelatory Text: Interpreting the New Testament as Sacred Scripture* (Collegeville, MN.: Michael Glazier Books, 1999), 131.

[8] Morgan, R., 'Review of A.C. Thiselton's *The Two Horizons*', *HeyJ* 22.3 (1981), 331.

[9] Wink, W., 'Review of A.C. Thiselton's *The Two Horizons*', *ThT* 37.4 (Jan. 1981), 506, 508.

[10] Moberly, R.W.L., 'Review of A.C. Thiselton's *New Horizons in Hermeneutics*', *Anv* 11.1 (1994), 71; cf. Mulholland Jr., M.R., 'Sociological Criticism', in *Interpreting the New Testament: Essays on Methods and Issues* (eds. D.A. Black and D.S. Dockery; Nashville, TN.: Broadman & Holman Publishers, 2001), 34.

[11] Watson, F., 'Review of A.C. Thiselton's *New Horizons in Hermeneutics*', *BibInterp* 4.2 (1996), 252.

[12] Moore, S.D., 'Review of A.C. Thiselton's *New Horizons in Hermeneutics*', *ThT* 50.2 (Jul. 1993), 287.

subsequently endorsed by N.T. Wright and others.[13]

Of course, Thiselton is not equally esteemed in every quarter. Thus whilst Linda Woodhead acknowledges Thiselton's 'undeniable insights and critical power', she regards his work *Interpreting God and the Postmodern Self* (1995) as 'triumphalist', and complains concerning the book's 'broad-brush characterizations of modernity' and 'postmodernity',[14] the latter point being echoed by D.R. Stiver.[15] M.W. Nicholson even accuses Thiselton of 'abusing Wittgenstein',[16] whilst W.J. Lyons numbers among several who criticize Thiselton's responses to the work of Stanley Fish, and D.R. Stiver numbers among several who criticize Thiselton's responses to the work of Jacques Derrida.[17] Mostly, though, Thiselton is highly esteemed, and even where he is not, he is *still* considered to be significant enough to merit attention.

(2) However, *despite* Thiselton's status as 'one of the major contemporary Christian authorities on hermeneutics', C.G. Bartholomew remarks in 1996 that, 'there has been surprisingly little *thorough* interaction' with Thiselton's work.[18] More ominously, in 1994, A.K.M. Adam asserted that 'Thiselton's overall premise' in *New Horizons in Hermeneutics* 'is that hermeneutical debate since *The Two Horizons* has not adequately understood the conceptual tools which that work made

---

[13] Carson, D.A., *New Testament Commentary Survey* (Leicester: IVP, 1984, 1993, 2001, and later), 80; cf.: Thiselton, A.C., *The First Epistle to the Corinthians* (eds. H. Marshall and D.A. Hagner; Series: The New International Greek Testament Commentary; Grand Rapids: Eerdmans; Carlisle: Paternoster, 2000); Wright, N.T., *The Resurrection of the Son of God* (Christian Origins and the Question of God; Minneapolis: Augsburg Fortress, 2003), 279; Gill, D.W.J., '1 Corinthians', in *Romans to Philemon* (ed. C.E. Arnold; Grand Rapids, MI.: Zondervan, 2002), 187; Bockmuehl, M., "To be or not to be': The Possible Futures of New Testament Scholarship', *SJT* 51.3 (1998), 291-292; Wenham, D., *Paul and Jesus: The True Story* (Grand Rapids, MI.: Eerdmans, 2002), xi; and many reviewers of this work by Thiselton (see our bibliography).

[14] Woodhead, L., 'Theology and the Fragmentation of the Self', *IJSTh* 1.1 (Mar. 1999), 68-69; cf. Thiselton, A.C., *Interpreting God and The Postmodern Self: On Meaning, Manipulation and Promise* (SJT: Current Issues in Theology; Edinburgh: T&T Clark, 1995).

[15] Stiver, D.R., 'The Uneasy Alliance Between Evangelicalism and Postmodernism: A Reply to Anthony Thiselton', in *The Challenge of Postmodernism. An Evangelical Engagement* (ed. D.S. Dockery; Grand Rapids, Mi.: Baker Books, 1997), 239-253.

[16] Nicholson, M.W., 'Abusing Wittgenstein: The Misuse of the Concept of Language-Games in Contemporary Theology', *JEThS* 39 (Dec. 1996), 617-629.

[17] Lyons, W.J., *Canon and Exegesis: Canonical Praxis and the Sodom Narrative* (Sheffield: Sheffield Academic Press, 2002), 108-115; cf. Stiver, 'TUA', 239-253; cf. Stiver, D.R., *The Philosophy of Religious Language: Sign, Symbol, and Story* (Oxford: Blackwell, 1996), 189-192, cf. 243; cf. Stiver, D.R., 'Review of A.C. Thiselton's *Interpreting God and the Postmodern Self*', *ChSRev* 26.2 (1996), 227-229; cf. those to whom we respond in Chapter 7.

[18] Bartholomew, C.G., 'Three Horizons: Hermeneutics from the Other End - An Evaluation of Anthony Thiselton's Hermeneutical Proposals', *EuJTh* 5.2 (1996), 122-123. Italics ours.

available'.[19]

That is, on the one hand, there is a question mark over whether Thiselton has been given a proper *hearing* – at least so far as *written* responses to his work are concerned. On the other hand, there is also a question mark over whether Thiselton has been adequately *understood* – at least so far as the *conceptual advances* made in *The Two Horizons* are concerned. Bartholomew and Adam, then, hint at a problem that has to do with how Thiselton's work has been *received*.

Digging into the archives, we find that Thiselton's paper, 'Understanding God's Word Today'[20] - presented at the second National Evangelical Anglican Congress in 1977 in Nottingham, UK (NEAC '77) - divided 'his audience'. Thus, whilst John King rejoiced in 'the drubbing given to that pretentious term "hermeneutics"' at the Congress,[21] C. Buchanan described Thiselton's address as 'a sensation' of 'apologetics' where, 'deep down, at the gut-level, something shifted' so that 'we cannot be quite the same again'.[22]

Twenty-three years later, W.J. Lyons alludes to a lesser but parallel stir caused by Thiselton's paper, 'Signs of the Times',[23] which was presented at Thiselton's inaugural presidential address at the 1999 meeting of the Society for the Study of Theology (SST) held in Edinburgh, UK. Lyons writes, Thiselton's 'audience was informed of the use of' 'the work of Richard Rorty and Stanley Fish' 'by American theologians but' 'encouraged to regard this as an inexplicable [i.e. unjustifiable] error… And in the ensuing discussion, nothing happened to alter that situation'. That is, Lyons is saying that Thiselton adopted a controversial audience-dividing stance in relation to the thought of Rorty and Fish and that, in the estimate of Lyons and of many others at the meeting, Thiselton did not establish adequate grounds for his belief that appeals to Rorty and Fish were unjustifiable. To Lyons, Thiselton almost seemed to commit a *faux pas* given the number of 'American theologians' present at the meeting: why had Thiselton been so openly aggressive towards 'American' thought? It was hardly surprising, then, that Thiselton later verbally reassured us from the SST platform: 'some of my best friends are

---

[19] Adam, A.K.M., 'Review of A.C. Thiselton's *New Horizons in Hermeneutics*', *ModTh* 10 (1994), 433-434.

[20] Thiselton, A.C., 'Understanding God's Word Today: Evangelicals Face the Challenge of the New Hermeneutic. Address at the Second National Evangelical Anglican Congress, Nottingham, 1977', in *Obeying Christ in a Changing World, Vol. 1* (ed. J.R.W. Stott; Glasgow: Collins/Fountain Books, 1977), 90-122, (henceforth the 'long' article with this title).

[21] Douglas, J.D., 'Hermeneutical Hazards. NEAC '77 Report', *CEN* 22 Apr. (1977), 9; cf. King, J., 'Decent Lack of Respect', *CEN* 6 May (1977), 10.

[22] Buchanan, C., 'The Shifts at Gut Level', *CEN* 6 May (1977), 11.

[23] Thiselton, A.C., 'Signs of the Times: Towards a Theology for the Year 2000 as a Grammar of Grace, Truth and Eschatology in Contexts of So-Called Postmodernity. Presidential Paper of the Society for the Study of Theology', in *The Future as God's Gift: Explorations in Christian Eschatology* (eds. D. Fergusson and M. Sarot; Edinburgh: T&T Clark, 2000), 9-39.

American'.[24]

Thus, there are clearly unanswered questions to do with the *controversial character* of Thiselton's work, and to do with the *reception* of Thiselton's work. We may even ask whether or not Thiselton has been adequately heard or understood *at all*.

(3) The questions surrounding the reception of Thiselton's work only become more pertinent once comments about his *style of writing* are considered. S.W. Sykes, responding to *The Two Horizons* in 1982, asked Thiselton to 'show us plainly the core of his argument'.[25] In 1983 D.S. Dockery warned that the work was 'in one sense too detailed and comprehensive for anyone but the specialist to understand'.[26] J. Bowden, similarly, viewed *The Two Horizons* as 'so crammed with "A says X about C" that the actual issues never have room to breathe'.[27] J.B. Webster likened the work to 'an over-stocked art-gallery: indigestible, tedious, with the attendant danger of passing over a pearl of great price',[28] and M.J. Erickson added, 'this is not a book for the novice'.[29] Similar objections to Thiselton's style of writing may be found in responses to Thiselton's contribution to *The Responsibility of Hermeneutics* (1985),[30] in responses to *New Horizons in Hermeneutics* (1992),[31] and in responses to Thiselton's contribution to *The Promise of Hermeneutics* (1999).[32]

---

[24] Lyons, W.J., 'Serious Man, Rhetorical Man, Straw Man: Just How Much of a Threat is Stanley Fish to Christian Theology?' (Oxford: Unpublished Paper Presented at the Conference of the Society for the Study of Theology, 2000), 1.

[25] Sykes, S.W., 'Review of A.C. Thiselton's *The Two Horizons*', *Chman* 96.2 (1982), 157.

[26] Dockery, '*R 2H*', 136.

[27] Bowden, J., 'Review of A.C. Thiselton's *The Two Horizons*', *Th* 84.697 (Jan. 1981), 56.

[28] Webster, J.B., 'Review of A.C. Thiselton's *The Two Horizons*', *FTht* 107.3 (1980), 220.

[29] Erickson, M.J., 'Review of A.C. Thiselton's *The Two Horizons*', *JEThS* 23 (Dec. 1980), 373.

[30] cf.: Snodgrass, K.R., 'Review of R. Lundin's, A.C. Thiselton's and C. Walhout's *The Responsibility of Hermeneutics*', *CovQ* 45 (Nov. 1987), 200; Turner, M., 'Review of R. Lundin's, A.C. Thiselton's and C. Walhout's *The Responsibility of Hermeneutics*', *FTht* 113 (Oct. 1987), 182; Bray, G.L., 'Review of R. Lundin's, A.C. Thiselton's and C. Walhout's *The Responsibility of Hermeneutics*', *Chman* 100.3 (1986), 260.

[31] cf.: Brown, C., 'Review of A.C. Thiselton's *New Horizons in Hermeneutics*', *CalThJ* 30 (Apr. 1995), 232; Moo, D.J., 'Review of A.C. Thiselton's *New Horizons in Hermeneutics*', *TrinJ* 13 (Fall 1992), 250; Osborne, G.R., 'Review of A.C. Thiselton's *New Horizons in Hermeneutics*', *CRevBRel* 7 (1994), 93; Moore, '*R NH*', 287; Papaphilippopoulos, R., 'Review of A.C. Thiselton's *New Horizons in Hermeneutics*', *SJT* 47.1 (1994), 143; Thomas, G.J., 'Telling a Hawk from a Handsaw? An Evangelical Response to the New Literary Criticism', *EvanQ* 71.1 (1999), 40, n.10.

[32] cf.: Dray, S., 'Review of R. Lundin's, C. Walhout's and A.C. Thiselton's *The Promise of Hermeneutics*', *EgeI*, 18.3 (Aut. 2000), 96; Pickett, T., 'Review of R. Lundin's, C. Walhout's and A.C. Thiselton's *The Promise of Hermeneutics*', *RelLit* 32.3 (Aut. 2000), 108; Parry, R., 'Review of R. Lundin's, C. Walhout's and A.C. Thiselton's *The Promise of Hermeneutics*', *EuJTh* 9.2 (2000), 203; Moberly, R.W.L., 'Review of R. Lundin's, C. Walhout's and A.C. Thiselton's *The Promise of Hermeneutics*', *ExTim* 111.7 (Apr. 2000), 237; Gruneberg, K.,

Of course, others disagree. Thus, W.A. Dyrness found *The Two Horizons* 'lucid' and 'highly readable',[33] whilst Robert Morgan described it as 'a model of clarity and fair-mindedness',[34] and V.S. Poythress spoke of Thiselton's 'remarkable clarity of expression'.[35] Morgan also commented on the 'wonderful lucidity' of *New Horizons in Hermeneutics*,[36] whilst R.W.L. Moberly noted the book's 'clearly structured and powerfully developing argument'.[37] Francis Watson found the 'exposition... usually lucid enough to meet the needs of non-specialist readers',[38] whilst J.S. Reist Jr. spoke of 'sustained argument that proceeds fluently and carefully',[39] and W. Russell of a 'structured... logical flow' of argument.[40]

Nevertheless, a question remains: are the issues pertaining to the reception of Thiselton's work – namely Thiselton's sometimes controversial character and the difficulties involved in understanding his thinking - at all related to his style of writing? This question would be all the more pertinent if it emerged that some of those championing the clarity of Thiselton's work had not, in fact, understood it. Thus, whilst noting the briefer summaries by the likes of B.J. Walsh and C.G. Bartholomew, a more thorough and extended engagement with Thiselton's work – and with its reception - is justified.[41]

## B. The Discipline of Hermeneutics

Indeed, a fresh study of Thiselton's hermeneutical theory is shown to be all the more necessary when six sets of observations about *the discipline of hermeneutics more broadly* are juxtaposed – as follows.

Thus, (1), hermeneutics is a *disorganized and confusing* discipline. Hermeneutics is traditionally likened to Cretan labyrinths, to Gordian knots, or to Morbius loops, and gives rise to a great deal of black humor. Thus, Roger Lundin cites Steven Weinberg's reminiscence that '"a physicist friend of mine... in facing death... drew some consolation from the reflection that he would never again have to look

---

'Review of R. Lundin's, C. Walhout's and A.C. Thiselton's *The Promise of Hermeneutics*', *Anv* 17.3 (2000), 223.

[33] Dyrness, W.A., 'Review of A.C. Thiselton's *The Two Horizons*', *CTday* 25 (Apr. 10, 1981), 94.

[34] Morgan, 'R *2H*', 331.

[35] Poythress, V.S., 'Review of A.C. Thiselton's *The Two Horizons*', *WThJ* 43 (Fall 1980), 179.

[36] Morgan, R., 'Review of A.C. Thiselton's *New Horizons in Hermeneutics*', *ExTim* 104.6 (Mar.1993), 186.

[37] Moberly, 'R *NH*', 71.

[38] Watson, 'R *NH*', 253.

[39] Reist, J.S., 'Review of A.C. Thiselton's *New Horizons in Hermeneutics*', *JEThS* 38.3 (Sep. 1995), 457.

[40] Russell, W., 'Review of A.C. Thiselton's *New Horizons in Hermeneutics*', *TrinJ* 17.2 (Fall 1996), 241.

[41] Walsh, B.J., 'Anthony Thiselton's Contribution to Biblical Hermeneutics', *ChSRev* 14.3 (1985), 224-235; cf. Bartholomew, '3H', 121-135.

up the word 'hermeneutics' in the dictionary'".[42] Gerald L. Bruns, at the time a 'Professor of English', recalls Hans Kimmerle's defence of 'Schleiermacher's conception of hermeneutics as a systematic, procedural approach to the texts of our cultural past against Hans-Georg Gadamer's idea of hermeneutics as a discipline of reflection in which our own historicality is what is at issue'. Bruns then admits, 'since that time, hermeneutics has been something I have been struggling to get clear about'.[43] More recently, Brevard S. Childs has written,

> for at least a decade it has become commonplace to speak of a crisis in biblical interpretation. Almost everyone engaged in the study of the Bible is fully aware that the enterprise has run into real difficulty. The present crisis has been described in different ways: methodological impasse, conflicting private agendas, loss of clear direction, extreme fragmentation, unbridgeable diversity, and even a deep sense of resignation.[44]

K.J. Vanhoozer adds, 'contemporary debates concerning theories of interpretation can be as intimidating to the lay-reader as discussions of non-Euclidean geometry or quantum mechanics'.[45] And the problem is not new. J.P. Pritchard, writing in 1968, comments: 'In this latter half of the twentieth century, students of literature may well feel bewildered in the maze of critical approaches that have been proposed. The problem lies not in a lack of value in many of the approaches presented; it is rather in the lack of a controlling over-all view'.[46]

Thus, there is real disorganization and confusion in hermeneutics. To use the language of Childs, Vanhoozer, and Pritchard, there is dread, 'resignation', and life-long struggle for clarity amongst experts. There are 'crises in biblical interpretation' related to methodology, divided interests, directionlessness, 'fragmentation', and 'diversity'. There is 'intimidating' debate and 'the lack of a controlling overall' paradigm. Therefore, to use the language of the later Wittgenstein and P.R. Keifert respectively, it makes sense to 'look and see' if a potentially unheard 'encyclopedic' thinker - namely Thiselton - can help us to bring order to this disorganized situation.[47]

---

[42] Lundin, R., 'Introduction', in *Disciplining Hermeneutics. Interpretation in Christian Perspective* (ed. R. Lundin; Leicester; Apollos, 1997), 1.

[43] Bruns, G.L., *Hermeneutics: Ancient and Modern* (Yale Studies in Hermeneutics; New Haven: Yale University Press, 1992), ix; cf. the back cover of this book.

[44] Childs, B.S., 'Foreword', in *Renewing Biblical Interpretation* (eds. C.G. Bartholomew, C. Greene and K. Möller; Scripture and Hermeneutics Series; Vol. 1; Carlisle: Paternoster, 2000), xv.

[45] Vanhoozer, K.J., *Is There a Meaning in This Text? The Bible, The Reader, and the Morality of Literary Knowledge* (Grand Rapids: Zondervan, 1998), 10.

[46] Pritchard, J.P., 'Preface', in *On Interpretation and Criticism* (A. Boeckh; trans. J.P. Pritchard; Norman, Oklahoma: University of Oklahoma Press, 1968), vii.

[47] Wittgenstein, L., *Philosophical Investigations* (trans. G.E.M. Anscombe; Oxford: Blackwell, 1953, 2001), 31e; cf. Keifert, '*R 2H*', 408.

(2) However, even without the issue of disorganization hermeneutics is, theoretically, a *complex discipline*, involving more than one philosophical, or other kind of, conversation or discourse. Thus, for example, Gadamer writes, 'our question... is how hermeneutics, once freed from the ontological obstructions of the scientific concept of objectivity, can do justice to the historicity of understanding'. In other words (*sic*), 'understanding' has a historical character, where the validation of this assertion presupposes an excursion into the philosophy of *history*. And the 'understanding' of 'understanding' itself (cf. hermeneutics) is hindered by 'the scientific concept of objectivity', where this hindering constitutes a problem that cannot be solved without excursions into *epistemology* and into the *history* of *epistemology*.[48]

In another example of hermeneutical complexity Gadamer writes, 'the linguisticality of understanding is the concretion of historically effected consciousness'. In other words (*sic*), 'understanding' has a *linguistic* character shaped by how history has conditioned interpreters' prior (largely) unconscious (pre-)judgments, thoughts, or attitudes.[49] Gadamer's statement thus presupposes conversations about *history*, *language* and *thought* that move beyond conversations about interpreting texts or about textuality.[50]

In still another example of hermeneutical complexity Jürgen Habermas writes, 'hermeneutic inquiry lends methodological form to a process of arriving at mutual understanding (and self-understanding) which takes place on the pre-scientific level in the tradition-bound structure of symbolic interaction'. In other words (*sic*), 'mutual understanding' and 'self-understanding' occur at 'the... level' of everyday language conditioned by traditions, whereas hermeneutics reflects a more technical level of discourse that supposedly describes and facilitates 'mutual understanding' and 'self-understanding'.[51] Habermas's comment thus introduces us to the notion of the close relationship between understanding and *discourse* or *dialogue*, to a further conversation about *self-understanding*, or about a hermeneutic of *human selves*, and to another conversation about the role of *traditions* in the broader context of history. Habermas's link to the issue of "methodology" also hints at the *practicalities of interpretation*, though no single "method" may be in mind.

Elsewhere, Habermas writes, 'I regard the hermeneutic paradox that vexes cultural anthropology as the methodological reflex of a failure to differentiate co-ordination of action by systemic means from co-ordination in terms of social integration'. In other words (*sic*), there are often clashes between the systems societies use to direct or co-ordinate 'action' and the ways in which peoples' actual life-worlds and 'social integration' direct their 'action'. "System" is rent asunder

---

[48] Gadamer, H.-G., *Truth and Method* (trans. J. Weinsheimer and D.G. Marshall; London: Sheed & Ward, 1975, 1989), 265.

[49] Gadamer, *TM*, 389.

[50] E.g., Jeanrond, W.G., *Text and Interpretation as Categories of Theological Thinking* (Dublin: Gill and MacMillan, 1988).

[51] Habermas, J., *Knowledge and Human Interests* (London: Heinemann, 1972), 191.

from "life-world", generating Habermas's 'hermeneutic paradox'. Hermeneutics, then, relates to cultural anthropology, or to a critical sociological hermeneutic (or interpretation) of *(Western) culture*.[52]

We could go on. But our point is that, whenever we quote sentences about hermeneutics written by hermeneutical theorists, several different kinds of conversation seem to be presupposed, making hermeneutical language-use more opaque than most other kinds of language-use. Thus, in using the phrase "in other words" several times, we have highlighted the need to critique the opacity of hermeneutical discourse *itself*. It makes sense, therefore, to "look and see" if Thiselton's relatively untapped "encyclopedic" resources can help us to bring clarity to a complex discipline through an explication of its various conversations. The complexities will not be resolved overnight, but perhaps Thiselton can help us to make a start.

(3) Hermeneutics is often charged with, or is sometimes even defined as, being *abstracted from actual practical interpretation*. Thus, Gerald Bruns, our longsuffering Professor of English, has written, 'I thought hermeneutics might help me bring my professional and intellectual lives together. But it was many years before anything like this sort of reconciliation took place'. Thus, for Bruns, hermeneutics for a long time seemed to be abstracted from historical-literary interpretation, such that 'hermeneutics plods along, as if it belonged to other sorts of history'. Bruns 'leaves open… the question of whether ignorance of hermeneutics among literary critics is invincible or merely strategic'.[53]

For some, hermeneutics actually seems to get in the way of practical interpretation. Thus, Stephen D. Moore criticizes Thiselton's supposedly 'interminable intellectual detour' between the Bible and its 'practical application',[54] and F. Watson enquires as to whether or not Thiselton's 'hermeneutics' can only serve 'interpretation indirectly'. Crucially, Watson enquires concerning the 'relation of hermeneutical theory to interpretative practice'.[55]

These kinds of issues, in the eyes of some (see Chapter 5), have implications for so-called "ordinary" (or so-called "non-academic") readers of the Bible. Does hermeneutics rob "ordinary" readers of access to the biblical texts? Does hermeneutics create an elite of experts - a new hermeneutical magisterium - who alone can know what the Bible says?

According to Paul Ricoeur 'the aim of all hermeneutics is to struggle against cultural distance and historical alienation… This goal is attained only insofar as

---

[52] Habermas, J., *The Theory of Communicative Action. Volume 2. Lifeworld and System: A Critique of Functionalist Reason* (trans. T. McCarthy; Cambridge: Polity Press, 1987), 164. "System" and "life-world", and this artificial split between them, are emphasized by the use of speech-marks here because this is one of Habermas' very famous theses. On our use of speech-marks in the present study, see our comments on "Presentation" below.

[53] Bruns, *Hermeneutics*, ix, x.

[54] Moore, 'R *NH*', 287.

[55] Watson, 'R *NH*', 255.

interpretation actualizes the meaning of the text for the present reader'.[56] If Ricoeur's point here is correct, though, then perhaps there *should* be a clear link between hermeneutical theory and practice. What we seem to find, however, is that texts on hermeneutics are so abstract that talk of direct links between hermeneutical theory and practice understandably generates 'ribald' retort.[57] It makes sense, then, to "look and see" if Thiselton's work can help us to clarify the relationship(s) between hermeneutical theory and practice.

(4) Hermeneutics is in *theoretical disunity* in several ways, and is in need of a new unifying framework. We have already noted Brevard S. Childs' comments about a 'crisis in biblical interpretation' and about 'extreme fragmentation' and 'unbridgeable diversity'.[58] We have also already noted J.P. Pritchard's less recent remarks about 'the lack of a controlling over-all view' or paradigm (though we are cautious about using the term 'controlling').[59] This problem of theoretical disunity, though, is complicated, and has at least three or four aspects to it, as follows.

First, Childs' remarks appear, significantly, in the Foreword to the first volume of the 'Scripture and Hermeneutics Series', where this volume and subsequent volumes in the 'Scripture and Hermeneutics Series' were produced annually - during the first decade of the millennium - by the Scripture and Hermeneutics Seminar held in Cheltenham, UK. Thus, the Seminar was established largely *in response to* the current 'crisis in biblical interpretation'. And it is our contention here that *part* of this current 'crisis in biblical interpretation' concerns the problem of finding a *new unifying framework for hermeneutics*.[60]

Thus, in the year 2000, C.G. Bartholomew, one of the editors of the 'Scripture and Hermeneutics Series', wrote, 'modernity is now in crisis, and through its rootage in modernity, biblical interpretation is unavoidably affected'.[61] What is needed, then, according to Bartholomew, is a new 'rootage' for 'biblical interpretation', a transformed philosophical and/or theological 'paradigm' (Bartholomew draws the term 'paradigm' from Thiselton here) or 'subtext' within which biblical interpretation, or even interpretation more broadly, can revise and re-establish its theoretical co-ordinates. Thus, for example, if 'the philosophical subtext of', say, 'the [predominant] historical-critical method' of/during the 1950s and 1960s was 'post-Enlightenment [especially broadly positivist] philosophies of

---

[56] Ricoeur, P., *Hermeneutics and the Human Sciences. Essays on Language, Action, and Interpretation* (ed. and trans. J.B. Thompson; Cambridge: CUP, 1981), 185.
[57] Douglas, 'HH', 9.
[58] Childs, 'Foreword', xv.
[59] Pritchard, 'Preface', vii.
[60] Bartholomew, C.G., C. Greene and K. Möller, eds., *Renewing Biblical Interpretation* (Scripture and Hermeneutics Series; Vol. 1; Carlisle: Paternoster, 2000); cf. Childs, 'Foreword', xv.
[61] Bartholomew, C.G., 'Uncharted Waters: Philosophy, Theology and the Crisis in Biblical Interpretation', in *Renewing Biblical Interpretation* (eds. C.G. Bartholomew, C. Greene and K. Möller; Scripture and Hermeneutics Series; Vol. 1; Carlisle: Paternoster, 2000), 4.

history', then we might *now* ask what the *transformed* 'philosophical subtext' for historical criticism - and for other dimensions of criticism - might or should look like.⁶²

Second, H.C. White, writing in 1988, argued that the reason 'the work of Rudolf Bultmann has exerted a major influence on modern Biblical studies' is 'primarily because he faced, and responded... to the two horns of the twentieth century hermeneutical dilemma'. On the one hand, Bultmann 'embraced the disciplines of the historical-critical method as a means of dealing with the text as an artefact of the past'. On the other hand, 'he... drew upon the philosophy of Martin Heidegger to provide an existential analysis in terms of which the message of the New Testament could be made understandable... in the cultural framework of the twentieth century'. Unfortunately, though, Bultmann thereby 'bequeathed to the subsequent generation a bifurcation between collective, objective history (*Historie*) and individual, existential history (*Geschichte*), which, in spite of numerous efforts, has not yet been overcome'.⁶³

Moreover, and as we shall see later, this *historical* dualism or dichotomy is *only one* of the *dozens* of theoretical dualisms or dichotomies that plague contemporary hermeneutical theory.

That is, to use B.S. Childs' and C.G. Bartholomew's language respectively, part of 'the crisis' in contemporary 'interpretation' is related to *philosophical (and indeed to other kinds of) dualisms or dichotomies* – i.e. to internal inconsistencies within existing interpretative theories. Any transformed 'paradigm' or 'philosophical subtext' for hermeneutics, therefore, may no longer *be* 'modern', but it still needs to grapple with the problems '*bequeathed*' *by* 'modernity' (however we choose to define or to use the word 'modernity' and its cognates).⁶⁴ This state of affairs gives the contemporary search for a unifying framework for hermeneutics a second aspect – an aspect that has to do with overcoming the *existing* problematic dualisms or dichotomies that plague *existing* interpretative theories.

Third, a further angle of view on the problem of theoretical disunity in hermeneutics concerns whether hermeneutics is unified through the philosophy of *history*, through the philosophy of *language*, or through *theology*.

In *older* debates still struggling with the legacies of Cartesian, transcendental,

---

⁶² Bartholomew, 'UW', 4, 12. See also: Thiselton, A.C., 'Communicative Action and Promise in Inter-Disciplinary, Biblical, and Theological Hermeneutics', in *The Promise of Hermeneutics* (R. Lundin, C. Walhout and A.C. Thiselton; Grand Rapids and Cambridge: Eerdmans; Carlisle: Paternoster, 1999), 137; Bartholomew, C.G., *Reading Ecclesiastes: Old Testament Exegesis and Hermeneutical Theory* (Bristol: Unpublished University of Bristol PhD Thesis, 1996), 97; but see, Thiselton, A.C., 'New Testament Interpretation in Historical Perspective', in *Hearing the New Testament: Strategies for Interpretation* (ed. J.B. Green; Grand Rapids: Eerdmans; Carlisle: Paternoster Press, 1995), 17.

⁶³ White, H.C., 'The Value of Speech-Act Theory for Old Testament Hermeneutics', *Sem* 41 (1988), 41. Italics White's.

⁶⁴ Childs, 'Foreword', xv; cf. Bartholomew, 'UW', 4, 12. Italics ours.

and/or phenomenological notions of "human selfhood" – notably debates preceding and/or featuring the thought of Husserl, Heidegger and Bultmann - understandings of the *"human self" also* played a central role in attempts to construct unified hermeneutical theories (see Chapters 3, 4, 6, and 7). *These days*, however, a human "self" is considered to be a dynamic historical contingency that is "historically" or "linguistically" "situated" and/or "constituted". Even notions of human selfhood that are consistent with Trinitarian theology – notions according to which each dynamic human self is an ontologically distinct unique unrepeatable "one-off" - are not necessarily inconsistent with a viewpoint according to which a hermeneutical critique of human selves is an *aspect of* a hermeneutical critique of history – so long as "history" is understood theologically, Christo-eschatologically and in a way that is respectful of "persons-in-relation" (see Chapters 3, 4, 6, and 7). Thus, *these days*, the question of hermeneutical unification *now* centers on the question: "Which is ontologically prior and thus more 'basic' conceptually: history, language, or theology?"[65]

In relation to this question J.C. McHann Jr. notes Gadamer's stance 'that *language* is' 'the ultimate "horizon of a hermeneutic ontology"'. But McHann Jr. also rightly *contrasts* Gadamer's stance with Pannenberg's insistence that, ontologically-speaking, 'universal *history*' is to be seen as being *more* 'ultimate' than 'language', provided that the *most* 'ultimate ontological ground of hermeneutical understanding' is understood to be *God* (as Trinity).[66]

Is hermeneutics, then, unified linguistically, historically, or theologically?

The theological aspect of this question is perhaps best addressed in the context of a discussion that focuses on the relationship between philosophy and theology in hermeneutics – a discussion that we will come to in a moment.

However, in the present context of discussion, we are then still left with the issue of questions concerning comparative assessments of the *relative ontological prioritizations of (conceptualizations of) history and language* in existing hermeneutical theories. It makes sense, then, to look and see whether or not Thiselton's work can help us to grapple with this issue, and with the previous two issues, to do with overcoming theoretical disunities in hermeneutics.

(5) Hermeneutics also suffers from *inter-disciplinary, inter-traditional and smaller-scale polarizations*. This problem may be seen as a fourth aspect of the problem of

---

[65] Thiselton, 'CAP', 212, following A. Plantinga's use of the term 'basic'. With respect to these "older debates" see: Thiselton, *2H*, 143-292; cf. Thiselton, *NH*, 204-236; cf. 237-271; cf. 272-282. We are not at all arguing that a hermeneutical critique of human selves is unimportant, but only that such a critique is made too central in anthropocentric approaches. Having said this, of course, the opposite error must also be avoided – that of "deconstructing" selves by "sublating" critiques of subjectivity and of inter-subjectivity into a hermeneutical critique of language (see Chapter 7).

[66] McHann Jr., J.C., *The Three Horizons: A Study in Biblical Hermeneutics with Special Reference to Wolfhart Pannenberg* (Aberdeen: University of Aberdeen Ph.D. Thesis, 1987), 252-253; 325; 326 (quoted); 334; see our discussion in Chapter 3. Our italics.

theoretical disunities in hermeneutics, but it is important enough for us to treat it separately here. Notably, this broad kind of hermeneutical disunity – i.e. that of inter-disciplinary, inter-traditional and smaller-scale polarizations - often emerges where there is a lack of adequate *dialogue* between the many disciplines, traditions, movements, thinkers and stances that are (or who are) of relevance to hermeneutics.

Thus, (a), in relation to *inter-disciplinary* polarizations then, (i), hermeneutics suffers from inter-disciplinary polarizations between 'theological hermeneutics' and 'philosophical hermeneutics', and does so without offering any unified agreement on how these two disciplines inter-relate.[67]

Of course, on the one hand, it is clear that there are *historical* overlaps between philosophical and theological hermeneutics. That "hermeneuticians" (to adopt A.K.M. Adam's phrase) are forced to deal with philosophical questions is a point that is too obvious to merit comment. That they have to deal with theological questions is also true, however - not least because of the multi-disciplinary *history* of hermeneutics.[68] Thus, Gadamer recalls how 'Heidegger's magnum opus, *Being and Time*', which focuses on the philosophical question of 'the meaning of Being', 'grew out of his... encounter with contemporary Protestant theology during his appointment at Marburg in 1923'.[69] Such historical inter-disciplinary overlapping, however, means that certain apparent and more recent dichotomous separations between "philosophical" and "theological" hermeneutics should perhaps strike us as being somewhat *artificial*, at least historically speaking.

On the other hand, though, there is a growing question-mark over whether or not these more recent dichotomous separations between "philosophical" and "theological" hermeneutics – however artificial these dichotomous separations are *historically*-speaking - will also ultimately turn out to be artificial *theoretically*-speaking.

Thus, Ernst Fuchs of the New Hermeneutic was, unlike Heidegger, a theologian. Fuchs writes, 'the awkward difficulty in Bultmann's program... resides less in the New Testament manner of speech than in the New Testament compelling us to examine our self-understanding by learning... to inquire in

---

[67] Thiselton, 'CAP', 133; cf.: Thiselton, A.C., 'The Use of Philosophical Categories in New Testament Hermeneutics', *Chman* 87.1 (1973), 91; Thiselton, A.C., "The Theologian Who Must Not Be Ignored'. Article Review of W. Pannenberg's *Basic Questions in Theology, Vol. 2*', *CEN* 25 Feb. (1972), 11.

[68] Adam, 'R *IGPS*', 438; cf.: Thiselton, *NH*, 6; Thiselton, A.C., 'Thirty Years of Hermeneutics: Retrospect and Prospects', in *International Symposium on the Interpretation of the Bible* (ed. J. Krašovec; Ljubljana: Slovenian Academy of Sciences and Arts; Sheffield: Sheffield Academic Press, 1998), 1159.

[69] Gadamer, H.-G., 'Heidegger's Later Philosophy', in *Philosophical Hermeneutics* (H.-G. Gadamer; ed. D.E. Linge; London: University of California Press, 1976), 214; cf. Heidegger, M., *Being and Time* (trans. J. Macquarrie and E. Robinson; Oxford: Blackwell, 1962, 2001), 1.

principle as to our alternatives for understanding ourselves'.[70] In other words (*sic!*), Bultmann was correct, in Fuchs' view, to highlight *both* the problem of interpreting so-called "mythical" language in the Bible *and* the problem of having to become self-critical. Bultmann's hermeneutics, then, emphasize, and indeed the New Testament commands us to engage in, self-critical "appropriation" as an aspect of obedience to God. Similarly, for Fuchs, God's Word interprets *"'us'"*, *"'as its object'"*. That is, Bultmann's and Fuchs's hermeneutics involve the theological or biblical interpretation *of human selves*.[71]

However, theoretically speaking, Bultmann's and Fuchs's hermeneutics – on this point at least - are distinct from the hermeneutics of Gadamer. Thus, Thiselton criticizes Gadamer for *artificially* reducing the "'consciousness'" of the self (or of selves) to 'a mere "flickering in the closed circuits of historical life"'.[72] Indeed, in relation to Gadamer's hermeneutics, D.J. Schmidt cites the motto, *'de nobis ipsis silemus'* ('of ourselves we remain silent').[73] By contrast, of course, Bultmann is *famous* for his theological interpretation of the self or of selves, specifically in relation to Pauline anthropology. Thus, in 1932 Bultmann asks, 'what exactly is the split in man's existence under the law that is portrayed in Rom. 7:14ff?'[74]

It is clear, then – even if Walter Wink turns out to be incorrect to assert that Bultmann's work is 'the foundation on which all subsequent interpretative theory must be built'[75] – that any *historical* study of hermeneutics cannot avoid questions related to both philosophy and theology. Any separation between these two sets of *historical* questions would be artificial.

It is not so clear, however, how philosophical and theological hermeneutics

---

[70] Fuchs, E., 'The New Testament and the Hermeneutical Problem', in *New Frontiers in Theology. Discussions among Continental and American Theologians, Volume II: The New Hermeneutic* (eds. J.M. Robinson and J.B. Cobb, Jr.; New York: Harper and Row, 1964), 117; cf. Fuchs, E., 'The Theology of the New Testament and the Historical Jesus', in *Studies of the Historical Jesus* (Studies in Biblical Theology; Naperville, Ill.: Alec R. Allenson, Inc, & Chatham: SCM Press Ltd, 1964), 178.

[71] cf.: Thiselton, A.C., 'Truth', in *The New International Dictionary of New Testament Theology, Volume 3* (ed. C. Brown; Exeter: Paternoster; Grand Rapids: Zondervan, 1978), 898; Thiselton, A.C., 'Understanding God's Word Today', *CEN* 15 Oct. (1976), 6; cf. Thiselton, A.C., 'The New Hermeneutic', in *New Testament Interpretation: Essays in Principles and Methods* (ed. I.H. Marshall; Grand Rapids: Eerdmans; Exeter: Paternoster Press, 1977), 313. Italics in speech-marks Fuchs's, cited by Thiselton; others ours.

[72] Thiselton, 'TY', 1565; cf. Thiselton, *2H*, 305.

[73] Schmidt, D.J., 'Gadamer', in *A Companion to Continental Philosophy* (eds. S. Critchley and W.R. Schroeder; Blackwell Companions to Philosophy Series; Oxford: Blackwell Publishers Ltd., 1998), 434. Italics Schmidt's.

[74] Bultmann, R., 'Romans 7 and the Anthropology of Paul', in *Existence and Faith. Shorter Writings of Rudolf Bultmann* (trans. and ed. S.M. Ogden; New York: Meridian Books, Inc., 1960), 147.

[75] Wink, 'R *2H*', 507.

relate to one another when we look at this relationship from a more *theoretical* angle of view. How are philosophical and theological hermeneutics to be related to one another *theoretically* when we are answering *theoretical* questions about "history", or about "language", or about "selves", and so on? Or, again, are the discontinuities between philosophical and theological hermeneutics that can be seen from a more *theoretical* angle of view as artificial as are those that can be seen from a more *historical* angle of view?

Further, if theoretical discontinuities *do* turn out to be artificial then, to use Wink's phrase, should we "build" – or rebuild - hermeneutical theory within a received *theological* framework that *also* warrants contributions from philosophy? Thus, Thiselton asks, 'why should the interpreter of the New Testament concern himself with philosophy?'[76] Or, should we build – or rebuild - hermeneutical theory within a received *philosophical* framework that *also* warrants contributions from theology? C.G. Bartholomew and F. Watson ask questions of Thiselton at this point. Does Thiselton invoke theological and eschatological considerations, or what Bartholomew calls 'hermeneutics from the other end', 'only at the end' of philosophical discussions?[77] That is, to use Watson's language, does Thiselton leave theology to 'the margins of the discussion'?[78]

Making a related point, David Tracy remarks, 'since the general issues of hermeneutical and historical interpretation can be argued on extra-theological grounds, it seems imperative for each theologian to render explicit her/his general method of interpretation'.[79] According to Tracy, then, there is an implicit question concerning at what point, if at all, theological considerations should be allowed to contribute to hermeneutical theory-construction. And, if a transformed "paradigm" for hermeneutics is being sought, then this question concerning the respective roles of theology and philosophy in relation to hermeneutical theory-construction becomes all the more urgent.

Of course, (ii), inter-disciplinary polarizations in hermeneutics are not confined to tensions between "philosophical" and "theological" approaches. To give another example of inter-disciplinary polarizations in hermeneutics, then we may observe that tensions also exist between "philosophical hermeneutics" and "literary theory". It is Thiselton himself who, in 1992, cites C. Norris's book, *The Contest of Faculties: Philosophy and Theory after Deconstruction*, in which Norris writes,

> Philosophy has tended to bypass the problems of coming to terms with its own textual or rhetorical constitution. Literary theory (at least since the advent of deconstruction) has made these problems its peculiar concern, and in this sense has

---

[76] Thiselton, *2H*, 3.
[77] Bartholomew, '3H', 131.
[78] Watson, 'R *NH*', 256.
[79] Tracy, D., *The Analogical Imagination: Christian Theology & the Culture of Pluralism* (London: SCM, 1981), 59.

moved into regions of enquiry closed off to "philosophy" as such.[80]

It is this situation, Norris argues, that has led to the 'contest of faculties' in which the temptation is for some literary theorists to view philosophy as merely a kind of rhetoric with no more of a "formal" 'anchorage' in reality (however "reality" is conceived) than any other form of literature.[81] From the other side, however, certain philosophical strands are far from being silent on the question of 'language-use', and would be far from happy with the notion of reducing all issues connected to questions of language-use to matters of "rhetoric". It is at this juncture that *non-idealist* developments in speech-act theory – both in relation to questions concerning the relationship of language to "reality" and in relation to critiques of epistemology - become relevant.[82]

Since, as we shall see in the present study, Thiselton takes up rather distinctive stances in relation to these kinds of issues – and also in relation to the tensions between "theological" and "philosophical" hermeneutics, and in relation to other tensions between "faculties" (for example, between "biblical studies" and "systematic theology", and between "biblical studies" and "pastoral theology") - then it seems unwise not to find out what he says. In short, can Thiselton's work help us to resolve the inter-disciplinary polarizations that vitiate hermeneutics?

(b) A different angle of view on the problem of "polarization" may be highlighted by the use of the phrase, "*inter-traditional* polarization". Thus, the well-known history of tensions between 'Continental' and 'Anglo-American' traditions of thinking (whether theological or philosophical) is one very important instance of inter-traditional polarization that is of relevance to hermeneutics. Thus, for example, C. Conroy writes 'that the Anglo-American *theological* tradition in general remained "extrêmement réfractaire à la tradition herméneutique continentale"' (i.e. "extremely resistant to the Continental hermeneutical tradition").[83]

Admittedly, S. Critchley bemoans the many 'problems with the *de facto* distinction between analytic [or Anglo-American] and Continental *philosophy*' – problems that include 'lingering cultural stereotypes' born out of 'a whole range of vexed ideological issues in cultural politics and political geography'. In Critchley's estimate, 'both Continental and analytic philosophy are, to a great extent, sectarian self-descriptions of philosophy that are the lamentable consequence of the professionalism of the discipline'. Nevertheless, Critchley is still forced to speak of a 'gulf that separates' 'Continental philosophy' from 'analytic… philosophy', and

---

[80] Norris, C., *The Contest of Faculties: Philosophy and Theory after Deconstruction* (London: Methuen, 1985), 11; cf. Thiselton, *NH*, 130-131.
[81] Norris, *Contest*, 1-18. Our use of the term 'anchorage' here is from Thiselton, 'TNI', 11.
[82] See, for example, Wittgenstein, *PI*, 11-12.
[83] Conroy, C., 'Review of A.C. Thiselton's *The Two Horizons*', *Greg* 62.3 (1981), 563. Italics ours.

of the need for a 'dialogue' that crosses that 'gulf'.[84]

Since, as we shall see, Thiselton, on the one hand, seeks to *widen dialogue* between polarized Anglo-American and Continental (and other) *theological* traditions and, on the other hand, seeks 'to draw equally on', and overcome the polarization between, 'the Anglo-American tradition of *philosophical* analysis and' the 'Continental European [*philosophical*] traditions', then it would seem odd not to consult Thiselton's *mediatory* work in relation to the overcoming of these broader kinds of inter-traditional polarization.[85]

(c) At a more specific or more particular level, one could also speak of tensions between smaller-scale *"movements"* of thought in cases where these movements of thought are of relevance to/for hermeneutics. (Such movements, as we shall see, can also be seen as being "traditions" that are smaller in spatio-temporal *extent* than so-called "Continental" and "Anglo-American" traditions. There is no scale-determined "formal" cut-off point between a "tradition" and a "movement", or "school", of thought).

Thus, there are certainly tensions between approaches pertaining to hermeneutically-relevant movements that are – broadly-speaking - *diachronically* separated from one another. Approaches that could safely be described as being "broadly positivist" generally pre-date, and are very different in character from, approaches that could safely be described as being "broadly neo-pragmatic" or, to use Thiselton's language, as being "broadly socio-pragmatic". Twentieth-century 'philosophical' or 'logical positivism' (as opposed to the nineteenth-century 'positivism' of A. Comte) 'had pretty much run its course' 'by the late 1960s'. But 'neo-pragmatism' only 'emerged' following R. Rorty's work, *Philosophy and the Mirror of Nature*, which was published in 1979.[86]

Conversely, very different movements may be broadly *synchronous* with one-another, as is so with respect to the case of the significant differences between, on the one hand, so-called "philosophical-hermeneutical" approaches, which emerged following the publication of Gadamer's major work, *Truth and Method*, in 1960 and, on the other hand, 'the various so-called poststructuralist Francophone' approaches of 'Derrida' and others, which also first emerged in the 1960s and

---

[84] Critchley, S., 'Introduction: What is Continental Philosophy?', in *A Companion to Continental Philosophy* (eds. S. Critchley and W.R. Schroeder; Blackwell Companions to Philosophy Series; Oxford: Blackwell Publishers Ltd., 1998), 6; cf. 8; cf. 14. First italics Critchley's, second italics ours.

[85] Thiselton, 'TY', 1560-1561. Italics ours.

[86] Fotion, N.G., 'Logical Positivism', in *The Oxford Companion to Philosophy* (ed. T. Honderich; Oxford: OUP, 1995), 507-508; cf. Lacey, A.R., 'Positivism', in *The Oxford Companion to Philosophy* (ed. T. Honderich; Oxford: OUP, 1995), 705-706; cf. Kögler, H.-H., 'Neo-Pragmatism', in *The Oxford Companion to Philosophy* (ed. T. Honderich; Oxford: OUP, 1995), 614; cf. Thiselton, *NH*, 536.

1970s.[87]

Since Thiselton, by 1992 at the latest, seeks to critique, to draw positively from, and to mediate between, *all four of these* traditions, movements, or schools – i.e. positivist, socio-pragmatic, philosophical-hermeneutical, and poststructuralist traditions, movements, or schools - then it makes sense to look and see if Thiselton can help us overcome some of the polarizations that exist between them (see, especially, Chapters 6 and 7).

(d) At an even more specific level, one could speak of tensions between the approaches of different "thinkers" who are of relevance to hermeneutics. Famous *polarized clashes or encounters* in the histories of traditions of relevance to hermeneutics include those between Gadamer and Habermas, between Gadamer and Derrida, between Derrida and Searle, between the later Wittgenstein and Popper, and so on.[88]

Conversely, there have also been famous *non-encounters* – scenarios where theorists have come to wonder why (insights derived from the thinking of) certain major contributors to hermeneutical theory have not been brought into dialogue with one another (or each other) earlier. Thus, as Thiselton himself points out, even by 1980 (when *The Two Horizons* was published) relatively few thinkers had allowed dialogue to develop between the thought of the later Wittgenstein and that of Heidegger and of Gadamer.[89]

And, of course, speaking of "non-encounters", then there can also be polarizations between over-selective *appeals to* specific thinkers or – on a slightly wider scale – between over-selective appeals to *specific groupings* of "already-sanctioned" thinkers (or sources) who (or that) support prior "already-sanctioned" conclusions.

Thus, in 1970, Thiselton criticizes W. Nicholls for neglecting 'Wittgenstein, and... Anglo-American achievements in linguistic philosophy' but, *in the same year*, Thiselton criticizes J. Pelikan for not giving 'more urgent priority' to 'Ebeling on hermeneutics'. That is, Thiselton opposes *over-selectivity* – regardless of whether its flavor is 'Continental', 'Anglo-American', or of any other kind.[90]

Similarly, D.A. Carson discusses R. Kysar's "survey" of 'the use of parallels in

---

[87] Linge, D.E., 'Editor's Introduction', in *Hans-Georg Gadamer: Philosophical Hermeneutics* (H.-G. Gadamer; trans. & ed. D.E. Linge; London: University of California Press, 1976), xi; cf. Critchley, 'Introduction', 4.

[88] On the debates between Gadamer and Habermas and between Gadamer and Derrida see, Grondin, J., *Hans-Georg Gadamer: A Biography* (trans. J. Weinsheimer; New Haven and London: Yale University Press, 2003), 301-311; cf. 324-329; cf. Schmidt, 'Gadamer', 437; on the debates between the later Wittgenstein and Popper and between Derrida and Searle respectively, see Chapters 6 and 7 of the present study.

[89] Thiselton, *2H*, 24-47.

[90] cf.: Thiselton, A.C., 'Theological Survey Has No Rival: Review of W. Nicholls' *The Pelican Guide to Modern Theology*', *CEN* 13 Feb. (1970), 12; Thiselton, A.C., 'Mixed Encyclopaedia of Continental Theology: Review of J. Pelikan's *Twentieth Century Theology in the Making, Volume 2*', *CEN* 3 Jul. (1970), 8.

the examination of the Johannine prologue (John 1:1-18) as undertaken by C.H. Dodd and Rudolf Bultmann'. Carson notes Kysar's finding that 'of the three hundred or so parallels' between 'the Johannine prologue' and other ancient sources 'that each of the two scholars adduced, the overlap' – i.e. the 'overlap' between the two sets of 'parallels' - 'was only 7 percent'. Carson remarks that 'one can only conclude that neither scholar had come close to a comprehensive survey of potential backgrounds'.[91]

Since, as we shall see, Thiselton's whole approach is *characterized* by "ever-widening dialogue" then it makes sense to look and see whether or not Thiselton's ever-widening dialogue could provide solutions that are of relevance to the problems caused by these – and other - kinds of over-selectivity.

Similarly, it makes sense to look and see whether or not Thiselton's *mediatory* approach helps us to resolve any of the polarizations that pertain to famous "encounters" - or to famous "non-encounters" - between specific thinkers relevant for/to hermeneutics.

(e) From still another angle of view, hermeneutics also suffers from polarizations that relate to opposing *stances* in relation to *specific approaches, issues or questions*. Even at this level of consideration, however, Thiselton may still be found mediating between, and attempting to overcome, unnecessary polarizations between "positions". It would seem odd, therefore, to ignore his work on such matters.

Thus, for example, Thiselton attempts to overcome undue polarization between approaches that over-emphasize *ancient textual horizons* and approaches that over-emphasize *present reader-horizons*. Thus if, traditionally, 'New Testament study' has often had 'an exclusively objectivistic concern with past facts… or… information for its own sake', then some 'Latin American' approaches to hermeneutics encourage a distorted 'activism' that over-emphasizes the 'present'.[92]

To give another example, we may note that Thiselton attempts to overcome the 'polarized' 'debate' between, on the one hand, W. Von Humboldt and B.L. Whorf, who (broadly-speaking) held to the view that 'thought' is determined by 'language', and, on the other hand, certain strands in 'general linguistics' that held to the view that 'thought' is almost completely independent of language.[93]

To give a final example, we may note how Thiselton attacks 'polarization'

---

[91] Carson, D.A., *Exegetical Fallacies* (Grand Rapids, MI.: Baker Book House Company, 1984), 43-44.

[92] Thiselton, 'UPC', 98; cf. Thiselton, 'U (long)', 95-97.

[93] Thiselton, A.C., 'Language and Meaning in Religion', in 'Word', in *The New International Dictionary of New Testament Theology. Volume III* (ed. C. Brown; Exeter: Paternoster; Grand Rapids: Zondervan, 1978; actually written by 1977), 1126-1127; cf.: Thiselton, A.C., *New Testament Hermeneutics and Philosophical Description: Issues in New Testament Hermeneutics with Special Reference to the Use of Philosophical Description in Heidegger, Bultmann, Gadamer, and Wittgenstein* (Sheffield: University of Sheffield Ph.D. Thesis, 1977; written by Dec. 1976), 186-192; Thiselton, *2H*, 133-139.

between "'hard'" ("'propositional'") 'and "soft"' ("'non-propositional'", "subjectivist", or "existentialist"') 'views' of 'biblical' "'truth'".[94]

We could go on. Historical and theoretical polarizations, differences and/or disunities of various magnitudes can be presented or highlighted on many levels of spatio-temporal scale - all the way from the inter-continental level down to the subtleties of inconsistency within single texts, or all the way from comparisons between ancient and recent approaches to interpretation to comparisons between the approaches and conclusions of writers who are working at the same time in the same academic settings.

Our point, though, is that given Thiselton's aforementioned attempts to *dialogue or mediate between* different disciplines, traditions (whether continental in scale or having a scale closer to that of movements or schools), thinkers, and stances on specific questions, then it does not make sense to ignore what he says on matters to do with *unnecessary polarizations* between the same.

(6) Contemporary hermeneutics is split in several ways over what actually happens, or over what should happen, during the processes of understanding or during *"responsible" 'interpretation'*. Robert W. Funk writes, 'he who lays a violent hand on his tradition must beware of falling statuary. Knowledge of the imminent hazard goes hand in glove with the right grasp of the temporality, the historicality, of that tradition. And such knowledge makes one circumspective'. Thus, Funk reasons, there is a 'responsibility for the past, which carries with it joint responsibility for the future'. The term 'responsibility' here is important. For what we actually *do* in any given instance of interpretation will likely be driven by what we think we *ought* to do in any given instance of interpretation. That is, interpretative responsibility and interpretative practice are closely inter-related.[95]

Having said this, we should note that Stanley Fish, in his 'Introduction' to his book, *Is There a Text in This Class?* (1980), admits that he 'gave up the project of trying to identify the one true way of reading'. For Fish, the only sense in which there could be 'the one true way of reading' would be if one were to come up with 'a way' others *in the present horizon* 'accepted'. And even then it would only be 'the one true way of reading' 'for a time'.[96]

However, to use the language of both Thiselton and Fish, what *then* happens to interpretative "responsibility" is that it becomes something relative to whatever "norms" define what constitutes "responsibility" in any given 'interpretative

---

[94] Thiselton, *2H*, 436-438; cf.: 432-434; 310; 371; cf. Thiselton, A.C., 'The Multi-Model Character of Holy Spirit Language', *CEN* 11 Apr. (1974), 8; cf. Thiselton, A.C., 'The Semantics of Biblical Language as an Aspect of Hermeneutics', *FTht* 103.2 (1976), 116, 117.

[95] Funk, R.W., *Language, Hermeneutic, and Word of God. The Problem of Language in the New Testament and Contemporary Theology* (New York: Harper and Row, 1966), xi; cf. Thiselton, 'U (long)', 121, 95, 119. Italics ours.

[96] Fish, S., 'Introduction, or How I Stopped Worrying and Learned to Love Interpretation', in *Is There a Text in This Class? The Authority of Interpretative Communities* (S. Fish; London: Harvard University Press, 1980), 16.

community'. But then, in such a scenario, if communities change, then 'norms' also change; and if 'norms' change, then "responsibility" changes; and if "responsibility" changes, then interpretative practice also changes.[97]

But this scenario is potentially very different to that presented by Funk. For Funk, 'responsibility for the future' *is a function of* 'responsibility for the past'. For Funk, responsible interpretation and appropriation, which shape the future, presuppose a 'right grasp [including a right textual grasp] of the temporality, the historicality, of [a] tradition'.[98]

Not surprisingly, Gadamer has also made a similar point. He writes, 'the general structure of understanding is concretized in historical understanding, in that the concrete bonds of custom and tradition [including those that are textually-transmitted] and the corresponding possibilities of one's own future become effective in understanding itself'. That is, for Gadamer, 'understanding' actualizes 'future' 'possibilities' from within the constraints (including the textual constraints) of 'tradition' – even if these 'future' 'possibilities' are *not* wholly determined by, or imprisoned within, such 'constraints'.[99]

That is, for Gadamer, the past – including that aspect of the past that is epistemologically-accessible through texts - lends *at least some* shape to what could count as 'responsibility' in the present and future. Irresponsible interpretations and appropriations, then, could "trip over" the past, just as robbing a bank "trips over" a pre-existing law, and could lead, to use Funk's phrase, to the 'imminent hazard' 'of falling statuary' (we might substitute the term "statutory"!).[100]

In short, (and again using the language of both Thiselton and Fish), is responsible interpretation a matter of conformity to an "interpretative community's" present "norms" only? Or, alternatively, is responsible interpretation a matter of conformity to "norms" that emerge *not only* from *present* communities, but also from *past* traditions that are largely *external to* any given present community and, potentially, from *past textually transmitted* traditions that are largely *external to all* present communities?

This question leads to another question, however: can past traditions and their norms even be *textually or epistemologically accessed at all* by any given present interpretative community? Some, in Stanley Fish's wake, would say not. W.J. Lyons, for example, urges that the 'important difference' between his hermeneutics and Thiselton's is 'the loss' (in Lyons' hermeneutics, but not in Thiselton's) 'of the adjudicative text'.[101] By contrast, Thiselton, after F. Mussner,

---

[97] Fish, 'Intro', 16; cf. Fish, S., 'Normal Circumstances, Literal Language, Direct Speech Acts, the Ordinary, the Everyday, the Obvious, What Goes without Saying, and Other Special Cases', in *Is There a Text in This Class? The Authority of Interpretative Communities* (S. Fish; London: Harvard University Press, 1980), 268.

[98] Funk, *Lang*, xi.

[99] Gadamer, *TM*, 264.

[100] Funk, *Lang*, xi.

[101] Lyons, 'SM', 3.

and drawing on Gadamer, allows that texts can – to some extent - constitute "'history as operative influence'".[102] In this view, to follow Thiselton and his adoption of Gadamer's language, texts *can* somehow potentially "speak" from the past, so as to actively contribute to the shape of or, to use Lyons' language, so as potentially and provisionally to "adjudicate" over and thus to lend some shape to, what counts as present (and future) "responsible interpretation".[103]

These points, though, lead to yet another question: even if a widely applicable notion of responsible interpretation could be formulated, what is it that would then actually be *done* during interpretation? Earlier on we noted C.G. Bartholomew's comments about unavoidable changes in 'the philosophical subtext' of 'historical-critical method[s]'.[104] But do these changes mean that interpretation can no longer use *any* form of historical criticism? Or, alternatively, do they mean that we need to use a *new* form of historical criticism? Peter Barry notes that the movement, the New Historicism, originating in the work of Stephen Greenblatt around 1980,

> accepts Derrida's view that there is nothing outside the text, in the special sense that everything about the past is only available to us in textualized form: it is "thrice processed", first through the ideology, or outlook, or discursive practices of its own time, then through those of ours, and finally through the distorting web of language itself.[105]

Is the "New Historicism", however, part of what *should* now be done in interpretation, or are there *other* "new" approaches to historical criticism?

Thus, questions about hermeneutical *practice* raise issues about hermeneutical *responsibility*, about textual *epistemological accessibility*, and ultimately about philosophical (and/or theological) *subtexts*. It makes sense, then, to look and see if Thiselton's work can help us to answer the question concerning what could count as "responsible interpretation" in any *transformed* hermeneutical paradigm.

Taking this last point together with our previous points about the state of the contemporary discipline of hermeneutics, and about Thiselton himself, then we may safely conclude that a fresh engagement with Thiselton's hermeneutical theory is warranted, and even urgently required.

## C. Scope, Approach, Presentation, and Comments on Language-Uses

Of course, though, such an engagement is easier said than done. Thus, (1), I had prepared and largely completed hefty analyses of *New Horizons in Hermeneutics*

---

[102] Cited in, Thiselton, *2H*, 45.

[103] Thiselton, *2H*, 310-313.

[104] Bartholomew, 'UW', 4.

[105] Barry, P., *Beginning Theory. An Introduction to Literary & Cultural Theory* (Manchester: Manchester University Press, 1995), 175, 173; cf. Dean, W., 'The Challenge of the New Historicism', *JRel* 66 (1986), 280.

(1992), *Interpreting God and the Postmodern Self* (1995), and of Thiselton's contribution to *The Promise of Hermeneutics* (1999) before I realized that the basic framework of Thiselton's hermeneutical theory was completed by the time of *The Two Horizons* (1980). After 1980, Thiselton was largely, *if not entirely*, responding to other thinkers from a theoretical platform established *prior* to that date.

Indeed, we recall A.K.M. Adam's observation that the 'premise' behind *New Horizons in Hermeneutics* was that the preceding 'hermeneutical debate' had 'not adequately understood' *The Two Horizons*.[106] Further, M.G. Brett adds that *New Horizons in Hermeneutics* 'builds on the philosophical foundations laid in the previous work' – i.e. in *The Two Horizons*.[107]

Thus, in relation to the question of the *scope* of the present study, I made the decision to re-focus on Thiselton's formative works (those published between 1965 and 1980) in order to get at the very heart of his thinking. Of course, my aim was still to evaluate these works within the diachronic context of understanding made possible by my analyses of later works by Thiselton. Nevertheless, my focus had become not so much issues such as, say, Thiselton's later attacks on thinkers such as R. Rorty; rather, my focus had become more directed towards the place *from which* those attacks were being carried out. In order to demonstrate that an understanding of *The Two Horizons* is the key to any assessment of that place, I shall seek – in the present study - to demonstrate *The Two Horizons'* crucial relevance in relation to my responses to even those amongst Thiselton's more *recent* critics, some of whom appeal to post-structuralist and/or to neo- or socio-pragmatic sources.

(2) It should also be pointed out that, in the present study, I was unable to adopt *Thiselton's approach* whereby he offers a nexus of historical responses to others' thinking. This was because my primary aim was to expound 'the core of' Thiselton's thought systematically in response to S.W. Sykes' request (see above) that Thiselton 'show us plainly the core of his argument'. Thus, on the one hand, I have employed a structuralist methodology (not a structuralist ideology) so as to break down or analyze Thiselton's responses – i.e. his responses to others' thinking - into their component 'semiotic elements', and so as then to reorganize these 'semiotic elements' in order (in Heidegger's language) to "gather together" or synthesize the "world" of Thiselton's own thought. On the other hand, and in order not to fall into the potential ahistoricisms of structuralist methodology, I have at all points preserved historical sensitivity such that this "gathered world" of Thiselton's thought – including the many actual or re-shaped text-strings from Thiselton's own texts that remain scattered throughout the text of the present

---

[106] Adam, 'R NH', 433-434.
[107] Brett, M.G., 'Review of A.C. Thiselton's *New Horizons in Hermeneutics*', *Th* 96.772 (Jul./Aug. 1993), 314.

study – is presented in terms of chronologically developing themes.[108]

Thus, in relation to the organization of the present study, then Chapters 1 and 2 are more historically oriented, though without overlooking theory, and examine, respectively, (a), Thiselton's earliest work between 1959 and 1970 and, (b), the historical context presupposed by Thiselton's major formative development as a thinker between 1970 and 1980. Chapters 3 to 7 are more theoretically oriented, and are divided into themes or hermeneutical "conversations", though in a historically sensitive way. Thus, Chapter 3 focuses on eschatology and epistemology; Chapter 4 focuses on language, Western culture, and on human selves; Chapter 5 focuses on understanding and/or on 'the hermeneutical task' and hermeneutical circle (and therefore on "responsible interpretation" and its outcomes); and Chapters 6 and 7 focus on dialogue, history, understanding, theology, objectivity, the unification of hermeneutics, and on the problem of hermeneutical foreclosure.[109]

Whilst my primary aim is to explicate the *value* of Thiselton's formative hermeneutical theory for the discipline of hermeneutics more broadly, I shall from time to time level constructive *criticisms* at Thiselton's formative work. Nevertheless, the constructive criticisms that I level at Thiselton's formative work are unique to this study, and will not be found elsewhere in the literature. Broadly speaking, I have concluded, and have attempted to thoroughly and exhaustively demonstrate, that Thiselton's work has often been grossly misunderstood and misrepresented in the literature. In the present study, therefore, I have constructively criticized Thiselton's formative work only after first attempting to properly listen to it for well over a decade.

Three of the *several* constructive criticisms that I will bring to bear on Thiselton's formative work, though, will emerge from an attempt to give Heidegger, Gadamer, and the later Wittgenstein a chance to reply to Thiselton's reading and use of their work (see Chapters 3 and 6).

(3) Several near-insuperable difficulties related to *presentation* arose during the writing of the present study. These difficulties emerged during my aforementioned attempts to rebuild the "gathered world" of Thiselton's thought synthetically and systematically from "actual or re-shaped text-strings from Thiselton's own texts" – i.e. from the "semiotic elements" present in Thiselton's texts. After wrestling with these difficulties for over a decade, I found that the following procedures were unavoidable *faute de mieux* (i.e. for want of better alternatives).

Thus, (a), the problem of constructing complex theoretical – *and yet simultaneously grammatically correct* - sentences from multiple (i.e. several hundred) sources forced me to combine straight citation (single speech-marks) with paraphrase (double speech-marks). The alternative would have been for me to

---

[108] Sykes, 'R 2H', 157. On 'semiotic elements' see, Thiselton, A.C., 'Keeping up with Recent Studies: II. Structuralism and Biblical Studies: Method or Ideology?', *ExTim* 89 (Aug. 1978), 332; on 'gathering' and 'world'; see, Thiselton, *2H*, 337-338.

[109] See, Thiselton, 'NH', 326.

borrow concepts or language-stretches from Thiselton and from other thinkers without highlighting the fact, which would have been unacceptable.

In addition, (b), since Thiselton *very often* presents his views indirectly through the use of *citations taken from the works of other thinkers*, then there was *no choice* but to use multiple speech-marks more often than would be normal in common practice. The alternative would have been to be seemingly attributing concepts or language-stretches from other thinkers – for example, Heidegger – directly to Thiselton, which *also* would have been unacceptable. Thiselton's approach is unique, and so a unique methodology had to be employed in the present study.

(c) There was also the problem (shared by all hermeneuticians) of highlighting various key hermeneutical concepts or other language-stretches - for various reasons determined by context and too numerous to list here – on occasions *where sometimes no act of citation was being performed*. I decided to use the convention of using double speech-marks in such instances – including instances where I was coining phrases, presenting hybrid-concepts, or positing rhetorical questions, paraphrases, or self-citations – so as to alert and instruct the reader *not necessarily* to look for a reference. The alternative – using single speech-marks without a footnote-marker – would have given the false impression that I was presenting unreferenced citations, which would have been unacceptable.

Admittedly, on occasions when there *are* acts of citation, *merely-highlighted* concepts and language-stretches on the one hand, and, *paraphrased* concepts and language-stretches on the other hand, could *potentially* be confused with one-another (an unavoidable *faute de mieux*). But reference to the cited sources and to context should be sufficient to clarify matters.

Occasional highlighted concepts or phrases *within* rhetorical or paraphrased stretches are highlighted by the use of single speech-marks. Being additionally embedded within double speech-marks, however, these concepts or phrases are always distinguishable from citations.

Finally, (d), the problem of constructing complex theoretical sentences from multiple sources also unavoidably led to footnotes that threatened to become too voluminous for comfort. I found that the *only* way to handle this problem was to combine *footnote-abbreviation* (a comprehensive key to footnote-abbreviations is provided in Appendix 1) with the practice of – sometimes - *gathering sources together under single footnotes at the end of some paragraphs*. The alternatives – both unacceptable - would have been *either* to omit some of my sources, *or* to have dozens of footnotes within single paragraphs and thus to "repeat-reference" sources in the footnotes so often as generate far more volume of footnote-text than of main-text on many pages.

In our view, the more a study moves *from the analytic to the synthetic*, the more it will have to grapple with precisely these cosmetic problems. Very many studies are (rightly) analytical. This study, however, is largely synthesis-built-post-analysis.

(4) Concerning some of my *language-uses* in the present study then, (a), it should be noted that whilst I follow Thiselton in using the term "narrow" – in a very specific sense - in relation to certain famous hermeneutical thinkers, neither of us

at all mean to say that such great historical figures were/are "narrowly read". Rather, we are saying that, in relation to these thinkers, there is a problem of "narrowness" that has to do with the number of traditions and disciplines that are allowed to contribute constructively to the dialogues implicit in the critical-theoretical syntheses that are operative at the level of their "pre-understandings" when they approach both hermeneutical theory-construction and practice – i.e. to do with the theoretical sublation-filters *through which* they critically assess and/or process and/or sublate that which emerges *from* their wide reading.[110]

I should also note that, (b), my uses of the phrases "hermeneutics" and "the discipline of hermeneutics" can include connotations of both "theory" and "practice", such that I sometimes depart from a common language-use in which the term, "hermeneutics", refers solely to "interpretative theory". J. Grondin admits both definitions of "hermeneutics" - and I use both. Further, the title of Professor F. Watson's book, *Paul and the Hermeneutics of Faith* (2004), which largely contains biblical exegesis rather than interpretative theory, suggests the acceptability of a practical connotation to the use of the term "hermeneutics".[111]

Nevertheless, as Professor Watson rightly noted in a verbal response to an earlier version of the present study, hermeneutical *theory* – including the *theory* of hermeneutical practice itself - is the present study's predominant focus. Of course, though, the present study remains very much a *practical* exercise in interpretation in that it performs an interpretation of *Thiselton's* formative works (and of other theoretical texts).

Ultimately, given the Conclusions at the end of the present study, we may be tempted to speculate as to whether or not all hermeneutics can be conceived of as "biblical interpretative events" in that the emerging philosophy that unifies theoretical hermeneutics appears to be a philosophy that "resonates" with Scripture. But this theoretical point does not necessarily mean that – at the practical level - it is always the Bible that is being interpreted (as we saw in relation to Ernst Fuchs' remarks earlier), which is why the phrase "biblical hermeneutics" is used only sometimes in the present study. Nevertheless, we sometimes do use just the term "hermeneutics" when, strictly speaking, it is "biblical hermeneutics" that is in view. It is hoped that the contexts of discussion for our uses of these terms will clarify any ambiguities.[112]

Indeed, what "hermeneutics" amounts to in practice will actually differ from case to case. Any single "paradigm" at the level of "philosophical and/or theological subtext" should not lead to a monopolization of interpretative practice by any single "paradigm" at the level of interpretative goals, strategies, critical tools, or models of texts or of textuality. And even different "subtexts" should

---

[110] See, Thiselton, *NTH*, xxv, conc. 6; cf. Thiselton, *2H*, 109, 114.

[111] Grondin, J., *Introduction to Philosophical Hermeneutics* (trans. J. Weinsheimer; Yale Studies in Hermeneutics; New Haven: Yale University Press, 1994), 17-18; cf. Watson, F., *Paul and the Hermeneutics of Faith* (London: T & T Clark International, 2004).

[112] cf.: Thiselton, 'CAP', 134; Reist, 'R *NH*', 459.

remain in dialogue with one another, which is why we were unhappy with J.P. Pritchard's notion of 'a *controlling* over-all view' or paradigm earlier.[113]

(c) We should also note that, in the present study, when we use the terms "theology", "theological", and their cognates, we mean either "biblical theology (provisionally understood)" or "theology provisionally taken to be *consistent with* Christian Scripture" – unless the context of discussion dictates otherwise. Thus, for example, sometimes it is clear from the context of discussion that our use of the word "theology" connotes a reference to "the discipline of Christian theology" more broadly – i.e. to a *larger-scale* discipline that includes *smaller-scale* disciplines such as biblical studies, systematic theology, pastoral theology, philosophical theology, and so on.

(d) Sometimes, certain concepts appear in both hyphenated and non-hyphenated forms (e.g. a-historical cf. ahistorical; pre-understanding cf. preunderstanding; post-modern cf. postmodern; post-structuralist cf. poststructuralist; and so on). In such instances there appears to be no universal agreement as yet with regard to which forms are to be adopted, and so the present study reflects this state of affairs. This approach may *appear* inconsistent, but it is in fact more *accurate* (historically-speaking).

And finally, (e), we prefer not to use the pronoun, "I", unless absolutely necessary and so we will endeavor not to do so in what follows. Nevertheless, this preference does not reflect any Gadamerian antipathy to the theoretical role of 'autobiography' in hermeneutics on our part.[114] Rather, for us, it is just a matter of an inherited (and preferred) style.

---

[113] Pritchard, 'Preface', vii. Italics ours.
[114] cf. Gadamer, *TM*, 276-277.

CHAPTER 1

# Widening Dialogue Towards Critical Synthesis: The Emergence of Thiselton's Hermeneutical Programme from 1959-1970

## A. Preliminary Comments: Where to Begin

Anthony C. Thiselton suggests that his article, 'Thirty Years of Hermeneutics: Retrospect and Prospects' (1998), is the place to begin if we are to understand his hermeneutical theory aright.[1] This 'short summary' outlines 'the content' of his writings on hermeneutics prior to 1998, together with their contexts – the 'universities' of Bristol, Sheffield, Durham, and Nottingham.[2]

In this 'summary', Thiselton divides his career into four periods. The first period, 1963-1970, is crowned by his article, 'The Parables as Language-Event' (1970), though Thiselton published another 58 writings during this time.[3] Thiselton's second period, 1971-1980, culminates with his most famous work, *The Two Horizons* (1980), which slightly modifies his PhD Thesis (Sheffield University, 1977). Yet, during this period, Thiselton published a further 106 writings beyond those mentioned in 'Thirty Years of Hermeneutics'.[4]

Similarly, Thiselton's third period, 1981-1992, culminates in Thiselton's second major book, *New Horizons in Hermeneutics* (1992).[5] Thiselton mentions two further

---

[1] Thiselton, A.C., 'Thirty Years of Hermeneutics: Retrospect and Prospects', in *International Symposium on the Interpretation of the Bible* (ed. J. Krašovec; Ljubljana: Slovenian Academy of Sciences and Arts; Sheffield: Sheffield Academic Press, 1998), 1559-1574; cf. Thiselton, A.C., 'Unpublished Bibliographic Letter to R. Knowles', 4th May 1999.
[2] Thiselton, 'TY', 1559.
[3] Thiselton, A.C., 'The Parables as Language-Event: Some Comments on Fuchs's Hermeneutics in the Light of Linguistic Philosophy', *SJT* 23.4 (Nov. 1970), 437-468.; cf. Thiselton, 'TY', 1559; cf. our bibliography.
[4] Thiselton, A.C., *The Two Horizons: New Testament Hermeneutics and Philosophical Description with Special Reference to Heidegger, Bultmann, Gadamer, and Wittgenstein* (Exeter: Paternoster Press, 1980); cf. Thiselton, A.C., *New Testament Hermeneutics and Philosophical Description: Issues in New Testament Hermeneutics with Special Reference to the Use of Philosophical Description in Heidegger, Bultmann, Gadamer, and Wittgenstein* (Sheffield: University of Sheffield Ph.D. Thesis, 1977; written by Dec. 1976); cf. our bibliography.
[5] Thiselton, A.C., *New Horizons in Hermeneutics: The Theory and Practice of Transforming Biblical Reading* (London: HarperCollins; Grand Rapids: Zondervan, 1992); Thiselton, 'TY', 1567.

publications from this period in 'Thirty Years of Hermeneutics', but this leaves another 46 writings unmentioned.[6]

Thiselton's fourth period, which in 'Thirty Years of Hermeneutics' is given as spanning from 1993 to 1996, may now be extended to its culmination in the publication of his major commentary, *The First Epistle to the Corinthians* (2000).[7] However, whilst in 'Thirty Years of Hermeneutics' Thiselton makes special note of two other major works from this time, we count a further 57 published writings from his fourth period.[8]

Since the beginning of 2001, during what we might here designate as being Thiselton's fifth period, Thiselton has published numerous further works – the vast majority of which appear in our bibliography. The three most notable of these works for our purposes are *Thiselton on Hermeneutics: Collected Works and New Essays* (2006), *The Hermeneutics of Doctrine* (2007), and *Hermeneutics: An Introduction* (2009). That is, with Thiselton's kind assistance, we have now identified well over 300 of his writings *so far*. Indeed in a recent verbal comment, Thiselton indicated that, during his retirement, he would be writing more and not less![9]

Thus, whilst we may *begin* with 'Thirty Years of Hermeneutics', comparison is immediately invited with many more writings if our aim is to understand Thiselton's developing hermeneutical 'programme' *as a whole*. Here in Chapter 1, however, our aim is to chart the historical *emergence* of this 'programme' between 1959 and 1970. Therefore, in the present chapter, we will constrain our

---

[6] Thiselton, A.C., 'Academic Freedom, Religious Tradition, and the Morality of Christian Scholarship', in *Their Lord and Ours: Approaches to Authority, Community and the Unity of the Church* (ed. M. Santer; London: SPCK, 1982), 20-45; cf. Thiselton, A.C., 'Reader-Response Hermeneutics, Action Models, and the Parables of Jesus', in *The Responsibility of Hermeneutics* (R. Lundin, A.C. Thiselton and C. Walhout; Grand Rapids: Eerdmans; Exeter: Paternoster, 1985), 79-113, 123-126; cf. our bibliography.

[7] Thiselton, A.C., *The First Epistle to the Corinthians* (eds. H. Marshall and D.A. Hagner; Series: The New International Greek Testament Commentary; Grand Rapids: Eerdmans; Carlisle: Paternoster, 2000).

[8] Thiselton, A.C., *Interpreting God and The Postmodern Self: On Meaning, Manipulation and Promise* (SJT: Current Issues in Theology; Edinburgh: T&T Clark, 1995); cf. Thiselton, A.C., 'Communicative Action and Promise in Inter-Disciplinary, Biblical, and Theological Hermeneutics', in *The Promise of Hermeneutics* (R. Lundin, C. Walhout and A.C. Thiselton; Grand Rapids and Cambridge: Eerdmans; Carlisle: Paternoster, 1999), 133-239. See our bibliography.

[9] cf.: *Thiselton on Hermeneutics: Collected Works and New Essays* (Aldershot: Ashgate; Ashgate Contemporary Thinkers on Religion; and, Grand Rapids: Eerdmans, 2006); Thiselton, A.C., *The Hermeneutics of Doctrine* (Grand Rapids: Eerdmans, 2007); Thiselton, A.C., *Hermeneutics: An Introduction* (Grand Rapids: Eerdmans, 2009). See our bibliography, which is *near-exhaustive* up to around the start of 2005, and which includes *almost all* of Thiselton's works after that date (until mid-late 2011 when the present project was submitted for publication). For the purposes of the present study, which concentrates largely on Thiselton's formative works, it was not necessary to locate every single one of his most recent lesser writings and book reviews – though it is hoped that, in later volumes, we might be able to address *all* of Thiselton's works.

observations to a consideration of Thiselton's writings from this, his first, period of hermeneutical endeavor.[10]

## B. Thiselton's "First Period" Hermeneutical Reflections: from 1959 to 1970

*1. 1959-1964: 1 Corinthians, Wittgenstein and Austin, and Continental Hermeneutics*

Anthony C. Thiselton (b. 1937) obtained his BD at London Bible College (LBC) in 1959, scoring '100%' in a 'history' exam, and being 'frustrated by the ease of the course'.[11] Even more notable, however, is the fact that Thiselton attended any degree course at all.

Specifically, Thiselton reports (in a personal communication to the present author) that he suffered from 'meningitis at the age of two which' severely damaged his 'eyesight' such that he has 'always found proof reading almost impossible'. The 'crisis' came during his 'last year at City of London School' when he 'had to leave… and work on A-levels at home'. In 1958, Thiselton's 'pre-ordination medical report' diagnosed his eyesight as being too poor for him to '"be able to read enough books to exercise a useful parish ministry"'. Nevertheless, since Thiselton 'had already studied Greek and Hebrew… and read numerous small-print books', 'the… Bishop of Southwark chose to ignore the report'. And so Thiselton's studies continued - after his move to LBC - and were supervised by his 'uncle, Dr. Ernest Kevan', the Principal of LBC (now, London School of Theology). In 1960, Thiselton became a Curate at Holy Trinity Church, Sydenham. After three years, he married and became a lecturer and 'Chaplain' at Tyndale Hall, Bristol University.[12]

Thiselton notes that 'from 1963 I had become increasingly familiar with the work of Wittgenstein and J.L. Austin'.[13] This increasing familiarity coincided with his interest in 1 Corinthians (cf. the title of his Masters thesis), and emerged from his discontent 'with more traditional… "biblical interpretation"'.[14] Thus, even by

---

[10] See also *Who's Who 1999: An Annual Biographical Dictionary* (151st Year of Issue; London: A&C Black, 1999), 1985; cf. on Thiselton's hermeneutical 'programme' see, Thiselton, A.C., 'Theology and the Future', *CEN* 23 Jan. (1970), 11. It will be noted that we have extended Thiselton's first period back from 1963 to 1959 in order to encompass his graduation.

[11] *WW*, 1985; cf. Thiselton, A.C., 'Personal Communication to Robert Knowles', 6th May 2007; cf. comments made to me verbally by a fellow student from Thiselton's undergraduate days. *WW* erroneously reports that Thiselton received his BD at King's College London – though it is true that Thiselton 'also attended some lectures' at 'Oak Hill College and King's College London'. Thiselton's current post-graduate qualifications are: M.Th. (London, 1964), Ph.D. (Sheffield, 1977), D.D. (Durham, 1993), D.D. (Archbishop of Canterbury at Lambeth, 2002), Hon. D.D. (Chester, 2012), F.K.C. (2010), F.B.A. (2010).

[12] Thiselton, 'PCRK', 6th May 2007; cf. Thiselton, *HD*, xii-xiii; cf. *WW*, 1985.

[13] Thiselton, 'TY', 1560; cf. *WW*, 1985.

[14] *WW*, 1985; cf. Thiselton, A.C., *Eschatology and the Holy Spirit in Paul with Special Reference to 1 Corinthians* (London: University of London Unpublished M.Th. Dissertation, 1964); cf. Thiselton, 'TY', 1559-1560.

1964, we find that Thiselton's interests had expanded beyond pastoral theology to include studies in 1 Corinthians, hermeneutics, and the philosophy of language. Subsequently, Thiselton's writings from 1965 indicate that, by 1964, he had begun to read Schleiermacher, Kierkegaard, De Chardin, Tillich, and the New Hermeneutic (notably, Ebeling).[15]

### 2. 1965: Mixed Response to Continental Hermeneutics

In 1965, Thiselton became a Recognised Teacher in Theology at Bristol University.[16] This appointment coincided with his first publications, in which we find his mixed response to Continental hermeneutics – a response precipitated by his engagement with Wittgenstein and Austin. Thus, Thiselton argues that Kierkegaard rightly emphasized 'the individual, personal, and subjective', but undervalued 'the collective and objective'.[17] Thiselton's publications from this time also reflect his interests in New Testament studies, biblical theology,[18] the biblical authority debate, and other faiths.[19]

### 3. 1966: Uniting the Pre-Cognitive and the Cognitive

In 1966 we again find that Thiselton's response to Continental hermeneutics is not entirely negative. Against unfortunate 'caricatures of conservative Evangelicals' emerging from the *'Honest to God Debate'*, Thiselton argues that Billy Graham's work, *World Aflame*, is 'categorical disproof… that only radical theologians' account for 'the world's' 'existential situation of despair'.[20] For Thiselton, though, Continental hermeneutics remains one-sided: there is no necessary antithesis between 'personal categories' and 'propositional categories' where, in Thiselton's view, M. Novak rightly stresses pre-cognitive '"subjectivity"', but wrongly

---

[15] Thiselton, A.C., 'Kierkegaard', *CEN* 5 Mar. (1965), 16; and Thiselton, A.C., 'Knights in Kierkegaard's Armour?', *CEN* 12 Mar. (1965), 16; cf.: Thiselton. A.C., 'Review of P.T. De Chardin's *The Making of a Mind: Letters from a Soldier-Priest'*, *Chman* 79.4 (1965), 313-314; Thiselton, A.C., 'Review of P. Tillich's *Systematic Theology: Volume 3'*, *CGrad* 18 (1965), 35; Thiselton, A.C., 'Review of G. Ebeling's *Word and Faith'*, *TSF* 42 (1965), 20-21.
[16] *WW*, 1985; cf. Thiselton, 'TY', 1560, 1561.
[17] Thiselton, 'KA', 16; cf. Thiselton, 'TY', 1560.
[18] Thiselton, A.C., 'Review of W.D. Davies' *The Setting of the Sermon on the Mount'*, *CGrad* 18 (1965), 38-39; and, Thiselton, A.C., 'Review of D.E.H. Whiteley's *The Theology of St. Paul'*, *TSF* 42 (1965), 17-18.
[19] Thiselton, A.C., 'Review of G.D. Yarnold's *By What Authority? Studies in the Relations of Scripture, Church and Ministry'*, *Chman* 79.1 (1965), 64-65; cf. Thiselton, A.C., 'Review of C. Isherwood's *Ramakrishna and His Disciples'*, *Chman* 79.2 (1965), 159-160.
[20] Thiselton, A.C., 'Reviews of J. Pollock's *Billy Graham: The Authorised Biography*, B. Graham's *World Aflame* and E. Hulse's *Billy Graham: The Pastor's Dilemma'*, *Chman* 80.2 (1966), 141.

undervalues cognitive 'concepts'.[21]

Also in 1966, Thiselton's interest in biblical studies broadens in his booklet, *Personal Suggestions about a Minister's Library*,[22] whilst his focus on 1 Corinthians re-emerges in his 'Tyndale Lecture',[23] which anticipates E. Käsemann's conclusion that 'Paul's struggle at Corinth' was against 'over-realized… eschatology'.[24]

### 4. 1967: Tensions Between Continental and Anglo-American Traditions

In 1967, Thiselton became a Senior Tutor at Tyndale Hall, Bristol University.[25] He recalls that 'a student asked my advice about English-language books on hermeneutics', prompting an almost 'fruitless literature search' in which 'only' R. Funk's *'Language, Hermeneutic and the Word of God* (1966) and' J.M. Robinson's and J.B. Cobb Jr.'s *'New Frontiers in Theology: II. The New Hermeneutic* (1964)' stood out. (Thiselton's subsequent career is clearly a successful attempt to address this problem).[26]

By 1967, Thiselton had also begun to critique the work of H.-G. Gadamer and E. Fuchs. Notably, Thiselton became 'entranced by the notion of projected "worlds"', '"narrative worlds"', or 'pre-cognitive value-systems' 'into which the reader was drawn' or 'seduced, only to find' his or her 'world' and 'expectations subverted and reversed'. Thiselton 'pressed on to explore "worldhood" in Heidegger's *Being and Time*' for himself, but found problems with Heidegger's 'philosophy of language'. Thus, Thiselton writes, 'whereas' 'Austin's "performatives" presupposed *institutional states of affairs* and specific contextual *conventions*… Heidegger and Fuchs regarded assertions, propositions, and conventions as at best derivative and secondary to a ['different'] kind of force'. Thiselton therefore experienced a 'combination of appreciation and unease' with Continental hermeneutics, where this mixed response reflected Thiselton's critical preference for 'Anglo-American' traditions (N.B. Thiselton had already seen the problem with Continental approaches to language by 1964-1965 – see above).[27]

This mixed response to Continental hermeneutics is evident throughout Thiselton's published writings from 1967, as is an implicit hint of a critical

---

[21] Thiselton, A.C., 'A Snappy Slogan, But…', *CEN* 11 Feb. (1966), 10; cf. Thiselton, A.C., 'Review of M. Novak's *Belief and Unbelief: A Philosophy of Self-Knowledge*', *Chman* 80.4 (1966), 320; cf. 321.

[22] Thiselton, A.C., *Personal Suggestions about a Minister's Library* (London: TSF, 1966, possibly 1967); cf. re. biblical studies, Thiselton, A.C., 'Review of J.R.W. Stott's *Men Made New: An Exposition of Romans 5-8*', *Chman* 80.3 (1966), 232-233.

[23] Unpublished.

[24] Thiselton, A.C., 'Review of E. Käsemann's *New Testament Questions of Today*', *Chman* 84.3 (1970), 229.

[25] *WW*, 1985; cf. Thiselton, 'TY', 1560.

[26] Thiselton, 'TY', 1559-1560.

[27] Thiselton, 'TY', 1560. Italics Thiselton's.

preference for the later Wittgenstein. Thus, Thiselton argues, G.W.H. Lampe and D.M. MacKinnon rightly hold 'historical enquiry' and 'existential impact' together: 'historical, philosophical, and theological problems are inextricably intertwined'.[28] For Thiselton, 'existentialism' should be held together with historical enquiry into 'the factual content of revelation'.[29] In Thiselton's view, H. Gollwitzer rightly rejects the antithesis between existential function and "mythological" or "objectifying" language in the 'existentialising talk of God' in the writings of Kant, Kierkegaard, Nietzsche, Jaspers, and Heidegger: in Thiselton's estimate, Christian language about God is 'not... mythical', 'but... analogical'.[30] Thiselton also notes the irony of E.J. Carnell's apparent alignment with Kierkegaard's notion that '"truth is subjectivity"': in Thiselton's view, Carnell provides 'the best *descriptive* treatment to date of Kierkegaard's thought as a Christian'.[31] Finally, with the later Wittgenstein in mind, Thiselton affirms V.A. Harvey's 'work' for its 'surprisingly few generalizations' and for its sensitivity to '"how"' '"theological terms"' are '"*variously used* in differing circumstances"'.[32]

In 1967 Thiselton's critique of Bultmann's hermeneutics is especially sharp. Thus, for Thiselton, 'the relationship between myth and analogy in Bultmann' is problematic, as are Bultmann's view of '"the historical Jesus"', his exclusion of the resurrection and '"the last judgment as mythological"', and his '"nature versus history... cosmology versus anthropology"', and '"being versus existence"' 'antitheses'. Thiselton rejects Bultmann's almost '"exclusively"' kerygmatic 'theology' with its near-Kierkegaardian notion of '"faith"' as bare '"decision"'. In Thiselton's view, faith and knowledge are actually closely related. Notably, Thiselton argues that Bultmann's appeal to 'philosophy is too narrow' (Thiselton is referring to Bultmann's *pre-understanding* here - see our Introduction for our comments on Thiselton's use of the word "narrow"), and that a wider appeal to 'philosophical traditions' and a more adequately 'eschatological' theology are required. Thiselton thus rejects 'Bultmann's philosophy of history', and argues that Bultmann's 'demythologization' exhibits 'acute problems... [to do with] criteria'.[33]

---

[28] Thiselton, A.C., 'Review of G.W.H. Lampe's and D.M. MacKinnon's *The Resurrection*', *Chman* 81.3 (1967), 232, 233.

[29] Thiselton, A.C., 'Review of C.F.H. Henry ed. *Jesus of Nazareth: Saviour and Lord*', *Chman* 81.3 (1967), 216.

[30] Thiselton, A.C., 'Review of H. Gollwitzer's *The Existence of God: As Confessed by Faith*', *TSF* 47 (1967), 17.

[31] Thiselton, A.C., 'Review of E.J. Carnell's *The Burden of Søren Kierkegaard*', *TSF* 48 (1967), 24. Italics Thiselton's.

[32] Thiselton, A.C., 'Review of V.A. Harvey's *A Handbook of Theological Terms*', *Chman* 81.1 (1967), 58; cf. Wittgenstein, L., *The Blue and Brown Books. Preliminary Studies for the Philosophical Investigations* (Oxford: Blackwell, 1958, 2002), 18-19. Italics Thiselton's.

[33] Thiselton, A.C., 'Review of C.W. Kegley ed. *The Theology of Rudolf Bultmann*', *Chman* 81.1 (1967), 59, 60; cf.: Thiselton, A.C., 'Review of C.W. Kegley ed. *The Theology of Rudolf Bultmann*', *TSF* 48 (1967), 21; Thiselton, 'R JN', 216.

## 5. 1968: Pannenberg, Wittgenstein, and Dialogue Between Traditions

Nevertheless, by 1968, Thiselton remains keen 'to draw equally on the Anglo-American tradition of philosophical analysis and on Continental European traditions'. Notably, Thiselton views 'Wittgenstein as a key figure who combined the incisiveness and rigor' of 'British analytical philosophy with the Continental suspicion of exclusively rationalist method and with a deeper concern about human subjectivity and life-worlds'.[34] Thus, for Thiselton, the later Wittgenstein serves as a mediator between these two traditions. Undoubtedly, Thiselton has the later Wittgenstein in mind when he complains concerning S. Lawton's 'questionable generalizations'.[35]

Pannenberg also serves as a mediator between traditions for Thiselton. Notably, Pannenberg alerts Thiselton 'further' 'to the problems left by the "devaluing" of assertions in Heidegger and Gadamer' (that is – and this is crucial – Thiselton was *already aware of this issue* – by 1964-1965 at the latest; see our next section in the present chapter).[36] Correlatively, Thiselton criticizes the virtual absence of reference to J.L. Austin and to P.F. Strawson in F.H. Cloebury's work.[37] Yet, with Pannenberg, Thiselton also retains an existential emphasis: Calvin's 'practical concern' rightly has an 'existential' character,[38] and M. Thornton rightly holds 'theology' and 'practice' together.[39] Contradicting J. Knox, Thiselton argues that 'the biblical creation-narratives and accounts of the resurrection' *unite* '"factual" and existential truth'.[40] In 1998, Thiselton retrospectively remarks that 'Pannenberg has always remained a major influence on my thinking'.[41]

Thus, an alliance between Pannenberg and the later Wittgenstein is forming in Thiselton's thinking as he addresses the need to mediate between Continental and Anglo-American traditions.

## 6. 1969: Widening Dialogue: Philosophical and Theological Traditions

Several developments in Thiselton's thinking first appear in 1969 when Thiselton

---

[34] Thiselton, 'TY', 1560-1561.

[35] Thiselton, A.C., 'New Practical Theology Series: Reviews of M. Thornton's *The Function of Theology*, and S. Lawton's *Truths that Compelled: Contemporary Implications of Biblical Theology*', *CEN* 4 Oct. (1968), 4; cf. Wittgenstein, *B&B*, 18-19.

[36] Thiselton, 'TY', 1560.

[37] Thiselton, A.C., 'Idealism etc.: Review of F.H. Cloebury's. *A Return to Natural Theology*', *CEN* 22 Mar. (1968), 4.

[38] Thiselton, A.C., 'Review of T.H.L. Parker trans. *Calvin's Commentaries: Galatians, Ephesians, Philippians and Colossians*', *TSF* 50 (1968), 28.

[39] Thiselton, 'Rs *FT, TC*, 4.

[40] Thiselton, A.C., 'Review of J. Knox's *Myth and Truth: An Essay on the Language of Faith*', *Chman* 82.3 (1968), 215. Italics ours.

[41] Thiselton, 'TY', 1560.

is still a Senior Tutor at Tyndale Hall.[42]

Thus, (1), criticizing 'Continental' thought, Thiselton widens his dialogue with *theological* mediators between traditions. Thiselton writes, 'in 1969 my wife and I had the great privilege of entertaining Professor and Frau Pannenberg in our Bristol home for a few days'. Having already read 'Pannenberg on hermeneutics' by 1968, Thiselton was 'convinced... [still] further' by Pannenberg's 'incisive oral comments' on 'the "devaluing" of assertions in Heidegger and Gadamer'. That is: (a), Thiselton was *already aware* of 'the "devaluing" of assertions in Heidegger and Gadamer' by 1967 – i.e. *prior to* his engagement with Pannenberg's thought on this matter; (b) Thiselton's publications from 1965 and 1966 suggest that Thiselton was aware of the problems with the Continental disparagement of cognitive language by 1964-1965 (if perhaps not specifically in relation to Heidegger and Gadamer); (c) Pannenberg 'further *alerted*' Thiselton to this problem within Continental hermeneutics in 1968; (d) Pannenberg's 'incisive oral comments' came later, in 1969, and 'further' *'convinced'* Thiselton in relation to this problem within Continental hermeneutics.[43]

Thiselton's praise for Pannenberg first appears in print in 1969 when Thiselton attacks H. Zahrnt's 'entirely one-sided discussion of Pannenberg' which 'grossly underestimates his significance'.[44] Drawing on Pannenberg and T.F. Torrance, Thiselton rejects both '"old fashioned"' 'language about God as Object' and the later Heidegger's 'attacks on conceptualizing' - though Thiselton maintains that 'some of the points made by Kierkegaard, Bultmann, and Tillich' are 'justified'. In Thiselton's view, 'Pannenberg, (with his impressive learning and his respect for rationality)', and Torrance promote 'a **right** kind of "objectification"'.[45]

---

[42] *WW*, 1985.

[43] Thiselton, 'TY', 1560. Italics ours. *Before* noting Pannenberg's visit to his residence in 1969, Thiselton speaks in the *pluperfect* when he says that he 'had been further alerted' 'by reading' Pannenberg in relation to the problems with Continental approaches to language. This point probably places the moment that Thiselton was 'further alerted' in this way into the time-frame of 1968 at the latest. And yet, the word 'further' here shows that Thiselton had *already* seen these problems for himself, which is why he places a paragraph that discusses these problems *prior to* his paragraph that mentions Pannenberg. In the former paragraph, Thiselton dates his "increasing familiarity" 'with the work of Wittgenstein and J.L. Austin' as being 'from 1963' onwards. Moreover, Thiselton's publications from 1965 and 1966 suggest that he was well aware of the language-related problems with Continental hermeneutics by 1964-1965. The absence of any mention of these problems in Thiselton's M.Th. thesis (1964 – see footnote 14 above) suggests that Thiselton had probably come to see the language-related problems with Continental hermeneutics for himself in his post-M.Th. period 1964-1965 – three to four years before Pannenberg 'further alerted' Thiselton to these problems.

[44] Thiselton, A.C., 'Continental Theology - Processed, Packaged and Branded: Review of H. Zahrnt's *The Question of God*', *CEN* 9 May (1969), 6.

[45] Bold type Thiselton's; cf. Thiselton, A.C., 'A Book Set Apart from the Ordinary Run of Books: Review of T.F. Torrance's *Theological Science*', *CEN* 12 Dec. (1969), 13.

In Thiselton's estimate, J. Macquarrie also rightly holds 'existentialist' insights, 'linguistic' philosophy, conceptualizing, 'biblical truth and Christian tradition' together. Thiselton approves of Macquarrie's 'fascinating comparison between Rudolf Bultmann and R.B. Braithwaite', who 'both... try to cash assertions about God as utterances about man, and... stress volition'. Thus, in Thiselton's view, Pannenberg, T.F. Torrance, and Macquarrie are alike in *facilitating dialogue between* 'existentialist' insights, 'linguistic philosophers', 'biblical' theology, 'and Christian tradition'.[46]

(2) Criticizing Continental thought, Thiselton also widens his dialogue with *philosophical* mediators between traditions. Thiselton approves of 'Wittgenstein's famous description of philosophy as a battle against the bewitchment of our intelligence by means of language'.[47] For Thiselton, 'linguistic philosophy offers not so much doctrines as techniques of investigation' that are 'increasingly fruitful... in theology' - though Thiselton applauds Cornelius de Deugd's 'well-timed plea for a more comprehensive philosophy of language' (cf. Chapter 4),[48] H.H. Price's 'linguistic philosophy', and W. Manson's 'excellent linguistic analysis'.[49] In Thiselton's estimate, N. Smart rightly follows the later Wittgenstein's 'shift away from' the positivistic aspects of his earlier thought, but misses 'Wittgenstein's... parallel shift away from... the individual ego, to the givenness of life-in-community'.[50]

Elsewhere, drawing on the later Wittgenstein, Thiselton complains concerning the 'breath-taking neatness' of H.W. Richardson's *a priori* 'historical generalizations' across many disciplines.[51] Thiselton criticizes Richardson's 'prescriptive views of language' (which fall foul of J.L. Austin's distinction between the 'logical' and the 'grammatical' in relation to 'actual language-uses') and his neglect of P.F. Strawson's 'careful account of the overlapping of M predicates and P predicates' in relation to a hermeneutic of the self (or selves).[52] Nevertheless, in Thiselton's view, Richardson rightly opposes Bultmann's elimination of 'the symbol-myth-image complex': 'symbols' are needed in order 'to

---

[46] Thiselton, A.C., 'Review of J. Macquarrie's *Studies in Christian Existentialism*', TSF 53 (1969), 24, 25.

[47] Thiselton, A.C., 'Resisting the Bewitchment of our Intelligence: Review of F. Ferré's *A Basic Modern Philosophy of Religion*', CEN 28 Feb. (1969), 4; cf. Wittgenstein, L., *Philosophical Investigations* (trans. G.E.M. Anscombe; Oxford: Blackwell, 1953, 2001), 47.

[48] Thiselton, A.C., 'Philosophy in Progress: Review of Royal Institute of Philosophy Lectures *Talk of God*', CEN 6 Jun. (1969), 5; cf. for example, Wittgenstein, L., *Zettel* (trans. G.E.M. Anscombe; Oxford: Blackwell, 1967, 1998), 80.

[49] Thiselton, A.C., 'Review of H.H. Price's *Belief*', Chn 11 Apr. (1969), x; cf. Thiselton, A.C., 'Review of W. Manson's *Jesus and the Christian*', Chman 83.1 (1969), 50-51.

[50] Thiselton, A.C., 'What after Death? Review of N. Smart's *Philosophers and Religious Truth*', CEN, 19 Dec (1969), 15; cf. for example, Wittgenstein, PI, 46-47.

[51] Thiselton, A.C., 'Theology for a New World: Review Article of H. Richardson's *Theology for a New World*', Chman 83.3 (1969), 200; cf. Wittgenstein, B&B, 18-19.

[52] Thiselton, 'NW', 201, 202; cf. Wittgenstein, PI, 39.

reach... beyond' the cognitive plane to 'Christian experience', though they require testing 'at the bar of discursive language' and 'analytical... reasoning'.[53]

Elsewhere, Thiselton argues that P. Van Buren rightly criticizes H. Ott's disparagement of '"conceptualizing"' or 'objectifying language',[54] but that he falsely applies contrasts 'between' 'stories' and 'statistics' and between 'facts' and 'fiction' to 'the Christian story'. Thiselton suspects that Van Buren has followed 'R.B. Braithwaite' and Bultmann; drawing on J.L. Austin and D.D. Evans, Thiselton prefers the distinctions 'between concrete and abstract, and between the logic of... description and the logic of self-involvement'.[55]

In Thiselton's estimate, Van Buren has wrongly followed 'the so-called open interpretation of the later Wittgenstein' despite the inconsistency between a '"world of multiplicity and relativity"' and one '"in which it matters what we do"'.[56] This point anticipates Thiselton's later critique of R. Rorty who 'stresses those aspects [of Wittgenstein's later work] which are compatible with a pragmatic behaviorism and which' supposedly 'encourage a consensus theory of truth'. Similarly, Thiselton complains that 'W. Hordern, Paul van Buren, and Henry Staten write as if Wittgenstein's language-games could be viewed as virtually self-contained contextual settings'.[57]

Hence, in Thiselton's view, Van Buren is hovering between a neo-Kantian dualism between fact and value (cf. Bultmann's 'impossibly difficult middle-of-the-road position'[58]) and the pragmatic relativism into which this threatens to decay. Thiselton cites Van Buren's own remark: 'I fully expect to spend my life making up my mind' - i.e. between positivism, existentialism, and neo-pragmatism.[59]

Thus, in Thiselton's view, the later Wittgenstein, J.L. Austin, D.D. Evans and others (such as P.F. Strawson, Cornelius de Deugd, H.H. Price, and W. Manson) are alike in *facilitating dialogue between Continental and Anglo-American traditions*. Others, however, in Thiselton's view, serve more to *perpetuate or accentuate polarizations between* these traditions.

(3) Thiselton's expanding mediatory, yet critical, dialogue between traditions does not negate his *cautious if qualified regard for Continental hermeneutics*. Thus, in Thiselton's estimate, J. Macquarrie *rightly* appeals to the work of Schleiermacher, Otto, and Tillich: '"religious feeling" involves more than subjective emotion... it "discloses" an awareness of that which evokes it'.[60] Further, Thiselton observes

---

[53] Thiselton, 'NW', 200-201.
[54] Thiselton, A.C., 'Review of P. Van Buren's *Theological Explorations*', *Chman* 83.3 (1969), 220.
[55] Thiselton, 'R *Exp*', 220-221; cf.: Thiselton, 'R *St*', 25; Thiselton, A.C., 'New Problems for Old: Article Review of J.A.T. Robinson's *The Human Face of God*', *CEN* 6 Apr. (1973), 8.
[56] Thiselton, 'R *Exp*', 220-221.
[57] Thiselton, *NH*, 395.
[58] Thiselton, 'R *Exi*', 17.
[59] Thiselton, 'R *Exp*', 220-221.
[60] Thiselton, 'R *St*', 24-25.

that P. Leon possesses 'a wider insight than even Kierkegaard gained into the self-deceptions and intricate subtleties of human nature'.[61] In Thiselton's view, H.W. Richardson *wrongly* neglects the later Heidegger's 'language theory behind the new hermeneutic' through a misplaced preoccupation with 'well-worn debates about demythologization'.[62] Nevertheless, contrary to Continental hermeneutics, Thiselton affirms D.T. Niles's stress on *both* 'practical contact and involvement' *and* 'historical issues'. For Thiselton, factual-historical and existential self-involving dimensions should be united.[63]

(4) Thiselton's expanding mediatory, yet critical, dialogue between traditions *accompanies* his heavily qualified 'conservative' "evangelicalism" (see Chapter 2). He writes, 'it is possible to remain faithful to conservative principles, without losing the capacity to draw from many other sources'. He asks, 'as evangelicals... can we learn to draw from... contemporary thought, so that we can present biblical truth in its rich variety and fullness both relevantly and imaginatively to our own generation?'[64]

*7. 1970: Thiselton's Hermeneutical Programme: Widening Dialogue Towards Critical Synthesis*

Whilst remaining a Recognized Teacher in Theology at Bristol University until 1971, Thiselton moved to Sheffield University in 1970 where he became a Sir Henry Stephenson Fellow - also until 1971.[65] However, his published works from 1970 still correspond to his Bristol period.[66] Four major themes emerge more fully in these works than previously – as follows.

(1) Thiselton outlines his *hermeneutical 'programme'* – his response to what he calls 'the hermeneutical problem'. In 'Theology and the Future' Thiselton argues, (a), that '"the hermeneutical problem"' 'concerns': (i), 'the complex relationship between language, meaning, understanding, and truth'; (ii), how 'our own cultural environment conditions... our words and... thinking'; and, (iii), the question, 'What does the Bible actually say to our own generation?'[67]

(b) Thiselton argues that the hermeneutical problem, however, 'cannot be solved by a theory, but only by a prolonged **programme**' of several steps: step one tested 'the usefulness of existential categories'; step two applied 'the results of hermeneutical philosophy'; and step three appropriates 'the enormous advances... in semantics, linguistics, and linguistic philosophy', where this appropriation

---

[61] Thiselton, A.C., 'Reviews of J.J. Vincent's *Secular Christ*, D.T. Niles' *Who is This Jesus?* and P. Leon's *The Gospel According to Judas*', *Th* 72.590 (Aug. 1969), 373-374.
[62] Thiselton, 'NW', 197, cf. 201.
[63] Thiselton, 'Rs *SC, TJ, GJ*', 373-374.
[64] Thiselton, A.C., 'Crossroads for Theology: Article on Canon Stafford Wright', *CEN* 19 Dec. (1969), 4.
[65] *WW*, 1985.
[66] See our bibliography.
[67] Thiselton, 'T&F', 11. Italics ours.

requires 'a... re-appraisal of the intended functions of language in specific biblical passages', and that we move beyond 'traditional... teaching on grammar and vocabulary'.[68]

(c) Following Moltmann, Thiselton argues that 'eschatology' can no longer be seen 'as a department of study': 'it... colors the whole of New Testament thought', 'provides a basis (together with other themes) for ethics, and constitutes a frame of reference' for Christology.[69]

Thus, (d), Thiselton argues that 'the theologian's task' is a matter of 'relating Biblical exegesis to "systematic theology"': pastors should keep up with 'changing... contemporary theology', since this affects 'pastoral work' and 'theological training'. Thiselton insists that fresh insights emerge from 'conservative' sources *and* from non-conservative sources, where Thiselton notes 'Bultmann's' work on Pauline anthropology and 'Kittel's *Theological Dictionary of the New Testament*' in this context.[70]

That is, (e), a new widened dialogue emerges in Thiselton's work between an eschatological hermeneutic of the New Testament and "the next step" of the philosophical 'hermeneutical programme' involving Wittgenstein, Austin, and Saussure. If 'Thirty Years of Hermeneutics' mostly looks *back* on Thiselton's hermeneutical programme from 1998, then 'Theology and the Future' largely looks *forward* to that programme from 1970.

(2) Thiselton moves beyond dialogue between traditions towards *a new critical hermeneutical synthesis*. The crowning article of Thiselton's first period is, 'The Parables as Language-Event: Some Comments on Fuchs's Hermeneutics in the Light of Linguistic Philosophy'.[71] We may reorganize the content of this complex paper so as to explicate Thiselton's framework, as follows.

(a) Aligning with Continental hermeneutics *and* with the later Wittgenstein, Thiselton rejects the Platonic idealist reduction of 'words' to 'imitations... of immaterial concepts' whose 'truth' is conveyed by 'propositions'.[72] Similarly, Thiselton rejects the 'Enlightenment'-rationalist, 'traditional', or 'ideational' reduction of language to 'information' that communicates *a priori* 'rational ideas'.[73]

(b) Thiselton also rejects the broadly positivist extension of this view of language and the *early* Wittgenstein's "picture theory": both 'generalize about propositions', reducing their function to "description", and thereby fragment 'reality' into 'concepts' to 'be manipulated' within 'formal' systems. For Thiselton, 'Gadamer' rightly views *these kinds of* propositions as 'isolating' 'what comes reflectively to individual consciousness', and as being '"antithetical to...

---

[68] Thiselton, 'T&F', 11. Bold type is Thiselton's.
[69] Thiselton, 'T&F', 11.
[70] Thiselton, 'T&F', 11. Italics in speech-marks are Thiselton's.
[71] Thiselton, 'Parab', 437-468.
[72] Thiselton, 'Parab', 448.
[73] Thiselton, 'Parab', 448, cf. 439, 452.

hermeneutical experience'".[74]

(c) Thiselton also questions the 'Cartesian' "scientific" epistemology of seeking 'knowledge... through observation, generalization', induction, and deduction.[75] After the later Wittgenstein and Heidegger, Thiselton argues that such a stance reduces '"understanding"' to 'conscious... logical inference' and to changes 'in... so-called mental states' or to the 'measuring' of one set of 'concepts' against another 'from the same source'. Thiselton, however, argues that 'understanding' actually 'involves' practicality, or, '"going on... independently"'.[76]

(d) Thiselton opposes the linguistic dualism of 'Heidegger', 'Gadamer', and 'Fuchs' since it too generalizes about 'propositions' - devaluing them as *only* the reduction of language to tools for manipulating 'concepts', 'ideas', or 'information' and, citing Heidegger, as 'not the primary "locus" of truth'. Conversely, Thiselton argues that pre-cognitive 'language-events' are artificially elevated - by these thinkers - as preceding and delimiting 'thought', and as permitting '"being to be present... in time"'. However, in Thiselton's view, 'propositions', 'assertions', and 'statements' should be reinstated against such dualism, though *without* a return to logical positivism.[77]

(e) Thiselton solves this linguistic dilemma through an appeal to the 'later... Wittgenstein'. Thiselton, after the later Wittgenstein, argues that 'propositions', like all 'language', are multi-functional and grounded in 'community' 'life'. Thiselton argues that *all* 'language... can be manipulated artificially' so as to bewitch (citing Wittgenstein, 'a *misunderstanding* makes it look... as if a proposition *did* something queer'), and that 'language without assertions... is a featureless waste, in which every meaning can be swallowed up by another'.[78]

Thus, whilst agreeing with Gadamer over the openness of 'horizons' of 'understanding' towards 'future experience', Thiselton rejects Gadamer's view that 'assertions' *necessarily* 'close', 'fix', or reduce such 'horizons' to abstractions that fail to 'attain the dimension of the linguistic experience of the world'.[79]

Rather, with the later Wittgenstein, Thiselton argues that 'what a proposition *is* is... determined by the rules of sentence formation... and... by the use of the sign in the language-game'.[80] Thiselton argues that 'language', '"proposition"', and 'parable' are 'concept[s] with blurred edges' (i.e. context-modifiable). For Thiselton, some propositions *align* with Gadamer's stress on the 'openness' of horizons

---

[74] Thiselton, 'Parab', 449-451; last citation from, Gadamer, H.-G., *Truth and Method* (trans. J. Weinsheimer and D.G. Marshall; London: Sheed & Ward, 1975, 1989), 468.

[75] Thiselton, 'Parab', 443.

[76] Thiselton, 'Parab', 451-453, 449.

[77] Thiselton, 'Parab', 440, 449, 448, 438, 451-454, 464; cf. 465; we cite, Heidegger, M., *Being and Time* (trans. J. Macquarrie and E. Robinson; Oxford: Blackwell, 1962, 2001), 269.

[78] Thiselton, 'Parab', 451-453, 464-465; cf. Wittgenstein, *PI*, 44. Italics in speech-marks are Wittgenstein's; other italics are ours.

[79] Thiselton, 'Parab', 450; last citation from, Gadamer, *TM*, 469.

[80] Wittgenstein, *PI*, 53. Italics ours.

towards 'future experience' (cf. S. Ullmann's notion of semantic '"vagueness"'), whereas others are almost 'completely closed'. Correlatively, Thiselton argues that there are 'family-resemblances' between *many kinds* of parables. For Thiselton, the problem is our contempt for '"the particular case"' and '"craving"' for 'easy generalization'.[81]

(Thiselton's appeal to K.-O. Apel's reading of Wittgenstein in this context may indicate an early interest in socio-critical theory – i.e. by 1970).[82]

(f) Thiselton also opposes linguistic dualism by appealing to J.L. Austin and D.D. Evans: for Thiselton, after Austin and Evans, for 'performative utterances' to operate effectively '"certain statements have *to be true*"'. Indeed, Thiselton argues, against Fuchs, that, far from undermining parable-'function', propositions attached to parables may both 'constitute a condition of effective performative force' and function variably 'themselves'. Thiselton argues that assertions in parables, therefore, may not be the result of 'unimaginative editing', 'but… part of a "language-family"'.[83] They do *not* 'function' as mere 'logia' 'appended' as if only 'to add a related lesson or injunction'.[84]

Of course, Thiselton observes that parallels between Fuchs' 'linguistic acts' and J.L. Austin's and D.D. Evan's speech-'acts' remain; but Thiselton prefers 'the more precise and developed terminology of linguistic philosophy', which avoids turning "distinction" into "dichotomy".[85]

(g) Arguably, Thiselton also implicitly appeals to post-Saussurian general linguistics in conjunction with his appeal to the later Wittgenstein. Thiselton argues that, synchronically (i.e. at a given point in time), various 'parables' form a 'family' linked by complex '"overlapping and criss-crossing"' '"similarities"' or '"family resemblances"'. Conversely, Thiselton argues that, diachronically (i.e. over time), several 'applications' may emerge for a given parable - 'applications' that are synchronically inter-linked at any given instant by 'secondary' 'logical connexions'.[86]

Thus, Thiselton argues that Jesus' hearers are not asked to "slavishly imitate" set 'examples', but are 'repeatedly', though 'freshly', directed into 'each new present' by 'roughly' similar 'paradigms' of 'appropriate' kinds 'of attitude and conduct' 'within certain limits'. Thiselton argues that Jesus' approach – in the parables - thus gives a 'hearer' 'freedom to "go on" for himself' – i.e. '"independently"'. Crucially, Thiselton observes how the notion of '"family resemblances"' explains how 'language' can 'function *creatively*' 'without… meanings' expanding 'arbitrarily'. Thiselton hopes that 'linguistic philosophy' may be of 'further' benefit to 'biblical'

---

[81] Thiselton, 'Parab', 450-456, 465-467, 459, 463.

[82] Thiselton, 'Parab', 463.

[83] Thiselton, 'Parab', 438-440. Italics Austin's, cited by Thiselton.

[84] Querying, Blomberg, C.L., 'Interpreting the Parables of Jesus: Where are We and Where Do We Go from Here?', *CBQ* 53.1 (1991), 57.

[85] Thiselton, 'Parab', 445-447, cf. 462-463.

[86] Thiselton, 'Parab', 455-456, cf.: 458-461; 468.

studies in the future.[87]

(h) Thiselton integrates or critically synthesizes an appeal to 'Pannenberg' with his appeals to traditions of language study, adopting Pannenberg's criticism that Gadamer has artificially abstracted '"statements"' from the '"background"' horizons that '"statements"' alone '"can"' '"grasp"'.[88]

(i) Using this critical synthesis, Thiselton challenges writers who presuppose either more "positivistic" or more "existentialist" (Continental) theories of language. Thus, for Thiselton, contrary to 'Jülicher's' "one point"' view, 'parables' cannot be flattened into single 'generalizing' assertions. Conversely, contrary to Fuchs' generalizations, Thiselton argues that 'all' parables are not as 'open-ended', 'vague', or 'non-cognitive as a Zen Buddhist *koan*' - they are not mere 'psychological stimulant[s]' designed to 'propel the hearer in any or every direction'.[89]

(j) Thiselton still appeals positively to Continental hermeneutics. With Heidegger, to an extent, Thiselton allows that 'language' "gathers" so as to establish 'worlds': 'the Being of beings is opened up in the structure of its gatheredness'.[90] Gadamer, in Thiselton's estimate, rightly relates 'understanding' to '"modes of *experience* in which truth comes to light"': the 'common world' of 'language', or of 'art' or games, is not 'a mere object' or "concept" for thought 'to manipulate', but creatively seizes readers 'at the deepest' "dispositional" 'level' – 'a player... adopts' its 'presuppositions', 'attitudes', or "roles" and, in Gadamer's words, is 'not' "allowed" 'to behave toward play as... an object'.[91]

Thiselton parallels Gadamer's points here with the later Wittgenstein's 'contrast between "interpreting 'from outside"', where one steps '"from one level of thought to another"', and 'participation', where one does '"not interpret"' but, rather, feels '"at home"'.[92]

Thiselton also adapts Gadamer's notion of a hearer's entering 'a new "world"': the 'hearer's' and the world's 'horizons' may interact, move, and begin 'to merge', to form a 'new', 'enlarged', 'integrated' horizon of 'understanding' or "fusion of horizons" – though this 'new' 'common world' only *links* two horizons, since Thiselton insists that the two horizons can *never fully* 'merge into one'.[93]

With Fuchs, Thiselton accepts that Jesus uses 'familiar' parable imagery to draw his hearers into active participation in various 'roles' corresponding with their own

---

[87] Thiselton, 'Parab', 456-457, cf. 468. Italics Thiselton's.

[88] Thiselton, 'Parab', 454.

[89] Thiselton, 'Parab', 454-455, cf. 467. Italics Thiselton's.

[90] Thiselton, 'Parab', 444; cf. Heidegger, M., *Introduction to Metaphysics* (trans. G. Fried and R. Polt; London: Yale University Press, 2000), 183.

[91] Thiselton, 'Parab', 443; cf. 447; cf. Gadamer, *TM*, 102. Thiselton's italics.

[92] Thiselton, 'Parab', 443-444; cf. Wittgenstein, *Z*, 42.

[93] Thiselton, 'Parab', 444-445; cf. later, Thiselton, A.C., 'The Use of Philosophical Categories in New Testament Hermeneutics', *Chman* 87.1 (1973), 87-88; cf. 93-94; see also Chapter 5 of the present study. Italics ours.

varying self-understandings. With Fuchs, Thiselton accepts that hearers are *then* drawn 'by' a parable's 'logic' into 'a strange world' (the parable '"content"' or '"truth"') that transcends or 'even' reverses 'conventional values and... criteria'. With Fuchs, Thiselton allows that hearers may thus become "outraged" or 'joyful', 'depending on' the roles 'adopted'; they no longer 'manipulate' 'the parable as an object of scrutiny', but 'become the object' of *its* 'scrutiny'. Thus, for Fuchs and Thiselton, Jesus, in '"love"', uses '"the artistic medium"' to create a '"sphere in which meeting takes place"'.[94] For Fuchs and Thiselton, some hearers may thereby be brought into the Christian 'community'. For Fuchs and Thiselton, then, self-involving parable language – in "striking home" at a "dispositional" 'level' to "expose" or "re-orientate" 'attitudes', 'presuppositions', and 'conscious thoughts' - is still *distinct* from - but is *not* dichotomously separated from - 'purely cognitive' 'language'.[95]

Summarizing: Thiselton appeals to a widened dialogue between linguistic philosophy, linguistics, and Pannenberg's thinking so as to form a critical-synthetic filter through which theory drawn from the Continental hermeneutical tradition is critically assimilated or 'sublated' (to use F. LeRon Shults' terminology – see Chapter 7), corrected, extended, or rejected. Thus, Thiselton notes that his 'combination of appreciation and unease' with Continental hermeneutics had come to light by '1970'.[96]

Notably, Thiselton *modifies* Gadamer's concepts of "horizons", "language-events", and of "transformation" *so as to embed the functioning of assertive language within the grammar of these concepts*. Thus, later, following 'Pannenberg', Thiselton *retains* that kind of "objectification" which 'transposes [the interpreter's] horizon "into an explicit statement"'.[97] Therefore, to use Thiselton's own later language, the "conceptual grammar" of Thiselton's use of Gadamerian terminology *is not simply "Gadamerian"*.[98]

In 1970 Thiselton's critical-synthetic appeal to linguistic philosophy and his mixed appeal to Continental hermeneutics emerge elsewhere. Thus, Thiselton queries E. Käsemann's neglect of "performative utterances or illocutions" in his (i.e. Käsemann's) exegesis of '"cursing and blessing"' 'in 1 Corinthians'. Thiselton also criticizes W. Nicholls for neglecting 'Wittgenstein, and... Anglo-American achievements in linguistic philosophy'; and Thiselton affirms S.C. Brown for his

---

[94] Thiselton, 'Parab', 440-442. Italics ours.
[95] Thiselton, 'Parab', 445-447, cf. 462-463.
[96] Thiselton, 'TY', 1560. On "sublation" (cf. *relever* in Derrida) see, Shults, F.L., *The Postfoundationalist Task of Theology: Wolfhart Pannenberg and the New Theological Rationality* (Grand Rapids, MI.: Eerdmans, 1996), 159-160, cf. 22-23, 104, 156; cf. Ingraffia, B.D., *Postmodern Theory and Biblical Theology: Vanquishing God's Shadow* (Cambridge: CUP, 1995), 168.
[97] Thiselton, *NH*, 335. Italics ours.
[98] For example see, Thiselton, A.C., Contribution to 'Flesh', in *The New International Dictionary of New Testament Theology, Volume 1* (ed. C. Brown; Exeter: Paternoster; Grand Rapids: Zondervan, 1975), 679. Italics ours.

thorough appeal to Wittgenstein. Conversely, Thiselton argues that J. Pelikan should have given 'more urgent priority' to 'Ebeling on hermeneutics'.[99]

(3) Thiselton's interest in a *hermeneutic of human selves* becomes clearer in 1970. He writes, 'the problem of selfhood has become increasingly important... for philosophers of religion' though, contrary to H.D. Lewis, he is not convinced 'that Strawson's [book] *Individuals* is incompatible with Biblical views about man'. In Thiselton's estimate, Lewis's 'distinction... between the mental and physical' fails to engage with the "post-Wittgensteinian" dismissal of 'dualism'.[100] Elsewhere, Thiselton approves of 'Bultmann's... accurate comments on Paul's understanding of man'. Thiselton particularly approves of Bultmann's work on 'Paul's **varied** uses of [the word] "flesh", and especially' of Bultmann's observations concerning the word's 'particular use' in which it "means" "'man in his self-sufficiency'".[101]

(4) Thiselton's new critical-synthetic hermeneutical approach *still assimilates - or rather sublates - traditional hermeneutical concerns*. By 1970 Thiselton had 'completely revised' his *Personal Suggestions about a Minister's Library*. This booklet thus became Thiselton's 'New Testament Commentary Survey'.[102]

In this survey, Thiselton argues, (a), that 'grammatical and linguistic commentaries help to ensure faithfulness to the meanings of words and phrases in their literary setting' and 'to the biblical message', so as to prevent the 'smuggling through' of 'one's own ideas under the cover of an authoritative text'. (b) Thiselton argues that 'theological commentaries set words and phrases in the wider context of *chapters and books*', where 'it can be seriously misleading to try to understand a word or concept in isolation from its linguistic and theological context'. (c) Thiselton argues that there is also a need for 'a *faithful and imaginative historical reconstruction* of events', 'actions', 'sayings', and their meaning 'in their original setting in the ancient world' that is preconditional for "cashing" them 'accurately... into today's currency'. However, Thiselton admits that 'it is disastrous when historical information becomes an end in itself'. Thus, (d), Thiselton argues that there is also a need for more pastoral 'guidance on the *legitimate range of... application*'.[103]

---

[99] cf.: Thiselton, 'R NTQs', 229; Thiselton, A.C., 'Theological Survey Has No Rival: Review of W. Nicholls' *The Pelican Guide to Modern Theology*', CEN 13 Feb. (1970), 12; Thiselton, A.C., 'Do Christian Concepts have Meaning Any More? Reviews of S.C. Brown's *Do Religious Claims Make Sense?*, and W.D. Hudson ed. *The Is/Ought Question*', CEN 19 Jun. (1970), 12; Thiselton, A.C., 'Mixed Encyclopaedia of Continental Theology: Review of J. Pelikan's *Twentieth Century Theology in the Making, Volume 2*', CEN 3 Jul. (1970), 8.

[100] Thiselton, A.C., 'Review of H.D. Lewis' *The Elusive Mind*', Chman 84.2 (1970), 150-151; cf. Thiselton, 'NW', 201-202.

[101] Thiselton, 'T&F', 11. Bold type is Thiselton's.

[102] Thiselton, A.C., 'New Testament Commentary Survey', TSF 58 (1970), 9-18, (revision of Thiselton, *Suggestions*); cf. Thiselton, A.C., 'Unpublished Bibliographic Letter to R. Knowles', 26th May 1999.

[103] Thiselton, 'NTCS', 9-10. Italics Thiselton's.

## C. Conclusion:
## "Widening Dialogue Towards Critical Synthesis"
## as a Hermeneutical Axiom

Imposing order on the account of Thiselton's development as a thinker from 1959 onwards given above, we arrive at the following "snap-shot" of where he had reached by 1970.

(1) Anglican churchmanship, biblical studies, biblical theology, systematic theology, pastoral theology, and Church mission constitute the background of interests against which Thiselton develops his hermeneutical programme. New Testament interpretation, Pauline studies, parable research, and 1 Corinthians are major emphases in Thiselton's thinking. Thiselton seeks to relate biblical studies to systematic theology - particularly to eschatology and Christology, which are key themes in 1 Corinthians and in Pannenberg's work. Thiselton's conservatism sharpens his focus on the biblical authority debate.

(2) This background contextualizes and precipitates Thiselton's hermeneutical programme. This programme is not a *once-for-all* theory, but nevertheless aims to contribute towards solving the hermeneutical problem *both* theoretically *and* practically. For Thiselton, the hermeneutical *problem* concerns: inter-relationships between major conversations (e.g. 'language, meaning, understanding, and truth'), the 'cultural' conditioning of language and thought, and 'what' 'the Bible' "says" to the present 'generation'. Thiselton's hermeneutical *programme* is part of a larger tradition, and cuts in *after* others' testing of categories from Continental-existential and Continental-philosophical hermeneutics. Thiselton's main concern is thus *to go on beyond Continental-existential and Continental-philosophical hermeneutics so as* to test categories from 'semantics, linguistics, and linguistic philosophy'.[104]

(3) Thiselton's hermeneutical programme *both* unites theological and philosophical concerns *and* widens dialogue between different theological and philosophical traditions – notably between the 'Anglo-American' and 'Continental' philosophical (and theological) 'traditions'.[105] Pannenberg is Thiselton's main *theological* mediator between traditions, but is joined by T.F. Torrance and by J. Macquarrie. The later Wittgenstein is Thiselton's main *philosophical* mediator between traditions, but is joined by J.L. Austin, D.D. Evans, and others. Thiselton is neither simply "Pannenbergian" nor simply "later-Wittgensteinian".

(4) Thiselton's hermeneutical programme seeks to advance biblical hermeneutics through appeals: (a) to the later Wittgenstein, J.L. Austin, D.D. Evans, and others; (b) to broader Anglo-American approaches to language and to hermeneutics of human selves and; (c) to post-Saussurian general linguistics and semantics. Thiselton follows the later Wittgenstein in relation to stressing "'the particular case'", in relation to rejecting *a priori* 'generalization', and in relation to noting "'blurred'" conceptual and semantic 'boundaries', the potential 'creative'

---

[104] Thiselton, 'T&F', 11. Italics ours.
[105] Thiselton, 'TY', 1560-1561.

functioning of assertions, and "'family resemblances'". Thiselton also adopts J.L. Austin's "logic of self-involvement", linking 'performative' function to "'true'" "'statements'", and views P.F. Strawson's hermeneutic of human selves as compatible with the Bible. Additionally, Thiselton implicitly adopts Saussure's distinction between synchronic and diachronic linguistics.[106]

(5) Thiselton's appeal to Continental hermeneutics is mixed, being critically-synthetically sublated into the framework of his appeals to the philosophy of language, general linguistics, semantics, biblical studies, and systematic theology. For Thiselton, Continental hermeneutics *rightly* stresses: individual subjectivity, personhood, creative *pre-cognitive* linguistic functions, projected or "gathered" "'narrative worlds'", "horizons", self-involvement, the "subversion" of horizons of "expectation", "language-events", transformation, faith, decision, and practice.[107]

However, Thiselton argues that Continental hermeneutics *undervalues*: corporate inter-subjective communication; "'performative utterances'" and the 'institutional' and conventional 'states of affairs' that their operation presupposes; certain forms of 'objectification'; cognitive or theoretical conceptualization; objective knowledge; discursive argument; historical-factual investigations into background; truth-criteria; description; truth-claims; and "propositions", "assertions", or "statements". Thus, Thiselton rejects Continental *historical, epistemological, linguistic, and anthropological dualisms or dichotomies*.[108]

(6) Thiselton's criticism of Bultmann is sharper still. Thiselton rejects: Bultmann's various dualisms or dichotomies; Bultmann's "'mythological interpretation'" of the resurrection and of Judgment Day; Bultmann's confusion 'between myth and analogy'; Bultmann's 'demythologization' programme and its problem 'with criteria'; Bultmann's overly kerygmatic 'theology'; Bultmann's Kierkegaardian notion of "'faith'"; Bultmann's view of "'the historical Jesus'"; Bultmann's 'philosophy of history'; and the "narrowness" of Bultmann's dialogue with 'philosophical traditions'. Nevertheless, Thiselton broadly affirms Bultmann's work on Pauline anthropology.[109]

We conclude that, by 1970, Thiselton's hermeneutical programme was underway, and that "widening dialogue towards critical synthesis" was an implicit hermeneutical axiom in his approach.

---

[106] Thiselton, 'Parab', 453, 454, 455, 456, 438.
[107] Thiselton, 'TY', 1560.
[108] Thiselton, 'Parab', 438, 454; cf. Thiselton, 'BSA', 13. Italics ours.
[109] Thiselton, 'R TB', 59, 60; cf. Thiselton, 'R TB', 21 (i.e. a different publication reviewing the same work); cf. Thiselton, 'R JN', 216.

CHAPTER 2

# Widening Dialogue of Historical Response vs. Hermeneutical Foreclosure: The Immersion of Thiselton's Hermeneutical Programme in the Processes of Traditions, 1970 to 1978/80

### A. Preliminary Comments: How to Continue

If, in Chapter 1, we examined the emergence of Thiselton's hermeneutical programme during his first period (1959-1970) then here, in Chapter 2, we begin our focus on his second period. Despite a comment by Thiselton concerning his 'Sheffield period from 1970 to 1985', his second period of hermeneutical *endeavor* falls between 1970 and 1978 or 1980 - depending on which criteria are considered.[1]

The *start* of Thiselton's second period is clearly his move to Sheffield University in 1970: this move was 'a decisive turning point' in his career.[2] Between 1970 and 1971, Thiselton was a Sir Henry Stephenson Fellow at Sheffield University whilst, in 1971, he became both a lecturer 'in Biblical Studies' at Sheffield University and a Member of the Church of England Faith and Order Advisory Group. Since Thiselton only publishes book reviews in 1971, then we may consider these as being representative of the start of his second period.[3]

The *conclusion* of Thiselton's second period of hermeneutical endeavor is more ambiguous, but probably occurs at the end of 1978 in relation to his *thinking*, or in 1980 in relation to his *publications and teaching*. Thus, the last publications from Thiselton's second period include his first responses to 'structuralist approaches' to biblical interpretation, which appear in 1978, 1979 and 1980.[4] In particular, *The*

---

[1] Thiselton, A.C., 'Thirty Years of Hermeneutics: Retrospect and Prospects', in *International Symposium on the Interpretation of the Bible* (ed. J. Krašovec; Ljubljana: Slovenian Academy of Sciences and Arts; Sheffield: Sheffield Academic Press, 1998), 1562.

[2] Thiselton, 'TY', 1561; cf. *Who's Who 1999: An Annual Biographical Dictionary* (151st Year of Issue; London: A&C Black, 1999), 1985.

[3] *WW*, 1985; and see the bibliography.

[4] See: Thiselton, A.C., 'Keeping up with Recent Studies: II. Structuralism and Biblical Studies: Method or Ideology?', *ExTim* 89 (Aug. 1978), 329; cf. 329-331; Thiselton, A.C., 'Review of R. Detweiler's *Story, Sign, and Self*', *ExTim* 90 (Jan. 1979), 119; Thiselton, A.C.,

*Two Horizons* (1980) slightly modifies Thiselton's PhD thesis (submitted 1976, awarded 1977) using material written by the end of 1978 – notably on "truth", on the later Wittgenstein and, as just noted, on structuralist approaches.[5]

Indeed, *The Two Horizons* aside, Thiselton publishes only a single book review in 1980,[6] hinting at a hiatus at the end of 1978, whilst in 1979 and 1980 Thiselton likely began work on articles published in 1981 and in 1982 that theoretically post-date *The Two Horizons*.[7] To include these articles in Thiselton's second period would contradict Thiselton's autobiographical remarks in 'Thirty Years of Hermeneutics' in which his second period of endeavor ends with the publication of *The Two Horizons*. Thus, Thiselton's illness in 1980-1 affects his third period of endeavor, not his second.[8]

But how should we *approach* Thiselton's 108 publications dated between 1971 and 1980? Flatly thematic approaches are susceptible to historical insensitivity, to anachronism, and to 'over-neat' "consumer-packaged" *a priori* categorization.[9] Conversely, strictly chronological approaches lack communicative clarity, tend to

---

'Review of N.R. Petersen's *Literary Criticism for New Testament Critics*', *ExTim* 90 (Feb. 1979), 153-154; Thiselton, A.C., 'Review of J.-M. Benoist's *The Structural Revolution*', *ExTim* 90 (May 1979), 248; Thiselton, A.C., 'Review of A.M. Johnson's *The New Testament and Structuralism*', *ExTim* 91 (Oct. 1979), 26-27; Thiselton, A.C., *The Two Horizons: New Testament Hermeneutics and Philosophical Description with Special Reference to Heidegger, Bultmann, Gadamer, and Wittgenstein* (Exeter: Paternoster Press, 1980), 428-431.

[5] Thiselton, *2H*; 428-431; cf.: Thiselton, A.C., *New Testament Hermeneutics and Philosophical Description: Issues in New Testament Hermeneutics with Special Reference to the Use of Philosophical Description in Heidegger, Bultmann, Gadamer, and Wittgenstein* (Sheffield: University of Sheffield Ph.D. Thesis, 1977; written by Dec. 1976); Thiselton, A.C., 'Truth', in *The New International Dictionary of New Testament Theology, Volume 3* (ed. C. Brown; Exeter: Paternoster; Grand Rapids: Zondervan, 1978), 874-902; cf. our footnote 4 above.

[6] Thiselton, A.C., 'Review of C.E.B. Cranfield's *A Critical and Exegetical Commentary on the Epistle to the Romans. Volume II: Commentary on Romans IX-XVI and Essays*', *Chman* 94.4 (1980), 356-357.

[7] Notably: Thiselton, A.C., 'Knowledge, Myth and Corporate Memory', in *Believing in the Church: Essays by Members of the Church of England Doctrine Commission* (ed. B. Mitchell; London: SPCK, 1981), 45-78; Thiselton, A.C., 'Academic Freedom, Religious Tradition, and the Morality of Christian Scholarship', in *Their Lord and Ours: Approaches to Authority, Community and the Unity of the Church* (ed. M. Santer; London: SPCK, 1982), 20-45.

[8] Thiselton, 'TY', 1561-1566; 1566-1569; cf. Thiselton, A.C., 'Unpublished Bibliographic Letter to R. Knowles', 4th May 1999.

[9] cf.: Thiselton, A.C., 'Review of K.J. Vanhoozer's *Is There a Meaning in this Text?*' *JThStud* NS51.2 (Oct. 2000), 705; Thiselton, A.C., 'Signs of the Times: Towards a Theology for the Year 2000 as a Grammar of Grace, Truth and Eschatology in Contexts of So-Called Postmodernity', *Unpublished Version of the Paper Given at The Society for the Study of Theology Annual Conference, Edinburgh*, Apr. 1999, 21-23; Thiselton, A.C., 'Theology for a New World: Review Article of H. Richardson's *Theology for a New World*', *Chman* 83.3 (1969), 200.

lose the "wholes" amidst the "parts", and would be too repetitious and voluminous since, occasionally, Thiselton repeats himself.[10]

Specifically, a strictly chronological approach would pay more attention to Thiselton's PhD Thesis (1976) than to the maturer version of this work, *The Two Horizons* (1980), which would seem odd. Thus, we defer treatment of the former until we address both it and *The Two Horizons* together in Chapters 6 and 7. Correlatively, in 'Thirty Years of Hermeneutics', Thiselton consigns comment on *The Two Horizons* to a separate section having *already* covered the period between 1970 and 1980 in relation to his teaching at Sheffield University.[11]

Therefore, in the present study, we offer a chronological-thematic approach: highlighting themes for clarity's sake, but retaining chronological sensitivity. This looks less neat, perhaps, but historical consciousness faces 'the "messiness" of it all'.[12] Here, in Chapter 2, we shall examine themes related to the *background context* of Thiselton's second period. Later, we shall examine themes to do with the *theoretical content* of Thiselton's second-period writings.

## B. The Background Context of Thiselton's "Second Period" Writings

Admittedly, the style of Thiselton's widening historical dialogue makes 'it... very difficult to actually isolate his own thought' from that of the other writers he cites.[13] Nevertheless, something of the character and 'importance of... Thiselton's' second period thinking emerges when observations concerning Thiselton as *an author, as an academic, and as an Anglican churchman* on the one hand, and observations concerning Thiselton's *historical context* or *'Sitz im Leben'* on the other hand, are juxtaposed – as follows.[14]

### 1. Thiselton as an Author, as an Academic, and as an Anglican Churchman: Thiselton's Relationship to Evangelicalism and to Anglicanism

Thus, to begin with, focusing on Thiselton as an *author, academic, and Anglican churchman*, then we may observe that Thiselton enjoyed a period of stability from 1971 until 1977, when four changes occurred. *First*, he became Examining

---

[10] E.g. Thiselton, A.C., 'Semantics and New Testament Interpretation', in *New Testament Interpretation: Essays in Principles and Methods* (ed. I.H. Marshall; Grand Rapids: Eerdmans; Exeter: Paternoster Press, 1977; actually written 1974), 79-89; cf.: Thiselton, A.C., 'Language and Meaning in Religion', in 'Word', in *The New International Dictionary of New Testament Theology. Volume III* (ed. C. Brown; Exeter: Paternoster; Grand Rapids: Zondervan, 1978; actually written by 1977), 1140-1142; Thiselton, 'SBS', 330-331.

[11] Thiselton, 'TY', 1563-1566, cf. 1561-1563.

[12] Thiselton, 'R *ITMITT*', 705.

[13] Verbal comments made by one of Thiselton's former students to me in October 2001.

[14] Conroy, C., 'Review of A.C. Thiselton's *The Two Horizons*', *Greg* 62.3 (1981), 563. Italics in speech-marks are Conroy's.

Chaplain to the Bishop of Sheffield. *Second*, he joined the Doctrine Commission of the Church of England. *Third*, Sheffield University awarded Thiselton his PhD, and *fourth*, his address, 'Understanding God's Word Today', created a stir at the second National Evangelical Anglican Congress (NEAC '77) held in Nottingham. Meanwhile, Thiselton remained on the Church of England Faith and Order Advisory Group, and continued as a lecturer 'in Biblical Studies' at Sheffield University. In 1979, Thiselton also became Examining Chaplain to the Bishop of Leicester, and was promoted to Senior Lecturer at Sheffield University.[15]

A) THISELTON'S HERMENEUTICAL CHALLENGE TO EVANGELICALS AT NEAC '77

His ecclesial and academic appointments and his PhD award aside, then only the impact of Thiselton's NEAC '77 address need concern us here since,[16] clearly, this event constituted a watershed in Thiselton's development as an author, as an academic, and as an Anglican churchman – as follows.

Thus, (1), in his NEAC '77 address, Thiselton argues that the *defence of biblical authority* depends on the Bible's 'practical cash-value' in 'use', and hence on 'hermeneutics', and not on 'abstract... theoretical' assertion. In Thiselton's estimate, 'the Bible' does 'authoritatively what it set out to do', where Thiselton argues that this statement coheres with 'Reformation' emphases, contrary to the charges of 'heresy' leveled at Thiselton by C.A.F. Warner. In Thiselton's view, 'evangelicals' 'may... have to... abandon some... cherished conceptions because they are not... truly biblical'. Thiselton insists he did not use 'the word "hermeneutics" from the platform at NEAC', but affirms others' use of the term 'to summarize' his 'subject'.[17]

S. Neill, however, remembers differently: Thiselton's 'introduction of this strange and barbarous word... set several cats among the pigeons'. Was Thiselton advocating the 'new hermeneutic' and 'a fresh bout of liberal scholarship'? R. Manwaring recounts that 'hermeneutics became the "shocker" at Nottingham and... Thiselton... produced the shock waves!', whilst W. Bebbington even implicates Thiselton and J.D.G. Dunn in a subsequent 'dispute' within Anglican circles over biblical 'authority'. Thiselton's appeal to hermeneutics so as to defend

---

[15] cf.: *WW*, 1985; Douglas, J.D., 'NEAC Remembers Church of Uganda. Charter of Evangelical Purpose', *CEN* 22 Apr. (1977), 1; cf. the reports in *CEN* 22 Apr. (1977), 1, 7-10, 14, 16; and, *CEN* 6 May (1977), 10, 11; Thiselton, A.C., 'Understanding God's Word Today: Evangelicals Face the Challenge of the New Hermeneutic. Address at the Second National Evangelical Anglican Congress, Nottingham, 1977', in *Obeying Christ in a Changing World, Vol. 1* (ed. J.R.W. Stott; Glasgow: Collins/Fountain Books, 1977), 90-122 (henceforth the 'long' article with this title).

[16] Thiselton, 'U (long)', 90-122; cf.: Thiselton, A.C., 'Understanding God's Word Today', *CEN* 15 Oct. (1976), 6, (henceforth the 'short' article with this title).

[17] Thiselton, A.C, 'Nitpicking at NEAC? Never: Reply Letter to C.A.F. Warner', *CEN* 17 Jun 1977, 9; cf. Douglas, J.D., 'Hermeneutical Hazards. NEAC '77 Report', *CEN* 22 Apr. (1977), 9.

biblical authority, then, was atypical given the evangelical setting of his address.[18]

(2) On the issue of *women's ordination* Thiselton, in his NEAC '77 address, 'offered two possible responses and invited his hearers to choose'. If we preserved 'the claims of the old creation order', there could be 'no women ministers'. If we took 'the view that the new age was crowding out the old', then there could 'definitely [be] women ministers' (N.B. the latter viewpoint emerges later as being Thiselton's stance). This 'left the audience (deliberately, on the part of the speaker) without any ready-made answer'.[19]

That is, Thiselton repudiates evangelical desires for fast 'neatly-packaged' solutions since they fall foul of Gadamer's and Wittgenstein's critiques of Enlightenment 'method' (see Chapter 3),[20] Kierkegaard's indirect '"dialectical"' approach,[21] Pannenberg's view that divine action changes "historical" 'truth' through time,[22] and Thiselton's own programmatic emphasis. That is, Thiselton sought to heighten 'awareness' that there was 'much work yet to be done' on women's ordination. Thus, for many, 'hermeneutics… preserved its forbidding image', and Thiselton's address was, again, atypical given its evangelical setting.[23]

(3) Thiselton's NEAC '77 address, furthermore, *confronted evangelical resistance to hermeneutics*. Aligning with Thiselton, J.D. Douglas, writing for the *Church of England Newspaper*, considered 'it… strange that… evangelicals' had only now 'stumbled upon such a vital topic'. Douglas writes, 'the reason' hermeneutics 'has suddenly come into prominence (though I don't think anybody really got the message delivered) is that non-Evangelicals have recently started interpreting the Bible in new ways' as in, for example, 'liberation theology'.[24]

Even in 1980, however, J. Macquarrie observed that, 'Thiselton has… to persuade Biblicists and evangelicals that… [hermeneutics] is worthwhile'. 'Evangelicals… too' readily 'ignore' historical 'distance', attempting 'to apply'

---

[18] Neill, S., 'Integrity of Approach: Review of I.H. Marshall ed. *New Testament Interpretation: Essays in Principles and Methods*', *CEN* 18 Nov. (1977), 20; cf.: Manwaring, R., *From Controversy to Co-Existence: Evangelicals in the Church of England 1914-1980* (Cambridge: CUP, 2002), 200; Bebbington, D.W., *Evangelicalism in Modern Britain: A History from the 1730s to the 1980s* (London: Routledge, 1989), 269, 352, n.166-168; Thiselton, 'NNN', 9; Dunn, J.D.G., 'The Authority of Scripture According to Scripture', *Chman* 96.2, 96.3, (1982), 104-122, and 201-255 respectively.

[19] Douglas, 'HH', 9; cf. Bebbington, *EIMB*, 269, 352, n.165.

[20] Thiselton, A.C., 'More Manageable Proportions. Review of J.W. Wenham's *The Goodness of God*', *CEN* 5 Apr. (1974), 8; 8; cf.: Thiselton, 'TY', 1560-1561; Thiselton, A.C., 'The Use of Philosophical Categories in New Testament Hermeneutics', *Chman* 87.1 (1973), 91-92.

[21] cf. Thiselton, A.C., 'Kierkegaard and the Nature of Truth', *Chman* 89.1 (1975), 98-99.

[22] cf.: Thiselton, A.C., 'The Theologian Who Must Not Be Ignored. Article Review of W. Pannenberg's *Basic Questions in Theology, Vol. 2*', *CEN* 25 Feb. (1972), 11.

[23] Douglas, 'HH', 9; cf. Thiselton, A.C., 'Theology and the Future', *CEN* 23 Jan. (1970), 11.

[24] Douglas, 'HH', 9.

biblical 'teachings directly'.[25] Similarly, in 1982, R.K. Johnston *also* has to urge evangelicals to adopt Thiselton's hermeneutics.[26] Historically, then, Thiselton is controversial, a trouble-shooter addressing the problems beleaguering evangelical biblical interpretation.

(4) We may even go as far as to say that, at NEAC '77, Thiselton *divided his evangelical audience over the issue of hermeneutics*. Negatively, many evangelicals reacted badly to perceived threats to existing interpretative practices. 'Hermeneutics' was 'lampooned and subject to ribald comment at almost every meeting', where 'many a clergyman... was found sheepishly avoiding anybody who might have pointed out to him that his hermeneutic had been defective for... years'.[27] John King writes, 'delegates will probably heave a sigh of relief' that 'the dreaded word "hermeneutic" does not appear in the' Congress 'statement'.[28] Indeed, King rejoices in 'the drubbing given to that pretentious term "hermeneutics"' at NEAC '77.[29] Possibly, King is still reacting to a rebuke from Thiselton two months previously in which Thiselton had argued that his (i.e. Thiselton's) sitting on 'four' 'NEAC' 'planning' 'committees' had given him 'a better vantage-point' for making 'judgments than' that of 'John King'. Contrary to what Thiselton had called 'King's journalese', Thiselton had argued – against King - that his (i.e. Thiselton's) occasional agreement 'with... John Stott' did not sacrifice 'intellectual integrity'.[30]

Positively, however, C. Buchanan hailed Thiselton's NEAC '77 address as 'a sensation' of 'apologetics'. Buchanan reported that whilst some saw 'hermeneutics' as 'either so trivial we all do it anyway, or so recondite we couldn't do it if we tried', for others, 'deep down, at the gut-level, something shifted'. Although some wanted to 'dodge the demands of hermeneutics', it 'is' now 'on our agenda. We have seen a shadow flit across a wall, and we cannot be quite the same again'. The 'hermeneutics swing' 'happened deep down', 'and... we can never go back'.[31] Indeed, J.R.W. Stott had predicted the 'crucial importance' of Thiselton's paper for NEAC '77,[32] and had fended off opposition to Thiselton's address,[33] (though

---

[25] Macquarrie, J., 'Review of A.C. Thiselton's *The Two Horizons*', *RelStud* 16.4 (Dec. 1980), 496.

[26] Johnston, R.K., 'Interpreting Scripture: Literary Criticism and Evangelical Hermeneutics', *ChLit* 32.1 (1982), 44-45.

[27] Douglas, 'HH', 9; cf. Bebbington, *EIMB*, 269, n.165.

[28] King, J., 'Congress Statement. NEAC '77 Report', *CEN* 22 Apr. (1977), 10.

[29] King, J., 'Decent Lack of Respect', *CEN* 6 May (1977), 10.

[30] Thiselton, A.C., 'Dissent from John King's Verdicts. Reply Letter to John King', *CEN* 11 Feb. (1977), 13. For links between Stott and Thiselton cf. Dudley-Smith, T., *John Stott: A Global Ministry: A Biography of the Later Years* (Leicester: IVP, 2001), 158.

[31] Buchanan, C., 'The Shifts at Gut Level', *CEN* 6 May (1977), 11.

[32] Stott, J.R.W., 'Obeying Christ in a Changing World', in *Obeying Christ in a Changing World. Vol. 1* (ed. J.R.W. Stott; Glasgow: Collins/Fountain Books, 1977), 21.

[33] Douglas, J.D., 'Question of Prophecy', *CEN*, 22 Apr. (1977), 7.

some neglected to mention it in their reports).[34] Thiselton spoke 'for quite a number', as an 'emerging' 'evangelical' leader,[35] and even John King, in his 'summary' of 'The Congress Statement', was forced to imply that hermeneutics *rightly* discouraged evangelicals from 'trying to force the Bible to answer distinctively modern questions to which the text does not refer'.[36]

(5) Thiselton's NEAC '77 address *criticized evangelical biblical hermeneutics at eight specific points* - i.e. for: (a) treating interpretative tradition as more 'authoritative' than 'the Bible'; (b) flattening 'the distinctiveness of different Biblical authors' through over-pressing biblical 'unity'; (c) flattening multiple language-functions into 'teaching' or 'information'; (d) making rushed '"applications"' prior to 'properly' listening to biblical texts;[37] (e) falling behind contemporary theology and its hermeneutical focus; (f) resisting hermeneutics; (g) making 'naïve' claims about "self-evident" textual meanings; and, (h), being ignorant of other interpretative approaches.[38] Nevertheless, Thiselton still defends evangelicals against undue criticism as we shall see later.[39]

Thus, (6), at NEAC '77, Thiselton addressed evangelicals on the familiar issue of biblical authority, but subverted 'cherished' evangelical beliefs by re-casting the issue in unfamiliar terms: "to defend the biblical authority you embrace, you need the hermeneutics you avoid". That is, Thiselton used "indirect communication" (see Chapter 3) to expose, enchant, or enrage different sections of his audience, successfully altering evangelical attitudes to hermeneutics (in some quarters) in the process.[40]

Yet, Thiselton is strangely silent in 'Thirty Years of Hermeneutics' about NEAC '77. Partly, this could be humility - a quality his pupils affirm in him.[41] Partly, however, it could be painful alienation. Thiselton was clearly misunderstood and rejected by many at the conference, and pursued a stance still

---

[34] Crowe, P., 'Developed and Improved Model', *CEN* 6 May (1977), 10; cf. Gladwin, J., 'Fear of What Change Will Mean?', *CEN* 6 May (1977), 11.

[35] Douglas, J.D., 'Where Did the Leaders Go?' *CEN*, 22 Apr. (1977), 9.

[36] King, 'CS', 10.

[37] Thiselton, 'U (short)', 6.

[38] cf.: Thiselton, *2H*, 3-4, 85-114; Douglas, 'HH', 9; King, 'CS', 10; King, 'DLR', 10; Thiselton, 'DJK', 13; Douglas, 'QP', 7; Thiselton, A.C., 'The New Hermeneutic', in *New Testament Interpretation: Essays in Principles and Methods* (ed. I.H. Marshall; Grand Rapids: Eerdmans; Exeter: Paternoster Press, 1977), 326-327.

[39] E.g. cf.: Thiselton, 'U (long)', 94-95; Thiselton, A.C., 'Distinctive Colleges. Reply Letter to Mrs Mable', *CEN* 12 Mar. (1971), 16; Thiselton, 'DJK', 13; Thiselton, 'NNN', 9.

[40] cf.: Thiselton, 'NNN', 9; Douglas, 'HH', 9; Carson, D.A., *Bible Interpretation. Parts 1-4. Tapes WA20-WA23. Word Alive 1993* (Eastbourne: ICC, 1993); Carson, D.A., *Bible Interpretation. Parts 1-4. Tapes WA12-1- WA12-4. Word Alive 1994* (Eastbourne: ICC, 1994).

[41] In personal communications, D. Olford, J. Thurgood, and M. Lovatt have all affirmed that humility is one of Thiselton's qualities.

unacceptable to many others during the 1980s.[42]

Thus, during his second period, Thiselton is an atypical evangelical, a controversial character - humble and prophetic to some, subversive to others, but certainly very important in introducing evangelicals to hermeneutics. He is not simply an academic, but an involved and leading churchman. And yet, he seems painfully alienated from "right wing" conservatives. Indeed, we might well ask: just how "evangelical" is Thiselton?

B) THISELTON'S SELF-CRITICAL, MODERATE, CONSERVATIVE EVANGELICALISM

Whilst Thiselton warns against easy 'consumer' "pigeon-holing" of 'thinkers' "'positions'", he nevertheless identifies himself as a "self-critical", 'moderate', 'conservative', 'evangelical' during his second period. Such "qualifiers" are important given the broad use of the term 'evangelical' recently, and Thiselton's conservatism should be held in tension with his stark criticisms of his own tradition – as follows.[43]

(1) As a *conservative* evangelical, Thiselton approves of G.E. Ladd's faithfulness to 'Scripture'[44] and of N. Anderson's 'evangelical conclusions about... doctrine' and 'the Bible'.[45] 'Being "under" Scripture',[46] Thiselton takes his 'cue from the theologians of the New Testament',[47] and also asserts 'that conservatives' pay more 'attention' to "non-conservatives" than vice versa.[48] C.K. Barrett's 'commentary' on '2 Corinthians' earns Thiselton's praise whilst,[49] for Thiselton,

---

[42] See, Adam, A.K.M., 'Review of A.C. Thiselton's *New Horizons in Hermeneutics*', *ModTh* 10 (1994), 433-434.

[43] Thiselton, A.C., 'The Theology of Paul Tillich', *Chman* 88.1 (1974), 86; cf.: Thiselton, 'S(un)', 22-24; Thiselton, A.C., 'Positive Role of Doubt', *CEN* 11 Jan. (1974), 8; Thiselton, A.C., 'Review of R.P. Martin's *New Testament Foundations: A Guide for Christian Students. Vol. 1: The Four Gospels*', *CGrad* 29.3 (Sep. 1976), 85; Thiselton, A.C., 'Conservative - and Intelligent With It. Review of N.A. Anderson's *A Lawyer Among the Theologians*', *CEN* 12 Oct. (1973), 9; Thiselton, A.C., 'The Multi-Model Character of Holy Spirit Language', *CEN* 11 Apr. (1974), 8; re. "evangelicalism": Carson, D.A., *The Gagging of God. Christianity Confronts Pluralism* (Leicester: IVP/Apollos, 1996), 444; cf. 444-461.

[44] Thiselton, A.C., 'Review of G.E. Ladd's *The New Testament and Criticism*', *CGrad* 24.3 (Sep. 1971), 86-87.

[45] Thiselton, 'CI', 9.

[46] Thiselton, A.C., 'Reply Letter to David Gregg about John Rosser', *CEN* 9 Feb. (1973), 11.

[47] Thiselton, A.C., 'Divine Friends. Reply Letter to an Article entitled 'Divine Friends'', *CEN* 4 Jun (1971), 7.

[48] Thiselton, 'DC', 16.

[49] Thiselton, A.C., 'Review of C.K. Barrett's *A Commentary on the Second Epistle to the Corinthians*', *TSF* 71 (Spr. 1975), 29-30.

A.T. Hanson wrongly and prematurely argues that the work of 'modern authors' can "replace" 'the creeds' just 'yet'.[50]

For Thiselton, 'the Christian... is... committed to... practical whole-hearted submission to the authority and truth of Christ'. Thiselton holds to the view that 'Christians' should 'stand in continuity with the New Testament' and 'believe that they have received an insight into truth which has the status of divine revelation'. This is neither 'arrogance' nor 'egotism', in Thiselton's view, but an 'honesty and integrity' that acknowledges 'the grace of God'.[51] Thiselton applauds the 'intellectual... integrity' of I.H. Marshall's affirmation of the historical authenticity of 'the New Testament evidence about Jesus'. In Thiselton's view, Marshall rightly invokes 'critical scholarship... in the *service* of Christian faith'.[52]

Thiselton was also involved in '"Dialogue 77"', an - at least partly - evangelical students' 'Christian outreach' at Sheffield University and,[53] furthermore, with R.C. Roberts, acknowledges 'objective grounds' for New Testament 'faith' 'in historical facts', 'miracles', and 'the resurrection of Christ'.[54] Elsewhere, Thiselton broadly affirms the work of W. Barclay, D.S. Russell, F.F. Bruce and C.E.B. Cranfield.[55]

(2) As a *moderate self-critical* 'conservative', however, Thiselton steers 'evangelicals... away from... short-cuts to "devotional" applications'. With Pannenberg, Thiselton rejects 'conservative' '"authoritarianism"', 'Platonism', fideism 'of the word', and separation of faith from rationality.[56] Thiselton argues that N. Anderson's attack on 'Bultmann's undue skepticism about... the historical Jesus' is valuable, but that 'many evangelicals' wrongly 'bypass' proper exegetical practice.[57] Thiselton argues that 'evangelical ordinands' should take 'Biblical criticism' and 'philosophical theology more seriously': 'Scripture' is not 'a bran-tub of timeless oracles'.[58] However, Thiselton complains that 'many evangelicals' avoid

---

[50] Thiselton, A.C., 'Reflections in the Current Debate. Review of A.T. Hanson's *Grace and Truth*', *CEN* 26 Dec. (1975), 9.

[51] Thiselton, A.C., 'Dialogue and the Dangers of Half-Truths', *CEN* 9 Apr. (1976), 8, 10.

[52] Thiselton, A.C. 'Review of I.H. Marshall's *I Believe in the Historical Jesus*', *CGrad* 30.4 (Dec. 1977), 117-118. Italics ours.

[53] Thiselton, A.C., 'Forget Image, Try Dialogue 77. Report on Outreach at Sheffield University', *CEN* 11 Feb. (1977), 2.

[54] Thiselton, A.C., 'Review of R.C. Roberts' *Rudolf Bultmann's Theology: A Critical Interpretation*', *Chman* 92.3 (1978), 267-268.

[55] cf.: Thiselton, A.C., 'Review of J.R. McKay and J.F. Miller eds. *Biblical Studies: Essays in Honour of William Barclay*', *Chman* 92.1 (1978), 62; Thiselton, A.C., 'Review of D.S. Russell's *Apocalyptic, Ancient and Modern*', *Th* 82.687 (May 1979), 218-220; Thiselton, A.C., 'Review of F.F. Bruce's *The Time is Fulfilled*', *CGrad* 32.4 (Dec. 1979), 30; Thiselton, 'R *Rom II*', 356-357.

[56] Thiselton, 'R *NTF*', 85; cf.: Thiselton, 'Doubt', 8; Thiselton, 'R *NTC*', 86-87; Thiselton, A.C., 'Review Article of W. Pannenberg's *Basic Questions in Theology, Vol. 1*', *Chman* 85.2 (1971), 120-122.

[57] Thiselton, 'CI', 9.

[58] Thiselton, A.C., 'Evangelical Dishonesty. Reply Letter to Editorial', *CEN* 3 Aug. (1973), 8.

the 'solemn obligation' of 'patient... careful theological debate'.[59]

Thus, Thiselton is clearly critical of his own evangelical tradition.[60] He commends 'evangelicals' for at last looking to 'broader' 'world problems and ethics', but neither for avoiding proper 'theological resources' and 'method', nor for 'one-sidedness' when addressing key contemporary 'questions'. Thiselton attacks 'naive pietistical' antipathy to 'doubt' since – in Thiselton's view - 'doubt' can engender 'self-criticism, change, and progress'. Some 'evangelicals', argues Thiselton, wrongly 'ransack the Bible... for isolated proof-texts...', or for 'a timeless oracle, cut loose from its' 'original historical and literary context'.[61]

Hence, Thiselton prefers 'the "ecclesiastical" type of church favored by Luther, Zwingli, and Calvin, and reflected in Lutheranism', over 'the "sectarian" churches of the evangelical radicals' or 'enthusiasts',[62] and applauds M.D. Goulder's challenge to 'traditional pietism'.[63] Further, in Thiselton's estimate, R.P. Martin's valuable 'conservative' New Testament scholarship will annoy '"right-wing" conservatives' but please 'moderate conservatives'.[64] Admittedly, in Thiselton's estimate, R.C. Roberts rightly attacks Bultmann's dualisms or dichotomies, his indebtedness 'to the spirit of the age', and his problematic 'view of language and meaning'. However, Thiselton complains that Roberts' 'one-sided' discussion misses Bultmann's 'complexity and subtlety' and 'his... debts to Hermann, Dilthey, Neo-Kantian epistemology, nineteenth-century Lutheranism and... dialectical theology'. And yet, in Thiselton's view, Roberts' work 'is one of the *better*' 'conservative' 'treatments of the subject'![65] As D.A. Carson puts it, Thiselton is an 'evangelical', but not 'simplistically partisan'.[66]

(3) By its very nature, Thiselton's historical-hermeneutical approach is a criticism of straightforward conservative evangelicalism. Again, Thiselton argues that evangelical desire for "fast answers" is bound up with a dated post-Enlightenment epistemology that neglects experiential, inter-subjective, and 'temporal' dimensions of understanding,[67] and that neglects the value of deliberate

---

[59] Thiselton, 'Gregg', 11.

[60] Thiselton, 'Doubt', 8; cf. Thiselton, A.C., 'Forsyth and his work brought to life. Review of A.M. Hunter's *P.T. Forsyth: per Crucem ad Lucem*', *CEN* 7 Jun. (1974), 6.

[61] Thiselton, 'Doubt', 8. Beginning in 1974, *The Church of England Newspaper* published a series of articles by Thiselton under the collective title of 'Theology and the Bible Today', though the individual titles of these articles are not Thiselton's titles (Thiselton, 'BL', 4th May 1999). 'Positive Role of Doubt' is one of these articles.

[62] Thiselton, A.C., 'Some Comments on the Anglican-Lutheran International Conversations', *Chman* 88.4 (1974), 289; cf. Thiselton, 'Till', 104-105.

[63] Thiselton, A.C., 'Cat Among the Pigeons. Review of M.D. Goulder's *Midrash and Lection in Matthew*', *CEN* 7 Feb. (1975), 10.

[64] Thiselton, 'R NTF', 85.

[65] Thiselton, 'R RBT', 267-268; cf. Thiselton, NTH, 288-316. Italics ours.

[66] Thiselton, A.C., *New Testament Commentary Survey* (Leicester: TSF, 1973, 1976); cf. D.A. Carson's later editorial comments (1976) on p. 1.

[67] cf.: Thiselton, 'UPC', 91-93; Thiselton, 'NH', 310-311; 317-321.

attempts to creatively initiate 'understanding' through "indirect" communication.[68] Such an "epistemology", then, in Thiselton's thinking, needs to be sublated into, and modified by, a larger framework of thinking (see Chapter 3).[69]

In other words, Thiselton cannot simply be caricatured as "evangelical" during his second period. And yet several reviewers perhaps fall into this trap.[70] J. Pereppadan, for example, caricatures Thiselton, writing 'the theological thinking of... ['the evangelical'] community seems to have exerted great influence on him...'[71] Thiselton, however, is not simply "evangelical", but is also – at least to an extent - a prophetic antagonist committed to *challenging* the "evangelical" church.

C) THISELTON'S SUBTLE RELATIONSHIP TO "ANGLICANISM" AND TO "LIBERALISM"

Indeed, Thiselton's "Anglicanism", as well as his "evangelicalism", also requires careful qualification. He actively contributes to ecumenical debates between 'Anglicans', 'Lutherans', and Methodists,[72] and recommends the 'Roman Catholic' writer 'Karl Rahner' to 'Protestant readers'. Yet, Thiselton regards himself 'as a loyal son of the Church of England in terms of its traditional Reformation doctrine'. Indeed, Thiselton writes, 'I am more "Anglican" in ecclesiology than some of my more charismatic brethren!'[73]

---

[68] cf.: Douglas, 'HH', 9; Thiselton, 'NH', 310-311, 320-321; Thiselton, 'KNT', 98-99, 104-105; Buchanan, 'Shifts', 11.

[69] cf.: Thiselton, 'UPC', 91-93; Thiselton, 'NH', 323-324; Thiselton, 'KNT', 103-105; Thiselton, 'Truth', 894-901; Thiselton, *2H,* 441, 4; Thiselton, A.C., *New Horizons in Hermeneutics: The Theory and Practice of Transforming Biblical Reading* (London: HarperCollins; Grand Rapids: Zondervan, 1992), 344.

[70] See: Pinnock, C.H., 'Climbing Out of a Swamp: The Evangelical Struggle to Understand the Creation Texts', *Interp* 43.2 (Apr. 1989), 144; Fackre, G., 'Evangelical Hermeneutics: Commonality and Diversity', *Interp* 43 (1989), 128; Fackre, G., 'Narrative: Evangelical, Postliberal, Ecumenical', in *The Nature of Confession: Evangelicals and Postliberals in Conversation* (eds. G.A. Lindbeck, D.L. Okholm and T.R. Phillips; Downers Grove, Ill.: IVP, 1996), 132, cf. 279, n.27; Dyrness, W.A., 'Review of A.C. Thiselton's *The Two Horizons*', *CTday* 25 (Apr. 10, 1981), 94; Bowden, J., 'Review of A.C. Thiselton's *The Two Horizons*', *Th* 84.697 (Jan. 1981), 55; Borsch, F.H., 'Review of A.C. Thiselton's *The Two Horizons*', *AThRev* 65 (Jan. 1983), 88-90; Poythress, V.S., 'Review of A.C. Thiselton's *The Two Horizons*', *WThJ* 43 (Fall 1980), 178; Rodd, C.S., 'Review of A.C. Thiselton's *The Two Horizons*', *ExTim* 91 (Jul. 1980), 289; cf.: Bray, G.L., *Biblical Interpretation: Past and Present* (Leicester: Apollos, 1996, 2000), 474; Klein, W.W., C.L. Blomberg, and R.L. Hubbard, *Introduction to Biblical Interpretation* (Nashville, TN.: Nelson Reference, 1993), 440.

[71] Pereppadan, J., 'Review of A.C. Thiselton's *The Two Horizons*', *JDh* 6.1 (Jan-Mar 1981), 89-92.

[72] Thiselton, A.C., 'The Ministry and the Church Union: Some Logical and Semantic Factors', *FUty* 18 (1974), 45-47; cf. Thiselton, 'A-LIC', 288-292.

[73] cf.: Thiselton, A.C., 'Shaping up to Tomorrow. Review of K. Rahner's *The Shape of the Church to Come*', *CEN* 7 Feb. (1975), 8-9; Thiselton, 'AF', 42-43; Thiselton, A.C., 'Personal Communication to Robert Knowles', 6th May 2007.

Nevertheless, whilst Thiselton notes 'the vast theological influence on Anglican thinkers of Bultmann, Tillich, Althous, Bornkamm, Käsemann, Ebeling, [and] Schlink',[74] he himself does *not belong to any* of these thinkers' respective traditions.[75] He diplomatically speaks of 'common ground among Anglicans', but is certainly not "Bultmannian". Ironically Thiselton writes, 'I lament the failure of much Anglican theology to engage with European Continental thought' – that is, with key aspects of its *own horizons or preunderstanding*. Conversely Thiselton, in explicating that preunderstanding, is *both* far more critical of it *and yet also*, at certain points, more accepting of certain Continental hermeneutical emphases where these constitute a right attack on the positivist excesses of the liberalism of the time.[76] Thus, for example, Thiselton rebukes certain Anglican scholars for "exaggerating" 'the problem of historical distance' between 'textual' and 'reader' 'horizons'.[77]

Thus, we reject *both* N.L. Geisler's caricaturing complaint about Thiselton's 'liberal tendencies'[78] *and* M.G. Brett's later caricaturing assertion that Thiselton's 'transcendental hermeneutic' is 'enshrined in Anglicanism'. Rather, in his second period, Thiselton has a critical relationship to the "liberalism" of the time and an emerging critical, if 'loyal', relationship to "Anglicanism". Thiselton must not be pre-dialogically "pigeon-holed" in an overly simplistic manner as being simply "evangelical", "Anglican", or "liberal". This kind of pre-dialogic categorization of

---

[74] Thiselton, 'A-LIC', 290.

[75] cf.: Thiselton, 'R *BQ1*', 120-122; Thiselton, A.C., 'Irrational Assumptions of Modern Theology Exposed. Review of T.F. Torrance's *God and Rationality*', *CEN* 19 Mar. (1971), 9; Thiselton, 'TNI', 11; Thiselton, 'CI', 9; Thiselton, A.C., 'Review of S.W. Sykes and J.P. Clayton eds. *Christ, Faith and History: Cambridge Studies in Christology*', *Chman* 87.1 (1973), 68-70; Thiselton, A.C., 'New Problems for Old: Article Review of J.A.T. Robinson's *The Human Face of God*', *CEN* 6 Apr. (1973), 8; Thiselton, A.C., 'Meaning and Myth. Review Article of W. Pannenberg's *Basic Questions in Theology, Vol. 3*', *CEN* 19 Oct. (1973), 8; Thiselton, 'UPC', 87-100; Thiselton, A.C., 'On the Logical Grammar of Justification in Paul. Paper Presented to the Fifth International Congress on Biblical Studies, Oxford, 1973', in *Studia Evangelica 7* (ed. E.A. Livingstone; Berlin: Akademie-Verlag, 1982), 491-495; Thiselton, A.C., 'The Meaning of SARX in 1 Corinthians 5:5: A Fresh Approach in the Light of Logical and Semantic Factors', *SJT* 26.2 (May 1973), 204-228; Thiselton, A.C., 'Myth, Mythology', in *The Zondervan Pictorial Encyclopedia of the Bible, Volume 4* (ed. M.C. Tenney; Grand Rapids, MI: Zondervan, 1975; written by 1973), 333-343; Thiselton, A.C., 'Head-On Challenge to Doubt: The Theology of Wolfhart Pannenberg', *CEN* 10 May (1974), 8; Thiselton, A.C., 'Review of A.D. Galloway's *Wolfhart Pannenberg*', *Chman* 88.3 (1974), 230-231; Thiselton, A.C., 'For Serious Students of St. Paul. Review of A.T. Hanson's *Studies in Paul's Technique and Theology*', *CEN* 9 Aug. (1974), 10; Thiselton, 'Till', 86-107; Thiselton, A.C., 'The Theological Scene: Post-Bultmannian Perspectives', *CGrad* 30.3 (Sep. 1977), 88-89; Thiselton, 'NH', 308-333.

[76] Thiselton, 'A-LIC', 291-292; cf. Thiselton, 'PCRK', 6th May 2007.

[77] Thiselton, 'U (long)', 94-95; cf. Thiselton, *2H*, 57; cf. 53-63, 74-84, 432-438.

[78] Geisler, N.L., 'Review of A.C. Thiselton's *The Two Horizons*', *BibSac* 138 (Apr.-Jun. 1981), 182-183.

thinkers and their "positions" re-emerges later in relation to how certain critics use the term "postmodern" and its cognates irresponsibly when referring to Thiselton (see Chapter 7 of the present study).[79]

D) WIDENING DIALOGUE WITH MULTIPLE TRADITIONS VS. HERMENEUTICAL FORECLOSURE

Clearly, then, Thiselton's widening dialogue with multiple traditions may be *contrasted* with the hermeneutical foreclosure of some of his critics, whether at NEAC '77 or in the literature. One begins to wonder: how well has Thiselton been heard? To avoid hermeneutical foreclosure ourselves, we may now shift the focus of our examination from Thiselton as an author, academic, and Anglican churchman to his second-period *Sitz im Leben*.

### 2. Historical Context: Thiselton's Immersion in Processes of Traditions

Thiselton's concern for widening dialogue steers his immersion in the *processes* of multiple traditions (with Gadamer, *'understanding'* involves *'participating in an event of tradition'*).[80] This approach also reflects Thiselton's later Wittgensteinian concern for multiple "angles of view" or a 'change of aspect' on any given issue.[81] Since *biblical interpretation* motivates Thiselton's hermeneutical programme, we shall begin by examining his immersion in multiple traditions in relation to that context.

A) TRENDS AND ISSUES IN BIBLICAL INTERPRETATION

In his second period, Thiselton responds to traditions, developments, debates, and issues in *biblical interpretation*, though overlap between biblical interpretation and philosophical themes is inevitable.[82] Thiselton's responses divide into *broader* responses to traditions, schools, trends, and associated debates, and *specific* responses to exegetical issues – as follows.[83]

(1) Thus, *broadly*, Thiselton responds to early 'twentieth century' 'biblical' studies - the "conservatism" of 'P.T. Forsyth', 'B.B. Warfield, H.C.G. Moule, and James Orr', the "liberalism" of 'Adolf von Harnack', 'Walter Rauschenbusch', 'Alfred Loisy', and 'R.J. Campbell', the '"history of religions" school', and the work of 'Albert Schweitzer' and 'Johannes Weiss'.[84] And yet, Thiselton normally

---

[79] Brett, M.G., 'Review of A.C. Thiselton's *New Horizons in Hermeneutics*', Th 96.772 (Jul./Aug. 1993), 314-315; cf. Thiselton, 'PCRK', 6th May 2007.

[80] Thiselton, *2H*, 306, cf. Gadamer, H.-G., *Truth and Method* (trans. J. Weinsheimer and D.G. Marshall; London: Sheed & Ward, 1975, 1989), 290. Gadamer's italics.

[81] E.g. cf.: Thiselton, 'SBS', 334; Wittgenstein, L., *Remarks on the Philosophy of Psychology. Volume 2* (eds. G.H. Von Wright and H. Nyman; trans. C.G. Luckhardt and M.A.E. Aue; Oxford: Blackwell, 1980), 80 (quoted).

[82] Thiselton, 'UPC', 87-89.

[83] e.g. Thiselton, 'NH', 308-333; cf. Thiselton, 'SARX', 204-228.

[84] Thiselton, A.C., 'An Age of Anxiety', in *The History of Christianity. A Lion Handbook* (eds. T. Dowley *et al*; Tring, Hertfordshire: Lion Publishing, 1977), 594-595; cf. 595-596.

only responds to *older* movements when their legacy can still be felt today in a way that is of particular relevance to his studies.[85] Consequently, he responds much more obviously to fourteen *more recent* movements, as follows.

(a) Thiselton has a mixed response to 'traditional' biblical interpretation[86] – whether 'evangelical' or positivist. Thus, he is critical of 'the biblical theology movement' ('1945'-'1968') upon which evangelicalism draws.[87] Similarly, Thiselton also critiques 'traditional historical-critical' methods, and does *not* merely supplement tradition with 'new' approaches 'which draw upon recent philosophical thought' (querying R. Van Voorst's reading of Thiselton).[88] Rather, Thiselton aligns more with 'recent attempts to go *beyond* historicism' whilst, at the same time, *retaining* a *thoroughly-revised* historical emphasis.[89]

Indeed, Thiselton, in *The Two Horizons*, reacts against 'the trauma… in theological circles over the impact of a certain type of historical-critical study of the Bible' that embodies 'a positivist philosophical bias' after 'Ernst Troeltsch (1865-1929)'.[90] Thus, Thiselton rejects D.E. Nineham's approach as dated, positivistic, ignorant of Continental hermeneutics, too pessimistic about 'the problem of historical distance', and too similar to an 'Enlightenment view of myth' in rejecting 'the supernatural' as belonging to 'a pre-critical world-view'. Thiselton argues that Nineham's approach only resembles supposedly 'value-neutral' 'phenomenology' 'superficially'.[91]

(b) Thiselton responds to 'Bultmann' and his 'demythologization programme',[92] which had 'dominated' 'Biblical hermeneutics in the [previous] three decades'.[93] Thiselton argues that 'most of the distortions in Bultmann's' approach 'come…

---

[85] e.g. Thiselton, A.C., 'Biblical Classics: VI. Schweitzer's Interpretation of Paul', *ExTim* 90 (Feb. 1979), 132-137; cf.: Thiselton, 'AA', 610-627.

[86] Thiselton, 'SNTI', 76; cf. Thiselton, A.C., "Important Achievement'. Review of G. Kittel and G. Friedrich eds. *Theological Dictionary of the New Testament, Volume 8*', CEN 10 Nov. (1972), 8.

[87] cf.: Thiselton, 'AA', 604-605; Thiselton, 'U (long)', 93-94.

[88] Querying, Van Voorst, R., 'Review of A.C. Thiselton's *The Two Horizons*', *RefRev* 34 (Spr. 1981), 220; cf. Thiselton, 'UPC', 87-100.

[89] Conroy, 'R *2H*', 563. Italics ours.

[90] McNicol, A.J., 'Review of A.C. Thiselton's *The Two Horizons*', *RestQ* 27.3 (1984), 187.

[91] Thiselton, A.C., 'Review of D. Nineham's *The Use and Abuse of the Bible*', *Chman* 91.4 (1977), 342; cf. 341-343; cf. Thiselton, NTH, 74-114; cf. Thiselton, *2H*, 51-83.

[92] See: Grech, P., 'Review of A.C. Thiselton's *The Two Horizons*', *Bib* 63.4 (1982), 572; Thiselton, 'UPC', 87, cf. 87-100; Thiselton, 'M&M', 8; Thiselton, A.C., *Language, Liturgy and Meaning* (Nottingham: Grove Books, 1975 and 1986); Thiselton, 'M,M', 333-343; Thiselton, A.C., 'The Parousia in Modern Theology. Some Questions and Comments', *Tyn* 27 (1976), 27-54; Thiselton, 'P-BP', 88-89; Thiselton, A.C., 'Myth, Paradigm, and the Status of Biblical Imagery', in *Using the Bible in Liturgy* (ed. C. Byworth; Nottingham: Grove, 1977), 4-12; Thiselton, 2H, 252-275.

[93] Grech, 'R *2H*', 572.

not from Heidegger... but from a neo-Kantian dualism of fact and value'.[94] Thiselton thus rejects 'Bultmann's "esoteric" conception of meaning' (or "value"), appealing instead to 'Wittgenstein's critique of "private language"': 'meaning' presupposes public 'criteria' that are inextricably linked to 'historical' facts.[95]

Thiselton complains that 'Bultmann' has 'drawn on too narrow a tradition of philosophy' at the level of critical-synthetic '"preunderstanding"' (see our Introduction).[96] Thiselton argues that Bultmann has thus generated 'skepticism about knowledge of the historical Jesus', that Bultmann has separated thought from language,[97] and that Bultmann has become guilty of "foreclosing" 'in advance certain' interpretative 'possibilities'.[98] In Thiselton's estimate, 'Bultmann's conclusions are read off from the *form* of the argument, not from the concrete particularities of exegesis'.[99] Thiselton dialogues with the two 'major' German volumes that respond to Bultmann's demythologization programme,[100] and D.F. Strauss thereby also comes under Thiselton's attack.[101]

Nevertheless, citing E. Schillebeeckx and B. Lonergan, Thiselton applauds Bultmann's insights into Pauline anthropology and into hermeneutical 'understanding',[102] and Thiselton defends Bultmann from conservatives who fail to appreciate his 'subtlety' as a thinker.[103] However, even in these contexts, Thiselton still rejects 'Bultmann's... individualism and radical subjectivism' (see especially

---

[94] Poythress, 'R 2H', 179; cf. Thiselton, 2H, 245-251.

[95] cf.: Torrance, A.J., 'The Self-Relation, Narcissism and the Gospel of Grace', *SJT* 40.4 (1987), 488; cf. 493, 510; Thiselton, NTH, 401-402, 545-553; Thiselton, 2H, 286-287, 379-385.

[96] Thiselton, 'UPC', 87; cf. Klein, W.W., 'Review of A.C. Thiselton's *The Two Horizons*', *TrinJ* 2 (Spr. 1981), 73.

[97] cf.: Thiselton, 'CI', 9; Thiselton, NTH, 344-350; Thiselton, 2H, 245-251; Thiselton, 'MP', 8-9; Thiselton, 'M&M', 8; Thiselton, 'Truth', 894-896; Thiselton, 'NP', 8; Thiselton, 'TNI', 11; Thiselton, 'IA', 9; Thiselton, 'P-BP', 88-89.

[98] Maddox, R.L., 'Review of A.C. Thiselton's *The Two Horizons*', *ThStud* 43.1 (Mar. 1982), 136; cf. Thiselton, 2H, 284.

[99] Klein, 'R 2H', 73; citing, Thiselton, 2H, 290. Italics Thiselton's.

[100] Thiselton, 'MP', 6; cf.: Hartlich, C., and W. Sachs, *Der Ursprung des Mythosbegriffes in der Modernen Bibelwissenschaft* (Tübingen: Mohr, 1952); Bartsch, H.-W., ed., *Kerygma und Mythos. Ein Theologisches Gespräch* (6 Volumes with Supplements; Hamburg: Reich & Heidrich, Evangelischer Verlag, 1948 and onwards); Thiselton, 2H, 448.

[101] Kaye, B.N., 'Strauss, D.F. and the European Theological Tradition - Der Ishariotismus unsere Tag', *JRelHist* 17.2 (1992), 175; cf. Thiselton, 2H, 255.

[102] Thiselton, 2H, 109-110; cf. 275-283; cf.: Thiselton, 'UPC', 87-88, 90-91; Thiselton, 'SARX', 208-209, 212, 217; Thiselton, A.C., Contribution to 'Flesh', in *The New International Dictionary of New Testament Theology, Volume 1* (ed. C. Brown; Exeter: Paternoster; Grand Rapids: Zondervan, 1975), 680-681; Thiselton, NTH, 386-397; Thiselton, 'NH', 312-313.

[103] cf. Thiselton, 'R RBT', 267-268; Thiselton, 2H, 291-292.

Chapter 6).[104]

(c) Thiselton attacks J.A.T. Robinson and M. Wiles of the British Bultmannian School for their 'Kantian' or Dilthey-type dualistic separations of "fact" and "value", "science" and "myth", and "non-objectifying" and "objectifying" language.[105] Further, Thiselton attacks the "New Morality" of J.A.T. Robinson and others.[106]

(d) Thiselton criticizes the Continental "Post-Bultmannian Movement" for failing to correct 'Bultmann's... approach to history'.[107] Thiselton's response to "the New Hermeneutic" of E. Fuchs and G. Ebeling is more extensive than his response to "the New Quest of the Historical Jesus" of E. Käsemann, E. Fuchs, G. Bornkamm, G. Ebeling, and H. Conzelmann.[108] Importantly, for Thiselton, Fuchs asks, 'what does the Bible actually say to our own generation?' and, "how does the message of 'the New Testament' 'strike home' 'today'?"[109] Thiselton esteems the New Hermeneutic in relation to parable interpretation and preaching, though he also criticizes its multiform one-sidednesses (see Chapters 3-6).[110]

(e) Thiselton responds to the American counterpart to the New Hermeneutic, and in this context values the work of R.W. Funk, D.O. Via, and J.D. Crossan on Jesus' parables,[111] and W. Wink's attack on contemporary New Testament studies[112] - though Thiselton's criticisms of the New Hermeneutic are also applied to these American thinkers.[113]

(f) Thiselton responds favorably to Pannenberg's biblical interpretation in relation to 'myth', 'history', and the relationship between apocalyptic and eschatology, accepting Pannenberg's modifications of B.S. Childs' 'conclusions' in this context.[114]

---

[104] Kleinig, J., 'Review of A.C. Thiselton's *The Two Horizons*', *RefThRev* 39 (Sep.-Dec. 1980), 90; cf. Thiselton, *2H*, 292.

[105] cf.: Thiselton, 'NP', 8; Thiselton, 'IA', 9; Thiselton, 'R *CFH*', 68-70; Thiselton, 'M&M', 8; Thiselton, 'SNTI', 86-88; Thiselton, 'Till', 101-102; Thiselton, 'Par', 41-44; Thiselton, 'AA', 607-608.

[106] Thiselton, 'KNT', 90, cf. 91-92.

[107] Thiselton, 'P-BP', 89.

[108] cf.: Thiselton, 'P-BP', 88-89; Thiselton, 'AA', 605-606; Thiselton, 'UPC', 95; Thiselton, A.C., 'Predictable, Domesticated and Tamed', *CEN* 8 Feb. (1974), 7; Thiselton, *NTH*, 480-496, 503-508; Thiselton, 'NH', 308-333; Thiselton, 'U (long)', 90-122; Thiselton, *2H*, 334-347, 352-356.

[109] Thiselton, 'T&F', 11; cf. Thiselton, 'NH', 308.

[110] Thiselton, 'NH', 311-312, 318-323, 308-309, 323-329.

[111] Thiselton, *2H*, 348; cf. 347-352; cf. Thiselton, *NTH*, 497-503.

[112] Thiselton, 'NH', 316-317.

[113] Thiselton, *NTH*, 503-508; cf. Thiselton, *2H*, 352-356.

[114] cf.: Thiselton, 'R *BQ1*', 120-122; Thiselton, 'TNI', 11; Thiselton, 'M&M', 8; Thiselton, A.C., 'Creativity of Heaven', *CEN* 8 Mar. (1974), 5; Thiselton, 'H-O', 8; Thiselton, A.C., 'No Horns on the Pope', *CEN* 14 Jun. (1974), 5; Thiselton, A.C., 'Looking for God's Triumph: The Role of Apocalyptic', *CEN* 12 Jul. (1974), 8; Thiselton, 'R *WP*', 230-231;

(g) Thiselton applauds the application of the work of the later Wittgenstein and J.L. Austin to biblical interpretation by 'D.D. Evans and... O.R. Jones'.[115] Thiselton believes himself to be the first 'New Testament scholar' to appropriate the later Wittgenstein's work,[116] though he is followed closely by D. Jasper and J.W. Voelz.[117] In particular, Thiselton appeals to the later Wittgenstein against arguments 'that early Christians merely inherited their authoritative view of Scripture "as a cultural presupposition... accepted uncritically"'.[118] A. Gibson approves Thiselton's introduction of 'logical topics to biblical linguistics' and his 'judgment that philosophical semantics can supplement linguistic semantics' (though, actually, "linguistic semantics" 'supplement' "philosophical semantics" in Thiselton - see Chapter 4. Notably, Thiselton later criticizes Gibson's work).[119]

(h) Thiselton responds to Saussure's 'linguistics' and their applications by J. Barr, J.F.A. Sawyer, and others. 'Traditional assumptions about language' and translation thereby come under Thiselton's critical eye; Thiselton clarifies the relationship between 'semantics' and 'hermeneutics'; and valuable insights emerge for academics and 'preachers'.[120]

(i) Thiselton approves 'conservative' reinstatements of the 'historical' Jesus by G.E. Ladd, C.K. Barrett, I.H. Marshall, F.F. Bruce, and others.[121] (j) We will consider Thiselton's response to structuralist approaches below. (k) Thiselton

---

Thiselton, A.C., 'Review of E.H. Cousins ed. *Hope and the Future of Man*', *Chman* 88.3 (1974), 232-233; Thiselton, 'M,M', 333-343; Thiselton, 'Par', 27-54; Thiselton, *NTH*, 101-114; Thiselton, 'MP', 8, 9; Thiselton, 'Truth', 900-901; Thiselton, *2H*, 74-83.

[115] Thiselton, 'LG', 493; cf. 491-495; cf.: Thiselton, 'SNTI', 75-76; Thiselton, 'UPC', 95-98; Thiselton, A.C., 'The Supposed Power of Words in the Biblical Writings', *JThStud* NS25.2 (Oct. 1974), 283-299; Thiselton, *LLM*; Thiselton, *NTH*, 562-606; Thiselton, 'MP', 10-11; Thiselton, 'LMR', 1123-1146; cf. Thiselton, *2H*, 386-427.

[116] Thiselton, *NTH*, 55; cf. Thiselton, *2H*, 26.

[117] Jasper, D., 'The New Testament and Literary Interpretation', *RelLit* 17.3 (Fall 1985), 8-9; cf. Voelz, J.W., 'Some Things Old, Some Things New: A Response to Wolfgang Schenk re. Paul's Letter to the Philippians', *Sem* 48 (1989), 162.

[118] Klein, 'R *2H*', 74; cf. Thiselton, *2H*, 434.

[119] Gibson, A., *Biblical Semantic Logic: A Preliminary Analysis* (Oxford: Blackwell, 1981), 1; cf. Thiselton, A.C., 'Review of A. Gibson's *Biblical Semantic Logic*', *Th* 85.706 (Jul. 1982), 301-303.

[120] Thiselton, 'SNTI', 77; cf. 76, 75-104; cf.: Thiselton, A.C., 'The Semantics of Biblical Language as an Aspect of Hermeneutics', *FTht* 103.2 (1976), 108; cf. 108-120; Thiselton, A.C., 'Enthusiasm Not Enough: Güttgemanns, Sawyer, and Barr on Biblical Research', *CEN* 13 Sep. (1974), 6; Thiselton, 'IAch', 8; Thiselton, *NTH*, 166-193; Thiselton, 'LMR', 1123-1146; Thiselton, *2H*, 117-139.

[121] cf.: Thiselton, 'R *NTC*, 86-87; Thiselton, 'R *IBHJ*', 117-118; Thiselton, A.C., 'Questions, but Not Enough Answers. Review of C.K. Barrett's *The Gospel of John and Judaism*', *CEN* 5 Dec. (1975), 7; Thiselton, 'R *2 Cor*', 29-30; Thiselton, 'R *TiF*', 30; Thiselton, 'AA', 604-611; Thiselton, 'Par', 41-44; Thiselton, A.C., 'Experience-Centred Religion: Harvey Cox on the Seduction of the Spirit', *CEN* 9 Aug. (1974), 8.

responds to 'Latin American liberation hermeneutics" appropriation of 'Marxist' thought, notably in his 'hermeneutics course' at Sheffield University (see below).[122] (l) Thiselton notes the contextualizing approaches to biblical interpretation in 'African' and 'Indian' theology.[123] (m) Thiselton criticizes the 'Death of God Movement' of T.J.J. Altizer and Harvey Cox, where M.A. Noll rightly records Thiselton's resistance to 'twentieth' 'century' "secular gospels".[124] And, (n), 'by 1980', Thiselton had covered 'Reader-Response Theory' in his 'course' on 'hermeneutics' at Sheffield University (see below).[125]

(2) Thiselton also engages with *specific* issues related to biblical exegesis. Thus, (a), in relation to *biblical studies as a whole*, we noted Thiselton's concern over Bultmann's approach to 'myth'.[126] Thiselton also applauds 'the growing interest in apocalyptic' literature from the 1950s to the 1970s. Thiselton argues that 'apocalyptic' is a 'widely misunderstood' genre, and that 'Pannenberg... and Moltmann' are important in this context.[127]

Moreover, Thiselton rejects problematic generalizations with respect to 'uses of *alētheia* and *alēthēs* in' classical 'Greek' and the supposed 'clear-cut contrast between' Greek 'and' Hebrew 'concepts of truth' (see Chapter 3).[128] In Thiselton's estimate, generalizing distinctions between '"Hebrew"' and '"Greek" thought... on the basis of... grammatical categories' presuppose erroneous approaches to language. Thiselton criticizes the work of T. Boman, J. Pedersen, G.A.F. Knight, and others in this context.[129]

Thiselton also attacks O. Procksch, G. von Rad, J. Pedersen, L. Dürr, H. Ringgren and others for relating the '"power"' of biblical (or any) language to a 'natural' view of the relation between 'words' and 'the world'.[130] Many writers endorse Thiselton's conclusions here, notably G.W. Ramsey who also summarizes Thiselton's arguments.[131] Thiselton also contributes word-studies on biblical terms

---

[122] Thiselton, 'TY', 1563, 1562; cf.: Thiselton, 'AA', 609-610; Thiselton, *NTH*, 153-156; Thiselton, *2H*, 111; cf. 110-113.

[123] Thiselton, 'AA', 610-611.

[124] Thiselton, 'AA', 608-609; cf. Thiselton, 'E-CR', 8; cf. Noll, M.A., 'Common Sense Traditions and American Evangelical Thought', *AmQ* 37.2 (1985), 238.

[125] Thiselton, 'TY', 1563, 1562.

[126] Thiselton, 'M&M', 8; Thiselton, 'M,M', 333-343; Thiselton, 'MP', 4-12; Thiselton, A.C., 'Review of T. Fawcett's *Hebrew Myth and Christian Gospel*', *TSF* 72 (Sum. 1975), 24.

[127] Thiselton, 'R *Apoc*', 218; cf. 219; cf. Thiselton, 'R *BS*', 62; cf. Thiselton, 'NHP', 5.

[128] Thiselton, 'Truth', 874. Italics and transliterations Thiselton's.

[129] Thiselton, 'SNTI', 86.

[130] Thiselton, 'Words', 284, 287-289, 292, 293-299; cf. Thiselton, A.C., 'The Parables as Language-Event: Some Comments on Fuchs's Hermeneutics in the Light of Linguistic Philosophy', *SJT* 23.4 (Nov. 1970), 448-451.

[131] E.g. cf.: Gibson, *BSL*, 93, cf. 151; Tosato, A., 'On Genesis 2:24', *CBQ* 52.3 (Jul. 1990), 390; Barr, J., 'Story and History in Biblical Theology', *JRel* 56 (1976), 3; Gunn, D.M., 'Deutero-Isaiah and the Flood', *JBLit* 94 (1975), 505; Ware, K., 'The Jesus Prayer', *Sob* G 2 (1980), 92-93; Brueggemann, W., 'Vine and Fig-Tree - A Case-Study in Imagination and

rendered 'flesh', and on those rendered 'explain, interpret, tell, and narrative'.[132]

Further, Thiselton criticizes the New Quest of the Historical Jesus for over-stressing biblical 'diversity', and criticizes evangelicals and the Biblical Theology Movement for over-stressing biblical 'unity'.[133] Finally, Thiselton criticizes trends in 'form criticism' and 'redaction criticism',[134] appealing to the later Wittgenstein to modify 'form criticism' in relation to '"logical function"'.[135]

(b) In *New Testament studies as a whole*, Thiselton criticizes J.D.G. Dunn for over-stressing 'New Testament' 'diversity' at the expense of its 'unity'.[136] Thiselton also argues that some writers over-stress passages that may seem to suggest that 'an *imminent* Parousia' was expected by the early Church.[137] Thiselton's 'New Testament Commentary Survey' responds to the needs of students and preachers,[138] and Thiselton also shows mixed favor towards the then-new Anglican 'lectionary'.[139]

(c) Thiselton shows a particular interest in *Pauline studies, Apocalyptic and the Parousia, and the Gospels*. In Pauline studies - 1 Corinthians aside - Thiselton is interested in debates surrounding 'Paul's doctrine of justification',[140] and also in A. Schweitzer's work, which precipitates 'debate' about 'the centrality and nature of justification in Paul'. In this context, Thiselton notes the work of Goguel and Bultmann, J. Moffatt, M. Werner, W.G. Kümmel, A. Wikenhauser, M. Bouttier, J.A.T. Robinson, E. Käsemann, D.E.H. Whiteley, and E.P. Sanders. Importantly, Thiselton counters Schweitzer's rejection of Paul's futurist eschatology.[141] In

---

Criticism', *CBQ* 43.2 (1981), 188-189; Ramsey, G.W., 'Is Name-Giving an Act of Domination in Genesis 2:23 and Elsewhere?', *CBQ* 50 (Jan, 1988), 31-32.

[132] cf.: Thiselton, 'Flesh', 678-682; Thiselton, 'SARX', 214-215, 204-205; Thiselton, A.C., 'Explain, Interpret, Tell, Narrative', in *The New International Dictionary of New Testament Theology, Volume 1* (ed. C. Brown, Exeter: Paternoster; Grand Rapids: Zondervan, 1975), 573-584.

[133] Thiselton, 'AA', 604-605.

[134] Thiselton, 'AA', 605-606.

[135] Grech, 'R *2H*', 574; cf. citation from Thiselton, *2H*, 396.

[136] Thiselton, A.C., '"Understanding the New Testament". Review of J.D.G. Dunn's *Unity and Diversity in the New Testament*', *CEN* 23 Dec. (1977), 8.

[137] Thiselton, 'Par', 31, 35; cf. 31-40, 41-44, 44-46. Italics Thiselton's.

[138] Thiselton, A.C., *Personal Suggestions about a Minister's Library* (London: TSF, 1966, possibly 1967); cf.: Thiselton, A.C., 'New Testament Commentary Survey', *TSF* 58 (1970), 9-18, (revision of Thiselton, *Suggestions*); Thiselton, *NTCS* (Leicester: TSF, 1973, 1976); Thiselton, A.C. 'New Testament Commentary Survey', *Them* 10.1 (Spr. 1974), 7-23; Carson, D.A., *New Testament Commentary Survey* (Leicester: IVP, 1984, 1993, 2001, and later).

[139] Thiselton, A.C., '"Towards Intelligent Preaching". Review of J. Gunstone's *Commentary on the New Lectionary, Vol. 2*', *CEN* 3 May (1974), 8.

[140] Thiselton, 'LG', 491; cf. 491-495; cf.: Thiselton, 'SNTT', 98-100; Thiselton, *NTH*, 593-599; Thiselton, *2H*, 415-427.

[141] Thiselton, 'Sch', 136, 135; cf. 132-137; cf.: Thiselton, 'Par', 35; cf. 31-35.

relation to 'Apocalyptic' and 'the Parousia',[142] Thiselton finds D.S. Russell's affirmation of the 'relevance' of 'apocalyptic' to 'our generation' both 'sober and very convincing'.[143] In relation to the Gospels,[144] Thiselton is particularly interested in parable research.[145]

(d) Thiselton's greatest 'second period' interest in biblical interpretation is *1 Corinthians*. Studies relating to this epistle constitute an important part of his historical context.[146] Ultimately, Thiselton published a massive commentary on 1 Corinthians (2000) and Thiselton is now considered to be a world authority on the epistle. However, his interest in the epistle dates back to his 1964 Masters degree and to his 1966 Tyndale Lecture.[147] In his 'second period', Thiselton pens three articles on 1 Corinthians,[148] where several writers follow his developed thesis on 'over-realized eschatology' 'at Corinth' – though, more recently, opinion is divided over the thesis.[149]

In relation to 1 Corinthians 5:5, J. Murphy-O'Connor aligns with Thiselton's thesis that for the Corinthians to applaud the incestuous believer, they must have 'considered themselves to' belong 'entirely to the new age' in such a way as to enable them to disparage 'the standards and values of the unredeemed world as

---

[142] Thiselton, 'R *Apoc*', 218-220; cf.: Thiselton, 'NHP', 5; Thiselton, 'LGT', 8; Thiselton, 'Par', 27-54.

[143] Thiselton, 'R *Apoc*', 219-220; cf. Thiselton, 'NHP', 5.

[144] Thiselton, A.C., 'Review of R.P. Martin's *Mark: Evangelist and Theologian*', *CGrad* 26.3 (Sep. 1973), 85; cf.: Thiselton, 'CATP', 10; Thiselton, 'Qs', 7; Thiselton, 'R *NTF*', 85; Thiselton, A.C., 'Review of N. Perrin's *Jesus and the Language of the Kingdom*', *Chman* 91.1 (1977), 85-86.

[145] cf.: Thiselton, 'UPC', 95; Thiselton, 'U (short)', 6; Thiselton, *NTH*, 490-503; Thiselton, 'NH', 318-323; Thiselton, 'U (long)', 90-92, 106-113; Thiselton, *2H*, 344-352.

[146] cf. those by C.K. Barrett, F.F. Bruce, Käsemann, E.E. Ellis, B.A. Pearson, W. Schmithals, Schweitzer, G.B. Caird, J. Moffatt, Conzelmann, Stendahl, Theissen, Bultmann, E. Schweizer, J.A.T. Robinson, Kümmel, Funk, Barth, S. Laeuchli, Bornkamm, C.F.D. Moule, J. Jeremias, K. Grobel, and many others.

[147] Thiselton, A.C., *The First Epistle to the Corinthians* (eds. H. Marshall and D.A. Hagner; Series: The New International Greek Testament Commentary; Grand Rapids: Eerdmans; Carlisle: Paternoster, 2000); cf.: Thiselton, A.C., *Eschatology and the Holy Spirit in Paul with Special Reference to 1 Corinthians* (London: University of London Unpublished M.Th. Dissertation, 1964); Thiselton, A.C., 'Review of E. Käsemann's *New Testament Questions of Today*', *Chman* 84.3 (1970), 229-230. On Thiselton as an authority on 1 Corinthians cf. flagged references in our bibliography. Thiselton's 1966 Tyndale Lecture was not published.

[148] Thiselton, 'SARX', 204-228; cf.: Thiselton, A.C., 'The 'Interpretation' of Tongues: a New Suggestion in the Light of Greek Usage in Philo and Josephus', *JThStud* NS 30.1 (Apr. 1979), 15-36; Thiselton, A.C., 'Realized Eschatology at Corinth', *NTStud* 24 (Jul. 1978), 510-526.

[149] Thiselton, 'REC', 510; cf. flagged references in our bibliography for references relevant to the debate following Thiselton's 'over-realized eschatology' thesis.

irrelevant'.[150] J.H. Neyrey accepts Thiselton's exposition of 'Paul's idea of a "spiritual body"', which contains 'the sense of "a total person controlled by God's Spirit"'.[151] J. Osei-Bonsu, however, departs from Thiselton's exegesis of '*sarx*', viewing the term as a reference to 'the physical body'.[152] Finally, for several writers, though not for W.O. Walker Jr., Thiselton rightly rejects the thesis 'that 1 Corinthians 11:2-16 is a post-Pauline interpolation'.[153]

B) TRENDS AND ISSUES IN SYSTEMATIC THEOLOGY

Thiselton also responds to traditions, developments, debates and issues in *systematic theology* during his second period, whilst simultaneously promoting 'dialogue' between 'biblical exegesis' 'and systematic theology'.[154] Five specifically theological aspects of Thiselton's context may be clarified, as follows.

(1) Thiselton names Barth, Reinhold Niebuhr, Bultmann, Bonhoeffer, and Tillich as five of 'the most important' theologians of the *mid-twentieth century*.[155] Yet, we shall demonstrate that none of these thinkers are pivotal for his formative hermeneutical thinking (though Barth, Niebuhr, and Bonhoeffer have secondary roles in Thiselton's later thought).[156] Indeed, in Thiselton's view, Karl Barth aside, the *later* twentieth century produced theologians of equal – or even greater – "importance" than these (see below).[157]

(2) Thiselton also responds to what were at the time *more recent* theological

---

[150] Murphy-O'Connor, J., 'Sex and Logic in 1 Corinthians 11:2-16', *CBQ* 42 (1980), 490; cf. Thiselton, 'SARX', 204-228.

[151] Neyrey, J.H., 'Body-Language in 1 Corinthians - The Use of Anthropological Models for Understanding Paul and his Opponents', *Sem* 35 (1986), 161.

[152] Osei-Bonsu, J., 'Anthropological Dualism in The New Testament', *SJT* 40.4 (1987), 575-577; citation from, 576. Italics and transliteration Osei-Bonsu's.

[153] cf.: Murphy-O'Connor, 'SL', 482; Murphy-O'Connor, J., 'Interpolations in 1 Corinthians', *CBQ* 48.1 (1986), 87; Meier, J.P., 'On the Veiling of Hermeneutics (1 Cor. 11:2-16)', *CBQ* 40 (1978), 218, n. 12; Thiselton, 'REC', 520-521. But cf.: Walker, W.O., 'The Theology of Woman's Place and the Paulinist Tradition (Reprinted)', *Sem* 28 (1983), 108, cf. 109; Fitzmyer, J.A., 'Another look at Kephale in 1 Corinthians 11:3', *NTStud* 35.4 (Oct. 1989), 504; Sterling, G.E., "Wisdom Among the Perfect": Creation Traditions in Alexandrian Judaism and Corinthian Christianity', *NovTm* 37.4 (1995), 377.

[154] Thiselton, *2H*, 315-326; cf. Ellingworth, P., 'Review of A.C. Thiselton's *The Two Horizons*', *EvanQ* 53 (Jul.-Sep. 1981), 179.

[155] Thiselton, 'AA', 597-599, 602, 604.

[156] cf.: Thiselton, 'KNT', 85-107; Thiselton, *NTH*, 386-397; Thiselton, *2H*, 88-90, 275-283, 315-318; Thiselton, 'UPC', 87-91; Thiselton, 'SARX', 208-212, 217; Thiselton, 'Flesh', 680-681; Thiselton, 'NH', 312-313; Thiselton, 'Till', 86; Thiselton, A.C., 'Authority and Hermeneutics. Some Proposals for a More Creative Agenda', in *A Pathway into the Holy Scripture* (eds. P.E. Satterthwaite and D.F. Wright; Grand Rapids: Eerdmans, 1994), 139; Thiselton, A.C., *Interpreting God and The Postmodern Self: On Meaning, Manipulation and Promise* (SJT: Current Issues in Theology; Edinburgh: T&T Clark, 1995), 19, cf. 21-25; 135-143.

[157] Thiselton, 'AA', 609; cf. later.

developments in the 1960s and 1970s, where we have already noted K. Rahner, J.A.T. Robinson and the New Morality, the New Hermeneutic, the New Quest of the Historical Jesus, the Death of God Movement, the Biblical Theology Movement, Latin American liberation theology, and African and Indian theology.[158] Most important for Thiselton, however, are the "Theologies of Hope" of Pannenberg and Moltmann,[159] "intelligent conservatism" (for example, that of C.K. Barrett, R.P. Martin, F.F. Bruce, I.H. Marshall, and of G.E. Ladd),[160] and T.F. Torrance's 'scientific' theology.[161]

(3) Thiselton specifically focuses on *Christology*, notably on debates about 'the Incarnation', Christ's 'pre-existence', and creedal 'Christology'.[162] Thiselton's response to J.A.T. Robinson's *The Human Face of God* is mixed, whilst his response to Moltmann's *The Crucified God* is more positive.[163] In Thiselton's view, A. Schweitzer underplays the importance of Christology relative 'to eschatology' in Pauline thought.[164]

(4) Thiselton's main theological focus is *eschatology*. We have already noted Thiselton's interest in biblical apocalyptic, Pauline eschatology (especially in 1 Corinthians),[165] and the Theologies of Hope.[166] Thiselton's eschatological dialogue is wide, however, and includes Schweitzer, Werner, Bultmann, Conzelmann, Tillich, J.A.T. Robinson, the 'process theology' of J. Cobb, S. Ogden, and D.D.

---

[158] Thiselton, 'AA', 608.

[159] cf.: Thiselton, 'Par', 46-53; Thiselton, 'R *BQT*', 120-122; Thiselton, 'TNI', 11; Thiselton, A.C., 'Theology Made Exciting. Review of W. Pannenberg's *The Apostles' Creed in the Light of Today's Questions*', *CEN* 19 Jan. (1973), 12; Thiselton, 'M&M', 8; Thiselton, 'CH', 5; Thiselton, 'NHP', 5; Thiselton, 'LGT', 8; Thiselton, 'R *WP*', 230-231; Thiselton, 'R *HFM*', 232-233; Thiselton, A.C., 'Great Compassion and Heart. Review of J. Moltmann's *The Crucified God*', *CEN* 10 Jan. (1975), 9; Thiselton, A.C., 'Review of J. Moltmann's *The Crucified God*', *Chman* 89.2 (1975), 148-149; Thiselton, A.C., 'Review of J. Moltmann's *The Experiment Hope*', *Chman* 90.3 (1976), 225-227; Thiselton, *NTH*, 101-114; Thiselton, 'AA', 609; Thiselton, 'Truth', 900-901; Thiselton, 'R *Apoc*', 218-220; Thiselton, *2H*, 74-83.

[160] cf.: Thiselton, 'CI', 9; Thiselton, 'AA', 604; Thiselton, 'R *NTC*', 86-87; Thiselton, 'MMP', 8; Thiselton, 'SS', 10; Thiselton, 'R *2 Cor*', 29-30; Thiselton, 'Qs', 7; Thiselton, 'R *NTF*', 85; Thiselton, 'R *IBHJ*', 117-118; Thiselton, 'UNT', 8; Thiselton, 'R *TiF*', 30; Thiselton, 'R *Rom II*', 356-357.

[161] cf.: Thiselton, 'RCD', 9; Thiselton, A.C., 'Review of R.G. Hamerton-Kelly's *Pre-Existence, Wisdom and the Son of Man*', *Chman* 87.2 (1973), 145-146; Thiselton, 'IA', 9; Thiselton, 'Truth', 900-901.

[162] Thiselton, 'NP', 8; cf.: Thiselton, 'M&M', 8; Thiselton, 'P-BP', 88-89; Thiselton, 'R *CFH*', 68-70; Thiselton, A.C., 'Review of B. Lindars and S.S. Smalley eds. *Christ and Spirit in the New Testament*', *CGrad* 27.2 (Jun. 1974), 55-56; Thiselton, 'GC', 9; Thiselton, 'R *TCG*', 148-149; Thiselton, 'RCD', 9; Thiselton, 'R *P-EWSM*', 145-146.

[163] Thiselton, 'NP', 8; Thiselton, 'GC', 9; Thiselton, 'R *TCG*', 148-149.

[164] Thiselton, 'Sch', 136.

[165] Thiselton, 'R *Apoc*', 218-220; cf. Thiselton, 'REC', 510-526.

[166] Thiselton, 'Par', 46-53; cf.: Thiselton, 'CH', 5; Thiselton, 'R *HFM*', 232-233.

*Widening Dialogue of Historical Response* 69

Williams, and the Teilhard de Chardin School of P. Hefner, D.P. Gray, and C. Mooney.[167] Specifically, in contrast to his own *eschatological* emphasis, Thiselton rejects the *futurological* 'evolutionary cosmologies of the nineteenth century'.[168]

(5) Another of Thiselton's theological interests is *biblical anthropology*, notably 'sin', and 'the problem of evil'. This interest largely emerges in his positive appeal to Bultmann,[169] and in his responses to Freud, Buber (see below and Chapter 4), and to A. Hodes and P.A. Bertocci. Thiselton considers the problem of evil in response to J.W. Wenham, and the importance of 'integrity' and of 'correspondence between word and deed' in his article, 'Truth'.[170]

c) Trends and Debates in Philosophy, Hermeneutics, and Philosophical Theology

A third major angle of view on Thiselton's second-period *Sitz im Leben* emerges in his responses to traditions and debates in *philosophy, hermeneutics, and philosophical theology*. For Thiselton, 'hermeneutics... is... "an absurdly neglected study in English theology at all levels"'.[171] Thus, *The Two Horizons* answers the 'desperate need of the English-speaking world for a sympathetic, thorough, yet critical survey of the German hermeneutical tradition and its relation to linguistic philosophy'.[172] That is, 'the Anglo-American theological tradition in general remained "extrêmement réfractaire à la tradition herméneutique continentale"', particularly in Britain.[173]

Specifically, Thiselton dialogues between theology, hermeneutics, and philosophical advances in relation to *seven major hermeneutical conversations* centered upon *widening dialogue* between historical traditions (including *theological* and *philosophical* traditions) *towards critical synthesis* (see Chapters 1, 2, 3 and 7), *history* (see Chapter 6), *epistemology* (see Chapter 3), *language, human selves, Western culture* (see Chapter 4), *and interpretative practice* (see Chapter 5).[174] R.L. Maddox notes

---

[167] cf.: Thiselton, 'Par', 27-35, 41-44; Thiselton, 'CH', 5; Thiselton, 'R HFM', 232-233.

[168] Noll, 'CST', 238.

[169] Thiselton, 'MMP', 8; cf.: Thiselton, 'SARX', 204-228; Thiselton, 'Flesh', 678-682; Thiselton, *2H*, 275-283.

[170] cf.: Thiselton, A.C., 'Man Longs for the Status and Dignity of a 'Thou'', *CEN* 9 Jan. (1976), 9; Thiselton, A.C., 'Sigmund Freud and the Language of the Heart', *CEN* 13 Feb. (1976), 12, 14; Thiselton, A.C., 'Review of A. Hodes' *Encounter with Martin Buber*', *Chman* 90.2 (1976), 138-139; Thiselton, A.C., ''Finding God in Personal Idealism'. Review of P.A. Bertocci's *The Person God Is*', *CEN* 9 Jul. (1971), 11; Thiselton, 'AA', 601-602; Thiselton, 'MMP', 8; Thiselton, 'Truth', 886.

[171] Sykes, S.W., 'Review of A.C. Thiselton's *The Two Horizons*', *Chman* 96.2 (1982), 156; cf. Thiselton, *2H*, 17-23.

[172] Maddox, 'R *2H*', 136-137.

[173] Conroy, 'R *2H*', 563. The French here translates as, 'extremely resistant to the Continental hermeneutical tradition'.

[174] cf.: Thiselton, *NTH*, 74-198; Thiselton, *2H*, 51-139; Thiselton, 'KNT', 85-107; Thiselton, 'Truth', 874-902; Thiselton, *LLM*; Thiselton, 'LMR', 1123-1146; Thiselton, 'SBL', 108-114; Thiselton, 'SNTT', 75-104; Thiselton, 'Words', 283-299.

Thiselton's foci on 'theology', 'history', 'and language' in *The Two Horizons*, though some wrongly imply that Thiselton's hermeneutics center *only* on these 'three... axes'.[175]

Historically, Thiselton finds *nine* points of departure in relation to philosophy, hermeneutics, and philosophical theology, as follows (our italicization shows the seven major hermeneutical conversations emerging as we proceed).

(1) Thiselton responds to the *Greek, Enlightenment, and positivist legacies* of 'traditional' hermeneutics. Thus, in relation to 'traditional' *theology* and *philosophy*, Thiselton attacks the notion of '"timeless" truth', approving J.A.T. Robinson's rejection of 'fifth-century' metaphysical '"substance" categories' and 'natural' versus 'supernatural' 'dualism'.[176] Against a 'positivist' view of *history*, Thiselton employs Pannenberg's critique of E. Troeltsch in order to reject D.E. Nineham's 'cynicism over... historical relativity' and distance.[177]

Thiselton also criticizes traditional *epistemological* '"objectivism"' and the 'correspondence', 'coherence', 'redundancy', 'semantic', and 'performative' "theories" 'of truth'. He is critical of 'the Cartesian' '"scientific method"' of classification and generalization',[178] though B.J. Walsh exaggerates matters when he suggests that Thiselton simply "rejects" the 'Cartesian tradition'.[179]

Thiselton largely rejects 'prescriptive', 'natural" (cf. 'dynamic'), "Lockean" (cf. 'dianoetic'), or 'positivist' (cf. 'logical') approaches to *language*.[180] For Thiselton, 'traditional' approaches to language rest on 'false assumptions', and over-stress 'vocabulary, grammar, and style'.[181] Thiselton argues that semantics must not presuppose 'referential' or 'ideational' "theories" 'of meaning' since,[182] following Gadamer and contrary to E.D. Hirsch, Thiselton argues that a text's 'meaning... always goes beyond its author'.[183] For Thiselton: '"communication"' is not primarily a matter of "informing statements" 'clothing' prior 'inner concepts';[184] and, for Thiselton, 'translation' does 'not' presuppose 'one-word/one-concept'

---

[175] Maddox, 'R *2H*', 136-137; cf.: Schneiders, S.M., 'Review of A.C. Thiselton's *The Two Horizons*', *JRel* 62.3 (Jul. 1982), 308; Pereppadan, 'R *2H*', 90.

[176] Thiselton, *2H*, 92-103; cf.: Thiselton, 'NP', 8; Thiselton, *NTH*, 131-143.

[177] Thiselton, *2H*, 60; cf. 51-84; cf.: Harrisville, R.A., 'Review of A.C. Thiselton's *The Two Horizons*', *Interp* 36 (Apr. 1982), 216; Roschke, R.W., 'Review of A.C. Thiselton's *The Two Horizons*', *CThM* 9 (Aug. 1982), 246; Thiselton, *NTH*, 74-121; Thiselton, 'R *UAB*', 341-343.

[178] Thiselton, *2H*, 22; cf.: Thiselton, 'Truth', 894-897; Thiselton, 'UPC', 91.

[179] Walsh, B.J., 'Anthony Thiselton's Contribution to Biblical Hermeneutics', *ChSRev* 14.3 (1985), 231.

[180] Thiselton, 'LMR', 1134-1136, 1125-1126; cf. Thiselton, 'Words', 297; cf. 286-298.

[181] Thiselton, 'Words', 289, 298; cf.: Thiselton, 'LMR', 1123, 1134; Thiselton, 'SNTI', 76; Thiselton, *LLM*, 3.

[182] Thiselton, 'Words', 287, 297; cf.: Thiselton, 'LMR', 1125, 1127-1130; Thiselton, *2H*, 124.

[183] Thiselton, *2H*, 315; cf. Gadamer, *TM*, 395.

[184] Thiselton, 'P-BP', 89; cf.: Thiselton, 'LMR', 1123; Thiselton, 'SNTI', 76; cf. 79.

'correspondence'.[185]

Both epistemological and linguistic concerns emerge in Thiselton's critique of *Western culture*,[186] and whilst Thiselton challenges Freud's positivist epistemology, he agrees with Freud's view that *human selves* are self-deceptive.[187]

Thiselton argues that interpretative *practice* should neither employ generalizing exegetical "'rules'" to perpetuate "'already-accepted'" understandings,[188] nor follow 'the fallacy of... atomizing exegesis which pays insufficient attention to context'.[189] For Thiselton, traditional 'theological' opposition to hermeneutics wrongly rejects the role of 'pre-understanding' in interpretation,[190] and wrongly argues that 'the Holy Spirit' replaces hermeneutics,[191] where M.I. Wallace notes Thiselton's critique of Karl Barth in this context.[192] Contrary to C. Van Til's views, Thiselton argues that his 'use of philosophical concepts and categories' does not "corrupt" the biblical message but elucidates it.[193] Thus, Thiselton defends 'the legitimacy and necessity of hermeneutics... against various biblicistic or fundamentalist objections'.[194]

(2) *Continental European traditions* of hermeneutics loom large in Thiselton's historical context.[195] Notably, Thiselton criticizes existentialist and philosophical hermeneutical traditions for their *historical, epistemological,* and *linguistic* "one-sidednesses", dichotomies, or "dualisms".[196] J. Bleicher speaks of 'three major "schools" of thought within the contemporary philosophical discussion of hermeneutics',[197] but Thiselton responds to *six* schools in Continental European hermeneutics during his second period *alone*.

Thus, (a), Thiselton later identifies the work of Schleiermacher, Dilthey, and Betti as a 'modern' 'hermeneutics of understanding', but engages with these thinkers in his second period, finding H. Kimmerle's work on Schleiermacher

---

[185] Thiselton, A.C., 'Review of D.H. Kelsey's *The Uses of Scripture in Recent Theology*', *Chman* 91.1 (1977), 88; cf.: Thiselton, 'SNTI', 96; Thiselton, *2H*, 132.

[186] cf.: Thiselton, 'Truth', 899-901; Thiselton, 'LMR', 1139; cf. 1142-1144.

[187] Thiselton, 'Freud', 12, 14; cf. Thiselton, 'AA', 601-602.

[188] Thiselton, 'NH', 310-311.

[189] Thiselton, 'SNTI', 79; cf. Walsh, 'TC', 224.

[190] Thiselton, *2H*, 103, cf. 103-114; cf. Thiselton, *NTH*, 143-157.

[191] Thiselton, *2H*, 85, cf. 85-92; cf. Thiselton, *NTH*, 122-130.

[192] Wallace, M.I., 'Karl Barth's Hermeneutic: A Way Beyond the Impasse', *JRel* 68.3 (1988), 396-397; cf.: Thiselton, *NTH*, 125-126; Thiselton, *2H*, 88 and onwards.

[193] Erickson, M.J., 'Review of A.C. Thiselton's *The Two Horizons*', *JEThS* 23 (Dec. 1980), 371; cf.: Thiselton, 'UPC', 87; Thiselton, *2H*, 9, on Thiselton's criticism of Van Til.

[194] Conroy, 'R *2H*', 564.

[195] Thiselton, 'TY', 1560. Italics ours.

[196] Thiselton, *2H*, 246; cf.: 245-251, 310-314 onwards; 352-356; cf.: Thiselton, *NTH*, xiv, xxiv-xxv, concs 5 - 5.2 onwards; Thiselton, 'NH', 323-329; Thiselton, 'TY', 1560.

[197] Cited in, Maddox, R.L., 'Contemporary Hermeneutic Philosophy and Theological Studies', *RelStud* 21.4 (Dec. 1985), 519.

'important'.[198] (b) Thiselton later includes broadly 'existentialist' thinkers within his 'hermeneutics of self-involvement':[199] "theological" and "secular" strands include Kierkegaard, Bultmann, and Tillich, and, Nietzsche, Heidegger, Jaspers, and Sartre respectively,[200] though Thiselton acknowledges that Heidegger is not strictly an 'existentialist thinker'.[201] In particular, Thiselton attacks the legacy of "Neo-Kantianism",[202] especially the "dualisms" or dichotomies pervading Bultmann's biblical hermeneutics, but also E. Cassirer's 'Enlightenment view of myth'.[203] Thiselton argues that 'neo-Kantianism' is linked to the *epistemological* and *linguistic* 'problem of' "objectification".[204]

(c) Thiselton appeals extensively to Gadamer's philosophical hermeneutics, but also responds to the New Hermeneutic of Fuchs, Ebeling, and H. Ott,[205] and its American counterpart in the work of R.W. Funk, W. Wink, D.O. Via, and J.D. Crossan.[206] (d) Thiselton *later* categorizes Ricoeur's work as a 'hermeneutics of suspicion and retrieval', but also responds to Ricoeur in his *second period*.[207] (e) J. Habermas and K.-O. Apel espouse what Thiselton later calls 'socio-critical hermeneutics', though Thiselton had appealed to Apel by 1970, and had taught on Habermas by 'the late 1970s'.[208]

(f) As noted earlier, Thiselton identifies Moltmann's and Pannenberg's respective socio-critical and epistemological eschatologies as Theologies of Hope where Hegel is not far in the background.[209] Pannenberg's belief in the *centrality of hermeneutics for theology* is important for Thiselton.[210] E. Schüssler-Fiorenza and J.P. Hogan note the *close links between theology and hermeneutics* in relation to 'Thiselton'

---

[198] Thiselton, *NH*, 194; cf.: 197, 204-271; cf.: Thiselton, *2H*, 103-107; cf. 234-240; 293, 308; Thiselton, 'NH', 310, 313-314.

[199] Thiselton, *NH*, 272, 274; cf. 272-282.

[200] Thiselton, 'KNT', 100-103; cf. Thiselton, 'Till', 86-107.

[201] Thiselton, *2H*, 143-144; cf. Keifert, P.R., 'Review of A.C. Thiselton's *The Two Horizons*', *WW* 1 (Fall 1981), 408.

[202] Thiselton, 'Truth', 899-900.

[203] Thiselton, *NTH*, 288-297; cf. 344-350; cf.: Thiselton, *2H*, 205-212; cf. 245-251; Thiselton, 'MP', 7.

[204] Thiselton, 'Truth', 899; cf.: Thiselton, *NTH*, 371-386; Thiselton, *2H*, 263-275.

[205] cf.: Thiselton, 'UPC', 91-95; Thiselton, *NTH*, 471-517; Thiselton, *2H*, 327-256; Thiselton, 'NH', 308-333.

[206] Thiselton, 'NH', 316-317, 320, 321, 322, 325; cf.: Thiselton, *NTH*, 497-508; Thiselton, *2H*, 347-356; Thiselton, 'R *JLK*', 85-86.

[207] Thiselton, *NH*, 344-378; cf.: Thiselton, 'SBS', 334; Thiselton, *NTH*, 10, 65, 151, 156-157, 170-172, 276; Thiselton, *2H*, 8, 46, 109, 113, 120-121, 201, 439.

[208] Thiselton, *NH*, 379-409; cf.: Thiselton, 'Parab', 463; Thiselton, 'TY', 1563.

[209] Thiselton, 'Par', 46-53.

[210] Thiselton, 'U (long)', 94; cf. Pannenberg, W., *Basic Questions in Theology. Collected Essays, Volume 1* (trans. G.H. Kehm; Philadelphia: Fortress Press, 1970), 188.

and 'Pannenberg' respectively.[211]

(3) Thiselton dialogues with 'the Anglo-American tradition of philosophical analysis'.[212] Thiselton argues that the later Wittgenstein, J.L. Austin, and D.D. Evans help inaugurate speech-act theory, which Thiselton later includes within his 'hermeneutics of self-involvement'.[213] However, Thiselton's 'horizon' is hardly *only* 'populated by the typically British concerns of philosophical analysis of *language*' (contradicting R.W. Roschke's reading of Thiselton).[214]

(4) Thiselton responds to 'general linguistics' and 'semantics' in Saussure's tradition, where J. Barr and J.F.A. Sawyer become important influences on Thiselton's thinking in this context.[215] Thiselton's contention is 'that New Testament exegetes have not availed themselves sufficiently of the fruit of semantic study', and 'have maintained false assumptions about *language*'.[216] Thiselton responds to this problem in his article, 'Semantics and New Testament Interpretation' where,[217] like A. Gibson, he 'felt compelled to reiterate Barr's work' since 'many' biblical scholars had 'not appreciated' its 'potential impact'.[218]

Thiselton also urges both preachers and colleges to note the 'immediate relevance' of the work of E. Güttgemanns and R. Kieffer on semantics although,[219] in 1978, he responds critically to 'structuralist approaches',[220] attacking the deterministic 'ideological' structuralism of Lévi-Strauss, R. Barthes, E. Leach, and Güttgemanns, but partly affirming "methodological" appropriations of the work of Saussure, V.I. Propp, and A.J. Greimas.[221] More "mid-range" or 'eclectic' 'structuralist approaches' (e.g. that of 'D.O. Via') receive a mixed response from Thiselton.[222]

---

[211] Schüssler-Fiorenza, E., 'Rhetorical Situation and Historical Reconstruction in 1 Corinthians', *NTStud* 33.3 (Jul. 1987), 386, 400; cf. Hogan, J.P., 'Hermeneutics and the Logic of Question and Answer - Collingwood and Gadamer', *HeyJ* 28.3 (Jul. 1987), 263; cf. 281.

[212] Thiselton, 'TY', 1560; cf.: Thiselton, *NTH*, 288-297; cf. 344-350; Thiselton, *2H*, 205-212; cf. 245-251; Thiselton, 'MP', 7.

[213] cf.: Thiselton, *LLM*, 17-18 and onwards; Thiselton, 'UPC', 89; cf. 96-98; Thiselton, 'SNTI', 76; Thiselton, *NH*, 274; cf. 283-307.

[214] Contradicting, Roschke, 'R *2H*', 246. Italics ours.

[215] cf.: Thiselton, A.C., 'Review of J.F.A. Sawyer's *Semantics in Biblical Research*', *TSF* 70 (Aut. 1974), 18; Thiselton, 'SNTI', 75; cf. 75-104; Thiselton, 'LMR', 1123-1146; Thiselton, 'SBL', 108-120; Thiselton, *NTH*, 164-198; Thiselton, *2H*, 115-139.

[216] Walsh, 'TC', 224; cf. Thiselton, 'SNTI', 76. Italics ours.

[217] Thiselton, 'SNTI', 75-104.

[218] Porter, S.E., '2 Myths, Corporate Personality and Language Mentality Determinism', *SJT* 43.3 (1990), 301-302.

[219] Thiselton, 'ENE', 6.

[220] Thiselton, 'SBS', 329; cf. 329-335; cf.: Thiselton, 'R *LCNTC*', 153-154; Thiselton, 'R *SSS*', 119; Thiselton, 'R *SR*', 248; Thiselton, 'R *NT&S*', 26-27; Thiselton, *2H*, 428-431.

[221] Thiselton, 'SBS', 331; cf. 331-332, 332-334.

[222] Thiselton, 'SBS', 329, 333, cf. 330-331.

(5) Thiselton responds to other philosophical or philosophical-theological trends in his second period. (a) By 1980, Thiselton had taught 'on Reader-Response Theory', though his main responses to American pragmatism and neo-pragmatism appear later.[223] However, in 1978, Thiselton rejects *'the pragmatic theory of truth'* originating with C.S. Peirce, W. James, and J. Dewey.[224] (b) Thiselton's responses to Freud and M. Buber are juxtaposed, hinting at Thiselton's ongoing interest in a hermeneutics of *human selves*.[225] (c) T.F. Torrance influences Thiselton's view of the relationship between Christianity and *rationality*.[226] (d) D. Cupitt's early Neo-Kantian look at Christology, W.W. Bartley III's work on 'religion and morality', and P.A. Bertocci's personalist perspectives also receive consideration from Thiselton.[227]

(6) Thiselton responds to debates on the relationships between *'language'*, 'thought', and 'power'. Thus, (a), Thiselton resolves the 'polarized' 'debate' between, on the one hand, the tradition of W. Von Humboldt and B.L. Whorf, and, on the other hand, certain strands in 'general linguistics'. The former tradition argues that 'thought' is determined by 'language', whereas the latter strands view 'thought' as almost completely independent of language (see Chapter 4).[228]

(b) Thiselton attacks both 'natural' accounts of language and "dualistic" accounts affected by 'natural' views. O. Procksch, G. von Rad, J. Pedersen, L. Dürr, O. Grether, and H. Ringgren come under fire from Thiselton on the one hand; Heidegger, Gadamer, Fuchs and Ebeling come under fire from Thiselton on the other.[229] In particular, 'the power of' 'models', 'metaphors', 'symbols', and

---

[223] Thiselton, 'TY', 1563; cf.: Thiselton, A.C., 'Reader-Response Hermeneutics, Action Models, and the Parables of Jesus', in *The Responsibility of Hermeneutics* (R. Lundin, A.C. Thiselton and C. Walhout; Grand Rapids: Eerdmans; Exeter: Paternoster, 1985), 79-113; Thiselton, *NH*, 471-555; Thiselton, A.C., 'Communicative Action and Promise in Inter-Disciplinary, Biblical, and Theological Hermeneutics', in *The Promise of Hermeneutics* (R. Lundin, C. Walhout and A.C. Thiselton; Grand Rapids and Cambridge: Eerdmans; Carlisle: Paternoster, 1999), 133-239; Thiselton, 'S (un)', 1-54.

[224] Thiselton, 'Truth', 896-897. Italics Thiselton's.

[225] Thiselton, 'ML', 9; cf.: Thiselton, 'Freud', 12, 14; Thiselton, 'R *EMB*', 138-139; Thiselton, 'AA', 601-602.

[226] Thiselton, 'IA', 9; cf. the earlier, Thiselton, A.C., "A Book Set Apart from the Ordinary Run of Books'. Review of T.F. Torrance's *Theological Science*', *CEN* 12 Dec. (1969), 13; cf.: Thiselton, 'Truth', 900-901; Thiselton, *NTH*, 129-130, 147, 220, 260-261, 452-455; Thiselton, *2H*, 91-92, 106, 188, 316, 318.

[227] Thiselton, A.C., 'Brink of Discovery. Review of D. Cupitt's *Christ and the Hiddenness of God*', *CEN* 1 Oct. (1971), 11; cf.: Thiselton, A.C., 'A Philosopher Without Inhibitions. Review of W.W. Bartley III's *Morality and Religion*', *CEN* 8 Oct. (1971), 10; Thiselton, 'FG', 11.

[228] Thiselton, 'LMR', 1126-1127; cf.: Thiselton, *NTH*, 186-192; Thiselton, *2H*, 133-139. Italics ours.

[229] Thiselton, 'Words', 283-286, 293; cf.: Thiselton, 'LMR', 1140; Thiselton, 'Parab', 440-451; Thiselton, 'NH', 325-326; Thiselton, 'SNTI', 75-104.

"pictures" concerns Thiselton, where M.E. Boring takes up Thiselton's warnings about "controlling pictures" (drawing on the later Wittgenstein).[230]

(7) Thiselton extends dialogue between Heidegger, Gadamer, the later Wittgenstein, Saussure and 'general linguistics',[231] and by 1978 brings 'structuralist approaches' into the 'discussion'.[232] Centrally, for Thiselton, 'Wittgenstein's view of language-games "has… parallels with Heidegger's understanding of "world" and… Gadamer's notion of… horizons"'.[233] Further, in Thiselton's estimate, Heidegger's notion of 'Saying' is analogous to the early Wittgenstein's notion of '"showing"' - both disclose the truly valuable.[234]

B.J. Walsh rightly commends Thiselton's 'unparalleled… crossing' of 'traditional barriers between Anglo-Saxon and Continental thought and' his 'appropriating and synthesizing' of 'insights' from 'both traditions while avoiding their respective pitfalls'.[235] Thiselton rejects 'the oft-mentioned incompatibility of the "German" philosophical tradition of Heidegger and the "English"… philosophical tradition of Wittgenstein… in favor of… fruitful comparison and interaction between the two'.[236]

Thus, Thiselton helps demolish the dividing 'wall' between 'English and Continental thought'.[237] Indeed, 'Many… have wondered why Wittgenstein and Heidegger have not been brought together' before.[238] Nevertheless, for Thiselton, 'British philosophy… provides finer tools with which to approach *language*' than Heidegger.[239]

(8) C. Conroy complains that, in *The Two Horizons*, Thiselton fails to respond to 'the "crisis of hermeneutics"… associated… with the Habermas-Gadamer debate', 'the… *Positivismusstreit* (H. Albert and others), and… the deconstructionist grammatology of J. Derrida'.[240] Also Conroy finds very little reference to 'Ricoeur' in *The Two Horizons* (as do R.E. Palmer, and S.M. Schneiders) and finds an

---

[230] cf.: Thiselton, 'M-M', 8; Thiselton, 'Till', 91-98; Thiselton, *2H*, 137, 432; Boring, M.E., 'The Language of Universal Salvation in Paul', *JBLit* 105.2 (Jun. 1986), 290; Thiselton, *LLM*, 25-27; Thiselton, 'MP', 12; Thiselton, 'LMR', 1123-1127; Wittgenstein, L., *Philosophical Investigations* (trans. G.E.M. Anscombe; Oxford: Blackwell, 1953, 2001), 44, 47, 48.

[231] Thiselton, 'LMR', 1123; cf.: Thiselton, *NTH*, 58-63; Thiselton, *2H*, 7, 24-47, 137, 159, 164-168, 180-181, 195, 199, 201, 292, 357-362, 370-372, 378-379, 406, 410-411, 440, 443.

[232] Thiselton, 'SBS', 329; cf.: Thiselton, 'LMR', 1123; Thiselton, *2H*, 428-431.

[233] Walsh, 'TC', 226-227; cf. Thiselton, *2H*, 33.

[234] Grech, 'R *2H*', 573; cf.: Thiselton, *2H*, 370; cf. 368-370.

[235] Walsh, 'TC', 235; cf. Thiselton, 'TY', 1560-1561.

[236] Maddox, 'R *2H*', 136.

[237] Macquarrie, 'R *2H*', 497.

[238] Dockery, D.S., 'Review of A.C. Thiselton's *The Two Horizons*', *GThJ* 4.1 (Spr. 1983), 135.

[239] Morgan, R., 'Review of A.C. Thiselton's *The Two Horizons*', *HeyJ* 22.3 (1981), 332. Italics ours.

[240] Conroy, 'R *2H*', 565. '*Positivismusstreit*' means, roughly, 'Positivism Debate'. Italics in speech-marks are Conroy's.

additional deficit of references to the 'Roman Catholic' hermeneutics of 'K. Rahner', 'E. Coreth', 'H. Cazelles and P. Grelot'.[241]

Partly, however, we must respond to Conroy by noting that *The Two Horizons* was not intended to be an exhaustive treatment of hermeneutical trends, unlike Thiselton's later work *New Horizons in Hermeneutics* (1992). Further, Thiselton's inter-disciplinary expansion during the 1970s was a period of ongoing discovery in which he 'began to see' Ricoeur's and Habermas' importance 'in the late 1970s' *after* his PhD thesis (completed in 1976).[242]

Nevertheless, it is crucial to note that, *The Two Horizons* (1980), and its predecessor, *New Testament Interpretation* (i.e. Thiselton's PhD Thesis, completed 1976/awarded 1977), were to become, and were even to some extent deliberately constructed *with a view to* becoming, the launch-pad *from which* Thiselton would respond to Habermas, Gadamer, Ricoeur, and Derrida later. During his second period Thiselton is, for the most part, *not* ignorant of the work of these thinkers, but is *deliberately preparing to critique* the work of these thinkers. 'Roman Catholic' hermeneutics are *also* brought more into Thiselton's ever-widening inter-disciplinary and inter-traditional dialogue in his later work. On Conroy's own reading: 'the importance of… Thiselton's' work can *only* become 'clear when one considers both its rich content *and its Sitz im Leben*'.[243]

(9) Central to Thiselton's dialogue with trends in philosophy is his engagement with the rise of '*historical* consciousness' through 'Herder, Hegel', 'Ranke', 'Dilthey', Collingwood, Heidegger, Bultmann, Gadamer, and Pannenberg.[244] Thiselton does *not* only stress 'the historicity of human existence', but *also* stresses 'the historical' and 'the historic' (contradicting E.S. Malbon's reading of Thiselton. Also, see Chapter 1).[245]

Clearly, then, and in conclusion, Thiselton neither simply follows Continental hermeneutics, nor simply succumbs to Gadamerian 'historical relativism' (contradicting C.S. Rodd's reading).[246] As R.E. Palmer notes, 'Thiselton's' 'reception… of Gadamer' is *"critical"* - though, qualifying Palmer's reading, we shall see that 'Thiselton's' 'reception… of Gadamer' is *not* simply 'a Pannenbergian

---

[241] Conroy, 'R *2H*', 565-566; cf.: Palmer, R.E., 'Review of A.C. Thiselton's *The Two Horizons*', *RevMet* 35.1 (1981), 173; Schneiders, 'R *2H*', 307.

[242] Thiselton, 'TY', 1563; cf. Thiselton, *NTH*, Title Page.

[243] Conroy, 'R *2H*', 563; cf. e.g. Thiselton, A.C., *The Hermeneutics of Doctrine* (Grand Rapids: Eerdmans, 2007), 150-156. Italics ours, except for the three words '*Sitz im Leben*', where they are Conroy's.

[244] Cahill, P.J., 'Review of A.C. Thiselton's *The Two Horizons*', *CBQ* 43.3 (Jul. 1981), 484; cf. Thiselton, *2H*, 63-69. Italics ours.

[245] Malbon, E.S., 'Structuralism, Hermeneutics, and Contextual Meaning', *JAARel* 51.2 (1983), 217; cf.: Thiselton, *NTH*, 101-114; Thiselton, *2H*, 74-83.

[246] Rodd, 'R *2H*', 290.

*Widening Dialogue of Historical Response* 77

critique... of Gadamer' (see Chapters 3 and 6).[247]

Nor does Thiselton simply follow the New Hermeneutic, but rather he offers a 'perceptive' critique of its 'deficiencies' (so M.E. Thrall).[248] J. Barr, however, wrongly urges that Thiselton accepts the New Hermeneutic 'quite cordially' in 'a profound abandonment of essential conservative territory'.[249] Conversely, W. Wink's insinuation that "belief", for Thiselton, does not go 'beyond mere "behavior" and "words"' seems ignorant of Thiselton's *positive* response to E. Fuchs' treatment of Jesus' parables in which the hearer is 'grasped' '"deep down"'.[250] Crucially, Thiselton only argues 'that at present there is more danger of neglecting the New Hermeneutic than of pressing its claims too far'.[251]

Some misreadings of Thiselton's work are admittedly trivial. Thus, D.J. Smit's comments concerning Thiselton being 'from the USA' may hark back to Thiselton's 'sabbatical' in North America from 1982 to 1984,[252] and N.L. Geisler is simply mistaken to record that Thiselton did his PhD in 'Aberdeen'.[253] Nevertheless, a detailed examination of Thiselton's *Sitz im Leben* has begun to expose more significant misreadings of his work.

D) TRENDS AND ISSUES IN THE CHURCH

A fourth angle of view on Thiselton's *Sitz im Leben* is his engagement with recent or contemporary issues, debates, trends, or situations within *the Church* – as follows.

(1) *Globally*, Thiselton detects unfortunate 'polarization... between' hermeneutical over-emphases on the 'past' and hermeneutical over-emphases on the 'present'. Thus, Thiselton argues that 'New Testament study' often has 'an exclusively objectivistic concern with past facts... or... information for its own sake', and 'traditional' 'preaching' often contrives 'artificial', over-'formal', and over-'generalized' '"applications"' almost as a postscript to historical interpretation. Conversely, Thiselton argues that 'the... "contextual" emphasis in the World Council of Churches', the modern 'charismatic' movement's stress on 'present experience', and the distorted 'activism' of some 'Latin American

---

[247] Palmer, R.E., 'The Scope of Hermeneutics: The Problem of Critique, and the Crisis of Modernity', *TRevCTLit* 3 (1984), 226-227; cf. Palmer, 'R *2H*', 172-174. Italics ours.

[248] Thrall, M.E., 'Review of I.H. Marshall ed. *New Testament Interpretation*', *SJT* 32.4 (Aug. 1979), 388; cf. Thiselton, 'NH', 323-329.

[249] Barr, J., 'Review of I.H. Marshall ed. *New Testament Interpretation*', *Th* 81.681 (May 1978), 234-235.

[250] Wink, W., 'Review of A.C. Thiselton's *The Two Horizons*', *ThT* 37.4 (Jan. 1981), 507; cf. Thiselton, 'NH', 320, 321.

[251] Thiselton, 'NH', 328; cf. Walsh, 'TC', 229.

[252] Smit, D.J., 'The Ethics of Interpretation: New Voices from the USA', *Scrip* 33 (May 1990), 16, 17, 18; cf. *WW*, 1985.

[253] Geisler, 'R *2H*', 182.

theology' all over-emphasize the 'present'.[254]

(2) Thiselton complains concerning 'the… individualism' of the *Western Church*, linking it to 'Kierkegaard' and Bultmann, and to whimsical and 'arbitrary' "'private interpretation'" apart from the 'community' of tradition.[255] (3) With Pannenberg and J.A.T. Robinson, Thiselton criticizes the Platonic legacy in the *traditional* (cf. 'orthodox', or 'conservative') Church.[256] R.K. Johnston takes up Thiselton's distress over 'traditional' "domestication" and "taming" of the Bible in 'reading', liturgy and 'preaching'.[257] We have already examined Thiselton's relationships with, (4), the *Anglican* Church and, (5), the *evangelical* church.

(6) Thiselton rejects several trends in the *Pentecostal and charismatic* movements, including experience-centeredness, naively labeling the "merely human" as the "Spirit's work", poor 'church order',[258] and abusing biblical 'metaphors' in preaching.[259] However, Thiselton does not interpret 'Paul' as wanting 'tongues' to 'be abolished'. Rather, for Thiselton, 'tongues' is a 'gift' for young Christians that should be replaced by 'the gift' of "'articulate speech'" as the speaker matures (contradicting W. Richardson's reading of Thiselton).[260]

(7) Thiselton criticizes the subsuming of genuine 'experience of God' beneath the "merely human", experience-centeredness, and poor church order in the *radical church* of Harvey Cox,[261] and the ethical problems of the New Morality of J.A.T. Robinson and H.A. Williams.[262] In conclusion, Thiselton neither provides hermeneutics in a vacuum, nor provides merely localized criticisms, but wishes to see a world-wide reform of biblical hermeneutics in the Church.

E) CONTEXTS AND ISSUES IN TERTIARY EDUCATION

A fifth angle of view on Thiselton's second period *Sitz im Leben* centers on his teaching context in the University of Sheffield and on his corresponding concerns for the tertiary education of, especially, pastors and preachers – as follows.

(1) Thiselton's second period encompasses an *inter-disciplinary expansion*. *Contextually*, Thiselton diversifies from teaching in the Department of 'Biblical Studies' and 'Theology' to also teaching in 'English', 'Linguistics', and 'Philosophy' Departments. In terms of *courses*, Thiselton diversifies from teaching 'Biblical Studies', to also teaching 'Biblical Studies and English', and 'Philosophy and Theology'. In relation to academic *content*, Thiselton 'offered public lectures on

---

[254] Thiselton, 'UPC', 98; cf. Thiselton, 'U (long)', 95-97.
[255] cf.: Thiselton, 'M&M', 8; Thiselton, 'EITN', 578-579.
[256] Thiselton, 'NP', 8; cf.: Thiselton, *2H*, 95-101; Thiselton, 'R *BQ1*', 120-122.
[257] Thiselton, 'PDT', 7; cf. Johnston, 'IS', 44-45.
[258] Thiselton, 'E-CR', 8; cf. Thiselton, 'UNT', 8.
[259] Thiselton, *LLM*, 25-27; cf.: Thiselton, 'M-M', 8; Thiselton, 'SNTI', 94-95.
[260] Richardson, W., 'Liturgical Order and Glossolalia in 1 Corinthians 14:26c-33a', *NTStud* 32.1 (Jan. 1986), 145-146; cf. Thiselton, 'TI', 17, 34-36.
[261] Thiselton, 'E-CR', 8.
[262] Thiselton, 'KNT', 90, cf. 91-92.

Wittgenstein in 1971-1972', and went on to teach 'literary theory' and 'semantics'. Thus, Thiselton recounts that 'the stage was set for teaching a full critical survey of hermeneutical theory'.[263]

(2) Specifically, this 'teaching' emerged in Thiselton's initiation of 'the first final-year Honours degree *course in hermeneutics*',[264] which developed between '1970' and '1980'. Initial foci included '[R.E.] Palmer's book *Hermeneutics* (1969) and several others, especially on Bultmann and myth'. During the early 1970s, the course expanded to include 'the origins and development of hermeneutics; the foundation of the modern discipline with Schleiermacher and Dilthey; Bultmann and demythologizing; Heidegger, Gadamer and the New Hermeneutic; functions of language with reference to Wittgenstein and to speech-acts in Austin'; the 'theological context and the status of the Bible as scripture'; and 'narrative theory and the relation between hermeneutics and semantics'. 'The mid 1970s' saw 'a fresh topic on Latin American Liberation hermeneutics' and, 'in the late 1970s', Thiselton included 'Ricoeur', 'Habermas', and Betti in his course. By this time, 'Ricoeur's *Freud and Philosophy*', 'Gadamer's *Truth and Method* and Bultmann's works' constituted 'part of the constant central core' of Thiselton's course, 'and by 1980', Thiselton had added 'a further unit on Reader-Response Theory'.[265] This widening dialogue in Thiselton's teaching aligns with our discussion of Thiselton's hermeneutical programme in Chapter 1.

(3) Light is shed on Thiselton's *Sitz im Leben* if we recall his concerns for the *proper education of pastors and preachers* – that they might avoid the pitfalls pointed out by Pannenberg and by Thiselton himself (see above)[266] and embrace 'Biblical criticism', 'theological debate', 'philosophical theology', and other aspects of responsible interpretative 'practice'.[267]

F) ISSUES IN THE BROADER SECULAR CULTURE OF BRITAIN AND THE WEST

A final angle of view on Thiselton's *Sitz im Leben* emerges from his response to recent trends in *Western culture*, in which he affirms Pannenberg and Tillich for having broader concerns beyond the church.[268] We will pick up this point in Chapter 4 rather than here, but for now we may briefly note L.P. Barnes' comments concerning Thiselton's particularly critical (though not *entirely* negative) responses to 'cultural', 'historical', and 'epistemological' relativisms.[269] We may now conclude by gathering together some key observations that emerge from the

---

[263] Thiselton, 'TY', 1561.
[264] Thiselton, 'TY', 1561. Italics ours.
[265] Thiselton, 'TY', 1562-1563. Italics Thiselton's.
[266] Thiselton, 'R BQI', 120-122; cf. Pannenberg, *BQ1*, 182-211.
[267] Thiselton, 'ED', 8; cf. Thiselton, 'Gregg', 11.
[268] cf.: Thiselton, 'Till', 104-105; Thiselton, 'TNI', 11; Thiselton, 'UPC', 87-100; Thiselton, *NTH*, xxii, xxx, concs. 1.4, 10; 4-12 onwards, 607-609; Thiselton, *2H*, 3-10, 445.
[269] Barnes, L.P., 'Light from the East? Ninian Smart and the Christian-Buddhist Encounter', *SJT* 40.1 (1987), 68-69; cf. Thiselton, 'Truth', 899-901.

present chapter.

## C. Conclusion:
### "Ever-Widening Dialogue of Historical Response" as Implicit Hermeneutical Axiom vs. Hermeneutical Foreclosure

We began by discussing the dating of Thiselton's second period of hermeneutical endeavor and our chronological-thematic approach to his writings. We noted the need to understand *both* Thiselton as an author, academic, and Anglican churchman *and* his *Sitz im Leben*, and we cited the "difficulties" of "isolating" Thiselton's 'own thought' as being part of the basis for our addressing of this need.[270]

Turning to focus on Thiselton as an author, academic, and Anglican churchman we found him to be a controversial character - to some humble and prophetic, to others heretical and subversive. He could not be caricatured as simply "evangelical", "liberal", or "Anglican"; but, rather, he stood out as a unique and independent thinker, particularly in relation to biblical authority, in relation to his implicit if embryonic promotion of women in ministry, and in relation to his theological distance from Bultmann, Tillich, and the Post-Bultmannian Movement. Thiselton's uniqueness lay partly in his widening dialogue with multiple traditions, which began to contrast sharply with the hermeneutical foreclosure of those who had caricatured him. We began to ask: "how well has Thiselton been heard?"

Next, turning to Thiselton's historical context or *Sitz im Leben*, we plumbed the true scope of his second period widened dialogue with multiple traditions. Thiselton was a complex thinker, responding to a whole range of traditions, trends, debates, and problems in biblical studies, systematic theology, philosophy, hermeneutics, philosophical theology, the church, tertiary education, and Western culture (though we deferred treatment of Thiselton's responses to Western culture until Chapter 4).

For Thiselton, broadly "traditional", "positivist", "existentialist", "philosophical hermeneutical", and "structuralist" schools of biblical interpretation needed a philosophical update that tackled their various Platonic, Cartesian, (post-) Enlightenment, Neo-Kantian (whether positivist or existentialist), and/or structuralist "ideologically deterministic" legacies. For Thiselton, the main (but not the only) sources of that updating were to be Pannenberg, the later Wittgensteinian and Saussurian traditions, and *aspects of* different traditions of Continental hermeneutics. Thiselton's criticisms emerged from his own practical involvement in biblical studies, particularly his studies in 1 Corinthians. This should alert us *against* seeing Thiselton as "assimilating biblical theology to philosophical traditions" – a point that we will take up again later.

That Thiselton meant business when he spoke about shaking off old

---

[270] Verbal comments made by one of Thiselton's former students to me in October 2001.

philosophical legacies emerged starkly in his *philosophical* distance from every one of the major *mid*-twentieth century theologians he had highlighted. Instead, philosophically and theologically, Thiselton was closest to the "new blood" of the time, namely Pannenberg and Moltmann (whom he now regards as the most important theologians of the twentieth century, alongside Barth),[271] T.F. Torrance's "scientific" theology, and "intelligent conservatism". His three main theological emphases were Christology, eschatology, and biblical anthropology. As Thiselton's second period progressed, seven major spheres of hermeneutical conversation began to emerge - in relation to (1) widening dialogue unto critical synthesis (presupposing immersion in multiple traditions), (2) history, (3) epistemology, (4) language, (5) Western culture, (6) human selves, and (7) responsible interpretative practice.

Thus, Thiselton's voice may be considered to be genuinely prophetic, in that it opposes problems in biblical interpretation at the levels of global, Western, traditional, Anglican, evangelical, charismatic, and radical Church - not to mention his critical concern for tertiary education and the beginnings of his mission-oriented and socio-critical engagement with Western culture (see Chapter 4).

However, Thiselton received a mixed reception, even being caricatured by J. Barr, R.E. Palmer, and W. Wink. Admittedly, some highlighted Thiselton's lack of dialogue with the likes of Derrida, Ricoeur, and others. We anticipated, however, that *The Two Horizons* was in fact – to some extent at least - a deliberately-constructed launch-pad for Thiselton's later responses to these thinkers (amongst others). In our view, Thiselton was ahead of the game and not behind by 1980.

We conclude that Thiselton practices an "ever-widening dialogue of historical response unto critical synthesis" as an implicit hermeneutical axiom, and we set this in opposition to the hermeneutical foreclosure that is beginning to emerge in some of the comments of his critics.

---

[271] Comments made to me by e-mail in July 2007.

CHAPTER 3

# Hermeneutics, Unity, and Epistemology: Unifying Hermeneutics Christologically and Eschatologically, and, Towards a Unified Hermeneutical Critique of Epistemology

### A. Preliminary Comments: Approach to Chapters 3 to 7

We now turn from the *'Sitz im Leben'* of Thiselton's second period work (Chapter 2) to 'its rich content' (Chapters 3 to 7), where both are relevant for an assessment of 'Thiselton's' 'importance' for the discipline of hermeneutics.[1]

In Chapter 2, we commented on Thiselton's *dialogic historical approach* and we acknowledged the reality of the problem of isolating 'his own thought':[2] to use the language of W.W. Klein, 'sometimes the trees obscure[d] the forest'.[3]

Nevertheless, J. Bowden's assertion that 'reading' Thiselton 'is... like trying to hold a serious conversation... in the middle of a noisy party' exaggerates matters.[4]

That is, the dialogic historical approach that Thiselton *rightly* adopts must be *taken into account*. "History" in all its dynamic diversity - in its embracing and engendering of moving contingent particularities - is not a neatly-ordered theme-park of already-finished quasi-Platonic categories. And so – as we said in Chapter 2 - historical consciousness must face 'the "messiness"' of history. To make this point is not at all to say that history and historical consciousness have "no developing orderedness" of *any* kind. And yet to make this point *is* to imply that there is necessarily an epistemological *delay* (*not* an absolute epistemological barrier) intrinsic to historical-hermeneutical understanding and to the hermeneutical circle – i.e. intrinsic to the understanding *of* history. That is, the developing orderedness or 'thematizing' of *responsible* interpretation will always *lag behind* the developing concrete orderedness of history because of the epistemological *delays* intrinsic *to* responsible interpretation. History never conforms to the pre-understandings that are operative initially during interpretation. During *responsible* interpretation, 'thematizing' *follows* "gathering", and "gathering" *follows* listening. In other words,

---

[1] Conroy, C., 'Review of A.C. Thiselton's *The Two Horizons*', *Greg* 62.3 (1981), 563. Italics Conroy's.

[2] Verbal comments made to me in October 2001 by an ex pupil of Thiselton's.

[3] Klein, W.W., 'Review of A.C. Thiselton's *The Two Horizons*', *Trinj* 2 (Spr. 1981), 75.

[4] Bowden, J., 'Review of A.C. Thiselton's *The Two Horizons*', *Th* 84.697 (Jan. 1981), 57.

Thiselton's expanding theoretical hermeneutics *quite rightly* lags behind his historical responses to other thinkers. Thus, for example, Thiselton had read 'Habermas' prior to '1980'. And yet Thiselton's main treatment of this thinker only appears in 1992 (Thiselton mentions Habermas only briefly in *The Two Horizons*), where we made a parallel point with respect to Thiselton's treatment of 'Ricoeur' in Chapter 2. What Bowden calls "noise", then, is really "Thiselton listening to historical particularity".[5]

Moreover, Thiselton's use of deliberate Kierkegaardian indirectness and "ambiguity" *invites* his readers into active thoughtful "self-involvement". Like the later Wittgenstein, Thiselton does "'not'" wish "'to spare'" his readers "'the trouble of thinking'".[6] Rather, Thiselton is like a mathematics professor who leaves his students to fill in missing intermediate steps between the key equations of a proof chalked on a blackboard. Admittedly, readers are 'left somewhat to' their 'own resources in formulating a solution' so far as re-organizing, and drawing implications from, Thiselton's material are concerned. And yet, there is no "noise" in Thiselton's writings. Everything he writes is integral to his arguments.[7]

In accepting Thiselton's invitation to self-involvement, therefore, we have applied an analytical Chomskian-like 'back-transformation' in order to render the components of the "'deep structure'" of Thiselton's thought. Then, we have applied a process of chronologically sensitive thematic re-organization or synthesis in order to "rebuild" the "gathered world" of Thiselton's thought systematically. This historical-structural approach avoids the pitfalls of a more straightforward

---

[5] Thiselton, A.C., 'Review of K.J. Vanhoozer's *Is There a Meaning in this Text?*' *JThStud* NS51.2 (Oct. 2000), 705 (quote regarding "'messiness'"); cf. Heidegger, M., *Being and Time* (trans. J. Macquarrie and E. Robinson; Oxford: Blackwell, 1962, 2001), 427 (the term 'thematizing' is Heidegger's, but we are not using this word in the way Heidegger used it); cf. Thiselton, A.C., *The Two Horizons: New Testament Hermeneutics and Philosophical Description with Special Reference to Heidegger, Bultmann, Gadamer, and Wittgenstein* (Exeter: Paternoster Press, 1980), 307 (on Habermas), 337 (our use of the term "gathering" harks back to Thiselton's treatment of Heidegger's notion of "gathering"; yet we are using the term differently - and in relation to *interpretations* rather than in relation to life-worlds or art-worlds); cf.: Thiselton, A.C., 'Thirty Years of Hermeneutics: Retrospect and Prospects', in *International Symposium on the Interpretation of the Bible* (ed. J. Krašovec; Ljubljana: Slovenian Academy of Sciences and Arts, Sheffield: Sheffield Academic Press, 1998), 1563; Thiselton, A.C., *New Horizons in Hermeneutics: The Theory and Practice of Transforming Biblical Reading* (London: HarperCollins; Grand Rapids: Zondervan, 1992), 379-393; Bowden, 'R *2H*', 57. Italics ours.

[6] Douglas, J.D., 'Hermeneutical Hazards. NEAC '77 Report', *CEN* 22 Apr. (1977), 9; cf. Thiselton, A.C., *Language, Liturgy and Meaning* (Nottingham: Grove Books, 1975 and 1986), e.g. 26; cf. Wittgenstein, L., *Philosophical Investigations* (trans. G.E.M. Anscombe; Oxford: Blackwell, 1953, 2001), viii.

[7] Erickson, M.J., 'Review of A.C. Thiselton's *The Two Horizons*', *JEThS* 23 (Dec. 1980), 373; Bowden, 'R *2H*', 57.

kind of 'back-transformation' – pitfalls that Thiselton himself notes.[8]

Admittedly, imposing order like this sometimes takes us beyond what Thiselton says explicitly. Some of our interpretative deductions reach *'behind'* Thiselton's text to a 'denotative' level; others are 'connotative', *'in front of* the text' - and it is impossible always to discern which is which. It is we, rather than Thiselton, for example, who speak of Thiselton's "hermeneutical critique of epistemology" or of his "second stratum" of thinking. And yet, in our view, even if our approach "goes beyond" Thiselton in the sense of building a structure that Thiselton does not explicitly build, then it is still emphatically *Thiselton* who has contributed the components *from which* that structure has been built. At the very least, then, as Thiselton himself notes in the Foreword to this project, what we have built here is entirely *consistent* with Thiselton's thinking, and is thoroughly "Thiseltonian". Thus, whilst Thiselton believes that we have "contributed" 'original thinking of… [our] own on the issue of a "unified" hermeneutical theory and practice', he rightly adds that 'the starting-point for this is true to [his] thinking'.[9]

In any case, our approach has yielded the chronological themes of Chapters 3 to 7, where we have organized these themes into three "strata", as follows.[10]

Thus, *ever-widening inter-disciplinary and inter-traditional (and smaller-scale) dialogue unto critical synthesis at the level of pre-understanding* is the focus of what we have called Thiselton's "first stratum" of thought. Themes that belong to this stratum of Thiselton's thinking concern the complex dialogic relationships between theology and philosophy, between philosophy and literary theory, between biblical studies, systematic theology, and hermeneutical philosophy, and between other disciplines, traditions, movements or schools of thought (and so on) that are of relevance for hermeneutics.

Themes belonging to Thiselton's "second stratum" of thought center upon his *five major theoretical hermeneutical critiques* of historical conceptualities related to history, epistemology, language, (Western) culture, and human selves respectively.

Themes belonging to Thiselton's "third stratum" of thought center on his *critique of hermeneutical understanding* – on his clarification of 'the hermeneutical circle' and of 'the hermeneutical' 'task' – and thus on "the problem of responsible interpretation". This stratum unites Thiselton's most *theoretical* works - which draw explicitly on Thiselton's five second-stratum theoretical hermeneutical critiques[11] -

---

[8] Thiselton, A.C., 'Semantics and New Testament Interpretation', in *New Testament Interpretation: Essays in Principles and Methods* (ed. I.H. Marshall; Grand Rapids: Eerdmans; Exeter: Paternoster Press, 1977; actually written 1974), 96.

[9] See, Thiselton, *NH*, 96-97; cf. 5, 363; cf. the Foreword to the present study. Italics in speech-marks Thiselton's, others ours.

[10] See also our comments on methodology in our Introduction and in Chapter 2.

[11] Thiselton, A.C., 'The Use of Philosophical Categories in New Testament Hermeneutics', *Chman* 87.1 (1973), 98; cf. Thiselton, *2H*, 4; cf. Thiselton, A.C., 'The New Hermeneutic', in *New Testament Interpretation: Essays in Principles and Methods* (ed. I.H. Marshall; Grand Rapids: Eerdmans; Exeter: Paternoster Press, 1977), 326, 327, 308-333.

with his simplest *practical* works, in which Thiselton's five second-stratum theoretical hermeneutical critiques are largely implicit.¹²

This three-stratum structure constitutes the basic steel-work of (our organization of) Thiselton's thinking.

Admittedly, Thiselton speaks of 'a systematic volume setting out [his] own hermeneutics', namely *New Horizons in Hermeneutics*.¹³ Yet, in mild disagreement with Thiselton, in our view *New Horizons in Hermeneutics* is still largely a systematization of trends emerging from Thiselton's historical responses to *others'* work, rather than an exposition of Thiselton's *own* views *per se*. Indeed, failure to appreciate Thiselton's work in ways that align with the character of, and interplay between, the "three strata" and various "critiques" emerging from our own imposed organization of Thiselton's thinking has produced questionable readings of Thiselton's work amongst others engaging with that work, as we shall demonstrate.

Thus, in the present chapter, we shall begin to expound Thiselton's first-stratum dialogue between theology and philosophy (important for the pre-understanding with which Thiselton approaches hermeneutical theory) before tackling his second-stratum hermeneutical critique of epistemology. Admittedly, the latter is less fundamental and/or less basic than Thiselton's hermeneutical critique of history. However, since Thiselton's hermeneutical critique of history only emerges in his PhD thesis and in *The Two Horizons*, then we shall defer our exposition of Thiselton's hermeneutical critique of history until Chapters 6 and 7 for the reasons that we have already outlined (see Chapter 2).¹⁴

In Chapter 4 we shall expound Thiselton's second-period second-stratum hermeneutical critiques of "language", "(Western) culture", and of "human selves" - though the latter two critiques only mature in the 1990s and later.¹⁵

And in Chapter 5, we shall expound Thiselton's second-period third-stratum

---

¹² e.g. Thiselton, A.C., 'Understanding God's Word Today: Evangelicals Face the Challenge of the New Hermeneutic. Address at the Second National Evangelical Anglican Congress, Nottingham, 1977', in *Obeying Christ in a Changing World, Vol. 1* (ed. J.R.W. Stott; Glasgow: Collins/Fountain Books, 1977), 90-122, (henceforth the 'long' article with this title).

¹³ Thiselton, 'TY', 1567.

¹⁴ See, Thiselton, A.C., *New Testament Hermeneutics and Philosophical Description: Issues in New Testament Hermeneutics with Special Reference to the Use of Philosophical Description in Heidegger, Bultmann, Gadamer, and Wittgenstein* (Sheffield: University of Sheffield Ph.D. Thesis, 1977; written by Dec. 1976), 74-121; cf. Thiselton, *2H*, 51-84.

¹⁵ cf.: Thiselton, A.C., *Interpreting God and The Postmodern Self: On Meaning, Manipulation and Promise* (SJT: Current Issues in Theology; Edinburgh: T&T Clark, 1995); Thiselton, A.C., 'Human Being, Relationality and Time in Hebrews, 1 Corinthians and Western Traditions. Paper presented at North Park Theological Seminary, Oct 17-19, 1997', *ExA* 13 (1997), 76-95; Thiselton, A.C., 'Can a Pre-Modern Bible Address a Postmodern World? (Public Lecture, University of St. Andrews)', in *2000 Years and Beyond: Faith, Identity, and the Common Era* (eds. P. Gifford, D. Archard, T. Hart, and N. Rapport; London: Routledge, 2003), 127-146.

critique of hermeneutical understanding - which builds on, but also goes beyond, his hermeneutical critique of epistemology.

In Chapters 6 and 7 we shall return again to our stratum-one discussion of theological and philosophical pre-understanding and, further, in this connection, we will contrast Thiselton's widening dialogues with the hermeneutical foreclosure(s) that may be found amongst his critics.

## B. Relating Theology and Philosophy during Hermeneutical Theory-Construction: Unifying Hermeneutics Christologically and Eschatologically

*1. Dialogue between Biblical Studies and Hermeneutics in Thiselton*

In Chapter 2, we noted the interwovenness of Thiselton's engagements with biblical interpretation, systematic theology, hermeneutics, philosophy and philosophical theology.[16] For Thiselton, understanding biblical texts necessarily involves philosophical hermeneutics. Otherwise, Thiselton argues, the genuine problems 'of historical distance', of readers' prior understandings (or preunderstandings), and of 'the rise of historical consciousness' are ignored. Thiselton argues that the Bible that merely reflects back readers' 'prior' traditions has not truly "spoken". Thiselton argues that such a Bible has become 'domesticated' in a way that makes reading dull, repetitive, or 'boring'.[17]

Hermeneutics, then, in Thiselton's estimate, need not "impose" alien 'philosophical doctrines' onto the Bible but,[18] rather, involves 'philosophical description'[19] 'of the hermeneutical task', clarification of the biblical 'texts' themselves, and a provisional liberation of the Bible's capacity to transform readers' self-understandings and (thence) readers' lives.[20]

Conversely, however, a provisionally-liberated Bible *also transforms Thiselton's hermeneutics*. Therefore, since 1 Corinthians constitutes Thiselton's main focus in biblical studies,[21] then we may outline its impact on his hermeneutics – as follows.

---

[16] cf.: Van Voorst, R., 'Review of A.C. Thiselton's *The Two Horizons*', *RefRev* 34 (Spr. 1981), 220; Conroy, 'R *2H*', 563; Nicholson, G., 'Transforming What We Know', *ResPhen* 16 (1986), 57.

[17] Thiselton, A.C., 'Predictable, Domesticated and Tamed', *CEN* 8 Feb. (1974), 7; cf.: Thiselton, *NTH*, 4-35; Thiselton, *2H*, xx, 3-23, 51; Thiselton, 'UPC', 87-88; Thiselton, 'NH', 308-315; Thiselton, 'U (long)', 90-105; Klemm, D.E., 'Review of A.C. Thiselton's *The Two Horizons*', *JAARel* 50.1 (Mar. 1982), 116.

[18] Thiselton, 'UPC', 87; 89; 98; cf. Thiselton, *2H*, 8.

[19] Palmer, R.E., 'Review of A.C. Thiselton's *The Two Horizons*', *RevMet* 35.1 (1981), 172-174; cf. Thiselton, *2H*, 3-10.

[20] cf.: Thiselton, *2H*, 4, 6; Thiselton, 'NH', 317; Thiselton, 'UPC', 87-100; cf. 89; cf. 98; Erickson, 'R *2H*', 371; Klein, 'R *2H*', 71.

[21] cf.: Thiselton, A.C., 'The Meaning of SARX in 1 Corinthians 5:5: A Fresh Approach in the Light of Logical and Semantic Factors', *SJT* 26.2 (May 1973), 204-228; Thiselton, A.C.,

Thus, to begin with, we should note that an argument highlighting a Pauline critique of 'over-realized eschatology' at Corinth is perennial in Thiselton's thinking.[22] During Thiselton's first and second periods, this argument appears in his Masters dissertation (1964),[23] in his 'Tyndale Lecture' (1966),[24] and in his article 'Realized Eschatology at Corinth' (written 1976, published 1978).[25] Even at the end of Thiselton's fourth period, the argument still appears in a qualified form in Thiselton's commentary on 1 Corinthians (2000).[26]

Certainly, in his second-period article 'Realized Eschatology at Corinth', Thiselton views Paul's critique of Corinthian '"enthusiastic"' and 'over-realized eschatology' as a key to interpreting 1 Corinthians.[27] Yet, this article also alludes to Thiselton's five major second-stratum hermeneutical critiques, hinting at the presence of a *dialogue between Pauline eschatology and Thiselton's hermeneutical theory.*

Thus, (1), in Thiselton's view, 'Paul' holds 'realized' and '"futurist"' 'eschatology' in tension. Corinthian 'over-realized eschatology', however, remains unqualified by 'the future'.[28] The point to note here is that this Pauline critique aligns with Thiselton's appeal to Pannenberg's eschatological *critique of history* and with Thiselton's criticisms of an over-focus on 'present' horizons in (to name just two examples), (a), 'charismatic' spirituality and in, (b), 'Bultmann's' non-futural eschatology and *'Geschichte'* versus *'Historie'* 'dualism'.[29]

(2) In Thiselton's exposition of 1 Corinthians, Paul holds definitive 'revelation'

---

'Realized Eschatology at Corinth', *NTStud* 24 (Jul. 1978), 510-526; Thiselton, A.C., 'The 'Interpretation' of Tongues: a New Suggestion in the Light of Greek Usage in Philo and Josephus', *JThStud* NS 30.1 (Apr. 1979), 15-36.

[22] Thiselton, 'REC', 510. Relevant articles are highlighted in the bibliography.

[23] Thiselton, A.C., *Eschatology and the Holy Spirit in Paul with Special Reference to 1 Corinthians* (London: University of London Unpublished M.Th. Dissertation, 1964); cf. *Who's Who 1999: An Annual Biographical Dictionary* (151st Year of Issue; London: A&C Black, 1999), 1985.

[24] Noted in, Thiselton, A.C., 'Review of E. Käsemann's *New Testament Questions of Today*', *Chman* 84.3 (1970), 229. The lecture is unpublished.

[25] Thiselton, 'REC', 510-526; cf. Thiselton, A.C., 'The Parousia in Modern Theology. Some Questions and Comments', *Tyn* 27 (1976), 43.

[26] Thiselton, A.C., *The First Epistle to the Corinthians* (eds. H. Marshall and D.A. Hagner; Series: The New International Greek Testament Commentary; Grand Rapids: Eerdmans; Carlisle: Paternoster, 2000), 99, 239, 345, 357.

[27] Thiselton, 'REC', 512; cf. 526.

[28] Thiselton, 'REC', 512; cf.: 520, 522-524, 526.

[29] cf.: Thiselton, 'UPC', 98; Thiselton, A.C., 'Review Article of W. Pannenberg's *Basic Questions in Theology, Vol. 1*', *Chman* 85.2 (1971), 120; Thiselton, 'Par', 36, cf. 37-41; Thiselton, *2H*, 246, 248; Thiselton, A.C., 'Experience-Centred Religion: Harvey Cox on the Seduction of the Spirit', *CEN* 9 Aug. (1974), 8; Thiselton, *LLM*, 25-27; Thiselton, A.C., 'The Multi-Model Character of Holy Spirit Language', *CEN* 11 Apr. (1974), 8; Thiselton, 'SNTI', 94-95; Thiselton, 'IT', 31; Gibson, A., *God and the Universe* (London: Routledge, 2000), 312. Italics in speech-marks are Thiselton's.

and ambiguous 'hiddenness' in tension. Thus, for Paul, valid truth-claims are possible, but 'future-oriented' open-endedness renders them provisional. Corinthian 'over-realized eschatology', by contrast, engenders over-certain and premature judgments and assessments.[30] Notably, though, this Pauline critique aligns with Thiselton's use of appeals to Pannenberg's eschatological *epistemology* (which combines "givenness" and 'hiddenness') in order to attack *both* Enlightenment 'objectivism',[31] *and* the various relativisms of Continental "existentialist", "post-structuralist", and American "neo-pragmatic" approaches.[32]

(3) In 'Realized Eschatology at Corinth', we also find that Thiselton draws on the later Wittgenstein in order to argue that 'Paul's' 'realistic' 'eschatology' provides the '"home" setting' that gives his (i.e. Paul's) language-uses their currency or meaning. Thus, for Paul, the term '"spirituality"' refers *both* to present 'day-to-day' human 'conduct' consistent with the Holy Spirit's transforming activity *and* to 'future'-orientation consistent with the Holy Spirit's transforming activity.[33] Corinthian 'over-realized eschatology', by contrast, re-defines terms through 'persuasive definition', up-anchoring them from their '"home"' settings such that, for example, the term 'spirituality' is then – artificially, abstractly, and ahistorically - made to refer primarily to *present "experience"'* of the Holy Spirit.[34] And again, in line with our previous two points, this Pauline critique aligns with Thiselton's more recent criticism of J. Derrida and S. Fish in relation to their "de-historicization" (our term) of *language and meaning* – a criticism that presupposes a non-idealist historico-philosophical sublation of insights drawn from the later Wittgenstein, from J.L. Austin, and from speech-act theory.[35]

(4) In Thiselton's exposition, 'Paul's' 'realistic' 'eschatology' also has implications for responsibility and 'freedom': "believers", despite being "new creations", 'still' "belong" 'to the natural order'. Thus, 'freedom' in Christ is qualified by the constraints of responsibility, both to contemporary social "conventions" and to 'eschatological' "imperatives" to embrace 'transformation'. Corinthian 'over-realized eschatology', however, by regarding 'law' and 'convention' as 'pre-eschatological', espouses 'freedom' as ethical licence and as

---

[30] Thiselton, 'REC', 514, 515.

[31] Thiselton, 'REC', 514; cf.: Thiselton, 'R *BQ1*', 120; Thiselton, A.C., 'The Theologian Who Must Not Be Ignored. Article Review of W. Pannenberg's *Basic Questions in Theology, Vol. 2*', *CEN* 25 Feb. (1972), 11; Thiselton, A.C., 'Head-On Challenge to Doubt: The Theology of Wolfhart Pannenberg', *CEN* 10 May (1974), 8; Thiselton, *2H*, 26-27.

[32] Thiselton, 'TNI', 11; cf. Thiselton, *NH*, 331-338, 80-141, 393-405, 529-550.

[33] Thiselton, 'REC', 515, 522-525; cf.: Thiselton, 'SARX', 215-218; Wittgenstein, *PI*, 48, 21-23, 42-43.

[34] Thiselton, 'REC', 515, 522-525; cf. Thiselton, 'SARX', 216, 217. Italics ours.

[35] Thiselton, A.C., 'Communicative Action and Promise in Inter-Disciplinary, Biblical, and Theological Hermeneutics', in *The Promise of Hermeneutics* (R. Lundin, C. Walhout and A.C. Thiselton; Grand Rapids and Cambridge: Eerdmans; Carlisle: Paternoster, 1999), 218-221; 154-158, (Fish); cf. 180-181, (Derrida).

autonomous 'liberation' from responsibility to others.³⁶ And again, this Pauline critique aligns with Thiselton's later critiques of so-called "modern" and 'postmodern' *Western Culture* in relation to "'autonomy'", 'power', and 'conflict'.³⁷

(5) Finally, in Thiselton's exegesis, as we noted and/or implied above, Paul holds together both divine transformation of *human selves* by the Holy Spirit and 'day-to-day conduct' that '"builds" towards' the same 'eschatological goal' as that pursued by the Holy Spirit.³⁸ Corinthian 'over-realized eschatology', however, stresses immediate 'experience' of the Spirit's "presence", but neglects '"building"' towards the Eschaton.³⁹ Not surprisingly, this Pauline critique aligns with Thiselton's later exposition of the 'narrative' (or "narratives") of 'self' (or of "selves") as being 'transformed' by divine "promise-fulfillment" within an anticipated 'larger' cosmic and corporate historico-eschatological 'narrative' *in contrast to* what Thiselton identifies as certain 'postmodern' interpretations of "selves" in which "selves" are forever being 'pre-determined' (and re-determined or "over-written") by fluxing socio-historical '"situatedness"' in (the immediate experience and reflexivity of) the 'fleeting' moment.⁴⁰

Hence, (6), in the context of Thiselton's biblical studies, we can see that Pauline theology and eschatology help to shape Thiselton's hermeneutical philosophy in/through a dialogue aimed at theoretical construction. If Thiselton's five second-stratum hermeneutical critiques are thereby eschatologically unified, then there is provisional evidence to justify our view that Thiselton's thinking does in fact *already* presuppose the 'more integral hermeneutic' that B.J. Walsh erroneously suggests is missing in Thiselton.⁴¹ Correlatively, in Chapter 6, we shall repudiate H.C. White's implicit assertion that Thiselton supposedly fails to 'overcome' the 'bifurcation between collective, objective history (*Historie*) and individual, existential history (*Geschichte*)' 'bequeathed' by 'Bultmann'.⁴²

Moreover, (7), if we can further demonstrate and confirm the validity of our argument that Thiselton's thinking involves a substantially *Pauline* eschatological unification of hermeneutics, then we may conclude that Thiselton's unification of hermeneutics, (a), stands in contrast to P.J. Cahill's 'literary' (cf. linguistic) and B.J.

---

³⁶ Thiselton, 'REC', 515, 516, 518, 520, 521.

³⁷ Thiselton, *IGPS*, e.g. 77-78, 161, 127-135; cf.: Thiselton, 'CAP', 133-239; Thiselton, A.C., 'Signs of the Times: Towards a Theology for the Year 2000 as a Grammar of Grace, Truth and Eschatology in Contexts of So-Called Postmodernity. Presidential Paper of the Society for the Study of Theology', in *The Future as God's Gift: Explorations in Christian Eschatology* (eds. D. Fergusson and M. Sarot; Edinburgh: T&T Clark, 2000), 9-39; cf.: Thiselton, *1 Cor*, 12-17, 33, 40-51, 75, 314, 548, 1002, 1054-1059, 1255; Thiselton, 'P-MB', 127-146.

³⁸ Thiselton, 'REC', 522, 523.

³⁹ Thiselton, 'REC', 520, 522, 524.

⁴⁰ Thiselton, *IGPS*, 74; cf. 151, 161; cf 122, 106; cf. 135.

⁴¹ Contradicting, Walsh, B.J., 'Anthony Thiselton's Contribution to Biblical Hermeneutics', *ChSRev* 14.3 (1985), 234.

⁴² White, H.C., 'The Value of Speech-Act Theory for Old Testament Hermeneutics', *Sem* 41 (1988), 41. Italics White's.

Walsh's "textual-ontological" and response-related suggestions regarding the unification of hermeneutics;[43] and, (b), contradicts numerous false charges that allege that Thiselton has supposedly succumbed to "Gadamerian" 'relativism',[44] to "Wittgensteinian" 'subjectivism' (cf. B.J. Walsh),[45] or to a neglect of 'the third horizon' (cf. J.C. McHann Jr.),[46] or that allege that Thiselton is simply 'Pannenbergian' (cf. R.E. Palmer).[47]

Admittedly, (8), Thiselton affirms Pannenberg's point that *Christ* is "'the proleptic'", 'provisional', and partial "anticipation" of the "'End'" of history[48] (even if Thiselton also criticizes Pannenberg's earlier 1970s Christology with reference to Hebrews).[49] Thiselton's complaint that A. Schweitzer over-stresses 'Paul's' 'eschatology' at the expense of Paul's 'Christology' also more than hints at the fact that Thiselton *ultimately* grounds and unifies his hermeneutics in *Christology* – as we shall see throughout the remainder of this study.[50]

### *2. Dialogue between Systematic Theology and Hermeneutics in Thiselton*

Thus, speaking about the relationship between biblical studies and hermeneutics in Thiselton's thinking inevitably brings us to systematic theology. That is, it can also

---

[43] cf.: Walsh, 'TC', 234; Cahill, P.J., 'Review of A.C. Thiselton's *The Two Horizons*', *CBQ* 43.3 (Jul. 1981), 484-485.

[44] cf.: Rodd, C.S., 'Review of A.C. Thiselton's *The Two Horizons*', *ExTim* 91 (Jul. 1980), 290; Dockery, D.S., 'Review of A.C. Thiselton's *The Two Horizons*', *GThJ* 4.1 (Spr. 1983), 135; Geisler, N.L., 'Review of A.C. Thiselton's *The Two Horizons*', *BibSac* 138 (Apr.-Jun. 1981), 183; Morgan, R., 'Review of A.C. Thiselton's *The Two Horizons*', *HeyJ* 22.3 (1981), 332; Poythress, V.S., 'Review of A.C. Thiselton's *The Two Horizons*', *WThJ* 43 (Fall 1980), 178-180.

[45] Walsh, 'TC', 235; cf.: McNicol, A.J., 'Review of A.C. Thiselton's *The Two Horizons*', *RestQ* 27.3 (1984), 188-189; Harrisville, R.A., 'Review of A.C. Thiselton's *The Two Horizons*', *Interp* 36 (Apr. 1982), 216-217; Geisler, 'R *2H*', 182; Wink, W., 'Review of A.C. Thiselton's *The Two Horizons*', *ThT* 37.4 (Jan. 1981), 507; Poythress, 'R *2H*', 178-180.

[46] cf.: Thiselton, *NH*, 26; 251; 337; McHann Jr., J.C., *The Three Horizons: A Study in Biblical Hermeneutics with Special Reference to Wolfhart Pannenberg* (Aberdeen: University of Aberdeen Ph.D. Thesis, 1987), 13-15; Klein, 'R *2H*', 72; Kleinig, J., 'Review of A.C. Thiselton's *The Two Horizons*', *RefThRev* 39 (Sep.-Dec. 1980), 89-90; Dyrness, W.A., 'Review of A.C. Thiselton's *The Two Horizons*', *CTday* 25 (Apr. 10, 1981), 94; Maddox, R.L., 'Review of A.C. Thiselton's *The Two Horizons*', *ThStud* 43.1 (Mar. 1982), 136-137; Borsch, F.H., 'Review of A.C. Thiselton's *The Two Horizons*', *AThRev* 65 (Jan. 1983), 90; Roschke, R.W., 'Review of A.C. Thiselton's *The Two Horizons*', *CThM* 9 (Aug. 1982), 246-247; Morgan, 'R *2H*', 331-333.

[47] Palmer, R.E., 'The Scope of Hermeneutics: The Problem of Critique, and the Crisis of Modernity', *TRevCTLit* 3 (1984), 226-227; cf. Palmer, 'R *2H*', 172-174.

[48] Thiselton, 'R *BQ1*', 121, 120; cf. Thiselton, 'Par', 49.

[49] Thiselton, 'Par', 50.

[50] Thiselton, A.C., 'Biblical Classics: VI. Schweitzer's Interpretation of Paul', *ExTim* 90 (Feb. 1979), 136.

be said that Thiselton's systematic theology, as well as his biblical studies, shapes his hermeneutical theory. Notably, his considerable second-period eschatological emphasis (see Chapter 2) was not a mere side-line, but was part of his *search for a unifying ground for hermeneutical theory* – as follows.[51]

Thus, (1), for Thiselton, both 'Tillich' and 'process theology' neglect 'the Parousia', where Thiselton also rejects J.B. Cobb's notion of 'the future... transcending of personality'.[52] Moreover, Thiselton complains that 'the Teilhardian' school similarly neglects 'the Parousia' and, in addition, Thiselton accepts Moltmann's criticism of its failure to '"begin"' with '"present"' '"transformation"'.[53] With Pannenberg and Carl Braaten, Thiselton argues that the Parousia, above all, shows that 'the future may confront, and even run counter to, the present' – and is not 'simply... a ["futurological"] development of present trends'. For Thiselton, then, emphases *on present transformation and on eschatological (not 'futurological') future must be held together* – against non-Christological 'evolutionary' approaches.[54]

(2) Positively, however, Thiselton applauds these same 'schools' of thought (i.e. Tillich, process theology, the Teilhardian school, and Theologies of Hope) for espousing a 'dynamic' 'heaven' and a 'living God' 'of the future', and for rejecting the more 'static', Platonic, 'timeless' views of 'traditional theology'. For Thiselton, these 'schools' rightly advocate 'a dynamic forward-looking... perspective in which' humanity 'is motivated and activated' '"from ahead"', where 'only the future gives genuine meaning to the present'. These 'schools' also – in Thiselton's view - rightly define 'the future' in terms of 'a cosmic-scale' 'kingdom of love', and not individualistically.[55] Thus, for Thiselton, the *eschatological future is cosmic, corporate, relational, and dynamic – and activates and gives meaning to the present from ahead.*

In Thiselton's view, (3), A. Schweitzer, F. Buri, and M. Werner rightly note 'the primitive' Church's belief in 'an *imminent* Parousia'. However, Thiselton also argues that these three thinkers: over-stress the influence of early belief in 'an *imminent* Parousia'; incorrectly claim that 'Jesus' held this 'belief';[56] and over-selectively cite the New Testament in order to bolster these erroneous perspectives.[57] Thiselton thus denies that *'the de-eschatologization of Christian doctrine'* followed in '"the... history"' 'of theology'.[58] Later, similarly, Thiselton bemoans the 'eschatological'

---

[51] See references flagged in our bibliography.
[52] Thiselton, A.C., 'Creativity of Heaven', *CEN* 8 Mar. (1974), 5; cf. Thiselton, 'Par', 28-29, cf. 31.
[53] cf.: Thiselton, 'CH', 5; Thiselton, A.C., 'Review of E.H. Cousins ed. *Hope and the Future of Man*', *Chman* 88.3 (1974), 232-233; Thiselton, 'Par', 29-30.
[54] Thiselton, 'R *HFM*', 232; cf. Thiselton, 'S (pub)', 9-10. Italics in speech-marks Thiselton's, others ours.
[55] cf.: Thiselton, 'CH', 5; Thiselton, 'R *HFM*', 232-233; Thiselton, 'Par', 28-30.
[56] Thiselton, 'Par', 31-35. Italics Thiselton's.
[57] Thiselton, 'Sch', 135.
[58] Thiselton, 'Par', 31-32. Italics Thiselton's.

splits projected between 'Paul' and 'Luke-Acts' by E. Käsemann.[59] And yet, in Thiselton's view, Schweitzer and Werner correctly relate 'apocalyptic' to 'the context of… Parousia-expectation'.[60] Thus, for Thiselton, *present eschatological expectation and a delayed Parousia are both biblical emphases.*

(4) Thiselton rejects Bultmann's view that 'supernatural' 'divine intervention' is 'myth' – partly because Bultmann thereby dualistically disparages the cognitive functions of biblical language relative to the self-involving functions of biblical language. In Thiselton's view, against Bultmann, the New Testament does not support demythologization and, again, Thiselton argues that Jesus did not "mistakenly" believe 'in an imminent Parousia'.[61] Thiselton also rejects H. Conzelmann's and J.A.T. Robinson's argument that 'the traditional doctrine of the Parousia… only' reflects 'later… New Testament thought'.[62] That is, for Thiselton, *Bultmannian and Post-Bultmannian attempts to demythologize the biblical notion of a delayed Parousia actually abuse biblical language in more than one way.*

(5) For Thiselton, then, biblical 'apocalyptic' is relevant 'today'. It 'safeguards the objective, public, act-of-God side of Christian theology' in which 'God' enters 'world-history' at the 'cosmic' level - against 'evil' - so as to bring 'new creation', 'judgment and resurrection'. With A. Nygren, Thiselton believes that 'history' moves 'towards a pre-destined goal', from 'the old age to' the 'new'.[63] In Thiselton's view, L. Morris, 'the Church' generally, and especially 'pietism' over-stress individualistic 'inner states'; conversely, Thiselton believes that K. Koch avoids this error. Nevertheless, Thiselton argues that 'apocalyptic' language is still "self-involving".[64] Thus, for Thiselton, *New Testament apocalyptic holds self-involving expectation and the objective delayed Parousia in tension.*

(6) In Thiselton's view, therefore, the Theologies of Hope of Pannenberg and Moltmann are 'visionary'. These thinkers help Thiselton to espouse a delayed Parousia and a future-oriented, eschatologically-structured Christianity.[65]

Thus, (a), with Moltmann, *first*, Thiselton argues that anticipations of 'history as a whole' should govern Christian attitudes, against Bultmann's anthropocentric 'individualistic' subjectivism.[66] *Second*, Thiselton argues, after Moltmann, that '"now"', the 'hidden' 'God' '"comes"' to us in our 'ambiguity', 'ignorance', and "fragmentation"; whereas at the "End", the "unveiled" 'God' brings 'truth', 'knowledge', integration, and 'rest'.[67] *Third*, after Moltmann, Thiselton argues that

---

[59] Thiselton, 'Sch', 135; cf. Thiselton, 'Par', 31-32; cf. 36-37.

[60] Thiselton, 'Par', 34.

[61] Thiselton, 'Par', 35-40.

[62] Thiselton, 'Par', 41; cf. 41-46.

[63] Thiselton, A.C., 'No Horns on the Pope', *CEN* 14 Jun. (1974), 5.

[64] Thiselton, A.C., 'Looking for God's Triumph: The Role of Apocalyptic', *CEN* 12 Jul. (1974), 8.

[65] Thiselton, 'Par', 47; cf. 50-53.

[66] Thiselton, 'Par', 49; cf. 47.

[67] Thiselton, 'Par' 47-48, 51.

the Christian's "'horizon of expectation'" is marked *both* by 'yieldedness', 'openness', 'acceptance', and 'faith in the' promise-fulfilling 'God', *and* by faith as activity, 'pilgrimage', 'exodus', 'change, readiness', and 'even unrest' - against the 'presumption' of "enthusiastic" over-'realized eschatology' and the 'despair' of Bultmann's non-futural "Kierkegaardian" eschatology.[68] Drawing on the later Wittgenstein, Thiselton adds that "'expectation'" is no mere 'state of mind', but an active practical 'attitude' consistent with "trust" in 'God'.[69]

(b) Despite these second-period appeals to Moltmann, however, Thiselton was also critical of Moltmann at that time – even though, today, Thiselton would not repeat these criticisms in relation to Moltmann's *later* work. Thus, in the mid 1970s, Thiselton complains that (the early) 'Moltmann often' seems to view 'nature as "hostile"… something to be overcome'; and, in Thiselton's estimate, (the early) Moltmann seems to disparage '"natural" gifts and cultural achievements'.[70] In Thiselton's view, Moltmann's earlier 'biblical' hermeneutics were 'precarious':[71] for Thiselton, against the early Moltmann, neither 'the cross' nor 'the Exodus' 'call us… to abandon our religious traditions *whatever* these' are, since such a 'call' would constitute 'a prescription for eternal flux'.[72]

Admittedly, Thiselton applauds 'Moltmann's… compassion for the suffering and oppressed, his desire for a theology that is socially and politically relevant, and his correlation of a theology of hope with that of the cross'. However Thiselton complains that, for the early Moltmann, 'the experience of poverty or suffering is almost a religious "work" which guarantees salvation'. And, in Thiselton's estimate, 'capitalism' *could* be 'combined with sufficient compassion to' negate the early Moltmann's call 'for a totally new social order'. Moreover, in Thiselton's view, the early Moltmann subsumes 'Christian identity' beneath 'contextual theology' when, in fact, we do *not* 'find Christian identity only when we lose it'.[73]

By contrast, (c), Thiselton's second-period appeals to Pannenberg are full of praise, and we recall Thiselton's comment in 1998: 'Pannenberg has always remained a major influence on my thinking'.[74] Thus, by the time of Thiselton's second period, Thiselton believes that Pannenberg is 'probably the most important of all the younger Continental theologians'[75] and one of 'the most

---

[68] Thiselton, 'Par', 47, 48, 51.

[69] Thiselton, 'Par', 52-53.

[70] Thiselton, 'R *HFM*', 232-233; cf. Thiselton, A.C., 'Personal Communication to Robert Knowles', 6th May 2007.

[71] Thiselton, A.C., 'Great Compassion and Heart. Review of J. Moltmann's *The Crucified God*', *CEN* 10 Jan. (1975), 9.

[72] Thiselton, A.C., 'Review of J. Moltmann's *The Crucified God*', *Chman* 89.2 (1975), 149. Italics Thiselton's.

[73] Thiselton, A.C., 'Review of J. Moltmann's *The Experiment Hope*', *Chman* 90.3 (1976), 225-227.

[74] Thiselton, 'TY', 1560.

[75] Thiselton, 'R *BQT*', 120.

important theologians' of the time.[76] For Thiselton, Pannenberg is 'one of the most constructive, stimulating, and important theologians of our time',[77] and (by the time of Thiselton's second period) 'has done more than anyone else in the last 20 years to open a new era in theology'.[78] Other praises for Pannenberg's work abound during Thiselton's second period.[79]

Nevertheless, (d), Thiselton remains critical of *both* Pannenberg *and* Moltmann during the 1970s (though, as in the case of Moltmann, Thiselton would not now repeat his criticisms of the early Pannenberg's work against Pannenberg's later work). Thus, for Thiselton, God's 'cosmic' arrival at the *'Parousia'* brings about 'history-as-a-whole' – a 'history-as-a-whole' to which the "unveiled" (*'apocalypsis'*) divine 'verdict' is applied so as to break through 'disguises, deceits', and '"misunderstandings"'.[80] Yet, for Thiselton, God's 'revelation' in Christ now has more "verdictive" finality than the early Pannenberg allows;[81] and, for Thiselton, there is a 'cosmic'- and ecclesial-level 'destruction of the negative' at 'the Parousia' that extends beyond what the early Moltmann's "socio-political" focus allows.[82]

Indeed, (e), in his second period, Thiselton argues that the early Pannenberg gives 'the impression... that even Christian revelation may... be called in question by the future'. For Thiselton, however, whilst 'the interpretation of revelation is... ongoing', '"in these last days God has spoken to us by his Son"'. Thus, Thiselton urges that it was 'revelation in the days of the prophets' that 'was "partial and piecemeal"' (Hebrews 1:1, 2).[83]

Thiselton applauds Pannenberg's view that 'the truth of God' 'is not... "finished"' in 'a Platonic' or mathematical sense,[84] but for Thiselton the "provisionality" of 'historical' "contingencies" does not subsume divine identity-stability or "the truth of God" in 'Christ'.[85] Rather, Thiselton argues that mutual qualification is required between viewing 'God' as 'a static... unchanging timeless Being' and viewing God as 'dynamic... moving ongoing love, who calls, invites,

---

[76] Thiselton, 'TNI', 11.

[77] Thiselton, A.C., 'Meaning and Myth. Review Article of W. Pannenberg's *Basic Questions in Theology, Vol. 3*', *CEN* 19 Oct. (1973), 8.

[78] Thiselton, 'H-O', 8.

[79] cf.: Thiselton, 'R *BQ1*', 120; Thiselton, 'TNI', 11; Thiselton, A.C., 'Theology Made Exciting. Review of W. Pannenberg's *The Apostles' Creed in the Light of Today's Questions*', *CEN* 19 Jan. (1973), 12; Thiselton, 'H-O', 8; Thiselton, A.C., 'Review of A.D. Galloway's *Wolfhart Pannenberg*', *Chman* 88.3 (1974), 230-231.

[80] Thiselton, 'Par', 52; cf. Thiselton, 'PCRK', 6th May 2007. Italics in speech-marks Thiselton's. Capitalization on 'Parousia' here – and from here on in our main text – is ours.

[81] Thiselton, 'Par', 50, cf. 52.

[82] Thiselton, 'Par', 50.

[83] Thiselton, 'Par', 50.

[84] Thiselton, 'TNI', 11.

[85] Thiselton, 'Par', 48, 49, 50; cf. Thiselton, A.C., 'Truth', in *The New International Dictionary of New Testament Theology, Volume 3* (ed. C. Brown; Exeter: Paternoster; Grand Rapids: Zondervan, 1978), 885, 890-892.

*Hermeneutics, Unity, and Epistemology* 95

and acts in ever-new ways'. Thiselton insists that 'God' does 'not suddenly change his nature'. Correlatively, Thiselton argues that 'heaven' is '"rest", finality, completion, goal', and promise-fulfillment, 'in contrast to all that is toilsome, laborious', and 'frustratingly incomplete'; but it is also 'vibrant, fresh, [and] creative', 'in contrast to... stagnation and decay'.[86]

Thus, (f), to summarize: Thiselton is neither simply Pannenbergian, nor simply Moltmannian. Rather, Thiselton transposes early Pannenbergian and early Moltmannian insights into a larger developing biblical-theological template.

Most notably, (g), Thiselton's positive appeals to Pannenberg are parallel to/with Thiselton's appeals to Paul's teaching in 1 Corinthians: both sets of appeals contribute to Thiselton's grounding and unifying of his five major second-stratum hermeneutical critiques.

Thus, *first*, following Pannenberg, Thiselton agrees that the biblical God does not simply reflect '"timeless"... Platonic ideas' or 'mathematical equations'.[87] For Pannenberg and Thiselton, the 'biblical' 'God' is *'living'*, against the purely static 'traditional notion of God as a transcendent being';[88] and, with Pannenberg, Thiselton argues that we are '"to understand all being in relation to God"'.[89] For Pannenberg and Thiselton, 'God' is *both* a 'God' 'of promise, purpose... meaning', 'the expected' and 'predicted', *and* 'of the "ever-new"' – where Christ's 'resurrection' *both* fulfils 'apocalyptic' 'expectation' *and* is 'radically new and unique'. Thus, biblically, and in Thiselton's *hermeneutical critique of history*, '"history"' juxtaposes '"continuity and unity"', and, '"contingency, novelty, and openness of the future"'.[90] That is, for Thiselton, after Pannenberg, history embraces '"the particular"' case, not *a priori* 'types'.[91] For Pannenberg and Thiselton, '"past"', '"present"', and '"future"' horizons are – or will be - linked by '"the totality of history"'[92] of 'New Testament eschatology', which is '"all [created] reality"',[93] or '"all temporal process"',[94] but which is not God - although God remains involved in it.[95] Against this background, Thiselton overcomes Bultmann's '"dichotomy between... *Historie* and *Geschichte*"' (see Chapter 6).[96]

---

[86] Thiselton, 'CH', 5.
[87] Thiselton, 'R *BQT*', 120.
[88] Thiselton, 'R *BQT*', 121; cf. Thiselton, 'TNI', 11. Italics Thiselton's.
[89] Thiselton, 'R *BQT*', 121.
[90] Thiselton, 'H-O', 8; cf.: Thiselton, 'R *BQT*', 121; Thiselton, 'TNI', 11.
[91] Thiselton, 'TNI', 11.
[92] Thiselton, 'R *BQT*', 120.
[93] Thiselton, 'TNI', 11.
[94] Thiselton, 'M&M', 8.
[95] Pannenberg, W., *Basic Questions in Theology. Collected Essays, Volume 1* (trans. G.H. Kehm; Philadelphia: Fortress Press, 1970); 15, 21; cf. Pannenberg, W., *Systematic Theology. Volume 1* (trans. G.W. Bromiley; Grand Rapids: Eerdmans, 1991), 331; cf. Pannenberg, W., *Systematic Theology. Volume 2* (trans. G.W. Bromiley; Grand Rapids: Eerdmans, 1994), 61.
[96] Thiselton, *2H*, 248; against, White, 'S-AT', 41. Italics Thiselton's.

*Second*, following Pannenberg, Thiselton urges that 'God' and the '"totality of history"' 'ground' '"the unity of truth"',[97] where '"the meaning of the present becomes clear only in the light of the future"'.[98] For Pannenberg and Thiselton, Christ's '"resurrection"' constitutes a '"proleptic"', '"provisional and anticipatory"' revelation of the '"end"' of history, and hence of 'the whole' of history, though present knowledge is necessarily *'provisional'*, correcting 'Hegel'.[99] Thus, in his *hermeneutical critique of epistemology*, Thiselton agrees with Pannenberg that 'truth' should be approached through 'Biblical history and eschatology',[100] 'beginning "from below", with historical enquiry'.[101] For Pannenberg and Thiselton, '"the meaning"' of an "event", '"text"', or "act", is its particular relationship to other 'events', texts, and 'acts' within "traditions" and within anticipations of the historical 'whole'. For Pannenberg and Thiselton, 'meaning' is not a separable human projection, against Bultmann's and Kähler's 'neo-Kantian' fact-value dualism, but is united with 'event'.[102] Contrary to 'Dilthey'[103] and to '"Troeltsch's... dependence upon known analogies to fix the limits of historical knowledge"', Pannenberg and Thiselton argue that 'meaning' and 'event' are 'unique',[104] being 'decisively conditioned by historical context'.[105] Yet, with 'Pannenberg' and 'Gadamer', Thiselton argues that historical 'continuity' allows overlap 'between two... horizons', and hence allows the '"fusion of horizons"' (though such '"fusion"' is never complete – see Chapter 5).[106]

*Third*, it is in *this* framework that Thiselton, following 'Pannenberg', and against Continental hermeneutics, reinstates 'propositions' *without* returning to 'the analytical abstractions of a timeless Platonism'.[107] This reinstatement contributes to Thiselton's *hermeneutical critique of language*. For Thiselton, if horizonal *overlap* allows some *access* to the historical past, horizonal *particularity* allows for the *difference* of the historical past. Hence, for Thiselton, historical propositions - as predicates conventionally presupposing historical-conceptual and extra-linguistic historical distinctions - can have meaning.[108]

---

[97] Thiselton, 'TNI', 11; cf.: Thiselton, 'R *BQ1*', 120; Thiselton, 'H-O', 8.
[98] Thiselton, 'R *BQ1*', 120; cf. Thiselton, 'TNI', 11.
[99] Thiselton, 'R *BQ1*', 121; cf. 120. Italics in speech-marks are Thiselton's.
[100] Thiselton, 'TNI', 11.
[101] Thiselton, 'H-O', 8; cf. Pannenberg, *BQ1*, 51-52.
[102] Thiselton, 'R *BQ1*', 121; cf. 120; cf. Thiselton, 'TNI', 11.
[103] Thiselton, 'R *BQ1*', 120; cf. 121.
[104] Thiselton, 'H-O', 8.
[105] Thiselton, 'TNI', 11; cf. Pannenberg, W., *Basic Questions in Theology. Collected Essays, Volume 2* (trans. G.H. Kehm; Philadelphia: Fortress Press, 1971), 61.
[106] Thiselton, 'R *BQ1*', 120; cf. 121.
[107] Thiselton, 'R *BQ1*', 121.
[108] cf.: Thiselton, 'TY', 1560; Thiselton, A.C., 'The Parables as Language-Event: Some Comments on Fuchs's Hermeneutics in the Light of Linguistic Philosophy', *SJT* 23.4 (Nov.

*Fourth*, Thiselton agrees with Pannenberg that "'historical reason'" assesses its "objects" in relation to anticipations of 'the whole' of 'history', and that "'historical reason'" therefore demands "serious" 'dialogue with' other 'world-religions', 'philosophy', 'biology, sociology and psychology' as 'an intellectual obligation'.[109] In Thiselton's view, 'Moltmann', 'Metz', and 'Pannenberg' rightly 'relate biblical teaching about the future to present political and social action'.[110] Thus, an eschatologically-framed epistemology grounds *both* Thiselton's *hermeneutical critique of Western Culture* (see Chapter 4)[111] *and* his rejection of Kierkegaard's and Bultmann's 'individualism'.[112]

*Fifth*, Thiselton agrees with Pannenberg that, in alignment with *the fall*, 'man's openness to his environment, his vulnerability and encounter with the future, and his centeredness upon himself' are 'expressed in defensiveness and self-assertion'. Yet, against Bultmann, Thiselton argues that, through *redemption*, 'faith' is linked both to past 'objective "historical"' "events" (cf. 'knowledge'), and to 'future' "promise-fulfillment" (cf. 'trust').[113] Thus, in Thiselton's *hermeneutical critique of human selves*, liberated or *redeemed* selves are not merely self-centered, defensive or assertive so as to reflect only 'bondage' to 'the past', but exhibit 'future-oriented' "'openness'" (see Chapters 4 and 6).[114] For Pannenberg and Thiselton, "'God'", as "'the power of the future'", and as "'the object of hope and trust'",[115] gives 'freedom' to humanity – 'the capacity to go beyond what [it] already has'. Therefore, Thiselton argues that 'Christian hope' is not evasive escapism but that such 'hope' involves active 'shaping [of] the future'.[116]

(7) Summarizing: Thiselton dialogues with several eschatological traditions, but favors Theologies of Hope, particularly Pannenberg and Moltmann. Whilst favoring the early Pannenberg over the early Moltmann, Thiselton is critical of both thinkers (though he would not level such criticisms at the later Pannenberg or at the later Moltmann). Nevertheless, Thiselton's appeals to Pannenberg's eschatology contribute to the grounding and unifying of Thiselton's five second-stratum major hermeneutical critiques in ways that parallel, supplement, and flesh-out the ways in which Thiselton's appeals to Paul's teaching in 1 Corinthians contribute to the grounding and unifying of Thiselton's five second-stratum major hermeneutical critiques. Therefore, 'biblical' studies, "'systematic theology'", and hermeneutics are combined in Thiselton's first-stratum inter-disciplinary and inter-

---

1970), 454; Thiselton, 'TNP', 11; Thiselton, *2H*, 77; cf. 79, 58; Thiselton, A.C., 'The Theology of Paul Tillich', *Chman* 88.1 (1974), 99-101; Thiselton, *NH*, 2.

[109] Thiselton, 'TNP', 11; cf. Thiselton, 'M&M', 8.

[110] Thiselton, 'CH', 5; cf. Thiselton, 'R *HFM*', 232-233.

[111] Thiselton, 'Truth', 900-901; cf. Thiselton, *NH*, 390-391; cf. 393-405.

[112] Thiselton, 'Par', 48-49.

[113] Thiselton, 'R *WP*', 230-231.

[114] Thiselton, *IGPS*, 128-129.

[115] Thiselton, 'TNP', 11.

[116] Thiselton, 'M&M', 8.

traditional dialogue, in alignment with his view of 'the theologian's task'.[117]

(8) This conclusion strengthens our earlier provisional argument that a unifying biblical Christological-eschatological framework grounds Thiselton's five major second-stratum hermeneutical critiques, and reinforces our earlier rejection of criticisms of Thiselton's work made by B.J. Walsh, H.C. White, P.J. Cahill, J.C. McHann Jr., R.E. Palmer, and numerous others. Notably, Walsh fails to appreciate some of the implications of Thiselton's appeals to Pannenberg, falsely suggesting that Thiselton is still under the spell of Continental 'dualisms'.[118] Further, J.C. McHann Jr. falsely suggests that Thiselton has not engaged sufficiently with 'Pannenberg's' 'eschatology'.[119]

In relation to this last point then, admittedly, in 1992, Thiselton recalls J.C. McHann Jr.'s criticism in 1985 that he (i.e. Thiselton) needed to pay 'more attention to Pannenberg's eschatological horizon',[120] and Thiselton 'did not dissent from' McHann's criticisms when Thiselton 'examined his [i.e. McHann's] doctoral dissertation'.[121] Thiselton even speaks of McHann's 'allowing some of my claims in *The Two Horizons* to interact with Pannenberg's theology'. Thiselton recalls that 'McHann argued that hermeneutical theory needed to move beyond the notion of "Two Horizons", to take account of the three horizons of "past, present, and future", and thereby to ground hermeneutics more adequately in ontology and eschatology'.[122]

However, as we have just seen, Thiselton's *other* second-period writings manifest his extensive engagement with Pannenberg's work *prior* to *The Two Horizons*,[123] the latter work being the 'mature *Summa* in which... [Thiselton] draws together his [second period] thinking'.[124] We have also noted Thiselton's retrospective comments that, 'Pannenberg has always remained a major influence on my thinking', at least from '1969'.[125]

Hence, Thiselton has deliberately glossed over a misreading of his work, probably in order to allow a valuable hermeneutical point to be reiterated more explicitly. McHann has missed what R.E. Palmer calls 'the reception - and at the

---

[117] Thiselton, A.C., 'Theology and the Future', *CEN* 23 Jan. (1970), 11.
[118] Walsh, 'TC', 234; cf. 231-232; cf. Thiselton, *2H*, 404.
[119] Thiselton, *NH*, 26; cf. 251, 337; cf. McHann Jr., *3H*, 13-15 especially.
[120] Thiselton, *NH*, 26; cf. McHann Jr., *3H*, 13-15.
[121] Thiselton, *NH*, 26.
[122] Thiselton, *NH*, 251; cf. 337.
[123] See flagged references in our bibliography, and also, Thiselton, A.C., 'The Ministry and the Church Union: Some Logical and Semantic Factors', *FUty* 18 (1974), 45-47; cf. Thiselton, A.C., 'Keeping up with Recent Studies: II. Structuralism and Biblical Studies: Method or Ideology?', *ExTim* 89 (Aug. 1978), 329-335.
[124] Ellingworth, P., 'Review of A.C. Thiselton's *The Two Horizons*', *EvanQ* 53 (Jul.-Sep. 1981), 178. Italics Ellingworth's.
[125] Thiselton, 'TY', 1560. But in Chapter 1, we deduced a date at *least* as early as 1967.

same time a Pannenbergian critique - of Gadamer in… *The Two Horizons*'.[126]

R.S. Hess thus *falsely* argues that 'Thiselton… follows his student' McHann (Hess mistakenly calls McHann 'Luckmann').[127] W.J. Heard Jr., similarly, *mistakenly* argues that 'it is in' McHann's 'work that Pannenberg's notion of eschatologically oriented ontology is wed with Thiselton's two horizons, resulting in a third horizon'.[128]

Actually, as we have just seen, this "wedding" occurs in Thiselton's *own* thinking around *a decade earlier*. Crucially, Thiselton's 'post-Wittgensteinian' and 'post-Gadamerian' framework *could never straightforwardly incorporate McHann's*, since McHann's framework builds - to a substantial extent at least - on E.D. Hirsch's work.[129]

Indeed, in Chapter 6 we propose that Thiselton's PhD Thesis and, subsequently *The Two Horizons*, radiate from modified Hegelian criteria in part-*revision* of Pannenberg's work. And yet, these two writings by Thiselton *pre-date* McHann's criticisms by nine and by five years respectively. Thus, we reject N.R. Gulley's comment that J.C. McHann Jr. 'goes one step further' than Thiselton's 'two horizons' by including 'the future'.[130] The future and eschatology are *central to Thiselton's thinking long before McHann's thesis* (contradicting W.J. Heard Jr.'s reading of Thiselton).[131]

Having said all this, (9), R.E. Palmer's comment about 'Thiselton's' 'Pannenbergian critique… of Gadamer' - whilst it sufficed in helping us to ward off McHann's (and others') mistakes - is probably also a caricature.[132] Palmer is correct in that B.J. Walsh, J.C. McHann Jr. and others falsely presuppose that Thiselton is under the spell of Continental hermeneutics, particularly Gadamer.[133] Yet, Palmer may have missed the complexity of Thiselton's critique of Continental hermeneutics, which is hardly simply "Pannenbergian" (see Chapter 6). Thus, H.C. White records Thiselton's 'incorporation of insights from Austin and Wittgenstein' to "strengthen" Ernst Fuchs' 'concept of language-event' (though even White's remark is inaccurate - see Chapter 4).[134]

---

[126] Palmer, 'Scope', 226-227; cf. Palmer, 'R *2H*', 172-174. Italics Palmer's.

[127] Hess, R.S., 'New Horizons in Hermeneutics: A Review Article', *Them* 18.2 (Jan. 1993), 23.

[128] Heard Jr., W.J., 'Eschatologically Oriented Psychology', in *God and Culture* (eds. D.A. Carson and J. Woodbridge; Grand Rapids: Eerdmans, 1993), 118.

[129] McHann Jr., *3H*, 13-15, 457, 463; cf.: Thiselton, *2H*, 25, 315; Thiselton, *NH*, 13, 37, 471.

[130] Gulley, N.R., 'Reader-Response Theories in Postmodern Hermeneutics', in *The Challenge of Postmodernism. An Evangelical Engagement* (ed. D.S. Dockery; Grand Rapids, Mi.: Baker Books, 1997), 208.

[131] Heard Jr., 'EOP', 118; cf. Thiselton, 'TY', 1560.

[132] Palmer, 'Scope', 226-227; cf. Palmer, 'R *2H*', 172-174.

[133] See footnotes 43-47; cf. Maddox, R.L., 'Contemporary Hermeneutic Philosophy and Theological Studies', *RelStud* 21.4 (Dec. 1985), 526.

[134] White, 'S-AT', 55.

(10) A question now arises: does Thiselton's dialogue between theology and philosophy – and in particular his eschatological (and ultimately Christological) unification and grounding of hermeneutics – lend any validity to the charge that he is straightforwardly "fideistic"?[135] Is S.D. Moore correct to assert that 'Thiselton's theological and pastoral interests dominate' Thiselton's later work, *New Horizons in Hermeneutics* (1992)?[136]

Here, in response to S.D. Moore, we may note that F. Watson's comment that 'theology' is often not 'the center' of Thiselton's 'discussion' is significant:[137] in our next section we argue that Thiselton attempts to philosophically *warrant* his theological appeals: he is *not* straightforwardly fideistic – as follows.

## C. Dialogic Theory-Construction:
## Towards a Unified Hermeneutical Critique of Epistemology

*1. Straightforward Fideism, or Warranted Inclusion of Theological Considerations?*

Superficially, admittedly, Thiselton occasionally *seems* straightforwardly fideistic. Thus, in the *longer* of his two articles entitled 'Understanding God's Word Today',[138] Thiselton argues, appealing to the later Wittgenstein, that if the 'biblical' texts were an '"ultimate" authority', then they could not appeal 'to a higher authority': self-attestation would be inevitable.[139] Hence, Thiselton argues that 'biblical writers' unavoidably affirm 'biblical authority',[140] and that 'biblical' and 'apostolic' authorities provide the only criteria sufficient to authenticate the genuinely 'Christian' *as* "genuinely Christian". Further, Thiselton argues that divine speech-action through 'the Bible *makes*' the Church and 'the Christian', and does not just "inform" them.[141]

Moreover, Thiselton argues that 'hermeneutics' confirms that biblical texts *can* operate authoritatively across 'historical distance' so as to transform today's "readers", despite 'the problem of "pre-understanding"' (on which, see Chapter 5).[142] Thiselton argues that 'the Holy Spirit' gives 'gifts' to facilitate exegetical 'scholarship' and 'creatively' 'inspires' 'understanding'. For Thiselton, 'the Spirit'

---

[135] cf. B.J. Walsh's comments in, Walsh, 'TC', 235.

[136] Moore, S.D., 'Review of A.C. Thiselton's *New Horizons in Hermeneutics*', *ThT* 50.2 (Jul. 1993), 287.

[137] Watson, F., 'Review of A.C. Thiselton's *New Horizons in Hermeneutics*', *BibInterp* 4.2 (1996), 255.

[138] Thiselton, 'U (long)', 90-122; cf. Thiselton, A.C., 'Understanding God's Word Today', *CEN* 15 Oct. (1976), 6, (henceforth the 'short' article with this title).

[139] Thiselton, 'U (long)', 114; cf. Wittgenstein, *PI*, 85.

[140] Thiselton, 'U (long)', 114-115; cf. 121; cf. Sykes, S.W., 'Review of A.C. Thiselton's *The Two Horizons*', *Chman* 96.2 (1982), 157.

[141] Thiselton, 'U (long)', 115-118, cf. 121. Italics ours.

[142] Thiselton, 'U (long)', 99-101, cf. 102-104, cf. 121.

does not undermine 'biblical authority' or 'hermeneutics', but acts *'through'* them.¹⁴³ For Thiselton, then, 'the Bible' - as authoritative multiform 'address' from 'God' - demands an 'obedient response' from its readers.¹⁴⁴

In his *shorter* article entitled 'Understanding God's Word Today', Thiselton identifies 'Christ' as 'God's Word'. For Thiselton, further, the biblical writings are *both* 'human' and historically conditioned *and* God's active 'word' of 'address', 'challenge', "judgment", "correction", "re-creation", and "transformation". For Thiselton the biblical writings should thus be thought of as "bringing" 'Christ and... salvation'.¹⁴⁵ Therefore, Thiselton argues that we must 'understand the Bible accurately', 'responsibly', 'faithfully', 'honestly', 'sensitively', 'and obediently', and that we must employ 'hermeneutics' to allow 'the Bible' to '"speak"' afresh today.¹⁴⁶ Thiselton criticizes 'evangelical' 'hermeneutics' in this context of discussion as we have already seen (see Chapter 2).¹⁴⁷

Thus, superficially, it seems that, for Thiselton, the Bible is authoritative because we experience God's help in interpreting it, and in changing us through it, and because it provides criteria that authenticate the genuinely "Christian" *as* "genuinely Christian". For Thiselton, moreover, these points are not undermined by arguments related to historical distance, to historical conditioning (cf. preunderstanding), to self-attestation, or to the Spirit's work.

We can imagine a critic's response: "Thiselton's stance, here, reflects merely the experience of being conformed to coherence with something accepted as 'true' or as 'authoritative' in a straightforwardly fideistic manner. But, epistemological warrant requires more than considerations of religious experience, conformity, internal coherence, and performative endorsement".¹⁴⁸

Whilst - to some extent – we accept this criticism of these two articles when they are taken in isolation, this criticism flounders once we consider the dialogic inter-relationships, in Thiselton's broader thinking, between biblical studies, systematic theology, and hermeneutics. Thiselton attempts to approach the Bible *through* hermeneutics, or '"from below"', 'in history'.¹⁴⁹

Thus, in relation to epistemology, Thiselton warrants or justifies the validity of his working hypothesis that the Bible can contribute positively to hermeneutical discourse by appealing to the Bible's resonance with, and to the Bible's anticipatory problem-solving cogency in relation to, criteria emerging through his dialogues with extra-biblical approaches to epistemology associated with 'the rise

---

¹⁴³ Thiselton, 'U (long)', 114, 116-120, cf. 121, cf. 99. Italics Thiselton's.

¹⁴⁴ Thiselton, 'U (long)', 105-106, cf. 121.

¹⁴⁵ Thiselton, 'U (short)', 6.

¹⁴⁶ Thiselton, 'U (short)', 6.

¹⁴⁷ Thiselton, 'U (short)', 6. We gave details in Chapter 2.

¹⁴⁸ Cf. Walsh, 'TC', 235.

¹⁴⁹ Thiselton, 'H-O', 8; cf.: Thiselton, 'UPC', 89, 98; cf. 87-100; Thiselton, 'NH', 328-329; Thiselton, 'U (long)', 115-117, cf. 119, 121.

of historical consciousness' in the Western philosophical traditions.[150]

That is, Thiselton in effect argues that if the Bible resonates with, or even improves upon, a properly historically configured epistemology that aligns with philosophical critiques emerging with/from 'the rise of historical consciousness', then it attains credibility in its role as a key contributor to a hermeneutical critique of epistemology. As we have already seen, for Thiselton, following 'Pannenberg', 'the theologian's' 'intellectual obligation' 'is to relate Christian thought to all truth, including… philosophy and the sciences',[151] where Thiselton begins to attempt to do this in his article, 'Truth' (1978), as we shall argue below.[152]

That is, Thiselton *avoids* a straightforward 'fideistic defence of the claim of religious language to its own realm' (affirming R.L. Maddox's reading of Thiselton).[153] His popular-level articles must be read against the background of his more theoretical works.[154] To the latter we now turn.

### 2. Philosophical Problem: Continental Epistemological Dualism and its Effect on the Character and Role of Conceptualization in Hermeneutics

(1) For Thiselton, 'hermeneutics', almost by definition, questions 'the Cartesian subject-object dichotomy' of traditional epistemology.[155] With Heidegger, Gadamer, and the later Wittgenstein Thiselton rejects 'the post-Cartesian… isolated worldless "I"': 'the human subject is always the participant in a community prior to… objectification and subjectivism'. Thus, Thiselton rejects 'objectivist epistemology, the correspondence theory of truth, and the referential theory of meaning':[156] 'knowing is grounded beforehand in a Being-already-alongside-the-world';[157] 'aesthetic consciousness… does not' simply "confront"

---

[150] Thiselton, *2H*, 51; cf.: Thiselton, 'TNI', 11; Thiselton, 'H-O', 8; Thiselton, 'UPC', 87; Thiselton, A.C., 'Kierkegaard and the Nature of Truth', *Chman* 89.1 (1975), 85-107; Thiselton, 'Truth', 874-902.

[151] Thiselton, *2H*, 51; cf. Thiselton, 'H-O', 8.

[152] Thiselton, 'Truth', 874-902.

[153] Maddox, 'R *2H*', 137.

[154] cf.: Thiselton, A.C., 'Irrational Assumptions of Modern Theology Exposed. Review of T.F. Torrance's *God and Rationality*', *CEN* 19 Mar. (1971), 9; Thiselton, 'UPC', 87-100; Thiselton, 'M&M', 8; Thiselton, 'Till', 86-107; Thiselton, 'KNT', 85-107; Thiselton, 'Par', 27-54; Thiselton, A.C., 'Sigmund Freud and the Language of the Heart', *CEN* 13 Feb. (1976), 12, 14; Thiselton, *NTH*; Thiselton, 'NH', 308-333; Thiselton, 'REC', 510-526; Thiselton, 'Truth', 874-902; Thiselton, *2H*.

[155] Walsh, 'TC', 230; cf.: Thiselton, *2H*, 87, 246.

[156] Walsh, 'TC', 231; cf.: Thiselton, *2H*, 38; Larkin Jr., W.J., *Culture and Biblical Hermeneutics. Interpreting and Applying the Authoritative Word in a Relativistic Age* (Grand Rapids: Baker, 1988), 36.

[157] Heidegger, *BT*, 88.

'an object';[158] and 'the concept of knowing is coupled with that of the language-game'.[159]

That is, *aligning* with Continental hermeneutics and with the later Wittgenstein, Thiselton argues that the epistemological "subject" and the epistemological "object" are already embedded in historical relationships with one another, and that they are not sharply or dichotomously separated from one another. Certainly, for Thiselton, against J.W. Montgomery's 'facile', 'naively objectivist' 'Cartesianism', an ahistorical notion of "subject-object conceptualization" cannot be imperialized.[160]

Nevertheless, (2), Thiselton refuses 'to replace' 'one dualism' 'with another': for Thiselton, 'Bultmann' over-stresses 'the subject side of the subject-object relation',[161] mirroring Heidegger's relativism and de-emphasizing the 'historical' 'past'. However, for Thiselton, "correct" *historical-factual* understanding must still accompany "deep" *historical-existential* understanding.[162] If, in Thiselton's estimate, Heidegger and Bultmann over-emphasize 'the possibilities' "afforded" 'for... understanding... human existence',[163] then Thiselton argues that hermeneutics must *unite* a properly historically-embedded subject-object conceptualization *with* "experiential" 'historical' 'understanding'.[164] Thus, B.J. Walsh's charge that Thiselton fails to steer clear of 'Bultmannian', "Heideggerian", "Gadamerian", or later "Wittgensteinian" 'subjectivism' may be rejected.[165]

That is to say, (a), for Thiselton, *with* Heidegger and Bultmann, *historically-embedded* subject-object conceptualization *replaces* a purely Cartesian *ahistorical* subject-object conceptualization. However, (b), for Thiselton, the former must not then be disparaged relative to, but must rather be united with, historical-existential "understanding", *since this approach thereby also more adequately re-historicizes historical-existential "understanding"* - *against* Heidegger's and Bultmann's epistemological "dualism" or "one-sidedness", which threatens to divorce persons from history.[166]

In other words, *with* Continental hermeneutics, Thiselton re-historicizes epistemology by letting *both* historical embeddedness *and* historical difference lend new configurations to *both* subject-object conceptualization *and* self-understanding *so as* to move away from Cartesian objectivism and away from a Kantian notion of

---

[158] Gadamer, H.-G., *Truth and Method* (trans. J. Weinsheimer and D.G. Marshall; London: Sheed & Ward, 1975, 1989), 101.
[159] Wittgenstein, L., *On Certainty* (trans. D. Paul and G.E.M. Anscombe; Oxford: Blackwell, 1969, 2001), 74e.
[160] Thiselton, 'UPC', 94, 95; cf. Thiselton, *2H*, 187-195, 375.
[161] Walsh, 'TC', 231; cf. Thiselton, *2H*, 38.
[162] Thiselton, 'UPC', 94, 95; cf. Thiselton, 'NH', 323-324.
[163] Thiselton, 'UPC', 93-95; cf. Bultmann, R., 'Bultmann Replies to His Critics', in *Kerygma and Myth. A Theological Debate* (ed. H.-W. Bartsch; New York: Harper and Row, 1961), 192.
[164] Thiselton, 'UPC', 91-94.
[165] Walsh, 'TC', 234-235.
[166] Thiselton, 'NH', 323-329.

the transcendental self. Yet, for Thiselton, *against* Continental hermeneutics, this re-historicization must not lead to the dualistic – *and still insufficiently historical* - disparagement of the "'comparative'" aspect relative to the 'existential' aspect of 'understanding'. But how does Thiselton achieve this?[167]

In B.J. Walsh's view, Thiselton *is* "dualistic" here, by which Walsh seems to mean that Thiselton supposedly merely qualifies "objectivism" by stressing "subjectivity", and 'subjectivism' by stressing 'objectivity', to create a 'balance' of 'objective' "testing" and "subjective" 'listening'.[168] However, as we will argue, Thiselton's correcting of multiple epistemological "one-sidednesses" (see below) occurs within a larger complex and unified "whole" that is neither, (a), "dualistic" nor, (b), compatible with Walsh's generalizing call for a move towards a unified hermeneutics in terms of, and/or through the means of, 'scriptural'-textual "'ontology'" or 'appropriate' 'interpretative stance'.[169]

Rather, (a), Thiselton's "whole" is the developing Christo-eschatological framework that unifies and grounds his five major second-stratum hermeneutical critiques. And, (b), Thiselton rejects even a generalized "'ontology'" of *parable* texts (see Chapter 1), let alone of the whole Bible. If even a single parable can engender multiple "appropriate responses", then how much more can the whole Bible?[170]

(3) But precisely *how* does Thiselton's developing Christo-eschatological framework unite "objective" but properly-historical subject-object conceptualization with historical-existential understanding (including self-understanding) whilst avoiding Continental epistemological dualism? How does Thiselton's *theology* address the *philosophical* problem of epistemological dualism?

Well, (a), first of all, and as we have already begun to argue, there can be no doubt that an *a-historical philosophical* framework produces deep problems - *both* for the conception of "subject-object conceptualization" *itself, and* for the conception of the *functioning of* "subject-object conceptualization" during interpretation.

Thus, Thiselton notes that, for Heidegger, 'subject-object' conceptualization became problematic - (i.e. 'a split perspective, in which subject becomes separated from object' developed) - when conceptualization was tied to a (post-) Platonic 'dualism' in which "'Being'", 'as *idea*, was exalted' relative to 'mere appearance'.[171] That is, Heidegger argued that the practice of imposing concepts onto "'Being'" ignores historical and linguistic 'conditionedness', and turns the "critical testing" of truth into a 'circularity' of 'artificial correspondence between' "sets" of 'concepts'. Thiselton, therefore, *aligns with* Heidegger's rejection of the Plato-

---

[167] See, Thiselton, 'NH', 314.

[168] Walsh, 'TC', 231; cf. 232, 234.

[169] Walsh, 'TC', 234; cf. Thiselton, 'NH', 324-325.

[170] Thiselton, 'Parab', 456-458, 468; cf. Walsh, 'TC', 229.

[171] Thiselton, 'NH', 323, cf. 318; cf. Heidegger, M., *An Introduction to Metaphysics* (New York: Yale University Press/Anchor Books, 1959), 89-90. Italics Heidegger's.

Descartes framework and of 'the correspondence theory of truth',[172] which merely amount to finding 'an agreement between "contents of consciousness"', and which miss 'the Being-uncovered... of' an 'entity itself'.[173] Indeed Thiselton asks:

> how do we escape the difficulty that when we try to test the truth of our judgment about a fact with the fact itself, all that we can really do is to compare our first judgment with some second *judgment*, not with "the fact itself" independently of any human judgment? To borrow a simile used by Wittgenstein... it is like buying a second copy of the morning paper in order to test whether what the first copy said was true.[174]

The *solution* to this difficulty, however, (b), does not lie in Heidegger's thinking according to Thiselton: for Thiselton, Heidegger sees the problem alright, but fails to offer an adequate solution. That is, for Thiselton, not only does an *ahistorical-*philosophical framework prove problematic for notions of subject-object conceptualization, but for Thiselton even *Heidegger's* attempt at an *historical-*philosophical framework proves problematic for notions of subject-object conceptualization. As we observed above, Thiselton argues that Heidegger's philosophy still dualistically and illegitimately disparages the role of re-historicized subject-object conceptualization.

Thus, Thiselton complains that Heidegger's thinking – in its outworking in the New Hermeneutic - tends to make '"what is true for me"' 'the' only 'criterion of "what is true"'.[175] In Thiselton's estimate, Heidegger rightly attempts to think more "historically", but Thiselton argues that Heidegger's notion of 'truth' as "eventful" disclosure somehow "passively" allows historical and linguistic conditioning (cf. '"linguisticality"' in the New Hermeneutic) to fatalistically trap thought, when the history and actual experience of *liberation* tell us that 'thinking' *can* release us from a given '"linguisticality"'.[176]

For Thiselton, then, against Heidegger, 'apprehending' is *not* just 'for the sake of being': "opposing" 'thinking to Being', "extending" 'its dominance... over Being', need not *always* be a Western distortion,[177] against Heidegger's "near - Zen Buddhist" 'pseudo-humility' and 'sheer irrationality', and against E. Fuchs' '"ontology"' of '"psychological illusionism"'. Thiselton argues that the New Hermeneutic *wrongly* adopts Heidegger's particular way of critiquing Cartesian subject-object conceptualization whereas, by contrast, Thiselton argues that 'the

---

[172] Thiselton, 'NH', 318-319, 323, 326; cf.: Thiselton, 'KNT', 102-103; Thiselton, 'Parab', 439, 443, 448-449; Thiselton, 'Truth', 894; Heidegger, *AIM*, 132.

[173] Heidegger, *BT*, 261.

[174] Thiselton, 'Truth', 895; cf. Wittgenstein, *PI*, 93-94. Italics Thiselton's.

[175] Thiselton, 'NH', 326.

[176] Thiselton, 'NH', 318-319, 323-324; cf. Heidegger, *BT*, 31, 41-49, 86-90, 427-430, 432-433, 436-455.

[177] Heidegger, M., *Introduction to Metaphysics* (trans. G. Fried and R. Polt; London: Yale University Press, 2000), 195 cf. 209.

New Testament' *rightly* emphasizes 'the [liberating] use of reason or "mind"'.[178]

Somehow, then, for Thiselton, (c), the New Testament encourages and enables a liberating use of the mind that involves "re-historicized" subject-object conceptualization in a way that Heidegger does not. But how does New Testament theology achieve this in Thiselton's thinking?

Well, (i), and in keeping with our argument that Thiselton is not straightforwardly fideistic, Thiselton does not initially appeal to theology at all in criticism of Heidegger, but rather appeals initially to the philosophy of Gadamer. Thiselton writes:

> Tradition may affect understanding either positively or negatively... The later Heidegger convincingly shows that... a given language-tradition may... distort truth... But Gadamer also convincingly shows that tradition may serve as a filter, passing on truth which has stood the test of time [cf. 'effective history']... Both sides must be taken into account... [and, against both thinkers, must qualify one another].[179]

In other words, first, Thiselton believes that Heidegger's attempt to replace an ahistorical philosophy with a historical philosophy was a good start, but that Heidegger *did not go far enough*. For Thiselton, Gadamer's philosophy of history provides a corrective to Heidegger's philosophy of history in that Gadamer's philosophy of history reinstates the capacity of "tradition" to transmit "truth". Thiselton argues that this point remains true even though Heidegger, in Thiselton's framework of thinking, retains a reciprocal corrective role in relation to Gadamer in that Heidegger rightly argues that "tradition" may 'distort truth'.[180]

However, second, Thiselton's point is that subject-object conceptualization – when conceived properly and historically – has a comparative function within interpretation of comparing and contrasting the *contents* of interpretative hypotheses against the received *contents* of transmitted traditions. Against Heidegger, Thiselton argues that the "contents" that re-historicized subject-object conceptualization compares are *not necessarily* the *abstract* "contents of consciousness" but may, rather, be the "contents" of *historical traditions* – whether of ancient texts themselves or of their interpretation - or 'reception' - histories.[181]

(ii) As we shall argue in Chapters 6 and 7, Thiselton's own philosophy of history is, ultimately, neither simply a "Gadamerian" correction of Heidegger's philosophy of history, nor simply a "Heideggerian" correction of Gadamer's philosophy of history, but is rather a multiform modification of Gadamer's philosophy of history that appeals to *several* philosophical traditions. Since, in Thiselton's thinking, the philosophy of history that emerges from this widened

---

[178] Thiselton, 'NH', 318-319, cf. 323-324.

[179] Thiselton, *NTH*, xxii, concs., 1.2, 1.2a-c.

[180] Thiselton, *NTH*, xxii, concs., 1.2, 1.2a-c; cf. Heidegger, *AIM*, 1, 2, 6, 12, 22, 29, 32, 36-42, 45, 46, 51; cf. Gadamer, *TM*, 291-300, cf. 300-307.

[181] See, Thiselton, 'CAP', 138-139.

*philosophical* dialogue also *resonates* with prior New Testament perspectives that are relevant for a philosophy of history, then New Testament *theological* content itself may be adopted as a working framework for the 'metacritical' testing of traditions without resorting to straightforward fideism. For Thiselton, the philosophical problem-solving cogency of received theological content becomes its provisional metacritical warrant.[182]

That is to say, it is by no means necessarily an act of straightforward fideism to argue that the "contents" of received New Testament traditions may provisionally be accorded metacritical status. Admittedly, interpretation must proceed from "within" history, and not from "above" it. But, as Thiselton later argues, Richard Rorty's

> mistake is to confuse the role of historical contingency and contextualism in challenging the status of some absolutized foundationalism outside time, place, and history, with a positive dialectical relation between contextual contingency and ongoing metacritical exploration and testing in the form of an open system. Habermas and Apel explore the possibility of such a system, in which neither contingent life-world nor explanatory system has the last word, but contribute to some interactive whole.[183]

In other words, Thiselton argues that a properly-developed philosophy of history does not dualistically exalt present contextual horizons (whether these are conceived individualistically, as in Heidegger, or corporately, as in Rorty) above or outside of the flow of the larger historical narrative to which they irrevocably belong so as to falsely imperialize present contextual horizons in their contribution to perception. That is, Thiselton argues that, only if present context is *artificially severed from* the larger historical flow does it achieve sole control over perceptions or over the contents of interpretative pre-understandings or (pre-)judgments.[184]

To put it another way, Thiselton believes that something more must be made of Heidegger's point that 'knowing is grounded beforehand in a Being-already-alongside-the-world' than Heidegger in fact makes of it.[185] For Thiselton, Gadamer begins to rectify Heidegger's unsuccessful attempt to avoid anthropocentricity when Gadamer argues that 'history does not belong to us; we belong to it'. For Gadamer, 'self-reflection and autobiography... are not primary and are... not an adequate basis for the hermeneutical problem, because through them history is made private once more'. Even if, in Thiselton's estimate, Gadamer overpresses this argument (see Chapter 6), Thiselton's point is that in *properly* historical thinking, human selves are *"de-centered"* relative to larger – if as yet incomplete - historical 'wholes'.[186]

---

[182] On metacriticism and criticism, cf. Thiselton, *NH*, 315-318.
[183] Thiselton, *NH*, 401.
[184] See, Thiselton, *IGPS*, 160, 163.
[185] Heidegger, *BT*, 88.
[186] Gadamer, *TM*, 276; cf. Thiselton, *IGPS*, e.g. 159-163.

And it is but an extension of this very point to argue that *incomplete* historical "wholes" – traditions say - must *necessarily* be de-centered – if only provisionally – relative to anticipations of *complete* historical "wholes" – anticipations that are emergent as "open systems" from within, or from comparisons between, those traditions themselves. That such anticipations *tend to emerge from within theological traditions* – notably those of the New Testament – only adds to the cogency of those theological traditions in relation to metacriticism.

We shall return to these issues in Chapters 6 and 7.

For now, (d), we may suggest that Thiselton's developing Christo-eschatological framework does indeed unite "objective" but properly historical subject-object conceptualization and historical-existential understanding whilst avoiding Continental epistemological dualism, and does so in a way that is consistent with a developed philosophy of history that we shall expound more fully in Chapter 6.

That is, for Thiselton, to embed subject-object conceptualization within history properly is to assign it comparative roles *both* in *critically* comparing the "contents" of interpretative hypotheses with those of received traditions *and* in *metacritically* comparing aspects of the "contents" of received traditions with "contents" pertaining to provisional, "open", anticipative metacritical systems emergent from within, or from comparisons between, those received traditions themselves. In both cases, the "contents" compared are historical, and not merely the abstract "contents of consciousness".

In Thiselton's reading of Heidegger, however, Heidegger's disparagement of tradition's capacity to transmit "truth" actually hinders the possibility of critical and metacritical testing. That is, Thiselton argues that Heidegger, in his setting of critical comparative testing in opposition to received traditions, fails fully to overcome the abstraction of critical testing *itself* that he (i.e. Heidegger) rightly perceives as being a problem within the Plato-Descartes framework. In Thiselton's view one has to ask: however rightly Heidegger approaches "conceptualization" *itself*, what *role is left* for *any* notion of "subject-object conceptualization" in Heidegger's hermeneutics?

To repeat the point in a different way, it is not so much Heidegger's *notion* of "subject-object conceptualization" that bothers Thiselton (for Heidegger at least *seeks* to make this notion properly 'historical'). What bothers Thiselton is the *lack of potential operative application of re-historicized "subject-object conceptualization" (in critical and metacritical testing)* that accompanies Heidegger's marginalization of those spheres in which comparative rationality operates. Again, Thiselton seems to ask: what *role is left* for re-historicized "subject-object conceptualization" to play or perform in Heidegger's approach to hermeneutics, regardless of how rightly Heidegger understands "conceptualization" *itself*?

At this point, (4), a short excursion is perhaps worthwhile in order to attempt to check whether or not Thiselton's reading of Heidegger is correct. We are aware that Roger Scruton writes of Heidegger's *'Being and Time'* that it 'is formidably difficult... I... have read no commentator who even begins to make sense of it'.[187] Thus, it is with some tentativeness that we present our reading of a small part of it here.

Of note, though, is the fact that Heidegger does indeed retain a notion of "conceptualizing" *per se*, but not that of the Western philosophical tradition which fails to presuppose an adequate phenomenological analytic of Dasein. Heidegger rejects a pre-phenomenological reduction of Dasein to a "subject" and "entities" to "objects" that ignores concrete "temporality" and "relationality".

Thus, for Heidegger, "conceptualization" 'is grounded beforehand in a Being-already-alongside-the-world'. Dasein must "hold" 'back... from any kind of producing [or] manipulating' and "put" 'itself into... the mode of just tarrying alongside' if it is to 'encounter entities... purely in the *way they look*'. Yet, for Heidegger, 'looking explicitly at what we encounter is possible' through 'dwelling autonomously alongside entities within-the-world' such that 'the *perception* of the present-at-hand is consummated' as 'an act of *making determinate*' 'expressed in propositions'.[188]

Thus, for Heidegger, "conceptualization" and "assertion" *can* belong to an authentic mode of knowing and describing that presupposes historical difference and relationality. "Knowing-persons" are not artificially abstracted from historical reality but are already embedded in history. Yet they may still perceive that which is "other". In "knowing", 'Dasein... does not somehow first get out of an inner sphere in which it has been proximally encapsulated, but... is always "outside" alongside' 'already discovered' 'entities'.[189]

Thus, for Heidegger, it is problematic 'to start with spatiality' – i.e. with a scenario in which "subject-object conceptualization" seeks to cross space, as in 'Descartes' ontology of the "world"'. Rather, for Heidegger, "conceptualization" operates within 'the "around"... constitutive for the environment' which is 'not... primarily "spatial"'. Of course, Heidegger readily admits that 'spatial character... incontestably belongs to any environment'. But, for Heidegger, this reality 'can be clarified only in terms of the structure of worldhood'. For Heidegger, "space" does not absolutely separate historical realities but is part of a world in which "knowing" links already-related historical realities.[190]

Initially, admittedly, Heidegger acknowledges that such "knowing" is 'not... bare conceptual cognition', but "manipulative" and instrumentalizing 'concern'. Thus, for Heidegger, 'achieving... phenomenological access to' encountered 'entities' 'consists... in [first] thrusting aside our interpretative tendencies'. 'To lay bare what is just present-at-hand... cognition must first penetrate *beyond* what is

---

[187] Cited in, Collins, J. and H. Selina, *Introducing Heidegger* (ed. R. Appignanesi; New York, NY.: Totem Books, 1999), 7. Italics Scruton's.
[188] Heidegger, *BT*, 88-89; cf., e.g., Thiselton, 'HB', 78. Italics Heidegger's.
[189] Heidegger, *BT*, 89.
[190] Heidegger, *BT*, 94-95.

ready-to-hand in our concern', our *'circumspection'*.[191]

Thus, for Heidegger, "conceptualization" is de-centered relative to "circumspection", and yet Heidegger still believes that 'observation... is just as primordial as... action'. For Heidegger, 'theoretical behavior is just looking, without circumspection'. Nevertheless, for Heidegger, 'cognition' is 'a *founded* mode of Being-in-the-world' that has 'ontological meaning'. Further, for Heidegger, 'the concept of Being' must be 'conceptually grasped' and, for Heidegger, science genuinely advances through revising 'its basic concepts'. Heidegger's notion of *'care'* (see Chapter 6) 'is' also 'an ontological structural concept'.[192]

This reading of Heidegger suggests that Thiselton remains too vague when he speaks simply of reinstating 'subject-object thinking in hermeneutics' as a *criticism* of Heidegger.[193] If Heidegger rejects only an *ahistorical* notion of "subject-object conceptualization", then Thiselton too rejects such a notion. If Heidegger *retains* a *historical* notion of "subject-object conceptualization", then how can Thiselton criticize Heidegger for *disparaging* such a notion?

Indeed, Thiselton acknowledges Heidegger's description of his own "conceptuality" and Thiselton acknowledges the consistency of Heidegger's early thought with a contemporary scientific paradigm, implying that Heidegger retains some form of "conceptualization" (see Chapter 7).[194] Thus, as already argued, it can only be with respect to the *roles played* by re-historicized "subject-object conceptualization" within *certain spheres of operation* that Thiselton means to criticize Heidegger. That this has to be *deduced* from Thiselton's writings, however, warrants a call for Thiselton to be more specific when he speaks of Heidegger's disparagement of "subject-object conceptualization".[195]

Moreover, Thiselton may go slightly too far regarding Heidegger's negative assessment of the capacity of 'tradition' to transmit truth. For Heidegger, the 'destruction' of Western metaphysics does not merely have 'the negative sense of shaking off the ontological tradition', but also "stakes" 'out the positive possibilities of that tradition'.[196]

Nevertheless, we cannot but agree with what Thiselton affirms: hermeneutics demands a properly historical overhaul of the Cartesian notion of subject-object conceptualization from the perspective of a properly developed philosophy of history. The latter, however, does not merely historically redefine or reconfigure the *notion* of subject-object conceptualization as in Heidegger. But rather, through its reinstatement of theological tradition, a properly developed philosophy of history *also* grounds, redefines and expands the *roles or spheres of operation of* re-

---

[191] Heidegger, *BT*, 95-96; cf. 101, cf. 98. Italics Heidegger's.

[192] Heidegger, *BT*, 99; 101; 25, 26; 29; 83-84. Italics Heidegger's.

[193] Thiselton, *2H*, 441.

[194] Thiselton, *2H*, 145, cf.: 155, 188, 194-196, 198-201, 203, 353.

[195] Thiselton, *2H*, 441.

[196] Heidegger, *BT*, 44; cf. Thiselton, *NTH*, xxii.

historicized subject-object conceptualization in criticism and metacriticism such that, against Heidegger, the comparative dimension is not disparaged relative to the historical-existential or historical-experiential dimension of "understanding" (cf. "self-understanding").

Moving on, (5), then this same area of discussion brings us into conflict with P.R. Keifert's response to Thiselton's reading of *Gadamer*. Keifert writes:

> Thiselton critiques Heidegger's emphasis on world-hood to the exclusion of subject-object thinking... However, in his critique of Gadamer, he transposes too much of this failing... onto Gadamer's concept of the fusion of horizons. The possibility for the historical and linguistic distanciation of the text in Gadamer's thought is far more prevalent than Thiselton suggests.[197]

Here, first, Keifert rightly notes Thiselton's critique of Heidegger's failure to stress both "worldhood" (see Chapter 6) and (re-historicized) "subject-object thinking" equally.[198] However, second, we must reject Keifert's view that Thiselton neglects Gadamer's notion of "distancing".[199] Rather, Thiselton asks how 'Gadamer', *given* his stress on '"distancing"', can completely reject 'the Cartesian model' 'in his third section' of *Truth and Method:* can the "other" really "assert" 'itself in its own separate validity' if we are *completely* "detaching" 'ourselves from the Cartesian basis of modern science'?[200]

Of course Thiselton argues, with 'Dilthey' and 'Gadamer', that 'the Cartesian' '"scientific method" of classification and generalization' *is* very limited in its scope, especially 'in the humanities'. Thiselton argues that Gadamer rightly highlights a broader notion of "rationality" in the history of Western philosophy that accounts for the roles of 'history', 'real-life experience', creative 'wit or ridicule', 'common sense', and 'intuition'.[201] Such "rationality" makes 'judgments' by "entering" and eventfully "experiencing" a 'situation', and by drawing on past 'experiences of life'. Such "rationality" operates 'within history' and in a manner that is conditioned by the unconscious 'pre-judgments' of 'tradition'. Such 'pre-judgments' are "filtered" through '"effective history"' (later translated as "history of effects"') and '"more"' "fundamentally" affect interpretation than 'conscious' '"judgments"' initially,[202] being 'justified prejudices productive of knowledge'.[203]

---

[197] Keifert, P.R., 'Review of A.C. Thiselton's *The Two Horizons*', *WW* 1 (Fall 1981), 408-409; cf. Gadamer, *TM*, 291-300.

[198] Thiselton, *2H*, 187-191; cf. Heidegger, *BT*, 86-90.

[199] Keifert, 'R *2H*', 408-409; contrast, Thiselton, 'UPC', 87-100; cf.: Thiselton, 'NH', 308-333; Gadamer, *TM*, 291-300.

[200] Thiselton, 'UPC', 91, 93, 94; cf.: Thiselton, 'NH', 317; cf. 320; Thiselton, *2H*, 306-308; Gadamer, *TM*, 299, 461.

[201] Thiselton, 'UPC', 91-94; cf.: Thiselton, *NH*, 318, 325-330.

[202] Thiselton, 'UPC', 91-93; cf. 95; cf.: Thiselton, 'NH', 317; cf. 323; Thiselton, *NH*, 318, 325-330; Thiselton, *2H*, 305-307; Gadamer, *TM*, 19-30, cf. 269-285, 300-307.

[203] Gadamer, *TM*, 279.

Thus, for Gadamer and Thiselton, 'understanding a work of *art*' involves '"modes of experience in which truth comes to light"' in 'real-life'. Such 'understanding... is... *progressive*', remaining '"incomplete"', even over centuries, and 'transcends... the conscious intentions of the artist'; - the 'literary' '"classic is... never fully understood"'. Such 'understanding' enters the '"world"' of an artwork, and 'the interpreter' is 'gripped *by* it' (i.e. by the '"world"' of the artwork), 'as' *its* 'object'. Similarly, 'the seriousness', 'purpose', and 'presuppositions of' 'a *game*' - not 'the conscious thoughts of' the 'players or spectators' – 'create the reality' or '"world"' that '"the player"' '"stands in"' and "experiences".[204] Thus, for Gadamer and Thiselton, 'play fulfils its purpose only if the player loses himself in play'.[205]

That is, in Thiselton's view, 'Heidegger', 'Gadamer', and 'the New Hermeneutic' rightly move beyond Cartesian 'knowledge' towards "deeper", "creative", "experiential", "historically-located" 'understanding'. And, in Thiselton's estimate, 'Gadamer' rightly highlights the need for a new "historical" 'paradigm' for 'rationality', 'practical knowledge', or '*phronesis*'.[206]

However, contrary to Keifert, Thiselton's *additional* stress on Gadamer's notion of '"distancing"' (i.e. on highlighting the historical particularity of textual horizons relative to that of reader horizons – see Chapter 5) demonstrates Thiselton's alignment with Gadamer's emphasis on historical "otherness", or 'strangeness'. Thus, Thiselton follows Gadamer's and the later Wittgenstein's attacks on 'Enlightenment' 'rationalist method' which seeks immediate interpretative answers that potentially conform to a system of foreclosed *a priori* categories.[207] For Gadamer, the later Wittgenstein and Thiselton, there is neither an 'antithesis between tradition and historical research'[208] nor '*a* philosophical method', but rather 'methods, like different therapies', that pertain to understanding historical *difference.*[209]

Conversely, it is again in the context of the issue of the 'metacritical' testing of traditions that Thiselton *criticizes* Gadamer, who caricatures 'the... prophet' as a

---

[204] Thiselton, 'UPC', 91-92; cf.: Gadamer, *TM*, 101-169; Gadamer, H.-G., 'Aesthetics and Hermeneutics', in *Philosophical Hermeneutics* (H.-G. Gadamer; ed. D.E. Linge; London: University of California Press, 1976), 98; Gadamer, H.-G., 'The Philosophical Foundations of the Twentieth Century', in *Philosophical Hermeneutics* (H.-G. Gadamer; ed. D.E. Linge; London: University of California Press, 1976), 125. Italics ours on 'art' and 'game', Thiselton's on 'progressive' and 'by'.
[205] Gadamer, *TM*, 102. Capitalization on 'Play' is Gadamer's.
[206] Thiselton, 'NH', 317, cf. 323; cf.: Thiselton, *NH*, 315, 318, 325-330; Heidegger, *BT*, 182-195; Gadamer, *TM*, 21, 101-169. Italics ours on 'phronesis'.
[207] Keifert, 'R 2H', 408-409; cf. Thiselton, 'NH', 317; cf.: Thiselton, 'TY', 1560-1561; Thiselton, *2H*, 294-309; Thiselton, 'UPC', 91-92; Wittgenstein, *PI*, 48-56; Gadamer, *TM*, 4-5, 295, 348-349.
[208] Gadamer, *TM*, 282.
[209] Wittgenstein, *PI*, 51e. Italics in speech-marks Wittgenstein's.

'Cassandra... preacher, or... know-it-all'.²¹⁰ To repeat our quotation from earlier, Thiselton writes:

> Tradition may affect understanding either positively or negatively... The later Heidegger convincingly shows that... a given language-tradition may... distort truth... But Gadamer also convincingly shows that tradition may serve as a filter, passing on truth which has stood the test of time [cf. 'effective history']... Both sides must be taken into account... [and, against both thinkers, qualify one another].²¹¹

Thus, in Thiselton's view, Gadamer's problem is more his failure to reinstate the grounds for the *role* of a properly-(re-)historicized subject-object conceptualization in relation to the *metacritique* of traditions than, contrary to Keifert, in relation to the *'critical'* distanciation of historical "otherness". Further, for Thiselton, neither of these comparative roles is *utterly* distinct from Cartesianism exhaustively and without remainder – even though both roles are now properly-rehistoricized in Thiselton's thinking.²¹²

That is – and placing Thiselton's second-period work in the larger diachronic context of his later work - for Thiselton, subject-object conceptualization (properly rehistoricized) is to be hermeneutically operative in at least three *historical* spheres: *'metacritical* evaluation', *'metacritical'* 'explanation', and *'critical'* "distancing" – where for Thiselton all three of these spheres/operations involve comparative 'testing'. In Heidegger, according to Thiselton, all three spheres are threatened. In Gadamer, according to Thiselton, 'critical' testing is partly safeguarded in Gadamer's notion of "distancing"; but Thiselton argues that metacritical evaluation and explanation are under threat in Gadamer's approach (even if, as we shall see in Chapter 7 (after E.A. Dunn), Gadamer's notions of 'dialogue' and 'tradition' respectively remain valuable for Thiselton in this context of discussion). In Thiselton's thinking, then, we are not at all dealing with an exhaustive rejection of Cartesian subject-object conceptualization (Thiselton asks questions of Gadamer in relation to this point), but rather with its hermeneutical sublation (see Chapter 7) into a historical key and into historical modes of operation.²¹³

In other words, stepping back, we are arguing that in order to reinstate a properly re-historicized subject-object conceptualization at what he calls 'the metacritical level', Thiselton invokes theology. Thus, for Thiselton, metacritical *evaluation* is, ultimately, the *potentially liberating comparative re-historicized subject-object evaluation or testing of traditions against transcendent 'criteria' with content*, where these 'criteria' are theological *and* historical. And, for Thiselton, metacritical *explanation* is, ultimately, the *comparative re-historicized subject-object explanation of how the historical*

---

²¹⁰ Gadamer, *TM*, xxxviii; cf. Thiselton, *NH*, 315-318.

²¹¹ Thiselton, *NTH*, xxii, concs. 1.2, 1.2a-c.

²¹² Thiselton, *NH*, 315-318; cf. Keifert, *'R 2H'*, 408-409. Italics in speech-marks Thiselton's, others ours.

²¹³ Thiselton, *NH*, 316, 338, 344; cf. Thiselton, *2H*, 16. Italics ours, except on the one phrase, *'metacritical* evaluation', where they are Thiselton's.

*"parts" relate to each other within eschatological anticipations of the historical "whole".* Conversely, Heidegger's and Gadamer's epistemologically dualistic philosophies fail to provide "'transcendent'" 'criteria' in Thiselton's estimate:[214] for Heidegger, 'the way of Being of the ideal, Objectivity… are opaque';[215] for Gadamer, 'the hermeneutic consciousness' is not 'eschatological'.[216]

For Thiselton, then, Continental hermeneutics rightly criticizes Cartesianism and, in Heidegger and Gadamer, rightly re-establishes a "historicized" "historically-embedded" notion of subject-object conceptualization at the level of its role in the comparative *critique* of historical difference relative to traditions (though Heidegger potentially marginalizes even this role in practice). Yet, Thiselton argues that Heidegger and Gadamer fail to provide a replacement "philosophical subtext" or framework of "metacriteria" that could re-ground a "re-historicized" "re-embedded" notion of subject-object conceptualization in relation to its roles in evaluative and explanatory *metacritiques* of traditions. Further, Thiselton argues that Heidegger and Bultmann fail to properly value the "public criteria" of traditions where, in Thiselton's view, these thinkers thus potentially undermine even *critical* testing relative to traditions.[217]

Thus, for Thiselton, theological exploration is warranted in order to resolve this problematic situation – in order to find provisional anticipative transcendent metacriteria against which traditions can be evaluated and explained and *hence* in order to access and mark out *valued* public criteria against which postulated historical facts, concepts, or interpretations can be meaningfully evaluated or explained or comparatively tested in their provisionality – not least in the context of discussions to do with socio-critical liberation. Of course, such a theological exploration could only retain philosophical credibility if its findings *also* dialogically resonated with philosophical concerns *and/or* provided credible solutions to philosophical problems. This point brings Thiselton back to Pannenberg.

*3. Towards a Warranted Theological Solution: Pannenberg's Eschatological Epistemology*

Broadly, then, we may affirm Thiselton's appeal to a theological framework so as to address the problem of the metacriticism of traditions - a problem left unaddressed by Heidegger and Gadamer. Thiselton appeals to Pannenberg's eschatological epistemology in this context - although, for Thiselton, whilst Pannenberg 'invites travel in the right direction', Pannenberg's early thought does not provide 'a final or definitive solution' in this context. Thiselton is not *only*

---

[214] Thiselton, *NH*, 25-26, 315-318, 383, 391, 440, 332; cf.: Thiselton, 'UPC', 91, 94; Gadamer, *TM*, 19-30, 291-307; Gadamer, 'PF', 119; Thiselton, *NH*, 25, 315-318. Thiselton's italics on *'criteria'*, others ours.

[215] Heidegger, *BT*, 198.

[216] Gadamer, *TM*, xxxviii.

[217] See, Thiselton, *2H*, 39; cf. Chapter 4.

'Pannenbergian'.[218]

Nevertheless, (1), following Pannenberg, Thiselton relates *'truth'* to 'the truth of God',[219] 'historical' "contingencies", human 'subjectivity', 'revelation' or manifestation, "appropriation",[220] and to divine *truth-claims and "verdicts"* (cf. Chapters 6 and 7 regarding metacritical *evaluation*).[221] *With* Continental hermeneutics' rejection of 'Platonic' idealism, Pannenberg and Thiselton argue that 'the truth of God' is thereby neither 'Platonic', nor '"already existing... as a finished product"' divorced from 'history', nor like the 'logical necessity' 'of geometrical theorems', nor 'simply an object of assent', nor like a '"thing... presently at hand"'. Similarly, Pannenberg and Thiselton argue that 'biblical truth' is neither 'detached from ordinary' 'life' like 'Plato's timeless ideas',[222] nor mere 'analytical definition', nor mere local *'salvation-history'*, nor merely "religious" 'truth'.[223] *Against* strands in Continental hermeneutics, however, Pannenberg and Thiselton argue that '"the unity"' of 'biblical' and historical 'truth' excludes 'Neo-Kantian' 'fact'-'value' or "event-proposition" dichotomies (where this exclusion facilitates *explanatory* metacriticism – see Chapters 6 and 7).[224]

(2) Following Pannenberg, and *with* Continental hermeneutics, Thiselton advocates *'"historical reason"'*:[225] – i.e. 'beginning "from below" with historical inquiry'[226] '"and the historicality of knowing"'. For Pannenberg and Thiselton, "historical" 'rationality' includes 'critical... judgment' relating to the past and present. *Against* some strands in Continental hermeneutics, however, Pannenberg and Thiselton argue that 'critical... judgment' *potentially involves re-historicized subject-object conceptualization relative to trans-temporal and trans-contextual public criteria* (cf. Chapters 6 and 7 regarding metacritical *explanation*). For Thiselton, following Pannenberg, historical rationality also involves ever-widening 'dialogue' and 'open-ended' "creative" 'imagination', relating to the 'future' and to "anticipations" of 'history as a whole'; and, in addition, for Pannenberg and Thiselton, historical rationality involves 'awareness of mystery', especially in relation to 'God'.[227]

*With* Continental hermeneutics, Pannenberg and Thiselton argue that '"reason"' is neither 'Platonic', nor a matter of 'preconceived categories and questions' into which Christianity must be fitted,[228] nor merely 'theoretical' 'rationalism', nor '"Protestant"' "orthodox" '"deductive reasoning"', 'nor the

---

[218] Thiselton, 'TNI', 11; cf. Palmer, 'Scope', 226.
[219] Thiselton, 'Par', 48. Italics ours.
[220] Thiselton, 'Par', 49-50; cf. Thiselton, 'TNI', 11.
[221] Thiselton, 'Par', 48, cf. 49-52. Italics ours.
[222] Thiselton, 'TNI', 11.
[223] cf.: Thiselton, 'Par', 48-50. Italics Thiselton's.
[224] Thiselton, 'TNI', 11.
[225] Thiselton, 'TNI', 11. Italics ours.
[226] Thiselton, 'H-O', 8.
[227] Thiselton, 'H-O', 8; cf.: Thiselton, 'TNI', 11; Thiselton, 'Par', 48-49.
[228] Thiselton, 'TNI', 11.

speculative reason of idealism'.²²⁹ *Against* strands in Continental hermeneutics, however, Pannenberg and Thiselton argue that a properly-unified notion of historical rationality is inconsistent with 'Neo-Kantian' historical dualism. Theologically speaking, Pannenberg and Thiselton argue that 'Neo-Kantian' historical dualism also fails to resonate with the '"unity"' of God's creation.²³⁰

(3) For Thiselton, following Pannenberg, and aligning *with* a Continental hermeneutical *critique of* positivism, *historical knowledge* of past and present historical "continuities" and particularities extends beyond "analogy" with present 'experience', and 'is provisional on future confirmation'.²³¹ *Against* strands in Continental hermeneutics, Pannenberg and Thiselton argue that the accessibility and pastness of the past (cf. Chapters 6 and 7 regarding the *explanatory* metacritical dimension) and the Christological anticipation of 'history as a whole' (cf. Chapters 6 and 7 regarding both *evaluative* and *explanatory* metacritical dimensions) preclude complete relativism or complete context-relativity²³² – though, for Pannenberg and Thiselton, historical relativity, '"subjectivity"', and 'human "historicity"' retain a place.²³³ For Thiselton, after Pannenberg, 'knowledge is' '"provisionally"' warranted not by 'logical necessity' but by *evaluations of truth-claims or verdicts* against as broad as possible a historical 'dialogue'²³⁴ – a dialogue that includes dialogues with and within comparative religion.²³⁵ For Thiselton, warrant also includes performative endorsement; and, for Thiselton, provisionally warranted claims become *criteria* against which relatively unwarranted claims are tested.²³⁶

(4) For Thiselton, following Pannenberg, *'faith'* (in one of its senses, and *against* strands in Continental hermeneutics), is structured like 'knowledge' in that 'faith' (in one of its senses) unites '"historical knowledge"' of the past, 'rational justification' or warrant, assent to cognitive content, 'trust' in relation to the present and future, *as well as* embodying (*with* Continental hermeneutics) future-oriented active commitment and 'decision'.²³⁷ *With* Continental critiques of objectivism, Pannenberg and Thiselton argue that 'faith' is not 'belief in' the 'absurd' justified by '"authoritarian"' or irrational "appeals" 'to the Holy Spirit';²³⁸ nor, is it '"absolutely certain"' 'belief',²³⁹ nor '"authoritarian"' 'belief in' a '"'self-authenticating' Word"'. In Thiselton's view, after Pannenberg, Barth makes '"a desperate evasion"' 'of Feuerbach's critique of religion': 'Christian' truth relates 'to

---

²²⁹ Thiselton, 'H-O', 8.
²³⁰ Thiselton, 'TNI', 11; cf. Thiselton, 'H-O', 8.
²³¹ Thiselton, 'H-O', 8.
²³² Thiselton, 'Par', 48-50; cf. Thiselton, 'H-O', 8.
²³³ Thiselton, 'TNI', 11.
²³⁴ Thiselton, 'TNI', 11; cf.: Thiselton, 'H-O', 8.
²³⁵ Thiselton, 'TNI', 11.
²³⁶ Thiselton, 'TNI', 11; cf.: Thiselton, 'H-O', 8.
²³⁷ Thiselton, 'Exc', 12; cf. Thiselton, 'TNI', 11; cf. Thiselton, 'H-O', 8. Italics ours.
²³⁸ Thiselton, 'Exc', 12; cf. Thiselton, 'H-O', 8; cf. Thiselton, 'TNI', 11.
²³⁹ Thiselton, 'Exc', 12.

all truth', 'including philosophy and the sciences', because '"God"... is the ground of all truth' as is shown by '"the abundance of analogies between biblical and non-biblical concepts of God"' (see Chapter 7).[240] *Contrary to* 'Kierkegaard' and Bultmann, Pannenberg and Thiselton argue that 'faith' is not 'sheer' 'decision' divorced from 'knowledge' and warrant.[241]

That is, (5), Thiselton in effect argues that an appeal to theology is warranted in order to attempt to address the Continental philosophical problems of, (a), dualisms associated with Neo-Kantianism, (b), a lack of metacriteria, and hence of, (c), *both* a lack of adequate tradition-criticism *and* a lack of critical testing or explanation of interpretative hypotheses, texts, events (and so on) relative to public criteria. Pannenberg's theology provides Thiselton with the potential evaluative metacriteria of revealed theological content whilst also embracing the explanatory frames of reference provided by accessible – if 'anticipatory' and provisional - historical trans-temporal "continuities" grounded '"in the unity"' of created '"history"'.[242]

In short, Thiselton's theology *resonates with philosophical criteria, yet also critiques philosophy and solves philosophical problems*. Thiselton's thinking, therefore, is hardly a case of straightforward '"fideism"'.[243]

*4. Philosophical Problem: The Spell of Kierkegaard's One-Sided Notion of Truth*

Moving on, then Thiselton highlights a second major problem in Continental philosophy that, in his view, provides a further arena in which theology proves its relevance to the epistemological discussion. That is, for Thiselton, Kierkegaard's legacy constitutes a "controlling picture" that "bewitches" subsequent broadly 'existentialist' approaches to truth.[244]

Admittedly, (1), Thiselton argues that Kierkegaard rightly reinstated two dimensions of 'truth' missing from 'the Danish Church of his day'.[245] Thus, (a), with Kierkegaard, Thiselton agrees that 'truth' relates to the self-involving "transformation" of the historical 'life' and 'subjectivity' of 'the individual' – (an emphasis also intermittently missing from Anglicanism in Thiselton's estimate).[246] Thiselton argues that this emphasis corrects: (i) Descartes' "artificial" abstraction of subjects from 'concrete' history and 'relationships' - an abstraction which reduces subjects to "reason"; (ii) Kant's 'generalizing', abstract, *a priori*, and

---

[240] Thiselton, 'H-O', 8; cf.: Thiselton, 'Exc', 12; Thiselton, 'TNI', 11.
[241] Thiselton, 'TNI', 11; cf.: Thiselton, 'Par', 49; Thiselton, 'H-O', 8; Thiselton, 'Exc', 12.
[242] Thiselton, 'Par', 49; cf.: Thiselton, 'H-O', 8; Thiselton, 'TNI', 11.
[243] Contradicting, Walsh, 'TC', 235.
[244] Thiselton, 'KNT', 85-107; cf. Thiselton, *2H*, 432; cf. Thiselton, 'UPC', 89.
[245] Thiselton, 'KNT', 89, 91, cf. 95, 101, 103.
[246] Thiselton, 'KNT', 103-105.

ahistorical 'universal' 'moral' 'law' and,[247] to an extent, (iii), 'Hegel's thought'.[248] (b) In Thiselton's view, 'Kierkegaard' rightly stressed the "'dialectical'" self-involving "indirect" manner in which 'truth' is often best 'communicated' – a mode of "communication" that may also be found in Jesus' Parables.[249]

Nevertheless, (2), Thiselton finds six deficiencies in Kierkegaard's approach to truth. Thus Thiselton argues, (a), that Kierkegaard's approach to truth, if separated from its appeal to theology, fails 'as a self-contained' philosophical epistemology,[250] and thus slides into 'skepticism' and 'relativism' in the thinking of 'Nietzsche', 'Heidegger', 'Jaspers', 'Sartre', and of 'the... new morality' of 'radical theology'.[251] (b) Thiselton argues that Kierkegaard is "individualistic" and that he neglects 'the community' and the dimension of corporate knowledge.[252] (c) Thiselton argues that Kierkegaard neglects 'rationality' and 'logical coherence' in relation to 'faith' and 'truth'-*'assessment'*.[253] (d) Thiselton argues that Kierkegaard neglects 'truth' as 'contingent historical events' because he (i.e. Kierkegaard) follows 'Lessing's' separation of 'reason' and 'the eternal' "'from the historical'".[254] Thus, Thiselton argues that Kierkegaard neglects modes of "'direct communication'", notably 'historical' report.[255]

(e) Thiselton argues, against Kierkegaard, that Christian truth involves 'both' 'rational' 'intellectual' "beliefs" with cognitive 'content' and 'practical response'. It is not either/or, but both/and.[256] (f) In Thiselton's estimate, Kierkegaard was too negative about 'Hegel's' 'historical' 'rationalism', which improved on 'earlier' "rationalisms".[257] The background here is Thiselton's juxtaposition of Pannenberg's qualified appropriation of Hegel's work with Pannenberg's criticism of Kierkegaard's 'anti-rational' 'individualism' and with Pannenberg's affirmation of some of Kierkegaard's other insights.[258] Through appeal to 'Pannenberg', therefore, Thiselton holds qualified appeals to 'Hegel' and to 'Kierkegaard' *together*.[259]

Having said this, (3), Thiselton still prefers Kierkegaard's approach to the

---

[247] Thiselton, 'KNT', 91, 93-95; cf.: Thiselton, 'Parab', 439, cf. 443, 448-449; Thiselton, *2H*, 208-217.
[248] Thiselton, 'KNT', 96-97.
[249] Thiselton, 'KNT', 98-99, cf. 103, 104.
[250] Thiselton, 'KNT', 91, cf. 100-102.
[251] Thiselton, 'KNT', 86, 90-92, 100-103.
[252] Thiselton, 'KNT', 90-91, cf. 104.
[253] Thiselton, 'KNT', 104, 105. Italics Thiselton's.
[254] Thiselton, 'KNT', 104, 105.
[255] Thiselton, 'KNT', 99, cf. 101.
[256] Thiselton, 'KNT', 95.
[257] Thiselton, 'KNT', 96-97.
[258] Thiselton, 'M&M', 8; cf. Thiselton, A.C., 'A Book Set Apart from the Ordinary Run of Books: Review of T.F. Torrance's *Theological Science*', *CEN* 12 Dec. (1969), 13.
[259] See, Thiselton, 'BSA', 13; cf. Thiselton, 'IA', 9; cf. Thiselton, 'TNI', 11.

broadly secular 'existentialism' of 'Nietzsche', 'Jaspers', 'Sartre', 'Camus' and 'Heidegger' (again, Thiselton knows Heidegger is not strictly-speaking an existentialist). Thus, (a), following 'Karl Barth', Thiselton argues that these thinkers misappropriate Kierkegaard's work. Thus, Thiselton observes that, for Kierkegaard, *'God'* calls 'Abraham' to *sacrifice* his 'hope' through a "paradoxical" 'decision to *obey*' that "contradicts" 'external' 'ethical' criteria. Yet, Thiselton observes that, for the 'secular' "existentialists", *the self* decides to *actualize* its "hope" in an 'egocentric' decision to *rebel* that contradicts 'external' 'ethical' 'criteria'.[260]

(b) Thiselton argues that 'Nietzsche', 'Jaspers', and 'Sartre' are "self-contradictory", and cites 'the… "paradox of skepticism"': if 'truth' is only *my* 'truth', and 'relativism' only *my* 'relativism', then 'the universal' claim that "all persons cannot know truly" cannot be made.[261] (c) We have already noted Thiselton's agreement with Heidegger's rejection of a 'correspondence theory of truth' and,[262] conversely, we have also already noted Thiselton's criticism of the "fatalistic" 'passivity' of Heidegger's notion of 'truth' – a notion according to which 'truth' is, predominantly, "eventful" disclosure. Thus, Thiselton argues that secular "existentialisms" - under Kierkegaard's "spell" - only *augment* Kierkegaard's problems in relation to "truth".[263]

Conversely, (4), Thiselton argues that 'Bultmann' and 'post-Bultmannian' "theological existentialisms" only *perpetuate* the strengths and weaknesses of Kierkegaard's approach (see above),[264] whereas Thiselton also argues that 'the… New Morality' of H.A. Williams and of J.A.T. Robinson *perpetuates* the problems of 'secular existentialism'. Thus, Thiselton observes that Williams views 'prostitution' as a potentially 'daring' 'faith'-'venture'. But Thiselton argues that Williams thereby reduces Kierkegaard's 'subjectivity' to an 'egocentric' subjectivism of doing 'what' seems 'true' '"for me"'. That is, Thiselton argues that Williams falsely makes the human subject the arbiter of truth.[265]

Hence, (5), Thiselton rejects 'secular' and theological 'existentialist' appropriations of Kierkegaard's epistemology as 'one-sided', and instead Thiselton sublates and holds Kierkegaard's and Hegel's positive insights together within a framework that appeals to Pannenberg. Thiselton argues that 'truth is multiform' and dependent upon its home '"forms of life"'; such 'forms of life include rationality, community… history… daily life… individual… subjectivity, and…

---

[260] Thiselton, 'KNT', 86-87, 90-92, 100-101; cf. Keifert, 'R *2H*', 408. Italics ours.

[261] Thiselton, 'KNT', 100, 101; cf. Thiselton, *NH*, 127.

[262] Thiselton, 'KNT',102-103; cf.: Thiselton, 'Parab', 448-449; Thiselton, 'NH', 318-319; Thiselton, 'Truth', 894-896.

[263] Thiselton, 'KNT', 102-103; cf.: Thiselton, 'NH', 323-324; our argument above.

[264] Thiselton, 'KNT', 94-97, 104-105; cf. Thiselton, A.C., 'The Theological Scene: Post-Bultmannian Perspectives', *CGrad* 30.3 (Sep. 1977), 88-89.

[265] Thiselton, 'KNT', 90, cf. 91-93, 100.

faith'.²⁶⁶ Thus, adapting later Wittgensteinian insights to a part-Pannenbergian frame, Thiselton again brings appeals to these two thinkers into juxtaposition.²⁶⁷

Summarizing: Thiselton argues that Kierkegaard's legacy in philosophy *and* theology presents difficulties in relation to "truth" and thereby presents us with a predicament that justifies or warrants further theological *and* philosophical explorations. Thiselton argues that widened dialogue between philosophy and theology is required in order to search for a *'multiform'* notion of "truth".²⁶⁸

### 5. Towards a Warranted Theological Solution: A Biblical Multiform Notion of Truth

Thiselton takes up this widened dialogue and search for a multiform notion of truth in his article, 'Truth' (1978).²⁶⁹ Thus, (1), Thiselton begins with a complaint:

> For many years there has been a tendency in biblical studies to over-generalize about the uses of *alētheia* and *alēthēs* in classical Greek… partly with a view to drawing a clear-cut contrast between Greek and Hebrew concepts of truth. It is then argued that whilst some NT writers preserve the Hebrew concept, other writers, especially John, achieve a fusion of these views.²⁷⁰

Thus, Thiselton continues, 'traditional… biblical scholarship' has understood the "classical *Greek*" notion 'of truth' as follows: (a) 'truth in contrast to mere appearance' ('in Hebrew the parallel word [''*met*] denotes stability or faithfulness'); (b) 'truth' as 'extra-historical' and 'timeless… above the temporal… material world'; (c) 'truth' as 'unhiddenness or unveiling'.²⁷¹

Whilst, in Thiselton's view, this understanding is 'valid up to a point',²⁷² Thiselton argues that two problems with this understanding emerge: (a) drawing on J. Barr's attack on "etymologizing" (see Chapter 4), Thiselton highlights the need to account for the 'different contexts in which ''*met* is employed in the OT'. Thus, Thiselton argues that, with respect to 'polysemy, or multiple meaning… ''*met* means "truth" in *some* contexts, and "faithfulness" in *other* contexts'.²⁷³ (b) Again drawing on 'Barr', Thiselton stresses that this 'semantic phenomenon' (i.e. of the 'polysemy' of '''*met*') 'does not' constitute a "distinctive Hebrew" "conceptual

---

²⁶⁶ Thiselton, 'KNT', 87, 92, 103, 105.

²⁶⁷ Thiselton, 'TY', 1560-1561; cf.: Thiselton, 'Parab', 450; Thiselton, 'UPC', 87-100; Thiselton, A.C., 'Myth, Mythology', in *The Zondervan Pictorial Encyclopedia of the Bible, Volume 4* (ed. M.C. Tenney; Grand Rapids, MI: Zondervan, 1975; written by 1973), 333-343.

²⁶⁸ Thiselton, 'KNT', 105. Italics ours.

²⁶⁹ Thiselton, 'Truth', 874-894.

²⁷⁰ Thiselton, 'Truth', 874-875. Italics and transliterations Thiselton's.

²⁷¹ Thiselton, 'Truth', 874, 875; cf. 877. Italics ours, except on '…'*met*…', where they are Thiselton's. The transliterations are Thiselton's.

²⁷² Thiselton, 'Truth', 875.

²⁷³ Thiselton, 'Truth', 877, 878. Italics Thiselton's.

*Hermeneutics, Unity, and Epistemology* 121

connection" between 'truth' and 'faithfulness'.[274]

In response to these problems, (2), Thiselton conducts a context-'specific' study of the 'uses' of the words translated as 'true', 'truth', 'truly', or 'to speak the truth' (i.e. the words *'alētheia'*, *'alēthēs'*, *'"met̲'* and their cognates) in classical Greek, Old Testament, inter-Testament, and New Testament writings.[275] Thiselton's resulting multiform biblical notion of truth may be systematized - as follows.

(a) For Thiselton, the 'comprehensive', unifying biblical notion 'of truth' is *'the truth of' God's 'Being'*, *'"reality"'*, *or 'actuality'*:[276] (i) this 'truth' is identified with '"the Father"', with 'Jesus Christ' (who *'is* the truth'), and with 'the Spirit of truth';[277] (ii) 'Jesus', as 'truth', is 'the Word made flesh' - a non-'abstract' 'personal' 'historical' 'life' and 'valid' 'witness' to 'the truth of God';[278] (iii) 'the truth of God' is *'personal'*, where God "loves", "creates", "judges", "wills", and is 'faithful' and '"just"'. Combining 'dynamic' and 'static' emphases, Thiselton argues that 'God' is creatively 'active', but also that God has a stable identity consonant with 'integrity': there is a 'correspondence' or "oneness" between God's "words" and "deeds", where 'God' is "faithful" to 'his covenant'.[279]

(iv) Thiselton argues that 'the truth of God' is *'revealed' 'publicly'* through his action (cf. "deeds") and speech-action (cf. "words" - including biblical speech-acts) in 'creation' and in the narrative of 'history' (especially 'in Jesus Christ'), "proving" '"itself anew in the future"'. For Thiselton, 'everything' does *not* rest 'on faith and decision'.[280] (v) Thiselton argues that 'the truth of God' is *"experienced"* by God's people and that,[281] (vi), 'the truth of God' is *'comprehensive'* in that it brings to unity and evaluates the other dimensions of 'truth'.[282] (vii) For Pannenberg and Thiselton, 'the truth of God' '"in Jesus Christ"' is the *anticipatory key to the truth of the eschatological fullness* 'of history'.[283] (viii) Thiselton argues that, biblically, 'the truth of God' *"contrasts" with* 'deceit', 'idolatry', 'dishonesty', 'concealment', 'falsehood',

---

[274] Thiselton, 'Truth', 878; cf. Thiselton, A.C., 'Language and Meaning in Religion', in 'Word', in *The New International Dictionary of New Testament Theology. Volume III* (ed. C. Brown; Exeter: Paternoster; Grand Rapids: Zondervan, 1978; actually written by 1977), 1126-1127. Italics Thiselton's.

[275] Thiselton, 'Truth', 878; cf. 874-877, 877-882, 882-883, 883-894. Italics and transliterations Thiselton's.

[276] Thiselton, 'Truth', 884-885, 890-893, 900; cf. Thiselton, 'TNI', 11. Italics ours.

[277] Thiselton, 'Truth', 890-891; cf. 892-893. Italics Thiselton's.

[278] Thiselton, 'Truth', 890-892, 900.

[279] Thiselton, 'Truth', 880-886, 892-893, 900; cf. Thiselton, 'CH', 5. Italics ours.

[280] Thiselton, 'Truth', 884-885, 891-892, 900-901; cf. Thiselton, A.C., 'The Supposed Power of Words in the Biblical Writings', *JThStud* NS25.2 (Oct. 1974), e.g. 292-293; cf. Thiselton, 'Till', 101. Italics ours.

[281] Thiselton, 'Truth', 880, 891, 888. Italics ours.

[282] Thiselton, 'Truth', 880, 891, 888, 893, 894, 900-901. Italics ours.

[283] Thiselton, 'R *BQ1*', 121, 120; cf.: Thiselton, 'TNI', 11; Thiselton, 'M&M', 8; Thiselton, 'H-O', 8; Thiselton, 'Par', 49-50; Thiselton, 'Truth', 900-901. Italics ours.

'and [with] the antichrist'.[284] (ix) In Thiselton's estimate, 'the truth of God' is the central or *'theological'* 'criterion of truth'. Thus, Thiselton argues that 'the truth of God' de-centers and repudiates all anthropocentric pretensions in which the role of central 'criterion of truth' might be falsely assigned to the human 'self' or selves.[285]

(b) For Thiselton, biblical 'truth' is also *'history' itself* - historical "contingencies", including "'the future'" and "'the eschatological'" gathering of "contingencies" into relation. (i) Thiselton argues that a *human 'self'* is itself a "historical contingent truth", and not divorced from other historical "contingencies", such as 'past' 'events'. (ii) For Thiselton, the truth of "'history'" is (or will be) ultimately *'history as a whole'*: 'past', 'present', 'future', 'process', 'movement', 'particular' "contingencies", "continuities", and "'eschatological'" "'End'". (iii) Thiselton, following Pannenberg, argues that "'history'" is *revealed 'proleptically in... Christ'* who is the "'eschatological'" 'revelation' 'of the' "'End'". (iv) For Pannenberg and Thiselton, "'history'" also *de-centers and repudiates anthropocentric approaches in which the human 'self' (or selves)* is falsely assigned a role as the central 'criterion of truth'.[286]

(c) For Thiselton, biblical 'truth' also encompasses *the divine 'speech-acts' of 'revelation'* - i.e. 'effective', "functional" (including 'descriptive' and "promissory") divine speech-action into human history, "paradigmatically" through 'the Bible'.[287] (i) Thiselton observes that, biblically, the 'truth' of 'revelation' includes the "authoritative", 'valid', 'authentic', 'effective', "non-provisional" speech-actions (including "verdicts" and "judgments") *of Jesus' and of 'the Spirit'*, which 'accord

---

[284] Thiselton, 'Truth', 884; cf. 885-886, 889-890, 893, 900. Italics ours.

[285] Thiselton, 'Truth', 893, 900; cf.: Thiselton, 'Par', 49; Thiselton, *2H*, 250, 443; Thiselton, 'KNT', 91, 100, 101. Italics ours.

[286] cf.: Thiselton, 'TNI', 11; Thiselton, 'Par', 48-50; Thiselton, *NTH*, 101-114; Thiselton, 'Truth', 893, 900-901; Thiselton, *2H*, 104, 246-251, 443; Thiselton, 'CH', 5; Thiselton, 'H-O', 8; Thiselton, 'U (long)', 95. All italics ours. See also, Rudman, S., *Concepts of Person and Christian Ethics* (New Studies in Christian Ethics; ed. R. Gill; Cambridge: CUP, 1997), 254-255. Rudman misleadingly argues that Thiselton seeks to overcome 'pluralism', 'diversity', and 'differences' between traditions, persons, interpretations, and ethical stances in the pursuit of universal agreement. By contrast, supposedly, Rudman argues that 'it is more important to interpret... diversity with historical accuracy and with ethical awareness'. Clearly, however, Thiselton's notion of 'history as a whole' presupposes the unity of the inter-relatedness of *diverse unique contingencies*. Rudman's assumption that historical interpretation *of* 'diversity' can be 'accurate' betrays that he too believes that understandings can eschatologically converge upon *the* truth *about* historical *diversities*. A false interpretation is admittedly a historical fact in that it *exists* – but it is not 'factual' in that it inaccurately *reports other* historical facts. Thiselton rightly distinguishes between *contingency* as that which truly *exists*, and *report* which may *truly exist* but which may simultaneously *report falsely*. False linguistic content cannot be rendered as 'true linguistic content' on the grounds that it truly exists within a historical diversity.

[287] cf.: Thiselton, 'Truth', 884-888, 891-893; Thiselton, *LLM*, 12, 13; Thiselton, 'Par', 51; Thiselton, 'SNTT', 76; Thiselton, 'LMR', 1135. Italics ours.

with' and shape historical 'reality'.[288]

(ii) Thiselton argues that 'revelation' includes the *"paradigmatic public traditions"* of *'the Bible'*: 'doctrine', precepts, "prophecy", "historical report", and 'promises' (cf. the later Wittgenstein's 'public criteria of meaning'). 'Revelation', Thiselton argues, thus includes 'cognitive' 'content', and presupposes "truth" as 'correspondence' to "states of affairs" (which Thiselton distinguishes from 'the correspondence theory of truth' since "truth" is not *only* 'correspondence' to "states of affairs").[289] (iii) Thiselton argues that, biblically, 'revelation' is specifically identified with *'the Gospel'*: its 'message', 'doctrine', historical 'report', "promises", and its "true to reality" character.[290]

(iv) For Thiselton, 'revelation' - as divine speech-action - is *functionally 'effective' to bring about human 'transformation' towards the future:* 'truth exposes lies' and 'falsehood'; it "cleanses" and 'consecrates' 'from sin', leading to "wholeness".[291] (v) 'Revelation', therefore, in Thiselton's estimate, *accords with 'authentic' human 'existence'* and,[292] (vi), *contrasts* with 'falsehood', 'deception', 'delusion', 'idolatry', 'mere' 'surface' 'appearance', 'concealment', 'mere human imaginings', and 'lies'.[293] (vii) Again, Thiselton argues that *the human 'self' (or selves) is thus de-centered* or disqualified from any role in which it might be falsely and anthropocentrically designated as being the central 'criterion of truth'.[294]

(d) For Thiselton, biblical "truth" also relates to 'individual' and corporate human *"subjectivity"'* and *"actualization":* i.e. to existentially, or "eventfully", *"encountering" 'reality'* - including being 'addressed by God' - in a way that is *experienced* as "transcending" the mere receiving of 'information'. In Thiselton's thinking, engaging with 'self-involving' textual 'language' also comes under this heading, though Thiselton argues that 'language' does 'not' communicate "'reality… itself'", but rather that 'language' potentially engenders engagement with or apprehension of the "'real'"- as in, for example, 'self-understanding'.[295]

Thus, (i), Thiselton's notion of the "truth" of "encountering reality"

---

[288] Thiselton, 'Truth', 883, 886, 890-892; cf. Thiselton, 'Par', 50. Italics ours.

[289] cf.: Thiselton, 'Truth', 884-885, 887-888, 879, 881-882, 892, 894; Thiselton, 'Par', 50, 51; Thiselton, *2H*, 247; Thiselton, 'NH', 317; Thiselton, 'UPC', 94, 96, 98; Thiselton, *LLM*, 4; Thiselton, NTH, 545-553, 565, 585-586; Thiselton, A.C., 'Myth, Paradigm, and the Status of Biblical Imagery', in *Using the Bible in Liturgy* (ed. C. Byworth; Nottingham: Grove, 1977), 11; Thiselton, 'LMR', 1126-1127, 1132, 1134-1135; Wittgenstein, *PI*, 24-25, 91, 98-99, 105, 116-117, 122. Italics ours.

[290] Thiselton, 'Truth', 884-888, 882; cf. 891; cf. Thiselton, 'Par', 51. Italics ours.

[291] Thiselton, 'Truth', 881-883, 885-887, 889, 892. Italics ours.

[292] Thiselton, 'Truth', 885; cf. 886-888, 892. Italics ours.

[293] Thiselton, 'Truth', 881; cf. 883-887, 889-893. Italics ours.

[294] Thiselton, *2H*, 250, 443; cf.: Thiselton, 'KNT', 91, 100, 101; Thiselton, 'Truth', 893; Thiselton, 'Par', 49. Italics ours

[295] cf.: Thiselton, 'Truth', 897-899; Thiselton, 'Parab', 446, 438, 440; Thiselton, *LLM*, 28, 16; Thiselton, 'U (long)', 116; Thiselton, *NH*, 11; Thiselton, 'KNT', 100; Thiselton, 'NH', 325; Thiselton, 'U (short)', 6; Thiselton, *2H*, 314. Italics ours.

presupposes existential 'self-involvement' in/as 'effective' 'communication' or *"actualization"*, both individually and corporately.[296] (ii) For Thiselton, "encountering reality" presupposes existential 'self-involvement' at 'pre-conscious', 'pre-cognitive', and 'pre-conceptual' - *and* at 'conscious', 'cognitive', and 'conceptual' - *"levels"*.[297] (iii) For Thiselton, "encountering reality" involves the eventful *'experience'* of the '"happening"' or "disclosure" of 'reality' (as in 'art') and of the 'truth' conveyed 'in' it though, again, Thiselton argues that language or art do not communicate '"reality"'... itself', but that they operate powerfully 'on the basis of convention'.[298] For Thiselton, 'parables' can '"grasp"' the reader 'deep down', drawing the reader into a hermeneutical 'world of new values', and engaging 'with... pre-cognitive attitudes and presuppositions'; Thiselton argues that the reader is thus 'addressed' and carried through a process of discovery, even '"transformation"'.[299]

(iv) For Thiselton, "encountering reality" involves 'creative' intuition and *hermeneutical 'understanding'* (in more than one of its senses – see Chapter 5), rather than merely 'theoretical' reason, and presupposes a broad notion of "rationality".[300] For Thiselton, "encountering reality" presupposes "listening" and 'openness' on the part of the reader, but not the abandonment of 'critical' assessment,[301] re-historicized 'subject-object thinking', or 'assertions'.[302] Thus, for Thiselton, the notion of "encountering reality" implies that *both* "distancing" *and* "fusion" between 'two' 'horizons' are facilitated as part of 'the process' of 'understanding'. Thiselton argues that 'the hermeneutical circle' or 'spiral' also involves both "movement" between 'parts' and "wholes" and 'the logic of question and answer' (see Chapter 5),[303] and thereby transforms '"pre-understanding"', 'presuppositions', or 'pre-judgments'.[304] (v) For Thiselton, "encountering reality", whilst being "existentially self-involving", does not reduce "truth" to '"what is true *for me*"' since "encountering reality" is *de-centered* relative to other truth-categories and criteria (see "(a)"-"(c)" above, and "(e)" below).[305]

(e) For Thiselton, biblical 'truth' also relates to *'authentic' human living* in

---

[296] cf. Thiselton, 'NH', 325-326; Thiselton, *LLM*, 28; Thiselton, 'U (long)', 116; Thiselton, *NH*, 11; Thiselton, 'M&M', 8. Italics ours.

[297] Thiselton, 'Truth', 898; cf. Thiselton, 'NH', 309-311, 321, 326. Italics ours.

[298] cf.: Thiselton, 'NH', 315, 317, 320, 325; Thiselton, 'UPC', 92; Thiselton, *2H*, 163. Italics ours.

[299] cf.: Thiselton, 'Parab', 441; Thiselton, 'Truth', 898-899; Thiselton, 'NH', 316; Thiselton, 'U (short)', 6. Italics ours.

[300] Thiselton, 'NH', 317; cf.: Thiselton, 'UPC', 91-94; Thiselton, *NH*, 318, 325-330. Italics ours.

[301] Thiselton, 'NH', 319, 320; cf. Thiselton, 'KNT', 102-103. Italics ours.

[302] Thiselton, *NTH*, xxv, conc. 5.2d; cf. xxviii, conc. 8.2b. Italics ours.

[303] Thiselton, *2H*, 104; cf.: Thiselton, 'UPC', 93-94; Thiselton, 'NH', 316-317. Italics ours.

[304] Thiselton, 'NH', 313; cf. Thiselton, 'UPC', 93; cf. Walsh, 'TC', 227. Italics ours.

[305] cf. e.g. Thiselton, 'NH', 326. Italics ours, except on *"for me"*, where they are Thiselton's.

accordance with 'divine revelation' and thereby,[306] (i), presupposes *trans-temporal* *'correspondence* between' 'actuality', 'words', and 'deeds': i.e. "enfleshed" 'word' as 'honesty', *'integrity'*, 'sincerity', and 'faithfulness'.[307] (ii) For Thiselton, 'authentic' living includes 'existential' 'self-involvement' as *"appropriation"* and *"application"* or as 'faithful' 'response' to God and to revelation, individually and corporately.[308] Thiselton argues that, in 'authentic' living, 'life' "backs", or 'gives' hard 'currency' to, 'words'.[309] For Thiselton, authentic living involves 'commitment to the… gospel' that brings 'transformation' towards the future.[310]

(iii) For Thiselton, 'authentic' living includes 'existential' 'self-involvement' in 'fully inter-personal' transparent *'relationships'*.[311] (iv) For Thiselton, 'authentic' living includes true or 'reliable' *'speech'*, where this speech includes 'factual' or 'historical' report, and "wisdom". Such speech presupposes 'honesty', transparency, and straightforwardness.[312] (v) For Thiselton, 'authentic' living presupposes 'reverence' for and *'submission* to truth', as in T.F. Torrance's "'scientific'" approach – i.e. 'authentic' living presupposes a 'readiness to submit all pre-conceptions to the test of truth'.[313]

(vi) For Thiselton, 'authentic' living stands *'in contrast to':* 'deceit', 'hypocrisy', 'idolatry', 'dishonesty', 'impurity', 'falsehood', secretiveness, 'lying', 'concealment', and manipulation;[314] the 'other-than-serious attitude to truth' of contemporary culture, 'mass advertising', 'party-political propaganda', and the 'mass media'; 'the pseudo-cynicism of our own age which tries to "unmask" everything'; denial of 'the possibility' of encounter with the real; unredeemed 'insecure' 'self-defensiveness and self-assertion' that 'give rise to falsehood'; and drawing from only 'one theological tradition'.[315] (vii) For Thiselton, 'authentic' living, in so far as it is a corporate and submitted response, places 'restraints' on 'the individual'; again, the human 'self' is *de-centered* and disqualified from performing any anthropocentric role – particularly an anthropocentric role in which it might be

---

[306] Thiselton, 'Truth', 892. Italics ours.

[307] Thiselton, 'Truth', 879; cf. 883-886; cf. 892. Italics ours.

[308] cf.: Thiselton, 'Truth', 892; cf.: 881, 898, 879; Thiselton, 'M&M', 8; Thiselton, 'KNT', 90-91, cf. 104; Thiselton, *LLM*, 16; Thiselton, 'NH', 316; Thiselton, A.C., 'Explain, Interpret, Tell, Narrative', in *The New International Dictionary of New Testament Theology, Volume 1* (ed. C. Brown; Exeter: Paternoster; Grand Rapids: Zondervan, 1975), 578-579; Thiselton, 'Par', 49; Thiselton, *NTH*, xxv, conc. 5.3b. Italics ours.

[309] Thiselton, 'Truth', 892; cf.: Thiselton, 'UPC', 95; cf. 97-98; Thiselton, *LLM*, 20; Thiselton, 'LMR', 1135; cf. 1143. Italics ours.

[310] Thiselton, 'Truth', 882-883; cf. 886-887; cf. 892. Italics ours.

[311] Thiselton, 'Truth', 881, 887, 892; cf. Thiselton, *LLM*, 16. Italics ours.

[312] Thiselton, 'Truth', 880; cf. 881, 883-887, 892, 894. Italics ours.

[313] Thiselton, 'Truth', 892; cf. 901. Italics ours.

[314] Thiselton, 'Truth', 880-881, 883-887, 889-893. Italics ours.

[315] Thiselton, 'Truth', 900, cf. 901. Italics ours.

falsely designated as being the decisive 'criterion of truth'.[316]

(f) For Thiselton, biblical "truth" also means *"correspondence" with 'the facts'*, or just 'the facts', where current 'factual truth' or 'historical truth' may be in view.[317] (i) This point, Thiselton argues, does not presuppose 'the correspondence theory of truth', or 'natural', 'referential', 'ideational', or broadly "positivist" theories of 'language' and 'meaning'.[318] Rather, for Thiselton, 'a biblical' "subtext" and approach to 'language' are presupposed (see Chapter 4).[319] (ii) For Thiselton, "truth as correspondence with the facts" presupposes an *interweaving of historical events and meaning* – and is *more secure* in a 'theological' context than in 'a secular' context (as we implied earlier).[320]

(iii) For Thiselton "truth as correspondence with the facts" presupposes that 'there is still a place for *re-historicized subject-object thinking* in hermeneutics'.[321] (iv) For Thiselton, "truth as correspondence with the facts" is *not free of "value-judgments"*, especially when such "truth" corresponds to human 'experience'.[322] Nevertheless, again, Thiselton argues that the human 'self' is not the only 'criterion of truth'. Thus, for example, Thiselton argues that 'internal coherence' and "correspondence" with 'the facts' are two other 'truth'-"criteria" that are relevant in relation to "historical report".[323] (v) For Thiselton, "truth as correspondence with the facts" stands *'in contrast to'* 'lies', 'false' report, 'mere' external 'appearances', and - sometimes – 'in contrast to' "human imagination".[324]

(g) For Thiselton, biblical 'truth' can mean 'logical' or 'internal *coherence*' - which is, (i), a notion of 'truth' that has *application* in abstract (and/or abstracted) truth-

---

[316] Thiselton, 'Truth', 892; cf.: Thiselton, 'REC', 521; Thiselton, 'Par', 48; Thiselton, *2H*, 250, 443. Italics ours.

[317] Thiselton, 'Truth', 883; cf. 884, 887, 888, 890, 892, 894. Italics ours.

[318] cf.: Thiselton, 'Truth', 894-896; Thiselton, A.C., 'Review of T. Fawcett's *The Symbolic Language of Religion*', *Chman* 85.3 (1971), 221; cf. 222; Thiselton, A.C., 'Language in a Haze. Review of T. Fawcett's *The Symbolic Language of Religion*', *CEN* 7 May (1971), 12; Thiselton, 'SNTT', 76; Thiselton, 'Words', 284, 287-289, 292-299; Thiselton, 'Parab', 448-451; Thiselton, 'NH', 325-326; Thiselton, 'Till', 88; cf. 98-101; Thiselton, *LLM*, 10-12; Thiselton, A.C., 'The Semantics of Biblical Language as an Aspect of Hermeneutics', *FTht* 103.2 (1976), 113-115; Thiselton, 'LMR', 1124-1130, 1135-1137; Thiselton, 'SBS', 330-331.

[319] cf.: Thiselton, 'CAP', 144; Thiselton, 'Words', 289-299; Thiselton, 'Till', 98-101; Thiselton, *LLM*, 6-7, 10-12, 18-21, 25, 29-31; Thiselton, 'LMR', 1126, 1132, 1137-1142.

[320] Thiselton, 'Truth', 894-896; cf. 899-900; cf.: Thiselton, 'KNT', 104; Thiselton, 'TNI', 11; Thiselton, 'MP', 10; Thiselton, A.C., 'Review of R.C. Roberts' *Rudolf Bultmann's Theology: A Critical Interpretation*', *Chman* 92.3 (1978), 267; Thiselton, *NTH*, 288-316. Italics ours.

[321] Thiselton, *NTH*, xxiv-xxv, conc. 5.2b; cf. Heidegger, *AIM*, 30, 89-90, 132. Italics ours.

[322] Thiselton, 'Truth', 894; cf.: Thiselton, 'SARX', 215-218; Thiselton, A.C., Contribution to 'Flesh', in *The New International Dictionary of New Testament Theology, Volume 1* (ed. C. Brown; Exeter: Paternoster; Grand Rapids: Zondervan, 1975), 681. Italics ours.

[323] Thiselton, 'Truth', 894, 896; cf. 883, 884, 887, 888, 890, 892; cf.: Thiselton, 'Par', 49; Thiselton, *2H*, 250, 443.

[324] Thiselton, 'Truth', 885; cf. 886, 888-890, 892-893. Italics ours.

'systems' - as in 'mathematics' and tautologies, as in *anticipatory* 'historical' truth-systems, and as in 'theological' truth-'systems'. (ii) For Thiselton, though, all truth-'systems' are 'corrigible, incomplete, and open-ended' towards the future; moreover, Thiselton notes that competing 'systems' can be "internally coherent". (iii) In Thiselton's estimate, this dimension of "truth" secures a place for "theoretical" 'reason', contrary to 'Kierkegaard', and again, (iv), has *more stability* within a 'theological' framework.[325]

(h) For Thiselton, biblical "truth" can relate to *the "genuine"*, *to the "real"*, *or to the 'valid'*, in contrast to the counterfeit.[326] (i) Thiselton argues that genuineness can be proven through 'critical' evaluation or *"testing"*.[327] Thus, to a limited extent and in a qualified way, Thiselton approves of A. Flew's falsification principle.[328] (ii) Thiselton argues that the genuineness of 'tradition' relative to biblical "paradigms" requires testing through a *metacritique of traditions*.[329] (iii) For Thiselton, the genuineness of a *'religious experience'* requires testing - through the employment of re-historicized subject-object thinking – relative to the same biblical "paradigms".[330] (iv) With 'T.F. Torrance', Thiselton argues that '"the [re-historicized] subject-object relationship"' is presupposed in '"all"' '"objectivity"', and in '"all knowledge"', even knowledge of 'God': what is needed is '"a scientific theology"'.[331] (v) In Thiselton's view, 'critical', 'comparative', "testing" is relevant to all understanding.[332]

(i) For Thiselton, "truth" has the functional sense of that which *facilitates 'liberation from' external manipulation or 'from self-deception'*. (i) For Thiselton, this dimension of "truth" need not only be associated with *divine speech-action*. (ii) Rather, Thiselton argues that this dimension of "truth" brings us back to the metacritique of traditions (cf. above). (iii) Thiselton warns us that that which *seems* to liberate in the *short term*, however, may not *ultimately* be liberating: against 'the pragmatic theory of truth', truly "liberating" "truth" requires *critical testing against trans-contextual and trans-temporal criteria*.[333]

(j) For Thiselton, "truth" also relates to the *'performative' dimension* of "asserting" the "truth", of making a truth-claim, or '"of using"' the 'adjective' '"true"'. (i) Thiselton argues that critical testing is required if 'an assertion' is to be given a

---

[325] Thiselton, 'Truth', 894-899; cf.: Thiselton, 'KNT', 104; Thiselton, *NH*, 25. Italics ours.
[326] Thiselton, 'Truth', 884; cf. 885, 888-891, 893. Italics ours.
[327] cf.: Thiselton, 'Truth', 894-896; Thiselton, 'TNP', 11; Thiselton, 'NH', 319, 323-324, 326-329; Thiselton, 'Till', 94; cf. 93; Thiselton, 'LMR', 1134; cf. 1135; Thiselton, *NTH*, xxv, conc. 5.2d. Italics ours.
[328] Thiselton, *NTH*, 407; cf.: Thiselton, *2H*, 290; Thiselton, 'LMR', 1137.
[329] Thiselton, *NTH*, xxii, conc. 1.2a; cf. Thiselton, 'LMR', 1135. Italics ours.
[330] Thiselton, 'E-CR', 8; cf.: Thiselton, 'Till', 92; Thiselton, 'LMR', 1134-1135. Italics ours.
[331] Thiselton, 'Truth', 900.
[332] cf. Thiselton, 'NH', 314, 320; cf. 323.
[333] Thiselton, 'Truth', 881, cf. 896-897. Italics ours.

status beyond a mere 'value-judgment' or speech-act.[334] (ii) Thiselton observes that linguistic 'performance' must not be "sharply" divided from 'linguistic content', since the former often presupposes the truth of the latter, as in J.L. Austin's and D.D. Evans' 'logic of self-involvement'.[335] (iii) Thiselton argues that the multi-functional character of language requires that attention be given to "what is going on" when an assertion is being made.[336] This ties in to Thiselton's later call for an *'extra-linguistic' critique of language.*[337]

Hence, (3), in view of this analysis, we must reject W.J. Larkin's view that Thiselton's notion of 'truth' is only *five*-fold and supposedly reducible to a 'correspondence theory of truth'.[338] Rather, comparing the first and second parts of Thiselton's article, 'Truth', implies that he, in effect, uses his *ten*-fold biblical multiform notion of truth to correct a whole *series* of "one-sided" approaches to "truth" in extra-biblical (or 'everyday', 'religious', 'philosophical', and 'theological') contexts of discussion – as follows.[339]

Thus, (a), Thiselton corrects a one-sided *over-abstract* or over-theoretical *generalizing* "formal" or "idealist" view of truth: truth is not a 'Platonic' ('timeless', "immaterial", 'eternal', 'changeless', "'finished'", 'extra-historical') 'reality' that contrasts with 'mere appearance'.[340] Nor does Thiselton follow 'Hegel' too closely but, after 'Pannenberg', transposes some of Hegel's insights into a different frame.[341] For Thiselton, 'biblical' truth is not identifiable with *a priori generalizations* about 'Greek' or 'Hebrew concepts of truth'; rather, for Thiselton, truth – even 'theological truth' – is tied in to *concrete "'history'"* and *'particularity'*.[342]

(b) Thiselton corrects a one-sided *"totalizing"* view of truth. For Thiselton, since 'a… comprehensive system' corresponding to 'the whole of reality' cannot be constructed, 'the coherence theory of truth' (from 'Leibniz, Spinoza, Hegel, and Bradley') that assesses 'statements' in relation to their 'coherence' with a prior 'system', cannot claim "comprehensiveness". Nevertheless, Thiselton allows that 'coherence' as a 'criterion' applies to provisional, expanding, 'open' systems "'on

---

[334] Thiselton, 'Truth', 894, 897. Italics ours.
[335] cf.: Thiselton, 'Truth', 897; Thiselton, 'LMR', 1126; Thiselton, 'Parab', 438, 463; Thiselton, 'UPC', 95; 97-98; Thiselton, 'MP', 8-9.
[336] Thiselton, 'Truth', 895; cf. 897; cf.: Thiselton, 'Parab', 450, 453, 454, 439-440, 465-467; Thiselton, 'Words', 297-298.
[337] Thiselton, *NH*, 367; cf. 598. Italics ours.
[338] Larkin Jr., *CBH*, 236-237.
[339] Thiselton, 'Truth', 974-894; cf. 894-902.
[340] Thiselton, 'TNI', 11; cf.: Thiselton, A.C., 'New Problems for Old: Article Review of J.A.T. Robinson's *The Human Face of God*', *CEN* 6 Apr. (1973), 8; Thiselton, 'Truth', 889, 875, 876. Italics ours.
[341] cf.: Thiselton, *2H*, 79; Thiselton, 'R *BQ1*', 121, 120; Thiselton, 'TNI', 11; Thiselton, 'M&M', 8; Thiselton, 'KNT', 96-97; Thiselton, 'BSA', 13; Thiselton, 'IA', 9; Thiselton, 'Par', 48-49; Thiselton, 'Truth', 900-901.
[342] Thiselton, 'TNI', 11; cf.: Thiselton, 'NP', 8; Thiselton, 'Truth', 874, 900; Thiselton, *2H*, 79. Italics ours.

the way to truth'", such as 'systematic' theologies, historical reconstructions, or 'mathematics'. Thus, Thiselton argues that 'historical truth' is *'incomplete'*; but also that abstract "rational" theorizing retains a place.[343]

(c) Thiselton corrects a one-sided emphasis on 'empirical... *correspondence*' by dislodging (with Heidegger) 'the correspondence theory of truth' which is tied to "formal" *"descriptive"* approaches to 'language'. Rather, Thiselton argues that language is both embedded in history and multifunctional. Here, Thiselton draws on the later Wittgenstein and, implicitly, on Pannenberg's critique of 'Neo-Kantianism': for Thiselton, 'the correspondence theory', even J.L. Austin's 'weakened version' of 'the correspondence theory', is still too tied in to an idealist philosophical subtext that is vulnerable to collapse into 'relativism'. Here, Thiselton also draws on 'Heidegger' and 'P.F. Strawson'. For Thiselton, though, as implied earlier, and against 'Heidegger', 'theology' more securely ensures that 'truth' *retains* a dimension of 'empirically informative' 'communication' (premised upon re-historicized 'subject-object' thinking) without collapse into 'relativism'.[344]

(d) Thiselton corrects a one-sided emphasis on individual *"'subjectivity'"* as "'truth'". For Thiselton, truth is not Kierkegaardian - though, in Thiselton's view, as we have said, Pannenberg rightly transposes some of Kierkegaard's 'insights' into a different frame.[345] Thiselton argues that human "'subjectivity'", or the 'self', is not the main 'criterion of truth' (against 'Kierkegaard', 'Heidegger', and 'Bultmann'), since 'theological' and 'historical truth' cannot be reduced to questions of "'subjectivity'" 'exhaustively and without remainder'.[346]

Indeed, Thiselton corrects *several* one-sided emphases in the Continental hermeneutical traditions during his 'second period'. Thiselton argues that, taken together, these traditions rightly emphasize: 'individual' active 'decision' and 'lived'-through "transforming" 'appropriation'; truth-as-"manifestation" and "'listening'" in 'openness'; 'practical' 'wisdom'; eventful 'experience' and "'actualization'" at the "'pre-conscious'", 'pre-cognitive level' of hermeneutical "worlds"; and 'self-understanding' (cf. 'subjectivity'). *However*, Thiselton argues that, taken together, the Continental hermeneutical traditions tend to marginalize: (re-historicized) 'subject-object thinking'; 'critical' 'testing"; 'theological truth'; the corporate dimension; 'historical knowledge'; 'public criteria of meaning' transmitted in "traditions"; multi-functional assertions; and "criteria of truth"

---

[343] cf.: Thiselton, 'Truth', 894-896; Thiselton, *NH*, 25; Thiselton, 'KNT', 104. Italics ours.

[344] cf.: Thiselton, 'Truth', 894-896, 899, 900; Thiselton, *2H*, 373-375; Thiselton, *NTH*, xxiv-xxv, conc. 5.2b; Thiselton, 'LMR', 1124-1126. Italics ours.

[345] cf.: Thiselton, 'TNP', 11; Thiselton, 'M&M', 8; Thiselton, 'PDT', 7; Thiselton, 'KNT', 90-92, 95, 98-105; Thiselton, 'Par', 48-49; Thiselton, 'LMR', 1142-1144; Thiselton, 'Truth', 897-898. Italics ours.

[346] cf.: Thiselton, 'TNP', 11; Thiselton, 'Truth', 898, 896, 894; Thiselton, *2H*, 250, 443; Thiselton, 'NP', 8; Thiselton, 'UPC', 87-88; cf. 90-95; Thiselton, 'NH', 312-319; cf. 323-327; Thiselton, 'Till', 98-102; Thiselton, 'KNT', 90-92, cf. 95, 98-105; Thiselton, 'Par', 49; Thiselton, 'MP', 8, 7, 9.

beyond the human 'self' or "selves". Thiselton argues that truth includes, but is broader than and *de-centers*, 'individual' 'subjectivity'.[347]

(e) Thiselton corrects the one-sided emphasis on 'practical' *usefulness* in 'the pragmatic theory of truth' by stressing trans-contextual "criteria" and 'critical' testing.[348] (f) Thiselton corrects the one-sided emphasis on the *'performative' action* of "making a truth-claim" in the 'redundancy', 'semantic', and 'performative' "theories" 'of truth' by emphasizing 'cognitive' content.[349]

(g) Thiselton corrects a potential or actual one-sided collapse into *'fragmentation'* or "multiformity" in 'everyday', 'pragmatic', and 'religious' notions of "truth" by stressing the 'comprehensiveness' of 'the truth of God which embraces all this particular variety'.[350] Thiselton, drawing on Pannenberg and T.F. Torrance, argues that the over-emphasis on '"subjectivity"' and the resulting 'fragmentation of truth' associated with the 'German' philosophical tradition needs correcting by the reinstatement of a unifying '"scientific theology"': truth is not fragmented, against Kantian or Neo-Kantian 'rational' vs. 'moral', fact vs. value, 'history' vs. 'faith', or 'thought' vs. 'will' dichotomies.[351] Nor, argues Thiselton, is truth a pluralistic competition between incommensurable contents; rather, for Thiselton, truth is a 'whole' consisting of complementary notions of truth that are inter-related in ways that are 'closer... than mere family resemblances', where the *strictly limited* application of the later Wittgenstein's thought in this area of Thiselton's epistemology must be noted.[352]

Thus, Thiselton argues that whilst the early 'Pannenberg' makes 'over-generalizing remarks about the contrast between Greek and Hebrew concepts of truth' (Thiselton would not make this criticism of the later Pannenberg), Thiselton also argues that Pannenberg 'has pointed the way forward to recovering a sense of the unity and comprehensiveness of truth in theology'.[353] Again, for 'Pannenberg' and Thiselton, 'the truth of God' '"embraces all other truth"', where 'Jesus Christ', as divine, and as 'the proleptic revelation of the End', links 'the truth of God' to 'the... truth' of 'history as a whole'.[354]

---

[347] cf.: Thiselton, 'Truth', 895-899; Thiselton, 'KNT', 85, 93, 86, 100-104; Thiselton, *2H*, 172, 176, 246, 379, cf. 382-385, 443, 250; Thiselton, 'Till', 90; Thiselton, 'NH', 323, 309; Thiselton, *NH*, 11; Thiselton, 'Parab', 464; Thiselton, 'Par', 48, 49; Thiselton, *NTH*, xxii-xxviii, concs. 5.2b-d, 5.3b-c, 6.1, 6.1a-b, 6.6b, 1.2a-c, all 8.2-8.3.

[348] Thiselton, 'Truth', 894, 896, 900-901; cf. Thiselton, 'NH', 320, 323-324.

[349] Thiselton, 'Truth', 896-897; cf.: Thiselton, 'NH', 324-326; Thiselton, 'Till', 100. Italics ours.

[350] Thiselton, 'Truth', 894, 896-897, 899-900. Italics ours.

[351] Thiselton, 'Truth', 898-900, 894.

[352] Thiselton, 'Truth', 894, 901; cf.: Walsh, 'TC', 234; Wittgenstein, *PI*, 31-32. Here, our exegesis directly contradicts Walsh's misleading inference that Thiselton supposedly espouses an epistemologically and linguistically dualistic hermeneutic.

[353] Thiselton, 'Truth', 900.

[354] Thiselton, 'Truth', 900-901; cf. Thiselton, 'Par', 48.

(h) Thiselton corrects *"skeptical"*, *"pessimistic"*, *and "trivializing"* attitudes to truth in popular *'secular'* culture in the West: for Thiselton, truth is not as elusive as contemporary 'skepticism and relativism' suggest, and "trivializing" "attitudes" 'to truth' should be discarded in favor of a biblical 'attitude' of epistemological seriousness. That is, for Thiselton, 'secular' 'theories of truth' need correcting by 'theological' approaches.[355]

In conclusion, (4), Thiselton's evaluation of extra-biblical approaches to truth through dialogue with "biblical" notions of truth - and vice versa - proves he is not straightforwardly "fideistic". On the contrary, the fact that a biblical multiform notion of truth can correct 'philosophical' and other extra-biblical approaches to truth warrants – in Thiselton's thinking - the acceptance of an exploratory working assumption that affirms the relevance of bringing biblical approaches to truth into epistemological conversations that pertain to hermeneutics. That is, in the context of his hermeneutical critique of epistemology, Thiselton's exposition of a biblical approach to truth further demonstrates the validity of bringing theological explorations into hermeneutical discussions in response to philosophical problems.[356]

### 6. *Mutual Dialogic Warrant: Rationality, Perception, and Self-Deception in Philosophy and Theology*

By now, it may appear that Thiselton perhaps still suppresses genuine two-way dialogue between theology and philosophy by only allowing theology to criticize philosophy in relation to epistemology and not vice versa. However, Thiselton *does* allow philosophy to function critically in relation to theological epistemologies that he considers to be unbiblical, and in relation to biblical interpretative problems. The validity of this point will emerge from what now follows.

A) HISTORICAL-SCIENTIFIC RATIONALITY IN PANNENBERG AND T.F. TORRANCE

Admittedly, in relation to *'rationality'*, Thiselton addresses philosophical problems from a theological stance, noting that T.F. Torrance's work "resonates" with and yet also critiques Continental philosophy. That is, Thiselton observes that Torrance, *with* strands in Continental hermeneutics, attacks *both* a Cartesianism of 'disinvolvement from one's task' (which denies historical embeddedness) *and* the 'general skepticism' commonly confused with 'objectivity'.[357] *Against* strands in Continental hermeneutics, however, Thiselton argues that Torrance rightly attacks the "rationality" of the Kantian/Neo-Kantian framework of 'Dilthey', 'Bultmann', 'Tillich', and 'J.A.T. Robinson' with its 'disastrous dualisms' or 'dichotomies' ('events' vs. 'values' or 'ideas'; 'object' vs. 'subject'; 'nature' vs. 'God'; historical

---

[355] Thiselton, 'Truth', 899-900, 901; cf. Thiselton, 'LMR', 1143. Italics ours.

[356] Thiselton, 'Truth', 894; cf.: Thiselton, 'H-O', 8; contradicting, Walsh, 'TC', 235.

[357] Thiselton, 'IA', 9. Italics ours.

'Jesus' vs. 'the Christ of faith') - since this framework denies historical unity.[358]

Conversely, in Thiselton's view, Torrance's notion of 'rationality' is properly "historical" in that it combines 'willingness to respect the claims of the given [i.e. the historical past] as over and against one's own prior assumptions' [in the present] with 'openness to the truth [including the future]', and in that Torrance's notion of 'rationality' also resonates with Pannenberg's notion of 'historical reason'.[359]

That is, in relation to the issue of a properly "historical" notion of "rationality", Thiselton observes that, in this context of discussion, there is *both* dialogic resonance *and* dissonance between philosophy and theology: i.e. for Thiselton, Torrance's notion of "rationality" satisfies biblical-theological criteria as expounded by Pannenberg, but also *both* satisfies philosophical criteria *and* addresses and corrects philosophical difficulties.

Hence, Thiselton affirms Torrance's work, *God and Rationality* as 'a book which should not be ignored' finding it strange, given the points just noted, that Torrance has not appealed to 'Pannenberg'.[360] Thiselton's discovery of *two* thinkers who come to similar "cogent" conclusions *independently* undoubtedly explains his excitement upon reading Torrance's work between 1969 and 1971.[361]

Elsewhere, however, Thiselton implicitly allows Continental thought to function critically in relation to unbiblical theological epistemology. Thus, Thiselton argues that the notion of "rationality" (or the 'rationalistic spirit of American old-style liberalism') implicit in P.A. Bertocci's 'personal idealism', and in Bertocci's appeal to 'process thought', *both* transgresses Continental philosophical criteria *and* transgresses the 'Hebrew-Christian conceptions of eschatology and history... exemplified in... Moltmann'.[362]

B) PERCEPTION IN THE LATER WITTGENSTEIN, D.D. EVANS, I.T. RAMSEY, AND C.S. LEWIS

Moving on to consider 'perception', which A. Morton identifies as an epistemological concern,[363] Thiselton argues that an appeal to philosophy is warranted because it provides solutions to theological problems, both (1) exegetically and (2) practically.

Thus, (1), exegetically, Thiselton argues that the later Wittgenstein's notion of

---

[358] Thiselton, 'IA', 9.

[359] Thiselton, 'IA', 9; cf. Thiselton, 'TNI', 11.

[360] Thiselton, 'IA', 9.

[361] Thiselton, A.C., 'Continental Theology - Processed, Packaged and Branded. Review of H. Zahrnt's *The Question of God*, CEN 9 May (1969), 6; cf.: Thiselton, 'BSA', 13; Thiselton, 'TY', 1560.

[362] Thiselton, A.C., 'Finding God in Personal Idealism. Review of P.A. Bertocci's *The Person God Is*', CEN 9 Jul. (1971), 11.

[363] Morton, A., *A Guide Through the Theory of Knowledge* (Oxford: Blackwell, 1977, 1997), e.g. 33-34.

"'seeing as'" and D.D. Evans' parallel notion of "'onlooks'"[364] resolve the supposed 'logical problems' 'associated with Paul's doctrine of justification': How can a 'believer' be both 'righteous, and' "sinful"? How is 'justification' both 'present' and 'future'? How can 'faith' exclude "'works'" yet remain in a different 'logical' 'category'?[365]

Rejecting existing solutions to these problems,[366] Thiselton draws on the later Wittgenstein to argue that how 'I see' something 'depends on' its 'function… within a system, frame of reference, or setting in life'. Thiselton argues that, with 'more than one… frame of reference', 'we… "see" something… *as* something'.[367] Thus, in Thiselton's estimate, whether we "'see'" 'Jastrow's duck-rabbit' drawing 'as' 'a duck' or 'as' 'a rabbit' 'depends on' whether we imagine ponds or fields.[368] For Thiselton, "frames-of-reference" render 'concepts intelligible'; for Thiselton, "'grammatical" statements' explicate or "extend" these "frames". Thus, Thiselton argues that 'the Old Testament' renders the concept of "redemption" 'intelligible' in terms of "deliverance from bondage".[369] (Thiselton's exposition of "'seeing as'" in *The Two Horizons*[370] appears in similar form in four further places in his second period).[371]

Similarly, Thiselton observes that, for D.D. Evans, "'x'" 'is "looked on"' "'as y'" when placed "'within a structure, organization… scheme'", or "'future… context'" and given "'a status, function, or role'". Thus, Thiselton argues, 'the logic' of 'valid or invalid' 'verdicts' contrasts with that of 'true-or-false' 'flat assertions'.[372]

Summarizing Thiselton's findings in this context, then we may observe that Thiselton argues that, in 'Paul's doctrine of justification', there is no 'contradiction' between 'assertions' about 'righteousness' and 'sinfulness'. Rather, Thiselton argues that these 'competing verdicts' are each 'valid' in their "frames of reference".[373] Thus Thiselton argues that, 'eschatologically', 'the believer' 'is "looked on" as righteous' – 'justification is a '""pre-dating" of… an eschatological act"'. Conversely Thiselton argues that, historically and legally, 'the believer' 'is

---

[364] cf.: Thiselton, 'UPC', 96-98; Thiselton, A.C., 'On the Logical Grammar of Justification in Paul. Paper Presented to the Fifth International Congress on Biblical Studies, Oxford, 1973', in *Studia Evangelica 7* (ed. E.A. Livingstone; Berlin: Akademie-Verlag, 1982), 491-495; Thiselton, 'SNTT', 98-100; Thiselton, *NTH*, 593-599; Thiselton, *2H*, 415-427.

[365] Thiselton, 'LG', 493; cf. 494, 492, 491.

[366] Thiselton, 'LG', 491-492 especially.

[367] Thiselton, 'LG', 493.

[368] Thiselton, 'LG', 493; cf. Thiselton, 'UPC', 96-97.

[369] Thiselton, 'LG', 493; cf. Thiselton, *2H*, 382-383; cf. Thiselton, 'UPC', 98.

[370] Thiselton, *2H*, 418, 419. Italics ours.

[371] Thiselton, 'UPC', 96-98; cf.: Thiselton, 'LG', 491-495; Thiselton, 'SNTT', 98-100; Thiselton, *NTH*, 593-599.

[372] Thiselton, 'LG', 493-494. Italics Thiselton's.

[373] Thiselton, 'LG', 492-493.

"seen as'" "sinful". Thiselton concludes that, since 'the eschatological' 'verdict' 'corresponds with future reality', then 'the eschatological' 'verdict' is 'decisive'.[374]

Thiselton argues that '"faith"', (in *this* 'context' of discussion), is 'part of the' "grammar" 'of the *concept* of justification', and involves a 'future-oriented outlook... effectively relevant in the present'. That is, for Thiselton, 'faith' (in *this* 'context' of discussion) steps from the 'historical' 'system' into the 'eschatological' 'system', accepting the 'righteous' 'verdict' of 'judgment day' as 'valid for faith now', and "appropriating" 'the eschatological future' 'in the present'.[375]

Conversely, Thiselton argues that '"works"' are part of' "the grammar" 'of the concept of law': since 'justification' and 'law' as 'concepts' 'stand in contrast to each other', then so do 'faith' and '"works"'; hence 'faith is not a special kind of work'.[376] Thiselton repeats these points elsewhere.[377] In conclusion: Thiselton argues that *the later Wittgenstein's and D.D. Evans' philosophy of perception aids biblical doctrinal interpretation.*

(2) Practically, and still in relation to epistemological considerations of "perception", Thiselton argues that the philosophy of language also provides solutions to the problem of irresponsible communication in 'preaching' and also to problems encountered in "translation", where in this context of discussion Thiselton links the later Wittgenstein's remarks on "controlling pictures" to I.T. Ramsey's comments on 'models and qualifiers'.[378]

Thus, Thiselton argues that 'models' have 'power' 'to help' 'or' to 'lead astray'. In Thiselton's estimate, preachers over-stressing 'the model of wind' for 'the Holy Spirit' may negate human effort, overlooking the qualifying model of the 'laborers in the vineyard'. That is, Thiselton argues that, when 'over-extended', each model contradicts the other, engendering contradictory 'attitudes'. Hence, Thiselton argues, following Ramsey: 'models must be qualified and their applications limited', since their over-extension transmits a false 'way of seeing the world', "beguiling" 'uncritical minds'. Thiselton argues that 'models and metaphors... are not just illustrations' but 'deliberately ambiguous devices' that help or allow 'us to see... new truth', or old truth differently. Therefore, Thiselton argues that they 'should' neither 'be used with total ambiguity', nor 'replaced by flat prosaic similes' that remove their 'power to' create 'new' vision. Thiselton argues that speech 'about God' must use 'models', but that it must do so 'responsibly', because of their 'power'. Thiselton agrees with Ramsey: 'every model requires its qualifier', since an unqualified 'picture', according to the later Wittgenstein and Thiselton, can "hold us captive".[379] Elsewhere, appealing to E. Bevan, Thiselton makes correlative remarks about symbols in critique of Paul Tillich: thus, for Thiselton,

---

[374] Thiselton, 'LG', 494-495.
[375] Thiselton, 'LG', 495; cf. 494, 493. First and third italics ours, second italics Thiselton's.
[376] Thiselton, 'LG', 495; cf. 493.
[377] Thiselton, 'SNTI', 98-100; cf.: Thiselton, *NTH*, 593-599; Thiselton, *2H*, 415-427.
[378] cf.: Thiselton, 'M-M', 8; Thiselton, *LLM*, 25; Thiselton, *2H*, 432.
[379] Thiselton, 'M-M', 8.

'the *power* of symbols... [is] no guarantee of their *truth*'.[380]

Similarly, Thiselton expounds C.S. Lewis's notion of "master's metaphors" as those that are used consciously and helpfully. Conversely, Thiselton observes that Lewis's "pupil's metaphors" may "captivate", 'bewitch', "seem like keys", or 'control' as unseen "axes" about which thought or '"action"' turns, causing us to speak 'nonsense'. Thiselton argues that since 'metaphor' potentially becomes 'doctrine' when its 'metaphorical status is forgotten', then metaphor needs to be used responsibly by combining multiple mutually-qualifying 'metaphors' with theological explanation. Thiselton argues that, in translation, very ambiguous or 'dead' metaphors require explanation, but that 'live' metaphors should be left alone, allowing them to provoke 'self-involvement'. For Thiselton, "bad" metaphor can over-extend meaning or involve inappropriate 'stylistic register' - like a bad 'joke'. Thus, the 'Spirit' searches us, 'but... is hardly... radar'.[381]

In conclusion: Thiselton argues that the later Wittgenstein's, D.D. Evans', I.T. Ramsey's, and C.S. Lewis's (among others') philosophies of perception help us to *address exegetical and practical concerns in theology*.

(3) Thiselton's appeal to the later Wittgenstein's notion of "pictures" in this context of discussion is not a return to linguistic formalism, epistemological positivism, or to philosophical idealism. With A. Kenny, Thiselton '*rejects*... "picture" and "use"... as contrasting slogans for the earlier and later writings' of Wittgenstein: the later Wittgenstein "*modified*" his 'picture theory'. Thiselton argues that propositions' 'relation to reality... differs from one language-game to another',[382] where Thiselton argues similarly in *The Two Horizons* and elsewhere.[383]

That is, Thiselton argues that, since 'language' is 'multi-functional' and 'performative', then 'what language... *is* depends on' what a speaker is doing in a 'particular language-game'.[384]

Hence, Thiselton insists that an 'extra-linguistic' critique of 'language-uses' is needed in order to prevent '"pictures"' (including 'religious' 'symbols') "holding" 'us captive', or in order to prevent 'language' from being used 'irresponsibly' without 'extra-linguistic' 'backing' or 'currency' in 'life'.[385] Thiselton argues that 'language'-'habits' can "perpetuate" spellbinding '"pictures"' that strongly condition 'thought'. For Thiselton, however, "spells" can be "broken". Thiselton argues that 'language-games' and "forms of life" are not "logically" isolated, as the

---

[380] Thiselton, 'Till', 102; cf. Thiselton, *LLM*, 22-24. Italics Thiselton's.

[381] Thiselton, *LLM*, 25-27.

[382] Thiselton, A.C., 'Review of A. Kenny's *Wittgenstein*', *Chman* 90.1 (1976), 72; cf.: Thiselton, 'SNTT', 93-95; Thiselton, 'M-M', 8; Thiselton, *LLM*, 25-26. Italics ours.

[383] cf.: Thiselton, *2H*, 432; Thiselton, 'MP', 12.

[384] Thiselton, 'TY', 1562; cf.: Thiselton, *LLM*, 18; Thiselton, 'LMR', 1131; Thiselton's linking of 'variety of different functions' and 'performs' at the top of 1126. Italics Thiselton's.

[385] Thiselton, *LLM*, 7; cf. Thiselton, 'LMR', 1127; cf. 1132, 1134-1135, 1137, 1138, 1143.

phenomenon of 'inter-translatability' shows.[386]

C) SELF-DECEPTION AS AN EMPHASIS IN FREUD'S PSYCHOANALYSIS

Moving on to consider 'self-deception' then, for Thiselton, 'biblical'-theological teaching on 'self-deception' resonates with but also improves upon Freud's approach. Negatively, Thiselton argues that Freud's "atheism" is not 'based on' 'scientific' 'psychological' 'observation' but on 'philosophical speculation' in the ancient skeptical tradition of 'Lucretius' and 'Hobbes'. Thiselton notes that this fact contradicts Freud's own positivist 'doctrine', drawn from 'Comte and... Feuerbach', according to which supposedly only 'scientific observation' yields 'valid knowledge'. Further, Thiselton speculates that Freud's hatred of 'his Jewish father' may have caused him to 'repress' God's 'reality... into his... unconscious'.[387]

Positively, however, Thiselton argues that Freud's expositions of 'the human' 'capacity' for 'self-deception', of 'the unconscious' as 'a reservoir of strong feeling' and inner urges, and of the need for 'rational' assessment of 'the unconscious' as 'part of... health and maturity' resonate with 'biblical' teaching about 'sin' and the human 'heart'.[388] Having said this, Thiselton argues that 'the Bible' is more skeptical and realistic than Freud about the human condition: given the divorce between 'self-consciousness' (i.e. conscious 'self-awareness') and 'self-understanding' (oneself truly understood), then only the Holy Spirit can unmask and heal the heart's 'self-deceptions' and 'inner conflicts' respectively. Thus, Thiselton argues that biblical theology is in no way an "unwarranted" dialogue partner with respect to the psychoanalytical tradition when it comes to hermeneutical reflection on the issue of self-deception.[389]

*7. Concluding Comments on Thiselton's Appeals to Mutual Dialogic Warrant*

In conclusion, Thiselton's theological explorations into historical rationality (including "re-historicized" subject-object conceptualization), historical knowledge, truth, faith, and self-deception are dialogically warranted in relation to emerging philosophical problems and criteria. Conversely, Thiselton's philosophical explorations into perception are dialogically warranted in relation to exegetical and practical theological problems and criteria. And, for Thiselton, Continental reflection on understanding provides correction in relation to the rationalism of "process" theology.

That is, Thiselton's "dialogical warranting" works in both directions: for Thiselton, theology and philosophy belong together in hermeneutical discussions

---

[386] Thiselton, 'LMR', 1126-1127; cf. Thiselton, *2H*, 137, 404, 374.
[387] Thiselton, 'Freud', 12, 14.
[388] Thiselton, 'Freud', 12, 14; cf. Thiselton, *IGPS*, 127.
[389] Thiselton, 'Freud', 12, 14; cf.: Gadamer, 'PF', 116; Achtemeier, P.J., *An Introduction to The New Hermeneutic* (Philadelphia: The Westminster Press, 1969), 88.

related to epistemology. Nevertheless, caution is needed at this point: Thiselton does not assimilate biblical theology to a philosophical worldview. Rather, Thiselton proves the cogency of *philosophy* in relation to the elucidation of a prior biblical and theological framework. And Thiselton proves the cogency of *a prior biblical and theological framework* in relation to the anticipation of philosophical criteria emerging from widening philosophical dialogues, and in relation to providing solutions of relevance to philosophical problems emerging from those same widening philosophical dialogues.

## D. Conclusion:
## Towards a Christological and Eschatological Unification of Hermeneutics and Towards a Unified Hermeneutical Critique of Epistemology, through Dialogue between Philosophy and Theology

We began the present chapter by explaining Thiselton's difficult style of writing in terms of his historical responses to others and in terms of his invitation to reader-involvement. Accepting this invitation, we outlined our historical-structural approach to Thiselton's work, and suggested that Thiselton's work connoted three "strata" of hermeneutical reflection: widening inter-disciplinary and inter-traditional (and smaller-scale) dialogue unto critical synthesis, five theoretical hermeneutical critiques, and a critique of hermeneutical understanding. We then related these three strata to Chapters 3-7 in the present study.

Next, we expounded Thiselton's widened dialogue(s) between biblical studies, systematic theology, and hermeneutics. Thiselton grounded and unified his hermeneutical theory in eschatology and Christology, contrary to charges of "disunity" or 'dualism', to other ways of unifying hermeneutics, and to charges of "Gadamerian" or "Wittgensteinian" relativism. Thiselton had neither neglected Pannenberg nor 'the third horizon' of eschatology. Nevertheless, calling Thiselton simply 'Pannenbergian' was also a caricature.[390]

Next, we demonstrated that Thiselton viewed his theological unification of hermeneutics as a provisionally warranted working assumption. Thiselton's popular writings on 'biblical authority' did not justify charges of straightforward 'fideism' when read against the background of his more theoretical works.[391]

Rather, (1), Thiselton warranted theological exploration on the ground that Continental philosophy, whilst rightly attempting to "re-historicize" understanding, failed to properly re-instate a re-historicized notion of "subject-object conceptualization" in relation to a metacritique of traditions, or even in relation to critical testing relative to traditional public criteria. Whilst Thiselton's reading of Heidegger in relation to conceptualization and tradition was open to mild criticisms, we could still affirm his overall point.

(2) Thiselton also demonstrated that theology, specifically a non-dualistic

---

[390] Contradicting: Walsh, 'TC', 234; McHann Jr., *3H*, 14; Palmer, 'Scope', 226-227.
[391] Thiselton, 'U (long)', 92; cf. again, we are contradicting, Walsh, 'TC', 235.

working biblical multiform notion of truth, cogently corrected various kinds of one-sidedness in extra-biblical approaches to "truth" and, in particular, corrected the 'controlling picture' of Kierkegaard's one-sided approach that had "bewitched" "secular" and "theological" 'existentialist' traditions. At the same time, Thiselton implicitly showed that extra-biblical approaches to "truth" sometimes genuinely "fleshed out" a 'biblical' approach to "truth".[392]

In addition, we might now add that Thiselton's approach to truth - being inconsistent with a pluralism of competing 'incommensurable' contents - *further* contradicts charges, emanating from some writers, that Thiselton supposedly succumbs to "Wittgensteinian" 'perspectivism', 'subjectivism', 'anti-essentialism', or 'relativism', or to "Gadamerian" 'relativism'.[393] Other writers rightly highlight Thiselton's *attacks* against 'relativism'.[394]

Moreover, Thiselton's approach to "truth" also helps to negate the caricature that Thiselton is 'Pannenbergian'. For Thiselton, in this context, the early Pannenberg 'invites travel in the right direction', but does 'not' provide 'a final or definitive solution'.[395]

(3) Thiselton's theological explorations also resonated with T.F. Torrance's properly-historical 'scientific' notion of 'rationality' and with Freud's emphases on 'self-deception', 'the unconscious', and on psycho-analysis. Conversely, Thiselton argued that solutions to exegetical and practical problems in theology were provided by theories of "perception" from the philosophy of language.[396]

Stepping back, (4), we propose that whilst Thiselton has looked into notions of "truth", "historical rationality", "historical knowledge", "perception", "faith", and so on - all "epistemological" concerns[397] - there is a string of epistemological terminology absent from his second period writings. This absence is partly accounted for by Thiselton's broader hermeneutical "language-game", by his "programmatic" approach (he engages with Alvin Plantinga and others in his "fourth" and "fifth" periods),[398] and by his move beyond the strictly-Cartesian

---

[392] Thiselton, *2H*, 432; cf.: Thiselton, 'KNT', 87; Thiselton, 'Truth', 900; again, contradicting, Walsh, 'TC', 234; cf. 231-232.

[393] cf.: McNicol, 'R *2H*', 189; Walsh, 'TC', 234; Grech, P., 'Review of A.C. Thiselton's *The Two Horizons*', *Bib* 63.4 (1982), 576; Poythress, 'R *2H*', 179; Rodd, 'R *2H*', 290; see also hints in, Dockery, 'R *2H*', 135; Geisler, 'R *2H*', 183; Morgan, 'R *2H*', 332.

[394] Barnes, L.P., 'Light from the East? Ninian Smart and the Christian-Buddhist Encounter', *SJT* 40.1 (1987), 68-69; cf.: Harrisville, 'R *2H*', 216; Van Voorst, 'R *2H*', 220; Conroy, 'R *2H*', 564.

[395] cf.: Thiselton, 'TNI', 11; Palmer, 'Scope', 226-227; Palmer, 'R *2H*', 172-174; Thiselton, 'Truth', 874-902.

[396] Thiselton, 'IA', 9; cf. Thiselton, 'Freud', 12, 14.

[397] Klein, 'R *2H*', 71.

[398] cf.: Thiselton, 'CAP', 209-214; Thiselton, A.C., 'Barr on Barth and Natural Theology: A Plea for Hermeneutics in Historical Theology. Review Article of J. Barr's *Biblical Faith and Natural Theology*', *SJT* 47.4 (1994), 522-523; Thiselton, A.C., *A Concise Encyclopedia of the Philosophy of Religion* (Oxford: One World, 2002), 228-230, 324-326.

"subject-object" model.[399] However, there are still epistemological issues that Thiselton has not addressed, for example 'Bayesianism' (which has to do with *probability*). This point suggests that there is still a need for a more extensive dialogue between Thiselton's hermeneutics and epistemological traditions.[400] C.G. Bartholomew's point that Thiselton has not adequately engaged with Spinoza's thought may have some relevance here – though, again, Thiselton considers Spinoza's thought later.[401]

In conclusion, and even before we move on to consider the hermeneutical circle, we can see that Thiselton's process of theoretical construction towards a unified hermeneutical critique of epistemology exposes different kinds of philosophical problems which – taken together – contribute to the provisional *warranting* of the exploratory widened dialogue between philosophy and theology that Thiselton pursues.

---

[399] e.g. Thiselton, 'NH', 312-313, 317-324; cf. Thiselton, 'CAP', 209-214.
[400] Morton, *Guide*, 190.
[401] Bartholomew, C.G., *Reading Ecclesiastes: Old Testament Exegesis and Hermeneutical Theory* (Bristol: Unpublished University of Bristol PhD Thesis, 1996), 9; but cf. Thiselton, *Encyclopedia*, 291-292.

CHAPTER 4

# Hermeneutics, Language, Cultures, and Selves: Towards Unified Hermeneutical Critiques of Language, Western Culture, and Human Selves

## A. Preliminary Comments: Justifying Our Approach

In this chapter we expound Thiselton's second-period thinking in relation to discussions about "language", "(Western) culture", and "human selves". We should note the following preliminary points.

(1) Our exposition will open up fresh angles of view on Thiselton's formative thinking, and will *expose several misreadings of his work in the literature* – notably misreadings relating to the character of Thiselton's appeals to the later Wittgenstein, to Heidegger, to Gadamer, and to the New Hermeneutic. In particular, we will demonstrate that Thiselton is neither simply "Wittgensteinian", nor simply "Gadamerian", nor simply a champion of "the New Hermeneutic".

(2) We address the question of "language" only after the question of "epistemology" for three reasons. (a) Thiselton's hermeneutical critique of epistemology relates "truth" to history, to eschatology, and to God (see Chapter 3). These, rather than "language", constitute 'the... ontological ground of' hermeneutics in Thiselton's thinking – where, on this point, Thiselton follows Pannenberg.[1] (b) Thiselton rejects Tillich's Heideggerian notion 'that language' may 'transcend... [re-historicized] subject-object' conceptualization. In Thiselton's

---

[1] cf.: Thiselton, A.C., 'Review of W. Pannenberg's *Basic Questions in Theology, Vol. 1*', *Chman* 85.2 (1971), 120-122; Thiselton, A.C., 'The Theologian Who Must Not Be Ignored. Article Review of W. Pannenberg's *Basic Questions in Theology, Vol. 2*', *CEN* 25 Feb. (1972), 11; Thiselton, A.C., 'The Use of Philosophical Categories in New Testament Hermeneutics', *Chman* 87.1 (1973), 96; Thiselton, A.C., 'Semantics and New Testament Interpretation', in *New Testament Interpretation: Essays in Principles and Methods* (ed. I.H. Marshall; Grand Rapids: Eerdmans; Exeter: Paternoster Press, 1977; actually written 1974), 76; Thiselton, A.C., 'Language and Meaning in Religion', in 'Word', in *The New International Dictionary of New Testament Theology. Volume III* (ed. C. Brown; Exeter: Paternoster; Grand Rapids: Zondervan, 1978; actually written by 1977), 1124-1130, 1135-1137; Thiselton, A.C., *New Horizons in Hermeneutics: The Theory and Practice of Transforming Biblical Reading* (London: HarperCollins; Grand Rapids: Zondervan, 1992), 337; McHann Jr., J.C., *The Three Horizons: A Study in Biblical Hermeneutics with Special Reference to Wolfhart Pannenberg* (Aberdeen: University of Aberdeen Ph.D. Thesis, 1987), 326 (quoted).

view, all intelligible 'language' involves 'conceptualization' grounded in 'semantic opposition or contrast'. Thiselton argues that, since 'thought' and 'language' are interwoven, then epistemological questions are not merely 'derivative' relative to linguistic questions.² (c) Thiselton draws on the later Wittgenstein in order to urge that a 'multi-level' extra-linguistic epistemological critique of 'language-uses' is required in order to avoid '"the bewitchment of our intelligence by... language"'. That is, Thiselton argues that *linguistic* actions are to be critically and metacritically evaluated relative to the larger and more basic spheres of *historical* traditions (including public criteria of meaning that embrace extra-linguistic *and* linguistic actions) and of *provisionally warranted and provisionally understood biblical-theological* metacriteria (see Chapters 3, 6 and 7).³

## B. Dialogic Theory-Construction:
## Towards a Unified Hermeneutical Critique of Language

In Chapter 3, we argued that Thiselton's second-stratum hermeneutical critiques were grounded in his first-stratum dialogues – particularly in his first-stratum dialogue between theology and philosophy. For example, we noted that, in Thiselton's view, 'philosophical description' – as well as having other functions – certainly *clarified* 'New Testament texts'. And yet, as we saw, biblical studies and systematic theology also *shaped* Thiselton's hermeneutics.⁴ In the present chapter, therefore, we will now revisit Thiselton's dialogue between theology and philosophy – this time with respect to his approach to *"language"*.

---

[2] Thiselton, A.C., 'The Theology of Paul Tillich', *Chman* 88.1 (1974), 88, 99, 100; cf.: Thiselton, 'LMR', 1126-1127; Thiselton, A.C., 'The New Hermeneutic', in *New Testament Interpretation: Essays in Principles and Methods* (ed. I.H. Marshall; Grand Rapids: Eerdmans; Exeter: Paternoster Press, 1977), 318-320; Heidegger, M., *Being and Time* (trans. J. Macquarrie and E. Robinson; Oxford: Blackwell, 1962, 2001), 195 onwards. Thiselton's italics removed from 'language' and 'conceptualization'.

[3] Thiselton, A.C., 'Truth', in *The New International Dictionary of New Testament Theology, Volume 3* (ed. C. Brown; Exeter: Paternoster; Grand Rapids: Zondervan, 1978), 881, cf. 896-897; cf.: Thiselton, 'UPC', 89; Thiselton, A.C., 'Thirty Years of Hermeneutics: Retrospect and Prospects', in *International Symposium on the Interpretation of the Bible* (ed. J. Krašovec; Ljubljana: Slovenian Academy of Sciences and Arts; Sheffield: Sheffield Academic Press, 1998), 1562; Thiselton, A.C., 'The Meaning of SARX in 1 Corinthians 5:5: A Fresh Approach in the Light of Logical and Semantic Factors', *SJT* 26.2 (May 1973), 210; Thiselton, A.C., *Language, Liturgy and Meaning* (Nottingham: Grove Books, 1975 and 1986), 10-16; Thiselton, *NH*, 367-368; Wittgenstein, L., *Philosophical Investigations* (trans. G.E.M. Anscombe; Oxford: Blackwell, 1953, 2001), 47; cf. Chapter 3 and our arguments below in the present chapter. Italics ours.

[4] Thiselton, 'UPC', 96-97; cf. 87-100; cf. Thiselton, A.C., *The Two Horizons: New Testament Hermeneutics and Philosophical Description with Special Reference to Heidegger, Bultmann, Gadamer, and Wittgenstein* (Exeter: Paternoster Press, 1980), 6; cf. 74-84.

*1. The Philosophical Clarification of a Prior Biblical and Theological Account of Language*

That is to say, (1), Thiselton's *hermeneutical critique of language* functions as philosophical description so as to clarify what he later calls 'a biblical and theological account of language'. Retrospectively he writes in 1999:

> one reviewer of my work appears to believe that my insistence on the major importance of speech-acts stems from being seduced by the later Wittgenstein. The reverse is the case. Since 1970... I have produced a series of writings urging that a biblical and theological account of language gives weight and currency to the importance of speech-acts.[5]

That is, from his second period (or even earlier) onwards, Thiselton moves dialogically between the Bible, 'the later Wittgenstein' and speech-act theory, noting – amongst other biblical speech-acts - biblical

> *acts of declaring* (kerygma);... *worship* (hymns and psalms),... *pronouncement and legal direction* (laws and commissionings); and... *acts of promise* (for Paul, Hebrews, Luther, and Tyndale, the... heart of... the liberating gospel). [Further, Thiselton notes that] in John and in 1 John, emphasis is put on "doing" the truth... on lifestyle.[6]

Thiselton then insists:

> It is not that Wittgenstein "invents" this view of language; he rescues it from its burial beneath an abstract Cartesian tradition that tends to equate language with argument or description alone. In Jesus Christ the Word was made *flesh*; Cartesian Protestantism threatens to turn flesh back into abstracted *word* again.[7]

Thus, contradicting J. Bowden, we can see that Thiselton's appeal to the later Wittgenstein *is* indispensable for biblical hermeneutics. Thiselton argues that, alongside speech-act theory, the later Wittgenstein facilitates a philosophical description that clarifies, and even 'rescues', 'a' prior 'biblical and theological account of language' that is grounded in 'Christ' as "enfleshed Word".[8]

Of course, Thiselton admits that this prior 'biblical and theological account of language' is not *exhaustively* clarified by philosophy. Thiselton allows that '"divine"' 'speech-acts' - contrary to what certain philosophical accounts of language might suggest in relation to human language - sometimes function with powerful 'causal

---

[5] Thiselton, A.C., 'Communicative Action and Promise in Inter-Disciplinary, Biblical, and Theological Hermeneutics', in *The Promise of Hermeneutics* (R. Lundin, C. Walhout and A.C. Thiselton; Grand Rapids and Cambridge: Eerdmans; Carlisle: Paternoster, 1999), 144.

[6] Thiselton, 'CAP', 144-145; cf. Thiselton, *NH*, 2, cf. 16, 17. Italics Thiselton's.

[7] Thiselton, 'CAP', 145; cf. Wittgenstein, *PI*, 189-192. Italics Thiselton's.

[8] Bowden, J., 'Review of A.C. Thiselton's *The Two Horizons*', *Th* 84.697 (Jan. 1981), 57; cf. Thiselton, 'CAP', 144-145; cf. later in the present chapter and also Chapter 6.

force' simply because they are "'divine'".⁹ Nevertheless, philosophical description remains very important for Thiselton, where Thiselton cites two works from his 'second period' that inter-relate 'theological' and 'philosophical' "accounts" 'of language'. His article on Paul Tillich is also relevant in this respect.¹⁰

Thus, (2), in 'The Supposed Power of Words in the Biblical Writings' (1974), Thiselton draws positively on the 'philosophy of language' (the tradition of the later Wittgenstein, J.L. Austin, and D.D. Evans), and on 'general linguistics' and 'modern semantics' (the Saussurian tradition - notably J. Barr), and notes resonances between these traditions and 'biblical' language.¹¹

(3) Thiselton also comments on 'biblical' language in critique of 'The Theology of Paul Tillich' (1974): (a) Thiselton draws on 'Saussure' and on 'general linguistics', arguing that biblical 'symbols' do not relate "naturally" to 'reality' but, like all 'language', are grounded in "conventional" 'speech-habits'.¹² (b) As already noted, Thiselton draws on the 'philosophy' of 'language' and on 'general linguistics' in order to argue that all intelligible 'language', including biblical language 'about God', involves 'conceptualization' grounded in 'semantic' differences. Therefore, Thiselton argues that Tillich's single allowed theological predicate, "'God is being-itself'", says nothing, since it is set in 'opposition' to nothing.¹³ (c) Thiselton argues, drawing on P. van Buren and W. Hordern, that God's unique personhood can only be distinguished by the '*particularizing* language' of biblical historical report and narrative, and not by 'symbols' alone: Thiselton argues that God acted specifically, in 'history', and therefore that God is not just an amalgamation of "qualities". Drawing on general 'linguistics' and on 'structural semantics', Thiselton insists that 'the fundamental unit of meaning' is not 'the word', but 'the' particular 'speech-act' in its context.¹⁴

(4) In *Language, Liturgy and Meaning* (1975), Thiselton draws positively on 'the philosophy of language', on general linguistics, on semantics,¹⁵ and sometimes positively on Continental traditions. Thiselton argues that the work of the later Wittgenstein – and sometimes also the work of Gadamer and of the New Hermeneutic - clarifies biblical language.¹⁶ Thiselton's friendliness towards Gadamer and the New Hermeneutic, however, is qualified by his criticisms of

---

⁹ Thiselton, A.C., 'The Supposed Power of Words in the Biblical Writings', *JThStud* NS25.2 (Oct. 1974), 290-291; cf. 296; cf.: Thiselton, 'TY', 1562; Thiselton, 'CAP', 144, cf. 203, 211, 213-214, 218, 221, 236; cf. our arguments below.
¹⁰ Thiselton, 'Words', 297 cf. 283-299; cf. Thiselton, 'CAP', 144; cf. Thiselton, *LLM*, 1-32; cf. Thiselton, 'Till', 86-107.
¹¹ Thiselton, 'Words', 286-287, 289-290, 293-294, 296-299; cf. Thiselton, A.C., 'The Semantics of Biblical Language as an Aspect of Hermeneutics', *FTht* 103.2 (1976), 108-120.
¹² Thiselton, 'Till', 98-101.
¹³ Thiselton, 'Till', 86, 99-100.
¹⁴ Thiselton, 'Till', 100-101. Italics Thiselton's.
¹⁵ Thiselton, *LLM*, 7, 18-19; cf. 6-7, 10, 12, 31.
¹⁶ Thiselton, *LLM*, 7, cf. 8-9.

both elsewhere,[17] whilst his responses to Heidegger, to Bultmann, and to 'R.B. Braithwaite' are more negative than positive in this context of discussion.[18]

That is, (5), Thiselton, *first*, draws positively on the philosophy of language, on general linguistics, and on modern semantics, but, *second*, has a mixed response to Continental approaches to language. Nevertheless, taken *together*, these two sets of appeals and/or responses constitute Thiselton's *hermeneutical critique of language* which, in turn, with very few exceptions, "philosophically describes" a prior 'biblical and theological account of language'.[19]

Thus, in 'Language and Meaning in Religion' (written 1977, published 1978), Thiselton combines appeals to 'Saussure', to 'general linguistics', to the later 'Wittgenstein', to Anglo-American 'linguistic philosophy', and to the Continental tradition of 'Heidegger and… Gadamer', and in effect argues that conclusions emerging from this *philosophical* dialogue resonate with, describe, and clarify a *prior* '*biblical and theological* account of language'.[20]

*2. The Theological Shaping of Thiselton's Hermeneutical Critique of Language*

Having said this, if Thiselton's hermeneutical critique of language helps to clarify a prior 'biblical and theological account of language', then the latter, in turn, also shapes the former. That is, as we have seen, Thiselton's Christo-eschatological framework "generatively" grounds and unifies his five major second-stratum hermeneutical critiques such that, for Thiselton, language (as well as epistemology) finds its ontological ground in Christology, eschatology, and history – as follows.[21]

Thus, (1), in his second period Thiselton *allies his appeals to Pannenberg with his appeals to the later Wittgenstein* in his (i.e. Thiselton's) approach to language. In Thiselton's view, (a), both these thinkers mediate between 'Anglo-American' 'analytical' traditions and 'Continental… traditions' where, in 1970, Thiselton combines appeals to both thinkers in his linguistic critique of certain characteristics of 'Continental hermeneutics'.[22] (b) In 1971, Thiselton notes that Pannenberg – like the later Wittgenstein - reinstates 'propositions…', but 'not the analytical abstractions of… timeless Platonism'. In Thiselton's view, these two thinkers 'above all others… cannot be dismissed with [Don Cupitt's] patronizing

---

[17] The relevant papers are, Thiselton, A.C., 'The Parables as Language-Event: Some Comments on Fuchs's Hermeneutics in the Light of Linguistic Philosophy', *SJT* 23.4 (Nov. 1970), 437-468; and, Thiselton, 'NH', 308-333.

[18] Thiselton, *LLM*, 15-16, 27-32.

[19] Morgan, R., 'Review of A.C. Thiselton's *The Two Horizons*', *HeyJ* 22.3 (1981), 331-333; cf. Thiselton, *2H*, 292; cf. Thiselton, 'CAP', 144.

[20] Thiselton, 'LMR', 1123, 1137-1142, 1130-1135; cf. 1126, 1132; cf. Thiselton, 'CAP', 144. Italics ours.

[21] Our use of the term "generatively" follows on from Thiselton's in, Thiselton, *NH*, 39.

[22] Thiselton, A.C., 'TY', 1560-1561; cf. Thiselton, 'Parab', 438; cf. 437-468; cf. 451-454.

nod'; they 'deserve criticism, if at all, only' after 'very long and careful discussion'.²³

(c) In 1973 Thiselton's defence of historical report anticipates his later appeals to Pannenberg and to the later Wittgenstein in the context of his (i.e. Thiselton's) arguments against positivism. Similarly, Thiselton approves of both thinkers' attacks on 'Kantian or Dilthey-type dualism'.²⁴ Elsewhere, implicitly accepting later Wittgensteinian insights into linguistic multi-functionality and Pannenberg's high estimate 'of apocalyptic', Thiselton rejects the reduction of 'apocalyptic' 'language' to existential categories.²⁵ Thiselton also interweaves Pannenberg's notion of 'typological' '"paradigmatic"' 'events' and the later Wittgenstein's notion of 'public criteria of meaning' (see below) – as, for example, in the case of Thiselton's later remarks about the disambiguation of the 'language' of '"redemption"'.²⁶ Finally, Thiselton appeals to both thinkers against 'Gadamer's' linguistic dualism and, implicitly, against Bultmann's notion of '"private language"' 'about… inner states'.²⁷

(d) Between 1974 and 1978, Thiselton juxtaposes implicit appeals to Pannenberg with explicit appeals to the later Wittgenstein in relation to 'eschatological futurity' and 'public criteria' respectively, and thereby distinguishes between "legitimate" and "illegitimate" 'vagueness' 'in theological formulations'.²⁸ Thiselton also interfaces Moltmann's 'eschatological' "expectancy" with Pannenberg's 'eschatological' epistemology, and with the later Wittgenstein's grammar of "expectancy".²⁹ Elsewhere, Thiselton combines an appeal to the later

---

[23] cf.: Thiselton, 'R BQ1', 121; Thiselton, A.C., 'Brink of Discovery. Review of D. Cupitt's *Christ and the Hiddenness of God*', *CEN* 1 Oct. (1971), 11; Thiselton, A.C., "Well-trampled'. Review of F. Ferré's *Language, Logic and God*', *CEN* 8 Jan. (1971), 12; Thiselton, A.C., "Language in a Haze'. Review of T. Fawcett's *The Symbolic Language of Religion*', *CEN* 7 May (1971), 12; Thiselton, A.C., 'Review of T. Fawcett's *The Symbolic Language of Religion*', *Chman* 85.3 (1971), 221-222.

[24] Thiselton, A.C., 'Review of S.W. Sykes and J.P. Clayton eds. *Christ, Faith and History: Cambridge Studies in Christology*', *Chman* 87.1 (1973), 69; cf. Thiselton, A.C., *New Testament Hermeneutics and Philosophical Description: Issues in New Testament Hermeneutics with Special Reference to the Use of Philosophical Description in Heidegger, Bultmann, Gadamer, and Wittgenstein* (Sheffield: University of Sheffield Ph.D. Thesis, 1977; written by Dec. 1976), 101-114; cf. Thiselton, *2H*, 74-84; cf. 359-361.

[25] Thiselton, A.C., 'New Problems for Old: Article Review of J.A.T. Robinson's *The Human Face of God*', *CEN* 6 Apr. (1973), 8; cf. Wittgenstein, *PI*, 6-7, 12.

[26] Thiselton, A.C., 'Meaning and Myth. Review Article of W. Pannenberg's *Basic Questions in Theology, Vol. 3*', *CEN* 19 Oct. (1973), 8; cf.: Thiselton, 'UPC', 98; Thiselton, 'LMR', 1135.

[27] cf.: Thiselton, 'UPC', 94, 96-98; Thiselton, *NTH*, 402, 545-553, 608; Thiselton, *2H*, 286-287, 379-385, 442, 444; Metzger, B.M., 'Review of A.C. Thiselton's *The Two Horizons*', *PSemB* NS3.2 (1981), 210.

[28] Thiselton, A.C., 'The Ministry and the Church Union: Some Logical and Semantic Factors', *FUty* 18 (1974), 46, cf. 45; cf. Wittgenstein, *PI*, 91, 98-99, 105, 116-117, 122.

[29] Thiselton, A.C., 'The Parousia in Modern Theology. Some Questions and Comments', *Tyn* 27 (1976), 46-48, 52-53.

Wittgenstein with a citation of 'Pannenberg' in validation of his (i.e. Thiselton's) "hermeneutical programme".[30] In Thiselton's view, further, 'Pannenberg' and the 'later' 'Wittgenstein' both rightly reject the 'Neo-Kantian' 'dualism' underlying 'Enlightenment' and 'existentialist' approaches to 'myth'.[31] Moreover, Thiselton's critique 'of structuralist approaches' combines appeals to the later Wittgenstein and to G. Schiwy, where Schiwy probably stands in for Pannenberg in this context.[32]

Summarizing: Thiselton allies his appeals to Pannenberg with his appeals to the later Wittgenstein. We may provisionally conclude that, for Thiselton, *language is ontologically grounded in history and eschatology, and not vice versa* (i.e. for Thiselton "history" and "eschatology" are *not* ontologically grounded in "language").

(2) Moving on, then the notion of 'Christ' as "enfleshed" 'Word' is a meta-criterion for Thiselton. In his article 'Truth' (1978), Thiselton links the notions of "enfleshed" 'Word' and 'correspondence between' "words", "deeds", and (revealed and/or historical) 'reality'.[33] For Thiselton, "enfleshed words", or "responsible" 'language-uses', have 'the… backing', hard 'currency', or 'cash value' of "actions" in 'authentic' historical 'life' - unlike "irresponsible", "self-deceptive" or "manipulative" 'language-uses'.[34]

Further, for Thiselton, regular 'patterns' of "enfleshed words" (interwoven 'social' 'behavior' and 'language-uses'), "experiences", 'events', and divine interventions, form 'historical' *"traditions"*. For Thiselton, 'language-uses' - for example, about 'God' – that lack consistency with "traditions" are "inauthentic" relative to those "traditions".[35] For Thiselton traditions, in turn, reside within a larger anticipated historical-eschatological 'narrative' framework,[36] and are subject to metacriticism: even tradition-backed words may not accord with 'Christ' as *the*

---

[30] Thiselton, A.C., 'Understanding God's Word Today: Evangelicals Face the Challenge of the New Hermeneutic. Address at the Second National Evangelical Anglican Congress, Nottingham, 1977', in *Obeying Christ in a Changing World, Vol. 1* (ed. J.R.W. Stott; Glasgow: Collins/Fountain Books, 1977), 114; cf. 94 (henceforth the 'long' article with this title); cf.: Thiselton, 'TY', 1560-1561; Thiselton, A.C., 'Theology and the Future', *CEN* 23 Jan. (1970), 11.

[31] Thiselton, A.C., 'Myth, Paradigm, and the Status of Biblical Imagery', in *Using the Bible in Liturgy* (ed. C. Byworth; Nottingham: Grove, 1977), 7, 8, cf. 9; cf. 10-11.

[32] Thiselton, A.C., 'Keeping up with Recent Studies: II. Structuralism and Biblical Studies: Method or Ideology?', *ExTim* 89 (Aug. 1978), 329, 334.

[33] Thiselton, 'Truth', 892, 883-886.

[34] Thiselton, 'LMR', 1142, 1127, 1134, 1143, 1135, 1132; cf. Thiselton, 'Truth', 892, 881.

[35] Thiselton, 'LMR', 1123; cf. 1134-1135; cf.: Thiselton, *LLM*, 4; Thiselton, A.C., 'Explain, Interpret, Tell, Narrative', in *The New International Dictionary of New Testament Theology, Volume 1* (ed. C. Brown; Exeter: Paternoster; Grand Rapids: Zondervan, 1975), 581; Thiselton, 'MP', 10-11; Thiselton, 'Truth', 892. Italics ours.

[36] Thiselton, 'R *BQ1*', 120-122; cf.: Thiselton, 'TNI', 11; Thiselton, 'M&M', 8; Thiselton, A.C., 'Head-On Challenge to Doubt: The Theology of Wolfhart Pannenberg', *CEN* 10 May (1974), 8; cf. Thiselton, *LLM*, 32.

"enfleshed Word".[37]

Later, Thiselton contrasts language embedded in concrete history (cf. "enfleshed word") with D. Cupitt's notion of "biology" embedded within language (cf. "en-worded flesh"). For Thiselton, a human "'self'" is not merely "'biological'" or "'animal'" "'energies and responses'" "'with cultural inscriptions [signs] written over its skin'", where Thiselton similarly criticizes Derrida (see Chapter 7).[38] Thus, the Christological notion of "enfleshed Word" remains pivotal in Thiselton's hermeneutical critique of language: *language is ontologically grounded in history understood eschatologically and Christologically, and not vice versa* (i.e. "history", "eschatology", and "Christology" are *not* ontologically grounded in "language").[39]

Summarizing: Thiselton's philosophy of language helps to clarify biblical texts, but biblical theology also shapes Thiselton's philosophy of language in which language is grounded in history, eschatology, and Christology. Thus, a dialogue emerges between philosophy and theology in Thiselton's hermeneutical critique of language, a dialogue to which we shall now turn in more detail.

*3. Thiselton's Appeal to the Later Wittgenstein and its Resonance with Theology, Eschatology, and Christology*

If, by the early 1970s, the later Wittgenstein's work had strongly influenced Thiselton because of what Thiselton's saw as being its 'hermeneutical' character then, by 1977, Thiselton views 'Wittgenstein' as 'one of the most original thinkers in twentieth-century philosophy', and always affirms Wittgenstein's later work.[40] Three preliminaries to our approach to Thiselton's second period appeal to the later Wittgenstein should be noted.

(1) In this context of discussion it is safe to treat Thiselton's second period texts "synchronically" (i.e. as though they were written simultaneously) since his stance in relation to the later Wittgenstein changes little throughout the 1970s. (2)

---

[37] cf.: Thiselton, A.C., 'The Multi-Model Character of Holy Spirit Language', *CEN* 11 Apr. (1974), 8; Thiselton, 'UPC', 89; cf. 98; Thiselton, A.C., 'On the Logical Grammar of Justification in Paul. Paper Presented to the Fifth International Congress on Biblical Studies, Oxford, 1973', in *Studia Evangelica 7* (ed. E.A. Livingstone; Berlin: Akademie-Verlag, 1982), 493 (para. 3); Thiselton, 'SNTT', 93-95; Thiselton, *LLM*, 25-26; Thiselton, 'MP', 11-12; Thiselton, 'LMR', 1123-1127, 1134-1138, 1143; Thiselton, 'Truth', 892, 881, 886, 896-897.

[38] Thiselton, A.C., *Interpreting God and The Postmodern Self: On Meaning, Manipulation and Promise* (SJT: Current Issues in Theology; Edinburgh: T&T Clark, 1995), 106; cf. Thiselton, *NH*, 127-129.

[39] With, Watson, F., 'Review of A.C. Thiselton's *New Horizons in Hermeneutics*', *BibInterp* 4.2 (1996), 254-255; contradicting, Poythress, V.S., 'Review of A.C. Thiselton's *New Horizons in Hermeneutics*', *WThJ* 55.2 (1993), 345.

[40] cf.: Thiselton, 'TY', 1560-1561; Thiselton, 'UPC', 89; quotation from, Thiselton, A.C., 'An Age of Anxiety', in *The History of Christianity. A Lion Handbook* (eds. T. Dowley *et al*; Tring, Hertfordshire: Lion Publishing, 1977), 600-601.

Our systematization of Thiselton's "later Wittgenstein" is provisional. Wittgenstein himself repeatedly failed to systematize his own later work, and we agree with his conclusion that no *formal* systematization of that work is possible. Nevertheless, a *"historical"* systematization or organization of "Thiselton's later Wittgenstein" may certainly be attempted, and we criticize the later Wittgenstein on a point not entirely unrelated to this kind of issue in Chapter 6.[41] (3) Importantly, for Thiselton, an appeal to insights drawn from the later Wittgenstein is dialogically warranted because of their resonance with theology, eschatology and Christology - and vice versa – as follows.

A) LINGUISTIC TRANS-CONTEXTUALITY, "ENFLESHED WORD", AND HISTORICAL ESCHATOLOGY

Thus, whilst following the later Wittgenstein's stress on 'the particular case', Thiselton does, with the later Wittgenstein, preserve a more general, historically *a posteriori* linguistic axis that is resonant with the notion of 'Christ' as "enfleshed Word" and with "trans-contextuality" in theology and eschatology. For the later Wittgenstein and Thiselton, language as "'language'" requires 'enough regularity' - *historically*.[42]

That is, (1), for the later Wittgenstein and Thiselton, 'language' is not "abstract", but "interwoven" with 'extra-linguistic', "active", "socio-historical" 'human' 'life' – "'only in the stream of thought and life do words have meaning'".[43] After the later Wittgenstein, Thiselton points out that many 'first-person utterances' are 'self-involving', and are 'not' just 'reports' or 'information' about 'inner' 'mental' 'states'. Hence, Thiselton, after the later Wittgenstein, observes that the "utterance" "'I am in pain'" is often 'pain-*behavior*' – 'the verbal expression of pain replaces crying'. Similarly, Thiselton argues that 'I "expect'" (cf. 'expecting'), "'I repent'", "'we praise thee'", "'I believe'" (cf. "'believing'"), "intending", and "'understanding'" presuppose an 'extra-linguistic' "grammar". Conversely Thiselton, following the later Wittgenstein, observes that the utterance, "I believe falsely", since it has no possible 'extra-linguistic' "behavioral" 'backing', is meaningless.[44]

Therefore, for Thiselton, 'language' is 'historical' 'communicative "*action*"' that involves 'different levels and dimensions of language *use*'. This point resonates

---

[41] Wittgenstein, *PI*, vii. Italics ours.

[42] cf.: Thiselton, 'SBS', 331-334; Thiselton, 'Truth', 892; Wittgenstein, L., *The Blue and Brown Books. Preliminary Studies for the Philosophical Investigations* (Oxford: Blackwell, 1958, 2002), 18-19; Wittgenstein, *PI*, 82 (quoted); Thiselton, *NH*, 395.

[43] Thiselton, 'LMR', 1130, 1131, 1143; cf.: Thiselton, 'UPC', 96; Thiselton, *LLM*, 7, 12, 9; Thiselton, 'SBS', 334, 333; Wittgenstein, L., *Zettel* (trans. G.E.M. Anscombe; Oxford: Blackwell, 1967, 1998), 30 (quoted).

[44] cf.: Thiselton, 'UPC', 95; cf. 97-98; Thiselton, *LLM*, 7, 10-13, 16-18, 20-21; Thiselton, 'Words', 297; Thiselton, 'Par', 52-53, cf. 27-54; Thiselton, 'NH', 316; Thiselton, 'LG', 495; Thiselton, *NH*, 223, 267, 559; cf. 559-561; Wittgenstein, *PI*, 89 (cited here), 91, 97, 102, 154, 181, 190, 192, 196. Italics ours.

with Thiselton's later 'action model' and with his rejection of Bultmann's 'fact'-'value' 'dualism' (see Chapter 6). For Thiselton, *prior* to interpretative considerations, "history" and "action" are more fundamental or more "'basic'" categories than "language".[45]

Hence, Thiselton argues that 'meaning' is not 'grounded in' 'vocabulary' or in 'surface-grammar' alone, but in an "interwoven" "'whole'" embracing 'language-uses', "actions", "particular" 'life'-"contingencies", "forms of life", and so on. That is, Thiselton concludes that 'meaning' is 'grounded in' 'how given words function within the total real life setting of a community'.[46]

Thus, Thiselton observes that the 'vocabulary' of the question "'what about the points?'" is simple, but asks: is 'the setting' 'railways', 'electric wiring', 'cricket', or otherwise? Similarly, Thiselton observes that 'the... surface-grammar' of "'this is poison'" is simple, but asks: is it 'an imperative... ("Quick! Fetch a doctor!")', 'a reproach: ("You forgot to put sugar in my tea")', 'or a warning: ("Look out!")?' The later Wittgenstein remarks, 'no wonder we find it difficult to know our way about'.[47]

(2) After the later Wittgenstein, Thiselton argues that 'the common behavior of mankind' grounds the historical *a posteriori* trans-contextual inter-relatedness of 'language-games' (see below) and, thereby, also grounds the "inter-translatability" of languages. Thus, Thiselton argues that language-"traditions" (in which cultural 'language-uses' are always embedded) condition but do not totally determine 'thought' or 'world-view'. Such trans-contextual inter-relatedness, however, is not *a priori* or 'formal' for Thiselton, but like *a posteriori* "'family resemblances'" about which no *a priori* "generalizing" assessment can be made. For Thiselton, specific "examples" of such trans-contextual inter-relatedness have to be considered *before any* kind of legitimate assessment can be made with respect to the "general" character of such trans-contextual inter-relatedness.[48]

(3) After the later Wittgenstein, Thiselton distinguishes between 'linguistic *form*', linguistic 'rules', linguistic *'uses'*, and linguistic 'content'. For Thiselton: 'form'

---

[45] cf.: Thiselton, *LLM*, 8; Thiselton, 'CAP', 133, 212; Thiselton, A.C., 'Reader-Response Hermeneutics, Action Models, and the Parables of Jesus', in *The Responsibility of Hermeneutics* (R. Lundin, A.C. Thiselton and C. Walhout; Grand Rapids: Eerdmans; Exeter: Paternoster, 1985), 107; cf. 79-113; Thiselton, *2H*, 247, 248, 211. Contradicting, Zuidervaart, L., 'Review of R. Lundin's, A.C. Thiselton's and C. Walhout's *The Responsibility of Hermeneutics*', *CalThJ* 21.2 (Nov. 1986), 296; the "action model" is a theoretical necessity *prior* to interpretation. Italics ours.

[46] cf.: Thiselton, A.C., 'Myth, Mythology', in *The Zondervan Pictorial Encyclopedia of the Bible, Volume 4* (ed. M.C. Tenney; Grand Rapids, MI: Zondervan, 1975; written by 1973), 338; Thiselton, 'SBS', 334, 333; Thiselton, *LLM*, 3, 4, 10, 12; Thiselton, 'LMR', 1131, 1127; Thiselton, 'UPC', 95-96.; Thiselton, 'TNI', 11. Italics Thiselton's.

[47] cf.: Thiselton, 'UPC', 95-96; Thiselton, *LLM*, 3, 10; Wittgenstein, *PI*, 6, 7, 11-12, 20-21, 168 (quoted).

[48] cf.: Thiselton, *LLM*, 6; Thiselton, 'LMR', 1126-1127; Thiselton, *NH*, 404; Thiselton, *2H*, 374, 372; Wittgenstein, *PI*, 82 (quoted). Italics ours.

embraces 'the "physical properties" of language' - notably 'vocabulary'; 'rules' are like '"rules"' '"in chess"' (cf. 'grammar' as *traditionally* understood); linguistic 'uses' are like 'chess' "moves" (cf. 'logical "grammar"' 'or function' as *philosophically* understood, or, 'questions' of 'style, genre' or "speech-action" - e.g. 'poetry' or '"promising"'); 'linguistic *content*' is "transmitted" by 'language' as in, for example, 'concepts' or 'historical' report. Thus, for Thiselton as for the later Wittgenstein, 'words can... be compared to chess men'.[49]

Notably, Thiselton argues that linguistic 'rules' presuppose the *sociality* of 'language': 'language' is 'public', 'not... "private" (in the later Wittgenstein's technical sense of the term)', contrary to the approach of *'Bultmann'*. Thiselton, after the later Wittgenstein, argues that 'it is' impossible 'to obey a rule "privately"'; and yet Bultmann opposes *'kerygma'* to 'general truths' and 'historical... facts'.[50]

(4) Thiselton argues that 'language' is dual-'level' and 'multi-functional'. After the later 'Wittgenstein', Thiselton distinguishes between 'surface-grammar' (cf. 'form', 'rules', 'content') and 'depth-grammar' (cf. 'uses', 'content'; – i.e. content relates to *both* "grammatical" "levels"), where both thinkers view 'language' as 'multi-functional' at the 'level' of 'depth-grammar'. Thus, Thiselton argues that texts may 'act' in a whole 'variety' of ways on readers, contrary to Cartesian views of texts as 'passive' "objects" 'of scrutiny' and to 'the idea that language always functions in one way'.[51]

On this basis, Thiselton criticizes 'form-criticism' for neglecting linguistic 'functions', though Thiselton acknowledges that 'performative' language may still convey 'information' or 'cognitive... content', as in 'New Testament' 'confessions'.[52] For Thiselton, 'meaning' *interweaves* 'self-involving' 'force' (multiple "overlapping" 'functions') and 'content' (cf. report, 'concepts'). Thus, Thiselton argues that 'liturgical' 'speech-acts' are not just 'flat' 'statements', but that such 'speech-acts' embody 'self-involving' "functions" of 'acclamation', 'proclamation', *'exclamation'*, 'pledge', 'phatic communion', and so on. And yet, as Thiselton insists,

---

[49] cf.: Thiselton, 'LMR', 1127, 1126, 1131-1132, 1138, 1134; Thiselton, *LLM*, 7, 3, 12, 18; Thiselton, 'SNTI', 79; Thiselton, 'M-M', 8; Thiselton, 'NH', 324; Wittgenstein, *PI*, 24; cf. 15, 20-21, 80-81, 231; Wittgenstein, *Z*, 16; Wittgenstein, *B&B*, 83-84 (quoted). Italics on 'form', 'uses' and 'content' Thiselton's, others ours.

[50] cf.: Thiselton, 'LMR', 1123, 1134-1135; Thiselton, 'UPC', 94, 96, 98; Thiselton, *NTH*, 402, 545-553, 608; Thiselton, *2H*, 286-287, 379-385, 442, 444; Wittgenstein, *PI*, 81 (quoted), 91, 98-99, 105, 116-117, 122; Bultmann, R., *Theology of the New Testament. Volume 1* (trans. K. Grobel; London: SCM Press Ltd., 1952), 307 (quoted). Italics in speech-marks are Thiselton's and Bultmann's respectively; other italics are ours.

[51] Thiselton, 'LMR', 1126-1127, 1134; cf.: Thiselton, *LLM*, 13, 10, 6; Thiselton, 'Words', 293; Thiselton, *NTH*, xxviii, conc. 8.2b; Thiselton, 'NH', 323, 312; Walsh, B.J., 'Anthony Thiselton's Contribution to Biblical Hermeneutics', *ChSRev* 14.3 (1985), 230; Thiselton, 'TY', 1562; Wittgenstein, *PI*, 6-7, 11-12, 102 (citation from 102), 168.

[52] Thiselton, *2H*, 396-397; cf. Grech, P., 'Review of A.C. Thiselton's *The Two Horizons*', *Bib* 63.4 (1982), 574; cf. Thiselton, 'UPC', 97-98.

such 'speech-acts' also include historical "report".⁵³

(5) Summarizing: for Thiselton, there are *a posteriori* "historical" – (not *a priori* "formal") - trans-contextual "universal" factors related to "language" (in all its 'variety'). In Thiselton's thinking, these factors constitute historical *"continuities"*. For Thiselton, the grounding of language in historical "'life'", as "enfleshed word" (cf. Christology), thereby resonates *both* with the grounding of language in the "'unity of history'" *and* with eschatological anticipations of "the totality of history" (see Chapter 6). That is, Thiselton argues that, *despite* the actuality of linguistic particularity and 'variety', language is still *always* grounded in historical "'life'" and *always* tends to exhibit certain features - whatever the linguistic activity, whatever the context, and at whatever point in history. In Thiselton's estimate, such trans-contextual and trans-temporal continuities – at the level of language-behavior – lend weight to, and find resonance with, *both* the notion of "historical unity" *and* the notion of "anticipated historical totality" (for the latter *presupposes* "historical unity").⁵⁴

B) LINGUISTIC TRANS-TEMPORALITY AND HISTORICAL TRADITION

For Thiselton, the later Wittgenstein's linguistic philosophy also resonates with theological views of tradition (cf. Chapters 6 and 7). Against "'logical positivism'", Thiselton, after the later Wittgenstein, argues that language is always interwoven with, and is always grounded in, trans-temporal and socio-historical "streams" or *'forms of life'*, "traditions", or "worlds" - where Thiselton notes that *'forms of life'* constitute "givens" in historical and linguistic criticism.⁵⁵

Notably, Thiselton observes that the later Wittgenstein's notion of "paradigmatic" 'language-uses' resonates with Pannenberg's notion of "'paradigmatic'" "typological'" 'events' in "traditions". Thiselton argues that, for both thinkers, further, "tradition" embraces "'continuity'" and 'change', 'stability' and "'openness'" towards "'the future'". In addition, for the later Wittgenstein and for Thiselton (and, by implication, for Thiselton's "Pannenberg"), 'there exists a correspondence between the concepts "rule" and "meaning'" that qualifies the "context-relativity" of meaning (see below).⁵⁶

Notably, (1), Thiselton argues that language-"traditions" embody trans-

---

⁵³ Thiselton, *LLM*, 10-17; cf. Thiselton, 'UPC', 97-98; cf. Thiselton, 'NH', 324. Italics in quotation marks Thiselton's.
⁵⁴ See also, Thiselton, *LLM*, 13, 4; cf. Thiselton, 'H-O', 8. Italics ours.
⁵⁵ Thiselton, *LLM*, 12, 3-6; cf.: Thiselton, 'LMR', 1136, 1127, 1123, 1134-1135; Thiselton, 'NH', 318; Wittgenstein, *PI*, 8-9, 11-12, 88, 174, 226 (quoted); Wittgenstein, *Z*, 30. Italics Wittgenstein's.
⁵⁶ Thiselton, 'M&M', 8; cf.: Thiselton, *2H*, 404-405; Thiselton, 'H-O', 8; Thiselton, *NH*, 393 onwards; Wittgenstein, L., *On Certainty* (trans. D. Paul and G.E.M. Anscombe; Oxford: Blackwell, 1969, 2001), 10e (quoted). Contradicting, Grech, 'R *2H*', 576. Grech confuses a properly historical "anti-essentialist" stance with a descent into relativism, and over-stresses the context-relativity of language-games.

temporal *'continuity'* – including "regular" 'patterns' of "language-uses". For Thiselton, existing 'vocabulary, grammar', and "structure" constitute non-'prescriptive' 'rules' that reflect 'past' concerns, 'language-habits', and "conceptuality", and that may be found strongly "influencing" but not 'absolutely' "determining" 'future' concerns, 'language-habits', and conceptuality. Again, for the later Wittgenstein and Thiselton, 'language' as "'language'" presupposes 'enough regularity' - *historically*.[57]

(2) Thiselton argues that language-"traditions" embody trans-temporal *change*, "purification", and "enrichment" - presupposing "open-endedness" 'towards future experience' and 'new' 'creative' 'language-uses' in a changing world. For Thiselton, after the later Wittgenstein, changes in 'vocabulary', 'grammar', and 'structure' demonstrate their 'conventionality': 'we alter them - as we go along'.[58]

(3) For Thiselton, language-"traditions" include *larger*-scale "discourses" - notably 'narrative', 'myth', "historical report", 'parables', or 'discursive' 'argument' - which "transmit" 'content' pertaining to *'public criteria of meaning'* (see below) and which potentially 'act' on readers.[59] Thiselton observes that language-'traditions' also embrace *smaller*, less extensive, phenomena – namely, "'language-games'" (see below). For Thiselton, the "concept" of "'language-games'" has parallels with other notions of 'frame-of-reference' – including "logical contexts", 'surroundings', "settings", or "contexts-in-life" (including 'culture'). Thus, contradicting P. Keifert's reading of Thiselton, we should conclude that Thiselton does *not* promote a 'facile equation' between 'Gadamer's [notion of] "language as tradition"' and the later Wittgenstein's notion of "'language-uses'".[60]

(4) Thiselton argues that all 'language', whether 'ordinary' or 'religious' ('religious' 'language' is *not* a "distinct" category in Thiselton, with G.J. Laughery), presupposes *'public criteria of meaning'* that,[61] (a), embrace *non-'prescriptive' 'rules'* ('regularities, customs', 'patterns', 'habits'): 'rules… are needed for establishing a practice';[62] (b) are *'observable'* and *'accessible'*, (not "'private'"): calling 'meaning a

---

[57] cf.: Thiselton, 'SNTT', 87-88; Thiselton, 'LMR', 1134-1135, 1127; Thiselton, *LLM*, 3-6; Wittgenstein, *PI*, 38-41, 82 (quoted), cf. 82-83. Italics ours.

[58] Thiselton, *LLM*, 4; cf.: Thiselton, 'SNTT', 85, 87-88; Thiselton, 'LMR', 1135, 1131; Wittgenstein, *PI*, 8, 39 (quoted).

[59] cf.: Thiselton, *LLM*, 4, 24-32; Thiselton, 'Till', 98-101; Thiselton, 'LMR', 1137, 1134, 1127; Thiselton, *2H*, 306; Thiselton, 'R-RH', 113. Italics in quotation marks Thiselton's.

[60] cf.: Thiselton, *LLM*, 3-6, 12; Thiselton, 'MP', 10; Thiselton, 'LG', 494; Thiselton, *2H*, 395. Keifert, P.R., 'Review of A.C. Thiselton's *The Two Horizons*', *WW* 1 (Fall 1981), 409. Italics ours.

[61] cf.: Thiselton, 'LMR', 1132, 1134-1135, esp 1134; Thiselton, 'UPC', 94, 96, 98; Laughery, G.J., 'Language at the Frontiers of Language', in *After Pentecost: Language and Biblical Interpretation* (eds. C.G. Bartholomew, C. Greene and K. Möller; Scripture and Hermeneutics Series; Vol. 2; Carlisle: Paternoster, 2001), 173, 180; Thiselton, *LLM*, 4-6; Thiselton, *2H*, 80-81, 370-385. Italics in quotations Thiselton's.

[62] Thiselton, 'LMR', 1134, 1127, 1135, cf.: Wittgenstein, *PI*, 80-81; Wittgenstein, *OC*, 21e (quoted). Italics ours.

"mental activity"... encourage[s] a false picture';[63] and, (c), are *trans-temporal*, exhibiting historical *'continuity'* and *'change'* - with the later Wittgenstein, Thiselton argues that we can follow 'definite rules at every throw' *or* 'alter them - as we go along'.[64]

(d) Thiselton argues that "public criteria of meaning" embrace the *'extra-linguistic'* dimensions of 'language'-'behavior', of historical 'events', and of kinds of 'situations' and "contexts" that "back", "give" hard 'currency to', and that are "conventionally" 'correlated' and interwoven with, certain 'language-uses'. As the later Wittgenstein puts it: this 'is the inherited background against which I distinguish between true and false'.[65] For Thiselton, against Bultmann, grounding 'meaning' in *'public criteria'* resonates with the interweaving of "event" and 'meaning' (see Chapter 6).[66]

(e) Thiselton argues that "public criteria of meaning" "transmit" 'linguistic', "conceptual" *'content'* subject to *'continuity'* and *'change'*: 'when language-games change, then there is a change in concepts, and... the meanings of words change'.[67] (f) For Thiselton, "'public criteria of meaning'" are exemplified in historical *"paradigm-cases"* or 'model' "language-games" - often in 'narratives': 'examples are needed for establishing a practice'.[68]

(g) Thiselton argues that "public criteria of meaning" constitute necessary "frames-of-reference" (cf. Gadamer's "'common world'", Fuchs' "'common understanding'") that are pre-conditional for the *'intelligibility'* and "communicability" of 'language-uses' or language-'behavior', where "patterned" "correlations" between 'language-uses and given situations' are pre-conditional for "understanding". The later Wittgenstein asks, "'how am I to know what he means, when I see nothing but the signs he gives?'"[69]

---

[63] cf.: Thiselton, 'LMR', 1134-1135; Thiselton, 'UPC', 94, 96, 98; Thiselton, NTH, 402, 545-553, 608; Thiselton, 2H, 381, 286-287, 379-385, 442, 444; Wittgenstein, PI, 39-40, 59-60, 72-73, 80-81, 89-100, 105-106, 151-154, 190-193, 223; Wittgenstein, OC, 21e, 23e, 70e-72e; Wittgenstein, Z, 4 (quoted), 12-16, 82. First italics ours, second Thiselton's.

[64] Thiselton, 'LMR', 1135; cf.: Thiselton, LLM, 6-7; Thiselton, 2H, 376, 405-407; Wittgenstein, PI, 11-12, cf. 39 (quoted)-40. Third set of italics Thiselton's, others ours.

[65] cf.: Thiselton, LLM, 6-7, 3; Thiselton, 'LMR', 1134, 1135, 1143; Thiselton, 'MP', 10, 11; Thiselton, 'SNTI', 85; Wittgenstein, PI, 39-40, 80-81, 92, 223; Wittgenstein, OC, 15 (quoted), 54, 61-62, 143-147. Italics ours.

[66] cf.: Thiselton, 'LMR', 1134-1135; Thiselton, 2H, 247-248. Italics Thiselton's.

[67] Thiselton, 2H, 306, 376, 405-407; cf. Thiselton, 'LMR', 1126, 1135; cf. Wittgenstein, PI, 34, 36; cf. Wittgenstein, OC, 10 (quoted). First and third italics Thiselton's, others ours.

[68] cf.: Thiselton, 'LMR', 1135; Thiselton, 'MP', 11; Wittgenstein, OC, 21e (quoted). Italics ours.

[69] cf.: Thiselton, LLM, 4, 12; Thiselton, 'LMR', 1135, 1140, 1131; Thiselton, 'MP', 4, 10-11; Wittgenstein, PI, 11-12, 26-27, 44, 139 (quoted); Wittgenstein, Z, 30. Thiselton's phrase here rendered, 'language-uses and given situations' (Thiselton, 'MP', 10), actually uses the compound word, 'language-users', not 'language-uses'. We have treated this as a typographical error. Italics ours.

(h) Thiselton argues that "public criteria of meaning" are pre-conditional for the "teaching" of, 'learning' of, and for *'training'* in, 'language-uses' or language-'behavior'. Conversely, Thiselton argues that '"private" language... unrelated... to observable... behavior' is 'necessarily unteachable'[70] - against 'Bultmann's "esoteric" conception of meaning' according to which 'all spiritual attitudes are unobservable'.[71] That is, for Thiselton, after the later Wittgenstein, '"one learns the game by watching how others play"' – 'there is no logical *a priori* "behind" training and upbringing in human life'. Similarly, Thiselton observes that, for Heidegger, 'Dasein is something prior to [re-historicized] subject-object thinking and to cognitive propositions': 'scientific research is not... the manner of Being... closest' to Dasein.[72]

(i) Thiselton argues that "public criteria of meaning" are pre-conditional for the possibility of "checking", testing, or *authenticating* 'language-uses' or language-'behavior'; notably, for Thiselton, "public criteria of meaning" provide "paradigm-cases" against which such "checking", testing, or authenticating can be carried out. Thus, after the later Wittgenstein, Thiselton in effect argues that 'the word "agreement" and the word "rule" are *related*'.[73]

(5) Thiselton applies the later Wittgenstein's notion of 'public criteria of meaning' to the question of so-called 'religious... language' *without* sharply distinguishing the latter from 'ordinary language' as a whole. Thiselton argues that 'experience', 'behavior', notions of 'identity' (human or divine), speech, and 'language-use' (e.g. 'symbols') are only authentically '"Christian"', and only have authentic Christian 'intelligible' 'teachable' 'meaning', if they relate positively to 'Old' and 'New Testament' '"public" criteria of meaning'.[74]

Therefore, Thiselton argues that 'Bible'-'reading' is important for clarifying 'paradigm' 'settings': 'Old Testament' 'paradigm-cases', 'regularities', or 'foundation events' render New Testament salvific 'events' 'intelligible', giving these and 'modern "Christian"... identity' and 'language-uses' their 'currency' and

---

[70] Thiselton, 'MP', 10-11; cf.: Thiselton, 'LMR', 1131, 1134-1135; Thiselton, *LLM*, 6, cf. 12-13; Wittgenstein, *PI*, 1-20, 26-27, 31-32. Italics ours.

[71] Torrance, A.J., 'The Self-Relation, Narcissism and the Gospel of Grace', *SJT* 40.4 (1987), 488, 493. Second citation from: Bultmann, R., 'A Reply to the Theses of J. Schniewind', in *Kerygma and Myth. A Theological Debate* (ed. H.-W. Bartsch; New York: Harper and Row, 1961), 102.

[72] Citing Wittgenstein in, Thiselton, 'LMR', 1135; cf.: Wittgenstein, *PI*, 21-23, 27; Thiselton, *2H*, 378; cited in, Grech, 'R *2H*', 573; cf. Heidegger, *BT*, 78-90; cf. 32 (quoted). Italics Thiselton's.

[73] Thiselton, 'LMR', 1134-1135, 1131; cf.: Thiselton, *LLM*, 12; Thiselton, 'Truth', 893; Thiselton, 'U (long)', 115-117; Wittgenstein, *PI*, 80-81, quoting 86. Second italics Wittgenstein's.

[74] Thiselton, *2H*, 379 onwards, 382; cf.: Thiselton, *LLM*, 4-6; Thiselton, 'LMR', 1132, 1135, 1134; Thiselton, 'U (long)', 115-119; Thiselton, 'Till', 99, 100; Thiselton, 'MP', 10-11.

'meaning'.[75] Thiselton argues that the "meaning" of 'New Testament' language is not dependent on "'inner'" 'mental' "processes" divorced from 'external events', against Bultmann's 'stripping away [of] the mythological garments' in his demythologization programme. In Thiselton's estimate, Bultmann "re-defines" terms, 'confusing' and 'undermining' 'Christian... identity'. But, with the later Wittgenstein, Thiselton argues that 'I must not saw off the branch on which I am sitting'. Against Tillich, Thiselton argues that 'symbols' require embedding 'within' and authentication 'against... broader' 'cognitive discourse'.[76]

Therefore, Thiselton argues that 'responsible' 'Christian' language-use has authentic 'backing' - a hard 'currency' of behavior aligning with 'public criteria of meaning' (cf. Christ as "enfleshed Word"). Conversely, in Thiselton's estimate, irresponsible or 'trivialized' language-use is "unbacked", having no 'anchorage in reality', and leads 'to... circularity and... relativism'. Contradicting P. Ellingworth's reading of Thiselton, we should conclude that Thiselton does *not* 'remove theological concepts to a safe place outside history'.[77]

Thiselton, therefore, prioritizes past 'settings' within a 'tradition' over 'present' 'settings' within a 'tradition', although Thiselton allows that *'both'* past 'settings' within a 'tradition' *and* 'present' 'settings' within a 'tradition' contribute to 'an overarching frame of reference' or 'hermeneutical arch' (after H. Ott). D.S. Dockery rightly stresses Thiselton's 'simultaneous emphasis upon both horizons', where Thiselton does *not* "ground" 'the hermeneutical circle' 'in the modern horizon' (see Chapters 5 and 6).[78]

(6) Thiselton's appeal to the later Wittgenstein to ground 'meaning' (partly) in the trans-temporal 'public' sphere of *'tradition'* resonates with traditional biblical hermeneutical concerns to do with authorial language-use, thought, and "intent" – though Thiselton *rejects* traditional 'psychologistic' or 'mentalist' approaches to 'intent'. With the later Wittgenstein, Thiselton agrees that 'nothing is more wrongheaded than calling meaning a mental activity!'[79] Contradicting L. Brodie's reading

---

[75] cf.: Thiselton, *LLM*, 4-6; Thiselton, *2H*, 381, 382, 384; Thiselton, 'LMR', 1134, 1135, 1131; Thiselton, 'MP', 10-11.

[76] cf.: Thiselton, 'MCU', 46; Thiselton, *2H*, 382, 381, 384; Thiselton, 'AA', 599; Thiselton, 'LMR', 1137; Thiselton, 'MP', 11; Thiselton, 'Till', 100, 98; Bultmann, R., 'New Testament and Mythology: The Problem of Demythologizing The New Testament Proclamation', in *New Testament and Mythology and Other Basic Writings* (ed. and trans. S.M. Ogden; Philadelphia: Fortress Press, 1984), 41; cf. Wittgenstein, *PI*, 27.

[77] Thiselton, 'LMR', 1142-1144; cf. Ellingworth, P., 'Review of A.C. Thiselton's *The Two Horizons*', *EvanQ* 53 (Jul.-Sep. 1981), 179.

[78] Dockery, D.S., 'Review of A.C. Thiselton's *The Two Horizons*', *GThJ* 4.1 (Spr. 1983), 135; contradicting, Thomas, R.L., 'Dynamic Equivalence: A Method of Translation or a System of Hermeneutics?' Essay Presented at the Fortieth Annual Meeting of the Evangelical Theological Society, Wheaton, IL, Nov. 1988, 158; but cf.: Thiselton, *2H*, 438; Thiselton, *LLM*, 4-6, 8-9. First italics Thiselton's.

[79] Thiselton, *LLM*, 4; cf.: Thiselton, *NH*, 223, 267, 559; cf. 559-561; Thiselton, 'LMR', 1130; Wittgenstein, *PI*, 91, 102, 153, 172 (quoted), 181, 196. Italics ours.

of Thiselton, we should note that Thiselton argues that '"the criteria"' involved in "discovering" '"what mental processes are going on"' during speech are not those presupposed in "understanding sentences".[80]

Later, after 'Schleiermacher', the later 'Wittgenstein', and 'Searle', Thiselton argues that authorial intention 'is… not' a mental 'action or process separable from the linguistic act or process itself'.[81] Rather, as F. Watson rightly observes, Thiselton argues that 'intention' turns on 'the "directedness" of the text within the linguistic conventions [cf. public criteria of meaning] with which it operates'; 'a text… constitutes a communicative action proceeding from an author'.[82]

Thus, whilst heavily qualifying G.R. Osborne's view that 'Thiselton remains firmly within the intentionalist camp', we still repudiate E.E. Johnson's view that 'Thiselton… rejects…' any appeal to 'authorial intention'. With K.R. Snodgrass, we should note that Thiselton *avoids* 'over-emphases on' readers.[83]

(7) Thiselton argues that language-"traditions" strongly condition '"the way we look at things"', and that they can 'hide or disclose reality', necessitating an 'extra-linguistic' critique of "traditions".[84] Negatively, Thiselton argues that language-traditions can "hold" '"us captive"' at a dispositional level, 'controlling' our "seeing" (see Chapter 3): 'forms of expression prevent us… from seeing' and have power over 'whole' "persons", not just over the "intellect".[85]

Positively, however, Thiselton, after the later Wittgenstein, argues that "strenuous thinking" can liberate 'us' – 'breaking the spell of' language-traditions, allowing 'us to *notice*' what was before 'unnoticed' though 'always before our eyes'. After the later Wittgenstein, Thiselton argues that 'linguistic philosophy' constitutes '"a battle against the bewitchment of our intelligence by means of language"' - '"a battle"' in which 'analytical or "grammatical" statements' liberate by 'extending' existing "frames of reference" so as to '"show the fly the way out of

---

[80] Thiselton, A.C., 'Review of A. Kenny's *Wittgenstein*', *Chman* 90.1 (1976), 72; cf. Brodie, L., 'Review of A.C. Thiselton's *The Two Horizons*', *Thom* 45.3 (1981), 486. Brodie seems to miss this point in his over-prioritizing of "the psychodynamics of composition".

[81] Thiselton, *NH*, 559.

[82] Watson, 'R *NH*', 254; but cf. 255: Watson cites a "Thiseltonian" point against Thiselton: Thiselton *agrees* with Watson re. the inaccessibility of psychological "motives".

[83] Osborne, G.R., 'Review of A.C. Thiselton's *New Horizons in Hermeneutics*', *CRevBRel* 7 (1994), 91; cf.: Johnson, E.E., 'Review of A.C. Thiselton's *New Horizons in Hermeneutics*', *BibSac* 150.600 (Oct.-Dec. 1993), 502; Thiselton, 'R-RH', 79-113; Snodgrass, K.R., 'Review of R. Lundin's, A.C. Thiselton's and C. Walhout's *The Responsibility of Hermeneutics*', *CovQ* 45 (Nov. 1987), 200.

[84] cf.: Thiselton, 'UPC', 89; Thiselton, *LLM*, 7; Thiselton, 'M-M', 8; Thiselton, *2H*, 402, 404, 405, 432, 444; cited in, Keifert, 'R *2H*', 409; cf. Borsch, F.H., 'Review of A.C. Thiselton's *The Two Horizons*', *AThRev* 65 (Jan. 1983), 89-90.

[85] cf.: Thiselton, 'R *W*', 72; Thiselton, 'SNTT', 93-95; Thiselton, *LLM*, 25-26; Thiselton, 'M-M', 8; Thiselton, 'MP', 12; Thiselton, 'LMR', 1123-1124, 1127, 1132-1138, 1143; Thiselton, 'LG', 493; Thiselton, *2H*, 198, 402, 404, 432; Wittgenstein, *PI*, 44 (quoted), 48.

the fly-bottle'".⁸⁶ Such statements, Thiselton observes, 'constitute the subject-matter of Wittgenstein's whole work'; they do not merely convey *'information'* but, 'directed at the scaffolding of our thinking', *'elucidate the logical grammar of a concept'*, "making" 'possible a new way of seeing', "expanding" '"the horizons of the reader's *understanding*"', and altering his or her *actions*. Notably, as the later Wittgenstein puts it, 'believing is not thinking. (A grammatical remark)'.⁸⁷ Therefore, in Thiselton's estimate, the later Wittgenstein's thinking is relevant for hermeneutics.⁸⁸

C) LANGUAGE-GAMES AND HISTORICAL SETTING

For Thiselton, the later Wittgenstein's approach to language also resonates with traditional emphases on socio-historical-linguistic context - and on historical reconstruction - in biblical hermeneutics. Thus, after the later Wittgenstein, Thiselton argues that, on a particular (as opposed to a general) axis, 'language' is "interwoven" with temporally located, sometimes culturally-specific, socio-historical 'surroundings', and with 'action' and '"thought"' within given "language-communities": the resulting "wholes" are "language-games", which are 'grounded' or *'embedded in* forms of life'. The later Wittgenstein remarks, 'look on the language-game as the *primary* thing'.⁸⁹

Thiselton, (1), observes that, in the later Wittgenstein's thinking, language-games may exhibit *trans-temporal* continuity. Yet, for the later Wittgenstein and for Thiselton, language-games 'are open-ended towards the future', and therefore may also 'change with time'. That is, in Thiselton's estimate, the later Wittgenstein's thinking is relevant for hermeneutics in a further sense (i.e. Gadamer of the Continental philosophical-hermeneutical tradition, like the later Wittgenstein, similarly stressed "open-endedness" 'towards the future' – see Chapter 1).⁹⁰

(2) Thiselton notes that language-games can sometimes be linked to cultural- or "contextual-relativity", but that they may also be *'trans contextual'*: 'lying', for example, 'is a language-game'. Language-games are not normally so extensive, however, as to allow B.J. Walsh's speech – in his responses to Thiselton – about

---

⁸⁶ cf.: Thiselton, *2H*, 30, 370-372, 404; Thiselton, *LLM*, 4; Thiselton, 'UPC', 89, 98; Wittgenstein, *PI*, 47-48, 101-103; Wittgenstein, *B&B*, 30; Wittgenstein, *Culture and Value* (trans. P. Winch; Chicago: The University of Chicago Press, 1980), 65e. Italics Thiselton's.

⁸⁷ Palmer, R.E., 'Review of A.C. Thiselton's *The Two Horizons*', *RevMet* 35.1 (1981), 174; cf.: Thiselton, *2H*, 386-392, 401-402; Grech, 'R *2H*', 574; quoting, Wittgenstein, *PI*, 152. Italics in speech-marks Thiselton's – final italics in speech-marks also Grech's.

⁸⁸ Thiselton, *2H*, 378.

⁸⁹ cf.: Thiselton, 'LMR', 1130-1135, 1127; cf. 1138; Thiselton, *2H*, 374; Thiselton, *LLM*, 7; Thiselton, *NH*, 439-452; Kleinig, J., 'Review of A.C. Thiselton's *The Two Horizons*', *RefThRev* 39 (Sep.-Dec. 1980), 90; Wittgenstein, *PI*, 5, 8-9, 11-12, 88, 167 (quoted), 174, 226; Wittgenstein, Z, 30. First italics ours, second italics Wittgenstein's.

⁹⁰ Thiselton, *2H*, 378; cited by Grech, 'R *2H*', 573; with, Harrisville, R.A., 'Review of A.C. Thiselton's *The Two Horizons*', *Interp* 36 (Apr. 1982), 216; cf.: Wittgenstein, *OC*, 34; Wittgenstein, *PI*, 11-12; cf. Thiselton, 'Parab', 450.

'the' *'whole'* 'Bible' 'as a particular kind of language-game'. Walsh, in his responses to Thiselton, also over-extends Heidegger's partly "parallel" category of 'world' (additionally confusing it with 'world-view') in speaking in the singular of 'the Bible' as 'a book with its own world', 'the biblical world'.[91]

(3) Thiselton, after the later Wittgenstein, notes that language-games are interlinked by 'a complicated network of similarities overlapping and criss-crossing' (cf. '"family-resemblances"'). Thus, with R.L. Maddox, we should note that Thiselton *avoids* straightforwardly 'interpreting Wittgenstein's "language-games" as a fideistic defence of the claim of religious language to its own realm'. Rather, Thiselton maintains a "general" axis at the level of "inter-linking between language-games" (as we saw above).[92]

Thiselton argues that links *between* language-games are *a posteriori* "historical" - *not a priori* "logical". For Thiselton, such links are thus *not* to be seen in "formal", "positivist", or in philosophically "idealist" terms. S.E. Fowl misleadingly posits a binary (*sic*) contrast between, on the one hand, R. Rorty's and J. Stout's 'therapeutic' development of the later Wittgenstein's and J.L. Austin's work, which focuses on "conventional" language-use 'in context', and, on the other hand, J.R. Searle's, K.J. Vanhoozer's, and Thiselton's "development" of the later Wittgenstein's and J.L. Austin's work, which supposedly seeks in 'a philosophy of language... a metaphysic or ontology'.[93] Thiselton, however, like K.-O. Apel, belongs to a *third* "metacritical hermeneutical" stream that rejects *both* "metaphysical" or "idealist", *and*, merely context-relative, 'therapeutic', or 'open' developments of the later Wittgenstein's and Austin's work. For Thiselton, a *properly "historical"* development of the later Wittgenstein's and Austin's work *retains* "trans-contextuality"; *and*, B. Russell's and K. Popper's "serious" philosophizing *differs sharply from* Thiselton's (see Chapter 6).[94]

(4) Thiselton argues that language-games are the proper 'logical' "homes" for specific 'concepts' and word-uses. Again, after the later Wittgenstein, Thiselton observes that '"when language-games change"', so do '"concepts"' and "wordmeanings". Hence, Thiselton argues that "viewing" 'concepts... *"outside* a particular language-game"' or 'frame of reference' "confuses" matters.[95] Thiselton,

---

[91] Thiselton, 'LMR', 1132; cf.: Wittgenstein, *PI*, 90; Walsh, 'TC', 226, 228-230, 233-234. First italics ours, second italics Walsh's.

[92] Thiselton, *LLM*, 6; cf.: Wittgenstein, *PI*, 32; Maddox, R.L., 'Review of A.C. Thiselton's *The Two Horizons*', *ThStud* 43.1 (Mar. 1982), 136.

[93] Thiselton, *LLM*, 6; cf. Fowl, S.E., 'The Role of Authorial Intention in the Theological Interpretation of Scripture', in *Between Two Horizons. Spanning New Testament Studies and Systematic Theology* (eds. J.B. Green and M. Turner; Cambridge: Eerdmans, 2000), 76. n. 10; cf. Ward, T., *Word and Supplement: Speech Acts, Biblical Texts, and the Sufficiency of Scripture* (Oxford: OUP, 2002), 191-192.

[94] Thiselton, *NH*, 393-405; cf.: Thiselton, A.C., 'Review of P. Van Buren's *Theological Explorations*', *Chman* 83.3 (1969), 220-221; Fowl, 'AI', 76. Italics ours.

[95] Thiselton, 'LG', 493; cf.: Thiselton, 'UPC', 96-97; Thiselton, *LLM*, 4; Wittgenstein, *OC*, 10e; Wittgenstein, *PI*, 21-23, 44. Italics Thiselton's.

after the later Wittgenstein, argues that "concern" for 'the particularities of specific language-situations' must displace 'the generalities of formal logic' which constitute 'a mythological description of the use of a rule'. This point reflects a further way in which the later Wittgenstein's work is relevant for hermeneutics in Thiselton's view. (We have already noted Thiselton's application of this point to 'Paul's doctrine of justification' in conjunction with the later Wittgenstein's notion of "'seeing as'").[96]

For Thiselton, "frames-of-reference" related to this more localized focus of discussion include, (a), 'the broader and narrower' 'linguistic' and 'conceptual' "context" (cf. 'universe of discourse', 'room', 'net', 'network' 'of co-ordinates'); (b) 'the extra-linguistic' historical 'situation', "setting", 'context-in-life', or 'context of situation' (cf. 'background'); and, (c), the (common) "'home'" or *'working'* "'language-game'" (cf. 'logical context') employed by 'the language… community' and 'tradition' - a "'language-game'" that embraces *both* speaker *and* hearer. Of course, for Thiselton, these more localized 'frames of reference' do not displace broader 'frames of reference', such as "traditions" and "anticipations" of 'history as a whole' (see above) but, rather, add further specificity. Notably, moreover, Thiselton also distinguishes between "textual" and "readers'" "language-games": a common "'language-game'" may *link* 'horizons', certainly, but this fact – in Thiselton's estimate - *neither* implies that 'horizons' are 'identical' *nor* that they can 'merge' fully.[97]

(5) Thiselton, after the later Wittgenstein, argues that "language-games" strongly condition "'the way we look at things'", and that "language-games" thus necessitate an 'extra-linguistic' critique of potentially 'context-relative' language-uses, or of 'what we do in our language-game', which 'always rests on a tacit presupposition'. That is, for Thiselton, the points made above in relation to "'bewitchment'" and "liberation" or "spell-breaking" also apply here, though on a more localized scale. That is, for Thiselton, traditions can potentially blind us; but, in Thiselton's estimate, local contexts that embrace language-games that are sheltered from external criticism can *also* blind us (the films The *Wicker Man* and *The Lord of the Flies* come to mind respectively).[98]

D) SPEECH-ACTION AND PARTICULAR "ENFLESHED WORD"

For Thiselton, at the most particular level, the later Wittgenstein's approach to

---

[96] Thiselton, *2H*, 378, 415; cf.: Grech, 'R *2H*', 573; Wittgenstein, *PI*, 85 (quoted); Wittgenstein, *B&B*, 18-19; Thiselton, 'LG', 491; cf. 493-494.

[97] cf.: Thiselton, 'LMR', 1123, 1132, 1135, 1138; Thiselton, 'SARX', 205, 212; Thiselton, 'SBL', 115; Thiselton, 'LG', 493, 494; Thiselton, 'Par', 49, 48; Thiselton, 'UPC', 93; Thiselton, *LLM*, 4, 9, 3; Thiselton, *2H*, xix; Wittgenstein, *OC*, 10e; Wittgenstein, *PI*, 21-23, 44. First italics Thiselton's.

[98] cf.: Thiselton, *2H*, 396, 404, 406-407, 434-436; Thiselton, 'UPC', 89; Thiselton, *LLM*, 7; Thiselton, 'NH', 323-324; Thiselton, 'M-M', 8; Thiselton, 'LMR', 1127; Wittgenstein, *PI*, 47-51, 179 (quoted); Wittgenstein, *Z*, 131-133.

language resonates with the biblical notion of "enfleshed Word", according to which Jesus' 'extra-linguistic' "action" disambiguates his specific utterances. Citing the later Wittgenstein, 'interpretations by themselves do not determine meaning'.[99] Thiselton approves of the later Wittgenstein's attack on 'the craving for generality and' on 'the contemptuous attitude towards the particular case' that afflict post-Enlightenment thought.[100] This point emerges in Thiselton's responses to F. Ferré, and to 'structuralist approaches' (see Chapter 5), both in *The Two Horizons*, and later.[101]

Specifically, (1), Thiselton, after the later Wittgenstein, argues that language manifests itself in *specific 'utterances'* (cf. "speech-acts"). For Thiselton, "the basic units of meaning" are not 'abstracted' 'words', 'sentences', or 'ideas' ('meaning' is not grounded in 'abstract' 'logic' or 'essential meaning'), but specific 'utterances' (cf. "speech-acts") in their 'particular' "frames-of-reference" 'in... life'.[102]

(2) Thiselton, after the later Wittgenstein, argues that specific utterances 'may *perform* several "*overlapping*" *functions*' *simultaneously* - not just "conveying" '"facts"' or 'concepts'. Thiselton argues, after the later Wittgenstein, that even 'propositions' can act 'creatively' on "hearers" (see also Chapter 1 of the present study).[103] Thiselton argues that 'cognitive', 'descriptive', and 'performative' dimensions of 'language' are interwoven. Thus, for example, Thiselton observes that 'the logic of description' and 'the logic of evaluation' are theoretically 'distinct', but tend to 'overlap' 'in practice'.[104] Thiselton argues that 'communication' does not depend on 'vocabulary alone', since a single 'surface-grammar' may represent a multiform 'depth-grammar'. The later Wittgenstein, followed by Thiselton, speaks of 'the multiplicity of... tools in language and of the ways they are used'.[105]

Thus, against B.J. Walsh's reading of Thiselton, we should stress that Thiselton's approach is not "dualistic", as though it only "balanced" Continental linguistic "dualism", but rather interweaves assertions with, and/or within, a larger linguistic 'multi-functional' whole.[106]

(3) Thiselton argues that specific utterances show that 'what language is *depends*

---

[99] Thiselton, 'Truth', 892; cf. 882-894; cf.: Thiselton, *LLM*, 7, 12; Wittgenstein, *PI*, 80.

[100] Thiselton, 'SBS', 334, 333; cf. Wittgenstein, *B&B*, 18-19.

[101] cf.: Thiselton, 'Well-trampled', 12; Thiselton, 'SBS', 329, 331, 333, 334; Thiselton, *2H*, 372-376; Thiselton, 'R-RH', 89.

[102] cf.: Thiselton, 'LMR', 1132, 1131, 1130; Thiselton, 'SNTT', 76; Thiselton, *NH*, 540; Thiselton, *2H*, 378; Thiselton, *LLM*, 4; cf. 5; Thiselton, 'SBL', 115; Palmer, 'R *2H*', 173; Wittgenstein, *PI*, 41-42; Wittgenstein, *Z*, 30. Italics ours.

[103] cf.: Thiselton, 'LMR', 1139-1140, 1131, 1126; Thiselton, *LLM*, 13, 11, 17; Wittgenstein, *PI*, 4, 6, 8, 109, 148-149, 13, 31-33; Thiselton, 'Truth', 894-896; Thiselton, 'NH', 326; Thiselton, 'Parab', 438, 456, 452-453, 465-467. Italics ours.

[104] cf.: Thiselton, 'UPC', 96, 94, 98; Thiselton, 'NH', 326; Thiselton, 'Parab', 438-440, 450-454, 465-467; Wittgenstein, *PI*, 13, 102, 105-106; Thiselton, 'SARX', 205-206, 207-210.

[105] Thiselton, *LLM*, 9, 10; cf. Wittgenstein, *PI*, 6-7, 12 (quoted), 13, 168.

[106] Walsh, 'TC', 234; cf. Thiselton, 'TY', 1562.

*on*' what a speaker '*is doing*' in a '*particular language-game*'. Thiselton argues that the meaning of 'a stretch of language' often cannot be disambiguated without considering 'extra-linguistic' "action". Therefore, for Thiselton, there can be 'no single', '"uniform"', or 'comprehensive' 'theory' or definition 'of language' in a philosophically idealist sense. The later Wittgenstein, followed by Thiselton, brings 'words back from their metaphysical to their everyday use', where 'for a *large* class of cases... the meaning of a word is its use...'.[107]

Thus, (4), Thiselton argues that 'the meaning' of an utterance or '"word is"' usually '"its use in"' its '"home"' '"language-game"' and language-'community'.[108] For example, Thiselton argues that 'the term... "God"' 'cannot' be defined "abstractly", but only in terms of "paradigmatic" "uses" by 'Christian' "communities" in "traditions of experiences" and language-'behavior', in 'life'. Thiselton admits that, 'in... certain particular' cases, 'meaning' can still be seen 'in terms of reference'; but, even then, 'many different kinds of thing are called "description"'.[109]

Thus, Thiselton may occasionally and superficially *seem* positive about a 'referential theory of meaning' (see below), but he rejects such theories at a 'comprehensive' level: there is *no* 'comprehensive theory of meaning' and no '"uniform"' relationship 'between language and meaning'. For Thiselton, as for the later Wittgenstein, 'one must... ask' how a 'word' 'is' 'used... in the language-game which is its original home'.[110]

(5) Thiselton observes that some words have several '"home"' 'language-games', where this point links with the later Wittgenstein's notion of '*polymorphous* concepts'. Thus, Thiselton notes that there is no one-to-one relationship between words and concepts.[111] Thiselton appeals to the notion of "polymorphous concepts" in relation to Paul's 'use of [the word] *sarx*' and in relation to uses of the terms 'oneness' and 'sameness' in 'ecumenical' debates.[112] As Thiselton observes, the later Wittgenstein's notion of "concepts with blurred edges" is not quite the same as the later Wittgenstein's notion of '*polymorphous* concepts': language-games can *change* which concept is associated with a word (cf. '*polymorphous* concepts') or

---

[107] cf.: Thiselton, 'Words', 297-298; Thiselton, 'LMR', 1131, 1126; Thiselton, *LLM*, 16, 3, 7, 12-13; Thiselton, A.C., 'Review of D.H. Kelsey's *The Uses of Scripture in Recent Theology*', *Chman* 91.1 (1977), 88; Wittgenstein, *PI*, 2-18, 20 (quoted)-21, 24, 31-32, 43-48 (quoted). First italics ours, second italics Wittgenstein's.
[108] cf.: Thiselton, 'LG', 493; Thiselton, 'SARX', 216; Thiselton, 'LMR', 1131; Thiselton, 'SBL', 115; Thiselton, 'UPC', 95-96; Thiselton, *LLM*, 13, 3, 10.
[109] cf.: Thiselton, *LLM*, 9, 13, 12; Thiselton, 'LMR', 1131; Wittgenstein, *PI*, 12 (quoted).
[110] Thiselton, 'LMR', 1128, 1131, 1130; cf. Wittgenstein, *PI*, 48 (quoted).
[111] Thiselton, 'SARX', 216; cf.: Thiselton, 'SNTT', 94; Thiselton, 'R *USRT*', 88; Wittgenstein, *PI*, 31-32, 106-111. Italics Thiselton's.
[112] Thiselton, A.C., Contribution to 'Flesh', in *The New International Dictionary of New Testament Theology, Volume 1* (ed. C. Brown; Exeter: Paternoster; Grand Rapids: Zondervan, 1975), 680, cf. 678-682; cf. Thiselton, 'MCU', 45; cf. 46. Italics Thiselton's.

merely *condition* a concept's "edges" (cf. "concepts with blurred edges").[113]

(6) Thiselton argues that the meaning of so-called 'religious language' depends on 'the relationship between everyday' 'words' and 'special' kinds of "use" in 'logically' "peculiar" language-games, 'settings', or "traditions", 'between' which there are 'unusual' "'family resemblances'". Thus, for Thiselton, as for the later Wittgenstein, "hearing God" reflects normal 'vocabulary' put to a 'special' use: "'you can't hear God speak to someone else'". Thiselton also considers the examples of "'birth'" (John 3), "'living... water'", "'meat'" (John 4), "bread", "eat and drink", and "come down'" (John 6).[114]

Thiselton argues that lifting language from "'its... home'" "'language-game'" and into an alien 'language-game' changes its 'meaning' illegitimately, where this process can be part of a manipulative maneuver called 'persuasive definition'. Thiselton, with reference to this point, expounds Paul's critique 'of the Corinthians' and attacks 'Bultmann's... demythologizing' programme. In Thiselton's estimate, therefore, whole passages can thus be given meanings irresponsibly – meanings that are incongruent with their "'home" setting[s]' (see Chapter 6).[115]

(7) Thiselton argues that specific utterances may employ 'metaphors', 'models', or 'symbols' that strongly "control" or condition "'the way we look at things'". Therefore, again, Thiselton argues that an 'extra-linguistic' critique of language-uses is necessary - at the level of "controlling pictures" - to 'investigate... the *application* of the picture'.[116] (Earlier observations need not be repeated, including those to do with responsible and irresponsible language-uses).[117]

To avoid problems related to "controlling pictures" (see Chapter 3), Thiselton advocates using multiple 'models' in mutually or reciprocally qualifying inter-relations – as in the Bible where 'Jesus' is simultaneously "'bread'", "'light'", "gate", 'shepherd', 'way', "truth", and so on. Thiselton observes that 'unwanted meanings' are thus "cancelled" by mutual qualification, and that remnant meanings are thus superimposed to form "'new'" 'semantic' fields or "markers". Thiselton argues that these "'new'" 'semantic' fields or "markers" can only be built by "communities", and not by "individuals", where here Thiselton also appeals to I.

---

[113] Thiselton, 'Parab', 466-467; cf.: Thiselton, 'SNTI', 94; Wittgenstein, *PI*, 34, 36. Italics in speech-marks Thiselton's.

[114] Thiselton, *LLM*, 4-6, 3; cf.: Wittgenstein, *PI*, 32; Wittgenstein, *Z*, 123; Thiselton, 'UPC', 96.

[115] cf.: Thiselton, 'SARX', 215-218; Thiselton, A.C., 'Realized Eschatology at Corinth', *NTStud* 24 (Jul. 1978), 514-525; Thiselton, 'MP', 11-12, 6; Thiselton, 'R-RH', 106.

[116] cf.: Thiselton, 'M-M', 8; Thiselton, *LLM*, 23, 25-26, 7; Thiselton, *2H*, 432; Wittgenstein, *PI*, 47, 48-51, 116 (quoted); Thiselton, 'UPC', 89; Wittgenstein, *Z*, 79, 81. Italics Wittgenstein's.

[117] cf.: Thiselton, 'M-M', 8; Thiselton, 'R W', 72; Thiselton, 'SNTI', 93-95; Thiselton, *LLM*, 25-26; Thiselton, 'UPC', 89, 98; Thiselton, 'LG', 493; Thiselton, 'LMR', 1123-1127, 1132-1138, 1143; Thiselton, 'MP', 12.

Ramsey, P. van Buren, J. Barr, and others. Notably, in this context, Thiselton approves of P. van Buren's 'suggestive picture' concerning how "communities" 'extend' language by 'using the edges of language'.[118]

E) THE LEGITIMACY OF THISELTON'S APPEAL TO THE LATER WITTGENSTEIN

In conclusion, and contradicting J. Bowden's reading of Thiselton, we can see that Thiselton *legitimately* employs the later Wittgenstein's insights, (1), to combat Cartesianism by "re-historicizing" language as "enfleshed word" with respect to speech-acts, language-games, forms of life, and "the common behavior of humankind", and, (2), as part of a philosophical description of 'biblical and theological' language-uses. Nevertheless, (3), contradicting N.L. Geisler's reading of Thiselton, we can also see that 'Thiselton's... presuppositions' are not 'Wittgensteinian' since – and here we are contradicting V.S. Poythress's and F. Watson's later readings of Thiselton - Thiselton does not "marginalize" 'theology' but rather,[119] as R. Papaphilippopoulos and R.W.L. Moberly rightly note, theology retains its decisive role for Thiselton.[120]

In Chapter 6, in our discussion concerning the ways in which Thiselton modifies Gadamer's hermeneutical circle, we shall evaluate Thiselton's appeal to the later Wittgenstein further.

*4. Thiselton's Appeal to Linguistic Philosophy and its Resonance with Theology, Eschatology, & Christology*

The later Wittgenstein aside, Thiselton also appeals to J.L. Austin, to D.D. Evans, and to the philosophy of language more broadly during his second period. In Thiselton's estimate, appeals to these thinkers and to this tradition are dialogically warranted partly because such appeals resonate *both* with 'biblical and theological... language' *and* with an appeal to the later Wittgenstein – as follows.[121]

Thus, (1), Thiselton draws on *Austin and Evans*. Indeed, (a), in the early 1970s, Thiselton's 'hermeneutics course' featured 'speech-acts in Austin'.[122] For Thiselton, further, Austin's and Evans' "logic of self-involvement" reinstates 'statements about the past', against 'post-Troeltschian theology', and contradicts J.A.T. Robinson's separation of '"descriptive"' 'statements' from 'interpretation'

---

[118] cf.: Thiselton, *2H*, 432; Thiselton, *LLM*, 4-7; Wittgenstein, *PI*, 8-9, 26-27, 31-32, 41-42.

[119] Contradicting: Bowden, 'R *2H*', 57; Geisler, N.L., 'Review of A.C. Thiselton's *The Two Horizons*', *BibSac* 138 (Apr.-Jun. 1981), 182; Poythress, 'R *NH*', 345; Watson, 'R *NH*', 255-256; and, Walsh, 'TC', 235. See also, Wittgenstein, *PI*, 82 (quoted); cf. Thiselton, *NH*, 404; cf. Thiselton, 'CAP', 144.

[120] Papaphilippopoulos, R., 'Review of A.C. Thiselton's *New Horizons in Hermeneutics*', *SJT* 47.1 (1994), 142-143; cf. Moberly, R.W.L., 'Review of A.C. Thiselton's *New Horizons in Hermeneutics*', *Anv* 11.1 (1994), 72.

[121] See, later, Thiselton, 'CAP', 144.

[122] Thiselton, 'TY', 1562-1563.

and from other linguistic "functions". Thiselton, drawing on Austin, also finds different speech-acts in 1 Corinthians.[123]

(b) In 1973, Thiselton's comparatively unqualified appeals to Austin and Evans contrast with his mixed appeals to Heidegger, Bultmann, and Gadamer.[124] For Thiselton, if 'traditional' approaches reduce language to 'flat assertion' and "information", "existentialist" approaches wrongly reduce language to 'performative' categories *'without factual remainder'*.[125] Following Austin and Evans, however, Thiselton argues that "effective" 'performative utterances' presuppose that 'appropriate' states of affairs and 'appropriate' 'circumstances and conventions' are '"true"': language interweaves 'cognitive' and 'performative' dimensions. In Thiselton's estimate, Austin speaks "hermeneutically" in that he argues that 'linguistic philosophy' "sharpens" our '"awareness of words"' (on Evans' notion of '"onlooks"', see Chapter 3).[126]

(c) In 1974, drawing on Austin and Evans, Thiselton agrees that language performs actions beyond speaking itself - though 'effective' illocutions presuppose *'accepted conventional procedure'*, an 'appropriate' authorized 'person' (or persons), and the 'appropriate situation'. Thiselton also relates Austin's illocutions to biblical language: for example, '"behabitives"' (e.g. "bless", "curse"), '"exercitives"' (e.g. '"proclaim"', '"warn"', and '"pardon"'), and '"commissives"' ('"promise"', '"swear"', and '"covenant"'). Further, Thiselton argues that 'effective' illocutions can have powerful '"conventional effect[s]"' (so 'Austin'), creating new '"institutional state[s] of affairs"' (so 'Evans').[127] With Austin, Thiselton argues that 'no single theory of language' can be comprehensive since 'language' is multifunctional, where the *'speech-act'* is 'the basic unit of meaning'.[128] With Austin, Thiselton argues that '"performative"' 'functions' presuppose 'descriptive' 'functions' – but *without* 'language' relating to 'reality' "naturally".[129] With Evans, Thiselton argues, against Tillich, that Christian 'commitment' aligns with biblical 'commissive language', 'such... as "I believe" or "I promise"'.[130]

(d) In 1975, Thiselton again agrees with Austin and Evans that language is multifunctional and grounded in multiform speech-action. Thiselton argues that Austin's 'commissives, behabitives, and exercitives' 'are... relevant to liturgy', and that Austin and Evans rightly urge 'that exercitives do not' operate with 'causal

---

[123] cf.: Thiselton, 'R *CFH*', 69; Thiselton, 'NP', 8; Thiselton, 'SARX', 222.

[124] Thiselton, 'UPC', 89, 96-98, 87-88, 90-91, 93-96.

[125] cf.: Thiselton, 'UPC', 94-98; Thiselton, *NTH*, 402, 545-553, 608; Thiselton, *2H*, 286-287, 379-385, 442, 444. Italics Thiselton's.

[126] Thiselton, 'UPC', 89, 96-98; cf.: Thiselton, 'Parab', 438; Thiselton, 'LG', 491-495; Thiselton, 'SNTP', 98-100; cf. Chapter 3.

[127] Thiselton, 'Words', 293-296. Italics Thiselton's.

[128] Thiselton, 'Words', 297-298; cf.: Thiselton, 'SNTP', 76, 101; Thiselton, 'TY', 1562. Italics Thiselton's.

[129] cf.: Thiselton, 'NH', 325-326; Thiselton, 'Words', 286, 293.

[130] Thiselton, 'Till', 102, 90, 95, 87.

force' as '"word-magic"' but presuppose "complete" execution of the 'relevant conventional procedure' by 'the' appropriate 'speaker'.[131] Drawing on the later Wittgenstein and Austin, Thiselton also extends semantic considerations beyond 'lexicography' to take authorial 'thought' and 'extra-linguistic' context into consideration. Similarly, Thiselton expounds the grammar of 'belief' in terms of "commissive" 'bodily' 'action'.[132]

(e) In 1977, Thiselton notes that 'Pannenberg', 'J. Macquarrie' and the Anglo-American tradition rightly reject the "dualisms" underlying 'existentialist' approaches to 'myth'. After Austin and Evans, and against Bultmann, Thiselton argues that 'the logic of self-involvement' presupposes 'the logic of... description'.[133] Thus, drawing on Austin, Thiselton argues that 'the power of' human "blessings and cursings" depends 'on the existence of certain accepted procedures'.[134] For Thiselton, "effective" illocutions 'depend on certain states of affairs' ('conventions', 'institutions', etc.) 'being true', 'not on... causal force'. For Thiselton, propositional content is thus connected to linguistic "performance" where, in Thiselton's view, eschatological language is both 'descriptive' and 'self-involving'.[135]

(2) Thiselton also makes appeals to *the philosophy of language more broadly*. Thus, (a), in 1973, drawing on V.H. Neufeld, Thiselton urges that 'primitive' 'New Testament' 'confessions' involve 'both' 'cognitive creedal content' and performance.[136] Thiselton also argues, after G. Ryle, that 'to say... that Africa was hot but the welcome was cold... is not to oppose two sets of things' but is, rather, the *language-behavior* of '"a poor joke"'.[137] Elsewhere, drawing on R.W. Hepburn, Thiselton argues that Bultmann's '"demythologizing"' is '"logically impossible"' since language about God 'must include symbol and analogy'. For Thiselton, 'Bultmann's' thought also manifests 'a flight from the evidential' and, furthermore, in Thiselton's estimate, Bultmann's 'definitions [of myth] are incompatible' with one-another.[138]

(b) In 1974, Thiselton makes appeals to philosophers of language (G. Ryle, G.E.M. Anscombe, A.R. White, S. Ullmann, I.T. Ramsey, M. Black, and W.P. Alston) in relation to '*polymorphous* concepts', and in countering 'natural' and 'ideational' views of language (see below): for Thiselton, language is 'conventional'

---

[131] Thiselton, *LLM*, 16, 18, 17, 19-21.
[132] Thiselton, 'EITN', 576; cf. Thiselton, 'Flesh', 679-680.
[133] Thiselton, 'MP', 8-9.
[134] Thiselton, 'LMR', 1125; cf. Thiselton, 'Words', 283-299.
[135] Thiselton, 'LMR', 1125, 1139, 1124; cf. Thiselton, 'Words', 294.
[136] Thiselton, 'UPC', 97-98; cf. Thiselton, *NH*, 19.
[137] Thiselton, 'SARX', 226.
[138] Thiselton, 'M,M', 340-341.

and multifunctional.[139] We have already noted Thiselton's appeal to I.T. Ramsey in relation to 'models and qualifiers'[140] and his appeals to P. van Buren and W. Hordern in relation to *'particularizing* language' and unique personhood.[141]

(c) In 1975, Thiselton again alludes to I.T. Ramsey's work on 'models and qualifiers' and, with P. van Buren, argues that only "communities" can 'extend' 'the edges of language'.[142] Further, after H.H. Price and V.H. Neufeld, Thiselton argues that '"belief"' is not 'primarily… an inner mental state', since cognitive and 'performative' dimensions of language are interwoven.[143] In Thiselton's view, several philosophers (namely, D.M. High, W. Hordern, and R. King) 'fruitfully' "explore" 'the broader implications of Wittgenstein's work for the language of religion' (though, as we noted earlier, so-called "religious" language is not separable from language as a whole in Thiselton's thinking).[144]

(d) In 1976, Thiselton draws on W. Hordern so as to argue that "falling in love" presupposes an 'I-Thou' 'relationship' between 'particular' 'persons', and not just the general "classes" 'female' and "male".[145] Further, for Thiselton, after P. van Buren, 'the meaning of' the word '"God"' is inseparable from its history of uses in Christian tradition and community '"life"'.[146]

(e) In 1977, drawing on S. Laeuchli, Thiselton warns of the semantic distortions and inversions that occur when 'biblical' language is lifted into alien frames of reference.[147] Further, drawing on D.M. High and J. Pelc, Thiselton again rejects 'ideational' theories of language and 'meaning' and,[148] drawing on I.T. Ramsey, makes additional comments about '"models and qualifiers"'.[149]

(f) In 1978, after 'P.F. Strawson', Thiselton cites J.L. Austin's '"failure to distinguish between"' '"empirically informative"' '"communication"' and the use 'of the word "true"', but Thiselton still rejects P.F. Strawson's own *'performative theory of truth'* (see Chapter 3).[150]

Thus, (3), and summarizing: resonances or agreements emerge between Thiselton's appeals to Austin, Evans, and to the philosophy of language more

---

[139] Thiselton, 'SNTI', 94, re. appeals to G. Ryle, G.E.M. Anscombe, and A.R. White cf. Thiselton, 'Words', 293, 294, 287; re. appeals to G. Ryle and S. Ullmann re. cf. 297-298 re. appeals to I.T. Ramsey, M. Black, and W.P. Alston. Italics Thiselton's.
[140] Thiselton, 'M-M', 8.
[141] Thiselton, 'Till', 100-101. Italics Thiselton's.
[142] Thiselton, *LLM*, 6-7.
[143] Thiselton, *LLM*, 12, 20-21.
[144] Thiselton, *LLM*, 7.
[145] Thiselton, A.C., 'Man Longs for the Status and Dignity of a 'Thou'', *CEN* 9 Jan. (1976), 9.
[146] Thiselton, 'SBL', 114-115.
[147] Thiselton, 'MP', 11-12.
[148] Thiselton, 'LMR', 1129-1130.
[149] Thiselton, 'LMR', 1132-1134.
[150] Thiselton, 'Truth', 894-896; but against P.F. Strawson, cf. 896-897. Italics Thiselton's.

broadly, and Thiselton's appeal to the later Wittgenstein – as follows: (a) for both (sets of) approaches language is extra-linguistically grounded, yet conventional. (b) For both (sets of) approaches language is multifunctional speech-action, against "comprehensive", "uniform", or "dualistic" theories of language. (c) Both (sets of) approaches would sympathize with the view that the interweaving of "cognitive" and "performative" functions of language and the "logic of self-involvement" account for "extra-linguistic" "textual" *'effects'* beyond the "intra-linguistic" dimension (see Chapters 5 and 6).[151] (d) Viewing "speech-acts" as "the basic units of meaning" resonates with the later Wittgenstein's stress on "use".[152] (e) For both (sets of) approaches language undergoes (trans-) temporal changes. (f) For both (sets of) approaches "frames of reference" involving both "extra-linguistic" and "(intra-)linguistic" dimensions shape meaning, perception, and conceptual grammar (see Chapter 3 on Wittgenstein's notion of "seeing as" and Evans' notion of "onlooks").[153] (g) For both (sets of) approaches the philosophy of language functions hermeneutically – clarifying biblical language.

Moreover, (4), and summarizing: further resonances or agreements emerge between Thiselton's appeals to Austin, Evans, and to the philosophy of language more broadly, and, 'biblical and theological… language' – as follows: (a) for both (sets of) accounts, interwoven linguistic functions are exemplified in language about God: God's personal identity links to the *'particularizing* language' of narrative and historical report, yet language about God cannot avoid symbols and analogy.[154] (b) An emphasis on multiform speech-acts is directly relevant for the analysis of biblical utterances. (c) Trans-temporal change in language resonates with trans-temporal modifications within biblical traditions of language-use.

In conclusion, Thiselton finds dialogic resonances between a prior 'biblical and theological account of language' and his appeals to the later Wittgenstein, J.L Austin and D.D. Evans, and to the philosophy of language more broadly.[155] For Thiselton, these theological and philosophical approaches to language mutually, dialogically, and reciprocally authorize or warrant one another.

## *5. Accommodation of the Saussurian Tradition to the Later Wittgensteinian Tradition*

Moving on, we now propose that Thiselton critically adjusts insights from the Saussurian tradition such that these critically-adjusted insights then resonate with, and are made to flesh out and to contribute to, a unified whole to which Thiselton's adopted insights from the later Wittgenstein, J.L. Austin, D.D. Evans, and from the philosophy of language more broadly, also contribute. The resulting fleshed-out "whole", in Thiselton's estimate, thereby resonates with a prior

---

[151] See, Thiselton, *LLM*, 7; and, Thiselton, *NH*, 2, 16. Italics Thiselton's.
[152] Thiselton, 'SNTP', 76.
[153] Thiselton, *LLM*, 4; cf. Thiselton, *NH*, 2.
[154] Thiselton, 'CAP', 144; cf. Thiselton, 'Till', 101. Italics Thiselton's.
[155] Thiselton, 'CAP', 144.

'biblical and theological account of language'.[156]

To start with, though, we should note that Thiselton's appeal to Saussure, to general linguistics, and to modern semantics is very complex.[157] In one article alone he draws on eleven writers positively,[158] on five writers in a qualified way,[159] and on a further seven writers in relation to biblical interpretation.[160] Elsewhere, Thiselton only *extends* the breadth of these appeals.[161] Notably, however, Thiselton speaks of the 'epoch-making' work of J. Barr, and even argues that J.F.A. Sawyer 'takes the discussion further than… James Barr' by providing 'principles… fundamental for all biblical exegesis'.[162] We begin by considering Thiselton's appeal to Saussure – as follows.

A) THISELTON'S APPEAL TO SAUSSURE'S FOUR PRINCIPLES OF GENERAL LINGUISTICS

Thiselton argues that Saussure's 'four principles are fundamental for' general 'linguistics', 'modern' 'semantics', and for 'all… structuralist' approaches, and that 'Barr' rightly adopts 'at least' 'three' of these 'principles'.[163]

Thus, (1), Thiselton adopts Saussure's *conventionalist approach to language*: "signs" (or 'vocabulary'-stock) and 'grammar' (i.e. surface-grammar) are '"arbitrary"';[164] they are rooted in 'use, social tradition, [and] rules of convention'; they are 'accidents' 'of word-history'; and they are not related "naturally" to 'the world'. This 'principle' of linguistic "conventionality", for Thiselton, is 'the first principle of language'.[165] That is, for Thiselton, language is grounded in extra-linguistic 'social' activity and in (largely) unconsciously-formed "habits" that display continuity yet 'admit… change', and that relate arbitrarily 'to the world' (cf. 'rules' in the later Wittgenstein and 'recursive' 'mechanisms' in N. Chomsky).[166] Against P.R. Keifert's reading of Thiselton, we should note that 'Thiselton' does not

---

[156] Thiselton, 'CAP', 144.

[157] Querying, Brett, M.G., 'Review of A.C. Thiselton's *New Horizons in Hermeneutics*', *Th* 96.772 (Jul./Aug. 1993), 315. Brett seems to miss this entire stratum of Thiselton's thinking.

[158] Thiselton, 'SNTI', 79-89 (Saussure); 83, 90 (Trier); 76, 84, 92 (Ullmann); 82 (Baskin); 75, 77, 80-85, 87-88 (Barr); 75, 83, 87 (Lyons); 76, 87 (Black); 90 (Ogden); 85 (Robins); 84 (Joos); 82, 87 (Crystal).

[159] Thiselton, 'SNTI', 83 (Stern); 78, 96-97 (Chomsky); 78, 84, 86, 90, 96-98 (Nida); 78, 95 (Wonderly); 96 and onwards (Taber); 90-98 (re. Trier & Nida).

[160] Thiselton, 'SNTI', 75, 77, 80-85, 87-88 (Barr); 75, 83, 88-89 (Güttgemanns); 75 (Kieffer); 75, 79 (Sawyer); 75, 83, 97 (Burres); 90 (Katz and Foder).

[161] Thiselton, 'LMR', 1124 (Korzybski); 1129-1130 (Pelc). The front cover of *LLM* reflects R. Jacobson's influence; cf. Thiselton, *LLM* more broadly; cf. Thiselton, *NH*, 487.

[162] cf.: Thiselton, 'SNTI', 84, 75; Thiselton, A.C., 'Enthusiasm Not Enough: Güttgemanns, Sawyer, and Barr on Biblical Research', *CEN* 13 Sep. (1974), 6; Thiselton, A.C., 'Review of J.F.A. Sawyer's *Semantics in Biblical Research*', *TSF* 70 (Aut. 1974), 18.

[163] Thiselton, 'SNTI', 79-80; cf. Thiselton, 'SBS', 330, 331.

[164] Thiselton, 'SNTI', 85.

[165] Thiselton, 'Words', 287, 289, 290; cf.: Thiselton, 'SBS', 330, 331; Thiselton, 'SNTI', 85.

[166] Thiselton, 'LMR', 1123, 1124, 1126, 1134.

ignore 'the relationship between language and reality';[167] rather, Thiselton defends Saussure's conventionalist stance on three grounds: considerations relating to, (a), translation,[168] (b), 'the relationship between' thought and 'language' and,[169] (c), 'everyday' linguistic 'phenomena' – as follows.[170]

Thus, (a), to begin with, Thiselton argues that 'the same semantic value' in two 'different languages' is generated by completely different 'vocabulary' stocks and grammatical structures.[171] Further, Thiselton argues that in order to render '"translation-equivalence between"' two '"languages"', 'both linguistic and extra-linguistic' "contexts" 'of... utterance" need to be considered.[172] Moreover, Thiselton notes that the same semantic force can be generated using different vocabulary and 'grammar' within the *same* language. Thiselton observes that '"the real"' 'logical' structure of an utterance may differ from its 'surface structure' or '"apparent logical form"', where "arbitrary" 'surface-grammar' is distinct from "depth-grammar".[173] Finally, Thiselton argues that if a '"language"' has no '"word for it"', '"it"' may still be 'said' in that language, even if a given concept is harder to express in one language than in another: languages are inter-translatable.[174]

(b) Thiselton argues that whilst existing vocabulary, grammar and structure 'reflect' a culture's *'past'* concerns, language 'habits', and 'thought' or conceptuality, 'they do not absolutely *determine*' these same spheres 'in the *future*', even though they may still strongly 'influence' them. For Thiselton, the possibility of 'creative' 'language-use' in a changing world demonstrates that language is 'conventional'.[175]

(c) Thiselton argues that certain 'everyday' linguistic 'phenomena' also demonstrate or prove the conventionality of language, where these 'phenomena' include *'homonymy'*, *'polysemy'*, *'opaqueness'* in vocabulary', 'diachronic *change*', 'hyponymy', 'arbitrariness in grammar', 'and the use of different words for the same object in different languages'.[176]

The conventionality of language, then, is not just a '"modern"... Western' view, but is 'absolutely demanded' in Thiselton's estimate.[177]

(2) Thiselton adopts what we call here Saussure's "second" axiom: *'langue'* - the community's 'language-system', 'linguistic' 'repertoire' or 'reservoir' - must be 'distinguished' from *'parole'*, or 'actual concrete speech-acts'. Thiselton notes that

---

[167] Keifert, 'R 2H', 409.
[168] Thiselton, 'SNTI', 75-78, 85-88, 96-98.
[169] Thiselton, 'SNTI', 87-88.
[170] Thiselton, 'SNTI', 85.
[171] Thiselton, 'SNTI', 85. After Saussure.
[172] Thiselton, 'SNTI', 87, 75.
[173] Thiselton, 'SNTI', 76-78; after B. Russell; 96. Thiselton, 'LMR', 1141, 1127, 1124.
[174] Thiselton, 'SNTI', 87. After D. Crystal and J. Lyons.
[175] Thiselton, 'SNTI', 87-88, 85. First and third italics ours, second italics Thiselton's.
[176] Thiselton, 'SNTI', 85; cf.: Thiselton, 'SBS', 330, 331; Thiselton, 'Words', 287, 289, 290; Thiselton, 'R SBR', 18. Italics Thiselton's.
[177] Thiselton, 'Words', 287.

*'langue'* embraces publicly agreed "'conventions'", is produced socially, is known completely "'only'" collectively, and is inferred from *'parole'*. Thiselton notes E. Güttgemanns' distinction between the synchronic laws of *'langue'* and the diachronic laws of 'the growth of oral traditions'. Thiselton also compares *'langue'* with N. Chomsky's category of 'competence' or "'generative grammar'", and *'parole'* with Chomsky's category of 'performance'. Similarly, Thiselton observes that E. Güttgemanns distinguishes between "'generative" matrix (competence)' and 'performance', though Thiselton adds the argument that the "'code'" versus "'message'" dichotomy of 'ideological' 'structuralism' distorts Saussure's *langue-parole* distinction (see Chapter 5).[178]

Interestingly, Thiselton concludes that 'tongues' ('as… practiced' by 'the Corinthians') cannot mean "foreign languages", since 'tongues' have neither "'surface-structure'" (cf. *parole*), nor "'symbolic code'" or "'deep-structure'" (cf. *langue*).[179] However, against W. Richardson and G.D. Fee, we should note that Thiselton does *not* read Paul as advocating the abolition of tongues.[180]

(3) Thiselton adopts what we call here Saussure's "third" axiom: a "'language is a self-contained'", 'self-justifying' *"structural" "system"* of *"interdependent parts"* that only "'function and acquire'" 'semantic' "values" "'through'" "'inter-relations'" within "'the [language-"system"' as a developing] whole'".[181] For Thiselton, this axiom precludes 'word-centered' approaches: 'meaning' depends on "'the simultaneous presence'" 'of two basic kinds' of "'inter-relationships'" (involving 'similarities and differences') between systemic 'elements' – as follows.[182]

Thus, (a), Thiselton notes that *"combining"* 'elements' creates 'syntagmatic' or juxtapositional 'relations' – as, for example, in the case of the 'relations' between 'words' in sentences.[183] Thiselton observes that a "term's" "'correct meaning… contributes least to the total context'", where combined words – or whatever combined 'linguistic units' are in view - limit each other 'reciprocally'.[184] (b) Thiselton notes that *substituting* one "element" for another – say, in a sentence - brings these two "elements" into 'associative' (cf. later, 'paradigmatic') 'relationship'. Thiselton thus argues that 'meaning' (partly) depends on 'choice' –

---

[178] Thiselton, 'SNTI', 88-89; cf.: Thiselton, 'SBS', 330, 331; Thiselton, 'LMR', 1131, 1142. Italics in speech-marks Thiselton's.

[179] Thiselton, A.C., 'The 'Interpretation' of Tongues: a New Suggestion in the Light of Greek Usage in Philo and Josephus', *JThStud* NS 30.1 (Apr. 1979), 31.

[180] Richardson, W., 'Liturgical Order and Glossolalia in 1 Corinthians 14:26c-33a', *NTStud* 32.1 (Jan. 1986), 145; cf. Fee, G.D., *The First Epistle to the Corinthians* (The New International Commentary on the New Testament; Grand Rapids, MI.: Eerdmans, 1987), 573-574; cf. Thiselton, 'IT', 34-35.

[181] Thiselton, 'SNTI', 82; cf.: Thiselton, 'LMR', 1140, 1141; Thiselton, 'SBS', 330, 331. Italics ours.

[182] Thiselton, 'SBS', 330.

[183] Thiselton, 'SBS', 330; cf. Thiselton, 'SNTI', 82. Italics ours.

[184] Thiselton, 'SNTI', 84-85; cf. Thiselton, 'LMR', 1141.

that is, on speakers' 'paradigmatic' selections from *"langue's"* possibilities. (c) Thiselton observes how R. Jakobson and "anthropological structuralism" "expound" these 'relations' (i.e. "syntagmatic" 'relations' and "paradigmatic" 'relations') 'in terms of metonymy and metaphor' respectively. (d) Thiselton notes that, 'in literary structuralism', systemic 'elements' include 'words', 'narrative' and "mythological" 'elements', 'or any unit of semantic significance'. Thus, (e), Thiselton broadly agrees with the view that "words" have 'meaning... only within a' 'semantic field', or '"in sentences"'.[185]

(4) Thiselton adopts what we call here Saussure's "fourth" 'axiom': *'synchronic'* considerations are prior to, pre-requisite to, and 'distinct' from *'diachronic'* considerations throughout interpretation. For Thiselton, as for Saussure, a word's 'meaning' in a given utterance 'at a given... time' is determined by 'investigations' into 'linguistic and extra-linguistic' "contexts" belonging to the same time, and not by 'investigations' into 'linguistic and extra-linguistic' "contexts" belonging to other times.[186]

B) THISELTON'S EXTENSION AND QUALIFICATION OF SAUSSURIAN INSIGHTS

Having noted Thiselton's indebtedness to Saussure, however, a careful reading of Thiselton's second-period writings reveals that he also espouses seven extensions and/or qualifications of Saussure's principles, especially through appeals to *the later Wittgenstein and to the philosophy of language*.

Thus, (1), Thiselton extends developments of what we have called Saussure's "third" axiom – developments to be found in J. Trier's 'field semantics' in which emphases on 'semantic relations' supplement valid 'traditional concerns' over 'historical and literary context'. Thus, Thiselton observes that, for Trier, 'a word has meaning' 'only' through 'semantic' "inter-relations" 'within a field', 'lexical' "sub-system", "system", or "whole"'. Thiselton notes that Trier establishes "fields" 'in terms of' 'syntagmatic relations', 'paradigmatic relations', *'similarity...* (synonymy)', 'opposition' ('complementarity', 'antonymy'), and in terms of "inclusion" ('hyponymy').[187]

Thiselton, however, extends and modifies these categories as follows: (a) 'synonymy' involves *'context-dependent'* or context-specific *'interchangeability'* (cf. the later Wittgenstein's emphasis on "use"). Thiselton notes that some terms 'are... synonymous' only in certain "contexts", at certain times in history, or 'cognitively' but neither "emotively" nor 'in terms of register' or "attitude".[188] (b) Thiselton notes that 'opposition' includes 'complementarity' ('two-way exclusion'; cf. C.K.

---

[185] Thiselton, 'SNTI', 82-89, 78-79; cf.: Thiselton, 'SBS', 330; Thiselton, 'LMR', 1141. Italics in speech-marks Thiselton's.

[186] cf.: Thiselton, 'SNTI', 80-82, 75; Thiselton, 'Words', 289; Thiselton, 'LMR', 1140; Thiselton, 'SBS', 330-331; Thiselton, 'R *SBR*', 18. Italics ours.

[187] Thiselton, 'SNTI', 90, 75, 83; cf.: Thiselton, 'SBS', 330-331; Thiselton, 'R *SBR*', 18. Italics Thiselton's.

[188] Thiselton, 'SNTI', 92-93. Italics Thiselton's.

Ogden's 'opposition by cut'), 'antonymy' ('one-way... opposition', 'gradable by scale'; cf. C.K. Ogden's 'opposition by scale'), and 'converseness' (e.g. "'buy'" cf. "'sell'").[189] (c) Thiselton observes that 'vagueness' embraces 'inclusiveness' or *'hyponymy'*, *'lack of specificity'*, *'lack of... clear cut-off point'*, *'polymorphous* concepts', and *'metaphor'.*[190]

In relation to 'vagueness', Thiselton argues that Paul's concept of 'faith' is 'polymorphous', and that this fact precludes 'generalizing' "formal" "definitions" of 'faith'. Further, Thiselton argues that 'New Testament' language is sometimes deliberately non-specific. Thiselton also argues that 'live metaphor' 'extends' accepted "uses" of terms 'in... logically odd' "ways", both creating 'a tension' that draws readers into active thought, and enabling them to "see" through 'a' new 'frame of reference'. Thiselton argues that 'live' 'metaphors' should not lose this 'ambiguity' and *force'* through translation, though Thiselton admits that 'dead metaphors' (i.e. metaphors no longer in common use) are better explained. Thiselton insists that 'metaphor' is not 'inferior to non-metaphorical discourse' and, against 'Bultmann', that 'metaphor' should not be confused with 'myth'. In Thiselton's view, Jesus' 'parables' may also 'function as metaphor'.[191]

That is, Thiselton argues that the semantic 'vagueness' of *'metaphor'* depends not only on *'linguistic'* considerations to do with intra-textual "codes" but also on *'extralinguistic'* considerations to do with reader *horizons*, where this point reminds us of Thiselton's appeal to the later Wittgenstein's work on perception (see Chapter 3). Thiselton's thought concerning the "context-dependency" of 'synonymy' also reflects later Wittgensteinian considerations to do with the particularities of linguistic *"use".*[192]

(2) Thiselton extends the *application* - in 'biblical' studies - of what we have called Saussure's "third" axiom. That is, Thiselton argues that "syntagmatically"-focused 'traditional' 'lexicology' requires an additional focus on 'paradigmatic' or "'associative'" 'relations' (cf. the later Wittgenstein's emphasis on "use"). In this context, Thiselton examines *'pneuma'*, *'hermēneuō'*, and *'mid̲rāš'*, and notes J.F.A. Sawyer's distinction 'between lexical fields and associative fields'.[193]

(3) Qualifying what we have called Saussure's "third" axiom, Thiselton agrees with S. Ullmann that, despite 'words' not being 'the basic unit[s] of meaning', they still often have "'a hard core of meaning'" that "'context'" "'only'" "'modifies'" to an *extent*. Thiselton argues that 'word-studies' have value - although Thiselton stresses that 'dictionary-entries... are' only 'rule-of-thumb generalizations based on assumptions about characteristic contexts'. With J.F.A. Sawyer, Thiselton

---

[189] Thiselton, 'SNTT', 90, 92.
[190] Thiselton, 'SNTT', 93, 90, 94-95. Thiselton's italics.
[191] Thiselton, 'SNTT', 93-95; cf. Thiselton, 'R *SBR*', 18. Italics Thiselton's.
[192] Thiselton, 'SNTT', 94, 75, 92; cf. Thiselton, 'SBS', 330. First italics Thiselton's, remaining italics ours.
[193] Thiselton, 'SNTT', 90; cf.: Thiselton, 'EITN', 580-581; Thiselton, 'R *SBR*', 18. Italics and transliterations Thiselton's, except for the italics on *"application"*, which are ours.

argues that 'generalizations about meanings always depend on particular uses of words in particular contexts' (cf. Thiselton's appeals to the later Wittgenstein's emphases on particularity and on use – see above).[194]

(4) Drawing on J.F.A. Sawyer, Thiselton extends what we have called Saussure's "third" axiom: 'linguistic' 'structural' considerations of 'context' (cf. 'verbal context', broader 'literary setting', genre, and 'structural semantics') must be *supplementary to* 'extra-linguistic' 'historical' considerations of 'context' (cf. '"context of situation"', '*Sitz im Leben*', and/or 'setting').[195] Thiselton argues that the '*speech-act*' is more strictly 'the basic unit of meaning' than '*the sentence*', and that '*parole*' actualizes possibilities allowed by '*langue*'.[196] Thiselton argues that, in 'biblical' 'studies', "cutting" "'propositions'" 'loose' from their 'situation' in life is *both* a lapse into '"Platonizing"' ('bad theology') *and* '"meaning-distorting"' ('bad linguistics').[197] References to Thiselton's applications of this extension of Saussure's thinking appear in the footnotes.[198] Thiselton thus critically adjusts Saussurian insights in order to ensure that they conform to/with his (i.e. Thiselton's) extended later Wittgensteinian approach to language.

(5) Commenting on E.A. Nida's and C.R. Taber's application of N. Chomsky's 'transformational grammar' 'in Bible translation', Thiselton affirms that 'back-transformation' (i.e. 'reducing' a complex sentence to a sequence of simple '"logical"' component 'sentences') reveals 'the arbitrariness of surface grammar' and the '"creativity"' of 'translation'. Thiselton allows that, in elucidating 'the contrast between surface grammar and deep grammar', 'back-transformation' '"eliminates ambiguities"' by highlighting what was previously 'implicit' (though Thiselton acknowledges that interpretative judgments may err during this process). Thus, Thiselton argues that 'translation… becomes *interpretation*', and is thus inseparable from hermeneutics.[199]

Against 'back-transformation', however, Thiselton argues that 'language' cannot simply 'be reduced to' a few '"basic structures"', 'transform[s]' or '"kernels"' of '"universal"' grammar' from which '"more elaborate"' '"structures"' are derived. For Thiselton, such '"kernels"' are too similar to the 'earlier' 'Wittgenstein's' 'elementary propositions'. And, for Thiselton, 'back-transformation' also loses 'emotive, cultural, or religious overtones', and wrongly views 'semantic equivalence… in' purely 'cognitive terms'.[200]

---

[194] Thiselton, 'SNTI', 83-84; cf. 76, 78-79; cf. Thiselton, 'R *SBR*', 18.
[195] Thiselton, 'R *SBR*', 18; cf. Thiselton, 'SNTI', 75, 76-79. Italics in speech-marks Thiselton's, others are ours.
[196] Thiselton, 'SNTI', 76, 88. Italics Thiselton's.
[197] Thiselton, 'SNTI', 79.
[198] cf.: Thiselton, 'SARX', 205-206, 210-212, 215; Thiselton, *LLM*, 9, 13; Thiselton, 'EITN', 576; Thiselton, 'SBS', 329-335; Thiselton, 'MP', 11-12.
[199] Thiselton, 'SNTI', 95-97; cf.: Thiselton, 'LMR', 1141-1142; Thiselton, 'R *SBR*', 18. Italics Thiselton's.
[200] Thiselton, 'SNTI', 95-98.

Thus, Thiselton frees 'back-transformation' from a quasi-positivist neglect of '"context of situation"' – again embedding extensions or qualifications of Saussurian insights into his later Wittgensteinian framework through a process of critical sublation (on sublation, see Chapters 7).[201]

(6) Thiselton extends and qualifies J. Barr's Saussurian point 'about the' negative 'relation between' 'surface-grammar' 'and thought'. With Barr, 'Saussure and' others, Thiselton agrees that 'surface-grammar and vocabulary-stock' (cf. linguistic rules and '*form*') 'have little' 'influence' on 'thought', being 'arbitrary' or 'accidental' 'conventions' (against B.L. Whorf). Thus, Thiselton applauds J. Barr's rejection of T. Boman's sharp surface-structural distinction between "Greek" and "Hebrew" thought, E.A. Nida's denial that (surface-)'grammar' shapes 'national' views of '"sex"' or '"time"', and D. Crystal's denial that the presence or absence of '"a word"' in a 'language' determines the presence or absence of a "concept" in that 'language'.[202]

And yet, Thiselton argues that 'tradition' and 'language-habits' (cf. 'linguistic *content*' and "use") *do* condition 'thought', 'world-view', or 'pre-understanding' (partly with Whorf), but without 'absolutely' "determining" them (against Whorf). After the later Wittgenstein (and 'Heidegger and Gadamer'), Thiselton argues that 'language-habits' 'may hold us captive', but that their 'spell' can be "broken" since they are not "logically" isolated. Thus, for Thiselton, 'the debate' between Whorf and Barr *et al* 'about the relation between language and thought' became unnecessarily 'polarized' through 'a failure to' distinguish between linguistic 'form', rules, 'content', and "use".[203] Querying P.J. Cahill's reading of Thiselton, we may conclude that Thiselton does not advocate 'the almost complete identification of language and thought'.[204] Rather, Thiselton only *qualifies* a trend in general 'linguistics', and only admits a '*half-truth*' in 'the Whorf hypothesis'. And Thiselton does this substantially – if not entirely - through an appeal to the later Wittgenstein.[205]

(7) Qualifying "ideological" 'structuralist' extensions of Saussure's notion of 'associative relation[s]', Thiselton urges that E. Güttgemanns rightly relates 'meaning' to "choices" 'between' 'deep structure' 'alternatives', but that Güttgemanns also wrongly identifies 'deep structure' 'alternatives' with the poles of the 'a-historical' 'binary' "oppositions" espoused by idealist 'anthropological' determinism (see Chapter 5). Drawing on the later Wittgenstein, Thiselton argues that the "choices" permitted by 'deep-structure' relate to (extra-)linguistic historical actions, and not to "formal" concepts.[206]

---

[201] Thiselton, 'SNTI', 96, 79.
[202] Thiselton, 'LMR', 1126-1127; cf. Thiselton, 'SNTI', 87. Italics Thiselton's.
[203] Thiselton, 'LMR', 1126-1127; cf.: Thiselton, *2H*, 133, 404; Thiselton, 'SNTI', 87. First italics Thiselton's.
[204] Cahill, P.J., 'Review of A.C. Thiselton's *The Two Horizons*', *CBQ* 43.3 (Jul. 1981), 484.
[205] Thiselton, 'SNTI', 87-88; cf. Thiselton, 'LMR', 1126, 1127, 1140-1141. Italics ours.
[206] Thiselton, 'LMR', 1142; cf. Thiselton, 'SBS', 329, 330, 334, 333, cf. 331-332.

C) "LINGUISTIC SEMANTICS" AS A "SUPPLEMENT" TO "PHILOSOPHICAL SEMANTICS"

Thiselton, then, critically sublates insights from the (post-)Saussurian tradition into his extended later Wittgensteinian approach to language. Other observations confirm this deduction. Thus, (1), Thiselton rejects approaches to 'semantics' that contradict the thinking of the later Wittgenstein (as we shall see shortly).[207]

(2) In Thiselton's view, the philosophy of language addresses the question of meaning more profoundly than general 'linguistics' does, though Thiselton allows that 'both' traditions "contribute" positively towards answering this question.[208] For Thiselton, 'hermeneutics… is' *not* 'part of the larger field of literary criticism'; the reverse is the case for Thiselton – where, here, we are contradicting M. Van Hamersveld's reading of Thiselton.[209] Thus, we also reject J. Barr's view that 'philosophical semantics' 'supplement' 'linguistic semantics' in Thiselton.[210] Rather, for Thiselton, 'linguistic'-'structural' considerations in relation to meaning 'supplement' those to do with "use", *'Sitz im Leben'*, 'public criteria' and 'tradition', and with eschatological anticipations of 'history as a whole' – where Thiselton grounds language and meaning in *nested 'historical' inter-relationships and contexts*. Thus, for example, Thiselton embeds appeals to the later Wittgenstein's semantics of "'expectation'" within eschatological co-ordinates (see Chapter 3).[211]

(3) We noted above that Thiselton's appeal to S. Ullmann's notion of "'hard-core'" word-meanings countered Saussurian linguistics for "taking the criticism" of 'words as units of meaning… too far'.[212] Similarly, Thiselton allies appeals to Ullmann and to the later Wittgenstein elsewhere: if some words have "hard-core" meanings that vary only a little from "'context'" to "'context'" (in mild correction of points from general linguistics), then so do certain "concepts with blurred edges" (though, again, Thiselton acknowledges that there is no "isomorphic" one-to-one relationship between 'words and concepts').[213]

In conclusion, then, Thiselton unifies his hermeneutical critique of language by critically accommodating the Saussurian tradition *to* the later Wittgensteinian tradition of the philosophy of language. Hence, Thiselton's appeals to the dialogic resonances and "mutual warranting" that exist between his appeals to philosophy and theology in this context of discussion remain undisturbed: Thiselton's

---

[207] Barr, J., 'Review of I.H. Marshall ed. *New Testament Interpretation*', Th 81.681 (May 1978), 233-234; cf.: Thiselton, 'SBL', 113-115; Thiselton, 'LMR', 1127-1129.

[208] Thiselton, 'SNTI', 98-100.

[209] Van Hamersveld, M., 'Review of R. Lundin's, A.C. Thiselton's and C. Walhout's *The Responsibility of Hermeneutics*', RefRev 40.3 (Spr. 1987), 252.

[210] Barr, 'R NTI', 234; cautioning, Gibson, A., *Biblical Semantic Logic: A Preliminary Analysis* (Oxford: Blackwell, 1981), 1.

[211] cf.: Thiselton, 'R SBR', 18; Barr, 'R NTI', 234; Thiselton, 'LMR', 1127, 1134; Thiselton, 'SNTI', 79, 75; Thiselton, 'Par', 52; Thiselton, 'TY', 1562; Thiselton, *LLM*, 9 cf. 13. First italics Thiselton's, second italics ours.

[212] Thiselton, 'SNTI', 83-84.

[213] Thiselton, 'SNTI', 84, 88; cf. Thiselton, 'Parab', 466-467.

philosophical description of 'biblical and theological language' has simply been fleshed out with further angles of view.[214]

### 6. Testing and Validating the Later-Wittgensteinian-Saussurian Alliance

Moving on, we propose that Thiselton tests, and thereby dialogically validates, what we may now designate as being his later-Wittgensteinian-Saussurian alliance. Thiselton does this by demonstrating the critical power of his later-Wittgensteinian-Saussurian alliance, first, in relation to 'traditional' and 'positivist' 'assumptions' and 'approaches' to 'language'; second, in relation to 'natural' and "Continental" "assumptions" and "approaches" to 'language'; and, third, through demonstrating the positive role of this alliance in relation to biblical interpretation, practical theology, and hermeneutical theory – as follows.[215]

A) CRITICISM OF TRADITIONAL AND POSITIVIST ASSUMPTIONS AND APPROACHES

Thiselton validates his later-Wittgensteinian-Saussurian alliance by using it to expose problems within broadly 'traditional' and/or broadly 'positivist' approaches to *'language'* that embrace 'referential', 'ideational', and/or 'positivist' approaches to *'meaning'*.[216]

Thus, (1), drawing on J. Barr and others, Thiselton rejects nine 'false' 'traditional' linguistic *'assumptions'* – as follows.[217] Thus, against 'traditional' linguistic 'assumptions': (a) Thiselton argues that "words" are neither 'the basic unit[s] of meaning', nor '"of translation-equivalence"', and (as we noted earlier) that there is no 'isomorphic' 'one word/one concept' 'relation between language and thought'. This point, in Thiselton's estimate, precludes 'atomizing' or '"word by word"' approaches to 'exegesis'.[218] (b) Thiselton argues that neither the 'arbitrary' and 'historical'-'accidental' 'distinctions' of (surface-)'grammatical' 'structure' and 'vocabulary-stock' (cf. *'langue'*), nor even the *scope* of *possible* 'language-use[s]' actualized by *'parole'*, allow "generalizing" 'conclusions' to be drawn 'about the distinctive thought of a' "nation" or 'people' (e.g. '"Greek"' cf. '"Hebrew"'), or 'about the… "richness" of' any given language.[219]

(c) Thiselton argues that 'surface-grammar' is not necessarily parallel to 'logical function' or '"depth-grammar"', against 'logico-grammatical parallelism'. Thus, Thiselton notes that the 'surface-grammar' of the utterance '"This is poison"' is 'indicative', but that the utterance may mean, '"Quick! Fetch a doctor!"' which is 'imperative'. Conversely, Thiselton argues that the utterance "rejoice in the Lord"

---

[214] Thiselton, 'CAP', 144.

[215] Thiselton, 'SNTI', 76; cf.: Thiselton, 'LMR', 1136, 1135, 1123; Thiselton, 'Words', 293.

[216] Thiselton, 'SNTI', 76; cf. Thiselton, 'LMR', 1124-1130; 1135-1137. Italics ours.

[217] Thiselton, 'SNTI', 76; cf. 75. Italics ours.

[218] Thiselton, 'SNTI', 75-78, 85-88; cf.: Thiselton, 'LMR', 1126; Thiselton, 'R SBR', 18.

[219] cf.: Thiselton, 'SNTI', 75-76, 86-89; Thiselton, 'LMR', 1126-1127, 1140-1141; Thiselton, 'Words', 287-290; Thiselton, 'SBS', 334. Italics in speech-marks are Thiselton's.

'is not necessarily a "command"'. Against 'Bultmann's' 'demythologizing', Thiselton argues that 'descriptive' "aspects" of 'language' 'cannot' always 'be reduced to' "imperatival" "aspects" of 'language' 'exhaustively and without remainder'.[220]

(d) Thiselton argues, after J. Barr, that a sentence's meaning is not the sum of the complete ranges of the possible meanings of its constituent words taken individually, against over-analytical "'word-by-word'" approaches. Thiselton argues that such *"illegitimate totality transfer"* fails to apprehend 'polysemy in language' - as though 'the "word" was 'an autonomous linguistic unit'.[221] (e) Thiselton, after J. Barr, argues that a word's 'meaning' is not found through 'etymologizing': 'etymology' only uncovers a word's "'history'".[222] (f) Thiselton argues that 'prescriptive' views of 'language' falsely relate 'language' logically (cf. 'positivist' approaches) or "naturally" (cf. 'natural' approaches – see below) 'to the world'.[223]

(g) Thiselton argues that a word's 'meaning' is not necessarily reducible to a "reference" to an 'object' or 'concept' (vs. 'referential' and 'ideational' approaches): not all 'words' are like "'names'" referring to "objects". Thiselton's counter-examples include - after the later Wittgenstein - words such as 'Water! Away! Ow! Help! Fine! No!'[224] Further, after G. Frege, Thiselton observes that 'words' with 'different meanings' can 'refer to the same object' and that word-meanings change in different contexts. After E. Schillebeeckx, Thiselton argues that a word's meaning is not its verifiable relation to an "object". Again, Thiselton argues that 'language' does not "operate" 'solely, or even primarily, on the basis of reference'; nor, argues Thiselton, is 'language' simply "external" "clothing" for "prior" 'inner concepts'.[225]

(h) Thiselton argues that viewing "statements", 'assertions', "propositions", "description", or "'information'" as 'the basic kind of language-use' (as in 'referential' and 'ideational' approaches) is also problematic.[226] Thiselton argues that such a practice tends towards "flattening" 'symbols' and 'metaphor' to "description", towards ignoring the 'self-involving' dimensions of language, and

---

[220] cf.: Thiselton, *LLM*, 10, 3, 29, 30; Thiselton, 'SNTI', 76, 77, 78; Thiselton, A.C., 'Sound, Devout Stodge. Review of W. Hendriksen's *Philippians*', *CEN* 1 Feb. (1974), 8; Thiselton, 'UPC', 96; Thiselton, 'Par', 38.

[221] Thiselton, 'SNTI', 84-85, 78; cf.: Thiselton, 'LMR', 1126, 1140-1141; Thiselton, 'Words', 290. Italics Thiselton's.

[222] cf.: Thiselton, 'SNTI', 76, 80-82; Thiselton, 'Words', 289; Thiselton, 'LMR', 1126, 1140-1141; Thiselton, 'SBS', 330-331; Thiselton, A.C., 'Sense and Nonsense in Interpreting Bible Words', *Ety* 27 (Mar. 1976), 16-17, 33-35.

[223] Thiselton, 'SNTI', 76; cf.: Thiselton, 'Words', 293; Thiselton, 'LMR', 1136.

[224] cf.: Thiselton, 'SNTI', 76; Thiselton, 'SBL', 114-115; Thiselton, 'LMR', 1127-1129; Wittgenstein, *PI*, 13 (quoted).

[225] Thiselton, 'LMR', 1127-1129; cf. Thiselton, 'Truth', 894-896; cf. Thiselton, 'SBL', 114-115; cf. Thiselton, 'SNTI', 76.

[226] cf.: Thiselton, 'SNTI', 76, 79; Thiselton, 'LMR', 1127, 1129.

towards becoming pre-occupied with 'generalizations', 'rules, guiding principles, universal maxims, classes and categories'. In this context, Thiselton unfavorably compares traditional assumptions about language and meaning with the early Wittgenstein's positivist-like assumptions about language and meaning.[227]

(i) Finally, Thiselton argues that 'language' is not "learned" primarily by 'ostensive definition' (against 'referential' approaches): as the later Wittgenstein observed, 'ostensive definition' remains ambiguous prior to 'linguistic training'. Thiselton notes that the later Wittgenstein asks, what does "'this is *tove*'" 'mean', when 'pointing to a pencil'? Does *"tove"'* mean "'wood'", "'hard'", or "'pencil'"? For Thiselton, as for the later Wittgenstein, 'meaning' is learnt by being "trained", 'by watching how others play' (see above). Thiselton concludes that 're-labeling' 'biblical' terms in 'liturgy' will *'not'* make them "'intelligible'" to modern readers.[228]

(2) Thiselton's critique of 'false' 'traditional *assumptions*' about language and meaning inevitably spills over into his critique of inadequate 'traditional' *"approaches"* to language and meaning – the latter reflecting an overlapping angle of view on the same nexus of problems. Thus, (a), for Thiselton, it is clear from what has already been said above that *'referential'* approaches cannot serve as 'comprehensive' approaches to 'meaning', against C.W. Morris, 'A. Tarski', and R. Carnap, who – Thiselton observes - "divide" "'semiotics'" or "'semantics'" (in a broader sense) 'into... syntax' (intra-linguistic relations), 'semantics' (narrower sense: *denotation, reference*), and 'pragmatics (...use...)'.[229]

Similarly, (b), Thiselton also rejects an *'ideational'* (in Locke) or 'dianoetic' (in O. Procksch and G. von Rad) approach in which 'language' is primarily seen as a vehicle for "expressing" 'intellectual' concepts, information, or 'psychological' 'inner' 'private mental states'. Following the later 'Wittgenstein... and... others', Thiselton argues that language is multifunctional, where the "conveyance" of conceptual or empirical content is only "'one'" possible "'function'" of language.[230]

Elsewhere, Thiselton again criticizes 'ideational' approaches for grounding 'meaning' in the relationship 'between' 'words', "concepts", and the "objects" to which both 'words' and "concepts" "refer". After the later Wittgenstein, Thiselton rejects such a sharp division between 'language and thinking'. After 'D.M. High', further, Thiselton argues that 'we do not always experience a' 'mental' "'motion picture'" parallel to speech since there are no 'causal' links between extra-linguistic "objects", 'mental' "concepts", and 'linguistic symbol[s]'. Thiselton concludes, contrary to 'C.K. Ogden', 'I.A. Richards', and others, that "approaches" in

---

[227] Thiselton, *LLM*, 10-11, 31-32, 25-26; cf. Thiselton, 'SNTT', 79.

[228] cf.: Thiselton, 'LMR', 1127-1129; Thiselton, 'Truth', 894-896; Thiselton, *LLM*, 11-12; Thiselton, 'SBL', 114; Thiselton, 'MP', 10, 12, 4; Wittgenstein, *PI*, 4, 27; cf. 1-20; Wittgenstein, *B&B*, 2-4. Italics ours.

[229] Thiselton, 'SBL', 113-115; cf.: Thiselton, 'LMR', 1127-1130; Thiselton, 'SNTT', 76. Italics ours.

[230] Thiselton, 'Words', 297-298. Italics ours.

"'semantics'" that presuppose 'ideational' "theories" inherit 'all... the' problems of 'referential' approaches or 'theories' and "add" the further difficulties of a 'mentalist' 'approach'.[231]

Consequently, (c), Thiselton rejects *positivist* (cf. '"logical'", 'empiricist') 'approaches to... language' that presuppose 'referential' or 'ideational' "approaches" to 'meaning'. Against 'G.E. Moore', B. Russell, and 'the Vienna Circle', Thiselton argues that meaning cannot be restricted to empirical 'facts' and 'tautologies'. Although A.J. Ayer also allowed *potentially* "verifiable" 'statements' to have 'meaning', Thiselton reminds us that Ayer's '"verifiability'" '"criterion'" was seen as 'empiricist' 'special pleading' in that it failed to have meaning on its 'own' terms. After 'H.J. Paton', Thiselton argues that Ayer's stance on this matter was merely skepticism '"in... linguistic dress'".[232]

Admittedly, Thiselton sympathizes with A. Flew's 'falsification... principle' because there are 'empirical' or 'cognitive' aspects of 'meaning' in many 'religious utterances'. However, Thiselton argues that discerning the 'meaning' of the utterance, '"God is love'", requires different criteria. Further, in Thiselton's view, 'referential', 'ideational', and 'positivist' "approaches" wrongly tend to disparage 'imagery' relative 'to so-called literal discourse' and, along with 'natural' "approaches" (see below), also wrongly tend to argue that revising 'Christian vocabulary' is the solution to 'the problem of' the lack of 'intelligibility' associated with using ancient 'religious language' in '"modern'" 'setting[s]'.[233]

B) CRITICISM OF "NATURAL" AND CONTINENTAL ASSUMPTIONS AND APPROACHES

Moving on, (1), Thiselton also applies his later-Wittgensteinian-Saussurian alliance in criticism of 'natural', 'primitive', or 'dynamic' approaches to language – which he dubs 'word-magic'.[234] Thiselton argues that 'language' may indeed be 'power-laden', but that language is not thereby '"a material'" 'force which irresistibly achieves its end'.[235] In Thiselton's view, 'words' should not be "confused" with the "material" '"thing'" (or 'names' with 'objects'), nor linguistic "effects" 'with... physical cause and effect'. Thiselton, following 'Saussure', argues that 'language' may be 'dynamic', but that 'language' remains '"conventional'".[236]

Thus, Thiselton argues that linguistic 'power' does not spring from 'a natural' relation between language and reality but from its potential to involve whole persons, 'not' just their '"intellects'", and from its capacity to connect "individuals" to "communities" ('past' or present) through potentially transforming communication. Criticizing Tillich, Thiselton argues that 'symbols' are not

---

[231] Thiselton, 'SBL', 115; cf. Thiselton, 'LMR', 1128-1130.
[232] Thiselton, 'LMR', 1135-1136, 1127, 1129, 1130. Italics ours.
[233] Thiselton, 'LMR', 1137, 1127, 1129, 1136, 1130, 1134; cf. 1135; cf.: Thiselton, 'Words', 293; Thiselton, 'MP', 10, 4; Thiselton, *LLM*, 3.
[234] Thiselton, 'Words', 293-294, 286-289, 296-298.
[235] Thiselton, 'Words', 297, 283.
[236] Thiselton, 'Words', 293, 294, 289, 296, 287, 297.

"naturally" related to the world despite 'their power' to facilitate 'the necessary interplay between conscious and unconscious', to resonate with 'childhood' or national 'memories', to "open up" '"the soul"', or to 'hold us' under their 'spell'. In Thiselton's estimate, not all 'powerful' 'symbols' appropriately symbolize 'God', but all such 'symbols' *do* require responsible authentication against the bar of *'public criteria'* and (thus) against the bar of 'broader' 'cognitive discourse'. Thus, contradicting P.R. Keifert's reading of Thiselton, we should again observe that 'Thiselton' does *not* neglect 'the relationship between language and reality'.[237]

(2) In 1971, Thiselton rejects T. Fawcett's *combining* of a 'naturalistic' view of language with 'a referential or ideational theory of meaning'. In Thiselton's view, Fawcett has 'virtually ignored' 'Wittgenstein', 'linguistic philosophy', and 'general linguistics'.[238]

Later, in 1974, drawing on 'Saussure' and J. Barr, Thiselton denies that the 'etymology' and 'semantics' of the Hebrew word *'dābār'* constitute any basis whatsoever for the view that 'the Old Testament' supposedly presupposes a 'natural' 'view of' language.[239] Crucially, applying his later-Wittgensteinian-Saussurian alliance, Thiselton rejects the *dualistic* prioritization of supposedly '"richer"' 'biblical' 'dynamic' aspects of language relative to supposedly '"impoverished"' '"Greek"' or '"modern"' Western 'dianoetic' aspects of language, contrary to O. Procksch, G. von Rad, 'Fuchs', 'Ebeling', and – by implication - Heidegger. Thiselton argues that this "dualism" presupposes 'false' 'alternatives'.[240] Thus, with 'Saussure', 'general linguistics', Austin, and 'Korzybski's "general semantics"', Thiselton urges that even 'performative language' is "conventional" and not 'natural'.[241]

In Thiselton's view, Continental linguistic dualism – apart from its 'false' 'alternatives' – also *'privatizes* language' so that it 'cannot be' '"tested"' against 'a public criterion of language intelligibility'. Thiselton, by contrast, urges that 'all language', including so-called 'religious language', 'relate[s] to human life in a public and observable way'.[242] Thus, against Continental thought, Thiselton reinstates 'assertions' and '"critical"' 'testing' (see also Chapters 1, 3, and 5), arguing that 'interpretation must be creative, but also faithful and true'.[243] Thiselton retains 'the theoretical, objective, and assertive side of language' which neither reflects 'a derivative mode of interpretation' (against Heidegger) nor 'one

---

[237] Thiselton, 'LMR', 1123-1124, 1127, 1134, 1137; cf.: Thiselton, *2H*, 404; Thiselton, 'Till', 102; Keifert, 'R *2H*', 409. Second italics Thiselton's.

[238] Thiselton, 'R *TSLR*', 221, 222; cf. Thiselton, 'Haze', 12.

[239] Thiselton, 'Words', 289-290, 286-287, 293; cf. Thiselton, 'SNTI', 85-88, 84. Italics and transliteration Thiselton's.

[240] Thiselton, 'Words', 296-298, 284, 287; cf. Thiselton, 'Parab', 448-451.

[241] Thiselton, 'NH', 325-326; cf. Thiselton, 'Words', 293, 283-299.

[242] Thiselton, 'Words', 297-298; cf.: Thiselton, *2H*, 379-385; Walsh, 'TC', 232-233. Italics ours.

[243] Thiselton, 'TY', 1560-1561; cf.: Thiselton, 'NH', 323-329; Walsh, 'TC', 232, 233, 234.

*Hermeneutics, Language, Cultures, and Selves* 181

of the relativities embraced by language's relation to the world' (against Gadamer).[244]

That is, (3), in the context of discussions about language, Thiselton's responses to Heidegger, Bultmann, Gadamer, and to the New Hermeneutic turn on the question of how each thinker (or movement) fares relative to his later-Wittgensteinian-Saussurian alliance.

Hence, (a), finding parallels in the later Wittgenstein (see above), Thiselton affirms 'Heidegger' for grounding 'language' in 'human' 'activity', and for relating 'meaning' to "horizonal" "concerns" and 'not' to abstract 'naked', 'present-at-hand' "objects": 'we come across "equipment" in signs'.[245] With Heidegger, Thiselton argues that 'language-habits' condition "world-view" without totally "determining" "world-view", being 'open-ended towards future experience'. Thus, Thiselton agrees with Heidegger that 'only… the temporality of discourse… can… make the possibility of concept-formation… intelligible'.[246] In Thiselton's view, 'Heidegger' also rightly bemoans 'Western' 'technological', 'functional', and "conceptual" "trivialization" and compartmentalization of 'language' for use as a 'mere' "tool", since this '"destroys our authentic relation to things"', in a 'progressive mutilation' of 'language'.[247]

Whilst acknowledging 'creative… eventful language' and whilst adapting Heidegger's notion of '"world"', however, Thiselton argues that Heidegger's 'view of language' is too like 'word-magic' (i.e. a too like a 'natural' view of 'language'), and too disparaging of 'cognitive' dimensions (e.g. 'assertions'). In Thiselton's view, Heidegger 'set[s] up a false antithesis' or dualism between a disparaged so-called 'ideational' dimension 'of language' and a promoted so-called 'dynamic' dimension 'of language'.[248]

(b) In Thiselton's view, 'Bultmann', like the later Wittgenstein, rightly rejects "abstract" treatments of 'language'. With Bultmann, Thiselton agrees that how a 'text' is "understood" or "questioned" relates to a reader's 'pre-understanding': 'the presupposition of understanding is the life relation of the interpreter to the subject matter'.[249]

---

[244] Walsh, 'TC', 231-232; cf.: Heidegger, *BT*, 195 and onwards; Gadamer, H.-G., *Truth and Method* (trans. J. Weinsheimer and D.G. Marshall; London: Sheed & Ward, 1975, 1989), 450; Thiselton, 'NH', 325-326.

[245] Thiselton, 'LMR', 1130-1131; cf.: Thiselton, *2H*, 155; Heidegger, *BT*, 107(quoted), 203-210.

[246] Thiselton, 'LMR', 1127, 1131; cf. Heidegger, *BT*, 400-401 (quoted).

[247] Thiselton, 'LMR', 1139, 1143; cf. Heidegger, M., *Introduction to Metaphysics* (trans. G. Fried and R. Polt; London: Yale University Press, 2000), 54 (quoted).

[248] cf.: Thiselton, 'LMR', 1139-1140; Thiselton, 'Words', 297, 293, 284, 287; Thiselton, 'NH', 320, 325-326; Thiselton, 'Parab', 440, cf. 451-452.

[249] Thiselton, 'LMR', 1138; cf. Bultmann, R., 'The Problem of Hermeneutics', in *New Testament and Mythology and Other Basic Writings* (ed. and trans. S.M. Ogden; Philadelphia: Fortress Press, 1984), 74 (quoted).

However, Thiselton argues that Bultmann's 'three' approaches to 'myth' are tied to false views of 'language'. Thus, (i), Bultmann complains that New Testament writers 'uncritically' "use" "mythical" "'imagery... to express'" – in "contradictory" ways – "'the other-worldly in terms of this world'": 'some... representations are mutually disharmonious'. But, in Thiselton's view, Bultmann's approach here "confuses" 'myth' and 'analogy'. Thiselton argues, by contrast, that New Testament writers *competently* employ 'a necessary diversity... of analogies, models', and 'metaphors'. (ii) In 'Bultmann's view', New Testament writers subscribed to the mythical 'world-view of a pre-scientific age' which masks the real *Kerygma*: their 'world-view' 'was not yet formed by scientific thinking'. But, in Thiselton's estimate, Bultmann's approach here 'presupposes too sharp a' distinction 'between' 'thought' and linguistic 'form'. Thiselton argues that the New Testament is not a decipherable 'code' to 'be discarded' once deciphered but an 'indispensable' 'masterpiece' inviting endless visits (Thiselton cites 'I. Hendersen' here). (iii) In Bultmann's view, 'myth' concerns self-understanding and "'not... an objective picture of the world'", and so requires 'anthropological' 'not' 'cosmological' "interpretation". But, drawing on the later Wittgenstein and Austin, Thiselton argues that eschatological 'language' is *both* 'descriptive' *and* 'self-involving' and so cannot be reduced to 'anthropological' terms exhaustively or without remainder.[250]

(c) In Thiselton's view, Gadamer, like the later Wittgenstein, rightly acknowledges: (i) distinctions between 'linguistic' "use", 'form', and 'content'; (ii) the way in which 'language-habits' condition, without totally "determining", 'thought' and 'world-view'; and, (iii), the "open-endedness" of 'language... towards future experience'. Citing Gadamer, 'tradition does not limit the freedom of knowledge but makes it possible'.[251] Thiselton also *adapts* (*sic*) 'Gadamer's notion[s] of' the 'fusion of horizons' and "'common world'". And yet, Thiselton argues that Gadamer, like Heidegger, falls victim to 'word-magic' (for Gadamer, 'whoever has language [supposedly] "has" the world') and dualistically disparages 'cognitive' dimensions of language (e.g. 'assertions').[252]

(d) In Thiselton's view, Fuchs and Ebeling, like the later Wittgenstein, rightly urge that 'language' 'does not merely inform', or 'convey concepts', but acts "creatively" on "hearers". Thiselton agrees with Fuchs and Ebeling that the New Testament 'does not' just speak *'about'*, but functions as part of, God's 'love' or 'salvation', and is 'not merely' to be sifted into pre-conceived 'concepts' by 'detached' "observers". Thus, after Fuchs and Ebeling, Thiselton argues that parable 'language' potentially 'draws' readers into Jesus' "'world'", "impacting" them 'deep down' through "language-events", and transforming their 'horizons'.

---

[250] Thiselton, 'LMR', 1138-1139; cf. Bultmann, 'NT&M', 10; cf. 3; cf. 9. Italics ours.

[251] Thiselton, 'LMR', 1126, 1131, 1127; cf. Gadamer, *TM*, 361(quoted)-379, 78, 383-405, 428-438, 456-491.

[252] Thiselton, 'LMR', 1140; cf.: Thiselton, *2H*, xix; Thiselton, 'NH', 320, 325-326; Thiselton, 'Parab', 451; Gadamer, *TM*, 306-307, 374-375, 105, 442-459 (quoting 453), 474.

And yet, in Thiselton's view, the problems 'of word-magic' and of the dualistic disparagement of the 'creative' role of 'cognitive' dimensions of language remain, such that the New Hermeneutic – in Thiselton's estimate - is only of hermeneutical 'use' for '*some* parts of the' New Testament.[253]

In conclusion, (4), Thiselton tests, and thereby dialogically validates, his later-Wittgensteinian-Saussurian alliance by using it to expose flaws in the Heideggerian-Gadamerian tradition of language-study, *whilst still drawing positively on that tradition*.

Admittedly, by 1977, Thiselton had stressed that positive dialogue with this 'third' tradition of language-study was required[254] in order to extend discussion beyond later Wittgensteinian and Saussurian traditions.[255] Nevertheless, J. Barr's claim that Thiselton "accepts" the New Hermeneutic 'quite cordially' is false.[256] Further, whilst H.C. White argues that, for Thiselton, 'insights from Austin and Wittgenstein' complement those drawn from E. Fuchs, *the reverse is actually the case*.[257] Certainly, contradicting C. Mercer's pre-dialogic categorizations, we should note that Thiselton does *not* simply "combine" 'postmodernist notions of language with more traditional representational perspectives'.[258]

c) Validating the Later-Wittgensteinian-Saussurian Alliance through Application

Moving on, we may briefly note that Thiselton further tests, and thereby dialogically validates, his later-Wittgensteinian-Saussurian alliance by putting it to positive use in biblical interpretation, in practical theology, and in hermeneutical theory – as follows.

Thus, (1), in his *biblical interpretation* - specifically in his paper on 1 Corinthians 5:5 (1973) - Thiselton combines appeals to: (a), Wittgenstein's notions of '"language-game"' and of the multi-functional character 'of language'; (b) distinctions – drawn from linguistic philosophy - 'between' 'evaluative' and 'descriptive' 'logic'; (c) the 'extra linguistic' embedding of language – as in Wittgenstein's thinking and in 'general... linguistics'; (d) notions of semantic 'opposition' drawn from post-Saussurian semantics; (e) notions of 'common

---

[253] cf.: Thiselton, 'LMR', 1139-1140; Thiselton, 'NH', 320, 324-326; Thiselton, 'Parab', 463-466. First italics Thiselton's, second italics ours.

[254] Thiselton, 'LMR', 1123; cf.: 1140-1142; 1130-1135; 1137-1140.

[255] So, Maddox, 'R 2H', 136; cf. Walsh, 'TC', 235.

[256] Barr, 'R NTI', 235; cf.: Thrall, M.E., 'Review of I.H. Marshall ed. *New Testament Interpretation*', *SJT* 32.4 (Aug. 1979), 388; cautioning, Klein, W.W., 'Review of A.C. Thiselton's *The Two Horizons*', *TrinJ* 2 (Spr. 1981), 74; contradicting, Hynson, L. O., 'Review of R. Lundin's, A.C. Thiselton's and C. Walhout's *The Responsibility of Hermeneutics*', *ChSRev* 18.1 (1988), 91.

[257] White, H.C., 'The Value of Speech-Act Theory for Old Testament Hermeneutics', *Sem* 41 (1988), 55.

[258] Mercer, C.R., 'Review of A.C. Thiselton's *New Horizons in Hermeneutics*', *CBQ* 56.1 (1994), 159.

"world" of understanding' drawn from R.W. Funk; (f) a notion of 'persuasive definition' drawn from linguistic philosophy; (g) Saussure's 'synchronic'-'diachronic' 'distinction'; and, (h), notions of semantic 'vagueness' drawn from post-Saussurian semantics.[259]

In 1978, Thiselton also combines an appeal to the synchronic-diachronic distinction with an appeal to J. Barr's comments on "etymologizing" and on the separation of 'arbitrary' 'surface-grammar' from notions of 'national' 'thought'.[260] Moreover, in 1979, Thiselton applies Saussure's synchronic-diachronic distinction with respect to authorial, "'linguistic'", socio-historical-situational, inter-authorial and inter-textual, literary, and anthropological considerations in his paper on 'tongues'.[261] Finally, in 1978 and 1980, Thiselton applies the later Wittgenstein's notions of 'language-games' and 'polymorphous concepts' in his (i.e. Thiselton's) interpretations of 1 Corinthians and of "'faith'" and "'truth'" in the New Testament.[262]

(2) In 1974, in his *practical theology* – and specifically in relation 'to preaching', "lecturing", and 'Bible study' - Thiselton appeals to notions of semantic 'opposition' 'and synonymy'.[263] Further, also in 1974, but this time in relation to 'ecumenical' issues, Thiselton combines appeals to Pannenbergian 'futurity', to 'polymorphous concepts', 'ambiguity' and 'vagueness', and to later Wittgensteinian and general linguistic critiques of 'meaning'.[264]

(3) In his *hermeneutical theory*, Thiselton emphasizes the role of 'language' study in 'elucidating' *both* "textual" 'horizons',[265] *and* readers' 'pre-understanding[s]'.[266] Thiselton argues that readers' 'pre-judgments' (cf. "'scaffolding'") and 'questions' are interwoven with, if not absolutely "determined" by, the 'language-habits' of the "traditions" in which they are situated. For Thiselton, 'hermeneutics' and 'translation' "concern" *'both'* sets of 'horizons'.[267] Thus, Thiselton addresses 'the multiform problem of the relation of language to understanding'.[268]

*7. Implications of this Exposition of Thiselton's Unified Hermeneutical Critique of Language*

Moving on, then this exposition of Thiselton's unified hermeneutical critique of

---

[259] Thiselton, 'SARX', 205, 216, 207, 209, 210, 212, 215, 217, 218, 224, 226, 227.

[260] Thiselton, 'Truth', 877-878; cf.: Thiselton, 'SBS', 330-331; Thiselton, 'LMR', 1126-1127.

[261] Thiselton, 'TT', 15-27, 31, 34-36.

[262] Thiselton, *2H*, 407-409, 411-415; cf. Thiselton, 'REC', 522-523.

[263] Thiselton, 'ENE', 6.

[264] Thiselton, 'MCU', 45-47.

[265] Thiselton, *2H*, 120-121, 133-139.

[266] cf.: Thiselton, *NTH*, 170-172, 186-193; Thiselton, *2H*, 120-121, 133-139.

[267] Thiselton, *2H*, 305, 74, 309-314, 120, 130-131; cf.; Thiselton, 'SNTI', 87-88; Thiselton, *LLM*, 3-6; Thiselton, 'LMR', 1134-1135, 1127. Italics ours.

[268] Webster, J.B., 'Review of A.C. Thiselton's *The Two Horizons*', *FTht* 107.3 (1980), 219; cf. Schneiders, S.M., 'Review of A.C. Thiselton's *The Two Horizons*', *JRel* 62.3 (Jul. 1982), 308.

language, (1), confirms our fears concerning the *inadequate "reception" of Thiselton's thinking in the literature* (see our Introduction). Continental traditions aside, sometimes only Thiselton's indebtedness to the later Wittgenstein is noted.[269] Others only note his indebtedness to the later Wittgenstein and to semantics;[270] or to the later Wittgenstein and Saussure;[271] or to 'Wittgenstein' and 'British philosophy';[272] or to Wittgenstein and general linguistics;[273] or to 'Wittgenstein' and '"speech-act"' theory;[274] or to 'Wittgenstein', 'Saussure', and "semantics";[275] or to 'Wittgenstein', G.E. Ryle, and 'James Barr'.[276] Even W.W. Klein only notes Thiselton's appeals to 'Wittgenstein', 'Saussure', 'modern linguistics', and to the semantics of J. Barr, J.F.A. Sawyer, and others.[277]

Indeed, our exposition yielded many further points of contention with numerous other Thiselton-readers (see our footnotes): Thiselton neither sat in 'the intentionalist camp' without qualification,[278] nor "rejected" authorial 'intention'.[279] Thiselton did not espouse 'hermeneutics' as a subset 'of literary criticism', but the reverse.[280] Thiselton did not "supplement" insights from 'linguistic semantics' with those from 'philosophical semantics', but the reverse.[281] Moreover, Thiselton is

---

[269] Cf.: Erickson, M.J., 'Review of A.C. Thiselton's *The Two Horizons*', *JEThS* 23 (Dec. 1980), 371-373; cf.: Rodd, C.S., 'Review of A.C. Thiselton's *The Two Horizons*', *ExTim* 91 (Jul. 1980), 289-290; Macquarrie, J., 'Review of A.C. Thiselton's *The Two Horizons*', *RelStud* 16.4 (Dec. 1980), 496-497; Poythress, V.S., 'Review of A.C. Thiselton's *The Two Horizons*', *WThJ* 43 (Fall 1980), 178-180; Palmer, 'R *2H*', 172-174; Wink, W., 'Review of A.C. Thiselton's *The Two Horizons*', *ThT* 37.4 (Jan. 1981), 506-507; Geisler, 'R *2H*', 182-183; Sykes, S.W., 'Review of A.C. Thiselton's *The Two Horizons*', *Chman* 96.2 (1982), 156-157; Roschke, R.W., 'Review of A.C. Thiselton's *The Two Horizons*', *CThM* 9 (Aug. 1982), 246-247; Harrisville, 'R *2H*', 216-217; Dockery, 'R *2H*', 133-136; Borsch, 'R *2H*', 88-90; Dyrness, W.A., 'Review of A.C. Thiselton's *The Two Horizons*', *CTday* 25 (Apr. 10, 1981), 94; Trocmé, E., 'Review of A.C. Thiselton's *The Two Horizons*', *RevHstPhRel* 61.2 (1981), 192-193. Italics ours.

[270] cf.: Keifert, 'R *2H*', 407-409; Brodie, 'R *2H*', 480-486; Klemm, D.E., 'Review of A.C. Thiselton's *The Two Horizons*', *JAARel* 50.1 (Mar. 1982), 116-117.

[271] cf.: Cahill, 'R *2H*', 484-485; McNicol, A.J., 'Review of A.C. Thiselton's *The Two Horizons*', *RestQ* 27.3 (1984), 187-189; Van Voorst, R., 'Review of A.C. Thiselton's *The Two Horizons*', *RefRev* 34 (Spr. 1981), 220-221; Schneiders, 'R *2H*', 307-309.

[272] cf.: Morgan, 'R *2H*', 331-333.

[273] cf.: Ellingworth, 'R *2H*', 178-179; Conroy, C., 'Review of A.C. Thiselton's *The Two Horizons*', *Greg* 62.3 (1981), 563-566.

[274] cf. Grech, 'R *2H*', 572-576.

[275] cf.: Metzger, 'R *2H*', 208-211; Metzger, B.M., 'Review of A.C. Thiselton's *The Two Horizons*', *ChSRev* 10.3 (1981), 262-265.

[276] cf. Bowden, 'R *2H*', 55-57.

[277] Klein, 'R *2H*', 71-75.

[278] Qualifying, Osborne, 'R *NH*', 91.

[279] Contradicting, Johnson, 'R *NH*', 502; and, Ward, *W&S*, 149; cf. Thiselton, *NH*, 59.

[280] Contradicting, Van Hamersveld, 'R *RH*', 252.

[281] Contradicting, Barr, 'R *NTI*', 233-234; and Gibson, *BSL*, 1.

not simply 'Wittgensteinian'. Nor does he fall into straightforward '"fideism"', context-relativity, 'subjectivism', or 'perspectivism' (McNicol uses the term, 'perspectival') on this basis.[282] Furthermore, Thiselton's appeals to Wittgenstein *cohere* with his theological framework.[283] The latter is not "marginalized" by Thiselton,[284] but is *more fundamental* to Thiselton's framework than Thiselton's appeals to Wittgenstein, as R. Papaphilippopoulos and R.W.L. Moberly rightly note.[285] Some writers over-emphasize Wittgenstein's role in Thiselton's thinking, when that role is largely (though not entirely) constrained to Thiselton's hermeneutical critique of *language* and not to his hermeneutical critique of *epistemology*.[286] Nor is Thiselton simply "Gadamerian"; and nor does he "accept" the New Hermeneutic 'quite cordially'. Rather, he is critical of Continental perspectives whilst still drawing positively on them.[287]

(2) Our analysis also furnishes a mild criticism of Thiselton, however. That Thiselton continues to use Continental terminology (i.e. "horizons", "world", "fusion" etc.) given his thoroughly mixed response to Continental traditions means that "the grammar(s)" of *Thiselton's* use(s) of this terminology is no longer that of its "home" "language-games". Afterall, in his moving *beyond* holding traditions in tension towards critical synthesis, Thiselton *reinstates* the role of a modified form of subject-object conceptualization (see Chapter 3), *reinstates* "transmitted truth-criteria", *reinstates* the "creative function" of certain kinds of 'assertions', and *reinstates* the ontological priority of history over language.[288] As we argue below Thiselton also, in effect, *transposes* the Heideggerian categories of 'historicality', "futurity", 'possibility', and 'potentiality' into an "eschatological" framework of 'prophetic promise'.[289]

Admittedly, we argue later that Thiselton *legitimately* changes the grammar(s) of Continental concepts through a process that we call "tradition-modification" – a process which should be clearly distinguished from illegitimate "persuasive definition". Admittedly, furthermore, Thiselton is still holding traditions in tension to some extent - in a way that reflects his "programmatic approach" (some of the critical synthesis is inevitably ours). Moreover, admittedly, it is difficult to improve on Continental terminology. And yet, despite these three important caveats, the grammatical changes implicit in Thiselton's critical synthesis require more explicit

---

[282] Contradicting: Geisler, 'R *2H*', 182; Poythress, 'R *NH*', 345; Walsh, 'TC', 235; Grech, 'R *2H*', 576; McNicol, 'R *2H*', 188-189.

[283] Answering, Bowden, 'R *2H*', 57.

[284] Correcting: Poythress, 'R *NH*', 345; Watson, 'R *NH*', 255-256; Walsh, 'TC', 235.

[285] Affirming: Papaphilippopoulos, 'R *NH*', 142-143; and, Moberly, 'R *NH*', 72.

[286] Contradicting: Geisler, 'R *2H*', 182; Walsh, 'TC', 235; Poythress, 'R *NH*', 345; Grech, 'R *2H*', 576; McNicol, 'R *2H*', 188-189.

[287] Contradicting, Rodd, 'R *2H*', 290; and, Barr, 'R *NTT*', 235.

[288] Thiselton, 'Till', 92; cf. Thiselton, 'Parab', 463, 464; cf. Chapter 3, and above.

[289] See our argument below and, cf.: Heidegger, *BT*, 424, 373, 310, 372; Thiselton, *2H*, 186, 183, 178, 80; Thiselton, 'Par', 47.

demarcation, where a partly parallel but much less significant argument could perhaps be offered with respect to Thiselton's use of Wittgensteinian terminology, such as "language-games", in theological contexts. This demarcation would liberate Thiselton from being falsely caricatured as being simply "Gadamerian", or as simply being "of the New Hermeneutic", or as being simply 'Wittgensteinian'.[290]

We will return to the question of the *legitimacy* of Thiselton's use of Continental terminology in Chapter 6. We may now turn to consider Thiselton's *hermeneutical critique of Western culture* before, finally, turning to consider Thiselton's hermeneutical critique of human selves.

## C. Dialogic Theory-Construction:
## Towards a Unified Hermeneutical Critique of (Western) Culture

Thiselton's *hermeneutical critique of (Western) culture* reaches maturity in the 1990s and so,[291] given our present focus on Thiselton's formative works (see our Introduction), our exposition here reflects only the embryonic form that Thiselton's hermeneutical critique of (Western) culture had developed into by 1980. Nevertheless, even prior to 1980, Thiselton again brings philosophy and theology into dialogue in a hermeneutical critique of (Western) culture that is not just socio-critical, but that also theorizes about (Western) culture along several other axes – as follows.

Thus, (1), after Pannenberg, Thiselton 'views' 'Western' 'culture' as '"part"' of a larger 'provisional' "frame(s)-of-reference", namely '"eschatological"' "anticipations" of global 'history as a whole'. In Thiselton's view, following Pannenberg, 'Western' 'culture' must be *explained and evaluated metacritically* through as wide a 'dialogue' as possible with 'other' "cultures", 'traditions', 'religions', "philosophies", and so on - for 'God' makes himself known through 'history'.[292] This first axis of consideration involves Thiselton's arguments for the legitimacy of including theology in the hermeneutical discussion – arguments that we have begun to outline in Chapter 3, and that we will continue to discuss in Chapter 7.

(2) With Moltmann, Thiselton argues that Western culture must be subjected to an *evaluative, metacritical socio-critique* of "traditions" and of human "experience" –

---

[290] cf. Chapter 3 and the present chapter; cf.: Rodd, 'R *2H*', 290; Barr, 'R *NTP*, 235; Geisler, 'R *2H*', 182.

[291] cf.: Thiselton, *IGPS*; Thiselton, 'CAP', 133-239; Thiselton, A.C., 'Signs of the Times: Towards a Theology for the Year 2000 as a Grammar of Grace, Truth and Eschatology in Contexts of So-Called Postmodernity. Presidential Paper of the Society for the Study of Theology', in *The Future as God's Gift: Explorations in Christian Eschatology* (eds. D. Fergusson and M. Sarot; Edinburgh: T&T Clark, 2000), 9-39.

[292] cf.: Thiselton, 'UPC', 93-94; Thiselton, 'NH', 314; Thiselton, 'TNI', 11; Thiselton, 'M&M', 8; Thiselton, 'R *BQT*', 120; Thiselton, 'Par', 48-50; Thiselton, *NTH*, 101-114; Thiselton, 'Truth', 900-901; Thiselton, 'Till', 104-105, 87-89.

primarily in relation to *biblical* metacriteria and paradigms.[293] Drawing on 'Heidegger' and the later Wittgenstein (among others), Thiselton argues that people require 'liberation' from "conventional" determinism, from external "manipulation", and from 'self-deception'[294] through an employment of 'linguistic philosophy' and of the 'truth'. In Thiselton's view, hermeneutics concerns how 'our own cultural environment conditions… our words and… thinking'.[295]

In relation to *mission* then, with Tillich, Thiselton argues that 'Church' mission should "frame" our understanding of Western 'culture'. With E. Fuchs, Thiselton asks, 'What does the Bible actually say to our own generation?' We also noted Thiselton's involvement in 'Dialogue 77' in Chapter 2.[296] In Thiselton's view, however, this *right* emphasis on Christian mission does not immunize the Church itself from the *same evaluative metacritical socio-critique* – especially in relation to biblical metacriteria and paradigms.[297]

Admittedly, Thiselton *contrasts* ephemeral "'cultural presupposition[s]'" or "culture-relativity" with the temporally-continuous, consciously thought-through, 'theological' 'convictions' of 'tradition', and also contrasts 'accidental' "cultural" 'linguistic *form*' with the trans-temporal 'language-habits' of 'tradition'. *Nevertheless* Thiselton argues that "culture", properly re-historicized, is inconsistent with *'a-historical'* notions of "culture-relativity" that divorce 'communities' from 'embeddedness within' and responsibility towards the historical-temporal 'continuities' of broader traditions and of "anticipations" of 'history as a whole'. That is, for Thiselton, "culture" is always a snap-shot of a superimposition of multiple trans-temporal, dynamic, inter-related and inter-relating "traditions". In this context of discussion, Thiselton later criticizes R. Rorty's *'a-historical'* 'socio-pragmatic hermeneutics' and their outworking in 'liberation hermeneutics' and/or 'in reader-response theories' (notably, that of S. Fish).[298] Nevertheless, Thiselton's hermeneutic of "traditions" is not "Thiselton's major hermeneutical axis". Rather, Thiselton's hermeneutic of "traditions" contributes *to* his broader *hermeneutical*

---

[293] cf.: Thiselton, A.C., 'Creativity of Heaven', *CEN* 8 Mar. (1974), 5; Thiselton, A.C., 'Review of J. Moltmann's *The Crucified God*', *Chman* 89.2 (1975), 148-149; Thiselton, A.C., 'Great Compassion and Heart. Review of J. Moltmann's *The Crucified God*', *CEN* 10 Jan. (1975), 9; Thiselton, A.C., 'Review of J. Moltmann's *The Experiment Hope*', *Chman* 90.3 (1976), 225-227.

[294] cf.: Thiselton, 'AA', 600; Thiselton, A.C., 'Kierkegaard and the Nature of Truth', *Chman* 89.1 (1975), 85-107; Thiselton, 'Truth', 881, 886; Thiselton, 'LMR', 1143.

[295] Thiselton, 'UPC', 89; cf. Thiselton, 'Truth', 881; cf. Thiselton, 'T&F', 11.

[296] Thiselton, 'Till', 104, 88; cf.: Thiselton, 'T&F', 11; Thiselton, A.C., 'Forget Image, Try Dialogue 77. Report on Outreach at Sheffield University', *CEN* 11 Feb. (1977), 2.

[297] Thiselton, A.C., 'Reflections in the Current Debate. Review of A.T. Hanson's *Grace and Truth*', *CEN* 26 Dec. (1975), 9; cf.: Chapter 2; Thiselton, *NTH*, xxii, conc. 1.2a.

[298] cf.: Klein, 'R *2H*', 74; Thiselton, *2H*, 434-436; Thiselton, 'LMR', 1126, 1127; Thiselton, 'SNTI', 87; Thiselton, *NH*, 401, 419, 515; cf.: 93-405; 410-427; 439-452; 529-550; Thiselton, 'CAP', 157; Thiselton, 'Par', 48-49. Italics in speech-marks are Thiselton's.

*critique of history* (see Chapter 6).[299]

(3) On *the specifics of a socio-critique of Western culture* then, for Thiselton, this axis of consideration includes the findings of metacritical *external* comparisons of Western culture with *other* cultures (cf. '(1)' above), and, the findings of metacriticism of characteristics *internal* to Western culture (cf. '(2)' above). Notably, Thiselton contrasts the "cosmological" and corporate dimensions of 'eschatology' with Western 'individualism', and appeals to 'African' and 'Latin American' 'theologians' both in critique of Western 'individualism' and in critique of Western over-'emphasis on... abstract theory'. With J. Miranda, Thiselton argues that 'Western Christians' tend to 'read' 'the Bible' 'theoretically', neglecting 'practical questions'.[300] With Moltmann, Thiselton also bemoans power abuse, "depersonalization" 'and alienation' in modern (especially Western) societies and, with M. Buber, attacks the instrumentalization of the 'other as an "it"' and the reduction of persons to 'anonymous' "units" 'of production', to "cogs" 'in the economic machine', or to "insignificants" in a "vast" impersonal 'universe'.[301]

Notably, Thiselton attacks contemporary Western 'relativism', 'extreme pessimism', and 'skepticism about truth'. In Thiselton's view, 'theories of truth' have wrongly been transposed 'into' 'an entirely secular context' and, lamentably, 'German' philosophy since 'Kant' has precipitated 'a fragmentation of truth' and a '*mood* of uncertainty' affecting Western 'theology', biblical studies, and culture more broadly. Thiselton argues that the unfortunate result of this situation (and - Thiselton would later add - of the influence of American neo- or socio-pragmatism) is that an 'other-than-serious attitude to truth' pervades 'mass advertising and party-political propaganda... through mass media'. Further, Thiselton argues that unredeemed and 'insecure' cultural 'self-defensiveness and self-assertion give rise to falsehood', and that cultural 'pseudo-cynicism... tries to "unmask" everything' – erroneously "believing" that 'no-one... can genuinely lay claim to truth'.[302] *With* Heidegger, Thiselton laments the "seductive", "trivial", "manipulative", and 'relativized' 'speech' of 'mass advertising' and 'social engineering' and, *with* Kierkegaard and the later Wittgenstein, Thiselton attacks "unbacked" irresponsible 'words' that produce 'circularity and... relativism' and that have 'no anchorage in reality'.[303]

Positively, against '*unduly* defensive... obscurantist... anti-scholarly, anti-intellectual' or 'anti-cultural' Christian 'pietism' and '"fundamentalism"', Thiselton urges that 'social' "conventions" may still *rightly* constrain individual "freedoms". Against the early Moltmann (though see our qualifications in Chapter 3), Thiselton

---

[299] Correcting a perspective on Thiselton's work encountered at the annual conference of the Society for the Study of Theology, 8th-11th April 2002, Lancaster University.

[300] Thiselton, 'AA', 609-610; cf.: Thiselton, 'Par', 47-52; Thiselton, *NTH*, 156; cf. 186-193.

[301] Thiselton, 'AA', 600; cf.: Thiselton, 'ML', 9; Thiselton, A.C., 'Review of A. Hodes' *Encounter with Martin Buber*', *Chman* 90.2 (1976), 138-139.

[302] Thiselton, 'Truth', 899-901. Italics Thiselton's.

[303] Thiselton, 'LMR', 1139; cf. 1142-1144.

argues that 'the Exodus' 'message' is not a call 'to abandon existing structures… regardless of whether' or not they 'may have built' something 'worthwhile already'. In Thiselton's view, 'capitalism… combined with… compassion', *could* still be viable.[304]

(4) Thiselton argues that *'Western culture' uniquely obscures hermeneutical 'understanding'.* Thiselton rejects "post-Enlightenment" approaches to 'history', "epistemology", 'language', human selves, and 'interpretation'.[305] With 'Fuchs and Ebeling' - following 'Gadamer' – Thiselton argues that '"understanding"' is *'not'* just a matter of applying *'"rules"'* akin to '"scientific"' '"method"'.[306] At best, Thiselton argues, '"method"' 'only' "prevents" 'false' 'understanding'; at worst it "imposes" prior alien 'categories' onto 'texts' (or onto persons, or onto whoever or whatever is being interpreted). In Thiselton's estimate, 'understanding' involves *both* "comparison" *and* '"intuitive"' or '"divinatory"' '"leaps"' '"into the hermeneutical circle"'; it 'is an *art*', and not just '"scientific"'.[307]

(5) Thiselton argues, drawing on Gadamer and on the later Wittgenstein, that *Western "traditions" – including 'culture' – "condition" the 'pre-understanding[s]' (cf. 'pre-judgments', '"scaffolding"') of 'modern' reading communities* through '"effective history"' and 'language-habits': "eliminating" the 'modern context' 'is impossible'. After the New Hermeneutic, Thiselton acknowledges that readers' 'attitude[s]' and 'unconscious' 'assumptions', being shaped by '"a changed situation"' and by 'a long' historical 'tradition of biblical interpretation', are very 'different' to those of 'the New Testament'.[308]

Negatively, Thiselton argues that '"pre-understanding[s]"' 'may' *"hinder"* 'genuine understanding' and 'communication'. Thus, Thiselton argues that 'modern readers' may inadvertently "reverse" a 'parable's' 'intended' 'function' by tearing parable language from its '"home"' '"language-game"' and by "re-embedding" it within 'modern' 'categories'. Therefore, Thiselton argues, 'the tyranny of pre-understandings' must 'be challenged' - through proper 'engagement' with 'the history of… fusions found in Christian tradition' – in order to prevent Bible reading becoming 'domesticated', dull, or 'boring'. In Thiselton's view, 'biblical' texts must be understood relative to 'biblical' 'public criteria of meaning', even if the latter are not objectivistically 'accessible' or immediately

---

[304] cf.: Thiselton, 'REC', 515-521; Thiselton, 'SARX', 214; Thiselton, A.C., 'Looking for God's Triumph: The Role of Apocalyptic', *CEN* 12 Jul. (1974), 8; Thiselton, A.C., "'Cat Among the Pigeons'. Review of M.D. Goulder's *Midrash and Lection in Matthew*', *CEN* 7 Feb. (1975), 10; Thiselton, 'R *TEH*', 225-227; Thiselton, 'AA', 595, cf. 596-597. Italics ours.
[305] Thiselton, 'NH', 319, 310-312, 318, 327, 317, 314, 323, cf. 326. Italics ours.
[306] Thiselton, 'NH', 310, cf. 314, cf. 317, cf. 323. Italics Thiselton's.
[307] Thiselton, 'NH', 317, 314, 310; cf. 319-320, 327-328; cf. Thiselton, 'UPC', 87, 88. Italics in speech-marks Thiselton's.
[308] cf.: Thiselton, 'NH', 308-309, 312; cf. 318-319; Thiselton, 'U (long)', 90; Thiselton, 'LMR', 1123-1124, 1127; cf. 1137; Thiselton, *2H*, 304-307, 395, 312, 315; Dockery, 'R *2H*', 134. Italics ours, except for *'pre-understanding[s]'*, where they are Thiselton's.

palatable. Thiselton argues that 'understanding' proceeds according to 'the hermeneutical circle' (or 'spiral') such that 'modern readers' in the West may increasingly "understand" themselves as being 'conditioned by' 'Western culture'. Thiselton argues that textual 'language' is thereby gradually "allowed" to 'function performatively', potentially "liberating" readers from "oppressive" aspects of 'Western' 'cultural' "conditioning", and "challenging" and "revising" readers' 'initial' 'questions'.[309]

Positively, Thiselton argues that '"pre-understanding[s]"', 'prior' '"common understanding"', or horizonal 'overlap… between', say, 'biblical' and 'modern… horizons', are *preconditional* for 'understanding' and 'communication'. For Thiselton, 'Western culture' constitutes one end of 'a hermeneutical arch' 'between… two sets of horizons'.[310] After 'Bultmann', Thiselton argues that any given reader's '"subjectivity"' cannot be "silenced" during '"understanding"'. Thus, when Thiselton asks, with 'Fuchs', 'How does the message of the New Testament strike home today?' his answer involves understanding 'Western culture'.[311]

(6) For Thiselton, *'Western culture' "conditions" contemporary actions – notably contemporary '"speech-acts"' – and vice versa*. Thiselton "grounds" 'language' and 'meaning' in 'historical' 'life', in "traditions" and *'public criteria'*, in 'context of situation' or *'Sitz im Leben'*, and in "horizonal" (and hence "culturally" 'conditioned') 'concern[s]'.[312] Thus, for Thiselton, 'meaning' is not simply 'culture-relative'. Rather, and, for example, in relation to 'religious' 'language'-'uses', Thiselton argues that *'both…* Biblical paradigms *and* contemporary life-experience… form part of an over-arching frame of reference within which

---

[309] cf.: Thiselton, 'NH', 313-317, 310-311, 319-324, 326-328; Thiselton, 'EITN', 583-584; Thiselton, A.C., 'Predictable, Domesticated and Tamed', *CEN* 8 Feb. (1974), 7; Thiselton, 'U (long)', 90-92, 97, 99, 101-102, 117-121; Thiselton, 'SARX', 216, 222; Thiselton, 'MP', 11, 4; Thiselton, *2H*, xix, 385, 437-438, 104, 105; Thiselton, *NH*, 450; Thiselton, 'Parab', 450; Thiselton, 'T&F', 11; Thiselton, 'UPC', 87-88, 92-94, 95; Thiselton, 'Truth', 881; Thiselton, 'Flesh', 680-682; Thiselton, 'KNT', 104-105; Thiselton, *NTH*, xxviii, conc. 8.2b; Thiselton, 'SBL', 109-111, 108, 116, 118; Thiselton, A.C., 'Understanding God's Word Today', *CEN* 15 Oct. (1976), 6, (henceforth the 'short' article with this title); Thiselton, 'REC', 524-525; Thiselton, A.C., 'The Theological Scene: Post-Bultmannian Perspectives', *CGrad* 30.3 (Sep. 1977), 88, 89; Thiselton, 'LMR', 1131-1135, 1139-1140; Thiselton, *LLM*, 8; Maddox, R.L., 'Contemporary Hermeneutic Philosophy and Theological Studies', *RelStud* 21.4 (Dec. 1985), 526, 528; contradicting, Thomas, 'DE', 10; re. objectivism, contradicting, Walsh, 'TC', 235. Italics ours.

[310] cf.: Thiselton, 'NH', 312-315, 319; Thiselton, 'U (long)', 102; Thiselton, *LLM*, 8-9; Thiselton, 'EITN', 583; Thiselton, 'SBL', 108-111, 118.

[311] cf.: Thiselton, 'NH', 312-315, 319; Thiselton, 'EITN', 583; Thiselton, 'LMR', 1138; Thiselton, 'P-BP', 89.

[312] cf.: Thiselton, 'NH', 319; Thiselton, 'U (long)', 90-91; Thiselton, 'LMR', 1123, 1129-1135, 1143; Thiselton, 'UPC', 94; Thiselton, *2H*, 156; Thiselton, 'SARX', 205-206, 210-212; Thiselton, 'SNTP', 78-79. Initial italics ours, remaining italics Thiselton's.

religious uses of language become intelligible'.³¹³ Thus, in Thiselton's view, 'Western culture' (or whatever contemporary culture is under consideration) contributes to a 'diachronic' "'whole'" against which 'past' *and 'present'* religious "'speech-acts'" have to 'be understood'. Conversely, however, Thiselton argues that "'contemporary'" actions, "'speech-acts'", and language-'habits' (*not* necessarily those initiated from *within* 'Western culture') also "condition", without totally "determining", 'Western culture' itself (or whatever contemporary culture is under consideration): the culture-language/action relationship is dialogic.³¹⁴

(7) In conclusion, we may see that whilst Thiselton's hermeneutical critique of (Western) culture has only developed to an embryonic level by 1980, it nevertheless *both* incorporates dialogue between theology and philosophy *and* provides axes of consideration that can be applied to *any* culture.

To summarize, these axes included: (a), hermeneutical argument for the possibility and legitimacy of metacritical comparative explanation and evaluation of any given culture *relative to other cultures* within the larger theological-eschatological narrative of anticipations of history-as-a-whole; (b), hermeneutical argument for the possibility and legitimacy of metacritical comparative explanation and evaluation at the level of the socio-criticism of *characteristics internal to any given culture*; (c), the details or findings of "(a)" and "(b)", which will be specific to a given culture; (d), the relationship between any given culture and the historical development of the (multi-)discipline of hermeneutics; (e), the relationship between cultural conditioning and the hermeneutical circle – where the former both hinders and facilitates the latter; and, (f), the dialogic relationship of mutual conditioning that ongoingly takes place between any given culture and actions (regardless of whether these actions are initiated from outside that culture *or* from within that culture) – notably speech-actions – in the present horizon.

Before concluding the present chapter, we may now turn to consider Thiselton's *hermeneutical critique of human selves.*

## D. Dialogic Theory-Construction:
### Towards a Unified Hermeneutical Critique of Human Selves

Like his hermeneutical critique of (Western) culture, Thiselton's *hermeneutical critique of human selves* also only reaches maturity in the 1990s.³¹⁵ And yet, the latter is more developed by 1980 than the former. Below, we offer a 'snap shot' reflecting where Thiselton's hermeneutical critique of human selves had reached in its development by 1980 (though we defer treatment of Thiselton's appeal to Heidegger in this

---

³¹³ Thiselton, *2H*, 81, 396; cf. Thiselton, *LLM*, 4. Italics Thiselton's.

³¹⁴ cf.: Thiselton, 'NH', 319; Thiselton, 'SNTI', 80, 81; Thiselton, *2H*, 19, 310, 18; Thiselton, 'UPC', 94; Thiselton, 'LMR', 1127, 1131. Italics ours.

³¹⁵ Thiselton, *IGPS*; cf. Thiselton, A.C., 'Human Being, Relationality and Time in Hebrews, 1 Corinthians and Western Traditions. Paper presented at North Park Theological Seminary, Oct 17-19, 1997', *ExA* 13 (1997), 76-95.

*Hermeneutics, Language, Cultures, and Selves* 193

context - see *The Two Horizons* - until Chapter 6).³¹⁶ Again, Thiselton's hermeneutical critique of human selves reflects a widened dialogue between philosophy and theology, as follows.

Thus, (1), Thiselton rejects the tradition running through 'Plato, Aristotle', 'Descartes', 'Kant', and 'the Enlightenment': *'the self'* is not an "ahistorical", "abstract", transcendental, 'isolated', "impersonal", 'static' amalgamation of *a priori* "generalizing" 'fixed properties'; nor are selves 'split' into 'soul'-'body', 'mind'-'body', 'reason'-'body' "dualisms"; nor are selves to be understood "individualistically".³¹⁷ Thiselton also rejects notions of "general" or of "transcendental" "humanness" 'in the later Schleiermacher' and in 'Dilthey'.³¹⁸

Notably, Thiselton repudiates the reductionism and determinism of 'ideological' 'structuralism' (see Chapter 5): 'everything' cannot be reduced to 'a self-referring system' of 'differential' 'relations'; "thought" does not consist of 'timeless', 'universal', 'natural', 'structures'; and theology, existential uniqueness, and openness towards the eschatological future cannot simply be dismissed.³¹⁹

(2) In Thiselton's thinking, selves are "situated" within a larger 'theological'-'eschatological' framework into which 'the' personal 'sovereign… God' 'acts' so as to shape 'history' according to divine 'promise'.³²⁰ In Thiselton's view, 'biblical' 'apocalyptic' warns of an 'objective' 'eschatological' "consummation" that extends beyond the 'Church', and beyond the 'individual', in its 'cosmic', corporate scope, and that includes both 'divine judgment' and 'the *fulfillment*' of 'a Kingdom of love'.³²¹ Thiselton argues that, against this backdrop, human subjects are 'fragile', "weak", 'fallible', finite in their *'creatureliness'* (cf. '"flesh"'), 'responsible', accountable, and unable to 'control' their 'own' "destinies".³²² In Thiselton's thinking, the larger *'narrative'* of 'Hebrew-Christian tradition', with its temporal 'contrast between' '"now"' and '"not yet"', situates all "human stories", precluding

---

³¹⁶ Thiselton, *2H*, 143-204.

³¹⁷ cf.: Thiselton, 'Parab', 439-449; Thiselton, 'UPC', 90-92, 95; Thiselton, 'SARX', 212-215; Thiselton, 'NH', 308-312, 314, 317-318, 320-321, 323-324; Thiselton, 'Truth', 898; Thiselton, 'Flesh', 680; Thiselton, 'H-O', 8; Thiselton, 'Till', 100-101; Thiselton, 'KNT', 91, 93-95; Thiselton, 'R *EMB*', 139; Thiselton, 'AA', 600; Thiselton, 'SBS', 334; cf. 329-335; Thiselton, *2H*, 246; Thiselton, A.C., 'Review of J.-M. Benoist's *The Structural Revolution*', *ExTim* 90 (May 1979), 248. First italics Thiselton's.

³¹⁸ Thiselton, 'NH', 311, 313, 314.

³¹⁹ Thiselton, 'SBS', 334, 331-332; cf. Thiselton, 'R *SR*', 248.

³²⁰ Thiselton, 'REC', 512, 517-518, 524-525; cf. Thiselton, 'Par', 47-53.

³²¹ cf.: Thiselton, 'LG', 495, 493; Thiselton, 'LGT', 8; Thiselton, 'REC', 510; Thiselton, 'Par', 47, 52; Thiselton, 'CH', 5; Thiselton, A.C., 'Review of E.H. Cousins ed. *Hope and the Future of Man*', *Chman* 88.3 (1974), 232-233; Thiselton, A.C., 'Biblical Classics: VI. Schweitzer's Interpretation of Paul', *ExTim* 90 (Feb. 1979), 134, 135. Thiselton's italics.

³²² Thiselton, A.C., 'Review of A.D. Galloway's *Wolfhart Pannenberg*', *Chman* 88.3 (1974), 230-231; cf. Thiselton, 'Flesh', 678-679; cf. Thiselton, 'LGT', 8. Thiselton's italics.

'over-realized eschatology'.[323]

Thiselton argues that selves are *also* "situated" within socio-"historical", "traditional", and "cultural" frameworks, and that selves are thereby 'historically' and "linguistically" 'conditioned' 'at a' predominantly 'pre-conscious level'.[324] In Thiselton's view, "traditions" "condition" selves' 'pre-judgments' (cf. "presuppositions", *'pre-understanding[s]'*, 'world[s]', "horizons", '"scaffolding"') and 'language-game[s]' (cf. '-habits', '-setting[s]'). Thiselton draws on Heidegger's notion of 'pre-conceptual' "worlds", according to which "world" '"is prior to and"' yet '"encompasses"' '"subjective"' and '"objective"' dimensions, and interweaves 'language', 'thought', 'life', 'understanding', 'conduct', 'attitudes', 'assumptions', 'experiences', "concerns", and 'reactions', being 'primarily... "linguistic"'.[325] Thiselton implicitly qualifies 'Heidegger's notion' of 'worldhood', however, by drawing on the later 'Wittgenstein's' less 'individualistic' and less "intra-linguistic" 'notion' of 'language-game[s]' in which 'community' 'surroundings', "action", 'language', and "thought" remain interwoven. For Thiselton, 'worldhood' and 'language-games' are only *partly* "parallel" 'concepts'.[326]

In Thiselton's thinking, "situatedness" ensures that selves are always already 'acted upon' from *'beyond'* their 'own... horizons' and that selves "experience" '"divine"' or others' 'creative' 'action' in "encounter", "address", "challenge", and "transformation", whether "individually" or corporately. In Thiselton's estimate, selves may experience divine 'promise'-"fulfillment" or speech-action, being "loved" by another, or being "creatively" "grasped" '"deep down"' at the 'pre-conscious' 'level' of 'values', 'presuppositions', or dispositions by 'art', 'games', or "texts". Thiselton argues that '"divine"' or others' speech-action potentially "involves" hearers' 'whole' persons.[327]

---

[323] cf.: Thiselton, LLM, 31-32; Thiselton, 'Par', 47-48, 51; Thiselton, 'REC', 510, 514, 515-518, 520-521, 522-523, 524-525; Thiselton, 'Sch', 133, 135. Thiselton's italics.

[324] cf.: Thiselton, 'Parab', 439, 443, 448-449; Thiselton, 'TNI', 11; Thiselton, 'UPC', 90-91; Thiselton, 'NH', 314, 318-319, 323-324; Thiselton, 'R WP', 230-231; Thiselton, 'KNT', 90-91, 93-95, 104, 85-107; Thiselton, 'M,M', 341, 339; Thiselton, 'AA', 600; Thiselton, 'Flesh', 678-679; Thiselton, 'U (long)', 90-92, 99, 102, 120 ('Thesis 4').

[325] cf.: Thiselton, 'Parab', 450; Thiselton, 'UPC', 87-88, 90-94; Thiselton, 'NH', 311-314, 318-320; Thiselton, 2H, 395, 155; Thiselton, LLM, 3; Thiselton, 'PDT', 7; Thiselton, 'KNT', 104-105; Thiselton, 'U (long)', 90, 92, 99, 102, 117-121; Thiselton, 'SBL', 108-111, 116-118; Thiselton, 'R EMB', 139; Thiselton, 'REC', 524-525; Thiselton, NTH, xxviii, conc. 8.2b; Thiselton, 'AA', 600; Thiselton, 'LMR', 1123-1127, 1135-1140; Thiselton, 'P-BP', 89. Italics Thiselton's.

[326] Thiselton, NTH, xxviii, conc. 8.2b; cf. 581-588; cf. Thiselton, 'LMR', 1130, 1131, 1127, 1134-1135, 1138; cf. Thiselton, 2H, 378, 202; cf. Thiselton, NH, 16.

[327] cf.: Thiselton, 'Parab', 439, 443-454; Thiselton, 'UPC', 90-91; Thiselton, 'Till', 101-102; Thiselton, 'LGT', 8; Thiselton, A.C., 'Experience-Centred Religion: Harvey Cox on the Seduction of the Spirit', CEN 9 Aug. (1974), 8; Thiselton, 'NP', 8; Thiselton, 'NH', 308-318, 320-325; Thiselton, 'M,M', 341, 339; Thiselton, 'U (long)', 90-91, 115-121; Thiselton, 'ML', 9; Thiselton, NTH, 581-588; Thiselton, 'Par', 47-53; Thiselton, 'LMR', 1123-1126,

Thiselton urges that "situatedness" precludes "'objectivism'" and 'subjectivism' in favor of 'historical' 'rationality': our "worlds", 'horizons', and 'conceptual' "frameworks" 'are shaped... by' 'God', by "anticipations" of "'the totality of history'", by "traditions", by 'language-habits', by 'shared' 'pre-judgments', and by "horizonal" 'concerns'.[328] In Thiselton's view, the sociality of 'language' means that 'world' and 'horizons' are always already partly 'shared', and not entirely "'private'". Thus, for Thiselton, the 'individual' self is not the central epistemological arbiter - since 'theological', "eschatological", socio-'historical', and 'linguistic' "situatedness" in "traditions" (and hence in "cultures") contributes to the "shape" of selves.[329]

(3) Thiselton's hermeneutical critique of human selves involves dialogue between philosophy and a theology of *creation* where, (a), by creation, selves are *'persons'* of great *worth and dignity*, not just "objects", because they are 'created... in' God's 'image'. In Thiselton's thinking, selves are *"uniquely" 'personal'* and vocationally "gifted" 'existential' "individuals", each self having a 'unique' *'story'* and 'history' "distinguishable" linguistically only by the *'particularizing* language' "'of historical'" 'narrative'. Thiselton argues that 'narrative' uniquely portrays 'unique' divine or human 'personhood' "personally", thereby uniquely 'involving' readers. Thus, Thiselton observes that 'biblical' "narratives" do not portray 'persons' through mere 'information', "'general truths'", or 'abstract treatise'. With W. Hordern, Thiselton observes that one 'does not fall in love with a' 'general' 'class', "male" or 'female', but with 'a *particular*' "'individual'". For Thiselton, 'persons' are *not* amalgamations 'of fixed properties', impersonal "types", 'categories', 'classes', "standardizing" 'rules', 'principles', or of 'universal maxims'.[330] (b) Thiselton argues that, by creation, the various 'characteristics' of selves are interwoven – where this point is reflected in Thiselton's concept of the *'whole' person.*[331]

(c) Thiselton argues that, by creation, selves have *"valued physicality"* (cf.

---

1131, 1135; Thiselton, 'Truth', 877-894; Thiselton, 'Sch', 134; Thiselton, 'KNT', 91-95; Thiselton, *LLM*, 31-32; Thiselton, 'Flesh', 680-682; Thiselton, 'SBL', 109-118; Thiselton, 'AA', 600; Thiselton, 'P-BP', 88-89; Thiselton, 'MP', 12. Italics Thiselton's.

[328] cf.: Thiselton, *2H*, 22, 156; Thiselton, 'TNI', 11; Thiselton, 'R *BQ1*', 121, 120; 'UPC', 90-93; Thiselton, 'H-O', 8; Thiselton, 'NH', 311, 308-309, 317-320, 323; Thiselton, 'KNT', 90-91, cf. 104; Thiselton, 'LMR', 1127.

[329] cf.: Thiselton, 'R *BQ1*', 121, 120; Thiselton, 'TNI', 11; Thiselton, 'NH', 311, 313-315, 320; Thiselton, 'KNT', 91-92, 85-107; Thiselton, *LLM*, 10; Thiselton, 'Par', 49; Thiselton, 'LMR', 1135; Thiselton, 'UPC', 93, 92; Thiselton, 'AA', 600; Thiselton, 'Truth', 883-893; Thiselton, *2H*, 314, 304-309, 82, 312, 387, 396-401.

[330] cf.: Thiselton, *2H*, 278, 277; Thiselton, 'Parab', 439-448; Thiselton, 'UPC', 89-91; Thiselton, 'NH', 311, 313, 314; Thiselton, 'Till', 100-101; Thiselton, 'H-O', 8; Thiselton, *LLM*, 31-32; Thiselton, 'ML', 9; Thiselton, 'U (long)', 117-121, cf. 99; Thiselton, 'R *EMB*', 139. First three italics ours, fourth, fifth, sixth, and seventh italics Thiselton's, remaining italics ours.

[331] Thiselton, 'P-BP', 89; cf. Thiselton, 'LMR', 1123-1124. Italics ours.

'"flesh"') or 'concrete' embodiedness - conceived individually and in relation to gender - where Thiselton appeals to P.F. Strawson's 'M' ('"material-bodily"') 'and P' ('"personal"') 'predicates'. Thiselton argues that 'incarnation' unites 'mutually interpreting' 'word and deed': 'obedience' is 'not an inner... psychological reality' 'or private affair', but a "consequence"-laden 'commitment to' public-sphere 'action'. Thiselton notes that embodiedness also shapes 'phonetic repertoire[s]'.[332]

(d) Thiselton argues that, by creation, selves exhibit 'creative', 'self-involving' 'decision' as *active agents* – "individually" and corporately - whether as 'response to God' or to others, or as initiative, where Thiselton comments on corporate 'language'-construction and on individual "speech-action".[333] (e) Thiselton argues that, by creation, selves exhibit *temporality*, being '"activated from ahead, by the unfinished, the unexpected, the ideal"', or by 'promise'. In Thiselton's thinking, Heidegger's notions of 'historicality', "futurity", 'possibility', and 'potentiality' are transposed into an "eschatological" framework 'of promise', thereby changing their grammar. For Thiselton, "openness" 'to the' "eschatological" 'future' liberates selves from "conventional determinism".[334] We expound Thiselton's appeal to Heidegger with respect to a hermeneutical critique of selves in more detail in Chapter 6.

(f) Thiselton argues that, by creation, selves are 'social', "relational", intersubjective, and corporate, fulfilling their individuality or "wholeness" of 'personhood' in sociality, *relationality*, 'communication', 'community', 'Church', and in "institution". Thiselton believes that M. Buber, whilst still too "individualistic", rightly stressed the *'lived-out... person-to-person encounter'* of 'I-Thou' 'dialogue' in which the 'other' is treated 'as a Thou' rather than instrumentalized and "depersonalized" 'as an it'. Thiselton argues that 'I-Thou' relationality, modeled by God as Trinity and evident in 'the biblical writings', involves "vulnerability", 'mutuality', 'reciprocity', 'dialogue', 'presence', "listening", and "giving and receiving".[335]

---

[332] cf.: Thiselton, 'HB', 82; Thiselton, A.C., "Theology for a New World'. Review Article of H. Richardson's *Theology for a New World*, *Chman* 83.3 (1969), 201; Thiselton, 'Parab', 443, 448-449; Thiselton, 'Flesh', 678-680; Thiselton, 'KNT', 91, 93-95; Thiselton, 'SBS', 331-332; contradicting, Osei-Bonsu, J., 'Anthropological Dualism in The New Testament', *SJT* 40.4 (1987), 575-577; Thiselton *does* allow '*sarx* to mean the physical body' *sometimes*. Italics ours.

[333] cf.: Thiselton, 'NH', 310; Thiselton, 'M,M', 341, 339; Thiselton, *LLM*, 16-21, 12, 4-6; Thiselton, 'ML', 9; Thiselton, 'CH', 5; Thiselton, 'U (long)', 104-106, 120-121; Thiselton, 'Truth', 883-894, 900; Thiselton, 'Sch', 135. Italics ours.

[334] cf.: Thiselton, *2H*, 186, 183, 178; Thiselton, 'UPC', 90-91; Thiselton, 'LG', 495, 493; Thiselton, 'CH', 5; Thiselton, 'H-O', 8; Thiselton, 'NH', 317, 323-324; Thiselton, 'Par', 29-30, 47-48, 50-51; Thiselton, 'AA', 600, 609; Heidegger, *BT*, 424, 373, 310, 372, 437; cf.: 279-311; 312-348. Italics ours.

[335] cf.: Thiselton, 'LGT', 8; Thiselton, 'CH', 5; Thiselton, 'KNT', 90-91, 104-105; Thiselton, 'NH', 314, 311; Thiselton, *LLM*, 31; Thiselton, 'Words', 296; Thiselton, 'Par', 48-49, 52; Thiselton, 'R *EMB*', 138-139; Thiselton, 'ML', 9; Thiselton, 'Truth', 900. First italics ours, second italics Thiselton's.

(g) Thiselton argues that, by creation, selves are "involved" in inter-subjective *"'understanding'"* as a 'fundamental' mode of *'existence'* (Thiselton draws on – but modifies – Heidegger's thought on "thrown projection" and/or on "historicality" here - see Chapter 6). After Bultmann, Thiselton argues that "'subjectivity'" is largely "pre-consciously" involved (not consciously "silenced") in 'understanding' at the 'level' of 'world[s]', 'horizons', "presuppositions", "'pre-understanding[s]'", and 'questions'. With Gadamer, Thiselton argues that unconscious 'pre-judgments are... more... fundamental for' understanding (i.e. for 'hermeneutics') *and for human identity* ('the historical reality of... being') 'than conscious' "'judgments'" (but see Chapter 6). After the later Wittgenstein, Thiselton argues that selves "see as" according to prior "'training'" (see above).[336]

Thus, in Thiselton's estimate, reader-'subjectivity', in 'understanding' and in 'communication', "shares" 'a prior' 'common' or "'mutual'" 'world', "languagecommunity", "'language-game'", "'pre-understanding'", "'agreement'", "'empathy'", "'involvement'", or *'Einverständnis'* with the speaker or writer 'at a' predominantly 'pre-conscious', 'pre-cognitive', "life-experiential" "eventful" 'level'. Thiselton argues that this point contrasts with the thought of 'the later Schleiermacher' and of 'Dilthey', who emphasize 'conscious' 'imagination and rapport', and with traditional emphases on 'conscious', 'cognitive exchange of language'. With Bultmann, Thiselton argues that "'understanding... presupposes a'" pre-existing 'life-relation' between the reader's 'subjectivity' and textual 'subject-matter[s]'.[337] We shall address the involvement of subjectivity in the hermeneutical circle in Chapter 5.

(h) Thiselton argues that, by creation, selves possess an 'unconscious' (cf. 'preconscious', 'heart') - the locus of "'existential forces'", 'strong feeling[s]' (e.g. 'fears', 'yearnings'), and "moods". In Thiselton's view, 'shared' "conceptualities" (cf. "'scaffolding'"), "ideologies", 'pre-judgments', "worlds", "horizons", "preunderstandings", "ways" of "asking" 'questions', "language games", 'orientations', 'attitudes', "perspectives", "dispositions", and 'concerns' are largely 'unconsciously inherited from' 'tradition[s]'. Further, for Thiselton, engaging with texts or with others may "transform" the unconscious.[338] (i) Thiselton argues that, by creation,

---

[336] cf.: Thiselton, *2H*, 161, 163, 173, 305, 417-419, 377; Thiselton, 'Parab', 453-454; Thiselton, 'UPC', 87-88, 92-93; Thiselton, 'NH', 311-314, 317, 320, 323; Thiselton, 'SBL', 108-111, 118; Thiselton, *NTH*, 581-588; Thiselton, 'U (long)', 104-106, 120-121; Thiselton, 'P-BP', 89; Thiselton, 'LMR', 1139-1140. First and third italics ours, other italics Thiselton's.
[337] cf.: Thiselton, 'UPC', 87-88; Thiselton, 'NH', 308-324; Thiselton, 'SARX', 205; Thiselton, 'Truth', 898; Thiselton, 'SBL', 108-111, 118; citing, Bultmann, 'PH', 75. Italics Thiselton's.
[338] cf.: Thiselton, 'Parab', 450-454; Thiselton, 'SARX', 205, 216; Thiselton, *2H*, 74; Thiselton, 'UPC', 87-88, 90-93; Thiselton, 'NH', 308-314, 317, 320, 323; Thiselton, 'Till', 92, 97-102; Thiselton, 'PDT', 7; Thiselton, 'EITN', 582; Thiselton, 'Flesh', 681-682; Thiselton, 'KNT', 103-105; Thiselton, A.C., 'Sigmund Freud and the Language of the Heart', *CEN* 13 Feb. (1976), 12, 14; Thiselton, 'U (short)', 6; Thiselton, 'SBL', 108-111, 116, 118; Thiselton, *NTH*, 496, 507-508, 581-588; Thiselton, 'R *EMB*', 139; Thiselton, 'U (long)', 104, 117-121,

selves function "pre-reflectively", "pre-cognitively", "pre-conceptually", or "pre-philosophically" 'at' the 'level' of 'life-experience', reflexivity, or of "'living-through'" - as when reading 'a novel' or playing 'a game' – where this "functioning" involves both unconscious and conscious aspects of 'subjectivity'.[339] (j) Thiselton argues that, by creation, selves consciously "reflect", exercising "historical rationality" - though Thiselton appropriates the Continental contrast between "'self-consciousness'" or 'self-awareness' and "'self-understanding'".[340]

(4) For Thiselton, selves participate in, and are afflicted by, "sin", 'evil', and "'divine judgment'", whether individually or corporately. Thus, (a), Thiselton relates 'the biblical' notion of *'the heart'*, as the "seat of evil", to 'the unconscious', as the locus of "'existential forces'" ('fears', 'yearnings'), chaotic "'lawlessness'", 'self-deception', counterfeit 'image' construction, and of potential "mental illness" (for Thiselton's response to Freud, see Chapter 3). In Thiselton's view, then, 'theological' 'criteria' are required 'to distinguish' between genuine 'experience of God' and "unconsciously" generated 'experience'.[341]

(b) As Thiselton notes, 'Paul' sometimes uses the Greek word translated as "*'flesh'*" to denote "sinful" "hostility" 'to God' as a "mode of existence" (not necessarily 'overt... public behavior'; not a 'quasi-Platonic' "'territory'" within "'human nature'"). Thiselton observes that the word translated as "'flesh'", which sometimes means "selfishness", is used variably, in order to denote a "multiform" polymorphous concept, but that the word may sometimes connote *pro-active* 'self-assertion' and/or *evasive* 'self-defensiveness'. Citing 'Bultmann', Thiselton agrees that the word translated as 'flesh' can denote 'trust in oneself as being able to procure life by the use of the earthly and through one's own strength and accomplishment' 'in... independence' from 'God'. In Thiselton's thinking, "self-sufficiency", 'self-reliance', self-definition, "self-orientation", and self-actualization are related notions. Thiselton observes that the word translated as "'flesh'" can also denote "self-righteous" "substitution" of one's own rights and wrongs for God's 'law', or a futile attempt to obey God's 'law' apart from 'God's grace in

---

99; Thiselton, 'P-BP', 89; Thiselton, 'MP', 12; Thiselton, 'SBS', 329, 331-332; Thiselton, 'Truth', 877-894; Thiselton, 'IT', 23-24.

[339] cf.: Thiselton, 'UPC', 90; Thiselton, 'NH', 320, 312; Thiselton, 'Truth', 898.

[340] cf.: Thiselton, 'TNI', 11; Thiselton, 'UPC', 89-92, 95; Thiselton, 'NH', 308-314, 317-318, 320-321, 323-324, 326-327; Thiselton, 'H-O', 8; Thiselton, 'Flesh', 680-682; Thiselton, 'EITN', 582; Thiselton, NTH, xxii, conc. 1.4; xxx, conc. 10; 4-12 and onwards, 496, 507-508, 581-588, 607-609; Thiselton, 'Freud', 12, 14; Thiselton, 'U (short)', 6; Thiselton, 'P-BP', 88-89; Thiselton, 'SBS', 329-335; Thiselton, *2H*, 113, 3-10, 445.

[341] cf.: Thiselton, 'Flesh', 680; Thiselton, A.C., 'More Manageable Proportions. Review of J.W. Wenham's *The Goodness of God*, *CEN* 5 Apr. (1974), 8; Thiselton, 'R HFM', 232; Thiselton, 'UPC', 90; Thiselton, 'Till', 92, 99, 101-102; Thiselton, 'E-CR', 8; Thiselton, 'Freud', 12, 14; Thiselton, 'P-BP', 88-89. Italics ours.

Christ'.³⁴² (c) We need not revisit Thiselton's critique of Western culture *corporately*.³⁴³

(d) For Thiselton, 'sin' results in *suffering or 'evil'*, notably 'predicament', 'estrangement', 'longing', 'anguish', 'alienation', "isolation", 'loneliness', '"insecurity"', 'loss of self-respect', escapism, and '"crisis"' involving adverse 'psychological', social, or even demonic 'pressures'. However, with J.W. Wenham, Thiselton argues that there is '"no... comprehensive water-tight"', 'neatly-packaged' '"system of answers"' that adequately addresses 'the moral difficulties of the Bible' or of 'the problem of evil'.³⁴⁴

(e) Commenting on *"divine judgment"'*, Thiselton notes sin's 'consequence' 'of vanishing possibilities' culminating in 'death'. In Thiselton's view, divine eschatological "verdicts" "unveil" all 'disguises, deceits' and '"misunderstandings"' and, for Thiselton, following 'Pannenberg', 'judgment' may partly '"consist"' of 'the final consequence[s] of' being '"left"' '"to the desires of"' our own '"hearts"'.³⁴⁵ J. Osei-Bonsu argues that, for 'Thiselton... punishment of the sinner ['in 1 Cor. 5:5'] may or may not have included physical suffering'. For Thiselton, though, God judges 'the incestuous man's... complacent self-sufficiency, not his physical body'.³⁴⁶

(5) Thiselton also emphasizes '"redemption"': (a) selves are 'acted upon' from *'beyond'* their "situatedness" by *divine loving, saving action*. In Thiselton's view, both the 'Christian' and the Church are "made" and "transformed" by divine speech-action, paradigmatically through 'biblical' writings liberated by 'hermeneutics' to 'strike home' '"afresh"' in interpreters' "worlds", "drawing" them into' 'biblical' '"worlds"', "exposing" truth, 'lies', and 'falsehood', and "consecrating" interpreters 'to authentic', 'health-giving' 'existence'. Thiselton draws on Fuchs in this context of discussion.³⁴⁷

With Tillich, Thiselton argues that 'symbols' may help 'integrate' a person, evoking 'responsive echoes' from 'the *unconscious'*. With 'Ricoeur', Thiselton accepts that 'the Exodus' 'narrative' may assist "the reader's" own "existential" "lived-through" '"wandering... from captivity to deliverance"'. With 'Fuchs',

---

³⁴² cf.: Thiselton, 'UPC', 90-91; Thiselton, 'Sch', 134; Thiselton, 'SARX', 209-215; Thiselton, 'Flesh', 680-681; Thiselton, 'KNT', 104; Thiselton, 'Truth', 901; citing, Bultmann, *TNT1*, 239. Italics ours.

³⁴³ See earlier in the present chapter.

³⁴⁴ cf.: Thiselton, 'UPC', 89-90; Thiselton, 'Till', 97, 101-102; Thiselton, 'MMP', 8; Thiselton, 'Flesh', 678-679; Thiselton, *IGPS*, 160; Thiselton, 'AA', 600; Thiselton, 'HB', 85, 92. Italics ours.

³⁴⁵ Thiselton, 'R *HFM*', 232-233; cf. Thiselton, 'Flesh', 681-682; cf. Thiselton, 'Par', 50, 52. Italics ours.

³⁴⁶ Osei-bonsu, 'AD', 576-577; cf. Thiselton, 'TY', 1561.

³⁴⁷ cf.: Thiselton, 'LMR', 1135; Thiselton, 'ML', 9; Thiselton, 'NH', 308-311, 320, 322; Thiselton, 'U (long)', 90-91, 115-118, 121; Thiselton, 'U (short)', 6; Thiselton, 'Par', 47; Thiselton, 'SBL', 108-111, 118; Thiselton, 'Truth', 883-894. First italics Thiselton's.

Thiselton urges that 'the Gospel' "strikes home" in interpreters' 'horizons', "taking hold of" and "actively" "transforming" interpreters, enabling them 'to see... differently'.[348] Thus, Thiselton argues that, in 'the parables', 'Jesus' "accounts" for, 'creates', and 'enters' "hearers'" "worlds", 'horizons', and 'interests', but 'draws them [i.e. his "hearers"] into his' 'world', "inviting" them 'to share' in his 'life', 'attitudes', 'reactions', and 'perspectives' at both 'pre-cognitive' and 'cognitive' "levels". Thiselton argues that hearers are thus "grasped" 'deep down', and that their 'horizons' are thus potentially "impacted" and "shattered" such that they experience disorientation, discovery, or "transformation". Thus, in Thiselton's view, any given hearer 'may... find' in 'the Bible' '"all"' that is needed '"for salvation"'.[349]

(b) In Thiselton's thinking selves, being saved by God, 'experience' 'the cleansing' event 'of coming to the end of oneself and of casting oneself on God alone', thereby *becoming a 'new creation'*.[350] With A. Schweitzer, Thiselton argues that Paul's notion of '"being-in-Christ"' denotes a "mystical" "relationship" between '"Christ"' and 'believers' that is prior to 'all other relationships'.[351] Drawing on Buber's notion of 'I-Thou' "relationality", Thiselton argues that 'God' "evaluates", "encounters", "loves", "names", and 'addresses' the believer. In particular, Thiselton argues that the believer ('not a mere case or number') receives 'full dignity' and 'the' only 'stable guarantee of personhood' in this 'relationship' of 'reciprocity' and 'mutual presence', "responding" "uniquely" and "personally" to 'God... as a Thou' in "address", "trust", and "obedience".[352]

(c) After Schweitzer, Thiselton argues that Paul's notion of '"being-in-Christ"' involves *'sharing in the death and resurrection of' Jesus*.[353] That is, (i), for Thiselton, believers live in two "eras" - that of the visible '"natural world"' and that of the hidden 'Kingdom' already 'inaugurated' in Christ's '"resurrection"'. In Thiselton's view, believers 'look back to... redemption' and "forwards" 'to... future' '"deliverance"', a scenario that implies a temporal contrast.[354] (ii) In Thiselton's view, "believers" also receive 'the verdict' "sinful" 'in the historical' *juridical context'*, but receive the 'verdict' 'righteous' 'in the' 'eschatological' 'context of

---

[348] Thiselton, 'Till', 97, 99; cf.: Thiselton, *LLM*, 23; Thiselton, 'SBL', 115-116; Thiselton, 'P-BP', 89; Thiselton, 'T&F', 11; Thiselton, 'UPC', 90; Thiselton, 'NH', 320. Italics Thiselton's.

[349] Thiselton, 'Parab', 447, 441, 453-454; cf.: Thiselton, 'UPC', 87-88; Thiselton, 'SBL', 109-110; Thiselton, 'P-BP', 89; Thiselton, 'LMR', 1139-1140; Thiselton, 'U (long)', 109, 99-101, 104, 120; Thiselton, 'Truth', 898-899.

[350] Thiselton, 'LGT', 8; cf.: Thiselton, 'REC', 515-521; Thiselton, 'Sch', 135. Italics ours.

[351] Thiselton, 'Sch', 134.

[352] Thiselton, 'ML', 9.

[353] Thiselton, 'Sch', 133-134. Italics ours.

[354] Thiselton, 'Sch', 133-135; cf. Thiselton, 'REC', 513.

justification' (see Chapter 3).[355] (iii) Thiselton argues that 'believers' also participate in two "modes" 'of existence' - the '"natural"' 'mode' (cf. '"flesh"') and '"the… Kingdom"' or 'resurrection mode' (cf. '"Spirit"'). In Thiselton's view, life '"in the Spirit"'' involves an already-inaugurated '"transformation"' in which 'believers' are helped 'to sit loose to the' '"sensuous, sinful"', "self-centered", '"transient world"' and to adopt the 'ethical response' of '"love"'.[356] Finally, (iv), Thiselton argues that believers experience both 'suffering' (even 'eschatological… tribulation') and "consolation" (even unto 'eschatological' glory).[357]

(d) Thiselton develops the "now" versus 'not yet' temporal 'contrast' of Pauline promissory 'eschatology' in terms of *responsibility and freedom*. Thus Thiselton argues that believers, belonging to the 'Kingdom' 'era' in which 'promise… fulfillment' has already begun but is 'not yet' complete, are "responsible" under the 'freedom'-constraining 'imperative' of "building" 'towards' the same 'eschatological' "goals" as those of '"the Spirit"' who "transforms" them. Yet Thiselton argues that "believers", in 'still' "belonging" 'to the natural' era, also remain "responsible" under the 'freedom'-constraining "imperatives" of corporate "conventions". Therefore, Thiselton argues that 'liberation' cannot be conceived of "individualistically" as "Kantian" ethical '"autonomy"' or as "Heideggerian" "possibility": rather, 'promise' and 'responsibility' *qualify* 'futurity' and "possibility".[358]

(e) Regarding believers' *"life"* *"in the Spirit"*, Thiselton urges that Paul's notion of the human '"spirit"' is not a 'quasi-Platonic' '"territorial"' '"point of contact"' within '"human nature"' (cf. '"soul"', '"mind"', or '"inner life"') for 'the' "work" "of the" Holy '"Spirit"', but a 'mode of existence' in alignment 'with… the Holy' Spirit's work in which the believer is "given" 'new desires', 'capacities', and 'horizons' that begin to transcend '"sinful"' '"existence"'.[359] In Thiselton's view, 'believers' begin to experience 'liberation from' the '"pre-conceptual"' "conflicting" '"forces"' and 'self-deceptions' of 'the heart' or 'unconscious'.[360] Eschatologically, in Thiselton's estimate, '"personhood"' is "intensified" and "enriched", not dissolved, "dispersed" or "transcended".[361] Thiselton also argues

---

[355] Thiselton, 'UPC', 96-98; cf.: Thiselton, 'LG', 491-495; Thiselton, 'SNTT', 98-100; Thiselton, NTH, 593-599; Thiselton, 2H, 415-427; Thiselton, 'Sch', 134, 136. Thiselton's italics.

[356] Thiselton, 'Sch', 133, 134, 135.

[357] Thiselton, 'Sch', 134.

[358] cf.: Thiselton, 'UPC', 90-91; Thiselton, NTH, xxv, conc. 5.3b; Thiselton, 'REC', 513, 515-518, 520-525; Thiselton, 'Sch', 133; Thiselton, 'R BQ1', 121; Thiselton, 2H, 203, 177-178; Thiselton, NH, 333; Thiselton, IGPS, 81-86.

[359] cf.: Thiselton, 'UPC', 90-91; Thiselton, 'SARX', 212-215; Thiselton, 'Flesh', 681-682; Thiselton, 'Sch', 133, 134. Italics ours.

[360] cf.: Thiselton, 'UPC', 90, 87; Thiselton, 'Sch', 134; Thiselton, 'Till', 101-102; Thiselton, 'Freud', 12, 14; Thiselton, 'P-BP', 88-89; Thiselton, 'Truth', 880-881.

[361] Thiselton, 'CH', 5; cf. Thiselton, 'Par', 29-30.

that 'the Holy Spirit' 'creatively' 'inspires' 'understanding', and gives "individuals" 'gifts'.[362] Moreover, in Thiselton's view, 'spirituality' recognizes 'eschatological' 'futurity' - against 'enthusiastic' 'over-realized' "eschatologies" that over-stress 'present' 'experience', that fall into epistemological absolutism, that appeal to 'manipulative' 'persuasive' (re-)'definition' of terms, and that conceive of 'freedom' in terms of 'individualistic' '"autonomy"'.[363]

(f) For Thiselton, the Christian's '"life"' '"in the Spirit"' is to be a '"life"' of *faith, hope, love, and truth*. We need not revisit Thiselton's points relating 'faith' (in one of its senses) to 'Paul's doctrine of justification' or, with 'Moltmann', to 'the eschatological' "promissory" 'contrast' between '"now" and… "not yet"'.[364] For Thiselton, 'faith' is 'polymorphous' - though, as B.M. Metzger notes, 'faith' in an important sense '"is *entailed* in being united with Christ as part of the new creation"'.[365] Nor is it necessary to revisit Thiselton's appeal to Moltmann in relation to 'hope' (see Chapter 3). For Thiselton, 'faith' and 'hope' are neither 'individualistic' nor wholly passive.[366]

For Thiselton, '"life"' '"in the Spirit"' also involves *loving* 'self-involvement' in 'fully inter-personal' transparent 'relationships' and in 'reconciliation' - in 'contrast' to manipulative 'deception', 'concealment', and "pietistic introspection". Earlier comments on Thiselton's appeal to Buber's 'I-Thou' 'dialogue' need not be revisited, and we have already examined Thiselton's notion of *'truth'* as 'authentic' human 'existence' – a notion according to which 'Christ', as "enfleshed Word", or as 'the truth', is the "paradigmatic" human being.[367]

Nevertheless, we may add that, in Thiselton's thinking, '"spirituality"' "backs" or gives hard 'currency' to 'words' - in 'honesty', 'integrity', 'sincerity', transparency, and straightforwardness.[368] For Thiselton, '"spirituality"' involves 'obedience' to God, 'reverence for' biblical 'truth', '"true" and/or 'reliable' 'speech',

---

[362] Thiselton, 'U (long)', 117-121, 99.

[363] cf.: Thiselton, 'REC', 514-525; Thiselton, 'Par', 47-51; Thiselton, *2H*, 177, 201; Thiselton, A.C., "Theology Made Exciting'. Review of W. Pannenberg's *The Apostles' Creed in the Light of Today's Questions*', *CEN* 19 Jan. (1973), 12; Thiselton, *IGPS*, 83, 4.

[364] cf.: Thiselton, 'Flesh', 681; Thiselton, 'LG', 495, 491, 493; Thiselton, 'UPC', 90-91; Thiselton, 'NH', 324-325; Thiselton, 'Till', 90, 95, 87, 102; Thiselton, *LLM*, 31-32; Thiselton, 'Par', 47-48, 51-53; Thiselton, 'REC', 518.

[365] Metzger, 'R *2H*', 210; cf. Thiselton, *2H*, 422, 423. Thiselton's italics.

[366] Thiselton, 'CH', 5; cf. Thiselton, 'Par', 29-30, 47-51.

[367] cf.: Thiselton, 'Flesh', 681; Thiselton, 'M&M', 8; Thiselton, 'UPC', 89-91; Thiselton, *LLM*, 16; Thiselton, 'LGT', 8; Thiselton, 'KNT', 90-91, 104; Thiselton, 'EITN', 578-579; Thiselton, 'Par', 49; Thiselton, *NTH*, xxv, conc. 5.3b; Thiselton, 'ML', 9; Thiselton, 'Truth', 880-891; cf. 892-893; Thiselton, 'MCU', 46; Thiselton, 'CH', 5; Thiselton, 'HB', 79. Italics ours.

[368] cf.: Thiselton, 'REC', 522; Thiselton, 'UPC', 95, 97-98; Thiselton, *LLM*, 16, 18-21; Thiselton, 'LMR', 1135, 1143; Thiselton, 'Truth', 878-879, 881-887, 892; Thiselton, 'M&M', 8; Thiselton, 'KNT', 90-91, 104; Thiselton, 'EITN', 578-579; Thiselton, 'Par', 49; Thiselton, *NTH*, xxv, conc. 5.3b.

future-oriented 'commitment', '"faithfulness"', and "critical testing" (including 'self-criticism') relative to 'theological' and biblical 'criteria'. Thiselton argues that Christ 'crucified', as 'criterion', exposes 'false' claims to 'apostolic authority'. Thiselton also argues that '"spirituality"' employs '"mind"' and 'rationality' to assess the 'true' versus the 'false', the 'correct' versus the 'incorrect', and the 'authentic' versus the 'inauthentic' – relative to 'truth'-'criteria'. With 'T.F. Torrance', Thiselton urges that 'spirituality' includes 'readiness to submit all preconceptions to the test of truth'. For Thiselton, '"spirituality"' also distinguishes between 'spiritual' "verdicts" and 'natural' "verdicts" (cf. the '"flesh"'), though Thiselton adds the caveat that the latter are 'not' all bad. In particular, Thiselton argues that 'spiritual' "verdicts" juxtapose 'thought', 'rational argument', a *'provisional'* biblical 'frame of reference', and "the Holy Spirit's" agency.[369]

(6) Summarizing: in conclusion, for Thiselton, theological considerations are warranted in relation to a hermeneutical critique of human selves: Thus, (a), Thiselton argues that theological-eschatological notions of *"temporality", "relationality", and of theo-socio-historical "situatedness"* qualify socio-historical "situatedness", rightly "de-centering" human "subjectivity" in a re-historicizing critique of Cartesian, Enlightenment, and "existentialist" traditions. Thiselton believes that, in these traditions, an isolated (and sometimes abstracted) "centered knower", "subjectivity", or *Dasein* problematically leads to epistemological objectivism, relativism, or dualism (see also Chapter 3).[370]

(b) In Thiselton's thinking, a theological notion of *unique personhood* with its *narrative* structure and great *worth* qualifies *both* "existentialist" notions of "uniqueness" and "wholeness" *and* deterministic or overly materialistic a-historical or transcendental Enlightenment perspectives of human selves. (c) In Thiselton's thinking, theological-eschatological notions of *temporality, promise, responsibility, the human heart, and of the "flesh"* qualify "existentialist" over-dependence on human futural active agency, and also qualify (post-)Enlightenment over-emphases on human ethical autonomy. (d) In Thiselton's view, theological notions of progressive sanctification and enlightenment *further* qualify epistemological objectivism and notions of ethical autonomy pertaining to the Enlightenment legacy.

(7) We will note later how Thiselton's sublation of historical categories into a Trinitarian theological-eschatological framework effectively ensures that "history" is understood *at least to a significant extent* in terms of the narrative(s) of "persons-in-relation". Thiselton thus rejects views of "history" that are associated with views of "selves" in which "selves" are "deconstructed" (see Chapter 7), *even if* Thiselton

---

[369] cf.: Thiselton, 'REC', 522; Thiselton, 'Flesh', 679-680; Thiselton, 'Truth', 901, 879-894; Thiselton, 'Till', 87-102, 87; Thiselton, 'Par', 47-51; Thiselton, 'P-BP', 88-89; Thiselton, 'NH', 323-324; Thiselton, 'E-CR', 8; Thiselton, 'U (long)', 115-121; Thiselton, 'LMR', 1135; Thiselton, 'TNI', 11; Thiselton, *2H*, 179, 188, 196-197; Thiselton, 'R *BQI*', 121. Italics Thiselton's.

[370] See, Thiselton, *2H*, 181; cf.: Thiselton, *IGPS*, 76; Thiselton, *NH*, 6. Italics ours.

*also* rejects views of "history" that are overly "anthropocentric" and/or sociopragmatic (see above and Chapters 6 and 7).

### E. Conclusion:
### Towards Unified Hermeneutical Critiques of Language, Western Culture, and of Human Selves, through Dialogues between Philosophy and Theology

Having justified our approach to/in the present chapter we then expounded Thiselton's *hermeneutical critique of language*. This critique *both* functioned as "philosophical description", clarifying a prior 'biblical and theological account of language',[371] *and* found its "ontological ground" in history understood eschatologically and Christologically. Thus a unifying dialogue between theology and philosophy existed at the level of theoretical-construction in Thiselton's hermeneutical critique of language. Correlatively, Thiselton's appeal to the later Wittgenstein resonated with theology – i.e. with theological concerns to do with eschatology, tradition, historical setting, and with 'enfleshed Word' – and constituted a re-historicizing of language in critique of Cartesianism and/or of Cartesian Protestantism. Thus, theology and philosophy had mutually dialogically warranted places in Thiselton's hermeneutical discussion in relation to language.

Next, we demonstrated that Thiselton's appeals to J.L. Austin, to D.D. Evans, and to the philosophy of language more broadly did not disrupt the unity provided by the resonances between biblical theology and Thiselton's appeals to the later Wittgenstein. Rather, Thiselton's appeals to J.L. Austin, to D.D. Evans, and to the philosophy of language more broadly resonated *both* with biblical theology *and* with Thiselton's appeals to the later Wittgenstein, serving primarily to "flesh-out" and add specificity to Thiselton's later-Wittgensteinian philosophical description of a prior "biblical and theological account of language".

We then argued that Thiselton critically allied his appeals to the later Wittgenstein and to the philosophy of language with his appeals to Saussure and general linguistics, but that Thiselton accommodated the latter tradition to the former, thereby *retaining* the unity of his hermeneutical critique of language. Thiselton dialogically justified this unified hermeneutical critique of language through critical application, finding *both* "referential", "ideational", "traditional", and/or "positivist" *and* "natural" and "Continental" assumptions and approaches relating to language and meaning inadequate – despite *also* drawing positively from both sets of traditions. Thiselton further validated his unified hermeneutical critique of language by applying it constructively in biblical interpretation, in practical theology, and in hermeneutical theory. The details of Thiselton's unified hermeneutical critique of language were too numerous to repeat here.

This analysis contradicted numerous other readings of Thiselton – which again raised the question of how well Thiselton's work had been received or understood

---

[371] Thiselton, 'CAP', 144.

in the literature. We also highlighted milder problems in relation to the unmarked (though legitimate) grammatical-conceptual changes implicit in Thiselton's continued use of Continental terminology given Thiselton's mixed response to the Continental traditions.

Moving on, we expounded the relatively embryonic hermeneutical critiques of Western culture and of human selves that pertained to Thiselton's formative second period framework, and showed that dialogue between theology and philosophy was present in both critiques.

In Thiselton's *hermeneutical critique of (Western) culture*, we discerned several axes of theoretical hermeneutical consideration that went beyond questions to do with Western culture *per se* and that could be applied to any culture. Notably, Thiselton "re-historicized" supposedly "culture-relative" contexts into relations of embeddedness and responsibility with respect to broader, trans-temporal traditions and even with respect to anticipations of history-as-a-whole. (In Chapter 3 we noted that, for Thiselton, philosophical considerations alone proved inadequate when it came to "evaluative" and "explanatory" socio-metacriticism).

Similarly, in relation to Thiselton's *hermeneutical critique of human selves*, we deduced that Thiselton's concern was to warrant the inclusion of theological contributions in the discussion on the grounds that theology, and its implicature, provided needed qualifications for a philosophical critique of anthropology or of "human selves" – even where that philosophical critique was also *already* concerned to "re-historicize" "selves" in contrast to approaches pertaining to (post-)Enlightenment and/or "existentialist" traditions. In particular, in Thiselton's thinking, (Trinitarian) theology provided needed qualifications for/of philosophical approaches in relation to "situatedness", epistemology, "wholeness, uniqueness, and worth", in relation to over-dependence on human futural active agency, in relation to notions of supposed "ethical autonomy" and, we anticipated, in relation to conceiving of "history" properly in relation to "narrative(s)" of "persons-in-relation" *without either* "deconstructing" persons *or* conceiving of "history" "anthropocentrically".

CHAPTER 5

# Hermeneutics and Responsible Interpretation: Towards a Unified Critique of Hermeneutical Understanding

### A. Preliminary Comments: Responsible Interpretation

In this chapter we shall expound Thiselton's third-stratum "critique of hermeneutical understanding" – a critique which includes Thiselton's conceptualizations of the hermeneutical circle (or spiral), of the hermeneutical task, and/or of responsible interpretation. Again, our concern is to expound Thiselton's formative second-period thinking, since later developments in Thiselton's hermeneutics presuppose this basis.[1] Three preliminary points may be

---

[1] Relevant second-period writings include: Thiselton, A.C., *New Testament Hermeneutics and Philosophical Description: Issues in New Testament Hermeneutics with Special Reference to the Use of Philosophical Description in Heidegger, Bultmann, Gadamer, and Wittgenstein* (Sheffield: University of Sheffield Ph.D. Thesis, 1977; written by Dec. 1976); Thiselton, A.C., *The Two Horizons: New Testament Hermeneutics and Philosophical Description with Special Reference to Heidegger, Bultmann, Gadamer, and Wittgenstein* (Exeter: Paternoster Press, 1980); Thiselton, A.C., 'Understanding God's Word Today: Evangelicals Face the Challenge of the New Hermeneutic. Address at the Second National Evangelical Anglican Congress, Nottingham, 1977', in *Obeying Christ in a Changing World, Vol. 1* (ed. J.R.W. Stott; Glasgow: Collins/Fountain Books, 1977), 90-122, (henceforth the 'long' article with this title); Thiselton, A.C., 'Myth, Paradigm, and the Status of Biblical Imagery', in *Using the Bible in Liturgy* (ed. C. Byworth; Nottingham: Grove, 1977), 4-12; Thiselton, A.C., 'Language and Meaning in Religion', in 'Word', in *The New International Dictionary of New Testament Theology. Volume III* (ed. C. Brown; Exeter: Paternoster; Grand Rapids: Zondervan, 1978; actually written by 1977), 1123-1146; Thiselton, A.C., 'The Use of Philosophical Categories in New Testament Hermeneutics', *Chman* 87.1 (1973), 87-100; Thiselton, A.C., 'The New Hermeneutic', in *New Testament Interpretation: Essays in Principles and Methods* (ed. I.H. Marshall; Grand Rapids: Eerdmans; Exeter: Paternoster Press, 1977), 308-333; Thiselton, A.C., 'Explain, Interpret, Tell, Narrative', in *The New International Dictionary of New Testament Theology, Volume 1* (ed. C. Brown; Exeter: Paternoster; Grand Rapids: Zondervan, 1975), 573-584; Thiselton, A.C., 'The Semantics of Biblical Language as an Aspect of Hermeneutics', *FTht* 103.2 (1976), 108-120; cf. Thiselton, A.C., 'Meaning and Myth. Review Article of W. Pannenberg's *Basic Questions in Theology, Vol. 3*', *CEN* 19 Oct. (1973), 8; Thiselton, A.C., 'Myth, Mythology', in *The Zondervan Pictorial Encyclopedia of the Bible, Volume 4*

made – as follows.

(1) Thiselton's critique of hermeneutical understanding overlaps with, but extends beyond, his hermeneutical critique of epistemology. Thus, in part, our focus on the hermeneutical circle in the present chapter continues on from our expositions in Chapter 3. And yet, for Thiselton, 'interpretation' also asks 'questions' alien to epistemology – for example, questions relating to 'literary genre'.[2]

(2) Thiselton's critique of hermeneutical understanding develops only slightly during his second period.[3] Thus, admittedly, Thiselton introduces appeals to 'Ricoeur' in his PhD thesis (1976/1977) and in his responses to 'structuralism' (1978). In these appeals, Thiselton introduces an anticipation of the Ricoeurian distinction between 'understanding' (more narrowly defined) and '"explanation"'. Otherwise, however, we may treat Thiselton's second-period writings synchronically in the present context of discussion (on this kind of approach, see our comments in Chapter 4).[4]

(3) Thiselton's third-stratum critique of hermeneutical understanding presupposes *both* his first-stratum emphasis on 'inter-disciplinary', inter-traditional, and smaller-scale 'dialogue(s)' ('dialogue(s)' through which he grounds hermeneutics in eschatology and Christology - see Chapters 3, 6 and 7), *and* his second-stratum hermeneutical critiques of (conceptualizations of) history, epistemology, language, (Western) culture, and of human selves. Thus, we may conclude that Thiselton's "programmatic" hermeneutical theory *as a whole* aims at "responsible interpretation" – *so long as* we also realize that, for Thiselton, "responsible interpretation" is configured in such a way as to embrace – additionally - the dimension of *"being interpreted"* (particularly in relation to the biblical texts, but not necessarily *only* in relation to the biblical texts).[5]

---

(ed. M.C. Tenney; Grand Rapids, MI: Zondervan, 1975; written by 1973), 333-343; Thiselton, A.C., *Language, Liturgy and Meaning* (Nottingham: Grove Books, 1975 and 1986).

[2] See: Thiselton, A.C., 'The 'Interpretation' of Tongues: a New Suggestion in the Light of Greek Usage in Philo and Josephus', *JThStud* NS 30.1 (Apr. 1979), 18, 20; Thiselton, 'NH', 327, 308-333; Thiselton, 'EITN', 582.

[3] For relevant writings, see footnote 1 above.

[4] cf.: Thiselton, *NTH*, 156-157; 170-172; Thiselton, A.C., 'Keeping up with Recent Studies: II. Structuralism and Biblical Studies: Method or Ideology?', *ExTim* 89 (Aug. 1978), 329-334; cf. Thiselton, A.C., *New Horizons in Hermeneutics: The Theory and Practice of Transforming Biblical Reading* (London: HarperCollins; Grand Rapids: Zondervan, 1992), 344-350.

[5] See: Thiselton, A.C., 'Thirty Years of Hermeneutics: Retrospect and Prospects', in *International Symposium on the Interpretation of the Bible* (ed. J. Krašovec; Ljubljana: Slovenian Academy of Sciences and Arts; Sheffield: Sheffield Academic Press, 1998), 1561; Thiselton, A.C., 'The Theologian Who Must Not Be Ignored. Article Review of W. Pannenberg's *Basic Questions in Theology, Vol. 2*', *CEN* 25 Feb. (1972), 11; Thiselton, A.C., 'Theology and the Future', *CEN* 23 Jan. (1970), 11; Thiselton, 'U (long)', 121; Thiselton, 'UPC', 87. Italics ours.

## B. The Need for a Transformed Hermeneutical Paradigm: Re-Addressing the Problem of Intelligibility Across Historical Distance

In his second period, Thiselton argues that a new critique of hermeneutical understanding – which involves/includes a new critique of responsible interpretation - is needed due to the 'inadequacy' of solutions offered by existing and/or earlier hermeneutical approaches to 'the problem' that 'historical distance' creates in relation to the *'intelligibility'* of the ancient 'biblical' "texts" to 'modern' readers 'today'.[6] Thiselton argues that since 'the modern' horizons of "today's" Bible-readers are shaped by 'long' "traditions" 'of... interpretation' and by modern "situations" (to name but two factors), then the 'original' purposes, 'content'(s), and "functions" of the "biblical texts" are often misunderstood 'today'. With E. Fuchs and G. Ebeling of the New Hermeneutic, Thiselton agrees that, for 'the biblical' message to 'strike home' 'today' as "effective" 'communication' of various kinds, '"the *same*"' thing must be '"said *differently*"'.[7]

### *1. The Inadequacy of Earlier Solutions to the Problem of Intelligibility Across Historical Distance*

The question, 'can there be fusion between... two horizons?' across great time-spans, however, 'is the hermeneutical... [question] of the twentieth century'. Indeed, in Thiselton's estimate, 'traditional', "positivist", "Bultmannian", "'post-Bultmannian'" (i.e. the New Hermeneutic in this context), and 'structuralist' traditions and approaches broadly *fail* to address 'the problem of' 'biblical' (un-) 'intelligibility' across 'historical distance' adequately. Thiselton may still draw positive insights from these approaches and traditions, but he also remains dissatisfied with them and sees them as having *flawed hermeneutical theories and practices* – as follows.[8]

Thus, (1), Thiselton bemoans the 'unexamined philosophical presuppositions' and 'philosophical naivety' of 'traditional' approaches to 'interpretation'. Thiselton argues that these approaches often presuppose 'classical' Platonic-Cartesian epistemology and that they therefore often reduce 'understanding' to 'subject-

---

[6] cf.: Thiselton, 'NH', 308-310; Thiselton, 'U (long)', 90-92; Thiselton, 'MP', 4; cf. 4-12; Thiselton, *2H*, 51; Bartholomew, C.G., 'Uncharted Waters: Philosophy, Theology and the Crisis in Biblical Interpretation', in *Renewing Biblical Interpretation* (eds. C.G. Bartholomew, C. Greene and K. Möller; Scripture and Hermeneutics Series; Vol. 1; Carlisle: Paternoster, 2000), 4, 12. Italics ours.

[7] cf.: Thiselton, 'NH', 308-310; Thiselton, 'U (long)', 91, 95, 90. First italics Thiselton's, second italics ours.

[8] Quoting, McNicol, A.J., 'Review of A.C. Thiselton's *The Two Horizons*', *RestQ* 27.3 (1984), 188-189; cf.: Thiselton, 'NH', 310; Thiselton, A.C., 'Review of D. Nineham's *The Use and Abuse of the Bible*', *Chman* 91.4 (1977), 342; Thiselton, 'MP', 4-12; Thiselton, A.C., 'The Theological Scene: Post-Bultmannian Perspectives', *CGrad* 30.3 (Sep. 1977), 88; Thiselton, 'SBS', 329; Thiselton, *2H*, 51.

object' "conceptualization". Correlatively, Thiselton argues that these approaches often also *reduce* 'language' to a "propositional" 'vehicle' for "transmitting" 'thought'-'content', 'communication' 'to a... conscious exchange' that *involves* primarily this *"reduced"* kind of 'language', and interpretation to a 'mere' 'mechanical' 'repetition' *of* 'biblical' 'language'. Thiselton argues that these approaches are often guilty of "prematurely appealing to the Holy Spirit's work", or to the Bible's capacity 'to interpret itself'. Thus, against A.K.M. Adam's later claim, Thiselton is hardly 'perpetuating a status quo' in 'biblical' hermeneutics.[9]

(2) Thiselton also broadly rejects the "positivist" approaches of E. Troeltsch and D.E. Nineham. Thiselton argues that 'Troeltsch' "imposes" 'a modern', 'personal horizon' 'on the past', and that Nineham's "pessimism" concerning 'bridging' 'historical distance' presupposes a 'positivistic' rejection of 'the supernatural' and a neglect of Continental 'hermeneutical' "traditions" where, in Thiselton's view, these problems persist in C.F. Evans' work. For Thiselton, however, 'the problem of the pastness of the' New Testament 'should' neither 'be ignored, nor... exaggerated'. Thiselton insists that the New Testament is an 'accessible source of authority'. (We shall go on to examine Thiselton's arguments for provisional and potentially progressive textual epistemological accessibility in Chapters 6 and 7).[10]

(3) Thiselton also broadly rejects 'Bultmann's' 'demythologizing' 'programme', which 'dominated' 'biblical' studies between the 1950s and the 1970s.[11] Admittedly, for Thiselton, Bultmann rightly argues that '"subjectivity"', '"pre-understanding"', and 'consciousness of... pre-understanding' are necessarily involved in 'accurate interpretation': Thiselton agrees with Bultmann's view that 'no exegesis is without presuppositions'.[12] Indeed, Thiselton would agree with S.M. Schneiders when she writes, 'Bultmann's... re-asking' of 'the hermeneutical question from the standpoint of contemporary philosophical thought and...

---

[9] cf.: Thiselton, 'NH', 308-317, 323-326; Thiselton, 'LMR', 1126-1130; Thiselton, *2H*, 312, 343; Thiselton, A.C., 'The Theology of Paul Tillich', *Chman* 88.1 (1974), 92, 96-98; (quoting) Brodie, L., 'Review of A.C. Thiselton's *The Two Horizons*', *Thom* 45.3 (1981), 480, 481; Sykes, S.W., 'Review of A.C. Thiselton's *The Two Horizons*', *Chman* 96.2 (1982), 156; Adam, A.K.M., 'Review of A.C. Thiselton's *New Horizons in Hermeneutics*', *ModTh* 10 (1994), 434. Italics ours.

[10] cf.: Thiselton, *2H*, 69-74; Thiselton, 'R *UAB*', 341-343; Thiselton, 'U (long)', 94-95; Brodie, 'R *2H*', 481; Metzger, B.M., 'Review of A.C. Thiselton's *The Two Horizons*', *PSemB* NS3.2 (1981), 210; Rodd, C.S., 'Review of A.C. Thiselton's *The Two Horizons*', *ExTim* 91 (Jul. 1980), 290; contradicting, Poythress, V.S., 'Review of A.C. Thiselton's *The Two Horizons*', *WThJ* 43 (Fall 1980), 179.

[11] cf.: Thiselton, 'MP', 4, 10-12, n.24; Grech, P., 'Review of A.C. Thiselton's *The Two Horizons*', *Bib* 63.4 (1982), 572.

[12] cf.: Thiselton, 'NH', 312-313; Thiselton, *2H*, 234-240; Cahill, P.J., 'Review of A.C. Thiselton's *The Two Horizons*', *CBQ* 43.3 (Jul. 1981), 484; quoting Bultmann, R., 'Is Exegesis Without Presuppositions Possible? (1957)', in *New Testament and Mythology and Other Basic Writings* (ed. and trans. S.M. Ogden; Philadelphia: Fortress Press, 1984), 149; 145-153.

[thereby from that of] historical consciousness' was 'of' 'real importance'.[13]

Nevertheless, Thiselton complains that Bultmann transposes 'Biblical' 'language' into alien "frameworks" and (therefore) out of the 'Biblical' "home" "traditions" that 'transmit' the very '"public" criteria' that render 'Biblical' 'language' "intelligible". Thus Bultmann writes, 'there is nothing specifically Christian about the mythical world picture' of 'the New Testament'. For Thiselton, though, Bultmann's 'demythologizing' programme creates misunderstanding, precipitates 'semantic' distortion and inversion, falls foul of '"private" language' arguments, and undermines the 'Biblical' "paradigms" that authenticate the genuinely 'Christian' *as* genuinely 'Christian'. Further, Thiselton argues that Bultmann's substitution of '"modern"' paraphrase for 'Biblical imagery' misconstrues the relationship 'between language and thought'.[14]

In Thiselton's argument, it is Bultmann's "narrow" critical-synthetic (our phrase) theological and philosophical 'pre-understanding' that causes these difficulties. Philosophically, Thiselton argues that Bultmann's *'hermeneutical theory'* is too narrowly 'shaped' by 'Neo-Kantianism' (see Chapter 6),[15] and that his dialogue with W. Hermann, Heidegger and others inadequately addresses '"the problem of history and historicality"' (on Bultmann, and on Heidegger's notion of '"historicality"', see Chapter 6) and collapses futural eschatology into (or at least towards) 'realized eschatology'.[16] In Thiselton's view, Bultmann demonstrates 'unwillingness to let his pre-understanding be... challenged by the text' and thus embraces an approach that *a priori* precludes 'certain' interpretative 'possibilities'.[17] Thus, Thiselton argues that Bultmann's hermeneutics become a 'threat to faith'. In Thiselton's estimate, a much '"broader"' dialogue than that entered into by Bultmann – i.e. a much '"broader"' dialogue (at the level of preunderstanding) *both* with theological traditions *and* with '"philosophical"' traditions - is required in order to enable '"the New Testament"' to '"speak more clearly in its own right"'.[18]

(4) Whilst Thiselton agrees with exponents of the New Hermeneutic who argue that 'hermeneutics' needs to progress both 'beyond historicism' and beyond

---

[13] Schneiders, S.M., 'The Paschal Imagination - Objectivity and Subjectivity in New Testament Interpretation', *ThStud*, 43.1 (1982), 55, 63; cf.: Thiselton, 'MP', 10-12; Thiselton, 'UPC', 87-89.

[14] cf.: Thiselton, 'MP', 4, 10-12, n.24; Thiselton, *2H*, 312; Thiselton, 'LMR', 1138; Bultmann, R., 'New Testament and Mythology: The Problem of Demythologizing The New Testament Proclamation', in *New Testament and Mythology and Other Basic Writings* (ed. and trans. S.M. Ogden; Philadelphia: Fortress Press, 1984), 3.

[15] Thiselton, *2H*, 283-285; cf.: Thiselton, 'MP', 10-12; Thiselton, 'UPC', 87-89. Italics Thiselton's.

[16] cf.: Thiselton, *2H*, 207-208, 213, 265; Thiselton, A.C., 'Realized Eschatology at Corinth', *NTStud* 24 (Jul. 1978), 520.

[17] cf.: Thiselton, *2H*, 284; (quoting), Morgan, R., 'Review of A.C. Thiselton's *The Two Horizons*', *HeyJ* 22.3 (1981), 332.

[18] cf.: Thiselton, *2H*, 445; Ellingworth, P., 'Review of A.C. Thiselton's *The Two Horizons*', *EvanQ* 53 (Jul.-Sep. 1981), 178-179; Schneiders, 'PI', 55, 63.

*Hermeneutics and Responsible Interpretation* 211

'Bultmann's' approach, it is crucial to note that Thiselton also *"moves beyond" the approach of the New Hermeneutic*.[19] Thiselton revises interpretation *per se*, and does *not* merely offer a 'hefty apparatus' in order 'to yield' minor adjustments in interpretative results (contradicting J. Kleinig's reading of Thiselton).[20] Thiselton argues, against the New Hermeneutic and against Continental hermeneutics more broadly, that "critical testing", 'cognitive discourse', 'tradition', 'rational' 'argument', 'historical' report, linguistic '"content"', 'description', and 'semantic' and "conceptual" 'opposition' remain important in relation to 'intelligibility'.[21]

Thus, again, Thiselton does not "accept" the New Hermeneutic 'quite cordially' (against what J. Barr suggests). Rather, as we shall demonstrate in Chapter 6, Thiselton appeals to the later Wittgenstein and to others in order to counter the New Hermeneutic's various problematic theoretical and practical dichotomies – particularly its 'fact'-'value' dualism: as the later Wittgenstein puts it, 'the possibility of a language-game is conditioned by certain facts'.[22] In Thiselton's view, notably, 'the New Hermeneutic, and… the work of Funk, Via, and Crossan [Thiselton identifies Funk, Via, and Crossan as the "American counterpart" to the New Hermeneutic – see Chapter 2], is… one-sided', too 'subjective', too 'selective in its choice of texts', and over-emphasizes 'the present' relative to 'the past'.[23]

(5) We defer comment on Thiselton's criticism of 'structuralist approaches' until later in the present chapter.

### 2. The (Ongoing) Urgent Need for a Transformed Paradigm for Hermeneutics

Moving on, then we have already noted that the critical responses given above were made by Thiselton, during his second period, in reply to earlier and/or existing *inadequate* attempts to resolve 'the problem' that 'historical distance' creates in relation to the present-day 'intelligibility' of the biblical texts. We said that these same earlier and/or existing *inadequate* attempts to resolve this 'problem' emerged from approaches and traditions that, in Thiselton's estimate, had *flawed hermeneutical theories and practices*. It is this historical situation, then, that precipitates Thiselton's sense – at the time of his second period (and later) - of *the "urgent" need*

---

[19] Thiselton, 'NH', 309-310; cf. Conroy, C., 'Review of A.C. Thiselton's *The Two Horizons*', *Greg* 62.3 (1981), 563; cf. Thiselton, 'P-BP', 88-89. Italics ours.

[20] See, Thiselton, 'MP', 4-12; and, Thiselton, 'SBS', 329-335; cf. Kleinig, J., 'Review of A.C. Thiselton's *The Two Horizons*', *RefThRev* 39 (Sep.-Dec. 1980), 90.

[21] cf.: Thiselton, 'NH', 323, 324, 328-329; Thiselton, 'Till', 100; Thiselton, 'MP', 4, 10-12; Thiselton, 'SBS', 334, 332.

[22] Brodie, 'R *2H*', 484; cf.: Barr, J., 'Review of I.H. Marshall ed. *New Testament Interpretation*', *Th* 81.681 (May 1978), 235; Thiselton, *2H*, 39; Thiselton, 'P-BP', 89; Thiselton, 'NH', 326; quoting, Wittgenstein, L., *On Certainty* (trans. D. Paul and G.E.M. Anscombe; Oxford: Blackwell, 1969, 2001), 82e.

[23] Brodie, 'R *2H*', 484 (quoted); cf.: Thiselton, 'NH', 323-329; Thiselton, *2H,* 352-356; Thiselton, 'SBS', 329.

*for a transformed framework or 'paradigm'* for biblical hermeneutics and for hermeneutics more broadly.[24]

Thus, (1), Thiselton argues that flawed hermeneutical theories and practices suppress biblical 'content and function' and, therefore, suppress "'God's Word'". Thiselton urges that if 'biblical authority' is genuine, then this suppression "urgently" needs to be overcome in order for the authoritative 'word of God' to be properly *"received"*. Thus, in Thiselton's view, a transformed hermeneutical 'paradigm' is urgently required.[25]

(2) For Thiselton, *if* flawed hermeneutical theories and practices suppress biblical 'content and function' - and hence suppress "'God's [authoritative] Word'" - partly *due to* the way in which flawed hermeneutical theories and practices *fail to resolve* 'the problem' that 'historical distance' creates in relation to the present-day *'intelligibility'* of the biblical texts, *then* a transformed hermeneutical 'paradigm' is "urgently" required in order *to address* 'the problem' that 'historical distance' creates in relation to the present-day 'intelligibility' of the biblical texts. That is, in Thiselton's view, a necessary *pre-condition* for the possibility of the proper 'reception' of "'God's [authoritative] Word'" is the addressing of 'the problem' that 'historical distance' creates in relation to the present-day 'intelligibility' of the biblical texts.[26]

(3) In Thiselton's view, dialogues between theological and philosophical traditions pertaining to the development of a transformed 'paradigm' for biblical hermeneutics demonstrate the problem-solving capacity of biblical theology to provide solutions of relevance to the theoretical difficulties that emerge in and/or through those very dialogues (see Chapter 3). That is, in Thiselton's estimate, deriving a transformed 'paradigm' for biblical hermeneutics will not only allow "'God's Word'" to be "intelligibly" "received": in Thiselton's estimate, the very processes pertaining to this derivation will also demonstrate the cogency of biblical theology in relation to solving the problems pertaining to the *construction of* a transformed hermeneutical 'paradigm'. And Thiselton argues that if transforming biblical hermeneutics thus begins to demonstrate the 'authority' of the 'biblical' texts – even indirectly - then transforming biblical hermeneutics becomes an 'urgent' task since, in Thiselton's view, the *'acceptance'* of the 'biblical' texts *as "authoritative"* is a necessary accompaniment to – or even (often) a necessary

---

[24] Thiselton, 'U (long)', 92; cf.: Thiselton, 'MP', 4, 10-11; Borsch, F.H., 'Review of A.C. Thiselton's *The Two Horizons*', *AThRev* 65 (Jan. 1983), 90; Thiselton, *2H*, 405-406; Thiselton, A.C., *The Hermeneutics of Doctrine* (Grand Rapids: Eerdmans, 2007), 136-137; cf.: 134-144; 162-173. Italics ours.

[25] Thiselton, 'U (long)', 95, 96, 92, 98, 101; cf. 92-99; cf.: Borsch, 'R *2H*', 90; Thiselton, A.C., 'Communicative Action and Promise in Inter-Disciplinary, Biblical, and Theological Hermeneutics', in *The Promise of Hermeneutics* (R. Lundin, C. Walhout and A.C. Thiselton; Grand Rapids and Cambridge: Eerdmans; Carlisle: Paternoster, 1999), 191-199. Italics ours.

[26] cf.: Thiselton, 'MP', 4, 10-11; Thiselton, 'CAP', 191-199; Thiselton, *2H*, 51; Thiselton, 'U (long)', 95, 96, 92; Borsch, 'R *2H*', 90. Italics ours.

precondition for - their "intelligible" reception.²⁷ For Thiselton, 'the problems addressed by philosophy and hermeneutics are issues raised by the [biblical] texts themselves'.²⁸

(4) A dialogue thereby emerges in Thiselton's thinking: biblical hermeneutics clarifies biblical texts that, in turn, feed into the hermeneutical discussions that yield the transformed paradigm according to which biblical hermeneutics itself proceeds and/or will proceed. For Thiselton, if biblical theology helps us to understand biblical hermeneutics itself, then the Bible needs to be understood urgently in order to refine the very 'interpretative' "strategies" with which it is approached. For Thiselton, 'urgent' biblical studies are thus *internal to the very grammar* of building a transformed paradigm for biblical hermeneutics. (N.B. in our use of the term "paradigm" we refer primarily to *strata one* and *two*, and do *not* refer to a single *stratum three* 'interpretative strategy' or "model" – see below).²⁹

(5) By implication, therefore, Thiselton's formative writings imply that urgent biblical studies *are also internal to the grammar of building a transformed so-called 'general'* hermeneutical paradigm. As we argued in Chapters 3 and 4, Thiselton's biblical theology feeds into and shapes his hermeneutical theory. For Thiselton, then, even so-called 'general' hermeneutical theorizing does not "put off" biblical studies, but rather presupposes it, dialogues with it, and facilitates it.³⁰

Therefore, (6), in relation to Thiselton's hermeneutics, we must carefully qualify any talk of distinctions between 'biblical' or 'special' and 'general hermeneutics'.³¹ Thus, (a), in one sense, Thiselton's 'general' "hermeneutic" – i.e. his overhaul of Continental hermeneutics – attempts to be "biblical". For example, Thiselton argues later that the 'biblical' Trinitarian principle of showing 'respect for the otherness of the' 'giving and given Other' applies to '*all* hermeneutics'.³²

Conversely, however, (b), Thiselton's "biblical" or 'special' hermeneutic is *not* 'general' in at least two senses: (i) Thiselton views the 'biblical texts' as unique in their potential to "function" as "'divine'" '*speech-acts*' that "build" 'Christians' and "*the Church*"'. For Thiselton, therefore, "responsible interpretation" in relation to the 'biblical texts' uniquely relates to questions to do with biblical authority,

---

²⁷ cf.: Thiselton, 'U (long)', 96, 92, 94, 115, 101-102, 95-97, 106; Thiselton, *2H*, xx; Thiselton, 'MP', 4; Borsch, 'R *2H*', 90. Italics ours.
²⁸ Roschke, R.W., 'Review of A.C. Thiselton's *The Two Horizons*', *CThM* 9 (Aug. 1982), 246; cf. Chapter 3.
²⁹ Thiselton, 'U (long)', 92; cf.: Thiselton, A.C., 'Review of W. Pannenberg's *Basic Questions in Theology, Vol. 1*', *Chman* 85.2 (1971), 120-122; Chapter 3.
³⁰ Thiselton, 'NH', 315; cf. Thiselton, 'U (long)', 94. Italics ours.
³¹ Thiselton, 'NH', 315; cf. Thiselton, 'U (long)', 94. Italics ours.
³² cf.: Thiselton, 'CAP', 189; cf. 133-135; Thiselton, *LLM*, 4-9; Thiselton, 'M,M', 333-343; Thiselton, 'P-BP', 88-89; Thiselton, 'R *UAB*', 341-343; Thiselton, 'MP', 4-12; Thiselton, 'SBS', 329-335; Thiselton, 'NH', 315, 308-310, 323-329. Italics ours.

submission, obedience, transformation, and mission (see below).[33] (ii) Thiselton rejects *a priori* "generalization" (re. 'categories', 'textual' 'models', notions of 'language', notions of 'truth', 'interpretative' "strategies", and so on). For Thiselton, "understanding", as a concept, is not just 'one' thing but, rather, is "'a concept with blurred edges'" that alters - at the very least - according to that which is being understood and according to interpretative aims (amongst other factors - see Chapters 3, 4, 6, 7, and also later in the present chapter). At the stratum-three level of conceptualizations of interpretative practice, Thiselton's notion of a 'general' "hermeneutic" only extends far enough to embrace *broader a posteriori* factors that pertain to most or 'all' responsible interpretation - for example, 'the hermeneutical circle'.[34]

Thus, (c), we must carefully qualify R. Papaphilippopoulos's later talk of Thiselton's 'desire to provide first a general... hermeneutic and then apply it to biblical texts'. That is, (i), with Papaphilippopoulos, we must conclude that Thiselton's transformed paradigm for hermeneutics is the same – at a *stratum-one and stratum-two* level - for *both* so-called "general" hermeneutics *and* so-called "biblical" or "special" hermeneutics. Moreover, (ii), with Papaphilippopoulos, we may even conclude – as noted above – that the *stratum-three* level of Thiselton's hermeneutical reflection embraces broad *a posteriori* factors – for example, the hermeneutical circle – that pertain to most or even 'all' responsible interpretation – whether "general" or "biblical"/"special".[35]

However, (iii), we must also conclude that Thiselton's transformed paradigm for hermeneutics as a "singular paradigm" *only extends so far* when it comes to

---

[33] cf.: Thiselton, A.C., 'The Supposed Power of Words in the Biblical Writings', *JThStud* NS25.2 (Oct. 1974), 291, 293-296; Thiselton, 'U (long)', 116, 118, 99-106, cf. 114-121; Thiselton, A.C., 'Understanding God's Word Today', *CEN* 15 Oct. (1976), 6, (henceforth the 'short' article with this title); Thiselton, 'REC', 522; Thiselton, 'Truth', 900-901; Thiselton, *LLM*, 12, 4, 5. Italics Thiselton's.

[34] cf.: Thiselton, 'NH', 315, 320-321, 326-327; Thiselton, 'CAP', 189; Thiselton, A.C., 'Well-trampled. Review of F. Ferré's *Language, Logic and God*', *CEN* 8 Jan. (1971), 12; Thiselton, *NH*, 33, 296, 562; Thiselton, 'UPC', 91, 94; Thiselton, A.C., 'Semantics and New Testament Interpretation', in *New Testament Interpretation: Essays in Principles and Methods* (ed. I.H. Marshall; Grand Rapids: Eerdmans; Exeter: Paternoster Press, 1977; actually written 1974), 78-79; Thiselton, *LLM*, 6, 31-32; Thiselton, A.C., 'Kierkegaard and the Nature of Truth', *Chman* 89.1 (1975), 91-95; Thiselton, 'EITN', 582-583; Thiselton, A.C., Contribution to 'Flesh', in *The New International Dictionary of New Testament Theology, Volume 1* (ed. C. Brown; Exeter: Paternoster; Grand Rapids: Zondervan, 1975), 681; Thiselton, 'U (long)', 95-97; Thiselton, A.C., 'The Parables as Language-Event: Some Comments on Fuchs's Hermeneutics in the Light of Linguistic Philosophy', *SJT* 23.4 (Nov. 1970), 453; Thiselton, 'P-BP', 88; Thiselton, 'MP', 5; Thiselton, 'SBS', 334; cf. 331-333; Thiselton, A.C., 'Truth', in *The New International Dictionary of New Testament Theology, Volume 3* (ed. C. Brown; Exeter: Paternoster; Grand Rapids: Zondervan, 1978), 874-875. Italics ours.

[35] Papaphilippopoulos, R., 'Review of A.C. Thiselton's *New Horizons in Hermeneutics*', *SJT* 47.1 (1994), 143.

*stratum-three* interpretative practices. That is, for Thiselton, as we shall see below, there is no single over-arching "hermeneutical paradigm" at the level of such factors as interpretative strategies, interpretative goals, models of texts, critical tools, reader-situations, and so on. For Thiselton, as we shall see below, such factors - in any properly "historical" approach to interpretation – must vary in line with changes in the historical particularities pertaining *both* to textual horizons *and* to reader horizons.

Therefore, as we shall see below, when we articulate Thiselton's "transformed hermeneutical paradigm (singular)", we must always present such factors as interpretative strategies, interpretative goals, models of texts, critical tools, reader-situations, and so on, as being irreducibly – but *responsibly* - plural. As we shall see below, Thiselton argues that "understanding" always reflects a dialectic diachronic dialogic dynamic relation between "two horizons" or between two sets of historical particularities. As we shall see below and in Chapter 7, Thiselton's line of argument here has *nothing to do with* what some might erroneously call a "sell-out to postmodernism". Rather, as we shall see, Thiselton distinguishes carefully between *legitimate* and *illegitimate* kinds of "pluralities of interpretative outcomes".

(7) Summarizing: (a) Thiselton broadly rejects (though still draws certain insights from) 'traditional', "positivist", "'Bultmannian'", 'post-Bultmannian' or 'Continental' (i.e. the New Hermeneutic), and 'structuralist' (see below) approaches to understanding the biblical texts. Conversely, (b), Thiselton argues that a transformed paradigm for 'biblical' and 'general hermeneutics' is thereby "urgently" required (though this "paradigm" is *not* a *single* stratum-three 'interpretative' "paradigm", "model", "tool", "goal", "situation", or 'strategy'). (c) In Thiselton's view, this transformed hermeneutical paradigm will facilitate the acceptance, the 'intelligibility', and the reception – i.e. the responsible interpretation and/or understanding - of the authoritative 'address' of "'God's Word'" through the 'biblical texts'. (d) For Thiselton, biblical studies, far from being suspended during the derivation and construction of this transformed hermeneutical paradigm, *remain integral to the conversations - between philosophical and theological traditions - through which this same "urgently"-required transformed paradigm for 'biblical' and 'general hermeneutics' is to be derived and constructed.*[36]

But what is Thiselton's transformed paradigm for hermeneutics practically speaking? What is his critique of hermeneutical understanding and how is it related to the hermeneutical circle (or spiral)? What does the hermeneutical task, or responsible interpretation, actually involve for Thiselton? And can any more light be shed on a "Thiseltonian" approach to interpretative *pluralities* – whether in relation to the variable inter-related and inter-relating particularities pertaining to the "two horizons", or in relation to legitimate and illegitimate "pluralities of interpretative outcomes"? These questions bring us to our next section.

---

[36] cf.: Thiselton, 'NH', 310, 315; Thiselton, 'R *UAB*', 342; Thiselton, 'P-BP', 88-89; Thiselton, 'TY', 1560; Thiselton, 'SBS', 329; Thiselton, 'U (long)', 92-96; Thiselton, *NH*, 296, 558; Thiselton, 'MP', 4; Thiselton, 'U (short)', 6; Thiselton, 'CAP', 189. Italics ours.

## C. Dialogic Theory-Construction:
## Towards a Unified Critique of Hermeneutical Understanding as Responsible Interpretation

Thiselton argues that hermeneutical 'understanding' *necessarily* involves human "subjectivities" in a *'progressive'*, practical *'process'* – namely 'the hermeneutical circle' or 'spiral' – but that hermeneutical 'understanding' involves human "subjectivities" in 'the hermeneutical circle' or 'spiral' *without necessarily* leading interpreters into absolute 'relativism' or 'subjectivism', or into 'solipsism', or into 'individualism'.[37]

*1. Involved Subjectivities vs. Absolute Relativism, Subjectivism, Solipsism, and Individualism*

Thus, (1), Thiselton broadly affirms Bultmann's stance that *"'understanding'" texts "'presupposes a'" 'life-relation' between "'the'" "'interpreter's'" "'subjectivity'"* (or, in Thiselton's case, less individualistically, *"'the'"* "subjectivities" of the community of "interpreters") *and "textual" 'subject-matter'*. Bultmann writes, 'I understand a novel only because I know from my own life what is involved, for example, in love and friendship'. Notably, Thiselton, after Bultmann, argues that "objectivity" cannot be "attained" by supposedly "silencing" "'subjectivity'"[38] through an attempt to adopt 'a' supposedly 'detached attitude' (here we are contradicting G.L. Bray's reading of Thiselton)[39] that appears "'scientific'",[40] since "'pure" exegesis, uncontaminated by philosophical and theological presuppositions', is impossible;[41] (regarding 'presuppositions', cf.: 'fore-sight' in Heidegger, "'pre-understanding'" in Bultmann, and "prejudice" and 'pre-judgments' in Gadamer).[42]

---

[37] Relevant writings include: Thiselton, 'Parab', 453-454; Thiselton, 'TNI', 11; Thiselton, 'UPC', 87-88, 92-93; Thiselton, 'NH', 308-327; Thiselton, 'SBL', 108-111, 118; Thiselton, *NTH*, 581-588; Thiselton, 'U (long)', 104-106, 120-121; Thiselton, 'P-BP', 89; Thiselton, 'LMR', 1135, 1139-1140; Thiselton, 'KNT', 85-86, 90-91, 104; Thiselton, *LLM*, 10; Thiselton, A.C., 'The Parousia in Modern Theology. Some Questions and Comments', *Tyn* 27 (1976), 48, 49, 52; Thiselton, 'Truth', 883-893; Thiselton, *2H*, 104, 304-307, 387, 396-401; Thiselton, 'M&M', 8; Thiselton, 'EITN', 578-579, 583-584; Thiselton, 'U (short)', 6; Walsh, B.J., 'Anthony Thiselton's Contribution to Biblical Hermeneutics', *ChSRev* 14.3 (1985), 227; Harrisville, R.A., 'Review of A.C. Thiselton's *The Two Horizons*', *Interp* 36 (Apr. 1982), 216. Italics in speech-marks Thiselton's, others ours.

[38] cf.: Thiselton, 'UPC', 87-88; Thiselton, 'NH', 312-313; Thiselton, 'P-BP', 88-89. Citing, Bultmann, R., 'The Problem of Hermeneutics', in *New Testament and Mythology and Other Basic Writings* (ed. and trans. S.M. Ogden; Philadelphia: Fortress Press, 1984), 75. Italics ours.

[39] Contradicting, Bray, G.L., 'Review of R. Lundin's, A.C. Thiselton's and C. Walhout's *The Responsibility of Hermeneutics*', *Chman* 100.3 (1986), 260.

[40] Brodie, 'R *2H*', 482.

[41] Conroy, 'R *2H*', 563.

[42] Citing, Heidegger, M., *Being and Time* (trans. J. Macquarrie and E. Robinson; Oxford: Blackwell, 1962, 2001), 191; cf. Bultmann, 'IEWPP', 149; cf. Gadamer, H.-G., *Truth and Method* (trans. J. Weinsheimer and D.G. Marshall; London: Sheed & Ward, 1975, 1989), 269; cf. Thiselton, *2H*, 305.

In Thiselton's estimate, arguing otherwise suppresses an awareness of one's own 'philosophical stance' and 'pre-understanding',[43] and so 'hinders' 'understanding'. Indeed, Thiselton stresses that, "initially", 'pre-understanding' constitutes 'an indispensable point of contact with the... text'.[44]

(2) Nevertheless, *and more adequately re-historicizing both Bultmann's notion of pre-understanding and Bultmann's notion of the role of pre-understanding during interpretation*, Thiselton argues that although "'understanding'" is necessarily 'conditioned by' "'subjectivity'" (or 'by' "subjectivities"), "'understanding'" *need not thereby be completely "relativistic" or "subjectivistic"*.[45]

Thus, (a), Thiselton admits that, since 'the rise of historical consciousness', the reality of *some* 'historical' "relativity" is undeniable: Thiselton admits that 'historicality' (see Chapter 6), "'linguisticality'", and "horizonal" 'concerns' "condition" 'understanding'.[46] With Heidegger, Thiselton agrees that "'historicality'"... is constitutive for Dasein's "historizing'" (see Chapter 6).[47]

However, (b), with Gadamer, Thiselton argues that the "'historically'"-mediated "unconscious" "'pre-judgments'" (cf. "prejudices") of 'tradition' "initially" "influence" 'interpretation' "'more than'" 'conscious' "'judgments'": for Gadamer and Thiselton, 'history does not belong to us; we belong to it'. Further, for Thiselton, drawing on Pannenberg, "Christological" and "'eschatological'" 'revelation' (including biblical 'revelation') and divine action qualifies 'historical consciousness', and thereby *further* de-centers and repudiates anthropocentric approaches in which individual 'subjectivity' is (or in which individuals' "subjectivities" are) falsely assigned roles as the central arbiter(s) of truth.[48] Thus, Thiselton argues that absolute 'relativism' and 'subjectivism', which imperialize "'what is true *for me*'", and 'hand-to-mouth pragmatism', which "imperializes" "'what works today'", are both precluded.[49]

Admittedly, (c), Thiselton also avoids *"objectivism"*, arguing that 'all'

---

[43] Thiselton, *2H*, 103-114; cf. Erickson, M.J., 'Review of A.C. Thiselton's *The Two Horizons*', *JEThS* 23 (Dec. 1980), 371, 372.

[44] cf.: Thiselton, 'U (long)', 120; Thiselton, 'UPC', 93; Thiselton, 'NH', 312-315; Thiselton, 'EITN', 583; Thiselton, 'Truth', 897-898.

[45] cf.: Thiselton, 'TNI', 11; Thiselton, 'NH', 313, 319, 326-327; Thiselton, 'U (long)', 90; Thiselton, 'KNT', 100-101; Thiselton, 'Par', 48-50; Thiselton, A.C., 'An Age of Anxiety', in *The History of Christianity. A Lion Handbook* (eds. T. Dowley *et al*; Tring, Hertfordshire: Lion Publishing, 1977), 600; Thiselton, 'LMR', 1142-1144; Thiselton, 'Truth', 899-901. Italics ours.

[46] cf.: Thiselton, *2H*, 51, 56, 186, 157, 164; Thiselton, 'TNI', 11; Thiselton, 'NH', 323, 318-319; Thiselton, 'U (long)', 90.

[47] Heidegger, *BT*, 41; cf. our Chapter 6.

[48] cf.: Thiselton, *2H*, 304-306, 51; Thiselton, 'UPC', 92-93; Thiselton, 'NH', 317, 323; Gadamer, *TM*, 265-277; citing, 276; Thiselton, 'TNI', 11; Thiselton, 'Par', 49, 48; Thiselton, 'Truth', 899-901.

[49] cf.: Thiselton, 'TNI', 11; Thiselton, 'NH', 319, 323, 326; Thiselton, 'Truth', 896-897; 899-901; Thiselton, *NH*, 27. Italics Thiselton's.

interpretations are 'provisional on future confirmation', and ultimately upon apocalyptic 'unveiling'.[50] Thus, Thiselton *acknowledges* 'the hiddenness or non-demonstrability of faith and its "objects"' (here we are contradicting R.A. Harrisville's reading of Thiselton),[51] and Thiselton rejects "evangelical" "authoritarian" "appeals" 'to "a block of... revealed truth"', Corinthian (and modern charismatic) 'enthusiastic' over-certainty, and the supposedly "self-evident truths" espoused by/in 'positivism'.[52]

Nevertheless, (d), Thiselton's hermeneutical 'programme' *counters* the 'relativism' and 'subjectivism' that 'reduce' 'the Gospel' to '"self-understanding"' or to an '"anthropocentric"' 'sell-out'. Against E.D. Hirsch, Thiselton argues that his (i.e. Thiselton's) acknowledgement of the existence of 'present meaning' 'does not' amount to a 'sell-out' to "subjectivism". For Thiselton, to accept 'legitimate interpretative impediments' is *not* to 'leap... to' a relativistic 'epistemological' stance and, for Thiselton, "respecting" 'both' "textual" and 'reader' "horizons" is not the same as granting them 'equal respect' authoritatively (here we are qualifying P. Ellingworth's reading of Thiselton).[53] Thiselton argues that 'the hermeneutical circle' unavoidably *"begins"* with 'the modern horizon', but that 'the hermeneutical circle' is *not* 'grounded' in 'the modern horizon'. Contradicting D.S. Dockery's reading of Thiselton, we should note that 'the goal of interpretation' for Thiselton is 'not... to do something to the text, but... to let the text do something to the interpreter'.[54]

(e) Thiselton thus appeals to Gadamer and to Pannenberg in his arguments against 'relativism'. But Thiselton *also* appeals – to a very limited extent - to the later Wittgenstein in his (i.e. Thiselton's) arguments against 'relativism'. Moreover, in the contexts of all these appeals, Thiselton *continues to modify the grammar both of 'Bultmann's' notion of 'pre-understanding' and of 'Bultmann's' notion of the role of 'pre-understanding' during interpretation*.[55]

---

[50] cf.: Thiselton, *2H*, 22; Thiselton, A.C., 'Head-On Challenge to Doubt: The Theology of Wolfhart Pannenberg', *CEN* 10 May (1974), 8; Thiselton, 'Par', 52, cf. 47-52; Thiselton, 'R BQ1', 120. Italics ours.

[51] Against, Harrisville, 'R *2H*, 216.

[52] cf.: Thiselton, 'TNI', 11; Thiselton, 'REC', 515; Thiselton, A.C., 'Sigmund Freud and the Language of the Heart', *CEN* 13 Feb. (1976), 12, 14; Thiselton, 'AA', 599-600; Thiselton, 'Truth', 900-901.

[53] cf.: Thiselton, 'T&F', 11; Thiselton, 'NH', 326-327; Thiselton, 'TNI', 11; Thiselton, 'AA', 594; Thiselton, 'P-BP', 89; Thiselton, 'LMR', 1139; Hirsch Jr., E.D., *Validity in Interpretation* (New Haven and London: Yale University Press, 1967), 209; quotes from: Russell, W., 'Review of A.C. Thiselton's *New Horizons in Hermeneutics*', *TrinJ* 17.2 (Fall 1996), 243; and from, qualifying: Ellingworth, 'R *2H*, 178.

[54] See previous footnote; cf. Thiselton, 'U (long)', 120; against, Dockery, D.S., 'Review of A.C. Thiselton's *The Two Horizons*', *GThJ* 4.1 (Spr. 1983), 135; with, Roschke, 'R *2H*, 246. Italics ours.

[55] cf.: Thiselton, 'TNI', 11; Thiselton, 'NH', 311-315, 320; Thiselton, *LLM*, 8-9; Thiselton, 'EITN', 583; Thiselton, 'LMR', 1138. Italics in speech marks, Thiselton's, others ours.

*Hermeneutics and Responsible Interpretation* 219

Thus, after the later Wittgenstein, Thiselton reinstates 'assertions' and *'public criteria'* (see Chapter 4), and thus avoids 'a hermeneutic' that falls into 'the trap of subjectivism and vacuous statements whereby faith has no content and revelation reveals nothing'. Thiselton complains that 'such a hermeneutic... privatizes language and therefore cannot be subjected to testing or have public meaning'.[56]

Further, Thiselton argues that 'pre-understanding' (cf. '"scaffolding"', '"training"', 'pre-judgments') need not embrace merely an 'uncritically' 'accepted' 'present cultural framework' or 'language-game', but that 'pre-understanding' may also embrace *'theological' 'criteria'* or the thought-through 'convictions' of 'tradition' and/or the corporate rational responses pertaining to "histories of effects" (to use Gadamer's, and then Pannenberg's, language alongside that of the later Wittgenstein).[57]

(3) *Continuing to more adequately re-historicize both Bultmann's notion of pre-understanding and Bultmann's notion of the role of pre-understanding during interpretation - and thereby continuing to alter Bultmannian grammar* – Thiselton argues that '"understanding"', despite being 'conditioned by' '"subjectivity"' (or 'by' subjectivities), is *not thereby "solipsistic"*. Thiselton's argument that this point is true *sits alongside* his acknowledgments that '"understanding"' presupposes 'communication' between "existentially" *'unique' 'persons'*, and that '"understanding"' does *not* presuppose so-called "transcendental" or *a priori* "general humanness".[58]

That is, (a), Thiselton argues that 'understanding', as "inter-subjective" "communication", presupposes 'a' *prior "shared" "world"'* (cf. *'Einverständnis'*; cf. '"language-game"') that 'provides and sustains' "over-lapping" 'horizons' where, for Thiselton, the "overlap" between these 'horizons' constitutes 'a hermeneutical arch' connecting these 'horizons'. Thiselton argues that his notion of '"world"', here, may presuppose 'shared' '"community"', 'shared' 'language', the 'shared' definitive 'settings' of a 'tradition', 'shared' "involvements", 'shared' 'experiences', and 'shared' attitudes' (cf. Thiselton's citation of E. Fuchs' example 'of a close-knit family'). We should also note - contradicting R.A. Harrisville's and others' readings of Thiselton – that, in Thiselton's thinking, "interpreters" are 'not' "locked" 'into a localized ethnocentric world' because, for Thiselton, 'inter-subjectivity reaches beyond particular communities'. For Thiselton, moreover, "traditions" and 'language-habits' positively "condition" '"worldhood"' such that the '"world"'

---

[56] See previous footnote; cf. Thiselton, 'Parab', 451; cf.: Thiselton, 'LMR', 1134; Walsh, 'TC', 232-233; Chapters 1 and 4. Italics Thiselton's.

[57] cf.: Thiselton, *2H*, 31, 33, 432-436, 383, 395, 322; Thiselton, 'UPC', 91-94; Thiselton, 'NH', 317, 323; Thiselton, 'LMR', 1131, 1134; Thiselton, 'CAP', 139; Thiselton, *NTH*, xxii, concs. 1.2a-c; Thiselton, 'Truth', 898-899; querying, Kleinig, 'R *2H*', 90. Italics Thiselton's.

[58] cf.: Thiselton, A.C., 'The Meaning of SARX in 1 Corinthians 5:5: A Fresh Approach in the Light of Logical and Semantic Factors', *SJT* 26.2 (May 1973), 205, 215; Thiselton, 'NH', 311, 313-315, 320; Thiselton, 'U (long)', 90; Thiselton, *LLM*, 8, 31; Thiselton, *2H*, 236; Thiselton, 'EITN', 583; Thiselton, 'UPC', 92-93; Harrisville, 'R *2H*', 216. Fifth italics Thiselton's (i.e. on *'unique' 'persons'*), others ours.

within which prior "shared" 'understanding' occurs can include the thought-through 'convictions' of 'tradition', as noted above. Thiselton's use of the notion of '"world"' thus *avoids* 'the solipsism lurking behind', and *changes the very grammar of*, Heidegger's notion of '"world"' (here we are contradicting R.A. Harrisville's reading of Thiselton).[59]

(b) Thiselton argues that 'understanding', as 'communication', presupposes "address" from *'beyond' the 'horizons' of 'the self'* – where, for Thiselton, this fact reflects *both* a "reversing" of the interpretative direction that is presupposed by Cartesianism *and* a limiting of the role of '"subjectivity"' (or of "subjectivities'") during interpretation and communication. In Thiselton's estimate, "interpreters" can '"be interpreted"' and "transformed" '"by"' '"divine"' speech-action through the biblical '"texts"' and, in Thiselton's estimate, 'ancient legal texts' may lead modern lawyers to new "applications".[60] These processes, in Thiselton's view, *both* presuppose 'openness', 'receptivity', "listening", and 'waiting', *and* preclude conceiving "interpretation" merely as the 'active' 'scrutiny' and "manipulation" of 'passive' texts whereby 'information' is sifted or "netted" into 'pre-conceived categories' by supposedly 'detached' "observers".[61]

(c) In his second period (and later) Thiselton normally sees hermeneutical 'understanding' as "inter-subjective" 'communication'. This angle of view on hermeneutical 'understanding' coheres with Thiselton's later 'model that locates texts in a nexus of responsible [authorial *and* interpretative] actions'. Further, in Thiselton's estimate, this same angle of view on hermeneutical 'understanding' *both* "avoids" 'the... dichotomy between... author-... and... reader-oriented' approaches (i.e. this same angle of view on hermeneutical 'understanding' thus potentially "links" 'interpretation and composition theory'), *and* forms the basis for Thiselton's later critiques of Ricoeur, Barthes and Derrida. That is, for Thiselton, understanding texts is inseparable 'from the life of the communities that produce

---

[59] cf.: Thiselton, 'NH', 311, 313-315, 320; Thiselton, NH, 13; Thiselton, LLM, 8-9; Thiselton, 'SARX', 205; Thiselton, 'EITN', 583; Thiselton, 'LMR', 1127; Thiselton, 'U (long)', 90; Thiselton, *2H*, 383, 395, 432-435; contradicting: Erickson, 'R *2H*', 371-373; Harrisville, 'R *2H*', 216; Walsh, 'TC', 228, 229; citing, Brown, C., 'Review of A.C. Thiselton's *New Horizons in Hermeneutics*', *CalThJ* 30 (Apr. 1995), 234; cf.: Klein, W.W., 'Review of A.C. Thiselton's *The Two Horizons*', *TrinJ* 2 (Spr. 1981), 74. Italics ours, except for Thiselton's on *'Einverständnis'*.

[60] cf.: Thiselton, 'NH', 311-313, 315-316, 320; Thiselton, 'Flesh', 680; Thiselton, 'UPC', 95; Thiselton, 'Par', 47; Thiselton, A.C., 'New Problems for Old: Article Review of J.A.T. Robinson's *The Human Face of God*', *CEN* 6 Apr. (1973), 8; Thiselton, 'U (long)', 90, 97, 101, 119; Thiselton, 'U (short)', 6; Thiselton, 'P-BP', 88-89. Italics: *'beyond'* (Thiselton's); *the 'horizons' of* (ours); *'the self'* (Thiselton's); *both, and, '"by"'* (ours).

[61] cf.: Thiselton, A.C., 'Irrational Assumptions of Modern Theology Exposed. Review of T.F. Torrance's *God and Rationality*', *CEN* 19 Mar. (1971), 9; Thiselton, 'Words', 295; Thiselton, 'NH', 312-316, 323, 319-320; Thiselton, 'LMR', 1139-1140; Thiselton, 'CAP', 134; Thiselton, 'TNI', 11.

and read literature'.[62]

(4) *Again continuing to more adequately re-historicize both Bultmann's notion of pre-understanding and Bultmann's notion of the role of pre-understanding during interpretation - and thereby again continuing to alter Bultmannian grammar* - Thiselton argues that '"understanding"', despite being 'conditioned by' '"subjectivity"' (or by subjectivities), is *not 'individualistic'*. For Thiselton, 'Gadamer' rightly views 'communal life and tradition', and not just 'the existential nature of the individual', as being preconditional for 'understanding'. Thus, for Thiselton, as well as for Gadamer, 'belonging to a tradition is a condition of hermeneutics'.[63]

For Thiselton, biblical interpretation is to be corporate. That is, in Thiselton's estimate, biblical interpretation is to be performed by 'the whole church' 'community' of 'tradition' in dialogue with '"full"' '"scholarly"' 'resources'. This corporate approach to biblical interpretation, in Thiselton's view, both aids 'faithfulness to the text', and avoids the pitfalls of individualistic '"private interpretation"'. In Thiselton's thinking, such pitfalls include: 'anti-rational' "authoritarian" interpretations; appeals to 'the Holy Spirit to' justify 'absurd' "beliefs"; the suppression of the 'dialogue' that rationally justifies biblical cogency (e.g. in relation to hermeneutical theory); appeals to a '"self-authenticating" Word'; "whimsical" and 'arbitrary' '"private"' '"interpretations"'; 'narrow' "pietistic" 'introspective' 'obsession with inner states'; and "self-centered" 'individualistic' interpretations of 'the future' or 'of the Parousia'. Nevertheless, Thiselton allows that "individuals" 'can' still 'find' '"all"' that is needed '"for salvation"' 'in the Bible'.[64] Moreover, Thiselton warns us that 'corporate' interpretations - despite

---

[62] cf.: Thiselton, 'NH', 311; Thiselton, *NH*, 13, 361, 68-132; Thiselton, A.C., 'Reader-Response Hermeneutics, Action Models, and the Parables of Jesus', in *The Responsibility of Hermeneutics* (R. Lundin, A.C. Thiselton and C. Walhout; Grand Rapids: Eerdmans; Exeter: Paternoster, 1985), 107-113; first quote from: Zuidervaart, L., 'Review of R. Lundin's, A.C. Thiselton's and C. Walhout's *The Responsibility of Hermeneutics*', *CalThJ* 21.2 (Nov. 1986), 291; second quotation from: Snodgrass, K.R., 'Review of R. Lundin's, A.C. Thiselton's and C. Walhout's *The Responsibility of Hermeneutics*', *CovQ* 45 (Nov. 1987), 200; third quote from: Weele, M.V., 'Review of R. Lundin's, A.C. Thiselton's and C. Walhout's *The Responsibility of Hermeneutics*', *ChLit* 35.4 (Sum. 1986), 48; fourth quote from: Van Hamersveld, M., 'Review of R. Lundin's, A.C. Thiselton's and C. Walhout's *The Responsibility of Hermeneutics*', *RefRev* 40.3 (Spr. 1987), 252.

[63] cf.: Thiselton, *2H*, 200; Thiselton, 'U (short)', 90; Thiselton, 'M&M', 8; Thiselton, 'NH', 313, 318-323, 326-327; Thiselton, 'KNT', 85-86, 90-91, 104; Thiselton, 'EITN', 578-579, 583-584; quoting: Maddox, R.L., 'Contemporary Hermeneutic Philosophy and Theological Studies', *RelStud* 21.4 (Dec. 1985), 523; Gadamer, *TM*, 346-379, 383-405, 438-474; citing, 291. Italics ours.

[64] cf.: Thiselton, 'U (long)', 99-104, 117-121; Thiselton, 'TNI', 11; Thiselton, 'M&M', 8; Thiselton, A.C., 'Academic Freedom, Religious Tradition, and the Morality of Christian Scholarship', in *Their Lord and Ours: Approaches to Authority, Community and the Unity of the Church* (ed. M. Santer; London: SPCK, 1982), 20-45; Thiselton, A.C., *Interpreting God and The Postmodern Self: On Meaning, Manipulation and Promise* (SJT: Current Issues in Theology;

their potential advantages - are *still not necessarily* "correct".⁶⁵

*2. Understanding as a Progressive Process: The Hermeneutical Circle (or Spiral)*

Moving on, then Thiselton argues that hermeneutical "'understanding'" (to use the broadest sense of this phrase) proceeds according to an 'ongoing' "'process'" called 'the hermeneutical circle' (or 'spiral'). For Thiselton, this "'process'" displaces a *strict* 'Cartesianism'. But Thiselton also argues that this "'process'" still allows a modified or *re-historicized* version of 'subject-object' "conceptualization" to remain operative during hermeneutical "'understanding'" (see below and Chapter 3).⁶⁶ Thiselton argues that 'interpretation' is neither 'a once-for-all act of knowledge' nor capable of rendering "'final'" 'abstract' formulations 'of truth'. Rather, Thiselton argues that 'interpretation' involves "continuous", 'progressive', "dialogic" "movements" within and 'between' multiple "polarities" or axes.⁶⁷ Contradicting B.J. Walsh's reading of Thiselton, we may observe that the superimposition of these axes in Thiselton's thinking constitutes a *non*-"dualistic" overall structure⁶⁸ - as follows.

A) RE-HISTORICIZED HISTORICAL-EXPERIENTIAL UNDERSTANDING AND RE-HISTORICIZED SUBJECT-OBJECT CONCEPTUALIZATION

Thiselton's 'hermeneutical circle' involves "continuous", 'progressive', "dialogic" "movements" 'between' *re-historicized* "eventful" "historical"-"experiential" hermeneutical 'understanding' (to use the median sense of the phrase "hermeneutical understanding") and *re-historicized* 'subject-object' "conceptualization", and often begins with the latter. For Thiselton, "creative" (cf. "deep") 'understanding' and 'critical' (cf. "correct") 'understanding' (cf. "testing")

---

Edinburgh: T&T Clark, 1995), 145-152; Thiselton, A.C., 'Theology Made Exciting. Review of W. Pannenberg's *The Apostles' Creed in the Light of Today's Questions*', *CEN* 19 Jan. (1973), 12; Thiselton, A.C., 'Positive Role of Doubt', *CEN* 11 Jan. (1974), 8; Thiselton, A.C., 'No Horns on the Pope', *CEN* 14 Jun. (1974), 5; Thiselton, A.C., 'Looking for God's Triumph: The Role of Apocalyptic', *CEN* 12 Jul. (1974), 8; Thiselton, A.C., 'Creativity of Heaven', *CEN* 8 Mar. (1974), 5; Thiselton, A.C., 'Review of E.H. Cousins ed. *Hope and the Future of Man*', *Chman* 88.3 (1974), 232-233; Thiselton, A.C., 'Enthusiasm Not Enough: Güttgemanns, Sawyer, and Barr on Biblical Research', *CEN* 13 Sep. (1974), 6; Thiselton, 'NH', 318-323, 326-327; Thiselton, A.C., 'Experience-Centred Religion: Harvey Cox on the Seduction of the Spirit', *CEN* 9 Aug. (1974), 8; Thiselton, 'H-O', 8; Thiselton, 'KNT', 85-91, 104; Thiselton, 'EITN', 578-584; Thiselton, 'Par', 48-53; Thiselton, 'U (short)', 6; Thiselton, 'AA', 602, 604, 610.
[65] cf.: Thiselton, *2H*, 314-319; Thiselton, 'NH', 323; Thiselton, *NH*, 392.
[66] cf.: Thiselton, 'UPC', 93-95; Thiselton, *2H*, 104; Thiselton, 'NH', 314-327; Thiselton, *LLM*, 8; Thiselton, 'EITN', 583-584; Thiselton, 'SBL', 113-118, 109; Thiselton, *NH*, 19-20.
[67] cf.: Thiselton, 'UPC', 93-95; Thiselton, 'TNI', 11; Thiselton, 'NH', 327, 315; cf. 323-329; Thiselton, 'SBL', 109; Thiselton, *2H*, 104.
[68] Contradicting, Walsh, 'TC', 234.

– united as *re-historicized* hermeneutical 'understanding' (to use the broadest sense of the phrase "hermeneutical understanding") - are the interwoven aims of theologically and eschatologically framed "'historical reason'" (see Chapter 3). For Thiselton, 'traditional' "imperialization" of Cartesian 'subject-object' "conceptualization" and Continental disparagement of the operative spheres and roles of (re-historicized) 'subject-object' "conceptualization" are *both* precluded.[69]

Continuing on from Chapter 3 then, (1), we should note that Thiselton's notion of a *more adequately re-historicized "historical"-"experiential" or 'hermeneutical' 'understanding'* (to use the median senses of the phrase "hermeneutical understanding"), with Gadamer, (a) involves – *but cannot be reduced to* (i.e. see also Chapter 3) – the "subjective", "'existential'", "self-involving" "'actualization'" (see also below) of the "effects", or "'truth'", of the "eventful" manifestation of 'reality', or of the "eventful" 'function' of "'texts'", and (b) "engages" with the 'pre-cognitive' "moods", 'attitudes', "dispositions", and "presuppositions" of "hearers'" 'hermeneutical' "'worlds'": for Gadamer and Thiselton, 'understanding is... participating in an event of tradition'. (c) Thiselton argues that interpretative 'openness', "listening", and 'creative intuition', rather than "theoretical reason" alone, are "'pre-conditional'" for "actualization". (d) Thiselton notes that such 'concrete' 'understanding', which is presupposed in all 'effective communication', is often "initiated" *apart from* abstract "theorizing". In Thiselton's estimate, Gadamer's examples of understanding 'art' and of playing 'games', Fuchs' example of 'understanding' 'a... cat' by "placing" 'a mouse in front of' it, Pannenberg's notion of God's "proving himself" in 'contingent' historical 'events', and M. Buber's view of eventful understanding during "counselling" are all relevant to this context of discussion.[70]

(e) Thiselton argues that corporate "actualizations", over time, constitute "histories of effects" that, on the one hand, are "filtered" through 'effective history' and that, on the other hand, contribute to the stable 'patterns' of 'tradition'. (f) For Thiselton, with Gadamer, 'effective history' thus "filters" the "'judgments'" and "'pre-judgments'" of historically-grounded 'practical' 'rationality' (cf. Thiselton's notion of "'historical'" 'rationality' - see Chapter 3). (g)

---

[69] cf.: Thiselton, 'UPC', 91-95; Thiselton, *2H*, 104; Thiselton, *NH*, 27; Thiselton, 'Parab', 465-468; Thiselton, 'NH', 310-320, 323-329; Thiselton, 'Truth', 895; Thiselton, *NTH*, xxii, concs. 1.2, 1.2a-c; Thiselton, 'U (short)', 6; Thiselton, 'TNI', 11; Thiselton, 'H-O', 8.

[70] cf.: Thiselton, 'IA', 9; Thiselton, 'TNI', 11; Thiselton, 'UPC', 90, 96; cf. 91-96; Thiselton, 'NH', 310-329; Thiselton, *NH*, 11; Thiselton, 'Parab', 450, 447; Thiselton, 'SBL', 116; Thiselton, 'CAP', 180; Thiselton, 'H-O', 8; Thiselton, A.C., 'Review of A.D. Galloway's *Wolfhart Pannenberg*', *Chman* 88.3 (1974), 230-231; Thiselton, 'Till', 100; Thiselton, 'KNT', 102-104; Thiselton, *LLM*, 26, 28, 8-9; Thiselton, 'EITN', 582-584; Thiselton, 'U (long)', 106-109; Thiselton, A.C., 'Review of A. Hodes' *Encounter with Martin Buber*', *Chman* 90.2 (1976), 139; Thiselton, 'U (short)', 6; Thiselton, 'P-BP', 89; Thiselton, 'LMR', 1123-1124, 1139-1140; Thiselton, 'Truth', 895, 898-899, 901; Thiselton, 'TT', 23-24; Gadamer, *TM*, 290, 101-169, 299-307, 19-30, 438-456, 269-277, 383-405 - citation from 290. Italics ours, except for Gadamer's on the word 'understanding'.

Thiselton, however, as noted already, also corrects 'Gadamer' here: for Thiselton, 'tradition' may either 'transmit' 'truth' (with 'Gadamer'), or 'distort' it (with 'Heidegger'). In Thiselton's view, responsible interpretation does not always reinforce 'tradition' because, in Thiselton's estimate, 'theological mistakes can be made'. Nevertheless, (h), Thiselton argues that Gadamer's stress on 'tradition' corrects Heidegger's and Bultmann's "individualism":[71] for Thiselton, 'both the historical text and the present-day interpreter stand in ongoing historical traditions and contexts'.[72]

(2) Thiselton argues that *since* his notion of historically-embedded or *re-historicized 'subject-object' "conceptualization"* is *no longer tied* to Platonic-Cartesian 'dualism', to 'Neo-Kantian epistemology', to 'the correspondence theory of truth', or to 'referential' and/or to 'ideational' "theories" of language and 'meaning' – but rather to 'tradition' and "theology" - *then* it no longer collapses into 'relativism'. For Thiselton, then, re-historicized 'subject-object' "conceptualization" is tied *both* to a 'rationality' broader than "Cartesianism", *and* to 'conscious' 'reflection', to 'cognitive' 'content', to 'public criteria', to 'description', and to "critical" (and to metacritical) "testing". Thiselton argues, with H. Jonas, that thought liberates us from Heideggerian "passive" situatedness. (We have already noted Thiselton's appeals to Pannenberg and to T.F. Torrance in relation to 'rationality' - see Chapter 3).[73]

For Thiselton, further, a Pauline notion of '"reason"' allows '"language"' to "extend" or "clarify" '"concepts for understanding"'. That is, in Thiselton's estimate, Pauline re-historicized subject-object conceptualization may function creatively.[74] Hence, contradicting J. Kleinig's and R.A. Harrisville's readings of Thiselton, we should note that Thiselton does not just re-assert 'subject-object' thinking as though 'Heidegger's' 'opposition' to it were merely 'excessive' but, rather, that Thiselton *re-historicizes* 'subject-object' thinking by embedding it (and its operation) within a different framework that is "historical" in a sense that is in line with biblical theology. Thiselton does not simply appeal to 'Heidegger' to overcome "Cartesianism" (see Chapter 3).[75]

(3) Thiselton argues that hermeneutical '"understanding"' (to use the broadest sense of this phrase) and/or 'communication' thus involve '"dialectical"' "movement" 'between' the 'concrete', 'practical', 'pre-conscious', 'pre-cognitive',

---

[71] cf.: Thiselton, 'UPC', 93, 91-94; Thiselton, 'NH', 317, 323; Thiselton, *NH*, 11; Thiselton, *IGPS*, 150; Thiselton, *2H*, 314, 307, 201, 292; Thiselton, *LLM*, 3-6; Thiselton, 'LMR', 1135; Thiselton, 'IA', 9; Thiselton, 'TNI', 11; Thiselton, *NTH*, concs. 1.2a-c, xxii; Thiselton, 'Truth', 898-899; Sykes, 'R *2H*', 156.

[72] See previous footnote; cf. Borsch, 'R *2H*', 89.

[73] cf.: Thiselton, *2H*, 213, 233, 314; Thiselton, 'IA', 9; Thiselton, 'LMR', 1126-1130, 1134; Thiselton, 'UPC', 93-95; Thiselton, 'NH', 310-311, 317-319, 323-326; Thiselton, 'KNT', 102-103; Thiselton, 'Truth', 894-901; Thiselton, *NTH*, xxii, concs. 1.2, 1.2a-c. Italics ours.

[74] Thiselton, *2H*, 400; cited in Grech, 'R *2H*', 574. Italics Thiselton's.

[75] Against Kleinig and Harrisville; cf. Kleinig, 'R *2H*', 90; cf. Harrisville, 'R *2H*', 216.

'pre-conceptual', and "experiential" 'level' (cf. 'pre-judgments' and 'attitudes') of human consciousness *and* the more 'abstract', 'theoretical', 'conscious', 'cognitive', 'conceptualizing', "reflective" 'level' of human consciousness.[76] Thiselton thus corrects 'the later' Schleiermacher's and Dilthey's over-emphasis on 'conscious' 'rapport' and on 'imagination' (as we noted earlier),[77] the *under*-emphasis on 'conscious' (e.g. "informing") dimensions of 'communication' in Continental hermeneutics, and the *over*-emphasis on 'conscious' dimensions of 'communication' in 'traditional' approaches.[78]

(4) Thiselton's broadest notion of "hermeneutical understanding", therefore, diverges from Gadamer's:[79] (a) Thiselton's two poles of "hermeneutical understanding" are interwoven *within a theological-eschatological framework*, against Gadamer's rejection of a so-called 'utopian or eschatological consciousness'.[80] We also noted in Chapter 3 that Thiselton's reinstating of a theologically and eschatologically framed re-historicized notion of subject-object conceptualization sought to correct what Thiselton perceived to be *Heidegger's* disparagement of the operative spheres and roles of (re-historicized) subject-object conceptualization.[81] Nevertheless, *with* Heidegger and Gadamer, Thiselton urges that hermeneutical understanding *both* 'seeks... a comprehensive alternative to the epistemological dualism between subject and object *and*... takes full account... of the autonomy of the object [cf. its historical difference] and the "historicality" of the subject' (on "historicality", see Chapter 6).[82]

(b) Drawing on Pannenberg and the later Wittgenstein, Thiselton reverses Gadamer's *'ontological' prioritization* of 'language' over 'history'. For Thiselton, as for the later Wittgenstein, 'the "bedrock" of language is human life'. Thiselton's approach, when compared to Gadamer's approach, thus *more adequately re-historicizes language, and thence more adequately re-historicizes understanding.*[83] For Gadamer, though,

---

[76] cf.: Thiselton, 'NH', 308-321, 324; Thiselton, 'Truth', 898; Thiselton, 'KNT', 98; Thiselton, 'UPC', 93; Thiselton, *2H*, 104; Thiselton, 'R *EMB*', 139. Italics ours.

[77] Thiselton, 'NH', 311, 313-314.

[78] cf.: Thiselton, 'UPC', 94-98; Thiselton, 'NH', 311-312, 323-329; Thiselton, A.C., 'Predictable, Domesticated and Tamed', *CEN* 8 Feb. (1974), 7; Thiselton, 'U (long)', 105-106, 121; Thiselton, 'P-BP', 88-89; Thiselton, 'LMR', 1139-1140; Thiselton, 'Truth', 894-896, 898-899.

[79] cf.: Thiselton, 'NH', 316; Gadamer, *TM*, 307-341.

[80] cf.: Thiselton, 'TNI', 11; Thiselton, 'NH', 317-319, 323-326; Thiselton, 'KNT', 102-103; Thiselton, 'Parab', 439, 443, 448-449; Thiselton, 'Truth', 895-896; Thiselton, *NTH*, xxii, concs. 1.2, 1.2a-c); Thiselton, 'UPC', 91-95; quoting, Gadamer, *TM*, xxxviii. Italics ours.

[81] Thiselton, 'UPC', 93, cf. 94-95; cf. Heidegger, *BT*, 86-90.

[82] Webster, J.B., 'Review of A.C. Thiselton's *The Two Horizons*', *FTht* 107.3 (1980), 219; cf. Thiselton, *2H*, 181-191; cf. 79; cf. 203-204. Italics ours.

[83] cf.: Thiselton, *2H*, 312-313, 360; Thiselton, *NH*, 251, 337; McHann Jr., J.C., *The Three Horizons: A Study in Biblical Hermeneutics with Special Reference to Wolfhart Pannenberg* (Aberdeen: University of Aberdeen Ph.D. Thesis, 1987), 326. Italics ours.

'the basic ontological view [is] that being is *language*'.[84] (c) Further, correcting Gadamer, Thiselton argues that understanding 'is… *conditioned* by' "revelatory" and "eschatological" factors (i.e. not just by revelation but also by the shaping of history by divine redeeming action), and not only by 'effective history'.[85] (d) Moreover, as already noted, Thiselton corrects Gadamer regarding *the ability of 'tradition' to 'distort truth'*.[86] This aspect of Thiselton's approach, when compared to Gadamer's approach, *also more adequately re-historicizes understanding in that Thiselton's approach more realistically accounts for historical-epistemological fallibility and provisionality*. (e) And, against Gadamer's *linguistic dualism*, and with 'the later' 'Wittgenstein', Thiselton regards 'language' as being 'multi-functional' where, for 'the later' 'Wittgenstein' and for Thiselton, *different linguistic "functions" are interwoven* within all language-uses (see Chapter 4). Thus, for Thiselton, 'assertions' play a role in "eventful" 'understanding'; and the later Wittgenstein notes the 'difference… between the utterance of fear, "I'm afraid!", and the report of fear, "I'm afraid"'.[87] Again, Thiselton's approach, when compared to Gadamer's approach, *more adequately re-historicizes language, and thence more adequately re-historicizes understanding.*

Hence, again, Thiselton's approach, when compared to Gadamer's approach, changes the grammar of a Continental terminology of "hermeneutical understanding" (e.g. "world", "horizons", "fusion", and "language-event") *through a kind of sublation that seeks to re-historicize understanding more adequately.* That is, Thiselton is less "Gadamerian" than some suggest. Further, Thiselton's 'critique… of Gadamer' is thus *far more complex* than R.E. Palmer's apparent suggestion that it is simply 'Pannenbergian'.[88]

However, if Thiselton changes Continental grammar, is he thereby guilty of acts of '"persuasive definition"' that are similar to those which he expounds 'Paul' as attacking in Corinth?[89] Shouldn't Continental terminology be left in its '"home"' 'language-games'?[90] Actually, in our view, Thiselton should be defended here. His stance is a critical 'synthesis of insights from broadly different… traditions'. Thiselton's stance is an instantiation of "tradition-modification" and not of

---

[84] Gadamer, *TM*, 487. Italics Gadamer's.

[85] cf.: Thiselton, 'U (long)', 90; Thiselton, *2H*, 307; Thiselton, 'TNI', 11; Thiselton, *NTH*, 440-441. Italics ours.

[86] cf.: Thiselton, *2H*, 314; Thiselton, *NTH*, xxii, concs. 1.2a-c; Thiselton, *NH*, 379-405. Italics ours.

[87] cf.: Thiselton, 'Parab', 450-451, 439, 466, 437-468; Thiselton, 'TY', 1562; Thiselton, *LLM*, 12-14; Wittgenstein, L., *Remarks on the Philosophy of Psychology. Volume 2* (eds. G.H. Von Wright and H. Nyman; trans. C.G. Luckhardt and M.A.E. Aue; Oxford: Blackwell, 1980), 121e. Italics ours.

[88] See, Maddox, R.L., 'Review of A.C. Thiselton's *The Two Horizons*', *ThStud* 43.1 (Mar. 1982), 136; cf. Watson, F., 'Review of A.C. Thiselton's *New Horizons in Hermeneutics*', *BibInterp* 4.2 (1996), 253; cf. Palmer, R.E., 'The Scope of Hermeneutics: The Problem of Critique, and the Crisis of Modernity', *TRevCTLit* 3 (1984), 226. Italics ours.

[89] Thiselton, 'TY', 1561; cf. Thiselton, 'SARX', 215-218.

[90] cf.: Thiselton, 'SARX', 216; cf. 215-218; Thiselton, 'REC', 514-518, 520-525.

"'persuasive definition'".[91] We will explain and justify this point later, in Chapter 6.

B) HERMENEUTICAL UNDERSTANDING AND SCIENTIFIC EXPLANATION, PARTICULAR AND GENERAL, AND PARTS AND WHOLES

Moving on, then Thiselton's 'hermeneutical circle' also involves "continuing", 'progressive', "dialogic" 'movement' 'between' hermeneutical 'understanding' (to use the median sense of this phrase) and 'explanation'. During Thiselton's second period, this 'movement' or polarity is largely manifest, (1), in relation to Thiselton's comments - after Gadamer, the later Wittgenstein and Ricoeur - on "movements" 'between' 'particular' and 'general' axes, and, (2), in relation to Thiselton's comments on traditional notions of "movements" 'between' 'parts' and "wholes".[92]

Thiselton's focus here has partially shifted from human *capacities* (conceptualization, and, intuition through experience) and *'performance'* ('textual' "effects", '"actualization"', 'critical' "testing", and so on – i.e. what we, including interpreters and authors, *do* with our capacities) to include inferences of *'historical' "structure"* ('parts'/"wholes" cf. historical "particularity"/historical 'continuity' or 'generality' cf. 'understanding'/ '"explanation"').[93]

Thus, (1), examining Thiselton's 'general' and 'particular' axes first, then we should note that whilst Thiselton allows for an *a posteriori* 'general' axis (see Chapter 6 on historical analogy), he rejects the *a priori* 'generalization' pertaining to 'idealist' and/or to "formalist" approaches. That is, Thiselton *re-historicizes the 'general' axis of hermeneutic process*. Notably, attacking (post-) 'Enlightenment' 'rationalist' pre-occupation with '"scientific method"' (cf. over-generalizing exegetical 'rules', 'principles', and 'abstract' "theory"), Thiselton reinstates 'historical' "particularity". For Thiselton, all 'generalization' that does not first respect 'historical' and 'textual' "particularity" is false – where, in relation to this point, Thiselton attacks 'traditional' approaches, early 'twentieth century' 'liberalism', and 'positivism'.[94]

Most notably, though, and in relation to this same point, Thiselton attacks 'ideological' 'structuralism' - from 'Lévi-Strauss' onwards - for disparaging

---

[91] Webster, 'R 2H', 220; cf. Thiselton, 'TY', 1561; cf. our Chapter 6.
[92] See footnote 94.
[93] See footnote 94. Italics ours.
[94] cf.: Thiselton, 'SBS', 334, 329, 331-333; Thiselton, 'TNI', 11; Thiselton, 'UPC', 93, 91, 94; Thiselton, *2H*, 104, 16, 294; Thiselton, 'TY', 1561; Thiselton, 'SARX', 213; Thiselton, 'SNTP', 76-79; Thiselton, 'Words', 293, 296; Thiselton, A.C., 'Review of J.F.A. Sawyer's *Semantics in Biblical Research*', *TSF* 70 (Aut. 1974), 18; Thiselton, 'NH', 320-329, 314-315; Thiselton, *LLM*, 28, 6, 31-32; Thiselton, 'KNT', 91, 93-95, 99; Thiselton, 'LMR', 1135, 1136; Thiselton, 'EITN', 582-583; Thiselton, 'Flesh', 681; Thiselton, A.C., 'Man Longs for the Status and Dignity of a 'Thou'', *CEN* 9 Jan. (1976), 9; Thiselton, 'U (long)', 95-97; Thiselton, 'AA', 594-595; Thiselton, 'P-BP', 88; Thiselton, 'MP', 5; Thiselton, 'Truth', 874-875, 881; Thiselton, A.C., 'Review of A.M. Johnson's *The New Testament and Structuralism*', *ExTim* 91 (Oct. 1979), 26-27; Thiselton, *NH*, 334-335, 344; cf. 344-378, 11. Italics ours.

'historical' and 'textual' "particularity".⁹⁵ Thiselton argues that the 'general' axis is not more 'objective' than the "particular" axis, and that "'biblical'" 'textual' "particularity" should not be subsumed by "mechanically applying" "generalizing" "'models'" derived "'from'" the "'narratives'" of "'folk, classical, or scholarly literature'".⁹⁶

Thiselton thus *also* argues that 'literary criticism' should not displace 'historical criticism' though, for Thiselton, the 'literary' 'distinction' between story... and plot', and R. Jacobson's 'model of addresser, context, message, code, and addressee', remain valuable – as, in Thiselton's estimate, do literary theories more broadly. Notably, however, whilst H. Frei is no 'ideological' "structuralist", Thiselton attacks Frei's 'history' versus 'history-likeness' 'distinction' for "presupposing" false "generalizing" alternatives between *either* 'report' "presupposing" 'referential theory' (then "excluded") *or* 'intra-linguistic' "constructs" divorced from 'history'.⁹⁷

Regarding 'ideological' 'structuralism', then Thiselton also argues that 'ideological' 'structuralism', in its pre-occupation with an *a priori* 'general' axis, artificially divorces 'texts' and 'meaning' from 'historical' 'particularity' by misappropriating 'Saussure's' thought. That is, in Thiselton's estimate, 'ideological' 'structuralism' wrongly up-anchors *'langue'* from 'history' in order to produce the ahistorical category, 'code', and wrongly disparages "historically" 'particular' *'parole'* as the category, 'message'.⁹⁸

Contrary to R. Barthes, however, Thiselton argues that 'message is not... a by-product of... code', but the pre-condition for "code's" derivation: in Thiselton's estimate, 'code' only partly shapes 'message'. Thiselton argues that appeals to 'Saussure's' "prioritization" of 'synchronic' 'linguistics' over 'diachronic' 'linguistics' cannot be used to justify the *neglect of* 'historical' 'particularity' since 'Saussure's' intention in this approach was to *guard* 'historical' 'particularity'. Moreover, Thiselton argues that since 'texts' are not just 'intra-linguistic' "phenomena" then, in Thiselton's estimate, 'meaning' is not just a matter of 'function within a self-referring system' 'of relations and' 'differences'. Rather, for Thiselton, 'meaning' "relates" irrevocably to 'historical' 'particularity' where, with the later Wittgenstein, Thiselton insists 'that... "...language is part of... a [historical] form of life'" (see Chapter 4).⁹⁹

Finally, in Thiselton's argument, 'ideological' 'structuralism' also reduces

---

⁹⁵ Thiselton, 'SBS', 331, 334, 329-330.

⁹⁶ Thiselton, 'SBS', 329, 331, 333-334.

⁹⁷ cf.: Thiselton, A.C., 'Review of N.R. Petersen's *Literary Criticism for New Testament Critics*', *ExTim* 90 (Feb. 1979), 153-154; Thiselton, 'SBS', 331; Thiselton, 'LMR', 1126-1129, 1131; Thiselton, *NTH*, xxviii, concs., 8.2, 8.2a-b, cf. 503-508; Thiselton, *NH*, 557. Italics ours.

⁹⁸ Thiselton, 'SBS', 329-334. Italics Thiselton's, except on the word, "*a priori*".

⁹⁹ cf.: Thiselton, 'SBS', 334, 329-331; Thiselton, 'LMR', 1123-1127; Thiselton, 'SNTI', 80; cf. 80-82; Thiselton, *NH*, 557; Thiselton, A.C., 'Review of J.-M. Benoist's *The Structural Revolution*', *ExTim* 90 (May 1979), 248.

*Hermeneutics and Responsible Interpretation* 229

theology to 'anthropology', 'historical' "continuities" and 'particularities' to "determinism" (excluding 'novelty' and 'eschatological' 'transformation'), and 'language-uses' to the "unconscious" "dimensions" of 'language'. But, in Thiselton's thinking, 'interpretation' cannot ignore theological, 'eschatological', 'historical', and 'conscious' "dimensions".[100]

Therefore, Thiselton argues that, during interpretative practice, "authorial" 'horizons' and "intentions", 'historical background', the 'results' 'of form criticism', 'message' content, 'textual' 'transmission', "authorial" 'language-uses' and '"actions"', and the 'public criteria' of 'tradition' cannot be ignored. For Thiselton, 'meaning' only relates secondarily to 'linguistic system'. Contradicting L. Zuidervaart's later criticisms of Thiselton (see Chapter 6), we should note that Thiselton's argument here qualifies his (i.e. Thiselton's) view of 'textuality' and his (i.e. Thiselton's) use of the phrase, '"the text itself"'. As F. Watson rightly summarizes: for Thiselton, 'a text is not… an autonomous, self-contained entity… separated from the broader context of the "life-world" within which it constitutes a communicative action'.[101]

(2) Moving on then, in Thiselton's view, after the 'early' 'Schleiermacher', the 'hermeneutical circle' involves "continuous", 'progressive', "dialogic" 'movement' 'between' 'parts' and "wholes". Thiselton argues that 'parts' are to be 'understood' in "relation" to "wholes", and vice versa, at various nested levels (e.g. 'words', 'sentences', "utterances", 'paragraphs', "language-games", "books", "authors", *'Sitz im Leben'*, "linguistic communities", "traditions" etc.). Ultimately, for Thiselton, drawing on 'Pannenberg', 'historical' 'parts' are to be '"understood"' in "relation" to "anticipations" of 'the eschatological' 'whole', and the latter – for both Pannenberg and Thiselton - is to be '"understood"' '"in relation to"' 'God'. For Thiselton, 'Christ', as the key to both 'the eschatological' and '"the divine"', is thus the key to the whole hermeneutical enterprise. Therefore, against B.J. Walsh's reading of Thiselton, we may observe that Thiselton does not succumb to '"Wittgensteinian"' 'subjectivism'. Thiselton's hermeneutical circle concludes at the Eschaton although, until then, admittedly, 'interpreters can never escape… the circle'. For Thiselton, 'movement' 'between' 'parts' and "wholes" is *'both'* 'critical' and '"intuitive"', where Thiselton argues that 'time' is needed to 'allow' "texts" 'to speak'. Notably, Thiselton argues that '"intuitive"' 'understanding' intuits "wholes" (for example, "authors" as "whole" "persons") and the *'relationships' 'between'* '"the parts"', and *'between'* '"the parts"' and whatever '"whole"' is under consideration. Clearly, though, for Thiselton, 'critical' '"comparative"' 'testing' of such 'relationships' is integral to 'explanation'. Thus, with 'Schleiermacher' and 'Dilthey', Thiselton argues that hermeneutical 'understanding is an *art* and a

---

[100] Thiselton, 'SBS', 331, 334, 330; cf. Thiselton, 'LMR', 1135, 1127; cf. Thiselton, *2H*, 79; cf. Thiselton, 'REC', 524. Italics Thiselton's.

[101] cf.: Thiselton, 'SBS', 334, 329-331; Thiselton, 'LMR', 1131-1135, 1123-1127; Zuidervaart, 'R *RH*', 296; Thiselton, *NH*, 57-58, 119, 17, 63; Thiselton, 'R-RH', 80-82, 113; Watson, 'R *NH*', 254.

*"science".* For Thiselton, drawing on H. Ott, 'movement' 'between' 'parts' and "wholes" also clarifies the 'relationships' 'between' 'exegesis' (cf. "parts"), 'systematic theology' (cf. 'pre-understanding', "whole"), and 'Scripture as a whole'.[102]

C) DISTANCING AND FUSION THROUGH QUESTION AND ANSWER: TOWARDS RE-HISTORICIZED OBJECTIVITY AND RE-HISTORICIZED SELF-INVOLVEMENT

Moving on, then Thiselton's 'hermeneutical circle' – in its adaptation of Gadamer's thinking - also involves "continuing", 'progressive', "dialogic" 'movement' 'between' the axes of "'distancing'" (cf. Gadamer's 'tension between the text and the present') and "'fusion'" (cf. Gadamer's 'fusion of horizons'). For Thiselton, "'distancing'" and "'fusion'" embrace "movements" 'between' 'textual' and 'reader' 'horizons' (cf. the 'two-sided' 'problem' and 'task of hermeneutics'), 'between synchronic and diachronic' considerations, 'between' various dimensions of ethical 'responsibility', 'between' considerations of different "levels" 'of context', 'between' 'textual' "action", 'actualization', 'appropriation', and 'application', and 'between' 'questions' "'and answers'". Thiselton's focus has now *largely* (though *not entirely*) shifted away from questions to do with human *capacities* and with *historical structure* and more firmly towards questions to do with *performance*, or towards questions to do with what *persons and texts do* during responsible interpretation.[103]

Thiselton argues that "'distancing'" and "'fusion'" presuppose that *both* "texts" *and* "interpreters" are "historically" 'conditioned', where Thiselton thus corrects "traditional" over-emphasis on the former. Hence, Thiselton both "respects" 'the integrity of the biblical text' (cf. 'distancing') and "explores" 'possibilities for responsible… appropriation' (cf. 'fusion'). This approach reflects Thiselton's later concerns to unite 'biblical interpretation and pastoral theology' and, in Thiselton's estimate, raises questions about the locus of 'meaning'.[104]

---

[102] cf.: Thiselton, *2H*, 103-104, 315; Walsh, 'TC', 227, 234-235; Thiselton, 'R *BQT*', 120, 121; Thiselton, 'SARX', 205; Thiselton, 'TNI', 11; Thiselton, 'UPC', 93-95; Thiselton, 'NH', 314-315, 323-327, 311; Thiselton, *LLM*, 8; Thiselton, 'LMR', 1135; Thiselton, 'EITN', 576; Thiselton, 'SNTI', 79; Thiselton, 'Par', 48-52; Thiselton, 'SBL', 113-118, 109; Thiselton, 'Truth', 900-901; Thiselton, *NH*, 215, 223, 344; Borsch, 'R *2H*', 89. Italics in speech-marks Thiselton's, except on *'relationships' 'between'* and on *'between'*.

[103] cf.: Thiselton, *2H*, 22, xix, 104, 309; Thiselton, 'UPC', 93, 87-88, cf. 91-94; Thiselton, 'NH', 310-329; Thiselton, 'SBS', 329, 334; Thiselton, 'SNTI', 80; Thiselton, 'SARX', 205; Thiselton, 'EITN', 576-577, 583-584; Thiselton, *LLM*, 8-9, 12; Thiselton, 'U (long)', 90-121; Thiselton, 'SBL', 108-118; Thiselton, *NH*, 11; Thiselton, 'R *UAB*', 341-343; Thiselton, 'MP', 4, 11-12; Thiselton, 'LMR', 1123-1125, 1135-1144; Thiselton, 'IT', 27, 31; Thiselton, 'TNI', 11; Thiselton, 'T&F', 11; Thiselton, 'Words', 293-296; Thiselton, *NTH*, 225-227; Gadamer, *TM*, 190-192, 265-266, 291-307, 374-375 - citations from 306.

[104] See previous footnote and: Thiselton, 'U (long)', 90, 91, 120; Thiselton, 'NH', 308; Morgan, 'R *2H*', 331; Thiselton, *2H*, 22, xix, 54, 60-63, 314-326; Thiselton, *NH*, 556, 557; cf. 556-619. Italics ours.

*Hermeneutics and Responsible Interpretation* 231

For Thiselton, 'distancing' relates to a "historically" re-configured or re-historicized (i.e. to a non-abstract, non-objectivistic, non-idealist) notion of 'objectivity' that respects historical *otherness* (see also Chapter 7) whilst, for Thiselton, 'fusion' relates to a "historically" re-configured or re-historicized (i.e. to a non-individualistic, non-anthropocentric, future-oriented, dynamic) notion of 'self-involvement' that respects historical *relationalities* (whether past, present, *or* future – see also Chapter 7). Querying D.W. Dayton's reading of Thiselton, Thiselton's dual-emphasis on "distancing and fusion" (1976 and earlier) *precedes*, and does not postdate, the dual-emphasis on "distancing and fusion" in C. Kraft's book, *Christianity and Culture* (1979).[105] We may now look at Thiselton's notions and employments of both distancing and fusion in more detail.

i) Distancing: Towards Re-Historicized or Historical Objectivity
For Thiselton, *distancing* (cf. "distanciation", "distanciations") elucidates the "objective" 'historical distance', "difference", '*otherness*', or 'tension' "'between'" 'textual' and 'reader' 'horizons' and/or "language-games"; and so, in Thiselton's estimate, distancing sheds light on 'intelligibility' 'problems'.[106] Thiselton argues that distancing – for the *most* part (unlike fusion) - demands "continuous" 'critical' 'study' and "testing", but that distancing *does also* involve 'creative' "'intuitive'" 'understanding'.[107]

Notably, (1), for Thiselton, distancing, 'in Biblical… hermeneutics', 'aims at' "understanding" 'the Bible' 'accurately', 'honestly', 'faithfully', 'responsibly', and 'obediently'.[108] Thus, for Thiselton, distancing aims to provide 'critical control over interpretation'. That is, for Thiselton, distancing aims to *avert "premature" "fusion of horizons"'* and/or to *avert* the projection or "imposition" of "interpreters"' 'prior' 'horizons' (including "generalizations") onto texts.[109]

---

[105] See previous three footnotes and: Thiselton, 'U (long)', 120; Thiselton, *2H*, 22; cf. Thiselton, 'NH', 326; Dayton, D.W., 'The Church in the World. The Battle for the Bible Rages On', *ThT* E37 (1980), 83. Italics ours.
[106] cf.: Thiselton, *2H*, 307-308; Thiselton, 'R *BQT*', 120, 121; Thiselton, 'UPC', 92-93; Thiselton, 'NH', 308-328; Thiselton, 'SBS', 329; Thiselton, 'SARX', 205; Thiselton, 'TY', 1564; Thiselton, 'PDT', 7; Thiselton, *LLM*, 16-21; Thiselton, 'EITN', 583-584; Thiselton, 'SBL', 111-116; Thiselton, 'U (long)', 99-104, 117-121; Thiselton, 'U (short)', 6; Thiselton, 'AA', 606-607; Thiselton, 'LMR', 1138; Thiselton, 'MP', 4, 10-12. First italics ours, second italics Thiselton's.
[107] cf.: Thiselton, 'UPC', 93; cf. 89-90; Thiselton, 'NH', 308-329; Thiselton, 'EITN', 583-584; Thiselton, *2H*, 309; Thiselton, 'U (long)', 104-105, 120-121.
[108] cf.: Thiselton, 'SBL', 113, 117-118; Thiselton, 'U (short)', 6; Thiselton, 'U (long)', 99-101, 104, 117-121.
[109] cf.: Thiselton, *2H*, xx, 326, 430, 319; Thiselton, 'UPC', 87-95, 98; Thiselton, 'SARX', 205, 215-218; Thiselton, 'NH', 308-329; Thiselton, 'PDT', 7; Thiselton, 'EITN', 582-584; Thiselton, *LLM*, 3-6; Thiselton, 'SBL', 108-113, 116-118; Thiselton, 'U (long)', 93, 97-105, 120-121; Thiselton, 'U (short)', 6; Thiselton, *NTH*, xxii, concs. 1.2a-c; Thiselton, 'AA', 595-597, 610-611; Thiselton, 'MP', 4, 11-12; Thiselton, 'LMR', 1138-1140; Thiselton, 'P-BP', 89;

Thiselton argues that the process of "premature fusion of horizons" (which Thiselton sometimes abbreviates to "premature fusion" or sometimes describes as "hermeneutical foreclosure") involves over-selective citation (cf. "proof-texting") in relation to, and fragmentation of, the textual message. Thus, in Thiselton's view, A. Schweitzer's and E. Käsemann's notions of an 'imminent Parousia' project splits between 'Paul' and 'Luke-Acts'.[110] Thiselton argues that, during reading or interpretation, premature fusion also "reflects" 'reader' 'horizons' 'back' from texts; and Thiselton argues that, during reading or interpretation, premature fusion thereby has the unfortunate result of "rendering" texts 'innocuous' and potentially 'boring'.[111] Thiselton warns that readers' "pre-understandings" may thus potentially stifle 'original' textual 'function' and 'effective communication'.[112] (Thiselton's examples of premature fusion are referenced in our footnotes).[113]

Thiselton readily admits that "interpreters" can 'only' "initially" approach texts 'with' existing "pre-understandings", but Thiselton insists that "interpreters" are 'not... [thereby] at the mercy of' a 'tyranny' of existing "pre-understandings".[114] For Thiselton, "absolutizing" 'one's' own (or one's community's own) 'cultural and philosophical assumptions' 'is' an 'idolatry' that suppresses 'the past'.[115] Thiselton argues that interpreters can be held under 'the spell of' 'narrow philosophical bases [biases?]' or under 'the spell of' "traditional" 'language', but that texts can still 'speak... *anew*' and "break" such "spells". For Thiselton, 'theological understanding' need not 'merely' serve 'prior' 'states of consciousness'.[116] Here, Thiselton's *re-historicized notions - both of pre-understanding and of the role of pre-understanding during interpretation - are in evidence:* for Thiselton, neither individual nor corporate pre-understandings should be imperialized since, in Thiselton's estimate, they are embedded within a *larger theological-historical whole.*

(2) For Thiselton, after 'Gadamer', distancing *"jogs"* readers *'into conscious awareness' of their previously unconscious 'pre-judgments':* for Gadamer and Thiselton 'encounter with a traditionary text can provide this provocation'. Thiselton thus rejects the socio-pragmatic practice of "imperializing" present "reader" 'horizons';

---

Thiselton, 'Truth', 898-899; Thiselton, 'SBS', 329, 331, 333-334; Klemm, D.E., 'Review of A.C. Thiselton's *The Two Horizons*', *JAARel* 50.1 (Mar. 1982), 116-117. Italics ours.

[110] Thiselton, A.C., 'Biblical Classics: VI. Schweitzer's Interpretation of Paul', *ExTim* 90 (Feb. 1979), 135; cf. Thiselton, 'Par', 34.

[111] Thiselton, 'NH', 328, 326, 316; cf.: Thiselton, 'SBL', 113, 117-118; Thiselton, 'PDT', 7; Thiselton, 'U (long)', 120.

[112] Thiselton, 'NH', 308-311; cf.: Thiselton, 'U (long)', 102, 90-92; Thiselton, 'U (short)', 6.

[113] cf.: Thiselton, 'U (long)', 90-92, 102-104, 120; Thiselton, 'MP', 7-8; Thiselton, A.C., 'Great Compassion and Heart. Review of J. Moltmann's *The Crucified God*', *CEN* 10 Jan. (1975), 9; Thiselton, 'U (short)', 6; Thiselton, 'SARX', 215-218; Thiselton, 'AA', 610-611.

[114] See previous footnote and, Thiselton, 'UPC', 93; cf. Thiselton, 'U (long)', 120, 102; cf. Thiselton, *2H*, xix; cf. Kleinig, 'R *2H*', 90; cf. Maddox, 'CHP', 526.

[115] See previous two footnotes and, McNicol, 'R *2H*', 188.

[116] See footnotes 113-114, and: Thiselton, *2H*, 432, 404; Thiselton, 'PDT', 7; Thiselton, 'NH', 309; McNicol, 'R *2H*', 188 (quoted); Borsch, 'R *2H*', 90. Italics Thiselton's.

*Hermeneutics and Responsible Interpretation* 233

for Thiselton, 'faithfulness to the… text' is an ethical 'responsibility' (see Chapter 7).[117] Thiselton argues that 'fresher, more accurate, and deeper understanding' emerges through a growing "awareness" 'of the modern context and its influence'.[118] With reference to Thiselton, F.H. Borsch rightly cites R.E. Palmer's illustration of the "invisibility" of 'water' to 'fish'. According to this illustration, the interpreter's 'task… is to make the contextual medium as visible as possible'.[119]

Thus, in Thiselton's thinking, clarifying "readers'" 'horizons' – 'horizons' that, in Thiselton's estimate, include "readers'" 'self-understanding[s]' - presupposes 'hermeneutics of selfhood', of 'Western culture' and of "traditions".[120] For Thiselton, hearing a text's 'challenge' without distortion involves "continuous" 'movement' 'between' assessments of 'the particularities' *both* of 'textual' 'horizons' *and* of "reader" 'horizons',[121] where Thiselton's approach thus transcends 'traditional' emphases on *"past"* 'historical and literary context'.[122]

(3) For Thiselton, distancing involves *'painstaking' 'exegesis' and 'critical scholarship'* (where, for Thiselton, 'critical scholarship' may be 'Biblical', 'theological', 'historical', 'linguistic', 'literary', 'sociological', "psychological", 'archeological', "philosophical" – and so on). Nevertheless, Thiselton still stresses that any 'modern reader' 'may' 'find in the Bible "all things necessary for salvation"'.[123] For Thiselton, drawing on the later Wittgenstein, distancing 'allows us to notice what was already there to be seen'.[124] Moreover, Thiselton urges that 'intellectual… integrity' need not undermine the 'Christian faith', but that 'intellectual… integrity' "serves" the 'Christian faith'.[125] Thiselton argues that distancing "prioritizes" 'synchronic' "investigations" over 'diachronic' "investigations". And Thiselton argues that distancing respects 'at least' *three over-lapping spheres* (B.J. Walsh blurs

---

[117] cf.: Thiselton, 'NH', 316-317, 311; Thiselton, 'UPC', 92-93; Thiselton, 'U (long)', 100, 121, 90, 97, 101, 119; Thiselton, *NH*, 27. Citation from, Gadamer, *TM*, 299. Italics ours.

[118] See previous footnote and, Dockery, 'R 2H', 134; cf. Poythress, 'R 2H', 178.

[119] Borsch, 'R 2H', 89.

[120] cf.: Thiselton, 'U (long)', 120; Thiselton, 'NH', 319, 317, 326-327; Thiselton, 'U (short)', 6; Thiselton, *IGPS*, 56.

[121] cf.: Thiselton, 'UPC', 93-94; Thiselton, *2H*, 104; Thiselton, 'NH', 323, 316-317, 327-328; Thiselton, 'PDT', 7; Thiselton, 'EITN', 583-584; Thiselton, 'SBL', 113, 117-118; Thiselton, 'U (long)', 99-101, 104, 120; Thiselton, 'SBS', 334, 329.

[122] Thiselton, 'SNTI', 90, 75, 83; cf. Thiselton, 'NH', 316. Italics ours.

[123] cf.: Thiselton, 'Doubt', 8.; Thiselton, 'AA', 604, 606; Thiselton, 'TT', 34; Thiselton, 'SNTI', 75, 79; Thiselton, 'ENE', 6; Thiselton, A.C., 'Review of C.K. Barrett's *A Commentary on the Second Epistle to the Corinthians*', *TSF* 71 (Spr. 1975), 29-30; Thiselton, 'EITN', 582-583; Thiselton, A.C., 'Review of R.P. Martin's *New Testament Foundations: A Guide for Christian Students. Vol. 1: The Four Gospels*', *CGrad* 29.3 (Sep. 1976), 85; Thiselton, 'U (long)', 99-101, 104, 117-121; Thiselton, 'U (short)', 6; Thiselton, 'MP', 5-6, 11-12; Thiselton, A.C. 'Review of I.H. Marshall's *I Believe in the Historical Jesus*', *CGrad* 30.4 (Dec. 1977), 117-118; Thiselton, 'REC', 511, 513. Italics ours.

[124] Thiselton, *2H*, 371; cf. quoting, Grech, 'R 2H', 573.

[125] cf.: Thiselton, 'R *IBHJ*', 118; Thiselton, 'AA', 609.

these into two) *of localized 'context'* that pertain (for the most part) to textual horizons. Thiselton thus argues that distancing is a process of "relating" language-use 'to its... environment' - as follows.[126]

Thus, (a), against "abstract" "generalizing" approaches, Thiselton inquires into *'extra-linguistic' 'historical' 'background' or 'context of situation'*, and thereby highlights 'historical' 'particularities'.[127] Thiselton employs the 'criteria' of 'logical' (i.e. internal) 'coherence' and of 'correspondence' to 'states of affairs' for the comparative 'testing' of the hypotheses offered by historical reconstructions.[128] Thiselton argues that textual and 'archeological' 'evidence', as well as socio-historical 'analyses', can correct historical inaccuracies.[129]

Against what Thiselton perceives to be contemporary over-emphases on 'present' 'horizons', Thiselton justifies his *re-historicizing approach to textual horizons* by making three appeals: (i) after 'J.L. Austin's' and D.D. Evans' 'logic of self-involvement', Thiselton argues that the "effective" "operation" of "speech-acts" presupposes the actuality of "'certain'" *'background' 'states of affairs'* (i.e. "institutional" or "'conventional'" 'procedures', "speakers", and 'circumstances').[130] (ii) Drawing on the later Wittgenstein, Thiselton reinstates *author-profiles*, including authorial 'orientations', 'pre-judgments', 'language-uses', and "interactions" with 'wider' 'cultural' 'settings' (see Chapter 4) though[131] - with Bultmann – Thiselton rejects "positivist" "generalizing" "biographies" of Jesus' 'psychological development': for Bultmann and Thiselton, *'interest in the personality of Jesus* is excluded'.[132] (iii) After Saussure, Thiselton makes broadly synchronic *inter-authorial and inter-textual comparisons* related to authorial "presuppositions" and "language-use", textual 'content', historical background, and "'directedness'" of authorial 'argument'.[133] In Thiselton's hermeneutics, after Saussure, 'diachronic' comparisons are of secondary importance. And yet, in Thiselton's estimate,

---

[126] cf.: Thiselton, 'SARX', 224, 205, 215; Thiselton, 'U (short)', 6; Thiselton, 'SNTI', 80-82; Thiselton, 'Words', 289; Thiselton, 'SBL', 111-112; Thiselton, 'SBS', 330-331; Thiselton, 'TI', 27; Walsh, 'TC', 224-225. Italics ours.

[127] cf.: Thiselton, 'SARX', 205, 212, 215; Thiselton, 'SNTI', 79; Thiselton, 'SBS', 334; Thiselton, A.C., "Understanding the New Testament'. Review of J.D.G. Dunn's *Unity and Diversity in the New Testament*, *CEN* 23 Dec. (1977), 8. Italics ours.

[128] cf.: Thiselton, 'SARX', 205-206, 210-212; Thiselton, 'Truth', 894-896.

[129] cf.: Thiselton, 'Sch', 136; Thiselton, 'AA', 606-607; Thiselton, 'TI', 17.

[130] cf.: Thiselton, 'UPC', 95-96, 98; Thiselton, 'Words', 293-296; Thiselton, 'AA', 611; Thiselton, 'U (long)', 104, 120; Thiselton, 'MP', 8; Thiselton, *LLM*, 16, 18, 20-21; Thiselton, 'LMR', 1139; Thiselton, 'SNTI', 76; Thiselton, 'Parab', 438; Thiselton, 'SARX', 212; Thiselton, 'Truth', 894; Thiselton, *NTH*, xxviii, concs. 8.2, 8.2b-c, 8.3. Italics ours.

[131] cf.: Thiselton, 'NH', 314; Thiselton, 'UPC', 92, 93; Thiselton, *LLM*, 3-6; Thiselton, 'Sch', 136; Thiselton, 'AA', 595-596. Italics ours.

[132] Thiselton, 'P-BP', 88-89; cf.: Thiselton, 'SNTI', 79; Thiselton, *2H*, 220-221; Bultmann, R., *Jesus and the Word* (trans. L.P. Smith and E.H. Lantero; London: Collins/Fontana Books, 1958), 13-14; quoting, 14. Italics Bultmann's.

[133] cf.: Thiselton, 'TI', 20-30, 15; Thiselton, *NH*, 13; Thiselton, *LLM*, 6. Italics ours.

*Hermeneutics and Responsible Interpretation* 235

'diachronic' comparisons still help establish textual relevance across historical distance.[134]

(b) Thiselton inquires into *'shared' 'working' "frames of reference"*, 'shared' "language-games" (cf. the later Wittgenstein), or into "common worlds" of "'understanding'" (cf. Fuchs).[135] Broadly speaking, Thiselton overcomes 'intelligibility' "problems" by highlighting the "'original'" "frames of reference", or the "language-games" and "traditions", in which 'Biblical language' "functions" - i.e. (in later Wittgensteinian terms) "'by watching how others play'". For Thiselton, this process involves clarifying "correlations" 'between… situations', 'behavior', 'and' 'language' in 'Biblical' "language-games" against 'the… background' of the 'public criteria of meaning' (including 'historical' 'report') embedded in 'Biblical' 'narratives'. Thiselton, drawing on Pannenberg and on the later Wittgenstein, argues that such 'narratives' disclose 'foundation events' that are "typologically" and "paradigmatically" "'normative'" for the 'intelligibility' and authentication of past and present 'Christian language-uses', religious 'experience[s]', and 'identity'.[136]

In this context, (i), Thiselton reinstates inquiry into texts' *"'original'" 'settings'*, and attacks 'persuasive definition', 'infinite polyvalency', 'irresponsible' "recontextualizations", 'abstract' "generalizing" treatments 'of meaning', and "'atomizing exegesis'".[137] Thiselton thus argues that word-meaning is not 'essential', but that word-meaning is normally related to 'use-context' and to 'the particularities of' 'language-uses'.[138] After the later Wittgenstein, Thiselton argues that "interpreters" must be "trained" in how 'words' and 'concepts' were "'used… in'" 'their "home"' 'language-games' and "communities" of 'tradition' (cf. "logical contexts", 'surroundings', 'settings', "'world'", "contexts-in-life"): for the later Wittgenstein and for Thiselton, 'the sense' is not 'an atmosphere accompanying the word'.[139]

In this context of discussion, Thiselton cites 'apocalyptic' and so-called

---

[134] cf.: Thiselton, *2H*, 126; Thiselton, 'SNTI', 80-82; Thiselton, 'IT', 26-27; 31; Thiselton, *LLM*, 8-9.

[135] Thiselton, 'SARX', 205, 215; cf. Thiselton, 'NH', 320, 311, 321-322. Italics ours, except: Thiselton's on *'working'*.

[136] cf.: Thiselton, 'MP', 4, 10-11; Thiselton, *LLM*, 3, 4; Thiselton, 'Truth', 894; Thiselton, 'SARX', 212; Thiselton, 'M&M', 8; Thiselton, *2H*, 437; Thiselton, 'U (long)', 117; cf. 115-120.

[137] cf.: Thiselton, 'MP', 11; Thiselton, 'SARX', 215-218; Thiselton, *NH*, 518; Thiselton, 'R-RH', 83, 109-113; Thiselton, 'REC', 514-518, 520-525; Thiselton, 'CAP', 137-139; Thiselton, *LLM*, 4, 9, 13, 31-32; Thiselton, 'UNT', 8; Thiselton, 'LMR', 1127-1130, 1138; Thiselton, 'SNTI', 78-79 - cited in, Walsh, 'TC', 224. Italics ours.

[138] See previous footnote and, Palmer, R.E., 'Review of A.C. Thiselton's *The Two Horizons*', *RevMet* 35.1 (1981), 173; quoting, Borsch, 'R *2H*', 90; cf. Thiselton, 'LMR', 1131.

[139] cf.: Thiselton, 'NH', 308; Thiselton, *2H*, 376; Thiselton, *LLM*, 3-6, 9, 12-13; Thiselton, 'LMR', 1131; cf. 1131-1135; Thiselton, 'SARX', 216; cf. 215-218; quoting, Wittgenstein, L., *Philosophical Investigations* (trans. G.E.M. Anscombe; Oxford: Blackwell, 1953, 2001), 48.

'"religious" language' (the latter is *not* a separate category in Thiselton – see Chapter 4) more broadly as examples.[140] Thiselton stresses that '"New Testament'" "concepts" should not be defined 'outside a given context or language-game'. Against P. Ellingworth's reading of Thiselton, we should note that Thiselton does *not* 'remove theological concepts to a safe place outside history'.[141] Rather, Thiselton argues, after the later Wittgenstein, that '"when language-games change, then there is a change in concepts, and with the concepts the meanings of words change"'.[142]

(ii) Thiselton also reinstates inquiry into *'linguistic' 'functions' 'within'* '"original'" 'settings'. Thiselton stresses that "interpreters" need to be aware of 'polysemy', 'polymorphous' "concepts", "concepts" '"with blurred edges"', the particularities of 'linguistic' 'functions', 'grammatical statements' that explicate 'concepts', and of other kinds of potentially 'creatively' "functioning" '"propositions"'.[143] Thiselton argues that "authorial" 'language-uses' need to be "placed" in their 'original' 'interpersonal' 'setting' of 'communication' with 'original' "audiences".[144] After the later Wittgenstein, Thiselton argues that the 'traditional' "reduction" of 'language' to 'information' fails to detect the "multiple" 'linguistic' 'functions' that often operate 'behind' 'surface-grammar': for the later Wittgenstein and for Thiselton, 'language' does *not* 'always' "function" 'in one way… to convey thoughts'.[145] (We have already corrected J. Barr on the relationship between 'philosophical' and 'linguistic

---

[140] Thiselton, 'NHP', 5; cf. Thiselton, 'LMR', 1132; cf. 1132-1137; Thiselton, 'H-O', 8; Thiselton, 'Par', 31-35; Thiselton, 'UPC', 96-98; Thiselton, *LLM*, 4-6; Thiselton, 'REC', 522-525; Thiselton, 'SARX', 215-218. Italics ours.

[141] Thiselton, *2H*, 407-415; quoting, Dyrness, W.A., 'Review of A.C. Thiselton's *The Two Horizons*', *CTday* 25 (Apr. 10, 1981), 94; second and third quotes from, Ellingworth, 'R *2H*', 179. Italics ours.

[142] Thiselton, 'UPC', 96-97; cf. Wittgenstein, *OC*, 10e.

[143] cf.: Thiselton, *LLM*, 4, 12; Thiselton, 'Words', 298, 287, 289-290; Thiselton, 'SARX', 216; Thiselton, 'NH', 308; Thiselton, 'Parab', 438, 456, 453; Thiselton, *2H*, 388; Thiselton, A.C., 'On the Logical Grammar of Justification in Paul. Paper Presented to the Fifth International Congress on Biblical Studies, Oxford, 1973', in *Studia Evangelica 7* (ed. E.A. Livingstone; Berlin: Akademie-Verlag, 1982), 493-495; Thiselton, 'Flesh', 681; Thiselton, 'LMR', 1124; cf. 1126-1127; Thiselton, 'Truth', 877; Thiselton, 'SNTI', 93-95, 98, 100; Thiselton, 'UPC', 98. Italics ours.

[144] cf.: Thiselton, A.C., 'Important Achievement. Review of G. Kittel and G. Friedrich eds. *Theological Dictionary of the New Testament, Volume 8*', *CEN* 10 Nov. (1972), 8; Thiselton, 'SNTI', 76, 80-82; Thiselton, 'ENE', 6; Thiselton, 'SBL', 109-112; Thiselton, 'Truth', 887, 874-878; Thiselton, *LLM*, front cover; Thiselton, 'SBS', 334, 329, 331; Thiselton, 'LMR', 1127; Thiselton, 'UPC', 97; Thiselton, 'SARX', 216; cf. 215-218; Thiselton, 'R-RH', 84; Thiselton, 'U (long)', 90; cf. 90-92, 97, 101, 119. Italics Thiselton's.

[145] cf.: Thiselton, 'SARX', 205-210; Thiselton, 'SNTI', 79; Thiselton, *LLM*, 10-14; Thiselton, 'UPC', 94-98; Thiselton, 'TY', 1562; Thiselton, 'NH', 312, 326; Thiselton, 'U (long)', 105-106, 121; Thiselton, *2H*, 396; Thiselton, 'Truth', 887; quoting, Wittgenstein, *PI*, 102.

semantics' in Thiselton).[146]

(iii) Thiselton reinstates inquiry into *"authorial" "intent"* – or into what Thiselton identifies as the 'linguistic' *'directedness'* of "authorial" 'argument'. That is, Thiselton reinstates this inquiry into *"authorial" "intent" without* conceiving 'purpose', 'intention', 'meaning', or 'thought' in 'psychologistic' or 'mentalist' terms (see Chapters 4 and 7).[147] Thus, contradicting E.E. Johnson's and B.J. Walsh's readings of Thiselton respectively, we should note that 'Thiselton' does not "reject" "authorial intent" or neglect textual 'purpose',[148] (cf. Gadamer):[149] Thiselton cites the ethical 'responsibility' of 'faithful' 'communication' as (part of the) grounds for a critique of authorial 'action', particularly – in addition - in relation to 'preaching', ecclesial 'language-uses', and 'Western' language-use more broadly. For Gadamer, however, 'subjective intentions' and/or 'the *mens auctoris*' are "left" 'behind'.[150]

(iv) Thiselton reinstates inquiry into *"transmitted" textual 'content'*, particularly into 'historical' "report" and 'assertions'.[151] Thiselton argues that "criteria" of 'logical' 'coherence' and of "authenticity" relative to 'public criteria' are relevant to 'testing' 'interpretative' 'hypotheses' (see, for example, Thiselton's second-period exegesis of 1 Corinthians).[152] For Thiselton, responsible interpretation addresses *specific*

---

[146] cf. Chapter 4; cf. Barr, 'R *NTT*, 234.

[147] cf.: Thiselton, A.C., 'The Ministry and the Church Union: Some Logical and Semantic Factors', *FUty* 18 (1974), 46; Thiselton, 'EITN', 582-583, 576; Thiselton, *NH*, 559-560, 223, 267, 559-561; Thiselton, 'U (long)', 90, 97, 101, 119; Thiselton, 'AA', 607; Thiselton, 'SBS', 334, 329, 331; Thiselton, 'IT', 35-36; Thiselton, A.C., 'Review of A. Kenny's *Wittgenstein*', *Chman* 90.1 (1976), 72; Thiselton, 'LMR', 1129-1130. Italics: *"authorial" "intent"* (ours), *'directedness'* (Thiselton's), *"authorial" "intent" without* (ours).

[148] See previous footnote and: Watson, 'R *NH*', 255; Johnson, E.E., 'Review of A.C. Thiselton's *New Horizons in Hermeneutics*', *BibSac* 150.600 (Oct.-Dec. 1993), 502; Walsh, 'TC', 234.

[149] See previous two footnotes and, Brodie, 'R *2H*', 484; cf. Gadamer, *TM*, 294-296, 276-277; cf. Gadamer, H.-G., 'Aesthetics and Hermeneutics', in *Philosophical Hermeneutics* (H.-G. Gadamer; ed. D.E. Linge; London: University of California Press, 1976), 103; cf. Gadamer, H.-G., 'The Philosophical Foundations of the Twentieth Century', in *Philosophical Hermeneutics* (H.-G. Gadamer; ed. D.E. Linge; London: University of California Press, 1976), 122.

[150] Thiselton, *NH*, 410-470; cf.: Thiselton, *2H*, 330; cf.: Thiselton, A.C., 'The Multi-Model Character of Holy Spirit Language', *CEN* 11 Apr. (1974), 8; Thiselton, 'U (long)', 100, 101; Thiselton, 'MCU', 45; Thiselton, 'LMR', 1143; quoting, Gadamer, 'Aesthetics', 103. Italics Gadamer's.

[151] cf.: Thiselton, 'Exc', 12; Thiselton, 'UPC', 87-88, 97-98; Thiselton, 'SARX', 215-218; Thiselton, 'H-O', 8; Thiselton, 'NH', 320-329, 311-312; Thiselton, 'Till', 98-99, 92-95, 90, 87, 102-103; Thiselton, 'TY', 1560; Thiselton, 'KNT', 95; Thiselton, 'SBL', 109-110; Thiselton, 'SBS', 334, 329, 331; Thiselton, 'Truth', 896-897; Thiselton, *NTH*, 4-6; Thiselton, 'IT', 36, 21. Italics ours.

[152] cf.: Thiselton, 'Truth', 894, 896-897, 892; Thiselton, 'IT', 16; Thiselton, 'Sch', 136; Thiselton, 'UPC', 94, 96, 98; Thiselton, 'E-CR', 8; Thiselton, 'Till', 92; Thiselton, 'Flesh',

*"debates"* in relation to 'content' (e.g. 'Paul's' view of 'tongues'), and employs 'theological', 'philosophical', and 'linguistic' 'tools'.[153] Conversely, Thiselton argues that 'Bultmann' wrongly disparages biblical 'content'. Thus, for example, Bultmann argues that 'Christian preaching… does not offer a doctrine which can be accepted either by reason or by a *sacrificium intellectus*'. Thiselton also argues that some writers "over-press" 'biblical' 'unity' and that other writers "over-press" 'biblical' 'diversity'.[154] Finally, querying L.O. Hynson's and J.W. Voelz's readings of Thiselton, we should note that Thiselton's stress on 'content' reflects *neither* an *over*-emphasis on 'reader-response' *nor* an *under*-emphasis on 'reader-response'.[155]

(c) Thiselton inquires into *'broader and narrower' 'literary' and 'linguistic contexts'* which, in Thiselton's view, are inseparable from 'extra-linguistic' 'considerations'.[156] Notably, (i), Thiselton repudiates *over-'generalization'* with respect to 'literary' "questions" about 'setting', "manuscripts", 'genre', 'style',[157] and about different text "types".[158] Admittedly, Thiselton allows that a text's communicative 'function' or 'style' can be more '"direct"' or more "indirect", more 'closed' or more 'open'.[159] However, Thiselton avoids both over-"generalizing" *'models' of 'texts'* that suppress "particularity" of 'function', 'content', or 'genre' (cf. 'language-games'),[160] and over-'generalizing' *"strategies of interpretation"* (cf. 'rules, guiding

---

681-682; Thiselton, 'U (long)', 115-117, 121; Thiselton, 'MP', 10-11; Thiselton, 'LMR', 1143, 1132, 1134-1135, 1137; Thiselton, *NH*, 260, 261; Thiselton, 'SBS', 334, 331.

[153] Thiselton, 'UPC', 89-91, 95-98; cf.: Thiselton, 'SARX', 224; Thiselton, 'IT', 15-18, 28-32, 34-36; Thiselton, 'Sch', 136. Italics ours.

[154] cf.: Thiselton, 'UPC', 96, 98; Thiselton, 'NH', 324-325; Thiselton, 'AA', 605; Thiselton, 'UNT', 8; Thiselton, 'R *IBHJ*', 117-118; Thiselton, 'U (short)', 6; quoting, Bultmann, R., *Jesus Christ and Mythology* (New York: Charles Scribner's Sons, 1958), 36. Italics Bultmann's.

[155] Querying, Hynson, L. O., 'Review of R. Lundin's, A.C. Thiselton's and C. Walhout's *The Responsibility of Hermeneutics*', *ChSRev* 18.1 (1988), 91; cf. Voelz, J.W., 'Multiple Signs, Levels of Meaning and Self as Text: Elements of Intertextuality', *Sem* 69-70 (1995), 157 n.12; cf. Thiselton, *NH*, 499, 501-502.

[156] Thiselton, 'SARX', 205, 215; cf. Thiselton, 'SNTI', 78-79. Italics ours.

[157] Thiselton, 'Parab', 466; cf.: Thiselton, 'UPC', 96; Thiselton, 'SNTI', 79; Thiselton, 'U (short)', 6; Thiselton, 'EITN', 582-583; Thiselton, *LLM*, 3. Italics ours.

[158] Thiselton, 'Till', 100-101; cf.: Thiselton, 'UPC', 89-90; Thiselton, *LLM*, 22-24, 29-31; Thiselton, *NH*, 557.

[159] Thiselton, *LLM*, 16; cf.: Thiselton, 'KNT', 99, 101; Thiselton, 'EITN', 577; Thiselton, 'Parab', 466; Thiselton, A.C., "'Behind' and 'In Front Of' the Text: Language, Reference and Indeterminacy', in *After Pentecost: Language and Biblical Interpretation* (eds. C.G. Bartholomew, C. Greene and K. Möller; Scripture and Hermeneutics Series; Vol. 2; Carlisle: Paternoster, 2001), 104.

[160] cf.: Thiselton, 'SBS', 334; Thiselton, *LLM*, 16; Thiselton, 'Parab', 462-468; Thiselton, 'EITN', 582; Thiselton, 'SARX', 216; Thiselton, 'Till', 92; Thiselton, 'NH', 324-325. Italics ours.

principles, universal maxims', or "'method'").[161]

(ii) Thiselton promotes the ethical 'responsibility' of finding an 'appropriate' 'interpretative strategy' (singular) through the 'testing' of *multiple 'models', "strategies", and 'critical' 'tools'* (plural) in each 'particular case' (i.e. in each 'particular' instance of interpretation and in relation to each 'particular' text or other "object" – even including readers themselves - being interpreted). In Thiselton's hermeneutics, different text-"types" - for example 'parables',[162] 'metaphors' and 'models',[163] biblical ("'broken'") 'myth',[164] 'narrative',[165] 'typology', 'allegory', 'analogy',[166] 'imagery',[167] and 'apocalyptic'[168] - require different approaches. Thiselton argues that 'the integrity of any particular literary genre… must be respected' where, later, Thiselton also stresses 'the particularities' of *'reading-situations'* and "goals".[169]

Therefore, against W.G. Jeanrond's and others' search for 'a *general* notion of 'textuality', Thiselton advocates using a plurality of 'models' of 'textuality'.[170] Thiselton also advocates using a plurality of "strategies of interpretation" and of "'critical'" "tools" *so as to* maximize the number of "vantage-points" on any given problem, maximize "'hermeneutical sensitivity'", and preserve "'faithfulness'" to "historical-textual particularity".[171] Later, Thiselton rejects the "imperializing" of 'single' 'models' as 'controlling' or "'overarching interpretative keys'": for

---

[161] cf.: Thiselton, 'NH', 310, 314, 317, 323; Thiselton, *LLM*, 32; Thiselton, *NH*, 296. Italics ours.

[162] cf.: Thiselton, 'Parab', 462-468; Thiselton, 'UPC', 95, 87; Thiselton, 'NH', 316, 311-312, 319-326; Thiselton, *NH*, 296; Thiselton, 'SBL', 109-110; Thiselton, 'U (long)', 121, 90-92; Thiselton, *NTH*, xxv, conc. 5.2d; Thiselton, 'SBS', 334; Thiselton, 'AA', 609; Thiselton, *LLM*, 22. Italics ours.

[163] Thiselton, 'M-M', 8; cf. Thiselton, *LLM*, 25-27.

[164] Thiselton, 'M&M', 8; cf.: Thiselton, *LLM*, 27-31; Thiselton, 'M,M', 333-343; Thiselton, 'MP', 4-12.

[165] Thiselton, 'Till', 98, 100-101; cf. Thiselton, *LLM*, 31-32; cf. Thiselton, 'SBL', 115-116.

[166] Thiselton, A.C., 'For Serious Students of St. Paul. Review of A.T. Hanson's *Studies in Paul's Technique and Theology*', *CEN* 9 Aug. (1974), 10; cf. Thiselton, 'M,M', 340; cf. Thiselton, *LLM*, 27-31; cf. Thiselton, 'LMR', 1132-1134.

[167] Thiselton, *LLM*, 31-32; cf.: Thiselton, 'MP', 4, 12; Thiselton, 'LMR', 1134.

[168] Thiselton, 'NHP', 5; cf. Thiselton, 'LGT', 8; cf. Thiselton, A.C., 'Review of D.S. Russell's *Apocalyptic, Ancient and Modern*', *Th* 82.687 (May 1979), 219.

[169] Thiselton, *NH*, 557-558, 618; cf. quoting, Walsh, 'TC', 226. Italics Thiselton's.

[170] See footnotes for previous paragraph and: Thiselton, *NH*, 129, xi, 557-558, 31-141; Jeanrond, W., 'Review of R. Lundin's, A.C. Thiselton's and C. Walhout's *The Responsibility of Hermeneutics*', *LitTh* 1.1 (Mar. 1987), 117; Papaphilippopoulos, 'R *NH*', 141. Italics Thiselton's.

[171] See footnotes for previous paragraph and: Thiselton, *NH*, 296; Thiselton, 'R-RH', 81, 89; Jensen, P.T., 'Review of R. Lundin's, A.C. Thiselton's and C. Walhout's *The Responsibility of Hermeneutics*', *Ety* 37.6 (Jun. 1986), 49; Thiselton, 'SBS', 334.

Thiselton, each 'model' is only "'exploratory'".[172]

Thiselton also "meta-criticizes" 'critical' practices in the light of his developing theoretical hermeneutical critiques. His meta-criticisms of 'positivist' 'historical-critical' "methods", of 'Bultmann's' "existentialist" *'Sachkritik'*, and of traditional 'form-criticism' are examples.[173] Later, Thiselton argues 'that neither one's interpretative tradition nor newer hermeneutical models should take precedence over the text of Scripture'. Thiselton stresses that each 'model... should' 'be tested and if necessary modified in the actual process of interpreting particular texts'.[174] In 1992 Thiselton adds the point that, 'we must... evaluate theories of texts on their own terms'.[175]

Thiselton's transformed framework for hermeneutics, then, *is not* a 'single' textual 'model', 'interpretative strategy', "reading-situation", "reading-goal", or 'critical tool'. Rather, Thiselton's transformed framework for hermeneutics is a dialogically-broadened theological-philosophical subtext or paradigm that *allows for historical particularity, and for historical plurality*, in relation *to* these practical aspects of interpretation – i.e. in relation to textual "models", 'interpretative' "strategies", "reading-situations", "reading-goals", and 'critical' "tools". That is, Thiselton's *re-historicizing approach to textual horizons* (which respects historical particularity and historical plurality) necessarily entails a *re-historicizing approach to "texts themselves", to models of texts, to reading situations, to reading goals, to interpretative strategies, and to critical tools*. For Thiselton, since *readers and texts* reflect historical particularity and historical plurality, then readers' *interpretative approaches to* texts must *also* reflect the historical particularity, and the historical plurality, of readers and texts.[176]

(iii) It is *in the context of this continued process of "re-historicizing"* that Thiselton *extends semantics* beyond 'traditional' "lexicographical" concerns 'about vocabulary' and 'surface-grammar' to include consideration of 'semantic' 'field' 'relations' (see Chapter 4).[177] Thiselton aims to clarify 'semantic systems', 'semiotic elements', 'oppositions', 'relations between oppositions' (Thiselton employs 'structuralist' 'methods' 'without' adopting 'structuralist ideology'), and the effects of "sign"-'relations' (*'langue'*) on 'possibilities' of 'language-*uses*' (*'parole'*).[178] Thiselton argues

---

[172] Thiselton, *NH*, 75, 27, 557-558; quoting, Zuidervaart, 'R *RH*', 294; cf.: Thiselton, 'R-RH', 100, 89; Thiselton, *2H*, 432; Brett, M.G., 'Review of A.C. Thiselton's *New Horizons in Hermeneutics*', *Th* 96.772 (Jul./Aug. 1993), 315.

[173] Thiselton, *2H*, 76, 70, 266, 396-397; cf. 69-84, 265-266; cf. Thiselton, *NH*, 316, 317. Italics Thiselton's.

[174] Thiselton, 'R-RH', 83; cf. 82, 89, 100-101; paraphrased in, Zuidervaart, 'R *RH*', 294.

[175] Thiselton, *NH*, 75; cf. quoted in, Moore, S.D., 'Review of A.C. Thiselton's *New Horizons in Hermeneutics*', *ThT* 50.2 (Jul. 1993), 288.

[176] Thiselton, 'R-RH', 100, 81; cf. Thiselton, *NH*, 32, 296, 618. Italics ours.

[177] Thiselton, 'LMR', 1123; cf. Thiselton, 'SNTI', 82-85, 90, 92-95; cf. Thiselton, *LLM*, 3, 10; cf. Thiselton, 'MCU', 45-47. Italics ours.

[178] Thiselton, 'SBS', 329, 330, 332; cf.: Klein, 'R *2H*', 74; Thiselton, 'LMR', 1127. Italics Thiselton's.

that semantic considerations aid "exegetical" 'precision', 'honesty', and 'faithfulness', 'providing... objective... scientific... control[s]' in relation to textual 'particularity'. Thus, Thiselton argues that it is necessary to discern 'semantic relations' in a "donor" "'language'" prior to translating to 'equivalents' in a 'receptor language'.[179]

Finally, in addition to the three more localized 'contexts' outlined here, Thiselton's notion of 'distancing' also sets "historical particularity" against broader "traditional", 'eschatological', and Christological/theological contextual backdrops (see Chapters 4, 6 and 7).[180]

ii) Fusion: Towards Re-Historicized or Historical Self-Involvement
Moving on then, for Thiselton, on the one hand, *'fusion'* allows 'readers' to be "addressed" and "transformed" from 'beyond' their 'own' 'historical' 'horizons'. However, Thiselton *also* argues, on the other hand, that asking "stereotypical" 'questions' "reflects" 'back', "supports", "clarifies", or "secures" *'prior* convictions', "understandings", or "traditions". Therefore, Thiselton insists that, in the context of biblical hermeneutics, 'fusion' should combat traditionalistic processes that involve the "domestication" or "taming" of the 'biblical' "texts" – processes that, in addition, render the 'biblical' "texts" 'predictable' or 'boring'. That is, in Thiselton's estimate, 'fusion' should *facilitate or liberate* textual "'action'" and "effects" *from traditionalism* (which *suppresses* textual "'action'" and "effects").[181]

Thus, in Thiselton's thinking, "fusion" is pre-conditional for 'genuine understanding',[182] and encompasses the 'existential' 'self-involvement' of 'readers' (individually or corporately) during "eventful", "continuing" 'movement' 'between' *textual "'action'"*, *"'actualization'"*, *'appropriation'*, *and "application"* (see below).[183] Thiselton sometimes uses the term 'understanding' almost synonymously with the term 'fusion', and thus develops Gadamer's notion of "'understanding'" in which "'understanding'" is "'always already applying'" where, for Gadamer and Thiselton, 'all reading involves application'.[184] That is, for Thiselton, 'fusion' avoids a dualism between "inner" and "outer" 'response'.[185]

---

[179] cf.: Thiselton, 'SBL', 113, 117-118; Thiselton, 'SNTI', 90; Thiselton, 'LMR', 1141-1142; Thiselton, *2H*, 120; Thiselton, 'R *SBR*', 18.

[180] Thiselton, 'SARX', 205; cf.: Thiselton, *2H*, 117; Thiselton, 'SBS', 334; Thiselton, 'LMR', 1135, 1127; Thiselton, 'Par', 51; cf. 46-53.

[181] cf.: Thiselton, 'UPC', 93; cf. 92-94; Thiselton, *LLM*, 16; Thiselton, 'Till', 101-102; Thiselton, 'NH', 316-317, 310-312, 320, 323, 328; Thiselton, A.C., 'Dialogue and the Dangers of Half-Truths', *CEN* 9 Apr. (1976), 8, 10; Thiselton, 'U (long)', 90, 97, 100-101, 119; Thiselton, 'PDT', 7; Thiselton, 'Words', 293-296. Italics ours.

[182] See previous footnote and, Kleinig, 'R *2H*', 89.

[183] cf.: Thiselton, 'NH', 312-316; Thiselton, *LLM*, 16; Thiselton, *2H*, 104; Thiselton, *NH*, 11; Thiselton, 'Words', 293; Thiselton, 'U (long)', 101, 120; Thiselton, 'UPC', 91-94; Thiselton, 'TNI', 11; Thiselton, 'U (short)', 6; Thiselton, 'CH', 5. Italics ours.

[184] Cited in Thiselton, 'NH', 316, 317; cf. Gadamer, *TM*, 307-341; quoting 340.

[185] Thiselton, 'NH', 317, 316; cf. Thiselton, 'PDT', 7.

Thiselton argues that 'fusion', like 'distancing', 'involves' *"continuous" 'movement' 'between' 'textual'* and *'reader' 'horizons'* (it would be *inconsistent with Thiselton's "re-historicizing" of understanding for either set of horizons to be over- or under-emphasized*). Thiselton also notes that 'fusion', for the *most* part (unlike 'distancing'), largely 'involves' *'creative'* 'intuitive' 'understanding', though Thiselton adds the caveat that 'critical' "testing" is *not absent* during 'fusion'.[186] Thiselton closely ties 'fusion' to the ethical 'responsibility' of 'practical' 'response' to texts, in line with his 'practical concern for the role of the Bible in the church and in the world'.[187] Thiselton's four-fold grammar of fusion requires further explication, as follows.

(1) For Thiselton, 'fusion' *liberates 'textual' "speech-action"* and *'intra-linguistic'* and *'extra-linguistic' "effects"* that *"transform" "readers"*. Thiselton retains, but also moves beyond or *re-historicizes*, concerns to do with 'semantics' and with 'intra-linguistic' "effects", but does so *without* "neglecting" 'critical' "testing". Following 'Ricoeur', Thiselton moves beyond the '"closed"' '"self-sufficient"' '"linguistic"' '"universe of"' 'the text' so as to account for '"the open state of"' 'textual' '"signs"' and for *'intra-linguistic'* "effects" that excite *'human'* 'possibility'. But Thiselton also stresses the *'extra-linguistic'* "effects" of *'speech-acts'*, (for example '"promise"'-'"fulfillment"'), which include the '"conventional"' "effects" of the creation of new '"institutional states of affairs"' (e.g. "baptism").[188] Thus, Thiselton argues that 'the Holy Spirit', to a large extent through 'the Bible', "transforms" human subjects in the 'extra-linguistic' domain 'towards' 'eschatological' "goals".[189]

Thiselton argues that 'textual' language does *'not' necessarily 'master'* or "affect" "readers" mechanically or "causally", however - querying 'the later... Heidegger' (for whom 'man speaks in that he responds to language') and against L. Langsdorf's reading of Thiselton.[190] Rather, for Thiselton, "readers", in 'openness', *may* "allow" a 'text to reshape' their 'horizons'. As Thiselton argues later, 'Jesus' own explanation of parabolic speech... suggests that his parables demand a

---

[186] cf.: Thiselton, 'U (long)', 120-121; Thiselton, 'UPC', 93-94; Thiselton, 2H, 104; Thiselton, 'SBS', 329; Thiselton, 'NH', 316-317, 323-324. Fourth italics Thiselton's, remaining italics ours.

[187] See, Thiselton, 'U (long)', 120, 121; cf. Thiselton, 'Truth', 899-901; cf. quoting, Mercer, C.R., 'Review of A.C. Thiselton's *New Horizons in Hermeneutics*', *CBQ* 56.1 (1994), 158.

[188] cf.: Thiselton, 'SBL', 115, 116; Thiselton, 'SBS', 329; Thiselton, 'LGT', 8; Thiselton, 'Words', 293-296; Thiselton, 'U (long)', 119; Thiselton, *NH*, 16; Thiselton, 2H, 148; Thiselton, 'Par', 47; Thiselton, *NTH*, 225-227; Thiselton, 'NH', 317, 323, 327-329; Thiselton, *LLM*, 7, 16, 18, 20-21. First, second, third, fourth, and sixth italics ours; fifth and seventh italics Thiselton's.

[189] Thiselton, 'REC', 512, 517-518, 524-525; cf. Thiselton, *LLM*, 7; cf. Thiselton, 'U (long)', 119, 115-117, 121.

[190] cf.: Thiselton, 'SBS', 329; Thiselton, *LLM*, 30-31; Thiselton, 'U (long)', 90; Thiselton, 'Words', 293, 288; Langsdorf, L., 'Current Paths Toward an Objective Hermeneutic. Review-Article of R. Lundin's, A.C. Thiselton's and C. Walhout's *The Responsibility of Hermeneutics*', *CrThRev* 2 (Fall 1987), 152-154. Heidegger citation from, Heidegger, M., *Poetry, Language, Thought* (trans. A. Hofstadter; New York: HarperCollins, 1971), 207. Italics ours.

readiness to respond'. Further, Thiselton argues that 'illocutions' 'are' 'only' 'effective' if 'certain states of affairs' are 'true'. Nevertheless, *partially* reinstating Langsdorf's reading of Thiselton, we should note that Thiselton readily admits that 'language' *may* 'trick' 'the… reader' into "self-involved" 'response' through its 'pre-cognitive' 'operation'. Langsdorf, though, in our estimate, still over-emphasizes the 'cognitive', 'conscious' aspects of 'understanding'.[191]

In Thiselton's thinking, 'fusion' – in the context of biblical hermeneutics - also presupposes both the 'diachronic' *relevance* of the 'biblical text[s]' to 'modern' 'horizons' and the '"rights"' or 'primacy' of the 'biblical text[s]' in relation to "addressing" 'the present'. Thiselton argues that non-biblical "texts" have the "right" to 'be heard', but that biblical-textual '"rights"' extend further. For Thiselton, 'fusion', in the context of biblical hermeneutics, liberates 'the Bible' to 'address' us "authoritatively" as "God's Word", and involves 'genuine encounter' with '"God's"' 'voice', 'a fresh coming-to-speech' (cf. *'speech-acts'*) of biblical-textual language 'in the… language' and "worlds" of "hearers", and "hearers" 'as… whole' persons as "the texts"' "objects".[192]

Against N.L. Geisler's reading of Thiselton, we should note that 'Thiselton' does not espouse a '"soft" view of' 'biblical' 'authority' here (see Chapter 7), but rather that in this context of discussion Thiselton "speaks" of *how 'biblical' 'authority' becomes 'concrete'*.[193] In Thiselton's view of fusion in biblical hermeneutics, "hearers" are sometimes 'drawn into' textual "worlds" that 'interpret', 'judge', and 'transform' their '"present"' '"life"'-"experiences", their 'conceptual frame[s]', and their 'self-understanding[s]'.[194] For Thiselton, 'biblical' "texts" 'act' "creatively" on "hearers", "bringing" 'Christ' 'and salvation', so that 'God' might "build" both '"the Church"' and 'Christians' themselves.[195]

The New Hermeneutic - particularly 'Fuchs's' 'work' on Jesus' 'parables' - is important for Thiselton in this context.[196] Further, after 'Ricoeur', Thiselton argues

---

[191] See previous footnote and: Thiselton, 'NH', 320, 317, 311; Thiselton, 'U (long)', 120, 121; Zuidervaart, 'R RH', 294; Thiselton, 'R-RH', 90, 83-84, 92; Thiselton, 'SARX', 222; Thiselton, 'Words', 294; Thiselton, 'LMR', 1139; Thiselton, 'TY', 1562; Thiselton, 'M-M', 8; Thiselton, *LLM*, 16; Thiselton, 'Truth', 899; Langsdorf, 'RA RH', 152-154. Italics ours.

[192] cf.: Thiselton, 'NH', 308-329; Thiselton, *2H*, 126, 60, 310; Thiselton, 'EITN', 583-584; Thiselton, 'UPC', 87-95; Thiselton, 'U (long)', 90, 97-106, 117-121; Thiselton, 'U (short)', 6; Thiselton, *LLM*, 12; Thiselton, 'P-BP', 88-89; Thiselton, 'PDT', 7; Thiselton, 'Truth', 898-899; Thiselton, 'LMR', 1123-1124, 1139-1140. First italics ours, second italics Thiselton's.

[193] Geisler, N.L., 'Review of A.C. Thiselton's *The Two Horizons*', *BibSac* 138 (Apr.-Jun. 1981), 183; cf. Thiselton, *2H*, 436. Italics ours.

[194] Thiselton, 'UPC', 87-88, 90, 92-93, 95, 98; cf.: Thiselton, 'NH', 320-322, 315, 326-327, 312-313; Thiselton, 'U (short)', 6; Thiselton, 'P-BP', 89.

[195] cf.: Thiselton, 'NH', 308, 311, 317, 320, 323-324; Thiselton, 'LMR', 1139-1140; Thiselton, 'Parab', 463-466; Thiselton, 'U (short)', 6; Thiselton, 'Words', 293; Thiselton, 'U (long)', 115-121; Thiselton, 'REC', 522.

[196] cf.: Thiselton, 'Parab', 437, 462-468; Thiselton, 'UPC', 90, 95; Thiselton, 'NH', 311-312, 320-326; Thiselton, 'SBL', 109-110; Thiselton, 'U (long)', 90-92.

that 'the Exodus' 'narrative' '"opens into"' "readers"' "existential" '"lived"'- '"through"' '"wandering... from captivity to deliverance"'. Yet, more than the New Hermeneutic, and more than 'Ricoeur', Thiselton emphasizes 'extra-linguistic' "effects" with origins *'behind'* 'the text' (see Chapter 6).[197]

(2) For Thiselton, 'fusion' involves *"actualization"'* or '"hermeneutical understanding" (to use the narrow sense of the phrase "hermeneutical understanding"). Without neglecting 'critical' "testing", Thiselton's *re-historicized or sublated notion of actualization* moves "beyond" 'hermeneutics' as '"rules"' or as (traditionalistic) indoctrination, and emphasizes 'effective communication' and individual and corporate 'self-involvement' in the "eventful" "transformation" *of* (individual or corporate) 'self-understanding' and in the "expansion" of (readers' and even of textual) 'horizons'. For Thiselton, '"actualization"' is similar – *if not identical* - to "hearing", and embraces and/or involves 'listening', 'openness', 'experience', "participation", *and* '"transformation"'.[198]

Thiselton urges that 'fusion' (including actualization) should not be "premature". For Thiselton, 'fusion' (including actualization) involves the 'active engagement', inter-'relation', 'dialogue', '"communion"', or increasing – though 'never' complete – 'merging' of (or between) "textual" and 'reader' 'horizons' (cf. Fuchs' notion, *'Einverständnis'*) such that – for Gadamer and Thiselton - there is "continual" "movement", 'enlargement', "transformation", and even "re-orientation" 'of' *both* 'textual' *and* 'reader' 'horizons'. Thiselton argues that, in 'genuine' 'fusion' (i.e. especially "actualization", in this context of discussion), 'each set of horizons... embraces what was initially beyond it' so as to expand *'towards...* fusion' 'into one' "new horizon" though, again, contradicting E.E. Johnson's reading of Thiselton, we should note that, for Thiselton, 'fusion' (including actualization) is 'never' complete. Thiselton argues that 'fusion' (including actualization) 'expands... texts' *as well as* 'the vision of the reader' since even texts are embedded and re-embedded as diachronic historical frames of reference expand through the continuous creation of new historical relationships.[199]

Following 'Schleiermacher', Thiselton moves *beyond* 'hermeneutics' conceived of as '"rules"' and *towards* 'the... *making... possible*' of - 'and' *towards* the

---

[197] Thiselton, 'SBL', 115-116; cf. Thiselton, 'UPC', 90; cf. Thiselton, *NH*, 363. See also our next footnote. Italics Thiselton's.

[198] cf.: Thiselton, 'M-M', 8; Thiselton, *LLM*, 16, 8-9, 27-31; Thiselton, 'P-BP', 89; Thiselton, 'NH', 308-329; Thiselton, 'PDT', 7; Thiselton, 'UPC', 87-88, 90-95; Thiselton, 'IA', 9; Thiselton, 'EITN', 583-584; Thiselton, 'U (long)', 99, 104-105, 117-121; Thiselton, 'R *EMB*', 139; Thiselton, 'U (short)', 6; Thiselton, *NH*, 11, 8. Italics ours.

[199] cf.: Thiselton, 'UPC', 87-88, 93-94; Thiselton, 'EITN', 583, 584; Thiselton, *2H*, 315, 307-309, 320, 326, xix; Thiselton, 'SBL', 109-110, 115-118; Thiselton, 'U (long)', 101-102, 119-120; Thiselton, *LLM*, 8-9; Thiselton, 'NH', 311-328; Thiselton, 'SBS', 329; Johnson, E.E., *Expository Hermeneutics* (Grand Rapids: Zondervan, 1990), 66, 226; quoting, Brodie, 'R *2H*', 483. First italics Thiselton's, remaining italics ours.

"deliberate" *'creative'* "initiation" of - 'new' *'understanding'*.[200] With 'Luther', Thiselton believes that 'verbal transaction' should have an 'inherent vitality' that "alters" 'the disputants:' "God's Word" may "come" to us uncomfortably *'as adversarius noster'* - in a manner that subverts our "worlds".[201] With 'Buber', Thiselton argues that, whereas 'education [cf. Thiselton's notion of actualization]... opens and expands' 'horizons', indoctrination (cf. 'propaganda') 'closes and stunts the mind... directing it to pre-packed answers', and/or to the mere 'mechanical repetition' of received systems (cf. traditionalism).[202]

Thiselton also argues that the liberating function of 'grammatical utterances' should be recognized. Following the later Wittgenstein, Thiselton argues that 'grammatical' "remarks" 'directed at' 'the *scaffolding* of our thoughts' "make" 'possible a... new understanding of things' that 'extends the horizons of the reader'.[203] That is, Thiselton argues that 'assertions' can 'function *creatively*' through "language-events". This point reflects one of the ways in which Thiselton's *re-historicizing sublation of Continental notions of actualization alters the grammar* of 'Fuchs's' notion of '"language-event"'.[204]

Finally, again correcting the New Hermeneutic, Thiselton 'critically' "tests" and "authenticates" 'actualizations', "language-events" or "interpretations" against 'cognitive' "criteria" – notably testing 'actualizations' for alignment(s) with a text's 'original' "purpose(s)" and 'function[s]' – as a matter of ethical 'responsibility'. Similarly, we noted in Chapter 2 that Thiselton criticized both H. Cox's 'radical' church and 'the charismatic movement' for neglecting the 'critical' "testing" of 'religious' "experiences". Thiselton argues that "experiential" "'actualization'" may also be under- or over-emphasized, against "traditional" and Corinthian practices respectively. For Thiselton, "deep" 'understanding' 'and' "correct" 'understanding' must be held together.[205]

(3) For Thiselton, 'fusion' 'involves... *appropriation*'. Thiselton argues - without "neglecting" 'critical' "testing" - that hermeneutical 'practice' should be *re-historicized* such that it moves *beyond* indulging merely in a form of "actualization" that could otherwise degenerate into '"a... hedonism" of' "self-affirming" 'event' and 'experience' and *towards* a form of "actualization" *that facilitates* "appropriation"

---

[200] Thiselton, 'NH', 310-311, 317, 321. Italics in speech-marks are Thiselton's.

[201] See previous footnote and, Cahill, 'R *2H*', 484; cf.: Thiselton, *2H*, 319; Thiselton, 'NH', 320-321; "adversarius noster" means "our adversary". Italics ours, except for Thiselton's on the single word *'as...'*.

[202] Thiselton, 'R *EMB*', 139; cf.: Thiselton, 'U (long)', 119, 99; Thiselton, 'PDT', 7.

[203] cf.: Thiselton, 'UPC', 89; Thiselton, *2H*, 406, 388; cf. 386-407; Wittgenstein, *OC*, 29e (first citation); Palmer, 'R *2H*', 174; Wittgenstein, *PI*, 222; Wittgenstein, L., *Zettel* (trans. G.E.M. Anscombe; Oxford: Blackwell, 1967, 1998), 123. Italics Wittgenstein's.

[204] Thiselton, 'Parab', 456, 462-464, 437-439. First italics Thiselton's, second italics ours.

[205] cf.: Thiselton, 'NH', 323-324, 314-317; Thiselton, 'Till', 88, 92-101; Thiselton, 'U (long)', 90-91, 121, 97, 101, 119; Thiselton, *NH*, 11; Thiselton, 'R-RH', 113; Thiselton, 'E-CR', 8; Thiselton, 'UPC', 92, 94-95; Thiselton, *2H*, 353.

or the individual and corporate 'self-involvement' of "obedient" 'commitment'. L. Brodie's reading of Thiselton, in which Brodie's "Thiselton" espouses 'the achievement of a new self-understanding', does not go far enough in this context of discussion. Rather, for Thiselton, 'appropriation' constitutes 'a changed relationship' *to* 'a new self-understanding' and *to* 'textual' 'function' and '"subject-matter"'. "Appropriation", then, for Thiselton, is akin to 'obedience' – at least in the context of biblical hermeneutics.[206]

Thus, later, Thiselton criticizes Stanley Fish for ahistorically reconfiguring interpretation into a form of "actualization" that *potentially* amounts merely to *'a phenomenology of religious self-discovery'*.[207] Thiselton also argues that 'biblical' "texts" should not be ahistorically "instrumentalized" as 'mere' 'information' or as 'mere' '"sources for"' (one-sidedly) "historical" "criticism". For Thiselton, such an approach would be like a "Pharisaic" power-bid for "sovereignty" in which "interpreters" refused to '"be"' the '"interpreted"' or refused to accept 'ethical' 'responsibility'.[208] However, in Thiselton's thinking, 'God', 'Christ', 'biblical' 'paradigms', 'the New Testament', and '"the Gospel"' *"authoritatively"* command 'trust' and 'practical', 'bodily', 'committed', "faithful" 'obedience',[209] and not 'mere intellectual assent' to 'concepts' or to 'information about' 'God'. Adapting the approaches of 'Kierkegaard', 'Heidegger' and 'Bultmann' to varying extents, Thiselton argues that "appropriation" 'involves' the 'corporate', *"subjective"*, "active", 'personal decision' and "lived-through" "transforming" "appropriation" of 'true knowledge' – though, clearly, Thiselton rejects these thinkers' 'individualism'.[210]

Admittedly, for Thiselton, "eschatologically"-oriented divine "promise-fulfillment" qualifies Heidegger's emphases – emphases presupposed by Heidegger's notions of 'futurity' and 'possibility' - on merely human brute "effort"

---

[206] cf.: Thiselton, 'NH', 313-317, 323-327; Thiselton, 'U (short)', 6; Thiselton, 'U (long)', 119; Thiselton, 'LG', 493; Thiselton, 'SBS', 332, 329; Thiselton, *NH*, 110, 550; Thiselton, 'E-CR', 8; Thiselton, *LLM*, 16, 13; Thiselton, 'Till', 98; Thiselton, 'TNI', 11; Thiselton, 'R 2 Cor', 30; Thiselton, 'Truth', 900; Thiselton, 'Flesh', 679-680; Brodie, 'R 2H', 482. Italics ours.

[207] Thiselton, *NH*, 550. First italics ours, second italics Thiselton's.

[208] cf.: Thiselton, 'UPC', 95; Thiselton, 'U (long)', 121; Thiselton, 'M,M', 341; Thiselton, 'KNT', 94; Thiselton, 'NH', 319, 322, 316; Thiselton, 'Sch', 135.

[209] cf.: Thiselton, 'Dial', 10; Thiselton, *LLM*, 32; Thiselton, 'U (short)', 6; Thiselton, 'R 2 Cor', 30; Thiselton, 'KNT', 95; Thiselton, 'Flesh', 679; Thiselton, 'UPC', 90; Thiselton, 'Truth', 884, 898. Italics ours.

[210] cf.: Thiselton, 'P-BP', 88; Thiselton, 'NH', 320, 321; Thiselton, 'PDT', 7; Thiselton, 'KNT', 90-93, 85-86, 103-105; Thiselton, *2H*, 203, 287, 292, 200; Thiselton, 'Truth', 898; Thiselton, A.C., 'Knowledge, Myth and Corporate Memory', in *Believing in the Church: Essays by Members of the Church of England Doctrine Commission* (ed. B. Mitchell; London: SPCK, 1981), 48, 49; Thiselton, 'UPC', 90; Thiselton, 'R EMB', 138-139; Thiselton, 'LGT', 8. Italics in speech-marks Kierkegaard's, cited by Thiselton.

or on 'resoluteness as *authentic Being-one's-self*'.[211] However, Thiselton argues that re-historicized "appropriation" is still 'authentic' "cruciform" 'human' 'existence', or a "living out" of the 'truth' (reminiscent of the approach of 'Kierkegaard', but not individualistic) – where, for Thiselton, the character of "appropriation" varies depending on the 'texts', 'readers', and 'situations' concerned.[212]

Thus, for Thiselton, re-historicized 'appropriation' places 'restraints' on 'human' "freedoms" - as over and against an 'individualistic' 'egocentric' "humanist" 'subjectivism' of doing 'what is true for me'.[213] Thiselton argues that "appropriation" presupposes 'openness' to, 'reverence' for, and 'humble submission to truth' - the displacement of 'the... subject' as arbiter of truth.[214] We need not revisit Thiselton's emphases on 'integrity' ('correspondence between' 'actuality', 'convictions', "deeds", and "words"),[215] 'love' ('fully inter-personal relationships' that manifest 'faithfulness', transparency, and "straightforwardness"),[216] 'faith',[217] 'hope',[218] and on 'truth' as 'authentic' living that involves 'true', 'reliable' '"speech"'.[219]

For Thiselton, re-historicized "appropriations" also require authentication via 'critical' "testing" - and via a 'readiness to submit all pre-conceptions to the test of truth'[220] - as a matter of 'ethical' 'responsibility' that goes beyond, but includes, *'pragmatic'* 'performative' endorsement (see Chapter 3).[221] Thus, against W. Wink's and V.S. Poythress's readings of Thiselton respectively, we should note that Thiselton neglects neither "appropriation" nor 'religious commitment'.[222]

(4) For Thiselton, 'fusion' involves *re-historicized "application"*. Thiselton - without "neglecting" 'critical' "testing" - argues that biblical 'hermeneutics' should move *beyond* 'Western' "individualistic" and overly abstract "theoretical" religion *towards* 'individual' and 'corporate' 'self-involvement' in redemptive action (including

---

[211] cf.: Thiselton, 'Par', 51; Thiselton, 'REC', 512, 517-518, 524-525; Thiselton, NTH, 247, 225 227, 254 260; Thiselton, 'Flesh', 681; Heidegger, BT, 344. Italics Heidegger's.

[212] cf.: Thiselton, 'Words', 293-296; Thiselton, 'PDT', 7; Thiselton, 'R EMB', 139; Thiselton, 'Truth', 898, 885-887, 891-892; Thiselton, 'NH', 321; Thiselton, 'U (long)', 90; Thiselton, 'R 2 Cor', 29; Thiselton, NH, 129, 558; Thiselton, LLM, 13.

[213] cf.: Thiselton, 'REC', 515-518, 520-521; Thiselton, 'Truth', 898; Thiselton, 2H, 200, 112; Thiselton, 'KNT', 100, 90-92; Thiselton, NTH, xxviii, conc. 8.2c.

[214] Thiselton, 'Truth', 898, 900, 901; cf. Thiselton, 'KNT', 90, cf. 91-92.

[215] Thiselton, 'Truth', 883-887, 892; cf. Thiselton, LLM, 19.

[216] Thiselton, 'Truth', 887, 881, 886, 877; cf. Thiselton, 'ML', 9.

[217] Thiselton, 'Par', 47, 48, 51; cf. Thiselton, 'Exc', 12; cf. Thiselton, 'REC', 512, 517-518, 524-525; cf. Thiselton, 'Doubt', 8.

[218] Thiselton, 'CH', 5; cf. Thiselton, 'Par', 29-30, 47, 48, 51.

[219] Thiselton, 'Truth', 878-879, 881-887, 892-893.

[220] Thiselton, 'Truth', 901, 896-898; cf. Thiselton, 'NH', 323.

[221] Thiselton, 'KNT', 93; cf. Thiselton, 'U (long)', 121, 118-119; cf. Thiselton, 'Truth', 896-897; cf. Thiselton, 'Sch', 136. Italics Thiselton's.

[222] Wink, W., 'Review of A.C. Thiselton's *The Two Horizons*', ThT 37.4 (Jan. 1981), 508; cf. Poythress, 'R 2H', 179, 180.

"liberating" 'socio-critical' '*praxis*'), or *towards* 'a changed relationship' to 'broader issues' in 'the' contemporary wider 'world'. For Thiselton, in the context of biblical hermeneutics, "application" is akin to "mission" (though, for Thiselton, "application" is *not reducible to* "mission").[223]

Since Thiselton's emphasis on "appropriation" remains in the background, however, then he has – in effect – extended and re-historicized the Jaussean-Ricoeurian distinction between 'understanding' (a term that abbreviates, and that has the narrow sense of, the phrase "hermeneutical understanding" – see above), "explanation", and 'application' in a way that prevents "'application'" from being reduced to mere "activism". For Thiselton, in the context of biblical hermeneutics, "appropriation" is "deep" 'existential' 'self-involving' 'obedience' to 'God's Word' ("individually" or "corporately"; and, *personally and/or relationally*); and yet, for Thiselton, in the context of biblical hermeneutics, "appropriation" must be accompanied by "application" which, for Thiselton, involves self-sacrificial tasks performed in 'the' 'external' wider 'world'. Thiselton still appeals to the three-way "understanding-explanation-application" distinction,[224] but his stress on 'appropriation' is never far away.[225]

In the context of 'biblical hermeneutics', Thiselton's practice of "application" involves a "'biblical *interpretation*'" of 'the world' in which 'eschatology' is essential to interpreting 'the present' and in which 'biblical… apocalyptic' remains "relevant" 'today'.[226] Thiselton argues that since 'culture' and "traditions" can 'distort truth' (with 'Heidegger', Thiselton allows that 'idle talk' involves 'gossiping and passing the word along') then, in Thiselton's estimate, 'a… socially and politically relevant' theological (meta-socio-)critique of 'culture' and of "traditions" is needed (see Chapter 4). Thus Thiselton asks, with E. Fuchs, 'what does the Bible actually say to our own generation?',[227] and Thiselton appeals to J. Moltmann and J. Miranda as already noted.[228] Similarly, later, 'Thiselton' "insists" 'on the

---

[223] cf.: Thiselton, 'Doubt', 8; Thiselton, 'NH', 317, 316, 323, 310; Thiselton, *2H*, 110, 111; Thiselton, *NH*, 379; Thiselton, A.C., 'Review of J. Moltmann's *The Crucified God*', *Chman* 89.2 (1975), 149; Thiselton, 'M&M', 8; Thiselton, 'Till', 98, 104-105, 87-89; Thiselton, 'CH', 5; Thiselton, 'R *HFM*', 232-233; Thiselton, A.C., 'Review of J. Moltmann's *The Experiment Hope*', *Chman* 90.3 (1976), 225-227; Thiselton, 'AA', 610, 609; Thiselton, 'Truth', 900-901; Thiselton, 'KMCM', 48-49; Thiselton, *LLM*, 16. Fourth italics Thiselton's, others ours.

[224] cf.: Thiselton, 'Truth', 898; Thiselton, 'CAP', 199; Thiselton, 'U (long)', 95, 121; Thiselton, 'NH', 323, 314; Thiselton, *2H*, 58; Thiselton, *LLM*, 16; Thiselton, 'R *2 Cor*', 30, 29; Thiselton, 'KMCM', 48; Thiselton, 'Doubt', 8; Thiselton, 'LGT', 8; Thiselton, 'SBS', 334. Italics ours.

[225] Thiselton, *2H*, 168, 172, 176, 267-270, 287; cf. 58, 308, 325, 376-377, 380.

[226] cf.: Thiselton, *2H*, 111, 113, 110; Thiselton, 'NH', 316; Thiselton, 'TNI', 11; Thiselton, 'NHP', 5; Thiselton, 'CH', 5; Thiselton, 'R *HFM*', 232-233; Thiselton, 'R *Apoc*', 219-220. Italics ours.

[227] Thiselton, *2H*, 436, 314; cf. Thiselton, *NTH*, xxii, concs. 1.2a-c; cf. Thiselton, 'R *TEH*', 227; cf. Thiselton, 'T&F', 11; cf. citation from Heidegger, *BT*, 212.

[228] Thiselton, 'AA', 600, 609-610; cf. Thiselton, 'Par', 50.

critical potential of Scripture',[229] and on 'the responsible use of Scripture in the modern world'.[230] Nevertheless, following 'Gadamer', Thiselton rejects complete iconoclasm and, therein, Gadamer and Thiselton also reject any notion of an *'antithesis between tradition and historical research'*. Gadamer and Thiselton argue that "traditions" can "transmit" tried and tested "convictions". Thiselton, combining appeals to Heidegger and to Gadamer, thus argues that a *properly re-historicized approach to tradition* is *neither* iconoclastic *nor* traditionalistic (for tradition can *both* transmit *and* distort truth) but is, rather, "tradition-modifying" or "tradition-refining". Thus, to use J. Grondin's language, we may conclude that Thiselton brings 'prophet *(prophetes)*' and *'hermeneus'* (interpreter) together in opposition to the iconoclast, to the traditionalist, and – we might add (drawing on Grondin and in line with Thiselton's attacks against authoritarian appeals to the Holy Spirit - see Chapters 3 and 7) - to *'mantike* (soothsaying)'.[231]

For Thiselton, in the context of 'biblical hermeneutics', "application" also involves "liberating" *'action'* or *'praxis'* in 'the [wider] world'. With 'Moltmann', Thiselton argues that '"hope"' "begins" with '"the transformation of the present"' where, ultimately, for Thiselton, "application" aims to "establish" 'God's Kingdom on earth' through mission and through '"building"' Church.[232] This approach to "application" contextualizes Thiselton's concerns for: proper 'liturgical' practice and "responsible" 'language-use' in the Church;[233] "honest" 'dealings with' one's "neighbors"; 'dialogue' between "the Gospel", 'modern' "hearers", and 'cultural' 'thought-forms'; 'social justice'; and for 'compassion' and 'solidarity with the poor', 'the suffering', 'and' 'with' the 'oppressed'.[234] Thiselton sets these practical concerns and actions in opposition to over-'abstract' '"Enlightenment"' 'rationalism', to 'Bultmann's' 'individualistic' subjectivism, to pietistic introspection (see Chapter 3), and to '"biblical studies"' that focus

---

[229] Thiselton, *NH*, 613-619; cf. Morgan, R., 'Review of A.C. Thiselton's *New Horizons in Hermeneutics*', *ExTim* 104.6 (Mar. 1993), 187. Capitalization ours.

[230] Thiselton, *NH*, 550; cf. Moberly, R.W.L., 'Review of A.C. Thiselton's *New Horizons in Hermeneutics*', *Anv* 11.1 (1994), 71.

[231] Thiselton, *2H*, 314, 306, 436; cf. Thiselton, *NTH*, xxii, concs. 1.2a-c; cf. Gadamer, *TM*, 277-307, quoting from 282; cf. Grondin, J., *Introduction to Philosophical Hermeneutics* (trans. J. Weinsheimer; Yale Studies in Hermeneutics; New Haven: Yale University Press, 1994), 21-23. Italics in speech-marks Gadamer's, except on *prophetes*, *hermeneus*, and *mantike*, where they are ours. Other italics are ours. Transliterations are Grondin's.

[232] cf.: Thiselton, *2H*, 113, 112; Thiselton, 'NH', 316; Thiselton, 'CH', 5; Thiselton, 'R HFM', 232; Thiselton, 'AA', 610, 608; Thiselton, 'REC', 518; Thiselton, 'U (long)', 115-117, 121. First italics ours, second italics Thiselton's.

[233] cf.: Thiselton, 'LMR', 1142-1144; Thiselton, *LLM*; 3, 6; Thiselton, 'MP', 4-12.

[234] cf.: Thiselton, 'AA', 607-610; Thiselton, 'Truth', 901; Thiselton, 'R HFM', 232; Thiselton, 'TNP', 11; Thiselton, 'U (long)', 90; Thiselton, 'NH', 308; Thiselton, 'R TCG', 149; Thiselton, 'R TEH', 227.

'exclusively' on 'past' 'horizons'.[235]

Conversely, and against calling anything and everything "praxis" for cosmetic reasons, Thiselton argues that "applications" should be critically tested and authenticated as a matter of ethical "'responsibility'". (Later, this consideration is reflected in Thiselton's comments on Aristotelian and on Marxist notions of *'praxis'*. Praxis – as *re-historicized* application - should not be divorced from historical traditions of wisdom or of theory).[236] Thus, for example, Thiselton argues, after 'J.W. Wenham', that 'Old Testament laws' "'should'" "'not'" "'be re-imposed today'". For Thiselton, therefore, "application" has *limits*.[237]

iii) The Dialogic Relationship between Distancing and Fusion

For Thiselton, a properly *re-historicized* approach to understanding demands that 'distancing and fusion are equally necessary', and that they are to be practiced together 'in… dialogue' "continuously" and "progressively" during 'interpretation', without over-stressing either "'distancing'" or 'fusion' or 'past' or 'present' 'horizons'. Therefore, (1), Thiselton criticizes Continental hermeneutics for viewing 'critical' "'distancing'" as 'a' mere 'preliminary' to 'interpretation', and 'liberation theology' for "evaporating" 'past meaning… in the horizon of the present'. In Thiselton's estimate, these approaches are *historically* inadequate in that they conceive of "understanding" in a way that fails fully to do justice to the way in which history as *properly* conceived affects, (a), the character of "understanding" and, (b), the way in which "understanding" must – broadly speaking - proceed (see also Chapters 6 and 7).[238]

Similarly, (2), for Thiselton, *'translation'* is inseparable from 'hermeneutics'. Thiselton argues that *'distancing'* should clarify textual 'particularity' prior to assessments "'of translation-equivalence'".[239] However, Thiselton also insists that such assessments - in relation to 'cognitive', 'emotive', 'cultural', and 'religious' factors - also involve the 'creative' "judgments" of *'fusion'*: for Thiselton, the aim in translation is 'effective communication', not 'surface-grammar' representation.[240]

(3) For Thiselton, *'the Holy Spirit'* gives "scholarly" 'gifts' relevant to the 'critical'

---

[235] cf.: Thiselton, 'H-O', 8; Thiselton, 'Par', 49; Thiselton, 'UPC', 98; Thiselton, 'PDT', 7; Thiselton, 'KNT', 97; Thiselton, 'NH', 316.

[236] Thiselton, 'R *TEH*', 226; cf. Thiselton, 'NH', 316; cf. Thiselton, *NH*, 380. First italics Thiselton's, second italics ours.

[237] Thiselton, A.C., 'More Manageable Proportions. Review of J.W. Wenham's *The Goodness of God*, *CEN* 5 Apr. (1974), 8; cf. Thiselton, 'NH', 316. Italics ours.

[238] cf.: Thiselton, 'NH', 320, 317, 323, 327-329; Thiselton, 'U (long)', 120, 99-102, 104; Thiselton, 'PDT', 7; Thiselton, 'UPC', 98; quoting from Dyrness, 'R *2H*', 94.

[239] cf.: Thiselton, 'R *SBR*', 18; Thiselton, 'SNTI', 87, 75, 95-98; Thiselton, 'IT', 15; Thiselton, *2H*, 119-120, 130-133. First italics ours, second italics Thiselton's.

[240] cf.: Thiselton, 'SNTI', 96-98; Thiselton, 'LMR', 1141-1142; Thiselton, 'NH', 317, 311; Thiselton, *2H*, 130-133; Thiselton, A.C., 'Review of D.H. Kelsey's *The Uses of Scripture in Recent Theology*', *Chman* 91.1 (1977), 88. Italics ours.

*Hermeneutics and Responsible Interpretation* 251

'models' employed during *'distancing'*, but also 'inspires' "creative", "transforming" 'understanding' during *'fusion'*. Thiselton argues that 'hermeneutics' cannot be "bypassed" by over-emphasizing "prophetic" "appeals to the Spirit": in Thiselton's view, 'the Spirit' mainly 'works *through*' - and 'not' apart from - 'the normal processes of... understanding'.[241] As Thiselton writes later, 'in a co-operative shared work, the Spirit, the text, and the reader [or readers] engage in *a transforming process*, which enlarges horizons and creates *new horizons*'.[242]

(4) For Thiselton, engagement with *"'interpretation'"* histories preserved in 'theological' "traditions" involves 'both distancing and fusion'.[243]

Thus, (a), Thiselton argues that 'academic integrity' considers 'both sides of' historically "debated" 'questions' – 'questions' that, in addition, relate *both* to textual 'content' (cf. 'distancing') *and* to appropriate 'response' (cf. 'fusion').[244] Thus, Thiselton assesses *both* A. Schweitzer's 'historical' approach to 'Pauline thought'-'content', *and* historical responses *to* 'Schweitzer'.[245]

And yet, (b), in *The Two Horizons*, 'Thiselton [also] argues that each generation requires its *own* fusion of horizons, and thus [that] hermeneutics remains an ongoing task'.[246] That is, for Thiselton, *'distancing'* that "elucidates" 'the history of... fusions found in Christian tradition' aids *present* 'fusion'.[247]

Thiselton's approach in this context anticipates his later stress on "post-histories" 'or' on 'reception' "histories" as part of a focus on 'the *full history* of the text'. But, for Thiselton, this *'full history'* also extends to embrace present interpreters: in Thiselton's view, present interpreters should not stop at distanciations concerning *past* fusions; rather, in Thiselton's estimate, present interpreters *themselves* should also *participate* in *present* fusions of horizons.[248]

---

[241] cf.: Thiselton, 'U (long)', 117-121, 99; Thiselton, 'NH', 309-310; Thiselton, *NTH*, xxv, Conclusion 5.2d; Thiselton, 'SBS', 334; Thiselton, *2H*, 92, 90; Thiselton, A.C., *The First Epistle to the Corinthians* (eds. H. Marshall and D.A. Hagner; Series: The New International Greek Testament Commentary; Grand Rapids: Eerdmans; Carlisle: Paternoster, 2000), 826. First, second, and third italics ours; fourth italics Thiselton's.

[242] Reist, J.S., 'Review of A.C. Thiselton's *New Horizons in Hermeneutics*', *JEThS* 38.3 (Sep. 1995), 459; cf. Thiselton, *NH*, 619. Italics Thiselton's.

[243] cf.: Thiselton, 'Doubt', 8; Thiselton, 'Sch', 135; Thiselton, 'CAP', 195, 194; Thiselton, 'U (long)', 120. Italics ours.

[244] cf.: Thiselton, 'Doubt', 8; Thiselton, 'R *IBHI*', 117-118; Thiselton, A.C., 'Review of R.C. Roberts' *Rudolf Bultmann's Theology: A Critical Interpretation*', *Chman* 92.3 (1978), 267; Thiselton, 'Sch', 135-136, 132-133; Thiselton, 'U (long)', 121; Thiselton, 'Till', 92. Italics ours.

[245] Thiselton, 'Sch', 132-133, 135-136; cf. Thiselton, 'Till', 92. Italics ours.

[246] Thiselton, *2H*, 95-101; cf. Klein, 'R *2H*', 72. Italics ours.

[247] Maddox, 'CHP', 528; cf.: Thiselton, *2H*, 120; Thiselton, 'Doubt', 8; Thiselton, 'Sch', 135. Italics in speech-marks are Thiselton's.

[248] cf.: Thiselton, A.C., 'Signs of the Times: Towards a Theology for the Year 2000 as a Grammar of Grace, Truth and Eschatology in Contexts of So-Called Postmodernity', *Unpublished Version of the Paper Given at The Society for the Study of Theology Annual Conference,*

iv) Question and Answer

Both "distancing" and 'fusion', for Thiselton, with 'Gadamer', and within Thiselton's properly re-historicized approach to understanding, involve "continuous", 'progressive', "dialogic" 'movement' 'between' 'question[s] and answer[s]'. For Gadamer and Thiselton, 'the essence of the *question* is to open up possibilities and keep them open'. That is, for Gadamer and Thiselton, this "opening" 'up' of 'possibilities', and this "keeping-open" of 'possibilities', involve a "dialogic" 'movement' 'between' 'question[s] and answer[s]' that is respectful towards the historical *other* (including the historically *past* "other" and the historically *present* "other") and towards the historical *future*. Querying B.J. Walsh's reading of Thiselton, this 'dialogue' 'between' 'question[s] and answer[s]' in Thiselton's thinking is thus *not* linked too exclusively to 'fusion'.[249]

"Initially", in Thiselton's thinking, "readers'" 'questions' 'yield' "inadequate" "understandings". But, Thiselton argues that the latter 'may… be' 'progressively' 'reshaped', 'questioned', 'challenged', and "revised" through 'an ongoing' 'dialogue' 'of' two-way 'question and answer' 'between' "interpreters" 'and… text' - requiring 'both' 'study and' "reflection" (cf. 'distancing'), and, 'openness', 'listening', and 'response' (cf. 'fusion'). Thiselton argues that intermediate and 'better' 'questions' and 'conclusions' then lead on to 'progressively' "clearer" or 'deeper' "understandings", and eventually to 'right questions' that "allow" 'the text' to 'come to speech' "and transform" "readers". Thus, in Thiselton's estimate, "texts" are 'not' mere "objects" 'of knowledge'.[250] Querying R.W.L. Moberly's reading of Thiselton, Thiselton does not ignore 'how transformation through openness to Scripture… affects the way Scripture is interpreted'.[251]

*3. In Anticipation of Later Discussions: A Brief Note On Plural Interpretative Outcomes*

Before going on to respond (more explicitly) to other readings of Thiselton's work in relation to his critique of hermeneutical understanding, it is worth making some brief comments now in anticipation of some of our arguments in Chapter 7 in which *interpretative outcomes* and – in particular - *the plurality of interpretative outcomes* will come into focus.

What follows here, though, cannot – for the most part - be read directly from Thiselton's "second period" writings or even from his later writings. Rather, what follows here – for the most part - *combines* points that may be *deduced* from the

---

*Edinburgh*, Apr. 1999, 44; Thiselton, 'CAP', 133-239; Barton, S.C., 'New Testament Interpretation as Performance', *SJT* 52.2 (1999), 206 (quoted); Thiselton, 'KMCM', 45-78; Thiselton, 'BTT', 105. Italics in speech-marks are Barton's, others are ours.

[249] cf.: Thiselton, 'NH', 317, 316, 104, 309; Thiselton, 'UPC', 93, 94; Thiselton, *2H*, 104, 309-310; Walsh, 'TC', 227; Gadamer, *TM*, 299 (quoted). Italics in speech-marks Gadamer's.

[250] cf.: Thiselton, 'UPC', 93, 94; Thiselton, 'U (long)', 119, 104-106; Thiselton, 'NH', 316-317, 311, 320; Thiselton, *2H*, 104, 309; Thiselton, 'EITN', 583.

[251] Moberly, 'R *NH*', 72.

*implicature* of our analyses above (or in earlier chapters) *with* points that may be *deduced* from the *implicature* of our analyses and arguments in Chapter 7 (or in Chapter 6).

*Chronologically or historically*, therefore, what follows really belongs towards the end of the present study – as a kind of conclusion or as a kind of set of emergent questions for further reflection. However, *thematically*, questions related to the plurality of interpretative outcomes often seem to be grouped – in popular hermeneutical parlance at least – with questions to do with what should actually be done during responsible interpretation. Thus, before we conclude our discussion in relation to the latter, a few comments on the former are perhaps best provided in the *present* chapter – in the form of a "pause for reflection".

And so, we may recall from earlier in the present chapter that, for Thiselton, such factors as interpretative strategies, interpretative goals, models of texts, critical tools, and so on, are irreducibly but responsibly plural because, in Thiselton's thinking, they must appropriately reflect *both* a plurality of historical particularities pertaining to different texts, *and* a plurality of historical particularities pertaining to different readers. We saw above that, for Thiselton, "understanding" – *in every particular instance of understanding* - always emerges through a dialectic diachronic dialogic dynamic inter-relationship between "two horizons" or between two sets of historical particularities.

As we may deduce from our observations in the present chapter, Thiselton *in effect* argues that interpretative interaction with or between these two sets of particularities *will indeed* always result in "a plurality of *legitimate responsible* readings or meanings". In Chapter 7, however, we shall imply that Thiselton does not lead us into an absolute relativism of interpretative outcomes at this point. Rather, as we shall see in Chapter 7, Thiselton argues that *this legitimate kind of* "plurality of interpretative outcomes" is to be *carefully distinguished from* the notion of artificially-abstracted "*infinitely* fluid meaning", *and from* the notion of "unnecessary *arbitrary* meaning-expansion". For Thiselton, as we shall see, these latter two notions reflect *illegitimate* "pluralities of interpretative outcomes".

Moreover, in Chapter 7, in the context of our responses to Thiselton's critics, we will highlight two further notions that reflect *illegitimate* "pluralities of interpretative outcomes" – notions that we may here summarize by using the phrases: "*mistaken* straightforward hermeneutical foreclosures" and "*obfuscating projections* of hostile criticism".

But can we really "legitimately" speak of a distinction between "legitimate" and "illegitimate" "pluralities of interpretative outcomes"? A few comments based on what we have observed so far, coupled with a few anticipations of later arguments, will suggest that we can – as follows.

Thus, (1), and with respect to the notion of "a plurality of *legitimate responsible* readings or meanings" then, (a), our observations in Chapters 1 and 4 of the present study imply that there is a link between the notion of "a plurality of *legitimate responsible* readings or meanings" and *literary genres and their potential (extra-) linguistic functions and self-involving effects*. Thus, for example, in Chapter 1, we saw how Thiselton argued that Jesus' parables were deliberately constructed so as to *allow, generate, or invite* plural, but inter-related, kinds of *self-involving response*. To give another example, the same kind of point was at least implicit in Thiselton's comments about deliberate "lack of specificity" and other kinds of potentially self-involving "vagueness" – especially "metaphor" - in relation to the biblical texts (see Chapter 4). Thiselton's thinking to do with extra-linguistic and intra-linguistic textual functions and self-involving effects is in the background in both these (sets of) examples (see Chapters 1, 4, 6, 7 and above).

Furthermore, (b), our arguments in Chapter 7 will suggest that there is a link between the notion of "a plurality of *legitimate responsible* readings or meanings" and potential *interpretative impediments*. One only has to read the larger biblical commentaries to see that many debates concerning the precise meanings of many biblical passages remain open on the grounds of ambiguities in relation to the availability (or not) of historical and/or other evidences that may or may not corroborate some readings of such biblical passages as over and against other readings of such biblical passages. Our findings above, in the present chapter, imply that the plural readings that legitimately emerge in the light of debates concerning historical and other evidences should not be prematurely collapsed into dogmatically-asserted singular readings through illegitimate hermeneutical foreclosure in relation to the processes involved in gaining a working knowledge of such debates.

(c) Our arguments in Chapter 7 will also be suggestive in relation to a link between the notion of "a plurality of *legitimate responsible* readings or meanings" and the issue of *"present meaning"* (although, in fact, considerations to do with literary genre, (extra-)linguistic and intra-linguistic functions and self-involving effects, and interpretative impediments *also* relate to "present meaning", though perhaps less directly). Since, as we shall see in Chapter 7, Thiselton argues that "present meaning" concerns the *relationships between* past and present horizons, then Thiselton also argues that "present meaning" is always changing in *legitimate* ways (see Chapter 7).

Thus, (i), we noted above that, as any given interpreter (or interpreters) reads any given text in accordance with the processes pertaining to the hermeneutical circle, then that interpreter (or interpreters) will – over time - arrive at a plurality of potentially increasingly "legitimate" or "accurate" readings, understandings, or "present meanings" in relation to the text being interpreted. If premature fusion of horizons, or hermeneutical foreclosure, is to be avoided, then the interpreter (or interpreters) has *no choice but* to interpret the text concerned in accordance with the processes pertaining to the hermeneutical circle. Therefore, in our view, the *unavoidability* of interpreting in accordance with the processes pertaining to the hermeneutical circle (if premature fusion is to be avoided) suggests that there is a broad "legitimacy" to the plurality of potentially increasingly mature, "legitimate" or "accurate" readings, understandings, or "present meanings" that thereby emerges *on the way to even-more-mature* readings, understandings, or "present meanings". Even famous commentaries on parts of the Bible are not "final understandings"; but nor would it be fair to describe such commentaries as "illegitimate" readings. Arguably, then, the notion of "a plurality of *legitimate responsible* readings or meanings" thus – in part - relates to what Thiselton calls *"hermeneutical deepening"* or *"hermeneutical growth"* (see Chapter 7).

Furthermore, (ii), in Chapters 6 and 7 we will note the existence of a link between the notion of "a plurality of *legitimate responsible* readings or meanings" and considerations related to *expanding historical horizons*. A simple example of our own will suffice to illustrate this link here. Thus, as history "moves on", the assassination of John F. Kennedy has ongoing effects on ever-later historical events. Since assessments of "meaning" relate "parts" to "wholes", however, then this history-of-effects implies that the "meaning" of JFK's assassination is still unfolding and altering as it relates to the ever-widening diachronic "whole" of expanding historical horizons (though this expansion is strongly qualified by eschatological convergence upon the horizons of biblical promise: 'the Scriptures must be fulfilled' – Mark 14:49 NIV). Thus, as JFK's assassination is interpreted and reinterpreted, there is more than potential "hermeneutical deepening" going on: the historical frame of reference *from within which* the assassination derives its meaning keeps altering. The "final meaning" of the assassination is perpetually deferred – at least until the Eschaton (see Chapter 7).

Moreover, (iii), we may link the notion of "a plurality of *legitimate responsible* readings or meanings" to considerations to do *with changing readers and with changing reader-situations*. Again, a simple example of our own will suffice to illustrate our argument. Thus, if Paul commands "generosity" in 2 Corinthians 8 and 9 but, on the one hand, a reader has just been miserly, then the passage could *legitimately* function as a *rebuke*. On the other hand, if a different reader has just been generous, then the *same* passage could *legitimately* function (at the *same* point in time) as an *affirmation*. As we moved between these simultaneous readings, the passage's "past meaning" would not change; only its "present meaning" would change. In Chapter 6 we will consider Thiselton's arguments in relation to distinctions between "past meaning" and "present meaning".

(iv) In Chapter 7 we will see that, arguably, W.J. Lyons alludes to another kind of "plurality of *legitimate responsible* readings or meanings". Thus, as we shall see, Lyons in effect points out that whilst *historians* might read the biblical texts with *a certain set* of questions, *theologians* will likely read the biblical texts with a *different* set of questions. And so, Lyons argues that the two sets of readers will have *different* notions of "full reading" and that *neither* notion of "full reading" is definitive (see Chapter 7). As we shall imply in Chapter 7, the valid aspect of Lyons' point here – *against* some of Lyons' other arguments - has very little to do with a Fishian epistemology. Rather, the valid aspect of Lyons' point here has far more to do with Thiselton's later Wittgensteinian comments to do with *"a change of aspect"*, *or to do with a change of "angle of vision" or "view"* (see Chapters 2, 4, and 6). That is, different interpreters will frequently – contrary to a strictly Fishian epistemology (see Chapter 7) - enquire into different aspects of *the same totality of historical otherness* that is reflected in and/or through an ancient text. These interpreters' "understandings" of the same ancient text will thus be different, but will not necessarily be incommensurable with one another (N.B. S. Fish and Lyons would acknowledge the truth of this last sub-point, but on different epistemological grounds – see Chapter 7). In order to clarify our point here, we need do no more than refer to the classic illustration according to which different blind-folded persons stand around an elephant in a serious attempt to identify the "object" before them. What each person perceives through touch will be very different. But the "plurality of readings or meanings" that results will be likely to be wholly legitimate and responsible – and yet will *have nothing to do with* (what Thiselton will later identify as) socio-pragmatic interpretative relativism. Again, we will address the issue of "present meaning" in Chapters 6 and 7.

(d) Of course, all six kinds of *legitimate* "pluralities of interpretative outcomes" noted above could be overlapping and superimposed in practice. Or rather, any given interpretation carried out will have its own individuality, but the ways in which any given interpretation *legitimately* differs from other interpretations of *broadly the same "object"* will be potentially multiform – i.e. up to six-fold - *prior* to any obvious mistakes, *apart from* any descent into what some might call "postmodernity", and *in stark contrast to* philosophically idealist or "formalist" notions of "fixed meaning".

(2) With respect to artificially-abstracted *"infinitely* fluid meaning", "unnecessary *arbitrary* meaning-expansion", *"mistaken* straightforward hermeneutical foreclosures" and the *"obfuscating projections* of hostile criticism", then our arguments in Chapter 7 will in effect distinguish Thiselton's thinking to do with *these* kinds of "pluralities" of meaning *from* Thiselton's notion of "a plurality of *legitimate responsible* readings or meanings".

Thus, (a), as we shall see in Chapter 7, the notion of "a plurality of *legitimate responsible* readings or meanings" reflects the kind of stratum-three "plurality" of meanings and readings that emerges when *there is respect, at the stratum-two level of hermeneutical theory, for the historico-philosophical criteria of historical particularity, historical continuity, historical unity, and historical dialectic – as well as for other historico-philosophical criteria that emerge from an adequate philosophy of history that resonates with a working knowledge of a prior biblical theology.*

However, (b), as we shall see in Chapter 7, the notion of artificially-abstracted *"infinitely* fluid meaning" that Thiselton associates with certain post-structuralist approaches reflects the kind of stratum-three "plurality" of meanings and readings that emerges when conceptualizations of "history" and of "language" - at the stratum-two level of hermeneutical theory - are inter-sublated in a way that reverses the relative ontological prioritizations that should be attributed to conceptualizations of "history" and of "language" respectively during theory-construction. In other words (*sic!*), when hermeneutical theory erroneously abstracts "language" from "history", then such hermeneutical theory sometimes lends credence to the supposed possibility that, during ongoing interpretations, the plurality of resulting interpretative outcomes or meanings will tend towards infinity in a way that is *unrelated to concrete historical particularity, to concrete historical*

*Hermeneutics and Responsible Interpretation* 257

*continuity, to concrete historical unity, and to concrete historical dialectic* (and to other historico-philosophical (and theological) criteria – see Chapter 7).

(c) As we shall see in Chapter 7, the notion of "unnecessary *arbitrary* meaning-expansion" that Thiselton associates with certain socio-pragmatic approaches reflects the kind of stratum-three "plurality" of meanings and readings that emerges when, during interpretations, the historical past is erroneously deemed to be *necessarily* epistemologically inaccessible through texts. We shall argue in Chapter 7 that this erroneous stratum-three assumption of textual-epistemological inaccessibility is grounded, at the stratum-two level of hermeneutical theory, in the historically-dichotomous notion of "absolute dissociation between historical horizons". This stratum-two notion, in turn, we shall argue, is uncritically adopted from post-structuralist thought at the level of pre-understanding (stratum one). In other words (*sic!*), Thiselton argues that certain socio-pragmatic hermeneutical theories erroneously abstract present horizons from past horizons (at least in relation to texts), and that such socio-pragmatic approaches thus only allow present horizons to provide constraints on meaning. In Thiselton's estimate, such approaches thus cause present meanings to become increasingly *arbitrary*, *however many meanings are in view, however "stable" the meanings are, and however "wide" or "global" the present-horizon interpretative community or communities become* (see Chapter 7).

(d) As we shall see in Chapter 7, our notion of "*mistaken* straightforward hermeneutical foreclosures" reflects *either*, (i), the kind of simple reading errors that anybody can make, regardless of their hermeneutical theory, *or*, (ii), what we will describe in Chapter 7 as a calculus of pre-dialogic (or historically *a priori*), over-generalizing, simplistic, and prescriptive "pigeon-holing". Both these kinds of "*mistaken* straightforward hermeneutical foreclosures" will lead to *illegitimate* "pluralities of interpretative outcomes".

The particular kind of "*mistaken* straightforward hermeneutical foreclosure" that we have called a "calculus of pre-dialogic (or historically *a priori*), over-generalizing, simplistic, and prescriptive pigeon-holing" is an erroneous interpretative practice that is not constrained to any particular hermeneutical-theoretical tradition. Rather, this kind of erroneous interpretative practice has to do with the bypassing of the processes of the hermeneutical circle and/or of the hermeneutical task of listening in openness to the other. As such, this kind of erroneous interpretative practice can result simply from *time-pressures*.

That is, whilst we will conclude in Chapter 6 – following Thiselton - that hermeneutical theory affects hermeneutical practice *directly*, we must also conclude here, on the basis of our observations in the present chapter, that – in Thiselton's estimate - hermeneutical practice is *a process that will always be interrupted before it is finished*. Hermeneutical practice is affected by *time-pressures as well as by hermeneutical theory* (see Chapters 6 and 7).

Having said this, however, hermeneutical processes can be interrupted earlier on some occasions than on others. The problem with "a calculus of pre-dialogic (or historically *a priori*), over-generalizing, simplistic, and prescriptive pigeon-holing" is that interpreters who fall into this kind of practice haven't yet listened *sufficiently* to the historical "other" for their own pre-understandings to be *sufficiently* enlarged by the historical "other", or for their interpretations to be *responsibly called "responsible"*.

Thus, "a calculus of pre-dialogic (or historically *a priori*), over-generalizing, simplistic, and prescriptive pigeon-holing" is closer in character to a "projected pre-understanding" than it is to an "understanding". And yet, as we shall see in Chapter 7, those interpreters who fall into this kind of practice *sometimes also* fall into *prematurely-dogmatic pronouncements* that *may sometimes* indicate an *unwillingness on the part of those interpreters to have their "projected pre-understandings" corrected by further listening*. In our view, this unwillingness – this "canonization" of hermeneutical foreclosure - is perhaps *sometimes* tied to *felt cultural pressures to project an impression of "expertise" in academic settings*.

Whilst we shall argue in Chapter 7 that "pseudo-post-structuralist" criticisms of Thiselton seem to indulge in a particularly "playful", "hedonistic" "side-stepping of conversation" that illegitimately "shelves" or "bins" Thiselton in the "idealist" or "formalist" "pigeon-hole", in our view such criticisms are really only a kind of *combination* of the problems pertaining to artificially-abstracted "infinitely fluid meaning" *coupled with* the problems pertaining to "unnecessary *arbitrary* meaning expansion" *and with* the problems pertaining to "a calculus of pre-dialogic (or historically *a priori*), over-generalizing, simplistic, and prescriptive "pigeon-holing".

(e) As we shall see in Chapter 7, our notion of the *"obfuscating projections* of hostile criticism" reflects scenarios in which stratum-three hermeneutical practice, which is properly a subset or an aspect of *Christ-like* relating, has been taken over by *hostile* relating. Hostile relating, as we are defining it, tends to play fast and loose with the truth, and can even engage in deliberate acts of lying that can amount to anything from disinformation and deception, to outright name-calling and defamation, to attempts to wound, undermine, or destroy. The possibility of provisionally, progressively "objective" or "truthful" interpretation, of course, is highlighted in part by the commonness of the opposite – namely "hostile criticism" that, through its indulgence in the telling of what amount to lies, *projects obfuscation*. This scenario very often leads *to counter-attacks and to conflicts* that have a different grammar to that of "robust debate" which, by contrast, *attempts to relate truthfully*. Such counter-attacks and conflicts, however, constitute *an illegitimate exchange between illegitimate "pluralities of interpretative outcomes"*. Whilst we shall argue in Chapter 7 that Thiselton is quite right to associate such a descent into conflict with the outworkings of broadly socio-pragmatic approaches to interpretation, we shall also argue that *anybody* can indulge in the *"obfuscating projections* of hostile criticism".

(3) Our points in "(1)(d)" and in "(2)(d)" above point to the conclusion that legitimate *and* illegitimate forms of "pluralities of interpretative outcomes" can also be combined in multiform ways in any given grouping of interpretative outcomes. Such are the historical complexities of the juxtaposed outcomes of diverse interpretative practices that manifest widely varying degrees of responsibility and irresponsibility.

*Hermeneutics and Responsible Interpretation* 259

(4) As we shall see in Chapter 7, the preceding points have relevance in relation to what is actually meant by different uses of the phrase, "conflict of interpretations". That is, we shall note in Chapter 7 that the grammar of the notion of a "conflict of interpretations" *alters markedly* in a manner that is directly dependent upon which *kind (or kinds)* of "plurality of meanings or readings" is presupposed *by any given use of* the phrase "conflict of interpretations".

This point allows us to speculate here that the five broad kinds of plural interpretative outcomes that we have noted – i.e. artificially-abstracted "*infinitely fluid* meaning", "unnecessary *arbitrary* meaning-expansion", "*mistaken* straightforward hermeneutical foreclosures", "*obfuscating projections* of hostile criticism", and "a plurality of *legitimate responsible* readings or meanings" – are associated with *five different broad kinds of* "conflict of interpretations". Combinations of different kinds of "pluralities of interpretative outcomes" will thus render the conceptual grammar of the notion of a "conflict of interpretations" involving such interpretative outcomes very complex indeed.

As we shall imply in Chapter 7, Thiselton supports only that notion of a "conflict of interpretations" that is associated with the "plurality of *legitimate responsible* readings or meanings" that emerges from what he would call "responsible interpretation". For Thiselton, other kinds of "conflicts of interpretations" emerge *either* as the "yeast" of inadequate hermeneutical theory works through the "dough" of irresponsible interpretative practice, *or* as time-pressures and/or attitudinal and relational factors cause interpretative practice to become irresponsible (see Chapter 7).

*4. Answering Critics in Relation to Thiselton's Critique of Hermeneutical Understanding*

To return to our main discussion, then we should note that our exegesis of Thiselton's second-period critique of hermeneutical understanding – i.e. our exegesis of his conceptualization of the hermeneutical task, of his conceptualization of the hermeneutical circle, and/or of his conceptualization of responsible interpretation[252] – stands in conflict with several other readings of Thiselton's work.

Thus, (1), some commentators miss Thiselton's *practical transformed* paradigm for hermeneutics. However, Thiselton *does* tell us 'what we *ought* to do' during "interpretation" (against B.M. Metzger's reading of Thiselton);[253] and Thiselton at least does not neglect a "practically"-oriented *consideration* of how 'pre-understanding' affects 'the interpretative process' (querying P. Keifert's reading of Thiselton).[254] Contradicting L. Brodie's and C.S. Rodd's readings of Thiselton, we

---

[252] These three are virtually synonymous in our exegesis of Thiselton's thinking.
[253] Metzger, 'R *2H*', 211. First and second italics ours; third italics Metzger's.
[254] Keifert, P.R., 'Review of A.C. Thiselton's *The Two Horizons*', *WW* 1 (Fall 1981), 409. Italics ours.

should note that 'Thiselton' does *not* 'state a problem rather than solve it'.[255] And contradicting M.J. Erickson's reading of Thiselton, we should conclude that the 'Thiselton' 'reader is' *not* 'left… to his own resources in formulating a solution to the [hermeneutical] problem' in *this* context of discussion.[256]

Further, querying D.E. Klemm's reading of Thiselton, we have seen that 'Thiselton' moves *beyond* existing 'philosophical description of the understanding process'.[257] Querying J. Kleinig's reading of Thiselton, we have seen that Thiselton has not merely demonstrated 'his grasp of the hermeneutically significant literature'.[258] And, querying R. Van Voorst's reading of Thiselton, we have seen that Thiselton has not simply shown 'that an understanding of recent hermeneutics is necessary for modern biblical study'.[259] Nor, contradicting V.S. Poythress's reading of Thiselton, is Thiselton's later work 'merely a matter of taming hermeneutical excesses'.[260] And contradicting W. Wink's reading of Thiselton, 'Thiselton's' work is not so much 'a monument to the conclusion of one stage in the hermeneutical debate' but, rather, presents us with *a new non-Bultmannian starting point*.[261]

F.H. Borsch believes that 'Thiselton' ushers in a 'hermeneutical' 'paradigm-shift' and yet, oddly, Borsch awaits 'a study' "presenting" 'more of [Thiselton's] own approach'.[262] Thiselton may not quite offer the 'death and resurrection of hermeneutical practice' hoped for by V.S. Poythress,[263] but Thiselton does indeed seek *and offer* a *practical* transformed paradigm so as to go beyond the inadequate 'traditional', "positivist", "Bultmannian", 'post-Bultmannian', and 'structuralist' "solutions" to 'the problem of' 'biblical' and/or 'textual' (un-)'intelligibility' across 'historical distance'.[264]

(2) Commentators sometimes realize that Thiselton offers solutions, but sometimes then argue prematurely that these solutions fail, or else misconstrue what Thiselton's solutions are, or what they could or should be. Thus, with L. Brodie, Thiselton does indeed respond 'to a crisis in biblical studies'. However, against Brodie, Thiselton's solution could not conceivably center on

---

[255] Brodie, 'R *2H*', 485; cf. Rodd, 'R *2H*', 290. Italics ours.
[256] Erickson, 'R *2H*', 373. Italics ours.
[257] Klemm, 'R *2H*', 117. Italics ours.
[258] Kleinig, 'R *2H*', 90.
[259] Van Voorst, R., 'Review of A.C. Thiselton's *The Two Horizons*', *RefRev* 34 (Spr. 1981), 220.
[260] Poythress, V.S., 'Review of A.C. Thiselton's *New Horizons in Hermeneutics*', *WThJ* 55.2 (1993), 345.
[261] Wink, 'R *2H*', 508. Italics ours.
[262] Borsch, 'R *2H*', 90.
[263] Poythress, 'R *NH*', 346.
[264] Thiselton, 'NH', 310, 308; cf.: Thiselton, 'R *UAB*', 342; Thiselton, 'MP', 4; Thiselton, 'P-BP', 88; Thiselton, 'SBS', 329; Thiselton, *2H*, 51. Italics ours.

'compositional psychodynamics' (see Chapter 6).[265] Nor, querying P. Grech's reading of Thiselton, does Thiselton try to 'cause a revolution in hermeneutics' merely by appeal to 'the *Tractatus* and the *Untersuchungen*'.[266] 'Thiselton's' new 'proposal' is neither "later Wittgensteinian" "perspectivism" (contradicting A.J. McNicol, who uses the word 'perspectival'),[267] nor later Wittgensteinian 'subjectivism' grounded in a straightforward "'fideism'" (contradicting B.J. Walsh's reading of Thiselton),[268] nor a 'distillation of speech-act theory and Wittgensteinian philosophy' (contradicting A.K.M. Adam's reading of Thiselton).[269]

W.W. Klein exclaims 'that', through Thiselton's work, 'hermeneutics has entered a new era'. However, against Klein's reading of Thiselton, we should conclude that Thiselton could never have simply offered 'new rules', 'results, steps, or techniques'.[270] Thiselton's philosophical dialogue neither merely "'identifies'" nor merely 'sort[s]... out' "pre-understanding" (contradicting A.J. McNicol's reading of Thiselton);[271] nor does Thiselton's philosophical dialogue merely suggest 'inquiry concerning presuppositions' (contradicting D.S. Dockery's reading of Thiselton); rather Thiselton's philosophical dialogue offers a modification and broadening of 'pre-understanding'.[272] Further, 'Thiselton' espouses neither an "objectivistic" view of the accessibility of biblical 'criteria' (contradicting B.J. Walsh's reading of Thiselton),[273] nor a mechanical-"causal" view of the functioning of speech-acts (contradicting L. Langsdorf's reading of Thiselton).[274]

Some writers (e.g. K.R. Snodgrass) later mistakenly characterize Thiselton's work as 'a new model for hermeneutics built upon the concepts of action and responsibility'.[275] However, during his second period, Thiselton revises the entire theoretical framework *within which* his later 'action... model' resides, attempting 'a major step forward in hermeneutics' (see Chapter 6).[276] As M. Van Hamersveld and L. Zuidervaart indicate, Thiselton does not appeal to his later 'action model' to "answer" 'all interpretative questions'.[277] Thiselton never simply presents 'an argument for doing hermeneutics by the action model' (contradicting R.L. Smith's

---

[265] Brodie, 'R 2H', 480, 485. Brodie's suggestion presupposes problems pertaining to the difficulties associated with asserting that all persons have a similar, and accessible, psychological "nature". See, Thiselton, 'NH', 314; cf. Thiselton, 'LMR', 1127-1130.

[266] Querying, Grech, 'R 2H', 575. Italics Grech's.

[267] McNicol, 'R 2H', 188, 189.

[268] Walsh, 'TC', 235.

[269] Adam, 'R NH', 433.

[270] Klein, 'R 2H', 75; cf. Thiselton, 'U (long)', 99-106, 120-121.

[271] McNicol, 'R 2H', 188.

[272] Dockery, 'R 2H', 134; cf. Erickson, 'R 2H', 371; cf. Klein, 'R 2H', 71.

[273] Walsh, 'TC', 235; cf. Thiselton, 2H, 22.

[274] Langsdorf, 'RA RH', 152-154; cf. Thiselton, 'Words', 293.

[275] Snodgrass, 'R RH', 199.

[276] Walsh, 'TC', 224; cf. Thiselton, 'R-RH', 113. Italics ours.

[277] Van Hamersveld, 'R RH', 252; cf. Zuidervaart, 'R RH', 296.

reading of Thiselton),²⁷⁸ as though this approach *replaced* 'language as the locus of meaning' (contradicting M.V. Weele's reading of Thiselton).²⁷⁹ For Thiselton, an 'action... model' cannot 'obviate the need first and foremost to look at the text itself in its linguistic and historical particularity'.²⁸⁰

(3) On behalf of those whom he refers to as 'non-academic readers', S.D. Moore bemoans 'the interminable intellectual detour' that Thiselton supposedly "interposes" 'between the biblical text and its practical application'.²⁸¹ However, we should reply to Moore by pointing out that, partly, Thiselton's 'detour' constitutes hermeneutical *theory-construction*, not excursions during interpretative *practice*. And, in Thiselton's view, only *some* in 'the Church' need take many of those "detours" that *do* remain part of practical interpretation – so as to provide appropriately pitched tools (e.g. commentaries) for others.²⁸²

Further, the category 'non-academic readers' *sometimes* seems patronizing. D.A. Carson records 'times' when shoe-makers 'learnt Greek' whilst they worked.²⁸³ Admittedly, 'by 1525', "disenchanted" with 'the Peasant's Revolt', 'Luther appears to have retracted his earlier view that anyone could interpret Scripture'.²⁸⁴ Nevertheless, Thiselton maintains that 'the modern enquirer may still find in Scripture "all things necessary to salvation"'.²⁸⁵ Sometimes though – and recalling Thiselton's complaint about the 'other-than-serious attitude to truth' in Western society - so-called 'non-academic readers' are far from innocent in this matter.²⁸⁶

Sometimes so-called "academics" are not innocent either. Later, Thiselton complains, 'I am *not* asking that the living address of the gospel today be buried under layers of dry academic argument'. Such a view 'of' 'hermeneutics' 'is based on misinformation and fallacy', in Thiselton's view, even though Thiselton refuses to reduce 'the Gospel' to 'cozy trivializing illustrations' 'toned down to the lowest level of memorable harmlessness', and even though Thiselton refuses to "popularize" 'the term *praxis*... in such a way as to threaten the balance between action and reflection'.²⁸⁷

---

²⁷⁸ Smith, R.L., 'Review of R. Lundin's, A.C. Thiselton's and C. Walhout's *The Responsibility of Hermeneutics*', *SWJTh* NS29.1 (Fall 1986), 64.

²⁷⁹ Against M.V. Weele; cf. Weele, 'R *RH*', 48. Italics ours.

²⁸⁰ Thiselton, 'R-RH', 113; cf. Koning, Jan. de., 'Review of R. Lundin's, A.C. Thiselton's and C. Walhout's *The Responsibility of Hermeneutics*', *PSChFJASA* 39 (Dec. 1987), 246.

²⁸¹ Moore, 'R *NH*', 287.

²⁸² Thiselton, 'U (long)', 92, 99-100; cf. Moore, 'R *NH*', 287. Italics ours.

²⁸³ Carson, D.A., *Bible Interpretation Part 1, Tape WA20, Word Alive 1993* (Eastbourne: ICC, 1993). Italics ours.

²⁸⁴ McGrath, A.E., 'Luther', in *A Dictionary of Biblical Interpretation* (eds. R.J. Coggins and J.L. Houlden; London: SCM, Philadelphia: Trinity Press, 1990), 416.

²⁸⁵ Thiselton, 'U (long)', 92.

²⁸⁶ Thiselton, 'Truth', 900-901; cf. Moore, 'R *NH*', 287.

²⁸⁷ Thiselton, A.C., 'Address and Understanding: Some Goals and Models of Biblical Interpretation as Principles of Vocational Training', *Anv* 3 (1986), 101, 112-113, 115-116; cf. Moore, 'R *NH*', 287. Italics Thiselton's.

Elsewhere, Thiselton rebukes those who 'irrationally regard hermeneutics as intrusive and inhibiting… as overlaying the text with unnecessary and intimidating theory'. Rather, after 'Terry Eagleton', Thiselton insists that 'antipathy towards theory usually means hostility towards other people's and oblivion of one's own'. Conversely, Thiselton argues that 'hermeneutics' "exposes" 'self-interest and the' "instrumentalization" 'of texts' that "serves" 'a will-for-power'. Therefore, in Thiselton's estimate, 'hermeneutics… liberates' 'texts' 'to speak not with the perlocutionary force of a seductive Hermes who has "thieved" the text, but with the illocutionary force of an authority appropriated in faith and validated finally at the last day'.[288]

We agree – except that we must insist that the discipline of hermeneutics still requires considerable organization, and that its distinct (though overlapping) and complex conversations still require considerable clarification.

## D. Conclusion:
## Towards A Unified Critique of Hermeneutical Understanding as Responsible Interpretation, through Dialogue between Philosophy and Theology

Since Thiselton's hermeneutics *as a whole* aims at "responsible interpretation" - *(where "responsible interpretation" here is to be understood to include the dimension of "being interpreted", particularly by or through the biblical texts)* - then we will slightly extend our concluding comments to the present chapter.

After preliminary remarks concerning definitions, theoretical and practical inter-relations, and approach, we highlighted Thiselton's major second-period concern to overcome "the problem of biblical (un-)intelligibility across historical distance" given (Thiselton's conclusions concerning) the failure of then-recent and/or then-existing interpretative approaches  notably "traditional", broadly "positivist", broadly "existentialist" (i.e. Bultmann and the New Hermeneutic), and broadly "structuralist" approaches - to address this problem. Thiselton "urgently" sought a theoretical *and* practical transformed paradigm for hermeneutics.

For Thiselton, the need for a transformed paradigm for hermeneutics was urgent because such a paradigm would liberate the Scriptures to function, and to be intelligibly received, as God's Word of authoritative transforming address to today's generation. For Thiselton, ongoing biblical studies were internal to the process of the derivation of such a transformed paradigm for hermeneutics in a manner that revealed the cogency of the Scriptures in relation to hermeneutical theory-construction. Thus, for Thiselton, the very process of hermeneutical

---

[288] Thiselton, A.C., 'Authority and Hermeneutics. Some Proposals for a More Creative Agenda', in *A Pathway into the Holy Scripture* (eds. P.E. Satterthwaite and D.F. Wright; Grand Rapids: Eerdmans, 1994), 140-141; cf. Eagleton, T., *Literary Theory. An Introduction* (Oxford: Blackwell, 1983, 2nd edition, 1996), x.

theory-construction *involved* in deriving a transformed hermeneutical paradigm would both "show" biblical authority and facilitate the acceptance of biblical authority. Thus, for Thiselton, the construction of a transformed paradigm for hermeneutics was urgent for this reason as well.

We also argued that, at stratum one and stratum two levels, Thiselton's "general" transformed paradigm for hermeneutics was the same as his "biblical" or "special" transformed paradigm for hermeneutics. Moreover, we argued that, even at a stratum-three level, Thiselton's "general" transformed paradigm for hermeneutics embraced broad *a posteriori* factors – notably, the hermeneutical circle - that were necessary in, and/or relevant for, *all* hermeneutics, including "biblical" or "special" hermeneutics.

Nevertheless, Thiselton argued that the *specific ways* in which broad *a posteriori* factors such as the hermeneutical circle would become operative during actual events of interpretation would differ from interpretative event to interpretative event. Thus, Thiselton argued that, in the case of "biblical" or "special" hermeneutics, "understanding" or "interpretation" was always to reflect the uniqueness of the Bible's status in relation to its formative and transformative functioning as the authoritative Word of God.

Furthermore, we argued that, at the stratum-three level of reading-situations, reading goals, interpretative strategies, models of texts, and critical tools (and so on), Thiselton banished the exclusive use of *any* single "controlling", imperialized, or monopolized hermeneutical "paradigm". At *this* level of hermeneutical practice, Thiselton insisted that every instance of interpretation and/or of understanding constituted a dynamic, dialogic, diachronic, dialectic inter-relating of two sets or pluralities of historical particularities (cf. Thiselton's "two horizons"). For "understanding" to be properly historical, Thiselton argued, it had to inter-relate – and thus accurately reflect - these two sets or pluralities of historical particularities. Thus, for Thiselton, reading-situations, reading goals, interpretative strategies, models of texts, and critical tools (and so on) remained *irreducibly*, but *responsibly*, plural.

Turning to our explication of Thiselton's transformed hermeneutical paradigm (in so far as it could be spoken of in a singular fashion), then we saw that Thiselton argued that Bultmann correctly insisted on the involvement of subjectivity (or of subjectivities) in understanding. Nevertheless, and to some extent against Bultmann, Thiselton argued that this fact did not necessarily lead to absolute relativism or subjectivism, to solipsism, or to individualism. That is, Thiselton – whether implicitly or explicitly - modified the grammar(s) of Bultmann's notion of "pre-understanding", and of Bultmann's notion of the role of "pre-understanding" during interpretation, by *more adequately re-historicizing both pre-understanding and the operation or role of pre-understanding during interpretation.*

Moving on, we saw that Thiselton argued that understanding was potentially progressive, and that understanding proceeded according to the hermeneutical circle or spiral, and embraced continuous, progressive, dialogic movements within and between multiple polarities. Whilst displacing a strict Cartesianism, Thiselton's critique of hermeneutical understanding still embraced *both* a *re-historicized* notion of subject-object conceptualization (see Chapter 3) *and* a *re-historicized* notion of historical-experiential understanding (see Chapter 3) – but Thiselton's critique of hermeneutical understanding incorporated these two dimensions of hermeneutical understanding into a larger complex whole that – against B.J. Walsh - "showed" that Thiselton's thinking was not epistemologically "dualistic".

Thus, first, in Thiselton's thinking, conceptualization, as a human *capacity* (and performance), was set into a dynamic, dialectic inter-relationship of dialogic converseness with/to the capacity (and performance) of receptive, creative, intuitive, historical-experiential, historical-existential – or "hermeneutical" – understanding (in the median sense of the phrase "hermeneutical understanding"). Again, it is important to note here that Thiselton *re-historicized both* subject-object conceptualization *and* historical-experiential understanding *beyond* the lesser "re-historicizations" of the same that pertained to the Continental hermeneutical traditions (see Chapter 3).

Second, in Thiselton's thinking, (re-historicized) conceptualization, in its comparative role of assessing historical differences and distinctions between particularities (cf. a "particular" axis), was set into a dynamic, dialectic inter-relationship of dialogic converseness with/to the creative intuitive "understanding" of "wholes", and of historical relationships between 'parts', and also between "parts" and "wholes". For Thiselton, however, the task of understanding historical "parts" and "wholes" engendered the need for an *a posteriori* "general" axis that could be invoked during the operation of a historically-reconfigured "scientific" comparative mode of "explanation" that, again, employed (re-historicized) conceptualization. Thiselton's focus had in part shifted from human interpretative capacities (and performance) to the historical structure and/or relationality of that which was to be perceived or understood.

Thiselton's historical *a posteriori* "general" interpretative axis was emphatically not a return to idealist or "formal" ahistorical *a priori* generalization. That is, Thiselton had *re-historicized the "general axis" of idealist hermeneutics* (thereby rendering this axis as *emphatically* "*non*-idealist"!) by embedding both "parts" and "wholes" in historical particularities and in *a posteriori* historical continuities. Thus, Thiselton repudiated "ideologically structuralist" dualistic approaches to texts and to meaning for exalting *a priori* generalizing, ahistorical, and deterministic approaches to linguistic structures at the expense of factors related to theology, to eschatology, to historical process and futurity, and to historical and linguistic particularity. In this context, Thiselton's later-Wittgensteinian-Saussurian alliance (see Chapter 4) exposed misappropriations of Saussure's work.

Regarding "parts" and "wholes", then Christ was the key to Thiselton's entire hermeneutical enterprise, being *both* the revelation of God (cf. metacritical evaluation) *and* an anticipatory revelation of history-as-a-whole (cf. metacritical explanation). Thiselton's "parts-wholes" emphasis also helped expound relationships between biblical exegesis, systematic theology, and the Bible "as a whole". Clearly, Thiselton had not succumbed to "Wittgensteinian subjectivism".

Third, for Thiselton, (re-historicized) conceptualization and receptive, creative, intuitive historical-experiential understanding were *both* involved *both* in "distancing" *and* in "fusion". Thiselton's focus had now shifted squarely towards *textual and interpretative* action or *performance*. If Thiselton's notion of "distancing" historically reconfigured notions of "objectivity" through his critique of Cartesian and/or broadly positivist objectivism, then Thiselton's notion of "fusion" historically reconfigured notions of "self-involvement" through his critique of broadly existentialist subjectivism. That is, Thiselton had *re-historicized objectivity and self-involvement*: historical *otherness* and historical *relationality* were *both* important. For Thiselton, textual horizons were distinct from reader horizons, and yet these two sets of horizons could always be "fused" or "related" to each other (though never perfectly). Thus, Thiselton's hermeneutical circle was grounded in the dynamic diachronic dialogue and/or dialectic between two sets of horizons, and *not* just in present horizons. Nevertheless, Thiselton argued that biblical texts were to be treated as authoritative, and that readers were to respond accordingly. Biblical interpretation was thus inseparable – in Thiselton's thinking - from pastoral theology.

For Thiselton, distancing aimed at preventing premature fusion of horizons or at preventing hermeneutical foreclosure – and did so in line with Thiselton's ethics of "responsible interpretation". Thiselton argued that readers' preunderstandings, whilst initially forming indispensable points of contact with texts, should not be allowed to tyrannize subsequent interpretation so as merely to affirm prior states of consciousness (whether individually or corporately). This point highlighted a further aspect of Thiselton's *re-historicization of both the notion of pre-understanding and of the role of pre-understanding during interpretation*: for Thiselton, a properly historical notion of pre-understanding – and of the role of pre-understanding during interpretation - could neither sanction an over-emphasis on *present-horizon individual* pre-understanding during interpretation (against Bultmann), nor sanction an imperialization of *present-horizon corporate* pre-understanding during interpretation (against, we may now add, S. Fish - see Chapter 7). In Thiselton's thinking, pre-understanding – together with the role or function *of* pre-understanding during interpretation - was embedded within a larger *diachronic historical and inter-subjective* whole.

Distancing, for Thiselton, involved painstaking exegesis and critical scholarship. In Thiselton's approach, these practices involved inquiries into extra-linguistic background or context of situation (cf. background states of affairs, author-profiles, and inter-authorial and inter-textual comparisons); into shared working frames of reference (cf. shared language-games or common worlds of understanding involving – amongst other considerations - original settings, linguistic functions, authorial intentions understood adverbially, and transmitted textual content); and into broader and narrower literary and linguistic contexts (involving, amongst other considerations, an extension of semantics beyond lexicographical factors). That is, Thiselton *re-historicized the textual horizon, re-embedding it within history* - against ahistorical and/or present-horizon-centric approaches.

Distancing, then, in Thiselton's thinking, repudiated ahistorical Western cravings for generality, and was, by definition, a matter of clarifying historical and linguistic particularities. Thus, Thiselton *employed* multiple interpretative strategies, multiple reading goals, multiple interpretative tools, and multiple models of texts. By contrast, and in line with Gadamer's rejection of any single "method", Thiselton *repudiated* single, imperialized, comprehensive, controlling, or overarching strategies, goals, tools, or models. Thus, as we noted above, Thiselton's transformed hermeneutical paradigm at *the level of theological-philosophical subtext* could not be transposed into a single controlling paradigm *at the level of practical "methods"*: texts and reading situations were much too variable, plural, and "particular" for that. Thiselton's *re-historicizing of interpretative processes* amounted to a *re-historicizing* not only of textual *horizons*, but also to a *re-historicizing* – in respect for all their historical particularity and historical plurality - of *"texts themselves"*, of models of texts, of reading situations, of reading goals, of interpretative strategies, and of critical tools.

Moving on, then fusion, for Thiselton, neither so over-emphasized past horizons that texts (especially the Bible's) were reduced to mere "historical sources" nor so over-emphasized present horizons that texts' (especially the Bible's) distinctive address as historically "other" was subsumed beneath present pre-understandings (whether individual or corporate). Thiselton's *re-historicizing of the hermeneutical problem and task* resulted in a two-horizon perspective that modified that of Gadamer (see also Chapter 6).

Fusion, for Thiselton, *re-historicized purely intra-linguistic notions of textual action and effects* by setting texts in the historical world of inter-subjective speech-acts and their extra-linguistic effects. Thiselton argued that texts sometimes gained the upper hand over readers, sometimes on account of the pre-cognitive aspect of their action. But Thiselton did not argue that this *necessarily* happened mechanically or causally. Nor did Thiselton's stress on the concrete *ways* biblically authoritative language operated during fusion constitute a "soft" view of biblical authority.

Fusion, for Thiselton, involved *re-historicized actualization*, and thus took readers *beyond* the mind-stunting indoctrination (cf. propaganda) of traditionalism, *beyond* the pre-packed answers of received systems, and *beyond* the application of hermeneutical "rules" that supported already-sanctioned interpretations, and *towards* educational actualization through deliberate, creative, initiation *both* of eventful transformation of self-understanding *and* (more broadly speaking) of expansion of horizons. Thiselton argued that biblical texts subverted readers' worlds, and did not just affirm readers' worlds. In Thiselton's thinking, even textual horizons expanded when they were properly re-historicized, since interpreters were then relating textual horizons to ever-widening diachronic frames of reference. Thiselton's re-historicization of Continental notions of actualization revised the grammar of Fuchs' "language-events", however. Thus, for Thiselton, religious experiences remained subject to critical testing because Thiselton respected the historical capacity of tradition to *distort* truth. And, for Thiselton, grammatical *propositions* could creatively extend understanding – *not only* because Thiselton respected the historical capacity of tradition to *transmit* truth, but *also* because Thiselton embedded *all* language within historical processes more effectively – notably within the *processes of tradition-refinement*.

Fusion, further, for Thiselton, also involved *re-historicized appropriation*. For Thiselton, "re-historicized appropriation" involved a changed relationship *to* a new self-understanding, and *to* textual content and function, that: neither allowed actualization/appropriation to degenerate into an individualistic hedonism of self-affirming event and experience; nor allowed actualization/appropriation to degenerate into an individual or corporate phenomenology of self-discovery; but, rather, aligned with historical dialectic, with tradition-refinement, and with personal and corporate transformation *as personal and corporate self-involvement in* historical dialectic and tradition-refinement. Thiselton argued that re-historicized appropriation in biblical hermeneutics, as public-world obedient cruciform self-involving commitment and action, was nevertheless not a matter of brute effort apart from divine grace. Furthermore, Thiselton's theologically-framed re-historicized practice of appropriation, in pursuing integrity, placed restraints on human freedoms and banished epistemological anthropocentricity. Moreover, Thiselton argued that biblical texts, properly re-historicized, were not just "sources" for historical criticism, not mere "objects" to be interpreted, and not simply "truths" for intellectual assent. Nevertheless, Thiselton also argued that re-historicized appropriation remained subject to critical testing, against unchecked pragmatism.

Fusion, for Thiselton, involved *re-historicized application*: a changed relationship to *the wider world*. However, Thiselton warned that if an inadequately-historical form of *appropriation* could degenerate into a kind of pietistic introspection that avoided broader issues in the wider world, then Thiselton also warned that an inadequately-historical form of *application* could degenerate into a distorted activism that misused the term "praxis" for merely-cosmetic reasons and that avoided reflection in relation to deeper personal, relational, and theoretical questions. Both emphases (i.e. re-historicized appropriation *and* re-historicized application) were needed in Thiselton's view, where Thiselton in effect thereby modified the Jaussean-Ricoeurian distinction between "understanding, explanation, and application". In Thiselton's approach, properly *re-historicized* application, in critique of the evasions of traditionalism, both *interpreted* the world and *changed* the world – not iconoclastically, and not through authoritarian appeals, but in tradition-respecting tradition-modification/tradition-refinement (this latter approach being the more adequately "historical" approach to traditions – see Chapter 6). For Thiselton, *re-historicized* application was corporate, concrete, and present – being neither individualistically subjectivistic, nor rationalistically over-abstracted from historical reality or life, nor over-fixated on past horizons. Moreover, for Thiselton, *re-historicized* application was future-oriented and activated from ahead - a matter of individual and corporate self-involvement in redeeming action (including, but not reducible to, the Church's mission) that in co-operation with the Holy Spirit, and by the grace imparted by the Holy Spirit, aimed towards the same future eschatological goals as the Holy Spirit. However, for Thiselton, *re-historicized* applications remained subject to critical testing and limits: *praxis* was divorced neither from historical (including biblical) traditions of wisdom nor from historical traditions of theory.

Thiselton appealed to the work of translation, of the Holy Spirit, and of engagement with interpretation histories in order to demonstrate that distancing and fusion, being mutually inter-dependent, should always be practiced together throughout the interpretative process. For Thiselton, distancing was no mere preliminary to interpretation: a properly *re-historicized* approach emphasized *both* ongoing distancing (cf. understanding of otherness) *and* ongoing fusion (cf. understanding of, and *formation* of, relationalities and/or relationships).

Indeed, in Thiselton's hermeneutics, distancing and fusion were inseparable from an interpretative dialogue between questions and answers that continuously revised its questions as texts continuously provided increasingly refined answers to those questions. In Thiselton's hermeneutics, the dialogue between questions and answers also presupposed a dialogue between listening in openness and critical reflection – both dialogues being true to a *properly re-historicized approach to the interpretative process*. Thiselton thus repudiated inadequately-historical approaches that treated texts as mere objects of knowledge.

Crucially, we concluded that Thiselton's hermeneutical circle was not simply "Gadamerian", even though it drew on Gadamer. Thus, (1), Thiselton framed conceptualization and intuitive-experiential understanding theologically as well as historically (thereby *providing better grounds for metacriticism* – see Chapter 3); (2) Thiselton prioritized history over language ontologically (thereby *more properly re-historicizing language and conceptualizations of language* such that the functioning of language throughout the processes of the hermeneutical circle could be better understood); (3) Thiselton modified the notion of the conditioning provided by effective history in that Thiselton also appealed to the "conditioning" effects of revelation and eschatology (i.e. for Thiselton, divine action shapes history towards eschatological goals); (4) Thiselton stressed traditions' capacity to distort truth (thereby being *more realistic about historical-epistemological fallibility and provisionality*); and, (5), Thiselton overcame linguistic dualism (again, *more properly re-historicizing language and conceptualizations of language* such that, for example, the creative tradition-refining role of some kinds of grammatical propositions could be properly acknowledged, understood, and facilitated). And these five modifications of Gadamer's thought were not just "Pannenbergian". Thiselton allied appeals to Pannenberg, to the later Wittgenstein, to J.L. Austin and D.D. Evans, to Saussure and modern semantics, and to Fuchs - amongst others.

And yet, didn't Thiselton's critique of Continental hermeneutics reduce his continued use of Continental terminology (such as "world", "horizon", "fusion", "language-event", and so on) to a case of misleading "persuasive definition" that up-anchored terms from their "home" language-games? We answered negatively: Thiselton's stance was a legitimate "tradition-modification" or "tradition-refinement" of Gadamer's approach – though we deferred further argument related to this point until Chapter 6.

Next, we anticipated our discussions in Chapter 7 during which we would observe first-hand some of the different "pluralities of interpretative outcomes", and (implicitly) some of the different "conflicts of interpretations", that Thiselton (or we) associated with different approaches to understanding (or to understanding Thiselton's work). In the present chapter we saw that, for Thiselton, "a plurality of legitimate and responsible readings or meanings" was the inevitable result of a properly-historical approach to understanding. We deduced from – for the most part – what we had observed so far, or else we anticipated, that, for Thiselton, superimposed and overlapping factors related to literary genre and (extra-) linguistic and intra-linguistic textual functions and self-involving effects, to interpretative impediments, to hermeneutical deepening or hermeneutical growth, to expanding historical horizons (qualified by eschatological convergence upon biblical horizons of promise), to changing readers and reading-situations, and to different interpretative angles of view (the last four of these six factors were perhaps more directly related to "present meaning") all led to "a plurality of *legitimate and responsible* readings or meanings" and to a certain kind (or kinds) of *legitimate* "conflict(s) of interpretations". Nevertheless, a few simple examples "showed" that Thiselton was not making a "turn towards the postmodern" at this point (here we are employing a later "Thiseltonian" use of the term "postmodern" – see Chapter 7). And certainly, Thiselton's stance stood in stark contrast to philosophically idealist or "formalist" notions of "fixed meaning".

Having said this, we also anticipated our arguments in Chapter 7 in which we would show that Thiselton argued that certain broadly post-structuralist approaches led to problems related to artificially-abstracted "infinitely fluid meaning", and that certain broadly socio-pragmatic approaches led to problems related to "unnecessary arbitrary meaning expansion". We also anticipated our own arguments in Chapter 7 in relation to kinds of "mistaken straightforward hermeneutical foreclosures" and in relation to the "obfuscating projections of hostile criticism". We anticipated that all four of these broad forms of "pluralities of interpretative outcomes", and (by implication) the kinds of "conflicts of interpretations" associated with them, would be illegitimate in Thiselton's view. Such outcomes and conflicts - and the approaches to interpretation associated with them - would not be properly "historical" in Thiselton's estimate.

Our exposition of Thiselton's second-period critique of hermeneutical understanding, and of some of its entailments, contradicted numerous other readings of Thiselton. Some commentators missed Thiselton's practical transformed paradigm for hermeneutics entirely. Others either misunderstood Thiselton's transformed hermeneutical paradigm, or prematurely offered alternatives. But Thiselton did not merely apply the later Wittgenstein's thinking and/or speech-act theory during interpretation. He was neither dualistic, nor straightforwardly fideistic, nor subjectivistic, nor objectivistic. He did not simply apply action models, new rules, results, steps, or techniques during interpretation.

Nor did he merely inquire into presuppositions or into preunderstanding. Nor did he espouse a mechanical-causal view of the functioning of speech-acts. And his far-reaching solutions could not be replaced by a one-sided focus on "compositional psychodynamics".

Importantly, Thiselton's hermeneutics did not constitute an impenetrable intellectual minefield or barrier between so-called non-academic readers and biblical texts. For Thiselton, the intellectual excursions required during interpretative practice (stratum three) were not the same as those required in hermeneutical theory-construction (strata one, two *and* three) and, in any case, could be undertaken by scholars who provided appropriately pitched tools for others. Thiselton argued that complaints about theory were often attempts to avoid self-criticism – to hide from one's own implicit theory and/or to indulge in hostile power-bids against others' theory. Nevertheless, we qualified Thiselton's approach by admitting that disorganized and complex hermeneutical discourses still required *considerable* organization and clarification.

Finally, again, we may conclude that the construction of a unified critique of hermeneutical understanding from Thiselton's formative work validates the promotion of working dialogues between theology and philosophy in the discipline of hermeneutics more broadly. Thiselton's unified critique of hermeneutical understanding – and/or of interpretative responsibility, the hermeneutical task, and the hermeneutical circle - *warrants* combined appeals to philosophy and theology.

CHAPTER 6

# Hermeneutics and History: Widening Dialogue Towards a New Historical Unification of Hermeneutical Theory as a Precondition for Responsible Interpretation

### A. Preliminary Comments:
### Justifying a Fresh Interpretation of *The Two Horizons*

Here, beginning in Chapter 6 and continuing on into the first three sections of Chapter 7, our primary task shall be to expound Anthony C. Thiselton's most famous work, *The Two Horizons* (1980), which is similar enough to his PhD thesis (1976/1977) for both works to be approached together (in the present chapter and in the first three sections of Chapter 7) as *"The Two Horizons"*.[1] Several preliminary considerations justify a fresh look at *The Two Horizons* – as follows.

(1) As we indicated in our Introduction, *The Two Horizons* deserves special attention because it is a major work by a leading but neglected thinker. Widely viewed in its day as 'authoritative'[2] – as 'the most important work' on hermeneutics,[3] as 'a classic',[4] and as 'a first-rate study'[5] 'of unusual scope and

---

[1] Thiselton, A.C., *The Two Horizons: New Testament Hermeneutics and Philosophical Description with Special Reference to Heidegger, Bultmann, Gadamer, and Wittgenstein* (Exeter: Paternoster Press, 1980); cf. Thiselton, A.C., *New Testament Hermeneutics and Philosophical Description: Issues in New Testament Hermeneutics with Special Reference to the Use of Philosophical Description in Heidegger, Bultmann, Gadamer, and Wittgenstein* (Sheffield: University of Sheffield Ph.D. Thesis, 1977; written by Dec. 1976).

[2] Smit, D.J., 'The Ethics of Interpretation: New Voices from the USA', *Scrip* 33 (May 1990), 18, cf. 16-18; cf.: Carver Jr., F.G., 'A Working Model for Teaching Exegesis', in *Interpreting God's Word for Today* (eds. W. McCown and J.E. Massey; Anderson, Ind.: Warner Press, 1982), 228; Hurding, R., *Pathways to Wholeness. Pastoral Care in a Postmodern Age* (London: Hodder and Stoughton, 1998), 104; Wells, R., *History Through the Eyes of Faith* (Christian College Coalition Series; New York: HarperCollins, 1989), 5; Blomberg, C.L., *Interpreting the Parables* (Leicester: IVP, 1990), 140, cf. 134.

[3] Carson, D.A., 'Church and Mission: Reflections on Contextualization and the Third Horizon', in *The Church in the Bible and the World. An International Study* (ed. D.A. Carson; Exeter: The Paternoster Press, 1987), 343, cf. 347.

[4] Hess, R.S., 'New Horizons in Hermeneutics: A Review Article', *Them* 18.2 (Jan. 1993), 22; cf.: Stott, J.R.W., *The Contemporary Christian: An Urgent Plea for Double Listening* (Leicester:

depth'[6] that addressed 'all the major issues that enter contemporary debates about interpretative theory'[7] - it was an exception amidst much "unimpressive" 'evangelical' scholarship.[8]

And yet, despite the possibility that *The Two Horizons* was 'the most comprehensive discussion of hermeneutical theory in print' for a number of years following its publication,[9] 'there has been surprisingly little thorough interaction with' both *The Two Horizons* and with 'Thiselton's work' more broadly (including his later work) – even today. Thiselton remains 'one of the major contemporary Christian authorities on hermeneutics'. And yet his thinking has been neglected – even today.[10]

(2) What 'little... interaction' there has been in the literature with *The Two Horizons*, and indeed with Thiselton's writings taken as a whole, has often produced and/or perpetuated a catalogue of misunderstandings of Thiselton's thinking. A.K.M. Adam even implies that Thiselton wrote his second major book - *New Horizons in Hermeneutics* (1992) - partly *because* he felt that his earlier 'work' (i.e. *The Two Horizons*) had been neglected or even misinterpreted. Indeed, as we shall demonstrate in Chapter 7, Adam's *own* reading of 'the Thiseltonian path' in terms of a 'distillation of speech-act theory and Wittgensteinian philosophy' is *itself* a misunderstanding of Thiselton's thinking.[11]

Some commentators even seem to miss the fact that *The Two Horizons* presents an argument at all, describing it simply as 'a comprehensive review', as 'a helpful' or 'introductory survey', as 'an overview', as one of five 'major surveys of contemporary hermeneutic reflection',[12] or as 'largely descriptive', almost a

---

IVP, 1995), 187-188; Young, F., 'The Significance of Third-Century Christian Literature', in *The Cambridge History of Early Christian Literature* (eds. F. Young, L. Ayres, and A. Louth; Cambridge: CUP, 2004), 245; Torrance, I.R., 'Gadamer, Polanyi and Ways of Being Closed', *SJT* 46.4 (1993), 497; Klein, W.W., C.L. Blomberg, and R.L. Hubbard, *Introduction to Biblical Interpretation* (Nashville, TN.: Nelson Reference, 1993), 83, 105, 340.

[5] Neill, S., and N.T. Wright, *The Interpretation of the New Testament: 1861-1986* (Oxford: OUP, 1988), 365.

[6] Ellingworth, P., 'Theory and Practice in Bible Translation', *EvanQ* 55 (Jul. 1983), 160.

[7] O'Collins, G., and D. Kendall, *The Bible for Theology: Ten Principles for the Theological Use of Scripture* (New York and Mahwah, N.J.: Paulist, 1997), 1.

[8] Pinnock, C.H., 'Climbing Out of a Swamp: The Evangelical Struggle to Understand the Creation Texts', *Interp* 43.2 (Apr. 1989), 144.

[9] Dockery, D.S., 'Review of A.C. Thiselton's *The Two Horizons*', *GThJ* 4.1 (Spr. 1983), 133.

[10] Bartholomew, C.G., 'Three Horizons: Hermeneutics from the Other End - An Evaluation of Anthony Thiselton's Hermeneutical Proposals', *EuJTh* 5.2 (1996), 122-123.

[11] Bartholomew, '3H', 123; cf. Adam, A.K.M., 'Review of A.C. Thiselton's *New Horizons in Hermeneutics*', *ModTh* 10 (1994), 433-434; cf. Thiselton, A.C., *New Horizons in Hermeneutics: The Theory and Practice of Transforming Biblical Reading* (London: HarperCollins; Grand Rapids: Zondervan, 1992).

[12] Silva, M., 'The New Testament Use of the Old Testament', in *Scripture and Truth* (eds. D.A. Carson and J.D. Woodbridge; Carlisle: Paternoster, 1995), 384; cf.: Fretheim, T.E.,

'philosophical biography'. One writer even asks, 'to what extent does... Thiselton... move beyond' expounding 'the [hermeneutical] problem to its solution?'[13] Another writer mistakenly views *The Two Horizons* simply as an exposition 'of the philosophical forces' behind 'the "New Hermeneutic"'.[14]

Other commentators, like Adam, rightly see that *The Two Horizons* presents hermeneutical 'solutions', but then misidentify these. Thus, as though finding 'solutions' to the problems associated with interpreting Paul's doctrine 'of "justification by faith"' was Thiselton's entire objective in *The Two Horizons*, J. Kleinig complains that such 'solutions' do not 'require the hefty apparatus fashioned to yield them'.[15] P.R. Keifert speaks of Thiselton's 'failure to develop the full range of implications of Heideggerian pre-understanding', as though Thiselton had no 'practical' hermeneutic, or as though Thiselton adopted 'Heideggerian pre-understanding' in an unqualified way.[16] In response to *The Two Horizons*, C.S. Rodd complains that, 'we have to descend from high philosophy and offer Christ... to those he came to save', as though Thiselton's concerns were unrelated to mission.[17]

(3) Some would doubtless blame the sometimes-difficult style of Thiselton's writing for such misunderstandings. After its publication, *The Two Horizons* was considered 'enigmatic',[18] 'tough going', 'daunting', 'unintelligible',[19] with 'insights... buried in scholarly rubble'[20] or 'stylistic clumsiness'.[21] Thus, 'it' was 'easy to lose one's way' in 'the barrage of encyclopedic details',[22] or in 'the labyrinth'.[23] Similar comments about Thiselton's style of writing appear in responses to Thiselton's contribution to *The Responsibility of Hermeneutics* (1985),[24] in responses to *Interpreting*

---

'Old Testament Commentaries: Their Selection and Use', *Interp* 36.4 (1982), 366; Libolt, C., 'Protestantism and Preaching', *MQRev* 22.3 (1983), 514; cf. 500-514; Hogan, J.P., 'Hermeneutics and the Logic of Question and Answer - Collingwood and Gadamer', *HeyJ* 28.3 (Jul. 1987), 281; Maddox, R.L., 'Contemporary Hermeneutic Philosophy and Theological Studies', *RelStud* 21.4 (Dec. 1985), 519.

[13] Harrisville, R.A., 'Review of A.C. Thiselton's *The Two Horizons*', *Interp* 36 (Apr. 1982), 216; cf. Rodd, C.S., 'Review of A.C. Thiselton's *The Two Horizons*', *ExTim* 91 (Jul. 1980), 290.

[14] Geisler, N.L., 'Review of A.C. Thiselton's *The Two Horizons*', *BibSac* 138 (Apr.-Jun. 1981), 182. Capitalization ours.

[15] Kleinig, J., 'Review of A.C. Thiselton's *The Two Horizons*', *RefThRev* 39 (Sep.-Dec. 1980), 90.

[16] Keifert, P.R., 'Review of A.C. Thiselton's *The Two Horizons*', *WW* 1 (Fall 1981), 409.

[17] Rodd, 'R *2H*', 290.

[18] Brodie, L., 'Review of A.C. Thiselton's *The Two Horizons*', *Thom* 45.3 (1981), 484.

[19] Klein, W.W., 'Review of A.C. Thiselton's *The Two Horizons*', *TrinJ* 2 (Spr. 1981), 75.

[20] Webster, J.B., 'Review of A.C. Thiselton's *The Two Horizons*', *FTht* 107.3 (1980), 220.

[21] Kleinig, 'R *2H*', 89.

[22] Keifert, 'R *2H*', 409.

[23] Bowden, J., 'Review of A.C. Thiselton's *The Two Horizons*', *Th* 84.697 (Jan. 1981), 56.

[24] E.g. Bray, G.L., 'Review of R. Lundin's, A.C. Thiselton's and C. Walhout's *The Responsibility of Hermeneutics*', *Chman* 100.3 (1986), 260.

*God and the Postmodern Self* (1995),[25] in responses to Thiselton's contribution to *The Promise of Hermeneutics* (1999),[26] and so on.

Thus, in the views of J.L. de Silva Goncalves and of D. Dawson respectively, 'one must plough through… to arrive at Thiselton's position',[27] or at 'his own thought'.[28] 'His method', in the view of P.D.L. Avis, 'is not… logical… but' dialogical, and consists of 'pitting one theologian or philosopher against another'.[29] Thiselton's 'structure', in G. Slater's view, 'is complex' and 'difficult to discern',[30] where these comments remind us of S.W. Sykes' plea, in relation to *The Two Horizons*, for Thiselton to 'show us plainly the core of his argument'.[31]

Admittedly, in our Introduction, we noted that some claimed to find *The Two Horizons* easy to understand. B.J. Walsh, for example, claims that 'Thiselton' 'cleared a path… through the jungle of contemporary hermeneutics',[32] whilst for V.S. Poythress, 'Thiselton's remarkable clarity of expression seems to make it easy'.[33] Similarly, F.H. Borsch claims to find Thiselton's 'arguments… remarkably lucid'.[34] Nevertheless, in our own study, we challenge each of these three thinkers' readings of Thiselton. There is perhaps *some* truth to the complaints about Thiselton's style of writing, even if these complaints are exaggerated.

And yet, (4), it is unfair to blame Thiselton alone for the misunderstandings. Hermeneutics is a complex problem-solving discipline that engages with difficult traditions of discourse. Substantially, 'the' intelligibility 'problem is not' Thiselton's fault, but is 'due… to the complexity of… hermeneutics' itself.[35] Indeed, 'philosophical hermeneutics' is 'notoriously complex',[36] and 'intrinsically difficult'[37]

---

[25] E.g. Debanné, M., 'Review of A.C. Thiselton's *Interpreting God and the Postmodern Self*', *ARC* 25 (1997), 163.

[26] E.g. Dray, S., 'Review of R. Lundin's, C. Walhout's and A.C. Thiselton's *The Promise of Hermeneutics*', *Egel*, 18.3 (Aut. 2000), 96.

[27] de Silva Goncalves, J.L., 'The Deconstructing of the American Mind', *Prem* 2.8 (Sep. 27 1995), 22.

[28] Dawson, D., 'Review of A.C. Thiselton's *Interpreting God and the Postmodern Self*', *PEcc* 7 (Sep. 1998), 249.

[29] Avis, P.D.L., 'Review of A.C. Thiselton's *Interpreting God and the Postmodern Self*', *ChTim* 8th Mar. (1996), 14.

[30] Slater, G., 'Review of A.C. Thiselton's *Interpreting God and the Postmodern Self*', *EpRev* 24 (Apr. 1997), 105, 104.

[31] Sykes, S.W., 'Review of A.C. Thiselton's *The Two Horizons*', *Chman* 96.2 (1982), 157.

[32] Walsh, B.J., 'Anthony Thiselton's Contribution to Biblical Hermeneutics', *ChSRev* 14.3 (1985), 235.

[33] Poythress, V.S., 'Review of A.C. Thiselton's *The Two Horizons*', *WThJ* 43 (Fall 1980), 179.

[34] Borsch, F.H., 'Review of A.C. Thiselton's *The Two Horizons*', *AThRev* 65 (Jan. 1983), 90.

[35] Brown, C., 'Review of A.C. Thiselton's *New Horizons in Hermeneutics*', *CalThJ* 30 (Apr. 1995), 233.

[36] Poythress, 'R *2H*', 179.

[37] Poythress, V.S., 'Review of A.C. Thiselton's *Interpreting God and the Postmodern Self*', *WThJ* 59 (Spr. 1997), 132.

– where this fact alone explains why *The Two Horizons* 'demands a serious intellectual effort', or why *New Horizons in Hermeneutics* is 'advanced and difficult'.[38] T.E. Pickett rightly contrasts 'the relentless demand' of the 'consumerist reader' for 'certainty', 'indeterminacy', and/or for 'the new', with 'the hard-won, hermeneutical *via media* put forth by Lundin, Walhout, and Thiselton' in *The Promise of Hermeneutics*.[39] Consumer-demand for *simplicity* may also be an issue, as we speculate in Chapter 7.

Therefore, if our arguments in the present study prove correct, then a fresh engagement with *The Two Horizons* is justified because *The Two Horizons* is a major work by a major thinker in the discipline of hermeneutics, and because *The Two Horizons* and, indeed, Thiselton's writings taken as a whole, have been neglected and misunderstood in the literature – regardless of whether or not this state of affairs has arisen because of the issue of Thiselton's difficult style of writing, or because of the issue of the complexity of hermeneutical discussions, or for other reasons.

Furthermore, if *The Two Horizons* captures the heart of Thiselton's thinking as a whole, and if the latter proves crucial to addressing the contemporary problems in the discipline of hermeneutics that we expounded in our Introduction, then a fresh engagement with *The Two Horizons* is *all the more urgently needed*. To this task we now turn.

## B. The Direct Affect of Theory on Practice:
### A Pre-Understanding of Broadening Philosophical and Theological Dialogues as a Precondition for Responsible Interpretation

*1. The Direct Affect of Theory on Practice: The Cruciality of Broadening Pre-Understanding*

To begin with, we should observe that *The Two Horizons* includes Thiselton's first-stratum argument for widening philosophical and theological dialogues in order to critically broaden the pre-understandings with which hermeneutical problems are approached. Primarily, Thiselton seeks to broaden such pre-understandings so that they extend beyond, and radically modify, those held by 'traditional', by broadly 'positivist', by '"Bultmannian"', by 'post-Bultmannian', and by 'structuralist' approaches and/or schools that are *engaged in biblical hermeneutics*. In Thiselton's view, it is the dialogic narrowness of the pre-understandings of these approaches and/or schools at the level of critical-synthesis (see our Introduction) that often causes them to misinterpret the Bible. But, for Thiselton, since 'the Bible' mediates "the Word of God", then this state of affairs becomes a problem that

---

[38] Van Voorst, R., 'Review of A.C. Thiselton's *The Two Horizons*', *RefRev* 34 (Spr. 1981), 220; cf. Kaiser, W.C. and M. Silva, *An Introduction to Biblical Hermeneutics: The Search for Meaning* (Grand Rapids: Zondervan, 1994), 287.

[39] Pickett, T., 'Review of R. Lundin's, C. Walhout's and A.C. Thiselton's *The Promise of Hermeneutics*', *RelLit* 32.3 (Aut. 2000), 109. Italics Pickett's.

requires an 'urgent' resolution.[40]

For Thiselton, then, '"hermeneutics"' is '"urgent"' and 'full of promise' because '"God speaks through the Bible today"'.[41] (Thus, contradicting J. Pereppadan's reading of Thiselton, we should note that Thiselton certainly *does* 'recognize the... presence of God in the universe').[42] Later, Thiselton urges that 'biblical' 'hermeneutics' 'relates to the very identity of Christian faith and stands at the heart of Christian theology', having importance in relation to 'theological integrity', and in relation to 'the nurture of faith and its communication in the modern world'.[43] So, Thiselton asks, why do '"English theology"' - and Western 'biblical studies' more broadly - continue to "neglect" 'hermeneutics', "attack" the hermeneutical importance of 'pre-understanding', misinterpret '"the Bible"', and thereby suppress God's Word?[44]

Notably, (1), Thiselton complains that '"purist"' "approaches" to interpretation dismiss even the *"category"* of 'pre-understanding'. Thiselton argues that these approaches advocate 'a' supposedly 'detached attitude to the Scriptures'[45] that, (a), naively equates 'self-understanding' with 'conscious' self-awareness and that, (b), thereby ignores 'philosophical and theological presuppositions'. For Thiselton, then, 'self-understanding' *includes* factors related to the unconscious – specifically factors related to *pre-understanding* and (therefore) to *'presuppositions'*. Nevertheless, for Thiselton, pre-understanding is not *only* a matter of presuppositions (see Chapter 5 and below).[46] Moreover, contradicting T. Longmann III's reading of Thiselton, presuppositions are not merely 'cultural and personal' in Thiselton's view, but relate to 'tradition'[47] – (though Thiselton argues later, *drawing on* S. Fish,

---

[40] Thiselton, *2H*, 117; cf.: 76; 283-284; 352-356; 428-431; 233; 443; 445; xix-xx; cf. Thiselton, A.C., 'The Theological Scene: Post-Bultmannian Perspectives', *CGrad* 30.3 (Sep. 1977), 88; cf. Thiselton, A.C., 'Keeping up with Recent Studies: II. Structuralism and Biblical Studies: Method or Ideology?', *ExTim* 89 (Aug. 1978), 329.

[41] Citing, Morgan, R., 'Review of A.C. Thiselton's *The Two Horizons*', *HeyJ* 22.3 (1981), 331 (first, second, and fourth quotes); cf.: Bartholomew, C.G., 'Introduction', in *After Pentecost: Language and Biblical Interpretation* (eds. C.G. Bartholomew, C. Greene and K. Möller; Scripture and Hermeneutics Series; Vol. 2; Carlisle: Paternoster, 2001), xxv (third quote); Thiselton, *2H*, xix-xx.

[42] Contradicting, Pereppadan, J., 'Review of A.C. Thiselton's *The Two Horizons*', *JDh* 6.1 (Jan-Mar 1981), 91. Italics ours.

[43] Thiselton, *NH*, 2; cf. Williams, P., 'Hermeneutics for Economists', *JACE* 22 (Dec. 1996), 16; cf. Russell, W., 'Review of A.C. Thiselton's *New Horizons in Hermeneutics*', *TrinJ* 17.2 (Fall 1996), 241.

[44] Thiselton, *2H*, 52; cf. 3-22; 108-114; xx, 356; cf. Thiselton, *NTH*, xxii, concs. 1.1-1.2a.

[45] Thiselton, *2H*, 8-10; cf.: 110; 236-238; 68; querying, Bray, 'R *RH*', 260. Italics ours.

[46] Conroy, C., 'Review of A.C. Thiselton's *The Two Horizons*', *Greg* 62.3 (1981), 563; cf. Thiselton, *2H*, 292; cf.: 304; 237; 27; 30-33, 313. Italics ours.

[47] Contradicting, Longman III, T., 'Literary Approaches to Biblical Interpretation', in *Foundations of Contemporary Interpretation* (ed. M. Silva; Grand Rapids: Zondervan, 1996), 120;

that 'the context-relative status of so-called "natural" meanings' cannot be ignored.[48] Thiselton is perhaps *both* less negative *and* less positive respectively about certain reader-response theories than R.S. Briggs and J. Ashton respectively seem to suggest).[49]

(2) Thiselton also attacks 'traditional' 'theological' 'objections' to 'hermeneutics' and to 'the category of pre-understanding'[50] – as follows. Thus, (a), Thiselton argues that 'the Holy Spirit works *through*', 'not' apart from, 'normal processes of... understanding'. Denying this, Thiselton argues, "misunderstands" the Spirit's 'work', falsely asserts that "'understanding'" proceeds directly to its "'object'", and unnecessarily risks "irrational" 'authoritarianism'.[51] Thus, for Thiselton, "'theological'" "'hermeneutics'" remains 'pneumatological',[52] but Thiselton argues that this fact does not discount 'rationality'[53] or hard "'thinking'".[54] In this context of discussion, Thiselton criticizes Karl Barth (see Chapters 3 and 7).[55]

(b) Thiselton argues that, since "'the Bible'" "creates" 'faith', then 'understanding' "'the Bible'" does *not* 'presuppose' only 'faith' (against what some claim) - even if, in Thiselton's estimate, 'pre-understandings' 'informed' by 'systematic' "theologies" (i.e. by the "received" 'faith') *do* facilitate 'exegesis'. (N.B. Thiselton's notion of 'pre-understanding' is not just pre-cognitive).[56]

(c) Against 'theological' "Platonizing" dismissals of hermeneutics, Thiselton argues that "'biblical... truth'" is neither "'timeless'" in the "strong" 'Greek' sense nor thereby necessarily easily intelligible to all as supposedly "'necessary' truth'.

---

cf. Thiselton, *2H*, 14-15, 19, 29-32, 44, 80-81, 137, 201, 305-307, 311-326; cf. Thiselton, *NTH*, xxii, concs. 7-7.3b.

[48] Thiselton, *NH*, 550, 533.

[49] Querying, Briggs, R.S., *Words in Action. Speech-Act Theory and Biblical Interpretation. Toward a Hermeneutic of Self-Involvement* (Edinburgh: T&T Clark, 2001), 21-22; and, Ashton, J., *Studying John: Approaches to the Fourth Gospel* (Oxford: Oxford University Press, 1998), 196; cf.: Thiselton, *NH*, 516-529, 495-508, 529-550; Thiselton, A.C., "'Behind' and 'In Front Of' the Text: Language, Reference and Indeterminacy', in *After Pentecost: Language and Biblical Interpretation* (eds. C.G. Bartholomew, C. Greene and K. Möller; Scripture and Hermeneutics Series; Vol. 2; Carlisle: Paternoster, 2001), 100-101.

[50] Thiselton, *2H*, 117, 109, 3-4, 18-23; cf.: 85-114, 103, 65, 90, 98, 102, 253, 288-289, 292.

[51] Thiselton, *2H*, 88-92; cf. Thiselton, A.C., 'Theology Made Exciting. Review of W. Pannenberg's *The Apostles' Creed in the Light of Today's Questions*', *CEN* 19 Jan. (1973), 12. Italics Thiselton's.

[52] Thiselton, *2H*, 88-92; cf. contradicting, Colwell, J.E., 'Perspectives on Judas: Barth's Implicit Hermeneutic', in *Interpreting the Bible: Historical and Theological Studies in Honour of David F. Wright* (ed. A.N.S. Lane; Leicester: Apollos, 1997), 169.

[53] Thiselton, *2H*, 91, 89. Contradicting, Ingraffia, B.D., 'Ontotheology and the Postmodern Bible', in *Renewing Biblical Interpretation* (eds. C.G. Bartholomew, C. Greene and K. Möller; Scripture and Hermeneutics Series; Vol. 1; Carlisle: Paternoster, 2000), 296.

[54] Thiselton, *2H*, 91-92.

[55] Thiselton, *2H*, 88-90.

[56] Thiselton, *2H*, 95, 92-94, 315; querying, Walsh, 'TC', 227-228.

Rather, Thiselton insists that "'biblical… truth'" is only 'timeless' 'in' the "'weak" sense' 'of' its "applicability" 'to… all generations'. And Thiselton argues that, since 'generations' 'change', then the discernment of the character of this "applicability" in the case of each "generation" still invokes and involves 'hermeneutical' 'considerations'.[57]

(d) Thiselton argues that "God's Word" only strikes home 'with… compelling force' when there are "'prior'" "'points of contact'" between "God's Word" and readers' pre-understandings. Thus, for Thiselton, considerations to do with "God's Word" "striking home" 'with… compelling force' are – against what some claim - necessarily still *'hermeneutical'* considerations.[58]

(e) Partly affirming the hermeneutical theory of 'Bultmann', Thiselton argues that, in the context of *responsible* interpretation, acceptance of the 'hermeneutical' 'category' of 'pre-understanding' is "unavoidable", despite the dangers that *potentially* accompany this acceptance (see Chapter 5 on subjectivism, relativism, solipsism, and individualism).[59] Further, Thiselton argues that since 'pre-understanding governs what one perceives in the text' initially, and that since 'inquiry concerning presuppositions is… the domain of philosophy' then, in Thiselton's estimate, Christian reflection must (for these, and for other, reasons) engage with "'secular'" thinking. For Thiselton, 'theology' is 'an inherently hermeneutical enterprise'.[60]

(3) Thiselton argues that broadly "positivist", "broadly" "'existentialist'", and broadly 'structuralist' approaches to 'biblical' hermeneutics artificially "'narrow'" "pre-understandings" by presupposing inadequately wide dialogues with 'philosophical' (and theological) 'traditions' at the level of critical-synthesis (on the notion of critical-synthesis, see our Introduction and also our discussions in Chapter 7). We may expound this point with reference to Thiselton's response to Bultmann in *The Two Horizons* as follows. (N.B. We will look at Thiselton's responses to the New Hermeneutic later in the present chapter. We have already considered Thiselton's responses to 'structuralist approaches' in Chapter 5, and we

---

[57] Thiselton, *2H*, 96, 95, 97-98, 101, cf. 88, 95-101; cf. Thiselton, A.C., 'Semantics and New Testament Interpretation', in *New Testament Interpretation: Essays in Principles and Methods* (ed. I.H. Marshall; Grand Rapids: Eerdmans; Exeter: Paternoster Press, 1977; actually written 1974), 79; contradicting, Klein, 'R *2H*', 72; and, Geisler, 'R *2H*', 182; and, Goldingay, J., *Models for Interpretation of Scripture* (Carlisle: Paternoster; Grand Rapids: Eerdmans, 1995), 33, cf. 167.

[58] Thiselton, *2H*, 101-103. Italics ours.

[59] Thiselton, *2H*, 284, 108, cf. 103-114.

[60] Thiselton, *2H*, 3 (third quote), 114; cf. Thiselton, A.C., 'The Theologian Who Must Not Be Ignored. Article Review of W. Pannenberg's *Basic Questions in Theology, Vol. 2*', *CEN* 25 Feb. (1972), 11; cf. first quote from, Dockery, 'R *2H*', 134; cf. second quote from, Erickson, M.J., 'Review of A.C. Thiselton's *The Two Horizons*', *JEThS* 23 (Dec. 1980), 371; cf.: fourth and fifth quotes from, Hogan, 'Q&A', 263.

defer further treatment of Thiselton's responses to 'positivism' until Chapter 7).[61]

Thus, (a), to begin with, positively, Thiselton argues, (i), that Bultmann rightly emphasized 'the category of pre-understanding' in his development of points from Dilthey's work. Citing Bultmann, 'any interpretation is… sustained by a… pre-understanding of the subject-matter'.[62]

As noted earlier, (ii), Thiselton agrees with Bultmann's point that '"a prior"' 'life-relation' 'between' an 'interpreter' 'and' an 'author' or 'text' is pre-conditional '"for understanding"' such that,[63] for Bultmann and Thiselton, 'interpretation always presupposes a life-relation'.[64]

With Bultmann, (iii), Thiselton argues that 'understanding' is an '"art"', '"involving"' '"the interpreter's"' '"subjectivity"' without excluding '"objectivity"', and that Bultmann rightly repudiates '"the… absurd"' 'demand that the interpreter has to silence his or her subjectivity… to achieve objective knowledge'.[65]

With Bultmann, (iv), Thiselton insists that '"prior"' '"shared"' '"understanding"' is the necessary 'starting-point' '"for"' the attainment of further '"understanding"', and that this axiom renders the notion of 'pre-understanding', and 'hermeneutics' more broadly, '"unavoidable"' – at least in the context of *responsible* interpretation.[66]

Notably, (v), with Bultmann, Thiselton argues that 'interpretation… involves self-understanding', since '"the interpreter"', and '"the interpreter's"' initial 'questions', can become "a text's" '"object"' (contrary to the Cartesian '"schema"'). With Bultmann (up to a point), Thiselton allows that – to *some extent* at least - 'the New Testament' 'word' 'is addressed directly to existential self-understanding'.[67]

Further, (vi), with Bultmann, Thiselton argues that interpreters' "pre-understandings" are to be 'enlarged' and 'informed' through 'dialogue with' 'traditions' 'of philosophy'. Thiselton argues that, if this principle of "enlargement" of "pre-understandings" through 'dialogue with' 'traditions' 'of philosophy' had not been endorsed by Bultmann himself, then 'Bultmann's' own 'fruitful' biblical hermeneutics 'would' have been 'lost'. Thiselton insists that such

---

[61] Thiselton, *2H*, 60; cf.: 244-245; 109-114; 283-292; 53-84; 428-431; cf. Thiselton, 'SBS', 329.

[62] Thiselton, *2H*, 109; cf.: 237; 379-385; 285-287; cf.: Bultmann, R., 'The Problem of Hermeneutics', in *New Testament and Mythology and Other Basic Writings* (ed. and trans. S.M. Ogden; Philadelphia: Fortress Press, 1984), 69-93; quote from 82.

[63] Thiselton, *2H*, 237; cf.: Bultmann, 'PH', 75; Bultmann, R., 'The Problem of Hermeneutics', in *Essays Philosophical and Theological* (trans. J.C.G. Greig; New York: The MacMillan Company, 1955), 242-243, 255.

[64] Bultmann, 'PH', 75.

[65] Thiselton, *2H*, 236-238; quoting, Bultmann, 'PH', 85.

[66] Thiselton, *2H*, 237, cf.: 238-239; 284; 114; cf.: Thiselton, A.C., 'The New Hermeneutic', in *New Testament Interpretation: Essays in Principles and Methods* (ed. I.H. Marshall; Grand Rapids: Eerdmans; Exeter: Paternoster Press, 1977), 311.

[67] Thiselton, *2H*, 237-238, 284; cf.: Thiselton, 'NH', 313; quoting, Bultmann, 'PH', 87-88.

an "enlargement" allows a biblical 'text' to 'speak more closely in its own right'.[68]

(b) Negatively, however, in what J.I. Packer describes as being Thiselton's 'masterly critique' of Bultmann, Thiselton argues that Bultmann, 'in *practice*' if not in *'theory'*, "absolutizes" a *"theological"* 'pre-understanding' that combines the following untenable *"theological" "dualisms"* or "dichotomies":[69] (i) 'God' beyond 'objectification' *versus* an 'objectified realm of knowing' (this dichotomy is 'Neo-Kantian' in Thiselton's estimate);[70] (ii) 'address' and 'justification through faith' *versus* 'works' as 'objectifying thought… in accordance with law' (in Thiselton's estimate, this particular dichotomy pertains to 'nineteenth-century Lutheranism' *combined with* 'Marburg Neo-Kantianism', and is not simply a dichotomy inherited from "existentialism" - M.A. Seifrid misreads Thiselton here);[71] (iii) 'Kerygma', '"revelation"', and 'faith' *versus* 'dogmatics', 'myth', and 'information' (in Thiselton's estimate, Bultmann inherited this particular dichotomy from 'liberal theology' and from then-'current' 'New Testament' 'scholarship');[72] (iv) the transcendent '"God"', divine '"action"', '"God's Word"', and Christian 'faith' *versus* '"this world"' (in Thiselton's estimate, Bultmann inherited this particular dichotomy from 'dialectical theology').[73]

Thiselton's juxtaposition of Bultmann's *four* theological dualisms or dichotomies in this context of discussion undermines W. Wink's misleading and over-simplistic assertion that Thiselton supposedly misunderstands 'Bultmann's distinction between this world and the beyond… in… spatial terms'.[74]

Notably, Thiselton recounts that, for Bultmann, so-called New Testament 'myth' failed the test of 'contemporary' '"cosmological correctness"' (cf. '"political correctness"') – a scenario that, in Bultmann's thinking, hindered his (i.e. Bultmann's own) evangelistic desire to "bridge" 'the gap between… the New Testament and the twentieth century'.[75] For Bultmann, modern 'Christian proclamation' could not 'expect [modern] men and women to acknowledge the

---

[68] Thiselton, *2H*, 292; cf.: xix; 94; 283-284; 206; 227-228; 315; 6-7; cf. quoting, Dockery, 'R *2H*', 135; cf. Thiselton, 'TNI', 11.

[69] Thiselton, *2H*, 283-284; cf. 246-247; cf.: quoting, Packer, J.I., 'Infallible Scripture and the Role of Hermeneutics', in *Scripture and Truth* (eds. D.A. Carson and J.D. Woodbridge; Carlisle: Paternoster, 1995), 415. First and second italics Thiselton's, remaining italics ours.

[70] Thiselton, *2H*, 210-212; cf. 285-286. Italics ours.

[71] Thiselton, *2H*, 217; cf.: 215; 210-211; 213-217, 219; cf. Seifrid, M.A., 'The Pauline Gospel in a Postmodern Age', in *The Challenge of Postmodernism. An Evangelical Engagement* (ed. D.S. Dockery; Grand Rapids, Mi.: Baker Books, 1997), 191. Italics ours.

[72] Thiselton, *2H*, 222, 228, 205-207; cf. 218-223. Italics ours.

[73] Thiselton, *2H*, 224; cf. 223-226. Italics ours.

[74] Wink, W., 'Review of A.C. Thiselton's *The Two Horizons*', *ThT* 37.4 (Jan. 1981), 506, 508.

[75] Thiselton, *2H*, 218-219, 288-290; cf.: quoting, Barton, S.C., 'Living as families in the light of the New Testament', *Interp* 52.2 (Apr. 1998), 140, 139; second quote from, Schneiders, S.M., 'Review of A.C. Thiselton's *The Two Horizons*', *JRel* 62.3 (Jul. 1982), 308.

mythical world picture as true'.[76]

For Thiselton, however, Bultmann's theological dichotomies almost "reduce" 'theology to anthropology' plus '"the 'word of the cross'"' where, for Bultmann, even 'the resurrection cannot be an authenticating miracle'.[77]

Indeed, argues Thiselton, Bultmann's theological dualisms or dichotomies seemed to him (i.e. to Bultmann) to make New Testament interpretation *center* upon 'de-objectification' or on 'demythologizing', where Thiselton thus argues that 'the terms of the hermeneutical problem were set for Bultmann *prior* to his engagement with Heidegger's philosophy' (for Bultmann, 'we may not see… [God] as we have conceived him').[78]

Nevertheless, Thiselton adds that the 'objectification' issue *did* make 'Heidegger's' 'conceptuality' 'seem' - to 'Bultmann' - to be tailor-made for biblical hermeneutics - especially given Bultmann's familiarity with H. Jonas' 'work' on 'myth'. Thus, Thiselton notes that Bultmann praised 'Heidegger's demonstration' that 'understanding… [is] something existential'.[79]

(c) Thiselton's point of departure, in relation to this last point, is not that Bultmann was wrong to dialogue with the early Heidegger, but that Bultmann's 'philosophical' 'dialogue' failed to widen *further* - towards a critique of its own Diltheyan, 'Neo-Kantian', early-Heideggerian shape.[80] The result of this state of affairs, in Thiselton's view, was that 'Bultmann's… pre-understanding' *also* became pervaded by '*philosophical*' "dualisms" or dichotomies, where 'Thiselton' criticizes these "dualisms" or dichotomies 'time after time'.[81]

Notably, (i), for Thiselton, 'Bultmann's' '*historical*' '*Geschichte*' versus '*Historie*' 'dualism' rightly stresses 'present' "individual" "subjective" 'existential' 'historical' "possibility" but wrongly disparages '"past"' '"historical"' "facts" and, additionally, fails "to relate" '"the[se] two"' poles to one another. Thiselton argues that Bultmann's appeal to R.G. Collingwood, who more properly interweaves '"the[se] two"' poles, fails to prevent Bultmann's sharpening of '"this problem"' – a '"problem"' that, in Thiselton's estimate, Bultmann inherited from 'Dilthey' and

---

[76] Bultmann, R., 'New Testament and Mythology: The Problem of Demythologizing The New Testament Proclamation', in *New Testament and Mythology and Other Basic Writings* (ed. and trans. S.M. Ogden; Philadelphia: Fortress Press, 1984), 3.

[77] Thiselton, *2H*, 223, cf. 291-292; cf. Bultmann, 'NT&M', 37.

[78] Thiselton, *2H*, 205, 233, 257, 259, 226, 230, 232, 291, 441-442; cf. quoting, Schneiders, 'R *2H*', 307; cf. quoting from Bultmann, R., 'Concerning the Hidden and the Revealed God', in *Existence and Faith: Shorter Writings of Rudolf Bultmann* (ed. and trans. S.M. Ogden; New York: Meridian Books, Inc., 1960), 26. Italics in speech-marks ours (originally Thiselton's, but removed by Schneiders).

[79] Thiselton, *2H*, 232, 442; cf. 222-223, 232-233, 256-257, 441-442; cf. Bultmann, 'PH', 234-261; cf. quoting, 251-252. Italics ours.

[80] Thiselton, *2H*, 291-292, 232-233, 239-240, 250-251; cf. Thiselton, 'TNI', 11. Italics ours.

[81] Conroy, 'R *2H*', 564; cf. Thiselton, *2H*, 284, 246; cf.: 245-251; 39, 75-76, 80-81, 385, 443. Italics ours.

from 'Heidegger'.[82] For Thiselton, then, a more unified philosophy of history is required: in Thiselton's estimate, 'Bultmann', being "cut" 'off from certain aspects of reality', fails to do 'justice to' a "text's" 'relationship to external events', and often disparagingly views biblical texts' 'content as objectifying representations'.[83]

(ii) Correlatively, for Thiselton, Bultmann's *epistemological* dualism, which reflects that of Heidegger, erroneously sets the 'truth' of '"subjectivity"', 'worldhood', 'feeling-states', and of 'ontological' "disclosure" (cf. '"encounter"', 'address', '"certainty"', '"decision"', and transformation) against the 'truth' of 'cognition', 'report', 'concepts' (including 'psychological' concepts'), '*and* critical testing' – and fails to relate '"the[se] two"' poles to one another. Thiselton argues, however, that "worldhood" and "feeling-states" (or 'states-of-mind') are not '"logically"' 'prior to', or 'more reliable' than, 'cognition'. Thiselton argues that, since 'epistemology' should include and "inter-relate" both pre-cognitive and 'cognitive' dimensions, then Bultmann is in error to sharply separate 'existential self-understanding' from 'existentialist knowledge', and, 'pre-scientific understanding' from 'objectifying procedure'.[84]

Indeed, Thiselton argues that 'Bultmann' has "merely" "replaced" 'the epistemological dualism between subject and object' with different dualisms, including the dualism between 'primary… and… secondary historical knowledge', and/or the dualism between 'genuine historical understanding' and '"objective" historical knowledge'.[85] Further, Thiselton argues that Bultmann has over-sharpened Dilthey's distinction between 'historical understanding' and "scientific" '"explanation"'. Conversely, Thiselton argues that 'Collingwood' rightly maintained a place for (some kind of notion of) '"subject"'-'"object"' 'reflection' in 'historical understanding'. Bultmann, however, in Thiselton's estimate, sharply separates 'existential understanding' from 'objectifying presentation'.[86]

Therefore we should note, against R.A. Harrisville's reading of Thiselton, that Thiselton does *not* simply "find" 'a way out of' 'subject'-'object' dualism 'in Heidegger' (see Chapter 3).[87]

(iii) Thiselton also argues against Bultmann's three-fold *linguistic* "dualisms". Thus, *first*, Thiselton argues that 'Bultmann', despite his appeals to 'Dilthey's

---

[82] Thiselton, *2H*, 279, 243-250; cf. 184-185. First italics ours, remaining italics Thiselton's.

[83] Thiselton, *2H*, 77, 81-84; cf. 245-251; cf.: Brodie, 'R *2H*', 483; last quote in, Bultmann, 'NT&M', 33.

[84] Thiselton, *2H*, 188-200, 163, 245-247, 286-291, 159, 274; cf. 232-233, 441; cf. Bultmann, R., 'Theology as Science', in *New Testament and Mythology and Other Basic Writings* (ed. and trans. S.M. Ogden; Philadelphia: Fortress Press, 1984), 45-67; cf. quotes from, 66 cf. 67; cf.: Bultmann, 'PH', 69-93; quote from 88. First italics ours, second italics Thiselton's.

[85] Walsh, 'TC', 231; cf.: Webster, 'R *2H*', 219; Thiselton, *2H*, 246-251, 205-217; Bultmann, R., 'Science and Existence', in *New Testament and Mythology and Other Basic Writings* (ed. and trans. S.M. Ogden; Philadelphia: Fortress Press, 1984), 131-144; quotes from, 138, 139.

[86] Thiselton, *2H*, 235; cf. 244, 243, 245; cf. 246; cf. quoting, Bultmann, 'S&E', 139.

[87] Contradicting, Harrisville, 'R *2H*', 216.

category of "'life'", fails "to relate" 'New Testament' '"meaning"' or 'value' to 'Old Testament' "objectifying" "traditions" or "facts". Therefore Thiselton argues, drawing on the later Wittgenstein's argument against "'private language'", that Bultmann's approach, in this way, renders 'revelation' "unintelligible". Thus, in affirmation of Thiselton's argument, we may note that Bultmann finds 'numerous instances where the Old Testament text only becomes of use' to 'the New Testament' 'when... understood... contrary to its original meaning'.[88]

*Second*, Thiselton argues that 'Bultmann' divorces 'self-involving' 'linguistic' "'functions'" from 'objectifying' 'linguistic' "'functions'" despite the fact that, in all speech-action, these two sets of 'linguistic' "'functions'" are actually interwoven. Thus, Thiselton observes that Bultmann argues that the kind (or kinds) of language that he (i.e. Bultmann) calls 'myth' (erroneously, in Thiselton's estimate) supposedly "wants" 'to be interpreted in existentialist terms'.[89]

*Third*, Thiselton argues that 'Bultmann' divorces 'thought' 'and inner' 'intention' from 'linguistic expression' despite the fact that, in life, 'thought', 'intention', and 'linguistic expression' are actually interwoven. Thus, for Bultmann, the 'real intention' of 'myth' 'is... obscured by' 'its' 'objectifying character'.[90]

(iv) Thiselton also rejects Bultmann's three-fold *anthropological* "dualisms": *first*, in Thiselton's estimate, Bultmann rightly stresses "individual" "'subjectivity'" but wrongly disparages corporate inter-subjectivity. Thus Bultmann argues that 'only in radical loneliness does man find himself'.[91] *Second*, Thiselton argues that, in Bultmann's thinking, 'worldhood' inappropriately displaces 'a logically prior concept of the whole person': for Bultmann, 'Paul... did not... describe man as a phenomenon in the... objectively perceptible world'.[92] *Third*, Thiselton argues that, in Bultmann's thinking, "imperatives" and "existential" questions about "'responsibility'" and "decision'" wrongly displace "'the material world'" in which they have their 'anchorage'. Admittedly, for Bultmann, 'eschatological existence... must actualize itself in the concrete deed'; and yet, Bultmann *also* argues that 'all

---

[88] Thiselton, *2H*, 39-40, 285-287, 234-248, 75-81, 382; cf. 211, 359-361, 385, 425, 442-444; cf. quoting, Bultmann, R., 'Prophecy and Fulfilment', in *Essays Philosophical and Theological* (trans. J.C.G. Greig; New York: The MacMillan Company, 1955), 185. Italics ours.

[89] Thiselton, *2H*, 195-196, 40, 292, 230-234, 313, 81, 372-373, 256-269; cf.: Bultmann, 'NT&M', 1-44; quoting, 9, cf. 10.

[90] Thiselton, *2H*, 271, 292, 442, cf. 311-314; cf.: Thiselton, A.C., 'Language and Meaning in Religion', in 'Word', in *The New International Dictionary of New Testament Theology. Volume III* (ed. C. Brown; Exeter: Paternoster; Grand Rapids: Zondervan, 1978; actually written by 1977), 1138-1139; Bultmann, 'NT&M', 1-44; quoting, 10.

[91] Thiselton, *2H*, 282-284, 238, 292; cf. quoting, Bultmann, R., 'Forms of Human Community', in *Essays Philosophical and Theological* (trans. J.C.G. Greig; New York: The MacMillan Company, 1955), 301. Italics ours.

[92] Thiselton, *2H*, 187-188, 191-194, 198, cf. 230-234; cf. quoting, Bultmann, R., *Theology of the New Testament. Volume 1* (trans. K. Grobel; London: SCM Press Ltd., 1952), 191.

spiritual attitudes are unobservable'.[93]

(v) Thiselton argues that Bultmann, on the one hand, "absolutizes", and claims comprehensiveness in relation to, his *generalizing* 'form criticism' and *'Sachkritik'* (cf. his "definitions", disparagement, and de-objectification/demythologizing of 'myth') and that, on the other hand, Bultmann neglects 'painstaking exegesis' 'of the *particular* case'. That is, Thiselton argues that Bultmann's approach involves an untenable *interpretative* dichotomy or dualism in practice. Thiselton argues that Bultmann thus wrongly monopolizes 'demythologizing as a hermeneutical method'.[94] But, Thiselton argues, Bultmann thereby 'so' "loads" 'the terms of the discussion that any exegetical conclusions would seem to support his [i.e. Bultmann's] claim'.[95] In Thiselton's estimate, Bultmann's approach to biblical interpretation thus reflects Bultmann's 'unwillingness to let his pre-understanding be sufficiently challenged by the text'.[96]

That is, Thiselton argues that Bultmann's hermeneutical theory – (i.e. *not* 'the role which Bultmann *formally* assigns to the concept of pre-understanding in hermeneutics' *but* the *theoretical content* of Bultmann's 'pre-understanding' that is *operative during* Bultmann's interpretative practice) - *directly affects* Bultmann's interpretative practice. Moreover, in Thiselton's estimate, '"Bultmann *absolutizes* his philosophical 'pre-understanding' in such a way that he decides in advance what the New Testament writings may or may not really say"'.[97]

(Later, extending his critique of 'Bultmann', Thiselton argues that 'the Christian story is not rightly called a "myth"', even if 'it' does 'contain mythical elements'.[98] Thiselton argues that since 'the term "myth"… suggests untruth', and that since

---

[93] Thiselton, *2H*, 195, 282, 292, 249-250; cf. quoting, Bultmann, *TNT1*, 337, cf. 190-352; cf. quoting, Bultmann, R., 'A Reply to the Theses of J. Schniewind', in *Kerygma and Myth. A Theological Debate* (ed. H.-W. Bartsch; New York: Harper and Row, 1961), 102.

[94] Thiselton, *2H*, 284, 288-291, 410, 219-223, 442, 252-283, 407; cf. quoting, Bultmann, R., 'On the Problem of Demythologizing (1952)', in *New Testament and Mythology and Other Basic Writings* (ed. and trans. S.M. Ogden; Philadelphia: Fortress, 1984), 105; cf. 95-130. Second italics Thiselton's, remaining italics ours.

[95] Thiselton, *2H*, 290; cf. Klein, 'R *2H*', 73.

[96] Thiselton, *2H*, 284, cf. 282-283; cf. Morgan, 'R *2H*', 332. Morgan's comment here is *consistent* with, and not a criticism of, Thiselton's argument – against Morgan.

[97] Thiselton, *2H*, 283; cf. Klein, 'R *2H*', 73. By the phrase "hermeneutical theory" here we mean "Bultmann's dualistic pre-understanding". Thiselton's use of the phrase "hermeneutical theory" in Thiselton, *2H*, 283, concerns only Bultmann's notion of the *role* of pre-understanding. In *this* sense Thiselton argues, 'we criticize not… [Bultmann's] view of pre-understanding'. Yet, Thiselton *does* reject the dualistic *content* of Bultmann's pre-understanding (see Chapter 5). Second italics Thiselton's, remaining italics ours.

[98] Macquarrie, J., 'Review of B. Mitchell ed. *Believing in the Church. The Corporate Nature of the Faith. A Report by the Doctrine Commission of the Church of England*', *Th* 85 (Mar. 1982), 126-127; cf. Thiselton, A.C., 'Knowledge, Myth and Corporate Memory', in *Believing in the Church: Essays by Members of the Church of England Doctrine Commission* (ed. B. Mitchell; London: SPCK, 1981), 70; cf. 67-72.

Bultmann views 'mythical thinking… [as] the opposite of scientific thinking', then 'the term "myth"' should be abandoned – at least in the context of biblical hermeneutics).[99]

Finally, (d), Thiselton argues that *even when* Bultmann's theologically and philosophically 'dualistic' 'pre-understanding' *helps to engender Bultmann's most 'fruitful' interpretative results* – then, *even then*, that 'pre-understanding' *still* only helps to engender *'one-sided'* biblical 'interpretation[s]'. That is, Thiselton argues that, in relation to '"Pauline anthropology"', even Bultmann's 'fruitful' exegeses of the 'unitary' human self (Bultmann: 'man does not have a *sōma*; he *is sōma*'), of "modes" 'of existence', and of '"possibility"' (Bultmann: 'a double possibility exists' for man – 'to be at one with himself [cf. *pneuma*] or… estranged from himself' [cf. *'sarx'*]) are flawed since, in Thiselton's estimate, *'sōma'*, *'sarx'*, and *'pneuma'* have a broader 'range of' meanings than Bultmann allows – (though some scholars disagree with Thiselton as to what those meanings are).[100]

Thiselton's main hermeneutical point, then, in this context of discussion, is that dialogically '"narrow"' 'pre-understandings' (at the "stratum one" "level" of critical-synthesis) generate unresolved theoretical dichotomies in relation to conceptualizations of history, epistemology, language, and, in Bultmann's case, of human selves (cf. 'stratum two'). Thiselton argues that these theoretical dichotomies, in turn, yield dichotomies within the theory and practice of interpretation itself, and thereby engender problematic interpretative results which, in turn, must inevitably lead on to problematic understandings, and to problematic outworkings of understandings (cf. 'stratum three'). That is, Thiselton argues that: (i) Bultmann rightly stresses 'the category of pre-understanding'; and that, (ii), Bultmann rightly *begins* 'philosophical' 'dialogue' at the level of 'pre-understanding'; but that, (iii), Bultmann wrongly absolutizes that 'dialogue' critically when that 'dialogue' is still too "narrow", and thereby ends up with problematic exegetical or interpretative results (cf. distanciations) – and so, by implication, also ends up with

---

[99] Thiselton, 'KMCM', 68-70, 72; cf. Davies, H., 'Review of B. Mitchell ed. *Believing in the Church. The Corporate Nature of the Faith. A Report by the Doctrine Commission of the Church of England*', *ThT* 39 (Jan. 1983), 464; cf. contradicting, Avis, P.D.L., *God and the Creative Imagination: Metaphor, Symbol and Myth in Religion and Theology* (London: Routledge, 1999), 132, 165-167; quoting, Bultmann, 'OPD(1952)', 95. Avis restates Bultmann's stance on "myth" without addressing the theological and philosophical problems entailed in using the term "myth" in relation to the biblical writings (so-called 'popular' views of 'myth' aside).

[100] Thiselton, *2H*, 284-285, 292, 277, 315, 279, 291, 282; cf. 275-283, 281-283, 291-292; cf. Osei-Bonsu, J., 'Anthropological Dualism in The New Testament', *SJT* 40.4 (1987), 576. But cf. Shults, F.L., *Reforming Theological Anthropology: After the Philosophical Turn to Relationality* (Grand Rapids, MI.: Eerdmans, 2003), 178; cf. Thiselton, A.C., 'Human Being, Relationality and Time in Hebrews, 1 Corinthians and Western Traditions. Paper presented at North Park Theological Seminary, Oct 17-19, 1997', *ExA* 13 (1997), 87; cf. 86-88; cf. Bultmann, *TNT1*, 190-352 (citations from 194, 196). First five sets of italics ours, sixth and seventh italics Bultmann's, remaining italics Thiselton's. Transliterations are Bultmann's and Thiselton's.

problematic understandings (cf. actualizations), and with problematic outcomes of understandings (cf. appropriations and applications). Bultmann, in Thiselton's estimate, thereby fails to realize that 'particular' 'philosophical' 'traditions' only yield 'particular… insights' and not 'comprehensive' "hermeneutical theories".[101] Thus, querying F. Watson's comments, we may observe that Thiselton shows that changes in 'hermeneutical theory' *do* 'lead directly' to changes in 'interpretative practice': *'theory' 'directly' affects 'interpretative practice', interpretative 'results', understandings, and the outworkings of understandings.*[102]

(4) In *The Two Horizons*, Thiselton's argument regarding pre-understanding progresses from a critique of Bultmann to a critique of the New Hermeneutic (i.e. the hermeneutics of E. Fuchs and of G. Ebeling) and of what Thiselton regards as being the American counterpart to the New Hermeneutic (i.e. the hermeneutics of R. Funk, of D.O. Via, and of J.D. Crossan). (In the present context of discussion, further, we may observe that Thiselton applies his *broader* criticisms of the New Hermeneutic to the American counterpart of the New Hermeneutic as well. In the present context of discussion, therefore, we may designate the New Hermeneutic and the American counterpart of the New Hermeneutic, taken together, as "the New Hermeneutic").[103]

Thus, (a), positively, Thiselton applauds how the New Hermeneutic – in effect if not always "explicitly" - extends philosophical dialogue at the level of pre-understanding to include the later Heidegger and 'Gadamer', where Thiselton, in addition, appeals to H. Diem, to H. Ott, and to P. Stuhlmacher in order to highlight the value of 'Gadamer's work' in relation to 'exegesis and' 'systematic theology'. Querying T.E. Van Spanje's reading of Thiselton, we should note that Thiselton does not simply imply that the New Hermeneutic is 'mainly built on R. Bultmann'.[104] Rather, Thiselton argues that, along with 'Gadamer', the New Hermeneutic emphasizes 'the linguisticality of understanding', or 'of Being', and that the New Hermeneutic attempts 'to *both correct and* carry forward the program of Bultmann' - though S.M. Schneiders seems to miss the fact that, in Thiselton's estimate, this attempt is to be viewed as an attempt 'to… correct' Bultmann's *multiple* dualisms, dichotomies, or 'one-sided' emphases along *multiple* axes of hermeneutical discussion.[105]

---

[101] Thiselton, *2H*, 109, 114, 315; cf. 291-292; cf. 284, 283, 354; cf. Thiselton, 'TNI', 11.

[102] Watson, F., 'Review of A.C. Thiselton's *New Horizons in Hermeneutics*', *BibInterp* 4.2 (1996), 255. Italics ours.

[103] Thiselton, *2H*, 327-356.

[104] Thiselton, *2H*, 337, 334-335, 314; cf. 319-356; cf. querying, Van Spanje, T.E., 'Contextualization: Hermeneutical Remarks', *BJRULibM* 80.1 (1998), 204.

[105] Thiselton, *2H*, 337; cf. 292; cf.: Thiselton, 'P-BP', 88; McHann Jr., J.C., *The Three Horizons: A Study in Biblical Hermeneutics with Special Reference to Wolfhart Pannenberg* (Aberdeen: University of Aberdeen Ph.D. Thesis, 1987), 224, 231; Gadamer, H.-G., *Truth and Method* (trans. J. Weinsheimer and D.G. Marshall; London: Sheed & Ward, 1975, 1989), 389; quoting, Schneiders, 'R *2H*', 308. Italics ours.

Thus, (i), Thiselton argues that the New Hermeneutic rightly tries to unite 'the Jesus of *history*' with 'the Jesus of faith' and, therefore, to some extent, to reinstate the '*past*' horizon.[106] Thiselton argues that, for the New Hermeneutic, as for 'Gadamer', '*respect for the otherness of the horizon of the other*' is rightly seen as being 'fundamental'.[107] Contradicting T.E. Van Spanje's reading of Thiselton again, we should observe that Thiselton does *not* espouse a view of the New Hermeneutic in which 'readers' are the only 'object' of 'interpretation'.[108] (ii) Furthermore, Thiselton argues that the New Hermeneutic rightly relates history to *epistemology*. In Thiselton's estimate, '*the truth*' of 'the' 'historical' 'past' – which is potentially capable of "transforming" interpreters' "worlds" "'from *beyond*'" their own 'horizons' - is better reinstated in the New Hermeneutic than in 'Bultmann'.[109] (iii) Thiselton argues that, 'with Gadamer', the New Hermeneutic rightly views '*language*' and 'thought' as being interwoven, and that the New Hermeneutic,[110] (iv), in relation to *anthropology*, rightly reinstates *corporate* '*community*' in correction of Bultmann's over-emphasis on '*individual*' "'subjectivity'".[111] In Thiselton's view, further, 'pre-cognitive' "dimensions" and "'existential'" questions are more firmly related to concrete 'life' in the New Hermeneutic than in Bultmann.[112] (v) In a related context, Thiselton approves of the later Heidegger's complaints *both* against "'standardization'" (cf. *generalization*) in '*Western*' culture, *and* (by implication, therefore, and in parallel with the later Wittgenstein) against the suppression of "'the *particular*'" in '*Western*' culture. In other words, *part* of Thiselton's hermeneutical argument in the context of his discussion in relation to the New Hermeneutic is that widening 'philosophical' 'dialogue' at the level of pre-understanding (cf. stratum one) *improves* interpretative theory in relation to the

---

[106] Thiselton, 'P-BP', 88; cf.: Thiselton, *2H*, 212, 221, 346; Fuchs, E., 'Preface to the English Edition', in *Studies of the Historical Jesus* (Studies in Biblical Theology; Naperville, Ill.: Alec R. Allenson, Inc, & Chatham: SCM Press Ltd, 1964), 7; quoting, Ebeling, G., 'The Question of the Historical Jesus and the Problem of Christology. To Rudolf Bultmann on his 75th Birthday', in *Word and Faith* (trans. J.W. Leitch; Philadelphia: Fortress Press, Chatham: SCM Press Ltd, 1963), 298. Italics ours.

[107] Thiselton, *2H*, 312-313, 318-319, 322, 324-326, 340, 342, 345, 349, 351, 356; cf.: Thiselton, A.C., 'Thirty Years of Hermeneutics: Retrospect and Prospects', in *International Symposium on the Interpretation of the Bible* (ed. J. Krašovec; Ljubljana: Slovenian Academy of Sciences and Arts; Sheffield: Sheffield Academic Press, 1998), 1564. Italics Thiselton's.

[108] Thiselton, *2H*, 353; contradicting, Van Spanje, 'CHR', 204.

[109] Thiselton, *2H*, 314; cf.: 347; 350-351; 356; 309-314; cf. Thiselton, A.C., 'Understanding God's Word Today: Evangelicals Face the Challenge of the New Hermeneutic. Address at the Second National Evangelical Anglican Congress, Nottingham, 1977', in *Obeying Christ in a Changing World, Vol. 1* (ed. J.R.W. Stott; Glasgow: Collins/Fountain Books, 1977), 119, (henceforth the 'long' article with this title). Italics ours.

[110] Thiselton, *2H*, 347, 314, 332; cf. 133-139. Italics ours.

[111] Thiselton, *2H*, 312, 324-326, 238, 339, 343-344. Italics ours.

[112] Thiselton, *2H*, 350, 351; cf. 294-296, 308, 313-315, 325-326, 338-339, 342-347, 356.

problem of "dualisms" or dichotomies (cf. stratum two).[113]

Nevertheless, (b), negatively, Thiselton warns that the 'dialogue' exercised by the New Hermeneutic, though broadened beyond that of Bultmann, is still too "narrow" at the level of the critical-synthesis implicit in its pre-understanding and, therefore, that the pre-understanding implicit in the New Hermeneutic still engenders problematic theoretical dichotomies and practical interpretative problems. Thiselton argues that, in the New Hermeneutic, only *some* of "'Bultmann's'" difficulties are resolved,[114] and that dualisms or dichotomies remain for the New Hermeneutic along most of the axes of hermeneutical discussion just noted (i.e. in "(a) (i)-(v)" immediately above).[115] That is, Thiselton is less "open" to the New Hermeneutic than W. Russell perhaps implies because, in Thiselton's estimate, the New Hermeneutic problematically perpetuates more than just the epistemological and linguistic 'dichotomies' that B.J. Walsh notes.[116]

Thus, (i), Thiselton argues that, in the New Hermeneutic, the *historical* 'present' still wrongly displaces 'the [historical] past' and that, in the New Hermeneutic, an untenable 'history' versus 'nature' dichotomy persists.[117] (ii) In relation to *epistemology*, Thiselton complains that, in the New Hermeneutic, "'what is true *for me*'" still subverts the "challenge" of 'truth' "'from beyond'" 'the horizons of the' self. Thiselton also complains that, in the New Hermeneutic, (re-historicized) 'subject-object' "conceptualization" is insufficiently restored. Moreover, Thiselton argues that, in the New Hermeneutic, the 'depth, creativity, and contemporaneity' of interpretation are rightly stressed, but only at the expense of a proper emphasis on the "correctness" of 'interpretation'.[118] In Thiselton's estimate, the New Hermeneutic also suffers from the following additional epistemological and/or historical-epistemological inadequacies: 'the problem of the status of objective historical knowledge persists';[119] 'tradition, the church... [and] history after the event of the cross' are still neglected;[120] and 'truth' "disclosed" *'through'* the self (or selves) 'is' still in danger of being 'reduced to disclosure *of* the self (or selves).[121]

---

[113] Thiselton, *2H*, 331; cf. 330-332, 372, 354; cf. Thiselton, 'TNI', 11. Italics ours.

[114] Thiselton, *2H*, 292; cf.: 354; 352-356; 109, 114; 293-356; cf. Thiselton, 'TNI', 11.

[115] Thiselton, *2H*, 352-356.

[116] Thiselton, *2H*, 352-356; cf.: Thiselton, 'P-BP', 88; Russell, 'R NH', 243; Walsh, 'TC', 234; cf. 232.

[117] Thiselton, *2H*, 314, 353, cf. 355-356; cf.: contradicting, Hynson, L. O., 'Review of R. Lundin's, A.C. Thiselton's and C. Walhout's *The Responsibility of Hermeneutics*', *ChSRev* 18.1 (1988), 91; Ebeling, G., 'The World as History. To Fritz Blanke on his 60th Birthday', in *Word and Faith* (trans. J.W. Leitch; Philadelphia: Fortress Press, Chatham: SCM Press Ltd, 1963), 365-366.

[118] Thiselton, *2H*, 353, cf. 355-356, 346, 314, 351; cf. Walsh, 'TC', 232. Second italics Thiselton's, first italics ours.

[119] Thiselton, *2H*, 355; cf. Palmer, R.E., 'Review of A.C. Thiselton's *The Two Horizons*', *RevMet* 35.1 (1981), 173.

[120] Thiselton, 'NH', 324-325; cf. Thiselton, *2H*, 354-355.

[121] Thiselton, *2H*, 200, 291-292, 355-356, 197; cf. McHann Jr., *3H*, 221. Italics Thiselton's.

(iii) Thiselton complains that, in the untenable *linguistic* dualism of the New Hermeneutic, so-called 'authentic' "'language'" - supposedly 'grounded in Being' - still falsely displaces the supposedly 'inauthentic' 'language' of "propositions". Thiselton complains that this linguistic dualism pervades *even Fuchs' most fruitful work on Jesus' parables* – which, in Thiselton's view, nevertheless still rightly "challenges" routinized "'repetition'" of 'religious' "statements".[122] That is, Thiselton rejects the New Hermeneutic's later Heideggerian notion 'of language as' "'the house of Being'",[123] and appeals instead to the later Wittgenstein - and to J.L. Austin and to D.D. Evans - so as to retain 'an extra-linguistic component that is necessary to check for correct understanding'.[124]

(iv) In relation to *anthropology*, Thiselton argues that, in the New Hermeneutic, "existential" predicament is still too sharply divorced from 'thought'. In Thiselton's estimate, this problematic dichotomy erroneously sets "'language-event'" in opposition to 'the discovery of objective truth' about the text – or about oneself or about one's community for that matter.[125] (v) Thiselton complains that, in the New Hermeneutic, "'distancing'" "'is reduced to'" 'a preliminary' during *interpretation*.[126] Further, Thiselton argues that the New Hermeneutic, when "applied" as a *generalizing* interpretative model, is found to be not suitable for all biblical genres.[127]

Thus, again, we may conclude that Thiselton espouses a hermeneutical axiom according to which foreclosing philosophical-theoretical dialogue at the level of pre-understanding harms interpretative practice and results – and, by implication, must also harm understandings and outcomes of understandings. Moreover, in conjunction with our arguments in Chapter 5, we may infer that, for Thiselton, this hermeneutical axiom must apply *both* to biblical hermeneutics *and* to hermeneutics more broadly.

(c) Positively, then, Thiselton argues that the New Hermeneutic demonstrates the validity of his argument for the widening of philosophical dialogue at the level of critical synthesis and/or pre-understanding but that, negatively, the New Hermeneutic also demonstrates the validity of his argument *against ceasing to continue* to widen such dialogue. This theme of "continuing widening dialogue" at the level

---

[122] Thiselton, *2H*, 345, 328-343; cf. 186, 195-197, 353-355, 99-101; cf. Thiselton, 'NH', 309; cf. Ebeling, G., 'The Meaning of "Biblical Theology"', in *Word and Faith* (trans. J.W. Leitch; Philadelphia: Fortress Press, Chatham: SCM Press Ltd, 1963), 93. Italics ours.

[123] Thiselton, *2H*, 337, cf. 341; contradicting Reist, J.S., 'Review of A.C. Thiselton's *New Horizons in Hermeneutics*', *JEThS* 38.3 (Sep. 1995), 459.

[124] Thiselton, *2H*, 379-385; cf. quoting, Dunn, E.A., *Beyond Dialogue and History: The Hermeneutical Pluralism of Anthony C. Thiselton and his Metacritical Use of the Cross and Resurrection of Christ* (Hamilton, Mass.: Gordon-Conwell Seminary M.A. Thesis, May 1998), 17, cf. 22.

[125] Thiselton, *2H*, 282, 353; cf. Thiselton, 'NH', 323-324, 341, 353; cf. Carson, D.A., *The Gagging of God. Christianity Confronts Pluralism* (Leicester: IVP/Apollos, 1996), 71. Italics ours.

[126] Thiselton, *2H*, 326, 353; cf. Thiselton, 'NH', 320, 323. Italics ours.

[127] Goldingay, *MIS*, 7; cf. Thiselton, *2H*, 353-354. Italics ours.

of pre-understanding persists throughout all Thiselton's writings: he constantly attacks 'the prevalence of hermeneutical foreclosure'.[128]

For Thiselton, therefore, the philosophical (and theological) pre-understanding that is presupposed by the New Hermeneutic is still too narrow or "foreclosed" – (i.e. too narrow or "foreclosed" in that too *few* 'philosophical' (and theological) 'traditions' are allowed to contribute positively to its implicit critical-synthesis prior to and/or during interpretation) - and so the pre-understanding that is presupposed by the New Hermeneutic must be 'enlarged' further. For Thiselton, moreover, widening dialogue "programmatically" with 'philosophical' (and theological) 'traditions' at the level of pre-understanding stands in opposition to 'hermeneutical foreclosure' and to interpretative irresponsibility (see also Chapters 5 and 7). Thus, Thiselton does not offer a *final* 'comprehensive' or 'normative' hermeneutical theory, but posits the principle that the practice of *ongoing broadening* philosophical and theological (and indeed other kinds of) dialogue at the level of pre-understanding is a necessary pre-condition for the possibility of even *beginning* to move in such a direction.[129]

In other words, (5), Thiselton concludes that artificially-narrowed (in the sense of ours and Thiselton's use of the term "narrow") "preunderstandings" (stratum one) produce problematic theoretical dichotomies (stratum two) that, in turn, lead – during/through interpretative practice - to 'one-sided', 'partial', or 'selective' 'New Testament' 'interpretations' (cf. "distanciations"). The implication, in Thiselton's estimate, is that the latter, in turn, will lead to inadequate understandings (cf. actualizations) and to inadequate outworkings of understandings (cf. appropriations and applications). That is, Thiselton argues that artificially-narrowed pre-understandings *prematurely* exclude valuable challenges from other philosophical or theological traditions and from past or present exegetical scholarship and that, as a result, such preunderstandings will tend to engender problematic distanciations, problematic understandings, and problematic outworkings of understandings *even when such preunderstandings are functioning as fruitfully as they can* during interpretation.[130]

That is, Thiselton demonstrates that hermeneutical theory *directly* affects

---

[128] See, Thiselton, 'TNI', 11; cf.: Thiselton, A.C., 'Meaning and Myth. Review Article of W. Pannenberg's *Basic Questions in Theology, Vol. 3*', *CEN* 19 Oct. (1973), 8; Thiselton, *NH*, 344-345; Thiselton, 'HB', 92; Thiselton, A.C., 'Communicative Action and Promise in Inter-Disciplinary, Biblical, and Theological Hermeneutics', in *The Promise of Hermeneutics* (R. Lundin, C. Walhout and A.C. Thiselton; Grand Rapids and Cambridge: Eerdmans; Carlisle: Paternoster, 1999), 133-135; cf. 209-218; qualifying, Klein, 'R *2H*', 74, 75; quoting, Briggs, *Words*, 17.

[129] Thiselton, *2H*, 354, 292, xix; cf.: Thiselton, A.C., 'Theology and the Future', *CEN* 23 Jan. (1970), 11; Briggs, *Words*, 17; querying, MacCammon, L.M., 'Review of R. Lundin's, C. Walhout's and A.C. Thiselton's *The Promise of Hermeneutics*', at http://www.bookreviews. org/bookdetail.asp?TitleId=406&CodePage=416,406; cf. http://www.bookreviews.org/pdf/406_964 .pdf, 1; cf. 3-4; and, Dockery, 'R *2H*', 135, 136.

[130] Thiselton, *2H*, 109, 114, 282-284, 315, 292; cf. 352-356. Italics ours.

interpretative practice and practical outcomes: in Thiselton's estimate, widening dialogue theoretically is *the only way* to avoid hermeneutical foreclosure practically and is therefore pivotal for preventing irresponsible interpretation. By implication, Thiselton has herein *proven the unity of hermeneutical theory and practice.*

### 2. Recovering Responsible Practice: Broadening Pre-Understandings Beyond Those of the New Hermeneutic (and Beyond Those of Later Approaches)

(1) (a) Part of Thiselton's whole aim in the *main* text of *The Two Horizons*, therefore, is: (i) to widen philosophical and theological dialogue – programmatically - beyond the place reached by the New Hermeneutic; (ii) to rectify – by means of this process of widening dialogue - the remaining theoretical dualisms or dichotomies that beleaguer the pre-understanding(s) presupposed by the New Hermeneutic; and, (iii), to ensure – by means of this rectification of dualisms or dichotomies - that improved biblical interpretations (cf. distanciations), improved biblical understandings (cf. actualizations), and improved outcomes of biblical understandings (cf. appropriations and applications) will emerge.

This three-fold aim is part of the whole point of Thiselton's initiation – in the *main* text of *The Two Horizons* and/or in the context of his second-period hermeneutical discussions more broadly - of his second-period dialogues with the later Wittgenstein, and with many other interlocutors.

(b) We saw, in Chapters 2 and 5, how Thiselton's second-period hermeneutical theory also constituted the basis for Thiselton's responses to *structuralist* approaches to biblical interpretation. In *The Two Horizons*, though, these responses are evident only in an Appendix, and not in the main text of the book, and so do not belong to the main line of argument that we are considering here. (Certain caveats in relation to *Saussure* should be noted in relation to this point, where some of these caveats *also* apply to the *Post-Saussurian* tradition of general linguistics and modern semantics - see our footnotes).[131]

---

[131] Caveats: (1) Thiselton's responses to Saussure in *2H* are not confined to an Appendix. But, (a), Thiselton associates Saussure more with the *origins* of "structuralism", than with structuralism itself. (b) Thiselton's responses to Saussure in *2H* add little to what has been said already in Chapters 4 and 5. What little *is* added in *2H* appears later in the present chapter. (c) Treating Thiselton's responses to Saussure in Chapters 4 and 5 enabled us to focus here on Thiselton's main argument in *2H* to do with crossing the historical distance between *two horizons* ("stratum three"). By contrast, (d), Thiselton's response to Saussure relates mainly (*if not exclusively*) either to a "stratum two" hermeneutical critique of language, or to a "stratum three" focus on a *single horizon* – the *textual* horizon (i.e. to a *subset* of the hermeneutical task). Theoretically, we examined "single horizon" considerations prior to "two horizon" considerations. (2) Points "(b)", "(c)", and "(d)", here, also apply to our treatments of Thiselton's second-period responses to "general linguistics" and "modern semantics" (i.e. the *(post-)Saussurian* tradition – see Chapter 4), and to *ideological* "structuralist approaches" (see Chapter 5). Whilst Chapter 5 focuses on the "two horizons", Thiselton's

Furthermore, (c), it will become apparent in Chapter 7 that Thiselton's thinking in *The Two Horizons also* constitutes the primary basis for Thiselton's later responses to broadly *post-structuralist* approaches and to broadly *socio-pragmatic* approaches.

(2) For now, though, we should note that, in line with Thiselton's *stratum-one* emphasis on widening inter-disciplinary and inter-traditional (and smaller-scale) dialogues, Thiselton's argument in *The Two Horizons* is cumulative, and involves 'comparative' appeals.[132] That is, Thiselton argues that hermeneutics must 'critically... compare what each' "tradition" (and each discipline, school of thought, and so on) has for or against it. Thus, F.H. Borsch rightly notes Thiselton's 'thesis that hermeneutics must be a multidisciplinary art', as do other writers.[133]

Moreover, in line with Thiselton's five *stratum-two* hermeneutical critiques (i.e. of "history", "epistemology", "language", "Western culture", and of "human selves") and with his *stratum-three* critique of hermeneutical understanding, Thiselton's argument in *The Two Horizons* corrects what R.S. Briggs calls 'false dichotomies' in the hermeneutical theory of Bultmann and of the New

---

second-period critique of ideological structuralist approaches was largely an argument that challenged these approaches' "one horizon" emphasis. (3) The exception to point "(2)", here, concerns Thiselton's second-period responses to "methodological" (cf. V.I. Propp, and A.J. Greimas) and "eclectic" (e.g. D.O. Via) structuralisms. In effect, we have already covered these responses: (a) Regarding *"methodological" structuralisms*, Thiselton: (i) applauds their potential to respect theology and historical particularity; (ii) agrees that semantic relations are fundamental to conceptualization and important in relation to meaning; (iii) argues that they provide a fresh vantage-point on hermeneutical questions that, (iv), should not be ignored by 'traditional' approaches; and, (v), argues that it would be premature simply to reject such approaches whilst they are still in their infancy (N.B. Thiselton said this in 1980!). Our point, though, is that we have *already introduced* Thiselton's second period discourses on theology, historical particularity, semantic relations, conceptualization, and meaning. "Vantage-points" are the same as "angles of vision"/"view" (cf. a "change of aspect"). (b) For Thiselton, *'eclectic' 'structuralist approaches'* tend to combine the positive aspects of "methodological" structuralism (see above) with *either* the negative aspects of ideological structuralism (see Chapter 5), *or* with 'Freudian or Jungian symbolism' (on symbols, see Chapters 1-4; on Freud, see Chapter 3), *or* with influences not expounded by Thiselton in his second period. (4) Thiselton associates D.O. Via with structuralism, but in *2H* introduces Via in connection with *the New Hermeneutic*. Overall, see: Thiselton, *2H*, 115-139, 347-352, 428-431 (Appendix); Thiselton, 'SBS', 329-335; on key thinkers in relation to structuralism see: Macey, D., *The Penguin Dictionary of Critical Theory* (London: Penguin Books Ltd., 2000), 342-343, 313-314, 227-229, 169-170; Hénaff, M., 'Lévi-Strauss', in *A Companion to Continental Philosophy* (eds. S. Critchley and W.R. Schroeder; Blackwell Companions to Philosophy Series; Oxford: Blackwell Publishers Ltd., 1998), 507-518, and onwards.

[132] Ellingworth, P., 'Review of A.C. Thiselton's *The Two Horizons*', *EvanQ* 53 (Jul.-Sep. 1981), 178; cf. quoting, Conroy, 'R *2H*', 564; cf. 565.

[133] Thiselton, *2H*, 292, cf.: 354, 84, 3-10; cf.: Borsch, 'R *2H*', 88; Conroy, 'R *2H*', 564; Jasper, D., 'The New Testament and Literary Interpretation', *RelLit* 17.3 (Fall 1985), 2.

Hermeneutic (and, either directly or by implication, in the hermeneutical theories of later approaches – see Chapters 5 and 7) along *six different axes* – (though Briggs almost exclusively focuses on the linguistic axis of Thiselton's thought, and S.M. Schneiders only speaks of 'the *three* major axes of the hermeneutical problematic' in relation to Thiselton's thinking).[134]

Crucially, these *six implicit axes* in Thiselton's hermeneutical criticisms, together with his first-stratum conversation on "dialogue", constitute *seven spheres of hermeneutical conversation or discourse* (i.e. "dialogue", "history", "epistemology", "language", "(Western) culture", "human selves", and "understanding") that, additionally, in our view, help *clarify hermeneutics as a complex multi-discourse discipline*.

Thus, (3), we must reject in the strongest terms J. Barr's view that *'The Two Horizons'* "builds" on 'the "New Hermeneutic"' 'entirely uncritically',[135] and we must at the very least heavily qualify W. Wink's assertions that Thiselton, in *The Two Horizons*, simply offers 'a corrective to Bultmann' and that 'Bultmann' is 'the foundation on which all subsequent interpretative theory must be built'.[136] Further, querying P. Grech's reading of *The Two Horizons*, we must conclude that Thiselton does not merely look for parallels or 'points of contact' between traditions. Nor, querying R.A. Harrisville's reading of *The Two Horizons*, can we conclude that Thiselton only presents a 'largely descriptive study'.[137] Nor, contradicting M.J. Erickson's reading of *The Two Horizons*, does 'Thiselton' simply provide 'four illustrations of the employment of philosophy in' hermeneutics that lack 'interconnection with one another'. And, querying B.M. Metzger's reading of *The Two Horizons*, we should stress that Thiselton does not only attempt to define 'the limits' of philosophical dialogue; rather, we must conclude that Thiselton also seeks to ongoingly broaden philosophical dialogue.[138]

Thus, (4), Thiselton's appeals – in *The Two Horizons* - to the later Wittgenstein and to others constitute an *attack on the dichotomies or dualisms in Continental hermeneutical theory that have greatly affected Continental (and other streams of) biblical interpretation in practice*. And yet, incredibly, even by 2001, 'relatively few writers' had applied later-'Wittgensteinian resources' 'to biblical interpretation'.[139] This state of affairs was indicative of a widespread problem in biblical hermeneutics - a problem that Thiselton's PhD Thesis had highlighted as much as *twenty-five years*

---

[134] Briggs, *Words*, 24; cf. Schneiders, 'R *2H*', 308. Italics ours.

[135] Thiselton, *2H*, 292, cf. 354; cf. Barr, J., 'Exegesis as a Theological Discipline Reconsidered and the Shadow of the Jesus of History', in *The Hermeneutical Quest: Essays in Honour of James Luther Mays* (ed. D.G. Miller; Princeton Theological Monograph 4; Allison Park, Pa: Pickwick Press, 1986), 38, 37. Italics Barr's.

[136] Wink, 'R *2H*', 508; cf. Keifert, 'R *2H*', 408.

[137] Querying, Grech, P., 'Review of A.C. Thiselton's *The Two Horizons*', *Bib* 63.4 (1982), 572; cf. querying, Harrisville, 'R *2H*', 216.

[138] Contradicting: Erickson, 'R *2H*', 373; and, Metzger, B.M., 'Review of A.C. Thiselton's *The Two Horizons*', *PSemB* NS3.2 (1981), 209.

[139] Briggs, *Words*, 12.

*earlier, but that was largely ignored even after the publication of The Two Horizons (1980).* Thus, contradicting W. Corduan's reading of Thiselton in the strongest terms, we must conclude that Thiselton's appeal to the later 'Wittgenstein' was, and is, most certainly *not* 'arbitrary', and that the 'omission' of this appeal from biblical hermeneutics *has been* 'a serious lack' - of historical proportions.[140]

Notably, (5), in *The Two Horizons*, Thiselton anticipates such reactions to his valuable and prophetic hermeneutical endeavors by justifying his appeals to the later Wittgenstein on four other grounds: (a) Thiselton observes that others - notably K.-O. Apel - have interfaced the work of 'Heidegger' with that 'of [the later] Wittgenstein'.[141] (b) Thiselton observes that others - notably B.I. Premo - have noted the later Wittgenstein's relevance for hermeneutics.[142] (c) Thiselton observes that others have noted 'affinities between' the early Wittgenstein's work and 'Continental' philosophy - thus, Thiselton observes that 'Neo-Kantianism' influences both 'Bultmann' and the *early* Wittgenstein.[143]

(d) Specifically, '"the Neo-Kantian"' background aside, Thiselton notes that '"parallels"' exist 'between' the *later* Wittgenstein's '"approach"' and 'the approaches of... Heidegger' and Gadamer. Thus, (i), Thiselton observes that, for the later Wittgenstein and *Heidegger*, our '"language"' '"discloses"' our '"world"', and '"determines our view of reality"'. Thiselton argues that, for 'both thinkers', our '"language... demonstrates and structures the things of"' our '"world"'. Moreover, Thiselton argues that, for 'both thinkers', '"the logical structure of the language of"' 'philosophy' (notably of '"metaphysics, or ontology"') 'is not representational [in a *formalistic* sense]', is inconsistent 'with' a 'traditional '"property"' theory of meaning' and, rather, 'is akin to... poetry', where 'meaning is contextually determined'. Furthermore, Thiselton observes that, for 'both thinkers', 'language'- 'uses' 'reflect... prior '"understanding"', where Thiselton notes that the notions of '"language-games"' and '"world"' are partly "parallel": for the later Wittgenstein and Heidegger, '"subjects"' '"participate"' '"in"' conditioning '"communities"' *"prior to... objectification and subjectivism"'*. Thiselton also notes that, for 'both thinkers', 'language' is '"powerful"', both negatively and positively, where '"Saying... in Heidegger"' '"parallels"' '"Showing in... [the later] Wittgenstein"'. And Thiselton argues that, for 'both thinkers', 'the method of philosophy is purely descriptive' (though *not* in an idealist way). (ii) Thiselton argues that, for the later Wittgenstein and *'Gadamer'* respectively, '"ahistorical"' approaches to language, and the ahistorical approach of "phenomenology", are inadequate. Further, Thiselton observes that parallels exist between the later Wittgenstein's notion of '"language-game"' '"rules"' and Gadamer's thinking concerning the '"inter-subjective"' '"institutional"' '"ways of seeing"' that characterize '"prejudice structures"' and

---

[140] Contradicting, Corduan, W., 'Humility and Commitment: An Approach to Modern Hermeneutics', *Them* NS11.3 (Apr. 1986), 87. Italics ours.

[141] Thiselton, *2H*, 33-34.

[142] Thiselton, *2H*, 34.

[143] Thiselton, *2H*, 34-36, 39, 359.

"'linguisticality'". Finally, Thiselton observes that, for "'both'" thinkers (i.e. for the later Wittgenstein and Gadamer), "'rules... are discovered only by observing... concrete'" "inter-subjective" language-uses.[144]

In Thiselton's view, therefore, including the later Wittgenstein in the hermeneutical discussion becomes a *historical* necessity – *a matter of keeping up with the debates*. But, for Thiselton, as we shall see later in the present chapter, including the later Wittgenstein (and others) in the hermeneutical discussion also emerges as a *theoretical and practical* necessity in relation to addressing the problem of dualisms or dichotomies in (especially but not exclusively) Continental hermeneutical theories and practices.

(6) As we have already begun to demonstrate, and as we shall continue to demonstrate in the remainder of the present chapter and in Chapter 7, Thiselton, in *The Two Horizons*, building on his other second-period writings, widens philosophical and theological dialogue (at the level of the critical synthesis within his pre-understanding) beyond that of the New Hermeneutic (and also, in some senses, beyond structuralist and later approaches – see Chapters 5 and 7) in *seven ways* that – in addition – do not *only* involve appeals to the later Wittgenstein.

Thus, (a), Thiselton - in his second-stratum hermeneutical critique of *history* (see later in the present chapter) - dialogues with a partly-Pannenbergian modification of three Hegelian axioms in order to expose difficulties *both* in broadly 'positivist' philosophies of history *and* in broadly "'existentialist'" philosophies of history. This dialogue, as we shall see below, has direct implications, (i), in relation to Thiselton's grounding of his hermeneutical critiques of epistemology, language, Western culture, and of human selves – and of his critique of hermeneutical understanding - in a hermeneutical critique of history, and thence, (ii), in relation to Thiselton's unification of hermeneutical theory. Later, C.G. Bartholomew notes 'Pannenberg's' "importance" for Thiselton's 'theology of history', but our point here - in the present context of discussion - primarily concerns Thiselton's *philosophy* of history, even though Bartholomew's point is *also* correct.[145]

(b) Continuing to ground his second-stratum hermeneutical critique of *epistemology* in his second-stratum hermeneutical critique of *history*, Thiselton critically synthesizes appeals to Pannenberg, T.F. Torrance, Heidegger, Gadamer, and to others in order to formulate an implicit *unified hermeneutical critique of historical "objectivity"* (see Chapter 7), and thereby – in relation to hermeneutics more broadly - further unites a philosophy of history with an historical approach to epistemology.[146]

Our discussion of these points (see Chapter 7) extends our arguments in

---

[144] Thiselton, *2H*, 33-38; cf. Chapter 4. Fourth italics Thiselton's, other italics ours.

[145] Thiselton, *2H*, 76; cf. 63-84, 244-251; cf. Bartholomew, C.G., 'Introduction', in *'Behind' the Text. History and Biblical Interpretation* (eds. C.G. Bartholomew, C.S. Evans, M. Healy, and M. Rae; Scripture and Hermeneutics Series; Vol. 4; Carlisle: Paternoster, 2003), 11.

[146] Thiselton, *2H*, 22, 26-33, 89-91, 113, 121, 158-160, 187-197, 228-237, 294-302, 316-320, 379, 411-415, 440-441. Italics ours.

Chapters 3 and 5 in relation to how Thiselton "re-historicizes" epistemology and understanding.

(c) Continuing to ground his second-stratum hermeneutical critique of *language* in his second-stratum hermeneutical critique of *history*, Thiselton further augments his appeals to his later Wittgensteinian-Saussurian alliance in order to qualify his reception of Continental hermeneutics still further, and thereby – in relation to hermeneutics more broadly - further unites a philosophy of history with a philosophy of language (see below).[147]

In this context of discussion, amongst other considerations, Thiselton argues that post-Saussurian linguistics and semantics provide "angles of vision" regarding language that are absent *both* from the later Wittgensteinian tradition *and* from Continental hermeneutical traditions.[148]

More broadly, we shall argue that Thiselton grounds language *both* in historical particularities *and* in historical continuities. This discussion (see below) extends our arguments in Chapter 4 in relation to how Thiselton "re-historicizes" language as "enfleshed word" with respect to speech-acts, language-games, forms of life, and with respect to "the common behavior of humankind".

(d) Continuing to ground his second-stratum hermeneutical critique of *(Western) culture* in his second-stratum hermeneutical critique of *history*, Thiselton makes further mutually-qualifying appeals to strands in 'Continental' and in 'Anglo-American' thinking, and thereby – in relation to hermeneutics more broadly - further unites notions of "history", "culture", and *"tradition"* as over and against an over-emphasis on "culture-relativity" (see below).[149]

Our discussion of these points (see below and Chapter 7) extends our arguments in Chapter 4 concerning how Thiselton "re-historicizes" perspectives on (Western) culture and on "culture-relativity" with respect to different kinds of situatedness and with respect to traditions.

(e) Continuing to ground his second-stratum hermeneutical critique of *human selves* in his second-stratum hermeneutical critique of *history*, Thiselton again makes mutually-qualifying appeals to strands in Anglo-American and in Continental thought, and thereby – in relation to hermeneutics more broadly - continues to unite notions of "history" with notions of "human selves" (see below).[150]

Our discussion of these points (see below) extends our arguments in Chapters 3 and 4 to do with how Thiselton – in critique of Continental anthropocentricity - "re-historicizes" and de-centers human selves with respect to different kinds of situatedness and with respect to traditions. However, as already noted in Chapter 4, and as we shall note again in Chapter 7, Thiselton's "de-centering" of human

---

[147] Thiselton, *2H*, 370-385, cf. 124-157, 419, 268-269, 337, 354-355, 437; cf. Chapter 4.

[148] Thiselton, *2H*, 115-139; cf. Thiselton, A.C., 'The Semantics of Biblical Language as an Aspect of Hermeneutics', *FTht* 103.2 (1976), 117.

[149] Thiselton, *2H*, 183-185, 229, 245-251, 304-314, 67, 81; cf. Thiselton, 'TY', 1560-1561. Italics ours.

[150] Thiselton, *2H*, 143-204, cf. especially 250.

selves in this way does not go so far as to constitute a "deconstruction" of human selves: Thiselton's sublation of a hermeneutical critique of history into a Trinitarian theological framework ensures that Thiselton's conceptualization of "history" is configured in such a way as to remain respectful of the narrative(s) of "persons-in-relation".

(f) Continuing to ground his third-stratum critique of *interpretative practice* (cf. hermeneutical understanding and/or responsible interpretation) in his second-stratum hermeneutical critique of *history*, Thiselton appeals to Dilthey, Pannenberg, the Saussurian tradition, Schleiermacher, Heidegger, Bultmann, the later Wittgenstein, J.L. Austin, D.D. Evans, and to the philosophy of language more broadly in order to modify Gadamer's hermeneutical circle (see below).[151]

Thiselton thus grounds the hermeneutical circle in a *very heavily modified* "'Hegelian dialectic'" that de-centers *both* individual subjectivity *and* culture-relativity (though *without* dismissing the historical reality of either). Our discussion of these points (see below) extends our argument, which we began in Chapter 5, concerning how Thiselton "re-historicizes" understanding in all its aspects so as *to modify* Gadamer's thought *considerably*.[152]

(g) Following, modifying, and/or even *revising* the approach of the early Pannenberg of the time (i.e. the time leading up to, and into, Thiselton's second period), Thiselton argues that a prior New Testament *theology* is consistent with, but also improves upon, insights drawn from a widened dialogue with *philosophical traditions* in that New Testament theology provides explanatory and evaluative metacriteria (see Chapter 3) along with other advantages – notably the

---

[151] Thiselton, *2H*, 104-107, 147, 166, 194-197, 284, 304, 307-308, 382, 386-407.

[152] Thiselton, *2H*, 183-185, 229, 245, 250-251, 304-308, 312, 314, 81; cf. 67. That is, in Chapter 5, we saw how Thiselton re-historicized and thereby corrected: (a) Bultmann's notion of pre-understanding; (b) Gadamer's linguistic dualism and ontological prioritization of language over history; (c) subject-object conceptualization; (d) historical-experiential understanding; (e) the "general" axis of the hermeneutical circle; (f) objectivity in relation to historical otherness; (g) self-involvement in relation to historical relationality; (h) the textual horizon; (i) "texts themselves", reader-situations, reading goals, interpretative strategies, critical tools, and models of texts; (j) *actualization* as: (i) intra-linguistic textual action and effects; (ii) mind-stunting indoctrination; (iii) Fuchs' notion of language-events; (iv) an individualistic hedonism of self-affirming event and experience; (v) an individual or corporate phenomenology of self-discovery; (k) *appropriation* as: (i) human brute effort alone; (ii) unrestrained human "freedom" or "autonomy"; (iii) unrestrained epistemological anthropocentricity; (iv) unchecked pragmatism; (v) pietistic introspection that avoided broader issues in the wider world; (vi) approaching texts as mere historical sources; (vii) approaching texts as mere objects of knowledge; (viii) approaching texts as mere sources of truths; (l) *application* as: (i) a distorted activism that avoided deeper personal, relational, and theoretical questions; (ii) iconoclasm towards traditions; (iii) traditionalism; (iv) individualistically subjectivistic; (v) rationalistically over-abstracted from historical reality or life; (vi) over-fixated on past or present horizons; (vii) "praxis" divorced from wisdom and/or from theory; (m) interpretation as an over-emphasis on distancing or on fusion.

interweaving of conceptualizations of "history" with those concerning "persons-in-relation" (see Chapters 4, 7 and above). Therefore, Thiselton unites philosophy and theology in hermeneutics *at the point at which hermeneutical theory as a whole is unified*. Thiselton, in line with his first-stratum axiom of critical-synthesis through ever-widening historical dialogue (see Chapters 1 and 2), argues that dialogue must ultimately be widened *beyond* philosophical traditions to include theological explorations (see Chapters 3 and 7).[153]

Our discussion of these points in Chapter 7 develops the point that, after Thiselton, we have been making from Chapter 3 onwards. This point concerns how a unified hermeneutical theory interweaves – and indeed *must* interweave (particularly if it is to be adequately meta-socio-critical) - appeals to philosophy *and* theology.

(7) If this analysis of Thiselton's seven second-period expansions of dialogue (at the level of pre-understanding) beyond the dialogue(s) implicit in the pre-understandings presupposed by the New Hermeneutic (and, in some respects, beyond the dialogues implicit in the pre-understandings presupposed by structuralist and later approaches) proves valid then: (a), for Thiselton, the four major theoretical second-stratum hermeneutical critiques and the third-stratum critique of hermeneutical understanding that we examined in Chapters 3, 4 and 5 – i.e. Thiselton's hermeneutical critiques of epistemology, language, (Western) culture, human selves, and his critique of hermeneutical understanding - come to unity in a fifth major theoretical second-stratum hermeneutical critique – namely Thiselton's hermeneutical critique of history. (b) Further, for Thiselton, (if our arguments prove to be correct), hermeneutical theory as a whole comes to unity in biblical theology. We shall attempt to prove the validity of these two points in the remainder of the present chapter and in Chapter 7 respectively.

Finally, (8), the following analysis will attempt to show that Pannenberg and Hegel are more fundamental to Thiselton's thinking than are the later Wittgenstein and Saussure: for Thiselton, history grounds language and not vice versa. We may now begin to expound Thiselton's extension of dialogue (at the level of pre-understanding) beyond that of the New Hermeneutic (and, in some senses, beyond that of structuralist and later approaches) in more detail – as follows.

### C. Dialogic Theory-Construction:
### Towards the Unification of Stratum Two and Stratum Three
### Hermeneutical Theory in a
### Unified Hermeneutical Critique of History

In the present section, speaking predominantly from a philosophical angle of view, we shall argue that Thiselton's second-stratum hermeneutical critique of history constitutes his unifying philosophical subtext for (stratum two and stratum three)

---

[153] Thiselton, *2H*, 74-84; cf. Pannenberg, W., *Basic Questions in Theology. Collected Essays, Volume 1* (trans. G.H. Kehm; Philadelphia: Fortress Press, 1970), 137-181.

hermeneutics (though Thiselton's biblical theology is *not* assimilated to this philosophical subtext, but rather anticipates, shapes, coheres with, and even improves upon this philosophical subtext). This philosophical subtext develops Pannenberg's qualified dialogue with Hegel – a dialogue that *avoids* 'Hegel's' dualistic and over-'abstract' 'idealism' and "totalization".[154]

Thus, from a philosophical angle of view, Thiselton's thinking in *The Two Horizons*, taken as a whole, implicitly unfolds from the following three inter-related *modified* Hegelian criteria: (1) 'History-as-a-whole' is the 'universal' 'context' for 'understanding', *but* (after Pannenberg) Thiselton's modification of this criterion is that 'history-as-a-whole' is '"anticipated"' from *within* '"history"', and not from the '"end"' of '"history"'.[155] (2) '"The unity of"' '"historical"' 'reality' grounds the "possibility" and unity of '"language"' and of 'understanding', *but* (broadly, *but not in every respect*, following Gadamer and Pannenberg) Thiselton's modification of this criterion is that 'historical understanding', concrete 'self-understanding' and concrete traditions are *interwoven*.[156] (3) The dynamic, '"dialectic"' 'process' of 'creative' 'historical' 'synthesis' generates 'historical' "particularities" and 'historical' "continuities", *but* (broadly, *but not in every respect*, following Gadamer and Pannenberg) Thiselton's modification of this criterion is that the "moving" '"historical"' 'dialectic' that this criterion depicts is *earthed* in the processes of concrete 'traditions' (i.e. 'traditions' that necessarily involve human selves).[157]

If the philosophical subtext of Thiselton's hermeneutical theory in *The Two Horizons* radiates from this basis, then his stance is neither a case of "later-Wittgensteinian perspectivism" or "perspectivalism" (against A.J. McNicol's reading of Thiselton), nor simply an "anti-essentialist" 'application of... the *Tractatus* and the *Untersuchungen*' (against P. Grech's reading of Thiselton).[158]

Nor, contradicting L. Brodie's reading of Thiselton, does Thiselton posit or espouse a Hobson's choice between 'a' 'failed' 'historical method' 'and a more recent hermeneutic which... tends to avoid or shelve [the] problems of history'. Rather, contradicting Brodie's reading of Thiselton, we should note that Thiselton *is* trying 'to improve', 'not... abandon', 'historical' criticism – by offering a widened philosophical dialogue (outlined above and expounded below) that transforms the entire hermeneutical paradigm, and centrally the "philosophy of history", bequeathed by Continental hermeneutics. This *historical* paradigm-transformation (see also Chapter 5) constitutes Thiselton's working provisional "solution" to the hermeneutical problem. In our estimate, this "solution" may be

---

[154] Thiselton, *2H*, 66-67, cf. 74-84, 248, 296, 302-303.

[155] Thiselton, *2H*, 82-83; cf. 66-67; cf. Thiselton, 'TNI', 11. Italics ours.

[156] Thiselton, *2H*, 83; cf.: 302; 243-251; 66-67; 75; 77-78, 80-81; 290. Italics ours.

[157] Thiselton, *2H*, 309; cf.: 302-313; 44-81; 181-183; 370-401; cf. Thiselton, A.C., 'Head-On Challenge to Doubt: The Theology of Wolfhart Pannenberg', *CEN* 10 May (1974), 8. Italics ours.

[158] Contradicting, McNicol, A.J., 'Review of A.C. Thiselton's *The Two Horizons*', *RestQ* 27.3 (1984), 188; and, Grech, 'R *2H*', 575, 576. Italics Grech's.

set over and against Brodie's counter-suggestion that posits a way forward through 'compositional psychodynamics': Brodie's counter-suggestion, in our estimate, is perhaps too close to Dilthey's over-emphasis on the continuity of 'human' 'psychology' - a solution proposed many years ago that has already failed.[159]

Again, as a note of caution, we should stress that everything that has been said so far, and everything that follows in the remainder of the present chapter and in Chapter 7, is *not* an argument to do with Thiselton supposedly "assimilating biblical theology to a philosophical worldview", but is, rather, true to Thiselton's aim of showing that a *prior* biblical theology is elucidated by, is consistent with, and has problem-solving cogency in relation to, *later* philosophical description and concerns emerging from *later* widening philosophical dialogues. Bearing this important background point in mind, we may now examine each of Thiselton's modified Hegelian criteria in turn, so as to demonstrate that they play a central role in Thiselton's thinking in *The Two Horizons*.

*1. Anticipations of History-as-a-Whole as the Universal Context(s) for Understanding*

Thus, Thiselton's *first* modified Hegelian criterion, following Pannenberg, is that 'history-as-a-whole' is, or rather will become, the 'universal' 'context' for 'understanding' where, in Thiselton's thinking - against 'Hegel's' '"idealist"' '"totalization"' - this historical '"whole"' is repeatedly '"anticipated"' from *within* 'expanding' "historical" 'horizons', and is not viewed as though from 'the end of history' or as though from "above history". That is, Thiselton argues that 'historical' "particularities" and "continuities" are to be "understood" '"in relation to"' "*anticipations*" of 'history-as-a-whole' and/or '"in relation to"' "*anticipations*" of 'the end of history' and/or (of) 'eschatology'.[160]

On the basis of this criterion, Thiselton argues that *both* broadly 'positivist' approaches to hermeneutics *and* broadly '"existentialist"' approaches to hermeneutics focus too exclusively on 'present' 'horizons' (though Thiselton acknowledges that Dilthey, 'Collingwood', and 'Bultmann' rightly associate '"meaning"' with '"historical relatedness"').[161] Thus, Thiselton argues that, in "positivist" approaches, 'the interpreter's own experience of life becomes the test of all historical truth' and/or 'the criterion of historical probability'.[162] Conversely, Thiselton argues that '"existentialist"' approaches so over-stress 'present' 'human' 'historicality' that they fail to maintain proper relationships between 'past', 'present', and 'future' (though Thiselton acknowledges that 'Dilthey',

---

[159] Contradicting, Brodie, 'R 2H', 485-486; cf. Thiselton, 2H, 240-242, 235, 302-303; cf. Thiselton, 'NH', 313-314. Italics ours.

[160] Thiselton, 2H, 66-67, cf.: 82-84; 302-303; 244, xix; 315; 372; cf.: Thiselton, 'TNI', 11. Italics ours.

[161] Thiselton, 2H, 76, 77-78, 82-84; cf. 235-237; cf. 244-245, 250; cf. Thiselton, A.C., 'The Parousia in Modern Theology. Some Questions and Comments', *Tyn* 27 (1976), 40, 39.

[162] Thiselton, 2H, 78, 77.

'Collingwood', and 'Bultmann' rightly insist that "interpretation" is 'never' final so long as 'historical... horizons' "expand").[163]

Thiselton, modifying Hegel's thought, also follows Pannenberg's clear distinction between 'history-as-a-whole' as '"the totality of all [created] reality"' and '"God"': for Pannenberg and Thiselton, 'history-as-a-whole' and '"God"' are '"not interchangeable"'. Nevertheless, Thiselton argues that 'speaking about God and speaking about the whole of [created] reality are not entirely different matters, but mutually condition each other' such that 'it is not... possible to speak of the whole of [created] reality without in some way thinking of God'. Thus, again, Thiselton rejects 'Bultmann's... sharp' separation 'between God and' the 'world'.[164]

### 2. The Unity of Historical Reality as the Ground for the Possibility and Unity of Language and of Understanding

Thiselton's *second* modified Hegelian criterion, which broadly (*but not in every respect*) draws on Pannenberg's thought (and more implicitly and less so on Gadamer's thought), is that '"the unity"' (not uniformity) '"of"' '"historical"' 'reality' grounds the "possibility" and unity of '"language"' and of 'understanding' though, against 'Hegel's' '"idealist"' '"abstraction"', Thiselton (after Pannenberg and, to some extent, after Gadamer) argues that 'historical understanding' is interwoven with concrete 'self-understanding' *and* with '"traditions"'. Thiselton, following Pannenberg and (to an extent) Gadamer, thus *modifies* Kierkegaard's "criticism" that 'Hegel... had forgotten existence'. Thiselton, following Pannenberg and (to *an extent*) Gadamer, argues that 'historical understanding' cannot become a pure, albeit "developing", '"system"' "abstracted" from the concrete 'life' of 'human' selves and of "traditions". Thiselton, drawing on Pannenberg, argues that '"the unity of"' '"historical"' 'reality' grounds '"the"' *a posteriori* '"universal correspondence"', '"correlative connections"', or "analogies" that exist between 'historical' "contingencies", and that '"the unity of"' '"historical"' 'reality' thus grounds 'the possibility' of a general axis of 'historical' inquiry.[165]

Thus, Thiselton, followed by J.I. Packer, argues that D.E. Nineham violates a *philosophical* axiom when he (i.e. Nineham) tries to appeal to the problem of 'historical distance' in order to justify his (i.e. Nineham's) argument against the possibility of making "ethical" appeals to biblical texts.[166] That is, contradicting F.H. Borsch's reading of Thiselton, we should note that the issue under discussion

---

[163] Thiselton, *2H*, 245; cf.: 250-251; 244; 186; cf. Thiselton, 'Par', 39-40.

[164] McHann Jr., *3H*, 341; cf.: Thiselton, *2H*, 82-83, 231, 233, 285-287; Pannenberg, *BQ1*, 156; cf. 137-181.

[165] Thiselton, *2H*, 77-84, 302-305, 243-251, 290, 66-67; cf. 72-73; citation from Kierkegaard in, Gadamer, H.-G., 'Heidegger's Later Philosophy', in *Philosophical Hermeneutics* (H.-G. Gadamer; ed. D.E. Linge; London: University of California Press, 1976), 214. Italics ours.

[166] Thiselton, *2H*, 57-58; cf. 60; cf. Packer, 'ISRH', 331. Italics ours.

here is *not* simply a case of Thiselton's 'hopes and optimism' versus 'Nineham's pessimism'.[167] Rather, for Thiselton, (to use G.H. Guthrie's language), 'the success of... communication' "depends" 'on... shared life-structures in... human experience', and *not* 'on spatial and temporal proximity'.[168] Three further sets of considerations concern us in this context of discussion – as follows.

(1) Thiselton outworks "the unity of historical reality" criterion in at least four ways that relate to his attack on "dualisms" or "dichotomies" (here, we develop our earlier points) – as follows: (a) Thiselton – drawing *in part* on Pannenberg - again rejects '*historical*' "dualisms" or "dichotomies", notably Bultmann's "dualisms" or "dichotomies" between 'history' ("human"' reality) and 'nature' (non-human, '"impersonal"' reality), and 'between *Geschichte*' ("human"' 'historicality' - see below) 'and *Historie*' ("facts", report).[169] By contrast, Thiselton argues that 'Collingwood' rightly softens Dilthey's "dualism" between '"human"' and '"natural... forces"'.[170] Thus, contradicting B.J. Walsh's and H.C. White's readings of Thiselton, we should note that 'Thiselton's' stance is not "dualistic",[171] specifically in relation to '*Geschichte*' versus '*Historie*',[172] but also in relation to 'subject and object' – though, in Thiselton's thinking, "distinctions" between these poles remain.[173] Following 'Pannenberg', Thiselton also rejects the 'salvation-history' versus 'world-history' dichotomy of 'the... salvation-history school'.[174]

(b) Thiselton – drawing *in part* on Pannenberg - again rejects "*epistemological*" dualisms or dichotomies, notably rejecting Bultmann's sharp separations of 'primary' 'historical' and "theological" 'knowledge' from 'secondary' 'historical' 'knowledge', and of 'faith' from '"its"' '"rational"', even "scientific", "basis"' in 'history'.[175] Thiselton thus argues that Bultmann wrongly follows G.E. Lessing's 'divorce of theology from history'.[176] For Thiselton, then, following Pannenberg, '"faith"' is not '"blind credulity"' to '"authoritarian"' truth-'"claims"'.[177] Moreover, Thiselton argues that Bultmann wrongly sharpens Dilthey's distinction between

---

[167] Contradicting, Borsch, 'R *2H*', 90.

[168] Thiselton, *2H*, 57-58; cf. Guthrie, G.H., 'Boats in the Bay: Reflections on the Use of Linguistics and Literary Analysis in Biblical Studies', in *Linguistics and the New Testament. Critical Junctures* (eds. S.E. Porter and D.A. Carson; Journal for the Study of the New Testament Supplement Series 168: Studies in New Testament Greek 5; Sheffield: Sheffield Academic Press, 1999), 33, who cites Thiselton's later work in this connection also.

[169] Thiselton, *2H*, 245-251, 186-187. First and second italics ours, other italics Thiselton's.

[170] Thiselton, *2H*, 243-244.

[171] Contradicting, Walsh, 'TC', 234.

[172] Contradicting, White, H.C., 'The Value of Speech-Act Theory for Old Testament Hermeneutics', *Sem* 41 (1988), 41. White's italics.

[173] Webster, 'R *2H*', 219; cf. Thiselton, *2H*, 187-191, 195, 199; cf.: 37-38; 440-441, 30-33.

[174] Thiselton, *2H*, 77, 56; cf. Pannenberg, *BQ1*, 39-46.

[175] Thiselton, *2H*, 246-248; cf. Thiselton, 'TNI', 11. Italics ours.

[176] Thiselton, *2H*, 64-65; cf. McHann Jr., *3H*, 163.

[177] Thiselton, *2H*, 248; cf. Thiselton, 'Exc', 12.

'historical understanding' and "scientific" "'explanation'".[178] In Thiselton's thinking, 'historical understanding' (including the "factual" dimension) and "'self-understanding'" are interwoven, though 'distinct'; and Thiselton, though critical of Heidegger in this context of discussion, still endorses Heidegger's critiques of, (i), Husserl's attempt to "dualistically" partition 'consciousness' from history, and of, (ii), 'Hegel's' "idealist" "abstractions". Thiselton argues that since "'history'" is a "'unity'" (not a uniformity), then modes of 'understanding' the "'historical'", whilst not uniform, are not "sharply" "divorced" from one-another either.[179]

(c) Thiselton – drawing *in part* on Pannenberg and the later Wittgenstein - again rejects *'linguistic'* "dualisms" or dichotomies. Notably, (i), Thiselton rejects Bultmann's 'value' versus 'fact' 'dualism' (which has 'historical', epistemological, *and* 'linguistic' aspects). Against Bultmann, Thiselton argues that 'an' 'event's'', or a "fact's", 'meaning' or 'value' - its internal structure aside - is its relation to its 'nexus' of 'historical' *'surroundings'*. Furthermore, for Thiselton, "transmitted" 'historical' report is thus indispensable in relation to assessments of meaning.[180]

Similarly, (ii), Thiselton opposes Heidegger's dualistic separation of *'Saying'* (cf. Bultmann's notion of 'value') from 'objectifying' 'propositions' (cf. Bultmann's notion of "'facts'"). Admittedly, Thiselton argues that Heidegger's notion of *'Saying'* - the 'non-objectifying letting-be-seen' of what "'cannot be put into words'" (cf. 'value') - has its merits. Yet Thiselton also argues that Heidegger's notion of *'Saying'* erroneously posits a view in which 'authentic' 'language' is supposedly 'grounded in Being' and supposedly dualistically exalted relative to and/or divorced from erroneously-disparaged 'objectifying language'.[181]

(iii) Thiselton also opposes the *early* Wittgenstein's partly parallel "dualistic" or dichotomous separation of "showing" (cf. Heidegger's notion of *'Saying'*) from "saying" (cf. Heidegger's notion of "objectification"). Nevertheless, Thiselton preserves *modifications* of these early-Wittgensteinian notions of "showing" and "saying" (*with* the *later* Wittgenstein) whilst at the same time insisting *both* that these *modified* notions *cannot* be dualistically separated theoretically *and* that these *modified* notions *cannot* be linked to any kind of formalism (*against* the *early* Wittgenstein). Thus, (iii.i), in relation to "saying", then Thiselton, in *The Two Horizons*, notes that the early Wittgenstein's notion of "saying" concerns the 'structural correspondence' of 'elementary propositions' to 'states of affairs', and that this notion relates to the early Wittgenstein's 'picture theory of meaning'. However, we have already seen that Thiselton *rejects* the early Wittgenstein's notion of 'elementary propositions' and that Thiselton's approach to the question of meaning is *inconsistent* with the early Wittgenstein's 'picture theory of meaning' (see Chapter 4). Nevertheless, we have *also* already noted Thiselton's *preservation* of a

---

[178] Thiselton, *2H*, 238; cf.: 208-211; 235; 243-244.
[179] Thiselton, *2H*, 235, 246-251, 191; cf.: 145; 302-303; 83; 80; cf.: McHann Jr., *3H*, 163.
[180] Thiselton, *2H*, 39-40, 75-81, 195, 211-217, 245-249, 268-274, 286-287, 292, 311-314, 359-361, 373, 385, 425, 442-444. Fourth italics Thiselton's, others ours.
[181] Thiselton, *2H*, 39; cf.: 367-370, 195, 328, 330-347, 354-355. Italics Thiselton's.

*Hermeneutics and History* 305

notion of 'empirically informative' 'communication' (see Chapters 3 and 4) and, later, we will briefly look at Thiselton's preservation of a *modified* notion of "saying" that is *consistent with* his preservation of a notion of 'empirically informative' 'communication'.[182]

(iii.ii) In relation to "showing", then Thiselton, in *The Two Horizons*, notes the early Wittgenstein's argument that, since '"language"'-'"limits"' determine '"world"'-'"limits"', then 'language' '"cannot"' '"say"' 'anything' about 'existence', the 'mystical', '"logical form"', or about 'language' itself - but *"can"* only '"show"' this 'realm' of 'value',[183] a 'realm' that the early Wittgenstein sought 'to protect... from reduction to the level of empirical propositions'.[184] Thiselton, therefore, observes that '"showing"', for the early Wittgenstein, meant "enabling" interpreters 'to notice' '"what cannot be said"'. Having said this, however, Thiselton then argues that 'there is a connection between "showing" in the earlier writings [of Wittgenstein] and Wittgenstein's later work on the relation between the formation of concepts and grammatical utterances'. Crucially, Thiselton observes that Wittgenstein's 'earlier work on tautologies stands in continuity with his later observations about analytical statements and formal concepts'. Nevertheless, at this point, it is important to note that the later Wittgenstein and Thiselton do *not* treat 'concepts' '"formally"'. Both the later Wittgenstein and Thiselton can assert that, '"it is our *acting* which lies at the bottom of the language-game"', and *not* '"logic"'. For the later Wittgenstein and for Thiselton, though, '"showing"' still involves the 'analytical' explication of 'concepts', and in *this* context has more to do with '"showing"' that which was *previously "unnoticed"* than with '"showing"' '"what cannot be said"'. Thiselton, therefore, argues that the *later* Wittgenstein's notion of '"showing"' has *'hermeneutical'* implications.[185] Taken together, these points are not 'remote from the main theme' of *The Two Horizons* (contradicting P. Ellingworth's reading of Thiselton),[186] but are *pivotal for Thiselton's modification of Gadamer's hermeneutical circle*, as we shall see below.[187]

In other words, (iii.iii), Thiselton rejects a notion of '"showing"' that is conceived of ahistorically and/or that is associated with a '"logical"' *'a priori'* (against the early Wittgenstein), or divorced from 'assertions' (against Heidegger). Rather, drawing on Pannenberg and the 'later' Wittgenstein, Thiselton transposes '"showing"' into a new unified '"historico-philosophical"' framework, reuniting it with 'assertions' (cf. "saying") where, for Thiselton, *both '"showing"' and "saying" are*

---

[182] Thiselton, *2H*, 39, 267, 370, 362-367; cf. Thiselton, 'SNTP', 95-98; cf. Thiselton, 'Truth', 894-896, 899, 900; cf. our Chapter 3. Second italics Thiselton's, other italics ours.

[183] Thiselton, *2H*, 362, 361, 367-370, cf. 39, 36. Italics in speech-marks Thiselton's.

[184] Jasper, 'NTLI', 4; cf. Thiselton, *2H*, 367, 369-370.

[185] Thiselton, *2H*, 361-362, 367-369, 371-372, 378. Italics on the word, '"*acting*"', are Wittgenstein's, and are preserved by Thiselton; remaining italics are ours.

[186] Contradicting, Ellingworth, 'R *2H*', 178. Italics ours.

[187] Thiselton, *2H*, 34, 39, 361; cf. Wittgenstein, L., *Tractatus Logico-Philosophicus* (trans. D.F. Pears and B.F. McGuinness; London: Routledge, 1961, 1974, 2001), 78. Italics ours.

*thus to be seen as 'historical' "actions".* Thus, querying R.A. Harrisville's and S.M. Schneiders' readings of Thiselton, it is not simply that 'in' the later 'Wittgenstein' Thiselton 'sees a deliverance from the dualism of fact and value'. Rather, the underlying historico-philosophical framework of 'life' is also at stake for Thiselton (drawing on Pannenberg): Thiselton's historico-philosophical framework-transformation *grounds* his linguistic framework-transformation. For Thiselton, the unity of language is grounded in 'the unity of history', though Thiselton argues that *neither* history *nor* language-uses are 'uniform'.[188]

(d) Thiselton argues that the criterion of 'the unity of history' prohibits dichotomous ahistorical over-emphases - *either* on *corporate "culture-relativity"* versus the rest of historical reality, *or* on *individual "subjectivity"* versus the rest of historical reality. As we noted in Chapters 3 and 4, Thiselton argues that cultures are but "snap-shots" of trans-temporal traditions in synchronic cross-section, and that "selves" cannot be conceived of in ways that presuppose an 'isolated' 'Cartesian' "'I'". For Thiselton, both "cultures" and "selves" are *embedded within* "'historical'" inter-relationships and are irrevocably "'historical'" themselves.[189]

We will expound Thiselton's critique of Heidegger in relation to historical *selves* a little later. But, in relation to *cultures*, we should note here that Thiselton's later criticism of the "ahistoricity" of approaches that, in some ways, over-stress and isolate present-horizon "culture-relativity" from diachronic history, is carried out on the *philosophical* basis of the "unity of historical reality" and emphatically not on a theologically dogmatic premise of "partisan" or "special" pleading.[190] We shall expand on this point in Chapter 7.

(2) Returning to points "(b)" and "(d)" immediately above, then we may now note that Thiselton develops his notion of the link between "historical understanding" and "self-understanding" in three ways – as follows.

(a) For Thiselton, 'historical understanding' *'begins'* 'with' or *emerges* 'through* self-understanding'. Here, Thiselton's notion of 'self-understanding' is to be understood with respect to its *relatedness to* Thiselton's notion of 'pre-understanding' - though, for Thiselton, 'pre-understanding' also includes "'a prior understanding of the subject'" as, for example, in the case of the subject-matter of, say, a text.[191] With 'Heidegger' and 'Bultmann', Thiselton argues that 'historical understanding' always *'begins'* 'with' 'self-understanding' – i.e. with "'the interpreter's'" 'questions', "life-experience'", or 'pre-understanding' - even if it then moves on.[192] Thiselton argues that, initially, 'understanding' "sees" 'something

---

[188] Thiselton, *2H*, 361-373, 39, 66-84, 245-251, 302-303, 195; querying, Harrisville, 'R *2H*', 216; contradicting, Schneiders, 'R *2H*', 307-309. First italics Thiselton's, remaining italics ours.

[189] Thiselton, *2H*, 299-314, 396, 238-245, 53-84, 434-436, 201, 250-251. Italics ours.

[190] Thiselton, *NH*, 393-405; cf.: 439-452; 529-550; cf. Thiselton, 'CAP', 157; cf. 152-182.

[191] Thiselton, *2H*, 105-107, 109-110, 149-176, 196-197, 228-244, 291. Italics in speech-marks are Thiselton's, others are ours.

[192] Thiselton, *2H*, 105, 107, 109-110, 197, 232, 235-237. Italics Thiselton's.

"as"' 'something' *'in relation to'* 'prior' 'horizons', and is not a matter of "neutral" 'detachment'. Hence, for Thiselton, 'speaking of God' "begins" 'with' 'speaking of man'.[193] However, in this context of discussion, Thiselton is critical of 'Dilthey', 'Heidegger', 'Bultmann', and of Fuchs and Ebeling of the New Hermeneutic since, in Thiselton's estimate, these thinkers 'too easily' *collapse* 'historical understanding' *into* 'self-understanding'. In Thiselton's view, 'Collingwood' better preserves the "distinction" 'between' "'I'" and "'Thou'".[194]

(b) For Thiselton, 'self-understanding' - understood with respect to its relatedness to Thiselton's notion of conscious self-awareness - emerges *'through'* a *detour into* 'historical understanding' and, in the context of this "detour", involves self-identification *'in relation to'*, and by contrast with, the historically 'other'.[195] Thiselton partly accepts 'Dilthey's' view that "'the I'" is "rediscovered" "'in the Thou'", but follows Collingwood's criticism that Dilthey comes too close to "identifying" "'the I'" with "'the Thou'". Similarly, Thiselton partly accepts Dilthey's view that 'self-understanding' does "'not'" come "'through introspection'", but through a "projection" of the self "'into… others'… past experience'" so as "'to re-live'" it.[196] Yet, following Collingwood's criticism of Dilthey again, Thiselton argues that such 'reliving' is not actual because of a changed 'context' - though Thiselton adds that such 'reliving' *is* "experiential" and 'existential' such that, for Thiselton, Dilthey's term 'life' (cf. Dilthey's notion of 'reliving') is more appropriate than Collingwood's term 'thought' (cf. Collingwood's notion of the "'re-enactment of a past thought'").[197] With G. Yorck, Thiselton agrees 'that history involves "critical self-examination"' via "texts", where Thiselton argues that this "'critical self-examination'" via "texts" leads to an "enlarging" of interpreters' "'experience'".[198] Similarly, with Gadamer, Thiselton argues that 'distancing' "jogs" unconscious "interpretative" 'pre-judgments' - which initially stand in contrast to explicit and implicit content embedded in "texts" - into 'conscious awareness', and that this process leads to 'self-understanding' and to "'transformation'".[199]

(c) For Thiselton, 'self-understanding' is *an 'aspect of'* 'historical understanding', since selves - as "whole" persons - are "'historical'": Thiselton grounds his hermeneutical critique of human selves in his hermeneutical critique of history. With 'Dilthey', Thiselton accepts that 'human life' is 'the subject-matter of history'

---

[193] Thiselton, *2H*, 39, 165-166, 237, 197, 155-156, 245, 230-233. Italics Thiselton's.
[194] Thiselton, *2H*, 239, 235, 308, 196-197, cf. 291-292, 242-243. Italics ours.
[195] Thiselton, *2H*, 236, 235, 197, 242-243, 107; cf. 237-238; cf. Thiselton, 'TY', 1564. First italics ours, second italics Thiselton's.
[196] Thiselton, *2H*, 235-237, cf. 242-243.
[197] Thiselton, *2H*, 242; cf. 241-244; cf. 293-299; cf. 285. Italics ours.
[198] Thiselton, *2H*, 238, cf. 235.
[199] Thiselton, *2H*, 326, 237, 306-308; cf.: Thiselton, 'NH', 316-317, cf. 311; Thiselton, A.C., 'The Use of Philosophical Categories in New Testament Hermeneutics', *Chman* 87.1 (1973), 92-93.

- though, more in line with 'Collingwood's' thought again, Thiselton adds the important caveat that 'human life' is not history's *only* 'subject-matter'.[200]

Notably, Chapters 6 and 7 of *The Two Horizons* - on the early Heidegger - continue Thiselton's 'philosophical' dialogue in relation to his hermeneutical critique of human selves (see Chapter 4).[201] Thus, as J.C. McHann Jr. notes, 'the early Heidegger focused primarily on man' (i.e. on Daseins);[202] and R. Morgan notes that Thiselton, 'in connection with… theologians influenced by' the early Heidegger (notably Bultmann, E. Käsemann, and others), provides 'valuable discussion of Paul's anthropology'.[203] Unable to 'accept' Heidegger's *"analytic of Dasein"* in every respect, however, Thiselton later considerably widens his dialogue in relation to a hermeneutical critique of human selves in order to include further appeals to Dilthey, to Ricoeur, and to many others. Nevertheless, in *The Two Horizons*, Thiselton is more critical of what Heidegger "neglects" to say than of much of what Heidegger does say. Thiselton argues that Heidegger correctly attempts to re-ground '"consciousness"' historically, in critique of 'Husserl' (and of 'transcendental' notions of "selfhood").[204] Thus, Thiselton refuses 'to approach Heidegger' 'through' 'Husserl':[205] citing Gadamer, Thiselton argues that just as the later Wittgenstein rightly "criticizes" '"Anglo-Saxon semantics"' for being '"ahistorical"', so Heidegger rightly "criticizes" '"the ahistorical art of phenomenological description"'.[206]

(3) In this context of discussion, it is worth expounding what D.S. Dockery refers to as being Thiselton's 'very complex' "discussion" 'of Heidegger' which, in Dockery's estimate, 'leaves the reader wanting further explanation'.[207] Crucially Thiselton, as noted above, uses a qualified appeal to Heidegger to ground his hermeneutical critique of human selves in his hermeneutical critique of history. In part thereby, correlatively, Thiselton modifies, "earths", or "makes concrete", the 'Hegelian' criterion of 'the unity of history' which, by itself, is too 'abstract'.[208] Bearing in mind Thiselton's rejection of dualisms or of dichotomies in Heidegger

---

[200] Thiselton, *2H*, 235, 242, 239-240; cf. 243-245; cf. 250-251. Italics ours.

[201] Thiselton, *2H*, 292, 143-204; this point is absent from most reviews of *2H*.

[202] McHann Jr., *3H*, 224.

[203] Morgan, 'R *2H*', 332; cf. Thiselton, *2H*, 275-283.

[204] Thiselton, A.C., *Interpreting God and The Postmodern Self: On Meaning, Manipulation and Promise* (SJT: Current Issues in Theology; Edinburgh: T&T Clark, 1995), 59-62, 73-78; cf. Thiselton, *2H*, 148, 145; cf.: 154-155; 199-204; 250; cf. Heidegger, M., *Being and Time* (trans. J. Macquarrie and E. Robinson; Oxford: Blackwell, 1962, 2001), 73, 86-90, 237; cf. Gadamer, *TM*, 255. Italics in speech-marks Heidegger's (preserved by Thiselton).

[205] Erickson, 'R *2H*', 372; cf. Thiselton, *2H*, 144-145.

[206] Thiselton, *2H*, 37. Citing, Gadamer, H.-G., 'The Philosophical Foundations of the Twentieth Century', in *Philosophical Hermeneutics* (H.-G. Gadamer; ed. D.E. Linge; London: University of California Press, 1976), 127.

[207] Thiselton, *2H*, 143-204; cf. Dockery, 'R *2H*', 134.

[208] Thiselton, *2H*, 302; cf. Thiselton, A.C., 'Kierkegaard and the Nature of Truth', *Chman* 89.1 (1975), 96-97.

*Hermeneutics and History* 309

and in Bultmann (see above), and bearing in mind our mildly critical responses to Thiselton's reading of Heidegger (see Chapter 3), then Thiselton's appeal to Heidegger in *The Two Horizons* is best summarized as follows.

(a) Thiselton argues that Heidegger *rightly grounds 'Dasein' in 'history'*, but that Heidegger *wrongly disparages the 'historical… past'*. With Heidegger, Thiselton agrees that 'history' includes "Dasein" (Thiselton would not use the term "Dasein" but the phrases, "human self" or "human selves") in that "Dasein" is a 'contingent' 'historical' 'reality' or 'truth', against "empiricist" notions of 'the self' as a "mere" "'object'", and against "rationalist" notions of 'the self' as an 'abstract' "'subject'". Yet, Thiselton argues that Heidegger's view, according to which 'Dasein's… historicality… is prior to… "history" (world-historical historizing)', is too dualistic or too dichotomous.[209]

With Heidegger, Thiselton agrees that 'historical' 'truth' 'is not' just 'abstract' 'propositions' or *"information"*, and that 'historical' 'truth' is neither the '"passive undergoing"' of 'present-at-hand' 'objects', nor a '"disowned"' "reified" 'temporality' split off from "Dasein's" '"reality"'.[210] Rather, for Thiselton, with Heidegger, "history" is the 'continually… created' '"happening"' of "contingencies", where these "contingencies" notably comprise of - and are partially "unveiled" to but also partially "hidden" to - historically "finite" selves (Thiselton does not "sacrifice" 'hiddenness', where here we are contradicting R.A. Harrisville's reading of Thiselton). By contrast, Heidegger argues, 'the theme of historiology is… the possibility which has been factically existent', where Heidegger argues that 'historiology' thus erroneously reduces 'history' to 'the *Object* of a science'.[211] For Heidegger, followed by Thiselton, '"history"' is *actually* pre-conditional for, and irrevocably tied to, the *concrete* '"possibility"' of '"the 'recurrence' of"' '"human"' *'existential'* '"possibility"' *prior* to the objectification involved in "historiological" 'thematizing'.[212] Whilst Thiselton departs from 'Heidegger's' near "reduction" of 'history' to 'Dasein', Thiselton accepts 'Heidegger's' argument that 'history' *does* include, and is interwoven with, "Daseins", or (to use Thiselton's language) with "selves".[213]

(b) Thiselton argues that Heidegger *rightly analyzes "Dasein" "temporally"* – *both* in terms of *"worldhood"*', which is more '"passive"' and which is grounded in the 'past' and 'present', *and* in terms of *'historicality'*, which is more '"active"' in that it is

---

[209] Thiselton, *2H*, 250-251; cf.: 175-186; 78-79; cf. Heidegger, *BT*, 86-90, cf. 439-455, 367-368, quoting 41. Italics ours.

[210] Thiselton, *2H*, 173-176, 182-187; contradicting Moorhead, D., 'Review of A.C. Thiselton's *Interpreting God and the Postmodern Self*', *JPsychTh* 27.4 (1999), 358. Italics Thiselton's.

[211] Thiselton, *2H*, 175-176, 186, 79; contradicting, Harrisville, 'R *2H*', 216. We quote, Heidegger, *BT*, 447, and 427. The capitalization and italics on *'Object'* are Heidegger's.

[212] Thiselton, *2H*, 175-176, cf. 186, 163; cf. Heidegger, *BT*, 447, and 427. Italics ours.

[213] Thiselton, *2H*, 250-251; cf. 143-149. Contradicting, Malbon, E.S., 'Structuralism, Hermeneutics, and Contextual Meaning', *JAARel* 51.2 (1983), 217. Italics ours.

conceived of as dynamically "relating to" 'past', 'present and… future'. However, in Chapter 3, we argued that, for Thiselton, Heidegger incompletely or inadequately "re-historicized" the Cartesian "knower" and that, for Thiselton, this problem was, (i), earthed in Heidegger's *historical* dualism or dichotomy (see also above) and, (ii), was a problem that outworked itself in Heidegger's epistemological, linguistic, and anthropological dualisms or dichotomies (see Chapters 3, 4, and below).[214] Nevertheless, for Heidegger, and in a qualified sense for Thiselton, 'worldhood' relates to 'the structure of that wherein Dasein as such already is'. And for Heidegger, and in a qualified sense for Thiselton, 'historicality' is 'the repetition of the heritage of possibilities by handing these down to oneself in anticipation'. Thus, for Heidegger and, in a qualified sense, for Thiselton, 'the horizon of temporality' is 'the ontological meaning' of 'Dasein's Being'.[215]

In other words(!), Thiselton argues that there is something right about Heidegger's analysis of Dasein in terms of "temporality", and thence in terms of "worldhood" and "historicality". However, for Thiselton, these categories require qualification and modification in relation to inter-subjectivity, conceptualization, cognitive language, tradition, history more broadly, and ultimately in relation to theology and eschatology.

(c) Thiselton, positively, broadly affirms Heidegger's thinking in relation to 'the… *existentialia*' that Heidegger calls *'feeling-states', 'understanding', and '"discourse"'* – which are in different ways linked to "historicality" and/or to "'worldhood'". Thus, (i), Thiselton argues that Heidegger rightly links 'pre-cognitive' *'feeling-states'* to 'truth'-"disclosure", and that, with Heidegger, a "feeling-state" is 'not' a "'mere feeling'" but a "'state-of-mind'" or "'mood'".[216] (ii) Thiselton also argues that Heidegger rightly links *'understanding'* 'to the hermeneutical circle', and to "'projected'" 'future' "possibilities" or to existential 'possibility', where existential 'possibility' is also linked to Dasein's *'concerns'*. Thiselton draws parallels between 'Heidegger's' notions of 'understanding' and "'world'" and the 'later' 'Wittgenstein's' notions of "'seeing as…'" and "'life'". Thus, for Thiselton, "'understanding'" is 'seeing' "'as'" "'for-the-sake-of-which'" in "relation to" 'the horizons' of "'world'" or of "'life'" (cf. "'life-world'"). To *an extent*, Thiselton agrees with Heidegger that 'understanding' is a "pre-cognitive" 'awareness' that is *'a priori'* to 'logic' and to 'conscious' 'interpretation'.[217] Finally, (iii), Thiselton argues that 'Heidegger' rightly links *"'discourse'"* (cf. 'language') to inter-personal *'communication'* – a point that, in Thiselton's estimate, also finds parallels in the

---

[214] Thiselton, *2H*, 182-186, 250; cf. 149, 172-173, 188, 154-155. Italics ours.

[215] Heidegger, *BT*, 120, 442, 416.

[216] Thiselton, *2H*, 161-164, 168, 191; cf. Thiselton, A.C., 'Truth', in *The New International Dictionary of New Testament Theology, Volume 3* (ed. C. Brown; Exeter: Paternoster; Grand Rapids: Zondervan, 1978), 898. First italics Thiselton's, remaining italics ours.

[217] See, Thiselton, *2H*, 163-166, 185, 473 (index), 417, 303, 378, 362, cf. 147; cf. Thiselton, 'NH', 311. First and third italics ours, remaining italics Thiselton's.

*Hermeneutics and History* 311

thinking of the later Wittgenstein.[218]

Negatively, however, Thiselton argues, in criticism of Heidegger, that 'feeling-states', 'understanding', and '"discourse"' are not simply or primarily only linked to 'pre-cognitive' factors and that, in practice, all three are closely and irrevocably tied to a re-historicized 'subject-object' "conceptualization" that is fully operative in critical and metacritical spheres (see Chapter 3), to "comparative" "testing" as fully operative in critical and metacritical spheres (see Chapter 3), and to "assertive" 'language' (see Chapters 3, 4, 5, and below), *against Heidegger's epistemological and linguistic dualisms*.[219]

(d) Focusing in then, for Thiselton, Heidegger *rightly affirms 'pre-cognitive' 'worldhood'* but, for Thiselton, Heidegger is *wrong* to do so *at the expense of 'cognitive' factors* (see Chapter 3). Drawing on, if slightly modifying, Heidegger's thinking, Thiselton broadly agrees with Heidegger that each 'historical' 'Dasein' manifests '"worldhood"', where '"worldhood"' is a 'pre-cognitive' *'a priori'* to 'reflection' and is 'conditioned by' 'Dasein's' 'historical' 'situatedness', 'facticity', and by Dasein's '"thrownness"' into a pre-'"given"' "concrete" 'historical' 'world' or 'heritage' of 'tradition', 'culture', 'attitudes', "perspectives", and of 'practical concerns'.[220]

With Heidegger, Thiselton (in a qualified sense) allows that 'Dasein's' '"thrownness"' reflects 'the *facticity of*' 'Dasein's' 'Being-delivered-over to the "there"' *a priori* to 'the factuality belonging to presence-at-hand'. For Heidegger, and in a qualified sense for Thiselton, Dasein's "situated" and 'conditioned' '"worldhood"' - closely linked to Dasein's 'possibilities' of 'understanding' - is 'provisionally bounded' by its 'pre-cognitive' 'horizons',[221] which are not (therefore) just a matter of 'world-view' (querying – in one place - J. Macquarrie's reading of Thiselton), or of 'perspective', or of 'understanding' (querying M.A. Noll's and D.F. Wells' reading of Thiselton).[222]

For 'Heidegger', and in a qualified sense for Thiselton, '"world"' and '"worldhood"' are *'existentialia'*, or 'fundamental' characteristics *'of Dasein, which has Being-in-the-world as its essential state'*.[223] For Thiselton then, despite his reservations about 'cognitive' factors (see Chapter 3), the 'notion of pre-cognitive "worlds"' is

---

[218] See, Thiselton, *2H*, 168, 195, 380-385; cf.: 157; 360-362; 406. First italics ours, second italics Thiselton's.

[219] See, broadly, Thiselton, *2H*, 160-168, 195, 198, 292, cf. 187-204; cf. Thiselton, 'NH', 323, 324. Italics ours.

[220] Thiselton, *2H*, 194, 200-201, 373, 52, 154-164, 184-187; cf. Thiselton, 'TY', 1563; cf. Thiselton, 'U (long)', 90, 91. First, second, and third italics ours, fourth italics Thiselton's.

[221] Thiselton, 'TY', 1563; cf.: Thiselton, *2H*, 185, 154-165, xix; Thiselton, 'U (long)', 90, 91; Heidegger, *BT*, 84, 183, 1, 416-417; 174 (cited). First italics Heidegger's, others ours.

[222] Macquarrie, J., *Theology, Church and Ministry* (London: SCM Press, 1986), 30; and, Noll, M.A., and D.F. Wells, 'Introduction: Modern Evangelicalism', in, *Christian Faith and Practice in the Modern World* (eds. M.A. Noll and D.F. Wells; Grand Rapids: Eerdmans, 1988), 17.

[223] Thiselton, *2H*, 154-155 cf.: 161, 169; cf. Heidegger, *BT*, 84, quoting 80. First italics Thiselton's, second italics Heidegger's.

'the earlier' "Heidegger's" 'most valuable' contribution to hermeneutics. For Thiselton, this contribution is rightly "developed" and modified 'later' in "Ricoeur's" work on 'narrative-worlds of *possibility*'.[224]

Still – in effect - expounding Heidegger's notion of "'worldhood'", Thiselton argues that 'the later Heidegger' *rightly stresses 'the capacity of language, tradition, and temporal distance to' distort 'truth'*, but that Heidegger *underplays their 'capacity' to "transmit" 'truth'* (see Chapter 3). Thus, correlatively, Thiselton notes that the *early* Heidegger stresses Dasein's "'fallenness'" ('not' the biblical ethical notion) or Dasein's "'Being-lost in the... "they'" of popular tradition and culture. Thiselton observes that Heidegger's notion of "'fallenness'" involves: (i) *'idle talk'*, or blinding 'language' that 'perpetuates' received 'perspectives'; (ii) *'curiosity'*, or the 'crowd'-pleasing 'supposed novelty' of "'what one 'must' have read or seen'"; (iii) *'ambiguity'*, or the sense of "familiarity" "'and'" "accessibility" associated with a counterfeit sense of "having" 'understood'; and, (iv), *"lostness"*, or being under 'the spell of' "'absorption in''" 'the... everyday' of 'inauthentic' "fascination" with "'the Dasein-with of Others'" (cf. "gossip").[225]

In other words, Thiselton finds Heidegger's analysis of how tradition *distorts* truth to be very valuable, but argues that Heidegger's work lacks a converse analysis of how tradition *transmits* truth. With respect to the latter analysis, we noted that Thiselton turned to Gadamer (see Chapter 3).

S. Perry cites 'idle talk' in critique of Stanley Fish's 'pragmatist hermeneutics', finding it 'curious' that Thiselton does not. In reply, however, we should note that 'idle talk' relates to distortions "perpetuated" by the 'language' of *traditions*, whereas Thiselton's later critique of Fish centers on the historical, epistemological, and linguistic problems of *"contextual-relativism"* - an approach that, in Thiselton's estimate, "ahistorically" attempts (at least in effect) to divorce itself – and its speech - *from* the matrices of traditions transmitted in texts. Nevertheless, Perry has made a very good point: one can speak "distortion" if one is in *ignorance* of a tradition because of isolationism; *and* one can speak "distortion" if one is under the *spell* of a distortion perpetuated *by* a tradition.[226]

(e) Thiselton argues, in a qualified way, that Heidegger is broadly right to argue that each 'Dasein' manifests *'historicality'* (see above and below), *'Existenz'*, and *"Ek-sistenz"*. Thiselton observes that, for Heidegger, *'Existenz'* (a term closely related to 'historicality' except that it has the sense of an external difference rather than that of an internal analytic) is Dasein's "'ontically'" "distinctive" 'mode of' 'existence' in contrast to that of 'mere' "objects". An *aspect of* this "distinctive" 'mode of' 'existence', according to Thiselton's observations in relation to Heidegger's thinking, is *"Ek-sistenz"'* - which is Dasein's unique ability to "'stand'"

---

[224] Thiselton, 'TY', 1563, 1564; cf. Thiselton, *2H*, 187-204. Italics Thiselton's.

[225] See, Thiselton, *2H*, 154, 312-314, 169-171, 404; cf. Heidegger, *BT*, 220-221, cf. 212. Italics ours.

[226] Perry, S., 'E-mail to Robert Knowles, 23rd May, 2000', 1; cf. Thiselton, *2H*, 169, 170; cf. Thiselton, *NH*, 541, cf. 537-550; cf. Thiselton, 'CAP', 157. Italics ours.

apart 'from itself to inquire about...' "'Being'". Thiselton's qualification of Heidegger's thinking in this context is that - in "unifying" "historical" 'reality' – Thiselton "distinguishes" 'ontological inquiry' into the 'Being' of selves from 'ontic inquiry' into 'beings' less sharply than Heidegger: for Heidegger, though *not* for Thiselton, 'ontological inquiry is... more primordial' than 'the ontical inquiry of the positive sciences'.[227]

(f) For Thiselton, Heidegger rightly views 'the... self' 'as *a unitary... whole*' with "'the historical motion'" of 'historicality'. However, (i), for Thiselton, Heidegger's notion of 'wholeness', in contrast to Thiselton's thinking in relation to *"ethics" and inter-personal 'relationality'*, underplays inter-subjective accountability and neglects submission to 'God' (i.e. for Thiselton, selves manifest internally self-consistent "wholeness" *only* in inter-subjective relations of love for God and neighbor – relations that also embrace a right attitude to the created environment as part of their grammar). Further, (ii), taking the extent of Thiselton's appeal to Pannenberg's eschatology during his second period into account, we must also conclude that Heidegger's view that 'Dasein reaches its wholeness in death' is unacceptable to Thiselton as it stands. This point emerges more explicitly in Thiselton's fourth period work in which Thiselton, combining appeals to 'Ricoeur and Pannenberg', argues that any notion of human 'wholeness' must be related to an *eschatological-historical 'temporal*' narrative'. Thiselton, then, argues that Heidegger's over-emphasis on Daseins excludes history understood in terms of such a larger 'temporal' or eschatological 'narrative'. In Thiselton's estimate, the problem of the lack of 'unity of' 'historical' 'reality' in Heidegger's thinking lies in the background at this point (i.e. for Thiselton, the narrative of a "whole" self is *united with* the narrative of the "whole of history" - which will be brought to an eschatological conclusion).[228]

Thiselton's dual sets of concerns (i.e. '(i)' and '(ii)' above) in relation to Heidegger's thinking on Dasein's "wholeness" – i.e. Thiselton's *ethical-relational* concerns and Thiselton's *eschatological-historical* concerns – are reflected in Thiselton's two-fold exegesis of, and/or in Thiselton's two-fold angle of view on, Heidegger's notion of "historicality", as follows.

Thus, (g), bearing Thiselton's (not Heidegger's) *ethical-relational* angle of view in mind, then we may observe that Thiselton notes that, for Heidegger, 'Dasein... in its wholeness' is 'care': for Heidegger, Thiselton observes, 'the Being of Dasein itself is... made visible as *care*', and is "brought" 'to light" by 'anxiety' (as opposed to 'fear'). Thiselton notes that, for Heidegger, 'care' thus binds *'existentialia'* 'into a' "unified" 'whole'. Notably, Thiselton observes that, for Heidegger, 'care' has three overlapping "'twofold'" "structures". Thus, expounding Heidegger's thought, (i),

---

[227] Thiselton, *2H*, 184, 147-148; cf.: 152-153; 302, 174, 172; 186-187; 245-251; cf. Heidegger, *BT*, 434-444, cf. 28-35, – final two quotations from 31. Second, third, fourth, and sixth italics Thiselton's, remaining italics ours.

[228] Thiselton, *2H*, 200-203; cf. 171-173, 185-186; 302, 250; Thiselton, 'HB', 77; cf. Thiselton, *IGPS*, 160; cf. citation from Heidegger, *BT*, 281. Italics ours.

Thiselton notes that "care's" "'twofold'" *'temporal'* "'structure'" is "'thrown projection'" or 'conditioned' 'historicality'. Thiselton observes that, for Heidegger, "'thrown projection'" is a temporalizing structure (i.e. "'thrown projection'" is a *movement* that that relates to *Dasein's own temporal structure*) according to which 'Dasein', whilst 'bound' by "finitude" and "conditioning" (cf. "worldhood"), nevertheless in its 'historicality' simultaneously instrumentalizes its 'heritage' (*relating "to itself"* in 'self-understanding'), reaching towards 'the future' and towards 'self'-"transcendence" or 'Being-ahead-of-oneself' (cf. Paul's contrast between 'body and spirit' – so Bultmann). Heidegger writes, 'self-projection upon the "for-the-sake-of-oneself" is grounded in the future and is an essential characteristic of *existentiality*. *The primary meaning of existentiality is the future*', where the dynamic of *'future'*-oriented 'self-projection' (cf. *'existentiality'*) constitutes 'the context…of' the 'ontological' 'structure' of 'Dasein's' 'existence'. 'Dasein' as 'essentially ahead of itself… has projected itself upon its potentiality-for-Being *before*… any mere consideration of itself'. Certainly, Thiselton *affirms* the broad notion of "'thrown projection'" in Heidegger's thinking here.²²⁹

(ii) Thiselton notes that, for Heidegger, the 'authentic' 'temporal' "'historical motion'" of "'thrown projection'", whilst being constitutive for Dasein's *self-relationality*, can become distorted (this point then takes on an ethical significance for Bultmann and for Thiselton, if not for Heidegger). Thus, Thiselton notes that, for Heidegger, "care's" "'twofold'" *self-relational* "'structure'" is such that Dasein *either* "falls" into "'self-betrayal'" and "evasion" (such that Dasein is "'estranged from'" itself and is thereby 'loaded down with the legacy of a "past" which has become unrecognisable') *or* obeys "'the call of care'" (such that Dasein is "'at one with'" itself in 'resoluteness against the inconstancy of distraction', in 'authentic' "'thrown projection'").²³⁰

Thiselton notes that, for Heidegger, "'the call of care'" is 'not' "abstract", but is part of 'Dasein' and is to be identified as 'the… silent' "'discourse'" of conscience'. This means 'that ethics' (in Thiselton's appropriation of Heidegger's thinking) has no "abstract" 'intellectual' "basis". Thiselton notes that, for Heidegger, *'Dasein'* is *'the caller of the call of conscience'*.²³¹ Thiselton observes that, for Heidegger, this "'call'" directs 'Dasein' *from* the "'forfeiture'" of 'the everyday they-self' (so far as is possible) *to* 'futurity' and, despite its 'uncanny mode of *keeping silent*', "'discloses'" to 'Dasein' *both* 'its [i.e. Dasein's]… historical heritage', *and*, its (i.e. Dasein's) "projected" 'possibilities' or 'the "whither"' (cf. counselling settings, where words

---

²²⁹ Thiselton, *2H*, 171, 161, 173, 185-186, 197; citations from Heidegger, *BT*, 83-84, 321, 181, 347-348, 243, 435, 237, 375-376, 33, and 458 respectively. First, fourth, fifth, sixth, and twelfth italics ours; third italics Thiselton's; remaining italics Heidegger's, except for the word *"relating"*, where they are ours.

²³⁰ Thiselton, *2H*, 185, 169, 155, 171-173, 177-180, 186, 277-280, cf. 153; cf. Heidegger, *BT*, 444, 442 respectively. Italics ours.

²³¹ Thiselton, *2H*, 179-181; cf. Thiselton, 'KNT', 91, 93-95; cf. Heidegger, *BT*, 310-311, 313-314, 319-325, 342-348, quoting 321. Italics Heidegger's.

are found to "disclose" *prior* or *present* 'silent' "uncanny" 'feeling-states', but with a view to "moving on" into the *future*).[232]

Nevertheless, Thiselton notes that, for Heidegger, 'the transcendence of Dasein's Being' *"distinctively"* involves 'radical *individuation*'.[233] Thus, Thiselton still regards Heidegger's notion of 'authenticity' as being too 'individualistic'. Indeed, were it not for Heidegger's "explicit warning" that he does 'not' intend to couple his points about 'authentic existence' with 'any overtones of ethical or theological judgment', then Thiselton would be *even more* sympathetic towards the view of 'Marjorie Green', for whom Heidegger's perspective constitutes a "double self-centeredness" that, as such, is marked by an absence of "accountability" "'to God'" and to "'others'". Thus, whilst affirming the existence (if not always the content) of 'the call of conscience', Thiselton *also* affirms *both* a 'divine' 'call' from *'beyond'* the 'horizons' of 'the... self' *and* 'the' *right* 'restraints' of *social* "conventions" 'not yet' left behind (see Chapters 3 and 4).[234]

In other words, in Thiselton's ethical appropriation and modification of Heidegger's thought, Thiselton acknowledges that ethics must have a concrete basis, and that the conscience of any given "self" can – in the context of that aspect of ethical behavior that involves "self-relationality" - "call" that "self" *from* one mode of "relating to oneself" *to* another mode of "relating to oneself". *However*, (ii.i), for Thiselton, ethics must move beyond (even if it still includes) an intra-subjective "self-relationality" towards an inter-subjective "relationality" of love for God (involving submission) and neighbor (involving at least some forbearance in relation to social constraints as opposed to an immediate assertion of personal rights); and, (ii.ii), for Thiselton, the ultimate "caller" is God, and not the human conscience, where the implication is that, for Thiselton, conscience can be corrupted (as in the cases of certain obsessive illnesses and of demonic influence) and can stand in contrast to the call of God that comes from "beyond the horizons of the self". At this point we may deduce that, in Thiselton's thinking, an ethics that focused entirely on internal self-relational factors (for example, "inner peace") could actually lead one into the path of *disobedience to God*. We may deduce that, in Thiselton's thinking, one must "discern between spirits" precisely because it is possible for *more than one spirit to influence* the self or selves (see also Chapters 2, 3, 4, and 7).

(iii) Admittedly, Thiselton acknowledges that Heidegger does not altogether neglect inter-subjectivity or 'Dasein-with'. Thus, Thiselton observes that, for Heidegger, "care's" "'twofold'" *inter-active* "'structure'" involves the following

---

[232] Thiselton, *2H*, 179-181, 177, 163, 183-186. The example from counselling is our own. Cf. Heidegger, *BT*, 321, 322, 326 respectively. Third italics Heidegger's, others ours.

[233] Heidegger, *BT*, 62. First italics ours, second italics Heidegger's.

[234] Thiselton, *2H*, 169, 179, 200-203; cf.: Thiselton, A.C., 'New Problems for Old: Article Review of J.A.T. Robinson's *The Human Face of God*', *CEN* 6 Apr. (1973), 8; Thiselton, 'NH', 311; Thiselton, A.C., 'Realized Eschatology at Corinth', *NTStud* 24 (Jul. 1978), 521, 517, 522. Fourth italics Thiselton's, other italics ours.

distinction: Dasein's "'caring *about*'" the non-human - a "'caring'" that Heidegger calls "'concern'" - is "distinct" from Dasein's "'caring *for*'" 'other Daseins' - a "'caring'" that Heidegger calls "'solicitude'". For Thiselton, however, Heidegger remains too 'individualistic', and, in Thiselton's estimate, a *"distinction"* 'between' "'concern'"… and… "'solicitude'" should not be sharpened into an anthropological *dichotomy* – or ultimately thereby into a historical dichotomy - that *under-emphasizes* inter-subjectivity by *disengaging Dasein from* inter-subjectivity.[235]

(h) We now turn from Thiselton's *ethical-relational* concerns to do with the implications of Heidegger's *individualistic* view of "'Dasein's'" 'wholeness' (cf. Thiselton's later more explicit focus on 'relationality') to Thiselton's *eschatological-historical* concerns to do with the implications of Heidegger's *temporal* view of Dasein's 'wholeness' (cf. Thiselton's later more explicit focus on selves' "narrative completion" - a different aspect of 'wholeness' that is related to Thiselton's later use of the term 'temporality'). That is, Thiselton *also* expounds Heidegger's closely related notions of 'conditioned' 'historicality', "'thrown projection'", and of "'Dasein's'" unique "'historical motion'" with a slightly *different* emphasis – as follows.[236]

Thus, Thiselton notes that, for Heidegger, obedience to "'the call of care'" is "'the historical motion'" of "'Geschichte'" (cf. 'historicality') in which, by "repeated" "decisions", Dasein "moves" through 'self-understanding' towards an "appropriation" of its 'historical heritage' that "transcends" that 'heritage'. Thiselton observes that, for Heidegger, "'Geschichte'" is 'the resolute taking over of one's factical "there"' (cf. Heidegger's notions of "'worldhood'" and 'resoluteness'). Thiselton notes that, for Heidegger, "'Geschichte'" is also 'freedom' – i.e. a "'free shouldering of a destiny'" in "'active… 'happening'"' "'self-extension'". Thiselton observes that, for Heidegger, 'freedom', despite being always "limited" by 'heritage' and by the 'practicalities' of 'finitude', "'projects'" 'possibilities' in 'openness towards the future' 'horizon' of 'death' – i.e. 'death' understood as the completion of a temporally-structured "whole". Thus, Thiselton observes that, for Heidegger, 'Dasein *hands* itself *down* to itself, free for death, in a possibility… it has inherited and yet… chosen'.[237]

Thiselton notes that "'Geschichte'" - for Heidegger - is thus 'Being-towards-death', or 'authentic' "'historical motion'" (cf. 'historicality') "'*in the face* of'" "'*the possibility of being itself*'", and "'*in the face* of'" the 'horizon' of one's "'ownmost… possibility'" understood "*as the possibility of the impossibility of… existence*'".[238] That is, Thiselton observes that, for Heidegger, "'Geschichte'" "'gives up'" the self-

---

[235] Thiselton, *2H*, 173, 200-203; cf. 302, 66-67, 77-78, 82-83, 250; cf. Heidegger, *BT*, 237. Second and third italics Thiselton's, remaining italics ours.

[236] Thiselton, *2H*, 171, 173, 185-186, cf. 182, 250; cf. Thiselton, 'HB', 76-77; cf. 79; cf. Heidegger, *BT*, 351-359, 432-437, 443-444, 449, quoting 434. Italics ours.

[237] Thiselton, *2H*, 185-186; cf. 181-182, 173-180, 204, 163, 149; 250; cf. Heidegger, *BT*, 281-286, 303-308, 310-322, 325, 342-348, 432, quoting 434, 435. Italics Heidegger's.

[238] Thiselton, *2H*, 177, cf.: 178-179, 185-186, 183, 149, 250. Italics Heidegger's.

protective hold on '"existence"' that characterizes the "evasions" of 'lostness in the everydayness of the they-self'.²³⁹ Thus, Thiselton concludes that, in Heidegger's thinking, '"Geschichte"' re-paradigms Dasein's 'mode of' 'existence' 'towards' 'futurity' - transforming "pre-occupations", "concerns", and 'discourse', and 'individualizing the self out of' '"lostness in the 'they'"', whilst simultaneously allowing Dasein to become "authentically" relational in 'solicitude'.²⁴⁰

Thiselton's perspective, however, implicitly anticipates J.C. McHann's application of Pannenberg's criticism here: against Heidegger, 'death does not "round out man's existence into a whole" but rather "breaks off our life… [where] even… the… successful life remains a fragment"… [and where] "human beings' intention toward wholeness, toward well-being, necessarily reaches beyond death"'.²⁴¹ Similarly, Thiselton's eschatological emphasis prevents him from linking '"wholeness"' '"with death"'.²⁴² Thus, later, he locates the 'narrative' of a '"human life"' within the 'larger' 'temporal' 'narrative' '"whole"' of the '"divine"' '"*fulfillment*"' of '"eschatological"' '*promise*'.²⁴³

In other words, Thiselton is implying (amongst other points) that, in effectively divorcing *human* temporal wholeness from the *broader horizons of historical and eschatological-historical* wholeness, Heidegger has *also* potentially transgressed the *philosophical* criterion of the unity of historical reality.

Moving on then, (i), Thiselton affirms Heidegger's stress on Dasein's *uniqueness and particularity*, though in Thiselton's estimate, against Heidegger, there is far more room for an *a posteriori* 'general' axis at the level of inter-subjectivity and of other 'historical' "continuities" than is allowed by Heidegger. With Heidegger, though, Thiselton agrees that since 'Dasein has *in each case mineness*… one must always use a personal pronoun… [for example, as in the utterances] "I am", [or] "you are"'. Thiselton, in a qualified affirmation of Heidegger's thinking, broadly agrees with Heidegger's point that 'Dasein is… more' '"*fundamental*"' 'than' 'subjectivity' in 'Kant or Kierkegaard', and with Heidegger's point that to speak of 'Dasein' as '"an object"' is '"depersonalization"'. With Heidegger, Thiselton would agree that any 'general' 'characteristics' of Daseins are strictly *a posteriori* to, and secondary to, that which is 'particular': for Thiselton, Heidegger does not offer a 'transcendental' notion of selfhood in the Kantian sense (though, with Gadamer, Thiselton admits that Heidegger 'does not completely escape the problematic of transcendental reflection').²⁴⁴ In this context of discussion, Thiselton rejects the later Dilthey's

---

²³⁹ Thiselton, *2H*, 185, 178-180, 186; cf. Heidegger, *BT*, 307.
²⁴⁰ Thiselton, *2H*, 183-185, 178; cf.: 179-181, 173, 170.
²⁴¹ McHann Jr., *3H*, 216.
²⁴² Thiselton, *2H*, 176; cf. Thiselton, A.C., 'Review of E.H. Cousins ed. *Hope and the Future of Man*', *Chman* 88.3 (1974), 232; cf. Thiselton, 'Par', 47-48, 51.
²⁴³ Thiselton, *IGPS*, 75-76; cf. Thiselton, 'NP', 8; cf. Thiselton, 'Par', 47, 49, 51. First italics Moltmann's (preserved by Thiselton), second italics Thiselton's.
²⁴⁴ Thiselton, *2H*, 77-78, 148, 153-154; cf. 182-183; cf.: Thiselton, A.C., 'The Theology of Paul Tillich', *Chman* 88.1 (1974), 101; Thiselton, 'H-O', 8; Thiselton, 'SBS', 334; citations

over-emphasis on the *a priori* "continuity" 'of human nature' but, in implicit criticism of Heidegger, does so *without* over-disparaging an *a posteriori* 'general' 'historical' axis as we have already argued (see Chapters 4 and 5 and below).[245]

(j) Thiselton gives qualified approval to Bultmann's adaptation of 'Heidegger's' thought in his (i.e. Bultmann's) work on "Pauline anthropology" - though Thiselton argues that Bultmann's exegesis remains 'one-sided' (see our arguments above). For Thiselton, Bultmann rightly overturns perennial 'quasi-Platonic' '"interpretations"' of 'Pauline' '"anthropology"' that emphasize *"'parts'"*, 'substance, nature… object', or '"properties"', or that emphasize 'mind' versus 'body dualism'. With Bultmann, Thiselton does not think in terms of 'the essence of persons' (here we are querying A. Tosato's reading of Thiselton), and Thiselton agrees with Bultmann that a '*person as a whole*, can be denoted by *sōma*'.[246]

Further, for Thiselton, 'Bultmann' rightly adapts Heidegger's 'two fundamental modes of existence' (though Thiselton again strongly qualifies an '*ethics*' *of "self-relationality"* with a stronger emphasis on *"inter-subjectivity" and on "obedience" to 'God'*). For Thiselton, Bultmann rightly notes that *"'sarx'"* can signify an 'inauthentic' '"self-reliant"' 'mode of existence' in which the '"self, at war with"' itself (in contrast to the 'futurity' of "authenticity"), clings to "evasive" strategies and to 'false' "securities", particularly to 'the past'.[247] Thiselton approves of the way in which Bultmann's 'Christian' can choose 'to live "according to the flesh" or… "according to the Spirit"' where, for Bultmann and Thiselton, the former of these two modes of existence embraces a 'sinful self-delusion that one lives out of the created world'.[248] Bultmann, in Thiselton's view, also rightly notes that the Pauline words translated as 'body and spirit' can signify the 'self' as a 'whole', "unified" '"person"': for Bultmann and Thiselton, 'when Paul speaks of the *pneuma* of man he' "means" 'simply his self' (on '*sōma*', similarly, see above).[249]

Thus, as R.W. Roschke points out, Thiselton notes that 'Bultmann saw in Heidegger a way of expressing the gospel in twentieth-century language: God speaks an existential word of address that calls humanity into grace-filled holistic living (*Dasein*)'. Nevertheless, Heidegger's "Daseins" are not identical to

---

from Heidegger, *BT*, 68; and, Gadamer, *TM*, 255. Third and fourth italics Heidegger's, other italics ours.

[245] Thiselton, *2H*, 235-243, 77; cf. Thiselton, 'H-O', 8; cf. Thiselton, 'Till', 101. Italics ours.

[246] Thiselton, *2H*, 276-281, 292; querying, Tosato, A., 'On Genesis 2:24', *CBQ* 52.3 (Jul. 1990), 390; cf. Bultmann, *TNT1*, 190-352, quote from 195. Italics and transliteration Bultmann's.

[247] Thiselton, *2H*, 202-203, 278-279, 183, 186; cf.: Thiselton, *NH*, 13; Thiselton, 'U (long)', 121; Owen, H.P., *Revelation and Existence. A Study in the Theology of Rudolf Bultmann* (Cardiff: University of Wales Press, 1957), 40, 42, 100; citation from 40; Achtemeier, P.J., *An Introduction to The New Hermeneutic* (Philadelphia: The Westminster Press, 1969), 63; cf. 67. First and second italics ours, third italics Thiselton's. Transliteration from the text cited.

[248] Bultmann, *TNT1*, 330-331, cf. 239.

[249] Thiselton, *2H*, 278-279, cf. 173, 171, 277, cf. 291; cf. Bultmann, *TNT1*, 206-207. First italics Bultmann's, second italics Thiselton's. Transliterations are from the texts cited.

Bultmann's "Daseins" or to Thiselton's "selves"; nor are Bultmann's "Daseins" identical to Thiselton's "selves". For Kierkegaard, Bultmann and Thiselton, though, a hermeneutic of human selves embraces an important 'goal of hermeneutics' – i.e. "obedience" *'to God'*, who "calls" "'from'" *'beyond'* a self's 'conscience'. 'Heidegger', however, as Bultmann observes, 'does not characterize the attitude of resolution as *submission*'.[250]

(k) Summarizing positively: Thiselton *appeals* to Heidegger and to Bultmann in relation to the understanding of human selves: (i) as "historically" "'contingent'" "truths"; (ii) as "historically" "'embedded'" and 'conditioned' (cf. "worldhood'"); (iii) as historically "self-transcending" or "moving" (cf. 'historicality', 'existentiality', 'disclosure', 'futurity', 'understanding', "'discourse'", 'possibility', 'freedom', 'decision', 'resoluteness'); (iv) as potentially historically "'whole'" – both *"ethically"* (after Bultmann rather than Heidegger, Thiselton allows that a concrete "basis" for 'ethics' links to a "self-relationality" that is either "authentically" self-consistent or "'at war with'" itself) and *'temporally"* (cf. selves' "activation" "'from'" the "'horizon'" of 'future' "completion"); and, (v), as historically unique (cf. 'particularity', "'mineness'", and difference, versus 'transcendental' notions of human selves).[251]

(l) Summarizing negatively: Thiselton *rejects* aspects of Heidegger's thinking: (i) against Heidegger's *'historical'* 'dualism', Thiselton argues that 'past' "'facts'" as well as human selves are "historically" 'contingent' "truths". (ii) Against Heidegger's *epistemological* and *linguistic* dualisms, Thiselton argues that 'historical' "conditioning" does not divorce "worldhood" and 'horizons' from *valued* 'cognitive' factors, including: 'the capacity of language, tradition, and temporal distance to' "transmit" 'truth'; re-historicized 'subject-object' "conceptualization" in its critical and metacritical roles; 'critical' and metacritical "comparative" 'testing'; and "assertive" 'language'. (iii) Neither – in Thiselton's estimate and against Heidegger - can "'historical'" "movement" or 'historicality' be divorced from the operation of these same *valued* 'cognitive' factors. We have already implied that, in Thiselton's estimate, Pauline "reason" shaped the future by extending conceptual frames of reference through the use of grammatical utterances (see Chapter 5, and also below). (iv) Against Heidegger, Thiselton argues that the 'wholeness' of selves, *"ethically"* speaking, cannot be divorced from love for or 'submission' "'to God'" (and to God's call from "beyond the horizons of the self" or of the corrupted conscience – in Thiselton's estimate, one must discern between spirits) and/or from accountability to "'others'" (including, to an extent, social constraints) in

---

[250] Thiselton, *2H*, xix, 179-180, cf. 200-203, 277-278, 292, 305-306, 314; cf.: Thiselton, *NH*, 321, 330; Thiselton, 'NH', 311; qualifying, Roschke, R.W., 'Review of A.C. Thiselton's *The Two Horizons*', *CThM* 9 (Aug. 1982), 246. Final quote from, Bultmann, 'NT&M', 28. First italics Roschke's, third italics Thiselton's, remaining italics ours.

[251] Thiselton, *2H*, 250, 79, 168-186, 383, 153-163, 278, 243, 235; cf.: Thiselton, A.C., 'Creativity of Heaven', *CEN* 8 Mar. (1974), 5; Thiselton, 'Par', 49, 48; Gadamer, *TM*, 255. Italics ours.

loving inter-subjective 'relationality' and 'responsibility' (though, for Thiselton, self-relationality retains a place). (v) Nor, in Thiselton's estimate, and against Heidegger, can the "'wholeness'" of selves, "temporally" speaking, be divorced from the 'larger narrative' of an *"'eschatology'"* of divine promise-fulfillment. (vi) Against Heidegger, Thiselton argues that the "historically" "'particular'" uniqueness of selves cannot be so emphasized as to neglect *a posteriori* historical "continuities", including inter-subjectivity. (vii) *All these points of criticism presuppose Thiselton's axiom or criterion of 'the unity of history'.* (It should be remembered that Thiselton's criticisms of Heidegger's thinking in the present context of discussion do not, in Thiselton's thinking, negate the fact that Bultmann's dialogue with the early Heidegger has proven useful in 'New Testament' "interpretation" in "relation to" "'Pauline anthropology'" – though Thiselton *does* remain critical of even this most fruitful aspect of Bultmann's biblical hermeneutics, as we noted earlier).[252]

In other words, Thiselton modifies the way in which Heidegger makes selves "'historical'" so as to preserve his (i.e. Thiselton's) modification of 'Hegel's' axiom or criterion of 'the unity of history'. Thiselton thus corrects Heidegger's and 'Bultmann's' *'Geschichte'* versus *'Historie'* and 'history' versus 'nature' (and several other of their) "dualisms". (And Thiselton also - we might add - moves into alignment with the biblical doctrines of creation, of the fall, and of redemption).[253]

This conclusion correlates with our arguments in Chapters 3 and 5: Thiselton departed from Continental hermeneutics because it had not made "understanding" "historical" *enough*. That is, for Thiselton, *truly* historical "understanding", and *truly* historical persons as those who understand, are not only consistent with departures away from ahistorical Cartesianism and away from transcendental Kantian notions of "selfhood"; they are also consistent with *an even more fully or more properly "'historical'" (or with an even more fully "re-historicized") framework than that of Continental hermeneutics.* This *more properly* "'historical'" or "re-historicized" framework – in Thiselton's thinking - has to grapple with conceptions of historical "'continuity'", of 'the unity of history', of a historical 'dialectic' earthed in concrete developing traditions, of eschatological "anticipations" 'of history-as-a-whole', and ultimately with theology and Christology. Therefore, for Thiselton, selves are "de-centered" relative to 'larger' *'public'* "realities" and their 'criteria' (though not at all de-emphasized entirely). For Thiselton, hermeneutics cannot be "Dasein-centric" because hermeneutics is more "'historical'", more *'public'*, more *trans-temporal*, more *relational*, and more *eschatological, theological, and Christological* than that. In particular, one cannot help but conclude that, for Thiselton, a biblical "Trinitarian" notion of "persons-in-relation" (cf. public *inter*-subjectivity) helps to correct Heidegger's more

---

[252] Thiselton, *2H*, 246-250, 171-203, 79, 155, 275-314, 441; cf.: Thiselton, 'HB', 77; Thiselton, *IGPS*, 76; Thiselton, 'Par', 47; Thiselton, 'H-O', 8; Bultmann, 'NT&M', 28. Italics ours.

[253] Thiselton, *2H*, 250, 302, 246. Italics Thiselton's.

individualistic "Dasein-centric" perspective (cf. private *intra*-subjectivity).[254]

*3. The Process of Historical Dialectic as Earthed in The Processes of Traditions*

Moving on, then Thiselton's *third* modified "'Hegelian'" criterion, following 'Pannenberg' (and, to an extent, Gadamer), embraces the notion that the dynamic, "'dialectic'" 'process' of 'creative' 'historical' 'synthesis' generates 'historical' "particularities" and 'historical' "continuities": for Pannenberg and Thiselton, 'historical' "'truth... is... not... timelessly unchangeable'" but "'full of contradictions'".[255] But Thiselton's modification in relation to, or internal to, this criterion - a modification *that draws on* Gadamer and Pannenberg - is that historical "'dialectic'" is earthed *in the processes of traditions* (N.B. Thiselton's *hermeneutical critique of traditions* is an *aspect of* Thiselton's hermeneutical critique of history).[256] Against Hegel, Thiselton believes that 'historical understanding' cannot pertain to a "pure", albeit "developing", 'system' 'abstracted from the' 'concrete' 'life' of 'human' "traditions". Citing Gadamer, we may observe that 'Hegel sees Bildung [culture] brought to completion through the movement of alienation and appropriation in a complete mastery of substance, in the dissolution of all concrete being'. However, for Thiselton, *with* Gadamer and Pannenberg, 'history' "ongoingly" and "creatively synthesizes" chronologically "developing" *'concrete' 'traditions'* that, in turn, constitute socio-historical extensions 'of the *hermeneutical circle*' (or 'spiral').[257]

Thiselton also *modifies Gadamer's* thinking, however - *both* in relation to tradition *and* in relation to the hermeneutical circle.

Thus, *first*, for Thiselton, as J.C. McHann Jr. puts it (nearly a decade later than Thiselton and, like Thiselton, following Pannenberg's criticism of Gadamer on this specific point): whilst 'language is the "medium of understanding"' (McHann *cites* Gadamer here), 'it is so via the intertwining of language with history in tradition-history, specifically the history of the transmission of traditions, in such a way that language is grounded in historical reality' (McHann, after Pannenberg, and like Thiselton, is *criticizing* Gadamer here).[258] Thus, for Thiselton, Gadamer's hint of something 'behind' 'spoken' 'language' in his adaptation of "'the *verbum interius*'" is simply inadequate. In other words Thiselton, following Pannenberg, ontologically prioritizes conceptualizations of "history" (cf. 'tradition-history')

---

[254] Thiselton, *2H*, 250, 302, 82, 382, 173, 379; cf. Thiselton, 'H-O', 8; cf. Thiselton, *IGPS*, 159, 76; cf. 159-163. Sixth and seventh italics Thiselton's, remaining italics ours.
[255] Thiselton, *2H*, 83, 66-67, cf. 19, 309-311, 175, 74-81, 44-45, 370-407, 95-101; cf. Thiselton, 'H-O', 8.
[256] Thiselton, *2H*, 67, 76-83, cf.: 44-45, 302-313; 321-322. Italics ours.
[257] Thiselton, *2H*, 321-326, 80-83, 66-67, 104; cf. Thiselton, *NH*, 540; cf. Thiselton, 'KNT', 96. Citation from Gadamer, *TM*, 15. Italics ours.
[258] McHann Jr., *3H*, 326; cf. Thiselton, *2H*, 310, 379-385, cf.: 392, 372-373, 337, 443; cf. Gadamer, *TM*, 389; cf. 383-405, cf. 438-491. Italics ours.

relative to conceptualizations of "language", and thereby *reverses* Gadamer's ontological prioritization of conceptualizations of "language" relative to conceptualizations of "history". As we have seen, and against R.S. Hess's, W.J. Heard Jr.'s, and N.R. Gulley's respective readings of Thiselton, we should again observe that Thiselton does *not* "follow" (Hess's term) McHann Jr. in this respect, but adopts this stance *at least a decade earlier* than McHann (see Chapter 3).[259] And as we shall see below, Thiselton's adoption of this stance is *not the only way* in which Thiselton modifies Gadamer's hermeneutic of traditions.

*Second*, Thiselton does not just "take over" 'Gadamer's phrase "the fusion of horizons"' (here we are querying D.J. Harrington's reading of Thiselton);[260] rather, Thiselton *modifies the very grammar* of Gadamer's notions of "fusion" and "distancing",[261] and thereby develops Gadamer's hermeneutical circle in a way that is *far more fundamental and important* than substituting 'the phrase' "hermeneutical spiral" for 'the phrase "hermeneutical circle"'.[262]

Reserving a separate section for our continuing exposition of Thiselton's modification of Gadamer's hermeneutical circle (see below, and continuing on from Chapter 5), we may first expound Thiselton's modification of a Gadamerian hermeneutic of *traditions*, as follows.

(1) For Thiselton, 'traditions' are *"interwoven wholes"* and/or 'life'-"contexts" 'for... understanding' that are subsidiary to 'history-as-a-whole' (N.B. the contrast with Gadamer here). For Thiselton, 'traditions' "interweave" "thought", 'culture', '"actions"', '"language"', 'events', "meanings", and "interpretations".[263] Notably, Thiselton argues that, in all traditions, 'facts' and "meanings" are "interwoven" in an inseparable unity. Thiselton thus argues against E. Troeltsch's broadly 'positivist' 'abstraction' 'of "brute facts"... from interpretation' and from 'meaning', and against "Kähler's and Bultmann's" "broadly" '"existentialist"' 'abstraction' of 'theological' or 'existential' 'interpretation' from 'historical facts' and from 'Old Testament' 'tradition'. For Thiselton, 'traditions' should not be artificially disintegrated in these ways.[264]

(2) For Thiselton, "traditions" also bridge 'past' and 'present' 'horizons'.

---

[259] Grondin, J., *Introduction to Philosophical Hermeneutics* (trans. J. Weinsheimer; Yale Studies in Hermeneutics; New Haven: Yale University Press, 1994), xiv; cf.: Thiselton, *2H*, 74-84, cf. 310, 379-385; cf. 392, 372-373, 337, 443; McHann Jr., *3H*, 326; Hess, 'RA NH', 23; Heard Jr., W.J., 'Eschatologically Oriented Psychology', in *God and Culture* (eds. D.A. Carson and J. Woodbridge; Grand Rapids: Eerdmans, 1993), 118; Gulley, N.R., 'Reader-Response Theories in Postmodern Hermeneutics', in *The Challenge of Postmodernism. An Evangelical Engagement* (ed. D.S. Dockery; Grand Rapids, Mi.: Baker Books, 1997), 208. Italics ours.

[260] Querying, Harrington, D.J., 'Biblical Hermeneutics in Recent Discussion: New Testament', *RelStudRev* 10 (Jan. 1984), 8.

[261] Thiselton, *2H*, 326; cf. 313, cf. 342-352, 386-407.

[262] Thiselton, *2H*, 104.

[263] Thiselton, *2H*, 44-45, cf.: 80-82, 303-312, 321-326, 379-385; cf. Gadamer, *TM*, xxxviii (i.e. Gadamer excludes eschatology). Italics ours.

[264] Thiselton, *2H*, 80-81, 245, 290, 286, 442, 379-385.

Thiselton argues that traditions are *diachronic 'frames of reference" for 'meaning'* such that, with 'Gadamer', Thiselton argues that '"meaning... goes beyond'" "authorial" "intent" without adding '"new'" textual '"content'": for Gadamer and Thiselton 'the *mens auctoris* does not limit the horizon of understanding' completely.[265] For Thiselton, the "dimension of" '"present'" 'meaning' is "unavoidable" since 'understanding' never "merely" "reproduces" 'the past', but "creates" 'new' "relationships" 'between' "texts" and successive "generations" of "readers" as "traditions" "develop".[266] Hence, with 'Gadamer', Thiselton argues that '"understanding is... placing... oneself'" in the "processes of traditions", and that '"understanding'" thus has 'a dialectic... emphasis... on... past' and 'present' 'horizons' that also, in line with Pannenberg's thinking, reaches towards 'the future': for Gadamer, Pannenberg and Thiselton *'understanding is... participating in an event of tradition*, a process of transmission'.[267]

This point grounds Thiselton's later criticism of Stanley Fish who – (along with, in Thiselton's estimate, 'some' approaches in 'pastoral theology') - locates meaning *solely* in "readers'" 'present' "horizons". In 1999 Thiselton, unfairly to himself, comments that he had previously 'failed to identify... the *fundamentally a-historical viewpoint of* [radical] *reader-response theory*'. However, in 1985 and 1992, Thiselton clearly notes Fish's loss of the 'two' 'horizon' perspective.[268]

Thiselton's '"dialectic'" emphasis on 'two horizons' also grounds his later attempt 'to steer between the Scylla of mechanical repetition and the Charybdis of radical polyvalency and unconstrained textual indeterminacy': for Thiselton 'a text is not restricted to one meaning; yet the text must be respected as Other, and it embodies communicative action, while its readers are situated in community and tradition'.[269]

For Thiselton, '"history'" retains its '"operative influence'" despite a right emphasis on "readers", where Thiselton argues that '"the biblical writings'" reflect this 'hermeneutic' of "traditions". Thus, Thiselton argues that 'New Testament writers' "placed" 'Old Testament texts in the context of the' Christ-event, but also vice versa (i.e. Thiselton argues that 'New Testament writers' also "placed" the

---

[265] Thiselton, *2H*, 18-23, 32, cf.: 44-45, 80-81, 293, 303-308; cf. Thiselton, A.C., *Language, Liturgy and Meaning* (Nottingham: Grove Books, 1975 and 1986), 4, 8-9; quoting, Gadamer, H.-G., 'Martin Heidegger and Marburg Theology', in *Philosophical Hermeneutics* (H.-G. Gadamer; ed. D.E. Linge; London: University of California Press, 1976), 210. First italics ours, second italics Gadamer's.

[266] Thiselton, *2H*, 114, 291, 18-23, 60-63, cf.: 67-68, 120-121, 298-300, 321-322.

[267] Thiselton, *2H*, 32, 19, 306, cf.: 67-68, 82-84, 44-45, 15-17, 309-310, 321-326; cf. Gadamer, *TM*, 254-264, cf. 290 (quoted), cf. 300-307. Italics Gadamer's.

[268] Thiselton, 'CAP', 157 (1999); cf. Thiselton, A.C., 'Reader-Response Hermeneutics, Action Models, and the Parables of Jesus', in *The Responsibility of Hermeneutics* (R. Lundin, A.C. Thiselton and C. Walhout; Grand Rapids: Eerdmans; Exeter: Paternoster, 1985), 105; cf. Thiselton, *NH*, 546, 556-558 (1992). Italics in speech-marks Thiselton's.

[269] Thiselton, *2H*, 67, xix; cf.: Thiselton, 'CAP', 137; Gruneberg, K., 'Review of R. Lundin's, C. Walhout's and A.C. Thiselton's *The Promise of Hermeneutics*', *Anv* 17.3 (2000), 223.

Christ-event 'in the context of' 'Old Testament texts'). For Thiselton, the '"double context"' for "interpreting" '"Scripture"' is '"God's"' '"past"' '"salvific action… and… contemporary happenings"'. Thus, Thiselton argues that 'in the' 'tradition' 'of prophetic promise', '"*events*"' "give" old '"*words*… new meaning"'.[270]

(3) For Thiselton, traditions are also chronologically 'developing' '*traditio*' or 'dialectic' "*processes*" of dialogue between '*traditum*' and 'community' that '"ground"', and constitute *socio-historical extensions of*, '*the hermeneutical circle*': for Thiselton, 'tradition… is not… a passive deposit'.[271] Thiselton argues that 'tradition' "moves on", through "communities"' 'active' corporate 'engagement ('*actus tradendi*') with' 'biblical' "texts", in a 'handed-on' 'process' of "reading and re-reading" 'the past' 'in the light of the present' (so N. Lash) that gives rise to 'new' '"subject-matter"' or "truths" that transform 'pre-understandings', 'tradition' itself, and 'the' wider 'world'. Readers, also, in Thiselton's thinking, are hardly 'passive'.[272]

With 'Gadamer', Thiselton agrees that '"past and present"' "horizons" '"are constantly fused"' in a 'history of… fusions' (Gadamer: 'past and present are constantly mediated'),[273] and in readers' quests to "understand" authors '"better than"' they "understood themselves" (in Thiselton's view, Gadamer's 'inquiry lends… new importance' to this argument).[274] Thiselton makes this point more explicitly later, as L.M. MacCammon summarizes: thus, for Thiselton, 'authors and readers collaborate in "communicative actions", generating a history of textual effects [cf. history of effects, '"post-history"', or reception-history] that… mediate judgments regarding textual content' (and/or speech-acts) and that "function" 'as a "conversation partner with the present community or with successive communities in the re-actualization of the text"'.[275]

Thus, contradicting C. Van Engen's reading of Thiselton, we should conclude that G.R. Osborne's "recognition" of 'a dynamic, constant interaction of text, community, and context through time' does *not* "go beyond" Thiselton's '"two-horizon" perspective'.[276] Further, challenging D.S. Dockery's reading of Thiselton, we must conclude that Thiselton's 'hermeneutical circle' '"begins from"', but is *not*

---

[270] Thiselton, *2H*, 11, 15-20, 44-45, cf. 80-82, 322-326. Italics Thiselton's.

[271] Thiselton, *2H*, 20, 67, 44-45, 306-326; cf. 82-83; cf. Ebeling, G., *Theology and Proclamation: A Discussion with Rudolf Bultmann* (trans. J. Riches; London: Collins, 1966), 25. First and third italics Ebeling's, remaining italics ours.

[272] Thiselton, *2H*, 321-324, 312-319, 345-352, 370, 372; cf. 286-291, 308; contradicting, Longman III, T., 'Storytellers and Poets in the Bible', in *Inerrancy and Hermeneutics: A Tradition, A Challenge, A Debate* (ed. H.M. Conn; Grand Rapids: Baker, 1988), 148; cf. Ebeling, *T&P*, 25-26. Italics Ebeling's.

[273] Thiselton, *2H*, 322-324, 306; cf.: Maddox, 'CHP', 528; citing, Gadamer, *TM*, 290.

[274] Thiselton, *2H*, 301; cf. citing Gadamer, *TM*, 296.

[275] MacCammon, 'R PH', 3 of 4; cf. Thiselton, 'CAP', 195.

[276] Van Engen, C., *Mission on the Way. Issues in Mission Theology* (Grand Rapids: Baker Books, 1996), 45; citing, Osborne, G.R., *The Hermeneutical Spiral: A Comprehensive Introduction to Biblical Interpretation* (Downers Grove: IVP, 1991/1992), 386 – or, in a later edition, 489.

'grounded in', 'the modern horizon'. Rather, Thiselton's 'hermeneutical circle' is "grounded in" a "'dialectic'" between "'past and present'" (a dialectic that grants more authority to the *past* horizon – *both* in the case of the biblical texts *and*, more broadly, and in a different way, with respect to *any* public criteria of meaning embedded in traditions – see Chapters 4 and 5).[277] Contradicting B. Kaye's reading of Thiselton, we must conclude that Thiselton's "two-horizon" approach is *not* 'simply a refinement' of "formulating" historical distance since, for Thiselton, "'openness to'" 'the *future*' and 'historical' *"relationality"* also remain in view.[278] Later in the present chapter, we shall expound Thiselton's modification of Gadamer's hermeneutical circle through his (i.e. Thiselton's) appeals to other thinkers.[279]

(4) For Thiselton, chronologically 'developing' "traditions" *generate and embrace a posteriori historical "continuities"* that include 'public criteria of meaning', 'convictions', and "judgments" – where, for Thiselton, these "continuities" relate closely *both* to the 'extra-linguistic' dimension *and* to the 'linguistic' dimension. (N.B. For Thiselton, the 'linguistic' dimension *is interwoven with* the 'extra-linguistic' dimension).[280]

Thus, (a), Thiselton argues that *'public criteria of meaning'* (see Chapter 4) interweave "'stable'" 'patterns' of 'extra-linguistic' 'events', 'behavior', and non-'prescriptive' 'linguistic' 'rules', *"customs"'*, or "habits".[281] We need not repeat our earlier points in relation to Thiselton's arguments that 'public criteria of meaning' are pre-conditional for the *'intelligibility'* and "teachability" of 'language', or that 'public criteria of meaning' provide authentic 'language-*uses*' with their 'logical grammar' (see Chapter 4).[282] For 'language' to *be* 'language', Thiselton argues, it must have "meaning" relative to accessible and/or observable corporate *'public'* "conventions" 'grounded' in *'tradition'* and 'life': for Thiselton, 'language' cannot be "based" upon an "individual's" *'experience'* alone.[283]

Later, Thiselton argues that 'language' can only "count as" "functioning" 'intelligibly' 'within' 'a… tradition' or '*Lebensform* (form of life)' *'on the basis of'* 'public criteria of meaning'. Thiselton argues that 'conceptual grammar' concerns 'extra-linguistic' *'stance rather than mental state'*. This point, Thiselton argues, renders *both* what Thiselton would call Bultmann's notion of "'private'" "'subjective'"

---

[277] Contradicting, Dockery, 'R *2H*', 135; cf. Thiselton, *2H*, 196-197, 67, 306.

[278] Kaye, B., 'Authority and The Interpretation of Scripture in Hooker's *Of the Laws of Ecclesiastical Polity'*, *JRelHist* 21.1 (1997), 89; cf. Thiselton, *2H*, 183, 244, 67-84, 44-45, 15-17, 309-326. Italics ours.

[279] For the hermeneutical circle in Gadamer see, Gadamer, *TM*, 190-192, 265-379.

[280] Thiselton, *2H*, 20, 379-385, cf.: 392-402, 303-307, 310-313, 315, 434-436, cf. 77; cf. Thiselton, 'H-O', 8; cf. Thiselton, 'LMR', 1135; cf. Thiselton, *LLM*, 7; cf. Thiselton, 'SNTI', 75. Italics ours.

[281] Thiselton, *2H*, 379-380, 381-382, 385, 311; cf. Thiselton, 'SNTI', 84; cf. Thiselton, *LLM*, 7. First italics Thiselton's, second italics Wittgenstein's.

[282] Thiselton, *2H*, 379-383, 437, 123; cf. Thiselton, 'LMR', 1143, 1127. Thiselton's italics.

[283] Thiselton, *2H*, 379-383, 134-135, 442, 385. First italics ours, other italics Thiselton's.

'language', *and* Bultmann's '"esoteric" conception of meaning', untenable and, in Thiselton's estimate, does so *despite* Bultmann's adoption of Dilthey's 'concept of "life"' (see above). 'New Testament' language, Thiselton argues, is only 'intelligible' against the background of 'Old Testament' 'criteria'.[284]

Further, questioning Heidegger, Gadamer, and Bultmann, Thiselton argues that 'public criteria of meaning' necessarily embody 'assertions' and can "guide" 'present action'.[285] Thiselton's appeal to 'public criteria of meaning' also informs his later attack on 'the Protestant' 'myth of the unbiased, private reader', where R. Lundin adopts Thiselton's argument in relation to this point.[286]

(b) Thiselton, drawing on the later Wittgenstein, argues that "traditional" "continuities" also include '"scaffolding"' *'convictions'* (see below) where, in Thiselton's estimate, contrary to D.E. Nineham and to '"pluralistic"' readings of the later Wittgenstein (see below and Chapter 7), these '"scaffolding"' 'convictions' may be "traditional" and 'theological' rather than merely *'culture-relative'*.[287] Thus, Thiselton argues that 'a given... language-game' – i.e. 'a given... language-game' that constitutes a "logical home" for such '"scaffolding"' 'convictions' - can occur in several theological 'traditions' over many centuries, where Thiselton relates this point to 'biblical authority' (see Chapter 7).[288]

(c) With 'Gadamer', Thiselton "stresses" the "stable" 'role of communal *judgments*, "the classic" and traditions of tested wisdom'. Thiselton argues that it is *'hermeneutically trained judgment'*, *'not... universal scientific method'*, that "grounds" 'respect for the horizon of the Other as *other* and... [that "grounds"] disciplined movement towards... fusion between... two horizons'. For Thiselton, 'historical consciousness must not rely' solely 'on... critical method'.[289] Thus 'Thiselton notes with Gadamer that a "hermeneutically trained mind" should "distinguish between those pre-judgments which are fruitful for the understanding of the text and those which are unfruitful"'. For Thiselton, with Gadamer, this 'filtering process... lets local and limited prejudices die away' and 'those that bring about genuine

---

[284] Thiselton, 'TY', 1566, 1565; cf. Thiselton, *2H*, 381-382, 379, cf. 383-385; cf. 285-287; cf. Thiselton, *LLM*, 7; cf. Torrance, A.J., 'The Self-Relation, Narcissism and the Gospel of Grace', *SJT* 40.4 (1987), 488, 493. Italics in speech-marks Thiselton's.

[285] Thiselton, *2H*, 379, 195, 196, 228, cf. 392-401; cf. Thiselton, A.C., 'The Parables as Language-Event: Some Comments on Fuchs's Hermeneutics in the Light of Linguistic Philosophy', *SJT* 23.4 (Nov. 1970), 465; cf. Thiselton, 'Till', 100.

[286] quoting, Lundin, R., 'Our Hermeneutical Inheritance', in *The Responsibility of Hermeneutics* (R. Lundin, A.C. Thiselton, and C. Walhout; Grand Rapids: Eerdmans; Exeter: Paternoster, 1985), 26; cf. Thiselton, *2H*, 379, 381-382.

[287] Thiselton, *2H*, 392, 395-396, cf. 434-436, cf. 358-359; cf. Thiselton, 'LMR', 1135. First italics ours, second italics Thiselton's.

[288] Thiselton, *2H*, 414, cf. 432, 434-436.

[289] See, Thiselton, 'TY', 1564-1565; cf.: Thiselton, *2H*, 293-296, cf. 304-312; Gadamer, *TM*, 271-307, 374-375, final quote from 361. First italics ours, remaining italics Thiselton's.

understanding... emerge'.²⁹⁰

Thus, we may conclude that whilst Thiselton retrospectively remarks that he 'perceived similarities between... Gadamer and... the later Wittgenstein' in relation to historical "continuities", Thiselton nevertheless "grounds" the "continuities" of 'tradition', including linguistic "continuities", firmly in 'extra-linguistic' history, and thus corrects Gadamer's more ambiguous 'intra-linguistic' mediation of historical "judgments" – a mediation according to which, *'Being that can be understood is language'*. Thiselton argues, rather, that *'language' 'is grounded', partly, 'in' 'extra-linguistic' 'historical' "continuities"*.²⁹¹

(d) Clearly, Thiselton's notion of "historical continuities" also closely relates to his notions of historical unity, *a posteriori* generality, historical analogy, and of the possibility of an *a posteriori* "general" axis of historical inquiry (see above). In Chapter 4, we also examined Thiselton's *a posteriori* "general" linguistic axis – which similarly links closely to Thiselton's notion of "historical continuities".

(5) For Thiselton, chronologically 'developing' "traditions" also *generate and/or embrace 'historical' "particularities" and "novelties", "uniqueness" and "difference"*. Having already noted Thiselton's affirmation of the "uniqueness" of human selves, we should observe that other implications related to this point are to be found in Thiselton's second-period thinking.²⁹²

Thus, (a), after Pannenberg, Thiselton argues that 'historical' 'particularities' are "unrepeatable", "'nonexchangeable'", and "'non-homogeneous'". For Thiselton, historical 'unity' *precludes "dualisms" or "dichotomies"*, but allows *"distinctions"* between one human and another, between human and non-human, between God and the world, between general and particular, between different historical particularities, and between 'historical understanding' and "scientific" "'explanation'".²⁹³ Thiselton argues that the "historically" 'other' is *not* so "'alien'" that it prohibits 'understanding', but Thiselton also argues that the "historically" 'other' *is* "'different'" enough to prohibit its complete "'assimilation'" into the "'modern'" 'horizons' of the individual or corporate "self'.²⁹⁴ For Thiselton, then, 'historical' 'particularity' limits the scope of 'historical analogy'. Certainly, Thiselton argues

---

²⁹⁰ McHann Jr., *3H*, 438, citing, Thiselton, *2H*, 306; cf. Gadamer, *TM*, 291-307, 341-379, final quote from 298.
²⁹¹ Thiselton, 'TY', 1565; cf.: Thiselton, *2H*, 373, 337, cf. 443, 305-313, 380-383; Thiselton, 'LMR', 1135, 1134; Thiselton, *LLM*, 7; Thiselton, 'SNTP', 75; Thiselton, 'H-O', 8; citing, Gadamer, *TM*, 474. N.B. We use the term "intra-linguistic" here in only *one* of the ways in which Thiselton uses the term: one sense carries the connotation of Thiselton's notion of 'word-magic' (see, Thiselton, *NH*, 16), another the connotation of imprisonment within linguistic 'worlds' (see, Thiselton, *NH*, 367). Only the first of these possibilities relates to Gadamer's work in Thiselton's understanding. First italics Gadamer's, second italics ours.
²⁹² Thiselton, *2H*, 20, 81, 372-373, 242, 66-67, cf. 79-84, 153-154, 370-379, 407-415; cf. 250-251; cf. Thiselton, 'H-O', 8. All italics ours.
²⁹³ Thiselton, *2H*, 378, 67, 79-80, 302, 246-247, 286-287, 77; cf. 239, cf. 291-292, 250-251, 235, 188, 158-161, 316, 318. Italics ours.
²⁹⁴ Thiselton, 'TY', 1564; cf. Thiselton, *2H*, 53-63, 103-104, 57, 308.

that, against E. Troeltsch and D.E. Nineham, 'analogy' with "interpreters'" 'present experience' is *not* 'the criterion of historical probability'.[295]

(b) Similarly, for Thiselton, "historical" 'particularity' ensures that *'historical understanding' and 'self-understanding', though linked, are still "distinct"*: "not self" cannot be 'reduced… to' "self".[296] And yet, Thiselton observes that Dilthey tends to subsume "'Thou'" beneath "'I'" and the "divine" beneath the "human",[297] and that Heidegger tends to subsume the 'past' beneath 'present' "'possibilities'", 'truth' encountered 'through' 'Dasein' beneath 'truth *about* Dasein', and "'collective destiny'" beneath "'individual destiny'".[298] Thiselton argues that Bultmann, as well as following Heidegger in these respects, also tends to subsume the eschatological "'not yet'" beneath 'the [historical] "now"', and "'objectivity'" beneath "'subjectivity'".[299]

For Thiselton, then, an erroneous conflating of 'historical understanding' with 'self-understanding' raises difficulties – notably, Thiselton argues, for 'liberation' 'theology' and for some 'reader-response' 'theories',[300] and particularly for 'neo-pragmatist philosophy' which, in Thiselton's estimate, 'reduces theology' and *'history'* 'to… a commodity shaped by consumer tastes'.[301] Thiselton insists that 'scholars' should not "neglect" 'the implications of their own world view for their work', and that 'pastors' should not "force" 'the biblical text to fit their own cultural and/or practical agendas'.[302] Notably, Thiselton attacks the "'polarization'" between *either* over-stressing "'present'" "horizons", as in these cases, *or* over-stressing "'past'" "horizons'", as in the case of 'the critical historical method as used in' Anglo-American 'New Testament studies'.[303]

(c) For Thiselton, an important implication of 'historical' 'particularity' is that *"'language'" and "meaning" 'are grounded in' 'life'-"diversities"* (for Thiselton, "'language'" and "meaning" are also 'grounded in' 'historical' 'life'-"continuities", where the latter constitute *a posteriori* regularities, or patterns, *of* historical particularities – see

---

[295] Thiselton, *2H*, 67, 77-78, cf. 79, cf. 72-73.

[296] Thiselton, *2H*, 235, 237, 242-243, 250-251, 197, cf.: 314, 199-200, 291-292. Italics ours.

[297] Thiselton, *2H*, 241-243, 235, cf. 239.

[298] Thiselton, *2H*, 250-251, 197, cf.: 199-200, 200-203. Italics Thiselton's.

[299] Thiselton, *2H*, 263-265, 291-292, cf. 236-237, 238.

[300] Thiselton, *2H*, 241-242, cf.: 243; 110-113; cf.: Thiselton, *NH*, 529, 546.

[301] Fergusson, D., 'Introduction', in *The Future as God's Gift: Explorations in Christian Eschatology* (eds. D. Fergusson and M. Sarot; Edinburgh: T&T Clark, 2000), 6; cf. Thiselton, A.C., 'Signs of the Times: Towards a Theology for the Year 2000 as a Grammar of Grace, Truth and Eschatology in Contexts of So-Called Postmodernity. Presidential Paper of the Society for the Study of Theology', in *The Future as God's Gift: Explorations in Christian Eschatology* (eds. D. Fergusson and M. Sarot; Edinburgh: T&T Clark, 2000), 15. Italics Thiselton's.

[302] Thiselton, *2H*, 107-114, cf. 60-63; citing, Moo, D.J., 'Review of A.C. Thiselton's *New Horizons in Hermeneutics*', *TrinJ* 13 (Fall 1992), 250.

[303] Thiselton, *2H*, 86-87; cf.: 241-243; 113; cf.: Thiselton, 'UPC', 98; Thiselton, 'NH', 316; also citing, Goldingay, J., 'Interpreting Scripture', *Anv* 1 (1984), 277.

above).³⁰⁴ With K.-O. Apel, and against the early Wittgenstein's approach, Thiselton follows the later Wittgenstein's shifting of 'the... *a priori* "ground" of 'language' *from* 'a single' 'abstract' 'formal logic', 'system', or 'calculus' of "self-evident" '"propositions"' and "generalizations" *"independent" 'of'* the *'future'*, *to* the "temporally changing" '"stream of... life"'-'diversity' ('historical' "particularities", "'forms of life'", 'training and upbringing', 'language-games', 'language'-'situations', "actions", "world"', 'life'-'settings', '"attitudes"', 'experience[s]', and so on).³⁰⁵ (Thiselton argues that 'Heidegger's belief that the world of Dasein is something prior to [re-historicized] subject-object thinking and to cognitive propositions' 'parallels' the later Wittgenstein's shifting 'of the... *a priori*'). Thus, Thiselton argues that '"surroundings"', 'training', and "applications" – 'which are [all] open-ended towards the future' - become important for assessments of 'meaning'.³⁰⁶

Drawing on the later Wittgenstein, 'Heidegger', and 'Gadamer', Thiselton argues that corporate and individual "creativity" and 'changes' in 'life-situations' generate "changes" in *'historical'* "particularities", 'language-*uses*', "linguistic worlds", and 'concepts' - and thus "free" us 'from' "imprisonment" 'within' the same.³⁰⁷ Nevertheless, Thiselton argues that all 'language-*uses*' belong to 'given' "language-games" and that, therefore, 'we cannot' ask 'questions' '"outside"' 'given' "language-games". Thiselton stresses that this point undermines 'earlier scholarship oriented towards finding the essential meaning of a key word or term, since the use-context is of decisive importance'.³⁰⁸ Thiselton applies this principle to the biblical 'polymorphous concepts' '"faith"... "flesh"... and "truth"', to the 'problems' associated with 'justification by faith in Paul', and to the inseparability of 'faith' and 'works' in 'James' as over and against the *'contrast'* between 'faith' and 'works' in 'Paul'.³⁰⁹

Thiselton notes that the early Heidegger, similarly to the later Wittgenstein, views 'signs' as '"ready-to-hand"' 'equipment', '"discourse"' as inter-"personal" "communicative" action, and 'meaning' as 'signs' '"ready-to-hand"' purpose. Again, Thiselton observes that, in Heidegger, the 'logic' 'prior to' 'life' relation is reversed to 'life' 'prior to' 'logic' – though, for Thiselton, the later Wittgenstein rightly avoids Heidegger's and Bultmann's historical, epistemological, linguistic, and anthropological "dualisms" – and also avoids Gadamer's linguistic dualism.³¹⁰

(d) For Thiselton, another implication of 'historical... particularity' is that

---

³⁰⁴ Thiselton, *2H*, 372-373, 379-383; cf. Thiselton, 'LMR', 1135. Italics ours.
³⁰⁵ Thiselton, *2H*, 360, 357-359, 372-379; cf. 361-362; cf. Thiselton, *LLM*, 3. Italics Thiselton's, except "*from*" and "*to*".
³⁰⁶ Thiselton, *2H*, 373, 376-378; citing, Grech, 'R *2H*', 573. Italics Thiselton's.
³⁰⁷ Thiselton, *2H*, 370-378, cf. 312; cf. Thiselton, 'LMR', 1127. Italics Thiselton's.
³⁰⁸ Thiselton, *2H*, 407-409, cf.: 376-378, 427, 360; cf. Thiselton, 'LMR', 1127; cf. citing, Palmer, 'R *2H*', 173. Italics Thiselton's.
³⁰⁹ Thiselton, *2H*, 407-415, 423: cf.: 415-427; cf. our Chapters 3 & 4. Italics Thiselton's.
³¹⁰ Thiselton, *2H*, 156-157, cf.: 168, 372-373, 378, 387, 360.

neither "action-models" nor 'speech-act' "models" 'provide a comprehensive model for the solution of all hermeneutical problems'. For Thiselton, 'no theoretical model provided by hermeneutical theory can obviate the need first and foremost to look at the text itself in its linguistic and historical particularity'.[311] Thus, B.D. Ingraffia and T.E. Pickett, in criticism of K.J. Vanhoozer's more overarching appeal to 'speech-act theory', caution Vanhoozer with reference to Thiselton's *refusal to "imperialize" any single 'hermeneutical... model'*.[312]

For Thiselton, then, links between '"language"' and 'historical... particularity' *preclude the "imposition" of 'generalizing models' 'onto' "texts"* – which is an erroneous practice that Thiselton criticizes in relation to the early 'Wittgenstein', general 'linguistics', and 'structuralist' approaches, though 'Thiselton' remains 'sympathetic' towards Saussure as we have seen.[313] In suggesting that Thiselton neglects 'a discussion of the purpose (or purposes) of the New Testament texts', B.J. Walsh may have under-estimated Thiselton's strong resistance to "generalization": for Thiselton, 'the multi-purpose nature of the biblical text[s] must be recognized'.[314]

(e) Thiselton's linking of '"meaning"' to 'historical... particularity' does not undermine his view that *'present meaning' reflects the "dialogic" "relationship" 'between two... horizons'*. For Thiselton, "present meaning", and even aspects of 'past' 'meaning', "change" as '"new"' "relationships" are forged between old and 'new' 'historical particularities'.[315]

In 2002, K.J. Vanhoozer rightly observes that, 'Thiselton explores Ricoeur's (and Hans Robert Jauss's) suggestion that the meaning of a literary work rests on the dialogical relation between the work and its audience in each age'. It is clear from the context in which Vanhoozer makes this observation that he here *rightly*

---

[311] Bartholomew, '3H', 128; citing, Thiselton, 'R-RH', 113. But cf. Thiselton, *2H*, 372, 281-283, cf.: 117-120, 353, 15.

[312] Ingraffia, B.D., and T.E. Pickett, 'Reviving the Power of Biblical Language: The Bible, Literature, and Literary Language', in *After Pentecost: Language and Biblical Interpretation* (eds. C.G. Bartholomew, C. Greene and K. Möller; Scripture and Hermeneutics Series; Vol. 2; Carlisle: Paternoster, 2001), 245; cf.: Thiselton, *2H*, 291, 292, 354; Thiselton, *NH*, 27; Vanhoozer, K.J., 'From Speech Acts to Scripture Acts', in *After Pentecost: Language and Biblical Interpretation* (eds. C.G. Bartholomew, C. Greene and K. Möller; Scripture and Hermeneutics Series; Vol. 2; Carlisle: Paternoster, 2001), 7; Vanhoozer, K.J., *First Theology. God, Scripture and Hermeneutics* (Leicester: Apollos, 2002), 164-165. Italics ours.

[313] Thiselton, *2H*, 373, 372, 430-431; cf. 119-120; citing, Moule, C.F.D., *The Birth of the New Testament* (London: A&C Black, 1981), ix. Italics ours.

[314] Walsh, 'TC', 234; cf. Thiselton, *2H*, 430-431, 372; cf. Hess, 'RA *NH*', 22.

[315] Thiselton, *2H*, 377, 372, 10-17, 19-20, 81, 244, 306-307, 15, 303, cf.: 80, 67, 175, 312; cf. Vanhoozer, *FT*, 164-165; cf. Thiselton, *NTH*, xxii, conclusions 1, 1.3, and 1.3b. How can aspects of "past meaning" change? For example, if JFK's assassination triggers a momentous historical event in the year 2149 then the "meaning" of the assassination cannot be dichotomously separated from the later event. Thus, the meaning of the past has not yet reached its fullness, but develops as history unfolds. Italics ours.

refrains from seeing Thiselton as espousing a view of the Bible in which the Bible is *only* 'a literary work'. As H. Jansen points out, Thiselton views the Bible as 'different... from other literary creations' – although not in the sense of a special category of "religious language" (against what Jansen seems to imply). Rather, for Thiselton, the Bible is 'different... from other literary creations' in that, first, it contains what certain philosophers would call '"everyday"' 'language' as well as more 'literary' language. Second, in Thiselton's estimate, God's Word operates through the biblical texts in a way that is unique to the biblical texts, and in so doing puts *normal language* (i.e. roughly speaking: thoroughly human in relation to surface-grammatical "rules" and "form") to *special use* (i.e. roughly speaking: divinely inspired in relation to depth-grammatical "content" and "use"). In referring to 'meaning' in terms of a 'dialogic relation', then, Vanhoozer *rightly* seems to notice Thiselton's notion of how present 'meaning' involves a *relationship between* two horizons – a relationship that, in the case of the biblical texts, involves God putting biblical language to "special use" in our lives - *relationally*.[316]

However, having said this, we may also ask whether or not Vanhoozer has missed the *full implications* of Thiselton's *earlier* development of this 'dialogical' "relational" approach to 'meaning' - in *The Two Horizons* and elsewhere in his (i.e. Thiselton's) second period writings. Admittedly, Vanhoozer complains that 'Thiselton misleadingly associates me with those who see meaning in terms of reference'. At first, this complaint may seem to suggest that Vanhoozer is saying that he too embraces a 'dialogical' "relational" approach to 'meaning' that is similar to Thiselton's. In response to Thiselton, however, Vanhoozer *then* outlines an aspect of his (i.e. Vanhoozer's) approach to meaning according to which he argues that 'what fixes the meaning of a text is what the author said/did...' – where the 'meaning' that is "fixed" by 'what the author said/did...' is a '"single determinate meaning"' 'that... does not change at the behest of the reader'.[317]

In our view, though, Vanhoozer here appears to depart from the *full sense* of Thiselton's more 'dialogical' "relational" approach to 'meaning' – especially "present meaning" - in *The Two Horizons* and elsewhere in his second period writings. That is, in Thiselton's estimate, Vanhoozer seems to be saying that 'what the author said/did', as *"referent"*, *fixes* the meaning of a text as a '"single determinate meaning"'.[318]

In other words, an author may perform a speech-act that is *not merely an act of*

---

[316] Vanhoozer, *FT*, 165; cf.: Thiselton, 'CAP', 191-199; Thiselton, *NH*, 503; contradicting, Jansen, H., 'Poetics and the Bible - Facts and Biblical Hermeneutics (Revisioning an 'Interpreted' Literary-Historical Approach to Holy Scripture)', *NZSThRelPh* 41.1 (1999), 23; cf. Chapters 4 and 5. Italics ours.

[317] Vanhoozer, *FT*, 164, 165; cf. Thiselton, 'BTT', 103-104; cf.: Thiselton, *2H*, 327-356; e.g. Thiselton, A.C., 'The Supposed Power of Words in the Biblical Writings', *JThStud* NS25.2 (Oct. 1974), 283-299; Chapter 4. Italics ours.

[318] Thiselton, 'BTT', 103-104; cf.: Vanhoozer, *FT*, 164; Thiselton, *2H*, 327-356; Thiselton, 'Words', 283-299; Chapters 4, 5, and 7. Italics ours.

*reference* – a rebuke against miserliness, say. However, a reader could then *objectify* *that rebuke against miserliness* as a "fixed historical fact" – as a "'single determinate meaning'" - that "fixed the meaning of the text". Thus, the meaning of the text, according to such a viewpoint, would be a "fixed *reference to* a rebuke against miserliness".[319]

A Thiseltonian argument, though, would say that the "rebuke against miserliness" could - *alongside* the objectification involved in distancing – *also* function *directly* as a rebuke against a reader who had just been miserly, or even as an *encouragement* for a reader who had just been generous.[320]

And, for Thiselton, a metaphorical speech-act – or other 'non-referential, non-representational, language' - could *relate directly* (*sic*) to readers in still more subtle self-involving ways that should not be reduced to a "fixed" or "'determinate'" reference *to* a metaphorical – or *to* a different kind of 'non-referential, non-representational' - speech-act.[321]

Thus, for example, if somebody says, "I love you", one does not normally respond by saying "you have just performed the speech-act of saying, 'I love you'" – for to respond this way would be to objectify, to distance oneself from, or to *step outside of*, the relational dynamic and treat it as a "referent".[322]

For Thiselton, then, the objectification pertaining to "'distancing'" cannot "fix" *present* meaning because "present meaning" emerges through "'distancing'" *and* 'fusion'. For Thiselton, 'fusion' involves "relating in all its variety", whereas "'distancing'" is primarily "objectification" – a small *subset of* "relating in all its variety". For Thiselton, then, to "fix" present meaning is to collapse relationality into objectification, and "understanding" into "'distancing'" – i.e. in Thiselton's estimate, to "fix" present meaning is to "'strike the text dead'" and stop it from functioning as a relational act that *involves* the reader or readers. If, for Thiselton, distancing *rightly* "strikes" "'the'" biblical "'text dead'", however, then, for Thiselton, 'fusion' *rightly* brings the biblical text *alive* as a relational act performed by God's Spirit.[323]

For Thiselton, further, it will not do to fatally-diminish the relationality of "fusion" and of "present meaning" by 'suggesting' that 'we resort to' the 'grossly over-simple, over-general, exhausted distinction between meaning and

---

[319] This example is our own; cf. Vanhoozer, *FT*, 164. Italics ours.

[320] E.g. Thiselton, *2H*, 436-437; cf. Chapters 4 and 5.

[321] Thiselton, 'BTT', 103-104; cf. Vanhoozer, *FT*, 164; cf.: Thiselton, *2H*, e.g. 43; cf. 436-437; Thiselton, A.C., 'The Multi-Model Character of Holy Spirit Language', *CEN* 11 Apr. (1974), 8; Thiselton, 'Till', 102; Thiselton, 'Words', 283-299; Thiselton, *LLM*, 22-24; Thiselton, 'SNTI', 93-95; Thiselton, A.C., 'Review of J.F.A. Sawyer's *Semantics in Biblical Research*', *TSF* 70 (Aut. 1974), 18.

[322] This example is our own.

[323] "'Distancing'" *should* "'strike the text dead'", yes, but fusion should bring the text *alive*; cf. (and citing) Thiselton, 'NH', 318-323; cf. Thiselton, *2H*, 307-308; cf. Thiselton, 'Words', 283-299; cf. Chapter 4. Italics ours.

significance' that was offered 'as a panacea for all hermeneutical headaches by the revered E.D. Hirsch' in his 'attempts to revitalize the humanist model of language'. Whilst, for Thiselton, Hirsch's approach was not without 'much of value', we may argue that, from a "Thiseltonian" perspective, the Hirschean category of "significance" – *however* much variety it allows - is *still* a matter of an *objectified* "variety" that *kills the relationality* of meaning.[324]

Thus, if somebody says "I love you", you would not normally respond by saying "the significance of your speech-act of love was that you love me", for this "frames" the *initiative of love* with the *response of reference*. Even if the depth-grammar of the phrase, "I love you", was really, "I want you as my partner-in-adultery", it would still be relationally odd (though, admittedly, normally much *safer - sic*) to reply, "the significance of your speech-act of seduction was that you want me as your partner-in-adultery". To reduce the relationality of fusion and of present meaning to objectification, then, even "strikes dead" *bad* relating! Whilst it is certainly "safer" (*sic*) and wiser to strike dead "bad relating", it is a different matter altogether when it is the *particularities of the immediate address of God's relational Word* that one is striking dead – or *de-relationalizing* - for the sake of "safety"; or, rather, we should say, for the sake of *a power-bid of relational avoidance*, or, alternatively, and to use Thiselton's language, for the sake of a Western over-'emphasis on… abstract theory'.[325]

(6) For Thiselton, chronologically 'developing' "traditions" also *"condition" "texts" and "readers"* where, in Thiselton's thinking, Gadamer's link between "conditioning" and "'tradition'" qualifies, and is qualified by, Heidegger's and Bultmann's stronger emphasis on the link between "conditioning" and 'Dasein' or "individual" "'subjectivity'" (cf. "concerns"). For Thiselton, *"'subjectivity'" is thus de-'centered', but not ignored:* that is, for Thiselton, traditions condition individuals, communities and texts; but, in Thiselton's estimate, individuals, communities, and texts *also* condition traditions (cf. Chapter 4, Section C, point "(6)", on speech acts and culture).[326] Several points should be made in our exposition of Thiselton's thinking in relation to this context of discussion, as follows.

(a) For Thiselton, *'historical conditioning is two-sided: the modern interpreter, no less than the text, stands in a given historical context and tradition'*.[327] Some writers, sometimes in criticism of Thiselton, try to extend the "two horizon" 'formulation' in order to include a *pastoral* 'third horizon' (not to be confused with an *eschatological* "third horizon" that, for Thiselton, *conditions history through divine promise-fulfillment*)

---

[324] Thiselton, 'BTT', 103-104; cf. Thiselton, 'NH', 320; cf. Thiselton, *2H*, 436-437.

[325] This example is our own, but we also cite, Thiselton, A.C., 'An Age of Anxiety', in *The History of Christianity. A Lion Handbook* (eds. T. Dowley *et al*; Tring, Hertfordshire: Lion Publishing, 1977), 609-610.

[326] Thiselton, *2H*, 20, 306, 155, 238, 305, 11-17; cf.: 15-33, 66-67, 111-114, 133-139, 145, 150-170, 200-203, 250-251, 292-354, 379-407, 434-436; cf.: Thiselton, 'Par', 49; Thiselton, 'TY', 1565; Thiselton, *IGPS*, 121, 159. Italics ours.

[327] See, Thiselton, *2H*, 11. Italics ours before the colon, italics Thiselton's after the colon.

pertaining to those "'to whom'" interpreters or pastors "minister" or preach. But, in defence of Thiselton's thinking, we should note that this supposed "extension" really only posits a *further* understanding (or "conditioning") event between '*two* horizons'. Moreover, Thiselton's work on translation at least strongly qualifies – and perhaps even disqualifies - W.C. Kaiser's criticism that Thiselton has, supposedly, neglected 'a cross-cultural perspective in the work of interpretation'.[328]

(b) For Thiselton, 'historical' "conditioning" *presupposes 'historical finitude'* or *"situatedness"* (cf. "embeddedness") within a larger socio-historical and (anticipated) theological-eschatological whole (in contrast to Gadamer's contra-eschatological stance – see Chapter 5). For Thiselton, "situatedness" is not just about 'culture-relative' identity 'bound up with the fashions of the day' (here we are contradicting R. Wade); rather, for Thiselton, "situatedness" actually *limits* an individual "subjectivity's" (or a community's) 'culture-relative' identity and "interpretative" arbitration since 'the... self' (or community) is always already "addressed" from '*beyond*' her or his (or its) 'own... horizons'. Thus, Thiselton argues - against an over-emphasis on 'individual' 'subjectivity' (or on Dasein) and/or on 'the' "'historical'" 'present' in 'Bultmann and Heidegger' (see above), or on "culture-relativity" in D.E. Nineham - that 'historical' "conditioning" forces *corporate 'tradition'* and 'the' 'historical' *'past'* to be taken into account. Thiselton's emphases on "divine" 'address' and on 'promise'-"fulfillment" extend this point *theologically* and towards the 'eschatological' *future*': for Thiselton, 'history' *itself* is "conditioned" or "shaped" 'by God'.[329]

(c) For Thiselton, with 'Gadamer' and the later Wittgenstein, *the "interweaving"* of *"action"* (*cf. "training"'*, '*praxis*'), '*language-habits*', *'and thought'* in 'relation' to "traditions" and "pre-understandings" is prior to and/or pre-conditional for the possibility of 'historical' "conditioning". With Gadamer and the later Wittgenstein, Thiselton argues that 'language-habits', "intentions", and "acts of" 'concept formation' "mutually" 'condition', or even "create", one-another - and 'are inseparable'. With Gadamer, Thiselton argues - against the notion of the supposed "scientific" "instrumentalization" of 'language' by 'thought' - that 'language-habits'

---

[328] Carson, D.A., 'A Sketch of the Factors Determining Current Hermeneutical Debate in Cross-Cultural Contexts', in *Biblical Interpretation and the Church. Text and Context* (ed. D.A. Carson; Carlisle: Paternoster, 1984), 17; cf.: Van Engen, *M*, 45; Caldwell, L.W., 'Third Horizon Ethnohermeneutics: Re-evaluating New Testament Hermeneutical Models for Intercultural Bible Interpreters Today', *AmJTh* 1 (1987), 314-333; Kaiser Jr., W.C., 'Obeying the Word', in *An Introduction to Biblical Hermeneutics: The Search for Meaning* (eds. W.C. Kaiser and M. Silva; Grand Rapids: Zondervan, 1994), 178-179; cf.: Thiselton, *2H*, 15-16, xix; Thiselton, 'SNTI', 75; cf. 76-78, 85-88, 96-98; cf. McHann Jr., *3H*, 14. Italics ours.

[329] Thiselton, *2H*, cf.: 57-63, 81-84, 162, 169-175, 185, 200-203, 217, 242-243, 250-251, 287, 292, 304-313, 319, 324-326, 342-356, 373, 388-389, 395-396, 440; cf.: Thiselton, 'Parab', 450; Thiselton, 'NH', 311; Thiselton, 'Par', 51, 47, 48, 50; Thiselton, 'CAP', 201; cf. 239; Heidegger, *BT*, 444-449; contradicting, Wade, R., 'Where Did 'I' Go? The Loss of Self in Postmodern Times', at *http://www.probe.org/docs/wheredid.html*. Third italics Thiselton's, other italics ours.

*Hermeneutics and History* 335

are '"the universal"' '"transmission"' '"medium"' for '"understanding"'. For Thiselton, against Bultmann's linguistic dualism, no '"pre-given"' 'abstract' '"system of"' 'thought'-'possibilities' 'exists' prior to 'language'; – though Thiselton's *partly*-Pannenbergian, *partly*-later-Wittgensteinian, *partly*-Austinian (along with other influences) *reversal* of Gadamer's '"ontological"' prioritization of 'language' relative to *'history'* (to use J.C. McHann Jr.'s language) constitutes part of the background to these arguments (McHann Jr. only offers this broad kind of argument about a decade later, and with less reference than Thiselton to the later Wittgenstein, and with no reference to J.L. Austin).[330]

(d) For Thiselton, with Gadamer, 'dialectical' *'interaction between'* a *"community's"* *'prior language'* *'and'* *an "interpreter's"* *(or "interpreters'")* *'prior consciousness'* is pre-conditional for the possibility of the 'historical' "conditioning" of that 'interpreter' (or "interpreters"): for Gadamer and Thiselton, 'tradition' 'comes to speech' '"only in"' the 'language' and 'concepts' of "the interpreter(s)".[331] With 'Ebeling and Fuchs' Thiselton agrees that 'the same thing must be said in a new time differently'. With W. Wink, Thiselton agrees that the '"common"' '"world"' 'of… tradition' is pre-conditional 'for the' possibility of 'language', communication, and 'fusion'. Thus, for Thiselton, "conditioning" involves multiple 'eventful' "fusions of horizons" through which "interpreters" are 'interpreted' 'and transformed'.[332]

Nevertheless, Thiselton argues that the fact that 'tradition' '"only"' 'comes to speech' '"in"' the 'language' and 'concepts' of "interpreters" does not prevent '"interpreters'" 'horizons' from being 'transformed' or extended *'beyond'* that kind of "transformation" that would be entailed in 'new' 'self-understanding'. For Thiselton, 'new' 'concepts' can be "formed" by 'interaction between' existing 'concepts' and, in turn, Thiselton argues that 'interaction between' 'new' 'concepts' can "create" still further 'concepts' that "transcend" readers' *'prior* horizons'. More than this, however: for Thiselton, after the later Wittgenstein, '"watching how others play"' can introduce readers to 'new' "correlations" between new language uses and behavior in such a way as to create concepts that are 'new' to those readers. Furthermore, for Thiselton, after the later Wittgenstein and Pannenberg, and in *criticism* of Gadamer, historical report can mediate such 'new' "correlations" and concepts *to* readers *from the past*.[333]

---

[330] Thiselton, *2H*, cf.: 39-40, 75-83, 111, 133-139, 145, 185, 211, 247-248, 268-271, 286-287, 292, 303, 310-314, 337, 346-349, 354, 359-361, 370-385, 404-407, 425, 442-444; cf.: Thiselton, 'Par', 454; McHann Jr., *3H*, 11; Chapter 4. Last italics McHann's, others ours.

[331] Thiselton, *2H*, 310-311, 312-313, 185. Italics ours.

[332] Thiselton, 'NH', 309; cf.: Thiselton, *2H*, 344, 326, 380-383, 185, 345-350, cf. 321-325, 306-307, 314-315; Thiselton, 'U (long)', 119; Borsch, 'R *2H*', 89.

[333] Thiselton, *2H*, 312, 309-310, 307, 313, 347, 370-379, 122-124, 291-292; cf.: Thiselton, 'U (long)', 119; Thiselton, 'NH', 311; Thiselton, 'LMR', 1135; Thiselton, A.C., 'Myth, Paradigm, and the Status of Biblical Imagery', in *Using the Bible in Liturgy* (ed. C. Byworth; Nottingham: Grove, 1977), 10-11; Thiselton, 'Parab', 454; Wittgenstein, L., *Philosophical*

(e) For Thiselton, similar considerations apply in relation to 'pre-cognitive' and non-conceptual "dimensions" (i.e. *as well as* in relation to the cognitive "dimension"). That is, for Thiselton, 'historical' "conditioning" "occurs" *both "non-cognitively" and "cognitively"*.[334] That is, (i), Thiselton argues that interpreters 'are conditioned' *"pre-cognitively"* through *'a priori'* "participation" in "traditions" 'and' "communities".[335] In this context of discussion, Thiselton draws "'parallels'" between' Heidegger's notion of "'world'", Bultmann's notion of "'pre-understanding'", Gadamer's "notions of" 'horizon', 'tradition', 'linguistic tradition', "'linguisticality'", 'pre-judgments' or "'prejudices'", and "institutional" 'signs', and the later Wittgenstein's "notions of" "'forms of life'", "'language-games'", "'training'", 'community', and "'scaffolding'".[336]

(ii) Thiselton argues that "interpreters" are "conditioned" *non-conceptually* through "practice", or through 'appropriation' and "'application'" (on 'appropriation' and "'application'", see Chapter 5). Thus, Thiselton is *not* only interested in 'dialogue between the... *mental* horizons of past and present'.[337] Finally, (iii), as already noted, Thiselton argues that interpreters are also 'conditioned' *cognitively* where, for Thiselton, 'pre-understanding' may include "systematic theologies" as well as 'attitudes'. These considerations concerning the "historical conditioning" of interpreters in no way undermine our earlier points - drawn from Thiselton - concerning the 'two-sided' nature of 'historical conditioning': for Thiselton, "texts" are *also* historically conditioned; and, for Thiselton, *readers historically condition future traditions*.[338]

(f) For Thiselton, 'historical conditioning' 'occurs', partly, through the operation of *both non-"assertive" and "assertive" 'linguistic' "functions"*, where Thiselton argues that these "functions" are interwoven (in contrast to Gadamer's linguistic dualism – see Chapter 4). In Chapter 1 we examined Thiselton's appeal to the later Wittgenstein in relation to the creative functioning of assertions, and later in the present chapter we shall look at the creative functioning of grammatical propositions, statements, or assertions in relation to Thiselton's hermeneutical

---

*Investigations* (trans. G.E.M. Anscombe; Oxford: Blackwell, 1953, 2001), 21-23, 27. First italics Thiselton's, other italics ours.

[334] Thiselton, *2H*, 350, 351, 185, 326, 315, cf. 111, cf. 310-311, cf. 305. Italics ours.

[335] Thiselton, *2H*, 185, 373, 31, 38, 382, 305-306, cf. 188-194; cf. 324-326. First italics ours, second italics Thiselton's.

[336] Thiselton, *2H*, 34, 30-38, 311, 305, 201. Citing: Heidegger, *BT*, 93; Bultmann, R., 'Is Exegesis Without Presuppositions Possible? (1957)', in *New Testament and Mythology and Other Basic Writings* (ed. and trans. S.M. Ogden; Philadelphia: Fortress Press, 1984), 149; Gadamer, *TM*, 245, 280, 389, 276, 155; Wittgenstein, *PI*, 11e, 5e, 4e; Wittgenstein, L., *On Certainty* (trans. D. Paul and G.E.M. Anscombe; Oxford: Blackwell, 1969, 2001), 38e, 29e; cf. Chapter 4.

[337] Thiselton, *2H*, 22, 111, 287, cf. 308, 314, 324-326, 347-352, 370-372, 385, 58, 376, 377; cf. in relation to Bultmann, 287-288; cf. correcting, Brodie, 'R *2H*', 481. Italics ours.

[338] Thiselton, *2H*, 185, 11, 315; cf. 321-322. Italics ours.

(g) For Thiselton, 'historical conditioning' 'may' *either facilitate or 'distort' 'understanding'*.[340] Thiselton argues that 'historical conditioning' negates neither '"historical"' 'difference' nor (therefore) 'the possibility of' historical 'objectivity'. For Thiselton, trans-historical 'unity' and inter-'"relatedness"' are *not* the same as trans-historical "identity" or "uniformity". Thiselton argues that 'the two horizons… never' fully 'merge' into one. Further, as we have already noted in Chapter 5, Thiselton argues that reader "pre-understandings" "initially" form "indispensable" 'point[s] of contact with' "texts", and that 'effective history' may *often* serve to "condition" readers through passing on "true" '"pre-judgments"'. *Nevertheless*, Thiselton also argues that factors related to historical "embeddedness" – and hence to 'historical conditioning' - 'may sometimes distort' understanding. For Thiselton, these factors include 'finitude'; "situatedness"; the genuine, if de-centered, factors of "culture-relativity" and '"subjectivity"'; the "interwovenness" of "action", 'language-habits', '"and thought"'; and "coming to speech" (but see our important qualifications of this point in Chapter 7, where we argue that, in Thiselton's estimate, such factors – long with other factors - may *either hinder* objectivity and understanding *or aid* objectivity and understanding).[341]

(h) Pausing momentarily, we propose that Thiselton's argument in *The Two Horizons* requires an extension in relation to considerations to do with the complexities of historical conditioning – an extension that, even now, Thiselton has not completely carried out. Admittedly, by the end of his "third period" (1992) Thiselton notes – and *partially* accepts - Stanley Fish's thinking in relation to multiple contexts (though this strand of thought is absent from *The Two Horizons*). Moreover, by the time of his "fourth period" (1993-2000) Thiselton certainly realizes that any given self is conditioned by complex arrays of '"traditions"' and 'communities' and not just by single '"traditions"' or 'communities'.[342]

Nevertheless, theologically speaking, we propose that different kinds and levels of fall-generated isolation – or what C.E. Gunton called 'disengagement' - make

---

[339] Thiselton, *2H*, 11, 326, 373, 273-274, 344-352; cf.: 40, 268-269, 292; 386-407, 195. Italics ours.

[340] Thiselton, *2H*, 11, 314-314; Thiselton, *NTH*, xxii, concs. 1-1.2c. Italics ours.

[341] Thiselton, *2H*, 11, 242-244, 316, 302, xix, 79-80, 383, 163, 369, 396, 190, 374, 307-314, 201, 292; cf.: Thiselton, 'NH', 312-317, 323; Thiselton, *NTH*, xxii, concs. 1-1.2c; Thiselton, 'U (long)', 120; Thiselton, 'UPC', 93; cf. 91-94; Thiselton, A.C., 'Explain, Interpret, Tell, Narrative', in *The New International Dictionary of New Testament Theology, Volume 1* (ed. C. Brown; Exeter: Paternoster; Grand Rapids: Zondervan, 1975), 583; Thiselton, 'Truth', 897-899; Thiselton, *LLM*, 3-6; Thiselton, 'LMR', 1135; Thiselton, A.C., 'Irrational Assumptions of Modern Theology Exposed. Review of T.F. Torrance's *God and Rationality*', *CEN* 19 Mar. (1971), 9; Thiselton, 'TNI', 11; Gadamer, *TM*, 300-307, 19-30, 265-285. Italics ours.

[342] Thiselton, *NH*, 542-543; cf.: Thiselton, *2H*, 342-347; Thiselton, *IGPS*; Thiselton, 'HB', 76-95.

historical conditioning even more complex.[343] Dysfunctional relationship, for example manipulative strategies, avoidance strategies, and the agendas they serve - and complex combinations and superimpositions of these strategies and agendas - are relevant to the issue of "historical conditioning" at both concrete and theoretical levels. As children, we are all "trained" by others' relational strategies, patterns of avoidance, and absences - as well as by our own decision-making. Considerations to do with *immediate concrete fallen human relationships* and to do with our *own decision-making* aside, then *biological factors to do with fallen human physicality* are *also* related to the grammar of "historical conditioning".

Admittedly, in *The Two Horizons*, Thiselton appeals to Heidegger and to M. Buber against the dynamic of "'depersonalization'" in which 'the I-Thou' 'relationship' "becomes" "'an'" 'I-It' 'relationship'.[344] Thiselton also shows qualified approval for Bultmann's development of Heidegger's notion of 'inauthentic existence' in which selves either avoid obedience to God or, more proactively, attempt "'to procure life'" apart from God.[345] Thiselton also looks at "'persuasive definition'" (which relates directly to manipulation), at Freud's emphasis on 'self-deception', and at the later Wittgenstein's notion of "'training'" ('every human being has parents').[346]

And yet, even in Thiselton's later work, including his socio-critical comments paralleling *'Corinthian'* and Western 'postmodern' societies,[347] there remains further scope for dialogues between Thiselton and pastoral theology in relation to the interaction - at a more immediate level - between historical conditioning and *both* a hermeneutic of fallen human relationships *and* a hermeneutic of fallen human physicality. We reject Nietzsche's view that, 'it is invisible hands that torment and bend us the worst'. Interpreters have relational and biological/medical "histories" of the kinds investigated by counsellors and doctors, and dialogue could be extended to include interlocutors such as R. Hurding, P.H. Ballard, S. Pattison, J. Woodward, D. Browning, E. Farley, P. Goodliffe, and many others. We will take up this point again in more detail in Chapter 7. Admittedly, though, Thiselton realizes the truth of this point and has *begun* this dialogue, notably with C.V. Gerkin and with D. Capps. Some of his more recent publications also show

---

[343] Gunton, C.E., *The One, the Three, and the Many: God, Creation, and the Culture of Modernity. The 1992 Bampton Lectures* (CUP, Cambridge, 1993), 13-16.

[344] Thiselton, *2H*, 154, 287.

[345] Thiselton, *2H*, 278, 171-172, 177-180, 186, 277-280, cf. 153.

[346] Thiselton, *2H*, 403-404; cf. 113-114, 376-379; cf. Wittgenstein, *OC*, 29e; cf. Thiselton, A.C., 'Sigmund Freud and the Language of the Heart', *CEN* 13 Feb. (1976), 14.

[347] Thiselton, A.C., *The First Epistle to the Corinthians* (eds. H. Marshall and D.A. Hagner; Series: The New International Greek Testament Commentary; Grand Rapids: Eerdmans; Carlisle: Paternoster, 2000), 14; cf. 12-17, 33, 40-43, 48-51, 75, 314, 548, 1002, 1054-1059, 1255; cf. Thiselton, A.C., 'Can a Pre-Modern Bible Address a Postmodern World? (Public Lecture, University of St. Andrews)', in *2000 Years and Beyond: Faith, Identity, and the Common Era* (eds. P. Gifford, D. Archard, T. Hart, and N. Rapport; London: Routledge, 2003), 127-146. Italics Thiselton's.

encouraging signs of movement in this direction.[348]

Having examined Thiselton's hermeneutical critique of history – which includes (but cannot be reduced to) his modification of Gadamer's hermeneutic of *traditions* - we may now turn to examine Thiselton's modification of Gadamer's *hermeneutical circle* – as follows.

### D. Widened Dialogue Towards Critical Synthesis: Thiselton's Transformed Hermeneutical Paradigm and Its Tradition-Refinement of Gadamer's Hermeneutical Circle

Having expounded Thiselton's second period "stratum two" hermeneutical critique of history, we shall now continue our exposition of Thiselton's second period "stratum three" critique of hermeneutical understanding. In his second period "stratum three" critique of hermeneutical understanding Thiselton – as we shall see below - sublates Gadamer's hermeneutical circle into a larger framework of wider philosophical and theological dialogue, and so both affirms Gadamer's thinking in some ways, and yet also modifies Gadamer's thinking in other ways.

We are well aware of Thiselton's later warnings in relation to 'declaring premature war between rival theories' or in relation to premature declarations concerning "'new philosophical paradigms nudging old paradigms aside'". It can indeed be a matter of "premature fusion of horizons" on a grand scale when theorists, who do not listen adequately to each other's contributions, prematurely "assign" 'thinkers into classificatory boxes as broad "types"' and "risk" 'nurturing a mind-set of conceiving of theology in terms of competing "schools"'. And so we *align* with Thiselton's later view that stresses the importance of "multiple voices" working together in relation to a "heuristically positive" environment for work in 'the hermeneutics of doctrine'.[349]

Nevertheless, it would also be a denial of the historical criteria of historical unity, historical continuity, and historical relationality if we argued that there was *no* general axis of historical enquiry or if we argued that there were no *a posteriori* historical trends.

And so, below, we shall demonstrate *a posteriori* that Thiselton, during his second period, *does indeed* usher in a transformed hermeneutical framework, or even a paradigm-shift in the discipline of hermeneutics, that moves well beyond a simple appeal to Gadamer.

---

[348] Thiselton, *NH*, 399, 410-470, 603, 615; cf. Thiselton, *IGPS*, 4-7, 11-15, 19-39, 53-54, 68-78, 108-109, 114-115, 125, 128-144, 150, 154-155, 158-163; cf. Nietzsche, F., *Thus Spoke Zarathustra. A Book for Everyone and No One* (trans. R.J. Hollingdale; London: Penguin, 1969), 69; cf. our bibliography. But cf. Thiselton, 'HB', 88-91; cf. e.g. Thiselton, A.C., *1 Corinthians. A Shorter Exegetical and Pastoral Commentary* (Grand Rapids and Cambridge: Eerdmans, 2006).
[349] Thiselton, A.C., *The Hermeneutics of Doctrine* (Grand Rapids: Eerdmans, 2007), 136-137; cf.: 134-144; 169; 162-173, see especially 169-170.

## 1. The Importance of Gadamer's Thought for Thiselton's Hermeneutical Circle

Certainly, as the title *'The Two Horizons'* suggests, 'Gadamer's' work *'is'*, of course, still very 'important for' Thiselton's 'formulation' 'of the hermeneutical circle': for Thiselton, '"understanding"' is a '"dialectic"' or "dialogic" 'process' that 'is never' '"final"'; for Thiselton, 'the hermeneutical circle' is simply 'true to... life' and involves 'the interplay of the movement of tradition[s] and the movement of... interpreter[s]'.[350] We need not revisit Thiselton's concerns to move beyond '"sterile"' interests in either 'historical'-'critical' or 'linguistic'-'critical' 'objectivity' - interests that, in Thiselton's estimate, neglect the equally necessary 'fusion of horizons'[351] - or to move beyond '"a single preoccupation with historical method"' that has dominated much interpretation since 'the Enlightenment'.[352]

We should note, however, that, in *The Two Horizons*, (1), Thiselton expounds Gadamer's notions of *'distancing'* (for Gadamer, 'distancing' involves "foregrounding" 'temporal distance and its significance for understanding') and *'fusion'* (for Gadamer, during 'fusion', 'old and new are always combining into something of living value') in relation to *'exegesis' and 'systematic theology'*. Thiselton argues *both* that 'systematic' "theologies" constitute 'the end process, to date' of "traditions" of 'biblical' 'exegesis' and 'fusion', *and* that 'systematic' "theologies" help "shape" the 'pre-understandings' out of which *subsequent* "exegeses" and "fusions" are initiated. Thiselton argues that the latter, in turn, "re-shape" 'pre-understandings' and "systematic theologies" that, in *their* turn, then help "shape" the 'pre-understandings' out of which *still further* "exegeses" and "fusions" are initiated, and so on, around 'the hermeneutical circle'. Thus, Thiselton bemoans the artificial 'separation of... biblical exegesis and systematic theology'.[353] We may conclude, particularly once our observations in Chapter 5 have been taken into account as well, that R.W.L. Moberly's later request – i.e. that 'Thiselton' provide a 'fuller treatment' of 'the' "relationships" 'between' the 'Bible', 'Christian tradition' and 'doctrine', 'reading', 'openness', and 'transformation' – seems to neglect Thiselton's second period thinking.[354]

---

[350] Thiselton, *2H*, 16-17, 323, 67, 296, 107; cf.: 307-310, 106, 197; cf. Gadamer, *TM*, 190-192, 265-379, quoting 293; cf. Thiselton, 'EITN', 583. First italics Thiselton's, others ours.

[351] Thiselton, *2H*, 14, 21-22, 67-69, 86, 117-121, 321, 322; cf. 443.

[352] Thiselton, *2H*, xix, cf. 206, 10-23; cf. Turner, M., and J.B. Green, 'New Testament Commentary and Systematic Theology', in *Between Two Horizons. Spanning New Testament Studies and Systematic Theology* (eds. J.B. Green and M. Turner; Cambridge: Eerdmans, 2000), 6, citing: Thiselton, A.C., 'New Testament Interpretation in Historical Perspective', in *Hearing the New Testament: Strategies for Interpretation* (ed. J.B. Green; Grand Rapids: Eerdmans; Carlisle: Paternoster Press, 1995), 10.

[353] Thiselton, *2H*, 315, 321-322, cf. 314-326, 307; cf.: Thiselton, 'EITN', 584; citing from Gadamer, *TM*, 296, 306; and from, Jeanrond, W.G., *Text and Interpretation as Categories of Theological Thinking* (Dublin: Gill and MacMillan, 1988), 75. Italics ours.

[354] Moberly, R.W.L., 'Review of A.C. Thiselton's *New Horizons in Hermeneutics*', *Anv* 11.1 (1994), 72.

(2) Some of Thiselton's major emphases with respect to *'distancing'* re-emerge in *The Two Horizons*. Thus, Thiselton argues, against D.E. Nineham's 'pessimism', that 'distancing' presupposes the *accessibility* of 'historical' 'knowledge'.[355] Thiselton also argues, against individualism, that 'distancing' employs *corporate* checks and accountabilities.[356] And Thiselton argues, against *'single controlling'* 'paradigms', that distancing must employ *multiple* 'models' so as to attain *multiple* "angles of vision" in relation to any interpretative problem.[357] For Thiselton, distancing involves *both* "'rigorous'" "'*historical*-critical'" - including 'sociological' -"reconstruction"[358] *and 'linguistic'* - including 'literary' - "criticism".[359] In the context of 'biblical' 'hermeneutics' Thiselton also employs *'theological'* criticism.[360] For Thiselton, 'distancing' at least *aims* at *"correct"* 'understanding' since, in Thiselton's estimate, 'the falsification of a text is, in principle, possible'.[361]

In Thiselton's thinking, however, as we have already seen, 'distancing' is not a process that simply "distances" "interpreters" from their 'own horizon' of 'cultural "baggage"'. D.A. Carson, we believe, would agree that it is impossible to 'leap out of' one's 'own' "horizons", which are not merely 'cultural' but also retain a diachronic component that pertains to "developing traditions".[362] Further, contradicting C.F.H. Henry's reading of Thiselton, we should observe that, for Thiselton, distancing is not a process that "removes" 'cultural baggage... from the text and from the interpreter" on route to philosophically-idealist 'objective truth'. Rather, as we have already seen, Thiselton argues that distancing is a process that *highlights* traditional and cultural *distinctions between* two sets of horizons *within history* (see Chapter 5).[363]

(3) In *The Two Horizons*, in relation to *'fusion'*, Thiselton again stresses 'openness' to 'textual' "action" and to "creative" reader effort. In *The Two Horizons*, Thiselton still implicitly holds to his four-fold grammar of 'fusion' (i.e. 'textual' "action",

---

[355] Thiselton, *2H*, 326, 60, 159, 57-58, cf. 59, cf. 316. Italics ours.

[356] Thiselton, *2H*, 326; cf.: our Chapter 5; Thiselton, 'NH', 318-323; cf. 326-327; Thiselton, A.C., 'Experience-Centred Religion: Harvey Cox on the Seduction of the Spirit', *CEN* 9 Aug. (1974), 8; Thiselton, 'KNT', 85-86, 90-91, 104; Thiselton, 'EITN', 578-579; cf. 583-584; Thiselton, 'Par', 48-52; Thiselton, A.C., 'Review of A. Hodes' *Encounter with Martin Buber*', *Chman* 90.2 (1976), 138-139; Thiselton, A.C., 'Understanding God's Word Today', *CEN* 15 Oct. (1976), 6, (henceforth the 'short' article bearing this title).

[357] Thiselton, 'R-RH', 100; cf. Thiselton, *2H*, 371, 291-292, cf. 403-405, 432-434, 115. Italics ours, except on the words, *'single controlling'*, where they are Thiselton's.

[358] Thiselton, *2H*, 14-15, 21, 68-69, 74-84, 86, 353; cf. Thiselton, 'Truth', 894; cf. Thiselton, A.C., 'The 'Interpretation' of Tongues: a New Suggestion in the Light of Greek Usage in Philo and Josephus', *JThStud* NS 30.1 (Apr. 1979), 34. Italics ours.

[359] Thiselton, *2H*, 116, 121, 115-124, cf. 386-427, cf. 11. Italics ours.

[360] Thiselton, 'U (long)', 99. Italics ours.

[361] Thiselton, *2H*, 326, 353; cf. 14; cf. Sykes, 'R *2H*', 157. Italics ours.

[362] Carson, *GG*, 120; cf. Thiselton, *2H*, 326, xix, 12, 16-17, 62, 114, 302, 304-307, 314-315.

[363] Henry, C.F.H., 'Postmodernism: The New Spectre?', in *The Challenge of Postmodernism. An Evangelical Engagement* (ed. D.S. Dockery; Grand Rapids, Mi.: Baker Books, 1997), 46.

'actualization', 'appropriation', and 'application' – see Chapter 5) where, in Thiselton's thinking in *The Two Horizons*, each aspect of 'fusion' should be understood corporately as well as "individually". This analysis of 'fusion' contributes to what Thiselton will later call his 'hermeneutics of self-involvement'.[364]

Notably, in *The Two Horizons*, (a), Thiselton argues that adequate or "responsible" 'fusion of horizons' cannot be expected simply to "happen" during 'distancing'.[365] Again, Thiselton attacks 'semantic' 'theories' that artificially narrow 'linguistic' 'function' to 'reference', or to the "transmission" of 'cognitive' 'content' or 'truth', although - in Thiselton's approach to language - such 'functions' 'remain... important'. That is, Thiselton insists that responsible fusion is *not comparable merely to the receipt of information or of knowledge*.[366] Again, though, Thiselton argues that even 'semantic' theories free from these problems of linguistic-functional reductionism still 'only' "concern" "textual" 'horizons', and not 'present meaning', and so 'cannot' constitute the whole 'task' 'of hermeneutics'. That is, for Thiselton, responsible fusion goes *beyond* respect for any given range of possible linguistic functions *within the textual horizon* and *towards* how textual language functions – (extra-)linguistically and/or intra-linguistically – in relation (*and in relationality*) to *readers' horizons "in front of the text"*.[367]

Conversely, (b), Thiselton argues that even 'translation' – which, in Thiselton's estimate, should not be marked by an erroneous stress on 'surface-structure' 'correspondence' - necessarily involves 'interpretative' "judgments" that amount to 'fusion'. That is, contrary to D.E. Nineham, Thiselton argues that 'fusion' *of some sort* is not only possible but unavoidable during interpretation - although Thiselton also argues that such 'fusion' then sometimes subsequently turns out to have been premature or irresponsible.[368]

Therefore, (c), as J.B. Webster puts it, Thiselton argues that '*both* hermeneutics [more narrowly defined] *and* linguistic and semantic investigation are' necessary during interpretation - though this important point is *not at all* Thiselton's 'underlying thesis' in *The Two Horizons*, as we have already implied.[369]

---

[364] Thiselton, *2H*, 324-326, 314, 309, 310, 353, 287; cf. Thiselton, *NH*, 33, 65, 11, 272-307; cf. Thiselton, 'NH', 323. Italics ours.

[365] Thiselton, *2H*, 319, 326, 304-308; cf.: Thiselton, 'U (long)', 121; contradicting, Clendenen, E.R., 'Postholes, Postmodernism, and the Prophets', in *The Challenge of Postmodernism. An Evangelical Engagement* (ed. D.S. Dockery; Grand Rapids, Mi.: Baker Books, 1997), 133.

[366] Thiselton, *2H*, 121-124, 312, 200, 268-269; cf. Thiselton, *LLM*, 3, 10. Italics ours.

[367] Thiselton, *2H*, 10, 117-121. Italics ours.

[368] Thiselton, *2H*, 130, 132, 124-133, cf. 59, cf. 60; contradicting, Ellingworth, 'T&PBT', 166. Ellingworth misses *Thiselton's* link between translation and hermeneutics – which is the inevitable involvement of performative distancing and fusion in both, not whether or not *further* acts of fusion distinguish cross-cultural reading from translation. Italics ours.

[369] Webster, 'R *2H*', 219. First and second italics Webster's, third and fourth italics ours.

## 2. Thiselton's Tradition-Modification of Gadamer's Hermeneutical Circle

Having said all this, however, 'Thiselton' does not simply "find" 'Gadamer's' hermeneutical circle 'persuasive' (querying C.G. Bartholomew's reading of Thiselton).[370] Rather, Thiselton *modifies* Gadamer's hermeneutical circle considerably – as follows.

Thus, (1), as R.E. Palmer notes, Thiselton's modification of Gadamer's hermeneutical circle involves Thiselton's appeal to *Pannenberg*. Initially, Thiselton appeals to Dilthey's "transposition" of 'Schleiermacher's' 'whole'-'parts' polarity 'into a temporal' 'historical' key; but then Thiselton further 'transposes' that polarity, after 'Pannenberg', into "eschatological" terms that, in addition, point to the Christ-event as an explanatory and evaluative metacriterion (see Chapters 3 and 7). And yet, correcting even Palmer, Thiselton's 'reception… of Gadamer' is not *only* 'a Pannenbergian critique' - as follows.[371]

Thus, (2), Thiselton appeals to the *Saussurian tradition* not only in relation to "language" (stratum two - see Chapter 4), but also – *if only to a lesser extent* - in relation to "understanding" (stratum three). That is, Thiselton does not neglect this tradition (here we are contradicting R.S. Hess's reading of Thiselton),[372] but appeals to it, partly, in the context of a modification of Gadamer's notions of 'distancing' and "fusion" that *allows the Saussurian tradition to contribute towards a fleshing out of, and/or a clarification of, what "distancing" and "fusion" actually involve during interpretative practice.*[373]

Thus, Thiselton argues that 'diachronic linguistics' (see Chapter 4) are 'valuable' for recovering 'lost' aspects of 'meaning'. In order to demonstrate the validity of this point, Thiselton cites 'Heidegger's' recovery of the notion of '"truth"' as 'unveiling'. Thiselton observes that, for Heidegger, the notion of '"truth"' as 'unveiling' relates to the idea of an event in which an 'entity… shows itself *just as* it is in itself'. Thiselton, of course, relates the idea of such an event to his notion of *fusion*.[374]

Conversely, Thiselton argues that 'synchronic linguistics' and "semantics" (see Chapter 4) extend the 'traditional' notion of '"literal sense"' in relation to those *aspects* of 'meaning' that are embedded *within* a "text's" own "horizon".[375] Thiselton thus argues that appeals to the Saussurian tradition aid *'distancing'* by helping to safeguard textual 'particularity' and prevent 'premature fusion'. Thus, for Thiselton, our interpretation of 'Jesus' '"must not… merely"' reflect '"our own

---

[370] Querying, Bartholomew, '3H', 123.
[371] Thiselton, *2H*, 5, cf. 67, 82-83, 166, 234-236, 302-303; cf. Thiselton, *IGPS*, 59-62, cf. 63-66; correcting, Palmer, R.E., 'The Scope of Hermeneutics: The Problem of Critique, and the Crisis of Modernity', *TRevCTLit* 3 (1984), 226-227; cf. Palmer, 'R *2H*', 172-174. Italics ours.
[372] Contradicting, Hess, 'RA *NH*', 24; cf.: Thiselton, *2H*, 116, 115; our Chapter 4.
[373] Thiselton, *2H*, 326, 119, 370-379, 379-385, 386-427; cf. 115-139. Italics ours.
[374] Thiselton, *2H*, 124-126; cf. Heidegger, *BT*, 261. First italics Heidegger's, others ours.
[375] Thiselton, *2H*, 125, 120, 115-116, cf. 117-120. Italics ours.

[prior] viewpoints and assumptions'" (so J. Macquarrie), since this would be 'idolatry' (so J.I. Packer). Hence, for Thiselton, 'meanings are' *not* 'grounded in pre-judgments' (here, we are contradicting H.M. Conn's reading of Thiselton).[376]

Enter Thiselton's major question in *'The Two Horizons'*: 'how do the two horizons of the ancient text and of modern readers actively *engage with each other creatively without merely bland, passive, domesticating assimilation?*'[377] Thiselton's answer to this question relates, partly, to 'distancing' which, for Thiselton, is a process that accounts for 'the effects of the intervention of a long tradition which separate[s] the two horizons historically'.[378]

Thus, as C.G. Bartholomew notes, 'Thiselton' affirms J. Barr's "mediation" of 'Saussure's influence into biblical studies', though our earlier observations contradict S.E. Porter's claim that 'Thiselton has' simply 'endorsed Barr's view'.[379] Further, most (indeed probably all) reviewers miss the *dialogue-widening significance* of Thiselton's appeals to the tradition of Saussure and Barr. Thiselton is concerned to expand, not merely to "see", "readers'" "pre-understandings" (here we are contradicting R. Van Voorst's reading of Thiselton).[380] 'Thiselton' does not just stress 'the limited roles of semantics' in relation to textual horizons; rather, Thiselton also stresses *the positive role of 'semantics' in relation to readers' horizons and in relation to widening dialogue at the level of critical-synthetic pre-understanding* (here we are qualifying D.E. Klemm's reading of Thiselton).[381]

(3) Thiselton appeals to *Schleiermacher* in order to counter what he (i.e. Thiselton) identifies as being Gadamer's under-emphasis on the roles of the 'individual' "subjectivities" of both authors and readers in relation to the processes pertaining to the hermeneutical circle (N.B. for Gadamer, 'subjectivity is a

---

[376] Thiselton, *2H*, 120, 119, 319, cf. 124-125, citing 57; cf. Macquarrie, *TCM*, 31; cf. Packer, J.I., 'In Quest of Canonical Interpretation', in *The Use of the Bible in Theology: Evangelical Options* (ed. R.K. Johnston; Atlanta: John Knox, 1985), 53. Contradicting, Conn, H.M., 'Normativity, Relevance, and Relativism', in *Inerrancy and Hermeneutics: A Tradition, A Challenge, A Debate* (ed. H.M. Conn; Grand Rapids: Baker, 1988), 187, 191. First italics Thiselton's, second italics ours.

[377] Thiselton, 'TY', 1563; cf. Thiselton, *2H*, 10-23; cf. 342-347. Italics Thiselton's.

[378] Thiselton, 'TY', 1563; cf. Thiselton, *2H*, 307-308; cf. 326.

[379] Bartholomew, C.G., 'Uncharted Waters: Philosophy, Theology and the Crisis in Biblical Interpretation', in *Renewing Biblical Interpretation* (eds. C.G. Bartholomew, C. Greene and K. Möller; Scripture and Hermeneutics Series; Vol. 1; Carlisle: Paternoster, 2000), 23; Bartholomew, however, is incorrect to suggest that 'Thiselton… does' not 'examine the philosophical subtext of de Saussure's semantics': all seven of Thiselton's points of appeal to Saussure are modified through a (largely, *but not exclusively*) later Wittgensteinian filter (see Chapters 4 and 7) which, in turn, is sublated into a theological-historical framework by Thiselton (see the present chapter); cf.: Porter, S.E., '2 Myths, Corporate Personality and Language Mentality Determinism', *SJT* 43.3 (1990), 302; Thiselton, *2H*, 125, 128, 133-139.

[380] Contradicting, Van Voorst, 'R *2H*', 220; cf. Thiselton, *2H*, 155, cf. 138-139.

[381] Qualifying, Klemm, D.E., 'Review of A.C. Thiselton's *The Two Horizons*', *JAARel* 50.1 (Mar. 1982), 117; cf. Thiselton, *2H*, 155, cf. 138-139. Italics ours.

distorting mirror').[382]

Thus, querying C.R. Mercer's reading of Thiselton, we should note that, in *New Horizons in Hermeneutics* (1992), Thiselton does not just show how 'Schleiermacher... changed the direction and content of hermeneutics'. Rather, in *New Horizons in Hermeneutics*, Thiselton defends 'Schleiermacher's' "interpretation" of 'texts' in relation to 'their' extra-linguistic backgrounds - including "their authors". We should note, contradicting J. Rieger, that Thiselton argues that Schleiermacher is not falling victim to the '"genetic"' fallacy at this point, but rather that Schleiermacher is showing 'concern' for the "other" where, according to Thiselton, Schleiermacher's work also "anticipates" Saussure's *'langue'-'parole'* 'distinction'.[383] As F. Watson summarizes, 'the quest for... authorial intention... does not attempt to reconstruct... [an] unknowable psychological process but investigates' a "text's" '"directedness"... within' its 'linguistic conventions'. This process, in Watson's estimate, 'can help... preserve a text's otherness against the self-absolutizing tendencies of hermeneutical pragmatism and of the (post-) structuralist proclamation of the death of the author'.[384] 'Thiselton' does *not* "focus" 'on... texts and reader-responses' 'instead' of on 'author's intention' (here we are contradicting E.E. Johnson's and M. Silva's readings of Thiselton). Rather, Thiselton stresses *'both'* 'horizons', *against* an over-emphasizing of 'the present' horizon that occurs, for example, in '"existentialist"' hermeneutics.[385]

Thiselton's reinstatement of Schleiermacher in *New Horizons in Hermeneutics* is present in embryo in *The Two Horizons*.[386] Thus, for Thiselton, admittedly, Schleiermacher's stress on 'the "strangeness" of the other which eludes "system"' anticipates Gadamer's *'respect for the... other'* and Gadamer's rejection of 'the imperializing "general method" of science'. Citing Gadamer, 'one does not...

---

[382] Thiselton, *2H*, 305; cf.: Thiselton, *NH*, 207, 320-321; Thiselton, *IGPS*, 61; Gadamer, *TM*, 276.

[383] Thiselton, *NH*, 206-208, 213-233; cf.: Thiselton, A.C., 'Language, Religious', in *The Blackwell Encyclopedia of Modern Christian Thought* (ed. A. McGrath; Oxford: Blackwell, 1993), 315; Watson, 'R *NH*', 254; Mercer, C.R., 'Review of A.C. Thiselton's *New Horizons in Hermeneutics*', *CBQ* 56.1 (1994), 159; cf. 158-160; Rieger, J., *God and the Excluded: Visions and Blindspots in Contemporary Theology* (Minneapolis, MN.: Augsburg Fortress, 2000), 40, 41. First and second italics ours, others Thiselton's.

[384] Watson, 'R *NH*', 254, but cf. 255; cf. also, Thiselton, *NH*, 223, 267, 559-561. Contradicting, Martin, F., 'Reading Scripture in the Catholic Tradition', in *Your Word Is Truth: A Project of Evangelicals and Catholics Together* (ed. C. Colson and R.J. Neuhaus; Grand Rapids, MI.: Eerdmans, 2002), 158.

[385] Johnson, E.E., 'Review of A.C. Thiselton's *New Horizons in Hermeneutics*', *BibSac* 150.600 (Oct.-Dec. 1993), 501, 502; cf. Silva, M., 'Contemporary Approaches to Biblical Interpretation', in *An Introduction to Biblical Hermeneutics: The Search for Meaning* (W.C. Kaiser and M. Silva; Grand Rapids: Zondervan, 1994), 234; cf. Thiselton, *NH*, 275; cf. 207-208, cf. 224-225; cf. Thiselton, *2H*, 16, 250-251, 245. Italics ours.

[386] Thiselton, *2H*, 67, 103-107, 113, 166, 300-301.

argue the other person down'.[387] Nevertheless, for Thiselton, Schleiermacher's emphasis on "authors" as 'whole' 'conscious' persons qualifies (and is qualified by) Gadamer's emphases on corporate 'tradition', on 'unconscious' 'pre-judgments', and on a de-centered '"individual"' '"subjectivity"'.[388] For Gadamer, though, 'tradition... is always part of us' such that selves are 'dominated by prejudices', where Gadamer makes this point in an argument against what he (in some ways *unlike Thiselton*) perceives to be Schleiermacher's 'psychological narrowness'.[389]

(4) For Thiselton, an appeal to the stress on 'individual' selves in *Kierkegaard, Heidegger and Bultmann* also qualifies Gadamer's hermeneutical circle.[390] For Heidegger, 'historiology... has Dasein's historicality as its presupposition'; for Bultmann, 'history' concerns 'the possibilities of... self-understanding'; (on Kierkegaard, see Chapter 3).[391]

Admittedly, Thiselton allows Gadamer to reciprocally correct 'individualism' in Kierkegaard, Heidegger, and Bultmann. For Gadamer, 'self-reflection and autobiography... are not primary'. We have also already noted Thiselton's attack on what one writer characterizes (rightly or wrongly) as Heidegger's 'solipsism' (see Chapter 5).[392] Thiselton argues that Heidegger neglects "inter-subjectivity" and corporate 'responsibility': for Thiselton, Heidegger's '"*hermeneutics*"' are still too 'rooted in' 'the orphaned Cogito' (see Chapter 3) and require a 'shift... to the interactive, relational self', who is ultimately 'rooted in the divine/human relation'. Thiselton would agree with Gadamer's view that 'Heidegger is not sufficiently aware of... the... dialectic that attaches to all... Heideggerian assertions'.[393]

*However*, Thiselton rejects Gadamer's reduction 'of "consciousness"' to 'a mere "flickering in the closed circuits of historical life"'.[394] Thiselton's hermeneutical circle is doubly grounded in '"tradition"' and in human selves or subjectivities. For Thiselton, 'understanding' is *both* a "community's" 'dialectic' inter-action with '*traditum*' in '*traditio*', *and* it is '"thrown projection"'. For Heidegger and Thiselton '"thrown projection"' is a 'future'-oriented '"historical motion"' that seeks to 'transcend' '"situatedness"'. For Heidegger and Thiselton, in '"thrown projection"'

---

[387] Thiselton, 'TY', 1564, cf. 1560-1561; cf. Thiselton, *2H*, 103-104, 106, 107; cf. 294, 295; cf. Gadamer, *TM*, 3-9, 348-349, 358-359, 362-379, quoting 367. Italics Thiselton's.

[388] Thiselton, *2H*, 106, 305, 306, 114, 103-107, cf.: 113-114; 304-306, 324-326.

[389] Gadamer, *TM*, 282, 360, 511.

[390] Thiselton, *2H*, 305, 304-308; cf. 163-166, 196-197; cf. 200-203; cf. 282-283, 284, 292.

[391] Heidegger, *BT*, 444; cf. Bultmann, R., 'On the Problem of Demythologizing (1961)', in *New Testament and Mythology and Other Basic Writings* (ed. and trans. S.M. Ogden; Philadelphia: Fortress, 1984), 157.

[392] See our argument in Chapter 5; cf. Thiselton, 'KNT', 90; Thiselton, *2H*, 200-203, 292; cf. Gadamer, *TM*, 276. Also, contradicting, Harrisville, 'R *2H*', 216.

[393] Thiselton, *2H*, 200-201, cf. 202-203, 282-283; quoting: MacCammon, 'R *PH*', page 3 of 4; Gadamer, H.-G., 'Heidegger and the Language of Metaphysics', in *Philosophical Hermeneutics* (H.-G. Gadamer; ed. D.E. Linge; London: University of California Press, 1976), 231-232. Thiselton includes Ricoeur's italics.

[394] Thiselton, 'TY', 1565; cf.: Thiselton, *2H*, 305.

'existence and understanding are co-terminous'. Thus, in 1981, possibly reflecting Ricoeur's influence, Thiselton speaks of 'the dialectic between the corporate and individual aspects' of 'understanding'. That is, for Thiselton, there is a reciprocal correction of Gadamer provided by Heidegger and Bultmann (and ultimately by Kierkegaard) in this context of discussion[395] – where this point is missed by some commentators. Thus, Thiselton does *not* simply present Gadamer's 'hermeneutics' as 'Heideggerian' (here we are contradicting D. McCartney's and C. Clayton's reading of Thiselton).[396]

Earlier observations concerning Thiselton's other reciprocal mutually qualifying appeals to 'Heidegger' and to 'Gadamer' regarding 'the capacity of language, tradition, and temporal distance to' 'distort' or "transmit" 'truth' respectively need not be revisited.[397] We should recall, however, that Thiselton's hermeneutical circle includes a stronger place for "critical" and/or for "metacritical" "testing" than do the hermeneutical circles of *both* Heidegger *and* Gadamer (see Chapters 3 and 5).[398]

(5) Thiselton's appeal to the *later Wittgenstein* also contributes towards Thiselton's modification of Gadamer's hermeneutical circle.[399] Thus, (a), Thiselton observes that the later Wittgenstein's *"way"'* of "conditioned" '"description"' (i.e. of approaching 'philosophical... puzzles', of "describing" 'language-uses' "philosophically" whilst acknowledging that '"description"' is "historically conditioned") embraces "notions" 'of' '"showing"' and "noticing". The later Wittgenstein asks, 'how can we *show* someone that we *know* truths?... conduct exhibits the thing we are concerned with'. Elsewhere the later Wittgenstein writes, 'noticing and seeing. One doesn't say "I noticed it for five minutes"'. For Thiselton, (b), this later-Wittgensteinian perspective allows him (i.e. Thiselton) to alter the grammar of Gadamer's notions of 'distancing' (cf. "noticing") and of 'fusion' (cf. '"showing"') because – in relation to "noticing" and '"showing"' *and more broadly* - the later Wittgenstein reinstates 'so-called "propositional"' language (*not* a '"propositional" view' of language or of 'revelation') and highlights what 'J.L. Austin' later calls its many varied 'performative' "functions". For the later Wittgenstein, a 'grammatical proposition' can, for example, 'shew [i.e. show]...

---

[395] Thiselton, *2H*, 306, 165-166, 324, 313, 173, 183, 185; cf.: Thiselton, 'TY', 1563; Ebeling, *T&P*, 25; Cahill, P.J., 'Review of A.C. Thiselton's *The Two Horizons*', *CBQ* 43.3 (Jul. 1981), 484; Thiselton, 'KMCM', 59, cf. 49, 54; qualifying, Dockery, 'R *2H*', 135. Italics in speech-marks Ebeling's, remaining italics ours.

[396] e.g. Morgan, 'R *2H*', 332; cf. Ellingworth, 'R *2H*', 178; cf. Maddox, 'CHP', 523; and, contradicting, McCartney, D., and C. Clayton, *Let The Reader Understand. A Guide to Interpreting and Applying the Bible* (Wheaton, Illinois: Bridgepoint, 1994), 297; cf. Thiselton, *2H*, 304-308; cf.: 163-166, 196-197; 200-203; 282-284, 292.

[397] Thiselton, *2H*, 314, 312; cf.: 250-251, 196-200; cf.: Thiselton, *NTH*, xxii, concs. 1.2ab.

[398] Thiselton, *2H*, 353, 200, cf.: 314, 195; Thiselton, *NH*, 315-317; cf. Heidegger, *BT*, 183-195, 200-201; cf. Gadamer, *TM*, 291-307.

[399] Thiselton, *2H*, 357-385, 386-427, 428-431, 432-438.

"the length of a rod"'.[400]

Admittedly, Thiselton is not unaware that "noticing" and "'showing'", *like* 'distancing' and 'fusion', contrast with hermeneutical foreclosure or with mere assent to prior categories.[401] Yet, Thiselton argues that - in presupposing the "active" "functioning" of "'grammatical propositions'" in "creatively" "extending" *'understanding'* - "noticing" and "'showing'" *cast doubt on* Gadamer's 'devaluing of assertions', where R.S. Briggs rightly notes 'Thiselton's' two precursor "articles" to *The Two Horizons* in relation to this argument.[402] For the later Wittgenstein and Thiselton, 'the role which propositions play in a language-game' is important whereas, for Gadamer, 'meaning... reduced to what is stated is always distorted'.[403]

Hence, (c), for Thiselton, as H.C. White notes, 'the concept of language event' is 'strengthened... by the incorporation of insights from Austin and Wittgenstein' (though see our qualifying comments in relation to White's point, in Chapter 4).[404] Similarly, Thiselton observes that 'Pauline' 'argument' uses 'propositions' to "clarify" and "extend" 'concepts', and that Paul's approach contradicts R. Funk's dualistic prioritizing 'of... parables as metaphor' as over and against 'discursive argument'.[405] Thus, for 'Thiselton... "showing" in the parables... and "argument" in... Paul are "two modes of discourse" quite related to one another'.[406] And Thiselton's 'discussion of parable and metaphor... is... relevant to Wittgenstein's concern to use language... to help others see what is already there'. For the later Wittgenstein and Thiselton, 'philosophy... leaves everything as it is' such that "'philosophical description'" (which unavoidably involves assertions, statements or propositions) does not alter its objects, but rather – provisionally and potentially progressively - "shows" them as they 'already' are.[407]

(d) Thiselton, as we have already noted, accepts that "propositions" may still "'say'". That is, Thiselton, after the later Wittgenstein, argues that "propositions"

---

[400] Thiselton, *2H*, 37, 29, 26-33, 373, 326, 307, 437, cf. 368-373; cf.: Edmonds, D., and J. Eidinow, *Wittgenstein's Poker: The Story of a Ten-Minute Argument between Two Great Philosophers* (London: Faber and Faber, 2001), 188; Wittgenstein, *OC*, 55e; Wittgenstein, L., *Remarks on the Philosophy of Psychology. Volume 2* (eds. G.H. Von Wright and H. Nyman; trans. C.G. Luckhardt and M.A.E. Aue; Oxford: Blackwell, 1980), 81e; cf.: Wittgenstein, *PI*, 47, 50, 57, 81, quotes from 90. Thiselton under-emphasizes Wittgenstein's later focus on philosophical puzzles in our view – see later in the present chapter. Italics in speech-marks Wittgenstein's.
[401] Thiselton, *2H*, 370, 371-373, 326; cf. 307-308; cf. Goldingay, *MIS*, 110-111.
[402] Thiselton, *2H*, 406, 387-388, 370-371; cf. 386-407, 195; cf. Thiselton, *NH*, 33; cf. Briggs, *Words*, 21. Thiselton's two relevant articles are, Thiselton, 'Parab', 466, 437-468; and Thiselton, 'UPC', 87-100. Italics in speech-marks Thiselton's.
[403] Wittgenstein, L., *The Blue and Brown Books. Preliminary Studies for the Philosophical Investigations* (Oxford: Blackwell, 1958, 2002), 82; cf. Gadamer, *TM*, 469.
[404] White, 'S-AT', 55; cf. Thiselton, *2H*, 195, cf. 353-355.
[405] Thiselton, *2H*, 399, 400, 396-401.
[406] Keifert, 'R *2H*', 409; cf. Thiselton, *2H*, 399.
[407] Borsch, 'R *2H*', 89-90; cf.: Wittgenstein, *PI*, 50, 47, 90, quoting 49e; Thiselton, *2H*, 29, cf. 30.

may still communicate 'information' or "arguments" *within* existing "frames of reference". Thiselton accepts 'the distinction between grammatical and factual utterance' *without* dismissing the latter. 'But', for Thiselton, 'propositions' may also '*show*': citing Wittgenstein, '"I can't imagine the opposite"' may 'look like an empirical proposition, but... is really a grammatical one'.[408]

(e) Thiselton – in effect – argues that "noticing" (cf. "seeing") and '"showing"' characterize the later Wittgenstein's 'whole' 'approach' which, therefore, in Thiselton's thinking, is very relevant in relation to the 'hermeneutical' circle and 'task'. Thus, Thiselton notes the later Wittgenstein's comment that, 'I should not like... to spare other people the trouble of thinking'.[409] Thiselton observes that - in contrast to Heidegger's 'passive yieldedness' but aligning with 'hermeneutics' more broadly - the later Wittgenstein "wishes" '"to stimulate"' "purposeful" 'strenuous thought' and '"inner change"' in his readers, and that the later Wittgenstein is thus interested in '"training"' his readers in '"a"' new '"way"' 'of seeing' that involves '"using"' *'conceptual tools'* to generate 'fresh' "angles" 'of vision'.[410]

Thiselton notes that the later Wittgenstein's goal, therefore, is to 'have changed your *way of seeing*'.[411] For the later Wittgenstein and for Thiselton, the goal is that the "familiar" is "re-arranged" (cf. 'gathering' in Heidegger), so as "to break" 'the spell of' "traditional" "ways" of "seeing" (cf. 'idle talk' in Heidegger), and so as 'to allow' the previously "unnoticed" to "show" itself and be "noticed" (cf. 'unveiling' in 'Heidegger'). Thus, Thiselton observes that "noticing" (cf. "seeing") and "showing" are not the same as the *'information'*, *"explanation"*, "deduction", or indoctrination of "saying".[412] Citing the later Wittgenstein, '"philosophy"' is 'description alone' *prior to* 'all new discoveries and inventions', and is a matter of abolishing 'grammatical illusions'.[413]

(f) Thiselton thus argues that '"showing"', which "elucidates" or 'extends' *'the logical grammar of'* "language-games", 'concepts', or "applications", is sometimes pre-conditional for '"finding... new information"' and is tied to *understanding*, to "extending" *"understanding"*, and to 'seeing... as'.[414] The later Wittgenstein writes, 'determine how long an impression lasts by means of a stop-watch. The duration of knowledge, ability, understanding, [cf. 'the grammar... of' these '"concepts"'] could not be determined [i.e. "shown", "understood"] in this way'. And if '"showing"' is tied to 'understanding' then, again, in Thiselton's thinking, it

---

[408] Palmer, 'R *2H*', 174; cf.: Thiselton, *2H*, 367, 421, 399, cf. 387-388, 124; Wittgenstein, *PI*, 90e. First and second italics ours, third italics Thiselton's.

[409] Thiselton, *2H*, 370-372, 417, 386; cf. Wittgenstein, *PI*, viii.

[410] Thiselton, *2H*, 371, cf. 370, 372, 138, 137, 417, 46, 9, 139. Italics Thiselton's.

[411] Wittgenstein, L., *Zettel* (trans. G.E.M. Anscombe; Oxford: Blackwell, 1967, 1998), 81. Italics Wittgenstein's.

[412] Thiselton, *2H*, 338, 371-372; cf.: 370, 388, 287; 337-340; 126, 368, 29, 367, 137, 403-404; 169-170; 175, 199-200. First italics Thiselton's, second italics Wittgenstein's.

[413] Wittgenstein, *PI*, 47, cf. 50.

[414] Thiselton, *2H*, 406, 388, cf. 374-378, 386, 401-407, 417-427. Italics Thiselton's.

"relates to" 'fusion'.[415]

(g) In relation to 'distancing', Thiselton appeals to the (post-) later Wittgensteinian notion of "'polymorphous concepts'" in order to enable readers "'to notice'" the variable "grammars" of the words translated as "'faith'", "'flesh'", 'and "truth'" in 'the New Testament'.[416] Thiselton also appeals to the later Wittgenstein's notion of "language-games" in order 'to allow' readers "'to notice'" 'conceptual clarifications' in relation to Paul's 'doctrine' of 'justification by faith' as compared to 'conceptual clarifications' of 'faith in James'. For Thiselton, 'distancing' should also "'notice'" how 'meaning' relates to "'depth-grammar'" (i.e. "'language-games'", *'uses'*, 'habits', *'content'* - see Chapter 4) *as well as* "noticing" how 'meaning' relates to 'accidental' 'surface-grammar'. Thus, Thiselton seeks to modify 'form criticism' and extends J.F.A. Sawyer's "parallels" 'between *Sitz im Leben*... and context of situation' to include "parallels" with 'language-games'.[417]

Summarizing: for Thiselton, 'distancing' includes "noticing" concept-uses, "concept-clarifications", and linguistic or 'logical' "functions" - including (in Thiselton's criticisms of 'Gadamer' and 'Heidegger') the (depth-)grammatical "functioning" of 'assertions', "propositions", and/or 'statements'. For Thiselton, therefore, the later Wittgenstein's notion of "noticing" *'shows'* the way in which Gadamer's notion of 'distancing' requires modification. Thiselton wishes 'to *notice*' 'biblical truths which are hidden only because we do not know how to look at them'. The later Wittgenstein asks, 'how do I *employ* the sentence?... a picture... can... serve a purpose'.[418]

(h) In relation to 'fusion' (cf. "showing") then, in *The Two Horizons*, Thiselton argues that Bible-readers should *'notice'* 'three classes of grammatical utterances' that "show". Thus, (i), Thiselton's "'class-one'" 'grammatical utterances' "show" by "allowing" readers 'to *notice*' trans-contextual 'rationality' or the "processes" within 'conceptualizing' itself. In this context of discussion, Thiselton gives the example of 'the... mutual exclusion' implicit in 'Paul's' 'grammatical utterances' concerning 'grace' and 'works'. Here, Thiselton is emphatically not returning to philosophical 'idealism' or to the epistemology of "logical positivism", but is, rather, invoking a trans-contextual and trans-temporal "historical rationality" that is operative in *'all'* 'historical' "traditions" and for which 'historical' 'life' is 'the... *a priori*'. Thiselton argues that *'all'* 'traditions' employ 'mutual exclusion': in the language of the later Wittgenstein, 'I cannot observe myself unobserved', or 'be in

---

[415] Wittgenstein, *R2*, 11e; cf. Thiselton, *2H*, 388, 406, 326.

[416] Thiselton, *2H*, 326, 371, 408-409, 409-411, 411-415.

[417] Thiselton, *2H*, 416, 371, 139, 417, 415, 326, 375, 387, 134, 137, 119-120, 396: cf. 415-427, 138, 66, 82-84; cf. Thiselton, 'LMR', 1126. Italics in speech-marks Thiselton's.

[418] Thiselton, *2H*, 326, 139, 376-378, 416, 313, 196, 380, 387-388, 372, 396-397; citing, Grech, 'R *2H*', 574-575; cf. Wittgenstein, *R2*, 114. First and second italics Thiselton's, third italics Wittgenstein's.

doubt at *will*.[419]

Thiselton is not saying that what "'class-one'" 'grammatical utterances' "show" or "conceptually" 'elucidate' about 'grace' and 'works' is "'universal'" or topic neutral', but that what they *'show'* about "historical rationality" is "'universal'" or topic neutral'. For Thiselton, "'class-one'" 'grammatical utterances' *secondarily* serve as 'an elucidation of the subject' that 'extends' *"understanding"*. P. Ellingworth, therefore, misses Thiselton's point to complain – in effect - that "'grace'" and "'works'" 'are… culture-relative', or (more properly) "traditional", 'concepts'.[420]

Thiselton argues that the *'distinctive'* "contexts" or 'settings' of 'class-one… utterances' are "dialogically" 'open-ended', "never-concluded", "arguments". Such "arguments", Thiselton observes, 'appeal' to "'common sense'", to "rationality", to "'strict intellectual probity'", to "'wisdom'", and to "'judgment'"; such "arguments", Thiselton observes, aim at 'effective understanding' and are "'uncommitted'" to any 'tradition' of "theology" or "ethics". Thiselton's 'examples' in this context of discussion include 'Old Testament' 'Wisdom literature' and 'Pauline' 'diatribe' as expounded by 'Bultmann'.[421]

For Thiselton, then, assertive language "shows". This point, in turn, "shows" us Thiselton's modification of the grammar of Gadamer's notion of 'fusion'. Moreover, for Thiselton, assertive language also "shows" (or "allows" readers 'to *notice*') the *very same kind of "broadened" "historical rationality" that Gadamer himself espouses and/or sees as being operative within* "'understanding'" or within *"hermeneutical consciousness"*. Thiselton thus argues (in effect) that Gadamer's disparagement of assertions, or of 'statements of various kinds', detracted from *his own* (i.e. Gadamer's own) work on the hermeneutical circle (see Chapters 3, 4, and 5).[422]

Our reading of Thiselton, here, contradicts that of S.E. Porter, who likens Thiselton's "'class-one'" 'utterances' 'to the analytical or *a priori* utterances of logical positivism' – '*a priori* utterances' which, Porter argues, are, thereby, on *that* basis, 'not culturally relative' in Thiselton's thinking.[423]

However, in reality, as we have "shown", Thiselton's "'class-one"… utterances' are 'analytical' *without* being '*a priori*', "positivist", or "formalist", since they occur in "'language-games'". As we argued earlier, Thiselton transposes "'showing'" into

---

[419] Thiselton, *2H*, 326, 139, 371-373, 91, 323, 198, 387-390, 302, 359-360, 65, 395-401; cf.: Thiselton, 'TNI', 11; Wittgenstein, *Z*, 123, quoting 102; quoting, Wittgenstein, *OC*, 29e. First italics ours, italics on the two occurrences of the word *'all'* are ours, last italics Wittgenstein's, remaining italics Thiselton's.

[420] Thiselton, *2H*, 389, 372, 396-400, 386-388, 392, 65, 91; cf.: Thiselton, 'TNI', 11; quoting, Grech, 'R *2H*', 573-574; Ellingworth, 'R *2H*', 179. First and third italics Thiselton's, second italics ours.

[421] Thiselton, *2H*, 396-401, 388. Italics Thiselton's.

[422] Thiselton, *2H*, 399, 326, 371, 139, 65, 91, 293-300, 313; cf. Thiselton, 'TNI', 11. First italics Thiselton's, remaining italics ours.

[423] Thiselton, *2H*, 389; cf. Porter, S.E., 'Wittgenstein's Classes of Utterance and Pauline Ethical Texts', *JEThS* 32 (1989), 88. First and second italics Porter's, others ours.

a *different* historico-philosophical framework and appeals to the *'later'* Wittgenstein in this context of discussion.[424]

Porter, however, misreads Thiselton as though Thiselton supposedly appealed to the *early* Wittgenstein and to 'A.J. Ayer' in this context.[425] On this false basis, Porter then erroneously imputes to Thiselton the notion 'that ethics should be based upon first-class utterances' or on abstract 'self-evident statement[s]'. Porter then argues that, since 'the verifiability principle itself is unverified' [i.e. since empiricism has been discredited], such a basis for ethics is untenable – where, in Porter's misunderstanding, this point contradicts "Thiselton's" view.[426] Porter, moreover, unwittingly *converges with* Thiselton's real stance when he (i.e. Porter) argues for the historicity of 'analytical' "statements" with reference to the 'faith'/'works distinction[s]' in Paul and 'James'.[427]

It is unclear as to whether Porter also unwittingly adopts Thiselton's *own resolution* of the 'apparent' Paul-James 'contradiction' – a resolution that distinguishes between 'different' "language-games".[428] Certainly, though, and contradicting Porter's reading of Thiselton, Thiselton does not regard '"class-one"… utterances' as 'self-evident' in a logical-positivist sense. Indeed, again, Porter's attack on Thiselton's supposed attempt to base 'ethics' on '"class-one"… utterances' actually *converges* with Thiselton's sympathies with Continental traditions in relation to a *non*-abstract "basis for" 'ethics'.[429]

(ii) Moving on, then Thiselton's 'class-two' 'grammatical utterances' *'show'* "the scaffolding'" 'convictions' (cf. "pre-judgments") of "traditions" – as, for example, in the case of the utterance, "God is good". Thiselton argues that, when "traditional" or 'theological content' is involved (i.e. the 'actual traffic' 'that… scaffolding sustains'), then 'class-two' 'grammatical utterances' are not merely 'culture-relative': for Thiselton, *'scaffolding'* 'convictions' may survive 'for unthinkable ages'.[430] And yet, in Thiselton's thinking, this point is unrelated to linguistic "formalism" or to the early Wittgenstein, but rather relates to *a posteriori* 'historical' trans-'temporal' "continuities". Indeed, Thiselton argues that, trans-contextually and/or trans-temporally, '"the same language-games *could* be

---

[424] Thiselton, *2H*, 389, 388, 387, 359, 361, 372, 399, cf. 396-401; cf. Wittgenstein, *PI*, vi. First italics ours, second italics Thiselton's, third and fourth italics ours.

[425] Porter, 'CoU', 88, 90.

[426] Porter, 'CoU', 89.

[427] Porter, 'CoU', 88, 89-90.

[428] Thiselton, *2H*, 420, 426-427.

[429] Porter, 'CoU', 89, 90; cf. Thiselton, *2H*, 389, 180, cf. 387.

[430] Thiselton, *2H*, 399, 392, 32, 33, cf. 395-396; cf.: Macquarrie, J., 'Review of A.C. Thiselton's *The Two Horizons*', *RelStud* 16.4 (Dec. 1980), 496; Thiselton cites, Wittgenstein, *OC*, 11e, 44e, 87e, 28e-29e (quoted), 13e, 20e, 22e, 30e, 21e, 17e. First italics Thiselton's, second italics Wittgenstein's.

employed in... [different] traditions'".⁴³¹

Thiselton endorses the later Wittgenstein's notion according to which "'scaffolding'" 'convictions' are interwoven 'axiomatic' 'assumptions' that may be likened to "twigs" in "'a'" bird's "'nest'". Thiselton follows the later Wittgenstein who argues that "'scaffolding'" 'convictions' reside on "'an unused siding'" and are thus "unconsciously" "'isolated from'" the normal "'traffic'" or "'route'" of "'enquiry'". "'Scaffolding'" 'convictions' – for the later Wittgenstein and for Thiselton – are "immobile" "'doctrines seen as facts'", and, 'are' typically "exempted" "'from doubt'", from 'denial', and/or from "testing". "'Scaffolding'" 'convictions' – for the later Wittgenstein and for Thiselton - 'are' "'not'" "seen", "'but'" "seen" "'through'", as "unconscious" *controlling* "frames of reference". "'Scaffolding'" 'convictions' – for the later Wittgenstein and for Thiselton - 'are' "foundational" 'for' subsequent 'inquiries', 'statements', "'and action'", and constitute the "'bedrock'" against which one's "'spade is turned'" (i.e. when searching for meaning in relation to, or for grounds for, subsequent 'inquiries', 'statements', "'and action'"). 'Outside' their 'tradition', "'scaffolding'" 'convictions' – for the later Wittgenstein and for Thiselton - lose their "'grammatical'" status of "showing" their 'tradition'. Thus, Thiselton endorses the later Wittgenstein's view that *'theology* [is] grammar' only *'within'* its 'tradition'.⁴³²

"'Scaffolding'" 'convictions' relate to Thiselton's discussions of *'public criteria of meaning'* and of 'paradigm cases' – where, for Thiselton, *'public criteria of meaning'* and 'paradigm cases' constitute the supporting "branches" that are preconditional for the 'intelligibility' and authentication of later 'language-*uses*' relative to given traditions.⁴³³ Thiselton notes that 'distinctive settings' for class-two utterances include "dialogic" 'argument' "presupposing" "'common'" "understandings", particularly 'theological' or 'ethical' 'argument'.⁴³⁴

For Thiselton, then, assertive language not only "shows" and not only, thereby, necessitates a modification of a Gadamerian notion of 'fusion', for Thiselton, assertive language also "shows" (or "allows" readers 'to *notice*') the *very 'pre-judgments' that 'Gadamer' himself 'insists' are operative initially – and indeed ongoingly to some extent - during the processes of "understanding"'*. Again, therefore, Thiselton argues (in effect) that Gadamer's disparagement of assertions or of 'statements of various kinds' detracted from *his own* (i.e. Gadamer's own) work on the hermeneutical circle.⁴³⁵

S.E. Porter, however, builds on his misunderstanding of Thiselton's 'class-

---

⁴³¹ Grech, 'R *2H*', 575. Grech is citing, Thiselton, *2H*, 414; cf. 361, 376-383, 77-78; cf. Thiselton, 'H-O', 8. First italics ours, second italics Thiselton's.

⁴³² Thiselton, *2H*, 396, 400-401, 392-395, 432, 418, 387. Italics Thiselton's.

⁴³³ Thiselton, *2H*, 392, 379-385, 434-438, 404-407; cf. Thiselton, 'LMR', 1127. Italics Thiselton's.

⁴³⁴ Thiselton, *2H*, 400, 389, 396-397, 399-401.

⁴³⁵ Thiselton, *2H*, 399, 326, 371, 139, 305, 306, 313. First italics Thiselton's, others ours.

one… utterances' in relation to this context of discussion.[436] Denying 'that every view of God qualifies as a second-class utterance', Porter views Thiselton's notion of 'class-two… utterances' as too 'culture-relative' 'and' as being – illegitimately – 'outside the parameters of investigation'.[437] Yet, we should observe that, for Thiselton, 'class-two… utterances' are not necessarily "relativized" just because they mediate "traditional" "'scaffolding'" 'convictions'. Porter also misconstrues Thiselton's thinking about "culture" and "tradition": in reality, Thiselton does not exalt "culture-relativity" to the exclusion of trans-contextual tradition in the way Porter suggests. Moreover, Porter confuses an utterance's "function" (cf. 'force') *'within* a… tradition' with its 'theological' 'truth-value' - a 'distinction' that Thiselton retains without descending into Bultmann's dualism. Indeed, as we have seen, for Thiselton, and according to the logic of self-involvement, an utterance's function – *regardless* of its level of *historically-qualified* "culture-relativity" - can *depend upon* its truth-value.[438] Furthermore, Thiselton does not immunize 'class-two… utterances' from criticism from outside their traditions in the way Porter suggests. Rather, for Thiselton, such utterances remain provisional and subject to correction.[439]

Porter also falsely argues that 'Thiselton equates' 'class-two… utterances' 'with… language-games'. However, for Thiselton, a 'class-two' "utterance" or a 'theological' or "traditional" 'conviction' may appear in *several* 'language-games'.[440] Nor, contradicting Porter, does Thiselton espouse the separateness or isolation of "'language-games'"; nor, contradicting Porter, does Thiselton "base" 'ethics' on 'class-two… utterances' thereby "relativized". Rather, Thiselton stresses *a posteriori* "'family resemblances'" or after-the-fact *'historical'* "'similarities'" between' 'traditions' and/or 'language-games', and for this, and for other, reasons *rejects* a 'socio-pragmatic' "basis for ethics" - though, admittedly, this latter point is clearer in Thiselton's later work.[441]

(iii) Moving on, then Thiselton's 'class-three' 'grammatical utterances' are 'linguistic recommendations' (i.e. for "redefining" 'certain *concepts*') that may alter "'scaffolding'" 'convictions' and that, therefore, may alter "traditions". For Thiselton, 'class-three' 'grammatical utterances' "show" *both* the process of alteration itself *and* the 'new' "recommended" 'way' of "seeing" 'things' where, for Thiselton, in this context of discussion, 'the predicate is not merely a tautology of the subject but its hermeneutical explanation' *and* "*redefinition*". The later

---

[436] Porter, 'CoU', 90-92, cf. 88-90; cf. Thiselton, *2H*, 397.

[437] Porter, 'CoU', 91-92; cf. Thiselton, *2H*, 397, 387-388.

[438] Thiselton, *2H*, 122-124, 397, 396, 392, 367. First italics Thiselton's, others ours.

[439] Porter, 'CoU', 92; cf. Thiselton, *2H*, 397, 392, cf. 393; cf. 405-406.

[440] Porter, 'CoU', 92; cf.: Thiselton, 'Parab', 453; Thiselton, *2H*, 397, 378, 396, 400-401, 435-436. Italics ours.

[441] Porter, 'CoU', 92; cf. Thiselton, *2H*, 134, 397, 396, 376, 414, 373-374; cf. 180; cf. later, Thiselton, *NH*, 401, 393-401, cf. 537-550. First and third italics ours, second italics Thiselton's.

*Hermeneutics and History* 355

Wittgenstein thus speaks of 'the use of *this* expression in connection with *these* criteria'. The utterance, "the *true* 'motorbike rider' *always* wears a crash-helmet" could be an example of a 'class-three' 'grammatical utterance' – or of a 'linguistic' "recommendation" - if it was uttered in a given context in which a different view of "motorbike riders" had been prevalent.[442]

Thiselton argues that 'class-three' 'grammatical utterances' 'often' presuppose extra-linguistic '"institutional facts"' and often cause "profound" but sometimes 'unnoticed' extra-linguistic effects on the '"ordering"' of 'life' and '"experience"'. Hence, with J. Searle, and contrary to 'A.J. Ayer', Thiselton argues that 'class-three' 'grammatical utterances' are 'not' just '"verbal"'. They also, Thiselton argues, presuppose and attack 'the power of linguistic' "habits" (cf. Thiselton's notions of 'pictures' and "spells") to "control" 'how' "things are" '"seen"' or "seen as" (see Chapter 3), where Thiselton argues that this 'power' is grounded in '"the"' interweaving '"of"' 'language-habits' '"and thought"'. In this context of discussion, Thiselton cites the later Wittgenstein's notion of a '"fly"' caught in a '"fly-bottle"'.[443]

Thiselton argues that it misses the point to look for 'formal' 'paradigms', "essential" '"*super*-concepts"', or for 'formal' *"ways" 'of'* '"seeing"' – whether 'in science' or in 'religion' – that are divorced from the history of 'paradigm-shifts' and from the 'linguistic recommendations' that 'paradigm-shifts' presuppose. Thiselton argues that even 'more true' – as opposed to "less true" - *"ways" 'of'* '"seeing"' are 'still' *"ways" 'of'* '"seeing"'. Thiselton argues that 'concepts' are "reformulated" as 'paradigms' "shift" - and also as 'language-games' "shift", as in the case of '"polymorphous concepts"'. Thus, in the context of biblical hermeneutics, Thiselton rejects Bultmann's and Jewett's attempts 'to suggest a unifying category which somehow binds together... varied uses of "flesh" into a single whole'.[444] Moreover, apparent "objectivity", in Thiselton's view, *may* be '"merely"' a matter of '"tracing round"' one's 'own' framework. Thiselton argues that "spells" may "perpetuate" "traditions", but that "spells" may also "perpetuate" 'confusion and ignorance'. Thiselton argues, citing the later Wittgenstein, that in the case of "spells" 'one thinks... one is tracing the outline of the thing's nature... and one is merely tracing round the frame through which we look at it'. Imposing order on Thiselton's thinking, we can detect four sub-categories within his view of 'linguistic recommendations', as follows.[445]

(iii.i) For Thiselton, 'linguistic recommendations' may *"break spells"* or "captivating pictures" and, in so doing, may '"show the fly the way out of the fly-bottle"'. For Thiselton, "spell-breaking" 'linguistic recommendations' engender

---

[442] Thiselton, *2H*, 406, 392, 396, 17-19, 399-407. Citing, Grech, 'R *2H*', 574; cf. quoting, Wittgenstein, *B&B*, 57. First italics Thiselton's; fifth and sixth italics Wittgenstein's; remaining italics ours.

[443] Thiselton, *2H*, 401-406, 432, 417-418; cf.: 137-139, 310-314; cf. Wittgenstein, *PI*, 103.

[444] Thiselton, *2H*, 361, 417, 402-411. Italics Thiselton's.

[445] Thiselton, *2H*, 404, 406-407, quoting, Wittgenstein, *PI*, 48e.

'new' "appraisal" and "insight" "'by'" "re-arranging" the "familiar" and by giving it 'new' "conceptual" 'grammar'. Thiselton argues that 'Paul' uses "spell-breaking" (cf. Thiselton's later use of the phrase, "'code-switching'") against "Corinthian" "'persuasive definition'" such that, in Thiselton's estimate, Paul modifies 'the audience's pre-understanding of what... [given] terms might mean' (cf. Thiselton's example in relation to 'the term "spiritual"'; see Chapter 3).[446] Thiselton also attempts "spell-breaking" in relation to "models" 'of biblical authority' and in relation to Paul's doctrine 'of justification' (see also Chapter 3 in relation to Thiselton's second period critique of the "spell" of Kierkegaard's approach to truth).[447] Heidegger's critique of "'the Western world'" is a parallel: for Heidegger, the West is under a "spell" such that 'everything... primordial gets glossed over'.[448]

For Thiselton, then, "spell-breaking" and 'the metacritical' 'epistemology' of 'socio-critical' 'liberation' are closely related. Meta-socio-critical 'liberation', however, involves the very aspect of the operation of 'distancing' and of 'fusion' that Thiselton - in his third period – will argue is under-developed in 'Gadamer's work'. (In this context of discussion, Thiselton will appeal to 'Habermas' only at a secondary level since, for Thiselton, secular socio-critical theory is *also* inadequate when it comes to the provision of metacriteria). Even in *The Two Horizons*, Thiselton in effect argues that since liberation involves a kind of coming to awareness that involves the processes of understanding and, therefore, involves the hermeneutical circle, then, again, in Thiselton's estimate, Gadamer's disparagement of assertions, or of 'statements of various kinds', detracts from *his own* (i.e. Gadamer's own) work on the hermeneutical circle.[449]

(iii.ii) Thiselton argues that 'linguistic recommendations' can *refine traditions* in a way that *both* preserves 'continuity' with a given 'tradition' 'against the background of' its 'institutional facts' *and* introduces a kind of "'novelty'" that is still "'positively related to'" that 'tradition'.[450] Thiselton's point, here, relates closely to Gadamer's notion of the 'new' "emerging" 'from the' dialogic 'process of' 'conversation' or "'of tradition'": for Gadamer, 'no one knows in advance what will "come out" of a conversation'.[451]

Thus, Thiselton argues, contrary to G.E. Moore, that 'public criteria' and 'paradigm cases' admit modification because, even as "'scaffolding'", they are 'still'

---

[446] Thiselton, 2H, 403-404, 406, 371, 386, 407; cf. Thiselton, 'TY', 1561; cf. McConville, J.G., 'Metaphor, Symbol and the Interpretation of Deuteronomy', in *After Pentecost: Language and Biblical Interpretation* (eds. C.G. Bartholomew, C. Greene and K. Möller; Scripture and Hermeneutics Series; Vol. 2; Carlisle: Paternoster, 2001), 333. Italics ours.
[447] Thiselton, 2H, 404, 432-434; cf. 415-422.
[448] Thiselton, 2H, 169-170, 330-335. Citing, Heidegger, BT, 165; cf. Heidegger, M., *An Introduction to Metaphysics* (New York: Yale University Press/Anchor Books, 1959), 1-61.
[449] Thiselton, 2H, 404, 326, 314, 307, 110-114; cf. Thiselton, NH, 381-385; cf. Gadamer, TM, 469, 298.
[450] Thiselton, 2H, 401-403, 81, cf. 405-406.
[451] Thiselton, 2H, 306, 309, 312-313; cf. Gadamer, TM, 367-388, quoting 383.

only "ways" 'of' "seeing". And yet, Thiselton argues that 'public criteria' and 'paradigm cases' should also be respected because they provide the 'rock-bottom' "currencies" of the *'grammar'* of terms. Thus, for example, Thiselton argues that Old Testament 'public criteria' and 'paradigm-cases' provide the 'rock-bottom' "currencies" of the *'grammar'* of genuinely "Christian" uses of the term "'redemption'". To disrespect 'public criteria' and 'paradigm cases' is, in Thiselton's view and in the later Wittgenstein's language, "'to saw off the branch on which I am sitting'".[452] Later, Thiselton argues that since 'such ways of seeing... function "as a [*non-idealist*, historical] *foundation* for research and action'", then 'American "non-foundationalism"... often mistakenly appeals to Wittgenstein'.[453] Notably, for Thiselton, the 'foundation reality' of the Christ-event is not merely "'symmetrical'" with subsequent moments in the hermeneutical process, least of all... [with] "the present situation'".[454]

Thiselton is not slipping into an absolute relativism of traditions here. Rather, Thiselton cites T.S. Kuhn and I. Barbour in relation to "scientific" 'paradigm-shifts' and 'Bultmann's work on' 'Paul's reappraisal of the terms "Jew", "son of Abraham", and "Jerusalem'" as examples of what he means.[455]

That is - and introducing an example of our own in order to explain Thiselton's thinking - then, *first*, since we have no absolute "objectivistic" access to the Christ-event that bypasses the interpretative process, then *what we have previously "seen as" the public criterion of the Christ-event will be modified* as histories of fusions gradually awaken us *towards an awareness of the fullness of the meaning of* the public criterion of the Christ-event. Further, *second*, as history unfolds, developing relationships between the Christ-event and new historical realities will actually *create* the fullness of the meaning of the Christ-event – not relativistically, but in convergence with "'eschatological'" "horizons" *'of promise'*.[456]

We have already said that, in Thiselton's estimate, the grammar of Gadamer's notion of 'fusion' is such that, for Gadamer, "statements" *obscure* 'the horizon of meaning'. Conversely, we have also already noted that, for Thiselton, the fact that assertive language *can "show"* 'the horizon of meaning' implies that the grammar of Gadamer's notion of 'fusion' requires modification. Now, though, we may add the point that, for Thiselton, assertive language also "shows" (or "allows" readers "'to notice'") the *very 'process' of tradition-refinement that is implicit in Gadamer's own notion 'of effective history'* in which 'temporal distance... performs [a] filtering process'. Thiselton argues that since tradition-refinement constitutes a socio-historical extension *of* the hermeneutical circle then, again, Gadamer's disparagement of

---

[452] Thiselton, *2H*, 379, 405, 401, 402, 406, cf. 437-438, cf. 382. Italics Thiselton's.

[453] Thiselton, 'S (pub)', 19. First italics ours, second italics Wittgenstein's (preserved by Thiselton).

[454] Watson, 'R *NH*', 254-255; citing, Thiselton, *NH*, 609; cf. 606.

[455] Thiselton, *2H*, 405-406, cf. 402-403.

[456] Thiselton, *2H*, 22, 419, 82; cf. Thiselton, 'Par', 49, 51. Final italics Thiselton's, remaining italics ours.

assertions, or of 'statements of various kinds', detracts from *his own* (i.e. Gadamer's own) work on the hermeneutical circle.[457]

(iii.iii) Thiselton argues that 'linguistic recommendations' can constitute 'manipulative' *'spell'-formation'* or '"persuasive definition"'. Thiselton notes that a 'term' 'with… favorable' (or unfavorable) connotations can be 'used' '"to carry a… different"' 'content' such that hearers are "seduced" 'into confusion and ignorance'. For Thiselton, the "spell-forming" procedure - of the 'manipulative' "re-definition" of "traditional" "terms" - "saws" '"off the"' supporting '"branch"' of public 'criteria' that gives these "terms" their observable and checkable meaning currency, and thereby in effect prohibits the critical testing of the contemporary uses of these same "terms", *such that* smuggled-in 'discontinuity' can thereby be passed-off as 'continuity'.[458]

Thus, for example, even though Bultmann's motivations were not at all manipulative in Thiselton's view, Thiselton still argues that Bultmann in effect carried out this same kind of "spell-forming" procedure. Thus, Thiselton attacks 'Bultmann's' rejection of 'Old Testament' 'criteria' (see above) because, in Thiselton's thinking, 'New Testament' terms, such as 'light, bread', or 'life', acquire their 'currency' 'from their Christological setting' and from their 'background of' 'Old Testament' 'institutional facts'.[459]

Thus, Thiselton's later positive valuation of '"illocutions"' grounded in 'institutional' 'facts' - as over and against 'self-assertive' "perlocutions" in which 'the self alone' 'acts' through 'causal' 'power' or through '"persuasive definition"' - hardly constitutes blindness to intra-"institutional" 'power-interests' (here we are contradicting Y. Dreyer's reading of Thiselton),[460] or even to the need to ethically evaluate public traditions themselves.[461] Thiselton merely distinguishes, say, the utterance, "I baptize", which presupposes the "institutional fact" of baptism, from, say, the utterance, "the resurrection is just an analogy for 'new life'", which subverts tradition by stealth. Dreyer confuses the metacriticism *of* traditions with criticism in relation *to* traditional criteria. And just because Thiselton espouses the latter in relation to *understanding*, it does not mean that he has neglected the former in relation to *epistemology* (see Chapter 3).[462]

For Thiselton, then, Gadamer's hermeneutical circle does not adequately

---

[457] Thiselton, *2H*, 406, 326, 371, 309, 307, 313; cf. Gadamer, *TM*, 469, 298. Italics ours.

[458] Thiselton, *2H*, 403-406, 37, 382, 379, cf. 437-438; cf. Thiselton, *1 Cor*, 804. Italics ours.

[459] Thiselton, *2H*, 382, 379, 405-406, cf.: 437-438; 285-287.

[460] Thiselton, *2H*, 406, 403; cf. Dreyer, Y., *The Institutionalization of Jesus' Charismatic Authority: 'Son of Man' as Case Study I* (Pretoria: Contributory PhD dissertation, Faculty of Theology, University of Pretoria; 2000), 13. Dreyer is citing, Thiselton, A.C., 'Christology in Luke, Speech-Act Theory, and the Problem of Dualism in Christology after Kant', in *Jesus of Nazareth. Lord and Christ* (eds. J.B. Green and M. Turner; Grand Rapids: Eerdmans; Carlisle: Paternoster Press, 1994), 463, 456.

[461] Thiselton, *NH*, 410-470; cf. Thiselton, *IGPS*, 137-144.

[462] Thiselton, *2H*, 402; cf. Thiselton, 'Christol', 461-463.

account for 'spell'-'formation' or for 'the capacity of' 'tradition' to 'distort truth'. Gadamer admits, 'I have emphasized the *assimilation* of what is past and of tradition'. Yet again, in Thiselton's estimate, Gadamer's disparagement of assertions, or of 'statements of various kinds', detracts from *his own* (i.e. Gadamer's own) work on the hermeneutical circle.[463]

(iii.iv) In our view, Thiselton's work in *The Two Horizons* implies that 'linguistic recommendations' can *'shatter' "worlds"* - though, admittedly, this link perhaps slightly extends Thiselton's thinking. The utterance, "his 'marital faithfulness' includes having affairs", can "break" a "'life-world'" and not just a 'spell'. As Thiselton observes then, for Heidegger, when a "world" 'is shattered', something's pre-cognitive 'ready-to-hand' "meaning" can suddenly be reduced to its 'present-at-hand' "properties". Thus, "the ring no longer means 'she loves me' - it is just a piece of metal". Citing Heidegger: 'circumspection comes up against emptiness'; '"we merely stare at something, our just-having-it-before-us lies before us *as a failure to understand it any more*"'.[464]

L. Langsdorf later questions 'Thiselton' in a way that relates to this context of discussion, asking, 'why would understanding the text as action... account' for 'its power to "mold and control" our lives?' Langsdorf complains, 'we can recognize... [a text's] appropriateness to a present situation and choose to adopt it, or not'. However, in our view, and with Thiselton, the utterance "your son/daughter has just been killed", with its "world-shattering" potential, undermines Langsdorf's point. Texts *can* have the "upper hand" over readers sometimes. As we argued earlier, Thiselton's notion of fusion involves all the self-involving variety of relationality between two horizons, and cannot be reduced to objectification *of*, or to reference *to*, variable speech-acts.[465]

Thus, 'Andrew Teele' writes of the "collapse" of the 'cult' of 'the Nine O'Clock Service' ('NOS') in 1980s-1990s Sheffield that, '"two worlds or realities"' "met" '"head-on, and as NOS reality met normality it simply collapsed"'.[466] R. Howard reports, 'NOS members' trauma was such that some people were hitting themselves against walls and mutilating themselves'.[467] "World-shattering", then, can be so "extra-linguistic" that it includes *physical or biological* "effects". Nevertheless, G.R. Osborne perhaps goes too far to write, 'Thiselton reasons that texts themselves control the process' of reading, 'some demanding a referential

---

[463] Thiselton, *2H*, 404, 37, 314; cf. Thiselton, *NTH*, xxii, concs. 1-1.2c; cf. Gadamer, *TM*, xxxvii, 469, 298. Italics ours.

[464] Thiselton, *2H*, 403, 345-347, 303, 404, 156, cf. 165; cf. Heidegger, *BT*, 105, 190. First and second italics ours, third italics Heidegger's.

[465] Langsdorf, L., 'Current Paths Toward an Objective Hermeneutic. Review-Article of R. Lundin's, A.C. Thiselton's and C. Walhout's *The Responsibility of Hermeneutics*', *CrThRev* 2 (Fall 1987), 152; cf. 154.

[466] Cited in, Howard, R., *The Rise and Fall of the Nine O'Clock Service. A Cult within the Church?* (London: Mowbray, 1996), 128, 5.

[467] Howard, *NOS*, 131.

interpretation, others a reader-oriented approach'. Rather, for Thiselton, 'textual' "particularity", interpretative 'goals', and *'reading-situations'* (along with other factors) *all* play a part in relation to the determination of reading "processes".[468]

"World-shattering", then, has a different 'grammar' to "spell-breaking". It is not so much "liberation" from a *false 'perspective'* as rude awakening to a *true 'perspective'* (as in the NOS case), or even to a new and unwelcome *true reality*. Sometimes the *world* changes, and at such times it is not just our 'convictions' that change. 'Linguistic recommendations' - as "world-shattering" utterances - involve unwelcome news that has a decidedly "extra-linguistic" functional 'grammar'. Again, Gadamer's notion of 'fusion' - in which 'the dimension of statements' falls short of 'linguistic experience' - is modified by Thiselton. In other words, the modification of Gadamer's hermeneutical circle that Thiselton brings to bear this time around relates to a better grounding for the functioning of (extra-)linguistic speech-acts, and for the operation of the extra-linguistic effects *of* (extra-)linguistic speech-acts, *during fusion*. Yet again, in Thiselton's estimate, Gadamer's disparagement of assertions, or of 'statements of various kinds', detracts from *his own* (i.e. Gadamer's own) work on the hermeneutical circle.[469]

Our reading of Thiselton's 'class-three… utterances' here contradicts that of S.E. Porter.[470] Porter argues as if, by the notion of 'linguistic recommendation', Thiselton only meant 'that one picture' (e.g. "a Jew is X") can 'simply' be "replaced" by 'another' (e.g. "a real Jew is Y") without regard for a picture's 'truth'-value in relation to traditional criteria. However, Porter thus misses the significance of Thiselton's comments on "scientific" and "religious" 'paradigm-shifts' in this context of discussion: for Thiselton, *more true* "pictures" *legitimately* 'replace' *less true* ones. Actually, Thiselton explodes Porter's reading of his work: Thiselton *attacks* '"persuasive definition"' *precisely because* '"persuasive definition"' *does* constitute 'misleading' violence against a 'tradition' (see above). The key distinction Porter misses in relation to Thiselton's thinking is the distinction between an "utterance's" 'grammatical' 'function' and an "utterance's" predicated 'content'.[471]

Porter, in criticism of Thiselton, also argues that whilst, for 'Paul', say, an 'utterance' could have "class-two status", it could have a "class-three status" for Paul's hearers. However, we should say in reply to Porter that, for Thiselton, the status of an "utterance" is not 'formal', but relates to its 'function' within a 'given' '"language-game"'. Porter again mistakenly ties Thiselton's thinking to the philosophy of the *early* Wittgenstein – a philosophy according to which 'a picture

---

[468] Thiselton, *2H*, 345; cf. Thiselton, *LLM*, 7; cf. Osborne, G.R., 'Review of A.C. Thiselton's *New Horizons in Hermeneutics*', *CRevBRel* 7 (1994), 92, 93; cf. Thiselton, *NH*, 49, cf. 557, 558. First and third italics ours, second italics Thiselton's.

[469] Thiselton, *2H*, 345, 396-404, 307; cf.: Thiselton, *LLM*, 7; Gadamer, *TM*, 469, 298. Italics ours.

[470] Thiselton, *2H*, 401; cf. Porter, 'CoU', 92-93.

[471] Porter, 'CoU', 92-93; cf. Thiselton, *2H*, 403-407, 392, 312, cf. 122-124. Italics ours.

is a fact'.⁴⁷²

(iv) Ironically, then, given Gadamer's 'undervaluing' of 'the range of logical functions that can be performed by statements of various kinds', Thiselton in effect argues that "grammatical utterances" (i.e. "grammatical" propositions or 'statements') "show" *strengths and weaknesses in Gadamer's own philosophy*. That is, for Thiselton, "grammatical utterances" "show": "broadened" "historical rationality"; 'pre-judgments'; 'socio-critical', "liberating", and/or "spell-breaking" "reformulations"; the "tradition-refinement" implicit in 'effective history'; 'manipulative' "spell-forming" 'perlocutionary' '"persuasive definition"' or 'propaganda' (though "spell-forming" can be well-intentioned, as in Bultmann's case); and that particular kind of "fusion" that is involved in rude-awakening through "world-shattering" news. That is, Thiselton appeals to the later Wittgenstein in order to *considerably modify Gadamer's hermeneutical circle*.⁴⁷³

We are now left with three further points in relation to Thiselton's appeal to the later Wittgenstein in this context of discussion – as follows.

Thus, (v), Porter asserts that 'Thiselton' later 'dismissed the central importance of... [the] formulation' of three 'classes of grammatical utterances' – supposedly in response to the 'several significant difficulties' pertaining to these utterance-classes that Porter claims to have exposed.⁴⁷⁴ However, the non-existence of these supposed 'difficulties' aside, what Thiselton actually "dismisses" in *The Two Horizons* itself is any "prescriptive" notion that the possible range of hermeneutical - or of grammatical - "functions" of "propositions" could supposedly be no wider than simply 'three classes of' 'grammatical utterances'.⁴⁷⁵

That is, speaking in "threes" can look "idealist" or conceptually 'formal', when in fact Thiselton argues against 'idealism' and against 'formal' approaches to concepts.⁴⁷⁶ Indeed, our explication of four 'types' of 'class-three... utterances' "shows" that *The Two Horizons* already heralds the collapse of the notion of a "triad" of 'utterance' 'types'. The 'three classes' are valid, but Thiselton acknowledges that there are many 'others'. For Thiselton, assertions 'function in' *many* 'ways that' can "show", 'that' can be "shown", and 'that' can be "noticed".⁴⁷⁷

(vi) Thiselton's continued use of 'favored' Continental 'terminology' (e.g. "fusion", "horizon", "language-event", etc.) carries with it 'grammatical' modifications that are consistent with tradition-refinement, not with '"persuasive definition"'. Gadamer's linguistic dualism, for example (see Chapter 4), *genuinely*

---

⁴⁷² Porter, 'CoU', 93; cf. Thiselton, *2H*, 361, 392, 373, 407-411, cf. 387-388. Citing, Wittgenstein, *Tr*, 10.

⁴⁷³ Thiselton, *2H*, 402-406, 313, 294, 65, 91, 305-307, 37, 287, 345; cf.: Thiselton, *NH*, 384, 385; Thiselton, 'TNT', 11; Thiselton, *1 Cor*, 804; Thiselton, 'Christol', 462. Italics ours.

⁴⁷⁴ Porter, 'CoU', 93, cf. 87.

⁴⁷⁵ Porter, 'CoU', 87; cf. Thiselton, 'SNTI', 76; cf. Thiselton, *2H*, 407, 386, 387.

⁴⁷⁶ Thiselton, *2H*, 302, 361, 387-388, 407-415.

⁴⁷⁷ Thiselton, *2H*, 407, 406, 139, 371.

*requires* modification.⁴⁷⁸ Had Thiselton further explicated his analysis of 'class-three… utterances', he may have seen the need to use "linguistic recommendations" in order to clearly mark these 'grammatical' modifications as "tradition-refinement" for his readers. As it is, he perhaps leaves himself open to the charge of '"persuasive definition"', even though this charge would be an *erroneous* charge.⁴⁷⁹

(vii) Having made this point, though, we may recall that we noted in Chapter 5 how several commentators fail even to perceive that Thiselton offers any transformed paradigm for hermeneutics at all. Thus, since R.L. Hubbard mistakenly views 'horizon' as 'Anthony Thiselton's metaphor', and since others, as already noted, mistakenly view Thiselton as merely "adopting" Gadamer's, Wittgenstein's, Fuchs's, or Ebeling's views, then we must question R.E. Palmer's use of the term 'explicitly' in his otherwise valid comment that 'Thiselton puts together so many things that needed to be explicitly related'.⁴⁸⁰

That is, Thiselton does not merely hold traditions in tension, but attempts a 'synthesis of insights from broadly different… traditions',⁴⁸¹ 'while avoiding their… pitfalls'.⁴⁸² For Thiselton, contrary to the linguistic dualism of Gadamer and of the New Hermeneutic, language-events can involve assertive language that "shows"; and, for Thiselton, contrary to Gadamer and to the New Hermeneutic, the '"linguisticality"' (see above) of "worlds" cannot presuppose a 'word-magic' that reverses the ontological priority of "history" over "language".⁴⁸³

(6) Moving on, then Thiselton also appeals to *the philosophy of language more broadly* – most notably to J.L. Austin and to D.D. Evans - in order to modify Gadamer's hermeneutical circle, particularly in relation to "fusion" – as follows.

Thus, (a), for Thiselton, with 'Gadamer', 'openness' 'to' *'textual activity'* involves '"placing… oneself"' into the "processes" 'of' "traditions" of textual 'effects' (cf. the later Heidegger's notion of *'Saying'*, and the later Wittgenstein's notion of '"showing"' - see above).⁴⁸⁴ We have noted this point before (see Chapter 5).

However, Thiselton's emphases on '"life"', 'tradition', inter-subjective 'communication', '"speech-acts"' (including divine 'speech-acts'), and on reader activity lead him to reject notions of "textual" 'autonomy' (i.e. notions that 'a text'

---

⁴⁷⁸ Trueman, C., 'Faith Seeking Understanding', in *Interpreting the Bible: Historical and Theological Studies in Honour of David F. Wright* (ed. A.N.S. Lane; Leicester: Apollos, 1997), 160; cf. Thiselton, *2H*, 406, 403, 195; cf. Gadamer, *TM*, 438-474.

⁴⁷⁹ Thiselton, *2H*, 406, 403.

⁴⁸⁰ Hubbard, R.L., 'Jai Alai, Hermeneutics, and Isaianic Peace', in *Conflict and Context. Hermeneutics in the Americas* (eds. M.L. Branson and C.R. Padilla; Grand Rapids: Eerdmans, 1986), 197; cf. Palmer, 'R *2H*', 174.

⁴⁸¹ Webster, 'R *2H*', 220.

⁴⁸² Walsh, 'TC', 235.

⁴⁸³ Thiselton, *2H*, 406, 347, 386-407, cf. 37, cf. 337; cf. Thiselton, 'NH', 311.

⁴⁸⁴ Thiselton, *2H*, 304, 306-307, 370-372; cf. Thiselton, *NH*, 33. First italics ours, second italics Thiselton's.

*Hermeneutics and History*

can *'act'* on its own). *Admittedly*, with Gadamer, Thiselton argues that 'texts' do still *'act'* on 'interpreters': for Thiselton, biblical texts may "draw" readers 'into' a textual 'world'; for Thiselton, interpretation 'cannot be reduced to mechanics';[485] and, for Thiselton, 'truth' may 'possess and remold the church'.[486] *And yet*, for Thiselton, 'fresh insights occur *within* reading traditions' (so R. Parry) in such a way that, as 'Thiselton' argues explicitly later, 'the "three metaphors"' 'of "behind", "within" and "in front of" the text', remain "inseparable" (so C.G. Bartholomew). Thiselton's later historically 'embedded' variant 'of... [the notion of] inter-textuality', coupled with his second-period employment of synchronous comparisons (see Chapter 5), implies that we could adopt a fourth "metaphor", "alongside the text" (e.g. two first-century texts could re-frame the same older text – say, the *Book of the Watchers* - differently) – a fourth "metaphor" that would *also* remain inseparable from the other '"three metaphors"' just noted.[487]

Hence Thiselton, potentially altering Gadamerian grammar, takes us more convincingly beyond a '"mimetic" world' of textual 'content' "projected" by "texts themselves" – and specifically beyond 'intra-linguistic' 'effects' associated with this 'world' – and into 'the life-world' of 'extra-linguistic' "speech-action" and *its* 'extra-linguistic' 'effects'. Thiselton's appeals to 'J.L. Austin' and to "D.D. Evans" are in 'the... background' here (see Chapter 4). Gadamer's remark, by contrast, that 'that which comes into language is not... pre-given before language' seems, perhaps, to be more ambiguous in this context of discussion.[488]

Notably, then, some writers rightly seem to deny that *any* notion of "textual" 'autonomy' can be found in Thiselton's thinking,[489] though others claim to find

---

[485] Traina, R., 'Inductive Bible Study Re-examined in the Light of Contemporary Hermeneutics', in *Interpreting God's Word for Today* (eds. W. McCown and J.E. Massey; Anderson, Ind.: Warner Press, 1982), 70-71; cf.: Thiselton, *2H*, 240, 306, 321-323, 293-300, 349, cf.: 234-240, 373; 304-326; 168; 129, 436-437; 335-352; Thiselton, *NH*, 32; First and third italics Thiselton's, second italics ours.

[486] Contradicting, Bloesch, D.G., *Holy Scripture: Revelation, Inspiration and Interpretation. Christian Foundations* (Downers Grove, Ill.: InterVarsity, 1994), 221; cf. Thiselton, *2H*, 436-437; cf. 323-326; cf. 348-350; cf. 401-407.

[487] Parry, R., 'Review of R. Lundin's, C. Walhout's and A.C. Thiselton's *The Promise of Hermeneutics*', *EuJTh* 9.2 (2000), 203; cf.: Bartholomew, 'Intro *AP*', xxxii; Thiselton, *2H*, 360, 312-313, cf. 322, 15, 117-120; Thiselton, 'BTT', 108; but cf.: Thiselton, A.C., 'On Models and Methods: A Conversation with Robert Morgan', in *The Bible in Three Dimensions: Essays in Celebration of Forty Years of Biblical Studies in the University of Sheffield* (eds. D.J.A. Clines, S.E. Fowl, and S.E. Porter; *JStudOT* Supplement Series 87; Sheffield: Sheffield Academic Press, 1990), 342; Thiselton, 'CAP', 202-203; Thiselton, A.C., 'Speaking and Hearing', in *Christian Faith and Practice in the Modern World* (eds. M.A. Noll and D.F. Wells; Grand Rapids: Eerdmans, 1988), 148. Second italics Parry's, others ours.

[488] Thiselton, *2H*, 436-437; cf. 337, 443; cf.: Thiselton, 'CAP', 201-203; Thiselton, *NH*, 16, 358, 360; Gadamer, *TM*, 306-307, 374-375, quoting 475. Italics ours.

[489] Watson, 'R *NH*', 254; cf. Thiselton, *2H*, 350, cf. 348-350.

such a notion in Thiselton.[490] Certainly, Thiselton does *not* reduce 'textual' 'performance' to 'the commissive realm', and does *not* reduce 'understanding' to 'locution' (here we are contradicting G.R. Osborne's reading of Thiselton).[491]

(b) Thiselton also espouses a *modified* Gadamerian grammar of *"actualization"*. For Thiselton, '"actualization"' is a process during which *historically-embedded* (not "autonomous") 'textual activity' (for example, "promising", "declaring", "convicting" etc.) "changes" "readers'" 'self-understanding' and their 'understanding' of textual 'subject-matter'. *Admittedly*, with Gadamer, Thiselton argues that truly 'new' "truth" "emerges" through 'conversation' with "texts", where 'both' 'reader' 'and' 'text' are "active" but 'not' '"in control"'. Citing Gadamer, 'a genuine conversation is never the one that we wanted to conduct'.[492]

And *admittedly*, with Gadamer, Thiselton argues that "readers" should exercise 'openness' to 'textual activity': citing Gadamer again, to '*question* is to open up possibilities and keep them open'. Having said this, of course, Thiselton argues that 'textual' 'forces' do not *necessarily* 'guide the reader to the text's "intended meaning"' or 'produce "intended" effects'. And so, in this respect, 'Thiselton' should not be placed 'firmly within the intentionalist camp'.[493] Thiselton's 'action-model' and his "adverbial" notion of 'intentionality' "rehabilitate" 'the author' whilst *avoiding* 'the old Cartesian… "…intentional fallacy"'.[494] Indeed, for Thiselton, aspects of 'present meaning' and/or of '"actualization"' could *never* have been foreseen by "authors".[495] Hence, Thiselton approves of 'Kierkegaard's' notion of 'understanding' as a '"repetition"' that is 'not' simply "repetition" and, similarly, Thiselton approves of Gadamer's point that 'fusion' 'can never' be complete, but 'is continually going on'.[496]

*And yet*, having said all this, Thiselton's emphasis on 'the logic of self-involvement' – in which 'effective' '"actualization"' in "broad" alignment with

---

[490] Vanhoozer, K.J., 'Review of R. Lundin's, C. Walhout's and A.C. Thiselton's *The Promise of Hermeneutics*', *ThT* 57.3 (Oct. 2000), 406; cf. Thiselton, *2H*, 168, cf. 436-437; cf. Thiselton, 'CAP', 154-156; cf. Osborne, 'R *NH*', 91-94.

[491] Thiselton, 'Words', 293-296; cf.: Thiselton, *NH*, 293; Osborne, 'R *NH*', 93.

[492] Thiselton, *2H*, 15, 309-314, 350, 342-352; cf.: Thiselton, *NH*, 11, 33; Thiselton, *LLM*, 18; Thiselton, 'Words', 296; Thiselton, 'Till', 98; Brodie, 'R *2H*', 482; contradicting, Longman III, 'Stor', 148; quoting, Gadamer, *TM*, 383. Italics ours.

[493] Gadamer, *TM*, 299; querying, Osborne, 'R *NH*', 91, 92; cf. Thiselton, *2H*, 15, 304, 12-17, 307-308; cf. Thiselton, 'EITN', e.g. 576; cf. Thiselton, A.C., 'Review of A. Kenny's *Wittgenstein*', *Chman* 90.1 (1976), 72; cf. later: Thiselton, *NH*, 33, 223, 267, 559-561. Second italics Gadamer's, remaining italics ours.

[494] Davies, M., 'Review of R. Lundin's, A.C. Thiselton's and C. Walhout's *The Responsibility of Hermeneutics*', *Th* 90 (Jan. 1987), 69; cf.: Thiselton, *2H*, 145, cf. 303, 436-437; Thiselton, 'EITN', 576; Thiselton, 'R *W*', 72; Dunn, J.D.G., 'What Makes a Good Exposition? The Expository Times Lecture, June 2002' *ExTim* 114.5 (Feb. 2003), 151; Thiselton, *NH*, 560, 559, 58-59. Italics ours.

[495] Thiselton, *2H*, 10, 307, 308-309; cf. Thiselton, *NH*, 11. Italics ours.

[496] Thiselton, *2H*, xix, 67-68, cf. 307-308, 317-318, 326; cf. Gadamer, *TM*, 306.

authorial 'purpose' "presupposes" the extra-linguistic "truth-value" of textual-linguistic 'reference' - again presupposes appeals to 'J.L. Austin' and to 'D.D. Evans' (see Chapter 4). '"Actualization"', for Thiselton, is not in *every* respect "comparable" to "involvement" in 'the performance of a... piece of artistic endeavor'. Reading the line, "there's a ship in trouble off Red Wharf Bay on Anglesey" in a novel is different to reading it in a current coast-guard's bulletin. Thiselton links '"actualization"' to 'extra-linguistic' "background" more firmly than Gadamer.[497]

Here, again, Thiselton's modification of Gadamer's thought cannot be identified as being simply 'Pannenbergian'. J.C. McHann Jr. notes how the early 'Pannenberg argues that the fusion of horizons is not... *produced by language*, but rather language is the result or "the expression of the fusion... accomplished by understanding"'.[498] However, appealing to Gadamer *and* to the philosophy of language, Thiselton refuses to sharply "separate" 'understanding and language' in this way. For Thiselton, 'fusion' only occurs when 'tradition' 'comes to speech' in the 'language' and 'concepts' 'of' "interpreters" (so Gadamer: in this respect 'the interpreter's own horizon is decisive, yet not as a personal standpoint that he maintains or enforces') even if, for Thiselton, 'language' remains part of a more fundamental "context" of inter-subjective historical 'action' (here Thiselton corrects Gadamer for whom 'man's relation to the world is absolutely and fundamentally verbal'). Thus, again, Thiselton alters Gadamerian grammar, but his 'critique' is hardly just 'Pannenbergian' where, here, we are correcting R.E. Palmer's reading of Thiselton.[499]

(c) Thiselton's view of *"appropriation"'* - according to which 'the community' or a "self" "changes" its 'relationship' *to* its 'new self-understanding' and *to* textual 'subject-matter' through 'self-involving' action - *admittedly* draws on Gadamer's and the later Wittgenstein's "concerns" for '"inner change"' and for outwardly "knowing" '"how to go on"':[500] for Gadamer, *'language games* exist where we, as learners... rise to the understanding of the world'; and, for the later Wittgenstein, 'an "inner process" stands in need of outward criteria'.[501] With Bultmann, Thiselton acknowledges that 'hermeneutics is "never *only* a matter of

---

[497] So, Kreitzer, L.J., and D.W. Rooke, 'Singing in a New Key: Philippians 2:9-11 and the 'Andante' of Beethoven's 'Kreutzer Sonata'', *ExTim* 109.8 (1998), 232; cf.: Thiselton, *2H*, 292, 123-124, 269, 386-407, cf.: 296-300, 353; Thiselton, 'NH', 311; Thiselton, *NH*, 11, 364; Thiselton, 'R-RH', 113; Thiselton, 'Parab', 464-465, 438-439. Italics ours.
[498] Correcting, Palmer, 'Scope', 226; cf. McHann Jr., *3H*, 321. Italics McHann Jr.'s.
[499] Thiselton, 'LMR', 1129-1130; cf.: Thiselton, *2H*, 137-139, 273-274, 310-326, 370-385; Gadamer, *TM*, 388, 475-476; Thiselton, *LLM*, 12, 20-21, after H.H. Price and V.H. Neufeld; Thiselton, 'Words', 294; Thiselton, 'Parab', 464-465, 438; Palmer, 'Scope', 226.
[500] Thiselton, *2H*, 287, 308, 309, cf. 314, 312, 324-326, 347-352, 370-372, 385; cf.: Thiselton, *LLM*, 20, 17, 30; Thiselton, 'Till', 98; Brodie, 'R 2H', 482; Thiselton, 'Parab', 452. First italics Thiselton's, remaining italics ours.
[501] Gadamer, *TM*, 490; cf. Wittgenstein, *PI*, 153e. Italics Gadamer's.

understanding [in the narrow sense of the term], but also of *hearing* and... *appropriation*'": for Bultmann and Thiselton, 'genuine obedience... includes a new understanding of oneself'.[502] Thiselton thus departs from 'modern hermeneutical approaches which isolate... reading... from the life of the communities that produce and read literature' (as M. Van Hamersveld rightly notes).[503]

*And yet*, to use J.C. McHann Jr.'s language (though to apply his point to Thiselton rather than to Pannenberg), Thiselton's "reversal" of Gadamer's 'ontological' prioritization of 'language' over 'history' (for Gadamer, 'the word gives' 'that which comes into language... its own determinateness')[504] firmly unites the "textual" '"world"' to the '"life-world"', '"behind"' the text', *and* to the '"life-world"' of 'appropriation'. Later, Thiselton explicitly links *'responsible'* 'recontextualization' (cf. 'appropriation') to *extra*-linguistic factors '"behind" the text' – including 'speech-acts'. Again, in this context of discussion, Thiselton invokes appeals to the philosophy of language.[505]

(d) Thiselton's view of *'application'*, in which "readers" "transform" 'the' wider 'world', is admittedly similar to the view of 'application' explicated in Gadamer's 'legal' examples in which 'a judge' 'has an orientation to his own history';[506] for Thiselton, 'application', like appropriation, is also closely linked to *'responsible'* 'recontextualization' – see above.[507]

Further, with Gadamer, Thiselton retains a 'tension', but not a sharp dichotomous categorical division, between 'past' 'meaning' and '"present meaning"'. With Gadamer, Thiselton *to an extent* agrees that there would be 'no such thing as... distinct horizons' were it not for 'temporal distance'. Thus B. Kallenburg, following D. Davidson, is mistaken to argue that the notion that the 'interpretative community... strives to embody [i.e. incarnate]... target language-games by conforming... to the underlying communal form of life' 'points us further' than Thiselton's thinking. Rather, Thiselton rightly notes that 'present' 'application' always remains *in 'tension' with* 'past' "forms of life".[508]

That is, for Thiselton, 'historical' or 'temporal distance' remains real, and Thiselton preserves the "distinction" between what a given 'text meant' at

---

[502] O'Brien, P.T., 'Principalities and Powers: Opponents of the Church', in *Biblical Interpretation and the Church. Text and Context* (ed. D.A. Carson; Carlisle: Paternoster, 1984), 115; citing, Thiselton, *2H*, 287, 277-281; cf. Bultmann, *TNT1*, 324. Italics Thiselton's.

[503] Van Hamersveld, M., 'Review of R. Lundin's, A.C. Thiselton's and C. Walhout's *The Responsibility of Hermeneutics*', *RefRev* 40.3 (Spr. 1987), 252, cf. Thiselton, *2H*, 324-326.

[504] E.g. McHann Jr., *3H*, 319; cf.: Thiselton, *2H*, 370-379, 379-385; Gadamer, *TM*, 475.

[505] Thiselton, *2H*, 347, 342-347, cf.: 350-351, 172, 176, 268-270, 287; 303; cf.: Thiselton, 'R-RH', 107-113; Thiselton, *NH*, 57. Second italics Thiselton's, remaining italics ours.

[506] Thiselton, *2H*, 308-309, cf. 58, 325, 376-377; cf.: Thiselton, 'R HFM', 232; Thiselton, A.C., 'Positive Role of Doubt', *CEN* 11 Jan. (1974), 8; Gadamer, *TM*, 328. Italics ours.

[507] Thiselton, 'R-RH', 110, 107-113. Italics Thiselton's.

[508] Gadamer, *TM*, 306; cf. Kallenberg, B., 'The Gospel Truth of Relativism', *SJT* 53.2 (2000), 192; cf. Thiselton, *2H*, 308, 124-126, 120, 58, 60. Italics ours.

different points in history and 'what it means *today*'. Whilst K. Duffy rightly notes that Thiselton later "criticizes" 'this distinction',[509] the apparent contradiction dissolves once it is realized that, in this later context of discussion, Thiselton is "criticizing" E.D. Hirsch's too 'clear-cut contrast between' '"past"... meaning' 'and "present" meaning' and his (i.e. Hirsch's) failure to explain 'the relation between' these aspects of meaning. Similarly, we may reject W.J. Larkin Jr.'s Hirschean attempt to argue for a 'clear' 'distinction' 'between' 'meaning and' present 'significance'. For Thiselton, '"past" and "present" meaning' are not separate *categories*, but "different" to one another only on account of the "continuous creation" 'of new' '"historical"' "relationships" (see our earlier discussion regarding 'significance' in the present chapter, and Chapter 7).[510]

That is, for Thiselton, '"past"... meaning' is a matter of 'semantic' and '"historical"' 'relationships' and "contexts", as is '"present" meaning'; it is just that, for Thiselton, these 'relationships' and "contexts" "develop" in the "processes of traditions".[511] Hence, Thiselton argues that a text's '"past"... meaning' "is prior to"' a text's '"present" meaning', but that 'meaning' still extends to "embrace" 'present' and 'future' 'horizons'.[512]

*And yet*, having said all this, Thiselton still modifies a Gadamerian grammar of 'application' in that Thiselton links 'application' to *divine* 'speech-acts'. Indeed, Thiselton also links divine 'speech-acts' to *'textual action'*, to '"actualization"', and to 'appropriation' – in part via appeals to Austin's and Evans' 'logic of self-involvement'. Thus, contradicting D.W. Hardy's reading of Thiselton, we should note that Thiselton does not sharply separate '"what God will do"' and 'the goodness of God', on the one hand, from the 'contingent historical' dimension of "transformation" or from '"what we will do"' on the other. Nor should Thiselton be contrasted with 'Moltmann' in this context of discussion (see Chapter 3).[513]

(7) We conclude that Thiselton substantially modifies Gadamer's hermeneutical circle. And yet, Thiselton's tradition-refinement of Gadamer's thought – and by implication his widening of philosophical and theological dialogue beyond that of the New Hermeneutic - is neglected in the literature.

---

[509] Duffy, K., 'The Ecclesial Hermeneutic of Raymond E. Brown', *HeyJ 39*.1 (Jan. 1998), 39; cf. Thiselton, *2H*, 57, 306, 117-118. Italics Thiselton's.

[510] Thiselton, 'R-RH', 109, 58, 175, 310, 312, 244, 248, 110, cf. 107-113; cf. Larkin Jr., W.J., *Culture and Biblical Hermeneutics. Interpreting and Applying the Authoritative Word in a Relativistic Age* (Grand Rapids: Baker, 1988), 311; cf. Hirsch Jr., E.D., 'Three Dimensions of Hermeneutics', *NLitHist* 3 (1972), 250. Italics ours.

[511] Thiselton, 'R-RH', 109; cf. Thiselton, *2H*, 119-121, 244, 127, 66, 306, 77-84, cf. 44-45.

[512] Thiselton, 'R-RH', 109; cf.: Thiselton, 'NH', 311; Thiselton, *2H*, 118-121, 307; Thiselton, 'UPC', 93-94.

[513] Thiselton, *2H*, 308, 287, 133, 292, 269; cf.: Thiselton, 'U (short)', 6; Thiselton, 'R-RH', 112; Thiselton, *NH*, 11; Thiselton, 'Parab', 464, 465; Hardy, D.W., 'Eschatology as a Challenge for Theology', in *The Future as God's Gift: Explorations in Christian Eschatology* (eds. D. Fergusson and M. Sarot; Edinburgh: T&T Clark, 2000), 152, cf. 157-158; Chapters 3, 4, and 5; third italics Thiselton's, others ours.

Thus, it is not simply the case that Thiselton's 'sympathies lie with the later… Wittgenstein… and… with… Gadamer'.[514] Nor is it true that 'Thiselton lets Gadamer down very lightly', as though Thiselton supposedly challenged only Gadamer's view 'of "effective history"'.[515] Thiselton is not simply "Gadamerian",[516] and his appeal to the later Wittgenstein is hardly "irrelevant" for 'biblical hermeneutics'.[517] Admittedly, one commentator observes that, 'Thiselton' has 'critiqued and adapted the "two-horizon" perspective', and another commentator observes that Thiselton has 'brought to light' the 'hermeneutical implications' of Wittgenstein's thought.[518] However, at best, commentators only seem to *hint* that Thiselton criticizes Gadamer's hermeneutical circle. Otherwise, comment in relation to Thiselton's multiform tradition-refinement of Gadamer's hermeneutics is *alarmingly absent from the literature*.

### 3. Thiselton's Transformed Paradigm as the Awaited Paradigm-Shift for Hermeneutics

But to what extent has Thiselton offered a transformed framework or paradigm for hermeneutics? Despite adding later caveats (see above), Thiselton broadly acknowledges the reality of predominant 'paradigms' and of 'paradigm-shifts' between them. But is F.H. Borsch really correct to suggest that Thiselton, by 1980, had "helped" 'accomplish' a 'hermeneutical' 'paradigm-shift'? Given that a correct appreciation of Thiselton's hermeneutical paradigm is (even today) nowhere to be found in the literature (including Borsch's review of *The Two Horizons*), then can we really trust such a remark?[519]

Well, certainly, (1), Thiselton – in his second period and later - contributes 'hermeneutical' "solutions"[520] – offering 'conceptual tools' that are new to the hermeneutical discussion,[521] and replacing 'philosophically illiterate' '"positivist"' and '"existentialist"' 'paradigms' associated with 'post-Enlightenment philosophies of history'[522] with a 'more solid status for historical knowledge'.[523] For Thiselton,

---

[514] Contradicting, Maddox, R.L., 'Review of A.C. Thiselton's *The Two Horizons*', *ThStud* 43.1 (Mar. 1982), 136.
[515] Contradicting, Packer, 'ISRH', 419; cf. Thiselton, *2H*, 307.
[516] Contradicting, Bartholomew, '3H', 125.
[517] Querying, Grech, 'R *2H*', 572; cf. 575-576.
[518] Van Engen, *M*, 44; cf. Conroy, 'R *2H*', 563.
[519] Borsch, 'R *2H*', 90; Thiselton, *2H*, 189, cf. 405-406; cf. Thiselton, *HD*, 145-173.
[520] McNicol, 'R *2H*', 188.
[521] Adam, 'R *NH*', 433.
[522] Bartholomew, 'UW' 4, 12; citing, Thiselton, 'CAP', 137; cf.: Thiselton, *NTH*, 123; Thiselton, *2H*, 245, 69-74, 74-84, 205-292.
[523] Palmer, 'R *2H*', 173.

*Hermeneutics and History* 369

in the words of T.C. Oden, 'the task of *historical studies* must now be reassessed',[524] and so Thiselton addresses 'the intricate... philosophical issues [that are] involved in an epistemology of historical knowledge'.[525]

Thus, for Thiselton, 'an ancient text should be read in [the] light of the philosophical problems emergent with the rise of historical consciousness'.[526] But, for Thiselton, even 'the rise of historical consciousness' is 'historical' in that it had, by the time of Thiselton's second period, become "entangled" with broadly 'positivist' and with broadly '"existentialist"' approaches – where, drawing on Pannenberg, Thiselton criticizes *both* E. Troeltsch and D.E. Nineham, *and*, Bultmann and the New Hermeneutic respectively.[527] Thus, Thiselton offers *a new larger critical synthesis or hermeneutical critique of history*, as argued above.

Moreover, (2), as already argued, Thiselton – by the conclusion of his second period of hermeneutical endeavor - in effect *employs* his new hermeneutical critique of history - extended eschatologically and Christologically - *to unify hermeneutics*, and thus conceives of *history as being ontologically prior to language* (see also Chapter 7).[528]

Not that Thiselton at all neglects 'the phenomenon of language', as we have seen.[529] But "history" is Thiselton's deepest philosophical focus,[530] and constitutes a more fundamental problem for Thiselton[531] than that of the issue of historical distance.[532] Thus, 'history is crucial to... [Thiselton's] topic'.[533] *The Two Horizons* 'is... an analytical discussion of the relationship of philosophy to hermeneutics with particular reference to how present knowing has to do with history and language'.[534]

Conversely, Thiselton argues that a linguistic or 'literary universe' cannot "unify" 'hermeneutics' (here we are contradicting P.J. Cahill).[535] Against M. Van

---

[524] Oden, T.C., 'So What Happens after Modernity?', in *The Challenge of Postmodernism. An Evangelical Engagement* (ed. D.S. Dockery; Grand Rapids, Mi.: Baker Books, 1997), 401. Italics Oden's.

[525] Martin, F., 'Review of J.B. Green and M. Turner eds. *Jesus of Nazareth: Lord and Christ*', *CBQ* 58 (Apr. 1996), 386; cf. Thiselton, *2H*, 74-84.

[526] Klemm, 'R *2H*', 116; cf. Thiselton, *2H*, 63-74.

[527] Klemm, 'R *2H*', 116; cf.: Thiselton, *2H*, 52, 84, 245, cf. 53-84, 245-251, 353; Thiselton, *NTH*, xxii, conc. 2.1, 2.1a.

[528] Snodgrass, K.R., 'Review of R. Lundin's, A.C. Thiselton's and C. Walhout's *The Responsibility of Hermeneutics*', *CovQ* 45 (Nov. 1987), 199-200; cf. Thiselton, *2H*, 74-84, cf. 370-379, 379-385. Our italics.

[529] Klein, 'R *2H*', 71.

[530] McNicol, 'R *2H*', 187-189; cf. Heyduck, R., *The Recovery of Doctrine in the Contemporary Church: An Essay in Philosophical Ecclesiology* (Waco, Texas: Baylor University Press, 2002), 47; cf. Thiselton, *2H*, 64.

[531] Thiselton, *2H*, 74-84, cf. 370-379, 379-385.

[532] Dockery, 'R *2H*', 133; but cf. Thiselton, *2H*, 66-67, 74-84.

[533] Van Voorst, 'R *2H*', 220.

[534] Borsch, 'R *2H*', 88.

[535] Contradicting, Cahill, 'R *2H*', 485; cf. Thiselton, *2H*, 370-379, 379-385.

Hamersveld's reading of Thiselton, we have concluded that 'hermeneutics' is not 'part of the larger field of literary criticism' for Thiselton; rather, the reverse is the case for Thiselton.[536] Indeed, Thiselton, in effect, *denies* that "all" historical 'experience' can be mediated *only* through language. The erroneous assumption that "all" historical 'experience' can be mediated only through language forced R. Hannaford, at the 2002 conference of the Society for the Study of Theology held at Lancaster University, England, to argue that to properly *"declare"* 'eschatological' "promises" was to actually *"experience"* their 'fulfillment'. However, in Thiselton's estimate, *linguistic* promises are effective only through *historical* promise-fulfillment: not even *God* fulfils a promise merely by making it.[537]

(3) As already argued, Thiselton, by appeal to the later Wittgenstein and others, *further* modifies a *predominantly* (but not exclusively) Gadamerian paradigm that the early Pannenberg had already *begun* to modify. Indeed, we might even argue that Thiselton doesn't so much build on Pannenberg's early work in this respect, but rather that Thiselton *restarts* it *with revisions.*

Admittedly, Pannenberg also dialogues with the later Wittgenstein in *Theology and the Philosophy of Science* (German: 1973). However, reference to this work is absent from *The Two Horizons*, suggesting that Thiselton had read the later Wittgenstein independently.[538] Indeed, *Theology and the Philosophy of Science* did not appear in English until 1976, the year *The Two Horizons* was largely completed. Whilst Thiselton could read German before 1976, he may have preferred to use English texts.[539] In any case, Thiselton writes: 'from 1963 I had become increasingly familiar with the work of Wittgenstein and J.L. Austin'. Thus, Thiselton's main appeals to the later Wittgenstein pre-date, and are independent of, those of Pannenberg (as J.C. McHann Jr. seems to imply).[540]

Thus, could Thiselton's transformed hermeneutical paradigm constitute the first truly 'post-Gadamerian', "post-later-Wittgensteinian" theological hermeneutic? Did Thiselton *revise or restart* Pannenberg's initiative by including appeals to the later-Wittgenstein so as to anticipate - by twenty-five years - C.G. Bartholomew's call for a replacement of 'outworn paradigms' or of "philosophical subtexts" in hermeneutics?[541] It would seem that the answer to both these questions is "yes".

---

[536] Contradicting, Van Hamersveld, 'R RH', 252.

[537] Hannaford, R., 'The Knowledge of Things Hoped For: Towards an Eschatology of Knowledge' (unpublished paper presented to the 2002 Conference of the Society of the Study of Theology at Lancaster University), 1, cf. 15. Italics ours.

[538] Conroy, 'R 2H', 563; cf.: Thiselton, NH, 331-338; Pannenberg, W., *Theology and The Philosophy of Science* (Philadelphia: Westminster Press, and London: Darton, Longman & Todd, 1976).

[539] Thiselton, NH, 331; cf. Thiselton, NTH, title page; cf. Thiselton, 'TY', 1560.

[540] See Chapter 1; cf.: Thiselton, 'TY', 1560; McHann Jr., 3H, 294-295.

[541] Thiselton, NH, 13; cf.: Bartholomew, 'UW', 4, 12; Thiselton, 2H, 74-84; Thiselton, 'CAP', 137; Thiselton, 'BTT', 107.

(4) That Thiselton's work signals the end of Gadamer's and the later Wittgenstein's mutual waiting for one another is a point that emerges unexpectedly when we allow Gadamer and the later Wittgenstein to respond to Thiselton's use of their work – as follows.

Thus, (a), beginning with Gadamer's work, *Truth and Method*, we find that, for Gadamer, 'subjectivity is a distorting mirror', and that, for Gadamer, 'the' "individual's" *'judgments'* and 'self-awareness… [are] only a flickering in the closed circuits of historical life'. Conversely, for Gadamer, *'prejudices'* primarily *'constitute the historical reality of his* [i.e. of an individual's] *being'*.[542] Earlier, we cited Thiselton's criticism that Gadamer was too reductionistic here: Thiselton views Gadamer's work as 'pointing towards a postmodern view of selfhood' 'as an opaque product of variable roles and performances… imposed… by… society and [of]… inner drives or conflicts'.[543]

H.H. Kögler, similarly, implicitly opposes Gadamer and Derrida because, in Kögler's view, these thinkers subsume the 'critical' 'reflexive subjectivity' of 'individual agents' beneath their [i.e. Gadamer's and Derrida's] criticisms of the 'untenable philosophy of consciousness' 'of… Western… metaphysics'. Kögler argues that, for these thinkers, "pervasive" 'trans-subjective background' 'structures' or 'forces' (i.e. 'being, language, dialogic event, *différance*, force fields of power' etc.) are "hypostatized" or "reified" 'into macrosubjects' "operating" 'independently of agency'. However, Kögler argues that these thinkers therein overlook their 'own… high level of reflexivity': for Kögler, 'transsubjective forces are… reproduced only through individual interactions'.[544]

Are Thiselton and Kögler fair to Gadamer here, though? Some observations in relation to Gadamer's thinking are helpful for our answering of this question - as follows.

*First*, following Heidegger, Gadamer argues that 'Dasein' and 'understanding' are only 'possible' because 'there is a "there", a clearing in being… between being and beings' called 'nothingness'. For Gadamer, '"nothing… is the veil of being"' and calls 'attention to' the 'being' or 'contingency of… beings', to 'their' 'possibility of… not being', and hence to '"the marvel of all marvels, that beings are"'. Further, for Gadamer, 'being' is also 'historic' in that it is "preconditional" for 'the possibility of the history of thought': for Gadamer, 'being' repeatedly 'clears out the underbrush of thinking… to make itself clear to thought'. Gadamer, then, against the background of 'being' and 'nothingness', admits the reality of

---

[542] Gadamer, *TM*, 276-277. Italics in speech-marks Gadamer's.

[543] Thiselton, 'TY', 1565; cf.: Thiselton, *2H*, 305; Thiselton, *IGPS*, 121. Thiselton's self-criticism in, Thiselton, 'TY', 1565, is too harsh. Whilst he did not explicitly point to Gadamer's reductionism regarding human selves in *2H*, his own considerable focus on selves in *2H* was at odds with what he had expounded as being Gadamer's perspective.

[544] Kögler, H.H., *The Power of Dialogue: Critical Hermeneutics after Gadamer and Foucault* (MIT Press: London, 1996), 271. Italics Kögler's.

"contingent" 'beings'.[545]

*Second*, for Gadamer, 'continuity' (common to all Daseins) includes 'self-understanding' and 'an experience... Heidegger calls *being* 'that transcends thinking' and 'subjectivism', that is "experienced" 'as limiting', and that frames dynamic 'human existence'. And yet, for Gadamer, this 'experience' neither eradicates 'the discontinuity intrinsic to aesthetic being and... experience', 'nor' heralds 'the extinction of one's self'. Gadamer thus *preserves* 'the discontinuity' of the 'aesthetic being and... experience' of *'the individual'* 'self'.[546]

*Third*, after Heidegger, Gadamer views 'understanding' as Dasein's 'mode of being'.[547] 'Understanding', for Gadamer, presupposes Dasein's 'fore-structure' of 'existential futurality',[548] and/or of 'potentiality-for-being and "possibility"',[549] and includes both '"thrownness"' and 'projection'[550] - though Gadamer admits "emphasizing" 'the assimilation of what is past and of tradition'.[551] Thus, for Gadamer, 'the concrete bonds of custom and tradition and the corresponding possibilities of one's own future become effective in understanding'.[552] "Projection", though, for Gadamer, involves 'transcendence... moving beyond the existent'. 'Thus', Gadamer argues that 'a person who understands, understands himself... projecting himself upon his possibilities'. That is, Gadamer preserves the 'projection' of the individual's future "possibilities" during 'understanding'. In Gadamer's thinking, these "possibilities" presuppose, yet also *"transcend"*, past 'tradition'.[553]

*Fourth*, for Gadamer, 'a hermeneutically trained consciousness' remains 'sensitive to... [a] text's alterity' through 'the foregrounding and appropriation of one's own fore-meanings and prejudices.... so that the text can present itself in all its otherness'.[554] Thus, Gadamer argues that 'historical knowledge... remains... adapted to the object', precluding '"homogeneity"'.[555] Yet, Gadamer also argues that 'both' 'the knower and the known' 'have the *mode of being of historicity*'; and for Gadamer, 'belonging to traditions belongs... to the historical finitude of

---

[545] Gadamer, *TM*, 257; cf. Robinson, J.M., 'The German Discussion of the Later Heidegger', in *New Frontiers in Theology. Discussions among Continental and American Theologians, Volume I: The Later Heidegger and Theology. A Dialogue on Important New Trends in Religious Thought Based on the Latest Works of Martin Heidegger* (eds. J.M. Robinson and J.B. Cobb, Jr.; New York: Harper and Row, 1964), 11 cf. 19 cf. 26.

[546] Gadamer, *TM*, 96, cf. 99-100, 269, 276. Second and fourth italics Gadamer's, others ours.

[547] Gadamer, *TM*, xxx.

[548] Gadamer, *TM*, 261.

[549] Gadamer, *TM*, 259.

[550] Gadamer, *TM*, 262.

[551] Gadamer, *TM*, xxxvii.

[552] Gadamer, *TM*, 264.

[553] Gadamer, *TM*, 260, 262, 259, 261, 264. Italics ours.

[554] Gadamer, *TM*, 269.

[555] Gadamer, *TM*, 261, cf. 262.

Dasein'.[556] Thus, Gadamer speaks of 'the interpreter's belonging to his object'.[557] Hence, for Gadamer, 'history does not belong to us; we belong to it'. Gadamer argues that 'self-reflection and autobiography... are not primary and are therefore not an adequate basis for the hermeneutical problem, because through them history is made private once more'. That is, Gadamer preserves heterogeneity, 'otherness', or 'alterity', even if he also "de-centers" 'self-reflection and autobiography'.[558]

Summarizing: Gadamer preserves 'individual' 'subjectivity' against the background of 'beings' (as opposed to 'being'), 'discontinuity' (as opposed to Daseins' "continuities"), "projected" 'possibilities' (as opposed to "'thrownness'"), and 'otherness' (as opposed to 'belonging'). And yet, Gadamer also de-prioritizes 'self-reflection and autobiography'. Does this analysis of a small part of Gadamer's thinking justify Thiselton's concerns about Gadamer making a move 'towards a postmodern' "self"? We may make three points in reply.[559]

*First*, Thiselton's *retention* of Gadamer's emphases on dialogue and on "'historical'" "'otherness'" seems to contradict his fears in relation to what he sees as being Gadamer's move 'towards a postmodern' "self". Admittedly, Gadamer remarks that 'what remains important is... that a self can be formed without breaking with or repudiating one's past'. And admittedly, with Thiselton, we should acknowledge those comments by Gadamer that we noted above: for Gadamer, 'subjectivity is a distorting mirror'; for Gadamer, 'the' "individual's" *'judgments'* and 'self-awareness... [are] only a flickering in the closed circuits of historical life'; and, for Gadamer, *'prejudices'* primarily *'constitute the historical reality of his* [i.e. of an individual's] *being'*. And yet, whilst Gadamer certainly seems to threaten notions of the individuality of the "'historical'" 'self' when he makes such remarks, his other emphases – i.e. on 'beings', 'discontinuity', "projected" 'possibilities' that "transcend" 'tradition' and that "transcend" "'thrownness'", and on 'otherness' - need to be held in tension with such remarks, as indeed Thiselton already does in relation to Gadamer's emphasis on 'otherness'. Moreover, it is *transcendental* subjectivity as an "idealist" metaphysical foundation – rather than *historical* notions of subjectivity - that Gadamer *most* firmly rejects.[560]

*Second*, nevertheless, defending Thiselton, individuality or 'private' 'autobiography' are "de-centered" *to an extent* for Gadamer. D.J. Schmidt observes 'the extraordinary reticence... with which Gadamer reveals himself to his readers', and in this connection cites Francis Bacon's 'motto', "*'de nobis ipsis silemus'*" ("of

---

[556] Gadamer, *TM*, 261, cf. 262. Italics Gadamer's.
[557] Gadamer, *TM*, 264.
[558] Gadamer, *TM*, 276, 269; cf. Thiselton, *IGPS*, 121.
[559] Gadamer, *TM*, 276, 100, 257, 96, 262, 260, 269; cf. Thiselton, 'TY', 1565.
[560] Weinsheimer, J., and D.G. Marshall, 'Translators' Preface', in *Truth and Method* (H.-G. Gadamer; London: Sheed and Ward, 1975, 1989), xii; cf. Thiselton, *2H*, 309; cf. Thiselton, 'TY', 1564, 1565; cf. Gadamer, *TM*, 99, 276-277; cf. 100, 257, 96, 259-262, 269, 264. Italics in speech-marks are Gadamer's, others are ours.

ourselves we remain silent")'.[561] Thus, there is indeed a tension in Gadamer between wanting to preserve individuality whilst simultaneously de-prioritizing 'self-reflection and autobiography'. Nevertheless, one cannot *entirely* discount Gadamer's conscious contribution to J. Grondin's biography of his life – despite Gadamer's numerous 'reservations' concerning the project![562]

*Third*, our own earlier emphasis on the complexity of historical conditioning in relation to immediate fallen relationships and in relation to immediate fallen human physicality perhaps reinstates "autobiography" (and biography) more than *both* Gadamer *and* Thiselton *without* losing sight of trans-contextual or trans-temporal factors. Admittedly, Thiselton later *affirms* the focus on personal and communal 'narrative-experience' in '*socio-pragmatic* hermeneutics' whilst still repudiating the lack of a 'metacritical dimension' in such approaches. Our emphasis was slightly different to this, however, in that we in effect argued for a reinstating of "autobiography" (and of biography) at the level of *a more complex theory of historical conditioning*. (Afterall, Francis Bacon's 'corruption', rather than any *solely* philosophical consideration, may have been one reason for his aforementioned silence!) We acknowledged, though, that Thiselton had certainly *begun* to move in the right direction in this respect.[563]

We may suspend further comment at this point until we have allowed the later Wittgenstein to reply to Thiselton – as follows.

Thus, (b), with Thiselton, we must agree that trans-contextual and trans-temporal categories are certainly present in the later Wittgenstein's work. Such categories, as we have seen, include (amongst others), 'the common behavior of mankind',[564] "forms of life",[565] "'family resemblances'",[566] "concepts with blurred edges", "'scaffolding'" 'convictions' and,[567] 'public criteria of meaning'.[568] We must therefore *approve* of Thiselton's rejection of any "neo-pragmatic" 'open' or

---

[561] Schmidt, D.J., 'Gadamer', in *A Companion to Continental Philosophy* (eds. S. Critchley and W.R. Schroeder; Blackwell Companions to Philosophy Series; Oxford: Blackwell Publishers Ltd., 1998), 434; cf. Gadamer, *TM*, 276; cf. Thiselton, *IGPS*, 121. Italics in speech-marks Schmidt's, others ours.

[562] Grondin, J., *Hans-Georg Gadamer: A Biography* (trans. J. Weinsheimer; New Haven and London: Yale University Press, 2003), ix; cf. Gadamer, *TM*, 276.

[563] Thiselton, *NH*, 462, 420, 440, 439; cf. 430-439; cf. Stokes, P., *Philosophy. 100 Essential Thinkers* (Leicester: Arcturus Publishing Limited, 2002), 64. Italics in speech-marks Thiselton's, others ours.

[564] Wittgenstein, *PI*, 82e.

[565] Wittgenstein, *PI*, 8e, 11e, 88e, 174e, 226e; cf. Wittgenstein, *OC*, 46e.

[566] Wittgenstein, *PI*, 32e, cf. 36e, 46e, 66e, 71e-73e; cf.: Wittgenstein, *R2*, 97e, 98e; Wittgenstein, *Z*, 5, 111; Wittgenstein, *B&B*, 17, 20, 33, 88, 98, 115, 117, 119, 125, 145, 152.

[567] Wittgenstein, *Z*, 67, 63; cf.: Wittgenstein, *OC*, 29e; Wittgenstein, *R2*, 107e; Wittgenstein, *PI*, 34e, 36e; Thiselton, *2H*, 396.

[568] Thiselton, *2H*, 39, 379-385; cf. Wittgenstein, *PI*, 38e-40e, 84e-120e.

'therapeutic' readings 'of the later Wittgenstein' that neglect such categories.[569]

Nevertheless, two sets of considerations suggest that Thiselton *slightly* over-extends the 'transcontextual' or trans-temporal side of the later Wittgenstein's thinking, as follows.[570]

*First*, the later Wittgenstein's epistemological observations focus mainly but not exclusively on present horizons. Thus, the later Wittgenstein writes that a 'figure can always *be* what I see it as'.[571] Or, the later Wittgenstein writes, 'don't say: "There *must* be something common, or they would not be called 'games'" - but *look and see*'.[572] Or, for the later Wittgenstein, 'metaphysical truths… are' just 'rules for the use of words',[573] so the later Wittgenstein argues that we should 'bring words back from their metaphysical to their everyday use'.[574]

Or, elsewhere, the later Wittgenstein argues that 'there' is 'no philosophical knowledge',[575] since 'problems attach to the words "to know"':[576] for the later Wittgenstein, 'the grammar of the word "knows" is… related to that of "can", "is able to"… "understands". ("Mastery" of a technique)'.[577] Thus, for the later Wittgenstein, 'one cannot guess how a word functions. One has to *look at* its use', though this is made "difficult" by 'the prejudice which stands in the way'.[578] Thus, the later Wittgenstein argues that "philosophy's" 'task… is conceptual clarification' and that "philosophy's" 'goal… is not knowledge but understanding'.[579]

Or, the later Wittgenstein argues that 'language' is not 'chained to the world of objects' but 'autonomous - it runs free'.[580] Thus, for the later Wittgenstein, 'philosophical questions… are' not 'problems' related to "Russell's" 'hidden logic' but 'puzzles' concerning 'how language is actually employed'.[581] We could go on.

That is, in other words, for the later Wittgenstein, 'strenuous' "puzzle"-solving can *'look and see'* or *'notice'* what is "shown" by *everyday immediate historically particular*

---

[569] Thiselton, *NH*, 329, 395-405; cf.: Thiselton, A.C., 'Review of P. Van Buren's *Theological Explorations*', *Chman* 83.3 (1969), 221; Fowl, S.E., 'The Role of Authorial Intention in the Theological Interpretation of Scripture', in *Between Two Horizons. Spanning New Testament Studies and Systematic Theology* (eds. J.B. Green and M. Turner; Cambridge: Eerdmans, 2000), 76, n.10.

[570] Thiselton, *NH*, 396.

[571] Wittgenstein, *R2*, 69e. Italics in speech-marks Wittgenstein's.

[572] Wittgenstein, *PI*, 31e. Italics Wittgenstein's.

[573] Hacker, P.M.S., 'Wittgenstein, Ludwig Joseph Johann', in *The Oxford Companion to Philosophy* (ed. T. Honderich; Oxford: OUP, 1995), 914.

[574] Wittgenstein, *PI*, 48e.

[575] Hacker, 'W', 915.

[576] Wittgenstein, *PI*, 15e.

[577] Wittgenstein, *PI*, 59e.

[578] Wittgenstein, *PI*, 109e. Italics Wittgenstein's.

[579] Hacker, 'W', 916.

[580] Edmonds and Eidinow, *WP*, 181.

[581] Edmonds and Eidinow, *WP*, 183.

*concrete language-uses* so long as "looking and seeing" and "noticing" address the problem of 'the prejudice' of '"seeing... as"'. Admittedly, here, there are hints of trans-contextuality and trans-temporality in the later Wittgenstein's uses of the terms "rules", 'technique', and 'prejudice'. But what about accessing, knowing, or understanding that which is *historically "past"*, or *historically "continuous"*, through *"report"?*[582]

*Second*, for the later Wittgenstein (as for Thiselton), Vienna-style 'metaphysical' '"problems"' are misleading. Primarily, for the later Wittgenstein (if less so for Thiselton) the 'puzzles' of immediate linguistic "confusions" are what matter. Karl Popper, however, likened the later Wittgenstein's 'interest in language to... cleaning spectacles' where, for Popper, and for other 'serious philosophers... the only point of... cleaning is to... see the world' better.[583] Bertrand Russell similarly 'dismissed' the 'view that... philosophical worries were merely puzzles': for Russell, '"we are... not"' "trying" '"to understand... only sentences"' but '"the world"'.[584] Citing the later Wittgenstein, though, and by contrast, our 'puzzlement' is, for example, supposedly about 'the use of the substantive "time"', 'not' about 'the nature of time'. For the later Wittgenstein, therefore, the 'facts about time' 'that concern us lie open before us'.[585]

For Thiselton, however, by contrast, there *are* '"serious philosophical problems"', '"not mere puzzles"', though *not in the sense meant by Popper and Russell*. For Thiselton, allowing "God's word" to '"strike home"' 'today' is a *"serious philosophical problem"* and 'not only a theological' issue.[586] Again, though, having said this, we should note that Thiselton's later 'historical' "dialectic" 'between' "contextually" 'contingent life-world' and "developing" 'metacritical' 'system' *attacks* 'positivism'.[587] Thus, whilst affirming 'Popper's' emphases on '"critical thought"', '"openness"' to' "revising" 'hypotheses', 'testing', and filtering out '"unwarranted"' 'metaphysical... assumptions', Thiselton approves of Pannenberg's appeal to T.S. Kuhn in criticism of Popper: for Kuhn, Pannenberg and Thiselton, 'theories' or 'hypotheses' involve '"anticipatory"' 'conjecture', and remain in 'dialogue with' other competing 'systems', 'contexts and bodies of knowledge'. For Kuhn, Pannenberg and Thiselton 'theories' or 'hypotheses' are not '"mirrors" of nature' but 'explanatory devices' that remain "distanced" from "the truth" of 'life-world'. That is, *Thiselton's "serious philosophy" is not "logical-positivist", but properly 'historical'*.[588]

---

[582] Thiselton, *2H*, 138, 139, 399, 417; cf. Edmonds and Eidinow, *WP*, 183; cf. Wittgenstein, *PI*, 31e, 109e, 80e, 59e. First italics Wittgenstein's, second italics Thiselton's, remaining italics ours.

[583] Edmonds and Eidinow, *WP*, 186, 183, 182; cf. Wittgenstein, *PI*, 48e.

[584] Edmonds and Eidinow, *WP*, 188.

[585] Wittgenstein, *B&B*, 6.

[586] Edmonds and Eidinow, *WP*, 186; cf. Thiselton, *2H*, xx, 342. Italics ours.

[587] Thiselton, *NH*, 401, 66, 334, cf. 25. Italics ours.

[588] Thiselton, *NH*, 334, 25, 401; cf. Thiselton, *2H*, 175. Italics ours.

*Hermeneutics and History* 377

In other words, the later Wittgenstein *opposes* Popper's "positivist" "seriousness", but would he *approve* of Thiselton's 'historical' "seriousness"? Admittedly, the later Wittgenstein is hardly disinterested in 'history'. He writes, 'perhaps one day this civilization will produce a culture. When that happens there will be a real history of the discoveries of the 18th, 19th and 20th Centuries, which will be deeply interesting'. The later Wittgenstein realizes that the recent war-time brutality and prevailing philosophical a-historicity of his own cultural context is not so conducive for the writing of 'real history'.[589]

However, the later Wittgenstein also believes that the Gospel 'should' only 'be... averagely historically plausible'. The Gospel's historicity, in the later Wittgenstein's estimate, is 'not... the essential, decisive thing' and 'should not be believed more strongly than is proper' 'because' this 'might distract attention from what matters', which is 'the *spirit*'.[590] The later Wittgenstein argues that even if 'the Gospels' were 'historically speaking... demonstrably false... belief would lose nothing... because historical proof... is irrelevant to belief'. For the later Wittgenstein, the 'believer's relation to' the Gospel 'is *neither* the relation to historical truth (probability), *nor yet* that to a theory consisting of "truths of reason"'.[591]

That is, the later Wittgenstein still suffers – at least to some extent - from the historically and epistemologically "dualistic" legacy of 'Neo-Kantianism' that Thiselton challenges in relation to 'Bultmann's' "value-versus-fact" and "*Geschichte* versus *Historie*" "dichotomies". And yet hasn't Thiselton appealed to the later Wittgenstein to oppose the very same "dichotomies"?[592]

Admittedly, the later Wittgenstein's emphases *both* on "historical contingency" *and* on "transcontextual" continuity leave an opening for Thiselton's approach. And yet, the later Wittgenstein fails to work out the *full historico-epistemological entailments of* his own trans-contextual categories and newer *non-dualist* emphases. The more trans-contextual his categories are, the less he develops them or their implications, such that he fails to properly establish the "dialectic" 'between' "looking and seeing" at the "contextually" 'contingent' 'practical' level of 'life-world' and "looking and seeing" at the level of '*historical*' 'truth'-'system', '*historical*' 'trans-contextual' '*tradition*' (or at the level of '*historical*' "anticipations" 'of history-as-a-whole'). *Unlike Thiselton, the later Wittgenstein is still awaiting Gadamer's (and Pannenberg's) philosophy of history*, and so largely - though not exclusively – the later Wittgenstein confines his epistemological concern to the momentary present and, correlatively, his historical thinking still reflects remnants of the dualistic Neo-Kantian legacy. The later Wittgenstein retrospectively attacks logical positivism as though looking back critically through the opening that he has created to

---

[589] Wittgenstein, *Culture and Value* (trans. P. Winch; Chicago: The University of Chicago Press, 1980), 64e; cf. Thiselton, *NH*, 334, 401; cf. Edmonds and Eidinow, *WP*, 186.
[590] Wittgenstein, *CV*, 31e. Italics Wittgenstein's.
[591] Wittgenstein, *CV*, 32e. Italics Wittgenstein's.
[592] Thiselton, *2H*, 39, 246, 247, 382. Italics ours.

something else. But the later Wittgenstein doesn't look far enough forwards through that same opening so to be able to see the *new* kind of "serious" philosophizing conducted by Thiselton - of which he may have approved.[593]

That is, Thiselton's "later Wittgenstein" actually looks like "the later Wittgenstein *made more consistent with his own new trans-temporal and trans-contextual insights* through an implicit appeal to Gadamer"!

In one place (in 1992) Thiselton allows K.-O. Apel's notion of "'meta-institution'" to be *potentially* equated with the later 'Wittgenstein's' notion of *"'language-game'"* (*as well as* with the later 'Wittgenstein's' notion of the "'common behavior of mankind'"), which is surprising. That is, Thiselton compares one of the later Wittgenstein's more *"particular-level"* emphases (though language-games *can* be trans-contextual as well - see Chapter 4) with Apel's *'transcendental* dimension'. Furthermore, interestingly, Apel's 'transcendental dimension' – as Thiselton himself points out - presupposes a 'dialogue with' *'Gadamer'*, C.S. Peirce and J. Royce that extends *beyond* his (i.e. Apel's) 'discussions of the later Wittgenstein'. This 'dialogue', therefore, embraces much fuller discussions of trans-contextuality and of trans-temporality than are present in the work of the later Wittgenstein (again, we are *not* saying that the later Wittgenstein ignores trans-contextuality or trans-temporality – far from it: see Chapter 4). Possibly, then, Thiselton imputes a little too much of the *fullness* of Gadamer's and Apel's developments of 'trans-contextual' and trans-temporal (cf. 'transcendental') emphases to the later Wittgenstein. Admittedly, though, the clues that support this speculation are subtle.[594]

Nevertheless, even if our speculations in relation to Apel in the paragraph immediately above can be discounted, we had *still* reached a rather interesting conclusion in the preceding paragraphs. That is, Thiselton *seems unwittingly to correct an imbalance in the later Wittgenstein*, who does not yet offer a *developed* "serious" philosophy of history like Thiselton's. Conversely, something of the later Wittgenstein's focus on communities' *and* selves' immediate present experience – *even though that is not the later Wittgenstein's only emphasis (in correction of some neo-pragmatist perspectives)* – may well contribute, along with Thiselton's appeals to other thinkers, to Thiselton's dissatisfaction with Gadamer's hermeneutical half-heartedness in relation to 'individual' selves.[595]

(c) Of course, Thiselton's appeals to the later Wittgenstein and J.L. Austin remain important for Thiselton's view that language is *'embedded' "within"* history. Drawing on these thinkers, Thiselton 'grounds language-use in something that is

---

[593] Thiselton, *NH*, 401, 396, 330, 25, 334; cf. Thiselton, *2H*, 382, 82; cf. Wittgenstein, *PI*, 31e; cf. Thiselton, 'Truth', 896. Fifth, sixth, and eighth italics Thiselton's, others ours.

[594] Thiselton, *NH*, 402-403, 404-405; cf. Apel, K.-O., *Towards a Transformation of Philosophy* (trans. G. Adey & D. Fisby; Milwaukee: Marquette University Press, 1998), 116-119. Italics ours.

[595] Gadamer, *TM*, 276; cf.: Thiselton, *2H*, 305; Thiselton, 'TY', 1565; Thiselton, *IGPS*, 61.

extra-linguistic, a... reality outside the language-event itself',[596] such that Thiselton thereby rejects 'Gadamer's... ontological turn toward language'.[597] Nevertheless, for Pannenberg and Thiselton, contrary to Gadamer and the New Hermeneutic, *and*, contrary to the later Wittgenstein and Austin, 'universal history' – and neither 'language' nor action – 'is the... horizon of a hermeneutic ontology' so long as 'the *ultimate* ontological ground of hermeneutical understanding' is understood to be 'God'.[598]

Thus, Thiselton's transformed-paradigm for hermeneutics is truly 'post-Gadamerian' and truly 'post-[later]-Wittgensteinian'. It follows neither thinker slavishly, but sublates appeals to both thinkers into a larger framework that – in addition – *also* considerably modifies *Pannenberg's* thinking. And in Thiselton's larger framework a hermeneutical critique of language is embedded within a hermeneutical critique of history that has *a greater sophistication than the mere notion that "language is embedded in history"*.[599]

Therefore, Thiselton is perhaps the first thinker to provide a transformed paradigm for theological hermeneutics that presupposes the end of the later Wittgenstein's and Gadamer's waiting for one-another, where Thiselton achieves this paradigm-transformation *before* anything of its ilk had had a chance to appear (or not) in Pannenberg's work - since Pannenberg's main appeals to the later Wittgenstein *post-date* Thiselton's. This point remains true *even if* Pannenberg's reading and modification of *Gadamer's* thought (but *not* of the *later Wittgenstein's* thought) has always been important for Thiselton since very early on in Thiselton's hermeneutical thinking (see Chapter 1). Admittedly, we saw in Chapter 1 that, by 1968, Pannenberg had 'further alerted' Thiselton 'to the problems left by the "devaluing" of assertions in Heidegger and Gadamer'. However, in Chapter 1, we deduced that Thiselton had been *independently* aware of these 'problems' by 1964/1965 and that, in any case, Thiselton had been aware of these 'problems' *from the perspective of a vantage-point that was quite different to Pannenberg's – a more "Anglo-American", less "Continental", vantage-point of "increasing familiarity" 'with the work of Wittgenstein and J.L. Austin' 'from 1963'* (see Chapter 1). In other words: *Thiselton, and not Pannenberg, has ushered in the fullest form of the required 'paradigm-shift' in*

---

[596] Dunn, *BD&H*, 19; cf. Thiselton, *2H*, 375; cf. 370-379, 379-385. Italics ours.

[597] Contradicting, McKnight, E.V., 'Old and New Horizons in Hermeneutics: Anthony C. Thiselton on Contemporary Developments in Hermeneutics. Review article of *New Horizons in Hermeneutics*', *PRelStud* 20 (Fall 1993), 299; cf. Thiselton, *2H*, 370-379, 379-385.

[598] McHann Jr., *3H*, 252-253, cf. 325; cf. citing 326, 334; cf. our Chapter 3; cf. Gadamer, *TM*, Section III Title-page 381, cf. 438-491; and, Robinson, J.M., 'Hermeneutic Since Barth', in *New Frontiers in Theology. Discussions among Continental and American Theologians, Volume II: The New Hermeneutic* (eds. J.M. Robinson and J.B. Cobb, Jr.; New York: Harper and Row, 1964), 50. See also our previous footnote. Italics in speech-marks McHann's.

[599] Thiselton, *2H*, 375; cf. Thiselton, *NH*, 13. Italics ours.

hermeneutics.[600]

(5) Thiselton's transformed hermeneutical paradigm cannot be reduced to "speech-act theory" or to "action models" – where this characteristic is one of the *defining* features of Thiselton's transformed hermeneutical paradigm.[601]

Thus, (a), according to K.J. Vanhoozer, 'Thiselton' argues 'that speech-act analysis is most helpful in understanding particular parts of the Bible'. Conversely, Vanhoozer, 'while not denying' this, views 'speech-act philosophy as contributing categories for a full-fledged interpretation theory that resonates well with properly theological themes'.[602] Similarly, according to R.S. Briggs, Vanhoozer views 'speech-act theory as an overarching perspective within which different genres are at work' whereas, by 'contrast', 'Thiselton's view' is 'that even without a vantage point exterior to the hermeneutical debate one may still make good use of speech-act theory in cases where it addresses issues appropriate to the texts in hand'. C.G. Bartholomew also notes this 'contrast' between the respective approaches of Vanhoozer and Thiselton.[603]

But whose approach to speech-act theory is correct? Certainly, Thiselton sometimes *seems* to align with 'Vanhoozer's… perspective': for Thiselton, since 'language' is "communicative" "action" of different 'particular' '"kinds"' with "multiple" '"functions"' then, for Thiselton, 'speech-act theory' is almost 'overarching' at one level, being almost always relevant.[604] And yet, Thiselton's emphasizing of this point is narrower than his broader view of hermeneutics as a whole. And in the latter context, Thiselton's argument for the *non*-"over-arching" status of speech-act theory seems irrefutable – as follows.

Thus, to begin with, on stratum one, Thiselton stresses the need for 'dialogue' with multiple disciplines, traditions and approaches, including *but not restricted to* speech-act theory which, therefore, cannot be "over-arching".[605] On stratum two, "language" is only *one* of Thiselton's five spheres of discourse (which focus on "history", "epistemology", "language", "(Western) culture", and "human selves") and, for Thiselton, is less fundamental than "history". So, again, for Thiselton, speech-act theory is not "over-arching".[606] During interpretative practice (stratum three), further, Thiselton employs multiple interpretative "models".[607] Thus, again, we should note, with B.D. Ingraffia and T.E. Pickett, that in Thiselton's thinking, speech-act theory cannot be 'imperialized' as 'a *single*' "over-arching"

---

[600] cf. Borsch, 'R 2H', 90; cf. Thiselton's comments in, Thiselton, *NH*, 13; cf. Thiselton, 'TY', 1560; cf. our Chapter 1. Italics ours.
[601] Thiselton, 'R-RH', 113.
[602] Vanhoozer, 'SA', 7; cf. Vanhoozer, *FT*, 164-165.
[603] Briggs, *Words*, 26-27; cf. Bartholomew, '3H', 134, n.55.
[604] Thiselton, *2H*, 168, 374, 372, 373; cf. 372-379, cf. 407-408; cf. Briggs, *Words*, 26.
[605] Thiselton, *2H*, 3-10, 291-292, cf. 354; cf.: Thiselton, 'LMR', 1123; cf. 1130-1135; cf. 1137-1142; Thiselton, 'TNI', 11; Thiselton, 'M&M', 8.
[606] McHann Jr., *3H*, 326; cf. Thiselton, *2H*, 51-84. Italics ours.
[607] Thiselton, *2H*, 291, 292; cf. 354; cf. 432-434; cf. Thiselton, 'R-RH', 113.

hermeneutical model. Thiselton's transformed hermeneutical paradigm is thus not reducible to speech-act theory.[608]

Again, therefore, Thiselton does not simply have later 'Wittgensteinian' 'presuppositions' (contradicting N.L. Geisler's reading of Thiselton);[609] and 'Wittgenstein and the speech-act theory of Austin and Searle' are *not* 'Thiselton's' 'central' 'conceptual tools' in New Testament "interpretation" (contradicting C.G. Bartholomew's reading of Thiselton).[610] Crucially, as we shall demonstrate in Chapter 7, Thiselton does *not* follow J.R. Searle's 'attempt to use Austin's work to develop… a metaphysic or ontology' (contradicting S.E. Fowl's reading of Thiselton).[611] And certainly, Thiselton's 'goal' is *not* simply to show 'how speech-act theory enables an understanding of how life can be transformed by communicative action in relation to the biblical text' (contradicting R.W.L. Moberly's point, though Moberly here brilliantly summarizes *one* of Thiselton's *many* aims).[612]

(b) A similar argument can be put forward with reference to Thiselton's 'action model', which he develops later in *The Responsibility of Hermeneutics* (1985). Whilst it is broader than speech-act theory in that it includes *interpretative* actions, Thiselton's 'action model' is still grounded – via Thiselton's hermeneutical critique of human selves - in the hermeneutical critique of history that Thiselton develops in *The Two Horizons*. It is ultimately this *even broader* hermeneutical critique of history that, for Thiselton, links 'an author-oriented hermeneutic and a reader-oriented hermeneutic' (here we are correcting K.R. Snodgrass's reading of Thiselton).[613]

Therefore, since L. Zuidervaart examines only Thiselton's critique of 'action', then it is no wonder that Zuidervaart fails to find "solutions" to 'any major problems', any 'new model of hermeneutics', or any "theoretical" (or qualifying) co-ordinates for Thiselton's notion of '"the text itself"'. (N.B. caution must be applied when relating *any* notion of '"the text itself"' to Thiselton – see above and also Chapter 7). Zuidervaart, then, has missed Thiselton's entire framework: the conceptual core of *The Two Horizons* is a *historical* unification of major hermeneutical critiques.[614] Contradicting G.R. Osborne's reading of Thiselton,

---

[608] Ingraffia and Pickett, 'Reviv', 245; cf. Thiselton, *2H*, 432, 291, cf. 292, cf. 354; cf. Thiselton, *NH*, 27. We are using the term "paradigm" at the macro-level of a (meta-) critical synthesis drawing on multiple dialogues with multiple traditions. Ingraffia and Pickett rightly *reject* using the term 'paradigm' (singular) for a single interpretative *model* (stratum three) *used as* an "over-arching paradigm" (stratum one). Italics Thiselton's.
[609] Contradicting, Geisler, 'R *2H*', 182.
[610] Contradicting, Bartholomew, '3H', 126.
[611] Contradicting, Fowl, 'AI', 76.
[612] Contradicting, Moberly, R.W.L., 'Review of R. Lundin's, C. Walhout's and A.C. Thiselton's *The Promise of Hermeneutics*', *ExTim* 111.7 (Apr. 2000), 237.
[613] Correcting, Snodgrass, 'R *RH*', 199, 200; cf. 199-202; cf. Thiselton, 'R-RH', 110-111; cf. 79-113. Italics ours.
[614] Zuidervaart, L., 'Review of R. Lundin's, A.C. Thiselton's and C. Walhout's *The Responsibility of Hermeneutics*', *CalThJ* 21.2 (Nov. 1986), 295, 291, 296. Italics ours.

then, we should note that Thiselton *neither* simply combines appeals to 'Wittgenstein', 'speech-act theory', and 'an "action model"'; *nor* does Thiselton simply follow 'a... middle ground between' a '"hermeneutics of suspicion"' 'and' E.D. Hirsch's approach.[615]

(6) Summarizing: Thiselton ushers in a hermeneutical paradigm-shift, a new larger critical synthesis grounded in a hermeneutical critique of history that ontologically subordinates a hermeneutical critique of language to itself. Whilst Pannenberg strongly influences Thiselton, it is Thiselton, and not Pannenberg who provides the first truly 'post-Gadamerian', 'post-[later]-Wittgensteinian' theological hermeneutic. Thiselton's fruitful appeal to the later Wittgenstein in order to correct Gadamer's thinking is relatively obvious: Thiselton appeals to the later Wittgenstein (and to others including, *subsequently*, Pannenberg) in order to correct Gadamer's linguistic dualism; and Thiselton combines appeals to Pannenberg and to the later Wittgenstein (and to others) in order to correct Gadamer's ontological prioritization of "language" relative to "history". However, Thiselton also implicitly appeals to Gadamer (and to Pannenberg) in order to flesh out the later Wittgenstein's under-developed philosophy of history. This latter point is, in part, ironically betrayed by what might well be slight Gadamerian distortions in Thiselton's reading of the later Wittgenstein. Finally, Thiselton's transformed paradigm for hermeneutics is not reducible to "speech-act theory" or to "action models".[616]

(7) This reading of Thiselton conflicts with that of other commentators. Thiselton, *without* regressing to logical positivism, does *not* align with H. Frei's approach (querying A.J. McNicol's reading of Thiselton).[617] Thiselton does not "move away" from "history" 'in *The Two Horizons*', contrary to S.E. Porter's reading of Thiselton, but grounds "action models" within his transformed historico-philosophical paradigm.[618] Thiselton's stance is *not* in alignment with Porter's attempt to reconcile a critique of W. Iser's 'formalism' with a plea that 'biblical scholars need to develop as "close readers" (... in formalist analysis)'.[619] 'Porter' (even more than the early Thiselton!) 'does not make his position at all clear' at this point.[620]

Nor does Thiselton merely seek 'to replace the... framework of meaning' of 'salvation-history' with a new focus on '"application"' (contradicting E. Schüssler-

---

[615] Contradicting, Osborne, 'R *NH*', 91, 93.

[616] cf. Thiselton, *NH*, 13; cf. Thiselton, 'R-RH', 113.

[617] Querying, McNicol, 'R *2H*', 187.

[618] Thiselton, 'CAP', 154; cf. Thiselton, 'R-RH', 113; cf. Porter, S.E., 'Why Hasn't Reader-Response Criticism Caught on in New Testament Studies?', *JLitTh* 4 (1990), 278-292; cf. Porter, S.E., 'Reader-Response Criticism and New Testament Study: A Response to A.C. Thiselton's *New Horizons in Hermeneutics*', *JLitTh* 8.1 (Mar. 1994), 94-102. Italics Porter's.

[619] Porter, 'R-RC', 100; cf. 97; cf. 99.

[620] Noble. P.R., 'Fish and the Bible: Should Reader-Response Theories Catch On?', *HeyJ* 37.4 (Oct. 1996), 467.

Fiorenza's reading of Thiselton).[621] Nor does Thiselton refuse to offer a unified hermeneutical *theory* (strata one and two) simply because he rejects 'a *single*' (stratum three) 'model' of *interpretation* (querying M. Turner's reading of Thiselton).[622] Nor does Thiselton *reduce* the relevance of the notion of '"paradigm shifts" in' recent New Testament 'interpretation' to 'the late twentieth century' '"shifts"' 'toward a "methodological pluralism"' (querying J.L. Boyce's reading of Thiselton) or to a supposed 'turn' from, say, 'historical' to 'literary' paradigms (though, in this context of discussion, we *affirm* C.G. Bartholomew's observation that Thiselton does indeed cite the importance of these "shifts" or "turns").[623]

Thiselton neither proceeds 'without any... reconceptualization of the task of exegesis' (contradicting R.S. Briggs's reading of Thiselton),[624] nor merely "accommodates" historical and linguistic 'biblical' studies to 'recent hermeneutics' (contradicting R. Van Voorst's reading of Thiselton).[625] Nor does Thiselton leave 'historical critical' "methods" unaltered (querying J. Ziesler's reading of Thiselton).[626] And it is false to argue that Thiselton in no sense offers 'a solution to the' hermeneutical 'problem' (contradicting M.J. Erickson's reading of Thiselton).[627]

Some commentators, further, largely emphasize Thiselton's responses to positivism,[628] whilst others largely emphasize his responses to "existentialism".[629] Admittedly, W.W. Klein and D.S. Dockery do at least rightly *note* or *allude to* both. Thus, Dockery notes that 'past' "scholarship" focused on 'the historical meaning of the text' (cf. traditional approaches, but also the influence of logical-positivism on the historiography implicit in historical-critical methodology), 'while... more... philosophical approach[es] have concerned themselves with the meaning for today' (cf. the "existentialism" of Bultmann and the New Hermeneutic).[630]

What is lacking in the literature, however, is any comment on how Thiselton definitively moves *beyond* both these - and also beyond broadly "structuralist" (and

---

[621] Schüssler-Fiorenza, E., 'Rhetorical Situation and Historical Reconstruction in 1 Corinthians', *NTStud* 33.3 (Jul. 1987), 386.

[622] Turner, M., 'Review of R. Lundin's, A.C. Thiselton's and C. Walhout's *The Responsibility of Hermeneutics*', *FTht* 113 (Oct. 1987), 182; cf. Thiselton, *2H*, 432, 292, 354, 115; cf. Thiselton, 'SBS', 333. Turner neglects to distinguish between different uses of the word "paradigm". Thiselton employs multiple models (cf. 'paradigms', stratum three) and yet can be said to offer an overall *working* "paradigm" that facilitates this employment (strata one, two and, to an extent, three – see Chapter 5). First and third italics ours, second italics Thiselton's.

[623] Boyce, J.L., 'Review of J.B. Green ed. *Hearing the New Testament*', *WW* 16 (Sum. 1996), 378; cf. Bartholomew, 'Intro *BTI*', 3, 4; cf. Thiselton, 'NTIHP', 11-37.

[624] Contradicting, Briggs, *Words*, 18.

[625] Contradicting, Van Voorst, 'R *2H*', 220; cf. Thiselton, *2H*, 66-67, 74-84, 103-107.

[626] Ziesler, J., 'Historical Criticism and a Rational Faith', *ExTim* 105.9 (1994), 270.

[627] Contradicting, Erickson, 'R *2H*', 373. Contradicting, Dockery, 'R *2H*', 136.

[628] For example, Grech, 'R *2H*', 572 and onwards.

[629] For example, Dockery, 'R *2H*', 133-136; cf. Thiselton, *2H*, 65.

[630] Klein, 'R *2H*', 72; cf. Dockery, 'R *2H*', 133-134.

later) - approaches *so as to usher in* a new historical unification of hermeneutics. Moreover, Thiselton's new historical unification of hermeneutics is not 'grounded in the Christian faith' fideistically (querying P.T. Jensen's reading of Thiselton). Rather, as already argued, straightforward '"fideism"' is absent from Thiselton's thinking (contradicting B.J. Walsh's reading of Thiselton).[631]

## E. Conclusion:
## Widening Dialogue Towards a New Historical Unification of Hermeneutical Theory as a Precondition for Responsible Interpretation

The arguments presented in the present chapter have been very involved. And so it is worth slightly extending our concluding section in order that these arguments may be presented with sufficient clarity.

We began the present chapter, (1), by attempting to justify our assertion that a fresh interpretation of Thiselton's *The Two Horizons* was needed.

We argued that *The Two Horizons* was a major work by a major thinker in the discipline of hermeneutics, and yet that it – and indeed Thiselton's writings taken as a whole – had been neglected and misunderstood in the literature. We speculated that the complexity of theoretical hermeneutics generally, and just possibly a mild issue to do with Thiselton's difficult style of writing at that time, probably lay behind this inadequate reception of Thiselton's work.

And yet, given the contemporary problems in the discipline of hermeneutics, and given the probable centrality of *The Two Horizons* in relation to the heart of Thiselton's thinking as a whole, an attempt had to be made to provide a fresh interpretation of *The Two Horizons*, and so we then progressed to this task.

Thus, (2), we started our fresh interpretation of *The Two Horizons* by expounding one of Thiselton's major arguments within it - as follows.

Thus, Thiselton argued that, in *biblical studies*, inadequate hermeneutical theory had led to problematic interpretative practice (and, by implication, to problematic understandings and to problematic outworkings of understandings).

Notably, Thiselton argued that "purist" and "traditional" approaches to biblical interpretation had often – on false grounds – chosen to ignore *both* the category of pre-understanding *and* the discipline of hermeneutics more broadly.

Conversely, Thiselton argued that broadly "positivist" and broadly "existentialist" approaches to biblical interpretation presupposed "narrowed" pre-understandings that were characterized by dialogues with philosophical (and theological) traditions - at the theoretical level of critical-synthesis - that were too restricted.

Thiselton showed that these overly restricted dialogues had led to the problem

---

[631] Thiselton, A.C., *A Concise Encyclopedia of the Philosophy of Religion* (Oxford: One World, 2002), 102; cf. Thiselton, *2H*, 428; cf. querying, Jensen, P.T., 'Review of R. Lundin's, A.C. Thiselton's and C. Walhout's *The Responsibility of Hermeneutics*', *Ety* 37.6 (Jun. 1986), 49; cf. contradicting, Walsh, 'TC', 235.

of "dualisms" or "dichotomies" *both* at the *theoretical* level of critical-synthesis within pre-understanding, *and* at the level of *practice* in biblical interpretation.

Thiselton in effect showed that this problem of "dualisms" or "dichotomies" had thereby, by implication, and in *the aftermath* of such biblical interpretation, led on to problematic understandings, and to problematic outworkings of understandings, that would adversely affect Bible-readers, the Church, and the wider world.

Thiselton thus sought a philosophical and theological dialogic widening of pre-understanding that went beyond the dialogically narrowed pre-understandings presupposed by "purist", "traditional", broadly "positivist", and broadly "existentialist" (i.e. Bultmann and the New Hermeneutic) approaches.

Thiselton sought this dialogic widening of pre-understanding for three reasons: (a) in order to attack problematic dualisms or dichotomies along six different axes in the pre-understandings and interpretative practices of Bultmann and the New Hermeneutic (who had already begun to progress beyond broadly positivist approaches); (b) in order to *replace* the pre-understandings and critical syntheses presupposed by Bultmann and by the New Hermeneutic – which were fatally dichotomous in multiple ways – with a *unified* pre-understanding and (therefore with a unified) critical synthesis; and, (c), in order – thereby - to *enable* (non-dichotomous) responsible interpretation – where, for Thiselton, responsible interpretation included, centrally, a liberation of the biblical texts that *freed* the biblical texts to function as God's Word in the interpretation, formation, and transformation of *Bible-readers, the Church, and the wider world.*

Thiselton thus showed that "widening dialogue" and responsible interpretation were inextricably linked. Conversely, by implication, Thiselton had in effect also shown that irresponsible interpretation and hermeneutical foreclosure were inextricably linked.

Thiselton had thus proven the direct relationship between - and hence the unity of - hermeneutical theory and practice.

However, (3), Despite Thiselton's conclusive demonstration of the importance of such "widening dialogue", his emphasis on "widening dialogue" had been missed by many critics who had responded to Thiselton, and had not been properly taken up or applied in biblical hermeneutics. One critic even viewed Thiselton's widening dialogue – notably Thiselton's widening dialogue that included the later Wittgenstein – as being "arbitrary".

(4) Anticipating our next section and Chapter 7, we then suggested that Thiselton widened philosophical and theological dialogue beyond that of Bultmann and of the New Hermeneutic (and, in some senses, beyond that of later approaches) in seven ways at the level of pre-understanding. We anticipated that Thiselton thereby unified second and third stratum hermeneutical critiques in a hermeneutical critique of history, and that Thiselton brought hermeneutics as a whole to unity in biblical theology.

(5) We acknowledged that, in *The Two Horizons*, Thiselton had *also* addressed the work of Saussure, the post-Saussurian tradition of general linguistics and modern

semantics, and (briefly) various "structuralist" approaches. However, we had covered Thiselton's treatment of these strands in earlier chapters because, within *Thiselton's* thinking, these strands were relevant primarily, but not exclusively, *either* to the study of language, *or* to the *textual* horizon, but not so much to considerations related to linking "the two horizons". Moreover, Thiselton had - during his second period - criticized some structuralist approaches *precisely because* they often failed to address the particularities of *either* of "the two horizons".

Thus, (6), moving on, we then explicated Thiselton's grounding and unification of his second and third stratum hermeneutical critiques in a hermeneutical critique of history that emerged from three inter-related modified Hegelian criteria.

Thus, (a), *first*, for Thiselton, eschatological anticipations of history-as-a-whole had to be made from within history. (Indeed, for Thiselton, all historical enquiry had to begin from "within history"). History-as-a-whole, in Thiselton's estimate, could not be viewed *either* from "the end of history", *or* from "above history". Totalization and objectivism were thus both precluded in Thiselton's estimate, and hence, in Thiselton's estimate, *some* historical relativity was unavoidable. Therefore, Thiselton argued that understanding was always provisional. Moreover, Thiselton emphasized past horizons, present horizons, *and* future horizons – *both* in contrast to approaches that focused too exclusively on past horizons *and* in contrast to approaches that focused too exclusively on present horizons.

(b) *Second*, for Thiselton, the unity of historical reality grounded the possibility and unity of language and of understanding. In Thiselton's estimate, over-abstraction was discounted in that historical understanding, existential self-understanding, and concrete traditions were thereby inextricably linked to one another and not sharply divorced from one another.

Indeed, Thiselton argued that the unity (not uniformity) of historical reality precluded historical, epistemological, linguistic, cultural, anthropological, and interpretative dualisms or dichotomies. In this context of discussion, Thiselton attacked dichotomies in the thinking of Dilthey, the early Wittgenstein, Heidegger and Bultmann.

One notable point that emerged from this discussion was that Thiselton followed the later Wittgenstein's transposition of "saying" and "showing" into a *non*-formalist "historical" key that, nevertheless, developed some of the early Wittgenstein's "analytical" emphases by highlighting the ways in which grammatical propositions could enable "understanding" through the explication and creative extension of concepts. (Here, in Thiselton's estimate, the later Wittgenstein aligned with a Pauline notion of rationality). Thiselton would go on to contrast the later Wittgenstein's positive evaluation of grammatical propositions in this respect with the linguistic dualism implicit in Gadamer's hermeneutical circle. Thus, for Thiselton, the later Wittgenstein's work was *very relevant indeed* for hermeneutics.

Moreover, in relation to epistemology, Thiselton argued that historical understanding and self-understanding were inextricably linked in three ways.

Thus, in Thiselton's estimate, historical understanding *began with* self-understanding - where, here, *pre-understanding* was the aspect of "self-understanding" that was under consideration. With Heidegger, Bultmann, and the New Hermeneutic, Thiselton acknowledged that there was no choice but *to begin* with pre-understanding – and hence with self-understanding - when embarking on the processes of historical understanding. And yet, against tendencies in Heidegger, Bultmann, and the New Hermeneutic, Thiselton argued that historical understanding could not be *reduced to* pre-understanding or to self-understanding.

For Thiselton, self-understanding – where this time self-understanding was understood in relation to conscious self-awareness - came through a *detour into* historical understanding. For Thiselton, one understood oneself only by identifying oneself *in relation to* the historical other. In this connection, Thiselton drew on Dilthey, Collingwood, G. Yorck, and Gadamer – but was again critical of Dilthey for tending to conflate the interpreter's "I" with the historical "Thou".

For Thiselton, self-understanding – where this time self-understanding was understood in relation to understanding "selves" as "whole" persons - was an *aspect of* historical understanding, since – in Thiselton's estimate - selves were "historical". With Heidegger, Bultmann, and Gadamer, and against Husserl, Thiselton agreed that "selves" were inextricably bound up with history. For Thiselton, there could be no return to "transcendental" idealist notions of selfhood. And yet, against Dilthey, Heidegger and Bultmann, Thiselton argued that "selves" were not the *only* subject-matter for historical enquiry. (N.B. in this context of discussion we noted Gadamer's point that Heidegger had not completely escaped idealist "transcendental reflection"; also: *idealist* "transcendence" is not to be confused with *historical* or *theological* transcendence!).

We then focused on the modifications of Heidegger's insights into Dasein that were implicit in Thiselton's embedding of a hermeneutical critique of human selves within a broader view of *historical unity* and in Thiselton's embedding of self-understanding within a broader view of *historical understanding*.

Thus, for Thiselton, drawing on Heidegger, selves were: historically contingent truths; historically embedded and conditioned pre-cognitively; historically self-transcending or moving *both* at the level of inward pre-cognitive processes associated with understanding *and* at the level of outward individuating actions; potentially "whole" (*partly* in terms of self-relationality and temporality); and historically unique.

And yet, for Thiselton, against Heidegger: past facts were *also* historically contingent truths (though of a different kind to selves); historical conditioning, historical self-transcendence, and historical movement *also involved cognitive processes* (including truth-transmission, conceptualization, critical and metacritical comparative testing, and the creative functioning of assertive language); selves became "whole" in the ethics-laden contexts of *submission to God and human inter-subjectivity* (cf. relationality), and in the context of *eschatology* (cf. temporality) – though *without* neglecting self-relationality; and emphases on Dasein's uniqueness and on historical particularity had to be *held together with* emphases on *inter-subjectivity* and on *historical continuity*.

(c) *Third*, for Thiselton, against over-abstract notions of historical process, history as dialectic process generated concrete historical particularities and concrete historical continuities that were earthed in the concrete processes of traditions that were understood (in the context of Thiselton's hermeneutical critique of traditions) as socio-historical extensions of the hermeneutical circle.

(i) Thiselton's hermeneutical critique of *traditions* modified Gadamer's hermeneutic of traditions primarily (but not exclusively) in that Thiselton *reversed* Gadamer's ontological prioritization of language (cf. language-traditions) over history (cf. tradition-history). (Thiselton's other modifications of Gadamer's hermeneutic of traditions would emerge as we proceeded).

(i.i) For Thiselton, as for Gadamer, traditions were interwoven wholes that could not be disintegrated into fact-value dichotomies (against broadly positivist approaches and against broadly existentialist approaches). However, unlike Gadamer, Thiselton framed traditions within anticipations of an eschatological notion of history-as-a-whole.

(i.ii) For Thiselton, as for Gadamer, traditions were diachronic frames of reference for meaning such that, for Gadamer and Thiselton, considerations of meaning were never a matter of mechanical repetition of the past, but always went beyond considerations of authorial intent so as to include considerations of present meanings. And yet, for Thiselton, understanding could neither be ahistorically reduced to individual or corporate self-understanding in the present horizon, nor allowed to "run free" as radical indeterminacy. For Thiselton, as for Gadamer, understanding was always a matter of immersion in the processes and events of traditions. For Thiselton, history retained its constraining operative influence on understanding and on present meanings – in accord (in Thiselton's estimate) with the biblical witness.

(i.iii) For Thiselton, as for Gadamer, traditions as *traditio* were chronologically developing in an active dynamic manner. In Thiselton's estimate, after Gadamer, ongoing interaction between past tradition (*traditum*) and communities of readers (*actus tradendi*) constituted a process called "effective history" that *both* produced histories of effects and of fusions *and* mediated pre-judgments, interpretative judgments, effects, and fusions through the *filter of* "effective history". Thus, as for Gadamer, Thiselton's hermeneutical circle was grounded in the dialectic of tradition, and not simply in the present horizon (though Thiselton also modified Gadamer's hermeneutical circle – see below).

(i.iv) For Thiselton, as for Gadamer, traditions generated historical continuities as they developed. For Thiselton, these continuities included (amongst other phenomena) public criteria of meaning, convictions, and judgments. For Thiselton, though, against Gadamer, such continuities were more firmly grounded in extra-linguistic history (given Thiselton's *reversal* of Gadamer's ontological prioritization of "language" relative to "history").

For Thiselton, after the later Wittgenstein, language was in part grounded in observable and accessible public criteria of meaning - public criteria of meaning apart from which – in the estimates of the later Wittgenstein and Thiselton -

*Hermeneutics and History* 389

language would be unintelligible, unteachable, and without grounds for authentication. For Thiselton, drawing on the later Wittgenstein, language could not be "private" (against Bultmann), meaning could not be "esoteric" (against Bultmann), Continental (including Gadamerian) linguistic dualism was banished on the grounds that public criteria of meaning necessarily embodied assertive language, and reading (including Protestant reading) could not be "detached or unbiased".

Thiselton, drawing on the later Wittgenstein and Gadamer, argued that convictions (cf. scaffolding, pre-judgments) were not necessarily "culture-relative", but could also be traditional and theological.

For Thiselton, as for Gadamer, the hermeneutically trained interpretative judgments of hermeneutical consciousness (judgments in part mediated by – and/or in relation to - "classic literature" and "traditions of tested wisdom") could not be produced by the errors of post-Enlightenment "universal scientific or critical method" (cf. *fixed* and *past* categories that *assimilate* historical particularity to *a priori* formal *generality*), but had to respect process (cf. "effective history"), anticipation of the future (cf. "newness"), and historical particularity (cf. "the uniqueness of the other").

Thiselton's notion of historical continuities was linked to his notions of: historical unity, *a posteriori* generality, historical analogy, an *a posteriori* axis of historical enquiry, and an *a posteriori* general linguistic axis.

(i.v) For Thiselton, as for Gadamer, traditions generated historical particularities as they developed. Having already considered the uniqueness of human selves in our discussion of Thiselton's responses to Heidegger, we examined other points in connection with historical particularity.

Thus, for Thiselton, historical particularity was inconsistent with historical dualisms or dichotomies, and also with epistemological dualisms or dichotomies, but – for Thiselton - *necessitated both* an emphasis on historical distinctions *and* emphases on distinctions between different kinds of "understanding" (i.e. for Thiselton, the grammar of understanding depended upon what was being understood). Thus, Thiselton argued that, given the absence of dualisms or dichotomies, a general axis of enquiry remained possible (cf. scientific explanation), even if Thiselton allowed that historical analogy was limited by historical particularity. Further, Thiselton argued that, given the absence of dualisms or dichotomies, the historical "other" was not too "alien" for understanding to begin, *even if* Thiselton *also* argued that historical particularity meant that the "other" could *not* be assimilated into one's own (or one's community's) horizons.

For Thiselton, self-understanding and historical understanding were thus linked, but also distinct. For Thiselton: historical otherness could *neither* be reduced to an (individual or corporate) "self"; *nor* to the present horizon; *nor* to a consumer-commodity or agenda shaped by an (individual or corporate) "self" (against – in Thiselton's estimate - neo-pragmatic philosophy, some reader-response theories, and some liberation theology). For Thiselton, God, others, the past, and the future had to be respected as "other". Nevertheless, for Thiselton, historical particularity was *also* a reality in relation to the "historical present" and, for Thiselton, included contemporary (individual or corporate) "selves", such that – in Thiselton's thinking - avoidance of "present (individual or corporate) selves" by over-focusing on the past was *also* excluded (here Thiselton argued against some trends in Anglo-American historical-critical practice). For Thiselton, polarization between past and present horizons was thus excluded.

For Thiselton, language was grounded in historical particularities as well as in historical continuities – and not formally or logically or independently of the future. For Thiselton, the moving historical particularities of life diversities grounded language such that language changed as history moved on. For Thiselton, after Gadamer, this dynamic scenario meant that the language of traditions did not *necessarily* imprison thought, although Thiselton allowed that the language of traditions could *potentially* hold us under a "spell". For Thiselton, meaning was not "formal" or "esoteric", but linked to the particularities of language-games. Thus, Thiselton argued for the "polymorphous" character of the biblical concepts of faith, flesh, and truth, and for the use of distinctions between language-games in order to resolve logical problems related to faith and works in Paul and in James respectively. Again, though, Thiselton's emphasis on historical particularity was *consistent with* his rejection of Continental dualisms and dichotomies (including Gadamer's linguistic dualism).

For Thiselton, historical particularity – specifically textual particularity - precluded the generalizing and imperializing use of single over-arching or monopolizing "comprehensive" models during interpretation. (Thiselton even refused to use his own "action models" and "speech-act models" in this way). Thiselton thus opposed such tendencies in the early Wittgenstein, in general linguistics, in (ideological) structuralist approaches, and in more recent approaches in biblical hermeneutics.

For Thiselton, historical particularity affected *both* sets of horizons during interpretation, and yet not in such a way as to imperialize *objectification or distancing*. For Thiselton, fusion between historically particular horizons embraced the full dynamics of inter-subjective relationality such that assessments of different speech-acts could not be confined *synchronically* to the textual horizon, but – for Thiselton - had to respect *diachronic* relational dynamics as well. Thiselton's approach, then, stood in contrast to approaches that reduced diachronic inter-relationality to "reference" or to "significance".

Thus, (and bringing in an example of our own), it would be inappropriate to respond immediately to a rebuke from one's boss at work by saying, "I notice that you have just rebuked me", or by saying, "the significance of your remark in relation to me was that it was a rebuke". Such responses kill the relational dynamic through "premature *distancing* between horizons" (our phrase) – or through a kind of objectifying "reference" that amounts to relational "avoidance" or to relational "playing it safe". Whilst this is good practice when one is being manipulated in the context of relational distrust, it is not good practice when one is being addressed by God's Word in the context of love. The *response of objectifying reference is inappropriate as a "total" relational response to the divine initiative of love through Scripture*.

(i.vi) For Thiselton, as for Gadamer, traditions also historically conditioned texts and readers. However, qualifying Gadamer's thinking, Thiselton perhaps related historical conditioning more to the concerns and agency of individual subjectivity - since Thiselton was concerned that Gadamer under-emphasized individual subjectivity.

For Thiselton, with Gadamer, historical conditioning was two-sided: both texts and readers were "conditioned" by tradition.

However, for Thiselton, individual persons and communities *also* conditioned traditions. And Thiselton even argued that the *eschatological* (and theological) "third" horizon "conditioned history" *itself* (from ahead).

Some critics of Thiselton argued that Thiselton had neglected a different kind of "third horizon" – a "third horizon" that was not eschatological, but pastoral. We may expand on what we said earlier at this point. Thus, according to this critical view of Thiselton, the Bible would constitute the first horizon, the horizons of – say – a missionary would constitute the second horizon, and the horizon of the culture in which the missionary was witnessing would constitute the third horizon. However, we argued - from a Thiseltonian perspective - that this viewpoint really only referred to *another* understanding or conditioning event between *two* horizons (real though that event was).

For Thiselton, historical conditioning presupposed historical finitude or situatedness. Against Gadamer, though, Thiselton again argued that history itself was situated and conditioned theologically and eschatologically. With Gadamer, Thiselton argued that situatedness limited individual or community interpretative arbitration and culture-relativity since selves and communities were already addressed (and conditioned) from beyond their own horizons. For Thiselton, then, historical conditioning thus necessarily involved *both* a focus on past corporate tradition *and* a focus on God and on eschatology.

For Thiselton, therefore, historical conditioning could not be used to ground subjectivism or radical culture-relativity - *even though* Thiselton *also* took *historically-embedded and historically conditioned* subjectivity and *historically-embedded and historically conditioned* "culture-relativity" into account.

For Thiselton, historical conditioning presupposed the interweaving of action, language-habits, and thought. With Gadamer, Thiselton argued that neither "scientific thinking" – nor indeed any other kind of thinking - could free itself from traditions of language-use so as to "instrumentalize" language in a "detached" fashion. Nevertheless, against Gadamer, Thiselton still ontologically prioritized "history" over "language".

For Thiselton, with Gadamer, historical conditioning presupposed dialectical interaction between the language and concepts of tradition and interpreters' prior consciousness, thoughts, and language. Thiselton, after Gadamer, argued that through this interaction, tradition "came to speech" in interpreters' horizons. For Thiselton, after W. Wink, the *common* world of tradition was the ground for this interaction. And yet, after Fuchs and Ebeling of the New Hermeneutic, Thiselton argued that the "same thing had to be said *differently*" to each generation if there was to be transformation through multiple fusions of horizons. With Gadamer, Thiselton argued that such a transformation came from beyond the present horizons of individuals or communities. Therefore, Thiselton argued that such a transformation could not be reduced to a transformation of self-understanding or to what individuals or communities already knew.

For Thiselton, with Gadamer, historical conditioning was both non-cognitive (i.e. pre-cognitive *and* performative or non-conceptual) and cognitive. In effect Thiselton thus corrected Continental under-emphases on cognitive conditioning.

For Thiselton, against Gadamer's linguistic dualism, historical conditioning occurred through the operation of both assertive and non-assertive language. Notably, drawing on the later Wittgenstein, Thiselton emphasized creatively functioning assertions – including grammatical propositions.

For Thiselton, historical conditioning could either distort or facilitate understanding. For Thiselton, historical conditioning did not banish historical particularity and so it did not banish historical difference or objective otherness. For Thiselton, additionally, historical conditioning also *presupposed* historical *relationality* and therefore allowed at least a degree of "access" *to* the historical "other". Thiselton also argued that, initially, readers' pre-understandings were indispensable points of contact with texts. Moreover, for Thiselton, after Gadamer, historical conditioning could pass on *true* pre-judgments. Nevertheless, after Heidegger, and in correction of Gadamer, Thiselton *did* still argue that historical conditioning, along with other historical factors, could also *distort* understanding. And yet, for Thiselton, these other factors, like historical conditioning, could also *aid* objectivity (see Chapter 7).

We then paused to argue that historical conditioning was even more complicated than Thiselton had yet allowed. Whilst Thiselton realized the reality of multiple overlapping conditioning contexts (e.g. traditions and communities), there were also factors to be taken into account that related to the isolations and distortions that pertained to the fallenness of human relationships. All manner of fallen relational patterns – including our own decisions - would have to be explored in order to link historical conditioning more adequately to concrete relationality. Fallen human physicality would also be a factor that "historically conditioned" readers. Thiselton had certainly begun to explore these kinds of issues, but there was much more work to be done. A broader dialogue with pastoral theology – and with disciplines of relevance to pastoral theology - was required.

(ii) Thiselton's widening dialogue not only led him to modify Gadamer's hermeneutic of traditions; Thiselton's widening dialogue also – (therefore) - led him to modify Gadamer's *hermeneutical circle*.

We saw how Pannenberg enabled Thiselton to transpose Gadamer's insights into a theological key, how the Saussurian tradition enabled Thiselton to flesh out Gadamer's notions of fusion and distancing, and how Schleiermacher,

Kierkegaard, Heidegger, and Bultmann allowed Thiselton to retain a greater stress on individual subjectivities than (in Thiselton's estimate) was preserved in Gadamer. We also saw how the later Wittgenstein enabled Thiselton to counter Gadamer's linguistic dualism by reinstating the role of grammatical propositions in understanding, and how J.L. Austin, D.D. Evans, and the philosophy of language more broadly enabled Thiselton to more properly relate aspects of fusion to "behind-the-text" extra-linguistic factors.

Notably, we saw how Thiselton's three-fold analytical application of the later Wittgenstein's work in relation to grammatical utterances or grammatical propositions both *corroborated* and yet also *challenged* Gadamer's thinking as Thiselton understood it.

Thus, on the one hand, in Thiselton's estimate, grammatical propositions "showed" – and thus *corroborated* – Gadamer's thinking: in relation to broadened historical rationality, in relation to the importance of the functioning of traditional pre-judgments in the processes of understanding, and in relation to the tradition-modification or "tradition-refinement" that occurred through the processes of effective history.

And yet, on the other hand, in Thiselton's estimate, grammatical propositions also "showed": the ways in which traditions could distort truth (cf. "spell-formation/persuasive definition"), the need to account for the possibility of an epistemology of socio-meta-critical liberation (cf. "spell-breaking"), and the need to account more convincingly for the extra-linguistic functioning and effects of speech-acts (cf. "world-shattering"). These latter three kinds of "showing" *challenged* Gadamer's thinking as Thiselton understood it.

Thus, the fact that grammatical propositions could "show" *both* strengths *and* weaknesses in Gadamer's thinking as Thiselton understood it *not only* – in Thiselton's estimate - raised problems in relation to what Thiselton saw as being Gadamer's dualistic disparagement of propositions, but *also* in Thiselton's estimate - raised problems in relation to what Thiselton saw as being Gadamer's neglect of the potentially creative (or destructive), experience-generating, understanding-transforming, multiformity and multifunctionality of grammatical propositions.

For Thiselton, then, against Gadamer, creatively functioning grammatical propositions were *integral to the hermeneutical circle, to the processes of traditions, and to historical dialectic.*

Having said this, however, that Thiselton's grammatical utterances admitted further modification and sub-division beyond any "formal" triadic notion of "utterance-types" might have alerted Thiselton to the necessity of *marking* the grammatical changes implicit in *his continued use* of Continental terminology more explicitly given his *criticisms* of Continental traditions. Thiselton *changed the grammar* of Gadamer's terminology *legitimately* in an act of tradition-refinement. And yet, Thiselton changed the grammar of Gadamer's terminology *almost covertly, as though* in an act of illegitimate "spell-formation" or "persuasive definition" (though Thiselton was in fact innocent in relation to such a charge).

In any case, (7), Thiselton's "widened dialogue" did indeed produce a needed "transformation" or "tradition-refinement" of the Gadamerian hermeneutical paradigm. Moreover, Thiselton's "tradition-refinement" of the Gadamerian hermeneutical paradigm effectively *re-started and revised* the early Pannenberg's transformation of that same paradigm.

Thiselton achieved this "re-start" or "revision" – we may now add - in alignment with "step three" of what he had, in 1970, identified as a broader 'hermeneutical programme' (see Chapter 1). For Thiselton, as we may recall, "step three" of this broader 'hermeneutical programme' was to appropriate 'the enormous advances… in semantics, linguistics, and linguistic philosophy'. And, for Thiselton, this appropriation of 'the enormous advances… in semantics, linguistics, and linguistic philosophy' required "widening dialogue" - at the level of critical synthesis and preunderstanding – to include more interlocutors.[632] And, for Thiselton, these interlocutors included - most notably, but by no means exclusively - the later Wittgenstein, J.L. Austin, the philosophy of language more broadly, the post-Saussurian tradition of general linguistics, and (to a very limited extent) structuralist approaches.

And so, we may conclude that Thiselton's work – in re-casting the broad kind of approach adopted by the early Pannenberg on a stronger footing in relation to the philosophy of language and general linguistics - thus *strengthened* the Pannenbergian conclusion that history was the ontological ground of language and not vice versa, and that hermeneutics came to unity in a hermeneutical critique of history and not in a hermeneutical critique of language.

Moreover, bearing in mind the fact that Thiselton's appeals to the later Wittgenstein (and to J.L. Austin, the philosophy of language more broadly, general linguistics, and so on – i.e. *to the predominantly "Anglo-American" tradition of analytical philosophy*) pre-dated those of Pannenberg, we can conclude that it was *Thiselton and not Pannenberg* who ushered in the *larger critical synthesis that united appeals to the major Continental and Anglo-American philosophical traditions*.

Thiselton understood that the problem of hermeneutics could not be solved until the artificial polarization between the major Continental and Anglo-American philosophical traditions had been overcome.

And so, we saw that Thiselton's larger critical synthesis embraced not only a later Wittgensteinian modification of Gadamer's thought, but also an implicitly Gadamerian correction of an imbalance in relation to the later Wittgenstein's under-development of the implications of his own new thinking for a philosophy of history – an implicit correction that also drew, later, on K.-O. Apel.

Thus, Thiselton was neither simply "Gadamerian", nor simply "later-Wittgensteinian", nor simply "Pannenbergian" but offered perhaps *the first* truly unified "post-Gadamerian", "post-later-Wittgensteinian" paradigm for theological hermeneutics (a mere sixteen years after the publication of Gadamer's *Truth and Method* we might add).

---

[632] Thiselton, 'T&F', 11.

Therefore, Thiselton's work constituted a genuine paradigm-shift in hermeneutics that *could not* be reduced simply to a mere "over-arching" stratum three hermeneutical "model" or "tool" based on speech-acts or on action-models. Rather, Thiselton altered the entire philosophical and theological *subtext* of hermeneutical theory – and, we may now add, *had already done so twenty-five years before* C.G. Bartholomew called *for* such a change to *begin*.

More than this, some of the main features of Thiselton's major achievement had been overlooked by *all* those who had commented on his work in the literature. This point *alone* calls for a *critique of hermeneutical foreclosure in academic settings* (see Chapter 7).

Furthermore, since stratum-one dialogue affects theory directly, and since theory affects interpretative practice and outcomes directly, then Thiselton's much needed, much awaited, and yet overlooked paradigm-shift towards a new philosophical-historical unification of hermeneutical theory now becomes *preconditional for responsible interpretation*. From now on, we have to at least begin by following in Thiselton's footsteps, even if his approach, in its turn, will inevitably eventually require further programmatic modification as he himself would argue.

(This further programmatic modification is, in our view, to begin with a widening dialogue with pastoral theology – and with disciplines relevant to pastoral theology – as we argued above).

Finally, the fact that Thiselton's unified theoretical construction emerges through his appeals to *both* philosophy *and* theology should not escape us. This point introduces us to the first subject addressed in our final chapter, to which we now turn.

CHAPTER 7

# Hermeneutical Unity, Objectivity and Foreclosure: Towards a Christological Unification of Hermeneutics, a Unified Hermeneutical Critique of Historical Objectivity, and a Critique of Hermeneutical Foreclosure

### A. Preliminary Comments:
### Hermeneutical Unity, Objectivity, and Foreclosure

In the present chapter, after our preliminary comments, we will begin by continuing our exposition of *The Two Horizons* from where we left off in Chapter 6. First of all, though, we may recall here that, in Chapter 6, we argued that Thiselton – during his second period (and from that time onwards) - brings his second and third stratum hermeneutical critiques to internal intra-critique unity, and to overall inter-critique unity, within the co-ordinates of his second-stratum hermeneutical critique of history.

Conversely, in Chapter 6, we saw that, for Thiselton, second- and third-stratum hermeneutical theory *cannot* be unified within the co-ordinates of a hermeneutical critique of "language".

This finding aligns with our argument, in Chapter 3, that Thiselton ultimately grounds and unifies hermeneutics in eschatology and in Christology. Further, in Chapters 3 to 6, we demonstrated that Thiselton everywhere combines philosophical and theological appeals in his theoretical reconstruction of hermeneutics. Thus, whilst Thiselton's work connotes a historical, rather than a linguistic, unification of/for hermeneutical theory, Thiselton understands "history" both eschatologically and Christologically. In the present chapter we will aim to provide further arguments that demonstrate that this is so.

We also argued, in Chapter 3, that Thiselton's mixing of philosophical and theological appeals was not a "straightforwardly fideist" accommodation of the former to the latter. Rather, Thiselton explored theological contributions to hermeneutics partly because of Heidegger's and Gadamer's failure to provide the provisional "metacriteria" (i.e. the provisional "transcendent" or *a posteriori* "trans-contextual and trans-temporal" metacriteria) required for liberation-oriented socio-meta-critiques of traditions – socio-meta-critiques that history and experience tell us are *both possible and necessary*.

Notably, Thiselton argued that Heidegger had unnecessarily diminished *the spheres of operation available* - during the processes pertaining to understanding - for the employment of re-historicized subject-object conceptualization in relation to comparative metacritical and critical testing. For Thiselton, this marginalization of re-historicized subject-object conceptualization in Heidegger's hermeneutics was a problem that required a solution.

Thiselton, therefore, argued that prior theological solutions to this problem were indeed available – solutions that allowed *both* provisional metacriteria *and* the provisionally accessible public criteria of tradition to function socio-critically – in the context of comparative metacritical and critical testing - *through* the employment and operation of properly reinstated re-historicized subject-object conceptualization.

We also saw that Thiselton's exposition of a biblical multiform notion of "truth" *corrected* extra-biblical approaches to truth – including Continental philosophical approaches to truth - along multiple axes.

It is the placing of these kinds of observations alongside the fact of the historical interwovenness of philosophy and theology in Western traditions (see our Introduction) that makes more recent inter-disciplinary polarizations between so-called "philosophical" hermeneutics and so-called "theological" hermeneutics look rather artificial.

But even if we allowed that an "independently-philosophical hermeneutics" could be constructed (a difficult stance given the histories of the concepts involved), then our findings in Chapter 6 would *still* engender the conclusion that such an "independently-philosophical hermeneutics" would come to unity *not* in a hermeneutical critique of language, but in a hermeneutical critique of history.

And *even this* "historically-unified" "independently-philosophical hermeneutics" would *still lack a metacritical dimension*, and so Thiselton's exploratory search for theological solutions to this problem would – even then - *still* be warranted.

Of course, as we have seen from Thiselton's work, any such theological solutions would only earn a place in the hermeneutical discussion – or would only be *philosophically warranted* – if they resonated with, or solved problems in relation to, issues emerging from widened and predominantly philosophical dialogues. Indeed, a viable theology – if it were to *unify hermeneutics as a whole* and thereby help to re-initiate dialogue between philosophy and theology more broadly in the Western traditions - would *not tend to easily disrupt the unity of a predominantly philosophical hermeneutic grounded in a hermeneutical critique of history*. A viable theology would likely tend to be *protective* of *this* kind of provisionally established historico-philosophical unity.

In the present chapter, therefore, we shall attempt to continue to show that Thiselton's work does indeed connote this kind of philosophically-warranted theological unification of hermeneutics, and that Thiselton's espousal of this kind of philosophically-warranted theological unification of hermeneutics constitutes *part* of the context in which Thiselton's high estimate of biblical authority should be understood.

Nevertheless, having said all this, it is crucial to note that Thiselton does *not* assimilate theology to a "philosophical worldview". Whilst Thiselton's hermeneutical critiques may certainly be seen from a philosophical angle of view, they also serve to elucidate resonances between philosophical traditions and a historically-*prior* biblical and theological framework. Further, we have already begun to see that Thiselton argues that widening dialogue – at the level of pre-understanding - with increasing numbers of philosophical (and other) traditions potentially produces greater and greater insights *into* – or greater and greater clarification *of* - this historically-prior biblical and theological framework. The implication of Thiselton's arguments in this context of discussion is that, as the process of widening dialogue continues, this historically-prior biblical and theological framework is revealed *both* as that which *historically anticipates* emerging philosophical unities *and* as that which *provides theoretical solutions to* emerging philosophical problems. One could say that, for Thiselton, the more philosophy one studies, the more of the content, authority, cogency, and profundity of the biblical writings one is able to see.

Moving on, then in the present chapter we shall also attempt, on the basis of *The Two Horizons*, to construct a Thiseltonian unified hermeneutical critique of historical objectivity – a critique in which Thiselton again unites appeals to philosophy and theology. This hermeneutical critique of historical objectivity constitutes a further aspect of Thiselton's hermeneutical critique of epistemology (on which, Chapter 3). The latter, in turn, contributes to Thiselton's developing unified hermeneutical theory as a whole in a way that we have already examined (see Chapters 3 and 6).

That is, we might ask: in the light of Thiselton's developing unified hermeneutical theory *as a whole*, how should we conceive of the possibility (or otherwise) of the "objectivity" of our understandings, interpretations or descriptions? The point of constructing a "Thiseltonian unified hermeneutical critique of historical objectivity" is to find an answer to this question. And the answer to this question that will emerge below is that, for Thiselton, responsible interpretation is properly *historical* – and is thus neither objectivistic nor purely relativistic.

Specifically, we shall argue that Thiselton posits eight overlapping axes of inter-related and mutually-qualifying historico-philosophical (and theological) criteria – criteria that, in the case of each axis, suggest that "history" affects "objectivity" *both* negatively *and* positively in ways that are (*to an extent*) distinctively shaped by the *character of* each axis, as we shall demonstrate. (Incidentally, these *"eight axes of criteria"* are derived from the theological and philosophical framework that emerges partly through Thiselton's sublation of his *"three inter-related modified Hegelian criteria"* into the co-ordinates of his expanding provisional biblical-theological understanding).

In other words, Thiselton's critique of hermeneutical understanding – which presupposes his hermeneutical critique of epistemology (along with his other second-stratum hermeneutical critiques) – brings to the hermeneutical task a developed and thoroughly "re-historicized" epistemology.

Moreover, the conclusion will emerge - as we proceed through the remainder of the present chapter – that Thiselton's epistemology is *not less* "re-historicized" than are the epistemologies pertaining to broadly "positivist", broadly "existentialist", broadly "structuralist", broadly "post-structuralist", and broadly "socio-pragmatic" traditions. Rather, Thiselton's epistemology is *more* "re-historicized" than are the epistemologies pertaining to these traditions.

Finally, in the largest section of the present chapter and, indeed, of the whole of the present study, we shall compliment our discussion concerning "responsible interpretation" by providing examples of the opposite. That is, we shall highlight a progression of kinds of irresponsible interpretation that are discernable in some of Thiselton's critics. As we shall demonstrate, these kinds of irresponsible interpretation range from straightforward hermeneutical foreclosure, through pseudo-"post-structuralist" canonization of hermeneutical foreclosure and broadly socio-pragmatic asserted "legitimization" of hermeneutical foreclosure, to hostile "disowned projections" of hermeneutical foreclosure.

Notably, we shall argue that pseudo-"post-structuralist" and broadly socio-pragmatic criticisms of Thiselton tend to presuppose - falsely – that Thiselton's stance is predicated upon the basis of a premise of linguistic-philosophical idealism or formalism, or upon the basis of a premise of philosophically idealist epistemological "foundationalism". In this context of discussion, therefore, and against these false criticisms, we shall attempt to *begin* to show that Thiselton's approach actually constitutes a genuine alternative to broadly post-structuralist approaches and to broadly socio-pragmatic approaches that is potentially *more* successful than these approaches in *leaving linguistic-philosophical idealism and/or formalism and/or philosophically idealist epistemological "foundationalism" behind*.

Moreover, we shall aim to show that broadly socio-pragmatic appeals to a Barthian epistemology of revelation merely complicate matters further in relation to the problems pertaining to theoretical (and practical) dichotomies that *already* beleaguer broadly socio-pragmatic hermeneutics.

Notably, we shall aim to show that when a Barthian epistemology of revelation is combined with a strictly "Fishian" approach to texts, then the result is a kind of "hermeneutics" that is internally fissured and disrupted by no less than *five sets of internal theoretical (and practical) dichotomies*. We shall contend – appealing to Pannenberg and Thiselton - that since Barthian-Fishian "argument" is internally disrupted to *this extent*, then "authoritarian assertion" *becomes the only remaining way* to promote a "Barthian-Fishian" approach to the biblical texts.

In particular, we shall argue that when a Barthian epistemology of revelation is combined with a strictly "Fishian" approach to texts, the outcome is that the authoritarianisms "of the Word" and "of the Spirit" that Pannenberg and Thiselton *already* associate with a Barthian epistemology of revelation threaten to focus increasingly towards a sharpened authoritarianism "of the Spirit" that could potentially lead communities affected by such an authoritarianism "of the Spirit" to try to immunize themselves from external criticism.

We shall also speculate as to whether or not hostile "disowned projections" of hermeneutical foreclosure constitute the beginnings of a fulfillment of Thiselton's third and fourth period prophetic predictions concerning the ways in which broadly socio-pragmatic culture inevitably (in Thiselton's estimate) decays into conflicts between competing groups.

### B. Towards a Provisional Christological Unification of Hermeneutics Embracing Metacritical Explanation and Metacritical Evaluation

*1. Thiselton's Critical Widening of Dialogue with Theological Traditions*

Against misleading charges that allege that Thiselton supposedly indulges in straightforward "'fideism'", we may observe that it is clear that Thiselton – in *The Two Horizons* - widens dialogue with theological traditions in a way that provisionally coheres with, but that retains the potential for criticism of, provisional conclusions emerging from his predominantly *philosophical* discussions. Correlatively, Thiselton attacks E. Troeltsch and D.E. Nineham for *'a priori'* "narrowing" or "excluding" *philosophically warranted* "'theological'" discussion in an "absolutist" manner. Again, Pannenberg's work is Thiselton's point of departure in this context of discussion: drawing on Pannenberg, Thiselton seeks to widen theological and philosophical dialogue - at the level of pre-understanding - beyond the places reached by the theological and philosophical dialogues that pertain to the pre-understandings presupposed by 'positivist' theology, by Bultmann, and by the New Hermeneutic. Nevertheless, Thiselton is not simply 'Pannenbergian' as we have already seen: rather, Thiselton, by independently appealing to *Anglo-American traditions of thought*, extends, revises, or even *restarts* (on a different footing) Pannenberg's earlier critique of *Continental traditions of thought*. Notably, Thiselton's first independent appeals to the later Wittgenstein *predate* Pannenberg's main published appeals to the later Wittgenstein. And so, the first truly "post-Gadamerian", "post-later-Wittgensteinian" *theological* hermeneutical paradigm emerges in the thinking of Thiselton, rather than in the thinking of Pannenberg. In our view, it is this "Thiseltonian" theological hermeneutical paradigm that constitutes the *philosophically-warranted* transformed hermeneutical paradigm that biblical hermeneutics – and even hermeneutics more broadly – has been waiting for. Thiselton's hermeneutics, then, are emphatically not a regression to an older Barthian "'fideism'" "of the Word", but move *away from* such "'fideism'".[1]

---

[1] Thiselton, A.C., *The Two Horizons: New Testament Hermeneutics and Philosophical Description with Special Reference to Heidegger, Bultmann, Gadamer, and Wittgenstein* (Exeter: Paternoster Press, 1980), 77-79, 60, 284; cf.: 53-84, 195, 274, 286-290, 322-325, 388-389, 396, 423-440. On the false charge of "'fideism'", cf. Walsh, B.J., 'Anthony Thiselton's Contribution to Biblical Hermeneutics', *ChSRev* 14.3 (1985), 235. On the caricature, 'Pannenbergian', cf. Palmer, R.E., 'The Scope of Hermeneutics: The Problem of Critique, and the Crisis of Modernity', *TRevCTLit* 3 (1984), 226-227. Third italics Thiselton's, remaining italics ours.

## 2. Contrasting Evaluations of Whether or Not Thiselton is Straightforwardly Fideistic

Some writers, however, falsely charge Thiselton with a straightforward "'fideism'" or with "privileging" 'theology'. Thus, according to A.J. McNicol, Thiselton supposedly espouses, to use R.L. Maddox's language, 'a fideistic defence of the claim of religious language to its own realm'.[2] Or, according to R.W.L. Moberly, Thiselton supposedly simply "privileges" 'the Bible' or 'Christian theology' over other religious texts or theologies.[3] Or, according to E.T. Charry, 'Thiselton' supposedly lacks 'a sustained… argument for the reclamation of theism';[4] or, according to R.L. Hall, Thiselton supposedly simply "defends" 'the traditional' 'theological enterprise';[5] or, according to B.R. Clack, Thiselton even supposedly "flees" 'from' 'postmodern' 'questions' to a 'Trinitarian' "'theology of promise'" as though Thiselton were, supposedly, a fideist who was unconcerned to relate these two spheres.[6]

However, against such cavalier misreadings of Thiselton, we should observe that P. Ellingworth rightly notes 'Thiselton's' 'dialogue' 'between philosophy', 'linguistics', 'systematic theology and biblical exegesis'. And we may observe that R. Morgan rightly accepts Thiselton's affirmation of 'the critical potential of Scripture' (though, elsewhere, Morgan is more ambiguous). Moreover, J.S. Reist astutely observes that - in Thiselton's estimate – "'Freud, Marx, and Nietzsche'" rightly highlighted "'human'" self-deception; and that, for Thiselton, this human characteristic "'resonates with biblical and theological assertions about the deceitfulness, opaqueness, and duplicity of the human heart'". That is, as we have already seen, and as we shall see even more clearly later in the present chapter, Thiselton's emphases on "dialogue", "resonance", and "critical potential" actually contribute to his *strong opposition to* straightforward "'fideism'".[7]

---

[2] Walsh, 'TC', 235; cf.: Moberly, R.W.L., 'Review of A.C. Thiselton's *New Horizons in Hermeneutics*', *Anv* 11.1 (1994), 72; Maddox, R.L., 'Review of A.C. Thiselton's *The Two Horizons*', *ThStud* 43.1 (Mar. 1982), 137; McNicol, A.J., 'Review of A.C. Thiselton's *The Two Horizons*', *RestQ* 27.3 (1984), 188-189. Maddox rightly argues that Thiselton *avoids* this – against McNicol.

[3] Moberly, 'R NH', 72.

[4] Charry, E.T., 'Review of A.C. Thiselton's *Interpreting God and the Postmodern Self*, *ThT* 54.1 (Apr. 1997), 108.

[5] Hall, R.L., 'Review of A.C. Thiselton's *Interpreting God and the Postmodern Self*, *IJPhRel* 42.2 (Oct. 1997), 121.

[6] Clack, B.R., 'Review of A.C. Thiselton's *Interpreting God and the Postmodern Self*, *RelStud* 32 (Sep. 1996), 428.

[7] Ellingworth, P., 'Review of A.C. Thiselton's *The Two Horizons*', *EvanQ* 53 (Jul.-Sep. 1981), 179; cf.: Morgan, R., 'Review of A.C. Thiselton's *New Horizons in Hermeneutics*', *ExTim* 104.6 (Mar. 1993), 187; Thiselton, *2H*, 84, 440; Morgan, R., 'Review of A.C. Thiselton's *The Two Horizons*', *HeyJ* 22.3 (1981), 332; Reist, J.S., 'Review of A.C. Thiselton's *New Horizons in Hermeneutics*', *JEThS* 38.3 (Sep. 1995), 459; citing, Thiselton, A.C., *New Horizons in Hermeneutics: The Theory and Practice of Transforming Biblical Reading* (London: HarperCollins; Grand Rapids: Zondervan, 1992), 14; contradicting, Walsh, 'TC', 235.

*3. Dialogic Warranting of the Inclusion of Theological Considerations in Hermeneutics*

Thus, in *The Two Horizons*, Thiselton's *actual* stance is that, since biblical theology resonates with, or even improves upon, conclusions emerging from widening philosophical dialogues, then biblical theology is warranted as a potential source of components that are of relevance in relation to the construction of a working framework of theoretical co-ordinates that pertains to the unification of hermeneutics. Thiselton argues that such theological components or considerations earn a place in hermeneutical discussions by addressing philosophical demands. For Thiselton, to deny this fact would be to evade the implications emerging from widening *philosophical* dialogue.[8]

Conversely, Thiselton argues that narrowing *philosophical* dialogue actually *hinders theology*. Thus, for example, Thiselton does not merely attempt to make the later Wittgenstein "fit" a prior understanding of biblical theology; rather Thiselton appeals to the later Wittgenstein in order to elucidate a *better* biblical theology – a biblical theology that is "more biblical" and that is consistent with and *made more visible by* the later Wittgenstein's writings concerning language (see Chapters 4 and 6). That is, Thiselton argues that philosophical description provides new angles of vision in relation to the biblical texts *themselves* – angles of vision that would otherwise not be available.[9]

Thiselton's whole work presupposes these kinds of arguments for *including both* theological *and* philosophical considerations in hermeneutical discussions. But Thiselton's whole work *also* presupposes arguments for allowing theological and philosophical traditions to *critique* one another in relation to hermeneutical questions (see also Chapters 3 and 4). Thus, K.J. Vanhoozer records that, in the 1990s, he, C.G. Bartholomew, F. Watson, and Thiselton 'argue for a theological hermeneutic... that is itself formed, informed, and reformed by Christian doctrine' (though Thiselton began this argument in the *1960s*). That is, again, Thiselton's use of 'philosophical description' to clarify biblical 'texts' is met with a counter-flow in which Thiselton allows biblical theology to shape and correct philosophical findings: for Thiselton, a dialogue takes place between philosophy and theology – a dialogue that is linked to warrant. For Thiselton, 'theology' is a 'hermeneutical enterprise'; but it is also true that, for Thiselton, hermeneutics is a theological 'enterprise'.[10]

And so, in some senses, Thiselton leaves 'theology' at 'the margins of the discussion',[11] and holds even his '"*metacritique*"' of '"the cross"' in tension with

---

[8] Thiselton, *2H*, 84, cf.: 440; 53-63; 74-84; 59.

[9] Thiselton, *2H*, 85-114; cf.: 386-427; 3-10; 445; querying, Bowden, J., 'Review of A.C. Thiselton's *The Two Horizons*', *Th* 84.697 (Jan. 1981), 57.

[10] Vanhoozer, K.J., *First Theology. God, Scripture and Hermeneutics* (Leicester: Apollos, 2002), 286; cf. Thiselton, *2H*, 6; cf. last quotation from, Hogan, J.P., 'Hermeneutics and the Logic of Question and Answer - Collingwood and Gadamer', *HeyJ* 28.3 (Jul. 1987), 263.

[11] Watson, F., 'Review of A.C. Thiselton's *New Horizons in Hermeneutics*', *BibInterp* 4.2 (1996), 256.

"'pluralities of readings'". His biblical theology is a working framework in progress, and is refined through his dialogue with philosophy.[12]

Conversely, Thiselton admits that 'from the standpoint of pluralism' his 'Christian' "interpretations" 'appear "privileged"', 'and' that 'a conflict of truth-claims may be inevitable'. Thiselton's "faith seeking understanding", however, should not blind us to his appeals to philosophical warrant. Admittedly, as J. Goldingay observes, in 1992 Thiselton speaks of Scripture as a '"gift"' from 'God'. However, the context of discussion here is Thiselton's demonstration of the resonance between "theological" "tradition" and philosophical views of 'textuality' even if, in turn, Thiselton allows textual '"givenness"' (on '"givenness"' see later) to become a reciprocal critique of *other* philosophies of 'textuality'. Philosophical warrant – i.e. allowing theological considerations to contribute to hermeneutical discussions because these theological considerations cogently address philosophical questions - is again implicit in Thiselton's approach.[13]

Nevertheless, as we have said on several occasions, Thiselton does not assimilate biblical theology to a philosophical worldview. As we shall see below, Thiselton's stance remains one of "faith seeking understanding". Thiselton allows his dialogues with different philosophical traditions *to refine his vantage-point in relation to* the received faith. But Thiselton also allows his refined vantage-point in relation to the received faith *to correct or re-shape real philosophical deficiencies* that he encounters *in the context of* his dialogues with different philosophical traditions.

### 4. *Christological Metacriteria and Broadened Philosophical Dialogue*

In *The Two Horizons*, then, Thiselton argues that theological considerations that are relevant to hermeneutics should not be *'a priori'* "excluded" from hermeneutical discussions. Crucially, following Pannenberg, Thiselton applies this argument, centrally, to the 'Christ'-'event'. That is, for Thiselton, the 'Christ'-'event' resonates with, or rather anticipates, and also *improves* upon, the three central inter-related modified Hegelian criteria that emerge from his (i.e. Thiselton's) widened dialogue with the philosophy of history (see Chapter 6).[14]

Thus, (1), Thiselton argues that the 'Christ'-'event', in "anticipating" *'history-as-a-whole'*, presupposes a 'universal' 'context' for 'understanding'. That is, for Thiselton, '"meaning"' partly turns on 'historical' "relationalities", and on 'historical' inter-relationships, within an anticipated historico-eschatological "whole". Thiselton would agree with J.C. McHann Jr. when McHann Jr., after Pannenberg, writes that, 'in... Jesus Christ we have a proleptic provision of a

---

[12] Reist, 'R *NH*', 459; cf. Thiselton, *NH*, 615. Italics Thiselton's.
[13] Thiselton, *NH*, 63-64; cf.: 55-132; 615; cf. Goldingay, J., *Models for Interpretation of Scripture* (Carlisle: Paternoster; Grand Rapids: Eerdmans, 1995), 36.
[14] Thiselton, *2H*, 78, 77, 82; cf. 74-84; cf. Thiselton, *NH*, 331-338, 604-619. Italics in speech-marks Thiselton's.

tentative conception of the terminus of the hermeneutical circle'.[15] E.A. Dunn rightly argues that, for Thiselton, the Christological anticipation of an eschatological notion of "history-as-a-whole" "extends" Gadamer's metacritical appeal to 'tradition' and to '"effective history"' and constitutes Thiselton's 'temporal metacritique' in relation to Christ's 'resurrection'. Dunn is correct to argue that Thiselton's eschatology, in following that of Pannenberg, "raises" 'history and tradition to the next level'. Dunn's exposition of Thiselton's hermeneutical critique of history is valuable (though he under-emphasizes Thiselton's other six hermeneutical axes), and he rightly observes Thiselton's *reversal* of Gadamer's 'ontological' prioritization of 'language' over 'history' (cf. Chapter 6).[16]

For Thiselton, the Christ-event also presupposes temporal distinctions between *past, present, and future*, and, in addition, engenders *provisionally-understood and potentially-progressive* "anticipations" of 'history-as-a-whole' – where these "anticipations" are projected *from within* '"history"'. Thus, Thiselton argues that the Christ-event was an '"historical"' actuality (i.e. a '"past"' event), that the Christ-event is the 'present' focus of 'faith' (cf. the 'present' "now"), and that the Christ-event was an '"eschatological… event"' with '"future"' significance (i.e. an anticipation of the '"future"' "not yet"). Thus, Thiselton argues that 'faith' (in three of its biblical senses) in the Christ-event rests on 'historical' 'events' (cf. the 'past'), involves repeated "decisions" based on a provisional 'progressive' 'understanding' of "experienced" divine "faithfulness" (cf. the 'present'), and involves '"trust"' without sight grounded in *'promise'* (cf. the 'future'). Thus, Thiselton argues that 'faith' (in three of its biblical senses) in the Christ-event resonates with *the "progressiveness", "provisionality", and "openness"' to "the future"' that characterize "the hermeneutical circle"'*. Moreover, Thiselton draws on Pannenberg in order to argue that 'faith' (in three of its biblical senses) in the Christ-event thereby also resonates with '"the proleptic structure of knowledge"'.[17]

---

[15] Thiselton, *2H*, 82-83, 77, 244; cf.: 66-67; 80-84; cf. McHann Jr., J.C., *The Three Horizons: A Study in Biblical Hermeneutics with Special Reference to Wolfhart Pannenberg* (Aberdeen: University of Aberdeen Ph.D. Thesis, 1987), 465. Italics ours.

[16] Thiselton, *2H*, 311, 307; cf.: 66-67; 74-84; 440-443; cf.: Dunn, E.A., *Beyond Dialogue and History: The Hermeneutical Pluralism of Anthony C. Thiselton and his Metacritical Use of the Cross and Resurrection of Christ* (Hamilton, Mass.: Gordon-Conwell Seminary M.A. Thesis, May 1998), 60; cf.: 61; 68-70; 22; McHann Jr., *3H*, 465, 326; Thiselton, *NH*, 330; Gadamer, H.-G., *Truth and Method* (trans. J. Weinsheimer and D.G. Marshall; London: Sheed & Ward, 1975, 1989), 301, 391, 438-491.

[17] Thiselton, *2H*, 82-84, 247-249, 274, 172, 103-104, 287, 409, 181; cf. 345-346, 179, 194, 382, 121, 264-266, 166, 197, 303-310, 315, 323; cf. Thiselton, A.C., 'The Parousia in Modern Theology. Some Questions and Comments', *Tyn* 27 (1976), 51; Thiselton, A.C., 'Communicative Action and Promise in Inter-Disciplinary, Biblical, and Theological Hermeneutics', in *The Promise of Hermeneutics* (R. Lundin, C. Walhout and A.C. Thiselton; Grand Rapids and Cambridge: Eerdmans; Carlisle: Paternoster, 1999), 223-231; quotation

Thus, Thiselton neither "sacrifices" 'the hiddenness... of faith and its "objects"' (here we are contradicting R.A. Harrisville's reading of Thiselton), nor so stresses 'hiddenness' that nothing is revealed now. Thiselton only writes that 'divine transcendence is disclosed *more openly* in a promised series of future events' than 'in... the cross'. Thiselton does not confine 'the cross' to 'the level of immanence', and does indeed view 'the cross [as] an *indirect* communication of divine transcendence' (here we are contradicting K.J. Vanhoozer's reading of Thiselton).[18]

For Thiselton, (2), biblical claims regarding the 'universal' "ethical" authority of the Christ-event presuppose *"'the unity of'" "'historical'" 'reality'*. Thiselton argues that there is no absolute dissociation of 'past' horizons from 'present' horizons that could make Jesus' teaching on 'love' irrelevant for 'today'. Philosophically-speaking, for Thiselton, such a dissociation would untenably "exaggerate" 'historical distance' *in that* such a dissociation would *transgress the philosophical criterion of* "'the unity of'" "'historical'" 'reality'. Furthermore, Thiselton argues that the strongly "relational" emphasis of the Christ-event (i.e. on 'love') also resonates with his (i.e. Thiselton's) critique of hermeneutical understanding – a critique that Thiselton supports by appealing (if critically) to 'Gadamer' and, later, to E. Betti. Thus, for Thiselton, as for Gadamer and Betti, "listening" in 'openness' to 'the other' contrasts sharply with 'manipulative' 'Enlightenment' "'method'". Therefore, Thiselton argues that, in part, hermeneutical understanding becomes an aspect of a *biblical or Christ-like way of relating* where, for Thiselton, this point extends questions about "validity" and "correctness" in relation to interpretations towards questions to do with "relational ethics". That is, for Thiselton, the Christ-event, as the primary anticipative paradigm for the coming eschatological 'kingdom of love', provides us with a dialogically-warranted working 'model' for an evaluative metacriterion for understanding that is (in part) predicated upon the ground of the premise of "'the unity of'" "'historical'" 'reality'.[19]

---

from, McHann Jr., *3H*, 384; cf. Tupper, E.F., *The Theology of Wolfhart Pannenberg* (London: SCM Press, 1974), 84. Fourth italics Thiselton's, remaining italics ours.

[18] Contradicting, Harrisville, R.A., 'Review of A.C. Thiselton's *The Two Horizons*', *Interp* 36 (Apr. 1982), 216; cf.: Thiselton, A.C., *Interpreting God and The Postmodern Self: On Meaning, Manipulation and Promise* (*SJT*: Current Issues in Theology; Edinburgh: T&T Clark, 1995), 147; Thiselton, A.C., 'Realized Eschatology at Corinth', *NTStud* 24 (Jul. 1978), 514; contradicting, Vanhoozer, *FT*, 371-372. First italics ours, second italics Vanhoozer's.

[19] Thiselton, *2H*, 82-83, 60-63, 302-304, 77-78, 53, 57, 422, 353; cf.: 80-84; 103-107; 200-203; 234-251; 294-295; 308-310; cf.: Thiselton, *IGPS*, 154, 13, 160; cf. 41-43, 47-51, 69-71, 153-163; Thiselton, A.C., 'Thirty Years of Hermeneutics: Retrospect and Prospects', in *International Symposium on the Interpretation of the Bible* (ed. J. Krašovec; Ljubljana: Slovenian Academy of Sciences and Arts; Sheffield: Sheffield Academic Press, 1998), 1564, cf. 1560-1561; Thiselton, *NH*, 252; cf. 247-253, 604-619; Thiselton, A.C., 'Reader-Response Hermeneutics, Action Models, and the Parables of Jesus', in *The Responsibility of Hermeneutics* (R. Lundin, A.C. Thiselton and C. Walhout; Grand Rapids: Eerdmans; Exeter: Paternoster, 1985), 113; Thiselton, A.C., 'Creativity of Heaven', *CEN* 8 Mar. (1974), 5. Italics ours.

In this context of discussion, Thiselton argues that "meaning" relates to *'verdictive' judgments regarding* - or to evaluative assessments of - the quality of 'historical' (including inter-personal) relationships (and "relationalities"). For Thiselton, such verdictive judgments - or evaluative assessments - emerge through a process of drawing comparisons between 'historical' relationships (and "relationalities"), and, Christ's 'historical' relating (i.e. love for God, neighbor, and – we might add – for the created environment). That is, Thiselton employs Christ's 'historical' relating as an evaluative metacriterion. Drawing on E.A. Dunn again, we should note that Thiselton here "extends" Gadamer's metacritical principle of understanding as 'dialogue' so as to embrace 'a Trinitarian' 'relationality' of 'love' in which the 'new' "emerges" through 'a critique' 'of power' or – more broadly - through 'a critique' of fallen 'relationality' and/or of fallen relationships. For Thiselton, dialogue *with* other traditions (stratum one) must be dialogue *as* 'love' for neighbors (stratum three). Moreover, Thiselton's focus on 'a Trinitarian' 'relationality' of 'love' – a 'love' made visible in the Christ-event - brings to the fore considerations to do with "personhood" (more properly, "persons") and with "persons-in-relation". For Thiselton, a unified conception of historical reality, once sublated into a 'Trinitarian' and Christo-eschatological theological framework, is rendered in such a way that it remains respectful - though not in an anthropocentric or socio-pragmatic way – *both* of individual "persons" (in their narrative-temporality) *and* of communities and their inter-subjective narrative-temporalities of "persons-in-relation".[20]

Therefore, Thiselton argues that historical-eschatological explanation and historical-eschatological evaluation are now one in Christ, since – in Thiselton's estimate - Christ "anticipates" *both* an explanatory *'view'* of the '"whole"' and 'parts' in relation to an "eschatological" '"third horizon"', *and* an evaluative *'critique'* of the '"whole"' and 'parts' in terms of an assessment of the quality of historical (including human) relationships and relationalities as judged by comparison with the 'public' "standards" of Christ's Trinitarian love.[21] Thus, Thiselton's 'theology of the cross and resurrection… criticizes human self-seeking and manipulation and opens the way for genuine transformation'.[22] For Thiselton, who draws on 'Jürgen Moltmann' at this point, 'the Cross of Christ… "becomes a socio-critical principle"' - a universally applicable epistemological metacriterion. Whilst Thiselton's appeal to Moltmann dates back to the mid 1970s (modifying E.A.

---

[20] Dunn, *BD&H*, 43-60; cf.: Thiselton, 'Par', 50, cf. 52; Thiselton, *2H*, 421, 313, 309, 60-63; Thiselton, A.C., 'Human Being, Relationality and Time in Hebrews, 1 Corinthians and Western Traditions. Paper presented at North Park Theological Seminary, Oct 17-19, 1997', *ExA* 13 (1997), 77; cf. 79-80; cf. 76-95; Thiselton, *IGPS*, 156, 161, 160; Thiselton, *NH*, 615; Gadamer, *TM*, 369, 383. See also Chapter 4. Italics on *'verdictive'* Thiselton's, others ours.

[21] Thiselton, *2H*, 82, 104; cf. Thiselton, *NH*, 251, 615; cf. Tulloch, S. ed., *The Reader's Digest Oxford Wordfinder* (Oxford: Clarendon Press, 1993), 108, where, in common parlance a 'bar' in a legal setting is 'a public standard of acceptability'. Italics ours.

[22] Moberly, 'R *NH*', 72; cf. Thiselton, *NH*, 334, 611-619.

Dunn's reading of Thiselton),[23] this appeal becomes more explicit and developed *after* Thiselton's later appeals to Jürgen Habermas' philosophy, in continuation of Thiselton's pattern of dialogic warrant. 'Admittedly', though, as J.C. McHann Jr. rightly remarks, ambiguities remain in relation to precisely 'how a "Christological principle"' of 'interpretation' should function.[24]

(3) Thiselton argues, in alignment with Pannenberg's thinking, that the Christ-event – in manifesting "continuities" 'with' 'Hebrew… tradition' whilst simultaneously paradigming the truly 'new' of "unrepeatable" 'historical novelty' - presupposes a kind of tradition-refinement that is resonant with the criterion of a dynamic, '"dialectic"' 'process' of *'creative' 'historical' 'synthesis'* that is grounded in the processes of concrete traditions (see Chapter 6). (Pannenberg's notion of 'plurality and unity in creation' may well contribute to the background of Thiselton's thinking here). In Chapter 6, we argued that, for Thiselton: (a) historical synthesis was grounded in the processes of concrete traditions; (b) that the processes of concrete traditions could be conceived of as socio-historical extensions of the hermeneutical circle; and, (c), that the hermeneutical circle thus had to take account of – *amongst many other things (see Chapters 5 and 6)* – the potential of the *processes* of traditions to "form spells", "break spells", "refine-traditions", and "shatter worlds". The implication that we may draw from these points here is that, in Thiselton's estimate, *if* the biblical accounts indicate that the Christ-event refined 'Hebrew… tradition' as noted above, *then* – in Thiselton's estimate - the Christ-event resonates with the hermeneutical circle (i.e. on account of the *philosophical* links that Thiselton finds between tradition-refinement and the hermeneutical circle). This conclusion only strengthens our points in '(1)' above to do with the resonances that Thiselton finds between faith (in three of its senses) in the Christ-event and the "progressiveness" of '"the hermeneutical circle"'. That is, for Thiselton, *faith in* the Christ-event, *and* the Christ-event *itself, both* resonate with '"the hermeneutical circle"'.[25]

Summarizing: the Christ-event, in Thiselton's hermeneutics, precedes, resonates with, but also anticipates and extends beyond, the three inter-related modified Hegelian criteria that emerge from Thiselton's widened dialogue with the philosophy of history. Therefore, for Thiselton, the use of *provisional* biblical-theological or Christ-centered systems in order to ground and unify *working* hermeneutical theory-constructions is *philosophically* warranted. Thiselton does not fail to warrant his "appeals" to 'divine intervention' in history (here we are querying F.H. Borsch's reading of Thiselton), 'to the cross', or 'to the "third horizon"' of eschatology (here we are contradicting R.S. Hess's reading of

---

[23] Dunn, *BD&H*, 46; cf.: 49; 54; 61; cf.: Thiselton, *NH*, 7, 606-615; Thiselton, 'Par', 47-53.

[24] Thiselton, *NH*, 379-393, cf. 336, 416-418, 606-614; cf. Thiselton, *IGPS*, 24-26, cf. 145-149, 154-158; cf. McHann Jr., *3H*, 386.

[25] Thiselton, *2H*, 19, 79-81, 66-67, 309, 104; cf.: 80-81; 17-19; 44-45; 322-326; 348-350; 401-407; cf. Thiselton, *NH*, 446; cf. Pannenberg, W., *Systematic Theology. Volume 2* (trans. G.W. Bromiley; Grand Rapids: Eerdmans, 1994), 61 onwards; cf. 136-146. Italics ours.

Thiselton).²⁶

Admittedly, the objection could be raised that since Hegel's philosophy is linked to Christian theology anyway, then it is not surprising that "inter-related modified Hegelian criteria" resonate with "the Christ-event" in Thiselton's hermeneutics. However, for Thiselton, the point is that these criteria *also unify a predominantly philosophical hermeneutics*. It is fitting, therefore, in Thiselton's view, that Hegel - whose thinking was *both* theological *and* philosophical - should contribute, albeit in *a heavily modified* way, to overcoming the present artificial divide between philosophical hermeneutics and theological hermeneutics – a divide bequeathed by Western traditions since Descartes and Kant.

*5. Dialogic Warrant as a Context of Understanding for Thiselton on Biblical Authority*

Against the charge of 'fundamentalism' that R.A. Harrisville inappropriately levels at Thiselton, we should note that Thiselton's comments on 'biblical authority' at the end of *The Two Horizons* should be viewed, at least partly, in the context of his warranted inclusion of theological considerations in hermeneutical discussions. It is partly in *this* context that Thiselton speaks of 'biblical authority' as being "independent of situations in the present horizon", or as presupposing 'the truth of' Jesus' divinity and of 'God's relationship to the world'. Thus, in his discussion on 'biblical authority', Thiselton's predominantly *philosophical* discussion often *also* surfaces, as when, for example, he argues – drawing on J.L. Austin's and D.D. Evans' "logic of self-involvement" - that 'God's' reality and Jesus' divinity are presupposed by the 'effective' operation of 'biblical' "'language'".²⁷

That is, broadly speaking, Thiselton's statements concerning "biblical authority" should be viewed partly in the light of his inclusion of theological considerations in the hermeneutical discussion on the basis of a *philosophical criterion of resonance with, or of problem-solving cogency in relation to, provisional conclusions and theoretical problems emerging from widening and predominantly philosophical dialogues*. Again, however, Thiselton's approach here is not an assimilation of biblical theology to a philosophical worldview. Rather, Thiselton shows that a *prior* biblical theology is *both* better elucidated by philosophical description *and* proven to be authoritative in the sense that it resonates with criteria emerging from, and cogently solves problems in relation to, *later* - and predominantly philosophical - hermeneutical dialogues or angles of view.

Thiselton also argues that 'Old Testament' "public" criteria are required to "identify" authentic (as opposed to inauthentic) "'Christian'" 'concepts or experiences'. On the one hand, for Thiselton, *inauthentic* "conceptuality and experience" – for example, the "conceptuality and experience" that Thiselton

---

²⁶ Thiselton, *2H*, 51-84, cf. 440; querying, Borsch, F.H., 'Review of A.C. Thiselton's *The Two Horizons*', *AThRev* 65 (Jan. 1983), 90; contradicting, Hess, R.S., 'New Horizons in Hermeneutics: A Review Article', *Them* 18.2 (Jan. 1993), 24.

²⁷ Thiselton, *2H*, 432; cf. 436-437; contradicting, Harrisville, 'R *2H*', 216. Italics ours.

argues are presupposed during '"persuasive definition"' (see Chapter 6) – '"saw off the"' supporting '"branch"' 'of... tradition' and artificially evade the 'process[es]' 'of... tradition'. On the other hand, Thiselton argues that *authentic* '"Christian"' "conceptuality and experience" are "continuous" with the "public" criteria and 'process[es]' 'of... tradition' (see Chapter 6).[28]

Thus, 'New Testament writers', in Thiselton's view, engage in tradition-refinement, and not in '"persuasive definition"', in that they *"critically"* adopt (and make tradition-modifying "linguistic recommendations" in relation to) "traditional" and *'theological'* '"scaffolding"' premises that are 'not... merely' *'culture-relative'*. Thiselton argues that his point, here, finds support in four places in the Bible: Jesus' critique of 'Moses'; "secularizing" in 'Jesus and Paul'; the debate about "Gentiles" and 'Jewish law'; and Paul's resistance to "Corinthian" 'enthusiasm'.[29]

That is, Thiselton in effect argues that the tradition-refinement found in the 'New Testament' resonates with, and anticipates, *both* a later *philosophical criterion of 'tradition' as '"dialectic"' 'process'*, *and* a later *philosophical criterion to do with the grounding of language and meaning (partly) in historical continuities.*[30]

For Thiselton, further, 'biblical' '"language"' is neither 'abstract', nor 'monolithic', nor "mere" 'information', but '"an activity"' '"in the stream of... life"' that is 'experienced' eventfully on 'different levels' as 'dynamic speech-acts' wherever 'inter-relation... between' authorial and '"readers"' 'language-games' 'occurs'. Thus, Thiselton argues that, in and through 'the Bible', 'divine' 'authority' 'comes to speech in' 'language-games' that employ 'human' language. Thiselton thus argues that 'the... Chalcedonian' 'Christological model' 'of biblical authority', whilst it accounts for 'human and divine' dimensions, is too 'static'. Further, Thiselton argues that 'the... Chalcedonian' 'Christological model' 'of biblical authority' also misses the 'polymorphous' character of 'biblical' '"truth"'. Thiselton argues that "multiple" "models" of 'biblical authority' are required so as to provide 'different' "angles" 'of vision' concerning 'biblical authority' because, Thiselton argues, *'single controlling'* "models" 'seduce', "blind", and "polarize" 'the debate' on 'biblical authority'. Thus, Thiselton attacks 'polarization' between '"hard"' ('"propositional"') 'and "soft"' ('"non-propositional"', "subjectivist", "existentialist") 'views' of 'biblical' '"truth"', and between wholly 'divine' and wholly 'human' 'models' pertaining to the question of the inspiration of the biblical texts (where Thiselton observes that these 'models' can be ancient and/or 'modern'). Hence, later, Thiselton argues 'that hermeneutical theory and the philosophy of language... draw... divergent' views of biblical 'authority'

---

[28] Thiselton, *2H*, 437-438, 403, 66, 322, 19. Italics ours.
[29] Thiselton, *2H*, 434-436, 403, 396; cf. Thiselton, 'REC', 521. First italics ours, remaining italics Thiselton's.
[30] Thiselton, *2H*, 434, 322, 67, 66; cf. 437-438, 403, 19, 379-385. Italics ours.

'together'.³¹

That is, Thiselton in effect argues that 'biblical' multiform textual "action" resonates with a *later philosophical criterion concerning the character and understanding of "language"*. Thus, *even in* Thiselton's language-game of "faith seeking understanding", Thiselton's language-game of philosophical warrant *also keeps surfacing*. This reading of Thiselton strongly contradicts the misleading view held by some commentators – the misleading view according to which Thiselton supposedly indulges in straightforward "'fideism'".³²

Again, though, Thiselton does not assimilate biblical theology to a philosophical worldview either. Rather, Thiselton shows that a *prior* biblical theology is elucidated by, is consistent with, and is of anticipative problem-solving cogency in relation to, *later* philosophical description and *later* philosophical concerns emerging from *later* widening philosophical dialogues.

*6. Problems with Broadly Positivist Approaches and with Broadly Existentialist Approaches*

Our exposition of Thiselton's dialogic warranting of the Bible's relevance for hermeneutics is validated further when we consider some more of Thiselton's second-period responses - *both* to "broadly" 'positivist' approaches to biblical hermeneutics *and* to "broadly" "'existentialist'" approaches to biblical hermeneutics. That is, Thiselton argues that, *unlike the New Testament*, 'the... positivism of' E. Troeltsch and D.E. Nineham and the "existentialism" of 'Kähler and Bultmann' *fail to satisfy the demands of, or the criteria emerging from, widening philosophical dialogue*.³³

Thus, Thiselton argues that both these traditions *'a priori'* endorse "'narrow'" "conceptions" "'of reality'" that "exclude" such categories as 'miracle' on 'the... basis of' outdated *'philosophical'* premises. That is, Thiselton argues that Troeltsch endorses an "empiricist" 'positivist metaphysic', that this 'metaphysic' is grounded in the philosophies of 'Vico' and "Hume", and that this 'metaphysic' is the 'product of' Troeltsch's own era. In Thiselton's view, Nineham endorses similar outdated philosophical assumptions to Troeltsch.³⁴ Conversely, Thiselton argues that Bultmann presupposes a dated "'pseudo-scientific view of a closed universe that'" almost transposes 'theology' into 'anthropology'. Thiselton argues that "'Dilthey'", before him (i.e. before Bultmann), *a priori* reduces "'God'" and

---

[31] Thiselton, *2H*, 436-438; cf.: 432-434; 310; 371; cf. Thiselton, A.C., 'The Multi-Model Character of Holy Spirit Language', *CEN* 11 Apr. (1974), 8; cf. Thiselton, A.C., 'The Semantics of Biblical Language as an Aspect of Hermeneutics', *FTht* 103.2 (1976), 116, 117; cf. Thiselton, A.C., 'Authority and Hermeneutics. Some Proposals for a More Creative Agenda', in *A Pathway into the Holy Scripture* (eds. P.E. Satterthwaite and D.F. Wright; Grand Rapids: Eerdmans, 1994), 114-117 and onwards. Italics Thiselton's.

[32] Thiselton, *2H*, 436-437; contradicting, Walsh, 'TC', 235. Italics ours.

[33] Thiselton, *2H*, 53, 81-84, 244-251; cf.: 69-84; 214-215; 254-263; 288-291. Italics ours.

[34] Thiselton, *2H*, 75-79, 53-58, 260; cf. 70-84. First italics Thiselton's, second italics ours.

*Hermeneutical Unity, Objectivity, and Foreclosure* 411

"'transcendent realities'" to humanly-"projected" "ciphers" that "serve" 'self-knowledge'.[35]

Thiselton readily admits that, from a *theological* angle of view, these various *a priori* 'philosophical' assumptions, premises, or presuppositions – regardless of whether they are "broadly" 'positivist' or "broadly" "'existentialist'" in flavor - all have "'anti-Christian'" "'implications'". *However*, Thiselton *also argues*, from an angle of view *grounded in an up-to-date philosophy of history*, that these *same a priori* 'philosophical' assumptions, premises, or presuppositions (of whichever flavor) *also all have anti-'historical'* "'implications'". Thus, Thiselton observes that Troeltsch, followed by Nineham, disparages historical "uniqueness" *per se* - and *not just* the 'unique' 'interventions' "'characteristic of... transcendental'" divinity (e.g. 'the resurrection', miracles, and so on). Moreover, Thiselton also argues that Troeltsch and Nineham *'a priori'* assign "'this-worldly'" 'mechanical... causation' to "'all... events'" such that only "'ordinary'" 'events' are allowed to "count as" 'historical'.[36] Thiselton replies, however, *from the perspective of an up-to-date philosophy of history*, 'that certain [historical] phenomena' suggest 'both... mechanical and... teleological... causation', and 'that' even 'natural "laws" are' "'only progress reports'" that constitute *'descriptive generalizations'* regarding the past that are 'not prescriptive' for an "open" future.[37] Conversely, Thiselton argues that 'Kähler and Bultmann' correctly defended "'the Biblical'" "'intention... to witness to'" divine "'acts'"; but Thiselton *also* argues that – *from the perspective of an up-to-date philosophy of history* - 'Kähler and Bultmann' were still too influenced by *historical* 'fact'-'value' 'dualism' (see Chapter 6).[38]

Therefore, Thiselton rejects 'positivist' claims concerning 'value-neutral' "description". *In line with* 'Dilthey', Thiselton argues that appeals to 'analogy with present' 'life-experience' can never 'be... value-neutral' where, in Thiselton's estimate, 'Wittgenstein's' critique 'of Sir James Frazer's... *The Golden Bough*' makes a similar point. That is, Thiselton argues that it is 'not... value-neutral' to *'a priori'*-*"exclude"* (from hermeneutical discussions) those *'theological considerations'* that are *warranted* by widening and predominantly *philosophical* dialogues.[39]

### 7. Responses to Critics of Thiselton's View of Revelation

Our preceding observations, in the current main section of the present chapter, force us to contradict several writers in relation to Thiselton's approach to revelation. Thus, Thiselton does not espouse a "'soft'" view of' Scriptural

---

[35] Thiselton, *2H*, 260-262, cf. 291-292; cf. 239. Italics ours.
[36] Thiselton, *2H*, 53, 244-245, 71-72, 75-84; cf. 260-261; cf. Thiselton, *NH*, 290. Last italics Thiselton's, others ours.
[37] Thiselton, *2H*, 260-261. Italics in speech-marks Thiselton's.
[38] Thiselton, *2H*, 75, 76. Italics ours.
[39] Thiselton, *2H*, 73, 78-79, 83-84. First italics ours, second and third italics Thiselton's, italics ours from the word *"exclude"* onwards.

'authority' (contradicting N.L. Geisler's reading of Thiselton). And Thiselton rejects 'a "propositional"' 'view' of Scriptural 'revelation' *without* rejecting 'propositions' or 'cognitive' language (contradicting B. Green's reading of Thiselton). Nor does Thiselton endorse an "existentialist" 'neo-orthodox encounter-view of Scripture' that disparages 'biblical' 'content' or 'propositional' 'truth' (contradicting L.L. Lichtenwalter's reading of Thiselton).[40] Admittedly, and to a limited extent affirming J. Bowden's reading of Thiselton, we may observe that Thiselton omits an *overt* 'discussion' on 'the place and significance of the New Testament in the Church' from *The Two Horizons*. However, we may also observe that Bowden ignores Thiselton's famous address at NEAC '77, which addresses Bowden's concerns. That is, we may now conclude that, historically, the precursor to *The Two Horizons* - Thiselton's PhD thesis – *must* have been the *theoretical* platform *from which* Thiselton made his address at NEAC '77 (see Chapter 2).[41]

D.G. Bloesch argues that, 'for Thiselton, revelation seems to be a progressive unfolding of eschatological wisdom as we move forward in the quest for greater understanding of God and the self through relating biblical texts to cultural change'. However, Bloesch's point, here, relates more closely to Thiselton's notion of human "transformation" *through* 'revelation'. For Thiselton, 'Christ' as the "enfleshed" 'Word' is central to 'revelation'. Furthermore, for Thiselton, 'the Bible', employed as divine 'speech-acts' by God's 'Spirit', together with an 'unfolding' 'history' in and through which 'the Scriptures must be fulfilled', serves as 'revelation' ongoingly in a manner that normally "transforms" believers *'through the normal processes of understanding'*. Thiselton argues that this view of the functioning of the Scriptures is compatible with 'God's' having 'spoken once for all in human history' '"by his Son"'.[42]

---

[40] Thiselton, *2H*, 436-437; 314, 386-407; cf.: 195; 354-355; cf.: Geisler, N.L., 'Review of A.C. Thiselton's *The Two Horizons*', *BibSac* 138 (Apr.-Jun. 1981), 183; Green, B., 'Richard Lints' Fabric and the Question of Postmodernity', *Prem* 4.3 (Oct. 1997), 7; Lichtenwalter, L.L., 'Review of A.C. Thiselton's *Interpreting God and the Postmodern Self*, *AUSStud* 36 (Aut. 1998), 312, 313. Italics ours.

[41] Quoting, Bowden, 'R *2H*', 57; cf. Thiselton, A.C., *New Testament Hermeneutics and Philosophical Description: Issues in New Testament Hermeneutics with Special Reference to the Use of Philosophical Description in Heidegger, Bultmann, Gadamer, and Wittgenstein* (Sheffield: University of Sheffield Ph.D. Thesis, 1977; written by Dec. 1976); cf. Thiselton, A.C., 'Understanding God's Word Today: Evangelicals Face the Challenge of the New Hermeneutic. Address at the Second National Evangelical Anglican Congress, Nottingham, 1977', in *Obeying Christ in a Changing World, Vol. 1* (ed. J.R.W. Stott; Glasgow: Collins/Fountain Books, 1977), 90-122, (henceforth the 'long' article with this title). Italics ours.

[42] Contradicting, Bloesch, D.G., *Holy Scripture: Revelation, Inspiration and Interpretation. Christian Foundations* (Downers Grove, Ill.: InterVarsity, 1994), 220, 221; cf.: Thiselton, *2H*, 90-92, 437, 66; cf.: 436-438; 66-67; 82-92; 302-303; Thiselton, A.C., 'Understanding God's Word Today', *CEN* 15 Oct. (1976), 6 (henceforth the 'short' article with this title); Thiselton, A.C., 'Truth', in *The New International Dictionary of New Testament Theology, Volume 3* (ed. C. Brown; Exeter: Paternoster; Grand Rapids: Zondervan, 1978), 892, 886, 901; cf. 874-902;

Bloesch himself views 'revelation as a decisive interruption of human interpretations by the self-disclosing God, who addresses sinful humanity'. By contrast, supposedly, according to Bloesch, Thiselton simply contradicts 'Barth's contention that the event of the Word of God is discontinuous with all human thought and experience'.[43]

However, we should note in reply that, actually, Thiselton merely argues that 'the Word of God' can only '"strike home"' when it 'comes to speech' in the hearer's developing 'language' and 'concepts'. That is, Thiselton argues that 'God' as Creator *is* 'discontinuous' with 'human' creatureliness; and, further, Thiselton argues that biblical 'revelation' *is* 'discontinuous' with that which is 'human' in that biblical 'revelation' comes from 'God', functions "authoritatively" to form and to transform believers, transmits 'a new' 'content', and is uniquely powerful in "subverting" "worlds" or "expectations". Thiselton only argues that 'God' and 'revelation' *are* "continuous" with that which is 'human' in that he argues (drawing on Bultmann) that 'God' and 'revelation' necessarily employ 'human language'.[44]

## C. Dialogic Theory-Construction:
## Towards a Unified Hermeneutical Critique of Historical Objectivity

Moving on, and extending the arguments that we put forward in Chapters 3 and 5,[45] we may now attempt to construct a unified hermeneutical critique of historical objectivity in such a way as to base our construction of this critique on Thiselton's second-period hermeneutical theory taken as a unified theological and philosophical "whole". Given Thiselton's theological-philosophical hermeneutical critique of history, and given his grounding of epistemology and understanding in that critique of history then – from a Thiseltonian viewpoint - how "objective" can even our most responsible interpretations of biblical texts - or of anything else for that matter - hope to become this side of the Eschaton?

We may begin to answer this question by noting that, broadly speaking, Thiselton's second-period transformed hermeneutical paradigm *further develops* certain reappraisals of (post-)'Enlightenment' thinking that were conducted by Heidegger, by Gadamer, and by the later Wittgenstein in relation to '"method"', '"certainty"', '"meaning"', and 'objectivity'.[46] (For Thiselton, these reappraisals

---

Thiselton, A.C., 'The Theologian Who Must Not Be Ignored. Article Review of W. Pannenberg's *Basic Questions in Theology, Vol. 2*', *CEN* 25 Feb. (1972), 11; Thiselton, 'Par', 50, cf. 52; Mark 14:49 (NIV); Hebrews 1:1, 2 (NIV); Thiselton, 'U (long)', 119. First italics ours, second italics Thiselton's.

[43] Bloesch, *HS*, 220, cf. 221; cf. Thiselton, *2H*, 88-92.

[44] Thiselton, *2H*, 88-92, 342, 310, 352; cf.: 310-314; 286-292; 382; 436-438; 342-347; 360; cf.: Bloesch, *HS*, 221; Thiselton, 'Truth', 892, 886; Thiselton, 'U (long)', 109. Italics ours.

[45] i.e. turning to an epistemological issue that constitutes an aspect of understanding.

[46] Thiselton, *2H*, 22-33, 58-91, 113-133, 149-168, 187-197, 228-251, 293-302, 310-320, 370-385, 392, 405-427, 435-441.

resonate with the 'Newtonian'-to-Einsteinian scientific 'paradigm-shift'.[47] 'Heidegger's philosophy', for example, in Thiselton's estimate, is 'not... antiscientific', but is 'highly compatible with *truly* modern science'. And this point is true, in Thiselton's view, *despite* Thiselton's conclusions concerning Heidegger's interpretative disparagement of the metacritical and critical spheres of operation of (re-historicized) 'subject-object' "conceptualization" - see Chapter 3).[48]

Thus, (1), as already noted, Thiselton applauds Heidegger's, Gadamer's, and the later Wittgenstein's repudiation – in criticism of (post-) 'Enlightenment' 'thought' - of any attempt to employ an *'a priori'* 'universal' "generalizing" "'method'" during interpretation. Thiselton argues that, for those pursuing responsible interpretation, *'methods'* are irreducibly 'multiform' because of the variable historical and linguistic particularities that may pertain to 'the [epistemological] *object*' being interpreted and to the 'frame of reference' 'of inquiry'. Certainly, with Heidegger, Thiselton argues that a "scientific" *'frame of reference'* must 'not' always be 'privileged'.[49] Of course, we have already seen how Thiselton *develops* this point in practice in Chapter 5 – notably in relation to how Thiselton argues that variable *reading goals* and variable *reading situations* potentially require that the "methods" employed during any interpretative process become *even more* multiform.

(2) With 'Heidegger' and 'the later Wittgenstein', Thiselton ties "'certainty'" not to a (post-) 'Enlightenment' notion 'of "scientific objectivity"', but 'to... attitudes', to 'life'-'practices', to concrete relationships with "others", and to 'subjectivity'. In what is, in effect, a *development* of this point, Thiselton thereby also links "'certainty'" to "appropriation" (here we are contradicting W. Wink's reading of Thiselton).[50]

(3) For Thiselton, with Heidegger, "'meaning'" is not' a secondary-level 'present-at-hand' "'significance'" that is "stuck" 'onto... naked' "objects", but is related to the irreducibly "multiform" "'ready-to-hand'" "'purpose... for the sake of which'" "'of *something*'", or of 'signs', in "relation" 'to' 'horizons' of *'concerns'* and of "experiences" 'in... life'. For Thiselton, the issue of 'present meaning' is unavoidable (L. Brodie rightly notes 'Heidegger's' significance for Thiselton here).[51] We need not repeat our earlier exposition of Thiselton's more *developed*

---

[47] Thiselton, *2H*, 159-160, 187-191, 406; cf.: 149-168; 293-300; 310-314; 370-385.

[48] McHann Jr., *3H*, 220, 263; cf. Thiselton, *2H*, 157-161, 187-200; 441. Italics in speechmarks McHann's. We are citing McHann's reading of Thiselton, which is correct at this point.

[49] Thiselton, *2H*, 78, 418; cf.: 187-189; 293-296; 370-373; 158-161; 200; 316; 404-406, 441; cf. Thiselton, A.C., 'The Use of Philosophical Categories in New Testament Hermeneutics', *Chman* 87.1 (1973), 91; cf. Thiselton, A.C., 'Kierkegaard and the Nature of Truth', *Chman* 89.1 (1975), 105. Italics Thiselton's.

[50] Thiselton, *2H*, 158-160, 294; cf. 370-371; contradicting, Wink, W., 'Review of A.C. Thiselton's *The Two Horizons*', *ThT* 37.4 (Jan. 1981), 508.

[51] Thiselton, *2H*, 164-166; cf.: 157-158; 181-188; 15-17; cf.: Thiselton, 'KNT', 105; Thiselton, *NTH*, xxii, conc. 1.3; Heidegger, M., *Being and Time* (trans. J. Macquarrie and E.

approach to the question of "meaning" (see Chapters 4, 5, and 6). However, we will return to the question of "present meaning" later in the present chapter.

(4) The question of Thiselton's notion of "objectivity" is not straightforward, since he nowhere presents such a notion systematically. Nevertheless, *The Two Horizons* is a very '"productive"' "text" in this respect, and questions concerning the problem of *'description'* are a major emphasis in *The Two Horizons*. Moreover, Thiselton's stress on 'the objectivity issue' pervades his later writings.[52]

Certainly, (a), for Thiselton, 'the interpreter' cannot simply 'eliminate his modern context'.[53] Thiselton argues, against "Cartesianism", that 'the... subject' 'cannot' leave '"behind"' its "finite", corporate, *'tradition'*-'conditioned' 'horizons' – or '"life-world"' - to become 'an isolated' 'worldless' '"I"'.[54] Notably, then, as we saw in Chapter 3, Thiselton does not overcome "Cartesianism" by "merely" 'reversing... the subject-object schema'. Rather, correcting B.J. Walsh's reading of Thiselton, we saw that Thiselton overcomes "Cartesianism" by replacing the entire framework *within which* conceptualization *itself* is conceived. In this way Thiselton goes beyond even the Continental traditions in moving *more thoroughly* from the "abstract" to the "historical" (see Chapter 3).[55]

In accounting for '"life-world"', (b), Thiselton also dismisses '"the knowing subject"' of '"Locke, Hume, and Kant"', and rejects 'the Cartesian' – and in some senses 'Kantian' - 'naïve "commonsense"' equation of 'truth with objectivity and error with subjectivity' in 'the' thinking 'of W. Wrede', 'A. Schlatter', and A. Von Harnack. Broadly speaking, Thiselton argues that the stance of the latter group of thinkers artificially "separates" "perceptions" '"from"' '"a "fixed"' '"world"'. Thiselton also rejects the over-'abstractions' of 'Hegel' and of 'Marburg Neo-Kantianism', and repudiates L. Von Ranke's illegitimate appeals to 'a... theology of history' – appeals through which Von Ranke, in Thiselton's estimate, tried to "escape" the problem of 'historical' 'finitude'. In Thiselton's view, 'Dilthey's... modified... idealism' similarly, but untenably, appealed to 'a standpoint "above" history'.[56]

---

Robinson; Oxford: Blackwell, 1962, 2001), 193; Brodie, L., 'Review of A.C. Thiselton's *The Two Horizons*', *Thom* 45.3 (1981), 482. First italics Heidegger's, second italics Thiselton's.

[52] Thiselton, *2H*, 113, 22-33, 158-161, 187-194, 236-246, 302-303, 316-325, 379, 441; correcting, Palmer, R.E., 'Review of A.C. Thiselton's *The Two Horizons*', *RevMet* 35.1 (1981), 174; quoting Langsdorf, L., 'Current Paths Toward an Objective Hermeneutic. Review-Article of R. Lundin's, A.C. Thiselton's and C. Walhout's *The Responsibility of Hermeneutics*', *CrThRev* 2 (Fall 1987), 146; cf. Thiselton, 'R-RH', 104-113; cf. Thiselton, *NH*, 41, 525, 393-405. Italics in speech-marks Thiselton's.

[53] Thiselton, *2H*, 22, 31, 157-161, 187-194, 236-246, 302-303, 316-325, 379, 441; cf. Poythress, V.S., 'Review of A.C. Thiselton's *The Two Horizons*', *WThJ* 43 (Fall 1980), 178.

[54] Thiselton, *2H*, 87, cf.: 154-155; 303-304; 324; 38; 15; 157-160; 174; 183; 188; 201; 295-296, 299, 353, 382, 441. Italics Thiselton's.

[55] Walsh, 'TC', 231-232; cf.: Thiselton, *2H*, 82-84; 440-441; Thiselton, 'UPC', 91-95; Thiselton, 'Truth', 895; Thiselton, *NTH*, xxii, concs. 1.2, 1.2a-c.

[56] Thiselton, *2H*, 189, cf.: 159-160; 319-323; 66-69; 302-303; 39; 358-360; 441.

(c) Accounting for merely the 'theological' and socio-historical "embeddedness" and/or "finite" '"situatedness"' of "knowers", however, is inadequate in Thiselton's view. Thiselton argues that "knowers" also exhibit historical *"motion"*, *change*, '"temporality"', 'historicality', "openness" 'to the future' and/or 'futurity' (see Chapter 6). Thus, Thiselton rejects 'nineteenth century' '"naturalistic"' accounts of '"the knowing subject"' – partly because these accounts focus on '"properties"'. Similarly, with 'R.G. Collingwood', Thiselton repudiates the 'pre-occupation with "statements" in British universities' that ignores historical *'process'*. That is, in relation to the question 'of objectivity', Thiselton argues that it is *simply 'naïve' to ignore factors emerging from 'the rise of historical consciousness'*.[57]

Thus, (d), Thiselton avoids *both* '"complete"' or 'radical relativism' *and* '"complete"' or 'naïve objectivism'. Clearly, on the one hand, Thiselton's 'two horizons' do not lead to absolute 'historical relativism' (here we are contradicting C.S. Rodd's reading of Thiselton): 'cultural', 'historical', and 'epistemological relativism[s]' are only inevitable *to an extent* in Thiselton's estimate, where this point qualifies L.P. Barnes's otherwise-correct observations concerning Thiselton's 'objections to… forms of relativism'.[58]

On the other hand, however, G.R. Osborne rightly highlights Thiselton's attacks against 'the "illusion of textual objectivism"'. Osborne cites four emphases or axes within Thiselton's thought that he (i.e. Osborne) sees as being evidences for the reality of Thiselton's attacks against '"objectivism"' – namely, 'pre-understanding', historical "distance", 'literary' language, and "a potential absence of shared understanding". Having said this, though, and in reply to Osborne, we should point out that, in our estimate, Thiselton in effect grounds his hermeneutical critique of *historical objectivity* – (which is an aspect of his hermeneutical critique of epistemology) - in his hermeneutical critique of *history*, and does so along no less than *eight* overlapping axes of polarities – polarities that are centered on *eight* sets of overlapping, inter-related, and mutually-qualifying historico-philosophical (and theological) criteria. Moreover, to a significant extent, we may *contrast* these eight axes with the 'four' axes expounded by Osborne in this context of discussion (see above). Thus, notably, considerations pertaining to each of Thiselton's *eight* axes show that *each* of Thiselton's eight sets of overlapping, inter-related, and mutually-qualifying historico-philosophical (and theological) criteria relate *both* negatively *and* positively to the possibility and 'problem of objectivity'. Our reading of Thiselton thus substantially qualifies Osborne's exclusively *negative* focus (at least in the context cited) on the *four hindrances* to

---

[57] Thiselton, *2H*, 302-303, 307, 181-188, 324-325, 66, 160, 383, 148, 153-154; cf.: 309; 63-69; cf. Thiselton, 'TY', 1563. Italics ours.

[58] Contradicting, Rodd, C.S., 'Review of A.C. Thiselton's *The Two Horizons*', *ExTim* 91 (Jul. 1980), 290; cf.: Barnes, L.P., 'Light from the East? Ninian Smart and the Christian-Buddhist Encounter', *SJT* 40.1 (1987), 68-69; Thiselton, *2H*, 70-74, 60, 26, 84, 387-388, 395-401. Italics ours.

understanding that he finds espoused in Thiselton's work.[59]

Thus, (i), for Thiselton, historical *'finitude'* and historical *'"situatedness'"* (cf. historical *"embeddedness"*) generate 'the problem of historical relativity' between 'provisional' interpretations. Thiselton argues that historical "hiddenness", 'the "now"' versus '"not yet"' tension, and '"the openness of the future"' render 'historical knowledge' 'provisional' upon 'fresh discoveries' where, as we have already seen, Thiselton argues that even 'natural "laws"' '"are only progress reports"' that constitute *'descriptive generalizations'* regarding the past that are 'not prescriptive' for the future. And again, as we have already seen, Thiselton argues that, prior to the Eschaton, interpreters are unable to stand at an eschatological "end-point" from which they could view 'history-as-a-whole'.[60]

*Nevertheless*, for Thiselton, the '"situatedness"' of historically-finite interpreters is also theological: for Thiselton, 'history-as-a-whole' 'is... proleptically' '"anticipated"' in the 'Christ'-'event' and 'in... [biblical] horizons' *'of promise'*. Theology aside, Thiselton argues that 'historical' 'unveiling' and tradition-development are – in some senses – 'progressive': in Thiselton's view, diachronic "frameworks" 'of reference' are not entirely "open" and, therefore, some '"objectivity"' is possible.[61]

(ii) For Thiselton, "historical" *'unity'* (not uniformity) limits '"objectivity"'. Thiselton argues that interpreters 'are' '"always"' 'already' 'immersed' or *'embedded'* (note a slightly different use of the word "embedded" here) in 'history' and 'tradition', that interpreters "belong" to 'history' and 'tradition' (to use 'Gadamer's' terminology), and that interpreters 'cannot' view 'history' from an 'Archimedean point' '"above" history'.[62]

*Nevertheless*, for Thiselton, "historical" 'unity' is pre-conditional for 'prior' "shared" 'understanding' which, in turn, in Thiselton's thinking, is pre-conditional for linguistic *'intelligibility'* (as well as for "ethical" 'relevance') - i.e. for further '"understanding"' to 'begin'. That is, Thiselton argues that '"objectivity"' *"depends*

---

[59] Osborne, G.R., *The Hermeneutical Spiral: A Comprehensive Introduction to Biblical Interpretation* (Downers Grove: IVP, 1991/1992; second edition, 2006), 489; cf.: Van Engen, C., *Mission on the Way. Issues in Mission Theology* (Grand Rapids: Baker Books, 1996), 45; Thiselton, *2H*, 113, 22, 31, 53-63, 103-114, 157-161, 187-194, 236-237, 246, 302-303, 316-325, 342-352, 379, 441. Italics ours.

[60] Thiselton, *2H*, 302-303, 66-67, 80-84, 265, 260-261; cf.: xix, 12-33, 107-114, 154-161, 196-197, 304-324, 372, 382; 175; 244, 260-265; cf.: Thiselton, 'TY', 1563; Thiselton, 'Par', 51; Thiselton, 'TNI', 11. Final italics Thiselton's, others ours.

[61] Thiselton, *2H*, 66-67, cf.: 82-84; 265; 17-23; 44-45; 53-63; 175, 104, 188-189; 304-310; 353; 440-441; cf.: Thiselton, 'TY', 1563; Thiselton, *IGPS*, 150; Thiselton, 'Par', 51, 52; Thiselton, 'UPC', 93; Thiselton, A.C., *Language, Liturgy and Meaning* (Nottingham: Grove Books, 1975 and 1986), 4, 8-9. First italics ours, second italics Thiselton's.

[62] Thiselton, *2H*, 302-316, 188, 375, 77-81, 157-174, 245-251, 367-368; cf. Thiselton, A.C., 'The New Hermeneutic', in *New Testament Interpretation: Essays in Principles and Methods* (ed. I.H. Marshall; Grand Rapids: Eerdmans; Exeter: Paternoster Press, 1977), 316; cf. Gadamer, *TM*, 261, cf. 262. Italics ours.

*on"* "historical" 'unity'. In Thiselton's view, further, the criterion of "historical" 'unity' (not uniformity) *contradicts* the absolute dismissal - in socio-pragmatic approaches *to texts* - of the possibility of any kind of checkable interpretative objectivity (see below). Primarily, in Thiselton's thinking, "historical" 'unity' (not uniformity) consists – or will consist - in the *inter-relatedness* of all aspects of history, or in what Pannenberg calls "'the universal correlative connections of... history'". That is, Thiselton argues that *relationships, relationalities, and "'relatedness'"* – *and thus the possibility of analogies* - *always* exist between historical horizons. Thiselton argues that this point remains true even though distinctions between horizons *also* always remain – distinctions that, in Thiselton's estimate, reflect what Pannenberg calls "'non-homogeneous'" "'non-exchangeable individuality and contingency'" (see also below).[63]

(iii) For Thiselton, historical *'process'* and/or *"'motion'"* (cf. *"movement", "change", "transformation"*) ensures *both* that responsible 'understanding' is not "'immediate'", *and* that responsible 'understanding' is 'never' 'once-for-all' or "'final'". Thiselton argues that initial understanding, or 'pre-understanding', is always "distorted" because it is impossible to proceed directly to "'the object'" "'of understanding'". With 'Schleiermacher', Thiselton argues that "'lack of understanding is never totally removed'". Thiselton argues that 'understanding' is always "'an incomplete'" 'process' – a 'process' that, in Thiselton's estimate, is further hindered (as G.R. Osborne rightly notes) when interpreting "'literary'", as opposed to "'everyday'", 'language'. Citing F. Watson, Thiselton's focus on 'originating historical context' can almost *seem* to result in a 'Derridean' "indefinite" "deferral" of 'meaning'.[64]

*Nevertheless*, for Thiselton, historical "processes" can aid "'objectivity'": Thiselton argues that only *"'final'"* 'understanding', and *not* 'progressive understanding', is perpetually 'deferred' – particularly, in Thiselton's view, once widening dialogue and multiple interpretative "models" are employed.[65] Thiselton argues that widening dialogue and multiple interpretative "models" yield: mutually and reciprocally cross-referenced and "correcting" "angles" 'of vision'; "clarification" 'of the hermeneutical task'; 'awareness' and modification of interpretative 'pre-judgments'; "enlargement" of interpreters' 'critical capacities' and "'experience'" 'in history'; and "clarification" 'of... biblical' 'texts'

---

[63] Thiselton, *2H*, 77-84, 165-166, 188, 302, 383, 15-19, 60-67; cf.: 103-104, 236-251, 302-307, 342-345, 379-385; cf. Thiselton, 'NH', 311, 327; cf. Thiselton, *NH*, 606. Second italics Thiselton's, remaining italics ours.

[64] Thiselton, *2H*, 103-106, 307, 89; cf.: xix, 88-92, 103-114, 163-166, 304-310, 147, 342-347; cf.: Thiselton, 'NH', 327; Thiselton, 'UPC', 92, 93; Thiselton, *NH*, 503; Osborne, *HS*, 489; Van Engen, *M*, 45; Watson, 'R *NH*', 255. Italics ours.

[65] Thiselton, *2H*, 66, 188, 238, xix, 104, 196-197, 309-324; cf.: 279-292, 115, 47, 354, 432-445; cf.: Thiselton, 'NH', 327; Watson, 'R *NH*', 255; Thiselton, 'R-RH', 113. Italics ours.

themselves.[66] For Thiselton, widening dialogue also precludes an *'a priori'* "absolutist" "narrowing" 'of' 'pre-understanding'. Thiselton argues that this "narrowing" often occurs through "blinkered" adherence to *'single'* over-'generalizing' interpretative 'models' that falsely "claim" "comprehensiveness", "polarize" "debates", and that paralyze and "control" understanding. Therefore, Thiselton argues that widening dialogue reduces the incidence of over-'selective' and 'partial' 'one-sided' 'interpretations'.[67]

(iv) For Thiselton, historical *"particularities"* – or 'the *other*' or the *"alien"'* – "resist" "assimilation". Thiselton argues that *"strangeness'"*, *"difference"*, *"uniqueness"*, *'distance'*, *"otherness"*, *'tension'*, or *'relativity'* (to use the limited historical sense of the term 'relativity' – a sense related to historical '"difference"', particularly differences between provisional interpretations) can inhibit '"objectivity"'. Earlier, we also noted Thiselton's respect for Pannenberg's comments about '"non-homogeneous"' '"non-exchangeable individuality and contingency"' – i.e. about historical characteristics that, similarly, in Thiselton's view, can inhibit '"objectivity"'. Thiselton insists that genuine "difference" cannot be "reduced" to '"sameness"' where, for Thiselton, this point means that '"historical"' 'analogy' has its limits. Thiselton argues that "distinctions" remain – for example - between 'cultures', traditions, 'horizons', 'language-games', linguistic "functions", "self" and "not self", 'theology' and 'anthropology', 'past' and 'present', 'pre-understanding' and prior 'conscious' self-'awareness', and between "truth" and '"what is true *for me*"'.[68]

*Nevertheless*, for Thiselton, largely after 'Gadamer', "historical" 'particularities' 'and tension' 'jog' interpretative 'pre-judgments into conscious awareness' (for Thiselton this is a process that involves historical 'objectification') through the operation of the juxtapositional contrasts that emerge between '"the past"' and the present during interpretation – particularly during comparative testing performed by the employment of re-historicized subject-object conceptualization. Thiselton argues that 'historical' 'distance' can thus actually "make" texts 'easier to interpret'.[69] Indeed, after F. Schelling, Thiselton argues that '"*encountering* the strange, the alien, the unfamiliar, the different… the Other, is"' *"pre-conditional"* '"for interpreting and understanding persons and selfhood"'. We need not revisit

---

[66] Thiselton, *2H*, 304-306, 400, 292, cf.: 4-7, 445; 303-308; 235-238; 386-427; cf. Thiselton, 'SBL', 116; cf. Thiselton, 'UPC', 93.

[67] Thiselton, *2H*, 78, 280-284, 109, 430-434; cf.: 290-292, 353-354; 266, 274, 410, 442. Italics Thiselton's.

[68] Thiselton, *2H*, 77-84, 103, 307-308, 82-84, 188, 291-292, 331, 376; cf.: 62-63, 153-154, 218, 241-243, 314-319, 370-379; 113-114, 355-356; cf.: Thiselton, 'TY', 1564; Thiselton, 'NH', 308, 327; Thiselton, *LLM*, 3, 9. Final italics Thiselton's, others ours.

[69] Thiselton, *2H*, 306-308, cf. 318-319; cf.: Thiselton, 'UPC', 92, 93; Thiselton, A.C., 'Keeping up with Recent Studies: II. Structuralism and Biblical Studies: Method or Ideology?', *ExTim* 89 (Aug. 1978), 334; quoting, Goldingay, J., 'Interpreting Scripture', *Anv* 1 (1984), 274. Italics ours.

points we made in Chapter 6 concerning how Thiselton inter-related "historical understanding" with "self-understanding", except to recall that Thiselton concluded that self-understanding emerges through a *detour into* "historical understanding" of historical otherness.[70]

(v) For Thiselton, historical *"continuities"* (cf. *similarity, analogy*) inhibit "'objectivity'", especially when 'hermeneutics' is primarily 'concerned with the formulation of "rules"' that are pre-designed "'to support, secure, and clarify an already accepted understanding'" – as, Thiselton argues, was sometimes the case "'in the history of'" the discipline of 'hermeneutics' prior to 'Schleiermacher'. Thiselton argues that *this* kind of "pre-Schleiermacherian hermeneutics" has the effect of merely 'perpetuating' "'fossilized'" "traditions" of interpretation and of preventing 'texts' from 'coming-to-speech' 'afresh' so as to refine traditions. Thus, Thiselton argues that, even today, 'Bible study' can – through the employment of *certain kinds* of "pre-Schleiermacherian hermeneutics" - 'become… tamed… predictable', or 'boring' – a matter of endlessly "repeating" "familiar" and potentially "distorted" interpretations.[71]

*Nevertheless*, for Thiselton, historical "continuities" – including 'pre-judgments', 'convictions', and *'public criteria'* - also aid "'objectivity'" in that they provide and/or constitute pre-conditions for the possibility of the *'intelligibility'* and "teachability" of 'language', and in that they provide and/or constitute 'paradigms' that delimit what may or may not *"count as"* 'genuinely' "objective" interpretation or *as* "authentic" interpretation. Furthermore, in Chapters 4 and 5, we saw that Thiselton argued that "'pre-understanding[s]'" (cf. 'pre-judgments'), 'prior' "'common understanding'", or horizontal 'overlap… between' two 'horizons' - for example, 'between' 'biblical' and 'modern… horizons' - were *preconditional* for the possibility of 'understanding' and 'communication'. For Thiselton, 'pre-understanding' constitutes 'an indispensable point of contact [cf. 'overlap'] with' the other or 'the… text'. That is, for Thiselton, this kind of 'point of contact' or 'overlap' is preconditional for the possibility of the *commencement of* the processes of 'understanding' that lead *towards* "'objectivity'".[72]

---

[70] Cited in, Wright, S.I., 'An Experiment in Biblical Criticism', in *Renewing Biblical Interpretation* (eds. C.G. Bartholomew, C. Greene and K. Möller; Scripture and Hermeneutics Series; Vol. 1; Carlisle: Paternoster, 2000), 243; citing, Thiselton, *IGPS*, 50; cf. Thiselton, *2H*, 103-104. First italics Wright's, others ours.

[71] Thiselton, *2H*, 404-407, 188, 392, 307-326, 342-343, 371; cf. 5-15; cf.: Thiselton, A.C., 'Language and Meaning in Religion', in 'Word', in *The New International Dictionary of New Testament Theology. Volume III* (ed. C. Brown; Exeter: Paternoster; Grand Rapids: Zondervan, 1978; actually written by 1977), 1135; Thiselton, A.C., 'Predictable, Domesticated and Tamed', *CEN* 8 Feb. (1974), 7; Thiselton, *NTH*, xxii, conc. 1.2a. Italics ours.

[72] cf.: Thiselton, *2H*, 406, 306, 396, 379, 188, 383, 438; cf.: 304-307, 379-385, 392-401; cf. Thiselton, 'LMR', 1134; Thiselton, 'NH', 312-315, 319; Thiselton, 'U (long)', 102, 120; Thiselton, *LLM*, 8-9; Thiselton, A.C., 'Explain, Interpret, Tell, Narrative', in *The New International Dictionary of New Testament Theology, Volume 1* (ed. C. Brown; Exeter: Paternoster;

(vi) In Thiselton's estimate, 'historical *conditioning*' – which, for Thiselton, is an entailment of a coupling between historical *"embeddedness"* and/or "situatedness" and historical process within the context of historical unity and historical relationalities - can 'distort truth'. Thiselton argues that interwoven practices, 'language-habits', 'and... thought' delimit "pre-cognitive" "worlds" and 'pre-judgments', and that interwoven practices, 'language-habits', 'and... thought' can thus "perpetuate" "disguised" "spells" or "distortions". Thiselton argues that the '*coming* to speech' 'of... tradition' is further "conditioned" by selves' 'life'- "experiences"', 'practical' "concerns", 'interests', "idiosyncrasies", and stages of development.[73]

Thiselton acknowledges that "language-events" can "misleadingly" suggest 'encounter' with '"objectivity"', and that the over-extended 'cognitive' 'emphasis' of 'modern' 'Western' "culture" both 'disguises' 'pre-cognitive' 'textual' "transforming" "action" in 'the present' and hinders the actualization of those aspects of '"objectivity"' that are yielded '*only*' by 'appropriation' and by 'application'.[74]

*Nevertheless*, for Thiselton, 'divine' "speech-action" "reshapes" hearers' "traditions". Further, after 'Gadamer', Thiselton argues that '"effective history"' potentially allows 'history' to become a 'source of correction' of "traditions" 'of... interpretation' (see Chapter 6).[75] Thus, Thiselton argues that 'pre-understanding[s]' may be '*informed*' by 'systematic' "theologies" which, for Thiselton, constitute 'the end process, to date, of "developing" "traditions".[76] Thiselton argues that 'critical' "comparative" "testing" against 'public criteria', and, 'fruitful' 'appropriations' and 'fruitful' "applications", can "transmit" '*fruitful*' 'pre-judgments' to be further refined '*through*' "fresh" "language-events" and through further 'critical' "comparative" "testing". Thiselton argues that dialogue or 'conversation' can "bring out" the truly 'new', and that 'distancing' can subject 'pre-judgments' to 'revision'. Thiselton argues that "spells" can be "broken", that '"persuasive definition"' can be "shown" for what it is, and that 'feeling-states' can '"disclose"'

---

Grand Rapids: Zondervan, 1975), 583; Thiselton, 'SBL', 108-111, 118; Thiselton, 'UPC', 93; Thiselton, 'Truth', 897-898. Second and third italics Thiselton's, others ours.

[73] Thiselton, *2H*, 11, 375, 133-145, 111, 310-314, 362, 169-170, 432-434, 236-238, 156, 106; cf.: 150-157; 36-38; 304-305; 404-407; cf.: Thiselton, *NTH*, xxii, conc. 1.2a; Thiselton, 'Par', 52; Thiselton, 'SBL', 109; Thiselton, A.C., 'The 'Interpretation' of Tongues: a New Suggestion in the Light of Greek Usage in Philo and Josephus', *JThStud* NS 30.1 (Apr. 1979), 26. First and second italics ours, third italics Thiselton's.

[74] Thiselton, *2H*, 404, 287, 188, 61, 308-309, 86, 342-354; cf. 370-372; cf.: Thiselton, 'NH', 324; Thiselton, A.C., 'An Age of Anxiety', in *The History of Christianity. A Lion Handbook* (eds. T. Dowley *et al*; Tring, Hertfordshire: Lion Publishing, 1977), 610; Thiselton, 'Par', 52; Thiselton, *NH*, 33; Thiselton, 'U (long)', 119. Italics Thiselton's.

[75] Thiselton, *2H*, 433, 437, xix, 306-307, 326, 382-383; cf.: 401-407, 436-437, 348-350, 314; cf.: Thiselton, 'NH', 308; citing, Dunn, *BD&H*, 36. Our italics.

[76] Thiselton, *2H*, 315, 94, 314, 66; cf.: 314-319; 94-95; 307. Our italics.

'truth'.[77]

Later, Thiselton criticizes R. Rorty for neglecting the *positive* side of the effect of "historical conditioning" on objectivity. Thiselton writes that, for 'Rorty', 'all *claims* [*sic*] to knowledge' "arise" 'only from within some given social tradition, in which the context of *convention* determines what is acceptable as "rational"'. (N.B. we saw in Chapter 6 that, for Thiselton, even properly "re-historicized rationality" had universal aspects to it that were common to *all* traditions – for example, "mutual exclusion").[78] K.J. Vanhoozer misidentifies Thiselton's criticism of Rorty, here, as Thiselton's complaint against 'Gadamerian' and 'Ricoeurian' "relativism"; however, Gadamer, Ricoeur, and Thiselton all note the possibility of tradition-*aided* objectivity.[79]

(vii) For Thiselton, "historical" *"individualism"* hinders objectivity. Thiselton observes that, in the practices of individualistic interpretation, a person's "idiosyncrasies", "interests", 'concerns', blind-spots, 'self-deception', lack of accountability, lack of 'dialogue' and cross-"referencing", lack of respect for 'tradition', lack of maturity, and lack of expertise remain unchecked.[80] Thiselton cites the legacy 'of Plato', 'Descartes', 'Hume', and 'the… Enlightenment', and argues that this legacy falsely exalted 'individual' 'critical reason' above supposedly 'unreliable… traditional' 'opinion'. For Thiselton, though, 'the dialectic between the corporate and individual aspects' of 'understanding' retains a place.[81]

*Conversely*, therefore, Thiselton notes that *contemporary* philosophy and science rightly stress the individual's (cf. subjectivity) dependency on 'other people's

---

[77] Thiselton, *2H*, 292; cf.: 353; 379-407; 287; 342-346; 304-314; 176; 437-438; 321-326; 161-163, 191-194; cf. Thiselton, *NH*, 222. First italics ours, second italics Thiselton's.

[78] Thiselton, *NH*, 395. Italics in speech-marks Thiselton's, except on our use of the term '*sic*'; other italics ours.

[79] Vanhoozer, K.J., *Is There a Meaning in This Text? The Bible, The Reader, and the Morality of Literary Knowledge* (Grand Rapids: Zondervan, 1998), 113; cf.: Thiselton, *2H*, 306-307; cf.: 120-121; 80-84; Thiselton, *NH*, 344, cf. 370-372; Gadamer, *TM*, 301; Ricoeur, P., *Time and Narrative. Volume 3* (trans. K. Blamey & D. Pellauer; London: The University of Chicago Press, 1988), 227-228. Our italics.

[80] Thiselton, *2H*, 94-95, cf.: 8-9, 80-81, 113-114, 154-156, 200-203, 282-292, 304-306, 404-406; cf.: Thiselton, 'IT', 26; Thiselton, A.C., 'Meaning and Myth. Review Article of W. Pannenberg's *Basic Questions in Theology, Vol. 3*', *CEN* 19 Oct. (1973), 8; Thiselton, A.C., 'Theology Made Exciting. Review of W. Pannenberg's *The Apostles' Creed in the Light of Today's Questions*', *CEN* 19 Jan. (1973), 12; Thiselton, A.C., 'Positive Role of Doubt', *CEN* 11 Jan. (1974), 8; Thiselton, 'CH', 5; Thiselton, 'NH', 318-327; Thiselton, 'EITN', 578-579; cf. 583-584; Thiselton, 'Par', 48, 49, 52; Thiselton, 'U (short)', 6; Thiselton, 'AA', 610. Our italics.

[81] Beckwith, R.T., 'Review of B. Mitchell ed. *Believing in the Church. The Corporate Nature of the Faith. A Report by the Doctrine Commission of the Church of England*', *Chman* 96.3 (1982), 251-252; cf.: Thiselton, A.C., 'Knowledge, Myth and Corporate Memory', in *Believing in the Church: Essays by Members of the Church of England Doctrine Commission* (ed. B. Mitchell; London: SPCK, 1981), 45-49; quoting 59, 55; cf. 54-55; Thiselton, *2H*, 200-203, cf.: 293-307.

acquired knowledge' 'transmitted' in "traditions".[82] Thiselton argues that interpretation should be *'corporate'* (cf. inter-subjectivity) so long as '"interpretative communities"' engage in widened 'dialogue' *'beyond'* their 'own... horizons'. This caveat is important, and Thiselton later attacks *'corporate* self-interest' and *'corporate'* "fallibility".[83] Thiselton argues that *'socio-pragmatic'* strands in 'liberation' hermeneutics and in 'feminist hermeneutics' fail to develop 'a... socio-critical' 'principle' and so fail to embrace *corporate* (meta-) self-criticism. A *considerable* wealth of literature proves that Thiselton's "interests" are not at all misogynistic at this point, but precisely the opposite (here we are contradicting E. Schüssler-Fiorenza's reading of Thiselton).[84]

(viii) For Thiselton, historical *fallenness* hinders objectivity. Thus, drawing on Kierkegaard and Bultmann, Thiselton argues that the New Testament word translated as 'flesh' can presuppose the 'self-deceptive' "suppression of" 'truth' through various '"evasions"', especially "hiding" '"in the crowd"'.[85] As we saw in Chapter 6, Thiselton also sympathizes in a qualified way with Marjorie Green, who criticizes Heidegger's '"resoluteness"' as being '"doubly self-centered"' in that it suppresses "responsible" relationship with others and 'the call of' 'God'. For Thiselton, a marginalization of these kinds of relationships, or of these aspects of relationality, could only ever affect "objectivity" negatively. Thiselton also argues that 'Heidegger's' 'later' emphasis on 'passive' 'listening' suppresses the 'strenuous thought' that is involved in "transformation", where *this* Heideggerian failing *too* could only affect "objectivity" negatively in Thiselton's view.[86]

Thus, Thiselton does not simply neglect the effect of 'sin' on 'understanding' (here we are contradicting V.S. Poythress's reading of Thiselton). Nor does Thiselton neglect divine judgment against sin (here we are contradicting K.J.

---

[82] Beckwith, 'R *Believing*', 251-252; cf. Thiselton, 'KMCM', 46, cf. 54-59; cf. Thiselton, *2H*, 304-307, cf. 314; cf. Thiselton, *NH*, 143. Italics ours.

[83] Thiselton, *2H*, 324-325, 53-63, cf.: 110-113, 314-319; cf.: Thiselton, *NH*, 392, 538; Thiselton, 'M&M', 8; Thiselton, 'NH', 311. Italics Thiselton's.

[84] Thiselton, *NH*, 462; cf.: 429-430; 440; 410-470. On the debate about Thiselton and feminism see, Schüssler-Fiorenza, E., *Rhetoric and Ethic: The Politics of Biblical Studies* (Minneapolis, MN.: Augsburg Fortress, 1999), 50; cf. Thiselton, *NH*, 442-452. But, against Schüssler-Fiorenza's view see flagged references in our bibliography. Also contradicting: Loader, W., *The Septuagint, Sexuality, and the New Testament: Case Studies on the Impact of the LXX in Philo and the New Testament* (Grand Rapids, MI.: Eerdmans, 2004), 100-102; cf. Doriani, D.M., *Women and Ministry: What the Bible Teaches* (Wheaton, IL.: Crossway Books, 2003), 76-82, cf. 188; cf. Tucker, R.A., and W.L. Liefeld, *Daughters of the Church: Women and Ministry from New Testament Times to the Present* (Grand Rapids, MI.: Zondervan, 1987), 445-446. First italics Thiselton's, others ours.

[85] Thiselton, *2H*, 277, 202; cf.: 277-281, 169-181; cf.: Thiselton, 'U (short)', 6; Thiselton, *NH*, 372; Thiselton, 'KNT', 85; Romans 1:18 (NIV).

[86] Thiselton, *2H*, 179, 202-203, cf.: 340-342, 370-371; cf.: Thiselton, *NH*, 185; Thiselton, 'U (long)', 119.

Vanhoozer's reading of Thiselton; cf. Chapter 4).[87] Thiselton attacks *both* the sin of reactive or "self-defensive" "'evasion'" *and* the sin of pro-active "self-reliance" or 'self-assertion'. Thiselton argues that both these sins involve 'deception', and that both these sins therefore hinder understanding and objectivity.[88] Correlatively, Thiselton later bemoans the "'evasions'" of "'virtual" reality',[89] and sympathizes with 'the postmodern ideology critique' of 'the motives of power and manipulation disguised in almost every discourse'.[90] Thiselton contrasts sinful *self-deceptive* relating with the truthfulness and integrity of the "Trinitarian" 'love' that is manifest in 'Jesus', and with the truthfulness and integrity of properly "relational" 'inter-personal' 'hermeneutics'.[91]

*Conversely*, Thiselton argues that historical *redemption* aids 'objectivity' by "liberating" interpretative capacities and 'attitudes' from the effects of sin. Thiselton argues that 'the... Spirit' gives exegetical 'gifts' and 'creatively' 'inspires' 'fusion'. For Thiselton, scholarly integrity proceeds in the direction that an 'inquiry itself... leads'. And, for Thiselton, scholarly integrity is always '*open* to' challenges to interpretative 'pre-understandings'.[92]

(5) Building on Thiselton's thinking in relation to this "fallenness-versus-redemption" axis of consideration - and also in relation to "historical conditioning" - we propose that every human relationship or discourse reflects the *influence* of varying instantiations, at both individual and corporate levels, of complex superimpositions of strategies of both evasion and manipulation (each involving self-deception) in relation to different aspects of life, depending (in relation to the details of this influence) on the person or group in view.

---

[87] Contradicting, Poythress, 'R *2H*', 180; and, Vanhoozer, *FT*, 188; cf.: Thiselton, A.C., 'On the Logical Grammar of Justification in Paul. Paper Presented to the Fifth International Congress on Biblical Studies, Oxford, 1973', in *Studia Evangelica 7* (ed. E.A. Livingstone; Berlin: Akademie-Verlag, 1982), 495; cf. 493; Thiselton, A.C., 'Looking for God's Triumph: The Role of Apocalyptic', *CEN* 12 Jul. (1974), 8; Thiselton, 'CH', 5; Thiselton, A.C., 'Review of E.H. Cousins ed. *Hope and the Future of Man*', *Chman* 88.3 (1974), 232-233; Thiselton, 'Par', 50, cf. 52; Thiselton, A.C., 'Biblical Classics: VI. Schweitzer's Interpretation of Paul', *ExTim* 90 (Feb. 1979), 134; cf. 135.

[88] Thiselton, *2H*, 202, 278; cf.: 277-281; 169-186, 229-230; cf.: Thiselton, 'Truth', 901; Thiselton, A.C., Contribution to 'Flesh', in *The New International Dictionary of New Testament Theology, Volume 1* (ed. C. Brown; Exeter: Paternoster; Grand Rapids: Zondervan, 1975), 681; Thiselton, *IGPS*, 128, 137; cf. 121-144.

[89] Thiselton, *NH*, 372; cf. Thiselton, *IGPS*, 132; cf. 111, 117, 131-132.

[90] Titans, N., 'Review of A.C. Thiselton's *Interpreting God and the Postmodern Self*', *CThM* 24.6 (1997), 521; cf. Thiselton, *IGPS*, 137-144.

[91] Thiselton, *IGPS*, 155, 163, 158; cf.: 153-163, 47-51; cf. Thiselton, 'Truth', 880-881, 883-887, 889-893, 900.

[92] Thiselton, *2H*, 88-92; cf.: 316, 304-305; cf.: Thiselton, 'Truth', 901; Thiselton, 'REC', 512, cf.: 517-518, 524-525; Thiselton, A.C., 'Sigmund Freud and the Language of the Heart', *CEN* 13 Feb. (1976), 14; Thiselton, 'U (long)', 117-121, cf. 99. Last italics Thiselton's, others ours.

Further, in line with Thiselton's comments on 'individualism', we suspect that the Western traditions have bequeathed a "de-relationalisation" effect that still shapes the kinds of questions asked during biblical exegesis in the West today. We suspect that this situation, in turn, has led to the suppression of the relational grammar of Scripture, and to the over-individualization of what interpreters mean by "sin" and by "righteousness".[93] However, if sin is self-deceptive, and yet falsely understood, then self-deceptive strategies of relating to God, to others, or to texts – strategies that undermine objectivity - will persist.

Thiselton hints at his awareness of this kind of consideration when he approves of the use of certain 'existentialist' 'categories' in biblical hermeneutics. Thus, for example, Thiselton approves of G.V. Jones' use of the categories 'estrangement', 'longing', and 'anguish' in order to interpret 'the Parable of the Prodigal Son'. For Thiselton, after Jones, "persons" are not "types" 'to be' treated 'by… standardized' "approaches" that deceptively deny particularity, personhood, and relationality. Moreover, we need not revisit Thiselton's appeals to M. Buber in relation to instrumentalization or Thiselton's comments concerning Paul's attacks against manipulative "persuasive definition" (see Chapters 4 and 6 respectively). That is, as we have seen, there can be no doubt concerning Thiselton's broad understanding of how the "relational" dynamics of sin at 'inter-personal' levels contrast with the "relational" dynamics that he espouses in relation to "Trinitarian" expositions of 'love'.[94]

Nevertheless, and aligning with our earlier argument (see Chapter 6), there remains still further scope for an even more developed hermeneutic of *fallen human relationships* and of *fallen human physicality* in relation to *the historical conditioning of understanding* - a hermeneutic that moves well beyond even Thiselton's work and that engages more deeply with pastoral theology and with other disciplines – disciplines that are of relevance *to* pastoral theology.

Thus, in relation to a hermeneutic of *fallen human relationships*, an exploration of the effects of *hysterical dissociation* on understanding, on self-deception, and on objectivity would be *one* example of an exploration that could be warranted in relation to such a hermeneutic. Similarly – and to follow L. Woolley's combining of language from J. Suler, J. Young, and transactional analysis - one could explore the effects of the projection or objectification of *prior "solipsistically-introjected" 'maladaptive schema'* (such as, for example, an internalized 'critical-parent' voice) onto external voices (whether divine, biblical-textual, or human, and so on) in such a way as to *overlay and seriously distort* those external voices. Such "projections" or "objectifications" tend, in practice, to seriously *hinder*, if not ultimately to prohibit, any level of objective apprehension *of* those external voices.[95]

---

[93] Thiselton, 'UPC', 88; cf. Thiselton, *2H*, 160, 303, 39; cf. Thiselton, 'AA', 610.
[94] Thiselton, 'UPC', 89, 90; cf. Thiselton, *2H*, 6; cf. Thiselton, *IGPS*, 158, 155.
[95] On hysterical dissociation see, Zangwill, O.L., 'Hypnotism, History of', in *The Oxford Companion to the Mind* (ed. R.L. Gregory; Oxford: OUP, 1987), 330-333; on the sub-point about "projection or objectification" see, Suler, J., 'The Online Disinhibition Effect',

Or, one could explore the implications of what Suler calls, in relation to *internet-use*, the 'online disinhibition effect'. In this context, Suler speaks of 'dissociative anonymity, invisibility, asynchronicity, solipsistic introjection, dissociative imagination, and minimization of authority'. Suler also adds the point that 'rather than thinking of disinhibition as the revealing of an underlying "true-self", we can conceptualize it as a shift to a constellation within self-structure, involving clusters of affect and cognition that differ from the in-person constellation'. That is, theologically-speaking, one may, in fallen alienation from oneself, misconstrue one's own created ontological uniqueness in terms of a "persona" that one may attempt to actualize in a particularly disinhibited way on the internet - to one's own (and others') harm. We might then ask: how does historical conditioning - mediated via a "shared world" of persona-related 'constellation[s] within self-structure[s]... involving clusters of affect and cognition that differ from... in-person constellation[s]' – *affect* progression towards objectivity via the operation of the hermeneutical circle?[96]

Alternatively, and in relation to a hermeneutic of *fallen human physicality*, one could inquire as to what extent Thiselton's problems with his eyesight "historically conditioned" his entire hermeneutical enterprise to date. One would have thought that this aspect of "historical conditioning" would have had a negative effect on that enterprise. However, when Thiselton's eyesight difficulty was *combined with Thiselton's reaction to* the comments made by a certain 'official Harley Street specialist' – (who, in Thiselton's 'pre-ordination medical report in 1958', concluded that 'this man will never be able to read enough books to exercise a useful parish ministry') – the resulting "historical conditioning" was something else entirely. It *now* looks as though the 'official Harley Street specialist' was trying to reconfigure the *very grammar* of the concept of "famous last words"! And so, we might ask: how does historical conditioning – as mediated via fallen human physicality - *hinder (or even help!)* progression towards objectivity via the operation of the hermeneutical circle?[97]

We could go on. Our point, though, is that "historical conditioning" is much more immediate, fallen, relational, and physical – and therefore much more complex - than hermeneutical notions of historical conditioning often *seem* to

---

*CyberPsychology & Behavior* 7.3 (2004), 321; cf. Young, J.E., Klosko, J.S., and Weishaar, M.E., *Schema Therapy: A Practitioner's Guide* (London and New York: the Guildford Press, 2003), 6. The sub-point about "projection or objectification" is our paraphrase of ideas communicated verbally to us by Louise Woolley. In her communication, Woolley combined the notions of "projection", "solipsistic introjection" (after Suler), "maladaptive schema" (after Young), "critical parent" (from transactional analysis), and of "overlaying or distorting" an external voice. Woolley also directed us to Suler's article and to the work of J.E. Young *et al.* On transactional analysis see, for example, Stewart, I., *Transactional Analysis Counselling in Action* (Sage Counselling in Action Series; ed. W. Dryden; London; Sage Publications, 2007). Italics ours.

[96] Suler, 'Online', 321.

[97] Thiselton, 'PCRK', 6th May 2007.

suggest. Without in any way departing from Thiselton's insights into historical conditioning, therefore, we would certainly suggest that the relationships between historical conditioning, fallen human relationships, and fallen human physicality need to be explored further. These explorations would also, of course, contribute to a developing hermeneutical critique of human selves *as well as* to questions related to historical conditioning and to historical objectivity.

These same explorations, furthermore, would require widening dialogue with pastoral theology, with psychology, with medicine, with psychiatry, with psychotherapy, with cognitive-behavioral therapy, with the philosophy of mind – and so on.

And, of course, the complex ways in which fallen human relationships and fallen human physicality *affect* "historical conditioning" will, in turn, *greatly affect each individual's (or community's) journey towards objectivity and wisdom as they develop (or not) in their responsible interpretation of life and of biblical (and other) texts.*

(6) An additional implication of our considerations to do with Thiselton's approach to historical conditioning may be noted: for Thiselton, the historical conditioning of "the historically finite" (texts, readers, events, actions, and so on) occurs against the background of, and *is itself conditioned by*, all the other overlapping, inter-related, and mutually-qualifying historico-philosophical (and theological) criteria that we have noted (i.e. historical unity, historical process and/or movement, historical particularities, historical continuities, historical individuals and communities, and historical fallenness and redemption). This point will become important in relation to our responses to socio-pragmatic criticisms of Thiselton's work later on.

(7) On the basis of our observations above we may conclude that, in Thiselton's thinking, all eight axes of overlapping, inter-related, and mutually-qualifying historico-philosophical (and theological) criteria are, in turn, derived from the theological-philosophical "whole" that emerges partly through Thiselton's sublation of his three inter-related modified Hegelian criteria into a provisional developing biblical-theological framework. And so, in Thiselton's thinking, the relationships between the "eight axes of criteria" and the "three inter-related modified Hegelian criteria" are complex.

Thus, on the one hand, we may conclude on the basis of our earlier observations in the present chapter that many of the criteria within Thiselton's "eight axes" are derived from, and explicate the grammar of, Thiselton's three modified Hegelian criteria. Thus, for Thiselton, historical continuity presupposes historical unity, and may also be seen in terms of historical relationality. For Thiselton, historical particularity presupposes the non-uniformity of historical unity, but also presupposes historical process (cf. change, transformation) and/or movement (cf. motion). For Thiselton, historical (human) subjectivity (cf. individuality) is a particular kind of historical particularity. For Thiselton, historical (human) inter-subjectivity (cf. community) is a particular kind of historical continuity that we might also see as a particular kind of historical relationality. For Thiselton, historical finitude reflects the relation between the historically particular and anticipations of history as a whole, and has a similar sense to the notions of historical embeddedness and historical situatedness, except that the latter two notions also have connotations of historical relationality, tradition and unity. For Thiselton, historical conditioning emerges as a result of historical unity, situatedness, embeddedness, relationality, particularity, and continuity being combined with historical movement and/or historical process. We could go on.

On the other hand, however, we may also conclude on the basis of our earlier observations in the present chapter that, for Thiselton, one of the main ways in which "theological sublation" alters, and improves upon, the three inter-related modified Hegelian criteria can be seen in that fact that theology provides grounds – in the evaluative metacriterion of the Christ-event - for ethical criteria related to historical fallenness and historical redemption. Further, in Thiselton's estimate, a biblical and theological framework provides grounds – in the eschatological-explanatory metacriterion of the Christ-event – for the eschatological-explanatory criterion of anticipations of history-as-a-whole. Moreover, for Thiselton, a biblical and theological framework, in its generative capacity in relation to the provision of a Trinitarian theology attained *through* Christology, more properly grounds multiform emphases related to "person" (cf. "subjectivity") and "persons-in-relation" (cf. "inter-subjectivity"), and thus – in Thiselton's thinking - forces conceptions of "history" to fully recognize and incorporate both persons and inter-personal relationality. This last point lies behind Thiselton's concerns about Heidegger's and Bultmann's individualisms and about Gadamer's potentially reductionistic "postmodern" approach to individual personhood (see Chapter 6). Finally, in Chapter 4, we noted how Thiselton used warranted theological contributions to the hermeneutical discussion – notably in relation to eschatology and promise - in order to modify philosophical notions of historical situatedness and of the role of human agency.

In conclusion, (8), by a process F. LeRon Shults describes as *"'Aufhebung"* or "sublation"' ('to cancel… to take up and use'; cf. *'relever'* in 'Derrida' – 'to relieve, to displace, to elevate, to replace and to promote, in one and the same movement') after "Hegel" and 'Pannenberg', Thiselton's historico-philosophical "'paradigm'"-transformation assimilates the question of 'objectivity', "bringing it" 'into itself' and into 'a… relation' of "dialectic" with 'itself', but 'without annihilating' that concern for 'objectivity'. Thus, Thiselton transcends the (post-)'Enlightenment' or "modern" framework of 'epistemology', and yet preserves (post-)'Enlightenment' or "modernity's" "concerns" for 'objectivity' and for the "justification" of 'knowledge'. Shults writes (with Thiselton and others in view): 'if we strip away any Hegelian overtones, this concept of sublation might be applied to the post-foundationalist attempt to relate epistemology and hermeneutics'. Thus Shults writes that, 'Thiselton uses language reminiscent of *"aufheben"*, without the Hegelian metaphysical baggage' (i.e. Thiselton also sublates "sublation" *itself*).[98]

---

[98] Shults, F.L., *The Postfoundationalist Task of Theology: Wolfhart Pannenberg and the New Theological Rationality* (Grand Rapids, MI.: Eerdmans, 1996), 159-160, cf. 22-23, 104, 156; cf.

Here, we depart from Shults' use of the generalization "post-foundationalism" to describe Thiselton. Thiselton affirms provisionally epistemologically-accessible *historical* (not idealist) foundations as we have seen (see Chapter 6). And yet, Shults' use of the term *"aufheben"* begins to capture what Thiselton does *both* with 'Hegel's' thought (again, Thiselton even sublates the notion of "sublation" itself) *and* with (post-) 'Enlightenment' or "modern" 'epistemology'. Thus, we query T.A. Hart's view that Thiselton "defends" 'Enlightenment ideals' 'as much... as' he "criticizes" 'them' in relation to 'objectivity'. Rather, Thiselton "sublates" such 'ideals' (i.e. "concerns") into a framework that is thoroughly historical, hermeneutical, and that is *not* philosophically idealist. Ultimately, this framework constitutes something much more ancient: 'the Judaeo-Christian faith matrix' that 'emerges... genuinely intact' 'from' the collapse 'of anthropocentric humanism'.[99]

Moreover, we may conclude that, for Thiselton, "philosophical description" neither presupposes sharp "fact-versus-value" or "description"-versus-'evaluation' dichotomies (querying V.S. Poythress's reading of Thiselton),[100] nor bypasses the hermeneutical circle (querying R.E. Palmer's reading of Thiselton). That is, whilst Thiselton certainly draws on Bultmann's thought to a very limited extent (e.g. in relation to pre-understanding – see Chapters 5 and 6), Thiselton nevertheless (and to use the language of R. Morgan) "avoids" 'the positivistic aspects of his [i.e. of Bultmann's] theology'. Nor does Thiselton's "philosophical description" 'impose... philosophical categories onto... biblical' "texts" (cautioning M.A. Noll's and D.F. Wells' reading of Thiselton).[101]

---

Thiselton, *NH*, 334; cf. Gadamer, H.-G., 'Heidegger and the Language of Metaphysics', in *Philosophical Hermeneutics* (H.-G. Gadamer; ed. D.E. Linge; London: University of California Press, 1976), 240; cf. Derrida's use cited in, Ingraffia, B.D., *Postmodern Theory and Biblical Theology: Vanquishing God's Shadow* (Cambridge: CUP, 1995), 168; cf. T.A. Hart's comments in, Gifford, P., D. Archard, T.A. Hart, and N. Rapport, 'Conclusion: Dialogue on the 'Common Era', in *2000 Years and Beyond. Faith, Identity and the 'Common Era'* (eds. P. Gifford, D. Archard, T.A. Hart, and N. Rapport; London and New York: Routledge, 2003), 173. Second italics Ingraffia's, others ours.

[99] Shults, *PTT*, 159, 160; cf.: T.A. Hart's and P. Gifford's comments in, Gifford, Archard, Hart, and Rapport, 'Conc', 173, 180; Thiselton, *2H*, 3, 302; Thiselton, A.C., 'Can a Pre-Modern Bible Address a Postmodern World? (Public Lecture, University of St. Andrews)', in *2000 Years and Beyond: Faith, Identity, and the Common Era* (eds. P. Gifford, D. Archard, T. Hart, and N. Rapport; London: Routledge, 2003), 127-146. Italics ours.

[100] Querying, Poythress, 'R *2H*', 179, 180; cf.: Thiselton, A.C., 'The Meaning of SARX in 1 Corinthians 5:5: A Fresh Approach in the Light of Logical and Semantic Factors', *SJT* 26.2 (May 1973), 205-210; Thiselton, *NTH*, 288-297; cf. 344-350; Thiselton, *2H*, 3, 205-212; cf. 245-251; Thiselton, A.C., 'Myth, Paradigm, and the Status of Biblical Imagery', in *Using the Bible in Liturgy* (ed. C. Byworth; Nottingham: Grove, 1977), 7; Thiselton, A.C., 'Review of W. Pannenberg's *Basic Questions in Theology, Vol. 1*', *Chman* 85.2 (1971), 120-122.

[101] Palmer, 'R *2H*', 174; cf. Morgan, 'R *2H*', 331-332; cf. Thiselton, 'UPC', 91-95; cf. Thiselton, *2H*, xx, 275-283, 427; cautioning, Noll, M.A., and D.F. Wells, 'Introduction:

Finally, the kind of "objective description" that Thiselton allies with responsible interpretation contrasts sharply with the various kinds of "hermeneutical foreclosure" that may be found in cases of irresponsible interpretation. But this point introduces our next section.

### D. Plea for Responsible Interpretation Against Kinds of Hermeneutical Foreclosure: *The Two Horizons* and a Response to Thiselton's Critics

In this section, we shall demonstrate that *The Two Horizons* is of pivotal importance in relation to the formulation of a response to Thiselton's critics, including some of his recent critics: Thiselton's emphases on widening dialogue and on responsible interpretation contrast with different kinds of hermeneutical foreclosure and/or of interpretative irresponsibility that can be found amongst some of his critics - as follows.

*1. Friendly Criticisms of Thiselton's Thinking: Straightforward Hermeneutical Foreclosure*

Thus, to begin with, (1), C.G. Bartholomew, (a), bemoans 'Thiselton's' failure to define 'philosophy'. Thiselton actually argues, however, that no "formal" definition of 'philosophy' could exist within a properly historical approach to language. For Thiselton, there are only diverse uses of the term, "philosophy" – uses that Thiselton primarily applies in various ways in relation to a diversity of particular thinkers. This point remains valid: (i) even though Thiselton's language-uses also include a general *a posteriori* use of the term, "philosophy", that *presupposes* such particularity and diversity; (ii) even though Thiselton certainly favors *to an extent* the later Wittgenstein's view of "'philosophy'" as 'description alone' *prior to* 'all new discoveries and inventions' - since, even with respect to *this* definition of philosophy, we have also argued that, in practice, Thiselton – unlike the later Wittgenstein – is not so keen to view "'philosophy'" as *only* a matter of abolishing 'grammatical illusions'; and, (iii), even though we have spoken in Chapter 6 about Thiselton's "serious historical philosophizing", since this practice cannot be reduced to one "formal" definition of 'philosophy', because philosophizing actions, *historically-speaking*, are not just one kind of action.[102]

More substantially, (b), we must reject Bartholomew's charge that 'Thiselton's' thinking embraces a 'faith'-versus-'reason' 'dichotomy'. Bartholomew seems to interpret Thiselton's thinking as though Thiselton were *either* "straightforwardly

---

Modern Evangelicalism', in, *Christian Faith and Practice in the Modern World* (eds. M.A. Noll and D.F. Wells; Grand Rapids: Eerdmans, 1988), 6, 19.

[102] Bartholomew, C.G., 'Three Horizons: Hermeneutics from the Other End - An Evaluation of Anthony Thiselton's Hermeneutical Proposals', *EuJTh* 5.2 (1996), 131; cf. Thiselton, *2H*, 3; cf. 361; cf. 407-415; cf. Wittgenstein, L., *Philosophical Investigations* (trans. G.E.M. Anscombe; Oxford: Blackwell, 1953, 2001), 47, cf. 50. Italics ours.

rationalist" (in the broader, popular sense of this term) *or* "straightforwardly fideist". We must respond in greater depth to this misleading charge, as follows.[103]

Thus, we may start by asking whether or not Bartholomew has missed Thiselton's 'polymorphous' view of "'faith'". Thiselton argues that the term "'faith'" cannot be defined "abstractly", but only in line with the "'language-game in which (it) is'" being used. Thus, (i), Thiselton argues that 'in Romans 4:5, "faith"' 'is' an 'activity or disposition of' "trusting" in God for "justification", and that "'faith'" in this sense is set in opposition to "'works'". (ii) Thiselton observes that, 'in 2 Corinthians 5:7', 'faith' is set in opposition to "'sight'" so as to imply 'a future orientation'. (iii) Thiselton argues that, 'in Romans 10:9 faith' combines 'intellectual conviction', 'self-involving confession' and, therefore, an appropriated "salvation". (iv) Thiselton observes that, 'in Galatians 1:23 "the faith" is 'simply "Christianity"'. And, (v), Thiselton argues that 'in 1 Corinthians 13:2 faith that can move mountains' is 'a gift... given... to' *some* 'Christians'.[104]

Moreover, we should note that none of these notions of "faith" are divorced from 'reason' in Thiselton's thinking. Thus, for Thiselton, "faith", in sense "(ii)" of the term's use (see above), coheres with "historical rationality". Thiselton argues that this kind of "faith" is not a matter of "seeing" 'a little way ahead', but of 'future'-"oriented" "'trust'" "grounded" partly in "'openness to'" 'promise' and to 'possibility', and partly in knowledge of "'past'" 'historical' "'events'".[105]

For Thiselton, "faith", in sense "(iii)" of the term's use (see above), amounts to "progressively", rationally, dialogically warranted - and "progressively" dialogically "understood" - 'belief' in 'revelation' (including "'received'" 'content'). As we noted above, Thiselton argues that such a notion of "faith" involves 'intellectual conviction' and embraces a choice to "confess" and, thereby, to appropriate "salvation". For Thiselton, this kind of "faith" – like the other kinds of "faith" - is consistent with the Spirit's "work".[106]

Thiselton argues that, "'faith'", as "'Christianity'" (i.e. sense "(iv)" of the term's use - see above) connotes the notion of the "'received'" "'faith'", which 'contributes' *a priori* 'to... [believers'] pre-understanding[s]'. Thiselton's own 'conscious' "reasoning", therefore, *'begins'* from "'faith'" 'as faith seeking

---

[103] Bartholomew, '3H', 131.

[104] Thiselton, *2H*, 408-409. The first set of brackets in this paragraph are Thiselton's.

[105] Bartholomew, '3H', 131; contradicting, Fackre, G., 'Narrative: Evangelical, Postliberal, Ecumenical', in *The Nature of Confession: Evangelicals and Postliberals in Conversation* (eds. G.A. Lindbeck, D.L. Okholm and T.R. Phillips; Downers Grove, Ill.: IVP, 1996), 132, 279; cf.: Thiselton, *2H*, 75, 79, 82-84, cf.: 265-266, 408-409, 421-422; Thiselton, 'R *BQ1*', 121; cf. 120; Thiselton, 'TNI', 11; Thiselton, 'Exc', 12; Thiselton, 'LG', 495; cf. 493; Thiselton, A.C., 'Review of A.D. Galloway's *Wolfhart Pannenberg*', *Chman* 88.3 (1974), 230-231; Thiselton, A.C., 'Head-On Challenge to Doubt: The Theology of Wolfhart Pannenberg', *CEN* 10 May (1974), 8; Thiselton, 'Par', 47-48, 51; Thiselton, 'Truth', 884-885; cf.: 891-893; 901.

[106] Thiselton, *2H*, 104, 90, 409, 314, 82-84, cf. 88-93; cf.: Thiselton, 'Par', 50; Thiselton, 'TNI', 11; Thiselton, 'Exc', 12; Thiselton, 'KNT', 104; Thiselton, 'Truth', 884-885; cf.: 891-893; 901; Bartholomew, '3H', 131.

understanding' - though Thiselton presupposes that *this* use of the term "faith" may presuppose sense "(iii)" (see above) of the use of the term "faith" also. Moreover, Thiselton argues that "'the scaffolding'" 'convictions' of "'received'" 'tradition[s]' are not necessarily "transmitted" or 'accepted uncritically', but that they are "filtered" through "'effective history'" in 'the past', that they are open to 'critical' "testing" in 'the present', and that they are (certainly in Thiselton's estimate) 'provisional on future confirmation' (see above and Chapters 4 and 6). With Gadamer, Thiselton insists that respect for the 'process of tradition' 'is not... irrational'. Rather, for Gadamer and Thiselton, such respect is profoundly more 'rational' than "self-deceptive" trust in the "limited" sight of an allegedly 'isolated' 'Cartesian "I"': for Gadamer and Thiselton, 'there is no... unconditional antithesis between tradition and reason'.[107]

For Thiselton, "'faith'", in sense "(i)" of the term's use (see above), may be an 'activity or disposition of' "trusting" in God that is grounded in senses "(ii)" and "(iii)" of the uses of the term "faith", and that is potentially also grounded in sense "(iv)" of the use of the term "faith". For Thiselton, 'faith', in sense "(v)" of the term's use (see above), may be treated as a special case of sense "(iii)" – as 'faith' for a "'particular'" outcome in "'particular'" circumstances.[108]

Therefore, contrary to Bartholomew's intended point in paralleling Thiselton's thinking with that of P. Jewett and with that of K.J. Vanhoozer, Thiselton does not espouse a straightforward fideism divorced from 'reason'. Nor – contrary to Bartholomew's reading of Thiselton - does Thiselton presuppose a 'nature-[versus-] grace dichotomy', as we have already seen. Conversely, whilst Bartholomew correctly argues that 'Christian scholarship in philosophy... should' 'always' 'operate as faith seeking understanding', he wrongly understands this principle to be a *criticism of Thiselton's stance* when he asks why 'Thiselton invokes... hermeneutics *from the other end* [i.e. theological and eschatological hermeneutics] only at the end of' philosophical dialogue. That is, in relation to Thiselton at least, Bartholomew seems to confuse the language-game of dialogic *theory-construction* with the language-game of dialogically *warranting* the practice of allowing biblical and 'theological considerations' to contribute *to* "hermeneutical discussions" or, more specifically, *to* hermeneutical theory-construction.[109]

In other words, in Thiselton's dialogic *theory-construction*, there is two-way dialogue between theology and philosophy "from the beginning", as we have demonstrated: Thiselton's pre-understanding ensures that he begins with 'faith seeking understanding'. Thus Thiselton is not simply "rationalist" (in the broader,

---

[107] Thiselton, *2H*, 409, 94-95, 154, 174, 237, 392, 353, 396; cf.: 305-307, 312, 314-315; 434-436; 114; cf.: Thiselton, 'H-O', 8; Thiselton, 'U (short)', 6; Bartholomew, '3H', 131; Gadamer, *TM*, 281. Second italics Thiselton's, others ours.

[108] Thiselton, *2H*, 408-409, cf. 396-400.

[109] Bartholomew, '3H', 131; cf. Thiselton, *2H*, 84; cf.: 66-67; 72-73; 77-84; 245-251. Second italics Bartholomew's, others ours.

popular sense of this term).[110] Conversely, however, in his "dialogic *warranting*" of theological contributions to hermeneutics, Thiselton first "listens" to 'the other' - that is, to philosophical traditions and concerns; and *then* Thiselton "shows" theology to be warranted as a dialogue partner *in relation to* these philosophical traditions and concerns. Thus, he is not simply "fideist" either.[111]

And again, as we noted earlier in the present chapter, Thiselton's aim is not to assimilate biblical theology to a philosophical worldview. Rather, Thiselton's aim is to show that a *prior* biblical theology is elucidated by, consistent with, or even of anticipative problem-solving cogency in relation to, *later* philosophical description and *later* philosophical concerns emerging from *later* ever-widening philosophical (and other inter-traditional and inter-disciplinary) dialogues.

(c) Bartholomew also speaks of Thiselton's 'too-ready appropriation of Gadamer' which, according to Bartholomew, lies behind 'Thiselton's' supposed problematic 'faith-[versus-] reason dichotomy'. And yet, in reply to Bartholomew, and as we have already argued, we should note that Thiselton – both in the context of his dialogic *theory-construction* and in the context of his dialogic *warranting of theological contributions to hermeneutical theory* - criticizes Gadamer on multiple levels, and does so *in line with* biblical theology. Thiselton *re-shapes the very grammar* of 'Gadamer's two horizons'.[112]

And so, (d), given these considerations, we must question whether or not Thiselton remains *either* "rationalist" *or* "fideist" in *any senses* of these terms.

Part of the confusion here perhaps turns on the fact that the "concept" of "reason" is 'polymorphous' and "historically changing", and so cannot be defined "formally" in an *idealist* sense (even though "reason" *can* have a certain *historical* shape with *some a posteriori* universal aspects, as we have seen). Indeed, in Chapter 3, we noted Thiselton's appeal to Pannenberg's rejection of all '"ahistorical"' notions of '"reason"' - regardless of whether these notions were described as 'Greek', or "rationalist", or "empiricist", or "idealist", and so on. For Thiselton, "rationality" has to take 'the rise of historical consciousness' into account if it is to be conceived of in a 'philosophically' "literate" way. Hence, we saw that Thiselton followed Pannenberg's thinking in relation to "historical rationality" or '"historical reason"', which is consistent with "faith" in its numerous senses, as we have just argued, and which sublates – *and therefore substantially modifies* - Gadamer's notion of "practical reason" by transposing this notion into a *different theological and philosophical framework*.[113]

---

[110] Bartholomew, '3H', 131; cf.: Thiselton, 'REC', 510-526; Thiselton, *2H*, 6-7; cf. 15, 304-306. Italics ours.

[111] Thiselton, *2H*, 399, 82-84; cf. Thiselton, 'TY', 1564. Italics ours.

[112] Bartholomew, '3H', 132, cf. 133; cf.: Palmer, 'Scope', 226-227; Thiselton, *2H*, 195, cf. 313, 314, 354; cf. (implicitly) the whole of 370-407; cf. 443. Italics ours.

[113] Bartholomew, '3H', 131; cf.: Thiselton, *2H*, 407-408, 376, 361, 37, 95, 76, 65-66; Thiselton, 'TNI', 11; Bartholomew, C.G., 'Uncharted Waters: Philosophy, Theology and the Crisis in Biblical Interpretation', in *Renewing Biblical Interpretation* (eds. C.G. Bartholomew, C.

Another part of the confusion perhaps turns on the fact that "faith" of *some* kind is *internal to the grammar of "historical rationality"*. Thus, for Thiselton, the 'proleptic' structure of 'knowledge' *"demands"* the operation of faith of some kind: for Thiselton, there is never a 'present' in which one can arrive at "rational" "'deductive'" closure concerning "knowledge" of an "open future". For Thiselton, then, 'faith' of some kind *is intrinsic to* "historical rationality". At worst, to use Roy Kearsley's language, such 'faith' only reflects 'other "fideisms" operating in critics of all persuasions'. That is, contrary to Bartholomew's reading of Thiselton, faith of *some kind* is operatively *part of the very grammar of Thiselton's – and in practice of anybody else's – "historical rationality"*. Thus, Thiselton argues that, short of the Eschaton, 'the hermeneutical circle' is simply 'true to… life'. Admittedly, Thiselton would *also* choose acts of 'faith' of a *specifically Christian* kind over acts of skepticism *in the face of* the inevitable failure of "'deductive'" "'historical'" "'reasoning'" in relation to "proving" an "open future". But, as we saw, Thiselton's 'faith seeking understanding' is *still consistent with* "historical rationality", even if it is *not always internal to the grammar of* "historical rationality". And so, for these reasons, and because of the common association of the term "fideism" with approaches to Christian belief that cohere with a Barthian epistemology of revelation, we doubt that the term "fideism" should be applied to Thiselton at all (*despite* the validity of Roy Kearsley's point). Later, we shall see that Thiselton follows Pannenberg's *strong opposition to* a Barthian epistemology of revelation (though both thinkers have great respect for Barth's *biblical theology*). Therefore, again, the term "fideism" should not be applied to Thiselton.[114]

(e) Bartholomew goes on to argue that, in *New Horizons in Hermeneutics* (1992), 'Thiselton, like Gadamer, will not outline a unified' 'hermeneutic'. Instead, according to Bartholomew's reading of Thiselton, Thiselton advocates multiple interpretative 'models'.[115] Similarly, E.A. Dunn speaks of Thiselton's 'hermeneutical pluralism', and W. Russell speaks of Thiselton's plural "'critical norms'".[116]

We should reply at this point, though, by observing that, whilst these comments are true with respect to *one aspect* of Thiselton's thinking, they could be misleading if they were applied to Thiselton's hermeneutics as a whole. That is, as we have already demonstrated, it is perhaps less confusing to say that Thiselton presupposes 'a unified' theological historico-philosophical hermeneutic (strata one, two, and *to an extent* stratum three) that *encompasses, generates, and demonstrates the*

---

Greene and K. Möller; Scripture and Hermeneutics Series; Vol. 1; Carlisle: Paternoster, 2000), 12; Thiselton, 'H-O', 8. Italics ours.

[114] Thiselton, *2H*, 84, 16-17, cf.: 307-310, 106, 197; cf.: Thiselton, 'Par', 49; Thiselton, 'H-O', 8; Thiselton, 'TNI', 11; Bartholomew, '3H', 131; R. Kearsley's comments were made in a personal communication. Third italics Thiselton's, others ours.

[115] Bartholomew, '3H', 129.

[116] Dunn, *BD&H*, 25; cf.: Russell, W., 'Review of A.C. Thiselton's *New Horizons in Hermeneutics*', *TrinJ* 17.2 (Fall 1996), 241-243; Thiselton, *NH*, 613.

*unavoidable necessity of* methodological diversity (stratum three).[117] For Thiselton, 'hermeneutics stands in relation to interpretation as a meta-discipline'.[118] Thus, for example, as we shall see below, Thiselton *meta*-critiques J. Derrida's and S. Fish's failure to submit interpretation to adequately historical criteria.[119]

Bartholomew, however, asserts that, 'the closest we get in either of Thiselton's two volumes [i.e. *The Two Horizons* and *New Horizons in Hermeneutics*] to a comprehensive... unified hermeneutic are chapters XV and XVI' of *New Horizons in Hermeneutics*. Actually, though, and for the reasons just stated, we should reply to Bartholomew by stressing that these methodological chapters are in fact the *furthest* we get from 'a unified hermeneutic' both in *The Two Horizons* and in *New Horizons in Hermeneutics*. Bartholomew thus seems to be completely unaware of Thiselton's *unifying* historical-eschatological understanding of 'the *third* horizon' since Bartholomew speaks only in terms 'of God and the world' in relation to 'Thiselton's' thinking in this context of discussion. However, against Bartholomew's reading of Thiselton, we should stress that the *unifying* eschatological *'third* horizon' *already is* 'integrated into' 'Thiselton's' *unified* 'hermeneutic' – *on a massive scale*. It is important to remember the extensive eschatological explorations that pervade Thiselton's second-period writings (see Chapter 3). And it is important to realize just how great an impression Pannenberg made on Thiselton a quarter of a century prior to *New Horizons in Hermeneutics* and in the entire period leading up to and surrounding its publication (see Chapters 1, 3, 6, and below). Bartholomew, then, along with J.C. McHann Jr., seems to have *completely missed Thiselton's historical-eschatological (and ultimately Christological) unification of hermeneutics in The Two Horizons* (and Bartholomew also misses this aspect of Thiselton's thinking in relation to *New Horizons in Hermeneutics*).[120]

(2) Moving on, then H.A. Harris's complaint about Thiselton's later, supposedly "unhermeneutical", categorical distinction 'between American... and European... postmodernism' also seems to be a case of straightforward hermeneutical foreclosure. Harris's complaint, (a), confuses Thiselton's *a posteriori* post-dialogic "categorizations" with polemical *a priori* pre-dialogic "categorizations" - where only the latter are fixed by prematurely foreclosing dialogue. Further, (b), Thiselton argues that since language *always* presupposes conceptual and categorical distinctions, the point is not to "overcome categorization", which is impossible, but rather the point is to ensure that any

---

[117] Thiselton, *2H*, 74-84, cf. 432-434; cf.: Thiselton, *NH*, 331-338; cf. 556-619; Thiselton, A.C., 'On Models and Methods: A Conversation with Robert Morgan', in *The Bible in Three Dimensions: Essays in Celebration of Forty Years of Biblical Studies in the University of Sheffield* (eds. D.J.A. Clines, S.E. Fowl, and S.E. Porter; *JStudOT* Supplement Series 87; Sheffield: Sheffield Academic Press, 1990), 341; Bartholomew, '3H', 129.

[118] Dunn, *BD&H*, 28, cf. 30, 31; cf. Thiselton, *NH*, 48, cf. 317.

[119] cf. Thiselton, 'R-RH', 79-113; cf. Thiselton, *NH*, 103-132, cf. 537-550.

[120] Bartholomew, '3H', 129; cf. 132, 133; cf. Thiselton, *2H*, 74-84, cf. 440. All italics ours, except in the phrases 'the *third* horizon' and '*third* horizon', where they are Bartholomew's.

"categorizations" used reflect historical particularities – *including* historically *real* distinctions or differences *between* particularities. That is, (c), for Thiselton, and against Harris's generalizing talk of 'the movement beyond dichotomies', *some* historical realities – if not others – are usefully described as being "two-fold" (for example, "thrown projection", which is described by Heidegger; see Chapter 3). (d) Thiselton argues that it is right to move beyond polemical *a priori* pre-dialogic "categorizations", whether these are two-fold, or three-fold, or four-fold, and so on. And it is right, in Thiselton's view, to move beyond untenable dualisms, dichotomies or internal contradictions in hermeneutical *theory (and practice)*. Moreover, Thiselton argues that it is also right to move beyond the *ahistorical* "formal" binary oppositions espoused in ideological structuralism or, more broadly, in Western – including Continental – idealist and formalist philosophy and/or metaphysics (see especially Chapters 5, 6, and below). However, (e), Thiselton's *a posteriori historically real* distinctions – in this case between historically-actual broad trends in American socio-pragmatism and historically-actual broad trends in European post-structuralism - should not be confused with *theoretical (or practical)* dichotomies that fail the test of rational internal coherence, or with *formal* linguistic binary oppositions that fail the test of linguistic conventionality, or (as in Harris's case) with polemical *a priori* pre-dialogic categorizations that suppress the hermeneutical circle and/or the hermeneutical task of listening in openness to the other. Nevertheless, (f), we will find a positive use for Harris's complaint later, though not in relation to Thiselton.[121]

(3) Moving on to another case of straightforward hermeneutical foreclosure, then we may note that W. Olhausen, (a), complains that Thiselton holds 'to a referential theory of meaning'. And yet, we must reply by observing that Olhausen simultaneously holds to a 'tradition' of 'semiotics' that Thiselton rejects *precisely because* it depends on 'the referential theory of meaning' (see Chapter 4 on Thiselton's rejection of 'the referential theory of meaning').[122]

(b) Olhausen also criticizes Thiselton for neglecting several matters that, in our estimate, Thiselton has *not* in fact neglected. Thus, against Olhausen's reading of Thiselton, we should point out that: (i) Thiselton *does* "pay" 'careful attention to "local" or pragmatic considerations [including language-uses] that... include the referential dimension of utterances'; (ii) Thiselton does *not* argue 'that the meaning of a sentence or... utterance... can be pursued apart from a real-life context of use'; (iii) Thiselton *already* relates '"meaning"' not to 'biblical' signs only, but also

---

[121] Harris, H.A., 'Living with Eschatological Hope. Conference Response', in *The Future as God's Gift: Explorations in Christian Eschatology* (eds. D. Fergusson and M. Sarot; Edinburgh: T&T Clark, 2000), 148; cf.: Thiselton, A.C., 'The Theology of Paul Tillich', *Chman* 88.1 (1974), 88; cf.: 99; 100. Italics ours.
[122] Olhausen, W., 'A 'Polite' Response to Anthony Thiselton', in *After Pentecost: Language and Biblical Interpretation* (eds. C.G. Bartholomew, C. Greene and K. Möller; Scripture and Hermeneutics Series; Vol. 2; Carlisle: Paternoster, 2001), 125; cf.: Thiselton, *2H*, 121-124; Thiselton, 'LMR', 1127-1130; Thiselton, 'SBL', 114-115. Italics ours.

to their *"'use'"* by 'God' (and to other persons and factors); (iv) Thiselton *already* maintains a 'dialogical or conversational emphasis'; (v) Thiselton *already* clarifies 'the role of the Holy Spirit' in interpretation; (vi) Thiselton *already* espouses something like C. Taylor's 'notion of "public space"' - thus, to give just one of many possible examples, Thiselton approves of Fuchs' notion – found in Fuchs' work on Jesus' parables - that *"'*love provides in advance the sphere in which meeting takes place'"; (see also Chapter 4 on "public criteria of meaning", and earlier in the present chapter on "objectivity" and inter-subjectivity).[123]

Finally, (c), it remains to be seen whether or not there are any philosophically idealist connotations pertaining to Olhausen's appeals to Brown's and Levinson's distinction between 'negative' and 'positive face'. For Thiselton, "communicative action" and effects are of *many* kinds where, historically speaking, these actions and effects (unlike *certain other* historical realities) cannot easily be reduced to two-fold distinctions. Admittedly, though, Olhausen may have rectified his problematic readings of Thiselton more recently, possibly in dialogue with a much earlier version of the present study.[124]

(4) D.R. Stiver's critique of Thiselton is a more serious example of a caricature based on a premature foreclosure of dialogue.[125]

Thus, (a), Stiver *rightly* argues 'that it is notoriously difficult to' derive 'criteria' to delineate the 'postmodern' since 'the positive shape of postmodernism has yet to be determined'. And yet, in accusing Thiselton of 'a common' 'misidentification of postmodernism', Stiver thereby implicitly and prescriptively delineates "postmodernism" *prior to* the dialogic resolution of "definitions" that he himself seeks.[126]

Indeed, in the "Introduction" to the book in which Stiver's critique of

---

[123] See, Olhausen, 'PR', 122; cf.: 124; 127, 128. But see, Thiselton, *2H*, 121-124, cf.: 370-379, 436 437; 168, 309-310; 407-408; 88-92; 345; cf. Thiselton, 'U (long)', 117-121; cf. 99; cf. Thiselton, A.C., 'The Spirit of Truth', in *We Believe in the Holy Spirit: A Report by the Doctrine Commission of the General Synod of the Church of England* (London: Church House Publishing, 1991), 112-133; cf. Thiselton, 'CAP', 133. Italics on the word, *"'use'"*, Olhausen's – other italics ours.

[124] Olhausen, 'PR', 126; cf.: Thiselton, 'UPC', 97-98; Thiselton, 'LMR', 1131; cf. 1126; Thiselton, *LLM*, 10-13, cf. 17; Thiselton, A.C., 'The Supposed Power of Words in the Biblical Writings', *JThStud* NS25.2 (Oct. 1974), 297-298; Thiselton, *2H*, 374-375; cf. 143-204; Thiselton, 'CAP', 150-151. An earlier version of the present study was sent to Olhausen at his request; cf. Olhausen, W.P., *Towards a Relational Hermeneutic: An Investigation in Historical Pragmatics with Special Reference to the Appropriation of Speech Act Theory in the Biblical and Theological Hermeneutics of Anthony C. Thiselton* (Chester: University of Chester Ph.D. Thesis; Liverpool Sydney Jones Library: Ph.D. Thesis 20710.OLHA, 2007).

[125] Stiver, D.R., 'The Uneasy Alliance Between Evangelicalism and Postmodernism: A Reply to Anthony Thiselton', in *The Challenge of Postmodernism. An Evangelical Engagement* (ed. D.S. Dockery; Grand Rapids, Mi.: Baker Books, 1997), 239-253.

[126] Stiver, 'TUA', 241-242, cf. 248-249; cf. Hammett, J.S., 'Review of D.S. Dockery ed. *The Challenge of Postmodernism*', *FMn* 14 (Spr. 1997), 93.

Thiselton appears, D.S. Dockery describes the '"postmodern"' as 'primarily... a time rather than... a distinct ideology'.[127] D. Okholm finds in 'the book' 'no agreement on what "postmodernism" is nor on how evangelicals should respond' where, in Okholm's estimate, Stiver tends to 'cast his net a bit wide in his enumeration of postmodernists' and stands 'at one extreme'.[128] J.S. Hammett remarks concerning the same publication, 'while all the essayists used the word "postmodernism", one does not clearly see that they are all speaking of the same phenomenon'.[129]

Thus, in relation to the identification of "postmodern" 'trends', even L.R. Bush's *critical* remark that 'evangelicals seem... better at analyzing trends than at detailing responses' is *prematurely positive*.[130] That is, as N. Titans concludes in a review of one of Thiselton's fourth-period works, postmodernism remains a 'phenomenon which many thinkers still continue to struggle to define'. And so, we must put the question to Stiver: if 'postmodernism' remains undefined, how can Thiselton be guilty of 'a common' 'misidentification of postmodernism'?[131]

As we shall see below, Stiver would probably respond to this question by saying that "even if we don't know what postmodernism *is* yet, we know what postmodernism *isn't*, and postmodernism isn't as narrowly defined as Thiselton says it is". We will address this potential rejoinder in "(b)" and "(c)" in what immediately follows, where we shall (in effect) argue that Thiselton's notion of "postmodernism" is in fact *much broader* than Stiver's notion of "postmodernism".

Thus, (b), whilst G. Chartier applauds 'Stiver's essay' as 'an excellent overview of the varieties of postmodernism',[132] Stiver's *own* premature pre-dialogic "definition" of postmodernity threatens to employ an untenable, simplistic and prescriptive *a priori* calculus of *largely epistemological* generalizations. Thus, he writes:

> All those pointing toward a middle way between objectivism and relativism that avoids the modernist criteria for knowledge are included... thinkers who do not use the term ["postmodern"] of themselves are ruled in, such as Gadamer, Ricoeur, Plantinga, and Placher. Those who still seek some objectivist criteria, like Jürgen Habermas and John Rawls, are ruled out.[133]

In response to these comments by Stiver, however, we should point out that, (i), the words 'objectivism and relativism' are both *epistemological* terms with *variable*

---

[127] Bush, L.R., 'Review of D.S. Dockery ed. *The Challenge of Postmodernism*', *FMn* 13 (Fall 1995), 129.

[128] Okholm, D., 'Review of D.S. Dockery ed. *The Challenge of Postmodernism*', *ChSRev* 26.2 (1996), 223; cf. 225.

[129] Hammett, 'R *TCP*', 93.

[130] Bush, 'R *TCP*', 129.

[131] Titans, 'R *IGPS*', 521; cf. Stiver, 'TUA', 249.

[132] Chartier, G., 'Review of D.S. Dockery ed. *The Challenge of Postmodernism*', *AUSStud* 35 (Spr. 1997), 113.

[133] Stiver, 'TUA', 245; cf.: Hammett, 'R *TCP*', 93; Okholm, 'R *TCP*', 225.

uses and that,[134] (ii), the notion of 'modernist criteria for knowledge' is an *epistemological generalization*.[135] Hence, (iii), to speak of "postmodernism" as 'a middle way between objectivism and relativism' is to suggest that the 'postmodern' resides in a ball-park lying between two poles of an artificial antithesis, or, between two supposedly "formal" generalizations that are each arbitrarily-defined as delineating the "modern" and that are each (seemingly or apparently) exclusively *epistemological* terms.[136] Moreover, (iv), the phrases "ruling in" and "ruling out" suggest an unfitting degree of *a priori* pre-dialogic prescription and categorization, given where the dialogue on the use of the term "postmodernity" (and its cognates) has reached historically. And, (v), it is inappropriate to attempt to pigeon-hole a thinker of Jürgen Habermas' caliber and sophistication by using terms in such a throw-away or potentially "sloganeering" manner – as, for example, in the case of Stiver's use of the term 'objectivist'.[137]

(vi) Thiselton's work, as we have seen, suggests that considerations of what could be counted as "modern" or as "postmodern" would have to engage with at least *seven* axes of critiques – critiques concerning conceptualizations of dialogic practice, of history, of epistemology, of language, of (Western) culture, of human selves, and of understanding (including the so-called *'aesthetic'* dimension). Stiver, however, on this particular occasion, as we have just seen, concentrates largely on *epistemological* factors in relation to his "inclusion" or exclusion of different thinkers in/from his pigeon-hole of 'postmodernism'. This fact is surprising, given 'the broader range' of 'thinkers' that Stiver has cited. Admittedly, as we shall see from what immediately follows (i.e. our point "(c)" just below), Stiver also addresses *linguistic* factors in relation to 'postmodernism'. Nevertheless, at the moment, Thiselton's notion of the "postmodern" is still looking much broader than Stiver's notion of the "postmodern".[138]

(c) Stiver, of course, as we have already begun to note, goes on to extend his employment of *a priori* generalizing calculus and/or of pre-dialogic categorization so as to use these to frame his reading of *Thiselton's* notion of 'postmodernism'. Thus, supposedly, in 'Thiselton', 'over and over, [Stiver] finds postmodernism

---

[134] Compare: Lyon, A.J., 'Objectivism and Subjectivism', in *The Oxford Companion to Philosophy* (ed. T. Honderich; Oxford: OUP, 1995), 631; Hepburn, R.W., 'Objectivism and Subjectivism, Ethical', in *The Oxford Companion to Philosophy* (ed. T. Honderich; Oxford: OUP, 1995), 631-632; Habermas, J., *Knowledge and Human Interests* (London: Heinemann, 1972), 69, 89; Thiselton, *2H*, 302, 81, 84; Thiselton, *NH*, 381; Stiver, 'TUA', 244, 245.

[135] But see, Stiver, 'TUA', 243-245; yet contrast, Carson, D.A., *The Gagging of God. Christianity Confronts Pluralism* (Leicester: IVP/Apollos, 1996), 58-64, 77; cf. Moore, G.E., *Principia Ethica* (Cambridge: CUP, 1959), 133-135.

[136] See, Stiver, 'TUA', 245; cf. Thiselton, *2H*, 302.

[137] Stiver, 'TUA', 245; contrast, Habermas, *K&HI*, 89.

[138] Stiver, 'TUA', 241, 245; cf.: 240-247; cf. Moore, S.D., 'The 'Post-' Age Stamp: Does it Stick? Biblical Studies and the Post-Modernism Debate', *JAARel* 57 (1989), 546. Second italics Moore's, remaining italics ours.

equated... with French post-structuralism'.¹³⁹ Elsewhere, Stiver misleadingly writes that, 'Thiselton uncritically identifies postmodernism simply with a radical reading of the French poststructuralists'.¹⁴⁰

However, our response to Stiver - in which we shall observe other generalizing hermeneutical foreclosures in his reading of Thiselton - is as follows.

Thus, (i), Thiselton does not at all use the term 'postmodern' (and/or its cognates) as narrowly as Stiver asserts. In *New Horizons in Hermeneutics*, for example, Thiselton uses the term 'postmodern' (and/or its cognates) in connection with one 'aspect' of 'Gadamer's work', as E.E. Johnson rightly observes.¹⁴¹ Further, as already noted, Thiselton defines what he calls "sociopragmatic" approaches as "postmodern".¹⁴² More broadly still, drawing on A. Huyssen, Thiselton argues that "postmodernity" is not so much 'a new... movement' as *a variety of different critiques of* "modernity". In this context of discussion, Thiselton *contrasts* the "postmodernity" of Habermas with that of Lyotard. This last point, in our estimate, demonstrates that Thiselton is not using the term "postmodernity" (and/or its cognates) in a generalizing or sloganeering manner, but as a polymorphous concept.¹⁴³

Taken together, all these uses of the term "postmodernity" (and/or its cognates) in Thiselton's third-period writings pave the way for his more recent *supplementary* stance of viewing 'postmodernity' – additionally and at the specific level of a *hermeneutical critique of Western culture* - 'as a "mood", attitude, or ethos'.¹⁴⁴

(N.B. The above considerations should caution us *against* using the term "postmodern" of Thiselton. We have already argued that whilst Thiselton draws on different traditions of philosophical thinking – including traditions that are commonly viewed as "postmodern" – Thiselton's aim in part is always to use widening dialogues between *many* traditions of philosophy so as to elucidate a *prior* biblical theology and so as to facilitate better "transforming biblical reading").

(ii) Stiver writes, '[P.]Bizzell indicates that the problem with [S.] Fish is not, as Thiselton indicates, that he is anarchistic but that he implies "total conformity and lack of change"'. Actually, however, Thiselton's view of Fish is much closer – though not identical - to what Stiver here purports to be Bizzell's view of Fish (on Thiselton and Stanley Fish, see below). Whilst Thiselton uses the term "postmodern" to describe the stances of R. Rorty and S. Fish (a point that Stiver must have missed given his erroneous view that, in Thiselton's thinking, 'postmodernism' is supposedly narrowly 'equated... with French post-

---

¹³⁹ Stiver, 'TUA', 242.

¹⁴⁰ Stiver, D.R., 'Review of A.C. Thiselton's *Interpreting God and the Postmodern Self*, *ChSRev* 26.2 (1996), 228, 229.

¹⁴¹ Thiselton, *NH*, 314 and onwards; cf. Johnson, E.E., 'Review of A.C. Thiselton's *New Horizons in Hermeneutics*', *BibSac* 150.600 (Oct.-Dec. 1993), 501.

¹⁴² Thiselton, *NH*, 393, 399; cf. 398-399.

¹⁴³ Thiselton, *NH*, 103.

¹⁴⁴ Thiselton, 'P-MB', 127.

*Hermeneutical Unity, Objectivity, and Foreclosure* 441

structuralism'), Thiselton does not simply associate Rorty and Fish with "anarchy". Whilst Thiselton allows that socio-pragmatic culture descends into conflict between competing groups, he also associates socio-pragmatism with "arbitrariness" and with "oppression" (as we shall see later).[145] (iii) In passing we may note that Stiver also misreads Thiselton's comments about Gadamer's "rejection" of 'post-Enlightenment' "'method'" as being comments about Gadamer's supposed "rejection" of "methods" *per se*. (iv) Against Stiver, we should also note that Thiselton's subtle reading of 'the French poststructuralists' should not be caricatured as being simply 'radical' or "uncritical".[146] This last point requires some further discussion, as follows.

Thus, we may note that Stiver contrasts what he regards as being Thiselton's "radical" reading of Derrida with his own (i.e. Stiver's) reading of Derrida. According to Stiver's reading of Derrida, 'a negative critique of language' – through a kind of *'via negativa'* – may 'protect the otherness of God and even the mystery of faith itself'. In effect, Stiver argues that Derrida "liberates" 'the "other"' from the 'oppressive' constraints of fixed language. Supposedly, in Stiver's estimate, 'authorial intent' may also be "protected" in this way. By contrast, according to Stiver, Thiselton supposedly 'fails to see a less radical reading of the post-structuralists... and the similarity of their work with the work of Gadamer, Ricoeur, and the later Wittgenstein, whom Thiselton affirms to a great extent'.[147]

We must respond, however, by noting that Stiver, in these criticisms of Thiselton, neglects to address the details of Thiselton's treatment – in relation to Derrida – of the philosophical questions pertaining to the relationship between language and the historical world, and to the relative ontological prioritizations of history and language with respect to one another (see below, and also Chapters 4 and 6). Stiver has failed - at least in his criticisms of Thiselton in the present cited context - to adequately address the question of whether Derrida's *philosophy* of language is tenable, and instead concentrates largely on Derrida's laudable *aims*. Moreover, even if Derrida's philosophy of language *did* help facilitate the kind of liberation that Stiver claims it does, then any philosophy of language that *improved* on that of Derrida would only potentially bring about a better, surer, kind of liberation. We are reminded of Thiselton's rejection of the 'the pragmatic theory of truth' and of the *apparent* short-term "liberation" that it can seem to bring. Partly, Thiselton rejects this approach to truth because, in Thiselton's estimate, *genuinely* "liberating" "truth" *also* requires *critical testing against trans-contextual and*

---

[145] Stiver, 'TUA', 252-253; cf. 242; cf. Thiselton, *NH*, 450; cf. 399; cf. 544-549.
[146] Stiver, 'TUA', 245, 246, 253; cf.: Stiver, D.R., *The Philosophy of Religious Language: Sign, Symbol, and Story* (Oxford: Blackwell, 1996), 189-192, cf. 243; Thiselton, 'R-RH', 94, 103, 105; Thiselton, *2H*, 188; Thiselton, *NH*, 6, 103-129; 314; 393-405; 499-508, 535-550; Thiselton, *IGPS*, 106.
[147] Stiver, *PRL*, 189, 192, 191, 243, 17. Italics Stiver's.

*trans-temporal criteria* (see Chapter 3).¹⁴⁸

In the context of Thiselton's discussion of Derrida then, from a Thiseltonian perspective (as we shall see later), there remains a serious question-mark over whether Derrida's philosophy of language actually achieves "liberation" through a provision of freedom from 'oppression'. For Thiselton, freedom *from* fixed and false labels and from *'controlling'* "pictures" is one thing (see Chapters 4 and 6). But, for Thiselton, the *positive* freedom to live out one's own identity - whether individually or corporately – on the grounds that that identity is broadly *correctly* recognized by others and thus broadly *promoted* by others, is quite another. For Thiselton, such positive freedom does not merely involve 'a *negative* critique of language' that, in any case, sometimes effectively *silences* the other. Rather, for Thiselton, such positive freedom also involves dialogically-derived true testimony to which the other contributes. As we have already seen, Thiselton argues that self-understanding emerges only *through* a detour into historical otherness – a detour that, in Thiselton's estimate, is made possible in part by the potential communicative efficacy of "enfleshed" language in relation to its potential unveiling *of* that historical otherness. That is, for Thiselton, language confers freedom *both* negatively *and* positively. Negatively - as we have begun to see and as we shall see further below - Thiselton argues that it is the *provisionality of the hermeneutical circle* that liberates the other from fixed and false labels, not the a-historical quasi-idealist abstraction of linguistic flux from the concrete grammars of dynamic historical contingencies (including selves) in traditions and in life (see below). Positively, Thiselton argues that it is the *identification of the other as a unique other* by the use of particularizing language in the context of *inter-subjective relationships in historical life-worlds* that liberates the other to *be* other (see Chapter 4), and *not* the "playful" ahistorical preclusion - or the intra-linguistic ostracism - of the other from concrete inter-subjective communication and understanding (see below). In our view, then, as we shall see later, Thiselton addresses these points, whilst Stiver – at least in his criticisms of Thiselton here - does not.¹⁴⁹

(v) In *partial* sympathy with Stiver's promotion of 'post-structuralism', we may observe that Thiselton's two sections in *New Horizons in Hermeneutics*, that are devoted – at least in part - to the *positive applications* of "post-structuralist" 'approaches to biblical' 'interpretation', prove that Thiselton is not as negative towards this tradition as Stiver suggests.¹⁵⁰

Thus, (vi), we must strongly reject Stiver's pre-dialogic pigeon-holing judgment that 'Thiselton' is 'a representative case of a negative evangelical response to postmodernism'. Rather, as we shall continue to demonstrate in the remainder of the present chapter, Thiselton's response to 'postmodernism' (given that we may

---

[148] Thiselton, *NH*, 103-113, 124-132; cf. Thiselton, 'Truth', 881, cf. 896-897; cf. Stiver, *PRL*, 192; cf. 181-184, 188-192. Italics ours.

[149] Thiselton, *2H*, 3; cf.: 432; 3-10, 26-33; Stiver, *PRL*, 192, 191, 189. Second italics Thiselton's, sixth italics Stiver's, remaining italics ours.

[150] Thiselton, *NH*, 114-123, 590-592; cf.: Stiver, *PRL*, 188-192; Stiver, 'TUA', 239.

even use such a term) is exceedingly and uniquely complex, and is both negative and positive, depending upon the thinker, tradition, and particular point of discussion in view.[151]

(d) Moving on, then we should note that D. Okholm seems to apply Stiver's kind of pre-dialogic categorization *to Stiver's own paper on Thiselton*. Thus, Okholm argues that Stiver steers 'evangelicals into a space between radical postmodern relativism and... modernist objectivism'. However, in making these comments, Okholm seems to miss the fact that Stiver relates 'radical... relativism' more closely to 'modernity' than to (what Stiver would see as being) the more authentically "postmodern".[152]

(e) D.A. Carson – in many senses rightly - speaks of Thiselton as "seeking" 'a new paradigm' that, 'with only a *handful* of self-described postmodernists... rejects relativism'. Interestingly, however, (i), Carson appeals to *Stiver's* article (see above) in order to make this largely correct point, when in fact Stiver, as we have seen, seems to argue for a view according to which *all* 'authentic' 'postmodernists' reject 'relativism'. Further, (ii), Carson, at least implicitly, appeals to the same article by Stiver (see above) in order to suggest that Thiselton has perhaps only had 'limited success' in his quest for 'a new paradigm', whereas in fact Stiver, whilst misunderstanding Thiselton in the ways we have just noted, is quite rightly more positive about Thiselton's achievements in this respect. Nevertheless, (iii), Carson, almost uniquely, is still entirely *correct* to identify Thiselton with 'a new paradigm' (though, as we noted above, we should not call Thiselton's 'new paradigm' "postmodern"; and, as we also noted above, we should not see Thiselton's 'new paradigm' as being *entirely* dismissive of *all* forms of "relativity"). Conversely, (iv), Stiver is entirely *incorrect* to suggest that Thiselton 'does not [consciously] recognize' 'a different paradigm' even though Thiselton, in Stiver's view, has achieved much by - supposedly - *unwittingly aligning with* such a 'paradigm'. On the contrary, (v), on the basis of our reading of Thiselton then, as far as theological hermeneutics goes, we have tried to demonstrate in the present study that it is Thiselton who has - completely *consciously* and completely *successfully* - *invented* the required 'new paradigm'.[153]

(5) Of course, having said all this, we should stress that since Bartholomew, Harris, Olhausen and Stiver would undoubtedly *agree* with Thiselton's resistance to hermeneutical foreclosure, then we should see their misreadings of Thiselton as being relatively straightforward. In the cases of these critics, there is misreading, confusion, and pre-dialogic categorization; but in the cases of these critics, there is no theoretical attempt to *justify* hermeneutical foreclosure.

In our next section, however, we will encounter some critics who consciously attempt – in effect – to theoretically *justify* hermeneutical foreclosure. Admittedly, other critics whom we will encounter in our next section would protest that they

---

[151] Stiver, 'TUA', 239-240.
[152] Okholm, 'R TCP', 224, cf. 225; cf. Stiver, 'TUA', 245; compare, Thiselton, *NH*, 314.
[153] Carson, *GG*, 460; cf. Stiver, 'TUA', 247. Italics ours.

*align* with Thiselton's resistance to hermeneutical foreclosure. And yet, as we shall see, even these other critics' viewpoints *still seem to presuppose more or less explicit appeals to* traditions that *would* indeed attempt – in effect – to theoretically justify hermeneutical foreclosure.

### 2. Pseudo-"Post-structuralist" and Broadly Socio-Pragmatic Criticisms of Thiselton's Thinking: Asserted, "Legitimized", and Canonized Hermeneutical Foreclosure

In *The Two Horizons* (1980), Thiselton responds neither to post-structuralist approaches, nor to radical reader-response theories.[154] And yet, 'by 1980', Thiselton had included 'Reader-Response Theory' in his 'course in hermeneutics' 'at Sheffield' 'University', and had responded to 'structuralist approaches'.[155]

Admittedly, speaking retrospectively of 'the 1970s and early 1980s', Thiselton acknowledges that 'reader-response criticism provided a valuable hermeneutical model for correcting' "traditional" over-emphases on 'historical reconstruction' and on 'conceptual or propositional content'. Nevertheless, in *The Two Horizons*, as we saw in Chapters 5 and 6, Thiselton's transformed hermeneutical paradigm *overcomes* the 'polarization... between' *either* focusing too 'exclusively' on 'past' 'horizons' *or* focusing too 'exclusively' on 'present' 'horizons'. It is likely, then, that the problem of focusing too 'exclusively' on 'present horizons' is a problem that Thiselton had associated with radical (i.e. broadly socio-pragmatic) reader-response theories *before* the end of his second period.[156]

In other words, broadly speaking, we may conclude that, in and by the time of *The Two Horizons*, Thiselton had *already* articulated a framework: (1) that was theoretically *a posteriori* to structuralist approaches (given their predominant focus on the *textual* horizon); (2) that was theoretically *alternative* (and in some senses even *a posteriori*) to post-structuralist approaches in that it constituted a *different kind of response* to broadly existentialist traditions and to ideological and other structuralisms; and that, (3), was theoretically *a posteriori* to radical or broadly socio-pragmatic reader-response theories – especially (though not exclusively) in relation to the issue of "the two horizons" (given the predominant focus - in such theories - on the *present* horizon).

*The Two Horizons*, then, rightly grounds our reply to post-structuralist (or,

---

[154] Contradicting, Fackre, G., 'Evangelical Hermeneutics: Commonality and Diversity', *Interp* 43 (1989), 128.

[155] Thiselton, 'TY', 1561-1563; cf.: Thiselton, 'SBS', 329; cf. 329-335; Thiselton, A.C., 'Review of R. Detweiler's *Story, Sign, and Self*, *ExTim* 90 (Jan. 1979), 119; Thiselton, A.C., 'Review of N.R. Petersen's *Literary Criticism for New Testament Critics*', *ExTim* 90 (Feb. 1979), 153-154; Thiselton, A.C., 'Review of J.-M. Benoist's *The Structural Revolution*', *ExTim* 90 (May 1979), 248; Thiselton, A.C., 'Review of A.M. Johnson's *The New Testament and Structuralism*', *ExTim*.91 (Oct. 1979), 26-27; Thiselton, *2H*, 428-431.

[156] Thiselton, 'CAP', 158; cf.: Thiselton, 'UPC', 98; Thiselton, *2H*, 19, 319; cf.: 10-17, 53-63, 86, 110-113, 314-319. Italics ours.

rather, as we shall see, to pseudo-"post-structuralist") and to broadly socio-pragmatic criticisms of Thiselton and/or, alternatively, to what G. Fackre calls 'contextual orthodoxies'.[157]

That is, *The Two Horizons* can, quite properly, be seen as constituting the *historico-philosophical* (and theological) launch-pad for Thiselton's later critiques of post-structuralist approaches and of broadly socio-pragmatic or radical reader-response theories.[158]

Notably, in these later critiques, Thiselton speaks of Jacques Derrida's *"docetic"* (i.e. historically "disembodied") "view" of 'texts' and of Stanley Fish's *'fundamentally a-historical viewpoint'*.[159] Much of the rest of the present study will be devoted to outlining a Thiseltonian response to these – or to similar - viewpoints. And again, whilst our Thiseltonian response will be grounded in *The Two Horizons*, we will from time to time cite some of Thiselton's later works as well.

A) RESPONSE TO A.K.M. ADAM IN RELATION TO S. FISH, J. DERRIDA, AND R. BARTHES

This context of discussion introduces our consideration of A.K.M. Adam's reading of Thiselton. In 1994, Adam urges that, in *New Horizons in Hermeneutics*, 'Thiselton overlooks the pertinent critiques of speech-act theory' by 'Stanley Fish' 'and' by 'Jacques Derrida'. Since, in Adam's view, 'Thiselton's' framework is supposedly a 'particular distillation of speech-act theory and Wittgensteinian philosophy', then Adam enquires as to why 'Thiselton' has "disregarded" Fish's and Derrida's 'pointed critiques' of this kind of framework. Adam wonders why Thiselton has replied to these 'pointed critiques' with only 'silence'. In 1997, Adam repeats this charge.[160]

We must reply to Adam, however, by arguing that he has misunderstood *The Two Horizons* and Thiselton's thinking as a whole. As we have already demonstrated, Thiselton's broadened dialogue with the philosophy of history is more central to his hermeneutics than are his appeals to 'speech-act theory' or even to the later Wittgenstein.[161]

Moreover, it is important to realize that Thiselton's later, qualified, appeals to J. Searle, to F. Recanati, and to J.G. du Plessis constitute a *sublation* of these thinkers' insights into the framework of Thiselton's *historical* critiques of ahistorical linguistic

---

[157] Fackre, G., 'The Use of Scripture in My Work in Systematics', in *The Use of the Bible in Theology: Evangelical Options* (ed. R.K. Johnston; Atlanta: John Knox, 1985), 210.

[158] See, for example, Thiselton, 'R-RH', 79-113; cf. Thiselton, *NH*, 103-132, cf. 537-550; cf. Thiselton, 'CAP', 133-239; cf. Thiselton, *2H*, 75.

[159] Thiselton, 'CAP', 157; cf. Thiselton, *NH*, 69, 7, 127-129. First italics ours, second italics Thiselton's.

[160] Adam, A.K.M., 'Review of A.C. Thiselton's *New Horizons in Hermeneutics*', *ModTh* 10 (1994), 433-434; cf. Adam, A.K.M., 'Review of A.C. Thiselton's *Interpreting God and the Postmodern Self*', *Interp* 51.4 (Oct. 1997), 438.

[161] Adam, 'R NH', 433; cf. Thiselton, *2H*, 51-84; cf.: 234-251; 304-326.

formalism and/or of philosophical idealism.[162]

Moreover, since 'the pertinent' essays 'by Derrida' ('"Signature, Event, Context"', and '"Limited Inc a b c..."') 'and Fish' ('"Normal Circumstances..."') cited by Adam *also* attack philosophical idealism and linguistic formalism, then they actually display certain *affinities* with Thiselton's stance.[163] The *differences* between the stances of Thiselton, Fish, and Derrida turn on what these three thinkers replace philosophical idealism and linguistic formalism *with*. Partly with reference to *The Two Horizons* and to Thiselton's later works, and partly with reference to the thinking of Derrida and of Fish, we may justify our responses to Adam, here, as follows.

Thus, (1), we may begin by turning to consider *Stanley Fish's* 'essay', 'Normal Circumstances, Literal Language, Direct Speech Acts, the Ordinary, the Everyday, the Obvious, What Goes without Saying, and Other Special Cases'.[164] Here, in this essay, we read that, for Fish, (a), *"meaning"* is "determined" by a given 'interpretative' 'community' in their 'context', and not by 'acontextual language or an independent world'. Fish states that such "meaning(s)" will be 'the ordinary' (cf. '"natural"', '"everyday"', 'literal', 'straightforward', or 'obvious') "meaning(s)" for the 'community', and that such "meaning(s)" will not be a matter 'of... free-play'. For Fish, though, as 'the' current 'context' - or sub-context – "changes", then so 'ordinary' "meaning(s)" *do* 'change'.[165]

For Fish, (b), readers' pre-existing, pre-cognitive, 'verbal and mental categories' *constitute the 'content'* of "perceived" 'entities'. Fish asserts that "perceptions" only *'seem'* to relate to 'the' external 'world' and that unconscious 'primary' 'interpretative activities' alone "produce" 'what is perceived to be "in the text"'.[166] Therefore, in Fish's estimate, 'content' is never 'independent of' or 'prior to interpretation'. Thus, Fish insists that 'Christ' 'was not "in the text"' 'of *Samson Agonistes*' 'for anyone' 'prior to' 'the typological interpretation of the poem'. Further, Fish urges that when 'a community' "changes", then textual 'content' "changes" such that no accessible 'irreducible content... survives the sea change of situations'.[167]

---

[162] Thiselton, *NH*, 283-307; cf. Thiselton, A.C., 'Speech-Act Theory and the Claim that God Speaks: Nicholas Wolterstorff's Divine Discourse. Review Article', *SJT* 50.1 (1997), 102, cf. 108.

[163] Adam, 'R *NH*', 434.

[164] Fish, S., 'Normal Circumstances, Literal Language, Direct Speech Acts, the Ordinary, the Everyday, the Obvious, What Goes without Saying, and Other Special Cases', in *Is There a Text in This Class? The Authority of Interpretative Communities* (S. Fish; London: Harvard University Press, 1980), 268; cf. 268-292.

[165] Fish, 'NC', 268; cf.: 271, 276-277; cf. Fish, S., 'Introduction, or How I Stopped Worrying and Learned to Love Interpretation', in *Is There a Text in This Class? The Authority of Interpretative Communities* (S. Fish; London: Harvard University Press, 1980), 11. Italics ours.

[166] Fish, 'NC', 271, 273. Italics ours.

[167] Fish, 'NC', 268, 271-272, 274, 277; cf. Fish, 'Intro', 11. Italics Fish's.

For Fish, (c), authorial *'intention'* is not accessible and so cannot 'yield' a *'correct'* 'literal reading' of 'a text'. Moreover, Fish urges that other textual sources brought in for comparative purposes cannot help 'yield' that "text's" authorial 'intention' either: since these other textual sources are *also* "interpreted" then they too, in Fish's estimate, are inaccessible 'to a literal reading'.[168]

For Fish, (d), only the *present extra-linguistic 'context'* can *'render'* "stable" 'plain' "meanings" – (until that 'context' "changes", that is). For Fish, 'no degree of ["'semantic'"] explicitness will ever be sufficient to disambiguate [a] sentence' so as to *'render it impossible to conceive of a set of circumstances in which its plain meaning would be other than it appears to be'*.[169] Indeed, Fish states that 'we never know a sentence except in the stabilized form a [readers'] context has *already* conferred'. For Fish, further, 'illocutionary force' is 'the way… ['a sentence'] is taken', which 'varies with circumstances'. Fish urges that 'listeners *always* know what speech act is being performed', 'but' that 'listeners' only 'know' this 'because… illocutionary force… will already have been determined' by the *listeners'* 'context'.[170]

Against this background, (e), Fish rejects J. Searle's 'distinction between direct and indirect speech-acts' since, in Fish's view, Searle's notion of 'direct' or 'normal' 'speech acts' or 'sentence' "meanings" erroneously 'reinstates… a class of utterances… that mean independently of situations, purposes, and goals'. In Fish's estimate, 'J.L. Austin' rightly tried to avoid this error.[171]

For Fish, then, any notion of what is '"normal" is context-specific', not 'transcendental' or independent of 'circumstances'. Fish states that H. and E. Clark also, like Searle, try 'to anchor language in… independent and formal constraints' such as 'literal meaning,… straightforward discourse,… direct speech acts,… the letter of the law,… normal circumstances, or the everyday world'. For Fish, though, such a stance presupposes 'that… constraints' are 'specifiable once and for all' when, in Fish's estimate, 'there are no inherent constraints on' 'sentence' 'meanings'. For Fish, 'meanings' cannot be 'objectively fixed'.[172]

We may turn now to our response to Fish. Notably, (f), we can see from our observations drawn from Fish's essay that Fish allows *present* historical context, but not *past* historical-textual context, to have a role in determining meaning. In assuming this stance, however, Fish suppresses the historical diachrony of "context", at least in relation to texts. He also suppresses the historical '"operative influence"' of textual action on readers' pre-understandings – an '"operative influence"' that occurs as part of the historical dialectic processes of traditions. As is the case in many instances of hermeneutical foreclosure, Fish prohibits progress – via the hermeneutical circle - beyond initial pre-understandings - *unless* this "progress" is seen only in terms of a growing understanding in relation to one's

---

[168] Fish, 'NC', 280-281. First and third italics ours, second italics Fish's.
[169] Fish, 'NC', 281-283. First italics ours, remaining italics Fish's.
[170] Fish, 'NC', 283, 284, 285, 292. First and second italics Fish's, third italics ours.
[171] Fish, 'NC', 285.
[172] Fish, 'NC', 287, 292.

own – or in relation to some other *present-horizon* - community's interpretative 'norms'. (When it is one's own community's norms that are in view Thiselton calls such "growth" a '*phenomenology of... self-discovery*'). To banish the "operative influence" of past textual horizons on present horizons, however, is – at the very least – to divorce textual horizons from the historical relationality and causality implicit in historical conditioning. To exclude texts from historical relationality and causality in this way, however, is to transgress the criteria of historical *unity* (not uniformity) and historical *continuity*. Indeed, only on the basis of a dismissal of historical unity, of historical continuity, and of the historical dialectic processes of traditions, could historical understanding be either sharply divorced from, or completely collapsed into, the corporate self-understanding of some present-horizon community (regardless of whether one's own community or somebody else's community is in view). That is, Fish's asserted *epistemological* dichotomy (which then leads to a *linguistic* dichotomy between transmitted and perceived "contents") presupposes an implicitly asserted *historical* dichotomy – regardless of whether the latter is seen as being between texts and the rest of historical reality or as being between the present and the past. Furthermore, Fish's stance must be a mere *assertion* since, presumably, on the grounds of his own thinking, he could not "access" the texts of the philosophers of history – philosophers against whom he would otherwise have to *argue* the case for his dichotomous hermeneutics.[173]

Moreover, of course, having said this, in practice it wouldn't actually do for Fish to say that the texts of the philosophers of history were also "inaccessible", for this too would presuppose that historical reality was supposedly split in that these texts, too, would then be - purportedly - split off from historical processes and unity. And since this premise would be, and is, absurd – (philosophically, it contradicts the criterion of historical unity; theologically, it contradicts the criterion of the unity of creation; and scientifically, it contradicts the criterion of the space-time continuum) - then any overly-dogmatic clinging to such a premise would necessarily be, and in the case of Fish certainly seems to be, authoritarian.

In other words, *by authoritarian assertion only*, Fish prohibits the re-shaping, by texts, of the pre-existing 'categories' of 'perception'.[174] That is, Fish splits historical understanding from perception, or, alternatively, he collapses historical understanding into "perception of the present horizon of corporate self-understanding" (regardless of which present-horizon community is in view and of how wide that community is), and Fish does this by – implicitly - splitting texts off from historical processes or dialectic. From a theological perspective, we could even say that Fish thereby *splits creation itself*.[175] Truly, in Fish, G.L. Bruns' fears are

---

[173] cf. Thiselton, *2H*, 45; cf.: 304-319; 44-45; 302-303, 77-82; cf. Thiselton, *NH*, 394, 550. Fifth italics Thiselton's, remaining italics ours.

[174] Fish, 'NC', 271; cf. Thiselton, *2H*, 304-310.

[175] cf.: Thiselton, *2H*, 260-261, 313, cf.: 354; 372-379; 66-67, 309; Thiselton, 'P-MB', 130-131, 140-143.

realized: 'hermeneutics plods along, as if it belonged to other sorts of history'.[176]

That is, by authoritarian assertion masquerading as argument, Fish "legitimizes" what is really a power-play that "imperializes" *present-horizon* voices and that dismisses the possibility of any level of "objectivity" in relation to authorial intention and/or textual content.[177] That is, Fish only allows present historical contexts to disambiguate, or to give any kind of meaning to, sentences. However, since all sentences are always already used prior to recontextualization then meaning is always at least a matter of historical relationships between two horizons. And, again, to deny the possibility of these historical relationships – even if only in terms of readers relating to texts - is necessarily to presuppose the preclusion of the historical unity (not uniformity) in which historical relationships and relationality are grounded. And again, where is Fish's argument from the philosophy of history to justify such a stance?[178]

Fish also only allows present historical context to determine illocutionary force. But if, historically, the utterance *was* a certain speech-act, how could present readers impute a different force to the utterance without misreading the text? Hermeneutical foreclosure is legitimized by Fish - almost canonized. But, yet again, Fish performs this maneuver without a detailed argument from the philosophy of history to justify his stance.[179]

Certainly, (g), Thiselton agrees with Fish's rejection of linguistic "formalism" (cf. idealist epistemological "foundationalism"), where Thiselton draws on the later Wittgenstein's rejection of an *'a priori'* 'transcendental' "logical" "ground" for language (see Chapters 4 and 6). However, rejecting ahistorical *a priori* "transcendental" philosophically idealist linguistic formalism (and/or philosophically idealist epistemological "foundationalism") need not lead to an *equally 'a-historical'* radicalized present-horizon contextual-relativism (no matter how wide the present context that is being posited is). Fish thus sets up a false antithesis, almost a formal binary opposition (*sic*), or "dichotomy", *between two ahistoricisms* (and in this instance, H.A. Harris' concerns that we noted earlier *would* be fully appropriate – though in relation to Fish, not Thiselton) - as though there were only two, or no properly *historical*, traditions in the history of the discipline of hermeneutics from which to argue. That is, ironically, Fish's quasi-formal binary "either/or" seems to fail to fully escape idealism, and thereby seems to presuppose an inadequate understanding of an entire recent non-idealist movement in the history of hermeneutics.[180]

---

[176] Bruns, G.L., *Hermeneutics: Ancient and Modern* (Yale Studies in Hermeneutics; New Haven: Yale University Press, 1992), x.

[177] cf. Thiselton, *2H*, 44-45, cf.: 66-67, 110-113; 302-303; 314; 245-251; 77-88; cf. Thiselton, *NH*, 27.

[178] Thiselton, *2H*, 10-17, cf.: 17-22, 44-45, 80-81, 304-326.

[179] cf. Thiselton, *2H*, 117-121; cf. 370-379, 379-385.

[180] Namely that of K.O. Apel, Pannenberg, and Thiselton; cf.: Thiselton, *2H*, 361, 407-415, 373, 370-379; cf. 386-388; Thiselton, *NH*, 296, 541-542; cf. 540-550; Thiselton, 'CAP', 157;

But, as Thiselton argues, 'what lies "behind the biblical text" will not go away' so easily since it is not "formal" but *historical*.[181] For Thiselton, 'the other' is historically 'particular' and is historically, *not formally*, '"objective"' as "not self" (though relationalities and relationships between historical *distinctions* remain).[182] Moreover, Fish's apparent asserted hermeneutical foreclosure of dialogue with the philosophy of history contrasts with Thiselton's widened dialogue with the philosophy of history.[183]

Thus, (h), in conclusion, A.K.M. Adam in effect misidentifies Thiselton as being "idealist" or "formalist" whilst Adam simultaneously misses Fish's failure to leave idealist formalism completely behind. Comparatively speaking, it is *Thiselton, and not Fish, who more successfully overcomes idealist formalism*.[184]

(2) In order to preserve the continuity of our response to A.K.M. Adam, it is necessary for us to defer until later our replies to those writers who appeal to Fish in their criticisms of Thiselton. Therefore, we may now turn to the other author whom Adam cites in critique of Thiselton, namely 'Jacques Derrida'. Regarding those of Derrida's essays that Adam cites, we may confine ourselves to a consideration of 'Limited Inc a b c…'. We may confine ourselves in this way because 'Limited Inc a b c…' reiterates key points from 'Signature, Event, Context', and sums up the well-known encounter between J. Searle and Derrida. According to Adam, this encounter is relevant to a critique of Thiselton. That is, Adam thinks that Thiselton's framework is similar to Searle's and, therefore, that Derrida's (and Fish's) criticisms of Searle also apply to Thiselton.[185]

To begin with, however, we should note that, (a), in 'Limited Inc a b c…' Derrida clarifies between fourteen and sixteen points of *agreement* with Searle who, in Derrida's estimate, has unwittingly 'borrowed *from*' '*Signature, Event, Context*' in order to criticize it. Derrida experiences 'perplexity at finding myself… often obliged to argue with a discourse moving *from/to Sec*, seeking to repeat against *Sec*

---

Fish, 'NC', 287; Harris, 'Living', 148. First italics Thiselton's, second italics ours, third italics ours (first word) and Thiselton's (second word), remaining italics ours.

[181] Bartholomew, C.G., 'Introduction', in *'Behind' the Text. History and Biblical Interpretation* (eds. C.G. Bartholomew, C.S. Evans, M. Healy, and M. Rae; Scripture and Hermeneutics Series; Vol. 4; Carlisle: Paternoster, 2003), 2; citing, Thiselton, A.C., "Behind' and 'In Front Of' the Text: Language, Reference and Indeterminacy', in *After Pentecost: Language and Biblical Interpretation* (eds. C.G. Bartholomew, C. Greene and K. Möller; Scripture and Hermeneutics Series; Vol. 2; Carlisle: Paternoster, 2001), 103. Italics ours.

[182] Thiselton, 'TY', 1564; cf. Thiselton, *2H*, 79, 188, 242; cf.: 370-385; 392-401; 304-307; 407-415; 79-80; 53-63; 244; 318. Italics ours.

[183] Thiselton, *2H*, 44-45, cf.: 51-84, 234-251; 304-326.

[184] Thiselton, *2H*, 370-379; cf.: 379-388.

[185] Adam, 'R NH', 434; cf.: Derrida, J., 'Limited Inc abc…', *Glyph* 2 (1977), 162-254; Derrida, J., *Limited Inc* (ed. G. Graf; Evanston, Il: Northwestern University Press, 1990); Derrida, J., 'Signature Event Context', *Glyph* 1 (1977), 172-197; Searle, J.R., 'Reiterating the Differences: A Reply to Derrida', *Glyph* 1 (1977), 198-208; Culler, J., *On Deconstruction. Theory and Criticism after Structuralism* (London: Routledge, 1983, 1998), 110-134.

what it has taken from *Sec* (N.B. *'Sec'* is *'Signature, Event, Context'* in Searle's hands).[186]

Of course, (b), Derrida still *attacks* Searle's untenable quasi-'phenomenological' "bracketing out" of those supposedly "parasitic" features of 'language' that "methodologically" aggravate the equally untenable philosophically "idealist", "abstract", "logical"', "formal" 'center' of his (i.e. of Searle's) '"theory"' of 'normal' 'speech-acts'. That is, in Derrida's view, Searle's whole approach is pervaded by certain problematic *'continental* metaphysical' 'presuppositions'.[187]

Nevertheless, (c), in Derrida's estimate, Austin's work on speech-acts was far subtler than Searle's. Derrida argues that Austin at least attempted to leave philosophical "idealism"/'formalism' behind, but that Searle's work goes backwards towards philosophical "idealism"/'formalism'. Thus, Derrida applauds Austin, admitting that his own thinking is *even more* in agreement with Austin's thinking than it is in agreement with Searle's thinking (though N. Murphy reminds us of the differences between Derrida's thinking and Austin's thinking).[188]

That is, whilst Derrida argues that 'speech acts theory' *of the Searlean variety* requires a 'general transformation' because of its attendant philosophical "idealism", Derrida *also argues that some kind of "theorizing" about 'speech-acts' is still legitimate.*[189]

(d) We should note that, like Derrida, but in contrast to Adam's pseudo-"post-structuralist" reading of Thiselton, Thiselton *also* rejects philosophical 'idealism' and "formalism" - though for Thiselton this maneuver is carried out *partly* through an appeal to the later Wittgenstein.[190] Thiselton, then, does not engage with Derrida's two essays because they *do not directly attack his stance*. What Thiselton *does* do, however, is *transpose* the early Wittgenstein's notions of '"showing"' and "saying" into a different historico-philosophical framework (see Chapter 6). Similarly, Thiselton sublates Searle's uses of the categories of *'force'*, 'content', *'background'*, and 'direction of fit' into *a non-formalist, non idealist frame*. Thiselton writes of Searle's categories of speech-acts: 'the value of the categories is *operational and pragmatic* [i.e. not "formal"] in relation to *given arguments and purposes*' (cf. language-games). Admittedly, Thiselton's non-formalist, non-idealist frame is not the same as Derrida's. And yet, *like* Derrida, as we have just noted, Thiselton still rejects "idealism" and/or "formalism". And again, *like Derrida*, Thiselton finds

---

[186] Derrida, 'LI', 162; cf.: 182-183, 187, 189, 191-193, 198-199, 202-203, 218, 242, 249. First italics ours, remaining italics Derrida's.

[187] Derrida, 'LI', 219, 233, 208, 236, 172, cf.: 193, 200-201, 210-211, 227, 237, 240. Italics Derrida's, except on "attacks".

[188] Derrida, 'LI', 208-209, 240; cf.: 169, 172, 178; 219; 227-228; 231; 233; 236-238; 241; cf. Murphy, N.C., *Anglo-American Postmodernity: Philosophical Perspectives on Science, Religion, and Ethics* (Boulder, Colo.: Westview Press, 1997), 142.

[189] Derrida, 'LI', 217; cf. 210, 211, cf.: 213; 214-215; 232-233; 240. Italics ours.

[190] Thiselton, *2H*, 302, 361, 370-379, 386-388, 407-415.

only *qualified* points of agreement with Searle.[191]

Thus, (e), the differences between Thiselton's thinking and Derrida's thinking do not center on "idealism" or "formalism" (both writers reject these). And, indeed, the differences between Thiselton's thinking and Derrida's thinking do not center on appeals to Searle either. Rather, as we will attempt to show, the differences between Thiselton's thinking and Derrida's thinking turn on Thiselton's grounding of language in history - that is, on Thiselton's relative axiomatic theoretical inter-sublationary prioritization of discourses on conceptualizations of "history" (and hence on conceptualizations of selves as historical agents) over discourses on conceptualizations of "language".[192]

Thus, (f), we may observe that, for Derrida, 'iterability' (i.e. susceptibility to 'repetition') and 'alterity' (i.e. susceptibility to 'alteration', to difference or otherness) contribute *internally* to 'the' intrinsic or 'functional structure *of the mark*' - where Derrida often makes related points.[193] Further, whilst recognizing present 'context', Derrida - conceptually speaking - marginalizes or sublates the selves who 'repeat' and who, by "repeating", "alter" language-stretches – arguing that 'the human subject is… "a function of language"'. Though '"absolutely indispensable"', 'the subject is', for Derrida, thereby *linguistically* "situated". Correlatively, again, Derrida ascribes roles to 'iterability' and to 'alterity' that are primarily 'inscribed in' or intrinsic to *the linguistic sphere*, where Derrida writes, 'the *graphics* of iterability inscribes alteration irreducibly in repetition'.[194]

Thiselton, however, (g), might write, "as historical horizons expand, historical selves, as agents constrained by 'the' *historicity* 'of iterability', 'irreducibly' "inscribe" both 'alteration' *and continuity* 'in' the historical processes or movements of 'repetition'". "Iteration", then, for Thiselton, is historical and concrete, and forms patterns of difference (cf. 'alterity') *and continuity* that, once they have become "past", become unalterable. Thus, for Thiselton, 'iterability' and 'alterity' are finite, if still open towards the future. Further, for Thiselton, 'alterity' is not a property or function of language or of writing or 'graphics' only (one discourse), but of *historical language-uses* by *persons* in *cultures* where, for Thiselton, cultures constitute snap-shots of traditions – traditions that, in Thiselton's estimate, potentially transmit and refine *knowledge* through *fusions of horizons* (six discourses). Thus, in a manner that reminds us of Foucault, Thiselton opposes Derrida's potential

---

[191] Thiselton, *2H*, 370, 367, 75; cf.: 360-361, 370-409; 82-84; 440; cf.: Thiselton, *NH*, 294-297, 301; cf.: 283-298, 307; Thiselton, A.C., *A Concise Encyclopedia of the Philosophy of Religion* (Oxford: One World, 2002), 26. Fourth and fifth italics Thiselton's, remaining italics ours.

[192] Thiselton, *2H*, 379-385; cf.: 123; 285-287; 195; 392-401; cf. Thiselton, 'TY', 1566.

[193] Derrida, 'LI', 184; cf.: 190; 195; 199-200; 219; 221; 223; 225; 231-233; 240; 250; cf. Derrida, 'SEC', 185. Italics ours.

[194] Derrida, 'LI', 220, cf. 200, 184; cf.: Stokes, P., *Philosophy. 100 Essential Thinkers* (Leicester: Arcturus Publishing Limited, 2002), 189; Schrag, C.O., 'Subjectivity and Praxis at the End of Philosophy', in *Hermeneutics and Deconstruction* (eds. H.J. Silverman and D. Ihde; Albany, N.Y.: State University of New York Press, 1985), 26. Italics ours.

abstraction of language – an abstraction that, in Thiselton's view, turns language into something 'docetic' through an unnecessary internalizing and/or sublating marginalization of certain discourses (notably those concerning history and selves) relative to discourses on language. Derrida does not at all oppose the notions of historical "speech-action", or of historical "contexts", or of human "subjects" in *every* sense, of course, as we have already noted. The point, though, concerns which hermeneutical critiques are prioritized during the sublations (cf. *relève*, in Derrida) performed within the language-games of hermeneutical theoretical discussions.[195]

(h) An analysis of Thiselton's critique – in *New Horizons in Hermeneutics* - 'of the kind of approach to texts associated with Derrida and with [the later] Barthes' seems to confirm our points about the differences between Thiselton's thinking and Derrida's thinking – as follows. Thus, for Thiselton, the *historical* 'extra-linguistic' 'embodiment' of 'language' qualifies any purely *'intra-linguistic'* 'process' that "places" 'signs' '"under erasure"'.[196] Further, for Thiselton, *historical* "inter-subjectivity" and particular *'judgments'* and speech-actions by 'human' "subjects" correct *ahistorical* emphases on 'subjectless' (in Thiselton's sense of this term, not Derrida's) "intertextual" 'systems'.[197] Moreover, Thiselton argues that *'concrete'* 'meaning' 'possibilities' "constrained by" *historical 'parole'* displace any notion of 'irreducible' "polyvalency" (what G. O'Collins and D. Kendall call 'an uncheckable range of alternative interpretations') that depends only on 'infinite' *'philosophical'* 'possibility'.[198]

Similarly, for Thiselton, the *"historical"* development of *'langue'* and *'parole'* overturns the *ahistorical 'philosophical'* notion of 'infinite series of' "dislocating" "systems" and *'différance'*.[199] Further, Thiselton argues that the *historical* "particularity" of "text type" and "function" displaces any "imperialization" of "hedonistic" 'play' and of 'deconstruction' as 'single' "models" of *'textuality'* and/or of interpretation – though Thiselton allows that "deconstruction" of a modified kind is a useful interpretative 'model' for *'some'* kinds of 'biblical texts'. Thiselton also argues that questions remain concerning Derrida's "prioritizing"

---

[195] Thiselton, *NH*, 7, 69, cf. 127-129; cf.: Derrida, 'LI', 200; 217; 211, 213; cf.: 214-215; 232-233; 240; 220; 184; Schrag, 'Sub', 26; cf. for the citation of Foucault, Palmer, R.E., 'Postmodern Hermeneutics and the Act of Reading', *NDEJ* 15.3 (1983), 68; cf. Derrida, J., *Margins of Philosophy* (trans. A. Bass; Brighton: The Harvester Press, 1982), 121; cf. Ingraffia, *PT&BT*, 168. All italics ours.

[196] Thiselton, *NH*, 113, 125, 129, 126, 108, 109; cf.: 103-132, 472-474, 582-592. Italics ours, Thiselton's italics removed from the term, 'process'.

[197] Thiselton, *NH*, 128, 127, 99, 102, 41; cf. 99-103, 127-129. Italics on 'judgments' Thiselton's, remaining italics ours.

[198] Thiselton, *NH*, 83, 100-101, 131; cf. O'Collins, G., and D. Kendall, *The Bible for Theology: Ten Principles for the Theological Use of Scripture* (New York and Mahwah, N.J.: Paulist, 1997), 20. All italics ours, except for Thiselton's italics on *'parole'*.

[199] Thiselton, *NH*, 83, 96, 101, 127, 97, 99; cf. 94-97, 125-129. All italics Thiselton's, except on *"historical"* and on *"ahistorical"*.

'of' 'writing' 'over' 'speech', and concerning [Roland] Barthes' prioritizing of 'connotative' 'system' over 'denotative system': for Thiselton, the latter half of each couplet must be retained in its *historical* (cf. 'inter-subjective world') *'otherness'*. Finally, theologically speaking, Thiselton questions whether or not 'biblical' 'promise' is consistent with the "indefinite" "deferral" of "meaning".[200]

For Thiselton, then, (i), *neither* an 'iconoclastic' approach to 'meaning', *nor* the complete "determination" of "'meaning'" by *present-horizon 'readers'*, could ever constitute "the only alternative(s)" to "positivistic" notions of "reference". For Thiselton, there is *another alternative* to positivism and/or idealism. Thus, it is not "positivistic" notions of "reference" or philosophically "idealist" "formal" "'concepts'" that "stabilize" "meaning" in Thiselton's hermeneutics. Rather, it is *historical* unity, *historical* "continuities", and *historical* dialectic that "stabilize" "meaning" in Thiselton's hermeneutics. That is, Thiselton in effect argues that, *in order* to promote either "iconoclasm" or the "imperialization" of present-day "reader"-'horizons', one does not simply have to overturn philosophical idealism or 'formalism' *legitimately*; one would also have to dismiss historical unity, historical 'continuity', and historical dialectic *illegitimately*. For Thiselton, then, *a posteriori* historical "continuities", and the resulting *"'constraints'"* on "meaning", cannot be dismissed simply on the basis of a critique of the *a priori* transcendental ahistorical reifications of "formalism" or of "idealism".[201]

Here, J. Goldingay's point about Derrida's anti-*theological* attack on "'homogeneity'" is plausibly relevant in relation to Thiselton's view that 'deconstruction is a worldview masquerading as an approach to interpretation' and semiotics. However, it would also be consistent with Thiselton's thinking to say that, in Derrida's attack on "'homogeneity'", Derrida has not retained adequate *philosophical* emphases on historical unity, on historical 'continuity', and/or on historical dialectic.[202]

(j) At this juncture, some of Hegel's thoughts are of interest in relation to our defence of Thiselton's thinking – particularly in relation to our arguments for the unity (not uniformity) of history and for the ontological prioritization of "history" over "language" during hermeneutical theory-construction. Hegel writes:

> The Now is pointed out; this Now. Now… it has already ceased to exist, when it is "pointed out". The Now that exists is **other** than the one that is pointed out; and we see that the Now is more precisely that-which-when-it-exists-is-already-to-exist-no-longer. The Now, as it is shown to us, is a *has-been*; and **this** is its truth. It does not

---

[200] Thiselton, *NH*, 557, 122, 123, 130-132, 590-592, 144, 558, 114, 112, 96, 97; cf.: 104-106, 120-123; 127-132, 101-102; cf.: Thiselton, 'TY', 1564; Watson, 'R *NH*', 255. Italics Thiselton's, except on the two occurrences of the word, *"historical"*.

[201] Thiselton, *NH*, 124-128, 538, 540-542, 27, 122, 546; cf.: Thiselton, 'LMR', 1135; Thiselton, *2H*, 407-411. Italics Thiselton's on *'readers'* and *"'constraints'"*, others ours.

[202] Goldingay, *MIS*, 27; cf.: Derrida, J., *Positions* (Chicago: University of Chicago Press, 1981), 63-64; Thiselton, *NH*, 92, 125-127; Thiselton, 'BTT', 110; Thiselton, 'LMR', 1135. Italics ours.

have the truth of existence. And thus, although it is, to be sure, true that this Now had existed, still what "had existed" is in fact no being. *It does not* EXIST. But our investigation was supposed to deal with existence.[203]

What we thus see in this pointing out is just a movement and its subsequent unfolding... The Now and the pointing-out of the Now is thus construed in such a way that neither the Now nor the pointing-out of the Now is an absolute simplicity, but a **movement**, which contains in itself various Moments...[204]

In reading Hegel here, one might deduce from Hegel's points that to isolate a "moment" in history is already an interpretative transposition or conversion *away from* a historical process or "movement" - a kind of conversion loosely analogous to that presented in some contexts as a conversion "from analogue to digital", a conversion that might be likened to a transposition that had the grammar of a Fourier transform (on Fourier transforms, see our footnotes).[205]

That is, certain interpretative acts, whilst being historical movements themselves, seem to "still" historical movement by creating a reflective space for the construction of models of the historical moment. Language-uses employed in the construction of "histories", then, do not exhaustively mediate "history" *per se*, but already constitute historical movements or actions themselves that nevertheless, in the reflective space, seem to suspend movement artificially so as to isolate "moments" - performing something akin to a Fourier transform in a concession to simpler model-construction. So, this kind of interpreting *is* action or movement but *also* seemingly suspends action or movement insofar as it describes moments or, indeed, stepping away from Hegel's abstractions, *horizons*.

Thus, with Hegel's points in the background, we might deduce that the historical reconstruction of what we would these days call past horizons – seen by Hegel more abstractly as "moments" – at the same time seems in *some* senses to negate "history" since it *both* stills historical "movement" artificially in the reflective space *and* artificially dissociates horizons from one-another in doing so.

---

[203] Hegel, G.W.F., *Phenomenology of Spirit*, Section 3.1, Paragraph 106, in *Hegel's Phenomenology of Spirit* (trans. H.P. Kainz; University Park, PA.: The Pennsylvania State University Press, 1994), 37. Bold type, capitalization, and italics theirs.

[204] Hegel, *PoS*, Sect. 3.2, Para. 107, 37-38. Bold type and capitalization theirs.

[205] A Fourier transform is a geophysical application in which complex 'analogue' wave-forms are broken down into superimpositions of simple wave-forms that are more easily stored 'digitally'. It is simpler to speak in terms of historical "difference" between historical "particularities" (cf. a digital analysis that ceases movement) than it is to see these as aspects of historical movement (cf. an analogue synthesis that preserves movement of different kinds – including continuities). On Fourier transforms see, Parasnis, D.S., *Principles of Applied Geophysics* (London: Chapman and Hall, 1979), 257-259; cf. Telford, W.M., L.P. Geldart, R.E. Sheriff, and D.A. Keys, *Applied Geophysics* (Cambridge: CUP, 1976), 370-372. Before returning to university to retrain in Christian Doctrine and in hermeneutics, the present author worked very briefly as a "geophysicist" in the oil industry.

The language of historical reconstructions, then, is historical, but partially negates history when it attempts to encapsulate history in that it artificially suspends historical movement and artificially reduces moments – or horizons - to dissociated quasi-simplicities. Our point, here, does not at all dismiss the possibility of "true historical report", but only acknowledges that "true historical report" *does not exhaustively mediate what historical reality is in its dynamics and unity.*

What we are really doing here, of course, is arguing for the unity of history and for the ontological prioritization, during hermeneutical theory-construction, of conceptualizations of history over conceptualizations of language. Any *radical* dissociation between "moments" or between "horizons" is really only an artefact of the interpretative process, and cannot be elevated to the status of an ontological hermeneutical axiom so as to dismiss, say, the possibility of historical report, or of historical understanding, or of historical operative influence. Further, language, being only an *aspect* of historical movement, seems to partially *negate* or "still" history when it attempts, but fails, to encompass it completely. Therefore, history – and hence historical action by selves - is ontologically prior to language.

Having said this, of course, historical "movement" itself cannot be reduced to an abstract quasi-formal concept with a singular grammar of the kind suggested in the caricatures of historical movement implicit in phrases such as "fleeting moment" or "flux". In line with Thiselton's second and third *modified* Hegelian axioms (see Chapter 6), historical "movement" and/or dialectic cannot be divorced from concrete historical "changes", "particularities" and "continuities". Crucially, historical continuities may all but *suspend certain movements* for a time (as, for example, in geological rock-formations), but in a way that *differs markedly in its grammar from the suspension of movement generated by certain interpretative actions in that the former suspension of movement (e.g. the geological) is neither artificial nor necessarily achieved by language.*[206]

That is, the ontological prioritization of conceptualizations of history over conceptualizations of language entails the subordination of linguistic flux and of the *intra-linguistic* suspension of historical movement *to extra-linguistic* historical movement and/or dialectic – and therefore to historical change, to historical particularities, to historical continuities, and to historical unity (not uniformity).

Thus, language is not simply in "flux", but rather is constrained to historically actual movements (*including those that engender continuities*) - of *various* locations, durations, distances, suspensions, velocities and accelerations - that belong to developing traditions. Again, Derrida's statement, 'the *graphics* of iterability inscribes alteration irreducibly in repetition' seems to us to be a half-truth.[207] It could also be said that, "the *historicity* of graphic iterability inscribes alterations *variably* in repetition", since the graphics of iterability is *always already* subordinated to the historicity of graphic iterability.

This point introduces an emphasis on *geographical location* – an aspect of

---

[206] Thiselton, 'LMR', 1135; cf. Thiselton, *2H*, 376.

[207] Derrida, 'LI', 200, cf. 220. Italics ours.

historicity that Derrida seems to under-emphasize in his prioritization of discourses on language – at least in 'Limited Inc a b c…'. We might ask: do the desks and studies where certain "broadly post-structuralist" texts are written constitute some of the only *geographical locations* where language-uses mimic the behavior of radically dissociating flux? Do certain "broadly post-structuralist" texts constitute an attempt to make actual a form of language-behavior that would not, otherwise, or often, come into existence? In other words, on a "Thiseltonian" view, the 'graphics of iterability' - being more convincingly subordinated to the historicity of (geo-)graphic (*sic*) iterability in Thiselton's thinking than seems to be the case in Derrida's thinking in 'Limited Inc a b c…'. - really depend on *who* is doing the inscribing, and *where*.

Thus, (k), in our view, Thiselton *rightly* concludes that Derrida's semiotics (and the later Roland Barthes' semiotics – see below) are not the only "possible" development of Saussurian semiotics, but rather that – certainly in relation to the philosophy of history - they constitute a '*semiotic*' cloaking of an *a priori* absolutized pre-understanding characterized by narrowed philosophical-theological dialogue - *at the level of critical-synthetic sublation-filter-construction* - with 'Nietzsche', 'Husserl', 'Heidegger', 'Freud', 'Saussure', and C.S. Peirce amongst others. This narrowed philosophical-theological dialogue brings with it a *mistaken conflating subduction of a developing hermeneutical critique of history beneath a critique of Western philosophical idealism*. In Thiselton's estimate, this subduction – and this conflation - has led to 'an antimetaphysical' '*world-view*' partly parallel '"to… Madhyamaka Buddhism"'. In effect, Thiselton concludes that Derrida and the later Barthes transgress criteria emerging from a widened dialogue with the philosophy of history – notably historical ontological priority, historical unity (including historical relationality), historical movement and/or dialectic, and historical continuity. That is, Thiselton argues that in the approaches of Derrida and the later Barthes: first, the respective ontological priorities of 'history' and 'language' are reversed; therefore, second, historical horizons are – implicitly and artificially – 'radically' "dissociated" from one another at a "stratum two" level of discourse (i.e. theoretically) rather than at a "stratum three" level of discourse (i.e. as an acknowledged artefact of the interpretative process); and, third, historical "subjects" are thereby reduced to "fluxing" linguistic "constructs" projected onto 'biological… drives'.[208] For Thiselton, moreover, fourth, Derrida's notion of 'radically' "dissociating" 'flux' threatens to presuppose a quasi-idealist temporal realm *divorced from* the actual

---

[208] Thiselton, *NH*, 125-126, 101-119, 82-84, cf.: 91-92, 125-127; cf. Thiselton, *IGPS*, 111. On radical historical dissociation and the prioritization of language, cf. Derrida, J., *Of Grammatology* (Eng. trans. G.C. Spivak; Baltimore, London: The Johns Hopkins University Press, 1974, 1976, 1997 corrected edition; Fr. 1967), 5, 6; cf. Derrida, J., *Writing and Difference* (Eng. trans. A. Bass; London: Routledge and Kegan Paul, 1978, 2001; Fr. 1967), 371, 373; cf. Derrida, J., 'Différance', in *Speech and Phenomena and Other Essays on Husserl's Theory of Signs* (trans. D.B. Allison; Evanston: Northwestern University Press, 1973), 140-160. Second and sixth italics Thiselton's, remaining italics ours.

grammars of historical movements in actual geographical locations. In Thiselton's estimate, therefore, historical (and other) dichotomies persist in Derrida's approach.[209]

By contrast, (l), for Thiselton, Christology and eschatology provide what we might here conceive of as being a unifying yet *tensorial* framework that, in turn, provides theoretical coordinates for all *seven* major hermeneutical *conversations* and, therefore, for all *six* major hermeneutical *critiques* (i.e. for critiques of conceptualizations of history, epistemology, language, (Western) culture, human selves, and of hermeneutical understanding). In particular, this tensorial framework "stretches" the six hermeneutical *critiques* apart so as to preserve their mutual distinctiveness (though they also overlap). But this tensorial framework also avoids dichotomies, preserving "directed" unifying mutual inter-relationships between - and thereby preserving unifying intra-relationships within - the critiques by correctly prioritizing, and by correctly inter-sublating, the different critiques conceptually in relation to ontology and/or in relation to their respective basicalities. (N.B. in biology, a tensor is a "stretching" muscle; in mathematics, a tensor is a vector, where vectors have "direction").[210]

That is, building hermeneutical theory is in some senses like constructing a Russian doll. Thiselton's Christological and eschatological tensorial framework preserves hermeneutical unity by allowing hermeneutical critiques to be built with, and into, the right inter-relationships of inter-sublation. We may liken this process of hermeneutical theory-construction to building a Russian doll in the normal manner, with less basic critiques (for example, "language") being properly nested within more basic critiques (for example, "history"). Conversely, attempting to build a theoretically more basic critique within the coordinates of a theoretically less basic critique is like trying to fit a larger doll within a smaller doll. To get any part of the larger doll into the smaller doll, the larger doll either has to be split into fragments (cf. dichotomies), or has to be collapsed out of shape, whilst the smaller doll has to be artificially over-extended (this notion of "over-extension" is from T.K. Seung – see below).

That is, if hermeneutical critiques of history, epistemology, language, (Western) culture, and of human selves – taken together with a critique of hermeneutical understanding - are wrongly inter-related, or wrongly inter-sublated, during theoretical discussions or during hermeneutical theory-construction then problems will result – as follows. *First*, the unity of the more-basic critiques - if the more-basic critiques are wrongly sublated into less-basic critiques - will potentially *shatter into dichotomies*. *Second*, the more-basic critiques, if wrongly sublated into less-basic critiques, will tend to *collapse in on themselves* (as well as, or instead of, shattering into

---

[209] McHann Jr., *3H*, 326; cf. Thiselton, *NH*, 113, 105, 125, 26; cf.: 251; 337; cf. Gadamer, *TM*, 301-302.

[210] See Chapter 3 and earlier in the present chapter; cf. Tulloch, *Wordfinder*, 1610. A 'tensor' is either "a muscle that tightens or stretches", or "a generalized form of vector involving an arbitrary number of indices". All vectors have direction.

dichotomies). *Third*, the less-basic critiques, if forced to conceptually accommodate the more-basic critiques, will show signs of *artificial over-extension or critique-over-extension* (so T.K. Seung – see below).

That is, broadly speaking, our study of Thiselton's thinking has led us to the provisional conclusion that these are three of the many problems that will tend to emerge when hermeneutical theorizing wrongly inter-sublates major hermeneutical critiques with respect to one another. Although space considerations with respect to the present study prevent us from carrying out a fuller treatment of these three problems here, we may nevertheless *begin* to demonstrate the validity of our tentative findings in regards to this matter by considering just a few critical responses by other writers to the thinking of the later Roland Barthes, as follows.

Thus, (m), with respect to the *first* of the three problems that we have just highlighted, then we have already argued that a "Thiseltonian" critique exposes the problem of *theoretical dichotomies* in relation to Heidegger, Bultmann, Gadamer, the New Hermeneutic, ideological structuralist approaches, Fish, and now in relation to Derrida also. Here, though, we may extend this argument still further through a consideration of some points made by the later R. Barthes and cited by B.D. Ingraffia. Thus, the later Barthes writes:

> writing ceaselessly posits meaning ceaselessly to evaporate it, carrying out a systematic exemption of meaning. In precisely this way literature (it would be better from now on to say *writing*), by refusing to assign a "secret", an ultimate meaning, to the text (and to the world as text), liberates what might be called an anti-theological activity… since to refuse to fix meaning is, in the end, to refuse God.[211]

Straight away, though, notably, when examining this citation, and in relation to the problem of *theoretical dichotomies*, we may observe, (i), that the later Barthes sets what amounts to completely fluid 'meaning' in opposition to "fixed" 'meaning', where the later Barthes closely associates "fixed" 'meaning' with 'God'.[212]

Of course, though, as Ingraffia rightly argues, the later Barthes is only able to dismiss 'God' in this manner by conceiving of God "ontotheologically", or in a philosophically idealist or formalist manner that ties 'God' artificially to "fixed" 'meaning'. 'Ontotheology', as Ingraffia explains, can be conceived of as a 'synthesis of Christianity and Neoplatonism' that 'always' 'leads… to a subordination of biblical revelation'.[213] Alternatively, Ingraffia argues that 'the god of ontotheology' is also 'the god which replaced the biblical God in Descartes'. 'In Descartes' ontotheology', Ingraffia argues, 'God is merely the metaphysical ground for the operation of the independent autonomous ego'. In other words, in Ingraffia's estimate, 'the god of ontotheology… is always the product of human

---

[211] Ingraffia, *PT&BT*, 6; cf. Ingraffia cites, Barthes, R., 'The Death of the Author', in *Image-Music-Text* (trans. S. Heath; New York: Hill and Wang, 1977), 147. Italics Barthes'.

[212] Ingraffia, *PT&BT*, 6; cf. Ingraffia cites, Barthes, 'DOA', 147.

[213] Ingraffia, *PT&BT*, 227, 6; cf. Ingraffia cites, Barthes, 'DOA', 147.

reason'.[214]

That is, we may agree with Ingraffia that the later Barthes' post-structuralist attack on the "god of ontotheology" succeeds only in undermining a philosophically idealist "god", and that the later Barthes unwittingly leaves the biblical God of *history* out of the discussion. Whilst Ingraffia employs generalizations such as 'modernism' and 'postmodernism' *without* invoking an argument for a dialogic resolution of definitions for such terms, we may nevertheless broadly agree with him when he writes, 'Christian faith has all too easily been conflated [*sic*] with ontotheology in modernism and then criticized for being ontotheology in postmodernism'. Crucially, (and here we are overlooking Ingraffia's over-generalizations), Ingraffia concludes that these "modern" and "postmodern" errors rest 'upon a profound misunderstanding of biblical revelation'.[215] In other words, the later Barthes' post-structuralism *overlooks the philosophy of history implicit in biblical revelation by conflating (sic) the latter with philosophically idealist ontotheology.*

Moving on, (ii), then another point related to problematic dichotomies emerges when we examine the later Barthes' comment that, 'writing ceaselessly posits meaning ceaselessly to evaporate it, carrying out a systematic exemption of meaning'. The other point that emerges is that, in this comment, the later Barthes *rightly* closely allies "language" (the later Barthes uses the term, "writing") and "meaning", but *wrongly* dissociates *both* "language" *and* "meaning" from a properly-developed notion or philosophy of *history*.[216]

That is, we have already seen that, for Thiselton, a hermeneutical critique of language and meaning is properly grounded in a hermeneutical critique of history (see Chapters 4 and 6). That is, for Thiselton, the question of meaning, whilst being irrevocably bound up with the question of *language*, is also irrevocably bound up with dialectically expanding *historical* relationalities - and/or historical relationships - between historical particularities and/or between historical horizons within diachronic historical and anticipatory 'wholes' (including traditions) against the background of the unity (not uniformity) of historical reality - and ultimately against the background of the *biblical* God and of the unity of the *biblical* God's creation (see Chapter 6 and earlier in the present chapter).

Thus, in Thiselton's thinking, as we saw in Chapter 4, certain kinds of literary semantics, which center on considerations of *linguistic* components of meaning, are only an *aspect of* philosophical semantics, which *also* take *historical* extra-linguistic factors into account – notably, the inter-subjective communicative actions of historical persons in developing traditions.

To return, though, to the later Barthes' comment - that, 'writing ceaselessly posits meaning ceaselessly to evaporate it, carrying out a systematic exemption of

---

[214] Ingraffia, *PT&BT*, 5, 4.
[215] Ingraffia, *PT&BT*, 6; cf. 4-5. Italics ours.
[216] Ingraffia, *PT&BT*, 6; cf. Ingraffia cites, Barthes, 'DOA', 147.

meaning'²¹⁷ – then one of our earlier examples may serve to highlight the falsehood of this comment, as follows.

Thus, investigators could, for example, write all manner of conspiracy theories about the assassination of John F. Kennedy. But, from a "Thiseltonian" stance, these investigators would not thereby 'evaporate' the 'meaning' of the event of the assassination. To write about the assassination would hardly be to "carry" 'out a systematic exemption of meaning' in relation to the assassination's unfolding historical relations of inter-subjective teleological causality with respect to subsequent historical events. *At worst*, such conspiracy theories would not 'evaporate' meaning or 'exempt' meaning from coming into existence but would, rather, only *obscure* the assassination's meaning for a limited time. *At best*, such conspiracy theories could even constitute mutually qualifying investigative angles of view on the assassination – angles of view that took investigators *towards* the *historical truth* of the matter.²¹⁸

The later Barthes, however, writes as though *writing itself* constituted an "over-writing" of *historical relationalities and/or of historical relationships*. Of course, *some* historical inter-relationships are more or less *linguistic*. Others, though, have decidedly *extra-linguistic* grammars, as in the case of the historical repercussions of JFK's assassination. That is, the later Barthes has erroneously sublated conceptualizations of "history" into conceptualizations of "language", and has then set up a quasi-formal binary opposition between, on the one hand, the sublation of conceptualizations of "history" into conceptualizations of "language" and, on the other hand, a philosophically idealist and/or formalist conception of God.²¹⁹

The later Barthes, of course, as Thiselton points out, is well aware of the distinctions between a philosophically idealist formalism that fixes meaning, a completely fluid notion of meaning, and something more in line with Thiselton's hermeneutics. And yet, because the later Barthes, in effect, unwittingly 'insists' on erroneously sublating a critique of history into a critique of language, then he is obliged to restrict the choice to an "either/or" that almost looks like a formal binary opposition – i.e. to a choice between idealist formalism and a completely fluid notion of meaning. Thus, Thiselton observes that the later 'Barthes insists' that the 'infinity of deferral is *not* to be identified… with the mere corrigibility of a "hermeneutic process of deepening, but rather with a serial movement of dislocations… variations… [with] an irreducible plurality"'.²²⁰

---

[217] Ingraffia, *PT&BT*, 6; cf. Ingraffia cites, Barthes, 'DOA', 147.

[218] Ingraffia, *PT&BT*, 6; cf. Ingraffia cites, Barthes, 'DOA', 147; cf. Thiselton, *2H*, 39, 40-45, 373, 75-77, 80-81, 115, 195, 211-212, 217, 244-249, 260-274, 286-292, 311-314, 359-361, 371, 385, 403-405, 425, 432-444; cf. Thiselton, 'R-RH', 100. Italics ours.

[219] In relation to "over-writing" see also, on Derrida, Thiselton, *NH*, 112; cf. 103-132.

[220] Thiselton, *NH*, 99; cf. Thiselton is citing, Barthes, R., 'From Work to Text', in *Textual Strategies: Perspectives in Post-Structuralist Criticism* (ed. J.V. Harari; Ithaca: Cornell University Press, 1979), 74. Italics Thiselton's.

Thiselton, though, by contrast, reverses the later Barthes' sublation-direction in relation to the inter-relationships between conceptualizations of "language" and of "history" without in any sense returning to formalism (see above and Chapters 4, 5 and 6). And it is this reversal that allows Thiselton to espouse the 'corrigibility of a "hermeneutic process of deepening'" whilst *agreeing* with the later Barthes' rejection of formalism. Afterall, *first*, it is not as though we are constrained to only two "formal" possibilities – "the later Barthes *versus* formalism" - when it comes to drawing on historical interpretative paradigms or on hermeneutical traditions. And, *second*, the later Barthes' mono-form conception of "plural interpretative outcomes" in terms of what amounts to artificially-abstracted "infinitely fluid meaning" is in fact a *gross over-simplification* when compared to the *six overlapping and superimposed kinds* of "pluralities of interpretative outcomes" that we associated with Thiselton's *properly historical approach* to hermeneutics in Chapter 5.[221]

(n) Moving on, then the *second* kind of problem that we highlighted earlier in the present context of discussion concerned the way in which more-basic hermeneutical critiques potentially *collapse in on themselves* when they are sublated into less-basic hermeneutical critiques.

Staying with Ingraffia's critical response to the work of the later Barthes, then we have already observed that, for the later Barthes, 'writing ceaselessly posits meaning ceaselessly to evaporate it, carrying out a systematic exemption of meaning'. In the later Barthes' thinking, this process constitutes 'an anti-theological activity... since to refuse to fix meaning is, in the end, to refuse God'. However, in the light of our study on Thiselton's thinking, and with some help from Ingraffia, we concluded above that the later Barthes had unnecessarily if unwittingly insisted that a stance that sublated conceptualizations of history into conceptualizations of language constituted the only alternative to philosophical idealism and/or formalism (where the latter, for the later Barthes, included the 'god' of ahistorical philosophical idealism, which the later Barthes erroneously conflated (*sic*) with the biblical God of history).[222]

Having said this, of course, it is not only the "ontotheological" 'god' of philosophical idealism that the later Barthes' critique of language "over-writes" or "collapses". Ingraffia comments that, 'if God is that which fixes human meaning, as ontotheology claims, then the absence of a God means that human meaning is unfounded and plays upon an abyss'. K.J. Vanhoozer adds that, 'for Roland Barthes, the disappearance of God leads to the death of the human author', where 'the author's absence means that there is nothing that fixes or stabilizes meaning'.[223] And the later Barthes, notably, does not exempt himself from this "absence". Barthes writes of himself: 'He wanted to write himself in RB. But

---

[221] Thiselton, *NH*, 99; cf. 540-546. Italics ours.
[222] Ingraffia, *PT&BT*, 6; cf. Ingraffia cites, Barthes, 'DOA', 147.
[223] Ingraffia, *PT&BT*, 6; cf. Vanhoozer, K.J., 'The Spirit of Understanding: Special Revelation and General Hermeneutics', in *Disciplining Hermeneutics: Interpretation in Christian Perspective* (Ed. R. Lundin; Leicester: Apollos, 1997), 136.

always there crept in the maxims. Were these to reassure others that this fragmentary creature had, after all, a bottom nature?'[224]

Thiselton, in his critical responses to the later D. Cupitt, makes a similar kind of point in relation to the "death of the self" or of "the subject". Thiselton writes that, in the later Cupitt's kind of thinking,

> the self... [is] largely a construct of the interaction between pre-conscious forces and social conventions. It is perceived as a "de-centered" construct within the sign-system, in which signs, not selves, occupy a privileged status. "Reality", if we may even use such a term, becomes only signs chasing signs.[225]

Here, of course, Thiselton does not at all mean to say that the later Cupitt dismisses the "concrete" aspect of our existence or of our environment. Thus, Thiselton draws our attention to two other citations from Cupitt's later work in which Cupitt writes: 'Today the self is an animal with cultural inscriptions [signs] written over its skin. Below it, there is only a trembling of biological energies and responses'... 'And that is what we are'.[226]

And yet, whilst these citations remind us that *both* Thiselton *and* the later Cupitt acknowledge that there is a "concrete" aspect to our reality (i.e. Cupitt speaks of "biological energies and responses"), these citations *also* remind us of the contrast that we observed in Chapter 4 between the notion of "enfleshed word" and the notion of "en-worded flesh". That is, when a hermeneutical critique of language – and hence of meaning – has erroneously usurped a hermeneutical critique of history from the latter's rightful role as the most-basic unifying hermeneutical critique in relation to ontology at the stratum two level of hermeneutical theory, then "enfleshed word" becomes "en-worded flesh".

In other words, and to extend our argument further, then *if* an approach is adopted in which a theoretically more-basic hermeneutical critique of history is erroneously sublated into a theoretically less-basic hermeneutical critique of language, then an internally consistent but ultimately artificial pattern or "logic" ensues – as follows.

To begin with, in such an approach, historical realities are erroneously subordinated to language (if not in a way that denies all notion of a "concrete" dimension, as we have seen). Therefore, language, though a historical reality itself, is thereby *also* erroneously cut free from history and subordinated only to a "docetic" version of itself. Thus language, despite actually being subordinated to historical movement in its every instantiation, is nevertheless - in such an approach - erroneously divorced from the geographically located concrete

---

[224] O'Neill, J., 'Homotextuality: Barthes on Barthes, Fragments (RB), with a Footnote', in *Hermeneutics: Questions and Prospects* (eds. G. Shapiro & A. Sica; Los Angeles: UMP, 1984), 166.
[225] Thiselton, *IGPS*, 105.
[226] Thiselton, *IGPS*, 106.

grammars of actual historical movements. This theoretical scenario then, as a result of this "divorce", erroneously allows linguistic movement to occupy a quasi-idealist temporal realm divorced from history in which the grammar of that linguistic movement is abstractly and ahistorically reduced to that of a privileged fictive mono-form linguistic flux. Other historical realities, aside from language, since they have *also* been erroneously subordinated to language in this problematic approach, are then *also* subordinated to this quasi-idealist linguistic flux.

This theoretical scenario thus also allows the artificial dissociation of historical horizons into quasi-simplicities that (in reality) pertains merely to the stratum-three interpretative activities of historical reconstruction (see above) to be *radicalized erroneously* into a supposedly theoretically-more-basic stratum-two phenomenon. In fact, though, as we saw earlier, the artificial dissociation of historical horizons into quasi-simplicities is only an artefact of the stratum-three interpretative process and is everywhere subordinated to historical movement. That is, again, as we saw earlier, artificial dissociation is only a function of a *stratum-three* conversion of historical movement and unity into the quasi-simplicities of "historical horizons" - a conversion, with a grammar analogous to that of a Fourier transform, that is performed solely for the sake of making a concession to simpler "short-hand" model-construction. (As we explained earlier, none of our argumentation here – or, we might add, anywhere else - contradicts the possibility of true historical report or of true historical reconstructions).

In other words, and to provide an illustration from the oil industry, just as "analogue" data collected during seismic surveys is *converted* (by the application of a Fourier transform – see above) into a "digital" format for the sake of ease-of-data-storage, so in historical reconstruction the "analogue" of historical movement is *artificially* "stilled" *by language* into reconstructions of discrete "horizons" which, then, may *appear* to be "radically dissociated from one-another *by the operation of language*". In reality, however, the historically-concrete remains a dynamic "analogue" unity. "History" is not *actually* "stilled", "encapsulated" or "dissociated from itself" by language any more than the geological formations beneath the North Sea are *actually* converted into electronic digital signals by Fourier transforms. "Radical dissociation" is only ever *seemingly* true of some interpreta*tions* (stratum three), and is *never* true of the interpret*ed* (stratum two).

By contrast, however, in the erroneous "logic" or "pattern" that we are exposing, those historical realities – including God (though God is more than, but not less than, "historical"), authors, and/or selves or subjects - that have been erroneously sublated into an erroneously ontologically-prioritized critique of language - and thus into the framework of an erroneously radicalized fictive quasi-idealist ahistorical mono-form internally-dissociative linguistic flux - are now erroneously seen as being, themselves, subject to radical internal dissociation through the supposed over-writing that pertains to such a fictive linguistic flux. This *ahistorical* "logic" or "pattern" then becomes the erroneous basis for arguments for the death of God, or for the death of authors, or for the death of human selves or subjects (see above).

Such arguments, however, as we have said, are flawed because they flow from the erroneous sublation of theoretically more-basic hermeneutical critiques of history into theoretically less-basic hermeneutical critiques of language. This erroneous sublation itself, further, has arisen from the still deeper problem of the conflating (*sic*) and concealing subordinating subduction of a non-idealist hermeneutical critique of history beneath philosophical (and structuralist) idealism and/or formalism within the context of broadly post-structuralist critiques *of* philosophical (and structuralist) idealism and/or formalism.[227] And this conflating (*sic*) and concealing subordinating subduction has occurred because of the inadequacies of broadly post-structuralist dialogues – not at the level of "breadth of reading" but at the level of the critical-synthetic sublation-filter-constructions operative within pre-understanding - with the philosophy of history and with biblical theology during or throughout the history of the rise of historical consciousness (see our arguments above).

Admittedly, arguably, biblical revelation aside, adequate philosophies of history may sometimes *post-date* the most influential tradition-defining broadly post-structuralist texts, the latter dating from the time-interval from 1964 to 1967 and later. Thus, for example, beginning in 1963, and culminating in 1976 – in a culmination just post-dating the advent of post-structuralism - Thiselton (rather than Pannenberg) appears to be the first emerging "theological hermeneutician" to employ an adequate post-Gadamerian philosophy of history that is *also* post-later-Wittgensteinian (see Chapter 6). And so it is perhaps no great surprise that critiques of language were mistakenly granted the status of having the primary theoretical basicality in the slightly earlier biblically-uninformed post-structuralist attempts to revolt – less successfully than Thiselton perhaps - against the "formal" categories and binary oppositions of Western idealist metaphysical traditions.[228]

(o) Moving on, then the *third* kind of problem that we highlighted earlier in the present context of discussion concerned the way in which the erroneous sublation of theoretically more-basic hermeneutical critiques into the coordinates of theoretically less-basic hermeneutical critiques would lead to the artificial over-extension of the latter. We need only note here that T.K. Seung finds this problem occurring in the later work of Barthes. That is, in Seung's estimate, the later

---

[227] cf. Ingraffia, *PT&BT*, 6; cf. 225-241.

[228] Thiselton, *NH*, 92-141; Thiselton indicates that "the most influential tradition-defining broadly post-structuralist texts" (our phrase) include: Barthes, R., *On Racine* (Eng. New York: Hill and Wang, 1964); Barthes, R., *Elements of Semiology* (Eng. London: Jonathan Cape, 1967); Barthes, R., *Writing Degree Zero* (Eng. London: Jonathan Cape, 1967); Barthes, R., *S/Z* (Eng. London: Jonathan Cape, 1975); Barthes, R., *The Pleasure of the Text* (Eng. London: Jonathan Cape, 1975); Barthes, R., *Criticism and Truth* (Eng. Minneapolis: University of Minnesota Press, 1987); Derrida, J., *Speech and Phenomena, and Other Essays on Husserl's Theory of Signs* (Eng. Evanston: North Western University Press, 1973; Fr. 1967); Derrida, J., *Of Grammatology* (Eng. trans. G.C. Spivak; Baltimore, London: The Johns Hopkins University Press, 1974, 1976, 1997 corrected edition; Fr. 1967); Derrida, J., *Writing and Difference* (Eng. trans. A. Bass; London: Routledge and Kegan Paul, 1978, 2001; Fr. 1967).

Barthes, in

> his doctrine of semantization... *overextends*... linguistic categories...[where the] central motivation is to regard nonlinguistic entities as extensions of language or as different kinds of language...[such that] language is accepted as the ultimate model of analysis...; everything else is investigated and interpreted through this universal model. Consequently, the science of linguistics becomes the arch science whose sphere of control and influence cannot be delimited.[229]

However, in Thiselton's view, as we have seen, it is *"history" (understood Christologically and eschatologically)*, and not "language", that comes closest to what Seung here refers to as an 'ultimate model', a 'universal model', or as an 'arch science'. That is, for Thiselton, as we saw, hermeneutics comes to unity in a hermeneutical critique of history (which includes historical selves or subjects), and not in a hermeneutical critique of language. Hence, Thiselton writes, against the later Barthes' radicalization of Saussure's thinking, that 'it is not the case, in Saussure, that *parole* can be generated by a subjectless system, in isolation from the *constraints* on possibility imposed by the purposive *choices of the* [historical] *speaking subject*'.[230]

(p) In concluding this sub-section, therefore, we might ask: has Thiselton perhaps more successfully left philosophical idealism behind than Fish and Derrida (and perhaps, also, than the later Barthes)? The answer to this question seems to be a resounding "yes".[231]

Thus, (3), we have now seen that the question of how conceptualizations of history and of language are inter-related or inter-sublated during hermeneutical theorizing resides close to the heart of Thiselton's hermeneutics. In our discussion of this question, we have found that even an *adequate* philosophy of *language* doesn't constitute the center of Thiselton's framework, but rather that a Christological and eschatological approach to *history* constitutes the center of Thiselton's framework. Certainly, philosophically idealist or formalist speech-act theory has no place at the heart of Thiselton's thinking. Rather, Thiselton sublates certain insights *from* this tradition *into* his properly *historical* hermeneutics.

Therefore, we must reject A.K.M. Adam's misleading caricature concerning Thiselton's supposed reliance on a 'particular interpretation of Wittgenstein' and on 'the unsurpassed cogency of speech-act theory'.[232] This misleading caricature of Thiselton, of course, shows us that Adam has failed to understand Thiselton. That is, in the case of Adam's reading of Thiselton, we are dealing with an example of

---

[229] Seung, T.K., *Structuralism and Hermeneutics* (New York: Columbia University Press, 1982), 125. Italics Seung's.

[230] Thiselton, *NH*, 99; cf. Seung, *S&H*, 125. First italics ours, other italics Thiselton's.

[231] Regarding Fish see, Thiselton, 'R-RH', 105; cf. Thiselton, *NH*, 393-405, cf. 515-550, 546; cf. Thiselton, 'CAP', 157; regarding Derrida see, Thiselton, *NH*, 124-132; cf.: 26; 251; 337; regarding Barthes see, Thiselton, *NH*, 99; cf. 92-103; cf. our comments in Chapter 6.

[232] Adam, 'R *NH*', 433.

hermeneutical foreclosure. Adam has interpreted Thiselton irresponsibly – where this conclusion becomes even more unavoidable when we consider some of the other points made by Adam in his responses to Thiselton.

Thus, Adam complains that 'over and over again' in *New Horizons in Hermeneutics* Thiselton cites J.L. Austin's utterance, '"he promises, don't you, Willie?"', when in fact this citation only occurs in two contexts in the book.[233]

Furthermore, Adam observes 'Thiselton's' use of the term *"'sic'"* in relation 'to the title of an article on Derrida and Barth'. In Adam's estimate, this observation supposedly implies 'that Thiselton is calling our attention to a misspelling of Roland Barthes's last name'. Adam then notes that, 'the article in question is not about Roland Barthes, it is about Karl Barth, a fact which Thiselton could hardly have missed if he were familiar with the article'. Surely, though, since Thiselton groups 'Derrida' and 'Barthes' together to some extent, then he is highlighting to the reader that the cited article *is* about 'Derrida and Barth', *in contrast to* his normal grouping of 'Derrida' with 'Barthes'. This is why Thiselton writes 'Barth' and *not* 'Barthes'! If Thiselton had 'missed' the 'fact' that the article was *about* 'Barth', then why did Thiselton *write* 'Barth' - and then *highlight* the 'fact'? Adam has projected his own hermeneutical foreclosure onto Thiselton.[234]

On a more serious note, Adam claims that 'Thiselton… fails… to' answer 'the hard question' posed by 'pragmatist hermeneutics', which is: 'how is a particular historical individual or community ever to reach a position from which it could recognize valid metacritical standards?' Of course, though, for Thiselton, it is *Jesus Christ* who is being talked about here where, for Thiselton, engagement with the philosophy of history *warrants* the provisional acceptance of progressively accessible Christ-centered theological metacriteria. The real question is, "why have socio-pragmatists so foreclosed dialogue *with* the philosophy of history that Adam cannot appeal *to* the philosophy of history to *warrant* a working provisional belief in a progressively accessible Christ?"[235]

Adam even asserts that *New Horizons in Hermeneutics* 'provides an impressive rationale not for "transforming biblical reading", but for perpetuating a status quo'. But Adam misses the whole point. In *New Horizons in Hermeneutics* Thiselton is further developing his historico-philosophical (and theological) hermeneutical paradigm-*transformation* – a paradigm-*transformation* that first emerges prior to and in *The Two Horizons*. Adam even accuses Thiselton of 'partisan pleading'. But it is *Adam's* remarkable succession of multiple misreadings and hermeneutical foreclosures that constitutes 'partisan pleading'. Such a phrase does not apply to Thiselton. Rather, it is the term 'warrant' that applies to Thiselton. Again, Adam projects his own interpretative irresponsibility onto Thiselton.[236]

---

[233] Adam, 'R *NH*', 434; cf. Thiselton, *NH*, 70, cf. 599, 600.
[234] Adam, 'R *NH*', 434; cf. Thiselton, *NH*, 642, cf. 80-141. Italics on '"*sic*"' Adam's.
[235] See Chapter 3 and earlier in the present chapter; cf. Adam, 'R *NH*', 433. Italics ours.
[236] Adam, 'R *NH*', 434; cf. Thiselton, *NH*, 99; cf. Thiselton, *2H*, 44-45, cf.: 51-84, 234-251; 304-326. Italics ours.

(4) Our responses to A.K.M. Adam also raise problems for other commentators who misunderstand Thiselton's relationships to Derrida's and/or to Searle's thinking. Thus, querying M.V. Weele's reading of Thiselton, we may conclude that Thiselton does *not* criticize Derrida primarily from a perspective that grounds 'hermeneutics' in 'speech-act theory' (presumably Searlean) or in an 'action' model.[237] Yes, for Thiselton, 'action is a larger and more basic category than language'; and, for Thiselton, 'language is… a product of human action'. Yet, Thiselton prioritizes *history*, not merely 'action', over 'language' (on Thiselton and Searle, see above).[238]

Thus, contradicting M. Van Hamersveld's reading of Thiselton, we may conclude that 'hermeneutics… is' *not* 'part of the larger field of literary criticism' for Thiselton. The reverse is the case since, as Thiselton argues, certain kinds of 'literary criticism' potentially consider only certain kinds of historical language-uses. For Thiselton, even where 'literary criticism' claims to address all kinds of language-uses, linguistic considerations *still* constitute only *one* of at least *seven* hermeneutical discourses.[239] Of course, our saying this is not to deny that hermeneutics may only constitute a small part of the curriculum in some university English departments. Sometimes, though, this state of affairs is likely to be the case because of the same kind of mistake as that made by Van Hamersveld.[240]

Moving on, and querying C. Brown's reading of Thiselton, we may conclude that J.R. Searle's 'work' - and even that of the later 'Wittgenstein' - does *not* constitute Thiselton's 'way forward' in rejecting post-structuralism. Brown misses Thiselton's more central emphasis on the philosophy of history.[241] Even leaving the question of the philosophy of history to one side, 'Thiselton's favored linguistic approach is' *not* simply 'through speech act theory', *especially* not 'through… Searle's' (here, R, Papaphilippopoulos, S.E. Fowl and T. Ward *also* misread Thiselton in ways parallel to A.K.M. Adam).[242] Indeed, in *The Two*

---

[237] Thiselton, *2H*, 370-388; cf. Weele, M.V., 'Review of R. Lundin's, A.C. Thiselton's and C. Walhout's *The Responsibility of Hermeneutics*', *ChLit* 35.4 (Sum. 1986), 48, 49. Italics ours.

[238] Smith, R.L., 'Review of R. Lundin's, A.C. Thiselton's and C. Walhout's *The Responsibility of Hermeneutics*', *SWJTh* NS29.1 (Fall 1986), 64; cf. Thiselton, *2H*, 370-388, 407-409. Italics ours.

[239] Contradicting, Van Hamersveld, M., 'Review of R. Lundin's, A.C. Thiselton's and C. Walhout's *The Responsibility of Hermeneutics*', *RefRev* 40.3 (Spr. 1987), 252; cf. Thiselton, *2H*, 372-378. Italics ours.

[240] Bruns, *Hermeneutics*, ix-x.

[241] Querying, Brown, C., 'Review of A.C. Thiselton's *New Horizons in Hermeneutics*', *CalThJ* 30 (Apr. 1995), 236.

[242] Contradicting, Papaphilippopoulos, R., 'Review of A.C. Thiselton's *New Horizons in Hermeneutics*', *SJT* 47.1 (1994), 142; cf. Fowl, S.E., 'The Role of Authorial Intention in the Theological Interpretation of Scripture', in *Between Two Horizons. Spanning New Testament Studies and Systematic Theology* (eds. J.B. Green and M. Turner; Cambridge: Eerdmans, 2000), 76. n. 10; cf. Ward, T., *Word and Supplement: Speech Acts, Biblical Texts, and the Sufficiency of Scripture* (Oxford: OUP, 2002), 191-192. Italics ours.

*Horizons*, Thiselton almost *completes* his hermeneutical critique of language with *hardly a reference* to Searle. In *New Horizons in Hermeneutics*, Searle is mentioned only *once* in Thiselton's chapter on post-structuralism. The philosophy of *history* to one side (which is Thiselton's real *philosophical* core as we have seen), the main *linguistic* influence on Thiselton's thinking is the work of the later Wittgenstein, and not that of Searle.[243]

Finally, contradicting R. Papaphilippopoulos's reading of Thiselton, we may conclude that Thiselton does not "make" 'a' mere 'philosophical move' in "favor" of 'speech-act theory' or in "favor" of 'realism' – as though Thiselton's stance was merely an un-argued or "rhetorical" stance. Thiselton's prolonged 'philosophical' dialogues (hardly simply 'a… move') preclude such implicit caricature. Furthermore, again, 'speech-act theory' is *not* the core of Thiselton's thinking.[244]

(5) In pseudo-"post-structuralist" hermeneutical foreclosure, then, there almost seems to be a canonization of foreclosure or of interpretative irresponsibility. A.K.M. Adam and perhaps others seem - hedonistically, playfully, and instantaneously – to shelve or bin Thiselton prematurely in the "idealist" or "formalist" pigeon-hole. To use David Tracy's language, 'conversation' almost seems to have broken down where, notably, Adam even potentially fails to 'recognize' Jesus Christ as the emerging 'metacritical' "standard".[245]

Having replied to Adam's misleading suggestion that the work of Derrida in 'Limited Inc a b c…' could constitute the grounds for a criticism of Thiselton's thinking, we may now pick up *where we left off* in replying to Adam's other misleading suggestion – his suggestion that the work of Fish in 'Normal Circumstances…' could constitute the grounds for a criticism of Thiselton's thinking.

B) Responses to a First Group of "Fishian" Criticisms: W.G. Jeanrond, M.G. Brett, V.S. Poythress, and S. Perry

Moving on, then we may begin this next section of the present chapter by noting that our preceding arguments can now help to ground our responses to critics who appeal to *Stanley Fish* in order to prematurely dismiss Thiselton's thinking. These critics form the most notable and vocal body of writers who oppose Thiselton's hermeneutics, and so we have had to defer our responses to these writers until now so as not to disrupt the flow of our responses to A.K.M. Adam. In reality, though, as we have just indicated, what follows now may still be viewed as an extension of our earlier arguments in which we opposed Adam's mistaken belief that Fish supposedly presents a serious threat to Thiselton's stance.

In this section and the next section, then, we shall focus on two groups of critics who appeal to Fish - whether implicitly or explicitly - in their criticisms of

---

[243] Thiselton, *2H*, 380, 402; cf. Thiselton, *NH*, 115; cf. 88-92, 102, 124-131. Italics ours.
[244] Contradicting, Papaphilippopoulos, 'R *NH*', 141-142.
[245] Adam, 'R *NH*', 433; cf. Thiselton's citation of David Tracy in, Thiselton, *NH*, 131.

Thiselton. Critics in the first group (see the present section of our study) make *less extensive* criticisms of Thiselton from stances that appear to be *influenced by* Fish. This first group includes W.G. Jeanrond, M.G. Brett, V.S. Poythress, and S. Perry. Critics in the second group (see the next section of our study) make *more lengthy* appeals to Fish in their criticisms of Thiselton. This second group includes W.J. Lyons and S. Woodman. We should note here, in advance, that we disagree with Perry, Lyons, and Woodman only reluctantly, since they graciously provided us with samples of their work. Further, we should stress that it is only their *hermeneutical theory*, and not other aspects of their work, that we are querying! To begin with, however, we respond to W.G. Jeanrond, to M.G. Brett, to V.S. Poythress, and also to S. Perry – as follows.[246]

Thus, (1), in 1987, *W.G. Jeanrond*, makes critical comments in relation to Thiselton's article, 'Reader-Response Hermeneutics, Action-Models, and the Parables of Jesus' (1985). In this article, Thiselton's approach to responsible interpretation includes the consideration of 'whether the primary action and the truth-claims in which... [the '*text*'] is embedded have been reduced or changed in different contexts' of 'interpretation'. That is, for Thiselton, responsible interpretation - involving "purposeful" 'performative act[s]' by readers in variable reading- 'situation[s]' - should be 'derivative from, and congruent with, the actions' belonging to a text's original 'context'. It is presumably this strand in Thiselton's thinking that Jeanrond criticizes when he argues that *since* Thiselton's 'criterion for interpretative responsibility... is... itself a result of (his own) interpretative activity', *and that since* Thiselton's 'criterion for interpretative responsibility' is 'open to... critique by other responsible acts of interpretation', *then* Thiselton supposedly leaves interpreters unable to 'free' themselves from 'this hermeneutical circle'. That is, what Jeanrond seems to be saying here is that Thiselton's 'criterion for interpretative responsibility' is only Thiselton's own construct, and that this

---

[246] See, Jeanrond, W., 'Review of R. Lundin's, A.C. Thiselton's and C. Walhout's *The Responsibility of Hermeneutics*', *LitTh* 1.1 (Mar. 1987), 115-117; cf.: Brett, M.G., 'Review of A.C. Thiselton's *New Horizons in Hermeneutics*', *Th* 96.772 (Jul./Aug. 1993), 314-315; Poythress, V.S., 'Review of A.C. Thiselton's *New Horizons in Hermeneutics*', *WThJ* 55.2 (1993), 343-346; Perry, S., 'A Proposed Model of Biblical Hermeneutics Incorporating the Work of Stanley Fish and Karl Barth' (Bristol: Unpublished Essay Submitted as Part of an MPhil Course at Trinity College, 1999), 1-27; Lyons, W.J., 'Serious Man, Rhetorical Man, Straw Man: Just How Much of a Threat is Stanley Fish to Christian Theology?' (Oxford: Unpublished Paper Presented at the Conference of the Society for the Study of Theology, 2000), 1-10; Lyons, W.J., *Canon and Exegesis: Canonical Praxis and the Sodom Narrative* (Sheffield: Sheffield Academic Press, 2002); Woodman, S., 'Untitled Contribution to MLitt Thesis. Personal Communication to Robert Knowles, 27th April 2000' (Bristol: Baptist College, 2000), 1-20. We are aware of the article by S.E. Porter – see Porter, S.E., 'Reader-Response Criticism and New Testament Study: A Response to A.C. Thiselton's *New Horizons in Hermeneutics*', *JLitTh* 8.1 (Mar. 1994), 94-102. However, as we noted in Chapter 6, it is not at all clear as to whether or not Porter is advocating a strong "Fishian" stance in this article, and so we omit it here.

construct necessarily leads to some kind of inescapable absolute interpretative relativism. Jeanrond then sets this reading of Thiselton's work in contrast to his own (i.e. Jeanrond's) emphases on a 'comprehensive theory of "text"', on 'the critique of ideologies', and on a 'pluralism of legitimate readings'. Presumably, Jeanrond is saying that he, unlike Thiselton, thereby or therein *avoids* the dangers of inescapable absolute interpretative relativism.[247]

On the basis of our exegesis of *The Two Horizons*, however, our reply to Jeanrond in relation to this criticism of Thiselton is as follows.

First, Jeanrond seems to confuse the *work* of interpretative activity with the *shape* or *content* of interpretations. An adequate philosophy of history allows 'the other' to contribute *both* to interpretative activity *and* to interpretative content. That is, 'address' from 'the' historical 'past' as *'beyond'*, or as "other", need not be suppressed, and certainly such 'address' has contributed to the content of Thiselton's 'criterion for interpretative responsibility'. This 'criterion', therefore, is not simply Thiselton's 'own' 'criterion' or Thiselton's 'own' "construct". To use Gadamer's terminology, Thiselton "belongs" to a developing hermeneutical tradition.[248]

Second, Thiselton's notion of 'the other', in the sense of the 'historical' '"past"' *as* 'other', promotes an emphasis on 'historical'-'textual' and 'linguistic' 'particularity' in a way that Jeanrond's search for a 'generalizing' 'comprehensive theory of "text"' seems potentially to suppress. Jeanrond also erroneously criticizes *The Two Horizons* in relation to this point.[249]

Moreover, third, we have also argued that 'Christ' plays an important *warranted* provisional evaluative metacritical role in Thiselton's hermeneutics from as early as 1976. 'Christ' – as *the* progressively accessible evaluative metacriterion - thus constitutes the core of Thiselton's biblical basis for 'the critique of ideologies' that Jeanrond prematurely fears is missing from Thiselton.[250]

And finally, fourth, contrary to Jeanrond's fears, Thiselton *accepts* that 'readers" contribution to the uniqueness of 'present meaning' generates a 'pluralism of legitimate readings' that reflects the uniqueness of readers and their situations (except that Thiselton might use the word "plurality" instead of the word

---

[247] Jeanrond, 'R RH', 116-117; cf. Jeanrond, W.G., *Text and Interpretation as Categories of Theological Thinking* (Dublin: Gill and MacMillan, 1988), 167; cf. Thiselton, 'R-RH', 111, 110, 113. Second italics Thiselton's, remaining italics ours.

[248] Jeanrond, 'R RH', 116; cf. Thiselton, *2H*, 66-67, 287; cf.: 53-63, 77, 107, 110-113, 120-121, 150-151, 297-298, 302-311, 314-319; cf. Thiselton, 'TY', 1564, 1565; cf. Thiselton, 'NH', 311; cf. Gadamer, *TM*, 261, 262. Nobody doubts the creative action of readers during interpretation. However, texts also act on readers so as to re-shape pre-understandings, *partly* through transmitted content. This two-way conversation coheres best with an understanding of historical dialectic and process, its possibility being grounded in historical unity. Italics are ours, except on the word *'beyond'*, where they are Thiselton's.

[249] Thiselton, 'TY', 1564; cf.: Thiselton, *2H*, 44, 372, 119; cf.: 117-120, 370-379; Thiselton, 'SBS', 329; Thiselton, 'R-RH', 82-83; cf.: Jeanrond, 'R RH', 117; Jeanrond, *T&I*, 167.

[250] Jeanrond, 'R RH', 117. Contrast, Thiselton, 'Par', 50, cf. 52.

'pluralism' in this context of discussion – see Chapter 5). Thiselton develops this point in *The Promise of Hermeneutics* (1999), but the philosophy of history that *allows* Thiselton's development of this point is central to his work, *The Two Horizons* (1980), as we have already seen.[251]

Taking these four responses to Jeanrond together then, against Jeanrond, we can see that Thiselton's notion and/or "criterion" of "interpretative responsibility" (to use Jeanrond's language - see above) does not lead to an inescapable absolute interpretative relativism.

Rather, and summarizing: *first*, an adequate philosophy of history allows that interpretative activity can - and therefore in the case of biblical hermeneutics must - relate congruently to actions and truth-claims that belong to texts' original contexts, such that interpretative activity is not necessarily shaped *only* by interpreters. *Second*, therefore, interpretative activity must be respectful of textual, historical, and linguistic particularity. This aspect of interpretative activity is certainly possible, and also accords with an adequate philosophy of history. *Third*, Christ, as a progressively accessible evaluative metacriterion, places additional constraints on interpretative activity.

Therefore, *fourth*, although reader-situations bring uniqueness to the dimension of 'present meaning' so as to allow for a "plurality" 'of legitimate readings', this "plurality" does not constitute an inescapable absolute interpretative relativism for Thiselton. Rather, to repeat a point from Chapter 1, we saw that Thiselton argued that a given parable, for example, may suggest several 'applications' diachronically, but that these 'applications' will be synchronically inter-linked at any given instant in time by 'secondary' 'logical connexions' that Thiselton likened to '"family resemblances"'. On the one hand, in this context of discussion, Thiselton argued that such 'applications' and/or 'meanings' do not expand 'arbitrarily'. On the other hand, in this context of discussion, Thiselton argued that readers are not made to "slavishly imitate" set 'examples'. Rather, in this context of discussion, Thiselton argued that readers are 'repeatedly', but 'freshly', directed into 'each new present' by 'roughly' similar 'paradigms' of 'appropriate' kinds 'of attitude and conduct' 'within certain limits'. Thus, in this context of discussion, Thiselton argued that a given 'hearer' has 'freedom to "go on" for himself' '"independently"'. Therefore, Thiselton concluded that the later Wittgenstein's notion of '"family resemblances"' explains how 'language' can 'function *creatively*' 'without... meanings' expanding 'arbitrarily'. These points, it may be added, also link questions to do with *literary genre and (extra-) linguistic functions* to the notion of a "plurality" 'of legitimate readings' (see also Chapter 5).[252]

---

[251] Thiselton, 'CAP', 133-135, 201; cf.: Thiselton, *2H*, 10, 120-121, cf.: 154-157, 244, 324-325, 348-349, 436-437; Thiselton, *NH*, 557-558; Thiselton, 'R-RH', 82-83; Jeanrond, 'R RH', 117.

[252] Jeanrond, 'R RH', 117; cf. Thiselton, A.C., 'The Parables as Language-Event: Some Comments on Fuchs's Hermeneutics in the Light of Linguistic Philosophy', *SJT* 23.4 (Nov. 1970), 455-457, cf.: 458-461; 468. Second italics Thiselton's, others ours.

The crux of the matter in relation to our response to Jeanrond, however, is that his erroneous comment that Thiselton's 'criterion for interpretative responsibility... is... itself a result of (his own) interpretative activity' seems to presuppose the influence of Fish, *even though Jeanrond seeks to avoid interpretative relativism himself*. Moreover, it is thus a Fish-type contextual relativism that Jeanrond falsely imputes to Thiselton. On this basis Jeanrond then falsely imputes to Thiselton a relativistic *distortion* of the 'hermeneutical circle' that leads *away from* objectivity, a circle from which interpreters can never 'free' themselves. Of course, though, *Thiselton's* hermeneutical circle leads *towards* objectivity. Whilst it is true that Thiselton argues that readers cannot 'free' themselves from *this* 'hermeneutical circle', why would they ever wish to do so?[253]

(2) In 1993 M.G. Brett complains that 'Thiselton' falls into the very trap of 'imperializing' that he (i.e. 'Thiselton') criticizes as being a problem in Fish's "socio-pragmatism". Moreover, Brett would have us believe that, supposedly, Thiselton's 'imperializing' involves "pressing" 'Wittgenstein, Searle, Eco, and Habermas... into the service of a corrigible yet transcendental hermeneutic'.[254]

However, we should reply to Brett by noting that, in Thiselton's view, Fish's "imperialization" proceeds via *assertion* and via the unnecessary and philosophically unviable *suppression* of the historical past as "other". Conversely, for Thiselton, a "non-imperializing" approach proceeds via *argument*, via *dialogue*, and via a philosophically warranted *respect* for the historical past as "other".[255] In both *The Two Horizons* and *New Horizons in Hermeneutics* Thiselton follows the latter "non-imperializing" route, and does so from the standpoint of a dialogue with the philosophy of history. Brett's pre-dialogic hermeneutically-foreclosing assertion overlooks these points, however, and - by implication - also threatens to suppress the historical past as "other". The "other" in this instance, of course, is Thiselton's actual thinking. In other words, it is not Thiselton who falls into Fish-type socio-pragmatic 'imperializing', but *Brett*. One particular aspect of the historical past as "other" that Brett suppresses is that fact that, as we have begun to see, 'Wittgenstein, Searle, Eco, and Habermas' *have very little to do with* Thiselton's 'corrigible yet transcendental hermeneutic' – though, in Thiselton's thinking, their works do reflect *varying* degrees of *consistency with* this hermeneutic.[256]

(3) Also in 1993, V.S. Poythress "argues" that, from a 'socio-pragmatic' perspective, Thiselton's supposed 'transhistorical and... transcendent' metacritique could be 'just one more idol... the illusion of transcendence... [being] all the more dangerous because it is masked'.[257]

---

[253] Jeanrond, 'R RH', 116-117; contrast, Thiselton, *2H*, xix, cf. 196-197, 305; cf. Thiselton, 'NH', 327; cf. Thiselton, 'Par', 50, cf. 52. Italics ours.
[254] Brett, 'R NH', 314-315; cf. Thiselton, *NH*, 393-405, cf. 537-550.
[255] Thiselton, *NH*, 27, 400, 418-419, 439-441, 450, 452, 543-546, 550. Italics ours.
[256] Thiselton, *2H*, 51-84, cf.: 181-187, 234-251, 304-314, 370-385, 392-415; cf. Brett, 'R NH', 314-315. Italics ours.
[257] Poythress, 'R NH', 344; cf. Thiselton, *NH*, 392.

But here, in our view, Poythress neglects to argue - via a widened dialogue with the philosophy of history – so as to justify or warrant the kind of historico-philosophical framework that such a charge would presuppose. It is only on the basis of such a particular kind of historico-philosophical framework that the "'operative influence'" of 'the' 'historical' 'other' could be discounted. And it is only on the basis of the discounting of the "'operative influence'" of 'the' 'historical' 'other' that the charge of "idolatry" cited by Poythress could stand.[258]

In other words, Thiselton, unlike Poythress, does *not* neglect to build his argument in the context of a widened dialogue with the philosophy of history. And the historico-philosophical framework that emerges from Thiselton's widened dialogue with the philosophy of history allows that 'the' 'historical' 'other' *can* impact selves. This means, however, that the interpretations or constructions that interpreters "construct" in their *work* of construction are not necessarily merely their "own" interpretations or "idols" so far as the *shape* or *content* of those interpretative constructs is concerned. That is, in even allowing that a supposedly "legitimate" charge of "idolatry" could be made against Thiselton from a 'socio-pragmatic' perspective, Poythress seems to be presupposing a Fish-type socio-pragmatism himself.[259]

Furthermore, since Thiselton's central dialogically warranted provisional - and progressively accessible - trans-contextual metacriterion is Jesus Christ, then to call Jesus an 'idol' would be a blasphemy that threatened to turn Poythress' objection into a polemic for sin.[260]

In the year 2000 this kind of consideration led me to ask Professor Thiselton - in his summation of our seminar group's findings at the Society for the Study of Theology's conference on 'Forgiveness and Truth' held at Oxford University in the UK - to cite Habermas' point "'that power'" abuse is "'distorted communication'". Without a metacritique that distinguishes between "'distorted'" relating and "'truthful'" relating, there can be no truth-based repentance, no truth-based "forgiveness", and no truth-based reconciliations.[261]

Poythress, however, does not seem so keen to explore the possibility of such a metacritique – except perhaps on fideist grounds. Poythress' mistake, partly, is his misidentification of Thiselton's 'transhistorical' transcontextual metacritique as being Thiselton's appeals to 'Wittgenstein, Austin, Searle, and Recanati'.[262] However, Wittgenstein and Austin, as we have seen, relate more to Thiselton's hermeneutical critique of *language* than to his hermeneutical critique of *epistemology*. And Searle and Recanati only contribute to Thiselton's hermeneutical critique of

---

[258] Thiselton, *2H*, 44-45, cf.: 66-67, 74-84, 309; cf. Thiselton, 'TY', 1564.
[259] Thiselton, *2H*, 45, 297-298, cf. 314; cf. Poythress, 'R *NH*', 344. Italics ours.
[260] Thiselton, 'Par', 50, 52; cf.: Thiselton, *2H*, 169-186, 229-230, 277-281, cf. 153; Thiselton, *NH*, 604-619; Poythress, 'R *NH*', 344.
[261] See, Thiselton, *NH*, 384; cf. Habermas, *K&HI*, 282.
[262] Poythress, 'R *NH*', 344-345.

*language* at a *secondary* level, as we have already begun to see in the case of Searle.[263]

Poythress also complains – in response to Thiselton - that 'almost without exception hermeneutical theorists want us to systematically forget' certain 'realities'. According to Poythress these 'realities' include "God's address" 'in the Bible and in general revelation', and 'that the eternal Word of God is the ontological foundation of language, and that the Holy Spirit invades the most personal space of our minds and our unconscious'.[264]

But we must reply by noting that Thiselton 'want[s] us to… forget' neither these emphases nor the 'biblical teachings about the Lordship of Christ over scholarship, and about God's wrath, sin, hell, heresy, and excommunication'.[265] Nowhere does Thiselton deny these doctrines, and in places he explicitly affirms many of them, as we have seen. In *The Two Horizons*, Thiselton clearly states that,

> our aim is certainly not to impose certain philosophical categories onto the biblical text. Indeed the point is precisely the reverse. A full awareness of the problems of hermeneutics provides a *defence against* the interpreter's so reading the text that he merely hears back echoes of his own attitudes or pre-judgments.[266]

(4) In 1999 *S. Perry* argues that Thiselton has misread Fish. Perry argues that this misreading appears in Thiselton's major work, *New Horizons in Hermeneutics* (1992). In Perry's estimate, the crux of this misreading is that Thiselton has misunderstood 'Fish' as 'arguing for the ultimate dominance of his [i.e. of Fish's own] cultural sub-group'. We must reply, however, that Thiselton, in *New Horizons in Hermeneutics*, actually challenges what Perry rightly regards as being Fish's real stance – which is 'that [present-horizon] communities' *alone* 'determine' and "construct" 'meaning'.[267]

That is, in *New Horizons in Hermeneutics*, Thiselton's argument - against the background of *The Two Horizons* again – is 'that [present-horizon] communities' should not and need not 'determine' and "construct" present 'meaning' in a way that denies all epistemological "access" to past 'meaning'. Thiselton argues that present-horizon "communities", rather, can and should "construct" *a "relation" (or relations) between* that which is potentially progressively epistemologically accessible as historically 'other' (whether past or present) and themselves. Thiselton argues that this constructed *"relation" (or relations) between* historically "particular" 'horizons' constitutes 'present meaning'. Certainly, in relation to *this latter* kind of construction of 'present meaning', Thiselton argues that it is largely 'the [present-horizon] community' that does the construction *work*. But, against Fish, Thiselton

---

[263] cf.: Thiselton, 'TNI', 11; Thiselton, 'H-O', 8; Thiselton, 'Truth', 874-902; Thiselton, *NH*, 283-307; Chapter 4.
[264] Poythress, 'R *NH*', 345.
[265] Poythress, 'R *NH*', 346.
[266] Thiselton, *2H*, xx. Italics Thiselton's.
[267] Perry, 'PM', 11; cf. Thiselton, *NH*, 544-546. Italics ours.

also argues that *the text* can and should contribute – not objectivistically but in line with a hermeneutical critique of historical objectivity (see above) - to the *content* and *shape* of the 'present meaning' that is constructed by the present-horizon community, since the text is potentially progressively epistemologically accessible as *historically* 'other'. That is, in Thiselton's view, Fish smuggles in baseless negative conclusions about *'epistemological... disclosure'*, and about other *historically-embedded textual actions*, beneath his (i.e. Fish's) notion of the present-horizon community's 'construction' of meaning. In other words, in Thiselton's estimate, Fish *ahistorically* suppresses the historical 'other' by arguing 'that [present-horizon] communities' *alone* 'determine' and "construct" 'meaning'. Thiselton's response to Fish on this point is to argue that, in responsible interpretation, *texts and their past meanings – and hence communities from the past* - *also* have a role to play in "determining" *present* 'meaning'.[268]

Thus, contrary to Perry's view, it cannot be 'in Fish's model that Thiselton's request for an overriding rank structure [i.e. for 'a metacritical ranking' of *'interpretative'* 'criteria'] is granted'. Thiselton's metacriteria – the basis for any subsequent 'metacritical ranking' of *'interpretative'* 'criteria' - resonate with a widened dialogue with the philosophy of *history*, as we have seen, and so could not possibly emerge from Fish's *'fundamentally a-historical'* and anti-metacritical stance.[269]

C) RESPONSES TO A SECOND GROUP OF "FISHIAN" CRITICISMS: W.J. LYONS AND S. WOODMAN

i) W.J. Lyons' "Oxford Article"

In a presentation from the year 2000 entitled, 'Serious Man, Rhetorical Man, Straw Man: Just How Much of a Threat is Stanley Fish to Christian Theology?', *W.J. Lyons* rejects the criticisms of Fish and of 'American neo-pragmatism' that appeared in Thiselton's 'address' at the 1999 meeting of the Society for the Study of Theology held in Edinburgh.[270] It is clear from our reading of Lyons' presentation (here designated as his "Oxford article") that he would similarly reject

---

[268] Thiselton, 'TY', 1564; cf.: Thiselton, *2H*, 10; cf.: 15-17, 45; 244; 77, 119; 300-308; 297-299, 314, 322, 324; Thiselton, *NH*, 501-502, cf.: 557-558; 535-550; Fish, 'NC', 280; Perry, 'PM', 11. Italics on *'epistemological... disclosure'* Thiselton's, remaining italics ours.

[269] Perry, 'PM', 23; cf.: Thiselton, *2H*, 74-84, Thiselton, *NH*, 317; cf.: 331-338; 535-550; Thiselton, 'CAP', 157. First, second and fourth italics Thiselton's, third italics ours.

[270] See, Lyons, 'SM', 1; cf.: Thiselton, A.C., 'Signs of the Times: Towards a Theology for the Year 2000 as a Grammar of Grace, Truth and Eschatology in Contexts of So-Called Postmodernity', *Unpublished Version of the Paper Given at The Society for the Study of Theology Annual Conference, Edinburgh*, Apr. 1999, 15; Thiselton, A.C., 'Signs of the Times: Towards a Theology for the Year 2000 as a Grammar of Grace, Truth and Eschatology in Contexts of So-Called Postmodernity. Presidential Paper of the Society for the Study of Theology', in *The Future as God's Gift: Explorations in Christian Eschatology* (eds. D. Fergusson and M. Sarot; Edinburgh: T&T Clark, 2000), 9-39; Thiselton, 'P-MB', 135. Lyons' presentation was given at the 2000 meeting of the Society for the Study of Theology (SST), Oxford University, England. The present author was in attendance both at this seminar in 2000, and at Thiselton's address at the 1999 meeting of the SST in Edinburgh.

W. Russell's view that Thiselton's critique of Fish in *New Horizons in Hermeneutics* is 'particularly devastating'.[271]

In his Oxford article, Lyons asserts that, 'the "text"… itself', including its historical 'horizon', cannot be epistemologically "accessed". In Lyons' thinking, then, whether or not he reads Fish correctly is a non-question. Rather, in Lyons' argument, what matters is which reading of 'Fish' is the 'more theologically relevant'.[272] In relation to these kinds of considerations, Lyons urges that Thiselton mistakenly and naively argues for the epistemological accessibility 'of the adjudicative text'[273] when, in Lyons' estimate, "the text" (and, therefore, 'the adjudicative text') is actually 'unapproachable' epistemologically.[274]

Lyons allows 'that there is… raw data out there', but insists that we cannot 'encounter it directly or… use "it" to adjudicate between interpretations'.[275] Rather, in Lyons' view, 'community' pre-understandings are determinative in 'interpretation'. Lyons allows that pre-understandings and/or interpretative 'constraints may change over time' but, in Lyons' estimate, this change comes from the present 'horizon' of the 'community', and not from the past 'horizon' of the text.[276] In Lyons' view, the community's pre-understandings cannot be altered *by* 'the text' so as to converge on those *of* 'the text'. In Lyons' estimate, 'assumptions' may clash 'between communities'; but, Lyons argues that 'assumptions' may *not* clash 'between communities' and 'texts'.[277]

Nevertheless, Lyons notes 'flaws' in Paul Noble's reading of Fish, and thus presupposes at least *some* textual 'access' to 'the real Fish' and to the "real Noble".[278] Further, at one point in the *text* of his Oxford article, Lyons asks 'please don't misunderstand me here', and Lyons then offers a *textual* clarification. Thus, Lyons presupposes – on behalf of any subsequent readers of his text - that at least a *partially* "accessible" "W.J. Lyons" is epistemologically "approachable" *through a text*.[279]

Attempting to rectify these performative self-contradictions, Lyons admits that it is only 'a neutral text' that is epistemologically inaccessible. Lyons argues that since 'the "text"' is always being viewed through community spectacles, it no longer exists as a separate, free entity which can be appealed to' for 'adjudicative' purposes.[280] 'Thiselton', though, in Lyons' estimate, still exhibits out-of-date epistemological naivety in that Thiselton - in Lyons' view - still tries to employ a

---

[271] Russell, 'R *NH*', 242.
[272] Lyons, 'SM', 8, 9, 2.
[273] Lyons, 'SM', 3.
[274] Lyons, 'SM', 4, 3.
[275] Lyons, 'SM', 5.
[276] Lyons, 'SM', 6, 7, 8.
[277] Lyons, 'SM', 8. Italics ours.
[278] Lyons, 'SM', 4, 9, 3. Italics ours.
[279] Lyons, 'SM', 9; cf. 4. Italics ours.
[280] Lyons, 'SM', 7, 3.

'"neutral text" to adjudicate between interpretations'.[281]

We must reply to Lyons, however, by stressing that Thiselton nowhere assumes *either* a '"neutral text"' free from "historical conditioning" *or* a '"neutral"' interpretative community free from "historical conditioning".[282] As we have already seen, the crux of the matter is that Thiselton rightly allows - in the context of, and as a precondition for the possibility of, interpretation - that the historical conditioning of "historically finite" texts and/or of "historically finite" readers prevents *neither* "distancing *towards* historical objectivity" *nor* "fusion *towards* historical understanding and/or historical self-involvement" (see Chapters 5, 6, and above).

In other words, Thiselton argues that if it is a *unified* (not uniform) historical reality (or creation) that conditions historically finite persons and/or texts, then the result of conditioning *cannot ever* be a radical dissociation between historical horizons. Thiselton argues that historical horizons, *however* they are "conditioned", *never* become so different to one another that they are unrelated to – or completely discontinuous with - one another, and *never* become so similar to one another that differences or juxtapositional contrasts between historical horizons are completely removed. And, for Thiselton, since historical horizons are related to one another so as to include *a posteriori* historical "overlaps" or *a posteriori* historical continuities with one another, then there can be *fusions* of horizons. And yet, for Thiselton, since historical horizons remain sufficiently distinct for juxtapositional contrasts between them to be preserved, then there is always an objectifying comparative role for historically-embedded, or re-historicized, subject-object conceptualization to play during *distancing* (see Chapters 3 and 5. N.B. Thiselton's notions of "historical horizons" and "horizons" are inter-changeable).

We saw earlier, in our responses to Derrida and to criticisms of the later Barthes, that, on the one hand, the misleading notion that historical horizons can supposedly be "radically dissociated" from one another is the result of a logic that begins from a set of false premises in relation to the ways in which conceptualizations of history and conceptualizations of language are inter-sublated with one another during hermeneutical theorizing. On the other hand, we saw that the same misleading notion – i.e. that historical horizons can supposedly be "radically dissociated" from one another - amounts to a baseless "second-stratum" hypostatization of a mere third-stratum artefact.

This third-stratum artefact consists merely of the way in which human subjects employ language during interpretative activity – notably during historical reconstructions. That is, since historical horizons are always subordinated to variable historical *movements* within a *unified* (not uniform) developing historical whole, then to reconstruct "a historical horizon" is really a simplification of the truth, even if that simplification *can still include true historical report*.

---

[281] Lyons, 'SM', 9.
[282] Lyons, 'SM', 9; cf.: Thiselton, *2H*, 15; cf.: 80-95, 120-121, 161-163, 191-194, 304-319, 321-322, 379-383, 386-407, 436-438, 348-353; Thiselton, *NH*, 315, 321-344, 370-372, 395.

This simplification can still include true historical report because this simplification only involves the artificial *suspension* or *"stilling"* of historical movement (when, in fact, historical movements continue) and the artificial treatment of historical horizons in *isolation* (when, in fact, historical horizons are always inter-related and *inter-relating*).

That is, during the third-stratum activity of *interpretation*, it is not necessary to detour into second-stratum *theoretical* considerations to do with historical movement or to do with historical inter-horizonal relationality in order to account for the possibility that a given state of affairs was so. So long as presupposed second-stratum theoretical considerations are *adequate* (since theory *does* directly affect practice and results), then the "stilling" and "isolating" of horizons is an acceptable concession for the sake of simplicity during historical reconstruction.

The "stilling" and "isolating" of horizons, then, is merely a feature of interpretative activity – a stratum-three artefact. The "stilling" and "isolating" of horizons does *not* constitute any kind of second-stratum conceptualization of a radical dissociation of historical horizons from one another at the level of historical ontology.

In other words, historical conditioning *does not* presuppose or engender a radical dissociation of historical horizons from one another at the level of ontology. Rather, the historical conditioning of "the historically finite" (whether we are speaking of texts, or of readers, or of events – and so on) *presupposes* the inter-related overlapping mutually-qualifying historico-philosophical (and theological) criteria of (created) historical unity (not uniformity), historical relationality, historical process, historical particularity, historical continuity, historical subjectivity, historical inter-subjectivity, historical fallenness, and historical redemption. In turn, as we saw earlier, these inter-related overlapping mutually-qualifying historico-philosophical (and theological) criteria – along with historical conditioning and historical finitude - *do not only have a negative effect* on "objectivity".

That is, against Lyons' thinking, the historical conditioning of historically finite readers, against the background of other historico-philosophical (and theological) factors or criteria, can also have a *positive* effect on "objectivity". It is thus "unhistorical" to proceed directly to present-horizon contextual relativism (however broad) just because one realizes that the historical conditioning of historically finite readers is a factor that interpretation has to take into account. This point remains valid even if we allow for an interpretative community that expands to embrace all of humanity and a world-wide consensus. For who is to say – on the basis of Lyons' approach – that such a consensus is not arbitrary in relation to historical truth? (Critiques of hermeneutical *understanding* and hermeneutical critiques of *epistemology* are related, but not identical).

Lyons though, on the sole basis of false notions of "historical conditioning" and "historical finitude" - in which "historical conditioning" and "historical finitude" are artificially abstracted from the *mutually-qualifying inter-related and overlapping* historico-philosophical (and theological) criteria of historical unity (not uniformity), historical relationality, historical process, historical particularity, historical continuity, historical subjectivity, historical inter-subjectivity, historical fallenness, and historical redemption - sports false ahistorical *epistemological* antitheses between objectivism and present-horizon context-relativity, and between *perfect* access to textual horizons and *no* access to textual horizons. In this way, Lyons actually transgresses *the very criteria that are preconditional for the possibility of* historical conditioning.[283]

To use an analogy in order to try to illustrate our point, then we are arguing that when Lyons says that texts cannot transform readers because of reader-conditioning, it is as though he were saying that food cannot transform the body because of taste. However, as the body alters in response to food, then so taste also alters with new food experiences. Food, taste, and the body, then, are brought into intimate inter-relationships with one another through the processes of *eating*.

Similarly, as we have seen, thought and language are intimately related (see Chapter 4). Therefore, since reading *introduces* readers' thinking to *new* language-uses, then reading can also *alter* readers' thinking. And since language *from the past travels forwards "with" time* on often-dusty book-shelves (or in computer memories, and so on), then readers do not have to achieve actual time-travel into the past in order to have their thinking altered by old texts! (And it won't do to say that old texts necessarily communicate nothing of their historical contexts either, for such an assertion transgresses: the historico-philosophical (and theological) criteria we noted above, the logic of self-involvement, and the criterion of the indispensability of public criteria of meaning in relation to the intelligibility of *all* language. One cannot *over-sharply* separate conditioning through texts from conditioning through speech).

Moreover, as we saw in Chapter 6, it is the very inter-relatedness of language and thought that constitutes *another* precondition for the possibility of historical conditioning. To a large extent, historical conditioning *is* the operation of language from the past on the thinking of readers in the present.

That is, just as food, taste, and the body are brought into intimate inter-relationships with one another through the processes of *eating*, so textual language, historical conditioning, and readers' thinking are brought into intimate inter-relationships with one another through the processes of *reading*. Perhaps the popular title, 'Readers' Digest', constitutes the most concise historical instantiation of this analogy!

We must reluctantly conclude, therefore, that Lyons' Oxford article seems to promote what W. Russell calls, an 'enormous leap… from legitimate interpretative impediments to epistemological dogma'.[284]

Moreover, notably, Lyons seems everywhere to presuppose Fish's polarizing distinction 'between "serious man" – the foundationalist – and "rhetorical man" – the non-foundationalist'. Lyons also employs the parallel polarizing distinction between "realism" and 'anti-realism'. These over-generalizing pre-dialogic

---

[283] Lyons, 'SM', 6, 7, 8, 9. Italics ours.
[284] Russell, 'R *NH*', 243.

distinctions, of course, are very similar to the distinction between 'formalism' and 'anti-formalism' that Thiselton addresses in *New Horizons in Hermeneutics*. Indeed, Lyons uses the term 'semi-formalist' *both* of Thiselton *and* of the 'early' Fish in order to set their respective approaches to texts in opposition to the approach of the later Fish. The clear implicature (*sic*) of Lyons' comments is that the later Fish has made the supposedly necessary transition to "anti-formalism", whilst Thiselton supposedly remains constrained to a significant extent by the errors of "formalism".[285]

Lyons, then, may indeed cite writers from many traditions – including Wittgenstein, Gadamer, Iser, Fish, and others. No doubt, Lyons is well-read. But, in the critical-synthetic sublation-filter Lyons employs at the stratum-one level of pre-understanding (the level that matters the most in this context of discussion) he seems – pre-dialogically - to hermeneutically foreclose or restrict the debate to a sphere that constrains or collapses conversation into an interface between only two traditions – namely epistemologico-linguistic 'formalism' and Fish's 'anti-formalism'.[286]

That is, Lyons' Oxford article everywhere seems to presuppose an artificial polarization or an absolutized "quasi-formal" binary opposition – between epistemologico-linguistic 'formalism' and 'anti-formalism' - that, ironically, in its very binary character, still echoes a philosophically idealist or formalist metaphysics. Even though a distinction remains between pre-dialogic categorizations and idealist binary oppositions (see our earlier response to H.A. Harris), these two phenomena seem oddly convergent in Lyons' Oxford article.

In other words, in a way that is analogous to how certain atheistic resistances to belief in God almost end up as being defined in terms of the shape of that which they are rejecting, then Lyons' Oxford article also seems to come close to being defined by what it is trying to resist.

By contrast, as we have seen, a *truly* "historical" approach like Thiselton's allows dialogue between *many* traditions during the process of critical-synthetic sublation-filter-construction at the level of pre-understanding. Lyons' framework, however, in its preservation of its quasi-formalist echo, in its transgression of historico-philosophical (and theological) criteria, and in its pre-dialogic categorizations and pre-dialogic stratum-one hermeneutical foreclosures, seems to *pre-date* rather than post-date Thiselton's more properly historical and more properly *dialogically-derived* framework.

In other words, whilst Thiselton widens his dialogue with the philosophy of history in *The Two Horizons*,[287] Lyons, by contrast, provides no engagement with the philosophy of history that could justify his historically dichotomous *dissociation* of the "'operative influence'" of the 'historical' *"past"* as 'other' (at least through texts) from the "historical conditioning" of the "interpretative community" in 'the

---

[285] Lyons, 'SM', 3, 10, 5, 9; cf. Thiselton, *NH*, 539; cf. 540-542. Italics ours.
[286] Lyons, 'SM', 9, 7; cf. 3, 10, 5, 9.
[287] Thiselton, *2H*, 51-84, cf.: 234-251; 304-326.

historical' "*present*".²⁸⁸

In effect, Lyons, like Fish, makes an assertion here (not an argument) that, again, transgresses the mutually-qualifying inter-related overlapping historico-philosophical (and theological) criteria of "'the unity'" (not uniformity), relationalities, "processes", particularities, finitudes, and continuities of 'historical' "'reality'" (alongside other such criteria) – as though communities, or at least texts, were adrift from the spacetime continuum or, indeed, from God's creation. Ironically, it is actually in *Lyons'* thinking (not in Thiselton's thinking) that the "text-as-historically-other" becomes 'a separate, free entity' – so separate, in fact, that it is assigned to a dissociated quasi-idealist realm, or to an imagined differently-created "reality" that we cannot reach (cf. the problem of dichotomies – see earlier). To create such textual epistemological inaccessibility, though, Lyons in effect, therefore, ironically *creates a form of idealism*. Conversely, *Lyons'* "text-as-corporate-projection" constitutes a text that is completely assimilated to the present horizon (cf. the problem of "critique-collapse" and the "death of the author" – see earlier). Thus, in Lyons' pre-understanding, the true epistemological "object" – the historically "other" - is utterly divorced from the epistemological "subject". Lyons' epistemological "subject" – which we understand to be communities in the present-horizon – then simply relates "within or to itself" in an act of corporate self-relationality. Admittedly, in fairness to Lyons, he rightly allows communities in the present horizon to challenge one-another's pre-understandings (as we noted above). However, Lyons' hermeneutics – at least when it comes to reading texts – still leaves us with a present-horizon that relates only to itself in a manner that excludes certain textual actions from the diachronic processes of historical dialectic. Lyons, then, at least when it comes to reading texts, seems to radicalize a corporate version of Cartesianism. In doing so, Lyons' pre-understanding seems to divide historical "object" from corporate "subject" so radically that only the corporate "subject" remains. In Lyons' hermeneutics, this corporate "subject" then seems to "construct" – in its own image - a fantasy version of the missing true historical "object". In Lyons' hermeneutics, it seems, this fantasy version of the missing true historical "object" then *replaces the* missing true historical "object"; and in Lyons' hermeneutics, it seems, it is then this fantasy version of the missing true historical "object" that the community calls "the text". In Lyons' hermeneutics, therefore, it is only this fantasy "text" that is allowed to speak, and only this fantasy "text" that is said to be the product of community interpretative norms and strategies.²⁸⁹

Moreover, Lyons' philosophically untenable *historical* dichotomy – which is *partially* analogous to Bultmann's *Geschichte* versus *Historie* dichotomy (see Chapter 6) despite the caveat that Lyons' dichotomy avoids individualism - results in an *epistemological* dissociation of historical understanding from present-horizon

---

[288] Lyons, 'SM', 6-8; cf.: Thiselton, *2H*, 15; 44-45, 77-80; Thiselton, 'TY', 1564. Italics ours.

[289] Lyons, 'SM', 6-8, 3; cf. Thiselton, *2H*, 302, 67, 174-175; cf.: 51-84, 234-251; 304-326. Italics ours.

corporate "self-understanding" when, in fact, corporate "self-understanding" can *only* emerge *through a detour into* historical understanding (see Chapter 6). Furthermore, Lyons also presupposes a *linguistic* dichotomy that disparages textual (extra-)linguistic functions – including, notably, textual epistemological disclosure functions - relative to the privileged present-context assertions (and other language-behaviors) of the interpretative community or communities.[290]

Thus, Lyons' hermeneutic disintegrates into historical, epistemological, and linguistic dichotomies. With respect to the *underlying philosophical problems – or even errors - that lead to such dichotomies,* then our allusions here to these problems (or even to these *errors*) presuppose our earlier responses to Fish, to Derrida, and to criticisms of the thinking of the later Barthes.

If we were to leave our criticism of Lyons's hermeneutics at this point, however, it would constitute an injustice against Lyons. Lyons provides us with a more extensive critique of Thiselton elsewhere – a critique to which we now turn.

ii) W.J. Lyons' *Canon and Exegesis*

Moving on, then in his book, *Canon and Exegesis: Canonical Praxis and the Sodom Narrative* (2002), Lyons responds to the 'criticisms of Fish' that appear in Thiselton's major work, *New Horizons in Hermeneutics* (1992).[291] In our view, Lyons presents a much more sophisticated argument in *Canon and Exegesis* than in his Oxford article. Nevertheless, we shall let our responses to Lyons' Oxford article stand, since they retain much of their relevance in relation to our responses to what Lyons says in *Canon and Exegesis* about Thiselton's thinking.

Turning now, (1), to consider *Canon and Exegesis*, we shall first present an analysis of Lyons' criticism of Thiselton in a full and ordered way so as to make sure that we have heard it properly - as follows.

Thus, (a), to begin with, in Lyons' view, 'prior' 'biblical' "readings", "perspectives", and 'interests' "influence" (and thus shape) everybody's 'biblical hermeneutics'. In Lyons' estimate, W.G. 'Jeanrond's', K.J. 'Vanhoozer's' and 'Thiselton's' 'interests' are largely 'theological', whereas Lyons argues that R.A. "Reese's" 'interests' are much less 'theological' than 'Jeanrond's', 'Vanhoozer's' and 'Thiselton's' 'interests'. Therefore, Lyons argues that these four thinkers' respective notions of '"full reading"' will reflect this difference of 'interests'. Therefore, Lyons (in effect) argues, against 'Jeanrond', that no single notion of '"full reading"' can really claim to be universally prescriptive.[292]

Nevertheless, (b), Lyons sees his own 'biblical hermeneutics' as *rightly* shaped by four legitimate hermeneutical 'interests' – i.e. 'by the desire' to give 'valid' "accounts" 'of' our 'plain experience' of, and/or 'of' our *'faith'* in relation to: (i)

---

[290] Lyons, 'SM', 6, 5. Italics ours.
[291] Lyons, W.J., *Canon and Exegesis: Canonical Praxis and the Sodom Narrative* (Sheffield: Sheffield Academic Press, 2002), 4.
[292] Lyons, *C&E*, 108-109.

'*God*' as 'a "Reality"' 'beyond interpretation' (vs. atheism);[293] (ii) 'the possibility' of present-horizon *inter-community* '*communication*' (vs. isolationism);[294] (iii) necessary hermeneutical '*constraints*' (vs. "relativism");[295] and, (iv), 'the possibility' of present-horizon '"hermeneutical *change*"', especially 'the possibility' of the 'reform' of 'evangelized' "communities" 'from... outside' 'by the... Church and its Bible' (vs. self-affirming idolatry). (N.B. In Lyons' view, his phrase '"hermeneutical *change*"' is a 'better' phrase than Thiselton's partly parallel phrase, 'hermeneutical *growth*').[296]

(c) Lyons argues, however, that 'Thiselton's' '"foundationalist"' hermeneutics - along with those of 'Jeanrond', 'Vanhoozer', R. 'Morgan', F. 'Watson', and C.L. 'Blomberg' - cannot give 'valid' "accounts" of these four legitimate hermeneutical 'interests' (cf. "desires", 'plain' "experiences", concerns, or 'basic' "needs" of 'the hermeneutical project'), even though Lyons acknowledges that Thiselton and these other thinkers still rightly '*desire*' to give 'valid' "accounts" of these four legitimate hermeneutical 'interests' (cf. "desires", 'plain' "experiences", concerns, or 'basic' "needs" of 'the hermeneutical project').[297]

Thus, (i), in Lyons' view, no-one has ever 'discovered' Thiselton's 'foundation' which, in Lyons' estimate, consists of '"raw"' '"unmediated"' '"data"' that is objectivistically "accessible" to 'all' in 'common human experience'.[298] Therefore, (ii), in Lyons' view, Thiselton's appeal to "philosophy" 'to justify' what Lyons perceives to be Thiselton's objectivism - as well as being futile – is 'circular' - an attempt to step 'outside of... interpretation' so as 'to justify' stepping 'outside of... interpretation'. In Lyons' estimate, Thiselton's attempt to step 'outside of... interpretation' so as 'to justify' stepping 'outside of... interpretation' is an "inconsistency" that even P.R. 'Noble' rightly avoids.[299]

Further, (iii), in Lyons' view, this state of affairs means that Thiselton cannot step 'outside of... interpretation' to speak of 'God', of 'common human experience' of 'Reality with a capital R', or of "texts" as 'objective', 'epistemologically solid', 'non-changing', 'free-standing', largely historically "other" historical contingencies (cf. Lyons' phrase, 'relatively objective'). Moreover, (iv), in Lyons' view, Thiselton is in error to suggest that such "texts" are, in 'common human experience', objectivistically "accessible" to 'all humanity'; or that such "texts" may thereby potentially "condition" 'all humanity'.[300] Rather, (v), in Lyons' 'Fishian' view, everything – including all texts and interpretations - is always "mediated" and "produced" by 'interpretation' and 'conditioning'. Indeed, in Lyons' view, 'the... Church' 'has always' treated 'the Bible' in a way that aligned

---

[293] Lyons, *C&E*, 108, 109; cf. 114, 70. First and third italics ours, second italics Lyons'.
[294] Lyons, *C&E*, 112; cf. 114, 113. Italics ours.
[295] Lyons, *C&E*, 111; cf. 114. Italics ours.
[296] Lyons, *C&E*, 112, 113, 114; cf. 109. Italics ours.
[297] Lyons, *C&E*, 108, 109. Italics ours.
[298] Lyons, *C&E*, 115; cf. 111; cf. 110.
[299] Lyons, *C&E*, 111; cf. 88-89.
[300] Lyons, *C&E*, 111; cf. 114; cf. 109, 110.

with (what is, in Lyons' estimate,) the truth of this point.[301]

Crucially, (d), if what Lyons perceives to be Thiselton's 'foundationalism' *cannot*, in Lyons' estimate, give 'valid' "accounts" of the aforementioned four legitimate hermeneutical 'interests' (cf. "desires", 'plain' "experiences", or concerns of 'the hermeneutical project'), then Lyons argues that a 'Fishian' 'non-foundationalist' "anti-realist" 'theory of hermeneutical commonality' *can* give 'valid' "accounts" of these four legitimate hermeneutical 'interests' (cf. "desires", 'plain' "experiences", or concerns of 'the hermeneutical project') – as follows.[302]

Thus, (e), in Lyons' estimate, a '"Fishian"' stance 'has nothing to say' about *'God'* as 'a "Reality"' 'beyond interpretation'. Therefore, Lyons argues that he is free to adopt a "postmodern" Barthian 'theology'.[303] In this context, Lyons cites his 'earlier discussion of' B.S. Childs' notion of biblical '"referentiality"' in which Lyons argues that "God", "God's actions", and 'history' (including '"historical background"') cannot be artificially "isolated" from their biblical interpretative and referential matrices so as to be either discarded, or reframed as mere '"facts"' for reinterpretation and redefinition, by anthropocentric or 'humanistic' power-bids for '"control"' by strands in 'Western' and 'eurocentric' '"modern"' 'thought'. That is, Lyons argues that 'epistemologically' anthropocentric 'interpretation' *cannot* reach 'God' on the grounds 'of an epistemologically solid text' (or on any other grounds), but that 'God' *can* "enter" 'our reality' – "revealing" himself and "speaking" 'to us' 'from… outside'.[304]

'The Church', then, in Lyons' view, must "encounter and know" "God's" 'revelation' *'only by faith'*; and, for Childs and Lyons, 'the "Bible"' must be allowed to "interpret" its own 'referents'. With Childs, Lyons 'sees the text and the referent as inseparable', meaning 'that it is only through the text that we have access to the theological reality'. For Childs and Lyons, this 'reality… is only available through the testimony of Israel and the early Church'. Nevertheless, at the same time, Lyons argues that the Church's 'reading strategy' and *'prior'* 'shared understanding of God, the Scriptures and its tradition' constitute the *preconditional 'setting' or 'basis' for "producing"*, (i), 'the Bible' as it is read now (or, more properly, in Lyons' view, "Bibles" as 'a series of "thin texts" that then function as Scripture within contextually differentiated Christian or Jewish communities') and, (ii), 'the' "Church's" 'concern' to proclaim 'the gospel' "truly".[305]

In Lyons' view, then, 'Thiselton' would be "ignoring" *both* the real implications of a '"Fishian"' stance *and* 'the' "Church's" 'concern' to proclaim 'the gospel' "truly" if he (i.e. Thiselton) contended that a '"Fishian"' stance "necessarily" - at best - led to an *atheistic* "D. Cupitt-style" 'projectionist "Sea of Faith" theology' that made '"grace or revelation [etc.]… illusory"' and that reduced *all* '"Reality"'

---

[301] Lyons, *C&E*, 115; cf. 111.
[302] Lyons, *C&E*, 114, 115; cf. 111; cf. 108, 109. Italics ours.
[303] Lyons, *C&E*, 114, 115; cf. 108, 109; cf. 70. Italics ours.
[304] Lyons, *C&E*, 114; cf. 69; cf. 70; cf. 71; cf. 68-71; cf. 275. Italics ours.
[305] Lyons, *C&E*, 114; cf. 71, 69, 70, 263. First italics Lyons', second and third italics ours.

'beyond interpretation' to 'a Nietzschean void'.[306]

(f) In Lyons' view, a 'Fishian' notion of '"universal commonality"' (Lyons' phrase) "accounts" for 'the possibility' of present-horizon inter-community '*communication*'.[307] Lyons argues, *with* the later Wittgenstein and 'Thiselton', that "language-game" "overlaps" within and between '"communities"' ensure that *both* '"trans-contextual bridges"' *and* more 'localized' "contextual" factors "shape" or "constrain" texts, '"meanings"', 'concepts', "concept-functions", 'interpretations', and 'interpretative strategies'. Lyons argues, *with* the later Wittgenstein and 'Thiselton', that 'communities"' "language-games" embrace *both* 'universal concepts' (cf. what Lyons identifies as being the later 'Wittgenstein's stable but fuzzy-edged concepts') *and* 'context-specific concepts'. Thus, *with* the later Wittgenstein and 'Thiselton', Lyons argues that since 'context-specific concepts' are still related to 'universal commonality', then such 'context-specific concepts' are *'not'* 'self-contained'.[308]

Consequently, Lyons argues that *some* 'interpretative strategies' are 'universal', where Lyons cites the example of the 'universal' "strategy" of the "ascription" of 'intention' to 'texts'. Against what Lyons sees as being 'Thiselton's misrepresentation' of 'Fish', however, Lyons argues that even 'universal interpretative strategies' can at best only engender 'wide' consensus concerning constructed 'interpreted reality' 'with a small "r"'. In Lyons' view, Thiselton and W. 'Iser' move illegitimately from trans-contextuality to espousing the objectivistic "accessibility" of '"raw data"' in '"the spacio-temporal world"' and to espousing 'universal' 'facts' respectively. Nevertheless, in sympathy with Thiselton's 'desire' 'to confront all humanity with the gospel', Lyons admits that 'the possibility' of wide consensus concerning 'constructed' 'interpreted reality' 'with a small "r"' potentially allows 'some interpretative communities' to expand 'to embrace all… humanity'.[309]

Having said all this, though, and against Thiselton, Lyons argues that 'communication' between very "different" 'communities' – *although always "possible"* – is more difficult 'than Thiselton' "allows". Lyons argues that 'context-specific concepts' – which, in Lyons' view, are less stable than 'universal concepts' - are more prevalent in *all* communities 'than Thiselton' "allows" - and that, therefore, 'translating' the languages of very different communities with respect to one another (*so that* they can communicate with one another) is often more "difficult" 'than Thiselton' "allows". In Lyons' view, the later Wittgenstein may have agreed with this point since, in Lyons' estimate, the later Wittgenstein was more "non-foundationalist" and 'localist' (like 'Fish') 'than Thiselton' "allows".[310]

In Lyons' view, then, Thiselton wrongly contends that a 'Fishian' stance

---

[306] Lyons, *C&E*, 114, 115. Italics ours.
[307] Lyons, *C&E*, 112; cf. 111, 109, 113. Italics ours.
[308] Lyons, *C&E*, 110; cf. 113, 114, 111. Italics ours.
[309] Lyons, *C&E*, 112; cf. 68, 109, 110, 113, 108. Italics ours.
[310] Lyons, *C&E*, 112, 113-114. Italics ours.

necessarily leads to an *isolationist* prohibition of 'the possibility' of present-horizon inter-community 'communication'.[311]

(g) In Lyons' view, a 'Fishian' notion of '"universal commonality"' accounts for necessary hermeneutical *'constraints'*. Lyons agrees - with what he perceives to be Thiselton's view - that Fish *does indeed* argue that – against the background of their *'prior'* 'interpretations' – 'interpretative' "communities"' 'interpretative practices' and 'interpretative strategies' *"construct"* or "constitute"' their "texts" and "interpretations" – and thence their "social realities" - "independently of raw data". Nevertheless, Lyons argues, against what he perceives to be Thiselton's view, that since communities' 'interpretative practices' and 'interpretative strategies' can be 'universal' *as well as* 'localized', then these 'practices' and 'strategies' can be 'stable' to the point that 'communities' cannot 'choose interpretations' freely: to them, argues Lyons, 'their texts' appear 'solid'.[312]

In Lyons' estimate, therefore, Thiselton *wrongly* contends that a 'Fishian' stance necessarily leads to a *'relativist'* removal of hermeneutical 'constraints'. In Lyons' estimate, therefore, Thiselton's *fears in relation to* what will happen if hermeneutical 'constraints' are removed by a 'Fishian' stance are unfounded. In Lyons' estimate these unfounded fears of Thiselton's are that 'an infinite number' of "infinitely" variable 'communities' will emerge that will: (i) draw 'indifferently' on all "perspectives"; (ii) construct 'infinite numbers of unchallengeable interpretations of any text' (and thence 'an infinite number of' 'unchallengeable' 'social realities'); (iii) turn 'the gospel' into any "tradition's"' 'linguistic construct plucked out of the air'; and, (iv), thereby '"rapidly dissolve"' 'Christian' "texts"', '"concepts"', 'interpretations', 'theology', and "traditions" into 'disastrous' 'infinite' '"indeterminacy"' and "instability".[313]

(h) In Lyons' view, furthermore, a 'Fishian' notion of '"universal commonality"' also "accounts" for 'the possibility' of present-horizon '"hermeneutical *change*"', and in particular for 'the possibility' of the 'reform' of 'evangelized' communities 'from outside' 'by the… Church and its Bible'. Lyons argues that if 'a critique of' a community's 'assumptions' 'from outside' is to 'be understood', then fresh 'communication' or "understanding"' can *necessarily* be initiated (cf. Fish: one '"never"' "starts"' '"from scratch"') by accessing (cf. 'the acquisition of' 'available' '"rubrics"' of which parties in '"agreement"' are 'aware') "close at hand"' '"shared"' "frames"' "of reference"' (cf. '"rubrics"', '"shared"' "bas[e]s for agreement"') or, if these cannot be accessed, by accessing '"shared"' "frames"' '"of reference"' that are further '"back"' and by then co-creating (cf. Fish: "fashioning"') '"a new… wider"', '"shared"' '"frame of reference"' (cf. '"basis for agreement"') from there.[314]

Admittedly, Lyons argues, 'only' ongoing 'praxis' (cf. the *future*), and not

---

[311] Lyons, *C&E*, 112, 113, 111, 114. Italics ours.
[312] Lyons, *C&E*, 111, 112, 109, 115, 113. Italics ours.
[313] Lyons, *C&E*, 111, 110, 114, 109. Italics ours.
[314] Lyons, *C&E*, 111, 112, 109, 113, 114. Italics ours.

"hermeneutical" 'theory' (cf. the *present*), could generate 'absolute certainty' that 'universal' 'Christian' '"hermeneutical change"' was 'possible'. However, Lyons argues that, since 'Christian theology' says that 'God' leaves 'no one unable to hear the gospel', then *'faith'* says that 'universal' 'Christian' '"hermeneutical change"' is definitely 'possible'. Lyons admits that he is 'wearing' 'two hats' at this point – one being "hermeneutical" 'theory', the other being 'Christian theology'.[315]

Lyons, therefore, argues that Thiselton is wrong to contend that a 'Fishian' stance necessarily leads to an idolatrous self-affirming prohibition of 'hermeneutical growth' (cf. '"hermeneutical change"') - as though the 'Fishian' community shut out other communities so as to "attend" '"carefully"' only to itself (C.L. Blomberg's words, cited by Lyons), or was *'"purely reader-oriented"'* (C.L. Blomberg's words, cited by Lyons), or turned 'gospel' proclamation into "preaching" that each community should '"construct"' its own 'gospel' 'plucked out of the air'.[316]

Moving on, (i), then the *implication* that Lyons draws from this 'non-foundationalist' 'Fishian' 'account' of the four legitimate hermeneutical 'interests' (cf. "desires", 'plain' "experiences", or concerns of 'the hermeneutical project') that he has outlined, is that if *Thiselton* were to 'account' for these same four legitimate hermeneutical 'interests' or concerns (etc.) *consistently*, then he would be compromising his own "foundationalism" (i.e. not 'remaining theoretically sound'), and would be 'falling into non-foundationalism'. In Lyons' view, this kind of 'falling into non-foundationalism' happened to T.S. 'Kuhn' (despite 'Kuhn's' denials) who, Lyons observes, is 'much quoted by Thiselton'.[317]

Furthermore, (j), the stance that Lyons has, in his estimate, 'demonstrated' to be *truly* 'Fishian' is very different to the 'badly skewed' false "caricature" 'of Fish' that, in Lyons' estimate, Thiselton promotes.[318] In Lyons' view, Thiselton's "caricature" of the 'Fishian' stance as being '"radical pragmatic anti-formalism"' is *not* the 'only' alternative to 'formalism' (N.B. in 'formalism' '"concepts"' are seen as having *a priori* ahistorical '"sharply-bounded crystalline purity"') that Fish offers, since Fish in fact offers *something else*.[319] Since Lyons has, in his estimate, 'demonstrated' that the true 'Fishian' 'position' does *not* lead to the consequences that Thiselton outlines, then 'Thiselton's' 'hermeneutical' and 'wider theological' 'concerns' to do with Fish's work are 'unfounded' in Lyons' view.[320]

(k) Lyons concludes that the *reason* Thiselton promotes what is, in Lyons' estimate, such a 'badly-skewed' false "caricature" 'of Fish', is that Thiselton's *right* hermeneutical 'interests' – which are, in Lyons' view, rightly directed towards attempting to 'account' for what we "plainly" 'experience' (cf. the aforementioned

---

[315] Lyons, *C&E*, 114, 112. First two italics ours, third italics Lyons'.
[316] Lyons, *C&E*, 113, 111, 109, 114, 112. Lyons' italics.
[317] Lyons, *C&E*, 114, 111, 109, 108, 86. Italics ours.
[318] Lyons, *C&E*, 112, 111, 88-89, 114, 109. Italics ours.
[319] Lyons, *C&E*, 114, 109, 111, 110. Italics ours.
[320] Lyons, *C&E*, 112, 111, 108; cf. 111-115. Italics ours.

four legitimate concerns of 'the hermeneutical project') - are corrupted by Thiselton's *wrong* traditionalist 'interests' to promote his own 'prior' 'epistemologically' '"foundationalist"' 'historical or theological' tradition (cf. Lyons' phrase, 'historical or theological necessity'). In Lyons' view, these corrupted 'interests' are shared also by 'Jeanrond', 'Vanhoozer', 'Morgan', 'Watson', 'Noble', and 'Blomberg'.[321]

(1) The problem with this state of affairs, in Lyons' view, is that *since Thiselton's* false "caricature" of Fish is 'easily the most important and influential critique of Fish' in 'Christian theology' and 'biblical hermeneutics', and *since* others (perhaps including, in Lyons' view, the present author) appeal "uncritically" to Thiselton's false "caricature" of Fish, *then Lyons'* promotion of the true 'Fish's' "usefulness" for 'theology', and thence of 'Childs's' "usefulness" for 'theology', is being obscured. Lyons fears that if 'Vanhoozer's' comparatively '"readable"' book, '*Is There a Meaning in This Text?* (1998)', "replaces" Thiselton's more difficult book, *New Horizons in Hermeneutics* (1992), 'as the standard "foundationalist" response to such as Fish' then, in Lyons' feared scenario, the '"foundationalist"' 'errors will be even more widely disseminated!'[322]

(2) Before we move on to our responses to Lyons, we may now similarly analyze and expound what Lyons refers to as his 'earlier discussion of' B.S. Childs' notion of biblical '"referentiality"' - as follows. (We noted above that Lyons indicated that this 'discussion' was relevant to his critique of Thiselton, and so it should not be overlooked).[323]

To begin with, then, (a), Lyons argues that strands in 'Western' and 'eurocentric' '"modern"' 'thought' - (strands alien to 'Asian and African Biblical Theologies') - have corrupted the shape of 'Western' and European '"science"', '"history"', and biblical studies. As a result, in Lyons' view, 'Western' and European biblical studies now reflect an attempted usurping of God's dominion - and of theocentric notions of 'truth', 'meaning', and '"interpretation"' – and thus also reflect an exaltation of human dominion and of anthropocentric (cf. 'humanistic') '"reason"' – a kind of '"reason"' that seeks to "redefine" 'truth', 'meaning', and '"interpretation"'.[324]

Consequently, (b), in 'Western' and European biblical studies, in Lyons' view, "truths" (cf. 'referents') are "isolated" from theocentric 'history' '"and interpretation"', and are reframed and reinterpreted (or "redefined") within anthropocentric perceptions of 'history'. Lyons argues that a less than '"truthful"' hermeneutical 'discourse' results that divorces 'truth' from '"interpretation"' – which means that, in Lyons' estimate, '"biblical"' 'referents' become artificially abstracted from their '"biblical"' '"interpretative"' and "referential" matrices. Consequently, Lyons argues, "Scripture's" primary 'theological' '"witness"' is

---

[321] Lyons, *C&E*, 88-89, 114, 109, 108; cf. 111. Italics ours.
[322] Lyons, *C&E*, 109, 114, 108; cf. 88-89, 115. Italics ours, book titles aside.
[323] Lyons, *C&E*, 114.
[324] Lyons, *C&E*, 71; cf. 275.

suppressed, "restricted", "distorted", or "flattened".[325]

Thus, for example, (c), Lyons argues that - in this particular broad 'Western' and 'eurocentric' context – "'interpretation'" is often stopped from "interpreting" 'truth', as in certain 'Yale'-style biblical hermeneutics, in the 'New Criticism', and in 'fully a-historical' "structuralism". Lyons argues that, in such schools of biblical criticism, 'divine', "'revelatory'", "'and... historical'" "backgrounds" are "'in principle'" disallowed from being treated in line with their true status as biblical 'referents' or "truths", even if they are still allowed to "exist" "extra-textually". In such schools of biblical criticism, in Lyons' estimate, "interpretation" is "redefined" anthropocentrically or "humanistically" as purely literary, or sometimes as 'fully a-historical'; and in such schools of biblical criticism, in Lyons' view, the biblical texts themselves are "redefined" as being the primary 'referent' - and as 'non-history', or as 'a-historical story', or 'as "historical fiction"'.[326]

Conversely, (d), Lyons argues that - in the same broad 'Western' and 'eurocentric' context – 'truth' is sometimes stopped from being "truly interpreted", as in "rationalistic", in 'demythologizing', and in certain 'modern historical-critical' approaches to biblical hermeneutics. Lyons argues that, in such approaches, 'divine', "'revelatory'" "'and... historical'" "backgrounds" (cf. "truths", 'referents') are reinterpreted "'ideally'" (cf. "rationalistic" approaches), or in relation to "'consciousness'" (cf. 'demythologizing' approaches), or in relation to a false anthropocentric 'historicity' that is preoccupied "'with overly ostensive'" "'correspondence'" and with "'absolute historical coherence'" (cf. certain 'modern historical-critical' approaches). Lyons argues that in certain 'modern historical-critical' approaches, for example, 'truth' becomes reduced to "'spacio-temporal'" "states-of-affairs" that "cohere" completely with one another.[327]

(e) Childs' approach, however, in Lyons' estimate (Lyons, in part, draws on R.R. Topping's reading of Childs), is much less affected by these problems (cf. "(a)-(d)" immediately above), and so Lyons argues that we should pay attention to Childs' approach (if still critically). Lyons argues that Childs' approach (unlike the 'Western' and 'eurocentric' strands Lyons has noted): (i) seeks submission to God's dominion and to a theocentric notion of "rationality"; (ii) seeks to retain theocentric notions of 'truth', 'meaning' (and "'interpretation'"); and, (iii), seeks to "define" 'truth' as properly "interpreted" within the framework of theocentric 'history'. In Lyons' view, the result of Childs' approach, 'from Childs' perspective', (and from Lyons' 'perspective' once Childs' approach has been subjected to certain lesser criticisms), is a 'more "truthful"' hermeneutical 'discourse' in which 'truth' "'and interpretation'" are "inseparable". That is, Lyons argues that, in this 'more "truthful"' hermeneutical 'discourse', "'interpretation'" is allowed to "interpret" 'truth', and 'truth' is allowed to be "truly interpreted". In other words, in Lyons' estimate, Childs' biblical hermeneutics rightly seeks to "understand"

---

[325] Lyons, *C&E*, 71; cf. 70, 69, 68.
[326] Lyons, *C&E*, 71; cf. 70, 69; cf. 275.
[327] Lyons, *C&E*, 71; cf. 68; cf. 69; cf. 70.

"biblical truths biblically interpreted", and thus rightly remains respectful of the "'subtle hermeneutic complexity'" and "'referentiality'" of Scripture'.[328]

Thus, (f), Lyons argues that Childs' biblical hermeneutics reinstate *biblical* 'referents' such that 'canonical texts' *are allowed* to "refer" "'in principle'" to "'God'", to God's "actions", and to 'history', and such that these "truths" are no longer subject to an anthropocentric (cf. 'humanistic') *disallowing of their status as* biblical 'referents'.[329]

Furthermore, (g), Lyons argues that Childs' biblical hermeneutics also reinstates the *"'biblical… interpretation'" of* biblical 'referents' or "truths", including the "'biblical… interpretation'" of "'God'", of God's "actions", and of 'history'. Thus, Lyons notes that Childs' biblical hermeneutics keeps the book of Exodus's *own* "'interpretation'" of God's "actions" in relation to "'the Exodus event'". Similarly, Lyons notes that 'J. Moltmann' keeps "'Paul's'" *own* "'gospel'" "'interpretation'" of "'the'" "'Christ'"-"'event'". In Childs' biblical hermeneutics, therefore, in Lyons' estimate, such 'referents' or "truths" are no longer subject to *anthropocentric false reinterpretation*, but are *"'rendered'" "inseparable" from their true interpretative framework* – 'the canonical texts'. (N.B. Lyons still holds that different interpretative communities' 'assumptions' will "produce" different "Bibles" in the sense of 'a series of "thin texts" that then function as Scripture within contextually differentiated Christian or Jewish communities').[330]

Moreover, (h), Lyons argues that Childs' biblical hermeneutics reinstates the biblical *prioritization* of biblical 'referents'. Childs, Lyons observes, argues that the Bible prioritizes *"'God'" and God's "actions"* (cf. "'divine'" and "'revelatory'" "'background'") over 'history' (cf. "'historical background'"), 'history' being only a *secondary* biblical 'referent' in Childs' view. Lyons argues that, for Childs, considerations of biblical "'historical background'", therefore, may 'inform', but 'must not replace or distort', the "rendering" 'of the *sensus literalis*' since, for Childs, Lyons observes, 'the *sensus literalis*' is "inseparable" from the Bible's 'theological' "'witness to'" its primary "'divine'" 'referent', namely "'God'". (N.B. Lyons holds that different interpretative communities' readings will produce 'different "Gods"').[331]

In addition, (i), Lyons argues that Childs' biblical hermeneutics reinstates the *true "complexities"* of "'biblical'" "'referentiality'". That is, Lyons argues (after Childs) that: *since* the Bible primarily "interprets" "'God'" and God's "actions", where "'God'" is a "'multi-dimensional… reality'" who *"'transcends'"* all "'historical'" "situations"; and *since* the Bible "interprets" 'history' theocentrically in a way that is very different to anthropocentric reinterpretations of 'history' and that involves 'the self-effacing [cf. non-anthropocentric] activities of' Scripture's

---

[328] Lyons, *C&E*, 71; cf. 70; cf. 68; cf. 69.
[329] Lyons, *C&E*, 69; cf. 70; cf. 71; cf. 275. Italics ours.
[330] Lyons, *C&E*, 71; cf. 69, 70, 68; cf. 110, 112, 114; cf. 263, 270. Italics ours.
[331] Lyons, *C&E*, 69; 70; cf. 68, 71; cf. 264. Italics Lyons' on the two occurrences of *'sensus literalis'*, others ours.

'tradents'; *then* the Bible has a '"subtle hermeneutic complexity"' and '"referentiality"'. Lyons argues (after Childs) that this '"subtle hermeneutic complexity"' and '"referentiality"', (i), *'necessarily'* involves the '"excessive"' '"history"'-"obscuring" or '"non-historical"' '"representative"' '"modes of depiction"' '"of the testimony of faith"' (reflecting '"the revelatory activity of God in space and time"') '"apart from which we have no independent access"' or "reference to" '"God"' or/and to God's past "actions". *Consequently*, (ii), Lyons argues (after Childs) that the Bible's '"subtle hermeneutic complexity"' and '"referentiality"' involves a multiform "complex" "reference" to '"historical background"' that is sometimes '"very loose"' and sometimes '"genuinely"' 'ostensive' (the implication, here, being that 'ostensive' 'historical' "reconstructions" retain a place in Lyons' hermeneutics).[332]

Finally, (j), Lyons argues that Childs' biblical hermeneutics also reinstate an awareness of the *limitations* of 'historical' "reconstructions". Thus, (i), *"in principle"*, for Childs and Lyons, 'texts' (including both 'canonical' and 'non-canonical' texts) *can* access, and can therefore contribute to "reconstructions" of, '"historical background"'. However, (ii), *in practice*, for both Childs and Lyons, 'historical' "reconstructions" of the biblical '"historical background"' are rendered '"tenuous and hypothetical"' at best *because:* (iii) for Childs and Lyons, biblical 'historical' "reference" is subordinated to biblical 'theological' "reference", making biblical 'historical' "reference" a very "complex" matter; and, (iv), *because*, for Childs and Lyons, 'non-canonical' 'historical' 'material' that is of potential relevance to reconstructions of biblical '"historical background"': (iv.i) interprets 'history' anthropocentrically; (iv.ii) hardly exists at all in any useful form; and, (iv.iii), is therefore doubly-subordinated to biblical theocentric 'historical' "reference" such that it very often cannot reliably be used to "test" or "independently" '"check"' biblical 'historical' "reference". (v) The clear implication of these points is that, in Lyons' estimate, a *lack of corroborative historical evidence* can produce what Thiselton would call a "plurality of legitimate readings" (see below and also Chapter 5).[333]

(3) In concluding his section on '"referentiality"' (which Lyons cites as being of relevance to his critique of Thiselton), Lyons adds that he will, in a later section, 'further' "consider" 'the use of constructions of "ostensive history" as a source of illumination for the shape of the final form' of the biblical canon. The implication is that there is 'further' content of potential relevance to Lyons' critique of Thiselton, and so we shall investigate this content briefly - as follows.[334]

Thus, (a), we should begin by underlining the fact that Lyons is far from being uncritical of Childs. Thus, in an "extension" of Childs' notion of 'illuminating the final form' of the canonical texts, Lyons argues that 'many' 'diverse sources' for 'illumination'[335]

---

[332] Lyons, *C&E*, 68; cf. 71, 70, 69. Third italics Lyons', others ours.
[333] Lyons, *C&E*, 69; cf. 70, 71. Italics ours.
[334] Lyons, *C&E*, 71; cf. 68-71.
[335] Lyons, *C&E*, 77; cf. 78.

have been woefully neglected, either because they were pre-critical interpreters (like Origen, Aquinas or Rashi), dogmatic theologians (like Barth, Tillich or Moltmann), or just non-historical-critical critics (like populist users of the Bible such as advertisers, comedians, film-makers and fiction-writers).[336]

In Lyons' view, different communities will, of course, "balance" or 'weigh the evidence' from 'the sources of illumination' 'differently'.[337]

Nevertheless, (b), since Lyons still approves of 'the use of constructions of "ostensive history" as a source of illumination' (albeit with the qualifications just noted from his section on '"referentiality"'), he adds that 'the cultural relativity' resulting from different communities 'balancing the sources of illumination' 'differently' *itself* 'needs to be balanced against the historical text'. That is, Lyons sees 'the need for some form of critical distancing', and for an 'emphasis on the canonical shape as restrictive'. That is, in Lyons' view, 'one must do justice to the texts as historical witnesses'.[338]

Having said this, (c), a further critical point that Lyons makes in relation to Childs' approach is that Childs fails to answer the question: 'when should historical information be… incorporated as illumination and when should it be rejected as "swamping" the text?'[339]

Lyons admits that this question cannot be fully answered since, in Lyons' estimate, R.W.L. 'Moberly's assertion that there is no one way to apply historical criticism to a canonical approach is correct'. In Lyons' view, though, 'two extremes are definitely to be avoided' and, in Lyons' estimate, are 'in practice' impossible in any case: 'first, that of asserting that no historical critical information that is not in the text may be added and, second, that of de-canonizing the text and reading it against a detailed historical critical construct'.[340] Crucially, Lyons argues that,

> the line between illuminating or distorting the final form is not ultimately a question of rule following but rather of the effect of that exegesis upon those who encounter it. If it is convincing and satisfying – and this does not have to mean inoffensive or culturally conforming – it is likely to be accepted as a correct application of historical criticism to the canonical text. If it is judged distracting and irrelevant by the community of the texts, it will be rejected. Only its acceptance over time will clarify such questions.[341]

Thus, in Lyons' view, 'the real question about the acceptability of' his 'particular interpretation' of 'the Sodom narrative' has to do with 'its momentary

---

[336] Lyons, *C&E*, 78.
[337] Lyons, *C&E*, 77-78; cf. 266.
[338] Lyons, *C&E*, 71; cf. 68-71; cf. 77; cf. 266; cf. 270. Italics ours.
[339] Lyons, *C&E*, 262.
[340] Lyons, *C&E*, 263.
[341] Lyons, *C&E*, 263.

rhetorical persuasiveness as to the moves [he has]... made and its general attractiveness to a believing community, rather than its correct application of a rigorous methodology'.[342]

That is, (d), and in a further criticism of Childs, Lyons argues that if *Childs'* 'canonical approach' seeks to "illuminate" 'a single' '"thick canonical text"' or 'singularity' that "holds" 'to' or "stands" 'in continuity with... the Christian tradition', *Lyons*, by contrast, sees that 'decisions about how deep the text should be investigated and the kind of extra-textual material invoked' will rarely be "identical" 'across cultural and temporal boundaries'. Nor, in Lyons' estimate, will such 'decisions' always reflect even 'a mutually reinforcing plurality'. Rather, Lyons argues that such decisions will, in practice, often be 'contradictory', especially 'across cultural and temporal boundaries'.[343]

The result of this scenario, in Lyons' estimate, is 'a series of "thin texts" that then function as Scripture within contextually differentiated Christian or Jewish communities, albeit with the – at least potentially – humbling proviso that they are not the "whole story"'.[344]

In other words, Lyons argues that 'different' interpretative communities will in fact construct *both* 'different' "Bibles" *and* 'different "Gods"', and will, by their 'assumptions', differently "define" 'the controlling function of the canonical shape'. In Lyons' view, this defining of 'the controlling function of the canonical shape' by communities' 'assumptions' 'must' go 'hand in hand' with 'the freedom inherent in the act of exegesis in all its contextuality' - 'with [in Lyons' estimate] both contributing to the meaning generated *wherever that position leads*'.[345]

(4) Turning now to *our response* to Lyons' critique of Thiselton in *Canon and Exegesis* then, (a), we may begin by noting that Lyons, (i), does not cite the whole of the paragraph in which Thiselton uses the phrase, 'raw data'.[346] The whole of Thiselton's paragraph is as follows:

> The fundamental philosophical weakness in Fish's polarizing of his two alternatives lies in failure to come to terms with *the major transcendental questions which stem from Kant, in which* very careful and rigorous attention is given to the working distinction between how the knowing human subject or agent conditions raw data and what this subject or agent constructs independently of raw data. Do social contexts condition or do they construct social realities, including texts? [Lyons' citation ends here, but Thiselton goes on to say that] *Beyond the Kantian philosophical tradition*, the *tradition of Hegel* which passes on through Gadamer to Habermas wrestles with a parallel tension between the contextually-historically finite and the broader continuum or frame

---

[342] Lyons, *C&E*, 266.
[343] Lyons, *C&E*, 269, 270; cf. 263. Italics ours.
[344] Lyons, *C&E*, 263.
[345] Lyons, *C&E*, 264; cf. 269-270. Italics in speech-marks Lyons'.
[346] Lyons, *C&E*, 110; cf. Thiselton, *NH*, 541-542.

which finite historical phenomena presuppose.[347]

From this paragraph it is clear that Thiselton's use of the phrase, 'raw data', reflects the thinking of 'the Kantian philosophical tradition'. Thiselton uses different language when commenting on the 'tradition of Hegel'. Crucially, though, we have seen that *Thiselton's tradition is more Hegelian than 'Kantian'* (see especially Chapter 6).[348]

More than this: we have demonstrated that even Thiselton's appeals to 'Hegel' are so heavily modified that the standard criticisms of Hegel to do with "totalization", "idealism", "ahistorical abstraction", and so on *simply cannot be leveled at Thiselton*. But if *even Thiselton's appeals to Hegel* are so "heavily modified" that the criticisms often leveled at the *'tradition of Hegel'* cannot be applied to Thiselton, then how much *less* can the criticisms often leveled at the *'Kantian… tradition'* be applied to Thiselton?[349]

The most that can be gleaned from the "raw data" paragraph about *Thiselton's* epistemology (as opposed to that of the 'Kantian… tradition') is an emerging point concerning "historical conditioning" and "interpretative construction" that subtends to a sublation-framework that transposes *aspects* from *both* the 'Kantian… tradition' *and* the 'tradition of Hegel' *into a new key*. Only by omitting Thiselton's juxtaposed reference to the 'tradition of Hegel' can Lyons hide Thiselton's implicit sublation-framework and make it seem as if Thiselton makes the "raw data" notion his own in this context of discussion. Lyons, then, is "proof-texting". Regardless of whether or not Thiselton "caricatures" Fish, Lyons certainly caricatures Thiselton.[350]

Thus, (ii), extending his caricature of Thiselton further and missing an entire sphere within Thiselton's thinking, Lyons asserts that it is the later Wittgenstein's 'trans-contextual bridges that give Thiselton the solid Bible he needs in order to confront all humanity with the gospel'.[351]

At this point, however, there is no need for us to repeat our arguments from Chapters 3, 4, 5, 6, and from earlier in the present chapter. We need only reiterate our point that Thiselton's epistemology is much more indebted to his widening dialogue with the philosophy of *history* - and to his hermeneutical critique of history (which is ultimately theological and biblical) – than to his widening dialogue with the philosophy of *language*, or to his hermeneutical critique of language.

It is, therefore, quite concerning that Lyons' critique of Thiselton seems to *hinge* on points about "raw data" and on a point about Thiselton's supposed grounding of a supposedly objectivist epistemology in the later Wittgenstein's 'trans-

---

[347] Thiselton, *NH*, 541-542. Thiselton's italics removed, ours added.
[348] Thiselton, *NH*, 542. Italics ours.
[349] Thiselton, *NH*, 542; cf. our Chapter 6. Italics ours.
[350] Thiselton, *NH*, 541-542; cf. Lyons, *C&E*, 110, 109, 114; cf. 108-115. Italics ours.
[351] Lyons, *C&E*, 110.

contextual bridges'.³⁵²

(iii) Lyons develops his caricature of Thiselton still further when Lyons argues that no act of reading or perception can bypass "interpretation" and when Lyons *then* presents *this* argument as a criticism of Thiselton's supposed notion of "objectivistic perception of raw data".³⁵³

We have already seen, however, that Thiselton argues: (iii.i) that the "two horizons" can *never* be *fully* fused into one horizon; (iii.ii) that initial pre-understandings are *always distorted;* and, (iii.iii), that (with Bultmann) a "life-relation" (i.e. 'shared life-structures in… human experience' or a *point of similarity or of analogy*) between readers' lives and a text's subject-matter is the necessary precondition for the possibility of the *commencement* of *both* the understanding of the text *and* the historical conditioning of readers by the text. For Thiselton, the *commencement* of understanding and of conditioning depends *neither* on 'spatial and temporal proximity' between readers' horizons and textual horizons, *nor* on an "objectivistic perception" of the text. That is, (iii.iv), Thiselton, along with Lyons, *also* believes that "objectivistic perception of raw data" is impossible (see Chapters 5, 6, and above). *Both* Thiselton *and* Lyons think that "interpretation" is *always involved* in perception. The difference between Thiselton's thinking and the Fishian aspect of Lyons' thinking, as we argued earlier, turns on whether or not *past* historical horizons, particularly those of ancient biblical texts, can *contribute* to the *shape* of, and thereby *contribute* to the constraints upon, the interpretations that present-horizon communities *work* to construct in the *present*.³⁵⁴

We will return to this point later, where we will add the caveat that this criticism of Lyons applies more to his "'Fishian'" stance than to his Barthian-Childsian stance. Against Lyons, we will argue that these two aspects of Lyons' thought – his "two hats" - are less compatible with each other than he would have us believe.³⁵⁵

(b) Lyons *subsumes* Thiselton's *actual* subtle hermeneutical critique of historical objectivity and of present meaning (see earlier and later in the present chapter and Chapters 3 and 5) *beneath* what Lyons erroneously supposes is Thiselton's "objectivistic excursion outside of interpretation so as to argue from philosophy

---

[352] Lyons, *C&E*, 109-111; but cf. our Chapters 3, 4, 5, 6, and 7. Italics ours.

[353] Lyons, *C&E*, 109, 110, 111; cf. 88-89. Italics ours.

[354] cf.: Thiselton, 'UPC', 87-88, 93-94; Thiselton, 'EITN', 583, 584; Thiselton, *2H*, 57-58, 315, 307-309, 320, 326, xix; Thiselton, 'SBL', 109-110, 115-118; Thiselton, 'U (long)', 101-102, 119-120; Thiselton, *LLM*, 8-9; Thiselton, 'NH', 311-328; Thiselton, 'SBS', 329; citing, Guthrie, G.H., 'Boats in the Bay: Reflections on the Use of Linguistics and Literary Analysis in Biblical Studies', in *Linguistics and the New Testament. Critical Junctures* (eds. S.E. Porter and D.A. Carson; Journal for the Study of the New Testament Supplement Series 168: Studies in New Testament Greek 5; Sheffield: Sheffield Academic Press, 1999), 33; Lyons, *C&E*, 110, 111; cf. 88-89. Italics ours.

[355] Lyons, *C&E*, 114-115.

for objectivistic access to raw data".[356]

Thus, our arguing (see above) that "*past* historical horizons, particularly those of ancient biblical texts, can *contribute* to the *shape* of, and thereby *contribute* to the constraints upon, the interpretations that present-horizon communities *work* to construct in the *present*", is emphatically *not* a case of "'foundationalism'" as Lyons has defined it.[357]

That is, as we have already begun to see, when Thiselton says that biblical texts are "accessible", or "given", he does *not* use the words "accessible" or "given" to mean anything consistent with "objectivistic access to texts" that supposedly only have 'fixed', or "'stable'", or 'inherent', or 'plain', or wholly pre-"determined" (cf. 'deterministic'), or solely "text-based" "meanings" (here we bring in language from S. Woodman's caricature of Thiselton which, as we shall see later, is parallel to Lyons's caricature of Thiselton).[358]

Rather, summarizing our prior findings: (i) Thiselton's notions of "the given" or of "givenness" have the implicature of potential *progressive* hermeneutic access to texts that have "given" (i.e. *historically prior*) *historico-linguistic particularity* and that *potentially* provide interpretative constraints that can and should prevent meanings from "expanding arbitrarily" at the behest of interpretative communities.[359]

At the same time, (ii), for Thiselton, a *non-objectivistically* "given" text, as historically "other" and as historically *prior*, also relates in a *developing* manner to expanding – though simultaneously eschatologically convergent - diachronic historical contexts of understanding that include various readers who are in variable reading situations and communities (see Chapters 5, 6, and the present chapter).[360]

Therefore, (iii), Thiselton's notion of "present meaning" is much more complex than Lyons' caricatures in relation to what Lyons sees as being Thiselton's supposedly 'epistemologically solid' text. For Thiselton, "present meaning" is a complex matter involving *both* stabilizing constraints (*some* of which come from the present-horizon corporate interpretative community) *and* dimensions of fluidity and/or plurality. Thiselton's stance certainly *cannot* be caricatured as entertaining any notion of "objectivistic access to texts and textual horizons", or as entertaining any supposedly 'deterministic' or 'fixed' or 'plain' or 'inherent' view of 'meaning' based solely in texts (to use S. Woodman's language again).[361]

---

[356] Lyons, *C&E*, 88-89; cf. 109-111. Italics ours.

[357] Lyons, *C&E*, 86, 109-111, 113, 114-115. Italics ours.

[358] Thiselton, *NH*, 548; cf. 279-280; cf. 63, 108-110, 395-398, 400, 502, 517, 522-523, 562; cf. Woodman, 'UC', 9. We are using Woodman's language here. Italics ours.

[359] Thiselton, 'Parab', 456-457, cf. 468; cf.: Thiselton, *NH*, 279-280; Chapters 3, 5, and 6. Italics ours.

[360] Thiselton, *NH*, 557-558; cf. Chapters 3, 4, 5, 6, and the present chapter. Italics ours.

[361] Lyons, *C&E*, 110, 114; cf. Chapters 3, 4, 5, 6, and earlier in the present chapter; cf. Woodman, 'UC', 9. We are still using Woodman's language here. Italics ours.

We may expand on each of these three points as follows.

Thus, (i), for Thiselton it is *not only* the present-horizon interpretative community that stabilizes meaning even though, as we shall see in our responses to S. Woodman later, Thiselton *does not deny* that reading communities can stabilize meaning. Rather, in Thiselton's view, there are several other "givens" (i.e. historical factors *other than* interpretative communities) within and behind – and sometimes even in front of - the biblical texts that can *also* stabilize meaning. These "givens" include *historically prior* "'linguistic'" "'rules'" and "'habits'", *historically prior* 'public criteria of meaning', *historically prior* historical "continuities", the concrete grammars of geographically located *historically prior* historical movements (including linguistic activities - see above), the insusceptibility of the past to alterity, the way divine 'promise' qualifies "futural" historical 'openness', factors related to the *historically prior* historical and linguistic particularities of texts and of various kinds of context, and so on. For Thiselton, these mostly *historically prior* "givens", because they belong to *our own* historical unity (not uniformity) as opposed to that of some radically dissociated alien world, can be potentially progressively – if never exhaustively or "neutrally" (i.e. never as "raw data") – understood.[362]

That is, again, Thiselton argues that these "givens" are not accessible objectivistically. Nevertheless, Thiselton argues that such "givens" *can* become *progressively* accessible in a *hermeneutically-qualified* way that does *not* involve any loss of epistemological sophistication. For Thiselton, history is simply not *so* "alien" that we cannot *begin* to understand it. We are reminded of Heidegger's view (which is hardly objectivistic) that, in its "knowing", 'Dasein [or we may now write, less individualistically, the "interpretative community"]... does not somehow first get out of an inner sphere in which it has been proximally encapsulated, but... is always "outside" alongside' 'already discovered' 'entities' (and, for Heidegger, to say this is not to say that these 'entities' are perceived "objectivistically").[363]

That is, Thiselton does not say that we can ever access "raw data" as we have already explained. But, for Thiselton, with Heidegger, we are 'always' already '"outside" alongside' 'already discovered' 'entities'. Thiselton does not think that we can ever perceive these 'entities' "just as they are". For Thiselton, we are always "interpreting them" such that the two horizons never "fuse into one". Nevertheless, it is to *over-sharpen the epistemological subject-object distinction into an a-historical dichotomy* if we say - as Lyons would seem to be saying when he is wearing his Fishian (as opposed to his Barthian-Childsian) 'hat' - that the "historically other" in the past is in no sense "historically related" - via texts - to us. That is, as we said in Chapter 3, Heidegger refuses 'to start with spatiality', as though "subject-object conceptualization" sought to cross space as in 'Descartes' ontology

---

[362] Thiselton, *2H*, xix, 15-17, 47, 53-63, 77-84, 104, 115, 133-139, 196-197, 265, 279-283, 291-292, 309-310, 324, 354, 374-385, 432-445; cf.: Thiselton, 'LMR', 1135; Thiselton, *NH*, 111, 335, 336; Woodman, 'UC', 9. Italics ours.

[363] Heidegger, *BT*, 89. Italics ours.

of the "world"'. Instead, for Heidegger, "conceptualization" operates within 'the "around"... which is constitutive for the environment' which, in turn, is 'not... primarily "spatial"'. Of course, Heidegger readily acknowledges that 'spatial character... incontestably belongs to any environment'. Nevertheless, Heidegger argues that 'spatial character' 'can be clarified only in terms of the structure of worldhood'. That is, for Heidegger and Thiselton, "space" does *not absolutely separate historical realities* (however these are perceived) but is part of a world in which "understanding" *progressively perceives the relations between already-related* historical realities. As we saw earlier, in Chapter 3, the Continental critique of Cartesianism demands that "subject-object conceptualization" is *"re*-historicized" - not *"de*-historicized" further as in the hermeneutics of Fish and Lyons. This *"re*-historicization" of comparative subject-object conceptualization is manifest in Heidegger, and then *still more so* in Gadamer, and then *still more so again in* Thiselton. And each re-historicization is a move *further away* from philosophical idealism: Thiselton is hardly uncritical of Heidegger and Gadamer, as we have seen.[364]

Lyons, however, at least when he is wearing his Fishian (as opposed to his Barthian-Childsian) 'hat', seems to *radicalize and de-historicize* a (corporate version of a) Cartesian subject-object distinction rather than progressively *re-historicize* that distinction. Thus, for Fish, and for the "Fishian" Lyons, there is no relationship between the present-horizon interpretative community (cf. "subject", or corporate "subject") and any 'prior' textual "object" because, for Fish and Lyons, 'any constraints' on interpretation 'are themselves either internal to the community or the products of interpretation'. In Fish's thinking, 'content' is never 'independent of' or 'prior to interpretation'. Thus, epistemologically-speaking, we could say that Fish and the Fishian Lyons, in their attempt to utterly separate "subject" and "object", try to go back to before Heidegger! Gadamer, though, recounts that 'Martin Heidegger changed the philosophical consciousness of the time with one stroke', and that 'Heidegger' powerfully affected 'every direction of scholarly research', making 'everything that preceded... seem feeble'. Of course, Lyons might argue, as he does with respect to Thiselton, that our appeal to philosophy is itself an objectivist attempt to "step outside of interpretation". Here, though, at this particular juncture if not elsewhere, Lyons presupposes a false dichotomy between "objectivist foundationalism" and "Fishian non-foundationalism". Seemingly, anybody who appeals to writers other than Fish and/or friends of Fish is "objectivist" and "'foundationalist'" in Lyons' view. Of course, though, all we are doing is "interpreting" some of Heidegger's texts. It is just that, in our use of the term, "interpreting", we are meaning something *different* to the two binary (*sic*) options to which Lyons (at such junctures as this) tries to constrain us. It is as though Lyons thinks that, historically, only a binary choice between two views of "perception" (and/or of "understanding") was ever proffered by thinkers. This structure within Lyons' approach looks like an imposed echo – if only a shadow -

---

[364] Heidegger, *BT*, 94-95; cf. our Chapter 3; cf. Lyons, *C&E*, 114. Italics ours.

of idealist formalism to us.[365]

(ii) Thiselton, in recognizing the reality of developing historical relationships - i.e. relationships between *non-objectivistically* "given" and *imperfectly-perceived* texts and successive generations of readers – allows for dimensions of meaning that are more fluid or plural. That is, as we noted in Chapter 5, Thiselton in effect espouses *a polymorphous notion of a 'plurality" 'of legitimate readings [cf. meanings]'* - a *polymorphous notion* that has a *six-fold grammar* and that therein takes into account: (ii.i) the effects of literary genre and (extra-)linguistic multi-functionality; (ii.ii) interpretative impediments; (ii.iii) hermeneutical deepening or hermeneutical growth; (ii.iv) expanding historical horizons and the openness of the future (qualified by eschatological convergence upon biblical horizons of promise); (ii.v) diverse readers and diverse reading-situations; and, (ii.vi), interpretative angles-of-view. The last four of these six factors relate *more explicitly* to "present meaning" than do the first two of these six factors (see Chapters 5, 6, and above).[366]

Of course, as we indicated in Chapter 5, Thiselton's notion of a "plurality" 'of legitimate readings [cf. meanings]' is a long way from the notion of "unnecessary arbitrary meaning-expansion" that Thiselton would undoubtedly see as being a problem with Fish's approach. For Thiselton, the notion of a "plurality" 'of legitimate readings [cf. meanings]' accords with criteria of interpretative responsibility and with respect for the historical "other". By contrast, for Thiselton, the notion of "unnecessary arbitrary meaning-expansion" *unnecessarily* "imperializes" (exalts) the present-horizon interpretative community (however wide), *unnecessarily* suppresses the historically-prior textual "other" (N.B. for Fish: 'content' is never 'prior to interpretation'), and is therefore a matter of irresponsible interpretation and of "bad relating".[367]

At this point, as we have seen, Lyons would no doubt interject by arguing that a 'Fishian' notion of '"universal commonality"' accounts for necessary hermeneutical *'constraints'*, and thus *prevents* "infinitely fluid meaning" – "infinitely fluid meaning" being what Lyons perceives Thiselton as fearing in the event of a Fishian view of texts taking hold in biblical studies. That is, in Lyons' estimate, since communities' 'interpretative practices' and 'interpretative strategies' can be 'universal' *as well as* 'localized', then these 'practices' and 'strategies' can be 'stable' to the point that 'communities' cannot 'choose interpretations' freely: to them,

---

[365] Lyons, *C&E*, 111; cf. 88-89; cf.: Fish, 'NC', 268, 271-274, 277; Fish, 'Intro', 11; Gadamer, H.-G., 'The Phenomenological Movement', in *Philosophical Hermeneutics* (H.-G. Gadamer; ed. D.E. Linge; London: University of California Press, 1976), 138-139; Lyons, *C&E*, 114. Italics ours.

[366] Jeanrond, 'R RH', 117; cf.: Thiselton, 'Parab', 455-457, cf.: 458-461; 468; Thiselton, *NH*, 557-558. Italics ours.

[367] Thiselton, 'CAP', 133-135, 201; cf.: Thiselton, *2H*, 10, 120-121, 154-157, 244, cf.: 324-325, 348-349, 436-437; Thiselton, *NH*, 557-558; Thiselton, 'R-RH', 82-83; Jeanrond, 'R RH', 117; Thiselton, 'Parab', 455-457, cf.: 458-461; 468; Fish, 'NC', 268, 271-272, 274, 277; Fish, 'Intro', 11. Italics ours.

Lyons argues, 'their texts' appear 'solid'.[368]

We saw that in Lyons' estimate, therefore, Thiselton *wrongly* contends that a 'Fishian' stance necessarily leads to a *'relativist'* removal of hermeneutical 'constraints' and to a situation in which 'an infinite number' of "infinitely" variable 'communities' can: draw 'indifferently' on all "perspectives"; construct 'infinite numbers of unchallengeable interpretations of any text' (and thence 'an infinite number of' 'unchallengeable' 'social realities'); turn 'the gospel' into any "tradition's" 'linguistic construct plucked out of the air'; and thereby '"rapidly dissolve"' 'Christian' "texts", '"concepts"', 'interpretations', 'theology', and "traditions" into 'disastrous' 'infinite' '"indeterminacy"' and "instability".[369]

We feel that there has been a misunderstanding at this point, however. That is, Lyons here tends to impute onto Thiselton's arguments in relation to *Fish* some of the language to do with "infinity" that Thiselton uses more in relation to the *later Barthes and Derrida*. That is, Lyons exaggerates and distorts Thiselton's argument in relation to Fish by bringing in Thiselton's language *from a different context*.[370]

But what *are* the consequences - in Thiselton's estimate - of a widespread acceptance of a Fishian notion of interpretative constraints? Well, the closest Thiselton comes to outlining a summary of the consequences of a widespread acceptance of *Fish's* notion of interpretative constraints is in his (i.e. Thiselton's) citation of C. West's observation of J. Dewey's "acknowledgment",

> that wholesale relativist historicism has only four possible consequences: either a paralyzing skepticism, or the view that "might is right", or sheer institutionism, or a self-situating contextualism. None of these four alternatives provides a critical theory for social action, as Rorty and Fish concede.[371]

This language, though, is quite different from Thiselton's language about 'infinite series of semiotic layers' in relation to the later Barthes, or about 'an endless series of "traces" or "tracks"' in relation to Derrida.[372]

That is, Thiselton would *not deny* the reality of the way in which communities' 'interpretative practices' and 'interpretative strategies' stabilize communities' interpretations of present meaning. Further, Thiselton acknowledges that *Fish* says this when Thiselton complains that 'socio-pragmatic reading... serves only to *affirm prior community norms*'. (Of course, Lyons would then interject by arguing that, here, Thiselton ignores the present-horizon inter-community 'communication' and '"hermeneutical change"' that a '"Fishian"' stance allows. We will answer this objection later as to do so here would take us away from our present point to do

---

[368] Lyons, *C&E*, 111, 112, 109, 115, 113. Italics ours.
[369] Lyons, *C&E*, 111, 110, 114, 109. Italics ours.
[370] Thiselton, *NH*, 92-132; cf. 393-405, 515-555; cf. Lyons, *C&E*, 111, 110, 114, 109. Italics ours.
[371] Thiselton, *NH*, 401.
[372] Thiselton, *NH*, 95; cf. 108.

with hermeneutical constraints).³⁷³

In other words, and gathering our points together, then whilst *Lyons* says that a Fishian perspective argues that 'interpretative practices' and 'interpretative strategies' (grounded in '"universal commonality"') prevent *"infinitely* fluid meaning", *Thiselton* argues that communities' 'interpretative practices' and 'interpretative strategies' *are not enough* to prevent "unnecessary *arbitrary* meaning-expansion". That is, Thiselton argues that *if* it is *only* 'the interpretative community' that stabilizes present meaning, then the danger is that, in relation to any given text, meanings could still "expand arbitrarily" – *either* as we move from community to community, *or* even as we stay within single communities that undergo temporal changes.³⁷⁴

At this point, then, on the one hand, it is important to distinguish *Thiselton's* notion of "unnecessary *arbitrary* meaning-expansion" from *Lyons'* caricature of Thiselton in which Lyons imputes to Thiselton's reading of Fish a notion that looks more like *"infinitely* fluid meaning". (Lyons, it will be remembered, achieves this caricature of Thiselton's reading of Fish by falsely attributing language drawn from Thiselton's responses to the later Barthes and Derrida to Thiselton's responses to Rorty and Fish). On the other hand, we *also* distinguished *Thiselton's* notion of "unnecessary *arbitrary* meaning-expansion" from Thiselton's acceptance of the polymorphous notion of a "plurality" '"of legitimate readings"'. (N.B. We mentioned this latter notion earlier, drawing partly on W.G. Jeanrond, and anticipated the same notion in Chapter 5). Thus there are *three different* notions under discussion here: "unnecessary *arbitrary* meaning-expansion", *"infinitely* fluid meaning", and a "plurality" '"of legitimate readings"'. Crucially, if the phrase "conflict of interpretations" is associated with each of these (and other related) notions of plural interpretative outcomes in turn, then it *changes its grammar as its association changes* (see Chapter 5).³⁷⁵

That is, Lyons, in effect, uses a strategy of code-switching in order to caricature Thiselton's points about "arbitrariness" as points to do with "infinity", and then sets the latter up as a straw man to be knocked down. Thiselton's use of the word 'arbitrary', however, carries with it the sense that it is not so much the *number* of "meanings" that is in view. Thiselton's use of the word 'arbitrary' carries with it the sense that if it is *only* the interpretative community or communities that *shape(s)* present meanings then, *no matter how many meanings are in view*, those meanings will still *tend towards arbitrariness (i.e. towards irresponsible discontinuity with the text's historical*

---

³⁷³ Thiselton, *NH*, 515; cf. Lyons, *C&E*, 111, 112, 109, 115, 113-114. Italics ours, except on the *three* words, *'prior community norms'*, where they are Thiselton's; italics on *'affirm'* are ours.
³⁷⁴ Thiselton, *NH*, 515; cf.: Thiselton, 'Parab', 455-457, cf.: 458-461; 468; Lyons, *C&E*, 111, 112, 109, 115, 113. Italics ours.
³⁷⁵ Thiselton, 'CAP', 133-135, 201; cf.: Thiselton, *2H*, 10, 120-121, cf.: 154-157, 244, 324-325, 348-349, 436-437; Thiselton, *NH*, 557-558; Thiselton, 'R-RH', 82-83; Jeanrond, 'R RH', 117; Thiselton, 'Parab', 455-457, cf.: 458-461; 468. Italics ours.

"*otherness*").³⁷⁶ We will return to this theme below.

(iii) Thiselton's *actual* notion of "present meaning", therefore, is much more complex than Lyons' pre-dialogic caricatures in relation to Thiselton's supposedly 'epistemologically solid' text or in relation to Thiselton's supposed fears concerning a supposedly "Fishian" notion of "infinitely fluid meaning". That is, for Thiselton, "present meaning" is actually a very complex matter that involves *both* stabilizing constraints (*some* of which come from the present-horizon corporate interpretative community, *some* of which come from the horizon of the text, and *some* of which come from elsewhere – see above) *and* dimensions of fluidity and/or plurality that are *neither* arbitrary *nor* infinite but that are, *rather*, related to the ways in which variable dynamic relationships between two sets of horizons, or between two sets of historical particularities, change diachronically as historical horizons expand in an eschatologically-qualified way (see Chapter 5).³⁷⁷

This point, (iii.i), therefore, leads us to reject a purely Fishian stance – the stance that Lyons seems to follow when he is wearing his Fishian "hat" - in which present meaning is constructed both *in and of* the present.

That is, for Fish, and so presumably for Lyons (who wants to treat 'the Bible' as a "'Fishian'" text(s)), *"meaning"* is "determined" by a given 'interpretative' 'community' in its 'context'.³⁷⁸ For Fish, readers' pre-existing pre-cognitive 'verbal and mental categories' *alone* constitute the *'content'* of "perceived" 'entities'; for Fish, "perceptions" only *'seem'* to relate to 'the' external 'world'; for Fish, unconscious 'primary' 'interpretative activities' *alone* "produce" 'what is perceived to be "in the text"'.³⁷⁹ For Fish, authorial *'intention'* is not accessible and so cannot 'yield' a *'correct'* 'literal reading' of 'a text'. For Fish, 'illocutionary force... will already have been determined' by the *readers'* 'context'. Similarly, for Lyons, 'any constraints' - on present meaning - 'are... either internal [*sic*] to the community or the products [cf. 'construction'] of interpretation'.³⁸⁰

Admittedly, if taken out of its context, the 'either internal... or' choice posited within this assertion by Lyons might at first seem to leave an opening for "external" textual constraints. However, Lyons' stated desire to be "Fishian" – which he highlights several times in *this* (as opposed to his Barthian-Childsian) context of discussion - implies that we have to interpret this 'either internal... or' choice in a *Fishian* way. And, for Fish, "perceptions" only *'seem'* to relate to 'the' external 'world'. Thus, the 'or' option denoted by the 'either internal... or' choice posited in Lyons' assertion here must - (given Lyons' often-stated desire to be Fishian – at least in *this* context of discussion) - simply refer to other *present-horizon constraints* that the present-horizon *community* – possibly in dialogue with other

---

³⁷⁶ Thiselton, 'Parab', 455-457, cf.: 458-461; 468; cf. Thiselton, *NH*, 540-546. Italics ours.

³⁷⁷ Lyons, *C&E*, 114; cf. our preceding argument. Italics ours.

³⁷⁸ Fish, 'NC', 268; cf.: 271, 276-277; cf. Fish, 'Intro', 11; cf. Lyons, *C&E*, 115. Italics ours.

³⁷⁹ Fish, 'NC', 271, 273. Italics ours.

³⁸⁰ Fish, 'NC', 280-281, 283, 284, 285, 292; cf. Lyons, *C&E*, 111. Second italics Fish's, remaining italics ours.

present-horizon *communities* - constructs.[381]

In our view, however, Thiselton rightly argues that: it is the *relationships between* the two sets of horizons that constitute present meaning, where these relationships are constructed by communities *in* the present, but where these relationships – and hence present meaning - can still be significantly *shaped* – at least in part – by the *past* meanings of texts. That is, for Thiselton, present meaning is a matter of relationships between two sets of horizons, and has a diachronic, dialectic, dynamic, and dialogical ground. For Thiselton, even an understanding-event between two sets of horizons that are both "present-day" horizons still presupposes this same diachronic, dialectic, dynamic, and dialogical ground since, in Thiselton's estimate, mature understanding is *never* instantaneous. For Thiselton, even the *'Einverständnis'* ("common understanding") pertaining to 'a close-knit family' presupposes a shared world that only becomes established *over time* (see Chapters 4, 5, and 6). For Thiselton, then, our historically-conditioned present horizons do *not necessarily prevent* the transformative '"operative influence"' of ancient textual language from becoming effective during our interpretative activities in the present. Rather, in Thiselton's estimate, our historically conditioned present horizons are *partly formed by* the present '"operative influence"' of textual language from the past. In part, for Thiselton, that is what historical conditioning *is*. Lyons, though, when wearing his Fishian hat, plays on the word "construct" (and its cognates) to subsume 'historical' '"operative influence"', and *this aspect* of the hermeneutical circle, beneath his notion of "meaning-construction".[382]

In this respect, we need not repeat our earlier points about confusing the *work* of meaning-construction with the *shape* or *content* of meaning-constructs. However, by way of providing an illustration that elucidates Thiselton's stance, then if I "construct" a very old purchased shelf unit, then it does not mean that I necessarily "construct" its design-content or instructions. No matter how old the shelf unit is, what I *do* is *still very* influenced by what comes *in* the box, or by what D. Patte calls – in the context of biblical hermeneutics - 'a plurality of textual constraints'.[383]

(iii.ii) Lyons would no doubt respond by arguing that since Fish allows for the 'plain experience' of '"hermeneutical change"' (on the grounds of '"hermeneutical commonality"'), then Thiselton is supposedly wrong to contend that a 'Fishian' stance necessarily leads to an idolatrous self-affirming prohibition of 'hermeneutical growth' as though the 'Fishian' community shut out other communities so as to "attend" '"carefully"' only to itself (C.L. Blomberg's words,

---

[381] Lyons, *C&E*, 111; cf. 108-115; cf. Fish, 'NC', 271, 273. Italics ours.

[382] Thiselton, *2H*, 44-45; cf. Thiselton, 'NH', 311; cf. Lyons, *C&E*, 111. Sixth italics Thiselton's, others ours.

[383] See, Thiselton, *2H*, 44-45, cf.: 51-84, 234-251; 304-326; cf.: Patte, D., 'Textual Constraints, Ordinary Readings, and Critical Exegesis: An Androcritical Perspective', *Sem* 62 (1993), 59, 76. Italics ours.

cited by Lyons), or was *"purely reader-oriented"* (C.L. Blomberg's words, cited by Lyons), or turned 'gospel' proclamation into "preaching" that each community should "'construct'" its own 'gospel' 'plucked out of the air'.[384]

However, in relation to our earlier analytical interpretation of Lyons' critique of Thiselton in *Canon and Exegesis* (and we are *not* compromising ourselves theoretically by acknowledging that we have "interpreted" this critique!) it will be noticed that, in this interpretation, we have inserted the term, "present-horizon", into our rendering of Lyons' notions of 'the possibility' of "present-horizon" inter-community 'communication' and of 'the possibility' of "present-horizon" "'hermeneutical change'". We have made this insertion because Lyons (when wearing his Fishian hat) still seems *to discount* the notion that *past* horizons can contribute to the shape of *present* horizons *through texts*. In our view, this point persists as a problem with Lyons' stance despite the fact that Lyons *potentially allows* any "present-horizon" community's "constructed texts" and 'assumptions' to become a "present-horizon" 'critique' of *any other* "present-horizon" community's "constructed texts" and 'assumptions'.[385]

That is, the Fishian side of Lyons' discussion seemed to allow "'hermeneutical change'" through *direct challenge from 'God'*, through *a community's own constructed "Bible"* (which could not be constructed from components that were from the historical past, since these components would be epistemologically inaccessible according to a Fishian argument), or through *challenge from other present-horizon communities who may have constructed Bibles* (which also could not be constructed from components that were from the historical past, since these components would be epistemologically inaccessible according to a Fishian argument).[386]

However, Lyons' discussion *did not* seem to allow "'hermeneutical change'" through the "'operative influence'" of *past* biblical language pertaining to *past* New Testament communities. That is, when Lyons is wearing his Fishian hat (*it is different when he is wearing his Barthian-Childsian hat*), he seems to imply that one's interpretative community could not be challenged, say, by *St. Paul's* language. To us, though, this side of Lyons' thinking again leaves us with the historical, epistemological, and linguistic dichotomies that we noted earlier in relation to his Oxford article.[387]

For Thiselton, however, as we have seen, neither the historical conditioning of texts nor the historical conditioning of readers takes place in some *alien* reality. Rather, for Thiselton, historical conditioning – of whatever kind - always takes place in *human* history. That is, we saw how Thiselton argued that - in *any* unified hermeneutical theory – the historical conditioning of "the historically finite" is grounded in the inter-related overlapping mutually-qualifying historico-philosophical (and theological) criteria of the unity, relationalities, dynamic

---

[384] Lyons, *C&E*, 109, 112, 111, 113, 114. Lyons' italics.
[385] Lyons, *C&E*, 111; cf.: 112, 113, 114. Italics ours.
[386] Lyons, *C&E*, 114-115; cf.: 112, 114, 263. Italics ours.
[387] Thiselton, *2H*, 44-45; cf. Lyons, *C&E*, 112-114; cf. 111. Italics ours.

processes, particularities, continuities, subjectivities, inter-subjectivities, fallenness, and redemption of historical reality (or creation). In other words, for Thiselton, historical horizons (including *past, present, and future* horizons) are always *related* and subject to *fusion*, but are always sufficiently *different* to one another to allow for *distancing* through comparisons related to juxtapositional contrasts. For Thiselton, historical self-involvement and historical objectivity are both potentially progressively possible and real.

Lyons' Fishian (if not his Barthian-Childsian) stance, however, presupposes that "understanding the past" (at least through texts) is *not a potential aspect of* "understanding *in* the present", which implies that these two dimensions of understanding (in Lyons' Fishian epistemology) must somehow be "unrelated", which constitutes an *epistemological* dichotomy. However, as we saw earlier, since the grammar of "understanding" is inseparable from considerations concerning that which is being understood, then Lyons is thereby unwittingly implying that "the past" (at least in relation to texts) is *unrelated* to "the present", which constitutes a *historical* dichotomy.

This aspect of the Fishian side of Lyons approach implies that if Lyons ever wishes to argue that God's creation is a unity (not a uniformity), and that history is therefore a unity (not a uniformity), then he has just contradicted himself. *At the very least* he has exempted "texts" from this created historical unity (not uniformity). That is, Lyons' Fishian stance (as opposed to his Barthian-Childsian stance) actually presupposes a historical dichotomy – despite what he may at some point *wish* to affirm about the unity (not uniformity) of God's creation.

(iii.iii) Stepping back for a moment, then what we have been trying to say is that history (or creation) is, in its "becoming", a dynamic unity (not uniformity) in which historical particularities, and hence historical horizons, are *related* to one-another in complex and changing ways that allow for degrees of *a posteriori* historical (not *a priori* formal or idealist) continuity – a kind of continuity that we may define here as consisting of "ontologically" (provided this term is sublated out of its idealist uses and into our historical use) stable realities that, nevertheless, as such, do not preclude, but are constituted in part by, historical movements.

The unity and relationalities of history (or, indeed, of creation) mean that those historical differences and particularities that remain alongside - and that also build together to form – these stable realities or continuities are not radically dissociated from one-another, even though distinctions remain. Thus, an understanding of selves in the present horizon is not a matter that is *entirely* different to understanding past horizons or to understanding textual horizons from the past. The two sets of horizons are always *related* - if still distinct.

That is, for Lyons (when wearing his Fishian hat) to presuppose that textual content and/or function from the past are "completely epistemologically inaccessible" is also to presuppose that, at a historical-ontological level, past horizons are "radically different", or "radically dissociated", from present horizons.

However, again, *first*, this Fishian presupposition transgresses the criteria of the unity (not uniformity), relationalities, continuities, and dynamic dialectic movements or processes of created historical reality (amongst other criteria).

And again, *second*, since the notion of a "radical dissociation" of historical horizons from one another is a falsehood grounded in a false set of premises (as we have argued in our earlier responses to Derrida and to criticisms of the later Barthes), then the notion of the "death" of certain historical realities – such as God (though God is more than "historical", if not less), authors, subjects, selves, *and any other historical reality that presupposes historical unity, relationality, continuity, and dialectic movements or processes* – is *also* a falsehood grounded in a false set of premises. That is, in post-structuralist approaches, a *right* attack on "formal" ahistorical idealist metaphysics has *wrongly* become an attack on *historical* unity, relationalities, continuities, and dynamic dialectic movements or processes – and so on.

In other words, Lyons' Fishian thinking seems, unwittingly, to an extent, to presuppose – partly – an inherited broadly post-structuralist pre-understanding and its attendant theoretical problems.

And so, we need only allude to our earlier arguments: Lyons provides no engagement with the philosophy of history to *demonstrate* that past horizons, or at least past textual horizons, are (supposedly) unrelated to present horizons.

(iii.iv) Lyons, of course, might argue that he could not in fact access the texts of the philosophers of history in order to justify his Fishian stance. In fact, as we saw, Lyons argued that, in his view, Thiselton's appeal to "philosophy" 'to justify' (what Lyons saw as being Thiselton's) objectivism was 'circular' – an attempt to step 'outside of... interpretation' so as 'to justify' stepping 'outside of... interpretation'. In Lyons' argument, further, Thiselton's supposed "stepping outside of interpretation" in order to appeal to philosophy so as to justify the "objectivistic accessibility of objective texts" was an "inconsistency" that even P.R. 'Noble' avoided.[388]

Of course, though, it is Lyons' *Fishian* (as opposed to his Barthian-Childsian) argument that is circular. Indeed, this "argument" is actually a *circular assertion* based on an *impossible historical dichotomy*. In effect, Lyons seems to argue: "Fish is right: the historical past is dissociated from the present; therefore we cannot access the texts of the philosophers of history so as to disprove the premise that the historical past is dissociated from the present; hence Fish is right". Or, we could say that Lyons seems to argue: "Fish is right; hence the past cannot address the present through texts; hence Thiselton's 'community' (in dialogue with other present-horizon communities) *alone* shapes his interpretations; hence Fish is right".

By contrast, as we have seen, Thiselton claims only to "interpret" philosophers' texts, and claims only to "interpret" Scripture. It is just that Thiselton's epistemology allows that interpretation can gain *a degree* of objective truthfulness. Unless *creation* is split into radically dissociated mutually-alien "realities" (cf. a theological perspective); or unless historical unity (not uniformity) is split into radically dissociated "fleeting moments" (cf. a philosophical perspective); or unless

---

[388] Lyons, *C&E*, 111; cf. 88-89.

the space-time continuum is catastrophically ruptured (cf. a scientific perspective), then interpretation *must potentially* be able to yield *a degree* of objective truthfulness.

As we have already seen, Thiselton readily acknowledges that we still only see "from below, from within history", and not from some Archimedean point "above" history, or from the eschatological "end-point" of history. But *neither* an Archimedean point *nor* an eschatological "end-point" are required for us to *begin* to interpret "truly". Epistemologically, one can *potentially* always *begin* to understand "the other" regardless of whether they are "past" or "present" – even if interpretative impediments (as opposed to hypostatized epistemological barriers) *may* prohibit such understanding. The "other" does not become unintelligible simply because of *the passage of time* - for space and time, and everything within them, are a *created unified (though not uniform) historical continuum*. Lyons' implicit assertion of radically dissociated horizons, therefore, as we have already said, seems to uncritically accept post-structuralist influences at the level of pre-understanding.

Of course, (iii.v), Lyons would object to our points above by arguing that, in his section on Childs' notion of "'referentiality'", he stood *with* Childs *against* those who "'in principle'" banished historical-textual reference.[389] Our response to this objection, however, is to question whether Lyons' *Barthian-Childsian* epistemology is at all compatible with his *Fishian* epistemology. This leads on to our next point.

(c) Lyons often compromises his own 'Fishian' epistemology[390] - *either* falling towards a more "Thiseltonian" stance, *or* falling towards a Barthian-Childsian epistemology of revelation that is less consistent with a Fishian stance than Lyons would have us believe. Thus, it is not *Thiselton* who has to compromise his thinking in order to account for the four legitimate "hermeneutical concerns" that Lyons highlights (see above), but *Lyons*.

That is, at times, Lyons seems to lapse into more performative self-contradictions of the kind we highlighted in relation to his Oxford article, such that he seems to break out of his own "Fishian non-foundationalism" versus "objectivist foundationalism" straightjacket.

Thus, (i), Lyons sees *Thiselton's* 'interests' as corrupted by (cf. 'driven by') "'foundationalist'" traditionalism (cf. 'historical and theological necessity'). Conversely, Lyons clearly *recommends* his *own* 'interests' as "right", where these 'interests' include 'the desire simply to offer a valid hermeneutical account of *plain experience*'. First, however, to us, Lyons' stance in this context of discussion looks empirical and evidentialist, rather than "Fishian". Second, Lyons' assignment of "rank" to 'interests' like this looks *metacritical,* which is not "Fishian" either. Notably the privileging of one set of interests over another *on objective grounds* like this epistemologically and *performatively contradicts* Lyons' immediately preceding point about how the relativity of different 'interests' *precludes* the privileging of 'theological' notions of "full reading" over and against less 'theological' notions of

---

[389] Lyons, *C&E*, 69; cf. 68-71. Italics ours.
[390] Lyons, *C&E*, 111; cf. 114-115.

"full reading".[391] That is, at this point, it would seem as though Lyons is *beginning* to move away from a Fishian stance and towards a more Thiseltonian stance.

Moving on then, (ii), in Lyons' estimate, he has 'demonstrated' that the 'content' of Fish's texts is other than that which is perceived by Thiselton. Surely, though, at this point, Lyons' notion of "demonstration" contradicts what we saw earlier to be a Fishian stance, in which readers' pre-existing pre-cognitive 'verbal and mental categories' constituted the *'content'* of "perceived" 'entities'. For Fish, "perceptions" only *'seem'* to relate to 'the' external 'world'. For Fish, unconscious 'primary' 'interpretative activities' *alone* "produce" 'what is perceived to be "in the text"'. For Fish, 'content' is never 'independent of' or 'prior to interpretation': for Fish, when 'a community' "changes", textual 'content' "changes", such that no accessible 'irreducible content… survives the sea change of situations'. And yet Lyons' '"Fishian" response to Thiselton' claims to *"demonstrate"* that the 'content' of Fish's texts is other than that which is "perceived" by Thiselton – which means that Lyons has committed *another performative self-contradiction!* Of course, further, Lyons' "demonstration" could not be objectivist in Lyons' view, for at another point Lyons says that he *'cannot* demonstrate' 'that raw data exists'. Lyons' "demonstration", then, *must* be provisional, corrigible, partial, and reflect, in Lyons' own language, 'the need for some form of critical distancing'. This point, though, looks very like what we have seen that Thiselton *actually* says (which is nothing like Lyons' "raw data" caricature of Thiselton). Not that we wish to be critical of Lyons' tendencies to slip from a Fishian epistemology towards a Thiseltonian epistemology. On the contrary, this situation is most encouraging![392]

Moving on, (iii), and developing our earlier point to do with Thiselton's careful distinctions between the notion of a "plurality of legitimate meanings" (though, actually, this notion is six-fold in Thiselton's thinking, as we have seen) and the notion of an "unnecessary arbitrary meaning-expansion", then we should observe that Lyons seems to conflate these two notions, despite the fact that they presuppose *different* epistemologies, as follows.

Thus, (iii.i), *on the one hand*, Lyons argues that 'historical criticism' serves as a "balancing" 'source' in the face of the 'cultural relativity' that results from different communities 'balancing… sources of illumination' 'differently'. That is, again, Lyons argues that 'the cultural relativity' resulting from different communities 'balancing the sources of illumination' 'differently' *itself* 'needs to be balanced against the historical text', in line with 'the need for some form of critical distancing', and in line with an 'emphasis on the canonical shape as restrictive'. That is, Lyons argues that 'one must do justice to the texts as historical

---

[391] Lyons, *C&E*, 109; cf. 108; cf. Thiselton, *NH*, 316-317, 549. Italics ours.
[392] Lyons, *C&E*, 112; cf. 111, 77; cf.: Fish, 'NC', 271-272, 273; cf. 268, 274, 277; Fish, 'Intro', 11. Italics ours (Lyons' italics removed from the word, "demonstrate", and ours added to the word "cannot", in the phrase *'cannot* demonstrate'; italicized word *"demonstrate"* is from a slightly different point in Lyons' text - italics ours on this word).

witnesses'.[393]

In Lyons' view, afterall, it is the likes of 'Yale'-style biblical hermeneutics, the 'New Criticism', 'fully a-historical' "structuralism" - and other such schools influenced by anthropocentric or 'humanistic' strands of 'Western' and 'eurocentric thought' - who *"'in principle'" disallow* the *genuine biblical* 'referents' or "truths" - whether "'divine'"/"'revelatory'" or "'historical'" - from *having the status of being* biblical 'referents' or "truths" (even if such schools still allow these "truths" to "exist extra-textually"). Lyons, like Childs, wishes to *distance* himself from humanists who wish to stop "'interpretation'" from "interpreting" 'truth'. Lyons does *not* wish to "redefine" "'interpretation'" as purely literary, or as 'fully a-historical'; and he does *not* wish to "define" the biblical texts *themselves* as the primary 'referent', or as *solely* 'non-history', or as *solely* 'a-historical story', or as *solely* "'historical fiction'".[394]

This side of Lyons' argumentation seems to favor the notion of what Thiselton would call a "plurality of legitimate meanings" and, again, *begins* to lean towards a Thiseltonian viewpoint. Such a "plurality of legitimate meanings" lends to any associated uses of phrases like "(a) conflict of interpretations" a *certain kind of grammar* that is broadly acceptable to Thiselton.

(iii.ii) *On the other hand*, however - *despite* Lyons' argument concerning the ways in which 'historical criticism' serves as a "balancing" 'source' in the face of the 'cultural relativity' that results from different communities 'balancing the sources of illumination' 'differently' - Lyons *then* seems to argue that 'historical criticism' is *itself* then offset (or unbalanced from its "balancing of differing balances" role) by a "conflict of interpretations" (our phrase, after Ricoeur and Thiselton) between 'a series of "thin texts" that then function as' different "Bibles".[395]

*This* "conflict of interpretations", though, in *this* side of Lyons' thinking, *has a different grammar*: that is, *this* "conflict of interpretations" is not the product simply of different readers or reading-situations or of interpretative impediments resulting from such factors as a dearth of historical sources or the referential complexity of the Bible. On the contrary, in relation to Lyons' "Bibles", then 'the controlling function(s) of the canonical shape(s)' is 'defined by the interpretative community's assumptions'. And communities are swayed more by 'momentary rhetorical persuasiveness... and... general attractiveness' 'than' by a 'correct application of a rigorous methodology' when it comes to the 'acceptability' of different "interpretations". This phenomenon is not at all seen as being a *problem* by Lyons, however, but as being *'the real question* about the acceptability of [his]... particular interpretation' of the Sodom narrative. It is almost as if Lyons says that the 'real question' concerning the 'acceptability' of his work is *not* related to its "methodological rigor", but more related to how much it is *liked by others*. That is, Lyons has turned an *empirical observation* - to do with how different communities

---

[393] Lyons, *C&E*, 71; cf. 68-71; cf. 77; cf. 266; cf. 270. Italics ours.

[394] Lyons, *C&E*, 71; cf. 70, 69; cf. 275. Italics ours.

[395] Lyons, *C&E*, 71; cf. 68-71; cf. 77; cf. 266; cf. 270; cf. 263. Italics ours.

interpret texts differently - into a *hermeneutical axiom or goal*. This stance, however, now looks much more Fishian (though there is still a nod towards historical "'referentiality'").[396]

Afterall, Lyons *doesn't* wish to be grouped with 'Western' and 'eurocentric' 'humanistic' strands – whether "rationalistic" or "demythologizing"; or whether "distortedly" 'historical-critical' in the sense of being preoccupied with an anthropocentric 'historicity' that over-stresses "'ostensive'" "'correspondence'" and "'absolute historical coherence'".[397]

And afterall, Lyons *does* wish to remain 'Fishian' and promote 'a "Fishian"… Bible' and 'A "Fishian" Response to Thiselton'.[398]

And, again, as we have said more than once, for Fish, readers' pre-existing pre-cognitive 'verbal and mental categories' constitute the *'content'* of "perceived" 'entities'. For Fish, "perceptions" only *'seem'* to relate to 'the' external 'world'. For Fish, unconscious 'primary' 'interpretative activities' alone "produce" 'what is perceived to be "in the text"'.[399] For Fish, 'content' is never 'independent of' or 'prior to interpretation': for Fish, when 'a community' "changes", textual 'content' "changes", such that no accessible 'irreducible content… survives the sea change of situations'.[400]

That is, *this* side of Lyons' thinking seems to favor not what *Thiselton* would call a "plurality of legitimate meanings", but what Thiselton would call an "unnecessary arbitrary meaning-expansion"; and so *this* side of Lyons' thinking is much more *non*-Thiseltonian.

In other words, (iii.iii), *sometimes* Lyons seems to argue for notions of present meaning (to use Thiselton's language) that are completely community-determined and more or less unrelated to textual-historical reference. In Thiselton's view, this scenario would lead to an "unnecessary arbitrary meaning-expansion". At *other times*, however, Lyons seems to argue for notions of present meaning (Thiselton's phrase) that presuppose biblical historical constraints, and that therefore would more likely be associated with a "plurality of legitimate meanings". *This* particular line of thought would link to Lyons' comments earlier (in his section on Childs' notion of "referentiality") about how genuine problems to do with historical evidence, or with a lack of it, could generate uncertainties to do with interpretative outcomes. *This* particular line of thought, however, would also be more true to what *Thiselton* thinks than to what *Fish* thinks – and so constitutes *another performative self-contradiction* by Lyons, given his desire to be "Fishian".

(iv) Moving on then, at another point, Lyons seems to use *four* words beginning with "a" ('acquisition', 'available', 'agreement' and 'aware'), in a desperate attempt to avoid using *one* word beginning with "a" (i.e. "access"). Thus, we saw that

---

[396] Lyons, *C&E*, 69; cf. 70; cf. 68; cf. 114; cf. 270; cf. 266, 263. Italics ours.
[397] Lyons, *C&E*, 69, 70.
[398] Lyons, *C&E*, 111, 115.
[399] Fish, 'NC', 271, 273. Italics ours.
[400] Fish, 'NC', 268, 271-272, 274, 277; cf. Fish, 'Intro', 11.

instead of speaking about "accessing shared frames of reference", Lyons (after Fish) spoke of 'the acquisition of' 'available' '"rubrics"' (i.e. '"shared"' '"bas[e]s for agreement"') of which parties in '"agreement"' are 'aware'!⁴⁰¹

For Lyons, then, 'Reality with a capital R' is *not* accessible, but '"rubrics"' *are* accessible. For Lyons, of course, there is no contradiction here since his notion of 'Reality with a capital R' has the connotation of "objectivistic access to unmediated raw data", whilst his '"rubrics"' are an aspect of agreed interpreted '"reality"' with a small '"r"'.⁴⁰²

In our view, however, Lyons' notion of 'Reality with a capital R' must have ontological as well as epistemological connotations. *What* could it *be* that Lyons says we cannot access objectivistically? Certainly, Lyons' notion of 'God' involves the connotation of a '"Reality"' 'beyond interpretation'. Lyons' notion of 'Reality with a capital R', however, must also connote "historical reality", or else it would be an idealist notion. Thus, Lyons' notion of 'Reality with a capital R' connotes 'God' and "historical reality", or else it is some kind of supra-historical idealist notion.⁴⁰³ We will expand on this point further, as follows.

Thus, (iv.i), if the *ontological* grammar of Lyons' notion of 'Reality with a capital R' is taken to relate to 'God', then the *epistemological* grammar of Lyons' notion of 'Reality with a capital R' changes from being "Fishian" to being "Barthian" in our view, and thereby compromises Lyons' desire for a fully-fledged "Fishian" biblical hermeneutics. That is, that which "*cannot* be accessed" becomes that which "cannot be *anthropocentrically* accessed, but which can be 'known' '*by faith*'" (to use Lyons' language).⁴⁰⁴

Since, for Fish, "perceptions" only '*seem*' to relate to 'the' external 'world', where unconscious 'primary' 'interpretative activities' alone "produce" 'what is perceived to be '"in the text"', then a Fishian notion of "perception" seemingly cannot be involved in "knowing God by faith".⁴⁰⁵ Thus, if Lyons were completely consistent with Fish, he would be forced to set a Fishian notion of "perception" over and against "knowing God by faith". Alternatively, if Lyons were completely consistent with his section on Childs' notion of '"referentiality"', a Fishian notion of "perception" would then be demoted, *on Lyons' own Childsian terms*, as being unfit for approaching 'Biblical Theology' due to its 'Western', 'modern', anthropocentric framework. But how could Lyons then still consider the *biblical* texts to be '"Fishian"'?⁴⁰⁶

That is, there is *another performative self-contradiction* in Lyons' thinking - between desiring to follow Barth and Childs in liberating the Scriptures *from*

---

⁴⁰¹ Lyons, *C&E*, 112-113; cf. 111. Italics ours.
⁴⁰² Lyons, *C&E*, 111; cf. 112-113. Italics ours.
⁴⁰³ Lyons, *C&E*, 111; cf. 114-115. Italics ours.
⁴⁰⁴ Lyons, *C&E*, 111; cf. 114-115; cf. 70-71; cf. 68-69. Italics Lyons' on '*by faith*', others ours.
⁴⁰⁵ Fish, 'NC', 271, 273; cf. Lyons, *C&E*, 114-115; cf. 70-71. Italics ours.
⁴⁰⁶ Fish, 'NC', 271, 273; cf. Lyons, *C&E*, 114-115. Italics ours.

anthropocentric interpretation on the one hand, and desiring to view the Scriptures *as* Fishian on the other hand.[407] Furthermore, an epistemological split emerges between a Fishian notion of perception (by which we can still perceive "'rubrics'") and whatever mode of perception is involved in "knowing God by faith".[408] (We will return to this epistemological dichotomy when we examine Pannenberg's criticism of a Barthian epistemology of revelation below).

(iv.ii) If the *ontological* grammar of Lyons' notion of 'Reality with a capital R' is taken to be inaccessible "historical reality", then it remains for Lyons to show us how "'rubrics'" - which he sees as being "accessible" (though he goes to great lengths to avoid using the word "access" and its cognates) – are *not* inaccessible "historical reality".[409]

If Lyons' answer is to turn to *epistemology* by saying that 'Reality with a capital R' is "uninterpreted history" (and is thus inaccessible) whereas "'rubrics'" are 'interpreted history' (and are thus accessible), then he is distinguishing between "uninterpreted history" and "interpreted history" and is still left with the task of showing how "interpreted history" is a different kind of historically contingent "other" to "uninterpreted history". That is, if we apply a Fishian notion of perception strictly, then "interpreted history" is really just another *inaccessible* "historical reality" that could only ever become accessible as "interpreted 'interpreted history'". This scenario, however, would make "'rubrics'" inaccessible, not accessible, against what we "plainly" 'experience' (to use Lyons' language). In our view, even if Lyons follows Fish faithfully at this point, then Fish's epistemology remains dichotomous and self-contradictory, and so does that of Lyons.[410]

If Lyons' answer is to turn to *ontology* by saying that "'rubrics'" are *present* "historical reality", and are thus "accessible", whereas 'Reality with a capital R' is *past* "historical reality", and is thus "inaccessible", then he has projected splits into created historical unity, since the grammar of the notion of "understanding" is dependant upon that which is being understood. Again, even if Lyons follows Fish faithfully here, then Fish's (and thus Lyons') epistemology remains dichotomous and self-contradictory.[411]

In other words, when Lyons allows that *some* notion of "reality" is accessible (i.e. "'rubrics'") but that *some* notion of "reality" is inaccessible (i.e. 'Reality with a capital R'), he is committing *another performative self-contradiction* and, also, is really still submitting to epistemological dichotomies that necessarily project absolute dichotomies onto historical reality or truth – whether these latter dichotomies are between God and history; or between the historical past and the historical present; or between "historical otherness as prior interpretations of history" and "historical

---

[407] Lyons, *C&E*, 68-71; cf. 114-115. Italics ours.
[408] Lyons, *C&E*, 114-115; cf. 112-113; cf. Fish, 'NC', 271, 273.
[409] Lyons, *C&E*, 111; cf. 112-113. Italics ours.
[410] Lyons, *C&E*, 111; cf. 112-113; cf. 109; cf. Fish, 'NC', 271, 273. Italics ours.
[411] Lyons, *C&E*, 112-113; cf. 111; cf. Fish, 'NC', 271, 273. Italics ours.

otherness *other than* prior interpretations of history"; or between "historical otherness as the contents of perception" and "historical otherness *other than* the contents of perception".[412]

Really, then, Fish and Lyons, despite what they *wish* to say, are in practice forced to work with the same non-objectivistic-but-nevertheless-real access ("acquiring available agreed awareness") to real historical contingency ("'rubrics'" in this case) as everybody else, but they disguise this fact by a change of language that reflects a dualistic defining of an unknowable 'Reality with a capital R' as being more real and less accessible than historical contingency. Of course, though, this "more real but unknowable Reality" then *potentially* begins to look unhistorical, empty, and philosophically idealist. This point reinforces our suspicion – noted earlier - that Lyons has ultimately failed to leave idealism behind. Indeed, Pannenberg notes the "connection" 'Heidegger' makes between, on the one hand, his own view in which 'being and nothingness coinhere' and, on the other hand, '*modern lyric poetry* and its "empty transcendence"', where Pannenberg sees 'a similar attitude' in 'Barth and Bultmann'.[413]

(v) Taking our points "(i)-(iv)" together, then we noted earlier that Lyons concluded that if *Thiselton* were to 'account' for Lyons' four legitimate hermeneutical 'interests', 'plain experiences', or concerns *consistently*, then Thiselton would be compromising his own "foundationalism" (i.e. not 'remaining theoretically sound') and, like T.S. 'Kuhn' in Lyons' view, would be 'falling into non-foundationalism'. Now, however, it looks like it is *Lyons* who is beginning to "fall" from one stance to another, and as though it is *Lyons*' hermeneutics that are internally compromised and that are thus not 'remaining theoretically sound'.[414]

That is, it is not Thiselton who is falling towards a Fishian stance, but Lyons who is falling sometimes towards a non-Fishian Thiseltonian stance, or sometimes towards a non-Fishian Barthian-Childsian stance.

Caution is needed at this point, however, for it seems to us that the main factor that generates the internal inconsistencies in Lyons' framework is not so much a move towards Thiselton's hermeneutics, but Lyons' desire to endorse *both* a modified Barthian-Childsian epistemology of revelation and theological hermeneutics *and* a Fishian approach to texts. That is, we are not as convinced as Lyons seems to be that a Fishian hermeneutical framework and a modified Barthian-Childsian epistemology of revelation and theological hermeneutics are mutually compatible.[415] Before we even consider this issue of incompatibility, however, we should note the problems that Pannenberg and Thiselton raise in relation to a Barthian epistemology of revelation – as follows.

---

[412] Lyons, *C&E*, 112-113; cf. 111; cf. Fish, 'NC', 271, 273. Italics ours.

[413] Lyons, *C&E*, 112-113; cf. 111; cf. our response to Lyons' Oxford article above; cf. Pannenberg, W., *Basic Questions in Theology. Collected Essays, Volume 2* (trans. G.H. Kehm; Philadelphia: Fortress Press, 1971), 198. Third italics Pannenberg's, other italics ours.

[414] Lyons, *C&E*, 114, 111, 109, 108, 86. Italics ours.

[415] Lyons, *C&E*, 114-115.

(d) The problems that Pannenberg highlights in relation to Barth's dialectical theology and its attendant epistemology of revelation have some relevance for our critical response to Lyons, particularly since Thiselton follows Pannenberg's critique of Barth at this point.[416]

In view of Lyons' stated commitment to a "postmodern" Barthian 'theology', then Lyons' Barthian notion of 'God' as 'a "Reality"' 'beyond interpretation' undoubtedly links to what Pannenberg describes as the 'early dialectical' 'emphasis' on 'the non-objectifiability of God'. For Pannenberg, however, there is 'no genuine solution to' the 'problem' of "speaking" about 'God' if 'God' is not "objectifiable": in Pannenberg's estimate, 'Bultmann retreated into existentialist interpretation' (though 'still' "spoke" "quasi-mythologically" about '"God's act"'), whilst 'Barth… effected a leap into the biblical supranaturalism of *Church Dogmatics*'. Lyons' notion of 'God' as 'a "Reality"' 'beyond interpretation', then, is his own version of Barthian 'biblical supranaturalism'.[417]

Thus, Pannenberg argues that 'Barth', for the most part, and followed by 'Gollwitzer', sharply divorced God's 'reality', God's 'self-disclosure', and 'the Christian proclamation' by '"the biblical writers"' (cf. 'Erich Schaeder's… *theocentrism*') from Feuerbach's 'anthropological' notion of 'man's self-deification', from 'all talk of God outside the Christian proclamation', or, from '"man's self-interpretation"'.[418]

Similarly, we noted how Lyons separated 'God' as 'a "Reality"' 'beyond interpretation' - which is a 'reality… only available through the testimony of Israel and the early Church' - from a '"Fishian"' stance that 'has nothing to say' about 'God' as 'a "Reality"' 'beyond interpretation'. And yet, a '"Fishian"' stance is (in Lyons' own view) still true to our 'plain experience' of inter-community 'communication' and of inter-community '"hermeneutical change"'. In our view, however, if a '"Fishian"' stance 'has nothing to say' about '*God*', then Fish must be talking about *us* – or to use Gollwitzer's language – Fish must be employing '"self-interpretation"'.[419]

Pannenberg also notes that 'Gollwitzer', like Barth, grounded 'the Christian proclamation' in the '"happening"' or '"concrete and contingent experience of being addressed by God"'.[420]

Similarly, again, we noted Lyons' appeal to 'plain experience'. That is, we noted above that, in line with a '"Fishian"' stance, Lyons seemed to argue that the Church's 'reading strategy' and *'prior'* 'shared understanding of God, the Scriptures

---

[416] Pannenberg, *BQ2*, 199-200; cf. 202-215; cf.: Pannenberg, W., *Basic Questions in Theology. Collected Essays, Volume 3* (trans. R.A. Wilson; Philadelphia: Fortress Press, 1973), 89, 99-102; Thiselton, 'H-O', 8; Thiselton, 'Exc', 12; Thiselton, 'TNI', 11; Chapters 3, and 6.

[417] Pannenberg, *BQ2*, 199; cf. Lyons, *C&E*, 114-115. Italics Pannenberg's.

[418] Pannenberg, *BQ2*, 203-204. Italics Pannenberg's.

[419] Pannenberg, *BQ2*, 203-204; cf. Lyons, *C&E*, 112, 114-115, 109; cf. 69; cf. 68-71; cf. our exposition above. Italics ours.

[420] Pannenberg, *BQ2*, 203-204.

and its tradition' constituted the *preconditional 'setting'* or *'basis' for "producing"*, (i), 'the Bible' as it is read now (or, more properly, in Lyons' view, "Bibles" as 'a series of "thin texts" that then function as Scripture within contextually differentiated Christian or Jewish communities') and, (ii), 'the' "Church's" 'concern' to proclaim 'the gospel' "truly". For Lyons, then, 'plain experience' would seem to be the ground since even the "first Bible" is presumably, in Lyons' estimate, still a "product" of the community that has "plainly experienced" God.[421]

In other words Lyons, *if* he were to remain true to both the Barthian and Fishian schools, would have to *sharply-separate* "theocentric biblical proclamation based in plain experience of divine address" *from* "anthropocentric interpretation based in plain experience that can 'say nothing' *about* 'God' and which must, therefore, be 'self-interpretation' – i.e. an addressing and 'hermeneutical changing' *of each other*".[422]

Pannenberg also notes that, for 'Gollwitzer', the Christian can only "assert", "'protest'", "'testify'", and "assure" that his or her proclamation is true and not another case of humanistic "'self-interpretation'" disguised in the 'theistic' terms of "'natural' theology'.[423]

Again, this point reminds us of Lyons' assertion that: *even though* a "'Fishian' stance 'has nothing to say' about 'God' as 'a "Reality"' 'beyond interpretation'; and *even though* Lyons cannot "test" or "independently" "'check'" biblical 'historical' "reference"; *he is nevertheless still free to assert* the existence of the 'God' who is 'beyond interpretation'.[424]

The problem, though, in Pannenberg's estimate, comes when *non-biblical* 'conceptions' of God – which, *for both Feuerbachian atheists and Barthians*, are mere humanistic 'self-interpretation' disguised in 'theistic' terms and are thus, for Barthians, 'out of the question' - are *also* "analogous" to 'biblical statements about God'. Then, in Gollwitzer's view, we have to take the latter 'simply on authority'.[425]

For Pannenberg, though, this stance is self-contradictory: for Pannenberg, if two 'theistic' assertions are broadly the same, then how can one be 'out of the question' whilst the other is "accepted" 'on authority'? In Pannenberg's estimate, such a stance is "authoritarian", 'irrational', and fails to escape Feuerbach's critique. Pannenberg asks: how could such a stance or view become "'binding upon society'"? Pannenberg answers that, since it could not, it becomes "'a matter of *private* belief. Genuine certainty is [then] excluded in faith because [from a Barthian viewpoint] there can be no objective criteria for the truth of the content of faith'". Pannenberg argues that 'if the idea of a personal God is everywhere else

---

[421] Lyons, *C&E*, 109; cf. 114-115; cf. 71, 69, 70, 263. Italics ours.
[422] Pannenberg, *BQ2*, 203-204; cf. Lyons, *C&E*, 114-115, 109; cf. 69; cf. 68-71; cf. our exposition above. Italics ours.
[423] Pannenberg, *BQ2*, 204; cf. Pannenberg, *BQ3*, 99-100.
[424] Lyons, *C&E*, 114-115; cf. 69; cf. 70, 71. Italics ours.
[425] Pannenberg, *BQ2*, 204. Italics ours.

judged to be a mythological self-interpretation of man', and if the same concepts appear in the biblical witness, then there is nothing to stop H. 'Braun's dissolution of the divine counterpart into existential relations, consistently thought through to the end', from leading to '"the end of theology"'.[426]

Putting it another way, Pannenberg writes that:

> In view of the extensive analogies between Christianity and the holy scriptures which it asserts as a testimony to revelation [on the one hand], and other religions and their documents [on the other hand], the postulate that in the case of Christianity we have something quite different, not a human religion but a divine revelation, could [to an atheist responding to a Barthian argument] only appear to be a bare assertion – and what is more a completely human assertion.[427]

As we saw in Chapter 3, Thiselton approves of Pannenberg's critique of Barth in which Pannenberg speaks of Barth's '"desperate evasion"' 'of Feuerbach's critique of religion' – a '"desperate evasion"' which, in Pannenberg's estimate, failed to relate 'Christian' truth 'to all truth', 'including philosophy and the sciences'. For Pannenberg and Thiselton, then, 'Christian' truth must relate 'to all truth' because '"God"… is the ground of all truth', as is evident, in Pannenberg's estimate, from '"the abundance of analogies between biblical and non-biblical concepts of God"'. For Pannenberg and Thiselton, therefore: to affirm 'Christianity and the Holy Scriptures' as true, one must *also* affirm that certain *extra-biblical* notions of God and of religion (from 'the history of religions' more broadly) are true. For Pannenberg and Thiselton, this argument is valid because certain *extra-biblical* notions of God and of religion overlap with, and are in agreement with, 'Christianity and the Holy Scriptures'. For Pannenberg and Thiselton, this line of argument implies that 'Christian' 'truth' is perceived in the same way as all other 'truth', and is not some "supra-historical" 'truth' or some quasi idealist realm of 'Reality with a capital R' (to use Lyons' language) that is supposedly "known" through a different kind of "perception". For Pannenberg and Thiselton, 'this [line of argument] means rejecting "the authoritarianism of the 'self-authenticating' Word as well as the authoritarianism that masquerades under the guise of the 'Spirit'"'. That is, for Pannenberg and Thiselton, we must reject these two authoritarianisms that spring from a Barthian epistemology of revelation. For Pannenberg and Thiselton, this rejection of authoritarianism 'means acknowledging the positive role of reason [in *Pannenberg's* sense of the term "reason" – see Chapter 3 and earlier in the present chapter] in Christian theology'.[428]

We will address the issue of '"the authoritarianism that masquerades under the

---

[426] Pannenberg, *BQ2*, 204-205, 206. Italics Pannenberg's.

[427] Pannenberg, *BQ3*, 100-101.

[428] Thiselton, 'H-O', 8; cf.: Thiselton, 'Exc', 12; Thiselton, 'TNP', 11; Pannenberg, *BQ2*, 199; Pannenberg, *BQ3*, 100-101; Pannenberg, *BQ2*, 200; Lyons, *C&E*, 111. Italics ours.

guise of the 'Spirit'"' when we come to S. Woodman's critique of Thiselton, since Woodman seems to invoke something like Lyons' notion of 'plain experience' when it comes to discerning the Spirit's adjudication between different biblical interpretations. Returning to our response to Lyons, though, then we may now provisionally conclude that it seems 'plain' that Lyons potentially espouses an "'authoritarianism of the 'self-authenticating' Word'".[429]

That is, in our exegesis of Lyons' section on Childs' notion of "'referentiality'", we saw that Lyons followed R.R. Topping's defence of Childs' view according to which the Bible primarily "interprets" "'God'" and God's "actions" where - for Childs, Topping, and Lyons - "'God'" is a "'multi-dimensional… reality'" who "'*transcends*'" all "'historical'" "situations". For Topping and Lyons this point implied that the Bible '*necessarily*' reflected the "excessive" "'history'"-"obscuring" or "'non-historical'" "'representative'" "'modes of depiction'" "'of the testimony of faith'" (which reflect "'the revelatory activity of God in space and time'") - "'modes of depiction'" "'apart from which we have no independent access'" or "reference to" "'God'" and to God's past "actions".[430]

In our view, though, there seems to be an epistemological dichotomy here – i.e. between the truth of God and the truth of history - when Lyons, after Childs and Topping, sees "'the testimony of faith'" as '*necessarily*' employing "excessive" "'history'"-"obscuring" or "'non-historical'" "'representative'" "'modes of depiction'".[431] For Pannenberg (and Thiselton), by contrast, 'the self-revelation of God, according to the biblical witnesses, did not take place directly, after the fashion of a theophany, but indirectly, through God's historical acts'.[432] Of course, in Thiselton's view, it is impossible to speak of God without using "analogies" and "symbols".[433] But Topping (and hence Lyons) seems to go further when using clauses like, "'the excesses of the testimony of faith which *obscures history*'", or, "'the revelatory activity of God in space and time *necessarily* gives rise to non-historical modes of depiction'". It is as though Topping and Lyons, true to the Barthian tradition, are setting the truth of God and of revelatory 'theophany' *over and against* historical truth – which would then lead to an "'authoritarianism of the 'self-authenticating' Word'".[434] Of course, with Thiselton, we must maintain that the truth of God is *distinct* from that of history. But this distinction is sharpened into a dichotomy in 'dialectical theology', as we saw – additionally - in relation to the case

---

[429] Thiselton, 'H-O', 8; cf.: Thiselton, 'Exc', 12; Thiselton, 'TNI', 11; Lyons, *C&E*, 68-71; cf. 109; Woodman, 'UC', 3, 4-5, 9-10.

[430] Lyons, *C&E*, 68; cf. 71, 70, 69. First italics Lyons', second italics ours.

[431] Lyons, *C&E*, 69-70. Italics ours.

[432] Tupper, *TWP*, 80; cf.: Thiselton, 'H-O', 8; Thiselton, 'Exc', 12; Thiselton, 'TNI', 11.

[433] Thiselton, A.C., 'Myth, Mythology', in *The Zondervan Pictorial Encyclopedia of the Bible, Volume 4* (ed. M.C. Tenney; Grand Rapids, MI: Zondervan, 1975; written by 1973), 340-341.

[434] Lyons, *C&E*, 69; cf. Tupper, *TWP*, 80; cf. Thiselton, 'H-O', 8. Italics ours.

of Thiselton's responses to Bultmann (see Chapter 6).[435]

In summary, then, a Barthian epistemology of revelation has its problems according to Pannenberg and Thiselton. These problems, as we have tried to show, also pervade the parallel Barthian aspect of Lyons' approach. Specifically, these problems include at least three sets of dichotomies, which may now be summarized as follows.

The *first* Barthian dichotomy (which is theo-historico-epistemological) can be presented as: the *truth* of Christianity (God, God's 'revelation', the Bible, biblical 'salvation history') *versus* 'all' other *truth* (extra-biblical 'history', humanity, 'philosophy and the sciences', the history of religious theistic concepts 'in "natural" theology').[436]

This dichotomy *redefines the truth of God* as being unrelated to 'philosophy', to 'the sciences', and to '"non-biblical"' 'history'; for Pannenberg and Thiselton, however, '"God"' 'is' actually 'the ground of all truth'.[437] Moreover, this dichotomy *redefines the truth of God's revelation* as a 'theophany'; for Pannenberg and Thiselton, however, God is revealed 'indirectly, through God's historical acts'.[438] Furthermore, this dichotomy *redefines the truth of the Bible* as being unrelated to 'the history of religions'; for Pannenberg and Thiselton, however, biblical truth and 'the history of religions' clearly overlap with multiple '"analogies"'.[439] Finally, this dichotomy thus falsely defines Christianity's uniqueness in a way that is easily undermined by the "demythologizers", and leads to what Pannenberg calls '"the end of theology"'.[440]

The *second* Barthian dichotomy (which is epistemological) can be presented as: "knowledge *'only by faith'*"[441] as the 'irrational' "authoritarian" assertion or 'proclamation' of perceptions grounded in 'theophany' or 'plain experience' (of the truth of God via God's 'Spirit', of the truth of God's 'revelation' as '"a self-authenticating Word"')[442] *versus* "knowledge" as warranted belief through rational 'historical critical' testing of the perceptions of 'plain experience' against '"objective"' '"truth"'-'"criteria"' - this side of the dichotomy being demoted as being anthropocentric 'modern' '"reason"' (by Lyons) and as humanity's '"self-interpretation"' (by Gollwitzer). In Lyons' approach, sometimes, a 'Fishian' viewpoint *replaces* the notion of '"objective"' '"truth"'-'"criteria"' altogether.[443]

---

[435] Thiselton, *2H*, 224; cf. 223-226. Italics ours.
[436] Thiselton, 'H-O', 8; cf. Tupper, *TWP*, 80; cf. Pannenberg, *BQ3*, 99-100. Italics ours.
[437] Thiselton, 'H-O', 8. Italics ours.
[438] Tupper, *TWP*, 80; cf.: Thiselton, 'H-O', 8; Thiselton, 'Exc', 12; Thiselton, 'TNI', 11. Italics ours.
[439] Thiselton, 'H-O', 8; cf. Pannenberg, *BQ2*, 200. Italics ours.
[440] Pannenberg, *BQ2*, 204-206.
[441] Lyons, *C&E*, 114. First italics ours, second italics Lyons'.
[442] Pannenberg, *BQ2*, 205, 204; cf.: Thiselton, 'H-O', 8; Tupper, *TWP*, 80; Lyons, *C&E*, 109.
[443] Lyons, *C&E*, 70, 71; cf. 109, 111; cf. Pannenberg, *BQ2*, 205, 204. Italics ours.

This dichotomy *exalts* two "authoritarianisms": "'the authoritarianism that masquerades under the guise of the 'Spirit'"' and the "'authoritarianism of the 'self-authenticating' Word'".[444] Conversely, this dichotomy *either* restricts critical testing against "'objective'" "'truth'"-"'criteria'" to 'non-Christian' or non-revealed 'truth', *or*, when *sometimes* sharpened still further, as in Lyons' Fishian approach, marginalizes critical testing against "'objective'" "'truth'"-"'criteria'" altogether. Broadly speaking, this dichotomy *redefines* religious "'belief'" as a matter of *"'private'"* religion that is not "'binding'" on *public* "'society'". We are reminded of Thiselton's objection to the views of 'Kierkegaard' and Bultmann – views according to which 'faith' becomes 'sheer' 'decision' divorced from 'knowledge' and warrant.[445]

The *third* Barthian dichotomy (which is linguistico-epistemological) can be presented as: the language of faith (biblical concepts 'of God', 'proclamation') *versus* language concerning everything else (including 'theistic' concepts of God – drawn from "'natural'" theology' – that are considered to be mere "'self-interpretation'").[446]

This dichotomy leads to the artificial and supposedly separate category of "religious language" (cf. Topping's notion of "'the excesses of the testimony of faith which *obscures history*'" – which seems to presuppose 'theophany' to us), which is then ring-fenced as being not open to challenge from "non-religious" sources, since the latter are over-readily dismissed as being anthropocentric and 'humanistic' "'self-interpretation'". Indeed, earlier, we noted Lyons' view that 'non-canonical' 'historical' 'material' that might otherwise be considered relevant to biblical studies: (i) interprets 'history' anthropocentrically; (ii) hardly exists in any useful form; and, (iii), is therefore doubly-subordinated to biblical theocentric 'historical' "reference" such that 'non-canonical' 'historical' 'material' very often cannot reliably be used to "test" or "independently" "check" biblical 'historical' "reference".[447] As Pannenberg puts it, Barth's approach,

> seemed to make it far too easy for theology to dismiss at a single stroke both atheist criticism and the encounter with non-Christian religions and with philosophy [cf. Lyons' over-easy dismissal of Thiselton's appeals to philosophy – see above]. Of course such considerations did not shake those followers of Barth who adopted the extreme position of the theology of revelation. The blows bounced off them.[448]

---

[444] Thiselton, 'H-O', 8; cf.: Thiselton, 'Exc', 12; Thiselton, 'TNI', 11; Lyons, *C&E*, 68-71; cf. 109; Woodman, 'UC', 3, 4-5, 9-10. Italics ours.

[445] Pannenberg, *BQ2*, 205; cf.: Thiselton, 'H-O', 8; Thiselton, 'TNI', 11; Thiselton, 'Par', 49; Thiselton, 'Exc', 12; Lyons, *C&E*, 69-70; but contrast, 77. Italics on the word "'private'" are Pannenberg's; remaining italics ours.

[446] Pannenberg, *BQ2*, 205; cf. Pannenberg, *BQ3*, 99-100. Italics ours.

[447] Lyons, *C&E*, 70; cf. 69, 71; cf. 275; cf.: Pannenberg, *BQ2*, 204-205; Tupper, *TWP*, 80. Italics ours.

[448] Pannenberg, *BQ3*, 101.

Admittedly, Lyons would no doubt protest that he has 'attempted carefully to chart a course between... two approaches to the canonical text'. One of these two approaches, according to Lyons, tries 'to work within the ideology of a text'. The other of these two approaches, according to Lyons, tries '*a priori* to resist the grain of the text', and 'would... be considered irrelevant by... Barth or... Childs'. In Lyons' view, only those following Barth and Childs whole-heartedly would be 'unimpressed by humanistic critiques of their practices and ideology'.[449]

In other words, Lyons has tried to steer clear of a fully-fledged Barthian-Childsian approach to the Sodom narrative. Whether or not one sympathizes with this strategy, however, one wonders where its *basis* is in *Lyons' hermeneutical theory*.

That is, it seemed clear – in the light of the particular section within *Canon and Exegesis* that was devoted to a critique of Thiselton's approach - that Lyons attempted to hold *both* to a '"Fishian"' view of 'the Bible' *and* to a Barthian 'Christian theology'.[450] The "Barthian" side of Lyons' thinking even seemed to be *reinforced* in Lyons' section on Childs' notion of '"referentiality"'.[451]

Conversely, though, we *also* found internal tensions within Lyons' epistemology in which he seemed to be moving towards a *Thiseltonian* perspective (*not* towards what Lyons *perceives* to be Thiselton's perspective, which is something alien to Thiselton). Now, at the end of *Canon and Exegesis*, Lyons seems to be *starting* to slip towards a more Thiseltonian hermeneutics again, even if the resemblances between Lyons' and Thiselton's respective approaches are only superficial. That is, Lyons at least seeks to combine "faith seeking understanding" (cf. reading 'within the' Bible's 'ideology') with "critical testing" (cf. "resisting" 'the grain of the text').[452]

Nevertheless, in many respects Lyons is still attempting to combine two incompatible viewpoints – the Fishian and the Barthian-Childsian. By contrast, Thiselton's hermeneutics are unified and consistent throughout, as we have demonstrated. Thus, as we said earlier, we must be very cautious not to over emphasize any superficial similarities that may sometimes appear to emerge between the approach of Thiselton and the approach of Lyons. Again, whilst Thiselton's approach is internally coherent and/or theoretically self-consistent, the problem that Lyons' approach faces is one of internal incoherence and/or of theoretical inconsistency. This conclusion brings us to our next point.

(e) In trying to hold *both* to a modified Barthian-Childsian approach to an epistemology of revelation and to biblical hermeneutics *and* to a '"Fishian"' approach to texts and to hermeneutical theory, Lyons effectively compromises both the Barthian-Childsian school of thought and the Fishian school of thought.[453] Lyons, though, resists any explicit argument for the construction of an

---

[449] Lyons, *C&E*, 275. Italics ours.
[450] Lyons, *C&E*, 114-115. Italics ours.
[451] Lyons, *C&E*, 68-71. Italics ours.
[452] Lyons, *C&E*, 275. Italics ours.
[453] Lyons, *C&E*, 114-115. Italics ours.

altogether different, *unifying*, hermeneutical framework into which insights from *both* these schools of thought could be sublated. Nevertheless, as we have seen, Lyons frequently seems to "slip" *towards* a more "Thiseltonian" viewpoint (a viewpoint that is *not* the same as the viewpoint that is presented in Lyons' caricature of Thiselton).

Thus, in our estimate, there is a real question-mark over whether or not a Barthian epistemology of revelation and a Childsian notion of "'referentiality'" - which do not "'in principle'" *epistemologically* banish textual-historical reference *despite* their emphases on those particular *interpretative impediments* that (in their framework) hinder 'historical reconstruction' – are really compatible with a Fishian epistemology, or with what we might here designate as being a *Fishian* notion of "'referentiality'" in which unconscious 'primary' 'interpretative activities' *alone* "produce" 'what is perceived to be "in the text"'.[454]

If, (i), on the one hand, Lyons chose to prioritize a *"Fishian"* notion of "'referentiality'", so as to sublate a modified Barthian-Childsian perspective into a "'Fishian'" framework, then in such a scenario Childsian *interpretative impediments* would be transformed into *epistemological barriers*. In such a scenario, the Church's "Bible(s)" would then (supposedly) become mere constructs of present-horizon communities.[455]

Admittedly, on the basis of Lyons' arguments, a community could still "project" a "referential" 'content' onto the "biblical" texts on the basis of its 'plain experience' of 'God'.[456] Lyons would no doubt argue that 'the Church' *'community'*, as the preconditional 'setting' for the creation of *its* biblical text, can impute to the text a 'referent' that it has *remembered "extra-textually"*.[457] For Lyons, when he is wearing his "'Fishian'" 'hat', then, it seems to be *"extra-textually"* transmitted corporate memories *of* the 'plain experience' of 'God' that produce a community's 'concern' to 'witness' truly *to* its 'plain experience' of 'God' - a 'concern' that then motivates that community to "produce" its "Bible" through a process of community-projected objectification.[458]

But the problem that would then arise in such a scenario would be that of an absence of "non-projected" criteria by which to distinguish between 'plain experience' of God and 'plain experience' of the merely human (or even of the demonic).[459] Lyons' category of 'plain experience' – and *remembered* 'plain experience' (or "extra-textually"-transmitted experience-generated theocentric memories) at that – would then become the only *source* of biblical 'content' (even though, in Lyons' thinking, presumably, one community's "extra-textually"-

---

[454] Lyons, *C&E*, 68-71; cf. Fish, 'NC', 271, 273; cf. our earlier expositions of both these texts. Italics ours.
[455] Lyons, *C&E*, 114; cf. 115; cf. 68-71; cf. 263; cf. Fish, 'NC', 271, 273. Italics ours.
[456] Lyons, *C&E*, 109; cf. 114-115; cf. Fish, 'NC', 271, 273.
[457] Lyons, *C&E*, 114; cf. 263; cf. 69, 70. Italics ours.
[458] Lyons, *C&E*, 115; cf. 114; cf. 70; cf. 109; cf. 263. Italics ours.
[459] Lyons, *C&E*, 109; cf. 114; cf. Fish, 'NC', 271, 273.

*Hermeneutical Unity, Objectivity, and Foreclosure* 523

transmitted memories could be challenged by another's).[460]

Such a scenario, though, would still subject "the Scriptures" to the effects of possible 'systematic' distortions of 'doctrine' and of practice, as Thiselton rightly argues.[461] We will address this issue when we respond to S. Woodman, since this issue relates to what Pannenberg and Thiselton call an "'authoritarianism that masquerades under the guise of the 'Spirit'".[462]

This "'authoritarianism… of the 'Spirit'"' is also generated by a more truly Barthian epistemology of revelation, as we have seen. But this authoritarianism "of the Spirit" would become further emphasized if Lyons sublated his Barthian-Childsian epistemology of revelation *into a Fishian framework* since, in such a scenario, we would then have not one "Bible" or "'thick text'" but many mutually 'contradictory' *and non-falsifiable* "Bibles" or "'thin texts'". These many mutually 'contradictory' and non-falsifiable "Bibles" or "'thin texts'" would constitute not so much a "*plurality* of interpretative outcomes" but would, rather, constitute a "*pluralism* of interpretative outcomes" (to borrow a phrase from W.G. Jeanrond – see earlier) that reflected what Thiselton would call an "unnecessary arbitrary meaning expansion".[463] In such a scenario, though, an "'authoritarianism that masquerades under the guise of the 'Spirit'"' would *no longer be kept in check even by an "'authoritarianism of the 'self-authenticating' Word'"*, since the latter would degenerate into a series of *arbitrarily* plural and mutually 'contradictory' "authoritarianisms" – "authoritarianisms" between which only the "experiences of the Spirit" *of those in power* could adjudicate.[464] We will address this issue further when we come to our responses to S. Woodman.

If, (ii), on the other hand, Lyons chose to prioritize a Barthian epistemology of revelation and a Childsian notion of "'referentiality'", so as to sublate a Fishian perspective into a modified Barthian-Childsian framework, then in such a scenario Fishian *epistemological barriers* would be demoted into becoming mere *interpretative impediments*.[465]

Lyons could then no longer say, with Fish, and against Childs, that biblical texts cannot "'in principle'" refer to a 'content' or "'historical background'" that exists 'prior' to the 'content' "produced" by the community. Lyons would have to repudiate Fish's view – i.e. that "textual reference and content" are solely "present-horizon community-projected perceptions" that only *'seem'* to relate to 'the' external 'world' (regardless of whether small or very large communities are doing the "perceiving") - in favor of the possibility of "*historical* textual reference

---

[460] Lyons, *C&E*, 109; cf. 114; cf. 70; cf. Fish, 'NC', 271, 273. Italics ours.
[461] Thiselton, *NH*, 549-550.
[462] Thiselton, 'H-O', 8.
[463] Lyons, *C&E*, 263; cf. Thiselton, 'Parab', 455-457, cf.: 458-461; 468; cf. Thiselton, 'H-O', 8. Italics ours.
[464] Thiselton, 'H-O', 8; cf. Lyons, *C&E*, 263. Italics ours.
[465] Lyons, *C&E*, 68-71; cf. 114-115. Italics ours.

to extra-textual realities".[466]

In such a scenario, a Fishian series of many mutually 'contradictory' *and non-falsifiable* "Bibles" or "'thin texts'" – which, from a Thiseltonian perspective, would reflect an "unnecessary arbitrary meaning expansion" – would then be reigned in to become *closer* to, but *not identical with*, a Thiseltonian "plurality of legitimate readings".[467] Caution is needed at this point, however: in a Thiseltonian framework, all "legitimate readings" remain "'in principle'" *falsifiable*. But Thiselton would argue that, in a Barthian-Childsian framework, "legitimate readings" would *still* be vulnerable to an "'authoritarianism of the 'self-authenticating' Word'" and to an "'authoritarianism that masquerades under the guise of the 'Spirit'''".[468]

Lyons, of course, (iii), might argue that he holds his 'two hats' in tension with one another.[469] From a modified Barthian-Childsian perspective, though, Lyons would then, in such a scenario, be merely espousing the co-existence of theocentric and anthropocentric epistemologies. However, whether or not one agrees with the view that these two epistemologies actually do co-exist in our 'plain experience' due to the dual realities of God's revelation and human finitude/fallenness, the problem with such a scenario, from a modified Barthian-Childsian perspective, is that a Fishian epistemology of human "referent-creation" and of human "assumption-construction" (which is hardly Barthian or theocentric) would *still* have to be designated as being "anthropocentric", and therefore as being erroneous. Such a scenario, though, would seem to compromise Lyons' plainly-stated desire to view 'the Bible' ('as the canonical Scriptures of the Christian Church') as 'a "Fishian" text'.[470]

(iv) In summary, then, if Lyons resolves the Barthian-Childsian versus Fishian tensions in favor of *Barth and Childs*, then he ends up with: (iv.i) problematic theo-historico-epistemological, epistemological, and linguistico-epistemological dichotomies; (iv.ii) the double authoritarianism - of the "experience of the Spirit" and of the "self-authenticating Word" – that has been exposed by Pannenberg and by Thiselton; and, (iv.iii), a demotion of Fish's "referent creation" and "assumption-construction" as being "anthropocentric".

Alternatively, if Lyons resolves the Barthian-Childsian versus Fishian tensions in favor of *Fish*, then he ends up with: (iv.i) the historical, epistemological, and linguistic dichotomies that we highlighted in our "Thiseltonian" response to Lyons' Oxford article; and, (iv.ii), a radicalized authoritarianism based on

---

[466] Lyons, *C&E*, 70; cf. 69; cf. 114; cf. Fish, 'NC', 271, 273. Italics ours.

[467] Lyons, *C&E*, 263; cf.: Thiselton, 'Parab', 455-457, cf.: 458-461; 468; Thiselton, 'CAP', 133-135, 201; Thiselton, *2H*, 10, 120-121, cf.: 154-157, 244, 324-325, 348-349, 436-437; Thiselton, *NH*, 557-558; Thiselton, 'R-RH', 82-83; Jeanrond, 'R *RH*', 117. Italics ours.

[468] Thiselton, *NTH*, 407; cf.: Thiselton, 'LMR', 1137; Thiselton, *2H*, 290, 326, 353; cf. 14; Sykes, S.W., 'Review of A.C. Thiselton's *The Two Horizons*', *Chman* 96.2 (1982), 157. Italics ours.

[469] Lyons, *C&E*, 114.

[470] Lyons, *C&E*, 68-71; cf. 109, 115; cf. Fish, 'NC', 271, 273; cf. our earlier expositions.

"experience of the Spirit".

Finally, if Lyons simply tries to hold Barthian-Childsian and Fishian viewpoints in tension, then he in effect ends up with a *further* set of dichotomies that reflects the incompatibilities between the two view-points. This further set of dichotomies is as follows: (iv.i) "*interpretative impediments* to historical-textual reference *vs. epistemological barriers* to historical-textual reference"; (iv.ii) "biblical historical-reference *vs.* community referent-creation and assumption-construction"; and, (iv.iii), "*theocentric* epistemology *vs. anthropocentric* epistemology".

And so, *whichever* of these three routes Lyons chooses, he *still* falls under a Thiseltonian critique - not under a critique based on an objectivistic foundationalism grounded in an idealist epistemology that appeals to "raw data" (since we have shown that Thiselton doesn't hold to such a stance), but to a critique grounded in Thiselton's properly historical-hermeneutical epistemology (which we have already expounded).

Lyons, though, as we stated above, resists any explicit argument for the construction of an altogether different, *unifying*, hermeneutical framework – a framework into which insights from *both* Barthian-Childsian and Fishian schools could be sublated. Rather, Lyons, as we have seen, seems to affirm one school one moment, and the other school another moment – as though largely oblivious of the contradictions that exist between these two schools. It is to be hoped, therefore, that Lyons will take note of that *fourth* set of dichotomies within his thinking (his performative self-contradictions) in which he – being forced to operate in the world of progressively accessible historical contingencies – sometimes slips *towards* a "Thiseltonian" hermeneutic (which is *not* the same as the hermeneutic presented in Lyons' caricature of Thiselton).

(f) We saw earlier that Lyons complained that Thiselton's work, *New Horizons in Hermeneutics*, misrepresented Fish by caricaturing Fish in several ways. We saw that Lyons made the point that *one* of the ways in which *New Horizons in Hermeneutics* misrepresented Fish related to the matter of hermeneutical 'constraints'.[471] We addressed this particular point earlier. However, we have still not addressed the other points raised by Lyons in relation to Thiselton's supposed caricature of Fish in *New Horizons in Hermeneutics*, and so we may do so now – as follows.

Thus, (i), Lyons argues that Thiselton is wrong to contend that a 'Fishian' stance: (i.i) necessarily leads to an *isolationist* prohibition of present-horizon inter-community 'communication'; and, (i.ii), necessarily leads to an *idolatrous* self-affirming prohibition of present-horizon inter-community "'hermeneutical change'".[472] We may now respond to these two charges as follows.

Thus, (i.i), in our view, Thiselton does not argue that Fish banishes the *possibility* of present-horizon inter-community 'communication'. Rather, Thiselton *acknowledges* Fish's recognition 'that the social roles which arise from contextual institutions may overlap and interpenetrate' in such a way as to ensure that

---

[471] Lyons, *C&E*, 111. Italics ours.
[472] Lyons, *C&E*, 111; cf. 112-113; cf. 114. Italics ours.

'practices and communities... are not "pure"'.⁴⁷³

What Thiselton *does* argue in *New Horizons in Hermeneutics*, however, is that if a Rortyan-Fishian epistemology spreads, then present-horizon inter-community 'communication' will steadily degenerate towards 'conflict' as agreed public-domain provisional objective truth-criteria become steadily eroded. In Thiselton's view, a Rortyan-Fishian epistemology dismisses "agreed public-domain provisional objective truth-criteria" (which presuppose consensus *and* some objectivity) in favor of "agreed public-domain 'assumptions'" or *mere consensus*. Mere consensus, however, in Thiselton's view, is far more vulnerable to disintegration into self-serving viewpoints - and thence into competing rhetorics, power-struggles, conflicts and violence - than are "agreed public-domain provisional objective truth-criteria", which involve *some acknowledgment* of, and therefore some *potential submission* to, provisional objectivity. Thiselton would argue that one *could* ignore human fallenness and cling naively to the hope that some kind of democratic utopia based *solely* on consensus will eventually emerge. However, Thiselton argues that, given the reality of human fallenness, the only *unity* likely to emerge from the spread of a Rortyan-Fishian epistemology is the unity of authoritarian "oppression".⁴⁷⁴

Of course, Lyons would call Thiselton's viewpoint, here, '"foundationalist"'.⁴⁷⁵ We have seen, however, that what Lyons *means* by his use of this label is so utterly unrelated to a Thiseltonian hermeneutical critique of historical objectivity (see above), or to a Thiseltonian viewpoint more broadly, that *Lyons' own viewpoint* (which is in part defined by its reaction *against* idealist "foundationalism"), when compared to a Thiseltonian viewpoint, is *actually the closer of the two viewpoints to idealist foundationalism*.

(i.ii) Thiselton does not argue that a Fishian stance banishes all *"possibility"* of present-horizon inter-community '"hermeneutical change"' originating 'from outside' (i.e. from other communities).⁴⁷⁶ What Thiselton *does* argue in *New Horizons in Hermeneutics* is that, on a Rortyan-Fishian basis, a community's *'only hope of change* is to imperialize other communities by extending its own boundaries until it disintegrates under its own weight and internal pluralism'. '"Hermeneutical change"', then, in Thiselton's view, is *possible* on a Rortyan-Fishian basis but – for the reasons just stated in "(i.i)" immediately above – Thiselton argues that fragmentation into self-serving viewpoints is a *more likely* outcome than a democratic utopia if a Rortyan-Fishian epistemology spreads.⁴⁷⁷

Admittedly, Thiselton *does* say that, in 'socio-pragmatic hermeneutics', 'the community cannot be *corrected* and *reformed* as Fish concedes, from outside itself' –

---

⁴⁷³ Lyons, *C&E*, 111-113; cf. Thiselton, *NH*, 543. Italics ours.
⁴⁷⁴ Lyons, *C&E*, 111-113, 114; cf. Thiselton, *NH*, 393-405; cf. 439-462; cf. 515-550. Italics ours.
⁴⁷⁵ Lyons, *C&E*, 109.
⁴⁷⁶ Lyons, *C&E*, 112-113. Italics ours.
⁴⁷⁷ Thiselton, *NH*, 27; cf. Lyons, *C&E*, 112-113. Italics ours.

where the notions of "correction" and "reformation", here, presuppose *provisional assessments of objective truth*. That is, Thiselton presupposes that 'change' 'from outside' *can* happen from a Fishian perspective – but not in the sense of "correction or reform" in relation to provisional assessments of objective truth.[478]

That is, in *New Horizons in Hermeneutics*, Thiselton certainly *does* argue that the spread of a *Rortyan-Fishian* (as opposed to a Barthian) epistemology would indeed make one community's 'reform' of another community's 'assumptions' *much less likely*. Thiselton in effect asks the question: *if* no group's interpretations can be said to be characterized by *any* "objective truthfulness" *then* what could constitute the *motivation* (other than pragmatic motivations) for one group to allow itself to be "imperialized" by, assimilated within, or even "reformed" by another group and its humanly-generated 'referent'-creations or 'assumption'-constructions?[479]

Indeed, we might ask, how could the word "reform" even be used if no group's views could be deemed to be "more correct" than any other group's views? Admittedly, one group may "see" another group's views "as" being "more correct" than their own views, and so could submit to "reform" or "correction" "from outside". But, *at that point, both* the submissive group *and* the reforming group would have *ceased to have a Fishian epistemology*. Indeed, at the point at which Lyons uses the word 'reform', it seems to us that he has moved from a Rortyan-Fishian epistemology to a Barthian epistemology. It is *Barth*, and not Fish, who allows Lyons to use the word 'reform'. Therefore, Thiselton's criticism stands, since it is *directed at Rorty and Fish and not at Barth*.[480]

Moreover, we should note that, in this context of discussion, Lyons slips into another of his tell-tale performative self-contradictions. Thus, on the one hand, Lyons says that his own phrase, "'hermeneutical *change*'" is a 'better' phrase than Thiselton's phrase, 'hermeneutical *growth*'.[481] On the other hand, however, it is interesting to note that Lyons *continues to use* Thiselton's phrase 'hermeneutical *growth*'. Surely, though, Lyons continues to use Thiselton's phrase 'hermeneutical *growth*' because, as we have seen, Lyons wishes to keep a notion of 'reform'. And yet, as we have argued, Lyons doesn't have any "grounds" in a *Fishian* approach *for* objective criticism and 'reform', which is precisely *why* Lyons *says* the phrase, "'hermeneutical *change*'", is a 'better' phrase than Thiselton's phrase, 'hermeneutical growth'![482]

Of course, Lyons would reply by arguing that since 'non-foundationalist' hermeneutics "says nothing" about whether or not *'God'* can change a community 'from… outside', whether directly or via other present-horizon communities, then a "'Fishian'" perspective *does not* in fact absolutely banish "correction or reform" in

---

[478] Thiselton, *NH*, 27; cf. Lyons, *C&E*, 112, 113, 114; cf. 109. Italics ours.
[479] Thiselton, *NH*, 393-405; cf. 439-462; cf. 515-550; cf. 27; cf.: Lyons, *C&E*, 114; cf. 69; Fish, 'NC', 271, 273. Italics ours.
[480] Lyons, *C&E*, 112-115; cf. our earlier arguments. Italics ours.
[481] Lyons, *C&E*, 112; cf. 113. Italics ours.
[482] Lyons, *C&E*, 114; cf. 112, 113. Italics ours.

relation to *revealed* 'truth'.[483]

We may respond, however, by pointing out that, *first*, on the basis of our prior arguments, it is highly questionable as to whether Lyons' *Barthian epistemology of revelation* can be reconciled with his *Fishian approach to texts*. If 'the Bible' mediates *revealed* 'truth' that a Fishian approach to texts can 'say' 'nothing' about, then how can 'the Bible' be treated *as* 'a "Fishian" text', when 'a "Fishian" text', *by definition*, must be characterized (as far as the issue of 'content' is concerned) *only* by community-*projected* 'content'?[484] Moreover, *second*, even in the case of a more *Barthian* stance then, according to Pannenberg and Thiselton, the Barthian basis for reform is *still* "evasive" epistemological "'authoritarianism'" when, from a Pannenbergian perspective, and also from a Thiseltonian perspective, the basis for reform *should* (and *can*) be "(meta-)critical testing against provisional truth-criteria in the public sphere" (N.B. we are not talking about Barth's profound *biblical theology* here, but about Pannenberg's critique of a Barthian *epistemology of revelation*).[485]

(ii) Lyons, in the context of his comments about inter-community 'communication', raises three other objections to Thiselton's thinking: (ii.i) Lyons again argues that Thiselton moves illegitimately from "later Wittgensteinian trans-contextuality" to "raw data" objectivism;[486] (ii.ii) Lyons argues that 'communication' (involving "translation") between very "different" 'communities' is more "difficult" 'than Thiselton' "allows"; and, (ii.iii), Lyons argues that the later Wittgenstein may be more "non-foundationalist" and 'localist' 'than Thiselton' "allows".[487]

The first two of these objections need not detain us. Thiselton's epistemology is neither objectivist nor grounded in the later Wittgenstein's thinking as we have already seen. And Thiselton fully respects the "difficulties" that can accompany translation, and would find points of *agreement* with Lyons in relation to this point (we are thinking, for example, of Thiselton's 48 years of wrestling with the translation of 1 Corinthians).[488]

Concerning the later Wittgenstein's supposed "non-foundationalism", then we

---

[483] Lyons, *C&E*, 114-115; cf. 112-113; cf. 68-71. Italics ours.

[484] Lyons, *C&E*, 114-115; cf. 68-71; cf. Thiselton, *NH*, 27; cf. 515-555; cf. Fish, 'NC', 271, 273. Italics ours.

[485] Thiselton, 'H-O', 8; cf. Pannenberg, *BQ2*, 199-206. Italics ours.

[486] Lyons, *C&E*, 110; cf. 112; cf. 113-114.

[487] Lyons, *C&E*, 112, cf. 113-114.

[488] e.g. Thiselton, A.C., 'Semantics and New Testament Interpretation', in *New Testament Interpretation: Essays in Principles and Methods* (ed. I.H. Marshall; Grand Rapids: Eerdmans; Exeter: Paternoster Press, 1977; actually written 1974), 87; cf.: Chapter 4; Lyons, *C&E*, 112, cf. 113-114; Thiselton, A.C., *Eschatology and the Holy Spirit in Paul with Special Reference to 1 Corinthians* (London: University of London Unpublished M.Th. Dissertation, 1964); Thiselton, A.C., *The First Epistle to the Corinthians* (eds. H. Marshall and D.A. Hagner; Series: The New International Greek Testament Commentary; Grand Rapids: Eerdmans; Carlisle: Paternoster, 2000). Italics ours.

have argued that whilst the later Wittgenstein moves away from *idealist* so-called "foundationalism" with its attendant objectivisms (which is where Lyons seems to think Thiselton is still coming from), the later Wittgenstein nevertheless still leaves an opening for notions of *"historical* foundations" that are *consistent with completely re-worked historical epistemologies* (which is where Thiselton is actually coming from). Thus, S.E. Fowl may be right to note that R. Rorty's and J. Stout's 'therapeutic' development of the later Wittgenstein's and J.L. Austin's work includes a focus on conventional language-uses in context. But Fowl mistakenly groups together J.R. Searle's, K.J. Vanhoozer's, and Thiselton's developments of the same tradition when Fowl implies (given Derrida's well-known responses to Searle in 'Limited Inc a b c...' – see above) that these three thinkers therein supposedly all seek an idealist 'metaphysic or ontology'. That is, against what Fowl seems to say here, there are *not just two* (*sic*) developments of the later Wittgenstein's and Austin's work, but at least three or more. We have argued that Thiselton's thinking is actually *further away* from "idealist foundationalism" *than that of Derrida and Lyons*. Again, Lyons' (and Fowl's?) dichotomous binary (*sic*) "foundationalism *versus* non-foundationalism" straightjacket is simplistic and unhistorical. Earlier in our argument we said that it was "as though Lyons thinks that, historically, only a binary choice between two views of 'perception' (and/or of "understanding") was ever proffered by thinkers", which looked "like an imposed echo – if only a shadow - of idealist formalism to us". Now, however, the idealist shadow is lengthening. Whereas a properly *historical* viewpoint like Thiselton's *immerses itself in multiple traditions*, Lyons sometimes seems to *project a binary either/or onto history so as to obscure its multiple traditions*. These "binary either/or" projections (see our earlier discussions) constitute a *fifth* set of dichotomies within Lyons' thinking.[489]

(iii) Finally, we saw that, in Lyons' estimate, 'Thiselton' would be "ignoring" *both* the real implications of a "'Fishian'" stance *and* 'the' "Church's" 'concern' to proclaim 'the gospel' "truly" if he contended that a "'Fishian'" stance "necessarily" - at best - led to an *atheistic* "D. Cupitt-style" 'projectionist "Sea of Faith" theology' that made "'grace or revelation [etc.]... illusory'" and that reduced *all* "'Reality'" 'beyond interpretation' to 'a Nietzschean void'.[490]

In response to Lyons, however, we may recall our earlier argument that Fish's notion of "referent-creation" and "assumption-construction" by *human* communities (however wide) *would* be considered anthropocentric and 'projectionist' from a Barthian perspective. We have also argued that even a *Barthian* stance is *already* vulnerable to anthropocentric 'projectionist' charges from the demythologizers, as Pannenberg has demonstrated.[491] Similarly, we saw in Chapter 3 how Thiselton argued that Kierkegaard's theological existentialism,

---

[489] Lyons, *C&E*, 113; cf.: Fowl, 'AI', 76. n. 10; Ward, *W&S*, 191-192; cf. our Chapter 6, and earlier in the present chapter. Italics ours.
[490] Lyons, *C&E*, 114, 115. Italics ours.
[491] Pannenberg, *BQ2*, 199-206; cf.: Lyons, *C&E*, 114-115; Thiselton, 'H-O', 8. Italics ours.

being unstable 'as a self-contained' philosophical epistemology,[492] slid into 'skepticism' and 'relativism' at the hands of 'Nietzsche', 'Heidegger', 'Jaspers', 'Sartre', and 'the... new morality' of 'radical theology'.[493] A Fishian stance does not at all banish, or protect against, such demythologizing, but merely undermines other groups' "right" to appeal to "objective grounds" when criticizing Christian communities. Crucially, a Fishian stance only achieves even *this* goal by recasting Christianity as *similarly divorced from objectivity* – i.e. as very likely (in the eyes of the demythologizers) a *merely human* objectification.[494]

Moreover, as we have seen, a Barthian epistemology of revelation leads to an "'authoritarianism of the 'self-authenticating' Word'" and to an "'authoritarianism that masquerades under the guise of the 'Spirit''".[495] Adding a Fishian stance to the mix just increases the problem of "'authoritarianism'" still further since its many "Bibles" and many "'Gods'" are likely to make its "'authoritarianism'" more and more Spirit-centric and less and less Word-centric.[496]

This conclusion is not just conjecture – it is related to what is already happening world-wide, which is why we have devoted so much space to our response to Lyons' work. Thus, P. Ward, following D.F. Wells, speaks of 'a sea change' in which 'confessional' 'evangelicalism' is giving way to a 'transconfessional evangelicalism' in which 'the emphasis has moved away from doctrine towards strategy and organizational power'. Ward continues: 'the emergence of' a 'third center, the charismatic' (with what Thiselton would call its over-emphasis on 'present' 'experience' of the 'Spirit') 'has merely served to emphasize these developments considerably whilst complicating the organizational picture'. In our view, the hermeneutical theory of S. Woodman potentially begins to reflect some of 'these developments'.[497] But this point introduces our next section.

iii) S. Woodman's Thesis Contribution

*S. Woodman* criticizes Thiselton's thinking in ways that are similar to the ways in which Lyons criticizes Thiselton's thinking – except that Woodman's criticisms of Thiselton's thinking also focus on *the role of the Holy Spirit* in biblical interpretation. Woodman's criticisms of Thiselton's thinking, like those criticisms provided by

---

[492] Thiselton, 'KNT', 91, cf. 100-102.
[493] Thiselton, 'KNT', 86, 90-92, 100-103.
[494] See our discussion of Fish earlier in the present chapter. Italics ours.
[495] Pannenberg, BQ2, 199-206; cf. Thiselton, 'H-O', 8.
[496] Thiselton, 'H-O', 8; cf. Lyons, C&E, 263; cf. 264.
[497] Ward, P., 'The Tribes of Evangelicalism', in *The Post-Evangelical Debate* (G. Cray *et al*, London: SPCK/Triangle, 1997), 26-27; cf.: Thiselton, 'UPC', 98; Thiselton, 'U (long)', 95-97; Thiselton, A.C., 'Experience-Centred Religion: Harvey Cox on the Seduction of the Spirit', *CEN* 9 Aug. (1974), 8; Thiselton, A.C., "Understanding the New Testament'. Review of J.D.G. Dunn's *Unity and Diversity in the New Testament*', *CEN* 23 Dec. (1977), 8; Thiselton, 'REC', 512; cf.: 520, 522-525, 526; cf. 514-515; Thiselton, 'SARX', 216, 217.

Lyons in *Canon and Exegesis*, constitute responses to the arguments in *New Horizons in Hermeneutics* that Thiselton brings against the approach of Fish. Woodman's criticisms of Thiselton's thinking originally appeared in a Thesis Contribution in the year(s) 2000/2001, and appeared again, with no significant changes, in a presentation in the year 2004 in a seminar forum that was attended by the present author. Woodman's recent article, 'The Dissenting Voice: Journeying Together Toward a Baptist Hermeneutic' (2011), repeats Woodman's Fishian arguments from a decade earlier, though without reference to Thiselton. Here, therefore, in the present study, we may confine our attention to Woodman's criticisms of Thiselton in his (i.e. Woodman's) Thesis Contribution (2000/2001). Indeed, we may confine our attention in this way for three reasons: *first*, Woodman's Thesis Contribution presents a Fishian stance that is almost identical to that presented again in Woodman's recent article from 2011; *second*, Woodman's Thesis Contribution constitutes the only written response by Woodman to Thiselton's work that is known to the present author; and, *third*, many of the multiple criticisms of Thiselton's stance that appear in Woodman's Thesis Contribution are also at least implicit or connoted in Woodman's recent article from 2011.[498]

Thus, focusing on Woodman's Thesis Contribution (2000/2001) then, (1), to begin with, against Woodman's reading of Thiselton, we should note that Thiselton does not hold 'that' 'formalism' and 'anti-formalism' 'both... function together'. Nor does Thiselton "travel" any distance on 'the road' between 'formalism' and 'anti-formalism'. Thiselton *does* say that, '*for Wittgenstein, as for F. Waismann*, "concepts with blurred edges" are situated on middle ground along the road from formalism to pragmatism'. However, as we have seen, Thiselton sublates insights from even the *later Wittgenstein's* thinking into a different historico-philosophical framework, and so it is incorrect simply to attribute every aspect of this comment directly to *Thiselton's* thinking.[499]

That is, in our estimate, Thiselton clearly views the "formalism/anti-formalism" distinction as an artificial pre-dialogic consumer-simplified quasi-formalist dichotomy that is both over-generalizing and *'a-historical'*. Even if Thiselton's arguments temporarily entertain the notions of a "formalism/anti-formalism" distinction and of a "road" between these two "movements", then Thiselton only tolerates this kind of language-use long enough to point to its error, and long enough to argue that, in any case, *both* "movements" (assuming that we

---

[498] Woodman, S., 'Untitled Contribution to MLitt Thesis. Personal Communication to Robert Knowles, 27th April 2000' (Bristol: Baptist College, 2000), 1-20; cf. Woodman, S., *The Christian Use of Apocalyptic Literature from the Perspective of Metaphor* (University of Bristol: MLit Thesis, 2001); cf. Woodman, S., 'The Dissenting Voice: Journeying Together Toward a Baptist Hermeneutic', in *The "Plainly Revealed" Word of God? Baptist Hermeneutics in Theory and Practice* (eds. H. Dare and S. Woodman; Macon, Georgia, USA: Mercer University Press, 2011), 213-229; cf. 223. Italics ours.

[499] Woodman, 'UC', 1, 2. Contrast, Thiselton, *NH*, 541; cf. 539-546. All italics ours.

can even use such a term) falsely de-historicize language.[500] Thiselton's own perspectives, by contrast, emerge from the *entirely different and thoroughly historical paradigm* put forward in *The Two Horizons*.[501]

(2) Woodman is also mistaken to argue that Thiselton holds to a notion of textual autonomy. As we saw in Chapters 4, 5, 6, and above, Thiselton firmly embeds texts and textual horizons *within larger* traditional, historical and theological horizons, and only employs the notion of 'the text itself' in a strictly qualified way. Woodman, however, *reverses* Thiselton's thinking by implying that Thiselton supposedly collapses theological horizons to the point that they are supposedly embedded *within* textual horizons. That is, Woodman sees Thiselton's stance in terms of 'the Spirit' supposedly *'only'* "speaking" *'through the'* "biblical texts", 'as if the word of God is contained within the text itself'. Indeed, in Woodman's view, Thiselton even comes 'close to equating the Bible with God'.[502]

But, as we saw in Chapters 3 and 4, Thiselton does not constrain "God's Word" to 'the text itself', but views "God's Word", *centrally*, as being Jesus Christ (and, therefore, as being "enfleshed"). We also saw in Chapters 3 and 4 that Thiselton does not argue that 'the Spirit' *'only'* 'speaks *through the*' "biblical texts".[503] Rather, for Thiselton, 'the... Spirit' imparts exegetical 'gifts', 'creatively' 'inspires' 'fusion', and sanctifies believers, operating "in front of" 'the... text', and not 'only' *'through'* 'the... text'.[504] Moreover, in Chapter 3 and earlier in the present chapter, we also saw that Thiselton does not almost "equate" 'the Bible with God', but rather that Thiselton holds to a Trinitarian view of God.[505]

Moving on, (3), then Woodman (reminding us of Lyons) appeals to the work of Karl Barth in order to argue that '"Scripture *becomes* 'authentic' and 'authoritative' for"' Christian readers '"through the work of the Holy Spirit"'. Since, in Woodman's estimate, 'the Spirit' belongs to 'the *interpretative community*' then, in Woodman's view, 'the *interpretative community*', rather than 'the text itself', is

---

[500] Thiselton, 'CAP', 156-157; cf. 211-213; cf.: Thiselton, *NH*, 540-546, 486; Thiselton, *2H*, 51-84, cf. 234-251, 304-326; Woodman, 'UC', 1-2. First italics Thiselton's, second italics ours.

[501] Thiselton, 'CAP', 156-157; cf. 211-213; cf.: Thiselton, *NH*, 486; Thiselton, *2H*, 51-84, cf.: 234-251; 304-326. Italics ours.

[502] Woodman, 'UC', 3-4, 6, 17. Contrast, Thiselton, *2H*, 234-240, cf.: 373; 304-308, 310-326; 168; 129, 436-437; 350; 335-352. Final italics Woodman's, other italics ours.

[503] Woodman, 'UC', 3-4, 6; cf. Smith, 'R RH', 64. Contrast, Thiselton, *2H*, 234-240, cf.: 373; 304-308, 310-326; 168; 129, 436-437; 350; 335-352. Last italics Woodman's, others ours.

[504] Thiselton, 'U (long)', 117-120, cf.: 121, 99; cf.: Thiselton, *2H*, 88-92; Thiselton, *NH*, 585-586; Woodman, 'UC', 3; Thiselton, A.C., 'Holy Spirit (A.C. Thiselton stresses: 'with additions by the editors')', in *Dictionary of Biblical Imagery* (eds. L. Ryken, J.C. Wilhoit, and T. Longman III; Leicester: Apollos, 1998), 393. See, Thiselton, 'TST', 116-117, 131, 133; cf. Thiselton, A.C., 'The Holy Spirit and the Future', in *We Believe in the Holy Spirit: A Report by the Doctrine Commission of the General Synod of the Church of England* (London, Church House Publishing, 1991), 170-171, 173-178. Italics Woodman's.

[505] Woodman, 'UC', 17. Contrast esp., Thiselton, 'Authority', 126.

the locus of 'interpretative' '"authority"'.⁵⁰⁶

We must reply to Woodman's points here, however, in two ways. (a) First, in our view, there is a problem with Woodman's assertion that 'the *interpretative community*' is supposedly the locus of 'interpretative' '"authority"'. To us, this viewpoint seems – potentially - to come close to transferring the Spirit's *divine* authority to the *human* members of the interpretative community. (b) Second, in our estimate, there is also a problem with Woodman's correlative negative assertion that, supposedly, there is *not* something "authentic" and "authoritative" about 'the [biblical] text itself' in its past horizons *prior to* the present-horizon '"work of the Holy Spirit"'. To us, this viewpoint seems to undermine the authority of the Scriptures by divorcing 'interpretative' '"authority"' from 'the' historically-embedded '[biblical] text itself'. We may expand on each of these two replies to Woodman, as follows.⁵⁰⁷

Thus, (a), we should note that Woodman seems to come close to contradicting his own viewpoint when he argues *not only that* 'the *interpretative community*' is supposedly the locus of 'interpretative' '"authority"', *but also that* 'the Spirit' is supposedly the *only* '*outside* influence... required' by 'the interpretative community' during biblical interpretation. That is, surely, the second of these two arguments implies that 'interpretative' '"authority"' is *not* actually grounded in 'the *interpretative community*', but rather that 'interpretative' '"authority"' belongs to the Spirit who *both* indwells *and transcends* the 'interpretative community'. That is, surely, the Spirit's *divine* 'interpretative' '"authority"' is not conferred to the *human* members of 'the interpretative community' just because the Spirit indwells that 'community'. Rather, in our estimate, the *human* members of 'the interpretative community' remain *under* the Spirit's '"authority"', and are not in *possession* of that '"authority"'.⁵⁰⁸ Admittedly, in fairness to Woodman, he may have intended to make this same point, and so the issue here may be no more than an issue to do with communicative clarity. Our next reply to Woodman, however, raises more involved issues, and so requires a more extended discussion, as follows.

Thus, (b), another part of the problem with Woodman's stance in this context of discussion is that he seems to divorce 'interpretative' '"authority"' from 'the [biblical] text itself'. Admittedly, it is doubtful whether Woodman's *aim* here is to divorce the Spirit's authority from the very language (i.e. the biblical texts) that the Spirit primarily uses. That is, in Woodman's thinking, the Spirit seems to be a "go-between" who stands between the biblical texts and modern readers, and who links modern readers to the Bible. Thus, Woodman allows that, in *some* sense, 'God' "communicates" '*through* the Bible as the individual [or 'community'] allows the Spirit to be active in the reading process'. Woodman continues, 'God *can* indeed be said to speak through the Bible, but in a different way to that as

---

⁵⁰⁶ Woodman, 'UC', 3, 4-5, 13. Italics Woodman's.

⁵⁰⁷ Woodman, 'UC', 3, 4-5, 13. First italics Woodman's, remaining italics ours.

⁵⁰⁸ Woodman, 'UC', 6, 7, 3, 4-5, 13. Italics ours, except on two occurrences of the phrase '...*interpretative community*', where they are Woodman's.

understood by Thiselton'.[509] That is, Woodman argues that,

> the Bible can be considered to be the text which God has chosen, by his grace, to be the means whereby he reveals his word to… readers. Just as the Spirit can be held to have been active in the writing of the text, so also Christians can see the Spirit active in its reading and interpretation.[510]

In response to Woodman at this point, however, we should note that Woodman's comments here now look very like Thiselton's own view, and it begins to look like Woodman is contradicting himself. That is, if 'the Spirit' was 'active in the *writing* of the' biblical 'texts', then can we still assert that there is not something '"authoritative"' *in* and *behind* 'the' biblical 'texts' that could have a role to play in adjudicating between interpretations?[511]

Woodman's reply to this rejoinder of ours, of course, is to argue - on the basis of the thinking of Stanley Fish - that even if the biblical texts *were* '"authoritative"', then even then we still could not epistemologically '*access*' the past horizons of the biblical texts or even the biblical texts themselves. Following Fish, Woodman writes, 'meaning is not found *within* the text, but is constructed at the interpretative stage in the act of communication'. Therefore we are, in Woodman's "Fishian" view, supposedly *epistemologically* constrained to the *present* horizon and to the Spirit's *present* adjudication between 'interpretations' – 'interpretations' that, additionally, in our view (though perhaps not in Woodman's – see below), are *potentially* entirely 'constructed' *in and of* the *present*.[512]

In response to Woodman, though, we should note that at least three sets of deeper difficulties still seem to plague Woodman's argument here, two of which we have already addressed in our responses to W.J. Lyons.

Thus, (i), first, there is the question of epistemological constraint - the question of whether or not authoritative texts or the past horizons of authoritative texts really cannot be "accessed" at all, epistemologically-speaking. This question gives rise to another: the question of how the Spirit's role in biblical interpretation is to be understood. Does the Spirit adjudicate between interpretations of texts, or do textual criteria *also* contribute to interpreters' adjudications between interpretations of texts and/or between discernments of spirits? It has been our argument, after Thiselton, that it is largely a hermeneutical critique of history - and the hermeneutical critique of epistemology that emerges in the context of that hermeneutical critique of history - that are determinative in relation to the answers to the epistemological aspects of these questions.

(ii) Second, there is the question of the construction of "present meaning". Is

---

[509] Woodman, 'UC', 6, 7, 3, 4-5, 13. Final italics Woodman's, preceding italics ours.
[510] Woodman, 'UC', 7.
[511] Woodman, 'UC', 7, 5; cf.: Thiselton, 'U (long)' 117-120, cf.: 121, 99; Thiselton, *2H*, 88-92, cf.: 436-437, 342-347. Italics ours.
[512] Woodman, 'UC', 5, 8, 9-10, 6. Third italics Woodman's, others ours.

present meaning constructed both *in and of* the present (so Fish, Lyons and – in our estimate - Woodman), or is present meaning constructed *in* the present but potentially *shaped* – at least in part – by *past* textual meaning (so Thiselton)? Alongside considerations to do with the role played by the Holy Spirit during interpretation, the answer to this question concerning the construction of present meaning constitutes another answer that depends, in its turn, upon the answer to the deeper epistemological question of whether or not the historical conditioning of our present horizons prevents the operative influence of ancient textual language from becoming effective and transformative in the context of our present-horizon interpretative activities.

(iii) Third, there is the question of how the Spirit's adjudication is *recognized*, if not through Scripture itself. The danger with Woodman's "Fishian" view here is that it seems to lead us to an unchecked relativism of interpretations that only becomes stabilized into "valid interpretations" by prior interpretative norms – norms shaped only by present-horizon communities, and not by the biblical texts. Such "norms", on the basis of Woodman's own view, would not be directly "checkable" against the bar of transmitted biblical-textual criteria, since the latter, on the basis of Woodman's own view, would be epistemologically inaccessible. Rather, such norms could, therefore, on the basis of Woodman's viewpoint, only emerge from prior assessments of what counted as "right interpretation" in the light of the "spiritual experiences" of those in the interpretative community whose "spiritual experiences" were deemed to be the "most convincing". However, those persons in the interpretative community who have "authoritative experiences of the Spirit", or who "deem" the "spiritual experiences" of others to be "convincing", are often those with the most power. And it is those with the most power who might also abuse that power by exercising, in Pannenberg's words, "'the authoritarianism that masquerades under the guise of the 'Spirit'" – an "'authoritarianism'" that we highlighted earlier as being a problem that could potentially also emerge from Lyons' approach to biblical hermeneutics. Thus, the arguments of Woodman (and of Lyons) do not adequately safeguard us from *experience-centered authoritarianism*.[513]

The first two of these sets of deeper difficulties have already been addressed in our responses to W.J. Lyons, and so we need only quickly summarize those prior responses in the present context of discussion. The third set of deeper difficulties was indeed an *implicit* entailment of Lyons' approach in our view, but this third set of deeper difficulties emerges *explicitly* in Woodman's Thesis Contribution, and so we will devote a little more space to it here.

Thus, (i), in relation to the *first* of these three sets of deeper difficulties that still plague Woodman's hermeneutics here, then we have seen that - against Fish, Lyons, and now against Woodman - hermeneutically-qualified epistemological "access" to the past horizons of the biblical texts – and to the biblical texts themselves - is possible. Emphatically, we saw that this possibility – a possibility

---

[513] Cited in, Thiselton, 'H-O', 8. Italics ours.

that emerges from a re-historicized epistemology of *perception* - is not dependent on idealist "foundationalism", but on multiple overlapping and inter-related mutually-qualifying historico-philosophical (and theological) criteria (which are all resonant with a prior biblical viewpoint) - most notably on the criterion of historical (cf. created) unity (not uniformity).

Woodman, like Lyons, misses Thiselton's subtlety here, however, and instead sets Thiselton up as supposedly espousing the possibility of 'perfect' "knowledge" of "authorial" "intent" - and of 'perfect access to the author's mind' - along the lines of out-of-date 'psychologizing' or 'mentalist' notions of "intent". That is, Lyons and Woodman *both* falsely caricature Thiselton as being naively objectivistic (in relation to perception), and *both* overlook Thiselton's "adverbial" notion of intent (in relation to meaning). Woodman, having set up his version of this caricature of Thiselton as a straw man, then sets this straw man into a disparaged position of antithetic binary opposition (*sic*) to his (i.e. Woodman's) own privileged "Fishian" notion of "no" possible "knowledge" of "authorial" "intent".[514]

Of course, though, Woodman, like Fish and Lyons, thereby dichotomously opposes "understanding *in* the present" to "understanding the past through texts". Woodman thus espouses a largely *epistemological* dichotomy that necessarily presupposes a *historical* dichotomy in which texts are exempted from created historical unity (not uniformity) - regardless of what Woodman may *wish* to affirm about the unity (not uniformity) of God's creation.[515]

As we have seen in the case of Lyons, an uncritically inherited post-structuralist influence (which erroneously espouses "radical dissociation" between historical horizons on the false grounds of an erroneous relation of "inter-sublation" between critiques of "history" and "language") is most likely at the root of this problem of historical and epistemological dichotomies, where the *unmarked presence* of this post-structuralist influence in Woodman's approach exposes a lack of *philosophical* (and theological) *argumentation* in Woodman's thinking.

Any protestation at this point involving a denial of the possibility of the epistemological accessibility of philosophical texts would, of course, as in Lyons' case, still be a *circular assertion* based on the *same impossible historical dichotomy*. Indeed, Woodman asserts that Fish's stance is confirmed because Thiselton's 'interpretative matrix' 'is determined by his own interpretative community'. Here, though, Woodman is really asserting that: "Fish is right; hence the past cannot address the present through texts [N.B. this point presupposes a historical dichotomy]; hence Thiselton's 'community' *alone* shapes his interpretations; and hence Fish is right". But, of course, we must reply to Woodman by pointing out that there is no argument from the philosophy of history here - just a circular assertion based on an impossible historical dichotomy.[516]

---

[514] Woodman, 'UC', 8-10; cf.: Lyons, 'SM', 3, 4, 9; Thiselton, *NH*, 559; Thiselton, 'LMR', 1130. Italics ours.

[515] Woodman, 'UC', 5, 8, 9-10, 6. Italics ours.

[516] Woodman, 'UC', 16; cf. Thiselton, *2H*, 44-45, cf.: 51-84, 234-251; 304-326. Italics ours.

Therefore, we conclude that the biblical texts, *as well as the Holy Spirit and the interpretative community*, may provide interpretative constraints. The Spirit's interpretative authority cannot be separated from the authority of the Spirit's *potentially progressively accessible* biblical language. Such a separation could potentially "gag God" (to use D.A. Carson's phrase) – as we shall see below.[517]

(ii) Turning to the *second* set of deeper difficulties that plague Woodman's hermeneutics, then we should note, (ii.i), that Woodman caricatures Thiselton as espousing a view of meaning in which meanings are 'fixed', 'stable', 'deterministic', 'inherent', 'plain', and solely text-based. Woodman then, (ii.ii), sets this caricature of Thiselton up as a straw man, and then sets this straw man into a position of disparaged binary opposition (*sic*) to what, in our estimate, amounts to a "Fishian" approach to meaning – a "Fishian" approach to meaning according to which meanings are constructed *in and of* the present and according to which meanings are thereby shaped *solely* by the interpretative community.[518]

In our response to Woodman here, however, (ii.iii), it is not necessary to repeat, but only to allude to, the exposition we gave in response to Lyons concerning the *exceptional* complexities that converge to shape Thiselton's approach to present meaning. In Thiselton's approach to present meaning, the *relationships between* two sets of historical horizons – relationships that are *constitutive for* present meaning - are constructed by communities *in* the present, but are potentially still significantly *shaped* – at least in part – by the *past* meanings of texts. If we are to avoid projecting splits into created historical unity (not uniformity), then present meaning *must* have a dialogical – *and also a diachronic dialectic dynamic* – ground. Admittedly, (ii.iv), Woodman might argue that since the Holy Spirit belongs to the interpretative community and that since, in his view, the Holy Spirit *links* the interpretative community *to* the biblical texts, then we are not being fair to his stance to argue that his "community" constructs meanings that are both *"in and of"* the present. However, our justification for our argument in relation to this particular matter will emerge from our next point.[519]

Thus, (iii), turning to the *third* set of deeper difficulties that plague Woodman's hermeneutics, then it is our view, (iii.i), that Woodman seems to elevate some kind of pietistically-introspective – or potentially solipsistically introjective or maladaptive - subjective and/or inter-subjective *experience* of the Spirit to the status of a "first port of call" with respect to interpretative authority. That is, Woodman

---

[517] See our bibliography. Italics ours.
[518] Woodman, 'UC', 9; cf. Dare, H. and S. Woodman, eds., *The "Plainly Revealed" Word of God? Baptist Hermeneutics in Theory and Practice* (Macon, Georgia, USA: Mercer University Press, 2011). Italics ours.
[519] Woodman, 'UC', 6; cf. 9; cf. 8-10; cf. 3, 4-5; cf.: Thiselton, *2H*, xix, 10, 15-17, 47, 53-63, 77-84, 104, 115, 120-121, 133-139, 154-157, 196-197, 244, 265, 279-283, 291-292, 309-310, 324-325, 348-349, 354, 374-385, 432-445; Thiselton, 'LMR', 1135, 1130; Thiselton, *NH*, 111, 335, 336; 540-546, 557-559; Thiselton, 'CAP', 133-135, 201; Thiselton, 'R-RH', 82-83; Jeanrond, 'R RH', 117; Thiselton, 'Parab', 455-457, cf.: 458-461; 468. Italics ours.

appears to be saying, "epistemologically speaking, Fish is right to say that we cannot access the biblical texts; but this problem doesn't really matter because the Spirit acts as a 'go-between' who is stationed between us and the biblical texts, and so the Spirit can simply 'let us know' which interpretation of any given biblical passage is 'valid for us'".

If Woodman is saying this, however, then the question becomes that of *how* the Spirit "lets us know" which interpretation of any given passage is "valid for us". With no epistemologically accessible textual constraints concerning "which interpretation is right", Woodman seems to be leading us into some kind of corporately and pietistically introspective – or potentially solipsistically introjective or maladaptive - experiential psycho-social impressionism. In turn, this scenario threatens to plunge us back into unchecked (if still corporate) subjectivism or interpretative relativism. *Admittedly*, as we saw in our responses to Lyons, interpretative constraints provided by any given community's interpretative norms may provide *some* limited *stability* in relation to what could count as "valid interpretations". *With* Fish and Lyons, such constraints or norms would indeed provide *some* checks upon the *number* of interpretations pertaining to that community. *However*, such constraints or norms would do little to prevent the problem of *arbitrariness* from afflicting the interpretations constructed by that same community. This is so because, on the basis of a Fishian view, such constraints or norms cannot be tested at the bar of *any* "texts" – (regardless of whether these texts are biblical or just historical texts that convey the content of interpretative norms or criteria) – and so must, ultimately, if a strictly Fishian stance is adopted, be far more vulnerable to distortion under the influence of subjective (or inter-subjective) experience, and thence under the influence of power-abuse or of objectified psychological pathologies.

Woodman, however, seems to deny this charge, arguing that the adjudication 'of the Holy Spirit', if not that of 'the text', *still* precludes the danger of 'relativism'. Thus, for Woodman, 'it is the Spirit who acts as the ultimate stabilizer of interpretative truth, not the text itself'. Woodman thus argues - in relation to any given interpretative activity involving the Church and the Bible – that "the correct reading" is that particular reading that is 'Spirit-filled', whatever that reading happens to be.[520]

However, Thiselton rightly argues that discernment *between* 'interpretations' or 'experiences' 'inspired' by 'the Spirit', and those 'inspired' by "personal" - or even 'community' - 'fears', 'wishes', or 'manipulative' 'power'-plays, *also* depends upon "theological" "criteria" embedded in the '*historical*' 'public criteria of meaning' found *in* and *behind* Scripture. Which "theological criteria" can Woodman invoke by which he can distinguish *between* constructs that are 'Spirit-filled' and "constructs" that are merely 'human' (or even demonic)? We have already said that appeal to "present-horizon community-norms" does not adequately safeguard against the problem of experience-centeredness. Now, though, we may add that

---

[520] Woodman, 'UC', 3, 4-5, 9-10; cf. Thiselton, *NH*, 547. Italics ours.

Derrida speaks of 'incorporation without introjection: a sort of indigestion more or less desired by the unconscious and provoked by the other or alien body which cannot yet be assimilated'. In addition, we also noted earlier L. Woolley's comments concerning the possibility of a "solipsistically introjected maladaptive schema being projected outwards so as to overlay an external voice". But, of course, these two points, taken together, imply that the *genuine* voice of God could "feel wrong". An interpreter who was as-yet able only to introject (cf. assimilate) a voice that aligned with their maladaptive schema could *potentially* experience 'incorporation without introjection' – commonly known as a "loss of peace" – in response to the *genuine* call of God! Conversely, the same interpreter could label their objectified maladaptive schema as being a "Spirit-filled voice" because it "felt right"! Therefore, in view of the dangers of experience-centeredness, we must conclude that biblical criteria are *also* needed in order to "test the spirits" (especially since some spirits only "*masquerade* as angels of light"). Furthermore, there is also a real question in this context of discussion over whether or not Woodman leaves any place in biblical hermeneutics – or even in hermeneutics more broadly - for the roles of metacritical and critical comparative testing and/or authentication. Unchecked interpretative relativism (at least in terms of *arbitrariness*) still seems to loom large if we accept Woodman's approach.[521]

Moreover, (iii.ii), it is clear that, for Thiselton, the Spirit's 'authority' is made 'concrete', to a large extent, through the Spirit's "in front of the text" employment of provisionally *intelligible* (and therefore provisionally "accessible") 'biblical' 'speech-acts'. Furthermore, as we have seen, Thiselton rightly argues that "'the logic of self-involvement'" demands that the *'effective'* 'authority' 'of… biblical' language employed as 'speech-acts' by 'the Spirit' "in front of the text" *depends upon* the "behind the text" 'authority' or 'truth' of 'biblical' truth-claims "within the text" (so J. Goldingay). As we noted in Chapter 5, the three metaphors "behind the text", "within the text", and "in front of the text" are inseparable in any viable hermeneutic of responsible interpretation. These metaphors are inseparable, of course, because history is a unity (if not a uniformity).[522]

In other words, *Geschichte* – even a modification of *Geschichte* that accounts for present-horizon corporate inter-subjectivity - should not be divorced from *Historie* again, as we saw from Thiselton's critique of Bultmann in *The Two Horizons*. If there is not something about *"within the text"* biblical 'content' and function that is *both* authoritative due to *"behind the text"* realities *and* accessible due to *"in front of the text"* intelligibility, then *even the Holy Spirit could not use biblical language to transform us.* In that case, why shouldn't the Church switch to another set of texts for its

---

[521] Thiselton, *NH*, 429, 549, 603, 430; cf.: Thiselton, 'E-CR', 8; Thiselton, 'Freud', 12; Woodman, 'UC', 9-10, 7; Thiselton, 'Till', 88; cf.: 99; 100; Thiselton, *2H*, 383; cf.: 379-385, 437-438, 353, 111-114, 90-91; Derrida, 'LI', 246-247; 2 Cor. 11:14. L. Woolley's comments were made in a verbal communication to me (see footnote 95 above). Italics ours.

[522] Woodman, 'UC', 3, 4-5, 13; cf.: Thiselton, *2H*, 436-437, cf.: 269, 355; Thiselton, *NH*, 274; Thiselton, 'TST', 130-131; so, Goldingay, *MIS*, 215. Italics ours.

formation and guidance - *War and Peace* perhaps?[523]

Woodman's implicit reply to such a question would seem to be that when he speaks of textual inaccessibility then he is talking about the impossibility of adjudicating between "legitimate" and "illegitimate" interpretations on textual grounds rather than about the supposed unintelligibility of biblical language itself.[524]

In our view, however, this argument – given that Woodman assumes a Fishian epistemology of perception - involves a sleight of hand that divorces notions of "intelligibility" from *biblical* linguistic functions – including linguistic epistemological content-*disclosures* - and that re-attaches notions of "intelligibility" to the *community's* linguistic-functional *projections* – including *content*-projections. Thus, in any *Fishian* argument that employed such a sleight of hand, it would not be *biblical* language-*uses* that were "intelligible", but the community's own preunderstandings expressed in up-anchored biblical *signs* that were "intelligible". So, our question stands: if a Fishian stance is adopted, why shouldn't the Church switch from the Bible to *War and Peace*?

(iii.iii) Woodman helpfully summarizes other aspects of Thiselton's thinking in relation to this kind of discussion, if only so as to oppose Thiselton. Thus, as Woodman rightly notes, Thiselton argues that, on account 'of the fall', divine redemptive action - i.e. '*grace* and *revelation*' - must initially be 'beyond the understanding of humankind' and must *not* be just a "re-ordering" of what people 'already' know - i.e. not just the "constructs" of 'the community'. In this context, as Woodman rightly notes, Thiselton argues that a Fishian 'pragmatism' "renders" '*grace* and *revelation*' 'illusory' since it allows 'no "givens"' and thus 'limits God' from 'acting... from beyond'. Further, Woodman helpfully cites Thiselton's related view that a Fishian 'pragmatism' 'leads to [a] Gnostic heresy', since 'it reduces' '"*the message of the cross*"' to a '"*linguistic construct* of a tradition"'.[525]

Woodman's reply to Thiselton in this context of discussion, however, is that Thiselton's argument 'hinges on' Thiselton's 'continued assertion that, if a pragmatic understanding is adopted, then God is limited, unable to speak into the human situation from beyond'. However, continues Woodman, 'this has been shown to be an unnecessary assertion': Woodman observes not only that many pragmatists believe in and 'describe' 'human' 'fallenness', but also that he and other pragmatists "*allow*" 'the Spirit to' 'transform' present horizons 'from beyond'. In other words, Woodman argues that his socio-pragmatic perspective is *consistent* with the view that 'the Spirit' 'speaks' '"from beyond"' the 'horizons' of the self or of 'the... community', and that Thiselton is supposedly clearly in error to say that socio-pragmatism is *inconsistent* with such a view. (N.B. Woodman's notion of "pragmatism" and Thiselton's notion of "socio-pragmatism" are almost

---

[523] Thiselton, *2H*, 245-251; cf. 312, 314. Italics ours.
[524] Woodman, 'UC', 3, 4-5, 6-7, 8, 9-10, 13.
[525] Woodman, 'UC', 10-12, 17, 6; cf. Thiselton, *NH*, 549-550. Third italics ours; remaining italics Thiselton's cited by Woodman.

completely synonymous in this particular context of discussion).[526]

Our reply to Woodman at this point, however, is that he now seems to have contradicted himself again since he also asserts that 'Thiselton',

> in his desire to preserve some notion of inherent authority within a text... overlooks the fact that no form of communication can truly transform "from outside". All that communication can do is to work with already defined conceptual systems.[527]

Woodman's statements here, however, seem to contradict, first, Woodman's own earlier point that the Spirit was the only *'outside* influence... required' by 'the interpretative community' in order for meanings to be "authoritatively" stabilized. And, second, Woodman seems to contradict his own point (which we noted just above) that a (socio-)pragmatic stance provides no barrier to the way in which the Holy Spirit addresses and transforms interpretative communities 'from beyond'.[528]

Woodman might try to argue, in response to this charge, that since the Spirit is "in" the interpretative community, then the Spirit is not truly transforming the community '"from outside"'. However, how is "from beyond" not also "from outside"? Woodman cannot have it both ways. On the basis of Woodman's own arguments then *either* the Spirit's address is entirely constructed from what the interpretative community 'already' thinks (in which case Thiselton's view that 'pragmatism' 'leads to [a] Gnostic heresy' is correct), *or* the Spirit's address is incommunicable.[529]

That is, it seems to us that Woodman contradicts himself when he argues *both* that 'God' *'can'* "act" and indeed 'speak, by his Spirit', 'within the human story from beyond' or from 'outside', 'breaking into humanity in a decisive way' that is 'beyond the understanding of human kind', *and* that 'Thiselton' supposedly 'overlooks the fact that no form of communication can truly transform "from outside"'.[530]

In our view, (iii.iv), this contradiction – or dichotomy – in Woodman's thinking emerges from the difficulties that come from his trying to hold a Barthian epistemology of revelation together with a Fishian view of texts.

We have already addressed this problem in response to Lyons. But, similarly, here, we may conclude that *if* Woodman *were* to argue that the biblical texts should be accepted as being authoritative on Barthian grounds, then he would be sacrificing his Fishian view of texts. Conversely, if Woodman were to subsume a Barthian epistemology of revelation beneath a Fishian view of texts – as would seem to be the case - then he would be rejecting the biblical texts as a progressively accessible source of public criteria of meaning. But, in *either* case

---

[526] Woodman, 'UC', 11, 12, 6, 16; cf. Thiselton, *NH*, 549-550. Our italics.
[527] Woodman, 'UC', 17.
[528] Woodman, 'UC', 6-7, 3, 11, 12, 16, 9-10. Italics ours.
[529] Woodman, 'UC', 3, 4-5, 13, 6, 7, 17. Italics ours.
[530] Woodman, 'UC', 3-7, 10, 11, 12, 13, 17. Second italics Woodman's, others ours.

(given Pannenberg's critique of Barth's epistemology of revelation – see earlier), how could Woodman's community *tell* the difference between what was 'from beyond' and what was *only* the community's 'linguistic construct'? Whether or not socio-pragmatists *believe* in address 'from beyond' is not the issue. The issue concerns how they *identify* address 'from beyond' *as* address 'from beyond'. That is, against Woodman, it is history – notably historical language and the horizons of the past - that identifies the "theologically from beyond" *as* '[theologically] from beyond' in the horizon of the present. History *alone* – and not theophany - identifies authentic theology *as* "authentic".[531]

Furthermore, (iii.v), Woodman's saying (when wearing his Fishian hat!) that 'no form of communication can truly transform "from outside"' is like saying that one cannot add bricks to a toy building-brick set. In fact, however, whilst the "rules" for connecting added bricks must initially be the same, the "form" of the bricks, the "content" of the set, the "habits" of "construction", and the *shape* (*sic*) of what is "constructed" may vary considerably and *may be changed from outside*. And builders can switch from toy building-bricks to woodwork, even learning new "rules of connection" as well.[532]

That is, for Thiselton, following Gadamer, 'tradition' 'comes to speech' 'in the… language' of "interpreters" *and* the truly 'new' '"emerges"' in 'conversation'. Drawing on the later Wittgenstein, Gadamer, I.T. Ramsey, and on others, Thiselton argues that "concept-formation" and "concept-extension" remain part of what historical understanding (and historical conditioning) *is*. Yes, Thiselton argues, there is 'prior' "shared" 'understanding'; but, in Thiselton's estimate, readers' 'horizons' can be 're-shaped and enlarged' *through reading texts*.[533]

(iii.vi) There is also the possible – though admittedly less certain – problem that Woodman *perhaps* seems at times to constrain the Spirit's "beyond-ness" or transcendence to a *quasi-spatial* transcendence within the temporal limitations associated with the isolated present horizon. Thiselton, by contrast, properly conceives of the Spirit's transcendence in a more 'trans-historical' diachronic manner in which the Spirit transcends not only 'present' horizons but also the horizons of 'the past' and of 'the future'.[534]

Moving on, (iii.vii), then Woodman's thinking manifests another problem that is closely related to the particular set of deeper difficulties that we are addressing here. That is, Woodman goes on to attack what he calls Thiselton's 'formalist

---

[531] Thiselton, 'M&M', 8; cf.: Thiselton, 'E-CR', 8; Thiselton, 'Till', 92; Thiselton, *2H*, 379-385, cf.: 437-438, 353, 111-114, 90-91; Woodman, 'UC', 12, 13, 10. Italics ours.

[532] Woodman, 'UC', 17. Italics ours.

[533] Thiselton, *2H*, 310-313, 400, xix, 165, 380-383, 123; cf.: 370-372; 386-407; 343-345; 121-124; cf.: Thiselton, *NH*, 317; Thiselton, 'NH', 311; Thiselton, *LLM*, 4-6; Woodman, 'UC', 10, 11, 12, 17. Italics ours.

[534] Woodman, 'UC', 6, 7, 3; cf.: Thiselton, *2H*, 53-63, cf.: 63-84, 88-92, 249-250, 265, 342-347; Thiselton, *NH*, 549; Thiselton, 'NH', 311; Thiselton, 'THS&TF', 170, 173, 185-186; Thiselton, 'REC', 512, cf.: 517-518, 524-525. Italics ours.

approach' to 'doctrine'. In this context Woodman rightly notes that, in Thiselton's estimate, a Fishian "'pragmatism'" is unable "'to determine what would *count as a systematic mistake in the development of doctrine*'". By supposed contrast, Woodman, after J. McClendon, argues that he (i.e. Woodman) ties 'doctrine' to 'church' 'practice', 'and… therefore… to the context of the interpretative 'community'. For Woodman, corporate interpretation 'provides a safeguard against rampant individualism and individualistic interpretations'.[535]

However, first, we must reply by noting that Thiselton is no 'formalist'. Thiselton may be found "embedding" *'texts'* in the *'two…* horizons' of 'communicative action' against the background of historical unity (not uniformity) and of historical relationalities, *and* "embedding" *"doctrine" both* in 'texts' *and* in the *corporate* 'horizons of' "church" 'community', 'interpretation', and practice.[536]

That is, second, as we implied in our responses to Lyons, Thiselton does not deny that there is some truth in Woodman's comment that 'the community can be seen to provide a stabilizing effect on the development of interpretation and doctrine'. The issue, though, concerns whether or not the corporate church body provides a *sufficient*, or the *only* "possible", guard against 'systematic' "doctrinal" "mistakes". And we must conclude, with Thiselton, that the corporate church body *does not* provide a *sufficient*, or the *only* "possible", guard against 'systematic' "doctrinal" "mistakes". We must come to this conclusion partly on the basis of human fallenness, and partly on the basis of Thiselton's historically-adequate – or re-historicized – epistemology (on which, see Chapters 3, 5, 6 and above).[537]

For Woodman, though, 'doctrine' is not 'text-dependent'. For Woodman, 'doctrine' is the 'context-dependent' 'way in which a given community of faith lives out and communicates the truths of their faith'.[538] However, for Thiselton, this kind of unnecessary artificial antithesis (i.e. between 'doctrine' and 'texts') falsely banishes from the community the very textual 'criteria' that *"identify"* 'the truths of their faith'. This scenario, in Thiselton's estimate, then leads to the problem that 'the context of *convention*' becomes the *only* 'criterion' establishing '"correct"' *'doctrine'*-in-'"practice"'. Since "conventions", however, are not – on the basis of a Fishian argument – *checkable* against textually-transmitted criteria, then

---

[535] Woodman, 'UC', 13-15. Woodman citing Thiselton's italics.
[536] Thiselton, *NH*, 541, 590; cf.: Thiselton, *2H*, 15, 375, 430, 168, 321, 314-316, 325, 308-309; cf.: 314-326; 110-113; Thiselton, 'CAP', 143. Our italics.
[537] Woodman, 'UC', 15; cf.: Thiselton, *2H*, 94-95, cf.: 8-9, 80-81, 113-114, 154-156, 200-203, 282-284, 292, 304-306, 404-406; Thiselton, 'M&M', 8; Thiselton, 'Exc', 12; Thiselton, 'Doubt', 8; Thiselton, A.C., 'No Horns on the Pope', *CEN* 14 Jun. (1974), 5; Thiselton, 'LGT', 8; Thiselton, 'CH', 5; Thiselton, A.C., 'Enthusiasm Not Enough: Güttgemanns, Sawyer, and Barr on Biblical Research', *CEN* 13 Sep. (1974), 6; Thiselton, 'NH', 318-327; Thiselton, 'E-CR', 8; Thiselton, 'H-O', 8; Thiselton, 'KNT', 90-91; 104; 85-86; Thiselton, 'EITN', 578-579; 583-584; Thiselton, 'Par', 48, 49; 52; Thiselton, A.C., 'Review of A. Hodes' *Encounter with Martin Buber*', *Chman* 90.2 (1976), 138-139; Thiselton, 'U (short)', 6; Thiselton, 'AA', 610; Thiselton, 'Sch', 135-136; Thiselton, *NH*, 544, 549, 601. Italics ours.
[538] Woodman, 'UC', 15.

"conventions" – in a Fishian community at least - become more easily subject to distortion at the hands of those in power. Thus, Woodman's Fishian stance does indeed potentially lead to a scenario in which there are no "checks" on 'corporate' 'power'-abuse, on '*corporate* self-interest', on 'corporate self-deception' or, indeed, on systematic doctrinal mistakes.[539]

In conclusion, (iii.viii), even if we overlook Woodman's self-contradiction concerning the Spirit's "communication from outside", then Woodman's stance of relying only on *experience* of the Holy Spirit and on the interpretative community itself to keep the interpretative community "on track" *still* carries with it a serious problem. This serious problem concerns the question of *how* the interpretative community could *check, test, authenticate, isolate, or identify* the "contents" and "functions" *both* of the Spirit's address *and* of its own corporate doctrine-in-practice. That is, how could these "contents" and "functions" be metacritically, or even critically, *checked, tested, authenticated, isolated, or identified?* How could *these* "contents" and "functions" be distinguished from *other* "contents" and "functions" - other "contents" and "functions" that were potentially psycho-social, pathological, or even demonic, in character and origin? How could the community "discern between spirits"? How could re-historicized subject-object conceptualization and juxtapositional comparative testing have any liberating socio-metacritical and/or critical role to play in Woodman's hermeneutics?

Moreover, against Woodman's argument, other insuperable problems emerge in Woodman's Fishian approach – problems that have to do with how the Spirit could in any sense "use" *biblical* language that was "within the text" to transform readers "in front of the text" if that language were epistemologically inaccessible (and presumably, therefore, unintelligible) and/or unrelated to true states of affairs "behind the text". On the basis of Woodman's approach, the Spirit would be "using" only the *community's own* "uses" of *up-anchored* biblical *signs*. Thus, in Woodman's "community", constructed present meanings would indeed be *both in and of* the present.

Of course, Woodman would reply – and has replied verbally in conversation - that since the past horizons of the biblical texts, and even the biblical texts themselves, are "inaccessible" epistemologically-speaking, then we have no choice *but* to rely only on *experience* of the Spirit and on the interpretative community itself for adjudications between interpretations. Woodman would perhaps disarmingly concede that Thiselton had *rightly* identified at least some of the problems that this situation brings. But, for Woodman, this situation and its problems are simply an unavoidable fact of life.[540]

This objection, however, has already been addressed and countered in our responses to the first and second sets of deeper difficulties that we found in

---

[539] Thiselton, *2H*, 353, 438; cf. 379-385; cf.: Thiselton, *NH*, 395, 440, 394, 544, 549, 413, 379, 386, 392; cf.: 399-401, 543-546; Thiselton, 'E-CR', 8; Woodman, 'UC', 15. First, third and fifth italics ours, remaining italics Thiselton's.

[540] Woodman, 'UC', 5, 8, 9-10, 6. Italics ours.

Woodman's stance in this context of discussion (see above).

(4) One final point raised by Woodman in his Thesis Contribution may now be addressed. Woodman argues that 'Thiselton's... mechanism' by which 'humanity can be addressed [by God through Scripture] from without' is merely 'a' 'rhetorical' 'personal crusade' based on 'theological' special pleading or assertion. In Woodman's estimate, Thiselton's stance is 'a hopeless idealization, held to for doctrinaire reasons'. Lyons, similarly, it will be remembered, argued that Thiselton's otherwise legitimate hermeneutical interests were corrupted by 'historical or theological necessity' (i.e. by a theology pervaded by an unconditionally-privileged philosophically idealist traditionalism).[541]

It would now seem, however, that these charges are false.

Thus, (a), the answer to the question of just who is being 'doctrinaire' is determined by finding out who is appealing to the philosophy of history so as to warrant "(meta-)critical testing against provisional truth-criteria in the public sphere", and who is appealing to epistemologically-evasive "'authoritarianism'". And, as we saw in our responses to Lyons, a Barthian epistemology of revelation leads to an "'authoritarianism of the 'self-authenticating' Word'" and to an "'authoritarianism that masquerades under the guise of the 'Spirit'"'.[542] As we saw, adding a Fishian stance into the mix only *sharpens* the problem of "'authoritarianism'" still further, since a Fishian stance's many "'Fishian'" "Bibles" (Lyons' notion) and many "'Gods'" (Lyons' language) are likely to make such "'authoritarianism'" more and more Spirit-centric and less and less Word-centric. Indeed, in our view, this "sharpening" of the problem of authoritarianism *is actually beginning to happen in Woodman's conceptualizations of biblical hermeneutics in his Thesis Contribution* (regardless of whether or not this "sharpening" of the problem of authoritarianism is beginning to happen *yet* in Woodman's *practice* in his biblical studies).[543]

Moreover, (b), it is difficult to see how Lyons and Woodman could possibly provide any kind of coherent *argument* for their Barthian-Fishian stance, given the five sets of internal inconsistencies that we have unearthed in their hermeneutics.

Thus, in relation to *Lyons*, (i), we saw how a *Barthian* stance led to theo-historico-epistemological, epistemological, and linguistico-epistemological dichotomies (see above).

(ii) We saw how Lyons' *Fishian* stance led to historical (present context *versus* past context, texts *versus* historical reality), epistemological (corporate self-understanding *versus* historical understanding), and linguistic (present – especially oral – linguistic constructs and assertions *versus* textually transmitted historical public criteria with referential and conceptual content, alongside other textual (extra-)linguistic functions) dichotomies.

(iii) We also saw how *tensions between* "Barthian" and "Fishian" stances in Lyons'

---

[541] Woodman, 'UC', 2, 3; cf. 6; cf. Lyons, *C&E*, 109.
[542] Pannenberg, *BQ2*, 199-206; cf.: Thiselton, 'H-O', 8; Woodman, 'UC', 2, 3; cf. 6.
[543] Thiselton, 'H-O', 8; cf. Lyons, *C&E*, 263; cf. 264. Italics ours.

thinking led to a *third* set of problematic dichotomies – dichotomies that were centered on questions to do with "interpretative impediments to historical-textual reference *versus* epistemological barriers to historical-textual reference", with "biblical historical-reference *versus* community referent-creation", and with "*theocentric* epistemology versus *anthropocentric* epistemology".

(iv) We found a *fourth* set of dichotomies in Lyons' thinking in which – in a series of performative self-contradictions - he seemed in *practice* to *begin* to slip from an unworkable Fishian epistemology *towards* a more Thiseltonian stance.

(v) We also found *interpretative* "straw-man-style" dichotomies between Lyons' own "non-foundationalism" and false charges concerning Thiselton's supposed idealist "foundationalism", and between Lyons' Fishian notion of "perception" and false charges concerning Thiselton's supposed objectivism. These dichotomies seemed to be a shadow of idealist "foundationalism" in that Lyons did not *immerse himself in multiple traditions (at the level of critical-synthetic sublation-filter-construction)* as Thiselton did, but *projected a binary either/or onto history so as to obscure its multiple traditions.* In our view, these "binary either/or" projections constituted an echo of idealist "foundationalism" *within* Lyons' perception of the current debate.

Similarly, in relation to Woodman then, (i), given Woodman's stated indebtedness to Barth's epistemology of revelation, then the *first* of these five sets of dichotomies must be flagged as being at least a *potential* problem in Woodman's hermeneutics. Moreover, (ii), given Woodman's Fishian points concerning textual epistemological "inaccessibility", then the *second* of these five sets of dichotomies is most certainly a problem in Woodman's approach. Furthermore, (iii), given Woodman's apparent desire to hold both to a Barthian epistemology of revelation and to a Fishian approach to texts, then the *third* of these five sets of dichotomies must also be flagged as being at least a *potential* problem in Woodman's hermeneutics.

In addition, (iv), we saw a couple of points where Woodman seemed to contradict himself and slip *towards* a Thiseltonian stance (cf. the *fourth* set of dichotomies we found in Lyons' approach – see above).

Thus, first, for Woodman, "no communication could truly transform from outside" (this was a point that Woodman made in *criticism* of Thiselton's thinking); and yet Woodman also argued that the Spirit was an "outside influence" who could speak and transform communities "from beyond" (Woodman's point here *aligns* with *an aspect of* Thiselton's thinking).

And, second, for Woodman, the Spirit was active during the "writing" of the biblical texts, which suggested that the biblical texts were authoritative (Woodman's point here *aligns* with *an aspect of* Thiselton's thinking); and yet Woodman also pursued the argument that the locus of interpretative authority was *not* "the [biblical] text itself" (this was a point that Woodman made explicitly as part of a *criticism* of an aspect of Thiselton's thinking).

Now, third, we may add a further observation in this context of discussion. This further observation concerns the way in which Woodman slips into a Lyons-style self-contradiction that may be said to be truly "performative". That is, in charging Thiselton with indulging in 'a' 'rhetorical' 'personal crusade' based on 'theological' special pleading or assertion, and in 'a hopeless idealization, held to for doctrinaire reasons', Woodman is actually presupposing that *he* – in *contrast to* Thiselton - has *argued* that his own stance is *warranted* on the ground of "testing against provisionally accessible provisional truth-criteria in the public sphere". That is, Woodman has unwittingly adopted a premise that is consistent *neither* with a Fishian epistemology *nor* with a Barthian epistemology of revelation. On the contrary, this premise is *Thiseltonian*.[544]

Finally, (v), the shadow of idealist foundationalism – the shadow that we found in a fifth set of dichotomies in *Lyons'* thinking - re-emerges in *Woodman's* thinking. That is, Lyons' "non-foundationalism *versus* the straw-man of foundationalism" dichotomy reappears in Woodman's Thesis Contribution as, (v.i), "anti-formalism *versus* the straw man of formalism"; as, (v.ii), "no access to texts and to authorial intent" *versus* the straw man of "absolute access to texts and to authorial intent along the old discredited psychologizing or mentalist lines of approach"; and as, (v.iii), "a Fishian view of meaning" *versus* the straw man of "a simplistic text-based 'deterministic', 'fixed', 'plain', or 'inherent' view of 'meaning'". This succession of antithetical over-generalized a-historical binary (*sic*) oppositions – which replaces assessments of actual multiple historical traditions – constitutes a binary-structured quasi-formalist interpretative content or grid that Woodman *roughly superimposes or projects onto the particularities of the history of hermeneutical traditions so as to obscure the latter*.

In other words, Lyons' and Woodman's internally inconsistent hermeneutic with its *five* sets of superimposed theoretical (and practical) dichotomies – once combined with a lack of criteria by which to distinguish between Spirit-sanctioned interpretations and interpretations of human and/or of demonic origin, and with a lack of criteria by which to distinguish between doctrine-in-practice and systematic mistakes in doctrine – could never form the basis of *any* coherent argument. Their stance could only ever lead – if pressed to its Fishian limits - to a post-theoretical *"authoritarianism that masquerades under the guise of the 'Spirit'"*. Lyons and Woodman, then, have *projected* their own 'rhetorical' 'personal crusade' based on 'theological' special pleading or assertion – or their own 'hopeless idealization, held to for doctrinaire reasons' – onto Thiselton, and have misleadingly marketed it for consumers as though it were "Thiselton's problem".[545]

This form of obfuscating projection, though, is a form of *hermeneutical foreclosure* that constitutes a dimension of hermeneutical foreclosure that is *additional* to that dimension of hermeneutical foreclosure that we have already highlighted in response to "Fishian" criticisms of Thiselton. That is, in "Fishian" criticisms of Thiselton, there is hermeneutical foreclosure through assertions to do with textual epistemological "inaccessibility". *Part* of the assertiveness of "Fishian" criticisms of Thiselton, however, *also* involves a projection or disowning *of* hermeneutical

---

[544] Woodman, 'UC', 2, 3; cf. 6; cf. Lyons, *C&E*, 109. Italics ours.
[545] Thiselton, 'H-O', 8; cf. Woodman, 'UC', 2, 3; cf. 6. Italics ours.

foreclosure, a projection or disowning of hermeneutical foreclosure in which *Thiselton* is falsely labeled as the one who has "not listened".

Whilst this "disowned projection" is still sometimes quite subtle in Lyons and Woodman (despite Woodman's explicit remarks about a 'rhetorical' 'personal crusade' based on 'theological' special pleading or assertion, or about 'a hopeless idealization, held to for doctrinaire reasons'), the presence of this "disowned projection" is in fact the beginning of a slide down a slippery slope towards a far less subtle form of retaliatory projection and hermeneutical foreclosure.

That is, as we shall see below, Thiselton predicted more than 15 years ago that, as socio-pragmatism works itself out in our academic university departments and in our societies more broadly, "rational debate" will descend towards a scenario in which competing groups – bereft of any acknowledged grounds or epistemological motivations for objective discussion, for criteria-based cross-referencing, for a call to relational civility, or for gathering together the world of rigorous argument in a patient manner that listens to the other – will find themselves at loggerheads with one another in increasingly hostile, overly-dramatic perlocutionary exchanges. As we shall see in our next section, Thiselton's predictions about such "bad relating" are beginning to come true – at least in *some* quarters.

D) CONCLUDING COMMENTS

Rounding off this present section, though, then we saw earlier that A.K.M. Adam's pseudo-"post-structuralist" criticism of Thiselton seemed almost to canonize hermeneutical foreclosure in that Adam simply "binned" or "shelved" Thiselton prematurely in the "idealist" or "formalist" pigeon-hole. Moreover, we saw that Adam seemed potentially to disallow Christ-centered metacriticism.

We also saw that, in socio-pragmatic hermeneutical foreclosure (notably, that of Fish, Lyons, and Woodman), there was much more at stake than straightforward misreading or confusion. Indeed, a whole nexus of problems converged to generate socio-pragmatic hermeneutical foreclosure – as follows.

(1) Socio-pragmatism's (pseudo)-theoretical *"legitimization"* of the notion of complete textual epistemological inaccessibility at the level of interpretative practice (stratum three) presupposed, (2), the theoretical "Fishian"-style *dichotomies* that beleaguered socio-pragmatism's implicit conceptualizations of history, epistemology, and language (stratum two).

(3) In socio-pragmatic approaches, these "Fishian"-style dichotomies, in turn, presupposed – and yet, in a *circular* fashion, were also in effect appealed to in order to warrant what was *thereby* only – an *asserted foreclosure* of dialogue with the philosophy of history at the *hidden* level of pre-understanding (stratum one).

(4) This socio-pragmatic pre-understanding was, in part, uncritically inherited and adopted from the post-structuralist tradition and, as such, presupposed the post-structuralist mistake of *reversing* the *proper* respective assigned basicalities, ontological prioritizations, or "sublation-relations" that *as a matter of course should* be applied to conceptualizations of "history" and of "language" during critical-synthetic sublation-filter-construction.

(5) Historically, this post-structuralist "mistake" occurred when a hermeneutical critique of history (consistent with a prior biblical theology and with an emerging philosophy of history) was erroneously conflated with, and subducted beneath, philosophically and ontotheologically "idealist" trends by post-structuralist language-based critiques of Western metaphysics.

(6) This conflating of the "philosophically idealist" with the "properly historical" occurred partly because, historically, post-structuralist language-based critiques of Western metaphysics emerged *just prior* to the watershed - in the development of an adequate theological philosophy of history - that is implicit in a later-Wittgensteinian-Gadamerian-Pannenbergian critical synthesis.

(7) This conflating of the "philosophically idealist" with the "properly historical" *persists* in the socio-pragmatic responses to Thiselton that we examined. By contrast, the later-Wittgensteinian-Gadamerian-Pannenbergian critical synthesis first emerges in *Thiselton's The Two Horizons*. Thus, *The Two Horizons*, heralds a more important development in Western thought than is commonly realized.

These findings, coupled with our earlier findings in response to Adam, tend to make Adam's – and perhaps others' - socio-pragmatic and pseudo-"post-structuralist" appeals to thinkers such as Fish and Derrida look like bluff, not theoretical sophistication. Has misreading descended towards *name-dropping?*

And yet, at the same time, the connections between post-structuralism and socio-pragmatism are quite real – though socio-pragmatism in fact presupposes what is, in effect, one of the main *weaknesses* of post-structuralism (i.e. its attempt to sublate a critique of history into an over-extended critique of language).

Moreover, we found that Lyons' and Woodman's attempts to integrate a broadly Barthian - or Barthian-Childsian - epistemology of revelation with a "Fishian" epistemology, and with a "Fishian" approach to the biblical texts, simply compounded the nexus of problems that we have just noted above. Thus, apart from the "Fishian"-style dichotomies noted above and the additional dichotomies that Pannenberg found *in* a Barthian epistemology of revelation, a third set of dichotomies was generated by tensions *between* Barthian and Fishian epistemologies. A fourth set of dichotomies emerged in the clash between a Fishian epistemology and the problem of having to function and interpret in the actual world. At such points, Lyons and Woodman *began* to slip towards a more *'Thiseltonian''* hermeneutic. A fifth set of dichotomies – that was ironically reminiscent of idealist "foundationalism" - emerged in a series of binary or "two-fold" interpretative antitheses – antitheses centered largely on questions to do with perception and meaning - that Lyons and Woodman *projected (sic) onto* history. This form of binary projection contrasted with a Gadamerian-Thiseltonian approach of *immersion in* multiple historical traditions. In the case of Lyons and Woodman, then, it was as though one had "to cease to listen to history" – it was as though Lyons and Woodman were *unshakably and pre-dialogically convinced* that only two broad sets of approaches (admittedly with various sub-categories) to perception and meaning had ever been offered in the history of thought.

Perhaps the most alarming feature of *theological* socio-pragmatic approaches, however, was their potential tendency to sharpen even the two authoritarianisms that emerged from a *Barthian* epistemological evasiveness into a radicalized authoritarianism that masqueraded as present experience of the Holy Spirit. If Pannenberg complained (see above) that "the blows bounced off" the *Barthians* then how much more will the *Fishians* – once the "yeast" of theory works through to the "dough" of interpretative practice - go on to immunize themselves from external criticism?

Moreover, as we shall see below, Thiselton's concerns - about the ways in which socio-pragmatism can lead to the fragmentation of society into competing interest-groups that indulge in hostile exchanges bereft of epistemological anchorage and, therefore, of "good relating" – cannot simply be ignored.

*3. Hostile Criticism: The Drama Triangle of Disowned Projected Hermeneutical Foreclosure*

Moving on, it is worth briefly observing another kind of hermeneutical foreclosure that appears in criticisms of Thiselton's work. As we indicated above, this further kind of hermeneutical foreclosure relates more to aggressive attack and *reaction* than it does to complex theoretical considerations. Whilst we have said that, in Thiselton's estimate, this kind of hermeneutical foreclosure can have its roots in socio-pragmatism, we shall see that it can emerge from so-called "right-wing" sources just as easily as it can emerge from so-called "left-wing" sources.

Indeed, it is not at all the case that all socio-pragmatists will necessarily descend immediately (or even eventually) into aggressive attack and reaction. Whilst theory affects practice directly, and whilst practice affects interpretative outcomes directly, it still takes time for the "yeast" to work through the "dough". Moreover, academic, cultural and traditional backgrounds are often such that strong etiquettes of "good relating" (stratum three) prevail *despite* the direction that *hermeneutical theory* (stratum two) is taking. Furthermore, it is also often the case – as we argued in relation to Lyons and Woodman - that interpreters' hermeneutical theories are internally inconsistent to such an extent that, when it comes to practice, there are different "yeasts" working through the "dough" simultaneously.

Admittedly, in our view, it is still *true* that serious problems are indeed emerging in the hermeneutical theory of Lyons and Woodman. And yet, at least biblical scholars like Lyons and Woodman sometimes make serious and laudable attempts to wrestle with the complexities of hermeneutical theory (or at least they have done in the past). Furthermore, and despite the dangers of socio-pragmatic isolationism, it is to be hoped that at least the etiquettes of *"good relating"* may be preserved between our two traditions, no matter how robust our *theoretical exchanges* become.

With respect to our next group of critics, however, "good relating" already seems to have descended into quasi-tabloid aggressive reaction and attack. Indeed, with respect to these critics, "good relating" seems to have been subsumed beneath the quasi-theatrical role-performances of a psycho-social "drama-triangle" of "victims", "persecutors", and "rescuers" (on "the drama triangle", see below) –

as follows.

Thus, (1), according to M.W. Nicholson, Thiselton's (and certain others') appeals to the later Wittgenstein are an "abuse" of the later Wittgenstein. In effect, Nicholson puts the later Wittgenstein forward as the "victim" of Thiselton's "abuse", Thiselton forward as the "abuser" or "persecutor" of the later Wittgenstein, and himself (i.e. Nicholson) forward as the "rescuer" who "rescues" the "victim" (i.e. the later Wittgenstein) *from* the "persecutor" (i.e. Thiselton). In this way, Nicholson so skews the terms of the debate that it is difficult for us even to *reply* to Nicholson without *our* looking like a "rescuer" "rescuing" a "victim" from a "persecutor"![546]

Nevertheless, our observations in Chapters 4 and 6 do in fact force us to repudiate *all* of the points that Nicholson makes in criticism of Thiselton. In our view, Nicholson has "reacted" to Thiselton by "disowning" his own hermeneutical foreclosure, by "projecting" his own hermeneutical foreclosure onto Thiselton, and by then "marketing" his own hermeneutical foreclosure as being "Thiselton's problem". That is, it is *Thiselton* who is misrepresented, *by Nicholson*; furthermore, it is *Nicholson*, and not Thiselton, who sometimes seems to misrepresent the later Wittgenstein – as follows.

Thus, (a), against Nicholson's reading of Thiselton, we should note that Thiselton's appeal to the later Wittgenstein does *not* simply "center" 'on… language-games', but is far more extensive than this as we saw in Chapter 4.[547] (b) Against Nicholson's reading of Thiselton, we should observe that Thiselton's later 'Wittgenstein' does *not* argue 'that "no gap occurs between 'the way the world is' and 'the way we see it'"', but speaks of '"seeing… as…"', "showing", "noticing", and '"scaffolding"' (see Chapters 4 and 6).[548] And, (c), Nicholson's 'reasonable extrapolation… that' '"form[s] of life"' is 'a socio-cultural term' that embraces 'customs' *supports*, and does *not* contradict, Thiselton's thinking. That is, as we noted in Chapter 4, Thiselton associates "forms of life" with "traditions".[549]

Moving on, then, (d), and against Nicholson's reading of Thiselton, we should note that 'Thiselton' does *not* simply espouse 'a Wittgensteinian framework'. Rather, Thiselton imports 'Wittgensteinian' insights into a broader historico-philosophical frame as we have seen. In Thiselton's thinking this frame, in turn,

---

[546] Nicholson, M.W., 'Abusing Wittgenstein: The Misuse of the Concept of Language-Games in Contemporary Theology', *JEThS* 39 (Dec. 1996), 617; cf. 617-629; on the drama triangle, cf. Karpman, S.B., 'Fairy Tales and Script Drama Analysis', *TAB* 7.26 (Apr. 1968), 39-43, also at: *http://www.karpmandramatriangle.com/pdf/DramaTriangle.pdf*. We are indebted to L. Woolley and H. McFarlane for bringing the "Drama Triangle" to our attention.

[547] Nicholson, 'AW', 617; cf. Thiselton, *2H*, 379-385. Italics ours.

[548] Nicholson, 'AW', 620; cf. for example, Thiselton, *2H*, 419, 372, 371, 392; cf. 415-422, 368-370, 7, 139, 361, 380-407. Italics ours.

[549] Nicholson, 'AW', 620-621; cf. Thiselton, *2H*, 378, 374, 382; cf.: 7-8, 32-33, 373-379. Italics ours.

elucidates – and is shaped by - a prior developing *biblical* framework.[550]

(e) Against Nicholson's reading of Thiselton, we may observe that Thiselton does *not* equate "'language-games'" with "'context'" and with *"'Sitz im Leben'"*, but only notes "parallels" 'between' these three concepts.[551] And, (f), against Nicholson's reading of Thiselton, we should note that 'Thiselton' does *not* thereby render "'language-games'" 'superfluous'. Rather, Thiselton rightly argues that the multiform concept of "'language-games'" has grammars that are different to the grammars that pertain to the concepts of "'context'" and *"'Sitz im Leben'"*. Thus, for example, Thiselton argues that the grammars of the multiform concept of "'language-games'" embrace connotations of *diachronic linguistic action by human agents*. That is, for Thiselton, "'language-games'" uniquely generate and shape human agents' *linguistic "'action'"* – where that "'action'" may include "'action'" *upon later readers who have a different "'context'" and "'Sitz im Leben'"*.[552]

(g) Against Nicholson's reading of Thiselton, we should observe that Thiselton does *not* argue that 'Wittgensteinian linguistics' can 'rise above relativism' unaided. As we saw in Chapters 3 and 6, and against Nicholson, we should note that Thiselton does *not* ground his hermeneutical critique of epistemology 'on a Wittgensteinian foundation'. Admittedly, Thiselton *does* argue that the later Wittgenstein's work is *consistent with historical and geographical trans-contextuality and trans-temporality*, where Thiselton also argues that historical and geographical trans-contextuality and trans-temporality (cf. historical continuity) are *two* of the factors that militate against radicalized views of culture-relativity or of context-relativity. That is, unlike Nicholson, Thiselton *rightly* notes the trans-contextual and trans-temporal connotations of the later Wittgenstein's thinking in relation to "language"-"'habits'", linguistic 'rules', 'forms of life", 'public criteria of meaning', "'scaffolding'" 'convictions', 'concepts with blurred edges', "'family resemblances'", 'the common behavior of humankind', and so on (see Chapters 4 and 6).[553] Thus, as E.A. Dunn notes, for example, 'the presence of... public rules... allows Thiselton to conclude that "effective language presupposes a distinction between correct and mistaken application of words"'. Again, as we saw in Chapter 4, Thiselton argues that this later Wittgensteinian point, amongst others that he (i.e. Thiselton) espouses, militates *against* radicalized views of culture-relativity or of context-relativity. Nevertheless, as we saw in Chapters 3, 6, and above, Thiselton's arguments in relation to historical and geographical trans-contextuality and trans-temporality are hardly the *basis* of Thiselton's

---

[550] Nicholson, 'AW', 622; cf. Thiselton, *2H*, 395-396. Italics ours.

[551] Nicholson, 'AW', 624-625; cf. Thiselton, *2H*, 396; cf. 66, 82-84. Italics in speech-marks Nicholson's, others ours.

[552] Nicholson, 'AW', 624-625; cf. Thiselton, *2H*, 376; cf.: 374-376; 388, 396-397, 326, 86. Italics ours, except for the two occurrences of the phrase "*'Sitz im Leben'*", where the italics are Nicholson's.

[553] Nicholson, 'AW', 625, cf.: 621, 628; cf.: Thiselton, *2H*, 358-359, 374-401; Thiselton, 'Parab', 466-467; Thiselton, *NH*, 516, 404; cf. 379-409, 381; cf. Chapter 3. Italics ours.

hermeneutical critique of epistemology.[554]

B.J. Walsh misreads Thiselton's work in ways that are analogous to Nicholson's misreadings of Thiselton's work in relation to this particular point (though Walsh is more of a "friendly" critic whose hermeneutical foreclosures in relation to Thiselton's thinking are relatively straightforward). That is, Walsh mistakenly argues that Thiselton simply extends the later Wittgenstein's notion 'of public criteria of meaning' in order to derive his (i.e. Thiselton's) working assumption that Christ's 'Cross' can function as 'a universal criterion of meaning'. Walsh then argues that because of the 'different language-games', 'forms of life, traditions, and corporate memories' that pertain to 'different people and communities', 'truly public criteria of meaning cannot be established' this 'easily'. Thus Walsh argues that 'Buddhists', for example, interpret 'the Cross' according to 'different' (i.e. non-biblical) 'criteria'. However, as we have seen, and against Walsh's reading of Thiselton, we should observe that Thiselton warrants his working belief that 'the Cross' can function as a universally applicable epistemological metacriterion primarily through his hermeneutical critiques of *history* and of *epistemology*, and not primarily through his hermeneutical critique of *language*. And the process by which Thiselton warrants his ascription of metacritical status to 'the Cross' is hardly an "easy" process, as we have seen (Thiselton is hardly straightforwardly "fideistic"). Moreover, Thiselton's use of the notion of 'public criteria of meaning' relates more closely to the question of intra-traditional and inter-traditional *intelligibility* than it does to the question of inter-traditional *consensus concerning truth-claims*. *Whatever* certain 'Buddhists' may believe about *truth*, they would have *failed to understand* ancient biblical language *on its own terms* if they interpreted that language according to their *own* 'public criteria of meaning' rather than according to *biblical* 'public criteria of meaning'.[555] As we noted in Chapter 5, a critique of hermeneutical *understanding* should not be confused with a hermeneutical critique of *epistemology* – even if the former presupposes *both* the latter *and other* hermeneutical critiques.

(h) Nicholson's assertion that the later Wittgenstein 'rejected any attempt at grounding language in a real world existing-in-itself apart from human linguistic interaction' presumably means that the later Wittgenstein – given his historical context of wrestling with, and of criticizing, positivistic Neo-Kantian approaches to language and meaning – 'rejected' logical positivist appeals to philosophically idealist and/or formalist 'referential' and/or 'ideational' theories. But, against Nicholson's reading of Thiselton, we should stress that this point cannot be turned into a criticism of *Thiselton*, since Thiselton *also* "rejects" philosophically idealist and/or formalist 'referential' and/or 'ideational' theories (see Chapters 4,

---

[554] Dunn, *BD&H*, 21; cf.: Thiselton, *NH*, 544, 549; Thiselton, *2H*, 380 (quoted by Dunn). Italics ours.
[555] Walsh, 'TC', 235, cf. 234, 233; cf.: Thiselton, *2H*, 74-84, cf.: 237, 306-310, 401-407; Thiselton, 'MP', 4-12; Thiselton, 'LMR', 1130-1135. Italics ours.

6, and above).[556]

(i) Nicholson's criticism of Thiselton in which Nicholson argues that, on the basis of the later Wittgenstein's thinking, there can be no "possibility" 'of passing judgment on any form of life, no matter how bizarre', cannot be legitimately applied to Thiselton. *To an extent*, Thiselton employs prior theological metacriteria (i.e. biblical metacriteria that already exist) *precisely because* he concludes that thinkers like the later Wittgenstein, Heidegger and Gadamer *fail* to provide the metacriteria that are urgently needed by liberation-oriented hermeneutics, as we saw in Chapter 3. For Thiselton: people *require* liberation from oppressive situations; philosophy *fails* to liberate such people from oppressive situations; and so metacriteria *have to be* derived from theological sources that, in addition, resonate with what philosophy *has* managed to achieve (see Chapter 3).[557]

Thus, R. Papaphilippopoulos notes that 'Thiselton offers... theological criteria' at *the end* of *New Horizons in Hermeneutics* – though, in a comment that reminds us of the misreadings of Thiselton by Nicholson and by B.J. Walsh, she erroneously suggests that Thiselton *relies* on the later Wittgenstein's notion of 'the "stream of life"' 'to provide' a 'trans-contextual' 'bridge between contexts'.[558] In reality, as we have seen, it is Thiselton's philosophy of *history* (and, ultimately, Thiselton's developing biblical framework) that, in Thiselton's hermeneutics, allows "bridges" to form – *both* 'between' historical 'contexts' *and* 'between' his appeals to 'theological' meta-criteria and his appeals to the later Wittgenstein. This latter point in no way invalidates our earlier arguments in relation to the *resonances* that Thiselton finds between *prior* theological emphases and the later Wittgenstein's approach to language and meaning (see Chapter 4).[559]

(j) Nicholson – in what appears to be a "socio-pragmatic style" criticism of Thiselton - seems to argue that 'language-games' are only *context-relative*, that linguistic *functions* are (therefore) only context-relative, and that the context-relative status of linguistic functions invalidates any *ascription* of trans-contextual 'truth'-*value* to 'concepts'.[560]

*First*, however, and in reply to Nicholson, we saw earlier that the later Wittgenstein's notions of "language"-"habits"', linguistic 'rules', "forms of life", 'public criteria of meaning', '"scaffolding"' 'convictions', 'concepts with blurred edges', '"family resemblances"', and 'the common behavior of humankind' (and so on) allowed Thiselton to argue that 'language-games' are *not necessarily only* context-relative. Therefore, in Thiselton's estimate, *concepts and linguistic functions* are not

---

[556] Thiselton, *2H*, 370-385, cf. 121-124; cf. Thiselton, 'LMR', 1129; cf. 1128-1137; cf. Nicholson, 'AW', 628-629. Italics ours.

[557] Nicholson, 'AW', 629; cf. Thiselton, *2H*, 74-84; cf. Thiselton, *NH*, 390-391, cf. 337, 611-619. Italics ours.

[558] Papaphilippopoulos, 'R *NH*', 142-143; cf. Thiselton, *NH*, 612-613. Italics ours.

[559] Papaphilippopoulos, 'R *NH*', 142; cf. Thiselton, *2H*, 74-84, cf.: 376, 382, 392-401. Italics ours.

[560] Nicholson, 'AW', 628, 629. Italics ours.

necessarily *only* context-relative either, but may *also* be traditional, or trans-contextual, or even trans-traditional or inter-traditional. From the perspective of Thiselton's theological philosophy of history, and against Nicholson, no historical context and/or language-game that belongs to a developing historical unity (or to a unity that is being created by God) can be *completely* isolated logically (N.B. here we are using the word "logically" with a *historical* sense, and *not* with an idealist or formalist sense).[561]

*Second*, as we have already seen, Thiselton argues that linguistic functions, or "force", are not unrelated to linguistic content, or to linguistic truth-value, or to questions of "reference". Nicholson seems to separate an utterance's function or force too sharply from its truth-value when, in fact, as Thiselton argues, certain linguistic functions *depend* on certain states of affairs being *true* – *regardless* of how narrow or wide the context of utterance is. Here, moreover, and possibly against Nicholson's reading of Thiselton, we can see that Thiselton's notion of "reference" presupposes appeals to *J.L. Austin, to D.D. Evans, and to others*, and not *only* to the later Wittgenstein (see Chapters 4 and 6).[562]

*Third*, as we have already seen, the issue of *ascribing trans-contextual truth-value* to concepts, and/or of cultures or traditions "seeing" something "as" something, takes us into the realm of socio-metacriticism. This issue is not simply a historico-linguistic issue, but is an issue that, in addition, presupposes considerations that pertain to a hermeneutical critique of *culture* and/or to a hermeneutical critique of *epistemology*. Nicholson seems to contradict his own earlier *valid* argument that historico-linguistic considerations by themselves cannot ground a *metacritical evaluation* of the truth-claims of different cultures. That is, if historico-linguistic considerations by themselves cannot ground a *metacritical evaluation* of the truth-claims of different cultures (*so* Nicholson), then historico-linguistic considerations by themselves cannot justify the *metacritical preclusion* of the truth-claims of different cultures *either* (*against* Nicholson).[563]

(2) Another "reactive" hermeneutical foreclosure in relation to Thiselton's work is that of L. Woodhead. Notably, Woodhead seems to be unaware that, in *Interpreting God and the Postmodern Self* (1995), and in some of his other fourth-period writings, Thiselton *widens* his *earlier* detailed dialogues in relation to hermeneutical critiques of human selves and of Western culture. Thus, for example, in *The Two Horizons*, Thiselton dialogues with Heidegger, with Bultmann, and with others in relation to a hermeneutical critique of human selves. However, in *Interpreting God and the Postmodern Self*, and in some of his other fourth-period writings, Thiselton

---

[561] Thiselton, *2H*, 392; cf.: 396; 434-436; 121-139; 358-359, 374-401; cf.: Thiselton, 'Parab', 466-467; Thiselton, *NH*, 404, 516; 379-409, 381; Wittgenstein, *PI*, 34, 36; Chapter 3. Italics ours.
[562] Nicholson, 'AW', 628, 629; cf.: Thiselton, *2H*, 392; cf.: 396; 392-401, 434-436; 121-124, 133-139; Thiselton, *NH*, 404, 516; Wittgenstein, *PI*, 34, 36. Italics ours.
[563] Nicholson, 'AW', 629; cf.: Thiselton, *2H*, 74-84; Thiselton, *NH*, 390-391, 337, 611-619. Italics ours.

*widens* these earlier dialogues such that they expand to include Thiselton's appeals to Dilthey, Ricoeur, and additional interlocutors. Correlatively, in *Interpreting God and the Postmodern Self*, and in some of his other fourth-period writings, Thiselton is not simply offering a set of *pre-dialogic* generalizing categorizations that could constitute – to use K. Cobb's misleading phrase - 'a *via media* between' 'modern… and… postmodern' notions of the human 'self'. Rather, in these fourth-period works, Thiselton is communicating *post-dialogic* or *a posteriori* assessments of historical trends in relation to hermeneutical critiques of human selves and of Western culture. Crucially, though, we should note that Thiselton is communicating these *post-dialogic* or *a posteriori* assessments *against the background of his detailed engagements with the particularities of the writings of widening numbers of different thinkers*.[564] This point has implications for our responses to Woodhead, as will become clear from what follows.

Thus, (a), Woodhead strongly rejects what she perceives as being 'Thiselton's blanket condemnation of' 'modernity', and of 'the postmodern world and the postmodern self' or 'quest for selfhood'. Woodhead also asserts that 'Thiselton's' supposed 'blanket condemnation' of 'the postmodern self "denies" 'the postmodern self' 'all possibility of agency'. Woodhead's only caveat in relation to these assertions is that she admits that Thiselton still 'allows postmodern suspicion and deconstruction a place'.[565]

However, we must reply to Woodhead by noting that, first, Thiselton's response to 'modernity' (cf. his thoughts on the "postmodern") is very complex, as we indicated in our critique of D.R. Stiver's response to Thiselton and as we indicated elsewhere in the present chapter (see above). Thiselton's response to 'modernity' cannot be caricatured as a 'blanket condemnation'. Second, Thiselton has only *redemptive* aims in view in relation to "postmodern selves",[566] and entertains no hostility towards, or 'blanket condemnation' of, *persons* influenced by "postmodern" culture. Admittedly, third, Thiselton also uses the phrase 'postmodern self' to mean 'postmodern' *interpretations* of selfhood, or of selves. But, even here, Thiselton only rejects *aspects* of such interpretations – which is hardly a case of 'blanket condemnation'.[567]

---

[564] Woodhead, L., 'Review of A.C. Thiselton's *Interpreting God and the Postmodern Self*, *ModTh* 13.4 (Oct. 1997), 537-539; cf.: Woodhead, L., 'Theology and the Fragmentation of the Self', *IJSTh* 1.1 (Mar. 1999), 53-72; Thiselton, *2H*, 143-204, 275-283; cf.: 250-251; 74-84; 302-307; Thiselton, *IGPS*, 53-62, cf.: 73-78, 145-163; Thiselton, 'HB', 76-95; contradicting, Cobb, K., 'Review of A.C. Thiselton's *Interpreting God and the Postmodern Self*, *JRel* 78.2 (1998), 304. Italics on the phrase "*via media*" Cobb's, remaining italics ours.
[565] Woodhead, 'T&FS', 69, cf. 72; cf. Woodhead, 'R *IGPS*', 538.
[566] Woodhead, 'T&FS', 69, 72; cf. Woodhead, 'R *IGPS*', 538; cf. e.g.: Thiselton, *2H*, xx, cf. 314-319; Thiselton, *NH*, 1-10, cf.: 410-470, 556-620; Thiselton, *IGPS*, ix, cf. 145-163. Italics ours.
[567] E.g. see, Thiselton, *IGPS*, 130; cf.: 130-135; 105-117; cf. Woodhead, 'T&FS', 69. Italics ours.

Indeed, fourth, Thiselton *affirms* aspects of "postmodern" culture; moreover, Thiselton *affirms* aspects of the work of Barthes, Derrida, and Foucault;[568] and, furthermore, Thiselton *affirms* aspects of "postmodern" 'critiques' 'of selfhood'. In addition, fifth, Thiselton does *not* argue that 'the postmodern self' has no 'possibility of agency'.[569] Indeed, for Thiselton, 'postmodern' 'hermeneutics of' a *'de-centered' - but potentially still manipulative or loving* (presupposing 'agency') - 'selfhood' are more "realistic" than their "modern" predecessors,[570] and are instructive for "theologians", "ministers", and "counsellors". Sixth, in relation to the "postmodern" more broadly, Thiselton is 'sympathetic yet critical',[571] particularly (as Woodhead herself allows) in relation to "deconstruction"[572] and in relation 'to a' "postmodern" 'hermeneutics of suspicion'.[573]

(b) Woodhead complains concerning what she perceives as being Thiselton's 'broad-brush characterizations... of modernity' and of 'postmodernity', in which Thiselton's supposed 'postmodernity... is a' 'unified', 'simple', yet self-contradictory 'whole' "constructed" from only an aspect of real 'postmodernity' and from a 'random selection of postmodern voices' (including 'Don Cupitt, Colin Hart and Anthony Freeman'). According to Woodhead, Thiselton then takes this untenable view of 'postmodernity' and sets it up as a straw man – only to be cast aside - by starkly and unfavorably contrasting it with a privileged "triumphal" 'Christianity'.[574]

However, in response to Woodhead, (i), we should note that Thiselton's meticulous generalization-free engagements with *specific thinkers* ground his *a posteriori* and historically valid comments, say, for example, about modernity's 'optimism'. That is, again, *a priori* or pre-dialogic stereotyping should not be confused with genuine *a posteriori* trends (see our response to H.A. Harris above). It is as if Woodhead accuses Thiselton of offering the former when he is really offering the latter. The reality, however, is that very few writers indeed attend to

---

[568] Thiselton, *NH*, 115-124, 590-592; cf.: Thiselton, *IGPS*, 117, 14-16, ix; cf.: 68-69, 132. Italics ours.

[569] Woodhead, 'T&FS', 69; cf.: Woodhead, 'R *IGPS*', 538; Thiselton, *IGPS*, 14, 8, 117; cf.: ix-x, 4-9, 13-15, 19, 28, 32, 127-135; 112-117. Italics ours.

[570] Woodhead, 'R *IGPS*', 538; cf.: Thiselton, *IGPS*, 117, 129, 124, 11-12, 14-15, cf.: 121-125, 132-133; 159-163; contradicting, Greene, C.J.D., *Christology in Cultural Perspective: Marking Out the Horizons* (Grand Rapids, MI.: Eerdmans, 2004), 95. Italics in speech-marks Thiselton's, others ours.

[571] cf. Fergusson, D., 'Review of A.C. Thiselton's *Interpreting God and the Postmodern Self*', *Th* 99.792 (Nov. - Dec. 1996), 463; cf. Thiselton, *IGPS*, 121-126.

[572] cf. Hart, T.A., 'Review of A.C. Thiselton's *Interpreting God and the Postmodern Self*', *ExTim* 107.9 (Jun. 1996), 282; cf.: Thiselton, *IGPS*, 14-16, 68-69, 122, 132-133; cf.: 39; 28, 29.

[573] Browning, P.D., 'Review of A.C. Thiselton's *Interpreting God and the Postmodern Self*', *Enc* 58 (Spr. 1997), 221; cf. Thiselton, *NH*, 344 onwards; cf. Thiselton, *IGPS*, 160.

[574] Woodhead, 'T&FS', 69; cf. also Woodhead, 'R *IGPS*', 537, 538.

particularities as rigorously as Thiselton.[575]

Further, (ii), Thiselton's view of 'postmodernity' includes strands in post-structuralism, Continental hermeneutics, socio-criticism, socio-pragmatism, reader-response theories, liberation hermeneutics, and cross-fertilizations of these. Moreover, earlier, we noted that Thiselton contrasts the "postmodernity" of Habermas with that of Lyotard. Indeed, even this complex view of the "postmodern" does not exhaust Thiselton's actual perspectives on the matter - as we saw earlier, in our responses to D.R. Stiver. That is, the complexities of Thiselton's perspectives on the "postmodern" can hardly be reduced to the 'simple' 'unified' 'whole' that Woodhead accuses Thiselton of offering. Moreover, (iii), if this 'whole' is not in fact 'simple', as Woodhead herself suggests, then how could there *not* be contradictions between different strands within it? Again, in *Interpreting God and the Postmodern Self*, Thiselton is offering *necessarily-briefer lectures (sic)* that cover *a posteriori* trends. Again, Thiselton's *background* attention to particularity in works such as *The Two Horizons* and *New Horizons in Hermeneutics* should neither be ignored nor doubted.[576]

Admittedly, (iv), at the time of Woodhead's writing, Thiselton had not systematically engaged with *every* 'postmodern' thinker or with '*all* postmodern rejections of theism'.[577] Thus, Thiselton had yet to dialogue significantly with 'Martha Nussbaum, Bernard Williams, [and] John Milbank',[578] or substantially with M.C. Taylor.[579] And yet, against Woodhead's reading of Thiselton, Thiselton does not just dialogue with a 'random selection of postmodern voices' (such as 'Don Cupitt, Colin Hart and Anthony Freeman'). Specifically, against N. Titans' reading of Thiselton, Thiselton does not dialogue 'only' with D. Cupitt and his associates. But even if Thiselton *had* dialogued (i.e. with 'postmodern voices') as narrowly as Woodhead and Titans falsely suggest, then Thiselton's philosophical-historical warranting of theological discussions and solutions *would still genuinely* expose the problems pertaining to Cupitt's various a-historical starting-points – a fact ignored by Woodhead.[580]

---

[575] Thiselton, *IGPS*, 12; cf. Thiselton, *2H*, 53-63, 70-74, 206, 218, 258-261; cf. Thiselton, *NH*, 380, 387, 389; cf. Thiselton, A.C., 'Barr on Barth and Natural Theology: A Plea for Hermeneutics in Historical Theology. Review Article of J. Barr's *Biblical Faith and Natural Theology*', *SJT* 47.4 (1994), 519-528. Italics ours.

[576] Woodhead, 'T&FS', 69; cf.: Thiselton, *NH*, 80-141, 314, 103-104, 393-405, 529-550, 410-470, 472; on *2H* see our arguments above. Italics ours.

[577] Woodhead, 'R *IGPS*', 538; cf. Browning, 'R *IGPS*', 221. Italics ours.

[578] cf. Dawson, D., 'Review of A.C. Thiselton's *Interpreting God and the Postmodern Self*, *PEcc* 7 (Sep. 1998), 249. But cf. Thiselton, *NH*, 26, 485-486, 500; cf.: 503-504, 557-558, 606; 317.

[579] cf. Titans, 'R *IGPS*', 521. But cf. Thiselton, *NH*, 88; cf. 80-141, 250-252, 330-338; cf. Thiselton, *2H*, 66-67, 82-84, 119-120.

[580] Contradicting: Woodhead, 'T&FS', 69; cf. Woodhead, 'R *IGPS*', 537, 538; cf.: Browning, 'R *IGPS*', 221; Titans, 'R *IGPS*', 521; Thiselton, *IGPS*, 34, cf.: 35-36, 47-78, 87-92; Thiselton, *2H*, 51-84, cf.: 234-251; 293-326, 370-385; cf. later, Thiselton, A.C., 'Cupitt, D',

That is, (v), Woodhead's comment that Thiselton has not dialogued with thinkers from *all* varieties of 'postmodernity' seems, unreasonably, to expect an "exhaustive" treatment of a field that no writer can yet exhaustively define hermeneutically speaking (on this last point see our critique of D.R. Stiver's response to Thiselton earlier in the present chapter). In a tell-tale *a priori* pre-dialogic generalizing comment, Woodhead falsely caricatures Thiselton's *SJT lectures (sic)* in *Interpreting God and the Postmodern Self* as an exhaustive 'reaction to *all* postmodernists and the *entire* postmodern scene'. Apparently, Woodhead offers this caricature or straw man so that she can then dismiss a claim that Thiselton *does not in fact make*. Indeed, Thiselton's emphases on ever-widening dialogue and on the "never-final" character of understanding mean that he would *never* make such an unhermeneutical claim. Finally, (vi), as we have already noted, Thiselton, *in part, appeals* to different *philosophical* traditions – *including* those considered to be "postmodern" - in order to *elucidate resonances between* these and a prior *biblical and theological* framework. Thus, Woodhead's claim that Thiselton sets "postmodernity" and "Christianity" in over-simplistic opposition to one-another is also false. Woodhead thus "projects" onto Thiselton's work *another* claim that Thiselton does not in fact make. Woodhead thus appears to be rather "socio-pragmatic" in her style of argument![581]

(c) Woodhead rejects what she perceives as being Thiselton's 'uncritical acceptance of the fragmentation thesis' in relation to 'postmodern' culture and selves.[582] Appealing to the 'empirical research' of S. Tipton and P. Heelas,[583] she then suggests that we consider – as an alternative to what she supposes is Thiselton's 'bestowed'/'authoritative' approach to 'modern selfhood' - 'four conflicting construals of modern selfhood': 'bestowed'/'authoritative', 'rational'/'liberal', 'boundless'/ 'expressive', 'and... effective'/'utilitarian'. In Woodhead's view, further, these *'conflicting* construals of modern selfhood' could somehow all still contribute to a more *integrated* 'Christian anthropology'.[584]

However, here, (i), we must reply to Woodhead by noting that Woodhead possibly confuses Thiselton's sophisticated hermeneutical critique of *human selves* with his hermeneutical critique of (Western) *culture*. Thiselton's hermeneutical critique of *human selves* engages with over a dozen thinkers - most importantly, with Heidegger, Bultmann and Ricoeur - and, in *this* context of discussion, Thiselton mostly favors the terms '"forces"' and 'conflicts' over the term 'fragmentation'.[585]

---

in *Dictionary of Historical Theology* (ed. T. Hart; Grand Rapids: Eerdmans, and Carlisle: Paternoster, 2000), 141-144. Italics ours.
[581] Woodhead, 'R *IGPS*', 537-538; cf. Woodhead, 'T&FS', 68. Italics ours.
[582] Woodhead, 'T&FS', 69.
[583] Woodhead, 'T&FS', 57; cf. 56-58, 62-65.
[584] Woodhead, 'T&FS', 53, cf. 69-70, 71. Italics ours.
[585] Thiselton, *2H*, 143-204, 275-283; cf. Thiselton, *NH*, 247-253, 556-620; cf. Thiselton, *IGPS*, 128; cf. 47-51, 53-57, 59-62, 67-71, 73-78, 127-163; cf. Woodhead, 'T&FS', 69. Italics ours.

Furthermore, (ii), Thiselton's argument *favors* a widening inter-disciplinary dialogue that embraces interaction between diverse "models" and "angles of vision". Thiselton would *agree* with Woodhead's call for the inclusion of 'socio-cultural' "models" 'of selfhood' in that dialogue.[586] (In our view, in making this call, Woodhead makes a valuable point that we call attention to in our conclusions at the end of the present study).

(iii) Woodhead herself, though, seems to lack such a widening dialogic pre-understanding in relation to philosophies of selfhood, or of selves. This apparent lack of a developed pre-understanding in relation to philosophies of selfhood, or of selves, suggests - (ironically, given her stated sympathies with the "postmodern") – that Woodhead might possibly be smuggling in a degree of uncritical 'value-neutral' objectivism behind her so-called 'empirical' appeals. That is, compared to Thiselton's heavily modified Ricoeurian framing of Heideggerian – and other – insights, Woodhead's sketchy notes about 'empirical' models seem almost cartoon-like. That is, again, the *public lectures (sic)* published in *Interpreting God and the Postmodern Self* must be understood against the background of *The Two Horizons* and of Thiselton's other second and third period works (i.e. works that *are not lectures*).[587]

Furthermore, (iv), Woodhead's *'conflicting'* 'construals of... selfhood' may *themselves* project a pre-dialogic "socio-ideological" 'fragmentation' onto 'historical reality' (her phrase) or, rather, onto conceptions of selfhood or of selves, despite her goal of integration. Thiselton, conversely, has been using dialogic appeals to various philosophical traditions in order to aim at elucidating an *integrated* biblical notion of the self, or of selves, since the 1960s (see Chapters 1 and 4) – which is hardly an 'uncritical acceptance of the fragmentation thesis'.[588]

Admittedly, (v), Thiselton's hermeneutical critique of *(Western) culture* allows that "societies" would indeed "fragment" 'into' *'competing groups'* driven by 'power-interests' if certain 'postmodern' socio-pragmatic trends were left unchecked. But this critique is also grounded in a widening dialogue – and is never presented by Thiselton as the 'whole' story. Indeed, this critique may even be proven to be correct by *the character of Woodhead's own responses to Thiselton*, as we shall see below.[589]

(d) Woodhead, (i), asserts that Thiselton (supposedly) neglects the tough 'questions' that are, in Woodhead's estimate, precipitated by his (i.e. Thiselton's) supposed acceptance 'of' a 'bestowed [/'authoritative'] selfhood' model. However, in this connection, and against Woodhead's reading of Thiselton, we should note

---

[586] Thiselton, *2H*, 291-292, cf.: 354; 143-204 (Heidegger); 432; cf.: Thiselton, *IGPS*, 59-62; cf. 73-78 (Dilthey, Ricoeur); Thiselton, 'SBL', 116, 117; Woodhead, 'T&FS', 53. Italics ours.

[587] Woodhead, 'T&FS', 57; cf. 56-58, 62-65; cf.: Thiselton, *2H*, 78-79, 291-292, 354; cf. 143-204 (Heidegger); Thiselton, *IGPS*, 47-62, 73-78 (Dilthey, Ricoeur). Italics ours.

[588] Woodhead, 'T&FS', 53, 56, 69, 71; cf. Thiselton, *2H*, 143-204, cf.: 250-251, 275-283. Our italics.

[589] Thiselton, *IGPS*, 135, 125, 131; cf.: 127-144, 73-78. Second italics Thiselton's, others ours.

that Thiselton does *not* neglect 'feminist' hermeneutics,[590] 'dependence upon God', 'freedom', 'human agency', 'relationality', 'dignity', or 'sinfulness' (see Chapters 4 and 6).[591] And, contrary to Woodhead's assertion, we should observe that Thiselton largely *accepts* Nietzsche's criticisms of 'power' 'abuse' in ecclesial 'institutions'.[592]

(ii) Admittedly, at the time of Woodhead's *writing*, Thiselton had yet to engage thoroughly with a 'specifically feminist contribution to the debate about selfhood', as Woodhead rightly notes.[593] And yet, by the time of Woodhead's *publication* of her responses to Thiselton, Thiselton had already aligned - at least partly - with Judith Gundry-Volf's 'interpretation of gender-identity' and, later, Thiselton writes more in this connection in his commentary on 1 Corinthians. Certainly, Thiselton is sensitive to this issue. Finally, (iii), against Woodhead, we should stress that Thiselton's sophisticated hermeneutical critique of human selves cannot be reduced to a notion that could ever be accurately captured merely by Woodhead's sloganeering use of the phrase, '"bestowed [/'authoritative'] selfhood" model" (see our last point above – and also Chapters 4 and 6).[594]

(e) Woodhead mistakenly views Thiselton's 'Christian conception of the self' as being 'the true organizing center' of *Interpreting God and the Postmodern Self*. According to Woodhead, moreover, Thiselton supposedly selects 'postmodern' 'protagonists' 'to serve as foil and mirror image' *relative to* this 'organizing center'.[595]

However, (i), as we have seen from our study of *The Two Horizons*, Thiselton's hermeneutical critique of human selves is grounded in his theological and philosophical hermeneutical critique of *history*. Of these two critiques the latter is much closer to being Thiselton's 'organizing center' since, in Thiselton's hermeneutical critiques of history and of epistemology, selves are "de-centered". (ii) *Thiselton's* "de-centering" of selves, of course, constitutes a theological and historical attack on *anthropocentricity* – an attack that draws on Pannenberg (see Chapter 3). This attack on anthropocentricity, though, is quite different to the "de-centering" of selves that Thiselton attacks in relation to *some* 'postmodern' interpretations of selves in which selves are *deconstructed* to the point of potentially becoming biological entities that are, in every sense other than biologically, perpetually partially reconstructed or over-written by shifting socio-linguistic forces that include imposed role-performances. (N.B. In Thiselton's thinking, this

---

[590] Thiselton, *NH*, 430-462; cf. Woodhead, 'T&FS', 70, 71. Italics ours.
[591] cf.: Chapter 4 above; Thiselton, *IGPS*, 73-78, cf. 145-163; Woodhead, 'T&FS', 70-71.
[592] Thiselton, *IGPS*, 4-9, cf.: 11-26; cf. Thiselton, *2H*, 275-283; cf. Woodhead, 'T&FS', 71. Italics ours.
[593] Woodhead, 'R *IGPS*', 537. Italics ours.
[594] Thiselton, A.C., 'Can Hermeneutics Ease the Deadlock? Some Biblical Exegesis and Hermeneutical Models', in *The Way Forward: Christian Voices on Homosexuality and the Church* (ed. T. Bradshaw; London: Hodder and Stoughton, 1997), 188; cf. Thiselton, *1 Cor*, e.g. 800-848; cf. Thiselton, *NH*, 430-462. Italics ours.
[595] Woodhead, 'R *IGPS*', 538. Italics ours.

"over-writing" does *not* overrule 'all possibility of agency', but merely tends to shape the parameters *within which* agency operates). (iii) Thiselton, by contrast, can be seen "appropriating" – in *some* respects - a 'Ricoeurian hermeneutic of detour' that is *as philosophical as it is theological*. That is, Thiselton "de-centers" human selves in relation to broader inter-subjective, historical, and theological contexts. We are saying that this "de-centering" is only 'Ricoeurian' in *some* respects because: with Ricoeur, Thiselton *agrees* that self-understanding comes through a detour into the historical realm of inter-subjectivity; *querying* Ricoeur, however, Thiselton more firmly "re-historicizes" the inter-subjective realm in terms of his (i.e. Thiselton's) affirming of the possibility of textual epistemological disclosures related to "behind-the-text" inter-subjective historical backgrounds. That is, for Thiselton, texts *too* are inter-subjective and, as such, are inseparable (historically, epistemologically, and linguistically) from the "behind-the-text" aspects of the broader diachronic contexts of inter-subjective communicative action.[596]

(iv) Woodhead – in her use of the phrase 'foil and mirror image' – uses persuasive definition in order to overstate, and thereby in order to misrepresent, the differences between Thiselton's supposed perspectives on 'Christian' and on 'postmodern' "conceptions" of "selves" respectively. Woodhead does this in order to caricature Thiselton in terms of his supposed espousal of a false antithesis between these two "conceptions". In reality, though, Thiselton clearly sees *both overlap and distinctions* between *numerous* 'Christian' and 'postmodern' "conceptions" of "selves". That is, Woodhead, by a process of implicit persuasive definition, misrepresents Thiselton's hermeneutical respect for *a posteriori* historical distinctions, and for *a posteriori* historical similarities, as a supposed employment of an *a priori* pre-dialogic categorization or antithesis. Again, her style of argument is beginning to look rather "socio-pragmatic"![597]

(f) Finally, Woodhead complains that Thiselton, in his supposed 'smug' power-play and one-upmanship, 'deliberately attack[s]' 'vast numbers of fellow Christians' and their 'different persuasions'.[598]

Surely, though, Woodhead herself is now in danger of indulging in a reactive polemic that amounts to a disowned socio-pragmatic projection of her own strategy. That is, here, Woodhead *again* uses persuasive definition – this time to misidentify "legitimate criticism" and "debate" as "personal attack". Moreover, we can see – in relation to Woodhead's persuasive definition – that Woodhead's clear respect for public-sphere debate *threatens* to decay *towards* conformity to the

---

[596] Woodhead, 'R *IGPS*', 538; cf.: Woodhead, 'T&FS', 69, cf. 72; Thiselton, *2H*, 250-251; cf.: 51-84; 234-251; 304-326; Thiselton, *NH*, 356-372; Thiselton, *IGPS*, 121-124; Debanné, M., 'Review of A.C. Thiselton's *Interpreting God and the Postmodern Self*, *ARC* 25 (1997), 163; contradicting, Titans, 'R *IGPS*', 521. Titans misses Thiselton's "originality" here. Italics ours.

[597] Woodhead, 'R *IGPS*', 538; cf. Thiselton, *IGPS*, 14, 8, 117; cf.: ix-x, 4-9, 13-15, 19, 28, 32, 127-135; 112-117. Italics ours.

[598] Woodhead, 'T&FS', 69, 70; cf. Woodhead, 'R *IGPS*', 537.

psycho-social "drama triangle" – a "drama triangle" that is marked by conflicting and/or colluding role-plays performed by "persecutors", "victims", and "rescuers". Woodhead thus tries to "rescue" Thiselton's "victims" from Thiselton - because Woodhead seems to view Thiselton as some kind of "persecutor".

Superficially, of course, refusal to "criticize" or "judge" others can sound "fair and humble" (though such a refusal would contradict the biblical traditions reflected in John 7:24 and 1 Corinthians 6:1-6). But disallowing criticism *of oneself* - or of one's *own tradition* – can reflect anything from self-deceptive denial, to authoritarian traditionalist self-assertion, to what Paul Tournier calls 'defensive aggressiveness'. These kinds of behavior, though, are precisely the kinds of behavior that Thiselton *rightly* exposes.[599]

This point, in our view, brings us to the real heart of Woodhead's and Nicholson's hermeneutical foreclosures in relation to their readings of Thiselton. Woodhead's and Nicholson's serial misrepresentations of Thiselton force us to conceive of a third broad kind of hermeneutical foreclosure – a kind of hermeneutical foreclosure that goes *beyond* straightforward misreadings and confusion, and that goes *beyond* purportedly "epistemologically-justified" – (though, in reality, anti-theoretical) – socio-pragmatic hermeneutical foreclosure and name-dropping. Is Woodhead's and Nicholson's more "reactive" kind of hermeneutical foreclosure the *beginning* of a descent *towards* a drama-triangle of *name-calling* in relation to "victims", "persecutors", and "rescuers"?

(3) R.L. Hall speaks in a self-contradictory manner about Thiselton's supposed 'English' 'contempt for' (cf. Thiselton the "persecutor"), and yet 'seduction by', 'postmodernism' (cf. Thiselton the "victim").[600] Hall also speaks of Thiselton's supposed failed *appeal* to 'Moltmann and Ricoeur' to "recover" 'theological truth'. Actually, however, Thiselton *criticizes* Ricoeur (and even the early Moltmann) in the context of this kind of discussion, as we have begun to see. Hall has almost *inverted* Thiselton's actual stance.[601]

Furthermore, Hall's unhermeneutical objection to Thiselton's '"working hypotheses" approach to' 'truth' and to 'theological claims' speaks volumes about Hall's own objectivism. Hall also sets his own objectivism in antithetical opposition to what he perceives as being Thiselton's supposedly simplistic "postmodern" epistemology. Again, though, this simplistic "postmodern" epistemology constitutes a product of *Hall's* thinking, *not* of Thiselton's.[602] *Obfuscating projection* has become the order of the day.

(4) Summarizing: in the cases of M.W. Nicholson, L. Woodhead, and R.L. Hall, a "reactive" "disowned" hermeneutical foreclosure – a kind of hermeneutical foreclosure that is *at times unrelated to these writers' contrasting relatively "left wing"* or

---

[599] Thiselton, *IGPS*, 115; cf. 111-117; cf. Tournier, P., *Guilt and Grace* (Crowborough, East Sussex: Hodder & Stoughton, 1962), 14. Italics ours.
[600] Hall, 'R *IGPS*', 121, cf. 123.
[601] Hall, 'R *IGPS*', 122, 123; cf. Thiselton, *NH*, 368-372; cf. Chapter 3. Italics ours.
[602] Hall, 'R *IGPS*', 123; cf. 121-123; cf. Thiselton, *IGPS*, 160. Italics ours.

*relatively "right wing" angles of attack* - is projected onto Thiselton as though it were being *marketed for consumers as being "Thiselton's* problem". Something is happening that is more reactive, aggressive, and misrepresentative than straightforward misreading or confusion, or than the socio-pragmatic name-dropping and quasi-theoretical (but ultimately theory-shunning) questioning of whether "texts" *can* "speak". In "reactive" or "hostile" hermeneutical foreclosure, misreading has *started* to degenerate *towards* a drama-triangle of *name-calling* by "rescuers" who are trying to liberate "victims" from "persecutors". Notably, Thiselton's predictions – predictions concerning the ways in which socio-pragmatism, contrary to its own aims, can (alongside other approaches) descend into conflict - thus seem to be starting to come true.

### 4. Interpretative Irresponsibility and Kinds of Hermeneutical Foreclosure

Thus, in conclusion, we have seen that there are several kinds of hermeneutical foreclosure or irresponsible interpretation. In relation to each kind of hermeneutical foreclosure, an adequate understanding of *The Two Horizons* has proven to be of central importance in answering Thiselton's critics – even Thiselton's recent critics.

In terms of the kinds of hermeneutical foreclosure that we have observed, then there is foreclosure through straightforward misreading and confusion; there is foreclosure through the canonized "dance" of playfully side-stepping conversation; there is foreclosure through a "quasi-theoretical" "legitimization" of "textual inaccessibility" that masks corporately authoritarian self-imperializing circularities, assertions, and theoretical dichotomies; and there is foreclosure through the reactive-aggressive "disowning projection" *of* foreclosure – a "disowning projection" that threatens to descend towards behaviors commonly associated with the psycho-social drama-triangle.

And, of course, all these kinds of hermeneutical foreclosure can be mixed together. Moreover, there must surely be other kinds of hermeneutical foreclosure as well. We are positing the "historical", rather than the "formal".

But, we may ask, what lies behind such hermeneutical foreclosures, historically speaking? Well, we may speculate as to whether the sheer busyness of over-stretched, under-staffed, and under-funded academic university departments contributes to *some* straightforward hermeneutical foreclosures. Have the *time-*pressures of "career" - in the face of the "over-loading" of too few staff - become the enemy of rigorous *listening?*

In relation to the case of socio-pragmatic hermeneutical foreclosure, we may speculate as to whether the sheer complexities of hermeneutical theorizing have contributed to a sudden demand for an emergency alternative – a knee-jerk market-demand for simple community-friendly or "inclusive" interpretations that, in relation to "theory", amounts to a "throwing of one's hands up in the air" that says "we give up". Have the consumer-demands of the market led to a dismissal of *complexity itself?* Has this dismissal of complexity, in turn, led to a resurgence of

"Barthian" appeals to *authoritarianisms* of the "Word" or of the "Spirit" that over-readily dismiss public-sphere critical and metacritical testing?

In relation to the case of "pseudo"-post-structuralist hermeneutical foreclosure, we may speculate as to whether certain socio-pragmatists have uncritically adopted certain aspects of "post-structuralist" thought whilst simultaneously appealing to the "inaccessibility" of philosophical (and biblical) texts so as to avoid the philosophical complexities – notably the need to criticize narrowed-dialogue (at the level of critical-synthetic sublation-filter-construction) - that adopting this kind of pre-understanding entails.

Could *some* socio-pragmatic appeals to post-structuralist thought even amount to a lazy post-theoretical "name-dropping" rather than to a *genuine widening of dialogue or of conversation*? It is one thing to be driven by the consumer-demands of the market for a dismissal of complexity itself. But it is quite another to *carry this off in a university setting*. One has to "*speak* simply, but still *look* clever in one's *writings*".

Probably, such speculations and questions in relation to socio-pragmatism, if left unqualified, seem too harsh to some. It is very likely that many who have adopted socio-pragmatic approaches - notably Lyons and Woodman - have done so with sincere and laudable aims. Moreover, many – including Lyons and Woodman – are perhaps genuinely wrestling with *some* of the complexities of hermeneutics.

Nevertheless, in our view, our speculations and questions still need to be made and/or asked because of the dire consequences – predicted by Thiselton - that could result if socio-pragmatism continues to become the global norm. This need to make speculations and ask questions remains real even if, at present, the socio-pragmatic "yeast" has not fully worked through the "dough", and even if, at present, there are still other "yeasts" mixed in with the "dough" that are slowing down the descent *towards* these dire consequences.

Speaking of such dire consequences, though, then in relation to the case of a reactive-aggressive hermeneutical foreclosure that employs disowned projection, we may speculate as to whether or not Thiselton's later prophetic predictions about competing and conflicting power-groups (see above) in an increasingly "postmodern" socio-pragmatic society have actually *already* begun to come true (whatever else the "postmodern" entails). Is it "postmodern" to avoid careful argument by resorting to *false obfuscating accusations against the other that potentially pertain to a drama-triangle that involves "rescuers" indulging in name-calling directed against "persecutors" so as to rescue "victims"*?

In contrast to the interpretative irresponsibilities of these different kinds of hermeneutical foreclosures, Thiselton teaches us that responsible interpretation takes *time to listen*, that responsible interpretation engages with the unavoidable historical reality of theoretical *complexities*, that responsible interpretation genuinely widens *dialogue or conversation* (notably at the level of critical-synthetic sublation-filter-construction), and that responsible interpretation is *respectful of the other*.

## E. Conclusion:
### Towards a Christological Unification of Hermeneutics, a Unified Hermeneutical Critique of Historical Objectivity, and a Critique of Hermeneutical Foreclosure

Having begun the present chapter by anticipating its main arguments, we then argued that the predominantly philosophical unification of "second" and "third stratum" hermeneutical critiques connoted by Thiselton's work *warranted* Thiselton's dialogue with theological considerations. Thiselton was not straightforwardly fideistic. Nevertheless, it was a mistake to think that Thiselton assimilated theology to a philosophical worldview. Rather, Thiselton showed that a *prior* biblical theology was elucidated by, was consistent with, and was an anticipative cogent problem-solving resource in relation to, *later* emerging and widening philosophical dialogues, unities, concerns, and descriptions.

In particular, Thiselton in effect argued that the *prior* Christ-event dialogically resonated with his three implicit *modified* Hegelian criteria and their entailments. Further, for Thiselton, the Christ-event surpassed and completed philosophical hermeneutics, providing (amongst other benefits) explanatory and evaluative meta-criteria that (as E.A. Dunn rightly observed) anticipated and extended Gadamer's notions of "tradition" and "dialogue" - in relation to eschatology and in relation to Trinitarian relating between persons respectively.

Thus, for Thiselton, the Christ-event unified hermeneutics as a whole (all three strata), linking "responsible interpretation" with inter-personal "Christ-like relating" in the context of a larger anticipated Christo-eschatological narrative. Moreover, Thiselton's view of biblical authority was not simply "fundamentalist" but, *in the context of the language-game of philosophical warrant*, was contextualized by the background of his philosophical appeals – notably his appeals to the philosophies of history and language. In this respect, Thiselton's philosophically-warranted approach to *prior* biblical authority produced a framework that genuinely exposed *philosophical* problems in broadly "positivist" approaches and in broadly "existentialist" approaches. Various misconceptions of Thiselton's view of authoritative revelation were highlighted.

Next, we rejected G.R. Osborne's ascription – at least in one context - of an entirely *negative four*-fold hermeneutical critique of historical objectivity to Thiselton. Thiselton's work actually implicitly connoted an *eight*-axis hermeneutical critique of historical objectivity that was centered on inter-related and overlapping mutually-qualifying historico-philosophical (and theological) criteria that affected public domain objectivity *both* negatively *and* positively. In Thiselton's thinking, post-Enlightenment or "modern" concerns for "objectivity" were sublated into a *transformed historical* framework that drew on both theology and philosophy.

Notably, in Thiselton's thinking, the historical conditioning of the historically finite (i.e. texts, readers, events, actions, and so on) was *itself conditioned by*, and occurred against the background of, the other inter-related and overlapping *mutually-qualifying* historico-philosophical (and theological) criteria (including historical unity and historical relationalities, historical processes and historical movements, historical particularities and historical continuities, historical subjectivities and historical inter-subjectivities, and historical fallenness and historical redemption). These criteria, in turn, resonated with (or, in the case of historical fallenness, at least related to) a *prior* biblical doctrine of a unified (not uniform) creation.

We also noted the complex ways in which these eight axes of historico-philosophical (and theological) criteria were related to the three modified Hegelian criteria that we had expounded in Chapter 6. Although most of the "eight axes of criteria" could be derived from the three modified Hegelian criteria, Thiselton's sublation of the latter into a theological framework had added – amongst other Christ-centered refinements - a dimension related to creation, fallenness and redemption and thus to metacritical ethical evaluation - a dimension that was under-developed in secular approaches to hermeneutics.

In relation to *fallenness*, however, we argued that – even in the light of Thiselton's more recent works - a more sophisticated hermeneutic of human selves was still required. In particular, we argued that explorations into *fallen human relationships* and into *fallen human physicality* would shed new light on the complexity of historical conditioning, and thence on the problem of historical objectivity.

In relation to *fallen human relationships*, and drawing on Zangwill, Suler, Young and Woolley, we speculated that hysterical dissociation, solipsistic introjection, maladaptive schema, and the ways in which internet-use could disinhibit users in relation to the harmful pursuit of (aspects of) their personas were just *some* of the factors that could be explored through a broadened dialogue with pastoral theology and with disciplines relevant to pastoral theology.

We also indicated that Thiselton's eyesight-related problems constituted just one example of how *fallen human physicality* could contribute to historical conditioning. We might add here, though, that the whole question of historical conditioning surely takes us into new territories for discussion and exploration – especially when we link historical conditioning to such issues as learning difficulties, various kinds of trauma, post-war syndromes, deafness, birth defects, and so on and so forth. Whilst Thiselton certainly links the particularities of individuals' personal "narratives" to hermeneutical questions by the end of his third period, there is perhaps more to be said in order to "flesh out" hermeneutical considerations that are related to how the particularities of different kinds of suffering shape the pre-understandings with which people approach the biblical texts – or texts more broadly, or other people, or the wider world.

Moving on, we focused next on Thiselton's contrast, implicit everywhere in *The Two Horizons*, between the ever-widening dialogue of responsible interpretation and the foreclosed dialogue of interpretative irresponsibility. In particular, we exposed several kinds of hermeneutical foreclosure amongst Thiselton's critics.

The hermeneutical foreclosures of those we called "friendly critics" were cases of straightforward misreading or confusion. In the cases of C.G. Bartholomew and W. Olhausen, we needed only to compare and contrast Bartholomew's and

Olhausen's readings of Thiselton with what Thiselton had actually said.

Admittedly, in the case of H.A. Harris, it became necessary to discern between different kinds of two-fold distinction. But this was still only a matter of clearing up a simple confusion. That is, Thiselton's *a posteriori historically real* distinctions were different to rationally incoherent *theoretical* dichotomies, to philosophically idealist *formal* linguistic binary oppositions, and (in relation to the case of Harris's criticisms) to polemical *a priori* pre-dialogic categorizations that suppressed the hermeneutical circle and/or the hermeneutical task of listening in openness to the other. Notably, we saw that *a priori* pre-dialogic categorizations could lead to a kind of domino-effect or calculus of serious misreadings. This was so in the case of D.R. Stiver's misreading of Thiselton's writings, even if Stiver's hermeneutical foreclosures were still relatively straightforward.

A.K.M. Adam's criticisms of Thiselton, however, introduced us to further kinds of hermeneutical foreclosure that were far from straightforward.

On the one hand, Adam's pseudo-"post-structuralist" appeal to Derrida falsely "shelved" or "binned" Thiselton in an "idealist" or "formalist" pigeon-hole without actually appreciating the similarities and differences between the thinking of Derrida and the thinking of Thiselton, or between the thinking of Thiselton and "idealism" or "formalism". In this respect, Adam almost seemed to canonize pre-dialogic, or hermeneutical, foreclosure.

On the other hand, Adam's socio-pragmatic appeal to Fish highlighted a possible *reason* for Adam's lack of appreciation of the similarities and differences between the thinking of Derrida and the thinking of Thiselton, or between the thinking of Thiselton and "idealism" or "formalism". Fish's socio-pragmatism amounted to a kind of *assertion* of hermeneutical foreclosure that banished "access" to texts on the grounds of an epistemology that bore no obvious relationship to the philosophy of history. That is, Fish's socio-pragmatic approach ostensibly attempted - "(a-)theoretically" - to *legitimize* the pre-dialogic foreclosure of pre-understanding (at least in relation to historical texts). But this approach presupposed a prior, *asserted*, hidden, and circular foreclosure of dialogue with the philosophy of history – a foreclosure of dialogue that presupposed an impossibly dichotomous approach to history.

In the end, Adam's stance led to his incredulity over the possibility of recognizing meta-criteria. This scenario meant, however, that Adam therein seemingly failed to allow metacritical recognition of *Jesus Christ*. It was from *this* place that Adam falsely – even hedonistically - "shelved" or "binned" Thiselton in an "idealist" or "formalist" pigeon-hole. Thus, we are reminded of a comment by J.W. von Goethe (cited by Schleiermacher): 'that much is created from little produces *only* pleasure'.[603]

Nevertheless, Adam's comments were still instrumental in taking us into much

---

[603] Schleiermacher, F.D.E., 'Manuscript 1'. Example of Hermeneutics', in *Hermeneutics: The Handwritten Manuscripts* (ed. H. Kimmerle; trans. J. Duke & J. Forstman; AAR Texts and Translations 1; Atlanta: Scholars Press, 1977), 65; cf. 243 n. 49. Italics ours.

deeper discussions. There were *genuine* broad differences between Thiselton's thinking and the thinking of Derrida, and between the thinking of Thiselton and "idealism" or "formalism". And there were *genuine* issues raised by a consideration of the false criticisms of Thiselton's thinking that were brought to the table by those who drew on the work of Fish – notably W.J. Lyons, S. Woodman, and other socio-pragmatists.

Crucially, our brief explorations in relation to Derrida and the later Barthes raised questions about how the various hermeneutical critiques "fitted" together. Our Russian Doll illustration tried to shed light on the problems of "theoretical dichotomies", on the problems of "critique-collapse", and on the problems of "critique-over-extension" that occurred when the various hermeneutical critiques were "inter-sublated" in the wrong order in relation to their respective historical-ontological basicalities.

For Thiselton, notably, it was ultimately a Christo-eschatological framework that prevented *both* these erroneous inter-sublations *and* the conflation of biblical - alongside developing Western hermeneutical - critiques of history with Western philosophical idealism – a conflation that was, in Thiselton's estimate, implicit in post-structuralist critiques of Western metaphysics, in post-structuralist erroneous inter-sublations, and in post-structuralist "over-extensions" of critiques of language.

In turn, this problem of post-structuralist erroneous inter-sublations and (the resulting) "over-extensions" of critiques of language had led to a false hypostatization of the notion of radically dissociating historical horizons, and thus on to the supposed "death of God", to the supposed "death of the author", to the supposed "death of the subject" or of the "self", and to the supposed "death" of any other historical reality that presupposed historical unity, relationalities, and dialectic movements or processes (amongst other historico-philosophical (and theological) criteria).

The socio-pragmatic criticisms of Thiselton by W.J. Lyons, S. Woodman, and perhaps others, seemed unwittingly to *presuppose* the false post-structuralist hypostatization of the notion of radically dissociating historical horizons. In turn, this scenario had led to further theoretical dichotomies in relation to epistemology and language. These dichotomies, in turn, had led to an assertion concerning the epistemological "inaccessibility" of texts or of the past horizons of texts. Thus, it seemed that Lyons, Woodman, and perhaps others had uncritically inherited aspects of post-structuralist thinking at the level of pre-understanding.

Any stance that admitted historical dichotomies, however, was inconsistent both with the philosophy of history and with the doctrine of creation (not to mention the space-time continuum). We are reminded of Ernst Fuchs' warning that, 'one must guard against certain naïvetés which all too easily establish themselves as a result of an undisturbed development' - (in this case, undisturbed by an adequate biblical and theological philosophy of history).[604]

Furthermore, Lyons' attempt to hold Barthian and Fishian approaches together merely led to a scenario in which the (broadly speaking) historical, epistemological, and linguistic dichotomies pertaining to Barth's "biblical supranaturalism" (to use Pannenberg's language) were *added* to those pertaining to a Fishian stance. This situation then led to a *third* set of dichotomies that emerged from the tensions that in fact existed *between* Barthian and Fishian approaches. A *fourth* set of dichotomies emerged as Lyons' attempt to operate in the actual world in which we cannot *but* "access" historical contingencies (for example, "rubrics") forced him to compromise his Fishian stance in a different direction – i.e. towards a *Thiseltonian* hermeneutic. A *fifth* set of dichotomies even emerged in Lyons' approach in which "immersion into multiple historical traditions" as a hermeneutical axiom was subsumed beneath a quasi-idealist straightjacket of binary "either/or" options – binary either/or options that were projected onto the history of ideas concerning (for the most part) perception and meaning. Many of these problems to do with these five sets of dichotomies re-emerged in the work of Woodman since Woodman, too, tried to unite a Fishian approach to texts with a Barthian epistemology of revelation.

In the end, we speculated as to whether *some* socio-pragmatic appeals to post-structuralist thought were really an instantiation of emergency "name-dropping" – a "name-dropping" that was precipitated by the awkward juxtaposition of a post-theoretical popular culture with so-called "academic" settings - rather than an instantiation of genuinely widening dialogue. Perhaps it was a deeper-level consumerist rejection of complexity itself that had, in turn, led to a resurgence of "Barthian" *authoritarianisms* of the "Word" or of the "Spirit" that dismissed public-sphere critical and metacritical testing over-readily.

The most concerning trend of all was the radicalization of the problem of authoritarianism that occurred when a "Barthian" epistemology of revelation was sublated into the framework of a Fishian view of texts. Where this occurred, even an erroneous authoritarianism of the "Word" could no longer hold an authoritarianism of the "Spirit" in check. The latter, in turn, could easily lead to new fanaticisms, extremisms or fundamentalisms in which God's voice could be confused with projected maladaptive schema(s). Truly, Pannenberg's fears concerning the ways in which Barthians exempted themselves from all criticism were potentially realized in the case of the "Fishian Barthians".

We admitted that such critical speculations and questions could seem over-harsh given the laudable aims and the sincere wrestling with complexity present in the work of Lyons and Woodman. However, the dire consequences that Thiselton predicted would emerge if socio-pragmatism spread globally at least warranted the *asking* of such difficult questions. Further, we speculated that, at present, the

---

[604] Fuchs, E., 'Response to the American Discussion', in *New Frontiers in Theology. Discussions among Continental and American Theologians, Volume II: The New Hermeneutic* (eds. J.M. Robinson and J.B. Cobb, Jr.; New York: Harper and Row, 1964), 235.

"socio-pragmatic yeast" had not yet spread all the way through the "dough" – at least when it came to Lyons and Woodman. An etiquette of "good relating" was potentially still possible between Lyons, Woodman and Thiselton despite the robust theoretical exchanges that occurred between their "schools".

Finally, turning to consider the actual beginnings of the emergence of the dire consequences just noted, we found examples of yet another kind of hermeneutical foreclosure that went still further than that of A.K.M. Adam and of Lyons and Woodman. Notably, this further kind of hermeneutical foreclosure could be described quite simply by the notion of a reactive-aggressive *disowning or projection of* hermeneutical foreclosure that indulged in the quasi-theatrical role-performances of a "drama-triangle" of "rescuers" and "victims" in opposition to Thiselton as "persecutor". In effect, M.W. Nicholson, L. Woodhead and R.L. Hall "consumer-marketed" their *own* hermeneutical foreclosures and attacks as *"Thiselton's* problem", and were beginning to write as if they were "rescuers" rescuing "victims" from "Thiselton the persecutor". Even to respond *at all* to such writings threatened to make *our own* writing look like that of a "rescuer" rescuing "Thiselton the victim" from "persecutors"!

Admittedly, we acknowledged that this further kind of hermeneutical foreclosure was not confined to the outworkings of socio-pragmatism. "Hostile critics" of all persuasions could indulge in the "bad relating" of obfuscating aggressive attack and reaction. Nevertheless, from a Thiseltonian perspective, a socio-pragmatism that "worked all the way through the dough" would indeed lead to a situation in which the "drama-triangle" became the inevitable conflict-laden consequence of the erosion of the acknowledged possibility of rational debate grounded in the possibility of provisional public sphere objectivity in relation to provisionally accessible truth-criteria. In the face of human fallenness, "mere consensus" and futile hopes for a democratic utopia were not enough. Some kind of metacritical basis for socio-critical liberation hermeneutics would *always* be needed.

We may conclude, therefore, that the hermeneutical complexities that have emerged in the various criticisms of (post-) Enlightenment thinking in the Western traditions have proven to be sufficiently overwhelming to produce the crisis in interpretation that we outlined in our Introduction. The straightforward hermeneutical foreclosures of misreading and of simple confusion have degenerated, *first*, into pseudo-theoretical name-*dropping* and now, *secondly*, in some cases at least, into false accusations and name-*calling* – a scenario that may be described as reactive, post-theoretical, and as being not too dissimilar to the scenario marked by the hostile exchanges that US President Barack Obama rightly highlighted in relation to *some* American political discourses in early 2011.

Thiselton, though, prophetically calls us back to responsible hermeneutics. We must *take time to listen*; we must *engage with the unavoidable historical reality of theoretical complexities*; we must *genuinely widen dialogue or conversation* (at the level of critical-synthetic sublation-filter-construction); and we must become *respectful of the other*.

CHAPTER 8

# Conclusions:
# The Value of Anthony C. Thiselton's Formative Thinking for the Discipline of Hermeneutics

In our Introduction we argued that a fresh study on the hermeneutical theory of Anthony C. Thiselton was required both on the grounds of observations related to Thiselton himself and on the grounds of observations related to the contemporary discipline of hermeneutics more broadly.

Certainly, Thiselton's world-ranking stature as a hermeneutical theorist, his status as an unresearched scholar, and his sometimes-difficult style of writing justified a fresh study of his work.

However, the current state of the discipline of hermeneutics more broadly made such a study an urgent priority.

Thus, the discipline of hermeneutics was disorganized, exceedingly complex, seemingly abstracted from interpretative practice, and in a state of internal theoretical disunity in several ways. The discipline (singular) of hermeneutics, whilst rightly being seen by many as "inter-disciplinary" and as "inter-traditional" in terms of the number of disciplines (plural) and traditions (plural) that *contributed* to its shape, was also suffering from the effects of artificial inter-disciplinary, inter-traditional and smaller-scale polarizations *between* and *within* those contributing disciplines and traditions. Finally, the discipline of hermeneutics was in crisis over what constituted "responsible interpretation".

These six sets of problems required solutions. And so it did not make sense to ignore the solutions offered by the world's most encyclopedic thinker in the discipline.

Having said this, it was not always easy to achieve an elucidation of the solutions that Thiselton offered to the discipline of hermeneutics. In order to elucidate Thiselton's solutions, we had to engage in a complex time-consuming historical-structural exegetical procedure that focused on the emergent formative core of Thiselton's thinking – on that basic steel-work of Thiselton's thinking that would become the theoretical platform *from which* the later Thiselton would critique even the most recent traditions, schools, and trends in the discipline of hermeneutics.

We made it clear that, in carrying out this exegetical procedure, we occasionally moved beyond what Thiselton *explicitly* said. Nevertheless it was still primarily the gathered world of *Thiselton's* formative thinking – rather than our own thought -

that we were attempting to elucidate. That is, our exegetical procedure involved us in the process of building hermeneutical theory from the components that *Thiselton* provided. And, arguably, our exegetical procedure allowed us to follow the kind of path of self-involvement into which *Thiselton* invited his readers.

Certainly, in the end, it was worthwhile following this path because the resulting programmatic movement towards a unified critical synthesis or hermeneutical theory did indeed provide solutions that were directly relevant to the six sets of problems beleaguering contemporary hermeneutics that we had expounded in our Introduction - as follows.

Thus, (1), Thiselton's formative work connoted a "three strata" scheme for *organizing* hermeneutical theory.

To begin with, (a), Thiselton's *first* stratum of formative hermeneutical reflection focused on *widening historical dialogue* to embrace as many hermeneutically-relevant disciplines, traditions, movements, schools, thinkers, and viewpoints and/or approaches as possible.

Thiselton's *goal* in this widening of historical dialogue was *both* to gain the *widest possible range* of "angles of view" on any and all problems related to hermeneutics *and*, thereby, to generate the *greatest possible depth of insight* in relation to any and all problems related to hermeneutics.

Thus, on the one hand, Thiselton's widening historical dialogue was *so extensive in scope* that it had to be understood from multiple "angles of view" *itself*. Indeed, we devoted an entire *chapter* (Chapter 2) *just* to the task of traversing the expanse of Thiselton's widening historical dialogue during *one* of his *five* periods of hermeneutical endeavor. For Thiselton, *immersion in the processes of multiple traditions* so as to *widen historical dialogue as much as possible* was an *utterly nonnegotiable hermeneutical axiom*.

Thus, Thiselton established broader *inter-disciplinary* dialogues between philosophy, theology, and literary theory, and – within theology between biblical studies, systematic theology, and pastoral theology. Thiselton also contributed to dialogues between philosophy, theology, psychology, anthropology, and sociology.

Moreover, Thiselton established wider *inter-traditional* dialogues. Sometimes these dialogues could be seen as being dialogues between *larger-scale* Continental and Anglo-American (and sometimes other) traditions. At other times, these dialogues could be seen as being dialogues between *smaller-scale* traditions, movements, and schools *within* the larger-scale Continental and/or Anglo-American (and sometimes other) traditions.

Furthermore, Thiselton established wider dialogues *both* between many of the *major individual thinkers* who were relevant to hermeneutics *and also* between many of the sharply contrasting *viewpoints* that pertained to the polarized debates that still beset many of the perennial issues and questions that were of importance in relation to hermeneutical theory and practice.

On the other hand, Thiselton's widening historical dialogue, whilst it was very broad, was also an attempt *to fathom the depths of the discipline of hermeneutics – to lay bare the heart of near-impenetrable theoretical questions and to divide joints from marrow in the pursuit of exacting answers*. Thiselton emphatically did *not* succumb to cheap predialogic pigeon-holing of thinkers and schools, but was quite content to spend several decades in the anatomizing pursuit of precision. For Thiselton, *fast* answers were almost always *wrong* answers.

Thus, *a single instance* of Thiselton's widening historical dialogue could be *simultaneously* inter-disciplinary, inter-traditional, an attempt to overcome a division between different schools or movements, an attempt to overcome a polarization between the stances of different individual thinkers, *and* an attempt to mediate between polarized viewpoints in relation to a single theoretical question. Thiselton's mediation between the respective approaches of the later Wittgenstein and Fuchs in relation to the creative functioning of language (see Chapter 1) was an example of a widening of historical dialogue that, *due to its depth*, could be understood from a wide range of *superimposed* angles of view.

In other words, Thiselton's widening historical dialogue opposed "hermeneutical foreclosure" *both* at the level of critical-synthetic sublation-filter-construction within preunderstanding *and* at the level of interpretative practice. That is, Thiselton opposed hermeneutical foreclosure *both* in that Thiselton opposed the problem of foreclosing, fixing, or absolutizing pre-understandings *and* in that Thiselton opposed the problem of coming to premature interpretative conclusions. Or, to put it another way, Thiselton *both* opposed a lack of proper listening to enough "angles of view" in relation to *theoretical* questions, *and* Thiselton opposed a lack of proper listening to enough "angles of view" during interpretative *practice*.

(b) The *second* stratum of hermeneutical reflection connoted by Thiselton's formative work centered on Thiselton's widening of existing dialogues pertaining to *five major theoretical axes* of philosophical and theological conversations of relevance for hermeneutics, where these axes or conversations centered on conceptualizations related to history, epistemology, language, (Western) culture, and human selves. We called Thiselton's contributions *to* these conversations Thiselton's "hermeneutical critiques".

Notably, again, Thiselton went beyond trendy citation of the word "dialogue", or of the "dialogic" theme of "question-asking" – often mere devices intended to serve a lazy pluralism – and towards an actual attempt to find provisional theoretical answers. Thiselton's programmatically widening inter-disciplinary, inter-traditional and smaller-scale dialogues were always conversations that were directed *towards new critical theoretical syntheses* – provisional though these syntheses remained.

(c) Thiselton's *third* stratum of formative hermeneutical reflection concerned *"responsible interpretation"* theoretically and practically, and included Thiselton's explication of the hermeneutical task and of the hermeneutical circle. We called this third stratum of hermeneutical reflection Thiselton's "critique of hermeneutical understanding" (cf. "historical understanding"). For Thiselton, hermeneutical theory was inseparable from his concerns regarding the obligation to allow the biblical texts to "strike home" afresh as authoritative divine address to each generation. This concern had academic, ecclesiological, and mission-related dimensions to it – dimensions that reflected Thiselton's own life-world involvements and practice.

Thus, our "three strata" explication of Thiselton's formative thinking turned on "the breadth of inter-disciplinary and inter-traditional (and other) dialogues" (where we normally left as implicit the fact that, in Thiselton's work, these dialogues also aimed at becoming deep and non-superficial), on the philosophical and theological "theoretical preconditions" or grounds for responsible interpretation, and on "responsible interpretation" (or historical/hermeneutical "understanding") itself respectively.

This scheme was not a "formal three-fold" philosophically idealist "essence of hermeneutics", but a historical organization of spheres of historical discussion within hermeneutics as a discipline in history.

Moving on, (2), this "three-strata" scheme already began to clarify hermeneutics as a *complex* discipline.

That is, (a), we immediately deduced from this scheme that Thiselton's formative work connoted not only these "three strata" but also *seven overlapping and inter-related hermeneutical conversations* – namely conversations centered on considerations to do with "dialogue", "history", "epistemology", "language", "(Western) culture", "human selves", and "responsible interpretation" or historical/hermeneutical "understanding". That is, since "wholes" are – to an extent - understood in relation to their constitutive "parts", then hermeneutical complexity – taken as a "whole" – is perhaps initially best approached and elucidated through attempts to identify and *name* its constituent conversations.

(b) To resolve hermeneutical complexity still further, however, we needed to move beyond hermeneutical conversation-*naming* and towards the actual *use* of different hermeneutical conversations so as to test and demonstrate their analytical power to resolve the intelligibility difficulties presented by existing hermeneutical writings.

Thus, (i), it is hoped that Chapter 6 achieved this aim in that, in Chapter 6, we used the "seven hermeneutical conversations" scheme to clarify Thiselton's responses – in *The Two Horizons* - to Bultmann and to the New Hermeneutic (and to what Thiselton designated as being the American counterpart to the New Hermeneutic).

Thus, in relation to "dialogue", Thiselton criticized Bultmann and the New Hermeneutic (including the latter's American counterpart) for presupposing inter-disciplinary and inter-traditional dialogues – particularly dialogues between different philosophical traditions - that were too narrow at the level of critical-synthetic pre-understanding.

Similarly, in relation to conversations pertaining to "history", "epistemology", "language", "(Western) culture", "human selves", and "(responsible) interpretation" (or historical/hermeneutical "understanding"), we were *both* able to expound Thiselton's attacks *against* the various theoretical and interpretative dichotomies that Thiselton found in Bultmann's thinking and in the thinking of the New Hermeneutic (and in the thinking of the latter's American counterpart), *and* able to expound Thiselton's *own* formative thinking.

(ii) Even in our responses in Chapter 7 - to D.R. Stiver's comments on "postmodernity", to broadly post-structuralist thinking, and to broadly socio-pragmatic thinking - we required only the "seven conversation" scheme to clarify the complexities we encountered.

Thus, broadly speaking, we suggested - in response to D.R. Stiver - that the term "postmodern" - in *one* of its wider senses - *could* denote changes in, or criticism of, "post-Enlightenment" thought and culture in accordance with conclusions emerging from the contexts of the *seven* axes of conversation that we had named using the headings "dialogue", "history", "epistemology", "language", "(Western) culture", "human selves", and "(responsible) interpretation" or historical/hermeneutical "understanding". "Postmodernity" – according to *this* particular use of the word – could not be reduced to critiques of epistemology and/or of language, even though it *included* these critiques.

More specifically, Thiselton's complaints concerning Derrida's "docetic" approach to language highlighted the importance of ascribing correct ontological prioritizations to/in theories of "history" and of "language" respectively. If "language" was ontologically prioritized theoretically, theoretical dichotomies (and other problems) ensued. If "history" was ontologically prioritized theoretically, theoretical dichotomies (and other problems) vanished. This finding, in turn, had implications for those socio-pragmatic approaches that tried to rely on (whether explicitly or implicitly), or at least pay lip service to, certain strands in post-structuralist thought.

In this context of discussion, *another* use of the term "postmodern" did not simply denote mere changes in, or criticism of, "post-Enlightenment" thought and culture in accordance with conclusions emerging from the seven hermeneutical axes of conversation noted above. Rather, this other use of the term "postmodern" denoted a *certain problematic kind of* criticism of "post-Enlightenment" thought and culture - a certain problematic kind of criticism *that did not accord with* conclusions emerging from the seven hermeneutical axes of conversation noted above. In this certain problematic kind of criticism, or in this kind of "postmodernity", theories of "history" and of "language" had been *wrongly* inter-related, or *wrongly* inter-sublated, with the result that a myriad of other problems had arisen in relation to all seven of the axes of hermeneutical conversation, reflection or discussion. *This* kind of "postmodernity" was certainly *not* characteristic of Thiselton's work. Rather, Thiselton's work *exposed the problems with* such "postmodernity".

(c) This last point, however, reflected our move (after Thiselton) *beyond* the *use* of different *named* hermeneutical conversations in order to *analyze* the complexities of hermeneutical texts, and *towards* the question of how the different named hermeneutical conversations should be *inter-related or inter-sublated* theoretically-speaking. Having named the "parts" of the hermeneutical "whole", and having then "used" the "parts" to clarify the complexities of hermeneutical texts, we had then, in turn, moved on towards *properly arranging* the "parts" *in relation to* one another.

The "seven conversation" model for analyzing hermeneutical discourse, then, emerged *from* Thiselton's formative thinking, but also had tremendous potential for clarifying the complexities of the discourses of *other* hermeneutical thinkers or trends, as well as for clarifying Thiselton's *own* work. More than this, however: the "seven conversation" model connoted by Thiselton's formative thinking *had its own internal grammar that could function metacritically* so as to expose problems with the ways in which other thinkers were *"building"* their hermeneutical theories.

(d) Still on the subject of clarifying hermeneutical complexity through naming, using, and through properly arranging the seven constituent conversations or discourses of hermeneutics then, notably, we found that, for Thiselton, "dialogue" *with* many disciplines, traditions (and so on) was also to be "dialogue" *after the fashion of* Christ-like relating. That is, we found that, in Thiselton's estimate, "widening dialogue" (stratum one) should have the form or *modus operandi* of "understanding as an aspect of Christ-like relating" (stratum three), such that the seven discourses thereby formed a loop.

That is, if we applied the "seven conversation" model to theological hermeneutics, then the "seventh conversation" – which centered on hermeneutical or "historical understanding" - engendered the conclusion that, for Thiselton, historical understanding converged *both* upon *eschatological* horizons (dialogue(s) *widened* to the maximum – stratum one) *and* upon *Trinitarian* horizons (dialogue(s) *sanctified* to the maximum – stratum three), and thence upon *Christ* who *both* anticipates *and* evaluates "history as a whole".

In other words, Thiselton argued that hermeneutics should aim at becoming: "Christ-like understanding - as an aspect of Christ-like relating - expanding in relation towards all history, and involving (amongst other characteristics) loving (if still critical) respect for the 'other', whether past, present, or future".

(e) Having made these points, of course, it would be stretching matters considerably to assert that we had completely resolved the problem of the difficulty and complexity of hermeneutical language. Many of the sentences in the present study could certainly benefit from further explication in the mode of "in other words (*sic*)"!

Indeed, it would be unprogrammatic - and a symptom of a consumerist demand for fast ready-packaged solutions - if we expected hermeneutical complexity to be resolved overnight. Even *to engage at all* with the major thinkers in hermeneutics unavoidably entails citing them. And the *extensions of existing* conceptualities generated by the insight-deepening grammatical processes of philosophical description, multi-level dialogue, and theoretical inter-sublation will inevitably and ongoingly lead to the formulation of *new hybrid* concepts.

Still, we hope that the present study has moved in the right direction by at least *beginning* to clarify the complexities of the discipline of hermeneutics through a study of Thiselton's formative writings.

(3) Thiselton's formative thinking also shed light on the problem of the

supposed *abstraction* of hermeneutical theory from interpretative practice. Thiselton constantly battled to convince biblical interpreters that they should attend to the issues raised by hermeneutical discussions as a matter of urgent priority on the grounds that these issues reflected factors that – during and/or after interpretation – *actually did* directly and greatly affect perceived textual functions, interpretative practices, and understandings (including exegetical results and practical outcomes).

Thus, (a), historically speaking, Thiselton demonstrated, with respect to the work of Bultmann and of the New Hermeneutic (including the latter's American counterpart), that their lack of "dialogue breadth" (at the stratum-one level of critical-synthetic preunderstanding) had adversely affected the conclusions emerging from their philosophical and theological discourses on history, epistemology, language, Western culture, and on human selves (stratum two) – and that these conclusions, in turn, had *directly* and often negatively affected their perceptions of textual functions, their interpretative practices, their exegetical results, their understandings, and their notions and practical outworkings of understanding(s) (stratum three). Thus, Thiselton argued that it was a historical fact that even Bultmann's and the New Hermeneutic's *most fruitful work in biblical studies* – in relation to Pauline anthropology and Jesus' parables respectively – had produced *one-sided results*.

Hermeneutics, then, in Thiselton's thinking, was not simply abstract theory divorced from practical interpretation and from understanding and its outcomes. Rather, for Thiselton, hermeneutics was a way of highlighting what existing interpretative practices, exegetical results, understandings, and practical outworkings of understandings potentially missed in, misconstrued from, or falsely authorized in relation to, texts themselves.

Thus, for example, broadly "positivist" and broadly "existentialist" approaches to interpretation might discount, say, "miracle" as being "only myth" *not* on the *often-asserted* grounds of painstaking historical-critical exegesis (stratum three), but on the *hidden* grounds of problematic exegesis-shaping theoretical dichotomies at the (stratum two) level of the philosophies of "history", of "epistemology", and of "language" (on this kind of point, see Chapter 7).

In other words, a principle emerged through our exposition of Thiselton's thinking: inadequate philosophical and theological dialogue at the critical-synthetic level of pre-understanding (stratum one) produces, or leaves unaddressed, problematic dualisms or dichotomies (and other theory-related problems) at the level of the five major theoretical axes of philosophical and theological reflection (stratum two). These problematic dualisms or dichotomies (along with other theory-related problems), in turn, *directly* cause interpretative and practical-outcome-related difficulties (stratum three).

This was the problem Thiselton sought to solve: narrow philosophical and theological dialogue leads to inadequate interpretative theory which, in turn, leads to misleading, one-sided, or over-selective interpretative results and to inadequate understandings and outcomes-of-understandings in practice. *Dialogue* affects *theory* affects *practice* (interpretative strategies) affects *exegetical results* (distanciations), *understandings* (actualizations), *and outcomes-of-understandings* (appropriations and applications) - *directly*.

This principle remains true *even if* sometimes – as in the case of internally inconsistent hermeneutical theories - *it takes time* for the "yeast" of newer theory to work through the "dough" of the remnants of older theoretical premises so as, in turn, to change interpretative practices, exegetical results, understandings and outcomes-of-understandings (actualizations, appropriations, and applications). One's biblical studies could remain "valuable" for a while *even after* the "rot" had set in with respect to one's hermeneutical theory. But it *would indeed* only be a matter of time before the "rot" worked through to the level of one's own – or, more worryingly, to the level of one's students' – interpretative practices, exegetical results, understandings and practical outcomes-of-understandings.

This, then, was the principle that emerged from Thiselton's formative thinking regarding the relationship between hermeneutical theory and practice: *Dialogue* (stratum one) affects *theory* (stratum two) affects *practice* (stratum three: interpretative strategies) affects *exegetical results, understandings, and outcomes-of-understandings* (stratum three: distanciations, actualizations, appropriations, and applications) - *directly*.

(b) Thiselton demonstrated that this principle did not conveniently disappear when considering the case of so-called "ordinary" or "non-academic" readers who wished to understand the biblical texts. Thiselton argued that the processes of broadening theoretical dialogues in the context of hermeneutical discussions could not be avoided merely because of consumerist demands for simplicity, novelty, or for immediate answers. Thiselton argued that it was all too possible for overly simplistic approaches to interpretation merely to reflect back the idiosyncrasies of the unexamined pre-understandings of the individuals or communities who employed such approaches. Thiselton argued that when this problem occurred – and Thiselton stressed that this problem often *did* occur – then the effective operative functioning of God's Word through the biblical texts could potentially be seriously distorted - or even silenced or inverted.

Nevertheless, Thiselton insisted that this state of affairs did not necessarily lead to undue pessimism with respect to the "abstractness" of much hermeneutical discourse. For Thiselton, the processes involved in hermeneutical *theory-construction* were different to those involved in *interpretative practice* – even though the former still *directly affected the latter*. Furthermore, when it came to interpretative practice, Thiselton argued that all manner of appropriately-pitched scholarly helps could be made available so as to enable any given reader or readers to progress beyond embryonic understandings of the Scriptures. Moreover, Thiselton argued that, even without such scholarly helps, readers could still find "all that was needed for salvation" through the Holy Spirit's speech-action through the biblical texts.

Thiselton's conclusions in relation to this matter, however, did *not* mean that he supposedly conceived of the Holy Spirit as "*only* working *through* the biblical texts" or as "*only* working from *behind* the biblical texts". Rather, Thiselton argued that the Holy Spirit *also* worked "*in front of* the biblical texts" as well as "through" and "from behind" the biblical texts so as to create faith, and so as to "build" Christians and the Church. Specifically, Thiselton argued that the Holy Spirit – working (in part) "in front of the biblical texts" - imparted the gifts needed for responsible biblical-critical scholarship, creatively inspired *understandings* that were *consistent with* responsible biblical-critical scholarship, and engendered *practical outcomes-of-understandings* that were *consistent with* responsible biblical-critical scholarship.

That is, for Thiselton, the Holy Spirit certainly *did* normally work *through*, and normally *not* apart from, the *normal* processes of human understanding. For Thiselton, the processes of broadening theoretical dialogues in the context of hermeneutical discussions could not be avoided merely on the grounds of super-spiritual or authoritarian appeals to the Holy Spirit's work any more than they could be avoided merely on the grounds of consumerist demands for simplicity, novelty, or for immediate answers. In this context of discussion, Thiselton also addressed several different "purist", "traditional", and "evangelical" objections to hermeneutics and/or to the category of pre-understanding (see Chapters 2 and 6).

Moving on then, (4), we may conclude - with respect to Thiselton's formative (and later) work - that Thiselton's provisional and programmatic solutions to the problem of *theoretical disunities* within hermeneutics embraced and presupposed four sets of considerations.

These four sets of considerations related - respectively – to the "theological-philosophical subtext" of hermeneutics, to "philosophical and theological dualisms or dichotomies" in hermeneutical theory, to the "relative ontological prioritizations or basicalities ascribed respectively to conceptualizations of history and of language" during hermeneutical theory-construction, and to "inter-disciplinary, inter-traditional and other polarizations" in hermeneutics.

The *fourth* of these four sets of considerations – i.e. that set of considerations to do with "inter-disciplinary, inter-traditional and other polarizations" in hermeneutics - has been reserved for our next heading, "(5)", since, in its focus on *external contextual reasons for* internal theoretical disunities, it reflects a slightly different kind of "problematic theoretical disunity", and so is best treated separately.

The *first three* of the above four sets of considerations relate more properly to *internal* theoretical disunities within hermeneutics, and are our focus here. The *relationships between* these first three sets of considerations can be highlighted by the question: "Which provisional working theological-philosophical subtext or overall meta-disciplinary 'paradigm' for hermeneutics best addresses the current problem of philosophical and theological dualisms or dichotomies in hermeneutical theory, and how are conceptualizations of *history* and of *language* inter-related or 'inter-sublated' within such a 'paradigm' in relation to their respective ascribed ontological prioritizations or basicalities?" (In our Introduction, we also noted how a hermeneutical critique of *human selves* related to the issues reflected in this question).

Of course, it was the complexity of this question, and of its answer, that precipitated our decision to split reflection on its attendant concerns into three sets of considerations under three headings – as follows.

Thus, (a), at the level of *"theological-philosophical subtext"* in hermeneutics, then Thiselton's provisional and programmatic *solution to* the problem of theoretical disunities in contemporary hermeneutics consisted of an implicit and predominantly – though not exclusively - *philosophical* unification of hermeneutical theory within a hermeneutical critique of history that was grounded in three inter-related modified Hegelian criteria.

In turn, in Thiselton's formative (and indeed in his later) thinking, this largely *philosophical* unification of hermeneutical theory elucidated, was resonant with, was anticipated and shaped by, and was further corrected and completed by, a prior developing *biblical and theological* framework.

That is, for Thiselton, hermeneutical theory – when considered from a predominantly *"philosophical"* angle of view – came to unity in a philosophy of history that radiated from three inter-related *modified* Hegelian criteria, where these three inter-related *modified* Hegelian criteria concerned "anticipatory conceptions of history-as-a-whole", "the unity (not uniformity) of historical reality", and "historical dialectic" (cf. "historical movement") respectively.

Crucially, however, in Thiselton's thinking, these three criteria were *not* indicative of any assimilation of a biblical-theological worldview to a philosophical worldview. Rather, in Thiselton's thinking, these three criteria constituted philosophical descriptions of *prior* biblical emphases. We may consider each of these three criteria in turn, as follows.

Thus, (i), Thiselton argued that "anticipatory conceptions of history-as-a-whole" could not be dispensed with as the largest diachronic contexts or frames-of-reference for understanding.

Thiselton's formulation of this criterion, however, drew on Pannenberg's *opposition to* Hegel's historical totalization. Thus, Thiselton argued that, prior to the Eschaton, "anticipatory conceptions of history-as-a-whole" were always themselves "historical" in that they were always (prior to the Eschaton) conceptualized from "below", or from "within" history. They could never (prior to eschatological consummation) be conceptualized as though interpreters stood at "the End of history". And so they could never (at least prior to eschatological consummation) be conceptualized as though interpreters viewed history from some "Archimedean point" "above history" *either*.

Thus, Thiselton argued that, prior to the Eschaton, all anticipations of historical "system" were necessarily provisional, "corrigible, incomplete, and open-ended". In turn, this fact meant that – in Thiselton's (formative and later) thinking – all conceptualizations of epistemology, of language, of (Western) culture, of human selves, and of understanding had – prior to the Eschaton - to be reconfigured in relation to historical *finitude and situatedness within* expanding (though still eschatologically convergent) historical horizons.

Moving on then, (ii), in Thiselton's (formative and later) thinking, his second modified Hegelian criterion was that "the unity (not uniformity) of historical reality" (and/or of creation) provided the basis for "horizonal overlap" or for inter-relationships between horizons, and thence for the possibility and unity of language and of understanding.

Nevertheless - bringing in a modification (that was in *some* senses Kierkegaardian) that was opposed to the way in which Hegel's philosophy of history embraced a view of history that was still too theoretically abstracted from life-worlds or from "existence" – Thiselton argued that "historical understanding" and concrete "self-understanding" (in several senses of the latter phrase) were *interwoven*.

Thus, (ii.i), for Thiselton, self-understanding (understood in relation to a "hermeneutic of selves") was an *aspect of* historical understanding; moreover, for Thiselton, historical understanding *began with* self-understanding (here, "self-understanding" was understood in relation to "pre-understanding"); and, finally, for Thiselton, self-understanding (understood in relation to expanding "conscious self-awareness") came *through a detour into* historical understanding.

Therefore, (ii.ii), Thiselton argued that historical understanding could neither be reduced to pre-occupation with the historical past, nor to preoccupation with "selves" or with "interpretative communities" in the historical present, nor even to preoccupation with historical future possibilities "as though future possibilities were present possibilities" (cf. "over-realized eschatology"). Rather, for Thiselton, historical understanding included emphases *both* on human selves and/or communities *and* on other aspects of historical reality and, furthermore, included emphases on the past, on the present, and on the future.

In particular, (ii.iii), Thiselton argued that historical horizons could not be radically dissociated from one another in any way. Indeed, in Thiselton's estimate, to posit such a radical dissociation would be to transgress and to ignore and/or to preclude historical unity (not uniformity), historical embeddedness, historical relationalities, historical analogy, and other historico-philosophical (and theological) criteria pertaining to historical unity (not uniformity). Conversely, Thiselton also argued that the criterion of historical particularity precluded any approach that "collapsed" or "assimilated" historical horizons into one-another: for Thiselton, historical unity did *not* amount to "historical uniformity".

Thus, (ii.iv), Thiselton argued, against socio-pragmatic approaches, that epistemology, language, and understanding could not be grounded in the a-historical collapse or assimilation of the particularities or "otherness" of *past* speech-actions-in-context – i.e. speech-actions by human (or divine or other) subjects - into the *present* horizons of interpretative communities (no matter how broad) on the false grounds of the artificial abstraction of either past or present horizons from historical unity, historical relationality, and historical embeddedness (and other historico-philosophical (and theological) criteria pertaining to historical unity).

*With* socio-pragmatic approaches, Thiselton freely admitted that conceptualizations of epistemology, of language, and of understanding had to be reconfigured in relation to the historical *conditioning* of the historically *finite* (where, for Thiselton, the historically finite included texts, readers, communities, actions, events, historical facts, and so on).

Yet, *against* socio-pragmatic approaches, Thiselton argued that this "reconfiguring" had to be carried out *without* transgressing the criterion of historical unity (not uniformity). Thiselton argued this way because he rightly saw that historical unity was *preconditional for the possibility of* historical embeddedness and historical relationalities which, in turn, were *preconditional for the possibility of* the historical conditioning of the historically finite.

This aspect of Thiselton's thinking, then, created historical, epistemological, linguistic, and hermeneutical problems for socio-pragmatic claims concerning supposed absolute "textual epistemological inaccessibility".

(iii) Thiselton's third modified Hegelian criterion, "historical dialectic", posited a dynamic process of creative historical synthesis or historical "movement" that – and bringing in a further modification (that was in *some* senses Gadamerian) that was opposed to the way in which Hegel's philosophy of history embraced a view of history that was still too theoretically abstracted from life-worlds or from "existence" - generated and embraced the historical particularities and historical continuities of the concrete traditions in which it was earthed.

Thus, for Thiselton, (iii.i), *traditions* – as interwoven wholes that precluded the abstraction of "fact" from "value" and vice versa – constituted expanding diachronic frames-of-reference for understanding that were subsidiary to but constitutive for anticipations of "history-as-a-whole", and that, in their dynamic of expansion, also constituted socio-historical extensions of the hermeneutical circle.

For Thiselton, *"culture"* – notably "Western culture" – was in effect a synchronic "snap-shot" of a cross-section of contemporary juxtaposed diachronically expanding and inter-relating traditions and their constituent language-games in their distinctions and overlapping similarities and cross-fertilizations with respect to one-another.

(iii.ii) Thiselton argued that *understanding* was thus irrevocably tied to the processes of traditions and to the hermeneutical circle. Thiselton argued that understanding was never final, but also that understanding was nevertheless potentially progressive in that it could reach a point at which it contributed to "tradition-modification". Thus, for Thiselton, understanding was not necessarily imprisoned within *past* traditions, but was involved in *shaping future* traditions.

Thiselton thus argued that understanding - in its *epistemological* aspect - could not only *perceive* historically-contingent "truths" that were *from the past and/or in the present*, but could also (to an extent at least) play a role in *shaping future* historically-contingent "truths". Thus, Thiselton "re-historicized" *both* subject-object conceptualization *and* historical-existential understanding.

That is, Thiselton reconfigured or re-historicized Cartesian (and later) notions of subject-object conceptualization along the lines of comparative testing in relation to *historical* differences; *and* Thiselton reconfigured or re-historicized historical-existential understanding in a manner that was consistent with a sublating of Heidegger's notion of "thrown projection" (which was *already* temporal, trans-temporal, and temporalizing) into a larger *historical* framework that had greater respect for corporate inter-subjectivity, for corporate interactions (*actus tradendi*) with tradition (*traditum in traditio*), and for *changing intuitive anticipations* of personal, inter-personal, traditional, historical and eschatological narrative "wholes" and "relationalities".

In other words, Thiselton's notion of "historical rationality" (where "historical rationality", for Thiselton, was a human *capacity* that was employed *during* hermeneutical understanding) embraced a double-dynamic. This double-dynamic involved *both* a community's dialectic inter-action with *traditum in traditio*, and "thrown projection". Thiselton's notion of "historical rationality" was *also* consistent with a transposition *of* this moving historical double-dynamic into a theological-eschatological key (a transposition that *simultaneously* corrected the problems with Continental approaches to language). Moreover, Thiselton *also* argued that it was only *within* the context of this theologically and eschatologically-framed *moving* historical double-dynamic that "re-historicized" subject-object conceptualization could become properly operative critically and metacritically.

Admittedly, in Chapter 7, we saw how historical reconstruction *artificially* stilled and isolated historical horizons. Nevertheless, we also argued that this "stilling" and "isolating" of historical horizons *in no way* precluded the possibility of "true" historical report. The "stilling" and "isolating" of horizons was an *acceptable* simplification for the sake of ease of model-construction. This simplification was acceptable *partly* because the pastness of the past placed constraints on alterity.

(iii.iii) Thiselton argued that *language*, being grounded in the moving life-world particularities and continuities of developing traditions, was *not* grounded "formally" or "logically" in a *static* positivist a-historical *a priori*. Nor, for Thiselton, was language grounded in some kind of Continental supra-historical quasi-mystical "house-of-Being" that supposedly enabled "history" to come into being through "speech". Nor, for Thiselton, was language grounded in a *mobile* a-historical *a priori* "temporal flux" divorced from the actual *variable* grammars of *concrete* geographically-located and traditionally-contextualized historical movements pertaining to speech-actions by persons or subjects (against, broadly speaking, post-structuralism).

Rather, for Thiselton, language was dynamic speech-action – or communicative action – that was embedded within, and inseparable from, larger dynamic and developing historical contexts. Thus, in correction of linguistically dualistic Continental approaches, Thiselton noted how *even propositions* could not only "say" in relation to the *past*, but could also function *creatively and dynamically* so as to "show" in a way that *transformed* readers' *future* actualizations, appropriations, and applications. Again, though, Thiselton did not say that language thereby "created history". Rather, for Thiselton, language was always already embedded within the larger framework of inter-subjective speech-action, a framework that was *always already* "historical" (and that *always already* had an extra-linguistic dimension).

(iii.iv) From a Thiseltonian perspective, therefore, conceptualizations of epistemology, of language, and of understanding had to be reconfigured in relation to *actual geographically-located* historical *processes or movements*, and *only thence in relation to continuity and difference.*

Thus, (iv), in Thiselton's thinking, hermeneutical critiques of history, epistemology, language, (Western) culture, human selves – and, therefore, of hermeneutical understanding - were brought to unity through "re-historicization" or, rather, through a non-idealist critical "sublation" of existing stratum-two theoretical hermeneutical discourses into a new historical key. Thiselton argued that "history" needed to be better understood philosophically; that "epistemology" was to be historically re-configured; that "language" was historically grounded; that (Western) culture was an instantiation or snap-shot of certain overlapping and juxtaposed traditions at given points in their histories; that human selves were to be understood *as* dynamic historically-structured historical contingencies; and that hermeneutical understanding was itself a historical process.

Thus, (v), Thiselton's work connoted that theoretical hermeneutics was brought to unity within a new modified Hegelian subtext that, in turn, resonated with *prior* biblical themes.

(vi) If, from a predominantly *philosophical* viewpoint, Thiselton's unifying "subtext" for hermeneutics centered on his three modified Hegelian criteria, then Thiselton's *sublation of* this predominantly "philosophical unity" into a *biblical-theological* key changed things for the better. This was so because the resulting "theological-philosophical unity" provided a better basis for linking "history" to "persons-in-relation", for the provision of explanatory and evaluative metacriteria, and for conceptualizations of human worth, identity and agency.

Moreover, this "theological-philosophical unity" connoted *eight* axes of inter-related and overlapping historico-philosophical (and theological) criteria that were of *relevance for a hermeneutical critique of historical objectivity*. These eight axes included the following sets of inter-related and overlapping historico-philosophical (and theological) criteria: (vi.i) finitude, situatedness, and embeddedness - in relation to anticipations of history-as-a-whole; (vi.ii) unity, relationality and embeddedness (in this context, the word "embeddedness" has a slightly different sense to the sense it has when it pertains to finitude and situatedness); (vi.iii) process and motion or movement; (vi.iv) particularity and difference (cf. otherness, strangeness, uniqueness, the alien, tension, distance, relativity, novelty, unfamiliarity etc.); (vi.v) continuities (e.g. traditions, public criteria, convictions, (pre-)judgments, transmitted content etc.) and similarity (cf. analogy, typology); (vi.vi) conditioning (cf. effects, change and transformation); (vi.vii) individual human subjectivity, and, corporate human inter-subjectivity (cf. community); (vi.viii) fallenness and redemption. (N.B. "creation" is reflected in "(vi.i) – (vi.vii)"!).

*Most* of these *eight axes* of criteria could be derived from Thiselton's *three* inter-related modified Hegelian criteria. *However*, the criteria that we called "historical fallenness" and "historical redemption" were uniquely grounded in Thiselton's biblical theology, and yet were still very relevant to his *hermeneutical critique of historical objectivity*. This point only further confirmed the truth of Thiselton's implicit argument that a *philosophically*-unified hermeneutical theory was *improved* when it was critically sublated into a *biblical-theological* key. Indeed, as we noted above, even Thiselton's *three* inter-related modified Hegelian criteria were, ultimately, *later* philosophical descriptions of *prior* biblical-theological emphases.

(b) Moving on, and with respect to the problem of *theoretical disunities* in relation to *"philosophical and theological dualisms or dichotomies"* in contemporary hermeneutics, then Thiselton's formative work brought multiple criticisms to bear against the dichotomies present in the work of Bultmann and of others (including, in effect, more recent approaches), as we have already begun to note.

In particular, (i), Thiselton tackled Bultmann's "historical", "epistemological", "linguistic", "anthropological", and "interpretative" dichotomies (note, here, five of our seven hermeneutical conversations) – as follows.

Thus, to begin with, Thiselton argued that the "unity of historical reality" criterion contradicted Bultmann's *historical* "history versus nature", "*Geschichte* versus *Historie*", and "value versus fact" dichotomies. Theologically speaking, Thiselton argued that the "unity of historical reality" criterion also contradicted Bultmann's "God and divine action versus 'this-world'" (cf. "grace versus nature") dichotomy along with Bultmann's other related theological dichotomies – though, for Thiselton, God as Creator remained distinct from, if still intimately involved in, the creation.

Similarly, Thiselton argued that the grounding of the unity of *understanding* in the "unity of historical reality" contradicted Bultmann's *epistemological* "pre-cognitive versus cognitive", "historical understanding versus scientific explanation", and "existential self-understanding versus existentialist knowledge" dichotomies. Further, Thiselton argued that the grounding of the unity of *language* in the "unity of historical reality" contradicted Bultmann's *linguistic* "meaning versus report", "self-involving functions versus objectifying functions", and "inner thought or intention versus linguistic expression" dichotomies.

Moreover, Thiselton argued that the grounding of *human selves* in socio-historical reality (on the basis of the criterion of "the unity of historical reality") contradicted Bultmann's *anthropological* "subjectivity versus concepts about 'self'", "subjectivity versus inter-subjectivity", and "decision versus material world" dichotomies.

Finally, Thiselton's uniting of historical continuities and historical particularities within a notion of tradition according to which tradition was conceived as an extension of the hermeneutical circle – and as a dynamic "historical dialectic" movement - contradicted what Thiselton saw as being Bultmann's dichotomous *interpretative* stress on "generalising" form criticism (and on *Sachkritik*) *at the expense of* painstaking exegesis of the "particular" case.

(ii) Thiselton's historico-philosophical (and theological) criteria also allowed Thiselton and/or the present study to address dualisms or dichotomies in the New Hermeneutic (and in its American counterpart), in "ideologically structuralist" approaches, and eventually in broadly "post-structuralist" approaches and in broadly "socio-pragmatic" approaches as well.

Thus, for example, we highlighted *both* Thiselton's implicit appeal to the grounding of the unity of language and of understanding in "the unity of historical reality" *and* Thiselton's implicit appeal to the notion of tradition as "historical dialectic" *so that* we (after Thiselton) could expose a historical-linguistic dichotomy in Derrida's broadly post-structuralist thought – i.e. so that we could expose a dichotomy, in Derrida's thinking, between a privileging of an "ahistorical abstracted temporality as a precondition for the possibility of linguistic flux" and a disparagement of "the grammars of actual geographically-located concrete historical movements pertaining to language-uses". Only on the basis of the former pole of this dichotomy - (itself a result of an erroneous attempt to build an ontologically more-basic critique of history within the co-ordinates of an ontologically less-basic critique of language) - could Derrida espouse radicalized historical dissociation and difference (*and* différance).

Furthermore, after Thiselton, we appealed to the same two historico-philosophical (and theological) criteria *in order to* oppose historical, epistemological, and linguistic dichotomies in socio-pragmatic approaches. Such approaches – in so far as they were strictly consistent with the approach of Stanley Fish - set present context in opposition to past context, and (in a particular way – see Chapter 7) set historical reality in opposition to historical texts. Such approaches – in so far as they were strictly consistent with the approach of Stanley Fish - also set corporate self-understanding in opposition to historical understanding through texts and, in addition, set present linguistic constructs and assertions (and other present-horizon linguistic behaviors) in opposition to textual (extra-) linguistic functions – where these textual (extra-) linguistic functions included (amongst other functions) the epistemological disclosure of textually-transmitted historical public criteria with referential and conceptual content.

In particular, we appealed to the same two historico-philosophical (and theological) criteria in order to defend Thiselton's view that "present meanings" could be *shaped* at least in part – by the *past* meanings of texts even if present-horizon communities contributed most of the *work* of meaning-construction. Socio-pragmatic approaches that saw "meaning" as shaped entirely by communities in present-contexts (no matter how wide) transgressed Thiselton's historico-philosophical (and theological) criteria – particularly Thiselton's criteria concerning, and pertaining to, historical unity (not uniformity) and historical dialectic.

(iii) Later on in Chapter 7 these kinds of arguments took on new levels of complexity as we applied not only Thiselton's three modified Hegelian criteria but also Thiselton's eight implicit axes of historico-philosophical (and theological) criteria (see above) in order to continue to expose, and to oppose, theoretical dichotomies in Fishian - and in Barthian-Fishian - socio-pragmatic approaches.

We have *already* noted above that *since* the "historical conditioning of the historically finite" is a process that *necessarily* occurs against the background of, and *is itself conditioned by*, all the other mutually-qualifying historico-philosophical (and theological) criteria – including historical unity (not uniformity) – *then* this process cannot be appealed to in order to justify the implicit notion of "radical dissociation between historical horizons" that is presupposed in socio-pragmatic assertions concerning textual-epistemological "inaccessibility".

However, in part by applying Thiselton's historico-philosophical (and theological) criteria taken as a whole, we *also* exposed the presence of no less than *five* sets of theoretical (and practical) dichotomies within certain Barthian-Fishian socio-pragmatic approaches. These dichotomies included: (iii.i) dichotomies pertaining to a Fishian approach (where at least one of these dichotomies was inherited from post-structuralist approaches); (iii.ii) dichotomies pertaining to a Barthian approach; (iii.iii) dichotomies pertaining to irreconcilable tensions *between* Barthian and Fishian approaches; (iii.iv) dichotomies between, on the one hand, Barthian and/or Fishian *theory* and, on the other hand, *actual interpretative practices* employed *by* the Barthian-Fishian socio-pragmatic approaches we considered; and, (iii.v), dichotomies pertaining to echoes or shadows of philosophical idealism.

We saw that this lack of proper theoretical (and practical) coherence within Barthian-Fishian socio-pragmatic approaches only *worsened* the problems related to authoritarianisms "of the Word" and to authoritarianisms "of the Spirit" that *already* afflicted older Barthian approaches: i.e. sublating a Barthian epistemology of revelation into the epistemology implicit in a Fishian approach to texts could only *adversely* alter these problems to do with authoritarianism such that they progressively degenerated into an authoritarianism (or, rather, into competing authoritarianisms) that masqueraded solely under the disguise of "experience of the Holy Spirit". In such a scenario, *even an authoritarianism "of the Word" could not keep an authoritarianism "of the Spirit" (with all the latter's attendant dangers in relation to experience-centeredness) in check.*

(c) With respect to the problem of *theoretical disunities* in relation to the *"respective ascribed ontological prioritizations or basicalities of history and language"* in contemporary hermeneutics, then Thiselton's "historical" - as opposed to "linguistic" - unification of hermeneutical theory (when viewed from a predominantly philosophical "angle of view") connoted the ontological priority of "history" over "language" and *not* vice versa. For Thiselton, all seven hermeneutical critiques or conversations were each profoundly *historical* and came to internal unity, and to unity with one another, within Thiselton's theologically-completed and theologically-anticipated modified Hegelian - and ultimately "biblical" – *historical* framework.

Notably, (i), Thiselton argued that the later Wittgenstein's unified (but not uniform) view of language resonated with the view that history was ontologically prior to language. Conversely, as noted above, we suggested – on the basis of Thiseltonian arguments - that an implicit historical-linguistic dichotomy potentially accompanied Derrida's attempt to prioritize language over history in relation to the processes of critique-sublation that were implicit within some of his theoretical discussions.

Drawing on Thiselton and on B.D. Ingraffia and others we also argued that, in the later Barthes' thinking, a similar attempt – i.e. to reverse the relationships or inter-sublation directions pertaining to the relative ontological basicalities ascribed, during hermeneutical theorizing, to conceptualizations of history and of language respectively - had led not only to the implicit historical-linguistic dichotomy just noted in relation to Derrida, but also to the closely-related problems of "critique-collapse" and of "critique-over-extension".

In Chapter 7, (ii), this kind of discussion – alongside that centered on "dichotomies" – *further* exposed the problems behind the socio-pragmatic hermeneutics of Fish and of writers following Fish's approach. It seemed that socio-pragmatic assertions concerning textual "inaccessibility" during interpretation (stratum three) were grounded in historical, epistemological, and linguistic dichotomies (stratum two) that, in turn, resulted from a pre-understanding (stratum one) that had – in part - been uncritically adopted from broadly post-structuralist approaches.

In the history of that (post-structuralist and, now, socio-pragmatic) pre-understanding, a developing *adequate* (biblical) hermeneutical critique of *history* had been erroneously subsumed beneath *language*-oriented critiques of Western idealist metaphysics. This theoretical-historical background had led – within, or in relation to, that same pre-understanding – (ii.i) to the problem of erroneously theoretically prioritizing (in effect) "linguistic basicality" over "historical basicality", and thence, (ii.ii), to the false problems of radical historical or horizonal dissociation (and other dichotomies), and thence, (ii.iii), to the false problems (cf. "critique-collapses") known as the "death of God", the "death of authors", the "death of selves", and so on - and thence also, (ii.iv), to the false problem of supposed textual-epistemological "inaccessibility".

At worst, however, as we noted above, "horizonal dissociation" was only an artificial artefact that resulted from simplifications employed during interpretative processes, and had very little to do with historical ontology. Correlatively, attributing ontological significance to "horizonal dissociation": (ii.i) transgressed the theological criterion of the unity of creation; (ii.ii) transgressed historico-philosophical (and theological) criteria – notably (but not exclusively) the unity, relationalities, continuities, and movements of historical reality; and, (ii.iii), in our view, also transgressed the scientific criterion of the space-time continuum.

Moving on then, (5), with respect to the problem of *inter-disciplinary, inter-traditional and other smaller-scale polarizations* in hermeneutics, we noted how Thiselton sought ever-widening dialogue unto provisional critical syntheses at every point within hermeneutics where it could be said that there were unnecessary polarizations – whether such polarizations were between different disciplines, traditions (whether inter-continental in scale, or closer in scale to "movements" or "schools"), thinkers (or appeals to specific thinkers or to groupings of specific thinkers or sources), stances in relation to specific practical approaches or specific theoretical philosophical problems, and so on.

Thus, (a), Thiselton attempted to overcome the *inter-disciplinary* polarization, in hermeneutics, between appeals to philosophy and appeals to theology. In this context of discussion we saw that Thiselton's predominantly-philosophical unification of hermeneutics in a hermeneutical critique of history *warranted* his adoption of a provisional working Christological and eschatological framework of coordinates for the unification of hermeneutics more broadly and as a (developing) whole.

Thus, for example, Thiselton argued that if a predominantly-philosophical unified hermeneutical theory lacked an adequate ground for metacritical explanation and evaluation (and for other key hermeneutical emphases), then New Testament theology did not.

Having said this, of course, (i), it was important to realize – again - that Thiselton never assimilated a biblical-theological worldview to a philosophical worldview. We concluded in Chapter 7 that Thiselton held two conversations in tension with respect to philosophy and theology.

Thus, on the one hand, there was Thiselton's conversation that could be seen as being "faith seeking understanding". This was a conversation in which Thiselton employed widening dialogue between different philosophical traditions so as to shed more and more light on Scripture. On the other hand, there was Thiselton's conversation according to which philosophy's *failure* to meet the demands emerging from certain of *its own philosophical concerns* - for example, its concerns regarding conceptualization, metacriticism and truth (see Chapter 3) - rationally *warranted* recourse to the prior biblical and theological solutions that were available, *regardless* of whether or not these prior biblical and theological solutions were *already* "received" in the case of any given individual or community.

That is, Thiselton in effect argued that *Christians* did not need to worry when it came to fears about the ways in which *widening* hermeneutical dialogues with philosophical traditions might affect perceptions of the cogency, and of the authority, of the Scriptures. On the contrary, Thiselton in effect argued that *philosophers* would need to be concerned if they thought that philosophical systems – or even combinations of philosophical systems - by themselves were wholly adequate hermeneutically or were somehow elevated "above" Scripture.

One context of discussion in which this point was driven home was Thiselton's epistemological discussion in relation to "truth" in which he showed how a prior multiform biblical notion of truth corrected different kinds of "one-sidedness" in various later extra-biblical and philosophical approaches to truth.

So, again, Thiselton did not (and does not) assimilate a biblical-theological worldview to a philosophical worldview. Rather, on the one hand, Thiselton demonstrated the great usefulness, but also the limitations, of philosophy in relation to hermeneutics. On the other hand, Thiselton demonstrated the cogency, authority, and superiority (relative to philosophical traditions) of the Christian Scriptures in relation to hermeneutics.

Thus, (ii), we saw that Thiselton's engagements with the philosophies of history, epistemology, and language - particularly his revision of Pannenberg's early stance - provided resonances with a *prior* biblical theology.

Thus, in relation to the philosophy of *history*, Thiselton argued that the *prior* Christ-event *already had* a character that *anticipated* the character of Thiselton's *later* three inter-related modified Hegelian criteria.

Thus, for Thiselton, the Christ-event, as an anticipation of "history-as-a-whole", anticipated and extended Gadamer's appeal to the notion of traditions as contexts for understanding (we drew on E.A. Dunn here). Moreover, for Thiselton, the Christ-event, in its claims concerning its ethical relevance for all humanity throughout all history, presupposed the unity (not uniformity) of historical reality. Thiselton also argued that the Christ-event, in being both related - as prophetic-fulfillment - to prior tradition and yet also genuinely unique, reflected "tradition" as a dialectic process that generated both "continuity" and "novelty".

That Hegel's philosophy was linked to Christian theology anyway only strengthened our arguments since it was the predominantly *philosophical* discussion that Thiselton's modified Hegelian criteria unified. It was, therefore, fitting that a qualified appeal to some of Hegel's thoughts could be used to overcome the artificial divide between philosophical and theological approaches that had arisen in the history of the discipline of hermeneutics.

In relation to a hermeneutical critique of *epistemology*, Thiselton argued that "faith" in Christ, in three or more of its several senses, was structured similarly to "historical rationality" and was thereby resonant with the progressiveness of the hermeneutical circle. More than this, however: for Thiselton, the Christ-event *itself*, in its resonance with historical dialectic and with "tradition-refinement", thereby also resonated with the hermeneutical circle. (The Creator is the ontological ground of the creation).

In relation to the philosophy of *language*, Thiselton argued that the notion of Christ as "enfleshed Word" resonated with appeals to the later Wittgenstein's philosophy of language which, in turn, could be grounded in a hermeneutical critique of history that was, ultimately, Christological and eschatological.

(iii) Thiselton also argued that bringing a theological discussion of metacritical explanation and evaluation into dialogue with philosophical criteria could be philosophically warranted as part of a working hypothesis and that – in addition - this theological discussion did not thereby necessarily project disunities into, or between, emerging philosophical and/or theological criteria.

Rather this theological discussion – far from projecting disunities into Thiselton's more "philosophical" critiques - infused Thiselton's hermeneutical critique of history with the notion of respect for the historical "other", his hermeneutical critique of epistemology with a meta-socio-critical principle and with a multiform notion of "truth" (including the "truth" of authentic humanity), and his hermeneutical critique of language with the notion of responsible speech "backed" by actions and by revealed reality. Similarly, Thiselton's hermeneutical critiques of (Western) culture and of human selves were infused with reflection on sin, judgment and redemption, and his critique of hermeneutical understanding was infused with a critique of human relationships and relating.

Notably, Thiselton argued that Christ's embodiment of love for God and neighbor provided the ethical "metacriterion" against which all other historical relationships and/or relationalities should (and would) be evaluated.

For Thiselton, practically speaking, and as we have already noted, proper understanding was an aspect of Christ-like Trinitarian relating. Theoretically speaking, Thiselton's notion of proper understanding thus extended Gadamer's notion of "dialogue" towards a notion that reflected the embodied Christ (again, we drew on E.A. Dunn here).

Thus, (iv), for Thiselton, the warrant for including theological considerations in the hermeneutical discussion was, in part, the introduction of a viable theological metacriterion for ethical evaluation – a metacriterion that resonated with, and improved upon, the fruits of extended philosophical dialogue. However, for Thiselton, the conversation of warrant, that brought theology in at the end, was qualified by, and was ultimately grounded in, the conversation of theory-construction, which brought theology in from the start as "faith seeking understanding".

Thiselton's hermeneutical approach involved a process that used philosophy in order to generate fresh understandings of the Bible. But, through that very process, Thiselton had also in effect begun to demonstrate the superiority of a developing biblical worldview that could *not* be assimilated to any single philosophical tradition, or even to any combination of philosophical traditions.

(v) We also alluded – both in the main body of our study and in our earlier conclusions above – to how Thiselton's sublation of predominantly "philosophical" hermeneutics into a Trinitarian and promissory theological whole resulted – in critique of (to an extent) Gadamer's and others' "postmodern" or "deconstructionist" approaches to "persons" - in a way of conceptualizing "history" that had to be respectful of, and indeed largely configured along the lines of, an anticipated eschatologically-promissory temporal narrative whole involving "persons-in-relation".

This way of conceptualizing "history" was true to Thiselton's thinking *despite* the ways in which Thiselton "decentered" individual subjectivity, individual agency, and individualistic epistemological arbitration in opposition to the anthropocentricity of Cartesian, transcendental, phenomenological, Heideggerian, Bultmannian, and broadly positivist and broadly existentialist approaches to selfhood and/or to subjectivity.

(vi) We also argued that Thiselton's Christological and eschatological extension of a historical unification of hermeneutics provided a "tensorial" ("tensor": *stretching* muscle in biology, cf. vector with *direction* in mathematics) framework of coordinates that held theoretical hermeneutical critiques in – or that stretched theoretical hermeneutical critiques out into - their proper directed inter-relationships, structure, or grammar.

This tensorial framework de-centered epistemology, language, Western culture, human selves and understanding relative to a history stretched out from the present horizon towards the past (cf. "two horizons") and towards the future eschatological horizon of divine promise-fulfillment (cf. "three horizons"). In this framework, problematic theoretical dichotomies disappeared from hermeneutics – a fact that only further warranted the inclusion of theological considerations in the hermeneutical discussion.

(vii) We likened Thiselton's biblical tensorial framework to a properly built Russian Doll in which the different sized dolls *within* the Russian Doll could be likened to the various hermeneutical critiques in their proper inter-relationships with one another. The implication of this way of viewing "the grammar of hermeneutics", however, was that any attempt to build the dolls/critiques together in the *wrong* order would produce, on the one hand, theoretical dichotomies and, on the other hand, two other problems closely related to theoretical dichotomies – problems that we called "critique-collapses" and "critique-over-extensions".

Thus, ultimately, it was Thiselton's biblical tensorial framework that grounded Thiselton's opposition to dualisms or dichotomies in the positivist, existentialist, Continental hermeneutical, structuralist, post-structuralist, and neo- or socio-pragmatic traditions. And it was the same biblical framework that formed the basis for Thiselton's more implicit opposition to "critique-collapses" and to "critique-over-extensions" in post-structuralist approaches and, by implication, in neo- or socio-pragmatic approaches.

Thus, for example, as we hinted at in our Introduction and argued more explicitly later, a Thiseltonian perspective led to the view that Heidegger, Bultmann, and even the New Hermeneutic, had made the human subject too central, and had thus fallen foul of historical, epistemological, and linguistic dichotomies. Notably, to allude to our Russian Doll illustration, we implied that Bultmann's construction of his philosophy of history "within" his anthropocentric Neo-Kantian epistemology had (alongside his appeals to Heidegger) helped him to split "history" into *Geschichte* and *Historie*.

Alternatively, and alluding to our Russian Doll illustration again, we observed how Thiselton suggested that Derrida had constructed "history" "within" a theory of language, and that Derrida had thus split history into a dichotomy between, on the one hand, an inaccessible ahistorical abstracted temporal realm that was preconditional for the possibility of linguistic flux and, on the other hand, successive "histories" as shifting intra-linguistic constructs.

Moreover – and still alluding to our Russian Doll illustration – we argued that a Thiseltonian perspective suggested that the later Barthes had also erroneously constructed a theory of "history" "within" a theory of "language", and that the later Barthes had thereby rendered certain historical realities – namely God (though God is more than just "historical", but is not less than "historical"), authors, subjects and/or selves – subject to the entailments of the "collapse" of a hermeneutical critique of history and to the entailments of the "over-extension" of a hermeneutical critique of language. This theoretical scenario had led to artificial "deconstructionist" conclusions concerning the supposed "death" of God and of authors and/or subjects or selves.

Finally – and again we are alluding to our Russian Doll illustration – we implied that a Thiseltonian perspective suggested that Fish (after Rorty) had constructed implicit theories of history, epistemology, and language "within" the present horizon of an imperialized corporate "selfhood" (however wide or "global", or, however "localist"), and that Fish (after Rorty) had thereby theoretically splintered "history", "epistemology", "language", and had (more than just theoretically) thereby potentially splintered "Western culture".

That is, drawing on Thiselton's thinking we argued that, in a Fishian approach: the historical past was dichotomously severed from the present, historical knowledge via texts was rendered impossible, and textual assertions (along with other textual functions) were disparaged. Thiselton predicted that the result of this collapse of the realm of qualified public objectivity would manifest itself as inevitable conflicts between competing sub-groups – conflicts that could ultimately fragment Western culture.

(viii) Thiselton's thinking concerning the relationship - in hermeneutics - between philosophy and theology now became clear: the predominantly philosophical subtext that unified hermeneutical theory was a highly modified Hegelian framework. However, Thiselton argued that this framework resonated with a *prior* biblical Christology and eschatology and thus warranted the inclusion of appeals to theology - both in relation to the provision of a working unifying ground for hermeneutics, and in relation to the provision of theoretical components during the processes of theory-construction.

For Thiselton, this inclusion of appeals to theology did not disrupt the unity of the hermeneutical critiques internally or in their inter-relations, but improved the situation - in part by infusing the "whole" with the metacriterion of ethical evaluation, namely the Christ-event, that had, until the inclusion of theology in the discussion, still been divorced from the "whole".

Thus, Thiselton argued that theology anticipated and extended the hermeneutical unity provided by philosophy. That is, we found that, for Thiselton, the emerging "philosophy" that unified theoretical hermeneutics was also the "philosophy" that cohered with Scripture. By contrast, Thiselton argued that philosophy that was dissonant with Scripture fragmented theoretical hermeneutics. For Thiselton, the unification of hermeneutics occurred when philosophy and a *prior* biblical theology that was elucidated by philosophy came to unity.

Further, (ix), far from simply "following" Pannenberg in relation to a qualified appeal to Hegel, Thiselton had actually "restarted" – on a stronger post-later-Wittgensteinian footing - the kind of theoretical construction that Pannenberg had attempted earlier. That is, it was safer to say that *Thiselton, rather than Pannenberg*, offered the first truly "post-Gadamerian-post-later-Wittgensteinian" *theological* hermeneutical synthesis – the "transformed paradigm" for hermeneutics (i.e. for *both* general hermeneutics *and* biblical hermeneutics) that the discipline had been waiting for.

That is, in twentieth-century hermeneutical discussion, it is as though a unified theoretical theological-philosophical hermeneutic could not be constructed until Gadamer and the later Wittgenstein had been allowed to mutually correct one another's thinking. And it was in Thiselton's work that Gadamer's and the later Wittgenstein's mutual "waiting for one another" first came to an end – at least in theological hermeneutics.

Of course, it would be unfair to under-estimate the great significance of Pannenberg's work for Thiselton. Hermeneutics would hardly be "theological" if it drew on Gadamer and on the later Wittgenstein alone. Thus, it is perhaps best to say that Thiselton provides the first unified and properly "post-Gadamerian, post-later-Wittgensteinian, post-early-Pannenbergian" theological hermeneutics.

Moreover, we should not neglect to observe the extent of Thiselton's second-period appeals to Heidegger and to Bultmann (and to Schleiermacher and Kierkegaard too) in relation to a hermeneutical critique of human selves. Thiselton's hermeneutics synthesize insights from *many* thinkers – and not just from Gadamer, the later Wittgenstein, and Pannenberg (see Chapter 6 especially).

Still in relation to the issue of *inter-disciplinary* polarization in hermeneutics then, (b), Thiselton also resolved the inter-disciplinary polarization in hermeneutics between philosophy and literary theory by embedding the latter within the former. For Thiselton, correlatively, linguistic semantics supplemented philosophical semantics and not vice versa, where Thiselton accommodated the post-Saussurian tradition *to* the later Wittgensteinian tradition.

Therefore, whilst "hermeneutics" might be only a *part* of "literary theory" courses in some university settings, Thiselton's ontological prioritization of the historical discussion over the linguistic discussion suggested that the reverse should be the case. This point was not at all intended to diminish literary theory, but rather to contextualize literary theory. Nevertheless, a Thiseltonian perspective says that to subjugate hermeneutics to literary theory is *to have misunderstood "hermeneutics" from the ground up*. In part, it was also G.L. Bruns and C. Norris who alerted us to the ways in which this kind of misunderstanding could affect certain university settings.

(c) We also noted how Thiselton's conception of the hermeneutical circle united biblical studies and systematic theology: for Thiselton, the latter (along with philosophical and other influences) contributed to the preunderstandings with/from which the former was carried out. Thiselton argued that biblical studies, in turn, reshaped systematic theology and thence reshaped pre-understandings – and so on around the hermeneutical circle. Thus, Thiselton argued that neither discipline could be carried out properly in ignorance of, or in isolation from, the other. Moreover, Thiselton argued that *both* these disciplines should enter into dialogue with the discipline of hermeneutics.

(d) Thiselton's conception of the hermeneutical circle also united biblical studies and pastoral theology. The latter was part and parcel of Thiselton's extended notion of "fusion" in which "understanding" was "always already actualizing, appropriating, and applying": only through its *operation in life* could the Bible be truly understood. Thiselton, therefore, argued (in his third period) that pastoral theologians should enter into dialogue with the disciplines of biblical studies, systematic theology, and hermeneutics.

(e) In relation to *inter-traditional* polarizations, then we saw early on that Thiselton explicitly sought to appeal *both* to Continental tradition(s) *and* to Anglo-American tradition(s). We saw that Thiselton *mediated between* these two major streams of Western thinking – whether in relation to theology or in relation to philosophy (or in relation to other disciplines) - and that Thiselton was keen to stress the existence of *parallels* between these two major Western traditions.

Of course, Thiselton's strong emphasis on historical particularity meant that he was highly resistant to all *a priori* generalization. Thiselton refused to subsume the particularities of the thinking of particular writers beneath broad-brush stereotyped characterizations of "Continental versus Anglo-American" thought. Nevertheless, Thiselton *did* allow for an *a posteriori* general axis of inquiry that admitted the possibility of after-the-fact historical trends or continuities – so long as historical particularity was always prioritized.

Thus, for Thiselton, mediation between "Continental" and "Anglo-American" thinking was always mediation between the writings of particular thinkers *before* it was mediation between "traditions". Nevertheless, for Thiselton, particular thinkers were always already shaped by prior traditions and, in their turn, went on to help re-shape those (and potentially other) traditions. For Thiselton, both individual and corporate dimensions had to be held together in a dynamic, dialectic, dialogic, diachronic inter-relationship of mutual historical conditioning.

Perhaps the most important instance of Thiselton's mediation between Continental and Anglo-American traditions was Thiselton's use of reciprocal qualifying appeals to Gadamer and to the later Wittgenstein – as we have already noted. Crucially, we saw that Thiselton assimilated neither of these two thinkers' philosophies to that of the other but rather, as we have already indicated, Thiselton in effect qualified the later Wittgenstein's approach to history by appeal to Gadamer, and qualified Gadamer's approach to language by appeal to the later Wittgenstein.

Similarly, we noted how Thiselton continued to use Continental terminology, but in a way that presupposed a conceptual grammar that had been modified by appeals to Anglo-American thought. (At all points, though, as we have already said, Thiselton refused to assimilate biblical theology to any single tradition of philosophy, or even to any combination of philosophical traditions. Rather, Thiselton mediated between philosophical traditions in order to better-elucidate a developing biblical-theological framework).

Of particular note, was Thiselton's use of appeals to Anglo-American traditions in order to reinstate what he identified as the "cognitive" dimension. This "cognitive" dimension included historical considerations related to report and to the textual transmission of conceptual content from the past, epistemological considerations to do with the character and role of conceptualization, and linguistic considerations to do with various kinds of assertive language - including empirically informative statements, creatively functioning assertions, and/or grammatical propositions that could "show".

Here, of course, Thiselton was not positing any "formal" distinctions between, say, assertive and non-assertive language, or between assertions, statements, and propositions. For Thiselton, as we saw, linguistic functions were always interwoven and very often multiform. Moreover, for Thiselton, the words "assertions", "statements", and "propositions" were often almost synonymous. And yet, at the same time, Thiselton argued, after the later Wittgenstein, that even so-called cognitive language was not just "one thing" but was, rather, pluriform and multifunctional.

(f) Thiselton also attempted to overcome polarizations between smaller-scale traditions, movements, or schools of thought. In this respect, however, Thiselton's thinking could not be reduced to a politically-motivated "both-and" approach that attempted to please all sides. Rather, Thiselton's approach attempted, first, to identify important issues or questions and then, second, to compare and contrast what each tradition had to say in relation to those issues or questions. Again, Thiselton moved beyond holding traditions in tension and towards new critical syntheses.

Thus, for example, and against J. Barr's reading of Thiselton in 1978, Thiselton did not simply try to affirm the New Hermeneutic in a partisan manner that "abandoned conservative territory". Rather, Thiselton accepted the emphasis on the *reversal of interpretative direction* that the New Hermeneutic had rightly highlighted, and then used that emphasis in order to highlight the "Pharisaic" refusal to become "the interpreted" that could be found in *some* more traditional and/or conservative circles of New Testament study. Conversely, Thiselton accepted the more traditional and conservative emphasis on the "cognitive" dimension and, having regrounded that emphasis on a stronger theoretical footing, allowed it to function as a criticism of the New Hermeneutic.

In relation to conservative approaches to biblical interpretation, therefore, those engaged in what some might characterize as being a "Proclamation Trust" approach to biblical exposition - in which it is predominantly *the text* that is being interpreted – could, from a Thiseltonian perspective, perhaps be vulnerable to temptations to suppress scenarios in which the text *interpreted the reader* in an *eventful way* that *inconveniently cut-across or even rudely interrupted pre-defined interpretative strategizing and time-tabling*.

This is *not at all* to say that Thiselton would "shelve" Proclamation Trust emphases on distanciation. On the contrary, it would be truer to say that, for Thiselton, Proclamation Trust emphases on distanciation were only *part* of what was needed – if still an *essential* part of what was needed – during interpretation. For Thiselton, though, the fusion of horizons cannot be reduced to objectifications of applications that are temporally and structurally consigned to exegetical end-points or postscripts in such a way as to subsume their potential to gain the upper hand over readers beneath reader-directed conceptualizing analytical consciousness. If one is suddenly rebuked by one's boss at work, one does not *initially* reply by asking "what truths can I glean from your rebuke in its historical context?" For Thiselton, hearing the other is a *relational* action that *also* involves objectification.

Our point, though, is that Thiselton always sought to listen to *both* sides of polarized debates and/or gulfs between traditions, movements, or schools. Notably, we rejected the assertions of W.J. Lyons and S. Woodman that stated that Thiselton's hermeneutics were driven by the "prior interests of his community". On the contrary, Thiselton has always been willing *both* to draw on *and* to criticize *any* tradition, movement, or school – including his own (much to the misguided exasperation of some of his contemporaries).

For Thiselton, then, *immersion in* the processes of *multiple* traditions *so as* to ever-widen dialogue unto *new* provisional critical syntheses was a hermeneutical axiom. For Thiselton, *neither* traditionalism *nor* iconoclasm could ever be consistent with hermeneutical consciousness, for traditions *both* distort truth *and* transmit truth. For Thiselton, ongoing tradition-modification or tradition-refinement through immersion in (i.e. dialogue between) multiple traditions was the only approach that was consistent with hermeneutical consciousness. For which person or community yet thinks as God would have them think? For Thiselton, both traditionalism and iconoclasm were/are idolatry.

Thus, Thiselton *also* in effect united prophet (*prophetes*) and interpreter (*hermeneus*) in opposition to soothsaying (*mantike*) – i.e. in opposition to super-spiritual authoritarian appeals to the Holy Spirit that bypassed immersion in multiple traditions and that bypassed thoughtful tradition-refinement. This particular point does not bode well for *some* of the forms of so-called "prophecy" that can be found in *some* church circles.

(g) We have already noted how Thiselton attempted to overcome *unnecessary* polarizations between the particularities of the thoughts of *different thinkers* whose writings were/are relevant for hermeneutics. Nevertheless, three other examples may be highlighted here.

Thus, (i), we saw how Thiselton's work helped to resolve the well-known tensions between the later Wittgenstein on the one hand, and Bertrand Russell and Karl Popper on the other. Thiselton's thoroughly *historical* approach to philosophy was in alignment with the later Wittgenstein's rejection of logical positivism's linguistic and epistemological formalism and/or philosophically idealist foundationalism. Against A.K.M. Adam, S.E. Porter, W.J. Lyons, and S. Woodman, Thiselton's approach could *not* simply be subsumed beneath approaches associated with the Vienna Circle, with the early Wittgenstein, with Popper, or with extensions of their thought. For Thiselton, as for the later Wittgenstein, Russell's and Popper's insufficiently-historical approaches were not the solution to the hermeneutical problem.

And yet, we also argued that Thiselton's approach *did* include a kind of "serious" philosophizing that – whilst being very different in character to that of Russell and Popper – *also* actually went *beyond* later Wittgensteinian emphases and towards a sophisticated philosophy of history that the later Wittgenstein *had not in fact* extensively developed (even if the later Wittgenstein had *begun* to point towards such a philosophy of history).

For Thiselton, as for Russell and Popper, philosophy *was* to be interested in describing and changing the world. For Thiselton, as for the later Wittgenstein, philosophy *was* to be concerned with "looking and seeing" at the level of how language is used today, in the present horizon. However, for Thiselton, "serious" historical philosophizing also – in effect – emphasized "looking and seeing" at the level of the historical *past*, at the level of the philosophy of *traditions*, and at the level of the search for *historically-grounded metacriteria* that could be employed in the *liberating socio-meta-criticism of* traditions. The later Wittgenstein certainly *had not* heavily developed this kind of "serious" historical philosophizing.

Thiselton's "serious" historical philosophizing thus had an epistemological edge to it that went beyond a "later Wittgensteinian epistemology". The later Wittgenstein's relevance for Thiselton's hermeneutical critique of epistemology was strictly limited - if *not absent altogether.*

Admittedly, the later Wittgenstein was important in relation to Thiselton's view of perception. And, admittedly, with the later Wittgenstein, Thiselton was concerned with identifying "mistaken applications of words" that were without the "backing" of "public criteria of meaning". For Thiselton, texts were in principle falsifiable, hermeneutical theories could be internally inconsistent in a manner that was not "true to historical life", and the particularities of historical *report* could at times be proven to be false. Thus, whilst respecting the *textual* particularities presented through/in the texts of particular writers and thinkers, Thiselton would not simply assume that these *textual* particularities were true – *either* to ongoing historical *life or* to prior *historical* particularity.

And yet, Thiselton's emphases on historical *metacriticism* took him beyond considerations to do with "mistaken applications of words", and even beyond respect for "public criteria of meaning". For Thiselton, even tradition-backed language-uses could be inconsistent with Christ as *the* "Enfleshed Word".

For Thiselton, then, the overcoming of the polarized debate between the later Wittgenstein, Russell, and Popper, meant taking something of Russell's and Popper's philosophical seriousness, and combining it with a *further development of* the later Wittgenstein's *move away from* the philosophical idealism of logical positivism and *towards* a more properly historical philosophy.

Thus, (ii), one of the implications of Thiselton's *historical* approach to "serious" philosophizing was that the search for hermeneutical unity was *not* necessarily a hangover from the legacies of out-dated approaches to philosophy. The search for a unified hermeneutical theory was emphatically *not* necessarily "formalist", "foundationalist", and/or philosophically "idealist".

On the contrary, it was *precisely* the rise of historical consciousness that was *preconditional for the possibility of* a new search for a unified hermeneutical theory. Inter-disciplinary, inter-traditional, and smaller-scale "polarizations" are *not* simply an emergent philosophical necessity governed by the unavoidable character of historical difference, but may sometimes reflect the *temporary state of confusion* that has resulted from the *suddenness* of the valid realization that hermeneutics needs to move away from all forms of "ahistorical" approach and towards thinking and interpreting in a thoroughly historical key.

That is, hermeneutics *does indeed* need to become thoroughly historical. But history is not simply an expanding horizon(s) of increasing plurality, dissociation and contradiction. Rather, biblically-speaking, history is, and/or will be, an eschatologically convergent anticipated narrative whole that has – and will have - a certain *historical and ethical* unity despite its non-uniformity ("the Scripture must be fulfilled").

This point, in turn, potentially transforms the current polarization between the hermeneutics of Fish, Adam, Lyons, and Woodman on the one hand and the hermeneutics of Thiselton on the other hand into a fruitful dialogue. Indeed, the current polarization is based largely on a misunderstanding of Thiselton.

That is, Adam, Lyons and Woodman speak as though Thiselton had *only just begun* to move towards the re-historicization of thought and interpretation. They wonder why Thiselton cannot "become historical" and thus respectful of historical finitude, difference, and relativity. However, the reality is that the situation is *the other way around*. Adam, Lyons and Woodman are still struggling with the legacies of ahistoricity, whilst it is *Thiselton* who has forged ahead with a new form of "serious" (re-)historicizing.

Indeed, even if it could be shown – as Lyons maintains - that Fish's perspective, and not Thiselton's, was the closest of these two thinkers' perspectives to that of the later Wittgenstein in this context of discussion (though we doubt that this can be shown), then it would *still* be Fish and the later Wittgenstein – *and not Thiselton* - who would have to become more thoroughly "historical". Thiselton is *even further* away from the ahistorical legacy of philosophical idealism than *both* the later Wittgenstein *and* Fish.

(iii) In relation to a Thiseltonian response to the polarized debate between Searle and Derrida, a parallel argument was offered. Thus, as we have already noted, whilst Thiselton *aligned with* Derrida's rejection of Searle's philosophical idealism, Thiselton *departed from* the alternative to Searle's philosophical idealism that Derrida espoused. It was our conclusion that Thiselton's construction of an approach to language *within* the co-ordinates of an approach to history was *truer* to the unity of created historical reality than was Derrida's destruction of historical unity through the sublation of a critique of history into the co-ordinates of a critique of language. That is, for Thiselton, *neither* Searle *nor* Derrida could be hailed as being "properly historical" and, for Thiselton, the polarized debate between (the traditions of) these two thinkers could *only* be overcome through a realization of the truth of this point.

Finally, (h), we noted several instances where Thiselton overcame smaller-scale polarizations at the level of specific issues and problems. One example concerned the way in which Thiselton overcame polarized "positions" concerning the relationship between language and thought by highlighting – in relation to language - the distinctions between "form", "use", "content", and "rules".

Another example concerned the way in which Thiselton overcame polarizations between views concerning "human" versus "divine" authorship of Scripture. For Thiselton, with Bultmann (to *an extent*), biblical revelation could only be intelligible if it was mediated by *human* language. Nevertheless, for Thiselton, God still acted upon readers through (as well as in front of) the Scriptures. For Thiselton, with Barth, the "truly new" could still emerge through conversation between interpreters and the Bible – i.e. God could (and did) still address humanity "from beyond" through the Scriptures. In this respect, we (in effect) saw how Thiselton overcame artificial polarization between appeals to Karl Barth on the one hand, and to Rudolf Bultmann on the other.

(6) Thiselton's critique of hermeneutical understanding – in clarifying the hermeneutical task and the hermeneutical circle – addressed the problem of what constituted *"responsible interpretation"* both theoretically and practically.

Theoretically, (a), all five of Thiselton's "second stratum" hermeneutical critiques – i.e. his critiques of conceptualizations of history, epistemology, language, (Western) culture, and of human selves – provided the ground for Thiselton's "third stratum" critique of hermeneutical understanding or for his approach to responsible interpretation.

Since these five "second stratum" critiques came to unity in Thiselton's hermeneutical critique of history, however, then his conceptualization of the hermeneutical circle was ultimately grounded in his hermeneutical critique of traditions (which was a subset of Thiselton's hermeneutical critique of history) and was, in Thiselton's thinking, constitutive in relation to the dynamic of historical process. Thiselton's hermeneutical critique of history, in turn, presupposed widened dialogue with and between philosophical and theological traditions. Thiselton's hermeneutical circle thereby substantially modified that of Gadamer – notably but by no means exclusively through appeals to Pannenberg and to the later Wittgenstein.

In practice, (b), Thiselton's hermeneutical circle constituted continuous movements within and between different overlapping polarities that reflected the kinds of human *capacities used*, the character of the *"objects"* (not in the Cartesian sense, but in historical structural-relational terms) *progressively encountered*, and the kinds of *tasks performed* (both by interpreters and by historically-embedded textual speech-actions) during interpretation.

Thus, for Thiselton, "historical rationality" (exercised during "hermeneutical understanding" – to use the broadest sense of the phrase "hermeneutical understanding"): (i) *employed* both historically-re-embedded "hermeneutical understanding" (to use the median sense of this phrase) and historically-re-embedded "subject-object conceptualization"; (ii) *encountered* both (inter-related and inter-relating) *historical* particularities and (inter-related and inter-relating) *a posteriori historical* continuities (cf. "particular" and "general"; "understanding" and "explanation"; cf. "parts" and "wholes"); and, (iii) *encompassed* both historically-re-embedded (not autonomous) "textual" speech-actions and interpretative actions (cf. "distancing" and "fusion"; cf. "noticing" and "showing"; cf. "question" and "answer"; cf. "acting" and "being acted-upon").

Thiselton argued, therefore, that historical rationality was, (iv), both *creative* and *critical*. For Thiselton, historical rationality was *creative* in that it *intuited*, on the basis of life-*experience* (cf. being acted-upon), (v), both *"wholes"* (especially: persons; "worlds" projected by – for example - art, narratives, parables and games; and historical contexts as "wholes") and *"relations"* *between* the past, the present, and anticipated futures – and/or *between* historical *"parts"* (events, texts, interpretations, semiotic elements, persons, and so on).

Conversely, Thiselton argued that historical rationality was *critical* in that it comparatively *tested* the cognitive (or otherwise) content of *"parts"* (i.e. "parts" understood, for example, as textual language-uses, historical reconstructions, persons' behaviors, or as events of fusion, and so on) against that of the *"wholes"* of traditions and, (vi), their transmitted-*critical* (cf. interpretative) criteria and emergent-*metacritical* criteria (cf. metacriteria).

Therefore, Thiselton argued that historical rationality was also, (vii), *experiential* and *conceptualizing*, and pre-cognitive and cognitive - where Thiselton argued that, (viii), interpretative questions and judgments proceeded from traditional *conditioning* (pre-understandings, pre-judgments, scaffolding, cf. "faith" in one of its senses) towards *transformation* (cf. fresh understanding, new outcomes of understanding, tradition-refinement). Inevitably, then, Thiselton argued that historical rationality was, (ix), both *corporate* and *individual*, and, (x), both *historical* and *theological*.

The sheer complexity of such numerous superimposed couplets - i.e. the couplets in these points "(i)" to "(x)" above taken together with other couplets in our other points below - contradicted B.J. Walsh's charge that Thiselton was somehow epistemologically "dualistic".

Still in relation to interpretative practice then, (c), Thiselton argued that, during interpretation, *interpreters'* "historical rationality" – operating from within moving historical horizons - potentially and progressively encountered the historical particularities, and *a posteriori* historical continuities, of texts, persons, and events (and so on) as originating from within the "otherness" of their historically situated, conditioned, conditioning, and moving horizons, and as irrevocably interwoven with their "meanings" understood as developing networks of historical and linguistic inter-relationships within the processes of traditions and within *anticipations* of history-as-a-whole.

Thiselton argued, against broadly positivist historical critical approaches and against ideologically structuralist approaches, that there was no place for the imperializing tyranny of a single "scientific method" that imposed *a priori* fixed categories onto the "other" since such an approach presupposed philosophical ineptitude in relation to the rise and historicity of historical consciousness. Nor, for Thiselton, was there any place for broadly existentialist, broadly post-structuralist, or broadly socio-pragmatic brands of "a-historicity".

Still in relation to interpretative practice then, (d), Thiselton's conceptualization of interpreters' actions and of "textual" or performative speech-actions taking place during interpretation embraced a modification of Gadamer's notions of "distancing" and "fusion" that took into account – amongst other factors – the later Wittgenstein's notions of "noticing" and "showing" according to which propositions and/or assertions of various kinds could function creatively.

Notably – and ironically, given Gadamer's linguistic dualism - *grammatical* propositions could creatively "show" aspects of Gadamer's own thinking – including Gadamer's notions of broadened rationality, of pre-judgments, and of effective history. Grammatical propositions, however, could also "show" problems with Gadamer's approach – problems related to: the capacity of tradition to distort truth, the need for "spell-breaking" meta-socio-critical liberation, and the need to account more convincingly for extra-linguistic effects.

In any case, (i), for Thiselton, distancing and fusion included movement between *textual* and *reader* horizons and thereby were identified neither as a sterile interest in texts as historical sources nor as a preoccupation with reader horizons alone. Thiselton argued that distancing and fusion also involved movement between *synchronic* and *diachronic* considerations and thereby neither divorced texts from questions to do with historical *particularity* nor from questions to do with historical *processes*. For Thiselton, synchronic considerations also allowed texts and authors (and so on) to be compared with other texts and authors (and so on) from the same period, whilst diachronic considerations could locate a text within the traditions of its composition, transmission, and reception histories.

(ii) In Thiselton's estimate, these aspects of interpretative practice could not be divorced from movements between considerations of several levels of *past and present* context – both *historical* and *linguistic* – though Thiselton established the need to focus on *past* "context" on the basis of widened philosophical dialogue rather than on the grounds of traditional preferences alone. In particular, we noted Thiselton's arguments for reinstating inquiries into background states of affairs, author profiles, inter-authorial and inter-textual comparisons, original settings, linguistic functions, authorial intent, and transmitted textual content.

For Thiselton, (iii), distancing and fusion also involved several dimensions of ethical responsibility. Thus, in Thiselton's estimate, there were obligations to be faithful to texts, to communicate faithfully, to use interpretative strategies appropriate to textual particularity and to appropriate interpretative goals, to practically respond to texts, and to test readers' responses at the levels of distanciation, actualization, appropriation, and application. Indeed, Thiselton argued that fusion (and - we might now add - to an extent, distancing) involved movements between textual action, actualization, appropriation, and application, and that fusion (and, to an extent, distancing) emphasized not only "eventful" interpretation intra-linguistically, but eventful interpretation at the extra-linguistic level of being acted-upon by "textual" speech-acts and of personal and corporate transformation, responses and actions in the wider world.

Thus, (e), Thiselton argued for moving *beyond* semantic concerns and concerns related to intra-linguistic effects and *towards* concerns to do with liberating textual speech-action and with extra-linguistic effects; for moving *beyond* hermeneutics as "rules" associated with indoctrination and *towards* widening horizons and education; for moving *beyond* a hedonism of self-affirming "event" and "experience" and *towards* appropriation and/or obedience; and for moving *beyond* Western individualistic and introspective religion and *towards* corporate involvement in the wider world.

(f) Thiselton argued that such interpretative movements also embraced further movements between *questions* and *answers*. Thiselton urged that these questions and answers could not take place where *a priori* generalizations replaced openness, listening, and respect for historical particularity. Responsible interpretation, then, in Thiselton's estimate, had to respect – and to ask questions of and receive answers from - multiple *text-types* and multiple textual *functions*, and had to employ multiple critical *tools* and multiple interpretative *models* and *strategies* – including extended semantic and structural considerations – that were in accordance with multiple appropriate interpretative *goals*. Thiselton argued that *no single* interpretative, critical, or textual *model* – and that *no single* interpretative *goal* and/or *strategy* - could claim to be comprehensive.

Overall, (g), Thiselton effectively corrected existing critiques of hermeneutical understanding by employing a process of *re-historicization* – a process which we unpacked in detail in Chapter 5. Again: since Thiselton's critique of hermeneutical understanding was grounded in his hermeneutical critique of history, then Thiselton's reconfiguration of the latter *profoundly reshaped* the former.

Thus, in particular, for Thiselton, interpretation involved the interpreter's subjectivity (or interpreters' subjectivities) but, for Thiselton, neither pre-understanding nor understanding could be conceived in subjectivistic, relativistic, solipsistic, or individualistic terms. That is, Thiselton's emphases on inter-subjectivity, objectivity, public shared worlds, and on corporate interpretation in effect re-historicized Bultmann's notion of pre-understanding and Bultmann's notion of the role of pre-understanding during interpretation.

Thiselton also re-historicized the textual *horizon* by re-embedding it within history and, thereby, within inter-subjective communicative action. Thus, Thiselton repudiated the notion of textual autonomy and only used the notion of "the text itself" in a qualified way that presupposed the embedding of texts and of textual horizons within broader historical (and theological) contexts. Thus, it could be said that Thiselton "re-historicized texts themselves".

In a slightly different sense, Thiselton could be said to have "re-historicized texts themselves" in his refusal to employ over-generalizing textual models, critical tools, interpretative strategies (cf. methods), or interpretative goals. That is, Thiselton re-historicized texts in that he respected their particularity to the point that it was the textual models, critical tools, interpretative strategies, and interpretative goals that had to be adjusted to suit the text, and not the other way around. Thus, for Thiselton, textual models, critical tools, interpretative strategies, and interpretative goals were *also* effectively "re-historicized" in that they were made to be respectful of particularity – and were thus unavoidably pluralized (i.e. made plural).

Moreover, Thiselton's embedding of intra-linguistic *textual action* (and inter-textuality) within extra-linguistic inter-subjective speech-action effectively re-historicized textual action.

And Thiselton's embedding of *actualization* within the dialectic of horizonal expansion effectively re-historicized actualization in that hermeneutics as "rules that *indoctrinated* interpreters into conformity with *past* traditions" was then replaced by hermeneutics as "*educational* initiation of new understandings that *modified* interpreters' traditions in accord with notions of historical dialectic".

Thiselton's embedding of *appropriation* within the historical dialectic of tradition-modification effectively re-historicized appropriation in that appropriation – when re-historicized in this way - could never merely "discover or affirm existing horizons", but always had to involve an obedient *change of relationship to* those horizons that then led to their *further* transformation.

Thiselton's embedding of *application* within the broader historical horizons of the wider world, within historical dialectic, and within historical traditions of wisdom and theory, effectively re-historicized application in that application could then neither be reduced to pietistic introspective concern only with oneself, nor aligned with the evasions of traditionalism, nor twisted into a self-affirming distorted activism that ignored or iconoclastically disparaged wisdom or theory, nor turned into something merely abstract and theoretical, nor subsumed beneath a fixation with past horizons.

Thiselton also re-historicized *understanding* by emphasizing *both* distancing *and* fusion, and by emphasizing past, present, and future horizons. To be properly historical, understanding had to be respectful of historical *differences, and* of historical *relationships, and* of historical *transformation* through the formation of *new* historical relationships through *ongoing* distancing and fusion.

(h) Thiselton's emphasis on "relationality" and on "relationships" with respect to the *two-way* interpretative interaction between "the two horizons" meant that speech-act dynamics could not be confined to the synchronic horizon of the text, but that speech-act dynamics – or relational dynamics – also operated diachronically between textual horizon(s) and readers' horizon(s).

Thus, for Thiselton, it would not do merely to "refer" to the multiform speech-action "within" the biblical texts, since it was inappropriate to respond to the divine initiative of love through the biblical texts with a mere act of reference. Thus, it is relationally odd to respond to somebody who says "I love you" by replying, "I notice that you have just uttered the illocution 'I love you'".

Whilst those who wished, like the Pharisees, to arrogate themselves to the status and role of "interpretative masters" - whilst simultaneously refusing to submit to becoming "the interpreted" - would certainly "objectify" or "de-relationalize" the Scriptures in this way, such a response to divine speech-action through the Bible was inappropriate for believers in Thiselton's view.

Certainly, a counselor or somebody facing harmful relational patterns in "the other" would be wise, for the sake of safety, to protect themselves by interrupting the harmful relational dynamic with objectifying reference. However, when responding to God's love through the Scriptures, such "playing it safe" really amounted to a sinful suppression of the proper functioning of God's Word.

And so whilst, for Thiselton, distancing rightly employed objectification (cf. reference) to "strike the biblical text dead", Thiselton also argued that fusion rightly "brought the biblical text alive" as a multiform relational dynamic that, first, could not be collapsed down into mere "distanciation" and that, second, *reversed the "interpretative direction"* so as enable the text to *relate as God's love to the reader or readers.*

God's love, of course, for Thiselton, was not just a matter of "imparting information", but involved the full range of relational dynamics, including encouragement, rebuke, correction, affirmation, declaration, promise, inspiration, and so on and so forth. Thus, for Thiselton, fusion was to bring Scripture alive as divine relational action that formed and transformed – or "built" – believers and the Church, with repercussions for mission in the wider world.

(i) Thiselton – in effect - argued that since understanding always emerged through a dynamic diachronic dialogic dialectic process that involved a relationship between two sets of horizons or historical particularities, then there would always be a *legitimate* plurality of interpretative outcomes and a *legitimate* conflict of interpretations.

Thus, for Thiselton, factors to do with literary genre and with linguistic and extra-linguistic functions and effects, factors to do with interpretative impediments, and factors more directly related to "present meaning" – such as hermeneutical deepening or "growth", expanding historical horizons, variable readers and changing reading-situations, and changes in interpretative goals and angles of view – would all produce a *legitimate* plurality of interpretative outcomes and a *legitimate* conflict of interpretations.

Nevertheless, if Thiselton allowed that a properly "historical" approach to understanding could produce a *legitimate* plurality of interpretative outcomes and a *legitimate* conflict of interpretations (without any so-called "turn towards the postmodern"), then Thiselton also argued that insufficiently historical approaches to understanding would produce *illegitimate* pluralities of interpretative outcomes and *illegitimate* conflicts of interpretations.

Thus, Thiselton associated broadly post-structuralist approaches with artificially-abstracted "infinitely fluid meaning", and Thiselton associated broadly socio-pragmatic approaches with "unnecessary arbitrary meaning-expansion".

In our responses to Thiselton's critics, we also identified "mistaken straightforward hermeneutical foreclosures" and "obfuscating projections of hostile criticisms" as sources and forms of *illegitimate* pluralities of interpretative outcomes associated with *illegitimate* conflicts of interpretations. We included the notion of "a calculus of pre-dialogic (or historically *a priori*), over-generalizing, simplistic, and prescriptive pigeon-holing" within our broader category of "mistaken straightforward hermeneutical foreclosures".

Such was the complexity and diversity of human interpretative approaches in history, however, that in practice "illegitimate" and "legitimate" forms of pluralities of interpretative outcomes and of conflicts of interpretations would be over-lapping and superimposed.

Nevertheless, for Thiselton, adequately *historical* hermeneutical theory would lessen the incidence of illegitimacy in relation to pluralities of interpretative outcomes and in relation to conflicts between interpretations.

That is, (j), for Thiselton, "hermeneutical foreclosure" or "premature fusion of horizons" was *still to be avoided at all costs.*

Notably, *first*, the problem of "hermeneutical foreclosure" became a theme in itself in the present study since Thiselton had not only been neglected in the literature, but had been seriously misunderstood in several ways in those instances where he *had* been cited.

Thus, Thiselton had been misleadingly caricatured as "Gadamerian", as "later Wittgensteinian", as "Pannenbergian", as simplistically "evangelical", or as typically "Anglican". Further, Thiselton had been misunderstood in relation to authorial intention, in relation to his philosophy of language, and in relation to his stance on the relationship between theology and philosophy.

Moreover, Thiselton's "third horizon" was also misunderstood, where the innovation of appropriating Pannenberg's thinking had been wrongly attributed to somebody else. Thiselton's philosophy of history was also unrecognized, despite his offer of a philosophically-transformed historical paradigm in *The Two Horizons*. Against the views of some commentators, we saw that Thiselton had *not* offered mere "action models" or a mere "hermeneutic of traditions".

Some commentators mistakenly thought that Thiselton grounded metacriticism in the later Wittgenstein's work, and so such commentators missed Thiselton's Christocentric perspective and his historical epistemology. Others falsely called Thiselton "subjectivist", "relativist", "perspective(al)ist", or "fideist", and thus missed his subtle notions of "objectivity" and "warrant". Notably, for Thiselton, "objectivity" was *not* only affected negatively by historical factors.

Other commentators misunderstood the place of J.R. Searle's work and of speech-act theory in Thiselton's thinking. Against such misunderstandings, however, Thiselton was *not* "formalist" or "idealist", but imported insights from Searle, Saussure, and others into a quite different non-idealist paradigm. Nor was Thiselton's thinking a case of idealist "foundationalism". This latter caricature was perhaps the worst of all the misreadings of Thiselton in that it then went on to completely miss the subtleties of Thiselton's hermeneutical critique of historical objectivity, of his views of perception, and of his complex view of present meaning.

Other problems related to hermeneutical foreclosure centered on misreadings of Thiselton's understanding of the hermeneutical task. Against such misreadings, however, Thiselton did not simply follow, but considerably modified, Gadamer's hermeneutical circle. In addition, Thiselton's views on textual content, on so-called "textual autonomy", on models of so-called "general textuality", on the role of the Holy Spirit in interpretation, and on the link between interpretation and appropriation had all been misunderstood. Further, the subtlety of Thiselton's engagement with notions of the "postmodern" had been missed.

There was also the false notion – presented as a criticism of Thiselton - that hermeneutical theory did not directly affect interpretative practice, when Thiselton had in fact demonstrated conclusively that it did - in positivist historical criticism, in Bultmann's demythologizing, in the New Hermeneutic, in structuralism, in post-structuralism, and in socio-pragmatism.

Nor did Thiselton's reinstatement of hermeneutical theory deny the Bible to so-called "ordinary" or "non-academic" readers. Only *some* in the corporate Church body would have to take "intellectual detours" in order to provide appropriately-pitched tools for others.

Finally, whilst problems with Thiselton's writing-style could not be *entirely* dismissed, the difficulty of Thiselton's writing was largely due to the complexity of the discussions at hand, and constituted an entirely correct repudiation of consumer-demands for novelty, indeterminacy, certainty, or simplicity.

In other words, *second*, the dialogue and careful listening exercised by Thiselton seemed *almost entirely absent from his critics*. In fact, the extent to which Thiselton had been misread and misunderstood was concerning – even alarming. This point even suggested that there was a need to critique academic settings *per se* as to their suitability (or not) for the promotion of rigorous reading.

Thus, to use Thiselton's terminology, we saw that the "irresponsible interpretation" pertaining to Thiselton's critics was – again - closely linked to various kinds of "hermeneutical foreclosure". These kinds of hermeneutical foreclosure included: straightforward misreading; the supposed "legitimization" (though this was only asserted) and hedonistic canonization of foreclosure in socio-pragmatic and (pseudo-)post-structuralist criticisms; and a drama-triangle of "disowned-projected" foreclosure in the case(s) of hostile critics.

We speculated that *straightforward* hermeneutical foreclosure was perhaps the result of the time-pressures of under-staffed and under-funded academic life, and was "straightforward" in the sense that it involved misreadings that often amounted to simple confusions or – at worst - to pre-dialogic categorizations or pre-dialogic pigeon-holing.

We speculated that *socio-pragmatic* hermeneutical foreclosure was perhaps sometimes the result of cultural rejections of hermeneutical complexity in favor of consumer-demands for instant community-friendly or "inclusive" interpretations.

We also speculated, however, as to whether or not the academic pressures of university contexts sometimes seemed to lead some socio-pragmatists to disguise this situation beneath a veneer of ostensibly "clever" appeals to post-structuralist thinkers. Such pseudo-"post-structuralist" appeals, however, were really just a matter of "name-dropping" in that, in the end, they lacked any serious engagement with the theoretical problems post-structuralism generated and/or presupposed.

Correlatively, theological socio-pragmatists seemed to resort to the authoritarianisms "of the Word" and "of the Spirit" that were attendant upon a Barthian epistemology of revelation – authoritarianisms that, when compounded by the promotion of a Fishian approach to texts, became potentially increasingly focused *solely* towards an authoritarianism that masqueraded as - and as being grounded in - present experiences of the Holy Spirit. We highlighted the dangers attendant upon such an approach – not only in terms of its authoritarian and isolationist self-immunization from external challenges, but also in terms of its potential collapse into dangerous fanaticisms, extremisms or fundamentalisms that – in addition – could potentially confuse the objectified "maladaptive schemas" (to use J.E. Young's language) of community-leaders with the voice of God.

We speculated as to whether or not *disowned-projected* hermeneutical foreclosure was perhaps often a case of hostile reaction and even of a kind of "name-calling" that pertained to a drama-triangle of "victims", "persecutors", and "rescuers". Thiselton's own prophetic remarks about the spread of a socio-pragmatic "epistemology" and about the consequent descent of public-sphere rational debate into fragmented sub-groups marked by competing power-interests and by a rhetoric of self-assertion and of misrepresenting "the other" in an obfuscating way had seemingly begun to come true.

Of course, "hostile criticism" was not *completely* confined to "left-wing" cases in which the socio-pragmatic "yeast" had thoroughly worked through the theoretical "dough" and into interpretative practice. "Right-wing" critics could *also* be equally hostile to Thiselton and could just as easily indulge in "obfuscating projections" – and indeed have done so ever since the attacks against Thiselton at NEAC '77.

(k) In any case, and in conclusion, no thorough engagement with Thiselton's hermeneutical theory existed in the literature. Thiselton had not been properly heard. In fact, Thiselton had been so misread and misrepresented that, again, we had - in effect - even begun to question the suitability of some kinds of present-day "academic" contexts in relation to the promotion of rigorous listening.

It was the aim of the present study, therefore, to give Thiselton a proper hearing. Only by avoiding the various kinds of hermeneutical foreclosure ourselves could we hope to find genuine constructive criticisms of Thiselton's work. Only eventually did we conclude that Thiselton's work left scope for further dialogue with epistemological traditions, with philosophies and models of human selves and of culture, with major "postmodern" thinkers, with pastoral theology, with theological anthropology, and with disciplines relevant *to* pastoral theology (for example, psychology, psychotherapy, cognitive-behavioural therapy, psychiatry, medicine, and so on).

Despite the numerous problems with L. Woodhead's criticisms of Thiselton's work, she was actually quite correct to suggest bringing further models of "human selfhood" and further engagements with major "postmodern" thinkers to the hermeneutical discussion. Thiselton would *agree* with this suggestion.

Indeed, in relation to a hermeneutical critique of "human selves", we ourselves suggested that a much more sophisticated hermeneutic of immediate fallen human relationships and of fallen human physicality was required, not least because a person's relationships and physicality were two of the main ways in which that person was historically conditioned – historical conditioning certainly wasn't *only* "philosophical", "traditional", and/or "cultural". This latter point, in turn, allowed us to argue that the conditioning of interpreters by fallen relationships and by the "maladaptive schemas" (to use J.E. Young's language again) associated with such fallen relationships could have constituted a factor that *added to* Thiselton's argument – in the context of his defence against theological socio-pragmatism - for the need to appeal to biblical and theological criteria, and *not only to* "present experience of the Spirit" or to conventional norms, when adjudicating/discerning between interpretations and/or spirits.

These constructive criticisms of Thiselton's hermeneutics remain true today - despite our focusing here mainly on Thiselton's formative work up until 1980, when Thiselton's hermeneutical critiques of "Western Culture" and of "human selves" were only embryonic; and despite Thiselton's later development of these critiques – which include the parallels he draws between Corinthian culture in St. Paul's day and contemporary Western "postmodern" culture.

We also found very minor problems with Thiselton's readings of Heidegger, of Gadamer, and of the later Wittgenstein. More specificity was required in relation to the kinds of "conceptualization" and their respective philosophical frameworks that Heidegger affirmed or rejected and in relation to Gadamer's heralding of a "postmodern" notion of selfhood given his emphases on "otherness" and on other criteria. Further, there was a real question concerning the *extent* to which the later Wittgenstein had outgrown his Neo-Kantian legacy so as to facilitate the kind of "serious" "historical" philosophizing about "problems" (as opposed to "puzzles") found in Thiselton. Also, recalling our concerns for the conditioning effects of immediate fallen human relationships and of fallen human physicality, we would perhaps go further than Gadamer *and* Thiselton in reinstating the *theoretical role* (or the stratum two significance) of biography and autobiography.

Perhaps the main difficulty with Thiselton's formative work, however, was that his important tradition-refinement of Continental hermeneutics was hidden behind his continued use of Continental terminology. He would potentially be open to the understandable, though thoroughly erroneous, charge of "persuasive definition" if it were not for the fact that his modifications of Continental grammar were both theoretically warranted and well hidden. Perhaps if Thiselton had provided a little more specificity in relation to his own analyses of grammatical utterances, it may have alerted him to the danger of the character of his own modifications of Continental grammar being misunderstood or missed altogether. In other words, Thiselton's main weakness was that he contributed towards the hiding of his own major achievement.

And what is Thiselton's "hidden major achievement"? It is his provision of the components for a long overdue paradigm-shift in, and thereby for a transformation and unification of, hermeneutics historically, eschatologically, and Christologically and, within these co-ordinates, for unifying each of its constituent theoretical conversations, both internally and in relation to one another, in the world's first truly integrated post-later-Wittgensteinian, post-Gadamerian, and post-early-Pannenbergian biblical and theological general hermeneutical paradigm.

Once systematized, Thiselton's hermeneutics provide a devastating exposure of the problems of philosophical dichotomies (amongst other problems) associated with broadly positivist approaches, with the Continental hermeneutical traditions, with broadly structuralist approaches, with broadly post-structuralist approaches, and with broadly socio-pragmatic approaches to interpretation. It is thus hoped that our initiation - in the present study - of that systematization, and of the use of "Thiseltonian" hermeneutics to expose dichotomies and other problems in existing traditions of hermeneutical theory and practice, has been worthwhile.

# Appendix 1: Footnote Abbreviations Other Than Journals

**Key to Footnote Abbreviations of Titles of Writings**

| | |
|---|---|
| '3H' | 'Three Horizons: Hermeneutics from the Other End' |
| 'AA' | 'An Age of Anxiety' |
| 'AD' | 'Anthropological Dualism in The New Testament' |
| 'AF' | 'Academic Freedom, Religious Tradition, and the Morality of Christian Scholarship' |
| 'AI' | 'The Role of Authorial Intention in the Theological Interpretation of Scripture' |
| 'A-LIC' | 'Some Comments on the Anglican-Lutheran International Conversations' |
| 'AW' | 'Abusing Wittgenstein' |
| 'BL' | 'Unpublished Bibliographic Letter to R. Knowles' |
| 'BSA' | 'A Book Set Apart from the Ordinary Run of Books' |
| 'BTT' | "'Behind' and 'In Front Of' the Text" |
| 'CAP' | 'Communicative Action and Promise in Inter-Disciplinary, Biblical, and Theological Hermeneutics' |
| 'CATP' | 'Cat Among the Pigeons' |
| 'CH' | 'Creativity of Heaven' |
| 'CHP' | 'Contemporary Hermeneutic Philosophy and Theological Studies' |
| 'CHR' | 'Contextualization: Hermeneutical Remarks' |
| 'Christol' | 'Christology in Luke, Speech-Act Theory, and the Problem of Dualism in Christology after Kant' |
| 'CI' | 'Conservative - and Intelligent With It' |
| 'Conc' | 'Conclusion: Dialogue on the 'Common Era'' |
| 'CoU' | 'Wittgenstein's Classes of Utterance & Pauline Ethical Texts' |
| 'CS' | 'Congress Statement, NEAC '77 Report' |
| 'CST' | 'Common Sense Traditions and American Evangelical Thought' |
| 'DC' | 'Distinctive Colleges' |
| 'DE' | 'Dynamic Equivalence' |
| 'Dial' | 'Dialogue and the Dangers of Half-Truths' |
| 'DJK' | 'Dissent from John King's Verdicts' |
| 'DLR' | 'Decent Lack of Respect' |
| 'DOA' | 'The Death of the Author' |
| 'E-CR' | 'Experience-Centred Religion' |
| 'ED' | 'Evangelical Dishonesty' |
| 'EITN' | 'Explain, Interpret, Tell, Narrative' |
| 'ENE' | 'Enthusiasm Not Enough' |

| | |
|---|---|
| 'EOP' | 'Eschatologically Oriented Psychology' |
| 'Exc' | 'Theology Made Exciting' |
| 'FG' | 'Finding God in Personal Idealism' |
| 'GC' | 'Great Compassion and Heart' |
| 'Gregg' | 'Reply Letter to David Gregg about John Rosser' |
| 'HB' | 'Human Being, Relationality and Time in Hebrews, 1 Corinthians and Western Traditions' |
| 'HH' | 'Hermeneutical Hazards, NEAC '77 Report' |
| 'H-O' | 'Head-On Challenge to Doubt' |
| 'IA' | 'Irrational Assumptions of Modern Theology Exposed' |
| 'IAch' | 'Important Achievement' |
| 'IEWPP' | 'Is Exegesis Without Presuppositions Possible? (1957)' |
| 'Intro AP' | 'Introduction', *After Pentecost* |
| 'Intro BTT' | 'Introduction', *'Behind' the Text* |
| 'Intro' | 'Introduction, or How I Stopped Worrying and Learned to Love Interpretation' |
| 'IS' | 'Interpreting Scripture' |
| 'ISRH' | 'Infallible Scripture and the Role of Hermeneutics' |
| 'IT' | 'The "Interpretation" of Tongues' |
| 'KA' | 'Knights in Kierkegaard's Armour?' |
| 'KMCM' | 'Knowledge, Myth and Corporate Memory' |
| 'KNT' | 'Kierkegaard and the Nature of Truth' |
| 'LG' | 'On the Logical Grammar of Justification in Paul' |
| 'LGT' | 'Looking for God's Triumph' |
| 'LI' | 'Limited Inc abc…' |
| 'LMR' | 'Language and Meaning in Religion' |
| 'M&M' | 'Meaning and Myth' |
| 'M,M' | 'Myth, Mythology' |
| 'MCU' | 'The Ministry and the Church Union' |
| 'ML' | 'Man Longs for the Status and Dignity of a "Thou"' |
| 'M-M' | 'The Multi-Model Character of Holy Spirit Language' |
| 'MMP' | 'More Manageable Proportions' |
| 'MP' | 'Myth, Paradigm, and the Status of Biblical Imagery' |
| 'NC' | 'Normal Circumstances…' |
| 'NH' | 'The New Hermeneutic' |
| 'NHP' | 'No Horns on the Pope' |
| 'NNN' | 'Nitpicking at NEAC? Never' |
| 'NP' | 'New Problems for Old' |
| 'NT&M' | 'New Testament and Mythology' |
| 'NTCS' | 'New Testament Commentary Survey' |
| 'NTIHP' | 'New Testament Interpretation in Historical Perspective' |
| 'NTLI' | 'The New Testament and Literary Interpretation' |
| 'NW' | 'Theology for a New World' |
| 'OPD(1952)' | 'On the Problem of Demythologizing (1952)' |

| | |
|---|---|
| 'Par' | 'The Parousia in Modern Theology' |
| 'Parab' | 'The Parables as Language-Event' |
| 'P-BP' | 'Post-Bultmannian Perspectives' |
| 'PCRK' | 'Personal Communication to Robert Knowles' |
| 'PDT' | 'Predictable, Domesticated and Tamed' |
| 'PF' | 'The Philosophical Foundations of the Twentieth Century' |
| 'PH' | 'The Problem of Hermeneutics' |
| 'PI', | 'The Paschal Imagination' |
| 'PM' | 'A Proposed Model of Biblical Hermeneutics Incorporating the Work of Stanley Fish and Karl Barth' |
| 'P-MB' | 'Can a Pre-Modern Bible Address a Postmodern World?' |
| 'PR' | 'A "Polite" Response to Anthony Thiselton' |
| 'Q&A' | 'Hermeneutics and the Logic of Question and Answer' |
| 'QP' | 'Question of Prophecy' |
| 'Qs' | 'Questions, but Not Enough Answers' |
| 'R 2 Cor' | 'Review of C.K. Barrett's *A Commentary on the Second Epistle to the Corinthians*' |
| 'R 2H' | 'Review of A.C. Thiselton's *The Two Horizons*' |
| 'R Apoc' | 'Review of D.S. Russell's *Apocalyptic, Ancient and Modern*' |
| 'R BQ1' | 'Review Article of W. Pannenberg's *Basic Questions in Theology, Vol. 1*' |
| 'R BS' | 'Review of J.R. McKay and J.F. Miller eds. *Biblical Studies*' |
| 'R CFH' | 'Review of S.W. Sykes and J.P. Clayton eds. *Christ, Faith and History: Cambridge Studies in Christology*' |
| 'R EMB' | 'Review of A. Hodes' *Encounter with Martin Buber*' |
| 'R Ex?' | 'Review of H. Gollwitzer's *The Existence of God*' |
| 'R Exp' | 'Review of P. Van Buren's *Theological Explorations*' |
| 'R HFM' | 'Review of E.H. Cousins ed. *Hope and the Future of Man*' |
| 'R IBHJ' | 'Review of I.H. Marshall's *I Believe in the Historical Jesus*' |
| 'R ITMITT' | 'Review of K.J. Vanhoozer's *Is There a Meaning in this Text?*' |
| 'R JLK' | 'Review of N. Perrin's *Jesus and the Language of the Kingdom*' |
| 'R JN' | 'Review of C.F.H. Henry ed. *Jesus of Nazareth*' |
| 'R LCNTC' | 'Review of N.R. Petersen's *Literary Criticism for New Testament Critics*' |
| 'R NH' | 'Review of A.C. Thiselton's *New Horizons in Hermeneutics*' |
| 'R NT&S' | 'Review of A.M. Johnson's *The New Testament and Structuralism*' |
| 'R NTC' | 'Review of G.E. Ladd's *The New Testament and Criticism*' |
| 'R NTF' | 'Review of R.P. Martin's *New Testament Foundations*' |
| 'R NTI' | 'Review of I.H. Marshall ed. *New Testament Interpretation*' |
| 'R NTQs' | 'Review of E. Käsemann's *New Testament Questions of Today*' |
| 'R P-EWSM' | 'Review of R.G. Hamerton-Kelly's *Pre-Existence, Wisdom and the Son of Man*' |
| 'R RBT' | 'Review of R.C. Roberts' *Rudolf Bultmann's Theology*' |
| 'R RH' | Review of R. Lundin's, A.C. Thiselton's and C. Walhout's *The |

| | |
|---|---|
| | *Responsibility of Hermeneutics'* |
| 'R *Rom II*' | 'Review of C.E.B. Cranfield's *A Critical and Exegetical Commentary on the Epistle to the Romans. Volume II*' |
| 'R *SBR*' | 'Review of J.F.A. Sawyer's *Semantics in Biblical Research*' |
| 'R *SR*' | 'Review of J.-M. Benoist's *The Structural Revolution*' |
| 'R *SSS*' | 'Review of R. Detweiler's *Story, Sign, and Self*' |
| 'R *St*' | 'Review of J. Macquarrie's *Studies in Christian Existentialism*' |
| 'R *TB*' | 'Review of C.W. Kegley ed. *The Theology of Rudolf Bultmann*' |
| 'R *TCG*' | 'Review of J. Moltmann's *The Crucified God*' |
| 'R *TCP*' | 'Review of D.S. Dockery ed. *The Challenge of Postmodernism*' |
| 'R *TEH*' | 'Review of J. Moltmann's *The Experiment Hope*' |
| 'R *TiF*' | 'Review of F.F. Bruce's *The Time is Fulfilled*' |
| 'R *TSLR*' | 'Review of T. Fawcett's *The Symbolic Language of Religion*' |
| 'R *UAB*' | 'Review of D. Nineham's *The Use and Abuse of the Bible*' |
| 'R *USRT*' | 'Review of D.H. Kelsey's *The Uses of Scripture in Recent Theology*' |
| 'R *W*' | 'Review of A. Kenny's *Wittgenstein*' |
| 'R *WP*' | 'Review of A.D. Galloway's *Wolfhart Pannenberg*' |
| 'RA *NH*' | 'New Horizons in Hermeneutics: A Review Article' |
| 'RA-*RH*' | '…Review-Article of R. Lundin's, A.C. Thiselton's and C. Walhout's *The Responsibility of Hermeneutics*' |
| 'RCD' | 'Reflections in the Current Debate' |
| 'REC' | 'Realized Eschatology at Corinth' |
| 'Reviv' | 'Reviving the Power of Biblical Language' |
| 'R-RC' | 'Reader-Response Criticism and New Testament Study' |
| 'R-RH' | 'Reader-Response Hermeneutics, Action Models, and the Parables of Jesus' |
| 'Rs *FT, TC* | '…Reviews of M. Thornton's *The Function of Theology*, and S. Lawton's *Truths that Compelled*' |
| 'Rs *SC, TJ, GJ*' | 'Reviews of J.J. Vincent's *Secular Christ*, D.T. Niles' *Who is This Jesus?* and P. Leon's *The Gospel According to Judas*' |
| 'S&E' | 'Science and Existence' |
| 'S(pub)' | 'Signs of the Times' (Published Version) |
| 'S(un)' | 'Signs of the Times' (Unpublished Version) |
| 'SA' | 'From Speech Acts to Scripture Acts' |
| 'S-AT' | 'The Value of Speech-Act Theory for Old Testament Hermeneutics' |
| 'SBL' | 'The Semantics of Biblical Language as an Aspect of Hermeneutics' |
| 'SBS' | 'Structuralism and Biblical Studies' |
| 'Sch' | 'Schweitzer's Interpretation of Paul' |
| 'SEC' | 'Signature Event Context' |
| 'SL' | 'Sex and Logic in 1 Corinthians 11:2-16' |
| 'SM' | 'Serious Man, Rhetorical Man, Straw Man' |
| 'SNTI' | 'Semantics and New Testament Interpretation' |

| | |
|---|---|
| 'SS' | 'For Serious Students of St. Paul' |
| 'Stor' | 'Storytellers and Poets in the Bible' |
| 'Sub' | 'Subjectivity and Praxis at the End of Philosophy' |
| 'T&F' | 'Theology and the Future' |
| 'T&FS' | 'Theology and the Fragmentation of the Self' |
| 'T&PBT' | 'Theory and Practice in Bible Translation' |
| 'TC' | 'Anthony Thiselton's Contribution to Biblical Hermeneutics' |
| 'THS&TF' | 'The Holy Spirit and the Future' |
| 'Till' | 'The Theology of Paul Tillich' |
| 'TNI' | 'The Theologian Who Must Not Be Ignored' |
| 'TST' | 'The Spirit of Truth' |
| 'TUA' | 'The Uneasy Alliance Between Evangelicalism and Postmodernism' |
| 'TY' | 'Thirty Years of Hermeneutics: Retrospect and Prospects' |
| 'U (Long)' | 'Understanding God's Word Today' (Longer Article) |
| 'U (Short)' | 'Understanding God's Word Today' (Shorter Article) |
| 'UC' | 'Untitled Contribution to MLitt Thesis' |
| 'UNT' | 'Understanding the New Testament' |
| 'UPC' | 'The Use of Philosophical Categories in New Testament Hermeneutics' |
| 'UW' | 'Uncharted Waters' |
| 'W' | 'Wittgenstein, Ludwig Josef Johann' |
| 1 Cor | *The First Epistle to the Corinthians* |
| 2H | *The Two Horizons* |
| 3H | *The Three Horizons* |
| AIM | *An Introduction to Metaphysics* |
| B&B | *The Blue and Brown Books* |
| BD&H | *Beyond Dialogue and History* |
| BQ1 | *Basic Questions in Theology: Collected Essays, Volume 1* |
| BQ2 | *Basic Questions in Theology: Collected Essays, Volume 2* |
| BQ3 | *Basic Questions in Theology: Collected Essays, Volume 3* |
| BSL | *Biblical Semantic Logic* |
| BT | *Being and Time* |
| C&E | *Canon and Exegesis* |
| CBH | *Culture and Biblical Hermeneutics* |
| CV | *Culture and Value* |
| EIMB | *Evangelicalism in Modern Britain* |
| FT | *First Theology* |
| GG | *The Gagging of God* |
| HD | *The Hermeneutics of Doctrine* |
| HS | *The Hermeneutical Spiral* |
| IGPS | *Interpreting God and The Postmodern Self* |
| K&HI | *Knowledge and Human Interests* |
| Lang | *Language, Hermeneutic, and Word of God* |

| | |
|---|---|
| LLM | *Language, Liturgy and Meaning* |
| M | *Mission on the Way* |
| MIS | *Models for Interpretation of Scripture* |
| NH | *New Horizons in Hermeneutics* |
| NOS | *The Rise and Fall of the Nine O'Clock Service* |
| NTCS | *New Testament Commentary Survey* |
| NTH | *New Testament Hermeneutics and Philosophical Description* |
| OC | *On Certainty* |
| PI | *Philosophical Investigations* |
| PoS | *Phenomenology of Spirit* |
| PRL | *The Philosophy of Religious Language* |
| PT&BT | *Postmodern Theory and Biblical Theology* |
| PTT | *The Postfoundationalist Task of Theology* |
| R2 | *Remarks on the Philosophy of Psychology, Volume 2* |
| S&H | *Structuralism and Hermeneutics* |
| T&I | *Text and Interpretation as Categories of Theological Thinking* |
| T&P | *Theology and Proclamation* |
| TCM | *Theology, Church and Ministry* |
| TM | *Truth and Method* |
| TNT1 | *Theology of the New Testament, Volume 1* |
| Tr | *Tractatus Logico-Philosophicus* |
| TWP | *The Theology of Wolfhart Pannenberg* |
| W&S | *Word and Supplement* |
| WP | *Wittgenstein's Poker* |
| WW | *Who's Who 1999* |
| Z | *Zettel* |

# Appendix 2: Anthony C. Thiselton's Degrees, Honors, Main Academic Posts and Involvements in Societies and on Editorial Boards

**Degrees**:

| | |
|---|---|
| B.D. | 1959 (LBC) |
| M.Th. | 1964 (King's College, University of London) |
| Ph.D. | 1977 (University of Sheffield) |
| D.D. | 1993 (University of Durham) |
| D.D. | 2002 (Archbishop of Canterbury at Lambeth) |
| D.Theol. | 2012 (University of Chester) |

**Honors**:

| | |
|---|---|
| 1998-2000: | President of the Society for the Study of Theology |
| 1995 - | Fellow of St. John's College, Durham |
| 2010 - | Fellow of King's College, London |
| 2010 - | Fellow of the British Academy |

**Main Academic Posts:**

| | |
|---|---|
| From 1969: | Society for the Study of Theology (Past President) |
| From 1976: | *Studiorum Novi Testamenti Societas* |
| From 1981: | Society of Biblical Literature |
| From 1965: | Tyndale Fellowship for Biblical Research |
| 1983-1997: | American Academy of Religion |
| 1976-1990; 1996-2006: | Church of England Doctrine Commission (Acting Chairman 1987) |
| 1983-present: | Editorial Consultant for *Ex Auditu* |
| 1984-1989: | Vice-Chairman, Board of Theological Studies, Council for National Academic Awards |
| 1989-1992; 1997-2005: | Church of England Committee for Theological Education and Training |
| 1992-2002: | Editorial Board of *Biblical Interpretation* (Brill, Leiden) |
| 1995-1999: | Member of Human Fertilization and Embryology Authority |
| 1995-present: | Elected to the General Synod of the Church of England (three terms) |
| 1999-present: | Editorial Board of *International Journal of Systematic Theology* |

| | |
|---|---|
| 2000-2007: | Member of Crown Nomination Commission |
| 2000-2005: | House of Bishops Clergy Discipline (Doctrine) Group (Consultant) |
| 2001-2005: | House of Bishops Working Party on Women in the Episcopate (Consultant) |
| 2004-2008: | Anglican Communion Working Party on Theological Education |
| 2005-2010: | Church of England Board of Education |
| 2004-present: | Editorial Board of *Ecclesiology* |

**Societies and Editorial Boards (Selection):**

| | |
|---|---|
| 1963-1970 | Recognized Teacher in Theology, University of Bristol, and Chaplain and Lecturer, Tyndale Hall Theological College, Bristol |
| 1970-1971 | Sir Henry Stephenson Fellow, University of Sheffield |
| 1971-1979 | Lecturer in Biblical Studies, University of Sheffield |
| 1979-1985 | Senior Lecturer in Biblical Studies, University of Sheffield |
| 1982-1983 | Professor and Fellow, Calvin College, Grand Rapids, Michigan |
| 1985-1988 | Principal of St John's College Nottingham and Special Lecturer in Theology, University of Nottingham |
| 1988-1992 | Principal of St John's College, University of Durham, and (from 1992) Honorary Professor of Theology, University of Durham |
| 1992-2001 | Professor of Christian Theology and Head of the Department of Theology, University of Nottingham |
| 2002- | Emeritus Professor of Christian Theology, University of Nottingham |
| 2003-2008 | Research Professor on Christian Theology (Chester College) now University of Chester |
| 2008- | Emeritus Professor of Christian Theology, University of Chester |
| 2006-2011 | Professor of Christian Theology, University of Nottingham; Emeritus Professor from Dec. 2011 |

| | |
|---|---|
| Also from 1994-2010: | Canon Theologian of Leicester Cathedral; Emeritus Canon Theologian from 2010 |
| 2000-2007: | Canon Theologian of Southwell Minster. From 2007: Emeritus Canon Theologian |
| Minor posts: | Taught on four continents and numerous countries. |

# Bibliography

## Writings by Anthony C. Thiselton, F.K.C., F.B.A.

*N.B. The following is the most complete bibliographic list of Thiselton's writings in existence to date, and is chronologically ordered and near-exhaustive up to the middle of 2011.*

*Eschatology and the Holy Spirit in Paul with Special Reference to 1 Corinthians* (London: University of London Unpublished M.Th. Dissertation, 1964).

'Review of G.D. Yarnold's *By What Authority? Studies in the Relations of Scripture, Church and Ministry*', *Chman* 79.1 (1965), 64-65.

'Kierkegaard', *CEN* 5 Mar. (1965), 16.

'Knights in Kierkegaard's Armour?', *CEN* 12 Mar. (1965), 16.

'Review of C. Isherwood's *Ramakrishna and His Disciples*', *Chman* 79.2 (1965), 159-160.

'Review of D.E.H. Whiteley's *The Theology of St. Paul*', *TSF* 42 (1965), 17-18.

'Review of G. Ebeling's *Word and Faith*', *TSF* 42 (1965), 20-21.

'Review of P. Tillich's *Systematic Theology: Volume 3*', *CGrad* 18 (1965), 35.

'Review of W.D. Davies' *The Setting of the Sermon on the Mount*', *CGrad* 18 (1965), 38-39.

'Review of P.T. De Chardin's *The Making of a Mind: Letters from a Soldier-Priest*', *Chman* 79.4 (1965), 313-314.

'A Snappy Slogan, But...', *CEN* 11 Feb. (1966), 10.

'Reviews of J. Pollock's *Billy Graham: The Authorised Biography*, B. Graham's *World Aflame* and E. Hulse's *Billy Graham: The Pastor's Dilemma*', *Chman* 80.2 (1966), 140-142.

'Review of J.R.W. Stott's *Men Made New: An Exposition of Romans 5-8*', *Chman* 80.3 (1966), 232-233.

'Reviews of M. Thornton's *The Rock and The River*, F.R. Barry's *Questioning Faith*, and G.B. Montini's (Pope Paul VI) *Man's Religious Sense*', *CGrad* 19 (1966), 38-39.

'Review of M. Novak's *Belief and Unbelief: A Philosophy of Self-Knowledge*', *Chman* 80.4 (1966), 319-321.

*Personal Suggestions about a Minister's Library* (London: TSF, 1966, possibly 1967).

'Review of V.A. Harvey's *A Handbook of Theological Terms*', *Chman* 81.1 (1967), 57-58.

'Review of C.W. Kegley ed. *The Theology of Rudolf Bultmann*', *Chman* 81.1 (1967), 58-60.

'Review of W. Künneth's *The Theology of the Resurrection*', *TSF*, 47 (1967), 14-16.

'Review of H. Gollwitzer's *The Existence of God: As Confessed by Faith*', *TSF* 47 (1967), 17-18.

'Review of C.W. Kegley ed. *The Theology of Rudolf Bultmann*', *TSF* 48 (1967), 20-21.

'Review of E.J. Carnell's *The Burden of Søren Kierkegaard*', *TSF* 48 (1967), 23-24.

'Review of C.F.H. Henry ed. *Jesus of Nazareth: Saviour and Lord*', *Chman* 81.3 (1967), 215-216.

'Review of L. Morris's *Glory in the Cross*', *Chman* 81.3 (1967), 231-232.

'Review of G.W.H. Lampe's and D.M. MacKinnon's *The Resurrection*', *Chman* 81.3 (1967), 232-233.

'Review of B. Martin's *Paul Tillich's Doctrine of Man*', *CGrad* 20.4 (1967), 25-26.

'Review of H. Flender's *St. Luke*', *Chman* 81.4 (1967), 280-281.

'Review Article of W.G. Kummel's *Introduction to the New Testament (1)*', *TSF* 49 (1967), 20-26.
'Review of T.H.L. Parker trans. *Calvin's Commentaries: Galatians, Ephesians, Philippians and Colossians*', *TSF* 50 (1968), 27-28.
'Idealism etc.: Review of F.H. Cleobury's *A Return to Natural Theology*', *CEN* 22 Mar. (1968), 4.
'Review Article of W.G. Kümmel's *Introduction to the New Testament (2)*', *TSF* 51 (1968), 15-24.
'Review of P. Tillich's *On the Boundary*', *CGrad* 21 (1968), 35.
'John Stott at Uppsala: Reply Letter to N. Mable's Critique of John Stott', *CEN* 6 Sep. (1968), 9.
'Review of J. Knox's *Myth and Truth: An Essay on the Language of Faith*', *Chman* 82.3 (1968), 215-216.
'New Practical Theology Series: Reviews of M. Thornton's *The Function of Theology*, and S. Lawton's *Truths that Compelled: Contemporary Implications of Biblical Theology*', *CEN* 4 Oct. (1968), 4.
'Review Article of W.G. Kümmel's *Introduction to the New Testament (3)*', *TSF* 52 (1968), 4-11.
'"Kaleidoscopes of Modern Theology.' Reviews of A.R. Eckardt's *The Theologian at Work*, and J. Macquarrie's *Contemporary Religious Thinkers*', *CEN* 29 Nov. (1968), 9.
'Resisting the Bewitchment of our Intelligence: Review of F. Ferré's *A Basic Modern Philosophy of Religion*', *CEN* 28 Feb. (1969), 4.
'Review of J. Macquarrie's *Studies in Christian Existentialism*', *TSF* 53 (1969), 24-25.
'Review of W. Manson's *Jesus and the Christian*', *Chman* 83.1 (1969), 50-51.
'Review of H.H. Price's *Belief*', *Chn* 11 Apr. (1969), x.
'Continental Theology - Processed, Packaged and Branded. Review of H. Zahrnt's *The Question of God*', *CEN* 9 May (1969), 6.
'Philosophy in Progress: Review of Royal Institute of Philosophy Lectures *Talk of God*', *CEN* 6 Jun. (1969), 5.
'Review of J.B. Cobb's *The Structure of Christian Existence*', *Chman* 83.2 (1969), 129-130.
'Review of E.A. Armstrong's *The Gospel Parables*', *Chman* 83.2 (1969), 138-139.
'Theology for a New World: Review Article of H. Richardson's *Theology for a New World*', *Chman* 83.3 (1969), 197-202.
'Review of P. Van Buren's *Theological Explorations*', *Chman* 83.3 (1969), 220-221.
'Reviews of J.J. Vincent's *Secular Christ*, D.T. Niles' *Who is This Jesus?* and P. Leon's *The Gospel According to Judas*', *Th* 72.590 (Aug. 1969), 373-374.
'A Book Set Apart from the Ordinary Run of Books: Review of T.F. Torrance's *Theological Science*', *CEN* 12 Dec. (1969), 13.
'Crossroads for Theology: Article on Canon Stafford Wright', *CEN* 19 Dec. (1969), 4.
'What after Death? Review of N. Smart's *Philosophers and Religious Truth*', *CEN*, 19 Dec. (1969), 15.
'Theology and the Future', *CEN* 23 Jan. (1970), 11.
'Theological Survey Has No Rival: Review of W. Nicholls' *The Pelican Guide to Modern Theology*', *CEN* 13 Feb. (1970), 12.
'"Excellent Basic Teaching on N.T.' Review of I.H. Marshall's *The Work of Christ*', *CEN* 8 May (1970), 8.
'Do Christian Concepts have Meaning Any More? Reviews of S.C. Brown's *Do Religious Claims Make Sense?*, and W.D. Hudson ed. *The Is/Ought Question*', *CEN* 19 Jun. (1970), 12.

'Review of H.D. Lewis' *The Elusive Mind*', *Chman* 84.2 (1970), 150-151.
'Mixed Encyclopaedia of Continental Theology: Review of J. Pelikan's *Twentieth Century Theology in the Making, Volume 2*', *CEN* 3 Jul. (1970), 8.
'Review of E. Käsemann's *New Testament Questions of Today*', *Chman* 84.3 (1970), 229-230.
'The Parables as Language-Event: Some Comments on Fuchs's Hermeneutics in the Light of Linguistic Philosophy', *SJT* 23.4 (Nov. 1970), 437-468.
'New Testament Commentary Survey', *TSF* 58 (1970), 9-18.
'Well-trampled. Review of F. Ferré's *Language, Logic and God*', *CEN* 8 Jan. (1971), 12.
'Distinctive Colleges. Reply Letter to Mrs Mable', *CEN* 12 Mar. (1971), 16.
'Irrational Assumptions of Modern Theology Exposed. Review of T.F. Torrance's *God and Rationality*', *CEN* 19 Mar. (1971), 9.
'Language in a Haze. Review of T. Fawcett's *The Symbolic Language of Religion*', *CEN* 7 May (1971), 12.
'Divine Friends. Reply Letter to an Article entitled 'Divine Friends'', *CEN* 4 Jun. (1971), 7.
'Review Article of W. Pannenberg's *Basic Questions in Theology, Vol. 1*', *Chman* 85.2 (1971), 120-122.#
'Finding God in Personal Idealism. Review of P.A. Bertocci's *The Person God Is*', *CEN* 9 Jul. (1971), 11.
'Review of G.E. Ladd's *The New Testament and Criticism*', *CGrad* 24.3 (Sep. 1971), 86-87.
'Review of T. Fawcett's *The Symbolic Language of Religion*', *Chman* 85.3 (1971), 221-222.
'Brink of Discovery. Review of D. Cupitt's *Christ and the Hiddenness of God*', *CEN* 1 Oct. (1971), 11.
'A Philosopher Without Inhibitions. Review of W.W. Bartley III's *Morality and Religion*', *CEN* 8 Oct. (1971), 10.
'The Theologian Who Must Not Be Ignored. Article Review of W. Pannenberg's *Basic Questions in Theology, Vol. 2*', *CEN* 25 Feb. (1972), 11.#
'"Charismatic Gifts.' Reply Letter to Mr. Dowling', *CEN* 6 Oct. (1972), 6.
'Important Achievement. Review of G. Kittel and G. Friedrich eds. *Theological Dictionary of the New Testament, Volume 8*', *CEN* 10 Nov. (1972), 8.
'Theology Made Exciting. Review of W. Pannenberg's *The Apostles' Creed in the Light of Today's Questions*', *CEN* 19 Jan. (1973), 12.#
'Review of S.W. Sykes and J.P. Clayton eds. *Christ, Faith and History: Cambridge Studies in Christology*', *Chman* 87.1 (1973), 68-70.
'The Use of Philosophical Categories in New Testament Hermeneutics', *Chman* 87.1 (1973), 87-100.
'Reply Letter to David Gregg about John Rosser', *CEN* 9 Feb. (1973), 11.
'New Problems for Old: Article Review of J.A.T. Robinson's *The Human Face of God*', *CEN* 6 Apr. (1973), 8.
'The Meaning of SARX in 1 Corinthians 5:5: A Fresh Approach in the Light of Logical and Semantic Factors', *SJT* 26.2 (May 1973), 204-228.
'Review of R.G. Hamerton-Kelly's *Pre-Existence, Wisdom and the Son of Man*', *Chman* 87.2 (1973), 145-146.
*New Testament Commentary Survey* (Leicester: TSF, 1973).
'Evangelical Dishonesty. Reply Letter to Editorial', *CEN* 3 Aug. (1973), 8.
'Review of R.P. Martin's *Mark: Evangelist and Theologian*', *CGrad* 26.3 (Sep. 1973), 85.
'Conservative - and Intelligent With It. Review of N.A. Anderson's *A Lawyer Among the Theologians*', *CEN* 12 Oct. (1973), 9.

'Meaning and Myth. Review Article of W. Pannenberg's *Basic Questions in Theology, Vol. 3*', *CEN* 19 Oct. (1973), 8.#
'Review of G. Ebeling's *Introduction to a Theological Theory of Language*', *Chman* 87.4 (1973), 295.
'Positive Role of Doubt', *CEN* 11 Jan. (1974), 8.
'The Theology of Paul Tillich', *Chman* 88.1 (1974), 86-107.
'Sound, Devout Stodge. Review of W. Hendriksen's *Philippians*', *CEN* 1 Feb. (1974), 8.
'Predictable, Domesticated and Tamed', *CEN* 8 Feb. (1974), 7.
'Creativity of Heaven', *CEN* 8 Mar. (1974), 5.#
'New Testament Commentary Survey', *Them* 10.1 (Spr. 1974), 7-23.
'More Manageable Proportions. Review of J.W. Wenham's *The Goodness of God*', *CEN* 5 Apr. (1974), 8.
'The Multi-Model Character of Holy Spirit Language', *CEN* 11 Apr. (1974), 8.
'Towards Intelligent Preaching. Review of J. Gunstone's *Commentary on the New Lectionary, Vol. 2*', *CEN* 3 May (1974), 8.
'Head-On Challenge to Doubt: The Theology of Wolfhart Pannenberg', *CEN* 10 May (1974), 8.#
'Forsyth and his work brought to life. Review of A.M. Hunter's *P.T. Forsyth: per Crucem ad Lucem*', *CEN* 7 Jun. (1974), 6.
'Review of B. Lindars and S.S. Smalley eds. *Christ and Spirit in the New Testament*', *CGrad* 27.2 (Jun. 1974), 55-56.
'No Horns on the Pope', *CEN* 14 Jun. (1974), 5.#
'The Ministry and the Church Union: Some Logical and Semantic Factors', *FUty* 18 (1974), 45-47.
'Looking for God's Triumph: The Role of Apocalyptic', *CEN* 12 Jul. (1974), 8.#
'Review of G. Ebeling's *Introduction to a Theological Theory of Language*', *TSF* 69 (Sum. 1974), 24.
'Experience-Centred Religion: Harvey Cox on the Seduction of the Spirit', *CEN* 9 Aug. (1974), 8.
'For Serious Students of St. Paul. Review of A.T. Hanson's *Studies in Paul's Technique and Theology*', *CEN* 9 Aug. (1974), 10.
'Enthusiasm Not Enough: Güttgemanns, Sawyer, and Barr on Biblical Research', *CEN* 13 Sep. (1974), 6.
'Review of A.D. Galloway's *Wolfhart Pannenberg*', *Chman* 88.3 (1974), 230-231.#
'Review of E.H. Cousins ed. *Hope and the Future of Man*', *Chman* 88.3 (1974), 232-233.#
'Review of J.F.A. Sawyer's *Semantics in Biblical Research*', *TSF* 70 (Aut. 1974), 18.
'The Supposed Power of Words in the Biblical Writings', *JThStud* NS25.2 (Oct. 1974), 283-299.
'Some Comments on the Anglican-Lutheran International Conversations', *Chman* 88.4 (1974), 288-292.
'Great Compassion and Heart. Review of J. Moltmann's *The Crucified God*', *CEN* 10 Jan. (1975), 9.#
'Kierkegaard and the Nature of Truth', *Chman* 89.1 (1975), 85-107.
'Shaping up to Tomorrow. Review of K. Rahner's *The Shape of the Church to Come*', *CEN* 7 Feb. (1975), 8-9.
'Cat Among the Pigeons. Review of M.D. Goulder's *Midrash and Lection in Matthew*', *CEN* 7 Feb. (1975), 10.

'Review of C.K. Barrett's *A Commentary on the Second Epistle to the Corinthians*', *TSF* 71 (Spr. 1975), 29-30.
'Explain, Interpret, Tell, Narrative', in *The New International Dictionary of New Testament Theology, Volume 1* (ed. C. Brown; Exeter: Paternoster; Grand Rapids: Zondervan, 1975), 573-584.
'Myth, Mythology', in *The Zondervan Pictorial Encyclopedia of the Bible, Volume 4* (ed. M.C. Tenney; Grand Rapids, MI: Zondervan, 1975; written by 1973), 333-343.#
'Review of J. Moltmann's *The Crucified God*', *Chman* 89.2 (1975), 148-149.#
Contribution to 'Flesh', in *The New International Dictionary of New Testament Theology, Volume 1* (ed. C. Brown; Exeter: Paternoster; Grand Rapids: Zondervan, 1975), 678-682.
*Language, Liturgy and Meaning* (Nottingham: Grove Books, 1975 and 1986).
'Review of T. Fawcett's *Hebrew Myth and Christian Gospel*', *TSF* 72 (Sum. 1975), 24.
'Review of R. Banks ed. *Reconciliation and Hope*', *CGrad* 28.3 (Aut. 1975), 84-85.#
'Questions, but Not Enough Answers. Review of C.K. Barrett's *The Gospel of John and Judaism*', *CEN* 5 Dec. (1975), 7.
'Reflections in the Current Debate. Review of A.T. Hanson's *Grace and Truth*', *CEN* 26 Dec. (1975), 9.
'Man Longs for the Status and Dignity of a 'Thou'', *CEN* 9 Jan. (1976), 9.
'Review of A. Kenny's *Wittgenstein*', *Chman* 90.1 (1976), 71-72.
'Sigmund Freud and the Language of the Heart', *CEN* 13 Feb. (1976), 12, 14.
'Sense and Nonsense in Interpreting Bible Words', *Ety* 27 (Mar. 1976), 16-35 (16-17, 33-35).+
*New Testament Commentary Survey* (Leicester: TSF, 1976).
'Dialogue and the Dangers of Half-Truths', *CEN* 9 Apr. (1976), 8, 10.
'The Semantics of Biblical Language as an Aspect of Hermeneutics', *FTht* 103.2 (1976), 108-120.
'Review of A. Hodes' *Encounter with Martin Buber*', *Chman* 90.2 (1976), 138-139.
'The Parousia in Modern Theology. Some Questions and Comments', *Tyn* 27 (1976), 27-54.#
'Review of R.P. Martin's *New Testament Foundations: A Guide for Christian Students. Vol. 1: The Four Gospels*', *CGrad* 29.3 (Sep. 1976), 85.
'Review of J. Moltmann's *The Experiment Hope*', *Chman* 90.3 (1976), 225-227.#
'Understanding God's Word Today', *CEN* 15 Oct. (1976), 6.
*New Testament Hermeneutics and Philosophical Description: Issues in New Testament Hermeneutics with Special Reference to the Use of Philosophical Description in Heidegger, Bultmann, Gadamer, and Wittgenstein* (Sheffield: University of Sheffield Ph.D. Thesis, 1977; written by Dec. 1976).#
'Review of N. Perrin's *Jesus and the Language of the Kingdom*', *Chman* 91.1 (1977), 85-86.
'Review of D.H. Kelsey's *The Uses of Scripture in Recent Theology*', *Chman* 91.1 (1977), 87-88.
'Forget Image, Try Dialogue 77. Report on Outreach at Sheffield University', *CEN* 11 Feb. (1977), 2.
'Dissent from John King's Verdicts. Reply Letter to John King', *CEN* 11 Feb. (1977), 13.
'Nitpicking at NEAC? Never: Reply Letter to C.A.F. Warner', *CEN* 17 Jun. (1977), 9.
'An Age of Anxiety', in *The History of Christianity. A Lion Handbook* (eds. T. Dowley *et al*; Tring, Hertfordshire: Lion Publishing, 1977), 594-611.#
'Myth, Paradigm, and the Status of Biblical Imagery', in *Using the Bible in Liturgy* (ed. C. Byworth; Nottingham: Grove, 1977), 4-12.#

'Semantics and New Testament Interpretation', in *New Testament Interpretation: Essays in Principles and Methods* (ed. I.H. Marshall; Grand Rapids: Eerdmans; Exeter: Paternoster Press, 1977; actually written 1974), 75-104.

'The New Hermeneutic', in *New Testament Interpretation: Essays in Principles and Methods* (ed. I.H. Marshall; Grand Rapids: Eerdmans; Exeter: Paternoster Press, 1977), 308-333.

'Understanding God's Word Today: Evangelicals Face the Challenge of the New Hermeneutic. Address at the Second National Evangelical Anglican Congress, Nottingham, 1977', in *Obeying Christ in a Changing World, Vol. 1* (ed. J.R.W. Stott; Glasgow: Collins/Fountain Books, 1977), 90-122.

'The Theological Scene: Post-Bultmannian Perspectives', *CGrad* 30.3 (Sep. 1977), 88-89.

'Review of I.H. Marshall's *I Believe in the Historical Jesus*', *CGrad* 30.4 (Dec. 1977), 117-118.

'Review of D. Nineham's *The Use and Abuse of the Bible*', *Chman* 91.4 (1977), 341-343.

'Understanding the New Testament. Review of J.D.G. Dunn's *Unity and Diversity in the New Testament*', *CEN* 23 Dec. (1977), 8.

'Review of J.R. McKay and J.F. Miller eds. *Biblical Studies: Essays in Honour of William Barclay*', *Chman* 92.1 (1978), 61-62.

'Language and Meaning in Religion', in 'Word', in *The New International Dictionary of New Testament Theology. Volume III* (ed. C. Brown; Exeter: Paternoster; Grand Rapids: Zondervan, 1978; actually written by 1977), 1123-1146.

'Truth', in *The New International Dictionary of New Testament Theology, Volume 3* (ed. C. Brown; Exeter: Paternoster; Grand Rapids: Zondervan, 1978), 874-902.#

'Realized Eschatology at Corinth', *NTStud* 24 (Jul. 1978), 510-526.#

'Keeping up with Recent Studies: II. Structuralism and Biblical Studies: Method or Ideology?', *ExTim* 89 (Aug. 1978), 329-335.

'Review of R.C. Roberts' *Rudolf Bultmann's Theology: A Critical Interpretation*', *Chman* 92.3 (1978), 267-268.

'Review of R. Detweiler's *Story, Sign, and Self*', *ExTim* 90 (Jan. 1979), 119.

'Biblical Classics: VI. Schweitzer's Interpretation of Paul', *ExTim* 90 (Feb. 1979), 132-137.#

'Review of N.R. Petersen's *Literary Criticism for New Testament Critics*', *ExTim* 90 (Feb. 1979), 153-154.

'The 'Interpretation' of Tongues: a New Suggestion in the Light of Greek Usage in Philo and Josephus', *JThStud* NS 30.1 (Apr. 1979), 15-36.

'Review of D.S. Russell's *Apocalyptic, Ancient and Modern*', *Th* 82.687 (May 1979), 218-220.#

'Review of J.-M. Benoist's *The Structural Revolution*', *ExTim* 90 (May 1979), 248.

'Review of A.M. Johnson's *The New Testament and Structuralism*', *ExTim* 91 (Oct. 1979), 26-27.

'Review of F.F. Bruce's *The Time is Fulfilled*', *CGrad* 32.4 (Dec. 1979), 30.#

*The Two Horizons: New Testament Hermeneutics and Philosophical Description with Special Reference to Heidegger, Bultmann, Gadamer, and Wittgenstein* (Exeter: Paternoster Press, 1980).#

'Review of C.E.B. Cranfield's *A Critical and Exegetical Commentary on the Epistle to the Romans. Volume II: Commentary on Romans IX-XVI and Essays*', *Chman* 94.4 (1980), 356-357.

'Review of J. Barr's *Explorations in Theology 7*', *Th* 84.698 (Mar. 1981), 133-135.

"Book Notes.' Short Reviews of C. Brown ed., *The New International Dictionary of New Testament Theology, Vol. 3*, F.C. Conybeare's and St. G. Stock's *A Grammar of Septuagint Greek*, E.E. Ellis's *Prophecy and Hermeneutic in Early Christianity*, B. Gerhardsson's *The Origins of the Gospel Traditions*, R.A. Guelich's *Unity and Diversity in New Testament Theology*, J.A. Kirk's *Liberation Theology* and *Theology Encounters Revolution*, J.D. Smart's *The Past, Present and Future of Biblical Theology*, S.H. Travis's *Christian Hope and the Future of Man*, and

J.A. Ziesler's *The Jesus Question*', *JStudNT* 12 (1981), 71-75.
'Knowledge, Myth and Corporate Memory', in *Believing in the Church: Essays by Members of the Church of England Doctrine Commission* (ed. B. Mitchell; London: SPCK, 1981), 45-78.
'Reviews of P.R. Wells' *James Barr and the Bible*, and J.I. Packer's *Under God's Word*', *Chman* 95.4 (1981), 340-341.
'Review of G. Theissen's *On Having a Critical Faith*', *SJT* 34.4 (1981), 376-377.
'On the Logical Grammar of Justification in Paul. Paper Presented to the Fifth International Congress on Biblical Studies, Oxford, 1973', in *Studia Evangelica 7* (ed. E.A. Livingstone; Berlin: Akademie-Verlag, 1982), 491-495.#
"Book Notes.' Short Reviews of J.R. Alsop ed. *An Index to the Revised Bauer-Arndt-Gingrich Greek Lexicon. Second Edition*, H. Berkhof's *Christian Faith*, G.L. Bray's *Holiness and the Will of God*, and D.J. Fox's *The 'Matthew-Luke Commentary' of Philoxenus*, M. Hengel's *The Atonement*', *JStudNT* 14 (1982), 125-127.
"Book Notes.' Short Reviews of P. Henry's *New Directions in New Testament Study*; and D.J. Bosch's *Witness to the World*', *JStudNT* 15 (1982), 125-126.
'Academic Freedom, Religious Tradition, and the Morality of Christian Scholarship', in *Their Lord and Ours: Approaches to Authority, Community and the Unity of the Church* (ed. M. Santer; London: SPCK, 1982), 20-45.
'From Existentialism to Post-Modernism', in *Eerdman's Handbook to the World's Religions* (eds. Beaver, R.P. *et al*; Grand Rapids, MI.: Eerdmans, 1982, 1994), 396-398.
'Søren Kierkegaard', in *Exploring The Christian Faith* (eds. R. Keeley *et al*; Nelson's Christian Cornerstone Series; Nashville, TN.: Nelson Reference, 1982, 1992, 1996), 449-450 (321-322 in 1996 edition).
'The Rise of Biblical Criticism', in *Exploring The Christian Faith* (eds. R. Keeley *et al*; Nelson's Christian Cornerstone Series; Nashville, TN.: Nelson Reference, 1982, 1992, 1996), 449 (320-321 in 1996 edition).
'Review of A. Gibson's *Biblical Semantic Logic*', *Th* 85.706 (Jul. 1982), 301-303.
'Review of H.A. Virkler's *Hermeneutics*', *EvanQ* 55 (Jan. 1983), 54-55.
"Book Notes.' Short Reviews of P.D.L. Avis's *The Church in the Theology of the Reformers*, D.A. Carson's *Divine Sovereignty and Human Responsibility*, R.H. Gundry's *A Survey of the New Testament*, M. Limbeck, ed. *Redaktion und Theologie des Passionsberichtes nach den Synoptikern*, and K.K. Schel's *Paulus. Leben-Brief-Theologie*', *JStudNT* 17 (1983), 124-126.
'Review of J.P. Louw's *Semantics of New Testament Greek*', *RefJ* 33.12 (Dec. 1983), 29-30.
'Review of C.K. Barrett's *Essays on Paul*', *EvanQ* 56 (Jan. 1984), 58-59.
'Review of E. Best's *Mark. The Gospel as Story*', *Them* 10.2 (Jan. 1985), 37.
'Review of R. Martin's *New Testament Books for Pastor and Teacher*', *Them* 10.2 (Jan. 1985), 40.
'Review of D. Tidball's *An Introduction to the Sociology of the New Testament*', *JThStud* 36 (Apr. 1985), 203-204.
'Reader-Response Hermeneutics, Action Models, and the Parables of Jesus', in *The Responsibility of Hermeneutics* (R. Lundin, A.C. Thiselton and C. Walhout; Grand Rapids: Eerdmans; Exeter: Paternoster, 1985), 79-113, 123-126.
'La Nouvelle Herméneutique', *Hok* 33 (1986), 1-36. French reprint of, Thiselton, A.C., 'The New Hermeneutic', in Marshall, I.H. ed., *New Testament Interpretation*, 308-333.
'The New Hermeneutic', in *A Guide to Contemporary Hermeneutics: Major Trends in Biblical Interpretation* (ed. D.K. McKim; Grand Rapids: Eerdmans, 1986), 78-107. Reprinted from, Marshall, I.H. ed., *New Testament Interpretation*, 308-333.
'Hermeneutics and Theology: The Legitimacy and necessity of Hermeneutics', in *A Guide to Contemporary Hermeneutics: Major Trends in Biblical Interpretation* (ed. D.K. McKim; Grand

Rapids: Eerdmans, 1986), 142-174. Reprinted from Thiselton, A.C., *The Two Horizons*, 85-114.
'Review of D.A. Carson ed. *Biblical Interpretation and the Church*', *ExTim* 97.5 (Feb. 1986), 154-155.
'Address and Understanding: Some Goals and Models of Biblical Interpretation as Principles of Vocational Training', *Anv* 3 (1986), 101-118.
'Postscript to 1986 Edition', in *Language, Liturgy and Meaning* (A.C. Thiselton; Nottingham: Grove Books, 1986), 33.$
'Sign, Symbol', in *A New Dictionary of Liturgy and Worship* (ed. J.G. Davies; London: SCM, 1986), 491-492.
'Review of S. Ogden's *Rudolf Bultmann, New Testament Mythology and other Basic Writings*', *ExTim* 97.10 (Jul. 1986), 316.
'Review of J.A. Davis' *Wisdom and Spirit*', *Them* NS 12.1 (Sep. 1986), 29.
Contribution (not specified) to 'the debate which informed the whole book', in *We Believe in God: A Report by the Doctrine Commission of the General Synod of the Church of England* (London: Church House Publishing, 1987).
'Reviews of J. Painter's *Theology as Hermeneutics*, and M.L. Branson's and C.R. Padilla's *Conflict and Context*', *ExTim* 99.3 (Dec. 1987), 87-88.
'Speaking and Hearing', in *Christian Faith and Practice in the Modern World* (eds. M.A. Noll and D.F. Wells; Grand Rapids: Eerdmans, 1988), 139-151.
'Hermeneutics', in *New Dictionary of Theology* (eds. S.B. Ferguson *et al*; Leicester: IVP, 1988), 293-297.
'Kierkegaard, Søren Aabye', in *New Dictionary of Theology* (eds. S.B. Ferguson *et al*; Leicester: IVP, 1988), 365-367.
'Tillich, Paul', in *New Dictionary of Theology* (eds. S.B. Ferguson *et al*; Leicester: IVP, 1988), 687-688.
'Wittgenstein, Ludwig Josef Johann', in *New Dictionary of Theology* (eds. S.B. Ferguson *et al*; Leicester: IVP, 1988), 726-728.
'Review of J. Painter's *Theology as Hermeneutics*', *EvanQ* 60 (Jul. 1988), 279-280.
'Review of G.E. Michalson's *Lessing's Ugly Ditch - a Study of Theology and History*', *SJT* 42.2 (1989), 253-255.
'Reviews of F. Young's and D.F. Ford's *Meaning and Truth in 2 Corinthians*, and, C.G. Kruse's *The Second Epistle to the Corinthians*', *Anv* 6.2 (1989), 167-168.
'Review of C. Tuckett's *Reading the New Testament*', *Anv* 7.1 (1990), 72-73.
'Review of M. Harvie ed. *Inerrancy and Hermeneutics*', *ExTim* 101 (May 1990), 249.
'Meaning', in *A Dictionary of Biblical Interpretation* (eds. R.J. Coggins and J.L. Houlden; London: SCM, Philadelphia: Trinity Press, 1990), 435-438.
'On Models and Methods: A Conversation with Robert Morgan', in *The Bible in Three Dimensions: Essays in Celebration of Forty Years of Biblical Studies in the University of Sheffield* (eds. D.J.A. Clines, S.E. Fowl, and S.E. Porter; JStudOT Supplement Series 87; Sheffield: Sheffield Academic Press, 1990), 337-356.
'Religious Language and Symbolism, Psychology of', in *Dictionary of Pastoral Care and Counselling* (ed. R.J. Hunter; Nashville: Abingdon Press, 1990), 1066-1068.
'Reviews of W.J. Larkin's *Culture and Biblical Hermeneutics*, and H.M. Conn ed. *Inerrancy and Hermeneutic*', *ExTim* 101.8 (1990), 249.
'The Holy Spirit and the Future', in *We Believe in the Holy Spirit: A Report by the Doctrine Commission of the General Synod of the Church of England* (London, Church House Publishing, 1991), 170-186.

'The Spirit of Truth', in *We Believe in the Holy Spirit: A Report by the Doctrine Commission of the General Synod of the Church of England* (London: Church House Publishing, 1991), 112-133.
'Review of C. Rowland's and M. Corner's *Liberating Exegesis*', *Anv* 8.3 (1991), 254.
'Review of K.J. Vanhoozer's *Biblical Narrative in the Philosophy of Paul Ricoeur*', *EvanQ* 63.4 (1991), 355-357.
'Review of G. Jones' *Bultmann*', *JThStud* NS 43.1 (Apr. 1992), 317-319.
*New Horizons in Hermeneutics: The Theory and Practice of Transforming Biblical Reading* (London: HarperCollins; Grand Rapids: Zondervan, 1992).
'Review of J.C. O'Neill's *The Bible's Authority*', *Th* 95.766 (Jul.-Aug. 1992), 295-296.
'Review of R.P. Burrows and P. Rorem eds. *Biblical Hermeneutics in Historical Perspective*', *ExTim* 104.6 (Mar. 1993), 187-188.
'Review of W.G. Jeanrond's *Theological Hermeneutics*', *JThStud* 44.1 (Apr. 1993), 463-466.
'Hermeneutics', in *The Oxford Companion to the Bible* (ed. B.M. Metzger; New York and Oxford: Oxford University Press, 1993), 279-280.
'Language, Religious', in *The Blackwell Encyclopedia of Modern Christian Thought* (ed. A. McGrath; Oxford: Blackwell, 1993), 315-319.
'Review of T.W. Randolph's *Biblical Interpretation*', *BibInterp*, 1.3 (1993), 384-386.
'Authority and Hermeneutics. Some Proposals for a More Creative Agenda', in *A Pathway into the Holy Scripture* (eds. P.E. Satterthwaite and D.F. Wright; Grand Rapids: Eerdmans, 1994), 107-142.
'Christology in Luke, Speech-Act Theory, and the Problem of Dualism in Christology after Kant', in *Jesus of Nazareth. Lord and Christ* (eds. J.B. Green and M. Turner; Grand Rapids: Eerdmans; Carlisle: Paternoster Press, 1994), 453-472.
'Review of C. Walhout and L. Ryken eds. *Contemporary literary Theory*', *LitTh* 8 (1994), 119-120.
'The Logical Role of the Liar Paradox in Titus 1:12,13: A Dissent from the Commentaries in the Light of Philosophical and Logical Analysis', *BibInterp* 2 (Jul. 1994), 207-223.
'Barr on Barth and Natural Theology: A Plea for Hermeneutics in Historical Theology. Review Article of J. Barr's *Biblical Faith and Natural Theology*', *SJT* 47.4 (1994), 519-528.
'New Testament Interpretation in Historical Perspective', in *Hearing the New Testament: Strategies for Interpretation* (ed. J.B. Green; Grand Rapids: Eerdmans; Carlisle: Paternoster Press, 1995), 11-37.@
> @The volume: "Green, J.B. ed., *New Testament Interpretation Today* (Grand Rapids: Eerdmans, 1995)" only appears quoted in the footnotes of: Thiselton, 'Authority and Hermeneutics', 128. According to Thiselton, this is the above reference under a then-proposed title that was not used in publication.
*Interpreting God and The Postmodern Self: On Meaning, Manipulation and Promise* (SJT: Current Issues in Theology; Edinburgh: T&T Clark, 1995).%
'James Atkinson: Theologian, Professor and Churchman', in *The Bible, The Reformation, and The Church* (ed. W. Stephens; Sheffield: Sheffield Academic Press, 1995), 11-35.
'Luther and Barth on 1 Corinthians 15: Six Theses for Theology in Relation to Recent Interpretation', in *The Bible, The Reformation, and the Church* (ed. W. Stephens; Sheffield: Sheffield Academic Press, 1995), 258-289.
'Wittgenstein, Ludwig', in *New Dictionary of Christian Ethics and Pastoral Theology* (eds. D.J. Atkinson and D.H. Field; Leicester: IVP, 1995), 897-898.
'Review of S.D. Moore's *Poststructuralism and the New Testament*', *ExTim* 106.10 (Jul. 1995), 309.
'Review of W.D. Edgerton's *The Passion of Interpretation*', *Them* 21.1 (Oct. 1995), 24.

'Reviews of J. Fitzmyer's *The Biblical Commission's Document, 'The Interpretation of the Bible in the Church': Text and Commentary*, and J.L. Houlden ed. *The Interpretation of the Bible in the Church*', *ExTim* 107 (Dec. 1995), 84-85.
'Review of F. Watson's *Text, Church and World*', *Anv* 13.1 (1996), 58.
'Review of W. Pannenberg's *Systematic Theology, Volume 2*', *Anv* 13.1 (1996), 77-78.
'Review of N. Richardson's *Paul's Language about God*', *Them* 21.3 (Apr. 1996), 23-24.
'Review of D. Patte's *Ethics of Biblical Interpretation*', *ExTim* 107.8 (May 1996), 249.
'Review of B. Witherington III's *Conflict and Community in Corinth*', *Anv* 13.2 (1996), 163-164.
'Review of J.D. Moores' *Wrestling with Rationality in Paul*', *JThStud* 47.2 (1996), 619-621.
'Review of J. Goldingay's *Models for Scripture*', *Th* 99.790 (Jul.-Aug. 1996), 309-310.
'Review of B.S. Rosner's *Paul, Scripture, and Ethics*', *EvanQ* 69.1 (Jan. 1997), 86-88.
'Speech-Act Theory and the Claim that God Speaks: Nicholas Wolterstorff's Divine Discourse. Review Article', *SJT* 50.1 (1997), 97-110.
'Review of F.F. Segovia's and M.A. Tolbert's *Reading from This Place, Volume 2*', *ExTim* 108.7 (Apr. 1997), 220.
'Biblical Theology and Hermeneutics', in *The Modern Theologians. An Introduction to Christian Theology in the Twentieth Century* (ed. D.E. Ford; Oxford: Blackwell, 1997), 520-537.
'Can Hermeneutics Ease the Deadlock? Some Biblical Exegesis and Hermeneutical Models', in *The Way Forward: Christian Voices on Homosexuality and the Church* (ed. T. Bradshaw; London: Hodder and Stoughton, 1997), 145-196.@
'Human Being, Relationality and Time in Hebrews, 1 Corinthians and Western Traditions. Paper presented at North Park Theological Seminary, Oct 17-19, 1997', *ExA* 13 (1997), 76-95.@
'Review of R.A. Harrisville's and W. Sundberg's *The Bible in Modern Culture*', *NLThT* 51.4 (1997), 325-326.
'Review of D.E. Demson's *Hans Frei and Karl Barth*', *ExTim* 109.3 (Dec. 1997), 90-91.
'Thirty Years of Hermeneutics: Retrospect and Prospects', in *International Symposium on the Interpretation of the Bible* (ed. J. Krašovec; Ljubljana: Slovenian Academy of Sciences and Arts, Sheffield: Sheffield Academic Press, 1998), 1559-1574.
'Biblical Studies and Theoretical Hermeneutics', in *The Cambridge Companion to Biblical Interpretation* (ed. J. Barton; Cambridge: CUP, 1998), 95-113.
'Holy Spirit (A.C. Thiselton stresses: 'with additions by the editors')', in *Dictionary of Biblical Imagery* (eds. L. Ryken, J.C. Wilhoit, and T. Longman III; Leicester: Apollos, 1998), 390-393.@

> @One other article was contributed to this volume, but A.C. Thiselton warns that it is 'too mangled to merit claiming it as mine' due to unwarranted editorial alterations, and so the article is omitted.

'Review of G. Fee's *Paul, the Spirit and the People of God*', *Them* 23.2 (1998), 68-69.
'Review of R.T. France's *Women in the Church's Ministry*', *EuJTh* 7 (1998), 74-75.
'Review of C. Forbes' *Prophecy and Inspired Speech in Early Christianity and its Hellenistic Environment*', *EvanQ* 70 (1998), 78-80.
'Hermeneutics, Biblical', in *Routledge Encyclopaedia of Philosophy, Volume 4* (ed. E. Craig; London and New York: Routledge, 1998), 389-395.
'Review of R. Lundin ed. *Disciplining Hermeneutics*', *Anv* 15.3 (1998), 230-232.
'Review of S.E. Fowl ed. *The Theological Interpretation of Scripture*', *JRel* 78.3 (1998), 447-449.
'Review of T.G. Stylianopoulos' *The New Testament, Volume 1*', *ExTim* 110.2 (Nov. 1998), 61.
'Review of L.E. Hahn ed. *The Philosophy of Hans-Georg Gadamer*', *Anv* 16.1 (1999), 71-73.

'Signs of the Times: Towards a Theology for the Year 2000 as a Grammar of Grace, Truth and Eschatology in Contexts of So-Called Postmodernity', *Unpublished Version of the Paper Given at The Society for the Study of Theology Annual Conference, Edinburgh*, Apr. 1999, 1-54.
'Unpublished Bibliographic Letter to R. Knowles', 4th May 1999.
'Unpublished Bibliographic Letter to R. Knowles', 26th May 1999.
'Review of M.T. Prokes' *Toward a Theology of the Body*', *Cru* 38 (Apr.-Jun. 1999), 135-136.
'Review of S.E. Fowl's *Engaging Scripture*', *IJSTh* 1.2 (Jul. 1999), 219-221.
'Communicative Action and Promise in Inter-Disciplinary, Biblical, and Theological Hermeneutics', in *The Promise of Hermeneutics* (R. Lundin, C. Walhout and A.C. Thiselton; Grand Rapids and Cambridge: Eerdmans; Carlisle: Paternoster, 1999), 133-239.
'Review of W.J. Wood's *Epistemology*', *Anv* 17.1 (2000), 62.
'Review of D. Ford's *Sin and Salvation*', *RevRelTh* 7.1 (Feb. 2000), 74-76.
'Signs of the Times: Towards a Theology for the Year 2000 as a Grammar of Grace, Truth and Eschatology in Contexts of So-Called Postmodernity. Presidential Paper of the Society for the Study of Theology', in *The Future as God's Gift: Explorations in Christian Eschatology* (eds. D. Fergusson and M. Sarot; Edinburgh: T&T Clark, 2000), 9-39.
'1 Corinthians', in *New Dictionary of Biblical Theology* (eds. T.D. Alexander and B.S. Rosner; Leicester: IVP, 2000), 297-306.
'Cupitt, D', in *Dictionary of Historical Theology* (ed. T. Hart; Grand Rapids: Eerdmans, and Carlisle: Paternoster, 2000), 141-144.
'Postmodernity', in *Dictionary of Historical Theology* (ed. T. Hart; Grand Rapids: Eerdmans, and Carlisle: Paternoster, 2000), 434-437.
'Review of A. Eriksson's *Traditions as Rhetorical Proof*', *Them* 25.3 (2000), 97-99.
'Unpublished Personal Letter to J.D.G. Dunn', 9th Oct. (2000).
'Review of G. Green's *Theology, Hermeneutics and Imagination*', *ExTim* 112.1 (Oct. 2000), 29.
'Review of K.J. Vanhoozer's *Is There a Meaning in this Text?*', *JThStud* NS 51.2 (Oct. 2000), 702-705.
*The First Epistle to the Corinthians* (eds. H. Marshall and D.A. Hagner; Series: The New International Greek Testament Commentary; Grand Rapids: Eerdmans; Carlisle: Paternoster, 2000).$%
'Review of H.-G. Gadamer's *Hermeneutics, Religion and Ethics*', *Anv* 17.4 (2000), 315-316.
'"Behind" and "In Front Of" the Text: Language, Reference and Indeterminacy', in *After Pentecost: Language and Biblical Interpretation* (eds. C.G. Bartholomew, C. Greene and K. Möller; Scripture and Hermeneutics Series; Vol. 2; Carlisle: Paternoster, 2001), 97-120.
'Review of S. Murray's *Biblical Interpretation in the Anabaptist Tradition*', *IJSTh* 3.3 (Nov. 2001), 341-344.
'Review of R.W.L. Moberly's *The Bible, Theology and Faith*', *RevRelTh* 8.4 (2001), 401-403.
'Review of J.N. Bremmer's *The Rise and Fall of the Afterlife*', *ChTim* 3 May (2002), 15.
*A Concise Encyclopedia of the Philosophy of Religion* (Oxford: One World, 2002).
'Review of D. Peterson ed. *Where Wrath and Mercy Meet*', *Anv* 19 (2002), 313-314.
with F. Bridger, D. Atkinson, N. Baines, T. Dakin: 'Ecclesiastical Support', *Guard* Tue. Oct. 8 (2002), 19.
'Review of B.L. Mack's *The Christian Myth: Origins, Logic, and Legacy*', *ExTim* 114 (Oct. 2002), 29.
'Review of H. Räisänen's *Challenges to Biblical Interpretation*', *ExTim* 114.3 (Dec. 2002), 101-102.
'Review of G.L. Byron's *Symbolic Blackness and Ethnic Difference in Early Christian Literature*', *ChTim* 13 Dec. (2002), 18.

'Review of S.G. Grenz's *The Social God and the Relational Self*', *Th* 106.830 (Mar.-Apr. 2003), 134-136.%
'Review of C.R. Seitz's *Figured Out*', *JThStud* 54 (Apr. 2003), 164-166.
'Can a Pre-Modern Bible Address a Postmodern World? (Public Lecture, University of St. Andrews)', in *2000 Years and Beyond: Faith, Identity, and the Common Era* (eds. P. Gifford, D. Archard, T. Hart, and N. Rapport; London: Routledge, 2003), 127-146.%
'Hebrews', in *Eerdmans Commentary on the Bible* (eds. J.W. Rogerson and J.D.G. Dunn; Grand Rapids and Cambridge: Eerdmans, 2003), 1451-1482.
'Review of J. Polkinghorne ed. *The Work of Love*', *Anv* 20.2 (2003), 147-148.
'Review of G.D. Fee's *New Testament Exegesis*', *ExTim* 114.11 (Aug. 2003), 388.
'Review of W. Baird's *History of New Testament Research, Volume 2*', *ExTim* 114.12 (Sep. 2003), 404.
'Review of R. Briggs' *Reading the Bible Wisely*', *ExTim* 115.2 (Nov. 2003), 52.
'Review of T. Work's *Living and Active*', *IJSTh* 6 (2004), 433-435.
'Review of B.W.R. Pearson's *Corresponding Sense*', *BibInterp* 12.2 (2004), 221-224.
'The Holy Spirit in 1 Corinthians: Exegesis and Reception-History in the Patristic Era', in *The Holy Spirit in the New Testament: Essays in Honour of James D.G. Dunn* (eds. G.N. Stanton, B.W. Longenecker, and S.C. Barton; Grand Rapids and Cambridge: Eerdmans, 2004), 207-228. Reprinted in *Thiselton on Hermeneutics*.
'Can the Bible Mean Whatever We Want it to Mean?' Unpublished Inaugural Lecture as Research Professor of Christian Theology, 29th October 2004, University College, Chester.
'Review of I.R. Kitzberger, ed., *Autobiographical Biblical Criticism*', *Th* 107 (Nov.-Dec. 2004), 436-437.
'Review of M. Gilbertson's *God and History in the Book of Revelation*', *Anv* 21.4 (2004), 300-301.
'From Existentialism to Post-Modernism', in *Eerdman's Handbook to the World's Religions* (eds. Beaver, R.P. *et al*; Grand Rapids, MI.: Eerdmans, 1982, 1994, 2005), 396-398.
'The Hermeneutical Dynamics of 'Reading Luke' as Interpretation, Reflection and Formation', in *Reading Luke: Interpretation, Reflection, Formation* (C.G. Bartholomew, J.B. Green, and A.C. Thiselton eds.; Carlisle: Paternoster Press and Grand Rapids: Zondervan, 2005), 1-52, (Published Conference Contribution, Jesus College, Oxford, August 2004).
with C.G. Bartholomew and J.B. Green, eds., *Reading Luke: Interpretation, Reflection, Formation* Carlisle: Paternoster Press and Grand Rapids: Zondervan, 2005).
'Review of J.M. Court ed., *Biblical Interpretation*', *Th* 108 (Mar.-Apr. 2005), 122-123.
*Can the Bible Mean Whatever We Want It to Mean? Inaugural Address as Research Professor of Christian Theology, University College, Chester, 29th October 2004* (Chester: Chester Academic Press, 2005).
'Biblical Interpretation', in *The Modern Theologians. An Introduction to Christian Theology in the Twentieth Century* (ed. D.F. Ford; Oxford: Blackwell, 2005, 3rd edition), 287-304.
'Richardson, Alan', in *The Dictionary of Twentieth-Century British Philosophers* (eds. S.C. Brown and A. Sell; Bristol: Thoemmes Press, 2005), page-numbers not ascertained.+
'Review of D.R. Hall, *The Unity of the Corinthian Correspondence*', *JThStud* 56 (2005), 599-601.
'Hermeneutics', and 'Hermeneutical Circle', in *Dictionary for Theological Interpretation of the Bible* (ed. K.J. Vanhoozer; London: SPCK and Grand Rapids: Baker Academic, 2005), 281-287.
'Review of D. Jasper's *A Short Introduction to Hermeneutics*', *Th* 108 (Jul.-Aug. 2005), 288-289.

'Goodness and Truth in the Bible: A Comparison with Truth in Hermeneutics and in Postmodernity', in *The Good, the True, and the Beautiful in the Twenty-First Century* (Conference of the C. S. Lewis Summer Institute, University of Cambridge, August 2005), page-numbers not ascertained.+

'Review of T. Holland's *Contours of Pauline Theology*', *ExTim* 116.12 (Sep. 2005), 425-426.

'Review of D. Patte ed. *The Global Bible Commentary*', *ChTim* 16 Sep. Issue 7436 (2005).+

'Review of R. Bauckham's *The Bible and Mission*', *Them* 30.2 (Wint. 2005), 84.

'The Significance of Recent Research on 1 Corinthians for Hermeneutical Appropriation of the Epistle Today', for *NeoT* (*JNTSSA* - Journal of the New Testament Society of Southern Africa) 40.2 (2006), 320-352, (Paper delivered at Kwa-Zulu University, Natal, January 2006).%

'Review of J. Zimmerman's, *Recovering Theological Hermeneutics*', *IJSTh* 8.2 (April 2006), 224-226.

'Introduction: Canon, Community, and Theological Construction', in *Canon and Biblical Interpretation: Scripture and Hermeneutics Series Volume 7* (eds. C.G. Bartholomew, S. Hahn, R. Parry, C. Seitz, and A. Wolters; Conference, the Gregorian Pontifical University, Rome, June 2005; Grand Rapids: Zondervan, & Carlisle: Paternoster, 2006), 1-30.

'Review of L.L. Welborn's, *Paul, the Fool of Christ*', *JThStud* 57 (2006) 277-279.

'Review of W. Loader's, *The Septuagint, Sexuality, and the New Testament*', *JThStud* 56.2 (2006), 633-635.

*1 Corinthians: A Shorter Exegetical and Pastoral Commentary* (Grand Rapids and Cambridge: Eerdmans, 2006).%

*Thiselton on Hermeneutics: Collected Works and New Essays* (Aldershot: Ashgate; Ashgate Contemporary Thinkers on Religion; and, Grand Rapids: Eerdmans, 2006).

'Review of James D. Hester and J. David Hester eds. *Rhetorics and Hermeneutics*' *ExTim* 118.3 (Dec. 2006), 136.

'Achaicus', in *The New Interpreter's Dictionary of the Bible Volume 1* (ed. K.D. Sakenfield *et al*; Nashville: Abingdon Press, 2006), 31.

'Anathema', in *The New Interpreter's Dictionary of the Bible Volume 1* (ed. K.D. Sakenfield *et al*; Nashville: Abingdon Press, 2006), 145.

'Chloe', in *The New Interpreter's Dictionary of the Bible Volume 1* (ed. K.D. Sakenfield *et al*; Nashville: Abingdon Press, 2006), 594.

'Corinthians, First Letter to', in *The New Interpreter's Dictionary of the Bible Volume 1* (ed. K.D. Sakenfield *et al*; Nashville: Abingdon Press, 2006), 735-744.

'Curse', in *The New Interpreter's Dictionary of the Bible Volume 1* (ed. K.D. Sakenfield *et al*; Nashville: Abingdon Press, 2006), 810-814.

'Biblical Interpretation in the Eighteenth and Nineteenth Centuries' and 'Biblical Interpretation in Europe in the Twentieth Century' in McKim, D.K. and G.T. Sheppard, eds. *Dictionary of Major Biblical Interpreters* (Downers Grove: Inter-Varsity Press, 2007), page-numbers not ascertained.+

'Review of C.C. Crocker's, *Reading 1 Corinthians in the Twenty-First Century*', *JThStud* 58.1 (April 2007), 230-232.%

'Review of J. Økland's, *Women in Their Place: Paul and the Corinthian Discourse of Gender and Sanctuary Space*', *JThStud* 58.1 (April 2007), 236-239.%

'Personal Communication to Robert Knowles', 6th May 2007.

'Bultmann, Rudolf', in *Dictionary of Biblical Criticism and Interpretation* (ed. S.E. Porter; London & New York: Routledge, 2007), 42-43.

'Schleiermacher, Friedrich D.E.', in *Dictionary of Biblical Criticism and Interpretation* (ed. S.E.

Porter; London & New York: Routledge, 2007), 329-330.

*The Hermeneutics of Doctrine* (Grand Rapids: Eerdmans, 2007).

'Review of J.L. Kovacs ed. & trans. *1 Corinthians Interpreted by Early Christian Commentators*', *JThStud* 58.2 (2007), 656-658.

'Review of J.L. González's *A Concise History of Christian Doctrine*', *Th* 110.857 (Sep. 2007), 369-370.

'Fortunatus', in *The New Interpreter's Dictionary of the Bible Volume 2* (ed. K.D. Sakenfield *et al*; Nashville: Abingdon Press, 2007), page-numbers not ascertained.+

'Head Covering', in *The New Interpreter's Dictionary of the Bible Volume 2* (ed. K.D. Sakenfield *et al*; Nashville: Abingdon Press, 2007), page-numbers not ascertained.+

'Devoted', in *The New Interpreter's Dictionary of the Bible Volume 2* (ed. K.D. Sakenfield *et al*; Nashville: Abingdon Press, 2007), 118.

'Review of R.H. Gundry's *The Old is Better: New Testament Essays in Support of Traditional Interpretations*', *JThStud* 59.1 (April 2008), 263-265.

'Review of A.L.A. Hogeterp's *Paul and God's Temple: A Historical Interpretation of Cultic Imagery in the Corinthian Correspondence*' *JThStud* 59.1 (April 2008), 445-446.

'Review of A.S. Jensen's *Theological Hermeneutics*', *RBL* 07/2008 at: http://www.bookreviews.org/pdf/6257_6732.pdf.

'Oath', in *The New Interpreter's Dictionary of the Bible Volume 4* (ed. K.D. Sakenfield *et al*; Nashville: Abingdon Press, 2009), page-numbers not ascertained.+

'Review of A. Munzinger's *Discerning the Spirits: Theological and Ethical Hermeneutics in Paul*, *JThStud* 60.1 (2009), 266-267.

*Hermeneutics: An Introduction* (Grand Rapids: Eerdmans, 2009).

*The Living Paul: An Introduction to the Apostle and his Thought* (London: SPCK, 2009).%

'Review of R.A. Horsley's *Wisdom and Spiritual Transcendence at Corinth: Studies in First Corinthians*', *RBL* 07/2009 at: http://www.bookreviews.org/pdf/6812_7381.pdf.

'Review of E.J. Epp's *Junia: the First Woman Apostle*', *Eccl* 5.2 (2009), 266-267.

'Review of M.A. Bowald's *Rendering the Word in Theological Hermeneutics: Mapping Divine and Human Agency*', *JThStud* 60.2 (2009), 587-589.

'Sosthenes', in *The New Interpreter's Dictionary of the Bible Volume 5* (ed. K.D. Sakenfield *et al*; Nashville: Abingdon Press, 2009), page-numbers not ascertained.+

'Review of D.J. Trier's Introducing Theological Interpretation of Scripture: Recovering a Christian Practice', *Th* 112.870 (Nov. 2009), 454-455.

'Review of D.C. Allison Jr.'s *The Historical Christ and the Theological Jesus*', *JThStud* 61 (Mar. 2010), 291-292.

*1 & 2 Thessalonians: Through the Centuries* (Blackwell Bible Commentaries; Maldon, MA, & Oxford, UK: Wiley-Blackwell, 2011).%

*Life after Death: A New Approach to the Last Things* (Grand Rapids: Eerdmans and London: SPCK, 2011 or 2012).

'Wisdom in the Jewish and Christian Scriptures: The Hebrew Bible and Judaism', *Th* 114.3 (May 2011), 163-172.

'Wisdom in the Jewish and Christian Scriptures: Wisdom in the New Testament', *Th* 114.4 (Jul. 2011), 260-268.

'Paul's Missionary Preaching in 1 Thess. 2: 1-16', in *Festschrift for Prof. I. Howard Marshall* (Grand Rapids: Eerdmans, 2011/2012, awaiting publication).

'Reception Theory, H.R. Jauss, and the Formative Power of Scripture: Plenary Paper Presented to the Society for the Study of Theology, York, 11th-13th April, 2011', for publication in either *IJST* or *SJT*.

## Additional Bibliographic Notes on Further Writings
## by Anthony C. Thiselton, F.K.C., F.B.A.

1. Thiselton has also reviewed the following works since 2005: N.T. Wright's *The Resurrection of the Son of God* (in *BibInterp*); G. Pattison's *A Short Course in Christian Doctrine* (in *Anv*); and J.A. Fitzmyer, S.J.'s *First Corinthians* (location not ascertained).
2. Thiselton also speaks of six papers delivered to seminaries and universities – also given to Korean universities and/or published in Korean, Seoul, May 2007. Thiselton also presented a keynote conference paper to the Old and New Testament Societies of Korea in 2007.
3. Thiselton has written further short entries to *ChTim* that are not listed here.
4. Students of Thiselton's writings are directed to the following academic journals with respect to the location of more-recent writings by Thiselton: *JThStud*, *ExTim*, *Anv*, *IJST*, *SJT*, *Eccl*, *BibInterp*, *Th*, *ChTim*, *RBL/SBL*, and *NeoT* (*JNTSSA*).
5. Thiselton is contracted for a book on *The Holy Spirit* (Grand Rapids: Eerdmans, 2012).

## Select Bibliography of Writings by Other Authors

Achtemeier, P.J., *An Introduction to The New Hermeneutic* (Philadelphia: The Westminster Press, 1969).

Adam, A.K.M., 'Review of A.C. Thiselton's *New Horizons in Hermeneutics*', *ModTh* 10 (1994), 433-434.

— 'Review of A.C. Thiselton's *Interpreting God and the Postmodern Self*', *Interp* 51.4 (Oct. 1997), 436-438.

Adams, J.W., *The Performative Nature and Function of Isaiah 40-55* (Library of Hebrew Bible/OT Studies [formerly JSOT]; Edinburgh: T&T Clark, 2006).+

Alexander, T.D., and B.S. Rosner, eds., *New Dictionary of Biblical Theology* (Leicester: IVP, 2000).

Apel, K.-O., *Towards a Transformation of Philosophy* (trans. G. Adey & D. Fisby; Milwaukee: Marquette University Press, 1980, 1998).

Arnold, C.E., ed., *Romans to Philemon* (Grand Rapids, MI.: Zondervan, 2002).

Ashton, J., *Studying John: Approaches to the Fourth Gospel* (Oxford: Oxford University Press, 1998).

Astley, J., 'Review of A.C. Thiselton's *A Concise Encyclopedia of the Philosophy of Religion*', *BritJRE* 26.2 (Jun. 2004), 203-205.

Austin, J.L., *How to Do Things with Words. The William James Lectures delivered at Harvard University in 1955* (eds. J.O. Urmson & M. Sbisà; Oxford: OUP, 1962, 1975).

— 'Performative Utterances', in *Philosophical Papers* (eds. J.O. Urmson & G.J. Warnock; Oxford: OUP, 1979), 234-241.

Avis, P.D.L., 'Review of A.C. Thiselton's *Interpreting God and the Postmodern Self*', *ChTim* 8th Mar. (1996), 14.

— *God and the Creative Imagination: Metaphor, Symbol and Myth in Religion and Theology* (London: Routledge, 1999).

Barclay, J., '1 Corinthians', in *The Oxford Bible Commentary* (eds. J. Barton and J. Muddiman; Oxford: OUP, 2001), 1108-1133.*

Barnes, L.P., 'Light from the East? Ninian Smart and the Christian-Buddhist Encounter', *SJT* 40.1 (1987), 67-83.

Barr, J., 'Story and History in Biblical Theology', *JRel* 56 (1976), 1-17.

— 'Review of I.H. Marshall ed. *New Testament Interpretation*', *Th* 81.681 (May 1978), 234-235.

— 'Exegesis as a Theological Discipline Reconsidered and the Shadow of the Jesus of History', in *The Hermeneutical Quest: Essays in Honour of James Luther Mays* (ed. D.G. Miller; Princeton Theological Monograph 4; Allison Park, Pa: Pickwick Press, 1986), 11-45.

Barry, P., *Beginning Theory. An Introduction to Literary and Cultural Theory* (Manchester: Manchester University Press, 1995).

Barthes, R., *On Racine* (Eng. New York: Hill and Wang, 1964).

— *Elements of Semiology* (Eng. London: Jonathan Cape, 1967).

— *Writing Degree Zero* (Eng. London: Jonathan Cape, 1967).

— *S/Z* (Eng. London: Jonathan Cape, 1975).

— *The Pleasure of the Text* (Eng. London: Jonathan Cape, 1975).

— 'The Death of the Author', in *Image-Music-Text* (trans. S. Heath; New York: Hill and Wang, 1977).

— 'From Work to Text', in *Textual Strategies: Perspectives in Post-Structuralist Criticism* (ed. J.V. Harari; Ithaca: Cornell University Press, 1979), 73-81.

— *Criticism and Truth* (Eng. Minneapolis: University of Minnesota Press, 1987).

Bartholomew, C.G., 'Three Horizons: Hermeneutics from the Other End - An Evaluation of Anthony Thiselton's Hermeneutical Proposals', *EuJTh* 5.2 (1996), 121-135.

— *Reading Ecclesiastes: Old Testament Exegesis and Hermeneutical Theory* (Bristol: Unpublished University of Bristol PhD Thesis, 1996).

— *Reading Ecclesiastes: Old Testament Exegesis and Hermeneutical Theory* (Rome: Pontifical Biblical Institute, 1998).

— 'Uncharted Waters: Philosophy, Theology and the Crisis in Biblical Interpretation', in *Renewing Biblical Interpretation* (eds. C.G. Bartholomew, C. Greene and K. Möller; Scripture and Hermeneutics Series; Vol. 1; Carlisle: Paternoster, 2000), 1-39.

— with C. Greene and K. Möller, eds., *Renewing Biblical Interpretation* (Scripture and Hermeneutics Series; Vol. 1; Carlisle: Paternoster, 2000).

— 'Introduction', in *After Pentecost: Language and Biblical Interpretation* (eds. C.G. Bartholomew, C. Greene and K. Möller; Scripture and Hermeneutics Series; Vol. 2; Carlisle: Paternoster, 2001), xxi-xxxvi.

— 'Before Babel and After Pentecost', in *After Pentecost: Language and Biblical Interpretation* (eds. C.G. Bartholomew, C. Greene, and K. Möller; Scripture and Hermeneutics Series; Vol. 2; Carlisle: Paternoster, 2001), 131-170.

— with C. Greene and K. Möller, eds., *After Pentecost: Language and Biblical Interpretation* (Scripture and Hermeneutics Series; Vol. 2; Carlisle: Paternoster, 2001).

— 'Introduction', in, *A Royal Priesthood? A Dialogue with Oliver O'Donovan* (eds. C.G. Bartholomew, J. Chaplin, R. Song, and A. Wolters; Scripture and Hermeneutics Series; Vol. 3; Carlisle: Paternoster, 2002), 1-45.

— with J. Chaplin, R. Song, and A. Wolters, eds., *A Royal Priesthood? A Dialogue with Oliver O'Donovan* (Scripture and Hermeneutics Series; Vol. 3; Carlisle: Paternoster, 2002).

— 'Introduction', in *'Behind' the Text. History and Biblical Interpretation* (eds. C.G. Bartholomew, C.S. Evans, M. Healy, and M. Rae; Scripture and Hermeneutics Series; Vol. 4; Carlisle: Paternoster, 2003), 1-16.

— 'Warranted Biblical Interpretation', in *'Behind' the Text. History and Biblical Interpretation* (eds. C.G. Bartholomew, C.S. Evans, M. Healy, and M. Rae; Scripture and Hermeneutics Series; Vol. 4; Carlisle: Paternoster, 2003), 58-78.

— with C.S. Evans, M. Healy, and M. Rae, eds., *'Behind' the Text. History and Biblical Interpretation* (Scripture and Hermeneutics Series; Vol. 4; Carlisle: Paternoster, 2003).

Barton, J., and J. Muddiman, eds., *The Oxford Bible Commentary* (Oxford: OUP, 2001).

Barton, S.C., 'Living as Families in the Light of the New Testament', *Interp* 52.2 (Apr. 1998), 130-144.
— 'New Testament Interpretation as Performance', *SJT* 52.2 (1999), 179-208.
Bartsch, H.-W., ed., *Kerygma und Mythos. Ein Theologisches Gespräch* (6 Volumes with Supplements; Hamburg: Reich & Heidrich, Evangelischer Verlag, 1948 and onwards).
Bauckham, R., *Gospel Women: Studies of the Named Women in the Gospels* (Grand Rapids, MI.: Eerdmans, 2002).*$
Bebbington, D.W., *Evangelicalism in Modern Britain: A History from the 1730s to the 1980s* (London: Routledge, 1989).$
Beckwith, R.T., 'Review of B. Mitchell ed. *Believing in the Church. The Corporate Nature of the Faith. A Report by the Doctrine Commission of the Church of England*', *Chman* 96.3 (1982), 249-252.
BeDuhn, J.D., '"Because of the Angels": Unveiling Paul's Anthropology in 1 Corinthians 11', *JBLit* 118.2 (1999), 295-320.*£
Black, D.A., and D.S. Dockery, ed., *Interpreting the New Testament: Essays on Methods and Issues* (Nashville, TN.: Broadman & Holman Publishers, 2001).
Bloesch, D.G., *Holy Scripture: Revelation, Inspiration and Interpretation. Christian Foundations* (Downers Grove, Ill.: InterVarsity, 1994).
Blomberg, C.L., *Interpreting the Parables* (Leicester: IVP, 1990).
— 'Interpreting the Parables of Jesus: Where are We and Where Do We Go from Here?', *CBQ* 53.1 (1991), 50-78.
— 'Appendix: Neither Hierarchicalist nor Egalitarian: Gender Roles in Paul', in *Two Views on Women in Ministry* (eds. C.L. Blomberg *et al*; Grand Rapids, MI.: Zondervan, 2001), 329-372.$
— *et al*, eds., *Two Views on Women in Ministry* (Grand Rapids, MI.: Zondervan, 2001).
Bockmuehl, M., '"To be or not to be": The Possible Futures of New Testament Scholarship', *SJT* 51.3 (1998), 271-306.
Boring, M.E., 'The Language of Universal Salvation in Paul', *JBLit* 105.2 (Jun. 1986), 269-292.
Borsch, F.H., 'Review of A.C. Thiselton's *The Two Horizons*', *AThRev* 65 (Jan. 1983), 88-90.
Bowden, J., 'Review of A.C. Thiselton's *The Two Horizons*', *Th* 84.697 (Jan. 1981), 55-57.
Boyce, J.L., 'Review of J.B. Green ed. *Hearing the New Testament*', *WW* 16 (Sum. 1996), 378-382.
Braaten, C.E., and R.W. Jenson, eds., *A Map of Twentieth-Century Theology. Readings from Karl Barth to Radical Pluralism* (Minneapolis: Augsburg Press, 1995).
Bradshaw, T., ed., *The Way Forward: Christian Voices on Homosexuality and the Church* (London: Hodder and Stoughton, 1997).
Branson, M.L., and C.R. Padilla, eds., *Conflict and Context. Hermeneutics in the Americas* (Grand Rapids: Eerdmans, 1986).
Bray, G.L., 'Review of R. Lundin's, A.C. Thiselton's and C. Walhout's *The Responsibility of Hermeneutics*', *Chman* 100.3 (1986), 259-260.
— *Biblical Interpretation: Past and Present* (Leicester: Apollos, 1996, 2000).
Brett, M.G., 'Review of A.C. Thiselton's *New Horizons in Hermeneutics*', *Th* 96.772 (Jul./Aug. 1993), 314-315.
Briggs, R.S., *Words in Action. Speech-Act Theory and Biblical Interpretation. Toward a Hermeneutic of Self-Involvement* (Edinburgh: T&T Clark, 2001).
Brodie, L., 'Review Article of A.C. Thiselton's *The Two Horizons*', *Thom* 45.3 (1981), 480-486.
Brown, A.R., 'Review of A.C. Thiselton's *The First Epistle to the Corinthians*', *Interp* 56.1 (Jan.

2002), 104, 106.

Brown, C., ed., *The New International Dictionary of New Testament Theology. Volume 1* (Exeter: Paternoster; Grand Rapids: Zondervan, 1975).

— ed., *The New International Dictionary of New Testament Theology. Volume III* (Exeter: Paternoster; Grand Rapids: Zondervan, 1978).

— 'Review of A.C. Thiselton's *New Horizons in Hermeneutics*', *CalThJ* 30 (Apr. 1995), 232-237.

Browning, P.D., 'Review of A.C. Thiselton's *Interpreting God and the Postmodern Self*, *Enc* 58 (Spr. 1997), 220-222.

Brueggemann, W., 'Vine and Fig-Tree - A Case-Study in Imagination and Criticism', *CBQ* 43.2 (1981), 188-204.

Bruns, G.L., *Hermeneutics: Ancient and Modern* (Yale Studies in Hermeneutics; New Haven: Yale University Press, 1992).

Buber, M., *I and Thou* (trans. R.G. Smith; New York: Charles Scribner's Sons, 1958, second edition).

Buchanan, C., 'The Shifts at Gut Level', *CEN* 6 May (1977), 11.

Bultmann, R., *Theology of the New Testament. Volume 1* (trans. K. Grobel; London: SCM Press Ltd., 1952).

— 'Prophecy and Fulfilment', in *Essays Philosophical and Theological* (trans. J.C.G. Greig; New York: The MacMillan Company, 1955), 182-208.

— 'The Problem of Hermeneutics', in *Essays Philosophical and Theological* (trans. J.C.G. Greig; New York: The MacMillan Company, 1955), 234-261.

— 'Forms of Human Community', in *Essays Philosophical and Theological* (trans. J.C.G. Greig; New York: The MacMillan Company, 1955), 291-304.

— *Essays Philosophical and Theological* (trans. J.C.G. Greig; New York: The MacMillan Company, 1955).

— *Jesus Christ and Mythology* (New York: Charles Scribner's Sons, 1958).

— *Jesus and the Word* (trans. L.P. Smith and E.H. Lantero; London: Collins/Fontana Books, 1958).

— 'Concerning the Hidden and the Revealed God', in *Existence and Faith: Shorter Writings of Rudolf Bultmann* (ed. and trans. S.M. Ogden; New York: Meridian Books, Inc., 1960), 23-34.

— 'Romans 7 and the Anthropology of Paul', in *Existence and Faith. Shorter Writings of Rudolf Bultmann* (trans. and ed. S.M. Ogden; New York: Meridian Books, Inc., 1960), 147-157.

— 'Is Exegesis Without Presuppositions Possible?', in *Existence and Faith: Shorter Writings of Rudolf Bultmann* (ed. and trans. S.M. Ogden; New York: Meridian Books, Inc., 1960), 289-296.

— *Existence and Faith: Shorter Writings of Rudolf Bultmann* (ed. and trans. S.M. Ogden; New York: Meridian Books, Inc., 1960).

— 'New Testament and Mythology', in *Kerygma and Myth. A Theological Debate* (ed. H.-W. Bartsch; New York: Harper and Row, 1961), 1-44.

— 'A Reply to the Theses of J. Schniewind', in *Kerygma and Myth. A Theological Debate* (ed. H.-W. Bartsch; New York: Harper and Row, 1961), 102-123.

— 'Bultmann Replies to His Critics', in *Kerygma and Myth. A Theological Debate* (ed. H.-W. Bartsch; New York: Harper and Row, 1961), 191-211.

— *et al*, *Kerygma and Myth. A Theological Debate* (ed. H.-W. Bartsch; New York: Harper and Row, 1961).

— 'New Testament and Mythology: The Problem of Demythologising The New Testament Proclamation', in *New Testament and Mythology and Other Basic Writings* (ed. and trans. S.M. Ogden; Philadelphia: Fortress Press, 1984), 1-43.
— 'Theology as Science', in *New Testament and Mythology and Other Basic Writings* (ed. and trans. S.M. Ogden; Philadelphia: Fortress Press, 1984), 45-67.
— 'The Problem of Hermeneutics', in *New Testament and Mythology and Other Basic Writings* (ed. and trans. S.M. Ogden; Philadelphia: Fortress Press, 1984), 69-93.
— 'On the Problem of Demythologising (1952)', in *New Testament and Mythology and Other Basic Writings* (ed. and trans. S.M. Ogden; Philadelphia: Fortress, 1984), 95-130.
— 'Science and Existence', in *New Testament and Mythology and Other Basic Writings* (ed. and trans. S.M. Ogden; Philadelphia: Fortress Press, 1984), 131-144.
— 'Is Exegesis Without Presuppositions Possible? (1957)', in *New Testament and Mythology and Other Basic Writings* (ed. and trans. S.M. Ogden; Philadelphia: Fortress Press, 1984), 145-153.
— 'On the Problem of Demythologising (1961)', in *New Testament and Mythology and Other Basic Writings* (ed. and trans. S.M. Ogden; Philadelphia: Fortress Press, 1984), 155-163.
— *New Testament and Mythology and Other Basic Writings* (ed. and trans. S.M. Ogden; Philadelphia: Fortress Press, 1984).
Bush, L.R., 'Review of D.S. Dockery ed. *The Challenge of Postmodernism*', *FMn* 13 (Fall 1995), 129.
Byron, J., 'Review of A.C. Thiselton's *The First Epistle to the Corinthians*', *ThStud* 63.1 (Mar. 2002), 164-165.
Byworth, C., ed., *Using the Bible in Liturgy* (Nottingham: Grove, 1977).
Cahill, P.J., 'Review of A.C. Thiselton's *The Two Horizons*', *CBQ* 43.3 (Jul. 1981), 484-485.
Caldwell, L.W., 'Doing Theology Across Cultures: A New Methodology for an Old Task', *IJFMn* 4 (1987), 3-7.
— 'Third Horizon Ethnohermeneutics: Re-evaluating New Testament Hermeneutical Models for Intercultural Bible Interpreters Today', *AmJTh* 1 (1987), 314-333.+
Carson, D.A., 'Editorial Comments', in *New Testament Commentary Survey* (A.C. Thiselton; Leicester: TSF, 1976), 1-2.
— *New Testament Commentary Survey* (Leicester: IVP, 1984, 1993, 2001, and later).
— 'A Sketch of the Factors Determining Current Hermeneutical Debate in Cross-Cultural Contexts', in *Biblical Interpretation and the Church. Text and Context* (ed. D.A. Carson; Carlisle: Paternoster, 1984), 11-29.
— ed., *Biblical Interpretation and the Church. Text and Context* (Carlisle: Paternoster, 1984).
— *Exegetical Fallacies* (Grand Rapids, MI.: Baker Book House Company, 1984).
— 'Church and Mission: Reflections on Contextualization and the Third Horizon', in *The Church in the Bible and the World. An International Study* (ed. D.A. Carson; Exeter: The Paternoster Press, 1987), 213-257, 342-347.
— ed., *The Church in the Bible and the World. An International Study* (Exeter: The Paternoster Press, 1987).
— with D.J. Moo, and L. Morris, '1 and 2 Corinthians', in *An Introduction to the New Testament* (D.A. Carson, D.J. Moo, and L. Morris; Grand Rapids, MI.: Zondervan, 1992), 259-287.*£
— with D.J. Moo, and L. Morris, eds., *An Introduction to the New Testament* (Grand Rapids, MI.: Zondervan, 1992).
— and J.D. Woodbridge, eds., *God and Culture* (Grand Rapids: Eerdmans, 1993).

— *Bible Interpretation. Parts 1-4.* Tapes WA20-WA23. *Word Alive 1993* (Eastbourne: ICC, 1993).
— *Bible Interpretation. Parts 1-4.* Tapes WA12-1 - WA12-4. *Word Alive 1994* (Eastbourne: ICC, 1994).
— and J.D. Woodbridge, eds., *Scripture and Truth* (Carlisle: Paternoster, 1995).
— *The Gagging of God. Christianity Confronts Pluralism* (Leicester: IVP/Apollos, 1996).
Carver Jr., F.G., 'A Working Model for Teaching Exegesis', in *Interpreting God's Word for Today* (eds. W. McCown and J.E. Massey; Anderson, Ind.: Warner Press, 1982), 221-247.
Charry, E.T., 'Review of A.C. Thiselton's *Interpreting God and the Postmodern Self*', *ThT* 54.1 (Apr. 1997), 106, 108, 110.
Chartier, G., 'Review of D.S. Dockery ed. *The Challenge of Postmodernism*', *AUSStud* 35 (Spr. 1997), 111-114.
Childs, B.S., 'Foreword', in *Renewing Biblical Interpretation* (eds. C.G. Bartholomew, C. Greene and K. Möller; Scripture and Hermeneutics Series; Vol. 1; Carlisle: Paternoster, 2000), xv-xvii.
Clack, B.R., 'Review of A.C. Thiselton's *Interpreting God and the Postmodern Self*', *RelStud* 32 (Sep. 1996), 428.
Clarke, A.D., *Serve the Community of the Church: Christians As Leaders and Ministers* (First-Century Christians in the Graeco-Roman World; Grand Rapids, MI.: Eerdmans, 2000).*£
Clendenen, E.R., 'Postholes, Postmodernism, and the Prophets', in *The Challenge of Postmodernism. An Evangelical Engagement* (ed. D.S. Dockery; Grand Rapids, Mi.: Baker Books, 1997), 132-147.
Cobb, K., 'Review of A.C. Thiselton's *Interpreting God and the Postmodern Self*', *JRel* 78.2 (1998), 304-305.
Collins, J. and H. Selina, *Introducing Heidegger* (ed. R. Appignanesi; New York, NY.: Totem Books, 1999).
Colson, C., and R.J. Neuhaus, eds., *Your Word Is Truth: A Project of Evangelicals and Catholics Together* (Grand Rapids, MI.: Eerdmans, 2002).
Colwell, J.E., 'Perspectives on Judas: Barth's Implicit Hermeneutic', in *Interpreting the Bible: Historical and Theological Studies in Honour of David F. Wright* (ed. A.N.S. Lane; Leicester: Apollos, 1997), 163-179.
Conn, H.M., 'Normativity, Relevance, and Relativism', in *Inerrancy and Hermeneutics: A Tradition, A Challenge, A Debate* (ed. H.M. Conn; Grand Rapids: Baker, 1988), 185-209.
— ed., *Inerrancy and Hermeneutics: A Tradition, A Challenge, A Debate* (Grand Rapids: Baker, 1988).
Conroy, C., 'Review of A.C. Thiselton's *The Two Horizons*', *Greg* 62.3 (1981), 563-566.
Corduan, W., 'Humility and Commitment: An Approach to Modern Hermeneutics', *Them* NS11.3 (Apr. 1986), 83-88.
Corley, J., 'The Pauline Authorship of 1 Corinthians 13' *CBQ* 66.2 (Apr. 2004), 256-274.*
Couser, G.A., 'God and Christian Existence in the Pastoral Epistles: Toward Theological Method and Meaning (Observations on Pauline Christological Sophistication and His Conception of Divinity)' *NovTm* 42.3 (2000), 262-283.*£
Craig, E., ed., *Routledge Encyclopedia of Philosophy* (London: Routledge, 1998).
Cray, G., *et al*, *The Post-Evangelical Debate* (London: SPCK Triangle, 1997).
Critchley, S., 'Introduction: What is Continental Philosophy?', in *A Companion to Continental Philosophy* (eds. S. Critchley and W.R. Schroeder; Blackwell Companions to Philosophy Series; Oxford: Blackwell Publishers Ltd., 1998), 1-17.

Crowe, P., 'Developed and Improved Model', *CEN* 6 May (1977), 10.
Culler, J., *On Deconstruction. Theory and Criticism after Structuralism* (London: Routledge, 1983, 1998).
Dare, H. and S. Woodman, eds., *The "Plainly Revealed" Word of God? Baptist Hermeneutics in Theory and Practice* (Macon, Georgia, USA: Mercer University Press, 2011).
Dautzenberg, G., 'Review of A.C. Thiselton's *The First Epistle to the Corinthians*', *BibZ* 46.1 (2002), 143-148.$
Davies, H., 'Review of B. Mitchell ed. *Believing in the Church. The Corporate Nature of the Faith. A Report by the Doctrine Commission of the Church of England*', *ThT* 39 (Jan. 1983), 462-464.
Davies, M., 'Review of R. Lundin's, A.C. Thiselton's and C. Walhout's *The Responsibility of Hermeneutics*', *Th* 90 (Jan. 1987), 68-69.
Dawson, D., 'Review of A.C. Thiselton's *Interpreting God and the Postmodern Self*', *PEcc* 7 (Sep. 1998), 248-249.
Dayton, D.W., 'The Church in the World. The Battle for the Bible Rages On', *ThT* E37 (1980), 79-84.
de Silva Goncalves, J.L., 'The Deconstructing of the American Mind', *Prem* 2.8 (Sep. 27 1995), 11-26.
Dean, W., 'The Challenge of the New Historicism', *JRel* 66 (1986), 261-281.
Debanné, M., 'Review of A.C. Thiselton's *Interpreting God and the Postmodern Self*', *ARC* 25 (1997), 161-163.
Deidun, T., 'The Bible and Christian Ethics', in *Christian Ethics: An Introduction* (ed. B. Hoose; Collegeville, MN.: Michael Glazier Books, 1998), 3-47.$
Deming, W., *Paul on Marriage and Celibacy: The Hellenistic Background of 1 Corinthians 7* (Grand Rapids, MI.: Eerdmans, 2004).*£
Derrida, J., 'Différance', in *Speech and Phenomena and Other Essays on Husserl's Theory of Signs* (trans. D.B. Allison; Evanston: Northwestern University Press, 1973; Fr. 1967), 129-160.
— *Speech and Phenomena, and Other Essays on Husserl's Theory of Signs* (trans. D.B. Allison; Eng. Evanston: North Western University Press, 1973; Fr. 1967).
— *Of Grammatology* (Eng. trans. G.C. Spivak; Baltimore, London: The Johns Hopkins University Press, 1974, 1976, 1997 corrected edition; Fr. 1967).
— *Writing and Difference* (Eng. trans. A. Bass; London: Routledge and Kegan Paul, 1978, 2001; Fr. 1967).
— 'Signature Event Context', *Gly* 1 (1977), 172-197.
— 'Limited Inc abc...', *Gly* 2 (1977), 162-254.
— *Positions* (Chicago: University of Chicago Press, 1981).
— *Margins of Philosophy* (trans. A. Bass; Brighton: The Harvester Press, 1982).
— *Limited Inc* (ed. G. Graf; Evanston, Il: Northwestern University Press, 1990).
Dockery, D.S., 'Review of A.C. Thiselton's *The Two Horizons*', *GThJ* 4.1 (Spr. 1983), 133-136.
— ed., *The Challenge of Postmodernism. An Evangelical Engagement* (Grand Rapids, Mi.: Baker Books, 1997).
— 'New Testament Interpretation: A Historical Survey', in *Interpreting the New Testament: Essays on Methods and Issues* (eds. D.A. Black and D.S. Dockery; Nashville, TN.: Broadman & Holman Publishers, 2001), 21-45.
Doriani, D.M., *Women and Ministry: What the Bible Teaches* (Wheaton, IL.: Crossway Books, 2003).
Douglas, J.D., 'NEAC Remembers Church of Uganda. Charter of Evangelical Purpose', *CEN* 22 Apr. (1977), 1.

— 'Question of Prophecy', *CEN*, 22 Apr. (1977), 7.
— 'Hermeneutical Hazards. NEAC '77 Report', *CEN* 22 Apr. (1977), 9.$
— 'Where Did the Leaders Go?' *CEN*, 22 Apr. (1977), 9.
Dowley, T., *et al*, eds., *The History of Christianity. A Lion Handbook* (Tring, Hertfordshire: Lion Publishing, 1977).
Dray, S., 'Review of R. Lundin's, C. Walhout's and A.C. Thiselton's *The Promise of Hermeneutics*', *Egel*, 18.3 (Aut. 2000), 96.
Dreyer, Y., *The Institutionalisation of Jesus' Charismatic Authority: 'Son of Man' as Case Study I* (Pretoria: Contributory PhD dissertation, Faculty of Theology, University of Pretoria; 2000), 1-19. At *http://www.up.ac.za/academic/theology/eng/*.
Dudley-Smith, T., *John Stott: A Global Ministry: A Biography of the Later Years* (Leicester: IVP, 2001).
Duffy, K., 'The Ecclesial Hermeneutic of Raymond E. Brown', *HeyJ 39*.1 (Jan. 1998), 37-56.
Dunn, E.A., *Beyond Dialogue and History: The Hermeneutical Pluralism of Anthony C. Thiselton and his Metacritical Use of the Cross and Resurrection of Christ* (Hamilton, Mass.: Gordon-Conwell Seminary M.A. Thesis, May 1998).
Dunn, J.D.G., 'The Authority of Scripture According to Scripture. Part 1', *Chman* 96.2 (1982), 104-122.
— 'The Authority of Scripture According to Scripture. Part 2', *Chman* 96.3 (1982), 201-225.
— 'What Makes a Good Exposition? The Expository Times Lecture, June 2002' *ExTim* 114.5 (Feb. 2003), 147-157.
— and J.W. Rogerson, eds., *Eerdmans Commentary on the Bible* (Grand Rapids, MI.: Eerdmans, 2003).
Dyrness, W.A., 'Review of A.C. Thiselton's *The Two Horizons*', *CTday* 25 (Apr. 10, 1981), 94.
Eagleton, T., *Literary Theory. An Introduction* (Oxford: Blackwell, 1983, 2nd edition, 1996).
Ebeling, G., 'The Meaning of 'Biblical Theology'', in *Word and Faith* (trans. J.W. Leitch; Philadelphia: Fortress Press, Chatham: SCM Press Ltd, 1963), 79-97.
— 'The Question of the Historical Jesus and the Problem of Christology. To Rudolf Bultmann on his 75th Birthday', in *Word and Faith* (trans. J.W. Leitch; Philadelphia: Fortress Press, Chatham: SCM Press Ltd, 1963), 288-304.
— 'The World as History. To Fritz Blanke on his 60th Birthday', in *Word and Faith* (trans. J.W. Leitch; Philadelphia: Fortress Press, Chatham: SCM Press Ltd, 1963), 363-373.
— *Theology and Proclamation: A Discussion with Rudolf Bultmann* (trans. J. Riches; London: Collins, 1966), 25-26.
Edmonds, D., and J. Eidinow, *Wittgenstein's Poker: The Story of a Ten-Minute Argument between Two Great Philosophers* (London: Faber and Faber, 2001).
Ellingworth, P., 'Review of A.C. Thiselton's *The Two Horizons*', *EvanQ* 53 (Jul.-Sep. 1981), 178-179.
— 'Theory and Practice in Bible Translation', *EvanQ* 55 (Jul. 1983), 159-167.
Ellis, E.E., 'Review of A.C. Thiselton's *The First Epistle to the Corinthians*', *SWJTh* 44.1 (Fall 2001), 113.
Ellwood, R., 'Review of A.C. Thiselton's *A Concise Encyclopedia of The Philosophy of Religion*', *TQuest* Jan./Feb. (2004), page-numbers not ascertained.+
Erickson, M.J., 'Review of A.C. Thiselton's *The Two Horizons*', *JEThS* 23 (Dec. 1980), 371-373.
Evans, D.D., The Logic of Self-Involvement. A Philosophical Study of Everyday Language with Special Reference to the Christian Use of Language about God as Creator (London: SCM Press, 1963).

Fackre, G., 'The Use of Scripture in My Work in Systematics', in *The Use of the Bible in Theology: Evangelical Options* (ed. R.K. Johnston; Atlanta: John Knox, 1985), 200-226, 241-248.
— 'Evangelical Hermeneutics: Commonality and Diversity', *Interp* 43 (1989), 117-129.
— 'Narrative: Evangelical, Postliberal, Ecumenical', in *The Nature of Confession: Evangelicals and Postliberals in Conversation* (eds. G.A. Lindbeck, D.L. Okholm and T.R. Phillips; Downers Grove, Ill.: IVP, 1996), 123-134, 278-279.
Fee, G.D., 'Εἰδωλόθυτα Once Again: An Interpretation of 1 Corinthians 8-10', *Bib* 61 (1980), 172-197.*£
— *The First Epistle to the Corinthians* (The New International Commentary on the New Testament; Grand Rapids, MI.: Eerdmans, 1987).*£
— *To What End Exegesis: Essays Textual, Exegetical, and Theological* (Grand Rapids, MI.: Eerdmans, 2001).*£
Fergusson, D., 'Review of A.C. Thiselton's *Interpreting God and the Postmodern Self*', *Th* 99.792 (Nov. - Dec. 1996), 462-463.
— 'Introduction', in *The Future as God's Gift: Explorations in Christian Eschatology* (eds. D. Fergusson and M. Sarot; Edinburgh: T&T Clark, 2000), 1-7.
— and M. Sarot, eds., *The Future as God's Gift: Explorations in Christian Eschatology* (Edinburgh: T&T Clark, 2000).
— 'Barth's 'Resurrection of the Dead': Further Reflections', *SJT* 56.1 (2003), 65-72.*£
Ferreira, J., 'Review of A.C. Thiselton's *The First Epistle to the Corinthians*', *ERevTh* 26.1 (Jan. 2002), 93-95.*£
Fish, S., 'Introduction, or How I Stopped Worrying and Learned to Love Interpretation', in *Is There a Text in This Class? The Authority of Interpretative Communities* (S. Fish; London: Harvard University Press, 1980), 1-17.
— 'Normal Circumstances, Literal Language, Direct Speech Acts, the Ordinary, the Everyday, the Obvious, What Goes without Saying, and Other Special Cases', in *Is There a Text in This Class? The Authority of Interpretative Communities* (S. Fish; London: Harvard University Press, 1980), 268-292.
Fisher, R., 'Review of A.C. Thiselton's *A Concise Encyclopedia of the Philosophy of Religion*', *RevRelTh* 10.4 (Sep. 2003), 473-475.
Fisk, B.N., 'ΠΟΡΝΕΥΕΙΝ as Body Violation: The Unique Nature of Sexual Sin in 1 Corinthians 6:18', *NTStud* 42.4 (1996), 540-558.*£
Fitzmyer, J.A., 'Another look at Kephale in 1 Corinthians 11:3', *NTStud* 35.4 (Oct. 1989), 503-511.
Forbes, C., *Prophecy and Inspired Speech in Early Christianity and Its Hellenistic Environment* (Philadelphia: Coronet Books, Inc., 1995).*£
Ford, D.F., ed., *The Modern Theologians. An Introduction to Christian Theology in the Twentieth Century* (Oxford: Blackwell, 1997 and 2005 editions).
Forrest, R., 'Review of A.C. Thiselton's *Interpreting God and the Postmodern Self*', *ERevTh* 22 (Jan. 1998), 82-83.
Fotion, N.G., 'Logical Positivism', in *The Oxford Companion to Philosophy* (ed. T. Honderich; Oxford: OUP, 1995), 507-508.
Fowl, S.E., 'The Role of Authorial Intention in the Theological Interpretation of Scripture', in *Between Two Horizons. Spanning New Testament Studies and Systematic Theology* (eds. J.B. Green and M. Turner; Cambridge: Eerdmans, 2000), 71-87.
Fretheim, T.E., 'Old Testament Commentaries: Their Selection and Use', *Interp* 36.4 (1982), 356-371.

Fuchs, E., 'Preface to the English Edition', in *Studies of the Historical Jesus* (Studies in Biblical Theology; Naperville, Ill.: A.R. Allenson, Inc, & Chatham: SCM Press Ltd, 1964), 7-8.
— 'The Theology of the New Testament and the Historical Jesus', in *Studies of the Historical Jesus* (Studies in Biblical Theology; Naperville, Ill.: A.R. Allenson, Inc, & Chatham: SCM Press Ltd, 1964), 167-190.
— 'The New Testament and the Hermeneutical Problem', in *New Frontiers in Theology. Discussions among Continental and American Theologians, Volume II: The New Hermeneutic* (eds. J.M. Robinson and J.B. Cobb, Jr.; New York: Harper and Row, 1964), 111-145.
— 'Response to the American Discussion', in *New Frontiers in Theology. Discussions among Continental and American Theologians, Volume II: The New Hermeneutic* (eds. J.M. Robinson and J.B. Cobb, Jr.; New York: Harper and Row, 1964), 232-243.
Funk, R.W., *Language, Hermeneutic, and Word of God. The Problem of Language in the New Testament and Contemporary Theology* (New York: Harper and Row, 1966).
Gadamer, H.-G., *Truth and Method* (trans. J. Weinsheimer and D.G. Marshall; London: Sheed & Ward, 1975, 1989).
— 'Aesthetics and Hermeneutics', in *Philosophical Hermeneutics* (H.-G. Gadamer; ed. D.E. Linge; London: University of California Press, 1976), 95-104.
— 'The Philosophical Foundations of the Twentieth Century', in *Philosophical Hermeneutics* (H.-G. Gadamer; ed. D.E. Linge; London: University of California Press, 1976), 107-129.
— 'The Phenomenological Movement', in *Philosophical Hermeneutics* (H.-G. Gadamer; ed. D.E. Linge; London: University of California Press, 1976), 130-181.
— 'Martin Heidegger and Marburg Theology', in *Philosophical Hermeneutics* (H.-G. Gadamer; ed. D.E. Linge; London: University of California Press, 1976), 198-212.
— 'Heidegger's Later Philosophy', in *Philosophical Hermeneutics* (H.-G. Gadamer; ed. D.E. Linge; London: University of California Press, 1976), 213-228.
— 'Heidegger and the Language of Metaphysics', in *Philosophical Hermeneutics* (H.-G. Gadamer; ed. D.E. Linge; London: University of California Press, 1976), 229-240.
Gaffin, R., 'Atonement in the Pauline Corpus: The Scandal of the Cross', in *The Glory of the Atonement: Biblical, Historical & Practical Perspectives: Essays in Honour of Roger R. Nicole* (eds. Hill, C.E., F.A. James, and R.R. Nicole; Leicester: IVP, 2004), 140-162.*
Geisler, N.L., 'Review of A.C. Thiselton's *The Two Horizons*', *BibSac* 138 (Apr.-Jun. 1981), 182-183.
Gerado, A., Review of A.C. Thiselton's *The First Epistle to the Corinthians*', *Kai* 33 (Jul.-Dec. 2003), 127-129.
Gibson, A., *Biblical Semantic Logic: A Preliminary Analysis* (Oxford: Blackwell, 1981).
— *God and the Universe* (London: Routledge, 2000).
Gifford, P., D. Archard, T.A. Hart, and N. Rapport, 'Conclusion: Dialogue on the 'Common Era'', in *2000 Years and Beyond. Faith, Identity and the 'Common Era'* (eds. P. Gifford, D. Archard, T.A. Hart, and N. Rapport; London and New York: Routledge, 2003), 147-190.
— with D. Archard, T.A. Hart, and N. Rapport, eds., *2000 Years and Beyond. Faith, Identity and the 'Common Era'* (London and New York: Routledge, 2003).
Giles, K., *The Trinity & Subordinationism: The Doctrine of God and the Contemporary Gender Debate* (Leicester: IVP, 2002).$
Gill, D.W.J., '1 Corinthians', in *Romans to Philemon* (ed. C.E. Arnold; Grand Rapids, MI.: Zondervan, 2002), 100-193.
Gladwin, J., 'Fear of What Change Will Mean?', *CEN* 6 May (1977), 11.

Goddard, J.M. ed., 'Review of A.C. Thiselton's *The First Epistle to the Corinthians*', *NB* 8.1 (Feb.-Apr. 2001), 4.

Goldingay, J., 'Interpreting Scripture', *Anv* 1 (1984), 261-281.

— *Models for Interpretation of Scripture* (Carlisle: Paternoster; Grand Rapids: Eerdmans, 1995).

Goldsworthy, G., 'Review of P.E. Satterthwaite and D.F. Wright eds. *A Pathway into the Holy Scripture*', *RefThRev* 55 (Jan.-Apr. 1996), 40-41.

Grech, P., 'Review of A.C. Thiselton's *The Two Horizons*', *Bib* 63.4 (1982), 572-576.

Green, B., 'Richard Lints' Fabric and the Question of Postmodernity', *Prem* 4.3 (Oct. 1997), 1-9.

Green, J.B., and M. Turner, eds., *Jesus of Nazareth. Lord and Christ* (Grand Rapids: Eerdmans; Carlisle: Paternoster Press, 1994).

— ed., *Hearing the New Testament: Strategies for Interpretation* (Grand Rapids: Eerdmans; Carlisle: Paternoster Press, 1995).

— and M. Turner, eds., Between Two Horizons. Spanning New Testament Studies and Systematic Theology (Cambridge: Eerdmans, 2000).

Greene, C.J.D., *Christology in Cultural Perspective: Marking Out the Horizons* (Grand Rapids, MI.: Eerdmans, 2004).

Grindheim, S., 'Wisdom for the Perfect: Paul's Challenge to the Corinthian Church in 1 Corinthians 2:6-16', *JBLit* 121.4 (Wint. 2002), 689-709.*

Grondin, J., *Introduction to Philosophical Hermeneutics* (trans. J. Weinsheimer; Yale Studies in Hermeneutics; New Haven: Yale University Press, 1994).

— *Hans-Georg Gadamer: A Biography* (trans. J. Weinsheimer; New Haven and London: Yale University Press, 2003).

Grudem, W.A., 'The Meaning of κεφαλη ('Head'): An Evaluation of New Evidence, Real and Alleged', in *Biblical Foundations for Manhood and Womanhood* (ed. W.A. Grudem; Foundations for the Family Series; Wheaton, IL.: Crossway Books, 2002), 145-202.§

— ed., *Biblical Foundations for Manhood and Womanhood* (Foundations for the Family Series; Wheaton, IL.: Crossway Books, 2002).§

Gruneberg, K., 'Review of R. Lundin's, C. Walhout's and A.C. Thiselton's *The Promise of Hermeneutics*', *Anv* 17.3 (2000), 222-223.

Gulley, N.R., 'Reader-Response Theories in Postmodern Hermeneutics: A Challenge to Evangelical Theology', in *The Challenge of Postmodernism. An Evangelical Engagement* (ed. D.S. Dockery; Grand Rapids, Mi.: Baker Books, 1997), 208-238.

Gunderson, S.R., 'Thiselton, Anthony C.', in *Dictionary of Biblical Criticism and Interpretation* (ed. S.E. Porter; London & New York: Routledge, 2007), 356-357.

Gunn, D.M., 'Deutero-Isaiah and the Flood', *JBLit* 94 (1975), 493-508.

Gunton, C.E., *The One, the Three, and the Many: God, Creation, and the Culture of Modernity. The 1992 Bampton Lectures* (CUP, Cambridge, 1993).

Guthrie, D., *New Testament Introduction* (Leicester: IVP, 1990).*£

Guthrie, G.H., 'Boats in the Bay: Reflections on the Use of Linguistics and Literary Analysis in Biblical Studies', in *Linguistics and the New Testament. Critical Junctures* (eds. S.E. Porter & D.A. Carson; Journal for the Study of the New Testament Supplement Series 168: Studies in New Testament Greek 5; Sheffield: Sheffield Academic Press, 1999), 23-35.

Habermas, J., *Knowledge and Human Interests* (trans. J.J. Shapiro; London: Heinemann, 1972).

— *The Theory of Communicative Action. Volume 2. Lifeworld and System: A Critique of Functionalist Reason* (trans. T. McCarthy; Cambridge: Polity Press, 1987).

Hacker, P.M.S., 'Wittgenstein, Ludwig Josef Johann', in *The Oxford Companion to Philosophy* (ed. T. Honderich; Oxford: OUP, 1995), 912-916.

Hall, R.L., 'Review of A.C. Thiselton's *Interpreting God and the Postmodern Self*', *IJPhRel* 42.2 (Oct. 1997), 121-123.

Hammett, J.S., 'Review of D.S. Dockery ed. *The Challenge of Postmodernism*', *FMn* 14 (Spr. 1997), 93-94.

Hannaford, R., 'The Knowledge of Things Hoped For: Towards an Eschatology of Knowledge' (unpublished paper presented to the 2002 Conference of the Society of the Study of Theology at Lancaster University).

Hardy, D.W., 'Eschatology as a Challenge for Theology', in *The Future as God's Gift: Explorations in Christian Eschatology* (eds. D. Fergusson and M. Sarot; Edinburgh: T&T Clark, 2000), 151-158.

Harrington, D.J., 'Biblical Hermeneutics in Recent Discussion: New Testament', *RelStudRev* 10 (Jan. 1984), 7-10.

Harris, H.A., 'Living with Eschatological Hope. Conference Response', in *The Future as God's Gift: Explorations in Christian Eschatology* (eds. D. Fergusson and M. Sarot; Edinburgh: T&T Clark, 2000), 145-149.

Harrison, J.R., 'The Fading Crown: Divine Honour and the Early Christians', *JThStud* 54.2 (Oct. 2003), 493-529.*£

Harrisville, R.A., 'Review of A.C. Thiselton's *The Two Horizons*', *Interp* 36 (Apr. 1982), 216-217.

Hart, T.A., 'Review of A.C. Thiselton's *Interpreting God and the Postmodern Self*', *ExTim* 107.9 (Jun. 1996), 282.

Hartlich, C., and W. Sachs, *Der Ursprung des Mythosbegriffes in der Modernen Bibelwissenschaft* (Tübingen: Mohr, 1952).

Hays, R.B., 'The Conversion of the Imagination: Scripture and Eschatology in 1 Corinthians' *NTStud* 45.3 (1999), 391-412.*£

Heard Jr., W.J., 'Eschatologically Oriented Psychology', in *God and Culture* (eds. D.A. Carson and J. Woodbridge; Grand Rapids: Eerdmans, 1993), 106-133.

Hegel, G.W.F., *Phenomenology of Spirit*, Sections 3.1 & 3.2, Paragraphs 106 and 107, in *Hegel's Phenomenology of Spirit: Selections* (ed. & trans. H.P. Kainz; University Park, PA.: The Pennsylvania State University Press, 1994), 37-38.

Heidegger, M., *An Introduction to Metaphysics* (New York: Yale University Press/Anchor Books, 1959). This is an earlier edition of the title, *Introduction to Metaphysics*.

— *Poetry, Language, Thought* (trans. A. Hofstadter; New York: HarperCollins, 1971).

— *Introduction to Metaphysics* (trans. G. Fried and R. Polt; London: Yale University Press, 2000).

— *Being and Time* (trans. J. Macquarrie and E. Robinson; Oxford: Blackwell, 1962, 2001).

Hénaff, M., 'Lévi-Strauss', in *A Companion to Continental Philosophy* (eds. S. Critchley and W.R. Schroeder; Blackwell Companions to Philosophy Series; Oxford: Blackwell Publishers Ltd., 1998), 507-518.

Henry, C.F.H., 'Postmodernism: The New Spectre?', in *The Challenge of Postmodernism. An Evangelical Engagement* (ed. D.S. Dockery; Grand Rapids, Mi.: Baker Books, 1997), 34-52.

Hepburn, R.W., 'Objectivism and Subjectivism, Ethical', in *The Oxford Companion to Philosophy* (ed. T. Honderich; Oxford: OUP, 1995), 631-632.

Hess, R.S., 'New Horizons in Hermeneutics: A Review Article', *Them* 18.2 (Jan. 1993), 22-24.

Heyduck, R., *The Recovery of Doctrine in the Contemporary Church: An Essay in Philosophical*

*Ecclesiology* (Waco, Texas: Baylor University Press, 2002).
Hill, C.E., F.A. James, and R.R. Nicole, eds., *The Glory of the Atonement: Biblical, Historical & Practical Perspectives : Essays in Honour of Roger R. Nicole* (Leicester: IVP, 2004).
Hirsch Jr., E.D., *Validity in Interpretation* (New Haven and London: Yale University Press, 1967).
— 'Three Dimensions of Hermeneutics', *NLitHist* 3 (1972), 245-261.
Hogan, J.P., 'Hermeneutics and the Logic of Question and Answer - Collingwood and Gadamer', *HeyJ* 28.3 (Jul. 1987), 263-284.
Honderich, T., ed., *The Oxford Companion to Philosophy* (Oxford: OUP, 1995).
Hoose, B., ed., *Christian Ethics: An Introduction* (Collegeville, MN.: Michael Glazier Books, 1998).
Horrell, D.G., 'Review of A.C. Thiselton's *The First Epistle to the Corinthians*', *JBLit* 121.1 (Spr. 2002), 183-186.*£
— 'Who are 'the Dead' and When was the Gospel Preached to Them? The Interpretation of 1 Peter 6:6', *NTStud* 49.1 (Jan. 2003), 70-89.*
Howard, R., *The Rise and Fall of the Nine O'Clock Service. A Cult within the Church?* (London: Mowbray, 1996).
Hubbard, R.L., 'Jai Alai, Hermeneutics, and Isaianic Peace', in *Conflict and Context. Hermeneutics in the Americas* (eds. M.L. Branson and C.R. Padilla; Grand Rapids: Eerdmans, 1986), 185-204.
Hurding, R.F., *Pathways to Wholeness. Pastoral Care in a Postmodern Age* (London: Hodder & Stoughton, 1998).
Hynson, L. O., 'Review of R. Lundin's, A.C. Thiselton's and C. Walhout's *The Responsibility of Hermeneutics*', *ChSRev* 18.1 (1988), 90-91.
Ingraffia, B.D., *Postmodern Theory and Biblical Theology: Vanquishing God's Shadow* (Cambridge: CUP, 1995).
— 'Deconstructing the Tower of Babel: Ontotheology and the Postmodern Bible', in *Renewing Biblical Interpretation* (eds. C.G. Bartholomew, C. Greene and K. Möller; Scripture and Hermeneutics Series; Vol. 1; Carlisle: Paternoster, 2000), 284-306.
— and T.E. Pickett, 'Reviving the Power of Biblical Language: The Bible, Literature, and Literary Language', in *After Pentecost: Language and Biblical Interpretation* (eds. C.G. Bartholomew, C. Greene and K. Möller; Scripture and Hermeneutics Series; Vol. 2; Carlisle: Paternoster, 2001), 241-262.
Jansen, H., 'Poetics and the Bible - Facts and Biblical Hermeneutics (Revisioning an 'Interpreted' Literary-Historical Approach to Holy Scripture)', *NZSThRelPh* 41.1 (1999), 22-38.
Jasper, D., 'The New Testament and Literary Interpretation', *RelLit* 17.3 (Fall 1985), 1-10.
Jeanrond, W.G., 'Review of R. Lundin's, A.C. Thiselton's and C. Walhout's *The Responsibility of Hermeneutics*', *LitTh* 1.1 (Mar. 1987), 115-117.
— *Text and Interpretation as Categories of Theological Thinking* (Dublin: Gill and MacMillan, 1988).
Jensen, P.T., 'Review of R. Lundin's, A.C. Thiselton's and C. Walhout's *The Responsibility of Hermeneutics*', *Ety* 37.6 (Jun. 1986), 49.
Jervis, L.A., "But I Want You to Know...' Paul's Midrashic Intertextual Response to the Corinthian Worshippers (1 Cor. 11:2-16), *JBLit* 112.2 (1993), 231-246.§
Johnson, A.F., *1 Corinthians* (ed. G.R. Osborne; The IVP New Testament Commentary Series; Downer's Grove, ILL.: IVP, 2004).§
Johnson, E.E., *Expository Hermeneutics* (Grand Rapids: Zondervan, 1990).

— 'Review of A.C. Thiselton's *New Horizons in Hermeneutics*', *BibSac* 150.600 (Oct.-Dec. 1993), 501-502.
Johnston, R.K., 'Interpreting Scripture: Literary Criticism and Evangelical Hermeneutics', *ChLit* 32.1 (1982), 33-47.
— ed., *The Use of the Bible in Theology: Evangelical Options* (Atlanta: John Knox, 1985).
Jones, I.H., 'Disputed Questions in Biblical Studies 4. Exile and Eschatology' *ExTim* 112.12 (Sep. 2001), 401-405.*£
— 'Review of A.C. Thiselton's *The First Epistle to the Corinthians*', *JThStud* 53.1 (Apr. 2002), 231-235.*£
Kaiser Jr., W.C., 'Obeying the Word', in *An Introduction to Biblical Hermeneutics: The Search for Meaning* (eds. W.C. Kaiser and M. Silva; Grand Rapids: Zondervan, 1994), 173-192.
— and M. Silva, eds., An Introduction to Biblical Hermeneutics: The Search for Meaning (Grand Rapids, MI.: Zondervan, 1994).
Kallenberg, B., 'The Gospel Truth of Relativism', *SJT* 53.2 (2000), 177-211.
Karpman, S.B., 'Fairy Tales and Script Drama Analysis', *TAB* 7.26 (Apr. 1968), 39-43, also at: *http://www.karpmandramatriangle.com/pdf/DramaTriangle.pdf*.
Kaye, B.N., 'Strauss, D.F. and the European Theological Tradition - Der Ishariotismus unsere Tag', *JRelHist* 17.2 (1992), 172-193.
— 'Authority and The Interpretation of Scripture in Hooker's *Of the Laws of Ecclesiastical Polity*', *JRelHist* 21.1 (1997), 80-109.
Kearney, P.J., 'He Appeared to 500 Brothers (1 Cor. 15:6)', *NovTm* 22 (1980), 264-284.*£
Kearsley, R., 'Review of A.C. Thiselton's *Interpreting God and the Postmodern Self*, *SBEvanT* 19.2 (Aut. 2001), 239-240.
Keeley, R, *et al*, eds., *Exploring The Christian Faith: A Contemporary Handbook of What Christians Believe and Why* (Nelson's Christian Cornerstone Series; Nashville, TN.: Nelson Reference, 1996).
Keifert, P.R., 'Review of A.C. Thiselton's *The Two Horizons*', *WW* 1 (Fall 1981), 407-409.
Kierkegaard, S.A., *Fear and Trembling. Dialectical Lyric by Johannes De Silentio* (trans. A. Hanney; London: Penguin, 1985).
— *The Sickness Unto Death. A Christian Psychological Exposition for Edification and Awakening, by Anti-Climacus* (trans. A. Hannay; London: Penguin, 1989).
Kimmerle, H., ed., *Hermeneutics: The Handwritten Manuscripts* (F.D.E. Schleiermacher; trans. J. Duke & J. Forstman; AAR Texts and Translations 1; Atlanta: Scholars Press, 1977).
King, J., 'Congress Statement. NEAC '77 Report', *CEN* 22 Apr. (1977), 10.
— 'Decent Lack of Respect', *CEN* 6 May (1977), 10.
King, M., *Heidegger's Philosophy. A Guide to His Basic Thought* (Oxford: Blackwell, 1964).
King, N., 'Review of A.C. Thiselton's *The First Epistle to the Corinthians*', *HeyJ* 44.4 (Oct. 2003), 498-499.
Klein, W.W., 'Review of A.C. Thiselton's *The Two Horizons*', *TrinJ* 2 (Spr. 1981), 71-75.
— with C.L. Blomberg, and R.L. Hubbard, *Introduction to Biblical Interpretation* (Nashville, TN.: Nelson Reference, 1993).
Kleinig, J., 'Review of A.C. Thiselton's *The Two Horizons*', *RefThRev* 39 (Sep.-Dec. 1980), 89-90.
Klemm, D.E., 'Review of A.C. Thiselton's *The Two Horizons*', *JAARel* 50.1 (Mar. 1982), 116-117.
Kloha, J., '1 Corinthians 6.5: A Proposal (Examining Textual Losses Within Greek Manuscript Traditions)' *NovTm* 46.2 (2004), 132-142.*

Kögler, H.-H., 'Neo-Pragmatism', in *The Oxford Companion to Philosophy* (ed. T. Honderich; Oxford: OUP, 1995), 614.
— *The Power of Dialogue: Critical Hermeneutics after Gadamer and Foucault* (MIT Press: London, 1996).
Koning, Jan. de., 'Review of R. Lundin's, A.C. Thiselton's and C. Walhout's *The Responsibility of Hermeneutics*', *PSChFJASA* 39 (Dec. 1987), 245-246.
Krašovec, J., ed., *International Symposium on the Interpretation of the Bible* (Ljubljana: Slovenian Academy of Sciences and Arts; Sheffield: Sheffield Academic Press, 1998).
Kreitzer, L.J., and D.W. Rooke, 'Singing in a New Key: Philippians 2:9-11 and the 'Andante' of Beethoven's 'Kreutzer Sonata'', *ExTim* 109.8 (1998), 231-233.
Lacey, A.R., 'Positivism', in *The Oxford Companion to Philosophy* (ed. T. Honderich; Oxford: OUP, 1995), 705-706.
Lambrecht, J., 'Paul's Christological Use of Scripture in 1 Corinthians 15:20-28', *NTStud* 28.4 (1982), 502-527.*£
Lane, A.N.S., ed., *Interpreting the Bible: Historical and Theological Studies in Honour of David F. Wright* (Leicester: Apollos, 1997).
Langsdorf, L., 'Current Paths Toward an Objective Hermeneutic. Review-Article of R. Lundin's, A.C. Thiselton's and C. Walhout's *The Responsibility of Hermeneutics*', *CrThRev* 2 (Fall 1987), 145-154.
Larkin Jr., W.J., *Culture and Biblical Hermeneutics. Interpreting and Applying the Authoritative Word in a Relativistic Age* (Grand Rapids: Baker, 1988).
Laughery, G.J., 'Language at the Frontiers of Language', in *After Pentecost: Language and Biblical Interpretation* (eds. C.G. Bartholomew, C. Greene and K. Möller; Scripture and Hermeneutics Series; Vol. 2; Carlisle: Paternoster, 2001), 171-194.
Libolt, C., 'Protestantism and Preaching', *MQRev* 22.3 (1983), 500-514.
Lichtenwalter, L.L., 'Review of A.C. Thiselton's *Interpreting God and the Postmodern Self*', *AUSStud* 36 (Aut. 1998), 311-313.
Limpitlaw, A., 'Review of A.C. Thiselton's *A Concise Encyclopedia of the Philosophy of Religion*', *American Theological Library Association Newsletter* 51.1 (Nov. 2003), 9-10.
Lindbeck, G.A., D.L. Okholm and T.R. Phillips, eds., *The Nature of Confession: Evangelicals & Postliberals in Conversation* (Leicester: IVP, 1996).
Linge, D.E., 'Editor's Introduction', in *Hans-Georg Gadamer: Philosophical Hermeneutics* (H.-G. Gadamer; trans. & ed. D.E. Linge; London: University of California Press, 1976), xi.
— ed., *Hans-Georg Gadamer: Philosophical Hermeneutics* (H.-G. Gadamer; trans. & ed. D.E. Linge; London: University of California Press, 1976).
Linss, W.C., 'Review of J.B. Green ed. *Hearing the New Testament*', *CThM* 23 (Dec. 1996), 456.
Livingstone, E.A., ed., *Studia Evangelica 7* (Berlin: Akademie-Verlag, 1982).
Loader, W., *The Septuagint, Sexuality, and the New Testament: Case Studies on the Impact of the LXX in Philo and the New Testament* (Grand Rapids, MI.: Eerdmans, 2004).
Longman III, T., 'Storytellers and Poets in the Bible', in *Inerrancy and Hermeneutics: A Tradition, A Challenge, A Debate* (ed. H.M. Conn; Grand Rapids: Baker, 1988), 137-149.
— 'Literary Approaches to Biblical Interpretation', in *Foundations of Contemporary Interpretation* (ed. M. Silva; Grand Rapids: Zondervan, 1996), 91-192.
Lundin, R., 'Our Hermeneutical Inheritance', in *The Responsibility of Hermeneutics* (R. Lundin, A. C. Thiselton, & C. Walhout; Grand Rapids: Eerdmans; Exeter: Paternoster, 1985), 1-29.

— with A.C. Thiselton and C. Walhout, *The Responsibility of Hermeneutics* (Grand Rapids: Eerdmans; Exeter: Paternoster, 1985).
— 'Introduction', in *Disciplining Hermeneutics. Interpretation in Christian Perspective* (ed. R. Lundin; Leicester; Apollos, 1997), 1-21.
— ed., *Disciplining Hermeneutics. Interpretation in Christian Perspective* (Leicester; Apollos, 1997).
— with C. Walhout and A.C. Thiselton, *The Promise of Hermeneutics* (Grand Rapids and Cambridge: Eerdmans; Carlisle: Paternoster, 1999).
Lyon, A.J., 'Objectivism and Subjectivism', in *The Oxford Companion to Philosophy* (ed. T. Honderich; Oxford: OUP, 1995), 631.
Lyons, W.J., 'Serious Man, Rhetorical Man, Straw Man: Just How Much of a Threat is Stanley Fish to Christian Theology?' (Oxford: Unpublished Paper Presented at the Conference of the Society for the Study of Theology, 2000), 1-10.
— *Canon and Exegesis: Canonical Praxis and the Sodom Narrative* (Sheffield: Sheffield Academic Press, 2002).
MacCammon, L.M., 'Review of R. Lundin's, C. Walhout's and A.C. Thiselton's *The Promise of Hermeneutics*', at *http://www.bookreviews.org/bookdetail.asp?TitleId =406&CodePage=416, 406*; cf. *http://www.bookreviews.org/pdf/406_ 964 .pdf*, 1; cf. 3-4.
Macey, D., *The Penguin Dictionary of Critical Theory* (London: Penguin Books Ltd., 2000).
Macquarrie, J., 'Review of A.C. Thiselton's *The Two Horizons*', *RelStud* 16.4 (Dec. 1980), 496-497.
— 'Review of B. Mitchell ed. *Believing in the Church. The Corporate Nature of the Faith. A Report by the Doctrine Commission of the Church of England*', *Th* 85 (Mar. 1982), 126-128.
— *Theology, Church and Ministry* (London: SCM Press, 1986).
— 'Review of The Doctrine Commission of the Church of England's *We Believe in the Holy Spirit*', *Th* 94 (Nov.-Dec. 1991), 454.
Maddox, R.L., 'Review of A.C. Thiselton's *The Two Horizons*', *ThStud* 43.1 (Mar. 1982), 136-137.
— 'Contemporary Hermeneutic Philosophy and Theological Studies', *RelStud* 21.4 (Dec. 1985), 517-529.
Malbon, E.S., 'Structuralism, Hermeneutics, and Contextual Meaning', *JAARel* 51.2 (1983), 207-230.
Manwaring, R., *From Controversy to Co-Existence: Evangelicals in the Church of England 1914-1980* (Cambridge: CUP, 2002).
Marshall, I.H., ed., *New Testament Interpretation* (Grand Rapids: Eerdmans; Exeter: Paternoster Press, 1977).
— 'The New Testament Does Not Teach Universal Salvation', in *Universal Salvation? The Current Debate* (eds. R.A. Parry and C.H. Partridge; Grand Rapids, MI.: Eerdmans, 2004), 55-77.*
Martin, F., 'Review of J.B. Green and M. Turner eds. *Jesus of Nazareth: Lord and Christ*', *CBQ* 58 (Apr. 1996), 385-386.
— 'Reading Scripture in the Catholic Tradition', in *Your Word Is Truth: A Project of Evangelicals and Catholics Together* (ed. C. Colson and R.J. Neuhaus; Grand Rapids, MI.: Eerdmans, 2002), 147-168.
McCartney, D., and C. Clayton, *Let The Reader Understand. A Guide to Interpreting and Applying the Bible* (Wheaton, Illinois: Bridgepoint, 1994).
McConville, J.G., 'Metaphor, Symbol and the Interpretation of Deuteronomy', in *After Pentecost: Language and Biblical Interpretation* (eds. C.G. Bartholomew, C. Greene and K. Möller; Scripture and Hermeneutics Series; Vol. 2; Carlisle: Paternoster, 2001), 329-351.

McCown, W., and J.E. Massey, eds., *Interpreting God's Word for Today* (Anderson, Ind.: Warner Press, 1982).
McGrath, A.E., 'Luther', in *A Dictionary of Biblical Interpretation* (eds. R.J. Coggins and J.L. Houlden; London: SCM, Philadelphia: Trinity Press, 1990), 414-416.
— ed., *The Blackwell Encyclopedia of Modern Christian Thought* (Oxford: Blackwell, 1993, 1995).
McHann Jr., J.C., *The Three Horizons: A Study in Biblical Hermeneutics with Special Reference to Wolfhart Pannenberg* (Aberdeen: University of Aberdeen Ph.D. Thesis, 1987).
McKnight, E.V., 'Old and New Horizons in Hermeneutics: Anthony C. Thiselton on Contemporary Developments in Hermeneutics. Review Article of *New Horizons in Hermeneutics*', *PRelStud* 20 (Fall 1993), 289-302.
McKnight, S., *1 Peter* (The NIV Application Commentary; Grand Rapids, MI.: Zondervan, 1996).
McNicol, A.J., 'Review of A.C. Thiselton's *The Two Horizons*', *RestQ* 27.3 (1984), 187-189.
Meier, J.P., 'On the Veiling of Hermeneutics (1 Cor. 11:2-16)', *CBQ* 40 (1978), 212-226.
Mercer, C.R., 'Review of A.C. Thiselton's *New Horizons in Hermeneutics*', *CBQ* 56.1 (1994), 158-160.
Metzger, B.M., 'Review of A.C. Thiselton's *The Two Horizons*', *ChSRev* 10.3 (1981), 262-265.
— 'Review of A.C. Thiselton's *The Two Horizons*', *PSemB* NS3.2 (1981), 208-211.
Meyer, L.R., 'Athanasius' Use of Paul in his Doctrine of Salvation', *VigCh* 52.2 (May 1998), 146-171.*£
Miller, D.G., ed., *The Hermeneutical Quest: Essays in Honour of James Luther Mays* (Princeton Theological Monograph 4; Allison Park, Pa: Pickwick Press, 1986).
Mitchell, B., ed., *Believing in the Church: Essays by Members of the Church of England Doctrine Commission* (London: SPCK, 1981).
Moberly, R.W.L., 'Review of A.C. Thiselton's *New Horizons in Hermeneutics*', *Anv* 11.1 (1994), 71-72.
— 'Review of R. Lundin's, C. Walhout's and A.C. Thiselton's *The Promise of Hermeneutics*', *ExTim* 111.7 (Apr. 2000), 237.
Moltmann, J., *Theology of Hope* (London: SCM, 1967).
— 'Theology as Eschatology', in *The Future of Hope: Theology as Eschatology* (J. Moltmann *et al*; ed. F. Herzog; New York: Herder & Herder, 1970), 1-50.
— *et al*, *The Future of Hope: Theology as Eschatology* (ed. F. Herzog; New York: Herder & Herder, 1970).
— 'Excerpt from *Theology of Hope*', in *A Map of Twentieth-Century Theology. Readings from Karl Barth to Radical Pluralism* (eds. C.E. Braaten & R.W. Jenson; Minneapolis: Augsburg Press, 1995), 160-168.
Moo, D.J., 'Review of A.C. Thiselton's *New Horizons in Hermeneutics*', *TrinJ* 13 (Fall 1992), 250.
Moore, G.E., *Principia Ethica* (Cambridge: CUP, 1959).
Moore, S.D., 'The Post-' Age Stamp: Does it Stick? Biblical Studies and the Post-Modernism Debate', *JAARel* 57 (1989), 543-559.
— 'Review of A.C. Thiselton's *New Horizons in Hermeneutics*', *ThT* 50.2 (Jul. 1993), 287-288.
Moorhead, D., 'Review of A.C. Thiselton's *Interpreting God and the Postmodern Self*', *JPsychTh* 27.4 (1999), 358.
Morgan, R.C., 'Review of A.C. Thiselton's *The Two Horizons*', *HeyJ* 22.3 (1981), 331-333.
— 'Review of A.C. Thiselton's *New Horizons in Hermeneutics*', *ExTim* 104.6 (Mar. 1993), 186-187.
Morris, L., *The First Epistle of Paul to the Corinthians: An Introduction and Commentary* (Tyndale

New Testament Commentaries, No. 7; Grand Rapids, MI.: Eerdmans, 1987).*£

Morton, A., *A Guide Through the Theory of Knowledge* (Oxford: Blackwell, 1977, 1997).

Moule, C.F.D., *The Birth of the New Testament* (London: A&C Black, 1981).

Mulholland Jr., M.R., 'Sociological Criticism', in *Interpreting the New Testament: Essays on Methods and Issues* (eds. D.A. Black and D.S. Dockery; Nashville, TN.: Broadman & Holman Publishers, 2001), 170-187.

Murphy, N.C., *Anglo-American Postmodernity: Philosophical Perspectives on Science, Religion, and Ethics* (Boulder, Colorado: Westview Press, 1997).

Murphy-O'Connor, J., 'Sex and Logic in 1 Corinthians 11:2-16', *CBQ* 42 (1980), 482-500.*£

— 'Interpolations in 1 Corinthians', *CBQ* 48.1 (1986), 81-94.

Neill, S., 'Integrity of Approach: Review of I.H. Marshall ed. *New Testament Interpretation: Essays in Principles and Methods*', *CEN* 18 Nov. (1977), 20.

— and N.T. Wright, *The Interpretation of the New Testament: 1861-1986* (Oxford: OUP, 1988).

Newcastle, A., *et al*, eds., *We Believe in the Holy Spirit: A Report by the Doctrine Commission of the General Synod of the Church of England* (London: Church House Publishing, 1991).

Newman, C.C., ed., *Jesus & the Restoration of Israel: A Critical Assessment of N.T. Wright's Jesus and the Victory of God* (Leicester: IVP, 1999).

Neyrey, J.H., 'Body-Language in 1 Corinthians - The Use of Anthropological Models for Understanding Paul and his Opponents', *Sem* 35 (1986), 129-170.*£

Nicholson, G., 'Transforming What We Know', *ResPhen* 16 (1986), 57-71.

Nicholson, M.W., 'Abusing Wittgenstein: The Misuse of the Concept of Language-Games in Contemporary Theology', *JEThS* 39 (Dec. 1996), 617-629.

Nietzsche, F., *Thus Spoke Zarathustra. A Book for Everyone and No One* (trans. R.J. Hollingdale; London: Penguin, 1969).

Noble. P.R., 'Fish and the Bible. Should Reader-Response Theories Catch On?', *HeyJ* 37.4 (Oct. 1996), 456-467.

Noll, M.A., 'Common Sense Traditions and American Evangelical Thought', *AmQ* 37.2 (1985), 216-238.

— and D.F. Wells, 'Introduction: Modern Evangelicalism', in, *Christian Faith and Practice in the Modern World* (eds. M.A. Noll and D.F. Wells; Grand Rapids: Eerdmans, 1988), 1-19.

— and D.F. Wells, eds., *Christian Faith and Practice in the Modern World* (Grand Rapids: Eerdmans, 1988).

Norris, C., *The Contest of Faculties: Philosophy and Theory after Deconstruction* (London: Methuen, 1985).

O'Brien, P.T., *Word Biblical Commentary Vol. 44, Colossians-Philemon* (eds. B.M. Metzger, D.A. Hubbard, and G.W. Barker; Nashville, TN.: Nelson Reference, 1982).*£

— 'Principalities and Powers: Opponents of the Church', in *Biblical Interpretation and the Church. Text and Context* (ed. D.A. Carson; Carlisle: Paternoster, 1984), 110-150.

O'Collins, G. and D. Kendall, *The Bible for Theology: Ten Principles for the Theological Use of Scripture* (New York and Mahwah, N.J.: Paulist, 1997).$

Oden, T.C., 'So What Happens after Modernity? A Postmodern Agenda for Evangelical Theology', in *The Challenge of Postmodernism. An Evangelical Engagement* (ed. D.S. Dockery; Grand Rapids, Mi.: Baker Books, 1997), 392-406.

Ogden, S.M., ed., *Existence and Faith. Shorter Writings of Rudolf Bultmann* (trans. S.M. Ogden; New York: Meridian Books, Inc., 1960).

Okholm, D., 'Review of D.S. Dockery ed. *The Challenge of Postmodernism*', *ChSRev* 26.2 (1996), 223-226.

Olhausen, W.P., 'A 'Polite' Response to Anthony Thiselton', in *After Pentecost: Language and Biblical Interpretation* (eds. C.G. Bartholomew, C. Greene and K. Möller; Scripture and Hermeneutics Series; Vol. 2; Carlisle: Paternoster, 2001), 121-130.

— *Towards a Relational Hermeneutic: An Investigation in Historical Pragmatics with Special Reference to the Appropriation of Speech Act Theory in the Biblical and Theological Hermeneutics of Anthony C. Thiselton* (Chester: University of Chester Ph.D. Thesis; Liverpool Sydney Jones Library: Ph.D. Thesis 20710.OLHA, 2007).+

O'Neill, J., 'Homotextuality: Barthes on Barthes, Fragments (RB), with a Footnote', in *Hermeneutics: Questions and Prospects* (eds. G. Shapiro & A. Sica; Los Angeles: UMP, 1984), 165-182.

Oropeza, B.J., 'Laying to Rest the 'Midrash': Paul's Message on Meat Sacrificed to Idols in Light of the Deuteronomic Tradition', *Bib* 79.1 (1998), 57-68.*ℓ

— 'Situational Immorality. Paul's 'Vice Lists' at Corinth', *ExTim* 110.1 (Oct. 1998), 9-10.

Osborne, G.R., 'Review of A.C. Thiselton's *New Horizons in Hermeneutics*', *CRevBRel* 7 (1994), 91-4.

— cited in: Goddard, J.M. ed., 'Review of A.C. Thiselton's *The First Epistle to the Corinthians*', *NB* 8.1 (Feb.-Apr. 2001), 4.

— *The Hermeneutical Spiral: A Comprehensive Introduction to Biblical Interpretation* (Downers Grove: IVP, 1991/1992; second edition, 2006).

Osei-Bonsu, J., 'Anthropological Dualism in The New Testament', *SJT* 40.4 (1987), 571-590.

— 'The Intermediate State in The New Testament and The Disembodied Soul in Christian Theology', *SJT* 44.2 (1991), 169-194.*ℓ

Owen, H.P., *Revelation and Existence. A Study in the Theology of Rudolf Bultmann* (Cardiff: University of Wales Press, 1957).

Packer, J.I., 'In Quest of Canonical Interpretation', in *The Use of the Bible in Theology: Evangelical Options* (ed. R.K. Johnston; Atlanta: John Knox, 1985), 35-55.

— 'Infallible Scripture and the Role of Hermeneutics', in *Scripture and Truth* (eds. D.A. Carson and J.D. Woodbridge; Carlisle: Paternoster, 1995), 321-356, 412-419.

Palmer, R.E., 'Review of A.C. Thiselton's *The Two Horizons*', *RevMet* 35.1 (1981), 172-174.

— 'Postmodern Hermeneutics and the Act of Reading', *NDEJ* 15.3 (1983), 55-84.

— 'The Scope of Hermeneutics: The Problem of Critique, and the Crisis of Modernity', *TRevCTLit* 3 (1984), 223-239.

Pannenberg, W., *Basic Questions in Theology. Collected Essays, Volume 1* (trans. G.H. Kehm; Philadelphia: Fortress Press, 1970).

— *Basic Questions in Theology. Collected Essays, Volume 2* (trans. G.H. Kehm; Philadelphia: Fortress Press, 1971).

— *Basic Questions in Theology. Collected Essays, Volume 3* (trans. R.A. Wilson; Philadelphia: Fortress Press, 1973).

— *Theology and The Philosophy of Science* (Philadelphia: Westminster Press, and London: Darton, Longman & Todd, 1976).

— *Systematic Theology. Volume 1* (trans. G.W. Bromiley; Grand Rapids: Eerdmans, 1991).

— *Systematic Theology. Volume 2* (trans. G.W. Bromiley; Grand Rapids: Eerdmans, 1994).

Papaphilippopoulos, R., 'Review of A.C. Thiselton's *New Horizons in Hermeneutics*', *SJT* 47.1 (1994), 141-143.

Parasnis, D.S., *Principles of Applied Geophysics* (London: Chapman and Hall, 1979).

Parry, R.A., 'Review of R. Lundin's, C. Walhout's and A.C. Thiselton's *The Promise of Hermeneutics*', *EuJTh* 9.2 (2000), 201-203.

— and C.H. Partridge, eds., *Universal Salvation? The Current Debate* (Grand Rapids, MI.: Eerdmans, 2004).

Passakos, D.C., 'Eucharist in First Corinthians: A Sociological Study', *RevBib* 104.2 (Apr. 1997), 192-210.*£

Patte, D., 'Textual Constraints, Ordinary Readings, and Critical Exegesis: An Androcritical Perspective', *Sem* 62 (1993), 59-79.

Pereppadan, J., 'Review of A.C. Thiselton's *The Two Horizons*', *JDh* 6.1 (Jan.-Mar. 1981), 89-92.

Perry, S., 'A Proposed Model of Biblical Hermeneutics Incorporating the Work of Stanley Fish and Karl Barth' (Bristol: Unpublished Essay Submitted as Part of an MPhil Course at Trinity College, 1999), 1-27.

— 'E-mail to Robert Knowles, 23rd May, 2000.'

Phillips, T.R., and D.L. Okholm, eds., *The Nature of Confession: Evangelicals and Postliberals in Dialogue* (Downers Grove, Ill.: InterVarsity, 1996).

Pickett, T., 'Review of R. Lundin's, C. Walhout's and A.C. Thiselton's *The Promise of Hermeneutics*', *RelLit* 32.3 (Aut. 2000), 103-109.

Pinnock, C.H., 'Climbing Out of a Swamp: The Evangelical Struggle to Understand the Creation Texts', *Interp* 43.2 (Apr. 1989), 143-155.

Porter, S.E., 'Wittgenstein's Classes of Utterance & Pauline Ethical Texts', *JEThS* 32 (1989), 85-97.

— 'Why Hasn't Reader-Response Criticism Caught on in New Testament Studies?', *JLitTh* 4 (1990), 278-292.

— '2 Myths, Corporate Personality and Language Mentality Determinism', *SJT* 43.3 (1990), 289-307.

— 'Reader-Response Criticism and New Testament Study: A Response to A.C. Thiselton's *New Horizons in Hermeneutics*', *JLitTh* 8.1 (Mar. 1994), 94-102.

— with P. Joyce and D.E. Orton, eds., *Crossing the Boundaries: Essays in Biblical Interpretation in Honour of Michael D. Goulder*. (Biblical Interpretation Series, 8; Leiden: E.J. Brill, 1994).

— and D.A. Carson, eds., *Linguistics and the New Testament. Critical Junctures* (Journal for the Study of the New Testament Supplement Series 168: Studies in New Testament Greek 5; Sheffield: Sheffield Academic Press, 1999).

Poythress, V.S., 'Review of A.C. Thiselton's *The Two Horizons*', *WThJ* 43 (Fall 1980), 178-180.

— 'Review of A.C. Thiselton's *New Horizons in Hermeneutics*', *WThJ* 55.2 (1993), 343-346.

— 'Review of A.C. Thiselton's *Interpreting God and the Postmodern Self*', *WThJ* 59 (Spr. 1997), 131-133.

Pritchard, J.P., 'Preface', in *On Interpretation and Criticism* (A. Boeckh; trans. J.P. Pritchard; Norman, Oklahoma: University of Oklahoma Press, 1968), vii-xv.

Ramsey, G.W., 'Is Name-Giving an Act of Domination in Genesis 2:23 and Elsewhere?', *CBQ* 50 (Jan, 1988), 24-35.

Ramsey, I.T., *Religious Language. An Empirical Placing of Theological Phrases* (London: SCM Press Ltd., 1957, 1993).

Reed, E.D., 'Review of A.C. Thiselton's *Interpreting God and the Postmodern Self*', *RevRelTh* 3 (1996), 69-71.

Reese, W.L., *Dictionary of Philosophy and Religion: Eastern and Western Thought* (New Jersey: Humanities Press, 1980).

Reist, J.S., 'Review of A.C. Thiselton's *New Horizons in Hermeneutics*', *JEThS* 38.3 (Sep. 1995), 457-459.

Richardson, W., 'Liturgical Order and Glossolalia in 1 Corinthians 14:26c-33a', *NTStud* 32.1 (Jan. 1986), 144-153.

Ricoeur, P., *Hermeneutics and the Human Sciences. Essays on Language, Action, and Interpretation* (ed. And trans. J.B. Thompson; Cambridge: CUP, 1981).

— *Time and Narrative. Volume 3* (trans. K. Blamey & D. Pellauer; London: The University of Chicago Press, 1988).

— 'Heidegger and the Question of the Subject', in *The Conflict of Interpretations. Essays in Hermeneutics* (P. Ricoeur; ed. D. Ihde; London: The Athlone Press, 1989), 223-235.

— *The Conflict of Interpretations. Essays in Hermeneutics* (ed. D. Ihde; London: The Athlone Press, 1989).

Rieger, J., *God and the Excluded: Visions and Blindspots in Contemporary Theology* (Minneapolis, MN.: Augsburg Fortress, 2000).

Robinson, J.M., 'The German Discussion of the Later Heidegger', in *New Frontiers in Theology. Discussions among Continental and American Theologians, Volume I: The Later Heidegger and Theology. A Dialogue on Important New Trends in Religious Thought Based on the Latest Works of Martin Heidegger* (eds. J.M. Robinson and J.B. Cobb, Jr.; New York: Harper and Row, 1964), 3-76.

— and J.B. Cobb, Jr., eds., *New Frontiers in Theology. Discussions among Continental and American Theologians, Volume I: The Later Heidegger and Theology. A Dialogue on Important New Trends in Religious Thought Based on the Latest Works of Martin Heidegger* (New York: Harper and Row, 1964).

— 'Hermeneutic Since Barth', in *New Frontiers in Theology. Discussions among Continental and American Theologians, Volume II: The New Hermeneutic* (eds. J.M. Robinson and J.B. Cobb, Jr.; New York: Harper and Row, 1964), 1-77.

— and J.B. Cobb, Jr., eds., *New Frontiers in Theology. Discussions among Continental and American Theologians, Volume II: The New Hermeneutic* (New York: Harper and Row, 1964).

— and J.B. Cobb, Jr., eds., *New Frontiers in Theology: Discussions Among Continental and American Theologians. Volume III: Theology As History. A Fresh Posing of Basic Questions on Jesus' Claim to Authority - The Ultimate Foundation of Faith and of the Christian Proclamation* (New York: Harper and Row, 1967).

Rodd, C.S., 'Review of A.C. Thiselton's *The Two Horizons*', *ExTim* 91 (Jul. 1980), 289-290.

Roschke, R.W., 'Review of A.C. Thiselton's *The Two Horizons*', *CThM* 9 (Aug. 1982), 246-247.

Rudman, S., *Concepts of Person and Christian Ethics* (New Studies in Christian Ethics; ed. R. Gill; Cambridge: CUP, 1997).

Russell, W., 'Review of A.C. Thiselton's *New Horizons in Hermeneutics*', *TrinJ* 17.2 (Fall 1996), 241-243.

Santer, M., ed., *Their Lord and Ours: Approaches to Authority, Community and the Unity of the Church* (London: SPCK, 1982).

Satterthwaite, P.E., and D.F. Wright, eds., *A Pathway into the Holy Scripture* (Grand Rapids: Eerdmans, 1994).

Schleiermacher, F.D.E., 'Manuscript 1': Example of Hermeneutics', in *Hermeneutics: The Handwritten Manuscripts* (ed. H. Kimmerle; trans. J. Duke & J. Forstman; AAR Texts and Translations 1; Atlanta: Scholars Press, 1977), 65; cf. 243 n. 49.

Schmidt, D.J., 'Gadamer', in *A Companion to Continental Philosophy* (eds. S. Critchley and W.R. Schroeder; Blackwell Companions to Philosophy Series; Oxford: Blackwell Publishers Ltd., 1998), 433-442.

Schneiders, S.M., 'The Paschal Imagination - Objectivity and Subjectivity in New Testament Interpretation', *ThStud*, 43.1 (1982), 52-68.
— 'Review of A.C. Thiselton's *The Two Horizons*', *JRel* 62.3 (Jul. 1982), 307-309.
— *The Revelatory Text: Interpreting the New Testament As Sacred Scripture* (Collegeville, MN.: Michael Glazier Books, 1999).
Schrag, C.O., 'Subjectivity and Praxis at the End of Philosophy', in *Hermeneutics and Deconstruction* (eds. H.J. Silverman and D. Ihde; Albany, N.Y.: State University of New York Press, 1985), 24-32.
Schrage, W., 'Review of A.C. Thiselton's *The First Epistle to the Corinthians*', *Bib* 83.2 (2002), 288-292.
Schreiner, T.R., *Paul, Apostle of God's Glory in Christ: A Pauline Theology* (Leicester: IVP, 2001).*£
— and A.B. Caneday, *The Race Set Before Us: A Biblical Theology of Perseverance & Assurance* (Leicester: IVP, 2001).*£
Schüssler-Fiorenza, E., 'Rhetorical Situation and Historical Reconstruction in 1 Corinthians', *NTStud* 33.3 (Jul. 1987), 386-403.
— *Rhetoric and Ethic: The Politics of Biblical Studies* (Minneapolis, MN.: Augsburg Fortress, 1999).
Searle, J.R., 'Reiterating the Differences: A Reply to Derrida', *Gly* 1 (1977), 198-208.
Seifrid, M.A., 'The Pauline Gospel in a Postmodern Age', in *The Challenge of Postmodernism. An Evangelical Engagement* (ed. D.S. Dockery; Grand Rapids, Mi.: Baker Books, 1997), 190-207.
Sell, A.P.F., 'Review of A.C. Thiselton's *A Concise Encyclopedia of the Philosophy of Religion*', *ThT* 60.1 (Apr. 2003), 145.
Seung, T.K., *Structuralism and Hermeneutics* (New York: Columbia University Press, 1982).
Sheehy, D., 'Review of A.C. Thiselton's *A Concise Encyclopedia of the Philosophy of Religion*', *ChTim* June 25th (2004), page-numbers not ascertained.+
Shults, F.L., *The Postfoundationalist Task of Theology: Wolfhart Pannenberg and the New Theological Rationality* (Grand Rapids, MI.: Eerdmans, 1996).
— *Reforming Theological Anthropology: After the Philosophical Turn to Relationality* (Grand Rapids, MI.: Eerdmans, 2003).
Silva, M., 'Contemporary Approaches to Biblical Interpretation', in *An Introduction to Biblical Hermeneutics: The Search for Meaning* (W.C. Kaiser and M. Silva; Grand Rapids: Zondervan, 1994), 229-250.
— 'The New Testament Use of the Old Testament', in *Scripture and Truth* (eds. D.A. Carson and J.D. Woodbridge; Carlisle: Paternoster, 1995), 143-165, 381-386.
— ed., *Foundations of Contemporary Interpretation* (Grand Rapids: Zondervan, 1996).
Silverman, H.J., and D. Ihde, eds., *Hermeneutics and Deconstruction* (Albany, N.Y.: State University of New York Press, 1985).
Slater, G., 'Review of A.C. Thiselton's *Interpreting God and the Postmodern Self*', *EpRev* 24 (Apr. 1997), 104-105.
Smit, D.J., 'The Ethics of Interpretation: New Voices from the USA', *Scrip* 33 (May 1990), 16-28.
Smit, J.F.M., 'Epideictic Rhetoric in Paul's 'First Letter to the Corinthians', Chapters 1-4', *Bib* 84.2 (2003), 184-201.*
Smith, R.L., 'Review of R. Lundin's, A.C. Thiselton's and C. Walhout's *The Responsibility of Hermeneutics*', *SWJTh* NS29.1 (Fall 1986), 64.

Snodgrass, K.R., 'Review of R. Lundin's, A.C. Thiselton's and C. Walhout's *The Responsibility of Hermeneutics*', *CovQ* 45 (Nov. 1987), 199-202.
Stephens, W., ed., *The Bible, The Reformation, & the Church* (Sheffield: Sheffield Academic Press, 1995).
Sterling, G.E., "Wisdom Among the Perfect': Creation Traditions in Alexandrian Judaism and Corinthian Christianity', *NovTm* 37.4 (1995), 355-384.*£
Stewart, I., *Transactional Analysis Counselling in Action* (Sage Counselling in Action Series; ed. W. Dryden; London; Sage Publications, 2007).
Stiver, D.R., 'Review of A.C. Thiselton's *Interpreting God and the Postmodern Self*', *ChSRev* 26.2 (1996), 227-229.
— *The Philosophy of Religious Language: Sign, Symbol, and Story* (Oxford: Blackwell, 1996).
— 'The Uneasy Alliance Between Evangelicalism and Postmodernism: A Reply to Anthony Thiselton', in *The Challenge of Postmodernism. An Evangelical Engagement* (ed. D.S. Dockery; Grand Rapids, Mi.: Baker Books, 1997), 239-253.
Stokes, P., *Philosophy. 100 Essential Thinkers* (Leicester: Arcturus Publishing Limited, 2002).
Stott, J.R.W., 'Obeying Christ in a Changing World', in *Obeying Christ in a Changing World. Vol. 1* (ed. J.R.W. Stott; Glasgow: Collins/Fountain Books, 1977), 9-31.
— ed., *Obeying Christ in a Changing World. Vol. 1* (Glasgow: Collins/Fountain Books, 1977).
— *The Contemporary Christian: An Urgent Plea for Double Listening* (Leicester: IVP, 1995).
Suler, J., 'The Online Disinhibition Effect', *CyberPsychology & Behavior* 7.3 (2004), 321-326.
Summer, S., *Men and Women in the Church: Building Consensus on Christian Leadership* (Leicester: IVP, 2003).§
Sykes, S.W., 'Review of A.C. Thiselton's *The Two Horizons*', *Chman* 96.2 (1982), 156-157.
Talbert, C.H., 'The Gospel and The Gospels', *Interp* 33 (1979), 351-362.*£
— 'Review of A.C. Thiselton's *The First Epistle to the Corinthians*', *PRelStud* 28.2 (Sum. 2001), 141-142.
Talbot, T., 'Christ Victorious', in *Universal Salvation? The Current Debate* (eds. R.A. Parry and C.H. Partridge; Grand Rapids, MI.: Eerdmans, 2004), 15-32.*
— 'Reply to My Critics', in *Universal Salvation? The Current Debate* (eds. R.A. Parry and C.H. Partridge; Grand Rapids, MI.: Eerdmans, 2004), 247-273.*
Telford, W.M., L.P. Geldart, R.E. Sheriff, and D.A. Keys, *Applied Geophysics* (Cambridge: CUP, 1976), 370-372.
Tenney, M.C., ed., *The Zondervan Pictorial Encyclopaedia of the Bible. Volume 4* (Grand Rapids, MI: Zondervan, 1975).
Thomas, G.J., 'Telling a Hawk from a Handsaw? An Evangelical Response to the New Literary Criticism', *EvanQ* 71.1 (1999), 37-50.
Thomas, R.L., 'Dynamic Equivalence: A Method of Translation or a System of Hermeneutics?' Essay Presented at the Fortieth Annual Meeting of the Evangelical Theological Society, Wheaton, IL, Nov. 1988.
Thrall, M.E., 'Review of I.H. Marshall ed. *New Testament Interpretation*', *SJT* 32.4 (Aug. 1979), 388-390.
— 'Review of A.C. Thiselton's *The First Epistle to the Corinthians*', *ExTim* 112.11 (Aug. 2001), 390.
Titans, N., 'Review of A.C. Thiselton's *Interpreting God and the Postmodern Self*', *CThM* 24.6 (1997), 520-521.
Tomlinson, D., *The Post-Evangelical* (Grand Rapids, MI.: Zondervan, 2003).
Torrance, A.J., 'The Self-Relation, Narcissism and the Gospel of Grace', *SJT* 40.4 (1987), 481-510.

Torrance, I.R., 'Gadamer, Polanyi and Ways of Being Closed', *SJT* 46.4 (1993), 497-505.
Tosato, A., 'On Genesis 2:24', *CBQ* 52.3 (Jul. 1990), 389-409.
Tournier, P., *Guilt and Grace* (Crowborough, East Sussex: Hodder & Stoughton, 1962).
Tracy, D., *The Analogical Imagination: Christian Theology and the Culture of Pluralism* (London: SCM, 1981).
Traina, R., 'Inductive Bible Study Re-examined in the Light of Contemporary Hermeneutics', in *Interpreting God's Word for Today* (eds. W. McCown and J.E. Massey; Anderson, Ind.: Warner Press, 1982), 53-83.
Trocmé, E., 'Review of A.C. Thiselton's *The Two Horizons*', *RevHstPhRel* 61.2 (1981), 192-193.
Trueman, C., 'Faith Seeking Understanding', in *Interpreting the Bible: Historical and Theological Studies in Honour of David F. Wright* (ed. A.N.S. Lane; Leicester: Apollos, 1997), 146-162.
Tucker, R.A., and W.L. Liefeld, *Daughters of the Church: Women and Ministry from New Testament Times to the Present* (Grand Rapids, MI.: Zondervan, 1987).
Tuckett, C.M., '1 Corinthians and Q', *JBLit* 102.4 (1983), 607-619.*£
— 'Jewish Christian Wisdom in 1 Corinthians?', in *Crossing the Boundaries: Essays in Biblical Interpretation in Honour of Michael D. Goulder* (eds. Porter, S.E., P. Joyce and D.E. Orton; Biblical Interpretation Series, 8; Leiden: E.J. Brill, 1994), 201-219.*£
Tulloch, S. ed., *The Reader's Digest Oxford Wordfinder* (Oxford: Clarendon Press, 1993).
Tupper, E.F., *The Theology of Wolfhart Pannenberg* (London: SCM Press, 1974).
Turner, M., 'Review of R. Lundin's, A.C. Thiselton's and C. Walhout's *The Responsibility of Hermeneutics*', *FTht* 113 (Oct. 1987), 180-182.
— and J.B. Green, 'New Testament Commentary and Systematic Theology: Strangers or Friends', in *Between Two Horizons. Spanning New Testament Studies and Systematic Theology* (eds. J.B. Green and M. Turner; Cambridge: Eerdmans, 2000), 1-22.
Van Engen, C., *Mission on the Way. Issues in Mission Theology* (Grand Rapids: Baker Books, 1996).
Van Hamersveld, M., 'Review of R. Lundin's, A.C. Thiselton's and C. Walhout's *The Responsibility of Hermeneutics*', *RefRev* 40.3 (Spr. 1987), 252.
Van Spanje, T.E., 'Contextualisation: Hermeneutical Remarks', *BJRULibM* 80.1 (1998), 197-217.
Van Voorst, R., 'Review of A.C. Thiselton's *The Two Horizons*', *RefRev* 34 (Spr. 1981), 220-221.
Vanhoozer, K.J., 'The Spirit of Understanding: Special Revelation and General Hermeneutics', in *Disciplining Hermeneutics: Interpretation in Christian Perspective* (Ed. R. Lundin; Leicester: Apollos, 1997), 131-165.
— *Is There a Meaning in This Text? The Bible, The Reader, and the Morality of Literary Knowledge* (Grand Rapids: Zondervan, 1998).
— 'Review of R. Lundin's, C. Walhout's and A.C. Thiselton's *The Promise of Hermeneutics*', *ThT* 57.3 (Oct. 2000), 403-406.
— 'From Speech Acts to Scripture Acts. The Covenant of Discourse and the Discourse of the Covenant', in *After Pentecost: Language and Biblical Interpretation* (eds. C.G. Bartholomew, C. Greene and K. Möller; Scripture and Hermeneutics Series; Vol. 2; Carlisle: Paternoster, 2001), 1-49.
— *First Theology. God, Scripture and Hermeneutics* (Leicester: Apollos, 2002).
Voelz, J.W., 'Some Things Old, Some Things New: A Response to Wolfgang Schenk re. Paul's Letter to the Philippians', *Sem* 48 (1989), 161-169.

— 'Multiple Signs, Levels of Meaning and Self as Text: Elements of Intertextuality', *Sem* 69-70 (1995), 149-164.

Vos, J.S., 'On the Relationship Between Argumentation and Situation in 1 Corinthians 15 (A Pauline Debate on the Resurrection of the Dead from his 'Letters to the Corinthians')', *NovTm* 41.4 (Oct. 1999), 313-333.*£

Wade, R., 'Where Did 'I' Go? The Loss of Self in Postmodern Times', at *http://www.probe.org/docs/wheredid.html.*

Walker, W.O., 'The Theology of Woman's Place and the Paulinist Tradition (Reprinted)', *Sem* 28 (1983), 101-112.

Wallace, M.I., 'Karl Barth's Hermeneutic: A Way Beyond the Impasse', *JRel* 68.3 (1988), 396-410.

Walsh, B.J., 'Anthony Thiselton's Contribution to Biblical Hermeneutics', *ChSRev* 14.3 (1985), 224-235.

Ward, P., 'The Tribes of Evangelicalism', in *The Post-Evangelical Debate* (G. Cray *et al*; London: SPCK/Triangle, 1997), 19-34.

Ward, R.S., 'Review of A.C. Thiselton's *The First Epistle to the Corinthians*', *RefThRev* 60.3 (Dec. 2001), 158-159.

Ward, T., *Word and Supplement: Speech Acts, Biblical Texts, and the Sufficiency of Scripture* (Oxford: OUP, 2002).

Ware, K., 'The Jesus Prayer', *Sob* G 2 (1980), 87-93.

Watson, F., 'Review of A.C. Thiselton's *New Horizons in Hermeneutics*', *BibInterp* 4.2 (1996), 252-256.

— *Paul and the Hermeneutics of Faith* (London: T & T Clark International, 2004).

Webster, J.B., 'Review of A.C. Thiselton's *The Two Horizons*', *FTht* 107.3 (1980), 219-220.

Wedderburn, A.J.M., 'The Problem of the Denial of the Resurrection in 1 Corinthians 15', *NovTm* 23.3 (1981), 229-241.*£

Weele, M.V., 'Review of R. Lundin's, A.C. Thiselton's and C. Walhout's *The Responsibility of Hermeneutics*', *ChLit* 35.4 (Sum. 1986), 48-49.

Weinsheimer, J., and D.G. Marshall, 'Translators' Preface', in *Truth and Method* (H.-G. Gadamer; London: Sheed and Ward, 1975, 1989), xi-xix.

Wells, R., *History Through the Eyes of Faith* (Christian College Coalition Series; New York: HarperCollins, 1989).

Wenham, D., *Paul and Jesus: The True Story* (Grand Rapids, MI.: Eerdmans, 2002).

White, H.C., 'The Value of Speech-Act Theory for Old Testament Hermeneutics', *Sem* 41 (1988), 41-63.

Who's Who Editorial Group, *Who's Who 1999: An Annual Biographical Dictionary* (151st Year of Issue; London: A&C Black, 1999), 1985.

Williams, P., 'Hermeneutics for Economists: Issues in Interpretation', *JACE* 22 (Dec. 1996), 13-37.

Wink, W., 'Review of A.C. Thiselton's *The Two Horizons*', *ThT* 37.4 (Jan. 1981), 506-507.

Winter, B.W., *After Paul Left Corinth: The Influence of Secular Ethics and Social Change* (Grand Rapids, MI.: Eerdmans, 2000).*£

Witherington III, B., *Jesus, Paul and the End of the World: A Comparative Study in New Testament Eschatology* (Leicester: IVP, 1992).*£

— *Conflict and Community in Corinth: A Socio-Rhetorical Commentary on 1 and 2 Corinthians* (Grand Rapids, MI.: Eerdmans, 1995).*£

Wittgenstein, L., *Culture and Value* (trans. P. Winch; Chicago: The University of Chicago Press, 1980).

— *Remarks on the Philosophy of Psychology. Volume 2* (eds. G.H. Von Wright and H. Nyman; trans. C.G. Luckhardt and M.A.E. Aue; Oxford: Blackwell, 1980).
— *Zettel* (trans. G.E.M. Anscombe; Oxford: Blackwell, 1967, 1998).
— *Tractatus Logico-Philosophicus* (trans. D.F. Pears and B.F. McGuinness; London: Routledge, 1961, 1974, 2001).
— *On Certainty* (trans. D. Paul and G.E.M. Anscombe; Oxford: Blackwell, 1969, 2001).
— *Philosophical Investigations* (trans. G.E.M. Anscombe; Oxford: Blackwell, 1953, 2001).
— *The Blue and Brown Books. Preliminary Studies for the Philosophical Investigations* (Oxford: Blackwell, 1958, 2002).
Woodhead, L., 'Review of A.C. Thiselton's *Interpreting God and the Postmodern Self*, *ModTh* 13.4 (Oct. 1997), 537-539.
— 'Theology and the Fragmentation of the Self', *IJSTh* 1.1 (Mar. 1999), 53-72.
Woodman, S., 'Untitled Contribution to MLitt Thesis. Personal Communication to Robert Knowles, 27th April 2000' (Bristol: Baptist College, 2000), 1-20.
— *The Christian Use of Apocalyptic Literature from the Perspective of Metaphor* (University of Bristol: MLit Thesis, 2001). *N.B. This was the thesis to which the above "Untitled" contributed.*
— 'The Dissenting Voice: Journeying Together Toward a Baptist Hermeneutic', in *The "Plainly Revealed" Word of God? Baptist Hermeneutics in Theory and Practice* (eds. H. Dare and S. Woodman; Macon, Georgia, USA: Mercer University Press, 2011), 213-229.
Wright, N.T., *The Resurrection of the Son of God* (Christian Origins and the Question of God; Minneapolis: Augsburg Fortress, 2003).*£
Wright, S.I., 'An Experiment in Biblical Criticism', in *Renewing Biblical Interpretation* (eds. C.G. Bartholomew, C. Greene and K. Möller; Scripture and Hermeneutics Series; Vol. 1; Carlisle: Paternoster, 2000), 240-267.
Young, F., 'The Significance of Third-Century Christian Literature', in *The Cambridge History of Early Christian Literature* (eds. F. Young, L. Ayres, and A. Louth; Cambridge: CUP, 2004), 239-250.
— with L. Ayres, and A. Louth, eds., *The Cambridge History of Early Christian Literature* (Cambridge: CUP, 2004).
Young, J.E., Klosko, J.S., and Weishaar, M.E., *Schema Therapy: A Practitioner's Guide* (London and New York: the Guildford Press, 2003).
Young, N.H., 'The Use of Sunday for Meetings of Believers in the New Testament. A Response (Observations on First Century Christian Assembly and Worship)' *NovTm* 45.2 (2003), 111-122.*
Zangwill, O.L., 'Hypnotism, History of', in *The Oxford Companion to the Mind* (ed. R.L. Gregory; Oxford: OUP, 1987), 330-333.
Ziesler, J., 'Historical Criticism and a Rational Faith', *ExTim* 105.9 (1994), 270-274.
Zuidervaart, L., 'Review of R. Lundin's, A.C. Thiselton's and C. Walhout's *The Responsibility of Hermeneutics*', *CalThJ* 21.2 (Nov. 1986), 290-296.

\*    *References relevant to Thiselton as an authority on 1 Corinthians.*
£    *References relevant to Thiselton as an authority on 1 Corinthians with particular reference to the debate following Thiselton's 'over-realized eschatology thesis'.*
\#    *Second Period works by Thiselton indicating his considerable eschatological emphasis at that time.*
$    *References militating against the view that Thiselton supposedly has "misogynist interests".*
%    *References of relevance to pastoral theology from amongst some of Thiselton's more recent works.*
+    *Small handful of references that either could not be obtained or that were discovered too late to be consulted in relation to the current project.*

# Author Index

Achtemeier, P.J. 136, 318, 633.
Adam, A.K.M. 1, 3-4, 13, 23, 54, 209, 261, 273-74, 368, 445-46, 450-51, 466-69, 548-49, 568, 571, 598, 600, 633.
Adams, J.W. 633.
Adey, G. 378, 633.
Albert, H. 75.
Alexander, T.D. 629, 633.
Allenson, A.R. 14, 288, 642.
Allison Jr., D.C. 632.
Allison, D.B. 457, 639.
Alsop, J.R. 625.
Alston, W.P. 165-66.
Althous, P. 58.
Altizer, T.J.J. 64.
Anderson, N.A. 54-55, 621.
Anscombe, G.E.M. 7, 36, 75, 83, 103, 141, 148, 151, 165-66, 211, 235, 245, 336, 349, 430, 658.
Apel, K.-O. 41, 72, 107, 158, 295, 329, 378, 394, 449, 633.
Appignanesi, R. 109, 638.
Aquinas, St. T. 493.
Archard, D. 85, 338, 429, 630, 642.
Aristotle 193, 250.
Armstrong, E.A. 620.
Arnold, C.E. 3, 633, 642.
Ashton, J. 278, 633.
Astley, J. 633.
Atkinson, D. 629.
Atkinson, D.J. 627.
Atkinson, J. 627.
Aue, M.A.E. 59, 226, 348, 658.
Austin, J.L. xvii, 30-32, 34-37, 39, 41, 45-46, 63, 73, 79, 88, 99, 128-29, 143, 158, 163-67, 180, 182-83, 204, 234, 269, 290, 298, 335, 347-48, 362-63, 365, 367, 370, 378-79, 381, 393-94, 408, 447, 451, 467, 474, 529, 555, 633.
Avis, P.D.L. 275, 286, 625, 633.
Ayer, A.J. 179, 352, 355.
Ayres, L. 273, 658.

Bacon, F. 373-74.
Baines, N. 629.
Baird, W. 630.
Ballard, P.H. xxiii, 338.
Banks, R. 623.
Barbour, I. 357.
Barclay, J. 633.
Barclay, W. 55, 624.
Barker, G.W. 650.
Barnes, L.P. 79, 138, 416, 633.
Barr, J. 31, 63-64, 73, 75, 77, 81, 120, 138, 143, 163, 168, 174-77, 180, 183-87, 211, 222, 236-37, 294, 344, 543, 558, 597, 622, 624-25, 627, 633.
Barrett, C.K. 54, 63, 66, 68, 233, 623, 625.
Barry, F.R. 619.
Barry, P. 22, 634.
Barth, K. 66-67, 71, 81, 116, 119, 138, 278, 379, 399-400, 413, 434, 467, 470, 485, 493, 496, 498-99, 501, 503, 505-08, 512-25, 527-30, 532, 541-42, 545-47, 549-50, 558, 565, 570, 587-88, 600-01, 608, 627-28, 635, 638, 641, 649, 652-53, 657.
Barthes, R. 73, 220, 228, 445, 453-54, 457, 459-63, 465-67, 478, 483, 501-02, 507, 557, 569, 588, 593, 634, 651.
Bartholomew, C.G. 3-4, 6-7, 10-11, 15, 22, 139, 152, 208, 238, 273, 277-78, 296, 330, 343-44, 356, 363, 368, 370, 380-81, 383, 395, 402, 420, 430-36, 443, 450, 567, 629-31, 634, 638, 645, 647-48, 651, 656, 658.
Bartley III, W.W. 74, 621.
Barton, J. 628, 633-34.
Barton, S.C. 252, 281, 630, 635.
Bartsch, H.-W. 61, 103, 154, 285, 635-36.
Baskin, W. 168.
Bass, A. 453, 457, 465, 639.
Bauckham, R. 631, 635.
Beaver, R.P. 625, 630.
Bebbington, D.W. 50-52, 635.
Beckwith, R.T. 422-23, 635.

BeDuhn, J.D. 635.
Benoist, J.-M. 48, 193, 228, 444, 624.
Berkhof, H. 625.
Bertocci, P.A. 69, 74, 132, 621.
Best, E. 625.
Betti, E. xviii, 71, 79, 405.
Bevan, E. 134.
Bizzell, P. 440.
Black, D.A. 2, 635, 639, 650.
Black, M. 165-66, 168.
Blamey, K. 422, 653.
Blanke, F. 289, 640.
Bleicher, J. 71.
Bloesch, D.G. 363, 412-13, 637.
Blomberg, C.L. 41, 57, 272-73, 484, 488-89, 504-05, 635, 646.
Bockmuehl, M. 3, 635.
Boeckh, A. 7, 652.
Boman, T. 64, 174.
Bonhoeffer, D. 67.
Boring, M.E. 75, 635.
Bornkamm, G. 58, 62, 66.
Borsch, F.H. 57, 90, 156, 185, 212-13, 224, 230, 232-33, 235, 260, 275, 293, 302-03, 335, 348, 368-69, 380, 407-08, 635.
Bosch, D.J. 625.
Bouttier, M. 65.
Bowald, M.A. 632.
Bowden, J. 5, 57, 82-83, 142, 163, 185-86, 274, 402, 412, 635.
Boyce, J.L. 383, 635.
Braaten, C.E. 91, 635, 649.
Bradley, F.H. 128.
Bradshaw, T. 561, 628, 635.
Braithwaite, R.B. 36-37, 144.
Branson, M.L. 362, 626, 635, 645.
Braun, H. 517.
Bray, G.L. 5, 57, 216, 274, 277, 625, 635.
Bremmer, J.N. 629.
Brett, M.G. 23, 58-59, 168, 240, 469-70, 473, 635.
Bridger, F. 629.
Briggs, R.S. 278, 291, 293-94, 348, 380, 383, 630, 635.
Brill, E.J. 652, 656.
Brodie, L. 155-56, 185, 209, 211, 216, 237, 244, 246, 259-61, 274, 283, 300-01, 336, 364-65, 414-15, 635.

Bromiley, G.W. 95, 407, 651.
Brown, A.R. 635.
Brown, C. 5, 14, 19, 43, 48-49, 61, 65, 94, 121, 125-26, 140-41, 146, 161, 206, 214, 220, 275, 284, 310, 337, 412, 420, 424, 468, 623-24, 636.
Brown, P. 437.
Brown, R.E. 367, 640.
Brown, S.C. 43-44, 620, 630.
Browning, D. 338.
Browning, P.D. 557-58, 636.
Bruce, F.F. 55, 63, 66, 68, 624.
Brueggemann, W. 64, 636.
Bruns, G.L. 448-49, 468, 595, 636.
Buber, M. 69, 74, 189, 196, 200, 202, 223, 245, 338, 341, 425, 543, 623, 636.
Buchanan, C. 4, 52, 57, 636.
Bultmann, R. xix, 1, 11-14, 19, 28, 33, 35-37, 39, 44, 46, 48, 55-56, 58, 60-62, 64-69, 72, 76, 78-80, 83, 85, 87, 89, 92-93, 95-97, 103, 114, 117, 119, 126, 129, 131, 141, 144-45, 149-50, 153-55, 162, 164-65, 172, 177, 181-82, 191, 197-99, 206, 208-11, 215-19, 221, 224, 234, 238, 240, 246, 249, 251, 260, 263-64, 266, 272, 276-77, 279, 280-89, 293-95, 298, 301-04, 306-09, 314, 318-20, 322, 324-26, 328-29, 333-36, 338, 346-47, 351, 354-55, 357-58, 361, 365-66, 369, 377, 383, 385-87, 389, 393, 400, 410-13, 423, 428-29, 459, 482, 496, 514-15, 519-20, 539, 555, 559, 575, 578, 586, 592-93, 595, 600-01, 604, 607, 619, 623-24, 626-27, 631-36, 640, 650-51.
Buri, F. 91.
Burres, K.L. 168.
Burrows, R.P. 627.
Bush, L.R. 438, 637.
Byron, G.L. 629.
Byron, J. 637.
Byworth, C. 60, 123, 146, 206, 335, 429, 623, 637.
Cahill, P.J. 76, 89-90, 98, 174, 185, 209, 245, 369, 347, 637.
Caird, G.B. 66.
Caldwell, L.W. 334, 637.
Calvin, J. 34, 56, 620.
Campbell, R.J. 59.

*Author Index*

Camus, A. 119.
Caneday, A.B. 654.
Capps, D. 338.
Carnap, R. 178.
Carnell, E.J. 33, 619.
Carson, D.A. xxiv, 2-3, 18-19, 53-54, 56, 65, 99, 262, 272-73, 281, 290, 303, 322, 334, 341, 366, 439, 443, 496, 537, 625-26, 637, 643-44, 650-52, 654.
Carver Jr., F.G. 272, 638.
Cassirer, E. 72.
Cazelles, H. 76.
Chaplin, J. 634.
Chardin, P.T. de 31, 69, 91, 619.
Charry, E.T. 401, 638.
Chartier, G. 438, 638.
Childs, B.S. 7, 10-11, 62, 485, 489-94, 496, 498-99, 503, 505-08, 510-12, 514, 518, 521-25, 549, 638.
Chomsky, N. 83, 168, 170, 173.
Clack, B.R. 401, 638.
Clark, E. 447.
Clark, H. 447.
Clarke, A.D. 638.
Clayton, C. 347, 648.
Clayton, J.P. 58, 145, 621.
Clendenen, E.R. 342, 638.
Cleobury, F.H. 34, 620.
Clines, D.J.A. 363, 435, 626.
Cobb Jr., J.B. 14, 32, 68, 91, 372, 379, 570, 620, 642, 653.
Cobb, K. 556, 638.
Coggins, R.J. 262, 626, 649.
Collingwood, R.G. 73, 76, 274, 282-83, 301-03, 307-08, 387, 402, 416, 645.
Collins, J. 109, 638.
Colson, C. 345, 638, 648.
Colwell, J.E. 278, 638.
Comte, A. 17, 136.
Conn, H.M. 324, 344, 626, 638, 647.
Conroy, C. 16, 49, 60, 69, 71, 75-76, 82, 86, 138, 185, 211, 216, 277, 282, 293, 368, 370, 638.
Conybeare, F.C. 624.
Conzelmann, H. 62, 66, 68, 92.
Corduan, W. 295, 638.
Coreth, E. 76.
Corley, J. 638.

Corner, M. 627.
Court, J.M. 630.
Couser, G.A. 638.
Cousins, E.H. 63, 91, 193, 222, 317, 424, 622.
Cox, H. 63-64, 78, 87, 194, 222, 245, 341, 530, 622.
Craig, E. 628, 638.
Cranfield, C.E.B. 48, 55, 624.
Cray, G. 530, 638, 657.
Critchley, S. 14, 16-18, 293, 374, 638, 644, 653.
Crocker, C.C. 631.
Crossan, J.D. 62, 72, 211, 287.
Crowe, P. 53, 639.
Crystal, D. 168-69, 174.
Culler, J. 450, 639.
Cupitt, D. 74, 144-45, 147, 463, 485, 529, 557-58, 621, 629.
Dakin, T. 629.
Dare, H. 531, 537, 639, 658.
Dautzenberg, G. 639.
Davidson, D. 366.
Davies, H. 286, 639.
Davies, J.G. 626.
Davies, M. 364, 639.
Davies, W.D. 31, 619.
Davis, J.A. 626.
Dawson, D. 275, 558, 639.
Dayton, D.W. 231, 639.
de Chardin, P.T. See "Chardin, P.T. de".
de Deugd, C. 36, 37.
de Koning, J. 262, 647.
de Saussure, F. See "Saussure, F. de".
Dean, W. 22, 639.
Debanné, M. 275, 562, 639.
Deidun, T. 639.
Deming, W. 639.
Demson, D.E. 628.
Derrida, J. xix, 3, 17-18, 22, 43, 75-76, 81, 88, 147, 220, 371, 428-29, 435, 441-42, 445-46, 450-54, 456-59, 461, 465-69, 478, 483, 501-02, 507, 529, 539, 549, 557, 568-69, 576, 587-89, 593, 600, 639, 654.
Descartes, R. 11, 40, 70, 80, 102-03, 105, 108-14, 117, 131, 138, 142, 150, 163, 193, 203-04, 208, 220, 222-24, 264, 266,

280, 306, 310, 320, 364, 408, 415, 422, 432, 459, 482, 498-99, 583, 592, 601.
Detweiler, R. 47, 444, 624.
Dewey, J. 74, 501.
Diem, H. 287.
Dilthey, W. 56, 62, 71, 76, 79, 96, 111, 131, 145, 193, 197, 225, 229, 280, 282-83, 298, 301, 303, 307-08, 317, 326, 328, 343, 386-87, 410-11, 415, 556, 560.
Dockery, D.S. 2-3, 5, 75, 90, 99, 138, 155, 185, 190, 218, 233, 261, 273, 279, 281, 291, 308, 322, 324-25, 341-42, 347, 369, 383, 437-38, 635, 637-39, 643-44, 650, 654-55.
Dodd, C.H. 19.
Doriani, D.M. 423, 439.
Douglas, J.D. 4, 10, 50-53, 57, 83, 639.
Dowley, T. 59, 147, 217, 333, 421, 623, 640.
Dray, S. 5, 275, 640.
Dreyer, Y. 358, 640.
Dryden, W. 426, 655.
du Plessis, J.G. 445.
Dudley-Smith, T. 52, 640.
Duffy, K. 367, 640.
Duke, J. 568, 646, 653.
Dunn, E.A. 113, 290, 379, 404, 406-07, 421, 434-35, 552-53, 566, 591-92, 640.
Dunn, J.D.G. 50-51, 65, 234, 364, 530, 624, 629-30, 640.
Dürr, L. 64, 74.
Dyrness, W.A. 6, 57, 90, 185, 236, 250, 640.
Eagleton, T. 263, 640.
Ebeling, G. 18, 31, 44, 58, 62, 72, 74, 180, 182, 190, 208, 287-90, 307, 324, 335, 347, 362, 392, 619, 622, 640.
Eckardt, A.R. 620.
Eco, U. 473.
Edgerton, W.D. 627.
Edmonds, D. 348, 375-77, 640.
Eidinow, J. 348, 375-77, 640.
Einstein, A. 414.
Ellingworth, P. 67, 98, 155, 185, 210, 218, 236, 273, 293, 305, 342, 347, 351, 401, 640.
Ellis, E.E. 66, 624, 640.
Ellwood, R. 640.
Epp, E.J. 632.
Erickson, M.J. 5, 71, 83, 86, 185, 217, 220, 260-61, 279, 294, 308, 383, 640.
Eriksson, A. 629.
Evans, C.F. 209.
Evans, C.S. 296, 450, 634.
Evans, D.D. xvii, 37, 41, 45, 63, 73, 128, 132-35, 143, 163-67, 204, 234, 269, 290, 298, 362-63, 365, 367, 393, 408, 555, 640.
Fackre, G. 57, 431, 444-45, 641.
Farley, E. 338.
Fawcett, T. 64, 126, 145, 180, 621, 623.
Fee, G.D. 170, 628, 630, 641.
Ferguson, S.B. 626.
Fergusson, D. 4, 89, 187, 328, 367, 436, 476, 557, 629, 641, 644.
Ferré, F. 36, 145, 160, 214, 620-21.
Ferreira, J. 641.
Feuerbach, L. 116, 136, 515-17.
Field, D.H. 627.
Fisby, D. 378, 633.
Fish, S. 3-5, 20-21, 88, 188, 246, 255-56, 266, 277, 312, 323, 337, 382, 399, 435, 440-41, 445-50, 459, 466, 469-70, 473-77, 480-89, 494-96, 498-509, 511-16, 519-31, 534-38, 540-50, 568-70, 587-89, 593-94, 600, 608, 641, 648, 650, 652.
Fisher, R. 641.
Fisk, B.N. 641.
Fitzmyer, S.J. J.A. 67, 628, 633, 641.
Flender, H. 619.
Flew, A. 127, 179.
Foder, J.A. 168.
Forbes, C. 628, 641.
Ford, D.E. 626, 628-30, 641.
Forrest, R. 641.
Forstman, J. 568, 646, 653.
Forsyth, P.T. 56, 59, 622.
Foucault, M. 371, 452-53, 557, 647.
Fowl, S.E. 158, 363, 375, 381, 435, 468, 529, 626, 628-29, 641.
Fox, D.J. 625.
France, R.T. 628.
Frazer, J. 411.
Freeman, A. 557-58.
Frege, G. 177.
Frei, H. 228, 382, 628.
Fretheim, T.E. 273, 641.
Freud, S. 69, 71, 74, 79, 102, 136, 138, 197-

98, 201, 218, 293, 338, 401, 424, 457, 539, 623.
Fried, G. 42, 105, 181, 644.
Friedrich, G. 60, 236, 621.
Fuchs, E. 13-14, 26, 28, 32, 39, 40-43, 62, 64, 72, 74, 77, 96, 99, 105, 144, 153, 180, 182-83, 188, 190-91, 199, 208, 214, 219, 223, 235, 243-45, 248, 267, 269, 287-88, 290, 298, 307, 326, 335, 362, 392, 437, 472, 569, 570, 574, 621, 642.
Funk, R.W. 20-21, 32, 62, 66, 72, 184, 211, 287, 348, 642.
Gadamer, H.-G. xvii-xviii, 1, 7-8, 12-14, 17-19, 21-22, 24, 27-28, 32, 34-35, 39-40, 42-43, 48, 51, 59, 70, 72-77, 79, 83, 85, 90, 96, 99, 102-03, 106-07, 111-14, 136-38, 140-41, 143-45, 152-53, 157, 163-64, 174, 181-83, 186-87, 190, 197, 206, 216-19, 221-27, 230, 232-33, 237, 241, 244, 249, 252, 267, 269, 272-74, 287, 288, 295-96, 298, 300, 302, 305, 307-08, 312, 317-19, 321-27, 329, 333-37, 339-40, 343-48, 350-51, 353, 356-68, 370-74, 377-79, 382, 386-94, 396, 400, 402, 404-06, 412-14, 417, 419, 421-22, 428-29, 432-34, 438, 440-41, 458-59, 465, 471, 481, 494, 499, 500, 542, 549, 554, 566, 583, 591-92, 594-96, 601-03, 607, 610, 623-24, 628-29, 642-43, 645, 647, 653, 656-57.
Gaffin, R. 642.
Galloway, A.D. 58, 94, 193, 223, 431, 622.
Geisler, N.L. 58, 77, 90, 138, 163, 185-87, 243, 274, 279, 381, 412, 642.
Geldart, L.P. 455, 655.
Gerado, A. 642.
Gerhardsson, B. 624.
Gerkin, C.V. 338.
Gibson, A. 63-64, 73, 87, 175, 185, 625, 642.
Gifford, P. 85, 338, 429, 630, 642.
Gilbertson, M. 630.
Giles, K. 642.
Gill, D.W.J. 3, 642.
Gill, R. 122, 653.
Gladwin, J. 53, 642.
Goddard, J.M. 1, 643, 651.
Goethe, J.W. Von 568.

Goguel, M. 65.
Goldingay, J. 279, 290, 328, 348, 403, 419, 454, 539, 628, 643.
Goldsworthy, G. 643.
Gollwitzer, H. 33, 515-16, 519, 619.
Goncalves, J.L. de Silva 275, 639.
González, J.L. 632.
Goodliffe, P. 338.
Goulder, M.D. 56, 190, 622, 652, 656.
Graf, G. 450, 639.
Graham, B. 31, 619.
Gray, D.P. 69.
Grech, P. 60, 65, 75, 138, 150-51, 154, 157, 159, 185-86, 209, 224, 233, 261, 294, 300, 329, 350-51, 353, 355, 368, 383, 643.
Green, B. 412, 643.
Green, G. 629.
Green, J.B. 11, 158, 340, 358, 369, 375, 383, 468, 627, 630, 635, 641, 643, 647-48, 656.
Green, M. 315, 423.
Greenblatt, S. 22.
Greene, C.J.D. 7, 10, 152, 208, 238, 277-78, 330, 344, 356, 420, 434, 436, 450, 557, 629, 634, 638, 643, 645, 647-48, 651, 656, 658.
Gregg, D. 54, 56, 79, 621.
Gregory, R.L. 425, 658.
Greig, J.C.G. 280, 284, 636.
Greimas, A.J. 73, 293.
Grelot, P. 76.
Grenz, S.G. 630.
Grether, O. 74.
Grindheim, S. 643.
Grobel, K. 66, 150, 284, 636.
Grondin, J. 18, 26, 249, 322, 374, 643.
Grudem, W.A. 643.
Gruneberg, K. 5, 323, 643.
Guelich, R.A. 624.
Gulley, N.R. 99, 322, 643.
Gunderson, S.R. 643.
Gundry, R.H. 625, 632.
Gundry-Volf, J. 561.
Gunn, D.M. 64, 643.
Gunstone, J. 65, 622.
Gunton, C.E. 337-38, 643.
Guthrie, D. 643.

Guthrie, G.H. 303, 496, 643.
Güttgemanns, E. 63, 73, 168, 170, 174, 222, 543, 622.
Habermas, J. 8-9, 18, 72, 75-76, 79, 83, 107, 356, 407, 438-40, 473-74, 494, 558, 643.
Hacker, P.M.S. 375, 644.
Hagner, D.A. 3, 29, 66, 87, 251, 338, 528, 629.
Hahn, L.E. 628.
Hahn, S. 631.
Hall, D.R. 630.
Hall, R.L. 401, 563, 571, 644.
Hamerton-Kelly, R.G. 68, 621.
Hammett, J.S. 437-38, 644.
Hannaford, R. 370, 644.
Hanney, A. 646.
Hanson, A.T. 55, 58, 188, 239, 622-23.
Harari, J.V. 461, 634.
Hardy, D.W. 367, 644.
Harnack, A. Von 59, 415.
Harrington, D.J. 322, 644.
Harris, H.A. 435-36, 443, 449-50, 481, 557, 568, 644.
Harrison, J.R. 644.
Harrisville, R.A. 70, 90, 138, 157, 185, 216, 218-20, 224, 274, 283, 294, 306, 309, 346, 405, 408, 628, 644.
Hart, C. 557-58.
Hart, T.A. 85, 338, 429, 557, 559, 629-30, 642, 644.
Hartlich, C. 61, 644.
Harvey, V.A. 333, 619.
Harvie, M. 626.
Hays, R.B. 644.
Healy, M. 296, 450, 634.
Heard Jr., W.J. 99, 322, 644.
Heath, S. 459, 634.
Heelas, P. 559.
Hefner, P. 69.
Hegel, G.W.F. 72, 76, 96, 99, 118-19, 128, 296, 298-302, 304, 308, 320-321, 386, 398, 403, 407-408, 415, 427-429, 454-456, 494-495, 566-567, 581-583, 585-588, 590-591, 594, 644.
Heidegger, M. 1, 11-13, 18-19, 23-25, 28, 32-35, 38, 40, 42, 48, 61, 72, 74-76, 79, 83, 85, 102-19, 126, 129, 137, 140-41, 144-45, 154, 158, 164, 174, 180-83, 186, 188-89, 192, 194, 196-97, 201, 206, 210, 216-17, 220, 224-25, 242, 246-49, 272, 274, 282-83, 287-88, 290, 295-96, 298, 302, 304-20, 323, 326, 328-29, 333-34, 336, 338, 343, 346-47, 349-50, 356, 359, 362, 371-72, 379, 386-87, 389-93, 396-97, 400, 412-15, 423, 428-29, 436, 457, 459, 498-99, 514, 530, 554-55, 559-60, 583, 592-93, 595, 610, 623-24, 638, 642, 644, 646, 653.
Hénaff, M. 293, 644.
Hendersen, I. 182.
Hendriksen, W. 177, 622.
Hengel, M. 625.
Henry, C.F.H. 33, 341, 619, 644.
Henry, P. 625.
Hepburn, R.W. 165, 439, 644.
Herder, J.G. Von 76.
Hermann, W. 56, 210.
Herzog, F. 649.
Hess, R.S. 99, 272, 322, 330, 343, 407-08, 644.
Hester, J. David 631.
Hester, James D. 631 (another J.D. Hester).
Heyduck, R. 369, 644-45.
High, D.M. 166, 178.
Hill, C.E. 642, 645.
Hirsch Jr., E.D. 70, 99, 218, 333, 367, 382, 645.
Hobbes, T. 136.
Hodes, A. 69, 189, 223, 341, 543, 623.
Hofstadter, A. 242, 644.
Hogan, J.P. 72-73, 274, 279, 402, 645.
Hogeterp, A.L.A. 632.
Holland, T. 631.
Hollingdale, R.J. 339, 650.
Honderich, T. 17, 375, 439, 641, 644-45, 647-48.
Hooker, R. 325, 646.
Hoose, B. 639, 645.
Hordern, W. 37, 143, 166, 195.
Horrell, D.G. 645.
Horsley, R.A. 632.
Houlden, J.L. 262, 626, 628, 649.
Howard, R. 359, 645.
Hubbard, D.A. 650.
Hubbard, R.L. 57, 273, 362, 645-46.
Hudson, W.D. 44, 620.

Hulse, E. 31, 619.
Humboldt, W. Von 19, 74.
Hume, D. 410, 415, 422.
Hunter, A.M. 56, 622.
Hunter, R.J. 626.
Hurding, R.F. 272, 338, 645.
Husserl, E. 12, 304, 308, 387, 457, 465, 639.
Huyssen, A. 440.
Hynson, L.O. 183, 238, 289, 645.
Ihde, D. 452, 653-54.
Ingraffia, B.D. 43, 278, 330, 380-81, 429, 453, 459-62, 465.
Iser, W. 382, 481, 486.
Isherwood, C. 31, 619.
Jakobson, R. 171.
James, F.A. 642, 645.
James, St. 329, 350, 352, 390.
James, W. 74, 633.
Jansen, H. 331, 645.
Jasper, D. 63, 293, 305, 630, 645.
Jaspers, K. 33, 72, 118-19, 530.
Jastrow, J. 133.
Jauss, H.R. 248, 268, 330, 632.
Jeanrond, W.G. 8, 239, 340, 469-73, 483-84, 489, 500, 502, 523-24, 537, 627, 645.
Jensen, A.S. 632.
Jensen, P.T. 239, 384, 645.
Jenson, R.W. 635, 649.
Jeremias, J. 66.
Jervis, L.A. 645.
Jewett, P. 355, 432.
John, St. 19, 63, 120, 142, 162, 278, 563, 623, 633.
Johnson, A.F. 645.
Johnson, A.M. 48, 227, 444, 624.
Johnson, E.E. 156, 185, 237, 244, 345, 440, 645.
Johnston, R.K. 52, 78, 344, 445, 641, 646, 651.
Jonas, H. 224, 282.
Jones, G. 627.
Jones, G.V. 425.
Jones, I.H. 646.
Jones, O.R. 63.
Joos, M. 168.
Joyce, P. 625, 656.
Jülicher, A. 42.
Kähler, M. 96, 322, 410-11.

Kainz, H.P. 455, 644.
Kaiser Jr., W.C. 276, 334, 345, 646, 654.
Kallenberg, B. 366, 646.
Kant, I. 33, 37, 56, 61-62, 72, 74, 80, 96, 103, 115-17, 129-31, 145-46, 189, 193, 201, 210, 224, 281-82, 295, 317, 320, 358, 377, 408, 415, 494-95, 553, 593, 610, 627.
Karpman, S.B. 551, 646.
Käsemann, E. 32, 43, 58, 62, 65-66, 87, 92, 232, 308, 621.
Katz, J.J. 168.
Kaye, B.N. 61, 325, 646.
Kearney, P.J. 646.
Kearsley, R. xxiv, 434, 646.
Keeley, R. 625, 646.
Kegley, C.W. 33, 619.
Kehm, G.H. 72, 95-96, 299, 514, 651.
Keifert, P.R. 2, 7, 72, 111-13, 119, 152, 156, 168-69, 180, 185, 259, 274, 294, 348, 646.
Kelsey, D.H. 71, 161, 250, 623.
Kendall, D. 273, 453, 650.
Kennedy, J.F. 255, 461.
Kenny, A. 135, 156, 237, 364, 623.
Kevan, E. 30.
Keys, D.A. 455, 655.
Kieffer, R. 73, 168.
Kierkegaard, S.A. 31, 33, 35, 38, 46, 51, 72, 78, 83, 93, 97, 102, 117-20, 127, 129, 138, 188-89, 214, 246-47, 302, 308, 317, 319, 346-47, 356, 364, 393, 414, 423, 520, 529, 582, 595, 619, 622, 625-26, 646.
Kimmerle, H. 7, 71, 568, 646, 653.
King, J. 4, 52-53, 623, 646.
King, M. 646.
King, N. 646.
King, R. 166.
Kirk, J.A. 624.
Kittel, G. 39, 60, 236, 621.
Kitzberger, I.R. 630.
Klein, W.W. 57, 61, 63, 82, 86, 90, 138, 183, 185, 188, 211, 220, 240, 251, 261, 273-74, 279, 285, 291, 369, 383, 646.
Kleinig, J. 62, 90, 157, 211, 219, 224, 232, 241, 260-61, 274, 646.
Klemm, D.E. 86, 185, 232, 260, 344, 369, 646.
Kloha, J. 646.

Klosko, J.S. 426, 658.
Knight, G.A.F. 64.
Knowles, R. xvii-xxi, xxiv, 28, 30, 44, 48, 57, 93, 312, 470, 531, 629, 631, 652, 658.
Knox, J. 34, 620.
Koch, K. 92.
Kögler, H.H. 17, 371, 647.
Koning, J. de 262, 647.
Korzybski, A. 168, 180.
Kovacs, J.L. 632.
Kraft, C. 231.
Krašovec, J. 13, 28, 47, 83, 141, 207, 288, 405, 628, 647.
Kreitzer, L.J. 365, 647.
Kruse, C.G. 626.
Kuhn, T.S. 357, 376, 488, 514.
Kümmel, W.G. 65-66, 620.
Künneth, W. 619.
Kysar, R. 18-19.
Ladd, G.E. 54, 63, 68, 621.
Laeuchli, S. 66, 166.
Lambrecht, J. 647.
Lampe, G.W.H. 33, 619.
Lane, A.N.S. 278, 362, 638, 647, 656.
Langsdorf, L. 242-43, 261, 359, 415, 647.
Lantero, E.H. 234, 636.
Larkin Jr., W.J. 102, 128, 367, 626, 647.
Lash, N. 324.
Laughery, G.J. 152, 647.
Lawton, S. 34, 620.
Leach, E. 73.
Leibniz, G.W. 128.
Leitch, J.W. 288-90, 640.
Leon, P. 38, 620.
LeRon Shults, F. see "Shults, F. LeRon".
Lessing, G.E. 118, 303, 626.
Levinson, S.C. 437.
Lévi-Strauss, C. 73, 227, 293, 644.
Lewis, C.S. 132, 135, 631.
Lewis, H.D. 44, 621.
Libolt, C. 274, 647.
Lichtenwalter, L.L. 412, 647.
Liefeld, W.L. 423, 656.
Limbeck, M. 625.
Limpitlaw, A. 647.
Lindars, B. 68, 622.
Lindbeck, G.A. 57, 431, 641, 647.
Linge, D.E. 13, 18, 112, 237, 302, 308, 323, 346, 429, 500, 642, 647.
Linss, W.C. 647.
Lints, R. 412, 643.
Livingstone, E.A. 58, 133, 147, 236, 424, 625, 647.
Loader, W. 423, 631, 647.
Locke, J. 70, 178, 415.
Loisy, A. 59.
Lonergan, B. 61.
Longenecker, B.W. 630.
Longman III, T. 277, 324, 364, 532, 628, 647.
Lössl, J. xxiv.
Louth, A. 273, 658.
Louw, J.P. 625.
Lovatt, M. 53.
Luckhardt, C.G. 59, 226, 348, 658.
Luckmann, T. 99.
Lucretius 136.
Luke, St. 92, 232, 358, 619, 625, 627, 630.
Lundin, R. 5-7, 11, 29, 74, 88, 142, 149, 156, 175, 183, 212, 216, 221, 238-39, 242, 262, 274-76, 289, 291, 323, 326, 359, 363-64, 366, 369, 381, 383-84, 404-05, 415, 462, 468, 470, 625, 628-29, 635, 639-40, 643, 645, 647-49, 651-52, 654-58.
Luther, M. 56-57, 142, 245, 262, 281, 622, 627, 649.
Lyon, A.J. 439, 648.
Lyons, J. 168-69.
Lyons, W.J. 3-5, 21-22, 255-56, 470, 476-532, 534-38, 541, 543, 545-50, 558, 565, 569-71, 597, 598, 600, 648.
Lyotard, J.-F. 440, 558.
Mable, N. 53, 620-21.
MacCammon, L.M. 291, 324, 346, 648.
Macey, D. 293, 648.
Mack, B.L. 629.
MacKinnon, D.M. 33, 619.
Macquarrie, J. 2, 13, 36-37, 40, 45, 51-52, 75, 83, 141, 165, 185, 216, 285, 308, 311, 344, 352, 414, 620, 644, 648.
Maddox, R.L. 61, 69-71, 75, 90, 99, 102, 158, 183, 191, 221, 226, 232, 251, 274, 324, 347, 368, 401, 648.
Malbon, E.S. 76, 309, 648.
Manson, W. 36-37, 620.

Manwaring, R. 50-51, 648.
Mark, St. 66, 255, 413, 621, 625.
Marshall, D.G. 8, 40, 181, 216, 287, 373, 404, 642, 657.
Marshall, I.H. 3, 14, 29, 49, 51, 53, 55, 59, 63, 66, 68, 77, 84, 87, 103, 140-41, 175, 183, 206, 211, 214, 233, 251, 279-80, 338, 417, 528, 620, 624-25, 629, 632-33, 648, 650, 655.
Martin, B. 619.
Martin, F. 345, 369, 648.
Martin, R. 625.
Martin, R.P. 54, 56, 66, 68, 233, 621, 623.
Marx, K. 64, 250, 401.
Massey, J.E. 272, 363, 638, 649, 656.
Matthews, H. xxiv.
Mays, J.L. 294, 634, 649.
McCarthy, T. 9, 643.
McCartney, D. 347, 648.
McClendon, J. 543.
McConville, J.G. 356, 648.
McCown, W. 272, 363, 638, 649, 656.
McFarlane, H. 551.
McGrath, A.E. 262, 345, 627, 649.
McGuinness, B.F. 305, 658.
McHann Jr., J.C. 12, 90, 98-99, 137, 140, 225, 287, 289, 302-04, 308, 317, 321-22, 327, 334-35, 365-66, 370, 379-80, 403-05, 407, 414, 435, 458, 649.
McKay, J.R. 55, 624.
McKim, D.K. 625, 631.
McKnight, E.V. 379, 649.
McKnight, S. 649.
McNicol, A.J. 60, 90, 138, 185-86, 208, 232, 261, 300, 368-69, 382, 401, 649.
Meier, J.P. 67, 649.
Mercer, C.R. 67, 649.
Metz, J.B. 97.
Metzger, B.M. 145, 185, 202, 209, 259, 294, 627, 649, 650.
Meyer, L.R. 649.
Michalson, G.E. 626.
Milbank, J. 558.
Miller, D.G. 294, 634, 649.
Miller, J.F. 55, 624.
Miranda, J. 189, 248.
Mitchell, B. 48, 246, 285-86, 422, 625, 635, 639, 648-49.

Moberly, R.W.L. 2, 5-6, 163, 186, 249, 252, 340, 381, 629, 649.
Moffatt, J. 65-66.
Möller, K. 7, 10, 152, 208, 238, 277-78, 330, 344, 356, 420, 434, 436, 450, 629, 634, 638, 645, 647-48, 651, 656, 658.
Moltmann, J. xvii-xviii, 39, 64, 68, 72, 81, 91-95, 97, 132, 145, 187-89, 202, 232, 248-49, 317, 367, 406, 491, 493, 563, 622-23, 649.
Montgomery, J.W. 103.
Montini, G.B. (Pope Paul VI) 619.
Moo, D.J. 5, 328, 637, 649.
Mooney, C. 69.
Moore, G.E. 179, 356, 439, 649.
Moore, S.D. 2, 5, 9, 100, 240, 262, 439, 627, 649.
Moores, J.D. 628.
Moorhead, D. 309, 649.
Morgan, R.C. 2, 6, 75, 90, 138, 144, 185, 210, 230, 249, 277, 285, 308, 347, 363, 401, 429, 435, 484, 489, 626, 649.
Morris, C.W. 178.
Morris, L. 92, 619, 637, 649.
Morton, A. 132, 139, 650.
Moule, C.F.D. 66, 330, 650.
Moule, H.C.G. 59.
Muddiman, J. 633, 634.
Mulholland Jr., M.R. 2, 650.
Munzinger, A. 632.
Murphy, N.C. 451, 650.
Murphy-O'Connor, J. 66-67, 650.
Murray, S. 629.
Mussner, F. 21.
Neill, S. 50-51, 273, 650.
Neufeld, V.H. 165-66, 365.
Neuhaus, R.J. 345, 638.
Newcastle, A. 650.
Newman, C.C. 650.
Newton, I. 414.
Neyrey, J.H. 67, 650.
Nicholls, W. 18, 43-44, 620.
Nicholson, G. 86, 650.
Nicholson, M.W. 3, 551-55, 563, 571, 650.
Nicole, R.R. 642, 645.
Nida, E.A. 168, 173-74.
Niebuhr, R. (Reinhold) 67.
Nietzsche, F. 33, 72, 118-19, 338-39, 401,

457, 486, 529-30, 561, 650.
Niles, D.T. 38, 620.
Nineham, D.E. 60, 70, 208-09, 302-03, 326, 328, 334, 341-42, 369, 400, 410-11, 624.
Noble, P.R. 382, 477, 484, 489, 507, 650.
Noll, M.A. 64, 69, 311, 363, 429-30, 626, 650.
Norris, C. 15-16, 595, 650.
Novak, M. 31-32, 619.
Nussbaum, M. 558.
Nygren, A. 92.
Nyman, H. 59, 226, 348, 658.
O'Brien, P.T. 366, 650.
O'Collins, G. 273, 453, 650.
O'Neill, J.C. 463, 627, 651.
Obama, B. 571.
Oden, T.C. 369, 650.
Ogden, C.K. 168, 171-72, 178.
Ogden, S.M. 14, 68, 155, 181, 209-10, 216, 280, 282-83, 285, 336, 346, 626, 636-37, 650.
Okholm, D.L. 57, 431, 438, 443, 641, 647, 650, 352.
Økland, J. 631.
Olford, D. 53.
Olhausen, W.P. 436-37, 443, 567-68, 651.
Origen 493.
Oropeza, B.J. 651.
Orr, J. 59.
Orton, D.E. 652, 656.
Osborne, G.R. 1, 5, 156, 185, 324, 359-60, 364, 381-82, 416-18, 566, 645, 651.
Osei-Bonsu, J. 67, 196, 199, 286, 651.
Ott, H. 37, 72, 155, 230, 287.
Otto, R. 37.
Owen, H.P. 318, 651.
Packer, J.I. 281, 302, 344, 368, 625, 651.
Padilla, C.R. 362, 626, 635, 645.
Painter, J. 626.
Palmer, R.E. 75-77, 79, 81, 86, 90, 98-99, 115, 137-38, 157, 160, 185, 226, 233, 235, 245, 289, 329, 343, 349, 362, 365, 368, 400, 415, 429, 433, 453, 651.
Pannenberg, W. xvii-xix, 12-13, 34-36, 42-43, 45, 51, 55, 58, 62, 64, 68, 70, 72-73, 76, 78-81, 87-88, 90-99, 102, 114-22, 128-32, 137-38, 140, 144-46, 151, 165, 184, 187, 193, 199, 202, 206-07, 213, 217-19, 222-26, 229, 235, 269, 278-79, 287, 291, 296, 298-306, 313, 317, 321, 323, 327, 335, 343, 365-66, 369-70, 376-77, 379, 382, 392, 394, 399-400, 403-05, 407, 413, 418-19, 422, 428-29, 431, 433-35, 449, 465, 513-20, 523-24, 528-30, 535, 542, 545, 549-50, 561, 570, 581, 590, 594-95, 601, 607, 610.
Papaphilippopoulos, R. 5, 163, 186, 214, 239, 468-69, 554, 651.
Parasnis, D.S. 455, 651.
Parker, T.H.L. 34, 620.
Parry, R.A. 5, 363, 631, 648, 651, 655.
Parsons, M. xxiv.
Partridge, C.H. 648, 652, 655.
Passakos, D.C. 652.
Paton, H.J. 179.
Patte, D. 504, 628, 631, 652.
Pattison, G. 633.
Pattison, S. xxiii, 338.
Paul, D. 103, 151, 211, 336, 658.
Paul, St. 3, 14, 26, 30-32, 39, 44-46, 58, 60-61, 63, 65-68, 75, 78, 87-90, 92, 95, 97, 133, 142, 147, 159, 161-62, 170, 172, 193, 198, 200-02, 224, 226, 232, 236, 238-39, 251, 255, 274, 281, 284, 286, 308, 314, 318-20, 329, 348, 350-52, 356-57, 360, 386, 390, 409, 424-25, 491, 505, 528, 578, 610, 619, 622, 624-25, 628, 631-32, 635-36, 638-39, 642-43, 645, 647, 649-52, 654, 656-57.
Pears, D.F. 305, 658.
Pearson, B.A. 66.
Pearson, B.W.R. 630.
Pedersen, J. 64, 74.
Peirce, C.S. 74, 378, 457.
Pelc, J. 166, 168.
Pelikan, J. 18, 44, 621.
Pellauer, D. 422, 653.
Pereppadan, J. 57, 70, 277, 652.
Perrin, N. 66, 623.
Perry, S. 312, 469-70, 475-76, 652.
Petersen, N.R. 48, 228, 444, 624.
Peterson, D. 629.
Phillips, T.R. 57, 431, 641, 647, 652.
Pickett, T.E. 5, 276, 330, 380-81, 645, 652.
Pinnock, C.H. 57, 273, 652.
Placher, W. 438.

Plantinga, A. 12, 138, 438.
Plato 39, 55, 78, 80, 82, 91, 94-96, 104, 108, 115, 128, 144, 173, 193, 198, 201, 208, 224, 278, 318, 422, 459.
Plessis, J.G. du – See "du Plessis, J.G."
Polanyi, M. 273, 656.
Polkinghorne, J. 630.
Pollock, J. 31, 619.
Polt, R. 42, 105, 181, 644.
Popper, K. 18, 158, 376-77, 598-99.
Porter, S.E. 73, 303, 344, 351-54, 360-61, 363, 382, 435, 470, 496, 598, 626, 631-32, 643, 652, 656.
Pott, J. xxiv.
Poythress, V.S. 6, 57, 61, 90, 138, 147, 163, 185-86, 209, 233, 247, 260, 275, 415, 423-24, 429, 469-70, 473-75, 652.
Premo, B.I. 295.
Price, H.H. 36-37, 166, 365, 620.
Pritchard, J.P. 7, 10, 27, 652.
Procksch, O. 64, 74, 178, 180.
Prokes, M.T. 629.
Propp, V.I. 73, 293.
Rad, G. Von – See "Von Rad, G."
Rae, M. 296, 450, 634.
Rahner, K. 57, 68, 76, 622.
Räisänen, H. 629.
Ramakrishna 31, 619.
Ramsey, G.W. 64-65, 652.
Ramsey, I.T. 132, 134-35, 163, 165-66, 542, 652.
Randolph, T.W. 627.
Ranke, L. Von – See "Von Ranke, L."
Rapport, N. 85, 338, 429, 630, 642.
Rashi 493.
Rauschenbusch, W. 59.
Rawls, J. 438.
Recanati, F. 445, 474.
Reed, E.D. 652.
Reese, R.A. 483.
Reese, W.L. 652.
Reist Jr., J.S. 6, 26, 251, 290, 401, 403, 652.
Richards, I.A. 178.
Richardson, A. 630.
Richardson, H.W. 36, 38, 48, 196, 620.
Richardson, N. 628.
Richardson, W. 78, 170, 653.
Riches, J. 324, 640.

Ricoeur, P. xvii-xix, 9-10, 72, 75-76, 79, 81, 83, 199, 207, 220, 227, 242-44, 248, 268, 308, 312-13, 330, 346-47, 422, 438, 441, 510, 556, 559-60, 562-63, 627, 653.
Rieger, J. 345, 653.
Ringgren, H. 64, 74.
Roberts, R.C. 55-56, 126, 251, 624.
Robins, R.H. 168.
Robinson, E. 13, 40, 83, 141, 216, 308, 414-15, 644.
Robinson, J.A.T. 37, 58, 62, 65-66, 68, 70, 78, 92, 119, 128, 131, 163, 145, 220, 315, 621.
Robinson, J.M. 14, 32, 372, 379, 570, 642, 653.
Rodd, C.S. 57, 76, 90, 138, 185-87, 209, 259-60, 274, 416, 653.
Rogerson, J.W. 630, 640.
Rooke, D.W. 365, 647.
Rorem, P. 627.
Rorty, R. 4, 17, 23, 37, 107, 158, 188, 422, 440-41, 501-02, 526-27, 529, 593-94.
Roschke, R.W. 70, 73, 90, 185, 213, 218, 318-19, 653.
Rosner, B.S. 628-29, 633.
Rosser, J. 621.
Rowland, C. 627.
Royce, J. 378.
Rudman, S. 122, 653.
Russell, B. 158, 169, 179, 375-76, 598-99.
Russell, D.S. 55, 66, 239, 624.
Russell, W. 2, 6, 18, 277, 289, 434, 477, 480, 653.
Ryken, L. 532, 627-28.
Ryle, G.E. 165-66, 185.
Sachs, W. 61, 644.
Sakenfield, K.D. 631-32.
Sanders, E.P. 65.
Santer, M. 29, 48, 221, 625, 653.
Sarot, M. 4, 89, 187, 328, 367, 436, 476.
Sartre, J.-P. 72, 118-19, 530.
Satterthwaite, P.E. 67, 263, 410, 627, 643, 653.
Saussure, F. de xix, 39, 46, 63, 73, 75, 143-44, 168-74, 179-80, 184-85, 204, 228, 234, 265, 269, 292, 299, 330, 344-45, 385, 457, 466, 607.
Sawyer, J.F.A. 63, 73, 168, 172-73, 185, 222,

227, 332, 350, 543, 622.
Sbisà, M. 633.
Schaeder, E. 515.
Schel, K.K. 625.
Schelling, F. 419.
Schenk, W. 63, 656.
Schillebeeckx, E. 61, 177.
Schiwy, G. 146.
Schlatter, A. 415.
Schleiermacher, F.D.E. 7, 31, 37, 71, 79, 156, 193, 197, 225, 229, 244, 298, 343-46, 392, 418, 420, 568, 595, 631, 646, 653.
Schlink, E. 58.
Schmidt, D.J. 14, 18, 373-74, 653.
Schmithals, W. 66.
Schneiders, S.M. 2, 70, 75-76, 184-85, 209-10, 287, 294, 306, 281-82, 654.
Schniewind, J. 154, 285, 636.
Schrag, C.O. 452-53, 654.
Schrage, W. 654.
Schreiner, T.R. 654.
Schroeder, W.R. 14, 17, 293, 374, 638, 644, 653.
Schüssler-Fiorenza, E. 72-73, 382-83, 423, 654.
Schweitzer, A. 59-60, 65-66, 68, 90-92, 193, 200, 232, 251, 424, 624.
Schweizer, E. 66.
Scruton, R. 108-09.
Searle, J.R. xvii, 18, 156, 158, 355, 381, 445, 447, 450-52, 468-69, 473-75, 529, 600, 607, 654.
Segovia, F.F. 628.
Seifrid, M.A. 281, 654.
Seitz, C.R. 630-31.
Selina, H. 109, 638.
Sell, A. 630.
Sell, A.P.F. 654.
Seung, T.K. 458-59, 465-66, 654.
Shapiro, G. 463, 651.
Shapiro, J.J. 643.
Sheehy, D. 654.
Sheppard. G.T. 631.
Sheriff, R.E. 455, 655.
Shults, F. LeRon 43, 286, 428-29, 572, 654.
Sica, A. 463, 651.
Silva, M. 273, 276-77, 334, 345, 646-47, 654.

Silverman, H.J. 452, 654.
Slater, G. 275, 654.
Smalley, S.S. 68, 622.
Smart, J.D. 624.
Smart, N. 36, 79, 138, 416, 620, 633.
Smit, D.J. 77, 272, 654.
Smit, J.F.M. 654.
Smith, L.P. 234, 636.
Smith, R.G. 636.
Smith, R.L. 261-62, 468, 532, 654.
Smuts, J. xxiv.
Snodgrass, K.R. 5, 156, 221, 261, 369, 381, 655.
Song, R. 634.
Spinoza, B. 128, 139.
Spivak, G.C. 457, 465, 639.
Stanton, G.N. 630.
Staten, H. 37.
Stendahl, K. 66.
Stephens, W. 627, 655.
Stephenson, H. 38, 47.
Sterling, G.E. 67, 655.
Stern, G. 168.
Stewart, I. 426, 655.
Stiver, D.R. 3, 437-43, 556, 558-59, 568, 576, 655.
Stock, St. G. 624.
Stokes, P. 374, 452, 655.
Stott, J.R.W. 4, 32, 50, 52, 85, 146, 206, 272, 288, 412, 619-20, 624, 640, 655.
Stout, J. 158, 529.
Strauss, D.F. 61, 646.
Strawson, P.F. 34, 36-37, 44, 46, 129, 166, 196.
Stuhlmacher, P. 287.
Stylianopoulos, T.G. 628.
Suler, J. 425-26, 567, 655.
Summer, S. 655.
Sundberg, W. 628.
Sykes, S.W. 5, 23-24, 58, 69, 100, 145, 185, 209, 224, 275, 341, 524, 621, 655.
Taber, C.R. 168, 173.
Talbert, C.H. 655.
Talbot, T. 655.
Tarski, A. 178.
Taylor, C. 437.
Taylor, M.C. 558.
Teele, A. 359.

Telford, W.M. 455, 655.
Tenney, M.C. 58, 120, 149, 207, 518, 623, 655.
Theissen, G. 66, 625.
Thiselton, A.C. xxi, xxiii-xxiv, 1-7, 9-26, 28-371, 373-446, 448-54, 456-63, 465-78, 481-89, 492, 494-511, 514-15, 517-32, 534-619, 625-31, 633-49, 651-58.
Thomas, G.J. 5, 655.
Thomas, R.L. 155, 191, 655.
Thompson, J.B. 10, 653.
Thornton, M. 34, 619-20.
Thrall, M.E. 77, 183, 655.
Thurgood, J. 53.
Tidball, D. xxiv, 625.
Tillich, P. 31, 35, 37, 54, 58, 67-68, 72, 79-80, 91, 97, 131, 134, 140-41, 143, 155, 164, 179, 188, 199, 209, 317, 436, 493, 619-20, 622, 626.
Tipton, S. 559.
Titans, N. 424, 438, 558, 562, 655.
Tolbert, M.A. 628.
Tomlinson, D. 655.
Topping, R.R. 490, 518, 520.
Torrance, A.J. 61, 154, 326, 655.
Torrance, I.R. 273, 656.
Torrance, T.F. 35-36, 45, 58, 68, 74, 81, 102, 118, 125, 127, 130-32, 138, 203, 220, 224, 296, 337, 620-21.
Tosato, A. 64, 318, 656.
Tournier, P. 563, 656.
Tracy, D. 15, 469, 656.
Traina, R. 363, 656.
Travis, S.H. 624.
Trier, D.J. 632.
Trier, J. 168, 171.
Trocmé, E. 185, 656.
Troeltsch, E. 60, 70, 96, 116, 209, 322, 328, 369, 400, 410-11.
Trueman, C. 362, 656.
Tucker, R.A. 423, 656.
Tuckett, C.M. 626, 656.
Tulloch, S. 406, 458, 656.
Tupper, E.F. 405, 518-520, 656.
Turner, M. 5, 158, 340, 358, 369, 375, 383, 468, 627, 641, 643, 648, 656.
Tutton, I. xxiv.
Tyndale, W. 142.

Ullmann, S. 41, 165-66, 168, 172, 175.
Urmson, J.O. 633.
Van Buren, P. 37, 143, 158, 163, 166, 375, 620.
Van Engen, C. 324, 334, 368, 417-18, 656.
Van Hamersveld, M. 175, 185, 221, 261, 366, 369-70, 468, 656.
Van Spanje, T.E. 287-88, 656.
Van Til, C. 71.
Van Voorst, R. 60, 86, 138, 185, 260, 276, 344, 369, 376, 383, 656.
Vanhoozer, K.J. 7, 48, 83, 158, 330-32, 364, 380, 402, 405, 422, 424, 432, 462, 483-84, 489, 529, 627, 629-30, 656.
Via, D.O. 62, 72-73, 211, 287, 293.
Vico, G.B. 410.
Vincent, J.J. 38, 620.
Virkler, H.A. 625.
Voelz, J.W. 63, 238, 656.
Von Goethe, J.W. 568.
Von Harnack, A. 59, 415.
Von Herder, J.G. See "Herder, J.G. Von".
Von Humboldt, W. 19, 74.
Von Rad, G. 64, 74, 178, 180.
Von Ranke, L. 415.
Von Wright, G.H. 59, 226, 348, 658.
Vos, J.S. 657.
Wade, R. 334, 657.
Waismann, F. 531.
Walhout, C. 5, 6, 11, 29, 74, 88, 142, 149, 156, 175, 183, 212, 216, 221, 238-39, 242, 262, 274-76, 289, 291, 323, 326, 359, 363-64, 366, 369, 381, 383-84, 404-05, 415, 468, 470, 625, 627, 629, 635, 639-40, 643, 645, 647-49, 651-52, 654-58.
Walker Jr., W.O. 67, 657.
Wallace, M.I. 71, 657.
Walsh, B.J. 6, 70-71, 73, 75, 77, 89-90, 98-104, 117, 124, 130-31, 137-38, 150, 157-58, 160, 163, 180-81, 183, 186, 191, 216, 219-20, 222, 229-30, 233-35, 237, 239, 252, 261, 265, 275, 278, 283, 289, 303, 330, 362, 384, 400-01, 410, 415, 553-54, 602, 657.
Ward, P. 530, 657.
Ward, R.S. 657.
Ward, T. 158, 185, 468, 529, 657.

Ware, K. 64, 657.
Warfield, B.B. 59.
Warner, C.A.F. 50, 623.
Warnock, G.J. 633.
Watson, F. xxiv, 2, 6, 9, 15, 26, 100, 147, 156, 163, 186, 226, 229, 237, 287, 345, 357, 363, 402, 418, 454, 484, 489, 628, 657.
Watt, J. xxiv.
Weaver, J. xxiv.
Webster, J.B. 5, 184, 225, 227, 274, 283, 303, 342, 362, 657.
Wedderburn, A.J.M. 657.
Weele, M.V. 221, 262, 468, 657.
Weinberg, S. 6.
Weinsheimer, J. 8, 18, 26, 40, 59, 103, 181, 216, 249, 287, 322, 373-74, 404, 642-43, 657.
Weishaar, M.E. 426, 658.
Weiss, J. 59.
Welborn, L.L. 631.
Wells, D.F. 311, 363, 429-30, 530, 626, 650.
Wells, P.R. 625.
Wells, R. 272, 657.
Wenham, D. 3, 657.
Wenham, J.W. 51, 69, 198-99, 250, 622.
Werner, M. 65, 68, 91-92.
West, C. 501.
White, A.R. 165-66.
White, H.C. 11, 89, 95, 98-99, 183, 303, 348, 657.
Whiteley, D.E.H. 31, 65, 619.
Whorf, B.L. 19, 74, 174.
Wikenhauser, A. 65.
Wiles, M. 62.
Wilhoit, J.C. 532, 628.
Williams, B. 558.
Williams, D.D. 68-69.
Williams, P. 277, 657.
Williams, H.A. 78, 119.
Wilson, R.A. 515, 651.
Winch, P. 157, 377, 657.
Wink, W. 2, 14-15, 62, 72, 77, 81, 90, 185, 247, 260, 281, 294, 335, 391, 414, 657.
Winter, B.W. 657.
Witherington III, B. 628, 657.
Wittgenstein, L.J.J. xvii-xviii, 1, 3, 7, 16, 18-19, 24, 28, 30-31, 33-37, 39-45, 48, 51, 59, 61, 63, 65, 73, 75, 79-80, 83, 85, 88, 90, 93, 99-100, 102-03, 105, 112, 120, 123, 129-30, 132-35, 137-38, 140-63, 165-68, 171-90, 194, 197, 204, 206, 211, 218-19, 225-29, 233-37, 245, 255, 261, 265, 269-70, 272-73, 284, 288, 290, 292, 294-300, 304-06, 308, 310-11, 325-27, 329-30, 334-36, 338, 344, 347-53, 355, 357, 360-62, 364-65, 368, 370-71, 374-79, 381-82, 385-86, 388-90, 392-94, 400, 402, 411-14, 430, 441, 445, 449, 451, 465-66, 468-69, 472-74, 481, 486, 495, 528-29, 531, 542, 549, 551-55, 574, 588, 591, 594-602, 607, 610, 623-24, 626-27, 640, 644, 650, 652, 657.
Wolters, A. 631, 634.
Wolterstorff, N. xvii, 446, 628.
Wonderly, W.L. 168.
Wood, W.J. 629.
Woodbridge, J.D. 99, 273, 281, 322, 637-38, 644, 651, 654.
Woodhead, L. 555-63, 571, 609, 658.
Woodman, S. 470, 476, 497-98, 518, 520, 523, 530-50, 565, 569-71, 597-98, 600, 639, 658.
Woodward, J. 338.
Woolley, L. 425-26, 539, 551, 567.
Work, T. 630.
Wrede, W. 415.
Wright, D.F. 67, 263, 278, 362, 410, 627, 638, 643, 647, 653, 656.
Wright, G.H. Von – See "Von Wright, G.H."
Wright, N.T. 3, 273, 633, 650, 658.
Wright, S.I. 420, 658.
Wright, S. 38, 620.
Yarnold, G.D. 31, 619.
Yorck, G. 307, 387.
Young, F. 273, 626, 658.
Young, J.E. 425-26, 567, 608-09, 658.
Young, N.H. 658.
Zahrnt, H. 35, 132, 620.
Zangwill, O.L. 425, 567, 658.
Ziesler, J.A. 358, 383, 625.
Zimmerman, J. 631.
Zuidervaart, L. 149, 221, 229, 240, 243, 261, 381, 658.
Zwingli, H. 56.

www.ingramcontent.com/pod-product-compliance
Lightning Source LLC
Chambersburg PA
CBHW071214290426
44108CB00013B/1175